High-Dimensional Data Analysis with Low-Dimensional Models

Connecting theory with practice, this systematic and rigorous introduction covers the fundamental principles, algorithms, and applications of key mathematical models for high-dimensional data analysis. Comprehensive in its approach, it provides unified coverage of many different low-dimensional models and analytical techniques, including sparse and low-rank models, and both convex and nonconvex formulations. Readers will learn how to develop efficient and scalable algorithms for solving real-world problems, supported by numerous examples and exercises throughout, and how to use the computational tools learnt in several application contexts. Applications presented include scientific imaging, communication, face recognition, three-dimensional vision, and deep networks for classification. With code available online, this is an ideal text for graduate students in electrical engineering, computer science, and data science, as well as for those taking courses on sparsity, low-dimensional structures, and high-dimensional data.

John Wright is an Associate Professor in the Electrical Engineering Department at Columbia University. He is also affiliated with Columbia's Department of Applied Physics and Applied Mathematics and the Data Science Institute.

Yi Ma is a Professor in the Department of Electrical Engineering and Computer Sciences at the University of California, Berkeley. He is a Fellow of the IEEE, ACM, and SIAM.

High-Dimensional Data Analysis with Low-Dimensional Models

Principles, Computation, and Applications

JOHN WRIGHT
Columbia University, New York

YI MA
University of California, Berkeley

CAMBRIDGE
UNIVERSITY PRESS

CAMBRIDGE
UNIVERSITY PRESS

Shaftesbury Road, Cambridge CB2 8EA, United Kingdom

One Liberty Plaza, 20th Floor, New York, NY 10006, USA

477 Williamstown Road, Port Melbourne, VIC 3207, Australia

314–321, 3rd Floor, Plot 3, Splendor Forum, Jasola District Centre, New Delhi – 110025, India

103 Penang Road, #05–06/07, Visioncrest Commercial, Singapore 238467

Cambridge University Press is part of Cambridge University Press & Assessment, a department of the University of Cambridge.

We share the University's mission to contribute to society through the pursuit of education, learning and research at the highest international levels of excellence.

www.cambridge.org
Information on this title: www.cambridge.org/9781108489737

DOI: 10.1017/9781108779302

First published 2022
3rd printing 2022

A catalogue record for this publication is available from the British Library

ISBN 978-1-108-48973-7 Hardback

Additional resources for this publication at www.cambridge.org/wright-ma.

To Mary, Isabella, and Mingshu (J.W.)

To Henry, Barron, and Diana,
and in memory of my father (Y.M.)

Contents

Foreword

I recall a moment, perhaps ten or fifteen years ago, of prodigious scientific activity. To give our reader a sense of this blessed time, consider a series of regular scientific workshops, each involving at most forty participants. Despite the small size and almost intimate nature of these workshops, they brought together an energized and enthusiastic mix of people from an array of disciplines, including mathematics, computer science, engineering, and the life sciences. What a privilege to be in a room with mathematicians such as Terence Tao and Roman Vershynin and learn about high-dimensional geometry; with applied mathematicians and engineers such as David Donoho, Joel Tropp, Thomas Ströhmer, Michael Elad, and Freddy Bruckstein and learn about the power of algorithms; with statistical physicists such as Andrea Montanari and learn about phase transitions in large stochastic systems. What a privilege to learn about fast numerical methods for large-scale optimization from computer scientists such as Stephen Wright and Stanley Osher. What a privilege to learn about compressive optical systems from David Brady, and Richard Baraniuk and Kevin Kelly (of single-pixel camera fame); about compressive analog-to-digital conversion and wideband spectrum sensing from Dennis Healy, Yonina Eldar, and Azita Emami Neyestanak; about breakthroughs in computer vision from Yi Ma, John Wright, and René Vidal; and about dramatically faster scan times in magnetic resonance imaging from Michael Lustig and Leon Axel. Bringing all these people – and others I regretfully cannot name for lack of space – together, with their different perspectives and interests, sparked spirited discussions. Excitement was in the air and progress quickly followed.

Yi Ma and John Wright were frequent participants to these workshops and their book magically captures their spirit and richness. It exposes readers to (1) a variety of real-world applications including medical and scientific imaging, computer vision, wideband spectrum sensing, and so on, (2) the mathematical ideas powering algorithms in use in these fields, and (3) the algorithmic ideas needed to implement them. Let me illustrate with an example. On the one hand, this is a book in which we learn about the principles of magnetic resonance (MR) imaging. There is a chapter in which we learn how an MR scan excites the nucleus of atoms by means of a magnetic field. These nuclei have a magnetic spin, and will respond to this excitation, and it is precisely this response that gets recorded. As for other imaging modalities, such as computed tomography, there is a mathematical transformation that relates the object we wish to infer and the data we collect. In this case, after performing a few approximations, this mathematical transformation is given by the Fourier transform.

On the other hand, this is a book in which we learn that most of the mass of a high-dimensional sphere is concentrated not just around the equator – this is already sufficiently surprising – but around any equator! Or that the intersection between two identical high-dimensional cubes, one being randomly oriented vis-à-vis the other, is essentially a sphere! These are fascinating subjects, but what is the connection? There is one, of course, and explaining it is the most wonderful strength of the book. In a nutshell, ideas and tools from probability theory, high-dimensional geometry, and convex analysis inform concrete applied problems and explain why algorithms actually work. Returning to our MR imaging problem, we learn how to leverage mathematical models of sparsity to recover exquisite images of body tissues from what appear to be far too few data points. Such a feat allows us to scan patients ten times faster today.

Through three fairly distinct parts – roughly, theory, computations, and applications – the book proposes a scientific vision concerned with the development of insightful mathematics to create models for data, to create processing algorithms, and to ultimately inspire real concrete improvements; for instance, in human health as in the example above.

The first part of the book explores data models around two main themes, namely, sparsity and low-rankedness. Sparsity expresses the idea that most of the entries of an n-dimensional signal vanish or nearly vanish so that the information can be effectively summarized using fewer than n data bits. Low rankedness expresses the idea that the columns of a data matrix 'live' near a linear subspace of lower dimension, thereby also suggesting the possibility of an effective summary. We then find out how to use these data models to create data processing algorithms, for instance, to find solutions of underdetermined systems of linear equations. The emphasis is on algorithms formulated as solutions to well-formulated convex optimization problems. That said, we are also introduced to nonconvex methods in Chapter 7 to learn effective empirical representations from data in which signals exhibit enhanced sparsity. All along, the authors use their rich experiences to communicate insights and to explain why some things work while others do not.

The second part reviews effective methods for solving optimization problems – convex or not – at scale; that is, involving possibly millions of decision variables and a possibly equally large number of constraints. This is an area that has seen tremendous progress in the last fifteen years and the book provides readers with a valuable point of entry to the key ideas and vast literature.

The last part is a deep dive into applications. In addition to the imaging challenges I already mentioned, we find a chapter on wireless radio communication, where we see how ideas from sparse signal processing and compressed sensing allow cognitive radios to efficiently identify the available spectrum. We also find three chapters on crucial problems in computer vision, a field in which the authors have brought and developed formidable tools, enabling major advances and opening new perspectives. Exposition starts with a special contribution, which also exploits ideas from compressed sensing, to the crucial problem of face recognition in the presence of occlusions and other nonidealities. (I recall an exciting *Wired* article about this work when it came out.) The book then introduces methods for inferring 3D structure from a series of 2D photographs, and to identify structured textures from a single photograph; solving the latter problem is often the starting point to recover the appearance, pose, and shape of multiple objects in a scene. Finally, at the time of this writing, deep learning (DL) is all the rage. The book contains an epilogue which establishes connections between all the better understood data models reviewed in the book and DL: the one hundred million dollar question is whether they will shed significant insights on deep learning and influence or improve its practice.

Who would enjoy this book? First and foremost, students in mathematics, applied mathematics, statistics, computer science, electrical engineering, and related disciplines. Students will learn a lot from reading this book because it is so much more than a text about a tool being applied with minor variations. They will learn about mathematical reasoning, they will learn about data models and about connecting those to reality, and they will learn about algorithms. The book also contains computer scripts so that we can see ideas in action and carefully crafted exercises making it perfect for upper-level undergraduate or graduate-level instruction. The breadth and depth make this a reference for anyone interested in the mathematical foundations of data science. I also believe that members of the applied mathematical sciences community at large would enjoy this book. They will be reminded of the power of mathematical reasoning and of the all-around positive impact it can have.

Emmanuel Candès
Stanford, California
December 2020

Preface

"The coming century is surely the century of data. A combination of blind faith and serious purpose makes our society invest massively in the collection and processing of data of all kinds, on scales unimaginable until recently."

– David Donoho, *High-Dimensional Data Analysis: The Curses and Blessings of Dimensionality, 2000*

The Era of Big Data

In the past two decades, our world has entered the age of "Big Data." The information technology industry is now facing the challenge, and opportunity, of processing and analyzing massive amounts of data on a daily basis. The size and the dimension of the data have reached an unprecedented scale and are still increasing at an unprecedented rate.

For instance, on the technological side, the resolution of consumer digital cameras has increased nearly ten-fold in the past decade or so. Each day, over 300 million photos are uploaded to Facebook;[1] 300 hours of videos are posted on YouTube every minute; and over 20 million entertaining short videos are produced and posted to Douyin (also known as TikTok) of China.

On the business side, on a single busy day, Alibaba.com needs to take in over 800 million purchase orders for over 15 million products, handle over a billion payments, and deliver more than 30 million packages. Amazon.com also operates at a similar scale, if not even larger. Those numbers are still growing and growing fast!

On the scientific front, super-resolution microscopy imaging technologies have undergone tremendous advances in the past decades,[2] and some are now capable of producing massive quantities of images with subatomic resolution. High-throughput gene sequencing technologies are capable of sequencing hundreds of millions of DNA molecule fragments at a time,[3] and can sequence in just a few hours an entire human genome that has a length of over 3 billion base pairs and contains 20 000 protein-encoding genes!

[1] Almost all of them are passing through several processing pipelines for face detection, face recognition, and general object classification for content screening, etc.

[2] For example, in 2014, Eric Betzig, Stefan W. Hell, and William E. Moerner were awarded the Nobel Prize in Chemistry for the development of super-resolution fluorescence microscopy that bypasses the limit of 0.2 micrometers of traditional optical microscopy.

[3] In 2002, Sydney Brenner, John Sulston, and Robert Horvitz were awarded the Nobel Prize in Physiology or Medicine for their pioneering work and contributions to the Human Genome project.

Figure 0.1 Images of Mary and Isabella: the resolution of the image on the left is 2500×2500, whereas the image on the right is down-sampled to 250×250, with only 1/100-th fraction of pixels of the original one.

Paradigm Shift in Information Acquisition, Processing, and Analysis

In the past, scientists or engineers have sought to carefully control the data acquisition apparatus and process. Since the apparatus was expensive and the process time-consuming, typically only necessary data (or measurements) were collected for a specific given task. The data or signals collected were mostly informative for the task and did not contain much redundant or irrelevant information, except for some uncontrollable noise. Hence, classical signal processing or data analysis typically operated under the following

$$\text{Classical Premise:} \quad \textbf{Data} \approx \textbf{Information}.$$

In this classical paradigm, practitioners mostly needed to deal with problems such as removing noise or compressing the data for storage or transport.

As mentioned above, technologies such as the Internet, smart phones, high-throughput imaging, and gene sequencing have fundamentally changed the nature of data acquisition and analysis. We are moving from a "data-poor" era to a "data-rich" era. As pointed out by Jim Gray (a Turing Award winner), "increasingly, scientific breakthroughs will be powered by advanced computing capabilities that help researchers manipulate and explore massive datasets." This is now heralded as *the Fourth Paradigm* of scientific discovery [HTT09].

Nevertheless, data-rich does not necessarily imply "information-rich," at least not for free. Massive amounts of data are being collected, sometimes without any specific purpose in advance. Scientists or engineers often do not have direct control of the data acquisition process anymore, neither in the quantity nor in the quality of the acquired data. Therefore, any given new task could be inundated with massive amounts of irrelevant or redundant data.

To see intuitively why this is the case, let us first consider the problem of *face recognition*. Figure 0.1 shows two images of two sisters. It is arguably the case that, to human eyes, both images convey the identity of the persons equally well, even though pixels of the second image are merely 1/100-th of the first one. In other words, if we view both images as vectors with their pixel values as coordinates, then the dimension of the low-resolution image vector is merely 1/100-th of the original one.

Figure 0.2 Detecting and recognizing faces in a large group photo, from the BIRS workshop on "*Applied Harmonic Analysis, Massive Data Sets, Machine Learning, and Signal Processing*," held at Casa Matemática Oaxaca (CMO) in Mexico, 2016.

Clearly, the information about the identity of a person relies on statistics of much lower dimension than the original high-resolution image.[4] Hence, in such scenarios, we have the following

$$\text{New Premise I:} \quad \textbf{Data} \gg \textbf{Information}.$$

For *object detection* tasks such as face detection in images or pedestrian detection in surveillance videos, the issue is no longer with redundancy. Instead, the difficulty is to find any relevant information at all in an ocean of irrelevant data. For example, to detect and recognize familiar people from a group photo shown in Figure 0.2, image pixels associated with human faces only occupy a very tiny portion of the image pixels (10 millions in this case) whereas the mass majority of the pixels belong to completely irrelevant objects in the surroundings. In addition, the subjects of interest, say the two authors, are only two among many human faces. Now imagine scaling this problem to billions of images or millions of videos captured with mobile phones or surveillance cameras. Similar "detection" and "recognition" tasks also arise in studying genetics: out of the nearly 20 000 genes and millions of proteins they encode, scientists need to identify which one (or handful of ones) is responsible for certain genetic diseases. In scenarios like these, we have

$$\text{New Premise II:} \quad \textbf{Data} = \textbf{Information} + \textbf{Irrelevant Data}.$$

[4] In fact, one can continue to argue that even such a low-resolution image is still highly redundant. Studies have shown that humans can recognize familiar faces from images with a resolution as low as around 7×10 pixels [SBOR06]. Recent studies in neuroscience [CT17] reveal that it is possible for the brain to encode and decode any human face using just 200 cells in the inferotemporal (IT) cortex. Modern face recognition algorithms extract merely a few hundred features for reliable face verification.

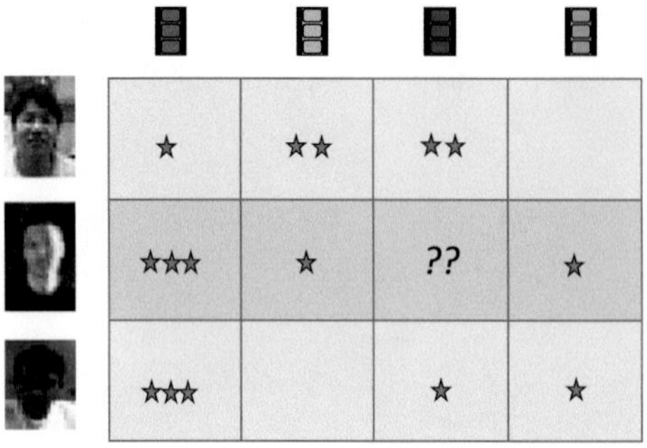

Figure 0.3 An example of collaborative filtering of user preferences: how to guess a customer's rating for a movie even if he or she has not seen it yet?

The explosive growth of e-commerce, online shopping, and social networks has created tremendous datasets of user preferences. Major internet companies typically have records of billions of people's preferences, across millions of commercial products, media contents, and more. By nature, such datasets of user preferences, however massive, are far from complete. For instance, in the case of a dataset of movie ratings as shown in Figure 0.3, no one could have seen all the movies and no movie would have been seen by all people. Nevertheless, companies like Netflix need to guess from such incomplete datasets a customer's preferences so that they could send the most relevant recommendations or advertisements to the customer. This problem in information retrieval literature is known as *collaborative filtering*, and most internet companies' business[5] relies on solving problems such as this one effectively and efficiently. The most fundamental reason why complete information can be derived from such a highly incomplete dataset is that user preferences are not random and the data have structure. For instance, many people have similar tastes in movies and many movies are similar in style. Rows and columns of the user preference table would be strongly correlated, hence the intrinsic dimension (or rank) of the complete table is in fact extremely low compared to its size. Hence, for large (incomplete) datasets drawn from low-dimensional structures, we have

$$\text{New Premise III:} \quad \textbf{Incomplete Data} \approx \textbf{Complete Information}.$$

As the above examples suggest, in the modern era of big data, we often face problems of recovering specific information that is buried in highly redundant, irrelevant, seemingly incomplete, or even corrupted[6] datasets. Such information without exception is encoded as certain low-dimensional structures underlying the data, and may only depend on a small (or sparse) subset of the (massive) dataset. This is very different from the classical settings and is precisely the reason why modern data science and engineering are undergoing a fundamental shift in their mathematical and computational paradigms. At its foundation, we need to develop a new mathematical

[5] Most internet companies make money from advertisements, including but not limited to Google, Baidu, Facebook, Bytedance, Amazon, Alibaba, Netflix, etc.

[6] Say due to negligence, misinformation, rumors, or malicious tampering.

framework that characterizes precise conditions under which such low-dimensional information can be correctly and effectively acquired and retained. Equally importantly, we need to develop efficient algorithms that are capable of retrieving such information from massive high-dimensional datasets, at unprecedented speed, at arbitrary scale, and with guaranteed accuracy.

Purposes of This Book

Over the past two decades, there have been explosive developments in the study of low-dimensional structures in high-dimensional spaces. To a large extent, the geometric and statistical properties of representative low-dimensional models (such as sparse and low-rank, and their variants and extensions) are now well understood. Conditions under which such models can be effectively and efficiently recovered from (a minimal amount of sampled) data have been clearly characterized. Many highly efficient and scalable algorithms have been developed for recovering such low-dimensional models from high-dimensional data. The working conditions, and data and computational complexities of these algorithms, have also been thoroughly and precisely characterized. These new theoretical results and algorithms have revolutionized the practice of data science and signal processing, and have had significant impacts on sensing, imaging, and information processing. They have significantly advanced the state of the art for many applications in areas such as scientific imaging,[7] image processing,[8] computer vision,[9] bioinformatics,[10] information retrieval,[11] and machine learning.[12] As we will see from applications featured in this book, some of these developments seem to defy conventional wisdom.

As witnesses to such historical advancements, we believe that the time is now ripe to give a comprehensive survey of this new body of knowledge and to organize these rich results under a unified theoretical and computational paradigm. There are a number of excellent existing books on this topic that already focus on the mathematical/statistical principles of compressive sensing and sparse/low-dimensional modeling [FR13, HTW15, Van16, Wai19, FLZZ20]. Nevertheless, the goal of this book is to bridge, through truly tractable and scalable computation, the gap between principles and applications of low-dimensional models for high-dimensional data analysis with

$$\text{A New Paradigm:} \quad \textbf{Principles} \xleftrightarrow{\textbf{Computation}} \textbf{Applications}.$$

Hence, not only does this book establish mathematical principles for modeling low-dimensional structures and understanding the limits on when they can be recovered, but it also shows how to systematically develop provably efficient and scalable algorithms for solving the recovery problems, leveraging both classical and recent developments in optimization.

[7] Compressive sampling and recovery of medical and microscopic images, etc.
[8] Denoising, super-resolution, inpainting of natural images, etc.
[9] Regular texture synthesis, camera calibration, and 3D reconstruction, etc.
[10] Microarray data analysis for gene–protein relations, etc.
[11] Collaborative filtering of user preferences, documents, and multimedia data, etc.
[12] Especially for interpreting, understanding, and improving deep networks.

Furthermore, through a rich collection of exemplar applications in science and technology, the book aims to further coach readers and students on how to incorporate additional domain knowledge or other nonideal factors (e.g., nonlinearity) in order to correctly apply these new principles and methods to model real-world data and solve real-world problems successfully.

Although the applications featured in this book are inevitably biased by the authors' own expertise and experiences in practicing these general principles and methods, they are carefully chosen to convey diverse and complementary lessons we have learned (often in a hard way). We believe these lessons have value for both theoreticians and practitioners.

Intended Audience

In many ways, the body of knowledge covered in this book has great pedagogical value to young researchers and students in the area of data science. Through rigorous mathematical development, we hope our readers are able to gain new knowledge and insights about high-dimensional geometry and statistics, far beyond what has been established in classical signal processing and data analysis. Such insights are generalizable to a wide range of useful low-dimensional structures and models, including modern deep networks, and can lead to entirely new methods and algorithms for important scientific and engineering problems.

Therefore, this book is intended to be a textbook for a course that introduces basic mathematical and computational principles for sensing, processing, analyzing, and learning low-dimensional structures from high-dimensional data. The *targeted core audience* of this book are entry-level graduate students in electrical engineering and computer science (EECS), especially in the areas of *data science, signal processing, optimization, machine learning*, and *applications*. This book equips students with systematic and rigorous training in concepts and methods of high-dimensional geometry, statistics, and optimization. Through a very diverse and rich set of applications and (programming) exercises, the book also coaches students how to correctly use such concepts and methods to model real-world data and solve real-world engineering and scientific problems.

The book is written to be friendly to both instructors and students. It provides ample illustrations, examples, exercises, and programs from which students may gain hands-on experience with the concepts and methods covered in the book. Materials in this book were developed from several one-semester graduate courses or summer courses offered at the University of Illinois at Urbana-Champaign, Columbia University, ShanghaiTech University, Tsinghua University, and the University of California at Berkeley in the past ten years. The main prerequisites for such a course are college-level linear algebra, optimization, and probability. To make this book accessible to a broader audience, we have tried to make the book as self-contained as possible: we give a crisp summary of facts used in this book from linear algebra, optimization, and statistics in the Appendices. For EECS students, preliminary courses on signal processing, matrix analysis, optimization, or machine learning will improve their appreciation. From our experiences, besides beginning graduate students, many senior undergraduate students at these institutes were able to take the course and read the book without serious difficulty.

Organization of This Book

The main body of this book consists of three inter-related parts: *Principles, Computation*, and *Applications*. The book also contains five *Appendices* on related background knowledge.

- *Part I: Principles (Chapters 2–7)* develops the fundamental properties and theoretical results for sparse, low-rank, and general low-dimensional models. It characterizes the conditions, in terms of sample/data complexity, under which the inverse problems of recovering such low-dimensional structures become tractable and can be solved efficiently, with guaranteed correctness or accuracy.
- *Part II: Computation (Chapters 8–9)* introduces methods from convex and nonconvex optimization to develop practical algorithms that are tailored for recovering the low-dimensional models. These methods show powerful ideas how to systematically improve algorithm efficiency and reduce overall computational complexity so that the resulting algorithms are fast and scalable to large-size and high-dimensional data.
- *Part III: Applications (Chapters 10–16)* demonstrates how principles and computational methods in the first two parts could significantly improve the solutions to a variety of real-world problems and practices. These applications also coach how the idealistic models and algorithms introduced in this book should be properly customized and extended to incorporate additional domain-specific knowledge (priors or constraints) about the applications.
- *Appendices A–E* at the end of the book are meant to make the book largely self-contained. The appendices cover basic mathematical concepts and results from linear algebra, optimization, and high-dimensional statistics that are used in the main body of the book.

The overall organization of these chapters (and appendices) as well as their logical dependence is illustrated in Figure 0.4.

How to Use This Book to Teach or to Learn

The book contains enough material for a two-semester course series. We have purposely organized the material in the book in a modular fashion so that the chapters and even sections can be easily selected and organized to support different types of courses. Here are some examples:

- *A One-Quarter Course on Sparse Models and Methods* for Graduate or Upper Division Undergraduate Students: the introduction Chapter 1 and two theoretical Chapters 2 and 3; the convex optimization Chapter 8, and two to three applications from Chapters 10, 11, and 13, plus some appendices will be ideal for an eight- to ten-week summer or quarter course for senior undergraduate students and early-year graduate students. That is essentially the red route highlighted in Figure 0.4.

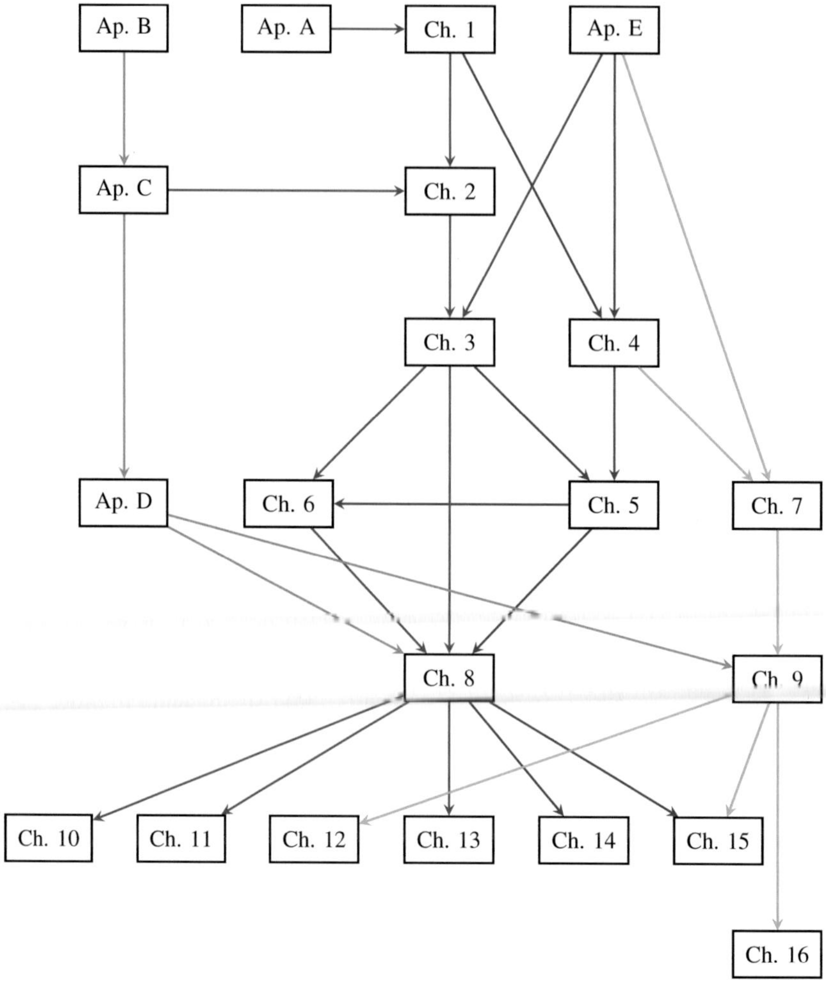

Figure 0.4 Organization chart of the book: dependence among chapters and appendices. Red route: sparse recovery via convex optimization. Blue route: low-rank recovery via convex optimization. Green route: nonconvex approach to low-dimensional models. Orange route: development of optimization algorithms.

- *A One-Semester Course on Low-Dimensional Models* for early-year Graduate Students: the introduction Chapter 1 and the four theoretical Chapters 2–5; the convex optimization Chapter 8, and the several application Chapters 10, 11, 13–15, plus the appendices will be adequate for a one-semester course on low-dimensional models for graduate students. That is essentially both the red and the blue routes highlighted in Figure 0.4.
- *An Advanced-Topic Course on High-Dimensional Data Analysis* for senior Graduate Students who conduct research in related areas: with the previous course as prerequisite, a more in-depth exposition of the mathematical principles, including Chapter 6 on convex methods for general low-dimensional models and Chapter 7

on nonconvex methods. One then can give a more in-depth account of the associated convex and nonconvex optimization methods in Chapters 8 and 9, and several application Chapters 12, 15, and 16 for nonlinear and nonconvex problems. Those are essentially the green and the orange routes highlighted in Figure 0.4. In addition, the instructor may choose to cover new developments in the latest literature, such as broader families of low-dimensional models, more advanced optimization methods, and extensions to deep networks (for low-dimensional submanifolds), say along open directions suggested in the epilogue of Chapter 16.

Certainly, this book can be used as a supplementary textbook for existing (graduate-level) courses on *signal processing* or *image processing*, since it offers more advanced new models, methods, and applications. It can also be used as a complementary textbook for more traditional courses on *optimization* as Chapters 8 and 9 give a rather complete and modern coverage of the first-order (hence more scalable) methods. For a conventional *machine learning* or *statistical data analysis* course, this book may serve as an additional reference for deeper and broader extensions to classic regression analysis, principal component analysis, and deep learning. For a more theoretical course on *high-dimensional statistics and probability*, this book can be used as a secondary text and provides ample motivating and practical examples.

In the future, we would very much like to hear from experienced instructors and seasoned researchers about other good ways to teach or study material in this book. We will share those experiences, suggestions, and even new contributions (examples, exercises, illustrations, etc.) at the book's website, which also contains demos, source code, and other supplementary materials:

https://book-wright-ma.github.io

Further information on the book can also be found on the Cambridge University Press website:
www.cambridge.org/9781108489737 (DOI: 10.1017/9781108779302)

Acknowledgements

Yi was first introduced to the subject of sparse representation by Professor David Donoho of Stanford when David visited the University of Illinois in 2005. During the dinner, David and Yi discussed Yi's research interests at that time: in particular *generalized principal component analysis* (GPCA) [VMS16], a subject that aims to learn an arbitrary mixture of low-dimensional subspaces from high-dimensional mixed data. David commented that GPCA in its most general setting would be an extremely challenging problem. He suggested starting with the simpler sparse model for which data are assumed to lie on a special family of subspaces.[13] Soon after that, Yi studied the subject of sparse representation systematically, especially during his sabbatical leave at Microsoft Research Asia in Dr. Harry Shum's group in 2006 and later at Berkeley in Professor Shankar Sastry's group in 2007. He was profoundly influenced and inspired by a series of seminal work at the time from Emmanuel Candès and Terence Tao on compressive sensing, error correction, and low-rank matrix recovery.

Since then, we have had the greatest fortune to work closely with many wonderful colleagues in this exciting new field. They are: Emmanuel Candès, Michael Elad, Guillermo Sapiro, Mario Figueiredo, René Vidal, Robert Fossum, Harm Derksen, Thomas Huang, Xiaodong Li, Shankar Sastry, Jitendra Malik, Carlos Fernandez, Julien Mairal, Yuxin Chen, Zhihui Zhu, Daniel Spielman, Peter Kinget, Abhay Pasupathy, Daniel Esposito, Szabolcs Marka, and Zsuzsa Marka. We would also like to thank many of our former colleagues from when we visited or worked at Microsoft Research and other places: Harry Shum, Baining Guo, Weiying Ma, Zhouchen Lin, Yasuyuki Matsushita, Zuowen Tu, David Wipf, Jian Sun, Kaiming He, Shuicheng Yan, Lei Zhang, Liangshen Zhuang, Weisheng Dong, Xiaojie Guo, Xiaoqin Zhang, Kui Jia, Tsung-Han Chan, Zinan Zeng, Guangcan Liu, Jingyi Yu, Shenghua Gao, and Xiaojun Yuan. These collaborations have broadened our knowledge and enriched our experience in this field. Many results featured in this book are conveniently borrowed from these years of fruitful collaborations.

We would like to send special thanks to our former students Allen Yang, Chaobing Song, Qing Qu, and Yuqian Zhang for directly helping with content in some of the chapters. Allen has been of great help during early germination of the book project,

[13] In the last chapter of this book, Chapter 16, we will see a rather unexpected connection between sparse models and GPCA, through an unexpected third party: *deep learning*. Concepts developed for GPCA such as lossy coding rates for clustering subspaces, in Chapter 6 of [VMS16], will play a crucial role in understanding deep networks.

back to early 2013. He has helped draft early versions of the application chapters on magnetic resonance imaging and robust face recognition. Chaobing has helped transform the optimization chapters with a unified parsimonious approach to optimization algorithm design and brought this classic topic to the modern context of scalable computation. We would also like to thank some of our colleagues who have generously shared some material for this book: Bruno Olshausen, Michael Lustig, Julien Mairal, Yuxin Chen, Sam Buchanan, and Tingran Wang.

We would like to thank many of our former and current students. Their research has contributed to many of the results featured in this book. Many of them have also kindly helped with proofreading drafts of the book during different stages or helped in developing exercises as they were taking or teaching assistants for the courses based on early drafts of this book. They are Allen Yang, Arvind Ganesh, Andrew Wagner, Shankar Rao, Zihan Zhou, Hossein Mobahi, Jianchao Yang, Kerui Min, Zhengdong Zhang, Yigang Peng, Xiao Liang, Xin Zhang, Yuexiang Zhai, Haozhi Qi, Yaodong Yu, Christina Baek, Zhengyuan Zhou, Chaobing Song, Chong You, Yuqian Zhang, Qing Qu, Han-Wen Kuo, Yenson Lau, Robert Colgan, Dar Gilboa, Sam Buchanan, Tingran Wang, Jingkai Yan, and Mariam Avagyan.

Last but not the least, we are grateful for generous financial support through all these years from the National Science Foundation, Office of Naval Research, Tsinghua Berkeley Shenzhen Institute, Simons Foundation, Sony Research, HTC, and VIA Technologies Inc.

1 Introduction

"*Entities should not be multiplied without necessity.*"

– William of Ockham, *Law of Parsimony*

1.1 A Universal Task: Pursuit of Low-Dimensional Structure

The problem of identifying low-dimensional structure of signals or data in high-dimensional spaces is one of the most fundamental problems that, through a long history, interweaves many engineering and mathematical fields such as system theory, pattern recognition, signal processing, machine learning, and statistics.

1.1.1 Identifying Dynamical Systems and Serial Data

The low dimensionality of real-world signals or data often arises from the intrinsic physical mechanisms from which the data are generated. Many real-world signals or data are observations of physical processes governed by certain generative mechanisms. For instance, magnetic resonance (MR) images[1] are generated by manipulating magnetic fields that obey Maxwell's equations; dynamics of any mechanical systems such as cars and legged robots follow Newton's laws of motion.

Mathematically such dynamics can often be modeled by a set of differential equations,[2] also known as a *state-space model* in system theory [CD91, Sas99]:

$$\begin{cases} \dot{\boldsymbol{x}}(t) = f(\boldsymbol{x}(t), \boldsymbol{u}(t)), \\ \boldsymbol{y}(t) = g(\boldsymbol{x}(t), \boldsymbol{u}(t)), \end{cases} \tag{1.1.1}$$

where $\boldsymbol{x} \in \mathbb{R}^n$ is the state, $\boldsymbol{u} \in \mathbb{R}^{n_i}$ is the input, and $\boldsymbol{y} \in \mathbb{R}^{n_o}$ is the (observed) output. Governed by such dynamical models, the output $\boldsymbol{y}(t)$ and state $\boldsymbol{x}(t)$ as functions in time t cannot be free and they are restricted to a certain *low-dimensional submanifold* in their respective functional space.

[1] That we will study in detail in Chapter 10.

[2] Here, for simplicity, we only consider ordinary differential equations. But the same argument carries over to data or signals associated with partial differential equations.

To see this more clearly, we consider the simplified case when the dynamical model is (discrete) linear time-invariant [CD91, OSB99]:[3]

$$\begin{cases} \boldsymbol{x}(t+1) = \boldsymbol{A}\boldsymbol{x}(t) + \boldsymbol{B}\boldsymbol{u}(t), \\ \boldsymbol{y}(t) \quad\;\; = \boldsymbol{C}\boldsymbol{x}(t) + \boldsymbol{D}\boldsymbol{u}(t). \end{cases} \tag{1.1.2}$$

According to the theory of system identification [VOdM96], the observed output $\{\boldsymbol{y}(t)\}_{t=1}^{\infty}$ is correlated with the input $\{\boldsymbol{u}(t)\}_{t=1}^{\infty}$ through a subspace of dimension no more than $n = \dim(\boldsymbol{x})$. To be more precise, let us define two *Hankel*-type matrices:

$$\boldsymbol{Y} \doteq \begin{bmatrix} \boldsymbol{y}(1) & \boldsymbol{y}(2) & \cdots & \boldsymbol{y}(N) \\ \boldsymbol{y}(2) & \boldsymbol{y}(3) & \cdots & \boldsymbol{y}(N+1) \\ \vdots & \vdots & \ddots & \vdots \\ \boldsymbol{y}(N) & \boldsymbol{y}(N+1) & \cdots & \boldsymbol{y}(2N-1) \end{bmatrix} \in \mathbb{R}^{n_o N \times N}, \quad \boldsymbol{U} \doteq \begin{bmatrix} \boldsymbol{u}(1) & \boldsymbol{u}(2) & \cdots & \boldsymbol{u}(N) \\ \boldsymbol{u}(2) & \boldsymbol{u}(3) & \cdots & \boldsymbol{u}(N+1) \\ \vdots & \vdots & \ddots & \vdots \\ \boldsymbol{u}(N) & \boldsymbol{u}(N+1) & \cdots & \boldsymbol{u}(2N-1) \end{bmatrix} \in \mathbb{R}^{n_i N \times N}.$$

Then from (1.1.2), the two matrices $\boldsymbol{Y}$ and $\boldsymbol{U}$ are related as

$$\boldsymbol{Y} = \boldsymbol{G}\boldsymbol{X} + \boldsymbol{H}\boldsymbol{U}, \tag{1.1.3}$$

where $\boldsymbol{G}$ and $\boldsymbol{H}$ are matrices with blocks of the form $\boldsymbol{C}\boldsymbol{A}^i$ and $\boldsymbol{C}\boldsymbol{A}^i\boldsymbol{B}$ respectively, and

$$\boldsymbol{X} = [\boldsymbol{x}(1), \boldsymbol{x}(2), \ldots, \boldsymbol{x}(N)] \quad \in \mathbb{R}^{n \times N}.$$

Let $\boldsymbol{U}^{\perp}$ be the orthogonal complement to $\boldsymbol{U}$.[4] We have

$$\boldsymbol{Y}\boldsymbol{U}^{\perp} = \boldsymbol{G}\boldsymbol{X}\boldsymbol{U}^{\perp}. \tag{1.1.4}$$

Hence we have:

FACT 1.1. (Linear system identification) *Regardless of the measurement sequence length N, the so-defined input–output matrix $\boldsymbol{Y}\boldsymbol{U}^{\perp}$ is always of rank less than or equal to the dimension n of the state space:*

$$\operatorname{rank}(\boldsymbol{Y}\boldsymbol{U}^{\perp}) \leq n. \tag{1.1.5}$$

In other words, the column vectors of the matrix $\boldsymbol{Y}\boldsymbol{U}^{\perp}$ span an n-dimensional subspace in an ambient space of $\mathbb{R}^{n_o N}$. From the theory of system identification [VOdM96, LV09, LV10], recovering this n-dimensional subspace associated with the input and output is the key to identifying the (unknown) parameters of the system $(\boldsymbol{A}, \boldsymbol{B}, \boldsymbol{C}, \boldsymbol{D})$ as they can subsequently be computed from the singular value decomposition[5] of the matrix $\boldsymbol{Y}\boldsymbol{U}^{\perp}$. In fact, system identification is one of the first problems that have inspired the convex approach for low-rank models [FHB01], which we will thoroughly study in Chapter 4.

[3] In many applications, linear time-invariant models can be viewed as a good approximation to real dynamical systems that could be mildly nonlinear or slowly time-varying. Or for many classes of nonlinear systems, they can be converted, either via feedback linearization [Sas99] or via a smooth nonlinear Koopman operator [Koo31, LKB18], to linear dynamical systems.

[4] That is, columns of $\boldsymbol{U}^{\perp}$ span the null space of $\boldsymbol{U}$. See Appendix A.

[5] For details on singular value decomposition, see Section A.8 of Appendix A.

Figure 1.1 From left to right: a texture image of regular pattern, a binary image of a Chinese character which is nearly symmetric, and an image of the Tiantan Temple of Beijing, which has a cylindrical body with its surface decorated with regular structural patterns.

EXAMPLE 1.2. (Recurrent neural network) *Notice that, in modern practice of* deep neural networks *(DNNs), variants to such state-space models*[6] *have been widely adopted, also known as* recurrent neural networks *(RNNs). A typical RNN model is of the so-called Jordan form [Jor97]:*

$$\begin{cases} \boldsymbol{x}(t+1) = \sigma_{\boldsymbol{x}}(\boldsymbol{A}\boldsymbol{x}(t) + \boldsymbol{B}\boldsymbol{u}(t) + \boldsymbol{b}), \\ \boldsymbol{y}(t) \quad\quad\; = \sigma_{\boldsymbol{y}}(\boldsymbol{C}\boldsymbol{x}(t) + \boldsymbol{d}), \end{cases} \tag{1.1.6}$$

where $\sigma_{\boldsymbol{x}}$ and $\sigma_{\boldsymbol{y}}$ are certain nonlinear activation functions.[7] *RNNs and their many variants have empirically proven to be very effective for modeling serial data such as speech signals, videos, and natural languages. The intrinsic low dimensionality of such models is the key to capturing structure or order in such serial data. Fundamental concepts, principles, and methods developed in this book will lead to a principled understanding of such deep models, as we will see in Chapter 16.*

1.1.2 Patterns and Orders in a Man-Made World

Of course, many other factors may contribute to the ubiquitous presence of low-dimensional structures in real-world data that do not necessarily involve natural dynamics or serial order. Another ample source of low-dimensional structures is due to human influence: almost all man-made objects are built by following simple code, rules, and procedures, for both economy and beauty. Those structures often visually manifest as repeated patterns in textures and decorations; symmetry in letters and characters; parallel, orthogonal, and regular shapes in man-made objects and architectures, etc., as shown by the few examples in Figure 1.1 and many more to be given in Chapter 15.

If we are to model such structures mathematically, low-dimensional models become the natural choices. For example, consider the leftmost image of a regular texture in Figure 1.1. We may view pixels of the 2D image array as the entries of a matrix $\boldsymbol{M}$,

[6] Usually with additional nonlinear activations introduced to places in the state space model.

[7] Popular choices of activation functions include the sigmoid function $\sigma(x) = e^x/(e^x + 1)$ or the rectified linear unit (ReLU) function $\sigma(x) = \max\{0, x\}$.

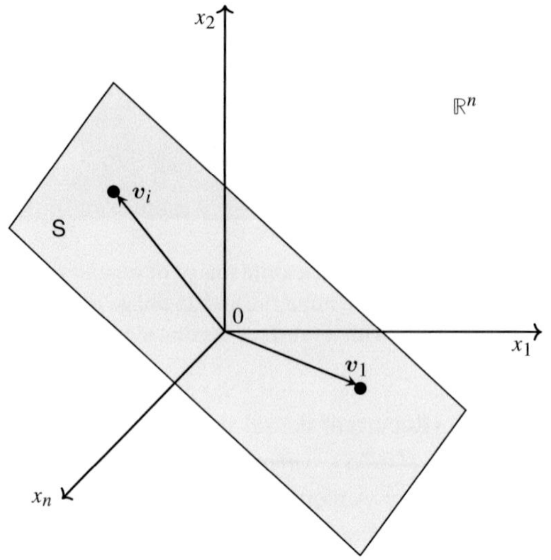

Figure 1.2 Column vectors $v_i \in \mathbb{R}^n$ of a low-rank $n \times n$ matrix span a low-dimensional subspace $\mathsf{S} \subset \mathbb{R}^n$.

say a matrix of $n \times n$ pixels. Obviously the column (or row) vectors of this matrix, viewed as vectors v_i in $\mathbb{R}^n$, are highly linearly dependent. They actually span only a very low-dimensional subspace S whose dimension, say d, is much less than n, as illustrated in Figure 1.2. That is

$$\operatorname{rank}(\boldsymbol{M}) = d \ll n. \tag{1.1.7}$$

Notice that this is the same type of low-rank condition that we have seen in the system identification problem (1.1.4). In the application Chapter 15, we will see how such natural low-rank regular textures would allow us to efficiently, accurately, and robustly recover geometric information encoded in such images – revealing the reason why we are able to accurately perceive 3D geometry of the Tiantan Temple and recover the rectified 2D texture from only a single image, shown on the right of Figure 1.1.

As a matter of fact, even for any generic 3D scene, when taking photos from multiple poses, the multiple 2D images of the same point, line, plane, or (symmetric) object in 3D are all related in such a way that a certain measurement matrix, known as the *multiple-view matrix* $\boldsymbol{M}$, becomes low-rank [MSKS04]. In fact, somewhat remarkably, the rank of such matrices will always be

$$\operatorname{rank}(\boldsymbol{M}) = 1 \text{ or } 2, \tag{1.1.8}$$

regardless of the number of views or the size of the matrix. A similar low-rank condition applies to multiple images of the same scene taken under different lighting conditions: $\operatorname{rank}(\boldsymbol{M}) = 3$, as we will study thoroughly in Chapter 14.

In general, we do not expect all data in human society to be equally regular and orderly. Nevertheless, many data that arise from societal, commercial, and financial

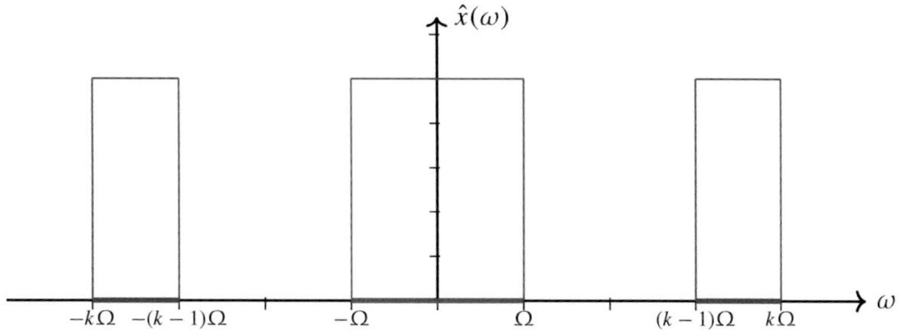

Figure 1.3 Functions with spectra supported in the red region are known as band-limited functions. They have the same size of spectral support as functions with spectra supported in the two blue regions.

activities or from social networks do exhibit very good patterns that can be well approximated by low-dimensional models, as we will see from plenty of examples in Chapters 4 and 5 and in the application Chapters 14–16. In this book we will establish the fundamental principles and algorithms that would allow us to exploit such low-dimensional structures in real data for correctly and efficiently recovering information from minimal (incomplete or imperfect) observations.

1.1.3 Efficient Data Acquisition and Processing

In classical signal processing, the intrinsic low dimensionality of data is mostly exploited for purposes of efficient sampling, storage, and transport [OSB99, PV08]. In applications such as communication, it is often reasonable to assume the signals of interest mainly consist of limited frequency components.[8] To be more precise, consider a signal $x(t)$ as a function of time t and its Fourier transform:[9]

$$\hat{x}(\omega) \doteq \int_{-\infty}^{\infty} x(t)\exp(-\mathrm{i}\omega t)dt. \tag{1.1.9}$$

Typically $\hat{x}(\omega)$ will be zero when $|\omega| \geq \Omega$ for some $\Omega > 0$. Let $\mathcal{B}_1(\Omega)$ be the set of *band-limited functions* whose Fourier transform vanishes outside of the spectrum $[-\Omega, \Omega]$:

$$\mathcal{B}_1(\Omega) \doteq \left\{ x \in L^1(\mathbb{R}) \mid \hat{x}(\omega) = 0 \;\; \forall\, |\omega| > \Omega \right\}, \tag{1.1.10}$$

as illustrated in Figure 1.3.

In other words, all functions in $\mathcal{B}_1$ have a maximal cutoff frequency $f_{\max} = \Omega/2\pi$. Notice that $\mathcal{B}_1$ forms *a subspace* in the space of all functions, just like the range of a low-rank matrix is a subspace in a vector space. This structure allows us to represent

[8] As analog and digital information is often physically carried by modulating periodic signals generated by resonant circuits, as we will elaborate more in Chapter 11.

[9] One may see Appendix A for a discretized version of the Fourier transform, equation (A.7.13), that can be applied to discretized signals or vectors.

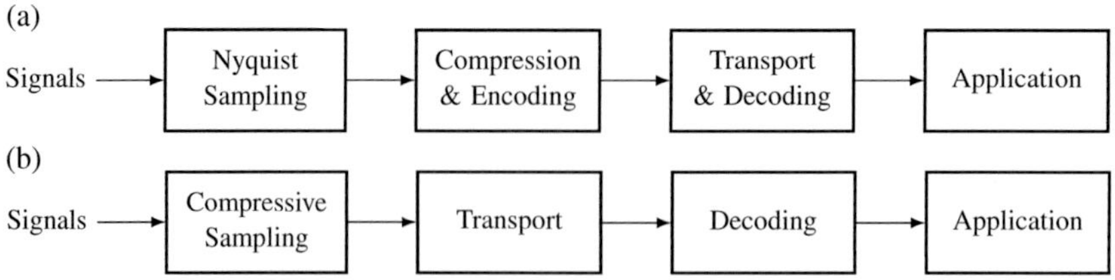

Figure 1.4 Comparison of classical signal acquisition and processing pipeline (a) and the compressive sensing paradigm to be introduced in this book (b).

such functions rather efficiently with their discrete samples. To see this, given $\hat{x}(\omega)$ the signal $x(t)$ can be expressed by the inverse Fourier transform:

$$x(t) = \frac{1}{2\pi}\int_{-\infty}^{\infty} \hat{x}(\omega)\exp(\mathrm{i}\omega t)d\omega = \frac{1}{2\pi}\int_{-\Omega}^{\Omega} \hat{x}(\omega)\exp(\mathrm{i}\omega t)d\omega. \tag{1.1.11}$$

So if we view $\hat{x}(\omega)$ as a periodic function in the spectral domain with a period 2Ω, it is fully determined by all its Fourier coefficients:

$$x\left(\frac{n\pi}{\Omega}\right) \doteq \frac{1}{2\pi}\int_{-\Omega}^{\Omega} \hat{x}(\omega)\exp\left(\mathrm{i}\omega\frac{n\pi}{\Omega}\right)d\omega, \quad n = 0, \pm 1, \pm 2, \dots. \tag{1.1.12}$$

Notice that the left hand side is precisely the values of the function $x(t)$ sampled with a period $T = \pi/\Omega$, or equivalently at a frequency

$$f = \frac{1}{T} = 2 \cdot \frac{\Omega}{2\pi}. \tag{1.1.13}$$

Hence we have:

FACT 1.3. (Nyquist–Shannon sampling) *To perfectly recover a band-limited signal $x(t)$, we need to sample it at a rate that is twice its maximal frequency $f_{\max} = \Omega/2\pi$.*

This is known as the classical *Nyquist–Shannon* sampling theorem [OSB99]. The sampled (hence discrete) signal can then be digitized and compressed based on its additional statistics. For images, such sampling and subsequent compression are done by the popular schemes such as JPEG or MPEG for videos. The compressed data are then used for storage, transport, and to be decoded later for various applications. Figure 1.4(a) illustrates a traditional pipeline for data acquisition and processing.

However, for signals that contain both low-frequency and high-frequency components, sampling at the Nyquist rate sometimes can be rather costly. For instance, as shown in Figure 1.3, for signals with their spectrum supported only in the red area, their maximum cutoff frequency is $\Omega/2\pi$; yet for signals with spectrum supported only in the blue areas, the maximum frequency is $k \cdot \Omega/2\pi$. So when k is very large (which is the situation in modern wideband wireless communication, see Chapter 11), the Nyquist sampling scheme would be rather expensive to realize. As an important example, in order to capture sharp edges or boundaries in natural images,[10] the number of pixels of imaging sensors in digital cameras has increased dramatically in recent

[10] A sharp edge can be represented by a step function which is not band-limited!

years. Such a *brute force* sensing scheme is obviously rather wasteful since sharp edges occupy only a very tiny fraction of the image and yet all the relatively smooth regions are sampled at the same rate! In medical imaging, such brute force increasing of sampling density is not even allowed due to patient comfort and safety [LDP07].

As we will see in this book, the number of samples truly needed to recover a signal should be proportional to the total width of its spectral support regardless of the location! For the examples shown in Figure 1.3, both types of signals would have the same effective bandwidth of 2Ω and in principle can be correctly recovered with effectively the same sampling rate. As a result, to acquire signals with spectrum supported in the blue regions, the sampling rate can be significantly lower than the Nyquist sampling rate [Tro10, ME10], hence the notion of "*compressed sensing*" or "*compressive sensing*," coined by [Don06a, Can06]. We will see in Chapter 11 precisely how such a new sampling scheme is realized in the context of modern wideband wireless communications.

In this book, we will systematically study the theoretical foundation for designing such compressive sampling schemes in a principled manner and develop algorithms for recovering the full signal from such samples correctly and efficiently. In general, such compressive samples of the signals are already compact enough for storage and transport, and the original signals can be fully recovered later when they are eventually being used. Figure 1.4(b) illustrates this new data acquisition and processing paradigm. In addition to wideband communications, we will also see a few striking applications of this paradigm at work. For instance, this new paradigm has revolutionized the field of medical imaging [LDP07], as we will elaborate more in Chapter 2 and further in Chapter 10.

1.1.4 Interpretation of Data with Graphical Models

In the practice of modern data science, we often deal with data that are not necessarily generated from any clear physical processes or artificial protocols. Their generative mechanisms can be hidden from us or are difficult to derive from first principles. Data such as customer ratings, web documents, natural languages, and gene expression data are such examples. Nevertheless, such data are by no means structureless, and there are usually strong and rich statistical correlation, dependence/independence, and causal relationships among the data.

To model such structure, one may view the observed data as samples of a set of random variables $\boldsymbol{x}_o \in \mathbb{R}^{n_o}$, which are generated through a certain conditional probability distribution given another set of hidden or *latent* variables $\boldsymbol{x}_h \in \mathbb{R}^{n_h}$. The structure of the data is fully described by the joint distribution of the random vector $\boldsymbol{x} = (\boldsymbol{x}_o, \boldsymbol{x}_h) \in \mathbb{R}^n$ with $n = n_o + n_h$. Now consider the n random variables $\{x_i\}_{i=1}^n$ in $\boldsymbol{x}$. For simplicity, let us assume that $\{x_i\}_{i=1}^n$ are jointly zero-mean Gaussian,[11] i.e., $\boldsymbol{x} \sim \mathcal{N}(\mathbf{0}, \boldsymbol{\Sigma})$ with a covariance matrix $\boldsymbol{\Sigma} \in \mathbb{R}^{n \times n}$. Let

[11] In practice, Gaussian can be used to approximate any distribution up to its second-order statistics.

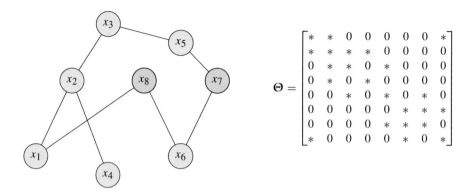

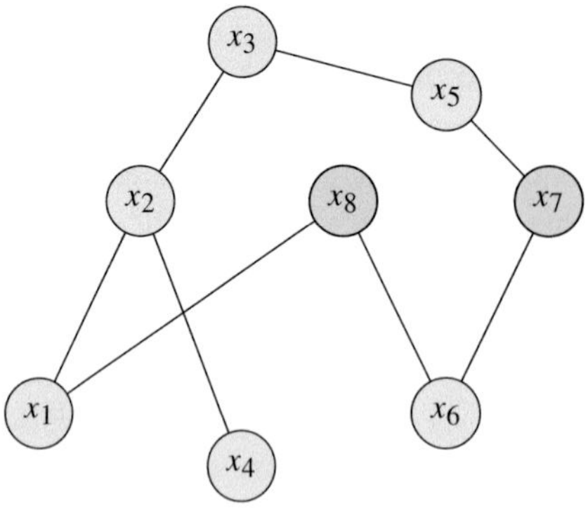

$$\mathbf{\Theta} = \begin{bmatrix} * & * & 0 & 0 & 0 & 0 & 0 & * \\ * & * & * & * & 0 & 0 & 0 & 0 \\ 0 & * & * & 0 & * & 0 & 0 & 0 \\ 0 & * & 0 & * & 0 & 0 & 0 & 0 \\ 0 & 0 & * & 0 & * & 0 & * & 0 \\ 0 & 0 & 0 & 0 & 0 & * & * & * \\ 0 & 0 & 0 & 0 & * & * & * & 0 \\ * & 0 & 0 & 0 & 0 & * & 0 & * \end{bmatrix}$$

Figure 1.5 Graphical model for a set of jointly Gaussian random variables. The inverse covariance matrix $\mathbf{\Theta}$ is often sparse if the dependence graph is sparsely connected. Suppose that gray nodes represent observed variables $\boldsymbol{x}_o = [x_1, x_2, \ldots, x_6]^*$ and blue ones $\boldsymbol{x}_h = [x_7, x_8]^*$ are hidden.

$$\mathbf{\Theta} \equiv \mathbf{\Sigma}^{-1} \quad \in \mathbb{R}^{n \times n}$$

be the inverse of its covariance matrix. From statistics, we have the following well-known fact:

FACT 1.4. (Conditional independence in graphical model) *Any two variables x_i and x_j are conditionally independent given all other variables $\{x_k \mid k \neq i, j\}$ if and only if the (i, j)-th entry of $\mathbf{\Theta}$ satisfies $\theta_{ij} = 0$.*

In machine learning, such dependences among random variables in $\boldsymbol{x} = \{x_i\}_{i=1}^n$ are often described with a *graphical model* [Pea00, Jor03, WJ08], denoted as $\mathcal{G} = (\mathsf{V}, \mathsf{E})$: The set of vertices V consists of all the random variables $\mathsf{V} = \{x_i\}_{i=1}^n$, and the set of edges $\mathsf{E} = \{e_{ij}\}$ indicate dependence among pairs of random variables (x_i, x_j) – there is an edge between x_i and x_j if and only if they are conditionally dependent. Figure 1.5 shows one such example. In fact, the state-space model (1.1.1) in Section 1.1.1 can be viewed as a special case of such latent variable graphical models.[12]

A fundamental and challenging problem in statistical learning is how to infer the joint distribution of $\boldsymbol{x}$ from marginal statistics of the observed variables $\boldsymbol{x}_o$ even if the number of latent variables and their relationships with the observed ones are unknown. In the most basic case when all the variables are jointly Gaussian, we may partition the covariance matrix $\mathbf{\Sigma}$ of $\boldsymbol{x} = (\boldsymbol{x}_o, \boldsymbol{x}_h)$ as

$$\mathbf{\Sigma} = \begin{bmatrix} \mathbf{\Sigma}_o & \mathbf{\Sigma}_{o,h} \\ \mathbf{\Sigma}_{o,h}^* & \mathbf{\Sigma}_h \end{bmatrix} \equiv \begin{bmatrix} \mathbf{\Theta}_o & \mathbf{\Theta}_{o,h} \\ \mathbf{\Theta}_{o,h}^* & \mathbf{\Theta}_h \end{bmatrix}^{-1} \in \mathbb{R}^{n \times n}. \tag{1.1.14}$$

[12] The input $\boldsymbol{u}$ and output $\boldsymbol{y}$ would be the observations and the (randomly initialized) state $\boldsymbol{x}$ would be the hidden latent variables.

Notice that in the above covariance matrix, only the covariance associated with the observed data $\boldsymbol{\Sigma}_o$ can be obtained from (statistics of) the data. Using facts from linear algebra, one can show that $\boldsymbol{\Sigma}_o$ is of the form

$$\boldsymbol{\Sigma}_o^{-1} = \boldsymbol{\Theta}_o - \boldsymbol{\Theta}_{o,h}\boldsymbol{\Theta}_h^{-1}\boldsymbol{\Theta}_{o,h}^* \quad \in \mathbb{R}^{n_o \times n_o}. \tag{1.1.15}$$

In the above expression, the first term $\boldsymbol{\Theta}_o$ will be sparse if the graph $\mathcal{G}$ is and the second term $\boldsymbol{\Theta}_{o,h}\boldsymbol{\Theta}_h^{-1}\boldsymbol{\Theta}_{o,h}^*$ has a rank less than the number of latent variables, which is often relatively small. For the example shown in Figure 1.5, there are only two hidden nodes; hence the rank of the second term would be at most 2 and the first term $\boldsymbol{\Sigma}_o$ would have the same pattern as the upper-left 6×6 submatrix of $\boldsymbol{\Theta}$ shown on the right of the figure. It has been shown that, in general, a graphical model is identifiable via tractable means *only if* the graphical model $\mathcal{G}$ is sufficiently sparse [CPW12]. Popular models such as trees and multilayer deep networks are representative examples of such graphical models.

Under such conditions, the covariance matrix $\boldsymbol{\Sigma}_o$ of the observed variables $\boldsymbol{x}_o$ always has the following *decomposable structure*:

$$\boldsymbol{\Sigma}_o^{-1} = \boldsymbol{S} + \boldsymbol{L} \quad \in \mathbb{R}^{n_o \times n_o}, \tag{1.1.16}$$

where $\boldsymbol{S}$ is a sparse matrix and $\boldsymbol{L}$ is a low-rank matrix. The rank of $\boldsymbol{L}$ is associated with the number of (independent) latent variables in the graph: $\operatorname{rank}(\boldsymbol{L}) = \dim(\boldsymbol{x}_h)$; the sparse matrix $\boldsymbol{S}$ is associated with the conditional dependence of the observed variables – an entry s_{ij} of $\boldsymbol{S}$ is zero if the two observed variables x_i and x_j are *conditionally independent* given the others.

So to a large extent, the problem of inferring the full graphical model $\mathcal{G}$, or the covariance matrix $\boldsymbol{\Sigma}$ in the Gaussian case, reduces to a problem of decomposing a matrix $\boldsymbol{\Sigma}_o^{-1}$ into a low-rank matrix $\boldsymbol{L}$ and a sparse matrix $\boldsymbol{S}$. Although this decomposition problem (1.1.16) is generally *NP-hard*,[13] we will see in Chapter 5, when both $\boldsymbol{L}$ and $\boldsymbol{S}$ are sufficiently low-dimensional, this problem actually becomes *tractable* and can be solved correctly and efficiently by methods introduced in this book.

1.2 A Brief History

Due to the ubiquity and importance of low-dimensional structures, there has been a long and rich history of studying, understanding, and exploiting them in science, engineering, statistics, and computation.

1.2.1 Neural Science: Sparse Coding

Through millions of years of evolution, the brain of humans and other animals, in particular the visual cortex, has adapted well to its living environment. The natural

[13] The well-studied "planted clique" problem [GZ19, BB20] in complexity theory is a special case of this problem, as we will discuss in Chapter 5.

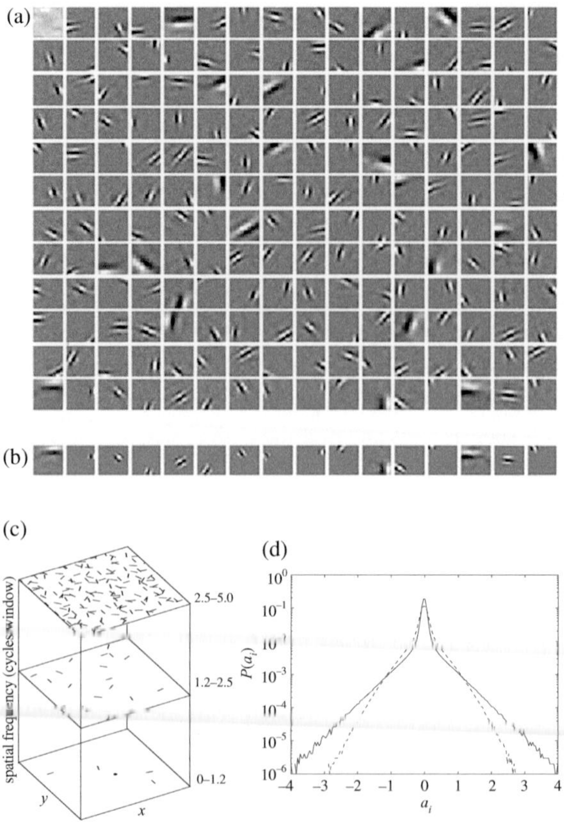

Figure 1.6 (a) Results from training a system of 192 basis functions on 16×16-pixel image patches extracted from natural scenes [OF96b]. (b) The receptive fields corresponding to the last row of basis functions in (a). (c) The distribution of the learned basis functions in space, orientation, and scale. (d) Activity histograms averaged over all coefficients for the learned basis functions (solid line) and for random initial conditions (broken line). Images reprinted with permission from Bruno Olshausen.

vision systems of primates are able to exploit statistics of natural images and achieve highly accurate visual perception with extreme efficiency in time and energy. This phenomenon has long been observed and studied extensively in neural science. Back in 1972, visual neuroscientist Horace Barlow proposed the following *dogma for natural vision* [Bar72]:

> "*. . . the overall direction or aim of information processing in higher sensory centres is to represent the input as completely as possible by activity in as few neurons as possible.*"

In 1987, David Field provided the first scientific evidence in support of this conjecture by showing that the oriented receptive fields of simple cells in the visual cortex are well suited to encode natural images with a small fraction of active units [Fie87]. His results support Barlow's dogma that *the goal of natural vision is to represent the information in the natural environment with minimal redundancy.*

Later in 1996, Bruno Olshausen and David Field had further hypothesized in their seminal work [OF97] that, in biological vision systems, visual sensory input data, say $\boldsymbol{y} \in \mathbb{R}^m$, are represented in terms of the linear combination of a set of elementary patterns (or features) $\boldsymbol{a}_i \in \mathbb{R}^m$:

$$\boldsymbol{y} = \sum_{i=1}^{n} x_i \boldsymbol{a}_i + \boldsymbol{\varepsilon} \quad \in \mathbb{R}^m, \tag{1.2.1}$$

where $\boldsymbol{x} = [x_1, x_2, \ldots, x_n]^* \in \mathbb{R}^n$ are sparse coefficients[14] and $\boldsymbol{\varepsilon} \in \mathbb{R}^m$ is some small modeling error. The collection of all patterns $\boldsymbol{A} = [\boldsymbol{a}_1, \boldsymbol{a}_2, \ldots, \boldsymbol{a}_n] \in \mathbb{R}^{m \times n}$ is called *a dictionary*, which is learned from statistics of the input. When adapted to a large collection of image patches extracted from natural images, the dictionary converges to a set of localized, oriented bandpass functions at different scales (or spatial frequencies) strikingly similar to the receptive fields found in the visual cortex (see Figure 1.6). Such a learned dictionary enables the vision system to reformat sensory information into a sparse code $\boldsymbol{x}$ during the early stages of visual processing. Subsequent studies of a wide range of animal (e.g., mouse, rat, rabbit, cat, monkey) and human brains have provided further evidence for sparse coding of sensory input in natural vision [OF04]. More recent studies of neurons in the monkey cerebellum by Reza Shadmehr's group at Johns Hopkins [HKSS15, HKSS18] further suggest that the same sparse coding dictionary organizes sensory motor control output and prediction errors which, in turn, organizes the entire closed-loop learning network for natural vision.

The fact that sparse coding becomes a central principle for natural vision sends two encouraging messages to engineers: first, seemingly complex real data, such as natural images, do have good intrinsic structures that can be exploited for compact and efficient representations [OF96a]; second, such structures and representations are already learned effectively and efficiently by nature [OF97, GS12, LLT18]. To mathematicians and computer scientists, the second message might seem a little surprising. It contradicts a known fact that finding the sparse code $\boldsymbol{x} \in \mathbb{R}^n$ for a given signal

$$\boldsymbol{y} = \boldsymbol{A}\boldsymbol{x} \quad \in \mathbb{R}^m \tag{1.2.2}$$

is in general an *NP-hard* problem even when the dictionary $\boldsymbol{A}$ is known but overcomplete, i.e., $m < n$ (see Theorem 2.8). Hence sparse coding can be computationally prohibitive and yet nature seems to learn to do it effortlessly. To a large extent, studies in this book reconcile this contradiction by characterizing conditions under which the sparse coding problem can be solved efficiently and effectively (Chapter 3). Furthermore, we will see in a later part of this book (Chapter 7) that, even when the dictionary $\boldsymbol{A}$ is not known in advance and needs to be learned (as in natural vision), given sufficient observations $\boldsymbol{Y} = [\boldsymbol{y}_1, \boldsymbol{y}_2, \ldots, \boldsymbol{y}_N]$,

$$\boldsymbol{Y} = \boldsymbol{A}\boldsymbol{X} \quad \in \mathbb{R}^{m \times N}, \tag{1.2.3}$$

[14] That is, most x_i are zeros.

both the correct dictionary $\boldsymbol{A}$ and associated sparse codes $\boldsymbol{X} = [\boldsymbol{x}_1, \boldsymbol{x}_2, \ldots, \boldsymbol{x}_N]$ can be learned correctly and efficiently, under fairly broad conditions! Eventually, towards the end of the last Chapter 16, we will see how mathematical and computational principles developed in this book might provide compelling mathematical justification for the need of sparse coding (even in nature), as well as other computational mechanisms that resonate more deeply with phenomena observed in neural science or cognitive science.

1.2.2 Signal Processing: Sparse Error Correction

The properties of sparse signals and data have long been studied by mathematicians and statisticians. Throughout history many have explored and proposed computationally efficient ways to exploit such properties. A classical problem in data analysis is to model an observation, say $y \in \mathbb{R}$, as a linear function of a set of known variables $\boldsymbol{a}^* = [a_1, a_2, \ldots, a_n] \in \mathbb{R}^n$:

$$y = f(\boldsymbol{a}) = \boldsymbol{a}^*\boldsymbol{x} = a_1x_1 + a_2x_2 + \cdots + a_nx_n, \tag{1.2.4}$$

where the $\boldsymbol{x} = [x_1, x_2, \ldots, x_n]^* \in \mathbb{R}^n$ are some unknown parameters to be determined. Given multiple, say m, observations of the form

$$y_i = \boldsymbol{a}_i^*\boldsymbol{x} + \varepsilon_i, \quad i = 1, 2, \ldots, m, \tag{1.2.5}$$

where ε_i is possible measurement noise or error, we may stack y_i as entries of a vector $\boldsymbol{y} \in \mathbb{R}^m$ and $\boldsymbol{a}_i^* \in \mathbb{R}^n$ as rows of a matrix $\boldsymbol{A} \in \mathbb{R}^{m \times n}$. The goal is then to find a set of parameters $\boldsymbol{x} \in \mathbb{R}^n$ such that $\boldsymbol{Ax}$ fits well with the given observation $\boldsymbol{y} \in \mathbb{R}^m$. In the classical setting, we usually have the number of measurements larger than the unknowns, i.e., $m \geq n$. Hence there may be no solution $\boldsymbol{x}$ that satisfies the equation $\boldsymbol{y} = \boldsymbol{Ax}$ precisely due to measurement errors.

Least Absolute Deviations versus Least Squares

As early as in 1750, French mathematician Roger Joseph Boscovich had proposed to solve for $\boldsymbol{x}$ that minimizes the absolute deviations between $\boldsymbol{y}$ and $\boldsymbol{Ax}$ [Bos50], namely

$$\min_{\boldsymbol{x}} \|\boldsymbol{y} - \boldsymbol{Ax}\|_1 = \sum_{i=1}^{m} |y_i - \boldsymbol{a}_i^*\boldsymbol{x}|, \tag{1.2.6}$$

where $\|\cdot\|_1$ is the ℓ^1 norm of a vector, which is the sum of absolute values of all its entries. This is also known as the *method of least absolute deviations*. According to a historical account [Pla72], this work had a significant influence on Laplace's conception of Laplace distribution [Lap74]; see Exercise 1.5. During the period which followed Boscovich and Laplace, mainly in the early 1800s, the *method of least squares* was proposed independently by Legendre in 1805 [Leg05] and Gauss in 1809 [Gau09]:

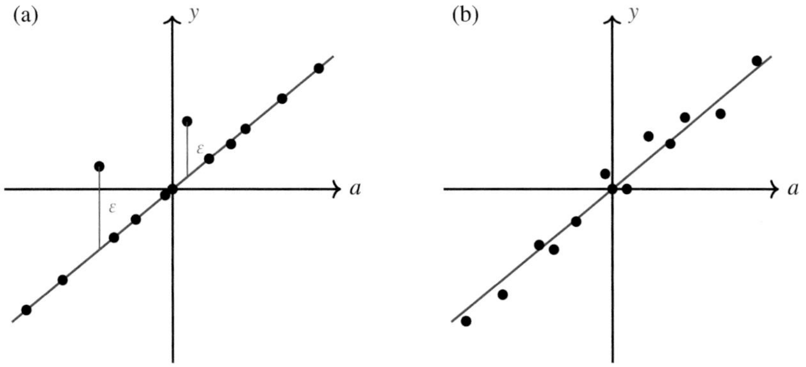

Figure 1.7 Data fitting with few but large errors versus small noise on almost every data point. The least absolute deviations (minimizing ℓ^1 norm of ε) is more suitable for the situation on the left whereas the least squares is for the right.

$$\min_{\boldsymbol{x}} \|\boldsymbol{y} - \boldsymbol{A}\boldsymbol{x}\|_2^2 = \sum_{i=1}^{m} (y_i - \boldsymbol{a}_i^* \boldsymbol{x})^2. \tag{1.2.7}$$

The method of least squares (or minimizing the ℓ^2 norm of errors) is known to be statistically optimal when the measurement errors ε_i are independent and identically distributed (i.i.d.) Gaussian noise.[15] In addition, the optimal minimizer $\boldsymbol{x}_\star$ admits a *closed-form* solution (which we leave as an exercise to the reader), hence was very appealing to practitioners before the age of computers.

At the time of Boscovich and Gauss, people intuitively knew that the least absolute deviations method (1.2.6) is more robust if the measurements contain *large but few* errors, as illustrated in Figure 1.7. However, the precise working conditions of ℓ^1 minimization were mostly not known or clarified, and unlike least squares, there is no closed-form solution to ℓ^1 minimization.[16] As a result, the method of least squares dominated data analysis for the next nearly three centuries! Nevertheless, as we will see in this book, the lack of closed-form solution for ℓ^1 minimization is very much alleviated by modern efficient optimization methods. With computers, solving ℓ^1 minimization is no longer a bottleneck even when the scale is very large (see Chapter 8). Advance in computation has paved the way for a strong return of methods based on numerical solutions such as ℓ^1 minimization. The remaining questions are when ℓ^1 minimization works and why.

Logan's Phenomenon

The theoretical analysis of ℓ^1 minimization for error correction has its earliest roots in work by Benjamin Logan[17] in the 1960s. His PhD thesis, completed at the Electrical

[15] To Gauss' credit, in his work [Gau09], he went beyond Legendre and established the connection between least squares and statistics, and showed its optimality for errors with Gaussian, also known as the normal, distribution. See Exercise 1.5.

[16] Nor were there computers at the time!

[17] Harmonic analyst and signal processor at Bell Labs, and also a renowned bluegrass fiddler.

Engineering Department of Columbia University, featured the following intriguing result:

> "*Suppose we observe a signal y which consists of a* band-limited *signal* x_o, *superimposed with an error* e_o *which is* sparse *in the time domain. If the product of the bandwidth of* x_o *and the size of the support of* e_o *is less than* $\pi/2$, *the true band-limited signal can be recovered by* ℓ^1 *minimization, no matter how large the error is in magnitude, or where its support is located.*"

This observation is known as *Logan's phenomenon*. To state this result slightly more formally, let $\mathcal{B}_1(\Omega)$ be the set of *band-limited functions* whose Fourier transform vanishes outside of $[-\Omega, \Omega]$, as previously defined in (1.1.10). A formal statement of Logan's theorem is as follows:

FACT 1.5. (Logan's theorem) *Suppose that* $y = x_o + e_o$, *with* $x_o \in \mathcal{B}_1(\Omega)$, $\|e_o\|_1 = \int_t |e_o(t)|dt < +\infty$ *and* $\text{supp}(e_o) \subseteq T$. *If*

$$|T| \times \Omega < \frac{\pi}{2}, \tag{1.2.8}$$

then x is the unique solution to the (conceptual) optimization problem

$$\begin{array}{ll} \min & \|x - y\|_1 \\ \text{subject to} & x \in \mathcal{B}_1(\Omega). \end{array} \tag{1.2.9}$$

Here, $|T|$ should be interpreted as the length of T (if T is an interval) or the Lebesgue measure of T (if T is a more general set). This result says that, no matter how large the error e_o is in magnitude, as long as it is sparse enough, it can be exactly corrected by ℓ^1 minimization. Figure 1.8 illustrates the implication of this result. It highlights three different areas (red, blue, and green) of the same size in the spectrum–time space for x_o and e_o, respectively. If the area size is less than $\pi/2$, then x_o and e_o can be separated by ℓ^1 minimization.

Logan was working with an eye towards applications in audio signal processing, in which a band-limited signal is the target of interest, and the corruption e_o is to be removed. Although Logan's result is stated for continuous-time signals, we will give a concrete example that shows how it works for discretized digital signals in Section 2.3.4 of Chapter 2. At this point, acute readers may have recognized the strong conceptual similarity between Logan's problem and the decomposition problem (1.1.16) that we have encountered in learning graphical models.

Logan obtained his result in the mid-1960s. It would be several decades before the modern theory of ℓ^1 minimization began taking form. However, practitioners in many applied computational disciplines were very actively practicing ℓ^1 minimization and related techniques for robust statistical inference with erroneous data, notably practice in the geosciences since the 1970s [CM73, SS86] as well as the work in robust statistics in the 1980s [Hub81, HRRS86]. In many cases, they observed intriguing phenomena, which seemed to parallel Logan's result: ℓ^1 minimization often exactly recovered sparse-enough solutions, and exactly corrected sparse-enough errors. Beginning in the early 2000s, a sequence of theoretical breakthroughs led to increasingly sharper and broader characterizations of the conditions under which ℓ^1 minimization succeeds

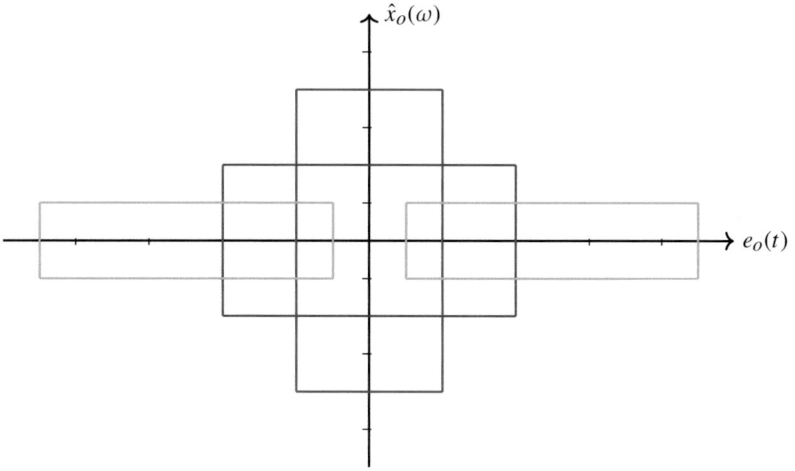

Figure 1.8 Illustration of Logan's Phenomenon: horizontal axis indicates support of e_o in time t, and vertical axis indicates support of the Fourier transform $\hat{x}_o$ of x_o in spectrum ω. All three colored areas have the same separability by ℓ^1 minimization according to Logan's statement.

in error correction (e.g., [CT05, WM10]). These are the conditions which we will develop thoroughly in this book.

1.2.3 Classical Statistics: Sparse Regression Analysis

A classical problem in statistical data modeling is to study how a given random variable, say $y \in \mathbb{R}$, depends on a set of predictive random variables (also known as predictors or features), say $\boldsymbol{a}^* = [a_1, a_2, \ldots, a_n] \in \mathbb{R}^n$. This is known as *regression analysis* [HTF09]. The most popular form is linear regression, in which we try to represent y as a linear superposition of (some or all of) the variables,

$$y = \boldsymbol{a}^*\boldsymbol{x} + \varepsilon = a_1x_1 + a_2x_2 + \cdots + a_nx_n + \varepsilon, \tag{1.2.10}$$

where ε is an error term whose variance is to be minimized:

$$\min \mathbb{E}\big[(y - \boldsymbol{a}^*\boldsymbol{x})^2\big]. \tag{1.2.11}$$

In practice, the problem becomes to find the coefficients $\boldsymbol{x} = [x_1, x_2, \ldots, x_n]^* \in \mathbb{R}^n$ from multiple, say m, samples $\boldsymbol{y} = [y_1, y_2, \ldots, y_m]^*$:

$$\boldsymbol{y} = \boldsymbol{A}\boldsymbol{x} + \boldsymbol{\varepsilon} \quad \in \mathbb{R}^m, \tag{1.2.12}$$

where the rows of $\boldsymbol{A} \in \mathbb{R}^{m \times n}$ are corresponding samples of the predictors. The method of least squares discussed earlier by Legendre and Gauss,

$$\min_{\boldsymbol{x}} \|\boldsymbol{y} - \boldsymbol{A}\boldsymbol{x}\|_2^2, \tag{1.2.13}$$

is arguably the earliest, and the most popular, form of regression in which all the variables $a_1, a_2, \ldots, a_n$ are used to predict y. See Figure 1.9(a) for an example. This is often a reasonable thing to do if the number of variables n is small and they are already chosen to be somewhat independent of one another. One may refer to the recent books [BV18, FLZZ20] for a more extensive exposition of this topic.

Best Subset Selection

In many settings of data analysis, the number of variables n can be very large. Many variables can be irrelevant for the prediction or there could be tremendous redundancy among the relevant ones.[18] Very often the number of predictors could even be larger than the number of available samples, i.e., $n > m$.[19] Hence, in addition to fitting the prediction $\boldsymbol{y}$ with $\boldsymbol{A}\boldsymbol{x}$, one often prefers to find a much smaller subset of the most relevant variables that can best fit $\boldsymbol{y}$ – the so-called *variable selection*. In other words, the coefficient vector $\boldsymbol{x}$ is desired to be a sparse vector with only a few, say $k \leq \min\{m,n\}$, of its entries being nonzero. A natural proposal to select $\boldsymbol{x}$ is to use the least-squares metric:

$$\min_{\boldsymbol{x}} \|\boldsymbol{y} - \boldsymbol{A}\boldsymbol{x}\|_2^2 \quad \text{subject to} \quad \|\boldsymbol{x}\|_0 \leq k, \tag{1.2.14}$$

where $\|\boldsymbol{x}\|_0$ indicates the ℓ^0 norm – the number of nonzero entries of a vector. This is called *the best subset selection problem* in regression analysis and was originally proposed by Hocking and Leslie [HL67] and Beale et al. [BKM67] in 1967. This notion of choosing the minimal subset of relevant variables is related to the more general *principle of minimum description length* proposed by Rissanen in 1978 [Ris78], which argues that, in choosing between various models, we should prefer models which can be encoded most efficiently [HY01].

Although this seems a sensible thing to hope for, directly solving the above subset selection problem is computationally intractable: when k and m become very large, the number of possible supports $\binom{m}{k}$ grows exponentially in k and m. In fact, we will soon see in the next chapter this problem is in general NP-hard. Hence, through its history, several other approaches have been proposed to address the variable selection problem via computationally tractable means.

Stepwise Regression

In 1966, Efroymson [Efr66] proposed a greedy forward (or backward) *stepwise regression* scheme for variable selection: start from an empty index set $\mathsf{I}_0 = \varnothing$, then at each step add to the index set I_k the index of a variable which gives the lowest squared error among all the remaining variables. To be more precise, let $\mathcal{P}_{\mathsf{I}}$ be the orthogonal projection on the range of the submatrix $\boldsymbol{A}_{\mathsf{I}}$ that consists of columns of $\boldsymbol{A}$ indexed by I.

[18] This is certainly the case with natural vision: to detect or identify an object in an image, the possible predictors can be of the same magnitude as the number of pixels. Hence dictionary learning and sparse coding become crucial in order to identify the most informative features that help with the detection.

[19] In the overdetermined case, the least-squares problem (1.2.13) no longer has a unique solution. A classical way to fix this is through introducing an additional Tikhonov-type regularization term $\lambda\|\boldsymbol{x}\|_2^2$, resulting in the so-called *ridge regression* $\min_{\boldsymbol{x}} \|\boldsymbol{y} - \boldsymbol{A}\boldsymbol{x}\|_2^2 + \lambda\|\boldsymbol{x}\|_2^2$. We leave this as an exercise for the reader; see Exercise 1.8.

The greedy selection at each step is given by

$$i_k = \arg\min_{i \notin \mathsf{I}_k} \|\boldsymbol{y} - \mathcal{P}_{\mathsf{I}_k \cup \{i\}}(\boldsymbol{y})\|_2^2, \tag{1.2.15}$$

and the index set is updated accordingly:

$$\mathsf{I}_{k+1} = \mathsf{I}_k \cup \{i_k\}. \tag{1.2.16}$$

This forward stepwise selection scheme is very much similar to more recent greedy algorithms proposed to solve the sparse coding problem, such as the *orthogonal matching pursuit* method that we will see in Chapter 8. Tools introduced in this book will allow us to clarify conditions under which such a greedy scheme succeeds in finding the optimal subset.

Lasso Regression

Notice that the main difficulty in solving the subset selection problem (1.2.14) is the ℓ^0 norm constraint: $\|\boldsymbol{x}\|_0 \leq k$. It makes the problem combinatorial hence challenging to optimize via conventional optimization methods.[20] In 1996, Tibshirani proposed to relax this constraint with the ℓ^1 norm: $\|\boldsymbol{x}\|_1 \leq k$. This leads to the so-called *Lasso regression* [Tib96]:

$$\min_{\boldsymbol{x}} \|\boldsymbol{y} - \boldsymbol{A}\boldsymbol{x}\|_2^2 \quad \text{subject to} \quad \|\boldsymbol{x}\|_1 \leq k. \tag{1.2.17}$$

A similar formulation, known as *basis pursuit*, was proposed in 1998 by [CDS98] which solves the following program:

$$\min_{\boldsymbol{x}} \|\boldsymbol{x}\|_1 \quad \text{subject to} \quad \boldsymbol{y} = \boldsymbol{A}\boldsymbol{x}. \tag{1.2.18}$$

Via convex duality, these problems are equivalent to an unconstrained *convex* optimization:

$$\min_{\boldsymbol{x}} \|\boldsymbol{y} - \boldsymbol{A}\boldsymbol{x}\|_2^2 + \lambda \|\boldsymbol{x}\|_1, \tag{1.2.19}$$

with $\lambda > 0$ a tuning parameter.[21] Compared to the greedy stepwise regression (1.2.15), the global nature of Lasso and basis pursuit leads to many favorable properties, and arguably, they have become the most popular regression methods since the method of least squares. In this book (Chapter 3), we will develop theoretical tools that allow us to fully understand the role of ℓ^1 norm minimization. These tools will help characterize the precise conditions when the above programs, or their variants, succeed in recovering the correct sparse coefficients. In Chapter 8 we further develop efficient algorithms that can solve these optimization problems in very large scale.

[20] Recently there has been some exciting progress in improving computation efficiency of the variable selection problem (1.2.14) via mixed-integer programming [BKM16].

[21] In contrast, the classical *ridge regression* considers an ℓ^2 norm regularization on $\boldsymbol{x}$: $\min_{\boldsymbol{x}} \|\boldsymbol{y} - \boldsymbol{A}\boldsymbol{x}\|_2^2 + \lambda \|\boldsymbol{x}\|_2^2$; see Exercise 1.8.

1.2.4 Data Analysis: Principal Component Analysis

In many applications, the observations can be modeled as samples from a multivariate random vector $\boldsymbol{y} = [y_1, y_2, \ldots, y_m]^* \in \mathbb{R}^m$. As the dimension m can be very high and there is often redundancy among these variables $y_1, y_2, \ldots, y_m$, a central problem in statistics or data analysis is to identify possible strong correlation among these variables and remove the redundancy.

Statistical Perspective
Principal component analysis (PCA) is a classical tool for this purpose. It was first proposed by Pearson in 1901 [Pea01] and later independently by Hotelling in 1933 [Hot33]. The main idea is to project the high-dimensional random vector $\boldsymbol{y}$ onto many fewer directions, represented by a sequence of mutually orthonormal vectors $\{\boldsymbol{u}_i \in \mathbb{R}^m\}_{i=1}^d$, such that the variances are maximized:

$$\boldsymbol{u}_i = \arg\max_{\boldsymbol{u}\in\mathbb{R}^m} \operatorname{Var}(\boldsymbol{u}^*\boldsymbol{y}) \quad \text{subject to} \quad \boldsymbol{u}^*\boldsymbol{u} = 1,\ \boldsymbol{u} \perp \boldsymbol{u}_j,\ \forall j < i. \tag{1.2.20}$$

The vectors $\boldsymbol{u}_i \in \mathbb{R}^m, i = 1, \ldots, d$, are called *principal directions* of $\boldsymbol{y}$ and the projections $w_i = \boldsymbol{u}_i^*\boldsymbol{y}$ are called *principal components* of $\boldsymbol{y}$. By construction w_i will be uncorrelated and they represent directions in which variables in $\boldsymbol{y}$ are most correlated.

Or equivalently, for a properly chosen d, the original high-dimensional random vector is best approximated by the $d \ll m$ principal components as

$$\boldsymbol{y} = \boldsymbol{u}_1 w_1 + \boldsymbol{u}_2 w_2 + \cdots + \boldsymbol{u}_d w_d + \boldsymbol{\varepsilon} \doteq \boldsymbol{U}\boldsymbol{w} + \boldsymbol{\varepsilon}, \tag{1.2.21}$$

where $\boldsymbol{U} = [\boldsymbol{u}_1, \boldsymbol{u}_2, \ldots, \boldsymbol{u}_d] \in \mathbb{R}^{m\times d}$, $\boldsymbol{w} = [w_1, w_2, \ldots, w_d]^* \in \mathbb{R}^d$, and the variance of the residual $\boldsymbol{\varepsilon} \in \mathbb{R}^m$ is minimized:

$$\min \mathbb{E}\big[\|\boldsymbol{y} - \boldsymbol{U}\boldsymbol{w}\|_2^2\big]. \tag{1.2.22}$$

Notice that both linear regression (1.2.10) and PCA minimize least squares of the fitting errors by a low-dimensional linear model. Nevertheless, in regression, one dimension of the data y is preferred and all other variables $a_1, a_2, \ldots, a_n$ are used to predict it, whereas in PCA, all dimensions $y_1, y_2, \ldots, y_n$ are treated equally and the principal components reveal their joint (low-dimensional) structure.[22] Figure 1.9 illustrates the relationship and difference between regression analysis and principal component analysis.

A classical result in statistics states a solution to PCA:

FACT 1.6. (Principal component analysis) *For a zero-mean random vector $\boldsymbol{y} \in \mathbb{R}^m$, its first d principal directions $\{\boldsymbol{u}_i \in \mathbb{R}^m\}_{i=1}^d$ are the d orthonormal eigenvectors of the covariance matrix $\boldsymbol{\Sigma}_{\boldsymbol{y}} = \mathbb{E}[\boldsymbol{y}\boldsymbol{y}^*] \in \mathbb{R}^{m\times m}$ associated with the largest d eigenvalues $\{\lambda_i\}_{i=1}^d$. Moreover, $\lambda_i = \operatorname{Var}(\boldsymbol{u}_i^*\boldsymbol{y}), i = 1, 2, \ldots, d$.*

[22] In terms of machine learning language, one may say that (linear) regression analysis is a *supervised learning* problem whereas principal component analysis is *unsupervised learning*.

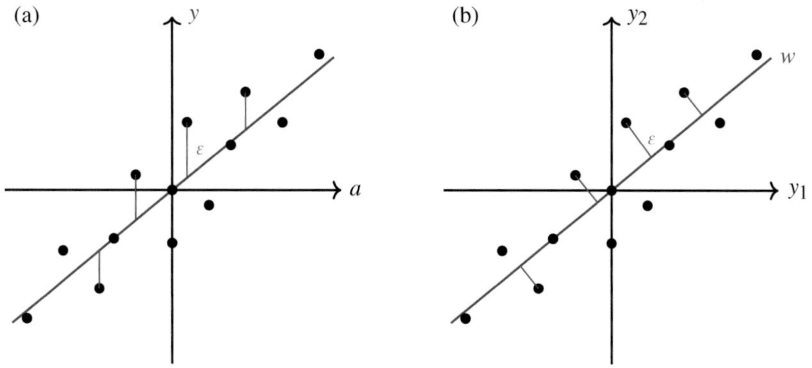

Figure 1.9 Illustration of linear regression (a) versus principal component analysis (b). Linear regression minimizes the least squares of ε, error in predicting the (one) variable y. Principal component analysis (PCA) minimizes the least squares of ε, distance to the estimated low-dimensional principal component w.

To estimate the principal directions $\boldsymbol{U}$ from samples of $\boldsymbol{y}$, we may stack the samples as columns of a matrix $\boldsymbol{Y} \doteq [\boldsymbol{y}_1, \boldsymbol{y}_2, \ldots, \boldsymbol{y}_n] \in \mathbb{R}^{m\times n}$. The covariance of $\boldsymbol{y}$ can be estimated by the sample covariance $\hat{\boldsymbol{\Sigma}}_{\boldsymbol{y}} \doteq (1/n)\boldsymbol{Y}\boldsymbol{Y}^* \in \mathbb{R}^{m\times m}$. So if

$$\boldsymbol{Y} = \boldsymbol{U}\boldsymbol{\Sigma}\boldsymbol{V}^* \tag{1.2.23}$$

is the singular value decomposition (SVD) of $\boldsymbol{Y}$, the estimated principal directions of $\boldsymbol{y}$ will be precisely the leading d singular vectors – the first d columns of $\boldsymbol{U}$. For a more detailed characterization of SVD, one may refer to Appendix A.

Low-Rank Approximation Perspective

Singular value decomposition of a matrix was initially developed in the numerical linear algebra literature by Eckart and Young in 1936 [EY36], independent of PCA.[23] The basic idea of singular value decomposition is to approximate a matrix with a superposition of a few rank-1 matrices (usually expressed in a bilinear outer product form):

$$\boldsymbol{Y} = \sigma_1\boldsymbol{u}_1\boldsymbol{v}_1^* + \sigma_2\boldsymbol{u}_2\boldsymbol{v}_2^* + \cdots + \sigma_d\boldsymbol{u}_d\boldsymbol{v}_d^* + \boldsymbol{E}, \tag{1.2.24}$$

where $\boldsymbol{E}$ is a matrix of small errors or residuals. In fact, the origin of matrix approximation by bilinear forms can be traced back as early as in the work of Beltrami [Bel73] and Jordan [Jor74] in the early 1870s.

To see the connection between SVD and PCA, let us consider the problem of approximating a given (sampled data) matrix $\boldsymbol{Y} \in \mathbb{R}^{m\times n}$ by a matrix $\boldsymbol{X} \in \mathbb{R}^{m\times n}$ of rank less than d in the least-squares sense:

$$\min_{\boldsymbol{X}} \|\boldsymbol{Y} - \boldsymbol{X}\|_2^2 \quad \text{subject to} \quad \operatorname{rank}(\boldsymbol{X}) \le d. \tag{1.2.25}$$

[23] So SVD is also known as the Eckart and Young decomposition [HMH00].

FACT 1.7. (Low-rank approximation) *Let* $Y = U\Sigma V^*$ *be the SVD of the matrix* $Y \in \mathbb{R}^{m \times n}$. *The optimal solution to the above low-rank matrix approximation problem* (1.2.25) *is given by*

$$X_\star = U_d \Sigma_d V_d^*, \tag{1.2.26}$$

where $U_d \in \mathbb{R}^{m \times d}$, $\Sigma_d \in \mathbb{R}^{d \times d}$, *and* $V_d \in \mathbb{R}^{n \times d}$ *are submatrices associated to the top d singular vectors and singular values in* U, Σ, *and* V, *respectively.*

While principal components were initially defined exclusively in a statistical sense [Pea01, Hot33], one can show that the above SVD-based solution gives asymptotically unbiased estimates of the true parameters in the case of Gaussian noise, according to the work of Householder and Young in 1938 [HY38] and then Gabriel in 1978 [Gab78]. A systematic and complete account of statistical properties of PCA can be found in the classic book by Jolliffe in 1986 [Jol86]. Generalization of PCA to models of *multiple* low-dimensional subspaces can be found in a more recent book by Vidal, Ma, and Sastry [VMS16].

Low-rank approximation by least-squares fitting (1.2.25) is a special case for which we have a simple tractable solution as stated in the Fact 1.7. This is in general not the case as rank minimization is typically NP-hard. In Chapters 4 and 5 we will study a much broader family of rank minimization problems and characterize conditions under which they can be solved efficiently.

1.3 The Modern Era

As we have seen in previous sections, low-dimensional structures arise ubiquitously in scientific, mathematical, and engineering problems. Many important instances have been long studied in various fields at different times in history. Many good ideas have been proposed and many effective computational methods have been developed for identifying and exploiting such structures.

1.3.1 From Curses to Blessings of High Dimensionality

In the classical era, due to limited computing resources, studies[24] had typically focused on formulations which allow closed-form solutions or on methods that are amenable to "hand computation," at least when the dimension is moderate (such as PCA, according to Pearson in 1901 [Pea01]). As a result, methods that rely on heavy numerical methods but conceptually superior formulations have been severely understudied and often ignored or forgotten. For instance, as we have seen in the previous section, for both sparse error correction or sparse regression, ℓ^1 minimization is conceptually the preferred formulation. However, its significant advantages have never been fully brought to light until very recently, thanks to efficient optimization methods and powerful computers. They have helped reveal striking properties and

[24] Especially studies that aim to reach at implementable algorithms or practical schemes.

phenomena of ℓ^1 minimization, especially *when the dimension becomes high enough*. Such empirical observations have motivated subsequent theoretical analysis and led to a rather complete and comprehensive theory featured in this book. This renewed understanding of many beneficial geometrical and statistical properties of sparse and many other low-dimensional models in high-dimensional space was celebrated as the "*blessings of dimensionality*" for data science, by Donoho in 2000 [Don00].

Speaking more broadly, in the classical settings, statistical methods and optimization methods were typically applied to data of relatively low dimension or to problems of relatively small scale. Although many profound (and useful) geometric and statistical properties of low-dimensional structure in high-dimensional space were long developed and known to mathematicians [Mat02], such properties had been completely out of reach for computation, hence oblivious to the practice of data analysis till very recently. Around the turn of this century, data science had entered into *a new era*, due to the rise of the Internet and social networks (and many other technological advancements mentioned in the Preface). There has been an explosively growing demand to solve ever larger-scale problems and compute with ever higher-dimensional data. To address such demand, powerful computing platforms and software tools have been developed to solve large-scale optimization problems. Nowadays data scientists and engineers are fully exposed to both good and bad traits of high-dimensional data. Understanding such traits is hence crucial for practitioners and researchers to develop more efficient and reliable algorithms and systems in the future.

As we are entering the new era of *big data computation*, many classical results and methods have become increasingly inadequate for modern data science in one crucial aspect: *lack of precise account of data complexity and computational complexity.*

As our previous survey of the fields and history has shown, many theoretical results have provided profound understanding and correct guidelines for approaching the problems of interest. However, many of the classical results do not directly translate to computationally tractable algorithms or solutions. Many of the statistical and information-theoretic concepts and analyses rely on conditions such as that the distributions of interest are generic. These concepts[25] often become *ill-defined* when the distributions become degenerate (low-dimensional) or *intractable* to compute when the ambient space is high. Most theoretical guarantees for correctness are *asymptotic* in nature. Straightforward implementation of such methods often leads to algorithms whose worst sample complexity or computational complexity grows exponentially in space or time, hence impractical for high-dimensional problems. Practitioners often find existing models and theory ineffective or even irrelevant to their real-world data and problems, hence resort to brute force, heuristic, and sometimes even *ad hoc* methods instead.[26]

Therefore, to provide practitioners in modern data science truly pertinent engineering principles and methodologies, we need to develop a new theoretical platform that

[25] Including some of the most basic quantities such as likelihood, entropy, and mutual information [CT91].

[26] In recent years, the gap between theory and practice has been significantly enlarged by the empirical success and popularity of deep learning, as we will try to address and resolve in Chapter 16.

can rigorously characterize the precise working conditions of a proposed method for low-dimensional structures in high-dimensional spaces:

- The theory would reveal the fundamental reasons why many seemingly intractable high-dimensional problems can be solved efficiently without suffering the curses of dimensionality: *because the intrinsic dimension of the data, hence solution, is very low relative to the dimension of the ambient state space.*
- The platform should also lead to tractable and scalable solutions and algorithms that work in the nonasymptotic regime: *giving precise characterization of the required data complexity*[27] *and computational complexity*[28] *for certain guaranteed accuracy or probability of success.*

Only through the lens of computation can we truly bridge the gap between theory and practice for high-dimensional data analysis and learning, which is the main purpose of this book. To a large extent, the main task of Part I of the book is to characterize precisely the data complexity; that of Part II is to characterize precisely the computational complexity; and that of Part III is to deal with other nonideal factors in real data and applications, such as nonlinearity.

1.3.2 Compressive Sensing, Error Correction, and Deep Learning

Compressive Sensing

Late 1990s regression methods such as Lasso or basis pursuit,

$$\min_{\boldsymbol{x}} \|\boldsymbol{x}\|_1 \quad \text{subject to} \quad \boldsymbol{y} = \boldsymbol{A}\boldsymbol{x}, \tag{1.3.1}$$

have been extensively experimented and practiced in statistics for sparse variable selection. Despite the fact that solving the sparsest solution to an under-determined linear system $\boldsymbol{y} = \boldsymbol{A}\boldsymbol{x}$ with $\boldsymbol{A} \in \mathbb{R}^{m \times n}$ $(m < n)$ is known to be NP-hard in general, overwhelming empirical evidence shows that the correct solution can be recovered effectively and efficiently under fairly broad conditions: for randomly chosen matrix $\boldsymbol{A}$, the above ℓ^1 minimization is able to recover a sparse vector $\boldsymbol{x}$ with support up to a constant fraction of n! This was eventually proven to be the case in 2006 by David Donoho [Don06b], and by Emmanuel Candès, Justin Romberg, and Terence Tao [CRT06b].

In a nutshell, these results suggest that, for a k-sparse signal $\boldsymbol{x}$ in an n-dimensional space $\mathbb{R}^n$, we only need to take approximately $O(k)$ general linear measurements in order to have all its information. In addition, the signal can be correctly and efficiently recovered by minimizing the ℓ^1 norm of $\boldsymbol{x}$ (see Chapter 3). One implication of this result is that if $\boldsymbol{x}$ is a signal that has a high bandwidth but is nevertheless sparse in its spectral domain (as shown in Figure 1.3), then one can sample and recover it at a rate much lower than the Nyquist sampling rate [Tro10, ME10], hence the

[27] Say in the number of samples or measurements, random or designed.
[28] Say in the number of evaluations of gradients.

notion of "*compressed sensing*" [Don06a] or "*compressive sampling*" [Can06]. We will give a real application of this new revelation to wideband wireless communication in Chapter 11.

Error Correction

As we have seen in the previous section, historically ℓ^1 minimization,

$$\min_{\boldsymbol{x}} \|\boldsymbol{y} - \boldsymbol{A}\boldsymbol{x}\|_1, \tag{1.3.2}$$

was proposed to correct (sparse) errors $\boldsymbol{e}$ in signal $\boldsymbol{y} = \boldsymbol{A}\boldsymbol{x} + \boldsymbol{e}$ by Boscovich and later by Logan. The connection between sparse signal recovery and sparse error correction reappeared in the seminal paper "*Decoding by linear programming*" by Candès and Tao in 2005 [CT05], in which more general conditions for the sparse error correction problem were derived. Their work has inspired many highly striking applications such as robust face recognition [WYG$^+$09] by the authors, which we will soon see in the next chapter and Chapter 13.

Ever since, the conditions under which ℓ^1 minimization recovers sparse signals or corrects sparse errors were quickly improved and extended to a broader family of settings and structures. For instance, both the compressive sensing and error correction results for sparse vectors were soon generalized to low-rank matrices [RFP10, CLMW11] (which will be studied in Chapters 4–5) and broader families of low-dimensional structures (see Chapter 6). Collectively, these results have started to reshape the foundation of modern data science, especially high-dimensional data analysis, which we will study systematically in this book.

Deep Learning

The above models are somewhat idealistic in the sense that the relationships between the measurements (output) $\boldsymbol{y}$ and the structured data $\boldsymbol{x}$ are linear and known. In many real-world problems and data, the mapping from $\boldsymbol{x}$ to $\boldsymbol{y}$ can be nonlinear or *unknown* and even the low-dimensional structures of the data $\boldsymbol{x}$ can be *nonlinear*. In this case, one may choose to *compose a sequence of simple maps* to incrementally approximate such a nonlinear and unknown mapping:

$$\begin{cases} \boldsymbol{z}_{\ell+1} = \phi(\boldsymbol{A}^{\ell}\boldsymbol{z}_{\ell}), \quad \boldsymbol{z}_0 = \boldsymbol{x}, \quad \ell = 0, 1, \ldots, L-1, \\ \boldsymbol{y} \quad\;\; = \phi(\boldsymbol{C}\boldsymbol{z}_L), \end{cases} \tag{1.3.3}$$

where $\boldsymbol{A}^{\ell}, \boldsymbol{C}$ are (unknown) matrices, representing linear mappings, and $\phi(\cdot)$ is some basic, typically *sparsity-promoting*, nonlinear activation. The RNN in (1.1.6) is one such example. Such models are also widely known as *deep networks*. Artificial (deep) neural networks have been proposed since the 1940s and 1950s [MP43, Ros58] and extensively studied in the following decades for a variety of problems in pattern recognition, functional approximation, and statistical inference, etc. (see [AB99] for a systematic introduction to this classic topic).

Due to the availability of big data and advancement in high-performance computation in the past decade, it has been shown in the seminal work of Krizhevsky,

Sutskever, and Hinton [KSH12] in 2012 that this class of models can be learned efficiently and effectively and give useful representations for large-scale real-world (visual) data. This has led to tremendous empirical successes of deep networks in a wide variety of applications such as computer vision, speech recognition, and natural languages [LBH15, GBC16]. Despite explosive technological advancements, the practice of deep networks has constantly been haunted by the lack of interpretability and understanding of the so-learned "black box" models, hence lack of rigorous performance guarantees.

Towards the end of the book in Chapter 16, we will see that the role of deep networks, together with their design principles and crucial properties, can be clearly explained, rigorously justified, and even derived as a "white box" from the perspective of learning discriminative low-dimensional representations for high-dimensional data. Therefore, concepts, principles, and methods covered in this book also serve as the foundation for a rigorous and deeper understanding of deep learning, or machine learning in general, in the future.

1.3.3 High-Dimensional Geometry and Nonasymptotic Statistics

To fully understand the reason why information about low-dimensional structure can be encoded by a nearly minimal number of (linear or nonlinear) measurements, and why it can be accurately and efficiently recovered by tractable methods such as convex and nonconvex optimization, we must resort to fundamental mathematical concepts and tools from high-dimensional geometry and nonasymptotic statistics. These are the tools that have enabled people to characterize the precise conditions under which the proposed methods are expected to work.

High-dimensional geometry and statistics are full of phenomena that are diabolically *counterintuitive*. Our geometric intuition developed in the familiar low- (two- or three-) dimensional space is completely useless for understanding what normally takes place in a high-dimensional space.[29] Actually our intuition may often be exactly opposite to the truth! Although many seemingly paradoxical properties of high-dimensional spaces have been long known to mathematicians and theoretical physicists in certain fields, they have stayed mostly alien to engineers and practitioners till not so long ago. This book aims to introduce some of the properties that are most pertinent to modern data science and engineering.[30] Here as a prelude, we give two examples of high-dimensional phenomena that, as we will see later, have a lot to do with explaining the magic of ℓ^1 minimization.

[29] While most people are rather presumptuous about their geometric intuition, be reminded that it took an Einstein to think correctly about the four-dimensional space and time!

[30] For mathematically oriented readers, we recommend the excellent recent books by Wainwright [Wai19] or Vershynin [Ver18] for a systematic exposition of nonasymptotic high-dimensional statistics and probability.

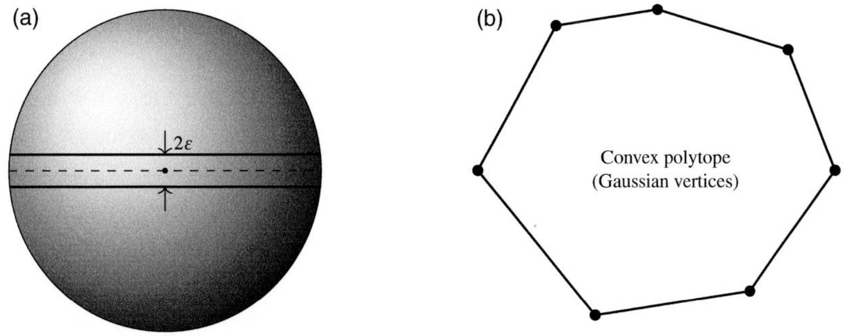

Figure 1.10 Two examples of rather counterintuitive high-dimensional phenomena. (a) Almost all the area of a high-dimensional sphere is concentrated in an ε-strip around its equator, and actually around any great circle! (b) Random samples of a high-dimensional Gaussian span a highly neighborly convex polytope, which is, however, impossible to illustrate with any 2D polytope.

Measure Concentration on a Sphere [Mat02]

Figure 1.10(a) shows an ε-strip around a great circle of a sphere $\mathbb{S}^{n-1}$ in $\mathbb{R}^n$. Here the great circle is the equator with $x_n = 0$. If we want the strip to cover the majority, say 99%, of the area of the sphere,

$$\text{Area}\{\boldsymbol{x} \in \mathbb{S}^{n-1} : -\varepsilon \leq x_n \leq \varepsilon\} = 0.99 \cdot \text{Area}(\mathbb{S}^{n-1}), \qquad (1.3.4)$$

our experience with low-dimensional spheres suggests that ε should be large (close to 1). However, simple calculation shows that, as dimension n increases, ε decreases in the order of $n^{-1/2}$. That is, the width of the strip 2ε can be arbitrarily small as n becomes large. Hence almost all the area of the sphere concentrates around the equator, as shown in Figure 1.10(a). If this is not strange enough, the area also concentrates on the ε-strip around *any* great circle! A rigorous statement will be given in Theorem 3.6 of Chapter 3. There are many bizarre implications of this fact and we encourage the readers to do some brain exercises of their own. We here point out one such implication which has something to do with our later study: If we randomly sample a point on the high-dimensional sphere, say $\boldsymbol{v} \in \mathbb{S}^{n-1}$, then with high probability, this vector will be very close to any of the equators. That is, the inner product of $\boldsymbol{v}$ with each of the standard base vectors (the poles) $\boldsymbol{e}_i \in \mathbb{R}^n$ will be

$$\langle \boldsymbol{v}, \boldsymbol{e}_i \rangle \approx 0, \quad i = 1, 2, \ldots, n. \qquad (1.3.5)$$

In other words, $\boldsymbol{v}$ will be simultaneously nearly orthogonal to all the base vectors $\boldsymbol{e}_i$, or highly *incoherent* to them, in terminology to be used in this book.

Neighborly Polytopes from Gaussian Samples [DT09, DT10]

Consider an m-dimensional Gaussian random vector $\boldsymbol{a} \in \mathbb{R}^m$ whose entries are i.i.d. Gaussian $\mathcal{N}(0, 1/m)$. Now take say $n = 5 \times m$ i.i.d. samples of this random vector and collect them into a matrix: $\boldsymbol{A} = [\boldsymbol{a}_1, \boldsymbol{a}_2, \ldots, \boldsymbol{a}_n] \in \mathbb{R}^{m \times n}$. This gives us a set of n random sample points in $\mathbb{R}^m$. When m is large, say $m = 1000$, then we have

$n = 5000$ points. Our experience with low- (two- or three-) dimensional Gaussian distributions suggests that many of the samples would be "close to the center" as the probability density is the highest there. However, as we will see later, with high probability, these 5000 random points span a convex polytope with every point being one of its vertices, as illustrated in Figure 1.10(b). No points would be inside the interior of the polytope at all! If this is not strange enough, try connecting every pair of the vertices with a line segment. Then none of the segments will be in the interior either and each is an edge of the convex polytope! Actually this is also true for any k vertices for k up to a certain large number. These vertices will span a k-face of the polytope. Such a polytope is called a *k-neighborly polytope* [DT09]. Neighborly polytopes are a rare breed in low-dimensional spaces[31] but are rather abundant and common in high-dimensional spaces. They are also very easy to construct (say by random sampling). As we will see later in Chapter 3 and Chapter 6, it is precisely such properties of high-dimensional polytopes that allow ℓ^1 minimization (1.3.1) to recover any k-sparse vector $\boldsymbol{x}$ from m random measurements $\boldsymbol{A}\boldsymbol{x}$, with m not so much larger than k.

1.3.4 Scalable Optimization: Convex and Nonconvex

The theoretical developments since the early 2000s mentioned above have offered exciting new prospects for practitioners of modern data science. They have provided theoretical guarantees that a very important family of problems, previously deemed as computationally prohibitive (NP-hard) to solve, can become *tractable* under fairly broad conditions. The studies also provide the mathematical tools needed to characterize the precise conditions under which this takes place, and hence provide practitioners very pertinent guidelines when such methods are expected to work.

There is one last hurdle though: just because a problem has become tractable, say being reduced to a tractable convex program, it does not mean the existing solutions or algorithms are already *practical* – meaning efficient enough for high-dimensional data and large-scale problems in the real world.

Return of First-Order Methods

Convex optimization is a classic topic and has been well developed in the literature, e.g., see the textbook by Boyd and Vandenberghe [BV04]. For small to medium-size problems, algorithms such as *the interior point methods* developed in the late 1980s [Wri87, Meg89, MA89a, MA89b] have proven to be extremely efficient and very much become the gold standard for convex programs. However, such algorithms rely on second-order information of the objective function, like the classic Newton's method. The computational and memory cost of computing the second-order derivatives, i.e., the Hessian matrix, can quickly become impractical when the dimension of

[31] Only the triangle in $\mathbb{R}^2$ and the tetrahedron in $\mathbb{R}^3$.

the problems becomes very large – say the number of variables is in the millions or billions.[32]

This has compelled people to use instead *first-order* optimization methods primarily for high-dimensional large-scale problems. The strive for ever growing scalability has shifted the study of optimization to more careful characterization of the computational complexity of the proposed algorithms, even within the family of first-order methods [Nes03, Nem07]. As a result, the acceleration techniques developed by Nesterov in 1983 [Nes83] have drawn significantly new attention. In fact, in recent years, almost all ideas that could have helped improve the convergence rate and reduce computational cost have been carefully reexamined and further refined, leaving almost no stone unturned. Because of this, we feel it is necessary to give a renewed account of optimization methods within the new context of supporting scalable computation: Chapter 8 is for the convex case and Chapter 9 for the nonconvex case.

Return of Nonconvex Formulation and Optimization

When we face a new class of challenging problems, the most natural approach is trying to reduce them to problems for which we already know a good solution. This is the case with the sparse and low-rank recovery problems. We are fortunate that in many cases they can indeed be reduced to convex programs which admit efficient solutions.

However, first of all, convexification has its theoretical limitations (as we will elaborate on in Section 6.3 of Chapter 6), and many problems we encounter in high-dimensional data analysis do not admit meaningful convex relaxation (as we will study in Chapter 7).

Second, the models considered in this book (e.g. sparse or low-rank) are idealistic for developing the fundamental concepts and core principles. They typically assume the low-dimensional data structures are *piecewise linear*. As we will see in the application Chapters 12, 15, and 16, real-world data often have *nonlinear* low-dimensional structures instead. Part of the data modeling and analysis process hence entails learning and undoing such nonlinear transforms if we want to apply principles from this book correctly and successfully.

Finally, very often in practice, we can be forced to adopt a nonconvex formulation due to computational constraints or implementation limitations. Let us consider the example of recovering a low-rank matrix, say $\boldsymbol{X} \in \mathbb{R}^{n \times n}$. When the dimension n becomes extremely high, it could become impossible to store the matrix as it is. We may have to represent the matrix as the product of two unknown low-rank factors,

$$\boldsymbol{X} = \boldsymbol{U}\boldsymbol{V}^*, \quad \boldsymbol{U} \in \mathbb{R}^{n \times r}, \boldsymbol{V} \in \mathbb{R}^{n \times r}, \tag{1.3.6}$$

[32] In addition to solving sparse coding problems, this is also the case for modern optimization methods for training deep neural networks which normally have millions or billions of parameters to tune. For an example, the latest GPT-3 model from OpenAI for natural language processing has a total of *175 billion parameters* to optimize [BMR+20] and the latest Switch Transformers model from Google has 1.6 trillion parameters [FZS21].

with $r \ll n$, in order to push for better scalability of the implementation. In such cases, we are forced to deal with the nonlinear nature of the representation or nonconvex nature of the program head-on [CLC19].

Interestingly enough, such somewhat forced choices lead to very nice surprises [SQW15]. It has been well known that, unlike convex optimization, it is very difficult to ensure global optimality or algorithm efficiency for general nonconvex problems. Nevertheless, as we will see in Chapter 7, for many families of problems that we encounter in high-dimensional data analysis, the problems have natural *symmetric* structure. For example, to represent the low-rank matrix $\boldsymbol{X}$ by two factors as in (1.3.6), there is an equivalent class of solutions: $\boldsymbol{U}\boldsymbol{V}^* = \boldsymbol{U}\boldsymbol{R}\boldsymbol{R}^*\boldsymbol{V}^*$ for any orthogonal matrix $\boldsymbol{R} \in \mathbb{R}^{r \times r}$ in the orthogonal group $\mathsf{O}(r)$. As a result, the associated nonconvex objective functions have extremely good local and global geometric properties. These properties make them amenable to extremely *simple and efficient* algorithms, such as gradient descent and its variants, detailed in Chapter 9. Under very benign conditions, these algorithms actually can converge to *the globally optimal solution* with high efficiency and accuracy [SQW15, MWCC18], quite atypical of nonconvex problems!

Although this is still a rather active research area, scalable nonconvex optimization algorithms used to solve such problems have been well developed for a long time and their computational complexities have been precisely characterized recently. So in Chapter 9 we give a rather complete and coherent survey of scalable nonconvex optimization methods as well as guarantees they offer in terms of the type of critical points converged to and the associated computational complexity. These algorithms are not only useful in the context of recovering low-dimensional structures but also essential to many modern large-scale machine learning problems such as constructing and training deep neural networks, which we will elaborate on more in the final Chapter 16.

1.3.5 A Perfect Storm

According to Wikipedia, "*a perfect storm is an event in which a rare combination of circumstances drastically aggravates the event.*" Then what has taken place in data science and technology in the last couple of decades can be precisely characterized as a "perfect storm," a good one that is. An unexpected combination of several factors has almost simultaneously advanced and contributed to a *revolution* in data science and technology: the massive high-dimensional data, rich scientific or technological applications, and powerful computational and data platforms (such as the cloud technology) have set an ideal stage for fundamental knowledge in high-dimensional geometry and statistics to be efficiently realized and exploited through scalable optimization algorithms. The confluence of these factors, as illustrated in Figure 1.11, has truly brought us into a new era of scientific discovery and engineering marvel.

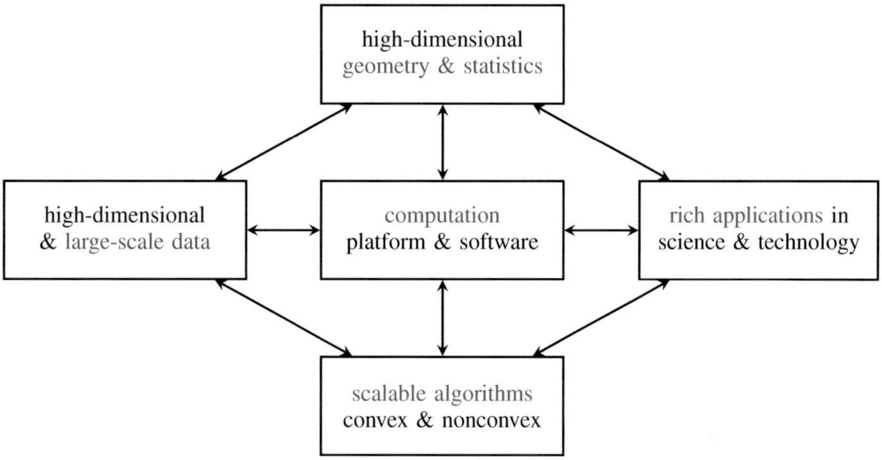

Figure 1.11 A perfect storm for revolutionary knowledge and technology advancement: confluence of the availability of massive data, powerful computational platforms, high-dimensional geometry and statistics, scalable optimization algorithms, and rich applications in science and technology.

1.4 Exercises

1.1. (Nyquist–Shannon sampling theorem) *Prove the Fact 1.3.*

1.2. (Conditional independence of gaussian variables) *Prove the Fact 1.4 for the case of a joint Gaussian vector with three variables* $\boldsymbol{x} = [x_1, x_2, x_3]^*$ *in which* x_1 *and* x_2 *are conditionally independent given* x_3.

1.3. *Given a jointly Gaussian random vector* $\boldsymbol{x} = (\boldsymbol{x}_o, \boldsymbol{x}_h)$, *prove that the structure of the covariance matrix of the observable part* $\boldsymbol{x}_o$ *has the structure given in* (1.1.15).

1.4. *Derive a closed-form solution to the method of least squares* (1.2.7).

1.5. (Maximum likelihood estimate with laplace or gaussian noise) *Recall that the probability density function of a Laplace distribution* $\mathcal{L}(\mu, b)$ *is*

$$p(x) = \frac{1}{2b} \exp\Big(-\frac{|x-\mu|}{b}\Big),$$

and of the Gaussian, or normal, distribution $\mathcal{N}(\mu, \sigma)$ *is*

$$p(x) = \frac{1}{\sqrt{2\pi}\sigma} \exp\Big(-\frac{(x-\mu)^2}{2\sigma^2}\Big).$$

Given a measurement model $\boldsymbol{y} = \boldsymbol{A}\boldsymbol{x} + \boldsymbol{\varepsilon}$, *consider the following two types of noise:*

(a) Entries of $\boldsymbol{\varepsilon} = [\varepsilon_1, \varepsilon_2, \ldots, \varepsilon_m]^*$ *are i.i.d. zero-mean Laplace.*
(b) Entries of $\boldsymbol{\varepsilon} = [\varepsilon_1, \varepsilon_2, \ldots, \varepsilon_m]^*$ *are i.i.d. zero-mean Gaussian.*

Derive the log maximum likelihood function for estimating $\boldsymbol{x}$ under these two noise models. Discuss their relationships to the ℓ^1 minimization and ℓ^2 minimization, respectively.

1.6. *Prove the Fact 1.6 for the case $d = 1$. That is, the principal direction of a random vector $\boldsymbol{y}$ is the eigenvector associated with the largest eigenvalue of its covariance matrix $\boldsymbol{\Sigma}_{\boldsymbol{y}}$. Furthermore, prove the Theorem A.29 in Appendix A.*

1.7. *Prove the Fact 1.7.*

1.8. (Ridge regression) *To solve a system of linear equations $\boldsymbol{y} = \boldsymbol{A}\boldsymbol{x}$, especially when the system is ill-posed (say underdetermined) or with (Gaussian) noise $\boldsymbol{y} = \boldsymbol{A}\boldsymbol{x} + \boldsymbol{\varepsilon}$, one popular way to estimate $\boldsymbol{x}$ is to consider the so-called* ridge regression*:*

$$\min_{\boldsymbol{x}} \|\boldsymbol{y} - \boldsymbol{A}\boldsymbol{x}\|_2^2 + \lambda \|\boldsymbol{x}\|_2^2, \tag{1.4.1}$$

for some $\lambda > 0$.[33] *This is also known as* Tikhonov regularization.[34]

(a) *Show that the optimal solution $\boldsymbol{x}_\star$ to the above optimization is given by*

$$\boldsymbol{x}_\star = (\boldsymbol{A}^*\boldsymbol{A} + \lambda \boldsymbol{I})^{-1}\boldsymbol{A}^*\boldsymbol{y}, \tag{1.4.2}$$

given that the matrix $\boldsymbol{A}^*\boldsymbol{A} + \lambda \boldsymbol{I}$ is invertible.

(b) *Discuss the conditions on the matrix $\boldsymbol{A}$ and λ so that the matrix $\boldsymbol{A}^*\boldsymbol{A} + \lambda \boldsymbol{I}$ is guaranteed to be invertible.*

Ridge regression is arguably the most widely studied and used form of regression in the classic statistical literature [HTF09]. There are many good properties of this type of regression, related to important methods such as the Wiener filter in signal processing. The reader may refer to the recent book [FLZZ20] for a more detailed study of ridge regression and many variants.

[33] This can be viewed as a Lagrangian formulation of the constrained optimization considered by Theorem A.25 in Appendix A.

[34] Strictly speaking, Tikhonov regularization may consider a more general class of regularization of the form $\|\boldsymbol{\Lambda}\boldsymbol{x}\|_2^2$ for some properly chosen positive definite matrix $\boldsymbol{\Lambda}$.

Part I

Principles of Low-Dimensional Models

2 Sparse Signal Models

"It is quite probable that our mathematical insights and understandings are often used to achieve things that could in principle also be achieved computationally – but where blind computation without much insight may turn out to be so inefficient that it is unworkable."

– Roger Penrose, *Shadows of the Mind*

This book is about modeling and exploiting *simple structure* in signals, images, and data. In this chapter, we take our first steps in this direction. We study a class of models known as *sparse models*, in which the signal of interest is a superposition of a few basic signals (called "atoms") selected from a large "dictionary." This basic model arises in a surprisingly large number of applications. It also illustrates fundamental tradeoffs in modeling and computation that will recur throughout the book.

2.1 Applications of Sparse Signal Modeling

Why do we need signal models at all? We give a pragmatic answer. Many problems arising in modern signal processing and data analysis are intrinsically *ill-posed*. Often, the number of unknowns vastly exceeds the number of observations. In this situation, prior knowledge is absolutely essential to solving the problem correctly.

To describe this phenomenon mathematically, consider the simple equation

$$\underbrace{\boldsymbol{y}}_{\text{observation}} = \boldsymbol{A} \underbrace{\boldsymbol{x}}_{\text{unknown}}. \tag{2.1.1}$$

Here, $\boldsymbol{y} \in \mathbb{R}^m$ is our observation, while $\boldsymbol{x} \in \mathbb{R}^n$ is unknown. The matrix $\boldsymbol{A} \in \mathbb{R}^{m \times n}$ represents the data generation process: the observed data $\boldsymbol{y}$ is a linear function of the unknown (or hidden) signal $\boldsymbol{x}$. This is a simple model; however, we will see that it is rich enough to bear on a vast array of practical applications.

Recovering the unknown $\boldsymbol{x}$ from observation $\boldsymbol{y}$ may appear trivial: we simply have to solve a linear system of equations! However, many practical applications raise a substantial challenge: the number of observations, m, can be significantly smaller than the number of elements, n, in the signal to be recovered. From linear algebra,[1] we

[1] Appendix A provides a detailed review of linear algebra and matrix analysis. In particular, Appendix A.6 reviews the existence and uniqueness of solutions to linear systems, which we use here to motivate our study of sparse approximation.

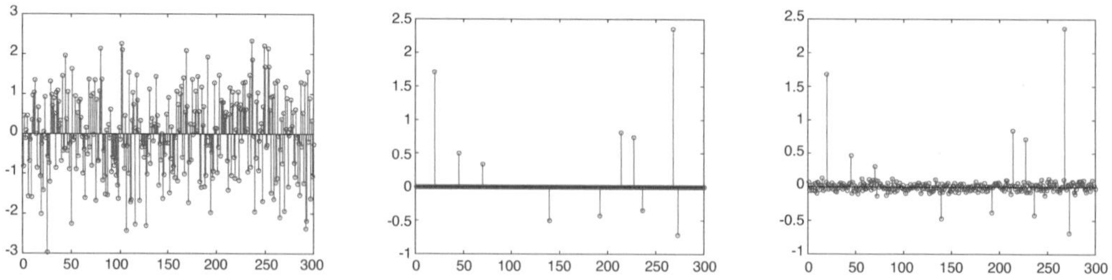

(a) dense vector (b) sparse vector (c) compressible vector

Figure 2.1 Dense versus sparse vectors. (a) A generic *dense* vector $\boldsymbol{x} \in \mathbb{R}^n$, with entries being independent standard normal random variables. (b) A *sparse* vector, with only a few nonzero entries. (c) A *compressible* vector, with only a few significant entries.

know that when $m < n$, the system of equations $\boldsymbol{y} = \boldsymbol{A}\boldsymbol{x}$ does not necessarily have any solution, but if it has any solution at all, then the solution space has at least dimension $n - m$. Hence, either there is no solution, or there are infinitely many solutions. Only one of them is the one we wish to recover! To make progress, we need to leverage some additional properties of the target solution.

Sparsity is one such property, which has strong implications on our ability to solve underdetermined systems. A vector $\boldsymbol{x} \in \mathbb{R}^n$ is considered *sparse* if only a few of its elements are nonzero. Figure 2.1(b) shows an example of such a vector. Some form of sparsity arises naturally in almost every type of high-dimensional signal or data that we encounter in practical applications. Below, we illustrate with a few representative examples.

2.1.1 An Example from Medical Imaging

Figure 2.2 shows a *magnetic resonance* (MR) image of the brain. This is a digital image $I \in \mathbb{R}^{N \times N}$. Each entry $I(\boldsymbol{v})$ (here, $\boldsymbol{v} \in \mathbb{R}^2$) corresponds to the density of protons at a given spatial location inside the brain. This essentially indicates where water is in the brain, and can reveal many biological structures that are important for disease diagnosis and monitoring. To caricature the magnetic resonance imaging (MRI) problem a bit, our goal is to estimate I, without opening up the brain! This is possible, if we subject the patient to a large, spatially and temporally varying magnetic field. The magnetic field causes the protons to oscillate at a frequency that depends on their locations and energy states. Each proton essentially acts as its own radio transmitter, and in aggregate they create a signal we can measure.

As we will see from a more detailed derivation of the physical model for MRI in Chapter 10, it turns out that the signal we observe is simply a sample of the two-dimensional Fourier transform of I:

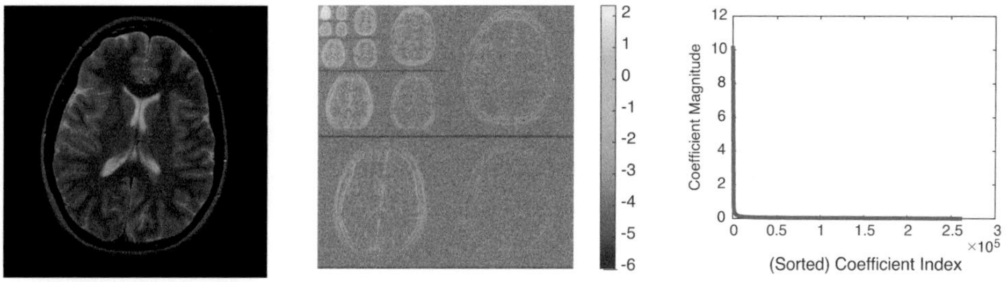

(a) image $I(\boldsymbol{v})$

(b) wavelet coefficients $\boldsymbol{x}$: $I = \Psi[\boldsymbol{x}]$.

Figure 2.2 A magnetic resonance image. (a) Target image of a human brain. (b) Coefficients in the wavelet decomposition $I = \sum_i \psi_i x_i$, and their magnitudes, sorted in descending order. The large wavelet coefficients concentrate around sharp edges in the image; wavelet coefficients corresponding to smooth regions are much smaller. The wavelet coefficients are highly compressible: their magnitude decays rapidly. Image reprinted with permission from Michael Lustig [Lus13].

$$y = \int_{\boldsymbol{v}} I(\boldsymbol{v}) \exp(-\mathrm{i}\, 2\pi\, \boldsymbol{u}^* \boldsymbol{v})\, d\boldsymbol{v}. \tag{2.1.2}$$

Here, $\mathrm{i} = \sqrt{-1}$ is the imaginary unit, and $(\cdot)^*$ denotes the (complex conjugate) transpose of a vector. The two-dimensional frequency vector $\boldsymbol{u}^* = [u_1, u_2] \in \mathbb{R}^2$ depends on how the magnetic field we applied varies over space. Here, letting $\mathcal{F}$ denote the 2D Fourier transform, the above expression is

$$y = \mathcal{F}[I](\boldsymbol{u}). \tag{2.1.3}$$

By changing the applied magnetic field, we can vary $\boldsymbol{u}$, and collect m samples of the Fourier transform, corresponding to different applied magnetic fields, parameterized by $\mathsf{U} = \{\boldsymbol{u}_1, \dots, \boldsymbol{u}_m\}$. We can concatenate all of our observations into a vector $\boldsymbol{y} \in \mathbb{C}^m$, given by

$$\boldsymbol{y} = \begin{bmatrix} y_1 \\ \vdots \\ y_m \end{bmatrix} = \begin{bmatrix} \mathcal{F}[I](\boldsymbol{u}_1) \\ \vdots \\ \mathcal{F}[I](\boldsymbol{u}_m) \end{bmatrix} \doteq \mathcal{F}_{\mathsf{U}}[I]. \tag{2.1.4}$$

Here, $\mathcal{F}_{\mathsf{U}}$ is simply the operator that obtains the Fourier samples of I, indexed by U. If you imagine the Fourier transform as acting by matrix multiplication, $\mathcal{F}_{\mathsf{U}}$ is simply the matrix we get if we discard all the rows of $\mathcal{F}$ that are not indexed by U.

One very basic property of the integral (2.1.2), and hence of the operator $\mathcal{F}_{\mathsf{U}}$, is that it is *linear* in its input I. This means that for any pair of inputs I and J and complex scalars α and β,

$$\mathcal{F}_{\mathsf{U}}[\alpha I + \beta J] = \alpha \mathcal{F}_{\mathsf{U}}[I] + \beta \mathcal{F}_{\mathsf{U}}[J]. \tag{2.1.5}$$

Because $\mathcal{F}_{\mathsf{U}}$ is a linear operator, the problem of finding I from $\boldsymbol{y}$ using the observation equation (2.1.4) "just" consists of solving a large linear system of equations.

There is a substantial catch though. In this system of equations, there are typically far more unknowns (here $n = N^2$) than observations m. This is necessary: it is generally too time- and energy-intensive to simply measure all N^2 Fourier coefficients. This is even more pressing of a concern in *dynamic MRI*, where the object being imaged is changing over time, and so acquisition needs to be time-efficient. So, in general, we need m to be as small as is just necessary to guarantee accurate reconstruction – and certainly significantly smaller than n.

This leaves us with a seemingly impossible situation: we have n unknowns and $m \ll n$ equations. Unless we can make some additional assumptions on the structure of I, the problem is ill-posed. Fortunately, real signals are not completely unstructured.[2] Figure 2.2(b) shows a *wavelet transform* of I. The wavelet transform expresses I as a superposition of a collection of basis functions $\boldsymbol{\Psi} = \{\psi_1, \dots, \psi_{N^2}\}$:

$$\underbrace{I}_{\text{image}} = \sum_{i=1}^{N^2} \underbrace{\psi_i}_{i\text{-th basis signal}} \times \underbrace{x_i}_{i\text{-th coefficient}}. \tag{2.1.6}$$

Here, $x_1, \dots, x_{N^2} \in \mathbb{R}$ are coefficients of the image I with respect to the basis $\boldsymbol{\Psi}$. The entries in Figure 2.2(b) are the magnitudes $|x_i|$ for the N^2 coefficients x_i. The important point is that many of these coefficients are extremely small. If we let $\mathsf{J} = \{i_1, \dots, i_k\}$ denote the k largest coefficients, we can approximate I as

$$\underbrace{I}_{\text{target image}} \approx \underbrace{\tilde{I}_k = \sum_{i \in \mathsf{J}} \psi_i x_i}_{\text{superposition of } k \text{ basis functions}}. \tag{2.1.7}$$

Figure 2.3 visualizes the reconstruction and reconstruction error $I - \tilde{I}_k$. It seems that even if we retain only a relatively small fraction of the coefficients, we still obtain an accurate approximation, and most of what remains is noise. This suggests that the sequence $\boldsymbol{x}$ is *compressible* – it is very close to a sparse vector.

In order to recover I, we can first try to reconstruct the sparse vector $\boldsymbol{x}$, using the observation equation

$$\begin{aligned}
\underbrace{\boldsymbol{y}}_{\text{observed Fourier coefficients}} &= \mathcal{F}_{\mathsf{U}}[I], \\
&= \mathcal{F}_{\mathsf{U}}\Big[\, \psi_1 x_1 + \cdots + \psi_{N^2} x_{N^2} \,\Big], \\
&= \mathcal{F}_{\mathsf{U}}[\psi_1] x_1 + \cdots + \mathcal{F}_{\mathsf{U}}[\psi_{N^2}] x_{N^2}, \\
&= \underbrace{\Big[\mathcal{F}_{\mathsf{U}}[\psi_1] \mid \cdots \mid \mathcal{F}_{\mathsf{U}}[\psi_{N^2}]\Big]}_{\text{matrix } \boldsymbol{A} \in \mathbb{R}^{m \times N^2},\ m \ll N^2.} \boldsymbol{x}, \\
&= \boldsymbol{A}\boldsymbol{x}.
\end{aligned} \tag{2.1.8}$$

[2] Indeed, we can construct a "generic" element I_{generic} of $\mathbb{R}^{N \times N}$, by choosing its entries at random – say from a standard Gaussian distribution $\mathcal{N}(0, 1)$. With very high probability, I_{generic} will simply look like noise. The target magnetic resonance image in Figure 2.2 certainly does not look like noise!

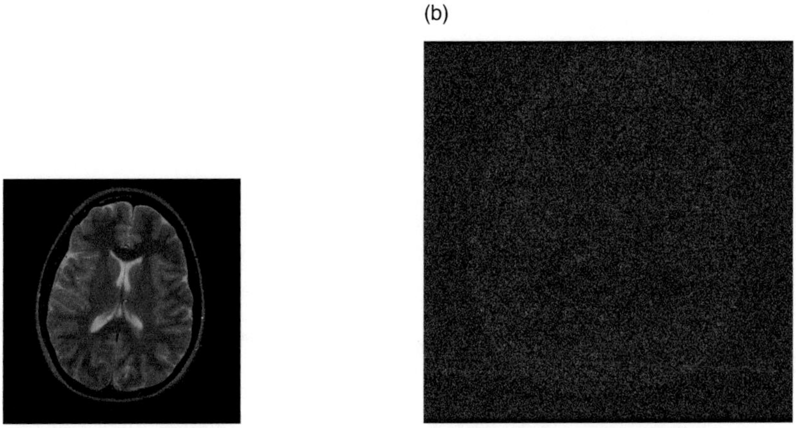

Figure 2.3 Wavelet approximation $\tilde{I}$ to I and approximation error. (a) Approximation to the image in Figure 2.2 using the most significant 7% of the wavelet coefficients. (b) Approximation error $|I - \tilde{I}|$. The error contains mostly noise, suggesting that most of the important structure of the image is captured in the wavelet approximation $\tilde{I}$.

After these manipulations, we end up with a system of equations $\boldsymbol{y} = \boldsymbol{A}\boldsymbol{x}$. The vector $\boldsymbol{x}$ contains the coefficients of the target image I in the wavelet basis. The i-th column of the matrix $\boldsymbol{A}$ contains a subset U of the Fourier coefficients of the i-th basis signal $\boldsymbol{\psi}_i$. To reconstruct I, we can look for a solution $\hat{\boldsymbol{x}}$ to this system, and then set

$$\hat{I} = \sum_{i=1}^{N^2} \boldsymbol{\psi}_i \hat{x}_i. \tag{2.1.9}$$

Because $\boldsymbol{x}$ has N^2 entries, but we only have $m \ll N^2$ observations, the system $\boldsymbol{y} = \boldsymbol{A}\boldsymbol{x}$ is underdetermined. Nevertheless, because the wavelet coefficients of I are (nearly) sparse – say, only its k largest coefficients are significant and others are negligible – the desired solution $\boldsymbol{x}$ to this system is sparse. To reconstruct I we need to find a sparse solution to an underdetermined system! In Chapter 10, we will illustrate how to actually apply such a "compressive sampling" scheme to real MRI images under more realistic conditions.

2.1.2 An Example from Image Processing

In the previous example, we used the fact that the image I had a good sparse approximation in terms of a "dictionary" of basic elements $\boldsymbol{\psi}_1, \ldots, \boldsymbol{\psi}_{N^2}$:

$$I \approx \sum_{i \in \mathsf{J}} \boldsymbol{\psi}_i x_i = \underbrace{\boldsymbol{\Psi}}_{N^2 \times N^2 \text{ matrix}} \underbrace{\boldsymbol{x}}_{\text{sparse vector}}, \tag{2.1.10}$$

where $x_i = 0$ for $i \notin \mathsf{J}$, and $k = |\mathsf{J}| \ll N^2$. Expressions of this form play a central role in lossy data compression. Image compression standards such as JPEG [Wal91] and

JPEG 2000 [TM01] leverage sparse approximations (in the discrete cosine transform (DCT) [ANR74] and wavelet bases [VK95], respectively). Generally speaking, the sparser the representation is, the more an input image can be compressed. However, sparse representations of images are not *just* useful for compression: they can be used for solving inverse problems, in which we try to reconstruct I from noisy, corrupted, or incomplete observations. We already saw an example of this in the previous section, in which we used sparsity in the wavelet domain to reconstruct MR images. To facilitate all of these tasks, we can seek representations of I that are as sparse as possible, by replacing $\boldsymbol{\Psi}$ with more general dictionaries $\boldsymbol{A}$. For example, we might consider *overcomplete dictionaries* $\boldsymbol{A} \in \mathbb{R}^{m \times n}$, $n > m$, which consist of several orthonormal bases (e.g., DCT and wavelets together). The idea is that each individual representation may capture a particular type of signal well – say, DCT for smooth variations and wavelets for signals with sharp edges. Together, they can represent a broader class of signals.

An even more aggressive idea is to simply *learn* $\boldsymbol{A}$ from data, rather than designing it by hand. Conceptually this leads to an even more challenging problem, known as *dictionary learning*, which we will study later in Chapter 7. This approach tends to produce better sparsity–accuracy tradeoffs for representing images I, and is also useful for a wealth of other problems, including denoising, inpainting, and super-resolution that involve reconstructing I from incomplete or corrupted observations. Each of these problems leads to an underdetermined linear system of equations; the goal is to use the prior knowledge that the target signal I has a compact representation in some dictionary $\boldsymbol{A}$ to make the problem well-posed. Figure 2.4 shows an example of this for the problem of color image denoising, from [MES08]. We observe a noisy image

$$I_{\text{noisy}} = \underbrace{I_{\text{clean}}}_{\text{target image}} + \underbrace{z}_{\text{noise}}. \tag{2.1.11}$$

We assume[3] that patches of the clean image have an accurate sparse approximation in some dictionary $\boldsymbol{A}$: if we break I_{clean} into patches $\boldsymbol{y}_{1\,\text{clean}}, \dots, \boldsymbol{y}_{p\,\text{clean}}$, then

$$\boldsymbol{y}_{i\,\text{clean}} \approx \underbrace{\boldsymbol{A}}_{\text{patch dictionary}} \times \underbrace{\boldsymbol{x}_i}_{\text{sparse coefficient vector}}. \tag{2.1.12}$$

In denoising, we do not actually observe $\boldsymbol{y}_{i\,\text{clean}}$. Rather, we observe *noisy* patches

$$\boldsymbol{y}_i = \boldsymbol{y}_{i\,\text{clean}} + \boldsymbol{z}_i = \boldsymbol{A} \times \boldsymbol{x}_i + \boldsymbol{z}_i, \quad i = 1, \dots, p.$$

Based on these patches $\boldsymbol{y}_1, \dots, \boldsymbol{y}_p$, we learn a dictionary $\hat{\boldsymbol{A}}$ such that

$$\underbrace{\boldsymbol{y}_i}_{i\text{-th image patch}} \approx \underbrace{\hat{\boldsymbol{A}}}_{\text{learned dictionary}} \times \underbrace{\hat{\boldsymbol{x}}_i}_{\text{sparse coefficient vector}} = \underbrace{\hat{\boldsymbol{y}}_i}_{\text{denoised patch}}.$$

[3] Of course, this assumption needs to be justified! See Exercise 2.16 and the notes and references to this chapter. We will also have ample examples in later chapters when we introduce methods to learn sparsifying dictionaries for real images.

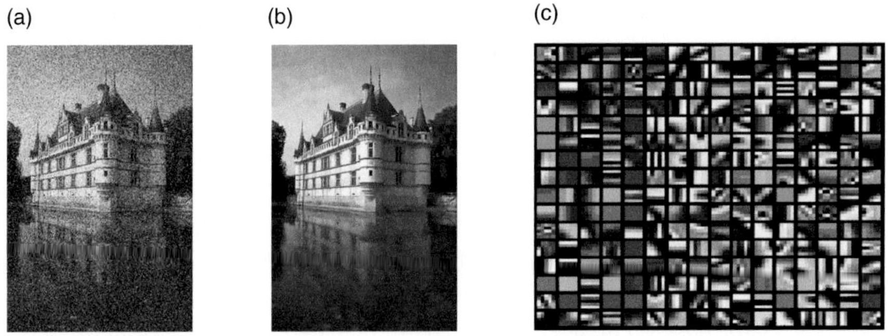

Figure 2.4 Image denoising by sparse approximation. (a) A noisy input image. The image is broken into patches $\boldsymbol{y}_1, \dots, \boldsymbol{y}_p$. A dictionary $\boldsymbol{A} = [\boldsymbol{a}_1 \mid \cdots \mid \boldsymbol{a}_n]$ is learned such that each input patch can be approximated as $\boldsymbol{y}_i \approx \boldsymbol{A}\boldsymbol{x}_i$, (b) Denoised image, reconstructed from the approximations $\hat{\boldsymbol{y}}_i = \boldsymbol{A}\boldsymbol{x}_i$. (c) Dictionary patches $\boldsymbol{a}_1, \dots, \boldsymbol{a}_n$. with $\boldsymbol{x}_i$ sparse. Figures from [MES08, WMM$^+$10]. Image reprinted with permission from Julien Mairal.

The dictionary $\hat{\boldsymbol{A}}$ and sparse coefficients $\hat{\boldsymbol{x}}_i$ can be learned by solving a nonconvex optimization problem, which attempts to strike an optimal balance between the sparsity of the coefficients $\hat{\boldsymbol{x}}_1, \dots, \hat{\boldsymbol{x}}_p$ and the accuracy of the approximation $\boldsymbol{y}_i \approx \hat{\boldsymbol{A}}\hat{\boldsymbol{x}}_i$. More detail will be given in Chapter 7. We take $\hat{\boldsymbol{y}}_i = \hat{\boldsymbol{A}}\hat{\boldsymbol{x}}_i$ as an estimate of $\boldsymbol{y}_{i\,\text{clean}}$.

Figure 2.4(a) shows the noisy input image; Figure 2.4(b) shows a denoised image constructed from $\hat{\boldsymbol{y}}_1, \dots, \hat{\boldsymbol{y}}_p$. Figure 2.4(c) shows the dictionary $\hat{\boldsymbol{A}}$ learned from the noisy patches. Although the sparse dictionary prior is relatively simple, and does not capture all of the global geometric structure of the image, it leads to surprisingly good performance on many low-level image processing tasks including image super-resolution [YWHM10] or restoration [MES08]. We discuss modeling and computational aspects of dictionary learning in detail in Chapters 7 and 9. For now, the key point is that the problem of reconstructing the clean image from noisy patches again leads us to an underdetermined linear system of equations, $\boldsymbol{y}_i \approx \boldsymbol{A}\boldsymbol{x}_i$.

2.1.3 An Example from Face Recognition

Sparsity also arises naturally in problems in which we wish to perform reliable inference from unreliable measurements. For example, due to sensor errors or malicious tampering, a vector-valued observation $\boldsymbol{y} \in \mathbb{R}^m$ might be grossly corrupted in a few of its entries:

$$\underbrace{\boldsymbol{y}}_{\text{observation}} = \underbrace{\boldsymbol{y}_o}_{\text{clean data}} + \underbrace{\boldsymbol{e}}_{\text{sparse error}}. \tag{2.1.13}$$

We illustrate this more concretely using an example from automatic face recognition. Imagine that we have a database consisting of a number of subjects. For each subject

i, we collect grayscale training images $I_{i,1}, \ldots, I_{i,n_i} \in \mathbb{R}^{W \times H}$, and vectorize them to form a base matrix $\boldsymbol{B}_i \in \mathbb{R}^{m \times n_i}$, with $m = W \times H$. We can further concatenate these matrices to form a large training "dictionary"

$$\boldsymbol{B} = \underbrace{[\boldsymbol{B}_1 \mid \boldsymbol{B}_2 \mid \cdots \mid \boldsymbol{B}_n]}_{\text{all training images}} \in \mathbb{R}^{m \times n}, \quad n = \sum_i n_i. \tag{2.1.14}$$

Suppose our system is confronted with a new image $\boldsymbol{y} \in \mathbb{R}^m$, taken under some new lighting condition, and possibly occluded – see Figure 2.5. For now, we can assume that the input $\boldsymbol{y}$ is well aligned to the training images (i.e., the faces occur at the same position in the training and test images).[4] There is a beautiful physical argument [BJ03] that shows that in an average case sense, images of "nice" objects taken under varying lighting conditions lie very close to low-dimensional linear subspaces of the high-dimensional image space $\mathbb{R}^m$.[5] This suggests that if we have seen enough training examples, we can approximate the input sample $\boldsymbol{y}$ as a linear combination of the training samples from the same class:

$$\underbrace{\boldsymbol{y}}_{\text{observed image}} \approx \underbrace{\boldsymbol{B}_{i_\star} \boldsymbol{x}_{i_\star}}_{\text{linear combination of training images from } i_\star\text{-th class}}. \tag{2.1.15}$$

Unfortunately, in practice, this equation is violated in at least two ways: First, we don't know the true identity $i_\star$ ahead of time. Second, nuisance factors such as occlusion

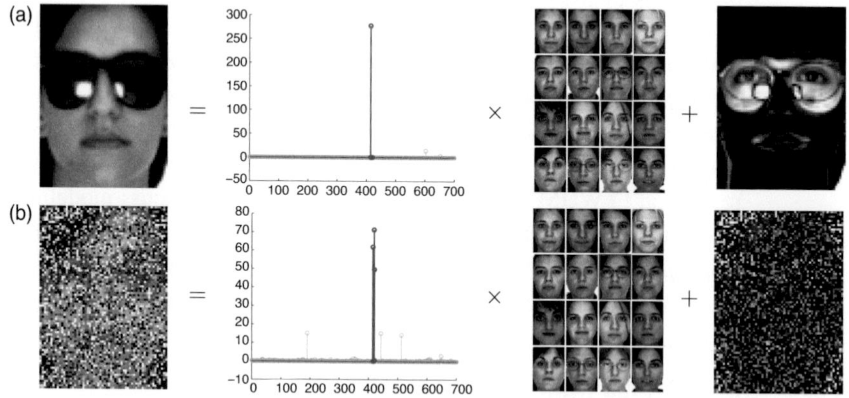

Figure 2.5 Face recognition via sparse representation. (a) Input face image $\boldsymbol{y}$ is wearing sunglasses. (b) Input face image $\boldsymbol{y}$ is with 50% pixels arbitrarily corrupted. Each test image $\boldsymbol{y}$ is approximated as a sparse combination $\boldsymbol{Bx}$ of the training images, plus a sparse error $\boldsymbol{e}$ due to occlusion. In this example, red coefficients correspond to images of the correct subject. Results and figures from [WYG$^+$09].

4 Relaxing this assumption is essential to building systems that work with unconstrained input images. We will talk about how to relax this assumption in Chapter 13.

5 We will give a more detailed justification for this fact in Chapter 14 based on a simplified physical model.

cause the equation to be badly violated on a portion of the image pixels (those that are occluded). For the first problem, we note that we can *still* write down an expression for $\boldsymbol{y}$ as a linear combination of elements of the database $\boldsymbol{B}$ as a whole: $\boldsymbol{y} \approx \boldsymbol{B}\boldsymbol{x}$. To deal with occlusion, we need to introduce an additional term $\boldsymbol{e}$, giving

$$\boldsymbol{y} = \boldsymbol{B}\boldsymbol{x} + \boldsymbol{e}. \tag{2.1.16}$$

Because the errors caused by occlusion are large in magnitude, this error $\boldsymbol{e}$ cannot simply be ignored or treated with techniques designed for small noise. Unfortunately, this means that the system is underdetermined: we have m equations, but $m+n$ unknowns $\bar{\boldsymbol{x}} = (\boldsymbol{x}, \boldsymbol{e})$. Writing $\boldsymbol{A} = [\boldsymbol{B} \mid \boldsymbol{I}]$, we again have a very large underdetermined system

$$\boldsymbol{y} = \boldsymbol{A}\bar{\boldsymbol{x}}. \tag{2.1.17}$$

If we did not have prior information about $\bar{\boldsymbol{x}}$, there would be no hope of recovering it from this observation. Fortunately, both $\boldsymbol{x}$ and $\boldsymbol{e}$ are very structured. The nonzero values of $\boldsymbol{x}$ should be concentrated only on those images of the true subject, $i_\star$, and so it should be a *sparse vector*. The nonzero values of the error $\boldsymbol{e}$ should be concentrated only on those pixels that are occluded or corrupted, and so it should also be sparse.[6]

Figure 2.5 shows two examples of a sparse solution to this system of equations for a given input image $\boldsymbol{y}$. Notice that the coefficients in the estimated $\hat{\boldsymbol{x}}$ are concentrated on images of the correct subject (red) and that the error indeed corresponds to the physical occlusion. The setting we have described so far is somewhat idealized – we will discuss both the modeling and system building aspects of this problem in the application section of this book, see Chapter 13. For our purposes here, it is enough to note that *if* we can somehow obtain a sparse $(\boldsymbol{x}, \boldsymbol{e})$, it should suffice to identify the subject, despite nuisances such as illumination, occlusion, and corruption.

2.2 Recovering a Sparse Solution

Suppose, as in the above examples, that we know the ground-truth signal $\boldsymbol{x}_o$ is sparse. How powerful is this knowledge? Can it render ill-posed problems such as MR image acquisition or occluded face recognition well posed? To answer these questions, we need a formal notion of sparsity. In the next two subsections, we begin by introducing the concept of a norm of a vector, which generalizes the concept of *length*. We then

[6] Of course, the goal is to correct as many errors as possible. One of the surprises of high dimensions is it is indeed possible to correct large fractions of errors using simple, efficient algorithms. Understanding precisely how many errors we can correct (and how dense the vector $\bar{\boldsymbol{x}}$ can be before our methods break down) will be a major theoretical thrust of this book. In Chapter 13, we will give a more precise characterization about how large a fraction of errors can be corrected for a system of linear equations, similar to those that arise in the robust face recognition setting.

introduce an "ℓ^0 norm," which counts the number of nonzero entries in a vector, a basic measure of how dense (or sparse) that vector is.

2.2.1 Norms on Vector Spaces

A *vector space* $\mathbb{V}$ consists of a collection of elements (vectors), a field such as the real numbers $\mathbb{R}$ or complex numbers $\mathbb{C}$ (scalars), and operations (adding vectors and multiplying vectors with scalars) that work in ways that conform to our intuitions from $\mathbb{R}^3$. Appendix A reviews the formal definition of a vector space, and gives examples. In the above application examples, our signals of interest consisted of collections of real or complex numbers – e.g., in MR imaging, the target image I was an element of $\mathbb{R}^{N\times N}$. We can view $\mathbb{R}^{N\times N}$ as a vector space, with scalar field $\mathbb{R}$ (written $\mathbb{V} = (\mathbb{R}^{N\times N}, \mathbb{R})$). In the other examples as well, the signals of interest reside in vector spaces.

A *norm* on a vector space $\mathbb{V}$ gives *a way of measuring lengths of vectors, that conforms in important ways to our intuition* from lengths in $\mathbb{R}^3$. Formally:

DEFINITION 2.1. (Norm) *A norm on a vector space $\mathbb{V}$ over $\mathbb{R}$ is a function $\|\cdot\| : \mathbb{V} \to \mathbb{R}$ that is*

(a) nonnegatively homogeneous: $\|\alpha \boldsymbol{x}\| = |\alpha|\|\boldsymbol{x}\|$ for all vectors $\boldsymbol{x} \in \mathbb{V}$, scalars $\alpha \in \mathbb{R}$,

(b) positive definite: $\|\boldsymbol{x}\| \geq 0$, and $\|\boldsymbol{x}\| = 0$ if and only if $\boldsymbol{x} = \boldsymbol{0}$,

(c) subadditive: $\|\cdot\|$ satisfies the triangle inequality $\|\boldsymbol{x} + \boldsymbol{y}\| \leq \|\boldsymbol{x}\| + \|\boldsymbol{y}\|$ for all $\boldsymbol{x}, \boldsymbol{y} \in \mathbb{V}$.

For our purposes, the most important family of norms are the ℓ^p norms (read "ell p norm"). We will use norms from this family to derive practical algorithms for finding sparse solutions to linear systems of equations, and for studying their properties. If we take $\mathbb{V} = (\mathbb{R}^n, \mathbb{R})$, and $p \in (0, \infty)$, we can write

$$\|\boldsymbol{x}\|_p \doteq \left(\sum_i |x_i|^p \right)^{1/p}. \tag{2.2.1}$$

The function $\|\boldsymbol{x}\|_p$ is a norm for any $p \geq 1$.[7] The most familiar example is the ℓ^2 norm or "Euclidean norm"

$$\|\boldsymbol{x}\|_2 = \sqrt{\sum_i |x_i|^2} = \sqrt{\boldsymbol{x}^* \boldsymbol{x}},$$

which coincides with our usual way of measuring length. Two other cases are of almost equal importance: $p = 1$ and $p \to \infty$. Setting $p = 1$ in (2.2.1), we obtain

[7] We leave as an exercise for the reader to show that for $0 < p < 1$, $\|\boldsymbol{x}\|_p$ is not a norm in the strict sense of Definition 2.1.

$$\|\boldsymbol{x}\|_1 = \sum_i |x_i|, \tag{2.2.2}$$

which will play a very large role in this book.[8] Finally, as p becomes larger, the expression in (2.2.1) accentuates large $|x_i|$. As $p \to \infty$, $\|\boldsymbol{x}\|_p \to \max_i |x_i|$. We extend the definition of the ℓ^p norm to $p = \infty$ by defining

$$\|\boldsymbol{x}\|_\infty = \max_i |x_i|. \tag{2.2.3}$$

To appreciate the distinction between the various ℓ^p norms, we can visualize their unit balls B_p, which consist of all vectors $\boldsymbol{x}$ whose norm is at most one:[9]

$$\mathsf{B}_p \doteq \left\{\boldsymbol{x} \mid \|\boldsymbol{x}\|_p \le 1\right\}. \tag{2.2.4}$$

The ℓ^2 ball is a (solid) sphere, the ℓ^∞ ball is a cube, and the ℓ^1 ball is a kind of diamond shape, also known as a *cross polytope* – see Figure 2.6.[10]

Notice that for $p \le p'$, $\mathsf{B}_p \subseteq \mathsf{B}_{p'}$. This is because when $p \le p'$, $\|\boldsymbol{x}\|_p \ge \|\boldsymbol{x}\|_{p'}$ for all $\boldsymbol{x}$.

REMARK 2.2. *This containment becomes even more striking in higher dimensions: in* $\mathbb{R}^n$, $\mathrm{vol}(\mathsf{B}_\infty) = 2^n$, *while* $\mathrm{vol}(\mathsf{B}_1) = 2^n/n!$ *(see, e.g., [Mat02]). So, in* $n = 2$ *dimensions* $\mathrm{vol}(\mathsf{B}_1) = (1/2) \times \mathrm{vol}(\mathsf{B}_\infty)$, *while in* $n = 1000$ *dimensions* $\mathrm{vol}(\mathsf{B}_1) \approx 10^{-2568} \times \mathrm{vol}(\mathsf{B}_\infty)$ *– a truly negligible fraction!*

REMARK 2.3. *This may seem to be in contrast to the mathematical fact that "in finite dimensions, all norms are equivalent" in the sense that they define the same topology for the space (see, e.g., Appendix A). Formally, this statement means that in a finite-dimensional vector space* $\mathbb{V}$, *such as* $\mathbb{R}^n$, *for any pair of norms* $\|\cdot\|_\diamond$ *and* $\|\cdot\|_\square$ *there exist numbers* $0 < \alpha, \beta < \infty$ *such that for every* $\boldsymbol{x} \in \mathbb{V}$,

$$\alpha \,\|\boldsymbol{x}\|_\square \;\le\; \|\boldsymbol{x}\|_\diamond \;\le\; \beta \,\|\boldsymbol{x}\|_\square. \tag{2.2.5}$$

So, the norms $\|\cdot\|_\square$ *and* $\|\cdot\|_\diamond$ *can be compared in size. However, as the example in Remark 2.2 shows, in high dimensions, the unit balls of the various* ℓ^p *norms can be very different – hence* α *and* β *can be very far apart. In applications involving high-dimensional signals, different choices in norm can lead to radically different solutions.*

8 Anyone who has traveled in Manhattan should have good appreciation for the distinction between ℓ^1 and ℓ^2 – in fact, the ℓ^1 norm is sometimes called the Manhattan norm! This example illustrates a'simple, but important point – the proper choice of norm depends quite a bit on the properties of the problem and design goals. Unless you can leap tall buildings in a single bound, measuring distance using the ℓ^2 norm would underestimate how much travel you need to reach your destination.

9 For a ball of radius ε in terms of ℓ^p norm, we denote it as $\mathsf{B}_p(\varepsilon)$ or $\varepsilon \cdot \mathsf{B}_p = \left\{\boldsymbol{x} \mid \|\boldsymbol{x}\|_p \le \varepsilon\right\}$.

10 To see this in action, you can run `Chapter_2_Illustrate_Lp_Balls.m`. All such referenced code will be available in a clearly accessible location on the book's website.

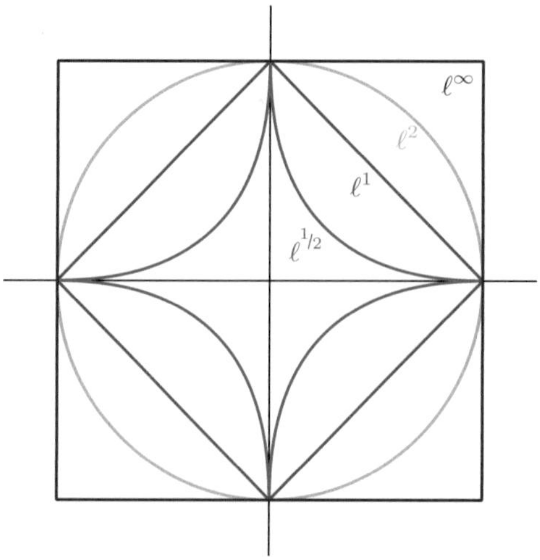

Figure 2.6 The ℓ^p balls $\mathsf{B}_p = \{x \mid \|x\|_p \le 1\}$ for $0 < p \le \infty$. For $p \ge 1$, B_p is a convex set, and $\|\cdot\|_p$ is a norm. For $p < 1$, $\|\cdot\|_p$ is not a norm, in the formal sense.

2.2.2 The ℓ^0 Norm

With the notion of a norm in hand, we are prepared to define a formal notion of sparsity. For this, we introduce a function, called the "ℓ^0 norm" (read "ell zero norm"), which is simply the number of nonzero entries in a vector $\boldsymbol{x}$:

$$\|\boldsymbol{x}\|_0 = \#\{i \mid \boldsymbol{x}(i) \neq 0\}. \tag{2.2.6}$$

Loosely speaking, $\boldsymbol{x}$ is sparse whenever $\|\boldsymbol{x}\|_0$ is small.

The ℓ^0 norm $\|\cdot\|_0$ is *not* a norm, in the formal sense of Definition 2.1: since for $\alpha \neq 0$, $\|\alpha\boldsymbol{x}\|_0 = \|\boldsymbol{x}\|_0$, it does not have the property of nonnegative homogeneity. It *does* have the other two properties, however. In particular, $\|\cdot\|_0$ is subadditive:

$$\forall\, \boldsymbol{x},\, \boldsymbol{x}', \qquad \left\|\boldsymbol{x} + \boldsymbol{x}'\right\|_0 \le \|\boldsymbol{x}\|_0 + \left\|\boldsymbol{x}'\right\|_0. \tag{2.2.7}$$

This is easily checked by noting that the set of nonzero entries for $\boldsymbol{x} + \boldsymbol{x}'$ is contained in the union of the set of nonzero entries of $\boldsymbol{x}$ and the set of nonzero entries of $\boldsymbol{x}'$.

Although the ℓ^0 norm is not a norm in the strict sense of Definition 2.1, it is related to the ℓ^p norm and can be viewed as a "continuation" of p from large to small. To understand this, note that for every $\boldsymbol{x} \in \mathbb{R}^n$,

$$\lim_{p \searrow 0} \|\boldsymbol{x}\|_p^p = \sum_{i=1}^{n} \lim_{p \searrow 0} |\boldsymbol{x}(i)|^p = \sum_{i=1}^{n} \mathbb{1}_{\boldsymbol{x}(i) \neq 0} = \|\boldsymbol{x}\|_0. \tag{2.2.8}$$

In this sense, the ℓ^0 norm can be considered to be generated from the ℓ^p norms, by taking p (infinitesimally) small. In the context of Figure 2.6, this can be understood as follows: in $\mathbb{R}^2$, the sparse vectors correspond to the coordinate axes. As p drops towards zero, the unit ball of the ℓ^p norm becomes more concentrated around the coordinate axes, i.e., around the sparse vectors.

The geometric relationship between the ℓ^0 and ℓ^p norms is useful for deriving algorithms, and for understanding why small p tends to favor sparse solutions. With this said, the formal notation $\|\boldsymbol{x}\|_0$ has a very simple meaning: *it counts the number of nonzero entries in* $\boldsymbol{x}$. In all of the applications discussed above, our goal is to recover a vector $\boldsymbol{x}_{\text{true}}$ with $\|\boldsymbol{x}_{\text{true}}\|_0$ small. In this book, we often use $\boldsymbol{x}_o$ as a shorthand for $\boldsymbol{x}_{\text{true}}$.

2.2.3 The Sparsest Solution: Minimizing the ℓ^0 Norm

Suppose we observe $\boldsymbol{y} \in \mathbb{R}^m$, with $\boldsymbol{y} = \boldsymbol{A}\boldsymbol{x}_o$, and that our goal is to recover $\boldsymbol{x}_o$. If we know that $\boldsymbol{x}_o$ is sparse, it seems reasonable to form an estimate $\hat{\boldsymbol{x}}$ by choosing the *sparsest* vector $\boldsymbol{x}$ that satisfies the equation $\boldsymbol{y} = \boldsymbol{A}\boldsymbol{x}$. That is, we choose the sparsest $\boldsymbol{x}$ that could have generated our observation. We can write this as an optimization problem

$$\begin{array}{ll} \min & \|\boldsymbol{x}\|_0 \\ \text{subject to} & \boldsymbol{A}\boldsymbol{x} = \boldsymbol{y}. \end{array} \tag{2.2.9}$$

How might we solve this problem numerically? Call

$$\operatorname{supp}(\boldsymbol{x}) = \{i \mid \boldsymbol{x}(i) \neq 0\} \subset \{1, \dots, n\} \tag{2.2.10}$$

the *support* of the vector $\boldsymbol{x}$ – this set contains the indices of the nonzero entries. The ℓ^0 minimization problem (2.2.9) asks us to find a vector $\boldsymbol{x}$ of smallest support that agrees with the observation $\boldsymbol{y}$. One approach to finding such an $\boldsymbol{x}$ is to simply try every possible subset of indices $\mathsf{I} \subseteq \{1, \dots, n\}$ as a candidate support. For each such set I, we can form a system of equations

$$\boldsymbol{A}_{\mathsf{I}}\boldsymbol{x}_{\mathsf{I}} = \boldsymbol{y}, \tag{2.2.11}$$

where $\boldsymbol{A}_{\mathsf{I}} \in \mathbb{R}^{m \times |\mathsf{I}|}$ is the column submatrix of $\boldsymbol{A}$ formed by keeping only those columns indexed by I, and similarly for $\boldsymbol{x}_{\mathsf{I}} \in \mathbb{R}^{|\mathsf{I}|}$. We can attempt to solve (2.2.11) for $\boldsymbol{x}_{\mathsf{I}}$. If such an $\boldsymbol{x}_{\mathsf{I}}$ exists, we can obtain a solution $\boldsymbol{x}$ to $\boldsymbol{A}\boldsymbol{x} = \boldsymbol{y}$ by filling in the remaining entries of $\boldsymbol{x}$ with zeros. This exhaustive search procedure is spelled out formally as Algorithm 2.1.

EXAMPLE 2.4. *Let us examine how the algorithm behaves numerically, using the code* `Chapter_2_L0_recovery.m` *and* `Chapter_2_L0_transition.m` *from the book's website. These examples generate random underdetermined linear systems* $\boldsymbol{y} = \boldsymbol{A}\boldsymbol{x}$*, with* $\boldsymbol{y} = \boldsymbol{A}\boldsymbol{x}_o$*, and* $\boldsymbol{x}_o$ *sparse. Apply Algorithm 2.1 (*`minimize_L0.m`*) to recover a vector* $\hat{\boldsymbol{x}}$*, and ask whether* $\hat{\boldsymbol{x}}$ *is equal to* $\boldsymbol{x}_o$ *up to machine precision. Fixing the system parameters* (m, n)*, varying the sparsity* $k = 0, 1, \dots,$ *and performing many random trials, we produce Figure 2.7, which shows that as long as k is not too large, the algorithm almost always succeeds.*

Algorithm 2.1 ℓ^0 Minimization by exhaustive search

Input: a matrix $\boldsymbol{A} \in \mathbb{R}^{m \times n}$ and a vector $\boldsymbol{y} \in \mathbb{R}^m$.
for $k = 0, 1, 2, \ldots, n$,
  for each $\mathsf{I} \subseteq \{1, \ldots, n\}$ of size k,
    if the system of equations $\boldsymbol{A}_{\mathsf{I}} \boldsymbol{z} = \boldsymbol{y}$ has a solution $\boldsymbol{z}$,
      set $\boldsymbol{x}_{\mathsf{I}} = \boldsymbol{z}$, $\boldsymbol{x}_{\mathsf{I}^c} = \mathbf{0}$.
      return $\boldsymbol{x}$.
    end if
  end for
end for

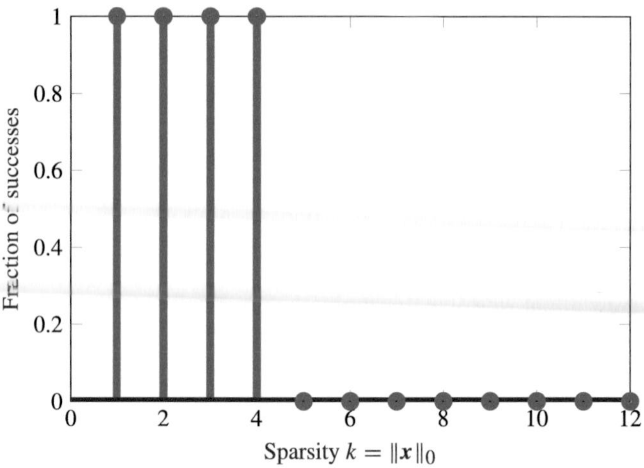

Figure 2.7 Transitions in ℓ^0 recovery. Fraction of correct recoveries across 100 trials, as a function of the sparsity of the target solution $\boldsymbol{x}_o$. The system is of size 5×12. In this experiment, ℓ^0 minimization successfully recovers all $\boldsymbol{x}_o$ with $k \leq 4$ nonzeros.

Is there any mathematical explanation for this phenomenon? To understand why ℓ^0 minimization succeeds, it is worth first thinking about when it would fail. Suppose that there is a nonzero k-sparse vector $\boldsymbol{x}_o \in \operatorname{null}(\boldsymbol{A})$. Then

$$\boldsymbol{A}\boldsymbol{x}_o = \mathbf{0} = \boldsymbol{A}\mathbf{0}. \tag{2.2.12}$$

Hence, for this $\boldsymbol{x}_o \neq \mathbf{0}$, when solving $\boldsymbol{y} = \boldsymbol{A}\boldsymbol{x}_o = \mathbf{0}$, the ℓ^0 minimizer is simply $\hat{\boldsymbol{x}} = \mathbf{0}$, and the true $\boldsymbol{x}_o$ is not recovered. Put simply: if the null space of $\boldsymbol{A}$ contains sparse vectors (aside from $\mathbf{0}$), ℓ^0 minimization may fail to recover the desired sparse vector $\boldsymbol{x}_o$.

In fact, the converse statement is also true: when the null space of $\boldsymbol{A}$ *does not* contain sparse vectors (aside from $\mathbf{0}$), ℓ^0 minimization *does* recover any sufficiently sparse vector $\boldsymbol{x}_o$. To state the argument simply, let us suppose that $\|\boldsymbol{x}_o\|_0 \leq k$, and assume:

($\star$) *the only* $\boldsymbol{\delta} \in \operatorname{null}(\boldsymbol{A})$ *with* $\|\boldsymbol{\delta}\|_0 \leq 2k$ *is* $\boldsymbol{\delta} = \mathbf{0}$.

Let $\hat{x}$ denote the solution to the ℓ^0 minimization problem, so $\|\hat{x}\|_0 \le \|x_o\|_0 \le k$. If we define the *estimation error*

$$\delta = \hat{x} - x_o, \tag{2.2.13}$$

then

$$\|\delta\|_0 = \|\hat{x} - x_o\|_0 \le \|\hat{x}\|_0 + \|x_o\|_0 \le 2k. \tag{2.2.14}$$

So, δ is a sparse vector. Moreover,

$$A\delta = A(\hat{x} - x_o) = A\hat{x} - Ax_o = y - y = 0. \tag{2.2.15}$$

So, δ is a sparse vector *in the null space of* A. Property $(\star)$ states that the only sparse vector in null(A) is $\mathbf{0}$. So, if $(\star)$ holds, $\delta = \mathbf{0}$, and so $\hat{x} = x_o$: ℓ^0 minimization indeed recovers x_o.

Property $(\star)$ is a property of the matrix A. The above reasoning suggests a slogan: *the "good"* A *for recovering sparse vectors* x_o *are those* A *that have no sparse vectors in their null space.* We can restate property $(\star)$ more conveniently in terms of the columns of A: property $(\star)$ holds if and only if every set of $2k$ columns of A is linearly independent.

DEFINITION 2.5. (Kruskal rank [Kru77]) *The* Kruskal rank *of a matrix* A*, written as* krank(A)*, is the largest number* r *such that every subset of* r *columns of* A *is linearly independent.*

From the above reasoning, if $\|x_o\|_0$ is at most half of krank(A), ℓ^0 minimization will recover x_o:

THEOREM 2.6. (ℓ^0 Recovery) *Suppose that* $y = Ax_o$*, with*

$$\|x_o\|_0 \le \tfrac{1}{2}\,\mathrm{krank}(A). \tag{2.2.16}$$

Then x_o *is the unique optimal solution to the* ℓ^0 *minimization problem*

$$\begin{array}{ll} \min & \|x\|_0 \\ \text{subject to} & Ax = y. \end{array} \tag{2.2.17}$$

Notice that Theorem 2.6 agrees with the behavior in Figure 2.7.[11] Theorem 2.6 predicts that as long as x_o is *sufficiently sparse*, it will be recovered by ℓ^0 minimization. The level of allowable sparsity depends on the Kruskal rank of the matrix A. It is not hard to see that, in general,

$$0 \le \mathrm{krank}(A) \le \mathrm{rank}(A). \tag{2.2.18}$$

[11] Actually, the behavior in Figure 2.7 is slightly better than what Theorem 2.6 predicts – with probability one the Kruskal rank of A is m, and so the theorem shows that ℓ^0 minimization succeeds when $k \le m/2 = 2$. However, in the experiment, success always occurs when $k \le 4$. Exercise 2.8 asks you to explain this discrepancy, by proving a modified version of Theorem 2.6.

For "generic" $\boldsymbol{A}$, the Kruskal rank is quite large:

PROPOSITION 2.7. *Let* $\boldsymbol{A} \in \mathbb{R}^{m \times n}$, $n \geq m$, *with* A_{ij} *independent identically distributed* $\mathcal{N}(0,1)$ *random variables. Then, with probability one,* $\operatorname{krank}(\boldsymbol{A}) = m$.

Proof Exercise 2.7 guides the interested reader through the proof. □

The intuition is that to have $\operatorname{krank}(\boldsymbol{A}) < m$, there must be some subset of m columns of $\boldsymbol{A}$ which are linearly dependent, i.e., there is some subset $\boldsymbol{a}_{i_1}, \boldsymbol{a}_{i_2}, \dots, \boldsymbol{a}_{i_m}$ which lies on a linear subspace of dimension $m-1$. For a Gaussian random matrix $\boldsymbol{A}$, the probability that this happens is zero. This is true of many other random matrices.[12] We can interpret this as saying that under generic circumstances, knowing that the target $\boldsymbol{x}_o$ is sparse turns an ill-posed problem into a well-posed one. The ℓ^0 minimization problem recovers vectors $\boldsymbol{x}_o$ whose number of nonzeros is as large as $m/2$. This level of sparsity is well beyond what is needed for most applications.

2.2.4 Computational Complexity of ℓ^0 Minimization

The theoretical results in the previous section show the power of sparsity: knowing that the target solution $\boldsymbol{x}_o$ is even moderately sparse can render the problem of recovering $\boldsymbol{x}_o$ well posed. Unfortunately, Algorithm 2.1 is not very useful in practice. Its worst-case running time is on the order of n^k, where $k = \|\boldsymbol{x}_o\|_0$ is the number of nonzero entries we wish to recover. For example, at the time of writing this book, to solve a problem with $m = 50$, $n = 200$, and $k = 10$, on a standard laptop, Algorithm 2.1 would require ≈ 140 *centuries*. This is still a very small problem by the standard of most modern-day applications!

Exhaustively searching all possible supports I may not seem like a particularly intelligent strategy for solving the ℓ^0 minimization problem (2.2.9). However, no significantly better algorithm is currently known that can solve this class of problems efficiently. Is this because we are not clever enough and have not found the correct (efficient) algorithm yet? Or is it the nature of this class of problems such that an efficient algorithm simply does not exist? To answer this question more rigorously, we need to borrow some formal tools and results from complexity theory.

Complexity Classes and NP-*Hardness*

If you don't have any background in complexity theory, you can loosely think of the situation as follows. The problem class **P** consists of problems that we can solve in time polynomial in the size of the problem. The problem class **NP** consists of those problems for which, if we are given a "certificate" describing the optimal solution, we can check that it is correct in polynomial time. That is, **P** contains problems for which *finding* the right answer is "easy," while **NP** contains problems for which *checking* the right answer is easy. Anyone who has ever struggled with a problem for days, only to have a colleague or teacher easily demonstrate an obviously correct solution

[12] For example, $\operatorname{krank}(\boldsymbol{A}) = m$ with probability one whenever $\boldsymbol{A}$ is distributed according to any absolutely continuous measure, i.e., there is a probability density function.

can appreciate the difference between finding the right answer and checking the right answer!

It turns out that amongst the **NP** problems, there are certain "NP-*complete*" problems to which *every* problem in **NP** can be reduced, in polynomial time, to each other. So, solving one of these problems efficiently would enable you to solve every problem in **NP** efficiently! It is remarkable that this class of problems exists, and that it is quite large. It includes famous examples such as the Traveling Salesman Problem and the Multiway Cut Problem.

To understand the phrase "NP-*hard*," we have to appreciate one technicality regarding the above definitions of **P** and **NP**: they pertain only to *decision* problems, in which the goal is to produce a YES/NO answer. For example, the decision version of the Traveling Salesman Problem asks: "Is it possible to visit all of the nodes of a given graph (cities) while traveling a distance at most $d_\star$?" The decision version of the ℓ^0 problem asks: "Does the system $\boldsymbol{y} = \boldsymbol{A}\boldsymbol{x}$ have a solution with at most k nonzero entries?"

Often in practice we care much more about *optimization problems* than *decision problems* – we do not just want to know whether a solution exists, we want to know the way to find it! Strictly speaking, optimization problems cannot be "NP-complete" – in the formal definition of **NP**, we only include decision problems. Nevertheless, we may call an optimization problem NP-*hard* if an efficient solution to that problem can be used to efficiently solve NP-complete problems. For example, the optimization version of the Traveling Salesman Problem asks: "Find the shortest path that visits all of the nodes in a given graph." If one can solve this problem efficiently, one can clearly also solve the decision version efficiently, just by checking whether the optimal path has length at most $d_\star$.

NP-complete problems are considered highly unlikely to be efficiently solvable (i.e., solvable on standard (model) computers polynomial in time and the size of the problem).[13] This class of problems includes notoriously difficult examples, such as the Traveling Salesman Problem. Fully appreciating the mathematical content of complexity theory requires formal modeling of computation (Turing machines, complexity theory for different problem classes, etc.) that is beyond the scope of this book. For interested readers, we refer to the book [GJ90] for a formal introduction to this important subject.

NP-*Hardness of ℓ^0 Minimization*

For our purposes here, we are interested in whether the ℓ^0 minimization problem (2.2.9) is equivalent (in its complexity) to certain known NP-hard problems. Indeed, we can show that:

THEOREM 2.8. (Hardness of ℓ^0 minimization) *The ℓ^0 minimization problem* (2.2.9) *is* NP-*hard.*

[13] This is known as the "**P** versus **NP**" problem, one of the most famous open problems in mathematics and theoretical computing. The Clay Mathematics Institute is offering a reward of 1 million dollars to anyone who has a formal proof that $\mathbf{P} = \mathbf{NP}$ or that $\mathbf{P} \neq \mathbf{NP}$.

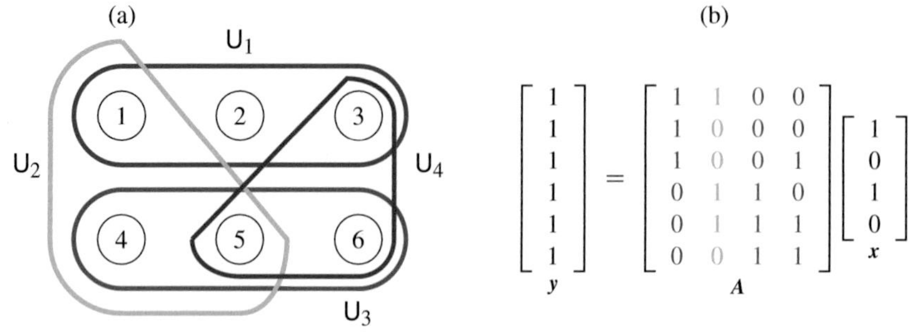

Figure 2.8 Exact three-set cover as a sparse representation problem. (a) A universe $\mathsf{S} = \{1, \ldots, 6\}$ and four subsets $\mathsf{U}_1, \ldots, \mathsf{U}_4 \subseteq \mathsf{S}$. $\{\mathsf{U}_1, \mathsf{U}_3\}$ is an exact three-set cover. (b) The same problem as a linear system of equations. The columns of $\boldsymbol{A}$ are the incidence vectors for the sets $\mathsf{U}_1, \mathsf{U}_2, \mathsf{U}_3, \mathsf{U}_4$, respectively, from left to right. The exact three-set cover $\{\mathsf{U}_1, \mathsf{U}_3\}$ corresponds to a solution $\boldsymbol{x}$ to the system $\boldsymbol{A}\boldsymbol{x} = \boldsymbol{y}$ with only $m/3 = 2$ nonzero entries.

Proof Hardness results are typically proved by reduction: we show that if we can solve the problem of interest efficiently, this would allow us to also efficiently solve some other problem, which is already known to be hard. For the ℓ^0 minimization problem, we do this by showing that ℓ^0 minimization can be used to solve certain (hard) set covering problems.

Consider the following problem:

> *Exact Three-Set Cover (E3C)*: Given a set $\mathsf{S} = \{1, \ldots, m\}$ and a collection $\mathcal{C} = \{\mathsf{U}_1, \ldots, \mathsf{U}_n\}$ of subsets $\mathsf{U}_j \subseteq \mathsf{S}$ each of which has size $|\mathsf{U}_j| = 3$, does there exist a subcollection $\mathcal{C}' \subseteq \mathcal{C}$ that exactly covers S, i.e., for all $i \in \mathsf{S}$ there is exactly one $\mathsf{U} \in \mathcal{C}'$ with $i \in \mathsf{U}$?

This problem is known to be NP-complete [Kar72, GJ79]. To reduce it to ℓ^0 minimization, suppose that we are given an instance of E3C: form an $m \times n$ matrix $\boldsymbol{A} \in \{0,1\}^{m \times n}$ by letting $A_{ij} = 1$ if $i \in \mathsf{U}_j$, and $A_{ij} = 0$ otherwise. Set $\boldsymbol{y} = \mathbf{1} \in \mathbb{R}^m$ (i.e., an m-dimensional vector of ones). Figure 2.8 illustrates this construction. We show:

> *Claim:* The system $\boldsymbol{A}\boldsymbol{x} = \boldsymbol{y}$ has a solution $\boldsymbol{x}_o$ with $\|\boldsymbol{x}_o\|_0 \le m/3$ if and only if there exists an exact three-set cover.

($\Leftarrow$) Suppose there exists an exact three-set cover $\mathcal{C}'$. Clearly, $|\mathcal{C}'| = m/3$. Set

$$x_j = \begin{cases} 1 & \mathsf{U}_j \in \mathcal{C}', \\ 0 & \text{else.} \end{cases}$$

Then $\|\boldsymbol{x}\|_0 = m/3$, and $\boldsymbol{y} = \boldsymbol{A}\boldsymbol{x}$.

($\Rightarrow$) Let $\boldsymbol{x}_o$ be a solution to $\boldsymbol{y} = \boldsymbol{A}\boldsymbol{x}$ with at most $m/3$ nonzero entries. Set $\mathcal{C}' = \{\mathsf{U}_j \mid \boldsymbol{x}_o(j) \neq 0\}$. We claim $\mathcal{C}'$ is the desired cover. Let $\mathsf{I} = \operatorname{supp}(\boldsymbol{x}_o)$. Since each column of $\boldsymbol{A}$ has exactly three nonzero entries, and $\boldsymbol{A}_\mathsf{I}$ has at most $m/3$ columns, the matrix $\boldsymbol{A}_\mathsf{I}$ has at most m nonzero entries. Since $\boldsymbol{A}_\mathsf{I}\boldsymbol{x}_{o\mathsf{I}} = \boldsymbol{y}$, each row of $\boldsymbol{A}_\mathsf{I}$ has at least one nonzero entry. Hence, each row of $\boldsymbol{A}_\mathsf{I}$ has *exactly* one nonzero entry, and the set $\mathcal{C}'$ gives an exact cover. □

In fact, the truth is even worse than Theorem 2.8 suggests: the ℓ^0 minimization problem remains NP-hard even if we only demand that $\boldsymbol{A}\boldsymbol{x} \approx \boldsymbol{y}$, in an appropriate sense. It is also NP-hard to find an $\boldsymbol{x}$ whose number of nonzero entries is within a constant factor of the smallest possible! See more discussions in the Notes Section 2.5. Based on our current understanding of complexity theory, it is extraordinarily unlikely that anyone will ever discover an efficient algorithm that solves any interesting variant of the ℓ^0 minimization problem for all possible inputs $(\boldsymbol{A}, \boldsymbol{y})$.

2.3 Relaxing the Sparse Recovery Problem

The rather bleak worst-case picture for ℓ^0 minimization has not stopped engineers from searching for efficient heuristics for finding sparse solutions to linear systems.[14] There is always some possibility for optimism:

> "Although the *worst* sparse recovery problem may be impossible to solve efficiently, perhaps my *particular* instance (or a subclass of instances) of interest is not so hard."

This optimism is occasionally rewarded in a rather striking fashion. In the next few chapters, we will see that many sparse recovery problems that matter for engineering practice *are* solvable efficiently. Our first step is to find a proper surrogate for the ℓ^0 norm which still encourages sparsity, but can be optimized efficiently.

2.3.1 Convex Functions

If our goal is efficient optimization, perhaps the most natural class of objective functions to consider are the *convex* functions. Smooth convex functions often appear "bowl shaped" – as in Figure 2.9(a). Indeed, a necessary and sufficient condition for a smooth function $f(x) : \mathbb{R} \to \mathbb{R}$ to be convex is that it exhibits nonnegative curvature – its second derivative $d^2 f(x)/dx^2 \geq 0$ at every point x.[15]

Iterative methods for optimization seek a minimizer of an objective function $f(\boldsymbol{x}) : \mathbb{R}^n \to \mathbb{R}$, by starting from some initial point $\boldsymbol{x}_0$,[16] and then generating a new point $\boldsymbol{x}_1$ based on the local shape of the objective function in the vicinity of $\boldsymbol{x}_0$. For a smooth function $f(\boldsymbol{x})$, the negative gradient $-\nabla f(\boldsymbol{x})$ defines the direction in which the objective function decreases most rapidly. A natural strategy for choosing $\boldsymbol{x}_1$ is to move in this descending direction:

$$\boldsymbol{x}_1 = \boldsymbol{x}_0 - t\nabla f(\boldsymbol{x}_0), \tag{2.3.1}$$

[14] As it has never stopped nature from learning and exploiting sparse coding.

[15] For a multivariate function $f(\boldsymbol{x}) : \mathbb{R}^n \to \mathbb{R}$, we need the Hessian of the function to be positive semidefinite: $\nabla^2 f(\boldsymbol{x}) \succeq \boldsymbol{0}$.

[16] In this book, we will use $\boldsymbol{x}_0$ to indicate the initial point of an iterative algorithm, which is not to be confused with $\boldsymbol{x}_o$, the desired ground truth.

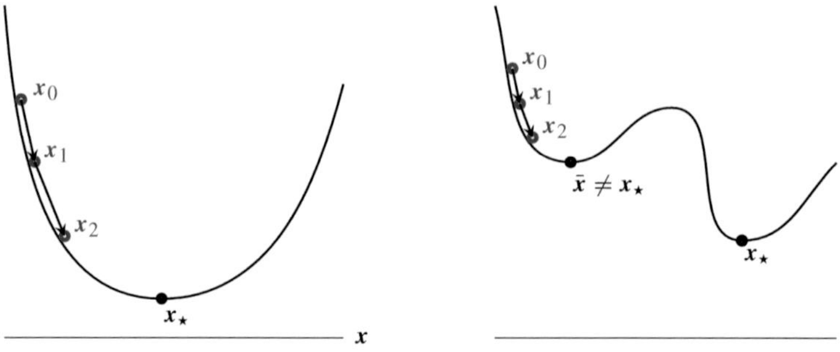

(a) convex (b) nonconvex

Figure 2.9 Convex and nonconvex functions. (a) A convex function. Local descent methods such as gradient descent produce a sequence of points $\boldsymbol{x}_0, \boldsymbol{x}_1, \dots$ which approach the global minimizer $\boldsymbol{x}_\star$. (b) A nonconvex function. For this particular function, depending on the initial point $\boldsymbol{x}_0$, local descent methods may produce the suboptimal local minimum $\bar{\boldsymbol{x}}$. Motivated by their good properties for optimization, in the first part of this book, we will seek convex formulations for recovering sparse (and otherwise structured) signals.

where t is a step size. Continuing in this manner to produce points $\boldsymbol{x}_0, \boldsymbol{x}_1, \boldsymbol{x}_2, \dots$, we obtain the *gradient descent* method,[17] a natural and intuitive algorithm for minimizing a smooth function $f(\boldsymbol{x})$. For the function f in Figure 2.9(a), assuming we choose the step size t appropriately, the iterates $\boldsymbol{x}_0, \boldsymbol{x}_1, \dots$ will converge to the global minimizer $\boldsymbol{x}_\star$. For the nonconvex function in Figure 2.9(b), this strategy only guarantees a local minimizer.[18]

Convex functions such as Figure 2.9(a) have the property that every local minimizer is a global minimizer.[19] Moreover, many convex functions arising in practice can be optimized efficiently using variants of gradient descent. Indeed, in Chapter 8, we will see that the particular convex functions that we encounter in computing with sparse signals (and their generalizations) *can* be efficiently optimized, even on a large scale and in high dimensions.

We review the properties of convex functions more formally in Appendix C. Here, we briefly remind the reader of the general definition of convex functions:[20]

[17] Gradient descent, also known as steepest descent, was first introduced by Cauchy in 1847 [Cau47]. Appendix C gives a more detailed account of optimization algorithms, including gradient descent.

[18] More precise conditions for convergence and complexity will be given in Chapters 8 and 9 for convex and nonconvex problems, respectively.

[19] It is worth noting that for many of the problems we will later discuss (e.g., MRI, spectrum sensing, face recognition), global optimality is very important – there is a *true* signal that we are trying to recover, and it is important to build algorithms that can do this reliably. In our simulated example of ℓ^0 minimization, we declared the solution $\hat{\boldsymbol{x}}$ correct, because it coincided with the true $\boldsymbol{x}_o$ that generated the observation $\boldsymbol{y}$. This is in contrast to some applications of optimization (e.g., in finance) where the objective function measures the goodness of the solution (say the expected rate of return on an investment), and locally improving the solution is meaningful, or even desirable, if the objective corresponds to dollars earned/lost!

[20] On the surface, this definition appears much more complicated than simply asking the second derivative to be positive. The reason for this complication is that we will need to work with convex functions that are not smooth; the general condition given in Definition 2.9 handles this situation as well.

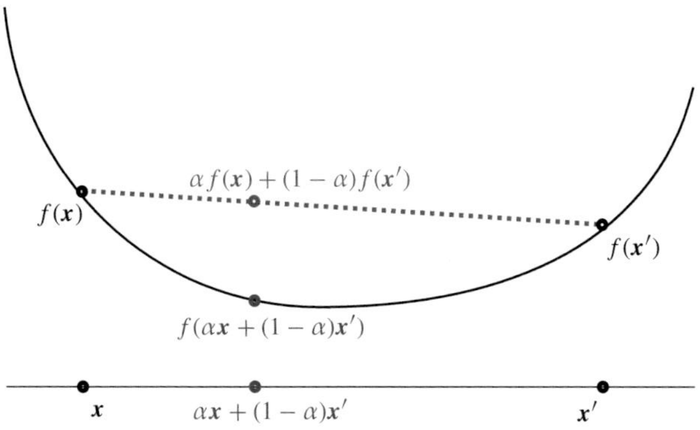

Figure 2.10 Definition of convexity. A convex function $f : \mathbb{R}^n \to \mathbb{R}$ is one which satisfies the inequality $f(\alpha x + (1-\alpha)x') \le \alpha f(x) + (1-\alpha) f(x')$ for all $\alpha \in [0,1]$ and $x, x' \in \mathbb{R}^n$. Geometrically, this means that if we take the points $(x, f(x))$ and $(x', f(x'))$ on the graph of f, and then draw a **line** joining them, the graph of the function falls below this line segment.

DEFINITION 2.9. (Convex function on $\mathbb{R}^n$) *A continuous function $f : \mathbb{R}^n \to \mathbb{R}$ is convex if for every pair of points $x, x' \in \mathbb{R}^n$ and $\alpha \in [0,1]$,*

$$f\big(\alpha x + (1-\alpha)x'\big) \le \alpha f(x) + (1-\alpha) f(x'). \tag{2.3.2}$$

This inequality can be visualized as follows. Consider two points $(x, f(x))$ and $(x', f(x'))$ on the graph of f. If we form the line segment joining these two points, this line segment lies above the graph of f. Figure 2.10 visualizes this inequality with an example.

A *convex combination* of a collection of points $x_1, \dots, x_k$ is an expression of the form $\sum_{i=1}^k \lambda_i x_i$, where the weights λ_i are nonnegative and $\sum_{i=1}^k \lambda_i = 1$. For example, for $\alpha \in [0,1]$, the expression $z = \alpha x + (1-\alpha)x'$ is a convex combination of the points x and x'. The definition (2.3.2) states that at the point z, the function f is no larger than the corresponding combination $\alpha f(x) + (1-\alpha) f(x')$ of the function values at the points x and x'.

This property of convex functions generalizes and gives the important Jensen's inequality, which states that the value of a convex function f at a convex combination of points is no greater than the corresponding convex combination of the function values:

PROPOSITION 2.10. (Jensen's inequality) *Let $f : \mathbb{R}^n \to \mathbb{R}$ be a convex function. Then for any k, any collection of points $x_1, \dots, x_k \in \mathbb{R}^n$, and any nonnegative scalars $\lambda_1, \dots, \lambda_k$ satisfying $\sum_{i=1}^k \lambda_i = 1$, one has*

$$f\left(\sum_{i=1}^k \lambda_i x_i\right) \le \sum_{i=1}^k \lambda_i f(x_i). \tag{2.3.3}$$

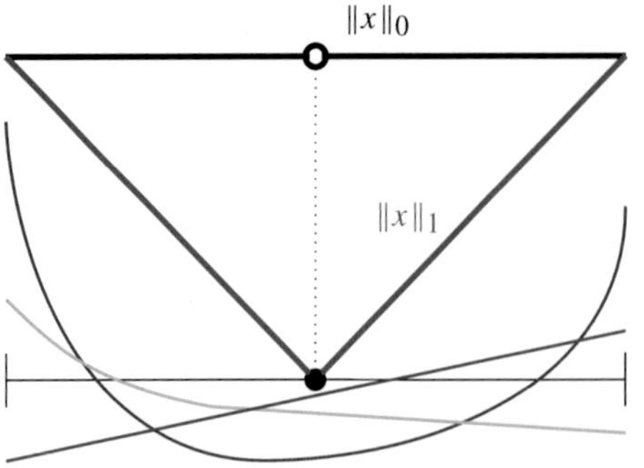

Figure 2.11 A convex surrogate for the ℓ^0 norm. In black, we plot the graph of the ℓ^0 norm of a scalar x, over the interval $x \in [-1, 1]$. This function takes on the value 0 at $x = 0$, and $+1$ everywhere else. In purple, green and blue, we plot various convex function examples $f(x)$ which underestimate $\|x\|_0$ on $[-1, 1]$, in the sense that $f(x) \le \|x\|_0$ for all $x \in [-1, 1]$. In red, we plot the function $f(x) = |x|$. This is the largest convex function which underestimates $\|x\|_0$ on $[-1, 1]$. We call $|x|$ the *convex envelope* of $\|x\|_0$ on $[-1, 1]$.

2.3.2 A Convex Surrogate for the ℓ^0 Norm: the ℓ^1 Norm

With the good properties of convex functions in mind, let us try to find a convex "surrogate" for the ℓ^0 norm. In one dimension, x is a scalar, and $\|x\|_0 = \mathbb{1}_{x \neq 0}$ is simply the indicator function for nonzero x. From Figure 2.11, it is clear that if we restrict our attention to the interval $x \in [-1, 1]$, the largest convex function which does not exceed $\|\cdot\|_0$ on this interval is simply the absolute value $|x|$. In the language of convex analysis, $|x|$ is the *convex envelope* of the function $\|x\|_0$ over the set $[-1, 1]$. This means that $|x|$ is the largest convex function f which satisfies $f(x) \le \|x\|_0$ for every $x \in [-1, 1]$, i.e., it is the largest convex underestimator of $\|x\|_0$ over this set. Thus, in one dimension, we might consider the absolute value of x as a plausible replacement for $\|x\|_0$.

For higher-dimensional $\boldsymbol{x}$ (i.e., $\boldsymbol{x} \in \mathbb{R}^n$), the ℓ^0 norm is[21]

$$\|\boldsymbol{x}\|_0 = \sum_{i=1}^{n} \mathbb{1}_{\boldsymbol{x}(i) \neq 0}. \tag{2.3.4}$$

Applying the above reasoning to each of the coordinates $\boldsymbol{x}(i)$, we obtain the ℓ^1 norm

$$\|\boldsymbol{x}\|_1 = \sum_{i=1}^{n} |\boldsymbol{x}(i)|. \tag{2.3.5}$$

As in the scalar case, this function is the tightest convex underestimator of $\|\cdot\|_0$, over an appropriate set of vectors $\boldsymbol{x}$:

THEOREM 2.11. *The function $\|\cdot\|_1$ is the convex envelope of $\|\cdot\|_0$, over the set $\mathsf{B}_\infty = \{\boldsymbol{x} \mid \|\boldsymbol{x}\|_\infty \le 1\}$ of vectors whose elements all have magnitude at most one.*

[21] In this book, we use $\boldsymbol{x}(i)$ to indicate the i-th entry of a vector $\boldsymbol{x}$. Also we often use the shorthand $x_i = \boldsymbol{x}(i) \in \mathbb{R}$.

Proof Let f be a convex function satisfying $f(\cdot) \leq \|\cdot\|_0$ on B_∞. We prove that $f(\cdot) \leq \|\cdot\|_1$ on B_∞ as well. Consider the cube $\mathsf{C} = [0,1]^n$. Its vertices are the vectors $\sigma \in \{0,1\}^n$. Any $\boldsymbol{x} \in \mathsf{C}$ can be written as a convex combination of these vertices:

$$\boldsymbol{x} = \sum_i \lambda_i \sigma_i. \tag{2.3.6}$$

Because $f(\cdot) \leq \|\cdot\|_0$, $f(\sigma_i) \leq \|\sigma_i\|_0 = \|\sigma_i\|_1$. Because f is convex,

$$\begin{aligned} f(\boldsymbol{x}) = f\left(\sum\nolimits_i \lambda_i \sigma_i\right) &\leq \sum_i \lambda_i f(\sigma_i) && \text{[Jensen's inequality]} \\ &\leq \sum_i \lambda_i \|\sigma_i\|_0 = \sum_i \lambda_i \|\sigma_i\|_1 && [\sigma_i \text{ are binary}] \\ &= \|\boldsymbol{x}\|_1 . \end{aligned} \tag{2.3.7}$$

Hence, $f(\cdot) \leq \|\cdot\|_1$ on the intersection of B_∞ with the nonnegative orthant. Repeating the argument for each of the orthants, we obtain that $f(\cdot) \leq \|\cdot\|_1$ on B_∞, and hence $\|\cdot\|_1$ is the convex envelope of $\|\cdot\|_0$ over B_∞. □

So, at least in the sense of convex envelopes, the ℓ^1 norm provides a good replacement for the ℓ^0 norm. Replacing the ℓ^0 norm in (2.2.9) with the ℓ^1 norm, we obtain a convex ℓ^1 minimization problem,

$$\begin{array}{ll} \min & \|\boldsymbol{x}\|_1 \\ \text{subject to} & \boldsymbol{A}\boldsymbol{x} = \boldsymbol{y}. \end{array} \tag{2.3.8}$$

In contrast to the ℓ^0 problem, this problem *can* be solved efficiently.

2.3.3 A Simple Test of ℓ^1 Minimization

Theorem 2.11 is a strong initial motivation for considering ℓ^1 minimization (2.3.8) for recovering a sparse solution – it says that in a certain sense, the ℓ^1 norm is the canonical convex surrogate for the ℓ^0 norm. Some care is in order, though. Theorem 2.11 does not say anything at all about the *correctness* of (2.3.8) – whether the solution to (2.3.8) is actually the desired sparse vector $\boldsymbol{x}_o$.

The easiest way to get some insight into this question is to do an experiment! For this, we will need to solve the problem (2.3.8) computationally and see how well it works. How do we solve the optimization problem (2.3.8)? Appendix D gives a quick introduction to some general optimization techniques that may help us solve problems of this kind. More specifically, since the objective function is convex, the geometry of a convex function in Figure 2.12(a) suggests that we should do quite well just using local information about the slope of the objective function. Indeed, if our objective function were differentiable, this would very naturally suggest the classical *gradient descent* method for solving problems of the form

$$\min \; f(\boldsymbol{x}). \tag{2.3.9}$$

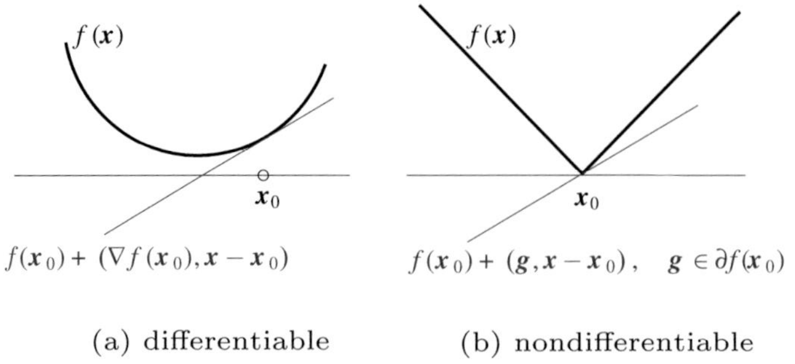

Figure 2.12 Subgradients of convex functions. (a) For a differentiable convex function, the best linear approximation at any point $\boldsymbol{x}_0$ is a *global* lower bound on the function. (b) For a nondifferentiable function, we say that $\boldsymbol{g}$ is a subgradient of f at $\boldsymbol{x}_0$ (and write $\boldsymbol{g} \in \partial f(\boldsymbol{x}_0)$) if $\boldsymbol{g}$ is the slope of a linear function that takes on the value $f(\boldsymbol{x}_0)$ at $\boldsymbol{x}_0$, and globally lower-bounds f.

This algorithm starts at some initial point $\boldsymbol{x}_0$, and then generates a sequence of points $(\boldsymbol{x}_0, \boldsymbol{x}_1, \ldots, \boldsymbol{x}_k, \ldots)$ by iteratively moving in the direction of greatest decrease of $f(\cdot)$:

$$\boldsymbol{x}_{k+1} = \boldsymbol{x}_k - t_k \nabla f(\boldsymbol{x}_k). \tag{2.3.10}$$

Here, $t_k \geq 0$ is a properly chosen step size.

There are two main difficulties that prevent us from directly applying the gradient descent iteration (2.3.10) to the ℓ^1 minimization problem (2.3.8).

- **Nontrivial constraints:** Unlike the general unconstrained problem (2.3.9), in the problem (2.3.8) we are only interested in $\boldsymbol{x}$ that satisfy $\boldsymbol{A}\boldsymbol{x} = \boldsymbol{y}$.
- **Nondifferentiable objective:** The objective function in (2.3.8) is not differentiable, and so at certain points the gradient $\nabla f(\boldsymbol{x})$ does not exist. Figure 2.12(b) shows this: the function is pointed at zero! Since zero is sparse, this is precisely one of the points we are most interested in.

Constraints

One approach to handle the first problem is to replace the gradient descent iteration with *projected gradient descent*. This algorithm aims at general problems of the form

$$\begin{array}{ll} \min & f(\boldsymbol{x}) \\ \text{subject to} & \boldsymbol{x} \in \mathsf{C}, \end{array} \tag{2.3.11}$$

where C is some constraint set. This algorithm is exactly the same as gradient descent, except that at each iteration it *projects* the result $\boldsymbol{x}_k - t_k \nabla f(\boldsymbol{x}_k)$ onto the set C. The projection of a point $\boldsymbol{z}$ onto the set C is simply the nearest point to $\boldsymbol{z}$ in C:

$$\mathcal{P}_{\mathsf{C}}[\boldsymbol{z}] = \arg\min_{\boldsymbol{x} \in \mathsf{C}} \tfrac{1}{2} \|\boldsymbol{z} - \boldsymbol{x}\|_2^2 \equiv h(\boldsymbol{x}). \tag{2.3.12}$$

For general C, the projection may not exist, or may not be unique (think about how this could happen). However, for closed, convex sets, the projection is well defined,

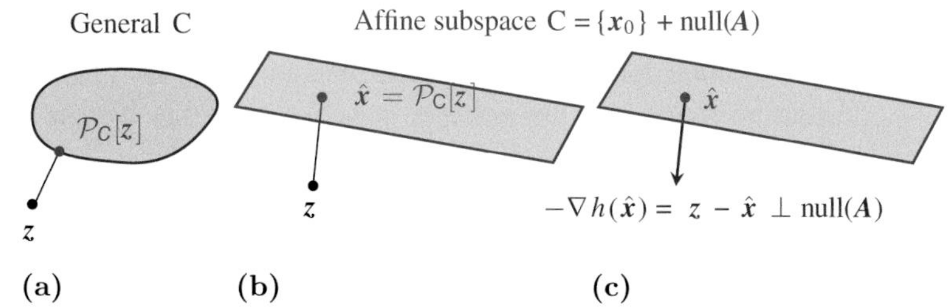

Figure 2.13 Projection onto convex sets. (a) Projection onto a general convex set. (b) Projection onto an affine subspace. (c) Projection onto the affine subspace can be characterized as the point $\hat{x}$ at which the gradient $\nabla h(\hat{x})$ is orthogonal to null(A).

and satisfies a wealth of useful properties. If A has full row rank, the projection onto the convex set $\mathsf{C} = \{x \mid Ax = y\}$ has an especially simple form:

$$\mathcal{P}_{\{x \mid Ax = y\}}[z] = z - A^* \left(AA^*\right)^{-1} \left[Az - y\right]. \tag{2.3.13}$$

Figure 2.13 visualizes the projection onto this particular C. This formula can be derived by noting two properties of the projection $\hat{x} = \mathcal{P}_{\mathsf{C}}[z]$:

1 **Feasibility**: $\hat{x} \in \mathsf{C}$, i.e., $A\hat{x} = y$.
2 **Residual is orthogonal**: $z - \hat{x} \perp \text{null}(A)$. Since $z - \hat{x} = -\nabla h(\hat{x})$, this condition can be stated as

$$-\nabla h(\hat{x}) \text{ is orthogonal to } \mathsf{C} \text{ at } \hat{x}.$$

Exercise 2.11 guides the interested reader through the derivation of this expression. For the general problem (2.3.11), with differentiable objective f, the *projected gradient algorithm* simply repeats the iteration

$$x_{k+1} = \mathcal{P}_{\mathsf{C}}\left[x_k - t_k \nabla f(x_k)\right]. \tag{2.3.14}$$

Nondifferentiability

The problem of nondifferentiability is slightly trickier. To handle it properly, we need to generalize the notion of derivative to include functions that are not differentiable. For this, we draw inspiration from geometry. Consider Figure 2.12(a). It displays a convex, differentiable function $f(x)$, as well as a linear approximation $\hat{f}(x)$, taken at a point x_0:

$$\hat{f}(x) = f(x_0) + \langle \nabla f(x_0), x - x_0 \rangle. \tag{2.3.15}$$

The salient point here is that the graph of f lies entirely above the graph of the approximation $\hat{f}$:

$$f(x) \geq f(x_0) + \langle \nabla f(x_0), x - x_0 \rangle, \quad \forall\, x \in \mathbb{R}^n. \tag{2.3.16}$$

It is not too difficult to prove that this property holds for *every* convex differentiable function and every point x_0, simply by using calculus and the definition of convexity.

This geometry opens the door for generalizing the notion of the gradient to nonsmooth functions. For nonsmooth functions such as $f(\boldsymbol{x}) = \|\boldsymbol{x}\|_1$, at a point of nonsmoothness $\boldsymbol{x}_0$, the gradient does not exist, but we can still make a linear underestimator

$$\hat{f}(\boldsymbol{x}) = f(\boldsymbol{x}_0) + \langle \boldsymbol{u}, \boldsymbol{x} - \boldsymbol{x}_0 \rangle, \tag{2.3.17}$$

as in Figure 2.12(b). Here, $\boldsymbol{u}$ replaces ∇f in the previous expression, and plays the role of the "slope" of the approximation. We say that $\boldsymbol{u}$ is a *subgradient* of f at $\boldsymbol{x}_0$ if the linear approximation defined by $\boldsymbol{u}$ is indeed an underestimator of f (i.e., it lower-bounds $f(\boldsymbol{x})$ at all points $\boldsymbol{x}$):

$$f(\boldsymbol{x}) \geq f(\boldsymbol{x}_0) + \langle \boldsymbol{u}, \boldsymbol{x} - \boldsymbol{x}_0 \rangle, \quad \forall\, \boldsymbol{x}. \tag{2.3.18}$$

Let us consider our function of interest – the ℓ^1 norm. For $\boldsymbol{x} \in \mathbb{R}$ (one dimension), $\|\boldsymbol{x}\|_1 = |x|$ is simply the absolute value. For $x < 0$, the slope of the graph of $|x|$ is -1, while for $|x| > 0$, it is $+1$. Convince yourself that if we take $\boldsymbol{x}_0 \neq 0$, then the only u satisfying the above definition is $u = \operatorname{sign}(x)$.

However, at 0 the function $|x|$ is "pointy," namely, nondifferentiable, and something different happens: at $x_0 = 0$, every $u \in [-1, 1]$ defines a linear approximation that underestimates f. So, in fact, every $u \in [-1, 1]$ is a subgradient. Thus, at points of nondifferentiability there may exist multiple subgradients. We call the collection of all subgradients of f at a point $\boldsymbol{x}_0$ the *subdifferential* of f at $\boldsymbol{x}_0$, and denote it by $\partial f(\boldsymbol{x}_0)$. Formally:

DEFINITION 2.12. (Subgradient and subdifferential) *Let* $f : \mathbb{R}^n \to \mathbb{R}$ *be a convex function. A* subgradient *of* f *at* $\boldsymbol{x}_0$ *is any* $\boldsymbol{u}$ *satisfying*

$$f(\boldsymbol{x}) \geq f(\boldsymbol{x}_0) + \langle \boldsymbol{u}, \boldsymbol{x} - \boldsymbol{x}_0 \rangle, \quad \forall\, \boldsymbol{x}. \tag{2.3.19}$$

The subdifferential *of* f *at* $\boldsymbol{x}_0$ *is the set of all subgradients of* f *at* $\boldsymbol{x}_0$*:*

$$\partial f(\boldsymbol{x}_0) = \left\{ \boldsymbol{u} \mid \forall\, \boldsymbol{x} \in \mathbb{R}^n,\ f(\boldsymbol{x}) \geq f(\boldsymbol{x}_0) + \langle \boldsymbol{u}, \boldsymbol{x} - \boldsymbol{x}_0 \rangle \right\}. \tag{2.3.20}$$

With these definitions in mind, we might imagine that in the nonsmooth case, a suitable replacement for the gradient algorithm might be the *subgradient method*, which chooses (somehow) $\boldsymbol{g}_k \in \partial f(\boldsymbol{x}_k)$, and then proceeds in the direction of $-\boldsymbol{g}_k$: $\boldsymbol{x}_{k+1} = \boldsymbol{x}_k - t_k \boldsymbol{g}_k$. Incorporating projection onto the feasible set C, we arrive at the following *projected subgradient algorithm*:[22]

$$\boldsymbol{x}_{k+1} = \mathcal{P}_{\mathsf{C}}[\boldsymbol{x}_k - t_k \boldsymbol{g}_k], \quad \boldsymbol{g}_k \in \partial f(\boldsymbol{x}_k). \tag{2.3.21}$$

To apply the projected subgradient method, we need an expression for the subdifferential of the ℓ^1 norm. Figure 2.14 visualizes this. In one dimension, $\|\boldsymbol{x}\|_1 = |x|$; this function is differentiable away from $x = 0$. For $x > 0$, $\partial|\cdot|(x) = \{1\}$, while for $x < 0$, $\partial|\cdot|(x) = \{-1\}$. At $x = 0$, $|x|$ is not differentiable, and there are multiple possible linear lower bounds. Figure 2.14 visualizes three of these lower bounds. It is

[22] Projected subgradient methods were first developed by Naum Shor [Sho85] and Boris Polyak among others in the 1960s.

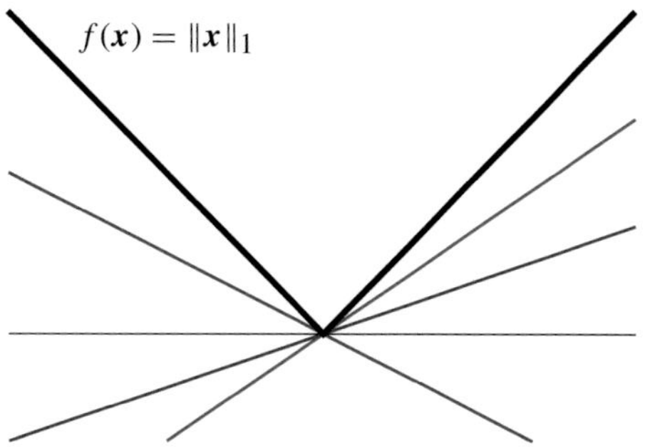

Figure 2.14 Subdifferential of the ℓ^1 norm. In black, $f(\boldsymbol{x}) = \|\boldsymbol{x}\|_1$. In blue, purple, and red, three linear lower bounds of the form $g(\boldsymbol{x}) = f(\boldsymbol{x}_0) + \langle \boldsymbol{u}, \boldsymbol{x} - \boldsymbol{x}_0 \rangle$, taken at $\boldsymbol{x}_0 = \boldsymbol{0}$, with slope $\boldsymbol{u} = -\frac{1}{2}, \frac{1}{3}$, and $\frac{2}{3}$, respectively. It should be clear that any slope $\boldsymbol{u} \in [-1, 1]$ defines a linear lower bound on $f(\boldsymbol{x})$ around $\boldsymbol{x}_0 = \boldsymbol{0}$. So, $\partial |\cdot|(0) = [-1, 1]$. For $\boldsymbol{x}_0 > 0$, the only linear lower bound has slope $\boldsymbol{u} = 1$; for $\boldsymbol{x}_0 < 0$, the only linear lower bound has slope $\boldsymbol{u} = -1$. So, $\partial |\cdot|(\boldsymbol{x}) = \{-1\}$ for $\boldsymbol{x} < 0$ and $\partial |\cdot|(\boldsymbol{x}) = \{1\}$ for $\boldsymbol{x} > 0$. Lemma 2.13 proves this formally, and extends to higher-dimensional $\boldsymbol{x} \in \mathbb{R}^n$.

not difficult to see that lower bounds at $x = 0$ can have any slope from -1 to 1; hence, the subdifferential is

$$\partial |\cdot|(x) = [-1, 1], \quad \text{at } x = 0.$$

The following lemma extends this observation to higher-dimensional $\boldsymbol{x} \in \mathbb{R}^n$:

LEMMA 2.13. (Subdifferential of $\|\cdot\|_1$) *Let* $\boldsymbol{x} \in \mathbb{R}^n$, *with* $\mathsf{I} = \operatorname{supp}(\boldsymbol{x})$,

$$\partial \|\cdot\|_1 (\boldsymbol{x}) = \left\{ \boldsymbol{v} \in \mathbb{R}^n \mid \boldsymbol{P}_{\mathsf{I}} \boldsymbol{v} = \operatorname{sign}(\boldsymbol{x}), \ \|\boldsymbol{v}\|_\infty \le 1 \right\}. \tag{2.3.22}$$

Here, $\boldsymbol{P}_{\mathsf{I}} \in \mathbb{R}^{n \times n}$ *is the orthoprojector onto coordinates* I*:*

$$[\boldsymbol{P}_{\mathsf{I}} \boldsymbol{v}](j) = \begin{cases} \boldsymbol{v}(j) & j \in \mathsf{I}, \\ 0 & j \notin \mathsf{I}. \end{cases} \tag{2.3.23}$$

Proof The subdifferential $\partial \|\cdot\|_1 (\boldsymbol{x})$ consists of all vectors $\boldsymbol{v}$ that satisfy

$$\sum_{i=1}^{n} |\boldsymbol{x}'(i)| \ge \sum_{i=1}^{n} |\boldsymbol{x}(i)| + \boldsymbol{v}(i) \left(\boldsymbol{x}'(i) - \boldsymbol{x}(i) \right) \tag{2.3.24}$$

for every $\boldsymbol{x}$ and $\boldsymbol{x}'$. A sufficient condition is that for every index i and every scalar z,

$$|z| \ge |\boldsymbol{x}(i)| + \boldsymbol{v}(i)(z - \boldsymbol{x}(i)). \tag{2.3.25}$$

Taking $\boldsymbol{x}' = \boldsymbol{x} + (z - \boldsymbol{x}(i))\boldsymbol{e}_i$ in (2.3.24) shows that (2.3.25) is also necessary. If $\boldsymbol{x}(i) = 0$, (2.3.25) becomes $|z| \ge \boldsymbol{v}(i) z$, which holds for all z if and only if $|\boldsymbol{v}(i)| \le 1$. If $\boldsymbol{x}(i) \ne 0$, the inequality is satisfied if and only if $\boldsymbol{v}(i) = \operatorname{sign}(\boldsymbol{x}(i))$. Hence, $\boldsymbol{v} \in \partial \|\cdot\|_1$ if and only if for all $i \in \mathsf{I}$, $\boldsymbol{v}(i) = \operatorname{sign}(\boldsymbol{x}(i))$, and for all i, $|\boldsymbol{v}(i)| \le 1$. This conclusion is summarized as (2.3.22). □

Algorithm 2.2 ℓ^1 Minimization by projected subgradient

Input: a matrix $A \in \mathbb{R}^{m \times n}$ and a vector $y \in \mathbb{R}^m$.
Compute $\Gamma \leftarrow I - A^*(AA^*)^{-1}A$, and $\tilde{x} \leftarrow A^\dagger y = A^*(AA^*)^{-1}y$.
$x_0 \leftarrow \mathbf{0}$.
$t \leftarrow 0$.
repeat many times
    $t \leftarrow t + 1$;
    $x_t \leftarrow \tilde{x} + \Gamma\,(x_{t-1} - (1/t)\,\mathrm{sign}(x_{t-1}))$;

The projected subgradient method alternates between subgradient steps, which move in the direction of $-\mathrm{sign}(x)$, and orthogonal projections onto the feasible set $\{x \mid Ax = y\}$ according to equation (2.3.13). We obtain a very simple algorithm that solves (2.3.8), which we spell out in detail as Algorithm 2.2.

REMARK 2.14. (Projected subgradient and better alternatives) *In many respects, this is a bad method for solving the ℓ^1 problem. It is correct, but it converges very slowly compared to methods that exploit a certain piece of problem-specific structure, which we will describe in later chapters. The main virtue of Algorithm 2.2 is that it is simple and intuitive, and also serves our exposition by introducing or reminding us of subgradients and projection operators.*[23] *The projected subgradient method for ℓ^1 minimization can be implemented in just a few lines of MATLAB code. In Chapter 8, we will systematically develop a number of more advanced optimization methods that can fully utilize the structures in this problem for better efficiency and scalability.*

To see how well ℓ^1 minimization (as implemented through the projected subgradient method) does perform, run `Chapter_2_L1_recovery.m` from the book's website. You may see an interesting phenomenon! Although the method does not *always* succeed, it *does* succeed whenever the target solution x_o is *sufficiently sparse*! Figure 2.15 illustrates this in a more systematic way. In the figure, we generate random matrices A of size 200×400 and random vectors x_o with k nonzero entries. We vary k from 1 to 200. For each k, we run 50 experiments and plot the fraction of trials in which ℓ^1 minimization correctly recovers x_o, up to numerical error. Notice that, indeed, ℓ^1 minimization succeeds whenever x_o is sufficiently sparse.

2.3.4 Sparse Error Correction via Logan's Phenomenon

In Section 1.2.2 of the introduction chapter, we have discussed the work of Benjamin Logan, who has shown that ℓ^1 minimization can be used to remove sparse errors in band-limited signals. To connect its content more closely to our setting here, let us consider a discretized analog of the result, in which we consider a finite-dimensional

[23] Also, we would like you to have a feel for at least one *very* simple way for implementing ℓ^1 minimization in code and to play with it. Our experience is that this helps to think more concretely about the optimization problem and its applications, rather than leaving it as a mathematical abstraction.

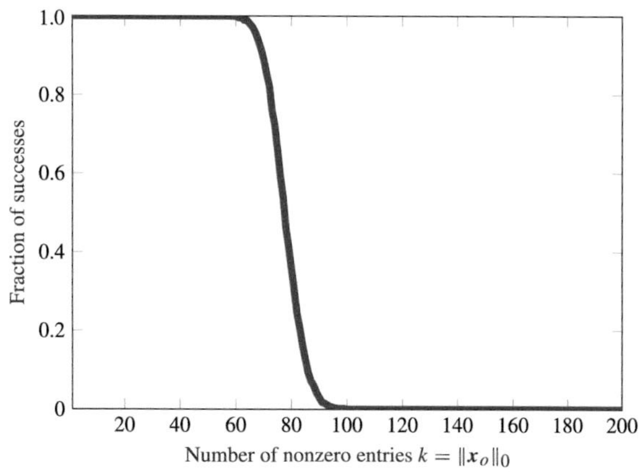

Figure 2.15 Phase transition in ℓ^1 minimization. We consider the problem of recovering a sparse vector $\boldsymbol{x}_o$ from measurements $\boldsymbol{y} = \boldsymbol{A}\boldsymbol{x}_o$, where $\boldsymbol{A} \in \mathbb{R}^{200\times 400}$ is a Gaussian matrix. We vary the number of nonzero entries $k = \|\boldsymbol{x}_o\|_0$ across $k = 0, 1, \dots, 200$, and plot the fraction of instances where ℓ^1 minimization successfully recovers $\boldsymbol{x}_o$, over 50 independent experiments for each value of k. Notice that this probability of success exhibits a (rather sharp) transition from 1 (guaranteed success) to 0 (guaranteed failure) as k increases. Notice, moreover, that *for sufficiently well-structured problems (k small), ℓ^1 minimization always succeeds.*

signal $\boldsymbol{y} \in \mathbb{C}^n$. Let $\boldsymbol{F} \in \mathbb{C}^{n\times n}$ be the discrete Fourier transform (DFT) basis for $\mathbb{C}^n$ (see equation (A.7.13) of Appendix A). That is, we have

$$F_{kl} = \frac{1}{\sqrt{n}} \exp\left(2\pi \mathrm{i}\frac{kl}{n}\right), \quad k = 0, \dots, n-1,\ l = 0, \dots, (n-1). \tag{2.3.26}$$

Let $\boldsymbol{f}_0, \dots, \boldsymbol{f}_{(n-1)}$ denote the columns of the DFT matrix:

$$\boldsymbol{F} = \left[\boldsymbol{f}_0 \mid \cdots \mid \boldsymbol{f}_{(n-1)}\right] \quad \in \mathbb{C}^{n\times n}. \tag{2.3.27}$$

Form a submatrix $\boldsymbol{B} \in \mathbb{C}^{n\times(d+1)}$, corresponding to the d lowest-frequency elements of this basis and their conjugates:[24]

$$\boldsymbol{B} = \left[\boldsymbol{f}_{-(d-1)/2} \mid \cdots \mid \boldsymbol{f}_{(d-1)/2}\right] \quad \in \mathbb{C}^{n\times(d+1)}, \tag{2.3.28}$$

where we use $\boldsymbol{f}_{-i}$ to indicate the conjugate of $\boldsymbol{f}_i$. Let us imagine that $\boldsymbol{x}_o = \boldsymbol{B}\boldsymbol{w}_o \in \mathrm{col}(\boldsymbol{B})$, and

$$\boldsymbol{y} = \boldsymbol{x}_o + \boldsymbol{e}_o, \tag{2.3.29}$$

where $\|\boldsymbol{e}_o\|_0 \le k$. Our task is to recover $\boldsymbol{x}_o$ (which is equivalent to removing $\boldsymbol{e}_o$). A discrete analog of the program suggested in Logan's theorem would be to solve[25]

[24] We use pairs of conjugate bases to represent real signals. One may view the range of $\boldsymbol{B}$ as the discretized version of the band-limited functions $\mathcal{B}_1(\Omega)$ introduced earlier in Logan's Theorem 1.5.

[25] For complex vectors, the ℓ^1 norm is simply the sum of absolute values of the real and imaginary parts. Or equivalently, we identify a complex vector in $\mathbb{C}^n$ as a real vector in $\mathbb{R}^{2n}$.

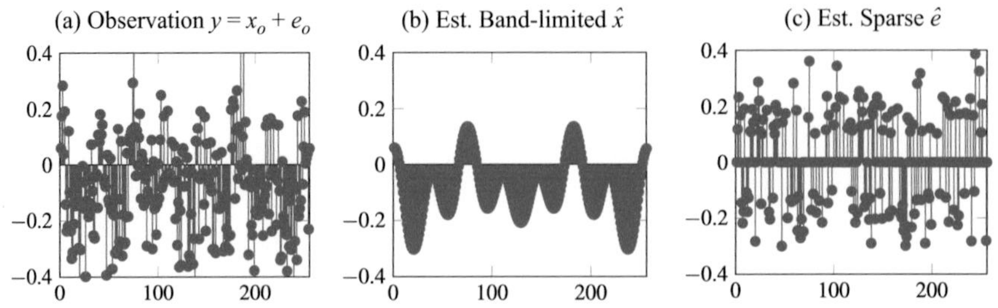

Figure 2.16 Logan's phenomenon. (a) The superposition $\boldsymbol{y} = \boldsymbol{x}_o + \boldsymbol{e}_o$ of a band-limited signal $\boldsymbol{x}_o$ and a sparse error $\boldsymbol{e}_o$. (b) Estimate $\hat{\boldsymbol{x}}$ by ℓ^1 minimization. (c) Estimate $\hat{\boldsymbol{e}}$ by ℓ^1 minimization. Both estimates are accurate to within relative error 10^{-6}.

$$\begin{array}{ll} \min & \|\boldsymbol{y} - \boldsymbol{x}\|_1 \\ \text{subject to} & \boldsymbol{x} \in \operatorname{col}(\boldsymbol{B}). \end{array} \tag{2.3.30}$$

This problem is actually very much equivalent to the sparse signal recovery problem discussed so far. To see this, let $\boldsymbol{A}$ be a matrix whose rows span the left null space of $\boldsymbol{B}$, i.e., $\operatorname{rank}(\boldsymbol{A}) = n - d$, and $\boldsymbol{A}\boldsymbol{B} = \boldsymbol{0}$. Then $\boldsymbol{A}\boldsymbol{x}_o = \boldsymbol{0}$, and our observation equation (2.3.29) is equivalent to

$$\bar{\boldsymbol{y}} = \boldsymbol{A}\boldsymbol{e}_o, \tag{2.3.31}$$

where $\bar{\boldsymbol{y}} = \boldsymbol{A}\boldsymbol{y}$. From this, it is not difficult to argue that the optimization problem (2.3.30) is equivalent to

$$\begin{array}{ll} \min & \|\boldsymbol{e}\|_1 \\ \text{subject to} & \boldsymbol{A}\boldsymbol{e} = \bar{\boldsymbol{y}}, \end{array} \tag{2.3.32}$$

in the sense that $\boldsymbol{e}_\star$ is an optimal solution to (2.3.32) if and only if $\boldsymbol{y} - \boldsymbol{e}_\star \in \operatorname{col}(\boldsymbol{B})$ is an optimal solution to (2.3.30). Figure 2.16 shows an example of this discrete analog of Logan's phenomenon. You can reproduce this result by running `E6886_Lecture2_Demo_Logan.m` from the book's webpage.

Given the examples we have seen thus far of how sparsity arises in application problems, the phenomenon associated with ℓ^1 minimization is certainly intriguing. In the coming chapters, we will study it first from a mathematical perspective, to understand *why* it occurs and what its limitations are; we will then investigate its implications for practical applications in later chapters.

2.4 Summary

Let us briefly recap what we have learned in this chapter. In many modern data analysis and signal processing applications, we need to solve very large, underdetermined systems of linear equations:

$$\boldsymbol{y} = \boldsymbol{A}\boldsymbol{x}, \quad \boldsymbol{A} \in \mathbb{R}^{m \times n},\ m < n.$$

Such problems are inherently ill posed: they admit infinitely many solutions.

Uniqueness of the Sparse Solution

To make such problems well posed, or to make the solution unique, we need to leverage additional properties of the solution that we wish to recover. One important property, which arises in many practical applications, is sparsity (or compressibility). This is a powerful piece of information: although the signals themselves reside in a very high-dimensional space, they have only a few intrinsic degrees of freedom – they can be represented as a linear superposition of just a few atoms from a properly chosen dictionary. As Theorem 2.6 shows, under fairly general conditions, imposing sparsity on $\boldsymbol{x}$ can indeed make the problem of solving

$$\min \|\boldsymbol{x}\|_0 \quad \text{subject to} \quad \boldsymbol{y} = \boldsymbol{A}\boldsymbol{x}$$

well conditioned: as long as the target solution $\boldsymbol{x}_o$ is sufficiently sparse with respect to *the Kruskal rank* of $\boldsymbol{A}$, the sparsest solution to $\boldsymbol{y} = \boldsymbol{A}\boldsymbol{x}$ is unique and is the correct solution.

Tractability of the Sparse Solution via Convex Relaxation

Computationally, however, finding the sparsest solution to a linear system is in general intractable (i.e., NP-hard, Theorem 2.8). To alleviate the computational difficulty, we relax the ℓ^0 minimization problem and replace the ℓ^0 norm of $\boldsymbol{x}$ with its convex envelope, the ℓ^1 norm:

$$\min \|\boldsymbol{x}\|_1 \quad \text{subject to} \quad \boldsymbol{y} = \boldsymbol{A}\boldsymbol{x}.$$

Projected Subgradient Descent

We have introduced a very basic subgradient descent algorithm (Algorithm 2.2) that solves the convex ℓ^1 minimization problem. From the results of the algorithm, we observe a striking phenomenon that ℓ^1 minimization can effectively recover the sparse solution under fairly broad conditions. We will explain why this is the case in the next chapter after we carefully characterize exact conditions under which ℓ^1 minimization gives the correct sparse solution.

2.5 Notes

Application Vignettes

Some of the early applications of sparse representation are in signal processing, such as medical imaging [LDP07], seismic signals [HH08], and image processing [YWHM08, MES08]. The three applications described in this chapter illustrate various aspects of sparse modeling and sparse recovery. The medical imaging application is described in the work of Lustig et al. [LDP07, LDSP08]. The denoising results shown in Section 2.1.2 are due to Mairal et al. [MES08]. The face recognition formulation in Section 2.1.3 is described in [WYG$^+$09]. The discussion in this chapter only touches the surface of these problems; we will revisit medical imaging in Chapter 10 and face recognition in Chapter 13. Please see these chapters and their references for broader context and related work on each of these problems. These are just a few of the vast array of applications of sparse methods; a few of these are highlighted in Part III of the book, such as Chapters 11–16.

NP-Hardness of ℓ^0 Minimization and Related Problems

The hardness result for ℓ^0 minimization, Theorem 2.8, is due to Natarajan [Nat95]; see also Davis, Mallat, and Avellaneda [DMA97]. Results of Amaldi and Kann [AK95, AK98] and Arora, Babai, Stern, and Sweedyk [ABSS93] show that ℓ^0 minimization problems are also NP-hard to approximate. Delineating the boundaries between tractable and intractable instances of sparse approximation remains an active topic of research: see, e.g., Zhang, Wainwright, and Jordan [ZWJ14] or Foster, Karloff, and Thaler [FKT15] for more recent developments. There are hardness results for a number of problems that relate closely to sparse approximation. These results also have implications for sparse error correction. There are also hardness results around the problem of *matrix sparsification* in numerical analysis, which seeks to replace a given matrix $\boldsymbol{A}$ with a sparse matrix $\hat{\boldsymbol{A}}$ such that range($\boldsymbol{A}$) $\approx$ range($\hat{\boldsymbol{A}}$): see McCormick [McC83], Coleman and Pothen [CP86], and Gottlieb and Neylon [GN16] for discussions of the hardness of this and related problems. Based on reduction techniques similar to that classical complexity theory, the most recent work of Brennan and Bresler [BB20] has systematically studied the gaps between statistical and computational complexity for a broad family of related problems such as sparse linear regression and sparse PCA, as well as many problems related to matrices and tensors that we will study in later chapters.

2.6 Exercises

2.1. (Convexity of ℓ^p norms) *Show that*

$$\|\boldsymbol{x}\|_p = \left(\sum_i |x_i|^p \right)^{1/p} \tag{2.6.1}$$

is convex for $p \geq 1$, and nonconvex for $0 < p < 1$.

2.2. *Show that for $0 < p < 1$, $\|\boldsymbol{x}\|_p$ is not a norm in the sense of Definition 2.1.*

2.3. (Relationship between ℓ^p norms) *Show that for $p < q$,*

$$\|\boldsymbol{x}\|_p \geq \|\boldsymbol{x}\|_q \tag{2.6.2}$$

for every $\boldsymbol{x}$. For what $\boldsymbol{x}$ is equality obtained (i.e., $\|\boldsymbol{x}\|_p = \|\boldsymbol{x}\|_q$)?

2.4. (Computing the kruskal rank) *Write a MATLAB function that takes as an input a matrix $\boldsymbol{A} \in \mathbb{R}^{m \times n}$, and outputs the Kruskal rank* krank($\boldsymbol{A}$). *There is no known way to efficiently compute the Kruskal rank. It is fine if your code takes time exponential in n. Corroborate the conclusion of Theorem 2.6, by generating a 4×8 Gaussian matrix $\boldsymbol{A}$, via* `A = randn(4,8)`, *and computing its Kruskal rank.*

2.5. (A structured matrix with small kruskal rank) *Consider a* 4×8 *dimensional complex matrix generated as*

$$A = [\, I \mid F \,], \tag{2.6.3}$$

where I *is the* 4×4 *identity matrix, and* F *is a* 4×4 *DFT matrix: in MATLAB,* `A = [ eye(4), dftmtx(4) ]`. *Using either your code from Exercise 2.4, or hand calculations, determine the Kruskal rank of* A. *You should find that it is smaller than 4! A general version of this phenomenon can be observed with the* Dirac comb, *which is sparse in both time and frequency.*

2.6. (The spark) *Results on* ℓ^0 *uniqueness are sometimes described in terms of the* spark *of a matrix, which is the number of nonzero entries in the sparsest nonzero element of the null space of* A*:*

$$\operatorname{spark}(A) \quad = \quad \min_{d \neq 0,\; Ad = 0} \|d\|_0.$$

What is the relationship between $\operatorname{spark}(A)$ *and* $\operatorname{krank}(A)$*?*

2.7. (Kruskal rank of random matrices) *In this exercise we prove that for a generic* $m \times n$ *matrix* A *with entries* $\sim_{\text{iid}} \mathcal{N}(0,1)$, $\operatorname{krank}(A) = m$ *with probability one.*

(a) Argue that for any $m \times n$ *matrix* A, $\operatorname{krank}(A) \leq m$.

(b) Let $A = [a_1 \mid \cdots \mid a_n]$ *with* $a_i \in \mathbb{R}^m$ *as column vectors. Let* span *denote the linear span of a collection of vectors. Argue that*

$$\mathbb{P}\left[a_m \in \operatorname{span}(a_1, \ldots, a_{m-1})\right] = 0. \tag{2.6.4}$$

(c) Argue that $\operatorname{krank}(A) < m$ *if and only if there exist some indices* $i_1, \ldots, i_m$ *such that*

$$a_{i_m} \in \operatorname{span}(a_{i_1}, \ldots, a_{i_m - 1}). \tag{2.6.5}$$

(d) Conclude that $\operatorname{krank}(A) = m$ *with probability one, by noting that*

$$\begin{aligned}
&\mathbb{P}\left[\exists\, i_1, \ldots, i_m \;:\; a_{i_m} \in \operatorname{span}(a_{i_1}, \ldots, a_{i_{m-1}})\right] \\
&\leq \sum_{i_1, \ldots, i_m} \mathbb{P}\left[a_{i_m} \in \operatorname{span}(a_{i_1}, \ldots, a_{i_{m-1}})\right] \\
&\leq m^n \times \underbrace{\mathbb{P}\left[a_m \in \operatorname{span}(a_1, \ldots, a_{m-1})\right]}_{=0} \\
&= 0.
\end{aligned}$$

2.8. (ℓ^0 minimization and typical examples) *We showed that there is a* worst-case *phase transition in* ℓ^0 *minimization at* $1/2\operatorname{krank}(A)$. *This means that* ℓ^0 *minimization recovers* every x_o *satisfying* $\|x_o\|_0 < 1/2\operatorname{krank}(A)$. *We also know that for a Gaussian matrix* $A \in \mathbb{R}^{m \times n}$, $\operatorname{krank}(A) = m$*, with probability one.*

Using code for ℓ^0 *minimization provided (or write your own!), do the following: generate a* 5×12 *Gaussian matrix* `A = randn(5,12)`. *What is* $\operatorname{rank}(A)$*? Generate a sparse vector* x_o*, with four nonzero entries, via* `xo = zeros(12,1);`

`xo(1:4) = randn(4,1)`. *Now, set* `y = A xo`. *Solve the* ℓ^0 *minimization problem, to find the sparsest vector* $\boldsymbol{x}$ *satisfying* $\boldsymbol{A}\boldsymbol{x} = \boldsymbol{y}$. *Is it the same as* $\boldsymbol{x}_o$? *Check whether* `norm(x - xo)` *is small, where* `x` *is the solution produced by your code.*

Notice that the worst-case *theory for* ℓ^0 *predicts that we can only recover vectors with at most two nonzero entries. But we have observed* ℓ^0 *succeeding with four nonzero entries! This is an example of a* typical case *performance which is better than the worst case.*

Please explain this! Argue that if $\boldsymbol{x}_o$ *is a fixed vector supported on some set* I *of size* $< m$, *then the probability that there exists a subset* $\mathsf{I}' \neq \mathsf{I}$ *of size* $< m$ *satisfying* $\boldsymbol{A}\boldsymbol{x}_o \in \operatorname{range}(\boldsymbol{A}_{\mathsf{I}'})$ *is zero.*

Does your argument imply that the worst-case theory based on rank *can be improved? Why or why not?*

2.9. (Subdifferentials) *Compute the subdifferentials for the following functions:*

(a) *The subdifferential for* $f(\boldsymbol{x}) = \|\boldsymbol{x}\|_\infty$ *with* $\boldsymbol{x} \in \mathbb{R}^n$.
(b) *The subdifferential for* $f(\boldsymbol{X}) = \sum_{j=1}^n \|\boldsymbol{X}\boldsymbol{e}_j\|_2$ *with* $\boldsymbol{X}$ *a matrix in* $\mathbb{R}^{n \times n}$.
(c) *The subdifferential for* $f(\boldsymbol{x}) = \|\boldsymbol{X}\|_*$ *with* $\boldsymbol{X}$ *a matrix in* $\mathbb{R}^{n \times n}$.

2.10. (Implicit bias of gradient descent) *Consider the problem of solving an under-determined system of linear equation* $\boldsymbol{y} = \boldsymbol{A}\boldsymbol{x}$ *where* $\boldsymbol{A} \in \mathbb{R}^{m \times n}$ *with* $m < n$ *and* $\boldsymbol{A}$ *is full rank. Of course the solution is not unique. Nevertheless, let us solve it by minimizing the least-squares error*

$$\min_{\boldsymbol{x}} f(\boldsymbol{x}) \doteq \|\boldsymbol{y} - \boldsymbol{A}\boldsymbol{x}\|_2^2,$$

say using the simplest gradient descent algorithm:

$$\boldsymbol{x}_{k+1} = \boldsymbol{x}_k - \alpha \nabla f(\boldsymbol{x}_k).$$

Show that if we initialize $\boldsymbol{x}_0$ *as the origin* $\mathbf{0}$, *then when the above gradient descent algorithm converges, it must converge to the solution* $\boldsymbol{x}_\star$ *of the minimal 2-norm. That is, it converges to the optimal solution of the following problem:*

$$\min_{\boldsymbol{x}} \|\boldsymbol{x}\|_2^2 \quad \text{subject to} \quad \boldsymbol{y} = \boldsymbol{A}\boldsymbol{x}.$$

This is a phenomenon widely exploited in the practice of learning deep neural networks. Although, due to overparameterization, parameters that minimize the cost function might not be unique, the choice of optimization algorithms with proper initialization (here gradient descent starting from the origin) introduces implicit bias for the optimization path and converges to a desirable solution.

2.11. (Projection onto an affine subspace) *In deriving the projected subgradient method for* ℓ^1 *minimization, we used the fact that for an affine subspace*

$$\mathsf{C} = \{\boldsymbol{x} \mid \boldsymbol{A}\boldsymbol{x} = \boldsymbol{y}\}, \tag{2.6.6}$$

where $\boldsymbol{A}$ *is a matrix with full row rank, and* $\boldsymbol{y} \in \mathrm{range}(\boldsymbol{A})$, *the Euclidean projection on* C *is given by*

$$\mathcal{P}_{\mathsf{C}}[\boldsymbol{z}] = \arg\min_{\boldsymbol{A}\boldsymbol{x}=\boldsymbol{y}} \|\boldsymbol{x} - \boldsymbol{z}\|_2^2 \tag{2.6.7}$$

$$= \boldsymbol{z} - \boldsymbol{A}^* \left(\boldsymbol{A}\boldsymbol{A}^*\right)^{-1} \left[\boldsymbol{A}\boldsymbol{z} - \boldsymbol{y}\right]. \tag{2.6.8}$$

Prove that this formula is correct. You may use the following geometric characterization of $\mathcal{P}_{\mathsf{C}}[\boldsymbol{z}]$: $\boldsymbol{x} = \mathcal{P}_{\mathsf{C}}[\boldsymbol{z}]$ *if and only if (i)* $\boldsymbol{A}\boldsymbol{x} = \boldsymbol{y}$ *and (ii) for any* $\tilde{\boldsymbol{x}}$ *satisfying* $\boldsymbol{A}\tilde{\boldsymbol{x}} = \boldsymbol{y}$, *we have*

$$\langle \boldsymbol{z} - \boldsymbol{x}, \tilde{\boldsymbol{x}} - \boldsymbol{x} \rangle \le 0. \tag{2.6.9}$$

2.12. *Projected gradient descent aims to:*

$$\min f(\boldsymbol{x}) \quad \text{subject to} \quad \boldsymbol{x} \in \mathsf{C}.$$

Show an example of when the projection onto set C*:*

(a) does not exist;

(b) is not unique.

(Tips: This problem does not have a unique solution; *you can either answer this question by drawing pictures or giving mathematical formula, so use your creativity!)*

2.13. (Sparse error correction) *In coding theory and statistics, we often encounter the following situation: we have an observation* $\boldsymbol{z}$, *which* should *be expressible as* $\boldsymbol{B}\boldsymbol{x}$, except that *some of the entries are corrupted. We can express our corrupted observation as*

$$\underbrace{\boldsymbol{z}}_{\text{observation}} = \underbrace{\boldsymbol{B}\boldsymbol{x}}_{\text{encoded message}} + \underbrace{\boldsymbol{e}}_{\text{sparse corruption}}. \tag{2.6.10}$$

Here $\boldsymbol{z} \in \mathbb{R}^n$ *is the observation,* $\boldsymbol{x} \in \mathbb{R}^r$ *is a message of interest,* $\boldsymbol{B} \in \mathbb{R}^{n \times r}$ $(n > r)$ *is a tall matrix with full column rank* r, *and* $\boldsymbol{e} \in \mathbb{R}^n$ *represents any corruption of the message. In many applications, the observation may be subject to corruption which is large in magnitude, but affects only a few of the observations, i.e.,* $\boldsymbol{e}$ *is a sparse vector. Let* $\boldsymbol{A} \in \mathbb{R}^{(n-r)\times n}$ *be a matrix whose rows span the left null space of* $\boldsymbol{B}$, *i.e.,* $\mathrm{rank}(\boldsymbol{A}) = n - r$, *and* $\boldsymbol{A}\boldsymbol{B} = \boldsymbol{0}$. *Prove that for any* k, (2.6.10) *has a solution* $(\boldsymbol{x}, \boldsymbol{e})$ *with* $\|\boldsymbol{e}\|_0 = k$ *if and only if the* underdetermined system

$$\boldsymbol{A}\boldsymbol{e} = \boldsymbol{A}\boldsymbol{z} \tag{2.6.11}$$

has a solution $\boldsymbol{e}$ *with* $\|\boldsymbol{e}\|_0 = k$. *Argue that the optimization problems*

$$\min_{\boldsymbol{x}} \|\boldsymbol{B}\boldsymbol{x} - \boldsymbol{z}\|_1 \tag{2.6.12}$$

and

$$\min_{\boldsymbol{e}} \|\boldsymbol{e}\|_1 \quad \text{subject to} \quad \boldsymbol{A}\boldsymbol{e} = \boldsymbol{A}\boldsymbol{z} \tag{2.6.13}$$

are equivalent, in the sense that for every solution $\hat{\boldsymbol{x}}$ *of* (2.6.12), $\hat{\boldsymbol{e}} = \boldsymbol{B}\hat{\boldsymbol{x}} - \boldsymbol{z}$ *is a solution to* (2.6.13)*; and for every solution* $\hat{\boldsymbol{e}}$ *of* (2.6.13)*, there is a solution* $\hat{\boldsymbol{x}}$ *of* (2.6.12) *such that* $\hat{\boldsymbol{e}} = \boldsymbol{B}\hat{\boldsymbol{x}} - \boldsymbol{z}$.

It is sometimes observed that "sparse representation and sparse error correction are equivalent." In what sense is this true?

2.14. (ℓ^1 versus ℓ^∞ minimization) *We have studied the* ℓ^1 *minimization problem*

$$\min \|\boldsymbol{x}\|_1 \quad \textit{subject to} \quad \boldsymbol{A}\boldsymbol{x} = \boldsymbol{y} \tag{2.6.14}$$

for recovering sparse $\boldsymbol{x}_o$*. We can obtain other convex optimization problems by replacing* $\|\cdot\|_1$ *with* $\|\cdot\|_p$ *for* $p \in (1, \infty]$*. For what kind of* $\boldsymbol{x}_o$ *would you expect* ℓ^∞ *minimization to outperform* ℓ^1 *minimization (in the sense of recovering* $\boldsymbol{x}_o$ *more accurately)?*

2.15. (Faces and linear subspaces) *Download* `face_intro_demo.zip` *from the book's website. Run* `load_eyb_recognition` *to load a collection of images under varying illumination into memory. The training images (under different lighting) will be stored in* `A_train`*, the identities of the subjects in* `label_train`*. Form a matrix* `B` *by selecting those columns of* `A_train` *that correspond to Subject 1. We will use the* singular value decomposition *to investigate how well-approximated the columns of* `B` *are by a linear subspace.*

Compute the singular values *of* `B` *using* `sigma = svd(B)`*. How many singular values r are needed to capture 95% of the energy of* $\boldsymbol{B}$*? That is, to ensure that*

$$\sum_{i=1}^{r} \sigma_i^2 > 0.95 \times \sum_{i=1}^{n} \sigma_i^2 \ ? \tag{2.6.15}$$

What about 99% of the energy? Repeat this calculation for several subjects.

3 Convex Methods for Sparse Signal Recovery

"Algebra is but written geometry; geometry is but drawn algebra."

– Sophie Germain

In the previous chapter, we saw many problems for which the goal is to find a sparse solution to an underdetermined linear system of equations $\boldsymbol{y} = \boldsymbol{A}\boldsymbol{x}$. This problem is NP-hard in general. However, we also observed that certain well-structured instances *can* be solved efficiently: in experiments, when $\boldsymbol{y} = \boldsymbol{A}\boldsymbol{x}_o$ and $\boldsymbol{x}_o$ was *sufficiently sparse*, tractable ℓ^1 minimization

$$\begin{array}{ll} \min & \|\boldsymbol{x}\|_1 \\ \text{subject to} & \boldsymbol{A}\boldsymbol{x} = \boldsymbol{y}, \end{array} \tag{3.0.1}$$

exactly recovered $\boldsymbol{x}_o$: $\boldsymbol{x}_o$ was the unique optimal solution to this optimization problem.

The experiments in the previous chapter are inspiring, and perhaps surprising. In this chapter, we will study this phenomenon mathematically, and try to precisely characterize the behavior of (3.0.1). The engineering motivation is simple: we would like to know whether the behavior in the previous chapter is some lucky instances or should be expected in general, and if it is the latter case, whether we can use it to build reliable systems.

3.1 Why Does ℓ^1 Minimization Succeed? Geometric Intuitions

Before diving into a formal proof that the ℓ^1 minimization (3.0.1) correctly recovers sparse signals, we describe two intuitive, geometric pictures of why this is the case.

Coefficient-Space Picture

We first visualize the problem in the space $\mathbb{R}^n$ of coefficient vectors $\boldsymbol{x}$. The set of vectors $\boldsymbol{x}$ that satisfy the constraint $\boldsymbol{A}\boldsymbol{x} = \boldsymbol{y}$ in (3.0.1) is an *affine subspace*[1]

$$\mathsf{S} = \{\boldsymbol{x} \mid \boldsymbol{A}\boldsymbol{x} = \boldsymbol{y}\} = \{\boldsymbol{x}_o\} + \operatorname{null}(\boldsymbol{A}). \tag{3.1.1}$$

[1] In (3.1.1), the set addition $\{\boldsymbol{x}_o\} + \operatorname{null}(\boldsymbol{A})$ is in the sense of Minkowski, i.e., for sets S and T, $\mathsf{S} + \mathsf{T} = \{\boldsymbol{s} + \boldsymbol{t} \mid \boldsymbol{s} \in \mathsf{S}, \boldsymbol{t} \in \mathsf{T}\}$.

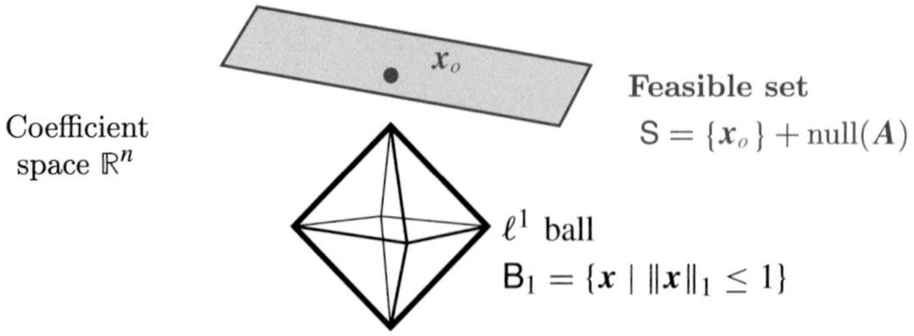

Figure 3.1 Coefficient-space picture. The set of all solutions x to the equation $Ax = y$ is an affine subspace S of the coefficient space $\mathbb{R}^n$. The ℓ^1 ball B_1 consists of all coefficient vectors x whose objective function is at most one.

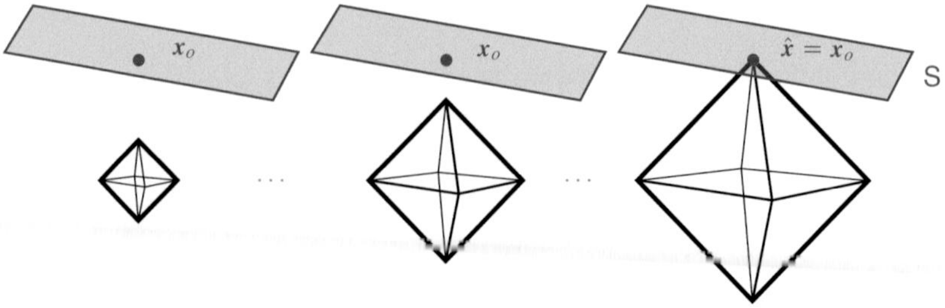

Figure 3.2 ℓ^1 Minimization in the coefficient-space picture. ℓ^1 Minimization can be visualized geometrically as follows: we squeeze the ℓ^1 ball down to zero, and then slowly expand it until it first touches the feasible set S. The point (or points) at which it first touches S is the ℓ^1 minimizer $\hat{x}$.

Figure 3.1 visualizes this set. The ℓ^1 minimization problem (3.0.1) picks, out of all of the points in the set S, the one (or ones) with smallest ℓ^1 norm. This can be visualized as follows. Consider the ℓ^1 ball of radius one:

$$B_1 = \{x \mid \|x\|_1 \le 1\} \quad \subset \mathbb{R}^n. \tag{3.1.2}$$

This contains all the vectors x with objective function at most one. Scaling this object by $t \ge 0$ produces the set of vectors x with objective function at most t:

$$t \cdot B_1 = \{x \mid \|x\|_1 \le t\} \quad \subset \mathbb{R}^n. \tag{3.1.3}$$

If we first scale B_1 down to zero, by setting $t = 0$, and then slowly expand it, by increasing t, the ℓ^1 minimizer is obtained when $t \cdot B_1$ first touches the affine subspace S. This contact point is the solution to (3.0.1) – see Figure 3.2. From the geometry of the ball, it seems that these contact points will tend to be the vertices or edges of B_1, which precisely correspond to the sparse vectors!

Observation-Space Picture

We can also visualize ℓ^1 minimization in the space $\mathbb{R}^m$ of observation vectors y. This picture is slightly more complicated, but turns out to be very useful. The $m \times n$ matrix

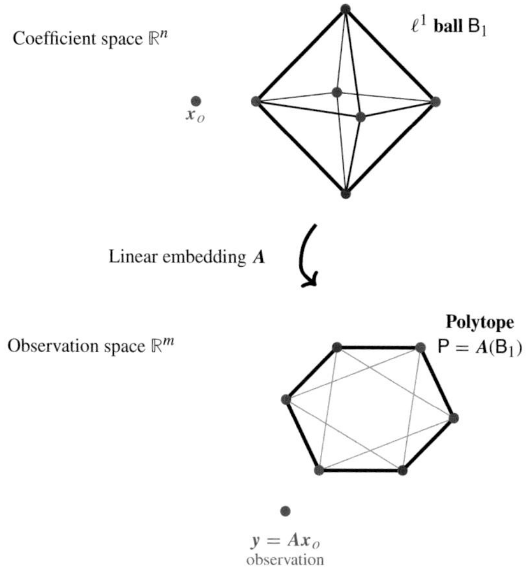

Figure 3.3 Observation-space picture. The ℓ^1 ball is a convex polytope B_1 in the coefficient space $\mathbb{R}^n$. The linear map A projects this down to a lower-dimensional set $\mathsf{P} = A(\mathsf{B}_1)$ in the observation space $\mathbb{R}^m$. The vertices v_i of P are subsets of the projections Av_j of B_1.

A maps n-dimensional vectors x to $m \ll n$ dimensional vectors y. Let us consider how the matrix A acts on the ℓ^1 ball $\mathsf{B}_1 \subset \mathbb{R}^n$. Applying A to each of the vectors $x \in \mathsf{B}_1$, we obtain a lower-dimensional object $\mathsf{P} = A(\mathsf{B}_1)$, which we visualize in Figure 3.3. The lower-dimensional set P is a *convex polytope*. Every vertex v of P is the image Av of some vertex $v = \pm e_i$ of B_1. More generally, every k-dimensional face of P is the image of some face of B_1.

The polytope P consists of all points y' of the form Ax' for some x' with objective function $\|x'\|_1 \le 1$. ℓ^1 Minimization corresponds to squeezing B_1 down to the origin, and then slowly expanding it until it first touches y. The touching point is the image $A\hat{x}$ of the ℓ^1 minimizer – see Figure 3.4.

So, ℓ^1 will correctly recover x_o whenever Ax_o is on the outside of $\mathsf{P} = A(\mathsf{B}_1)$. For example, in Figure 3.3, all of the vertices of B_1 map to the outside of $A(\mathsf{B}_1)$, and so ℓ^1 recovers any one-sparse x_o. However, certain edges (one-dimensional faces) of B_1 map to the inside of $A(\mathsf{B}_1)$. ℓ^1 Minimization will not recover these x_o.

From this picture, it may be very surprising that ℓ^1 works as well as it does. However, as we will see in the remainder of this chapter, the high-dimensional picture differs significantly from the low-dimensional picture (and our intuition!) in ways that are very useful – a "blessing of dimensionality." In particular, if we are in m dimensions and n is proportional to m, not only do all of the vertices of B_1 map to the outside of $A(\mathsf{B}_1)$, so do all the one-dimensional faces, and all of the two-dimensional faces, and so on, all the way up to k-dimensional faces with k proportional to m!

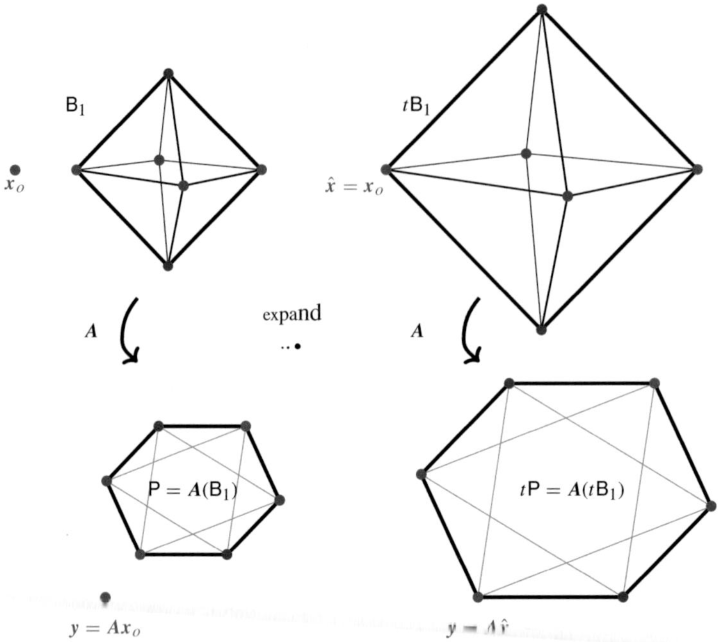

Figure 3.4 ℓ^1 Minimization in the observation space picture. ℓ^1 Minimization corresponds to scaling B_1 down to zero, and then slowly expanding it. As B_1 expands, so does $P = A(B_1)$. The optimal value for the ℓ^1 minimization problem is the first scalar t such that $tP = A(tB_1)$ touches the observation vector y. The first point that touches y is the image $A\hat{x}$ of the ℓ^1 minimizer $\hat{x}$. This means that ℓ^1 *minimization recovers point* x_o *if and only if* $Ax_o/\|x_o\|_1$ *lies on the boundary of* P.

3.2 A First Correctness Result for Incoherent Matrices

With solid empirical evidence and a bit of geometric intuition at hand, our next task is to develop some rigorous understanding of this phenomenon.

3.2.1 Coherence of a Matrix

What determines whether ℓ^1 minimization can recover a target sparse solution x_o? Our discussion on ℓ^0 minimization isolated two key factors: how structured the target x_o is (i.e., how many nonzero entries) and how nice the map A is (measured there through the Kruskal rank). Moreover, there was a tradeoff between the two factors: *the nicer* A *is, the denser* x_o *we can recover.*

In fact, this qualitative tradeoff carries over to tractable algorithms such as the ℓ^1 relaxation as well. However, we need a slightly stronger notion of the "niceness" of A to guarantee that the tractable relaxation succeeds. Our first notion measures how "spread out" the columns of A are in the high-dimensional space $\mathbb{R}^m$:

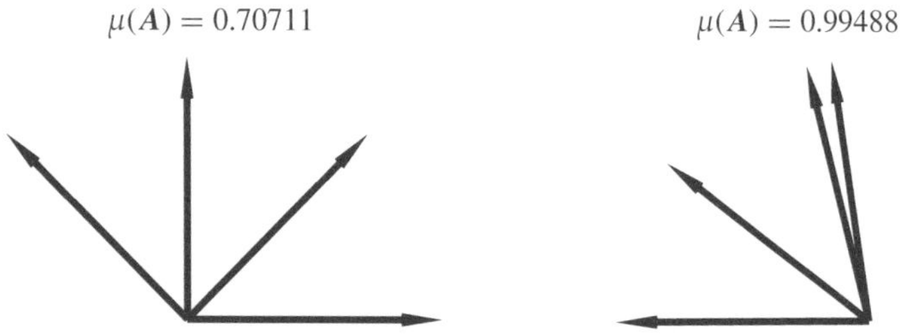

Figure 3.5 Mutual coherence for two configurations of columns of A. (a) Well-spread vectors in $\mathbb{S}^2$: $\mu(A) \approx 0.707$. This is the smallest achievable μ for four vectors in two dimensions. In higher dimensions, the mutual coherence can be *much* smaller: for example, a random $m \times 2m$ dimensional matrix has coherence on the order of $\sqrt{\log(m)/m}$, which diminishes to zero as m increases. (b) Here $\mu(A) \approx 0.995$. Mutual coherence depends on the closest pair a_i, a_j, and so in this example it is very large.

DEFINITION 3.1. (Mutual coherence) *For a matrix*

$$A = \Big[\, a_1 \mid a_2 \mid \cdots \mid a_n \,\Big] \quad \in \mathbb{R}^{m \times n}$$

with nonzero columns, the mutual coherence $\mu(A)$ *is the largest normalized inner product between two distinct columns:*

$$\mu(A) = \max_{i \neq j} \left| \left\langle \frac{a_i}{\|a_i\|_2}, \frac{a_j}{\|a_j\|_2} \right\rangle \right|. \tag{3.2.1}$$

As the mutual coherence only depends on the direction of the column vectors, for simplicity, we typically assume the columns are normalized to be of unit length.

The mutual coherence takes values in $[0, 1]$. If the columns of A are orthogonal, $\mu(A)$ is zero. If $n > m$, the columns of A cannot be orthogonal. The quantity $\mu(A)$ captures how close they are to orthogonal, in the worst-case sense. Matrices with small $\mu(A)$ have columns that are more spread out; we will see that such matrices tend to be better for sparse recovery, in the sense that ℓ^1 succeeds in recovering denser x_o. Figure 3.5 visualizes the columns A and displays the coherence, for two examples of $A \in \mathbb{R}^{2 \times n}$.

One intuition for why small $\mu(A)$ is helpful is the following: Suppose that $y = Ax_o$, with x_o sparse, and I the support of x_o. Then $y = \sum_{i \in \mathsf{I}} a_i x_o(i)$. Intuitively speaking, it should be easier to "guess" which columns a_i participate in this linear combination if distinct columns are not too similar to each other.

To connect the mutual coherence more formally to sparse recovery, we will show that whenever $\mu(A)$ is small, the Kruskal rank krank(A) is large. Recall that krank(A) $\geq k$ if and only if every subset of k columns of A is linearly independent, i.e., every k-column submatrix A_{I} has full column rank. In fact, if the coherence $\mu(A)$ is small, then column submatrices of A not only have full column rank – they are even *well conditioned*, in the sense that their smallest singular value $\sigma_{\min}$ is not far from their largest singular value $\sigma_{\max}$. To see this, let $\mathsf{I} \subset [n]$ with $k = |\mathsf{I}|$. Write diagonal and off-diagonal entries as

$$A_I^* A_I = I + \Delta. \tag{3.2.2}$$

Because $\|\Delta\| \le \|\Delta\|_F < k\,\|\Delta\|_\infty \le k\mu(A)$,[2] we have

$$1 - k\mu(A) < \sigma_{\min}(A_I^* A_I) \le \sigma_{\max}(A_I^* A_I) < 1 + k\mu(A). \tag{3.2.3}$$

In particular, if $k\mu(A) \le 1$, A_I has full column rank. Combining this observation with our previous discussion of the Kruskal rank, we obtain:

PROPOSITION 3.2. (Coherence controls kruskal rank) *For any* $A \in \mathbb{R}^{m\times n}$,

$$\operatorname{krank}(A) \ge \frac{1}{\mu(A)}. \tag{3.2.4}$$

In particular, if $y = Ax_o$ *and*

$$\|x_o\|_0 \le \frac{1}{2\mu(A)}, \tag{3.2.5}$$

then x_o *is the unique optimal solution to the* ℓ^0 *minimization problem*

$$\begin{array}{ll} \min & \|x\|_0 \\ \text{subject to} & Ax = y. \end{array} \tag{3.2.6}$$

Thus, provided $\mu(A)$ is small enough, ℓ^0 minimization will uniquely recover x_o.

3.2.2 Correctness of ℓ^1 Minimization

The previous result showed that if $\mu(A)$ is small, then ℓ^0 minimization recovers sufficiently sparse x_o. The next result shows that under the same hypotheses, if $\mu(A)$ is small, the *tractable* ℓ^1 minimization heuristic also recovers x_o. This implies that sparse solutions can be reliably obtained using efficient algorithms! The result is as follows:

THEOREM 3.3. (ℓ^1 succeeds under incoherence) *Let* A *be a matrix whose columns have unit* ℓ^2 *norm, and let* $\mu(A)$ *denote its mutual coherence. Suppose that* $y = Ax_o$, *with*

$$\|x_o\|_0 \le \frac{1}{2\mu(A)}. \tag{3.2.7}$$

Then x_o *is the unique optimal solution to the problem*

$$\begin{array}{ll} \min & \|x\|_1 \\ \text{subject to} & y = Ax. \end{array} \tag{3.2.8}$$

[2] The first inequality comes because the operator norm is always bounded by the Frobenius norm: $\|\Delta\| = \max_i \sigma_i(\Delta)$ and $\|\Delta\|_F = \sqrt{\sum_i \sigma_i^2(\Delta)}$. The second inequality arises because $\|\Delta\|_F^2 = \sum_{ij} |\Delta_{ij}|^2$. The diagonal entries of Δ are zero, and so in this case, $\|\Delta\|_F^2 = \sum_{i\ne j} |\Delta_{ij}|^2 \le k(k-1)\,\|\Delta\|_\infty^2$.

REMARK 3.4. *It is possible to improve the condition of Theorem 3.3 slightly, to allow recovery of* $\boldsymbol{x}_o$ *satisfying*

$$\|\boldsymbol{x}_o\|_0 \le \frac{1}{2}\left(1 + \frac{1}{\mu(\boldsymbol{A})}\right). \tag{3.2.9}$$

This is the best possible statement of this form: there exist examples of $\boldsymbol{A}$ *and* $\boldsymbol{x}_o$ *with* $\|\boldsymbol{x}_o\|_0 > 1/2\left(1 + 1/\mu(\boldsymbol{A})\right)$ *for which* ℓ^1 *minimization does not recover* $\boldsymbol{x}_o$*. Nevertheless, we will see later in this chapter that for certain classes of* $\boldsymbol{A}$ *of practical importance, far better guarantees are possible, and that this has important implications for sensing, error correction, and a number of related problems.*

Proof Ideas for ℓ^1 *Recovery*

Before embarking on a rigorous proof of Theorem 3.3, we sketch our approach. Recall from the previous chapter that for any $\boldsymbol{v} \in \partial \|\cdot\|_1 (\boldsymbol{x}_o)$ and $\boldsymbol{x}' \in \mathbb{R}^n$, the subgradient inequality

$$\left\|\boldsymbol{x}'\right\|_1 \ge \|\boldsymbol{x}_o\|_1 + \left\langle \boldsymbol{v}, \boldsymbol{x}' - \boldsymbol{x}_o \right\rangle \tag{3.2.10}$$

lower-bounds the ℓ^1 norm of $\boldsymbol{x}'$. Notice that if $\boldsymbol{x}'$ is feasible for (3.2.8), then $\boldsymbol{y} = \boldsymbol{A}\boldsymbol{x}'$ and so $\boldsymbol{A}(\boldsymbol{x}' - \boldsymbol{x}_o) = \boldsymbol{0}$. Hence, for any $\boldsymbol{\lambda} \in \mathbb{R}^m$,

$$\left\langle \boldsymbol{A}^*\boldsymbol{\lambda}, \boldsymbol{x}' - \boldsymbol{x}_o \right\rangle = \left\langle \boldsymbol{\lambda}, \boldsymbol{A}(\boldsymbol{x}' - \boldsymbol{x}_o) \right\rangle = 0. \tag{3.2.11}$$

So *if* we can produce a $\boldsymbol{\lambda}$ such that $\boldsymbol{A}^*\boldsymbol{\lambda} \in \partial \|\cdot\|_1 (\boldsymbol{x}_o)$, plugging into (3.2.10) we necessarily have

$$\left\|\boldsymbol{x}'\right\|_1 \ge \|\boldsymbol{x}_o\|_1 \tag{3.2.12}$$

for every $\boldsymbol{x}' \in \mathbb{R}^n$. This implies that $\boldsymbol{x}_o$ is *an* optimal solution. Figure 3.6 visualizes this construction geometrically.

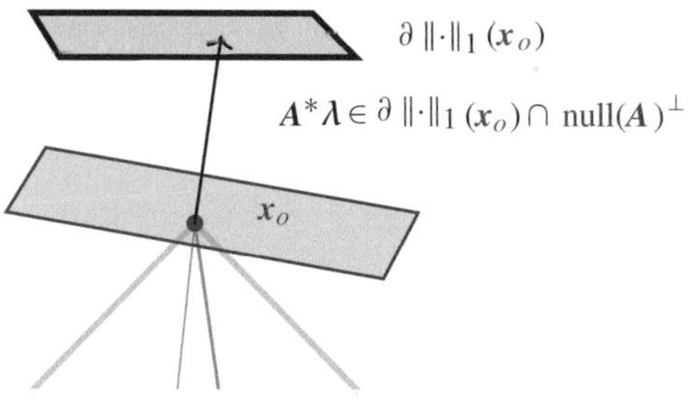

Figure 3.6 Geometry of the proof of ℓ^1 recovery. We prove that $\boldsymbol{x}_o$ is an optimal solution to the ℓ^1 minimization problem, by demonstrating that there exists $\boldsymbol{\lambda}$ such that $\boldsymbol{A}^*\boldsymbol{\lambda}$ is in the subdifferential of $\partial \|\cdot\|_1 (\boldsymbol{x}_o)$. In this picture, there is a *subgradient* of the objective which is orthogonal to null($\boldsymbol{A}$). This generalizes the condition for projecting onto an affine subspace (Figure 2.13), in which the gradient of the approximation error is orthogonal to null($\boldsymbol{A}$).

Let I denote the support of $\boldsymbol{x}_o$, and $\boldsymbol{\sigma} = \mathrm{sign}(\boldsymbol{x}_{o\mathsf{I}}) \in \{\pm 1\}^k$. Recall that the subdifferential $\partial \left\|\cdot\right\|_1(\boldsymbol{x}_o)$ consists of those vectors $\boldsymbol{v}$ such that

$$\boldsymbol{v}_{\mathsf{I}} = \boldsymbol{\sigma}, \tag{3.2.13}$$

$$\|\boldsymbol{v}_{\mathsf{I}^c}\|_\infty \le 1. \tag{3.2.14}$$

Hence, the condition $\boldsymbol{A}^*\boldsymbol{\lambda} \in \partial \left\|\cdot\right\|_1(\boldsymbol{x}_o)$ places two conditions on the vector $\boldsymbol{A}^*\boldsymbol{\lambda}$:

$$\boldsymbol{A}_{\mathsf{I}}^*\boldsymbol{\lambda} = \boldsymbol{\sigma}, \tag{3.2.15}$$

$$\left\|\boldsymbol{A}_{\mathsf{I}^c}^*\boldsymbol{\lambda}\right\|_\infty \le 1. \tag{3.2.16}$$

The first condition is a linear system of k equations, in m unknowns $\boldsymbol{\lambda}$. The second is a system of $n-k$ inequality constraints. The system of equations (3.2.15) is underdetermined. Our approach will be to look at the simplest possible solution to this underdetermined system,

$$\hat{\boldsymbol{\lambda}}_{\ell^2} = \boldsymbol{A}_{\mathsf{I}}(\boldsymbol{A}_{\mathsf{I}}^*\boldsymbol{A}_{\mathsf{I}})^{-1}\boldsymbol{\sigma}. \tag{3.2.17}$$

This putative solution automatically satisfies the equality constraints (3.2.15). Moreover, $\hat{\boldsymbol{\lambda}}_{\ell^2}$ is a superposition of the columns of $\boldsymbol{A}_{\mathsf{I}}$. Because $\mu(\boldsymbol{A})$ is small, the columns of $\boldsymbol{A}_{\mathsf{I}^c}$ are almost orthogonal to the columns of $\boldsymbol{A}_{\mathsf{I}}$, and so $\left\|\boldsymbol{A}_{\mathsf{I}^c}^*\boldsymbol{\lambda}\right\|_\infty$ is also small.

Below, we make the above discussion rigorous. The details are slightly more complicated than the above sketch, because we wish to prove that $\boldsymbol{x}_o$ is not just *an* optimal solution, but actually *the unique* optimal solution. We will see that if we can ensure that $\boldsymbol{A}_{\mathsf{I}}$ has full column rank and $\left\|\boldsymbol{A}_{\mathsf{I}^c}^*\boldsymbol{\lambda}\right\|_\infty$ is strictly smaller than one, this follows.

Proof of theorem 3.3 Let $\mathsf{I} = \mathrm{supp}(\boldsymbol{x}_o)$ and $\boldsymbol{\sigma} = \mathrm{sign}(\boldsymbol{x}_{o\mathsf{I}}) \in \{\pm 1\}^k$. Notice that $\sigma_{\min}(\boldsymbol{A}_{\mathsf{I}}^*\boldsymbol{A}_{\mathsf{I}}) > 1 - k\mu(\boldsymbol{A})$, and so under our assumption $\boldsymbol{A}_{\mathsf{I}}$ has full column rank. Suppose that there exists $\boldsymbol{\lambda}$ such that

$$\boldsymbol{A}_{\mathsf{I}}^*\boldsymbol{\lambda} = \boldsymbol{\sigma}, \tag{3.2.18}$$

$$\left\|\boldsymbol{A}_{\mathsf{I}^c}^*\boldsymbol{\lambda}\right\|_\infty \le 1. \tag{3.2.19}$$

Consider any $\boldsymbol{x}'$ which is feasible, i.e., satisfies $\boldsymbol{A}\boldsymbol{x}' = \boldsymbol{y}$. Let $\boldsymbol{v} \in \mathbb{R}^n$ be a vector such that $\boldsymbol{v}_{\mathsf{I}} = \boldsymbol{\sigma}$, and $\boldsymbol{v}_{\mathsf{I}^c} = \mathrm{sign}([\boldsymbol{x}' - \boldsymbol{x}_o]_{\mathsf{I}^c})$. Notice that $\boldsymbol{v} \in \partial\left\|\cdot\right\|_1(\boldsymbol{x}_o)$, and so by the subgradient inequality,

$$\left\|\boldsymbol{x}'\right\|_1 \ge \|\boldsymbol{x}_o\|_1 + \left\langle \boldsymbol{v}, \boldsymbol{x}' - \boldsymbol{x}_o\right\rangle. \tag{3.2.20}$$

Since $\boldsymbol{x}' - \boldsymbol{x}_o \in \mathrm{null}(\boldsymbol{A})$, $\left\langle \boldsymbol{A}^*\boldsymbol{\lambda}, \boldsymbol{x}' - \boldsymbol{x}_o\right\rangle = 0$, and the above equation implies that

$$\begin{aligned}
\left\|\boldsymbol{x}'\right\|_1 &\ge \|\boldsymbol{x}_o\|_1 + \left\langle \boldsymbol{v}, \boldsymbol{x}' - \boldsymbol{x}_o\right\rangle \\
&= \|\boldsymbol{x}_o\|_1 + \left\langle \boldsymbol{v} - \boldsymbol{A}^*\boldsymbol{\lambda}, \boldsymbol{x}' - \boldsymbol{x}_o\right\rangle \\
&= \|\boldsymbol{x}_o\|_1 + \left\langle \boldsymbol{v}_{\mathsf{I}^c} - \boldsymbol{A}_{\mathsf{I}^c}^*\boldsymbol{\lambda}, [\boldsymbol{x}' - \boldsymbol{x}_o]_{\mathsf{I}^c}\right\rangle \\
&\ge \|\boldsymbol{x}_o\|_1 + \left\|[\boldsymbol{x}' - \boldsymbol{x}_o]_{\mathsf{I}^c}\right\|_1 - \left\|\boldsymbol{A}_{\mathsf{I}^c}^*\boldsymbol{\lambda}\right\|_\infty \left\|[\boldsymbol{x}' - \boldsymbol{x}_o]_{\mathsf{I}^c}\right\|_1 \\
&= \|\boldsymbol{x}_o\|_1 + (1 - \left\|\boldsymbol{A}_{\mathsf{I}^c}^*\boldsymbol{\lambda}\right\|_\infty) \left\|[\boldsymbol{x}' - \boldsymbol{x}_o]_{\mathsf{I}^c}\right\|_1.
\end{aligned} \tag{3.2.21}$$

Since $\left\| A_{\mathsf{I}^c}^* \lambda \right\|_\infty < 1$, either $\left\| x' \right\|_1 > \| x_o \|_1$, or $\left\| [x' - x_o]_{\mathsf{I}^c} \right\|_1 = 0$. In the latter case, this means that $\operatorname{supp}(x') \subseteq \mathsf{I}$, and $x'_{\mathsf{I}} - x_{o\mathsf{I}} \in \operatorname{null}(A_{\mathsf{I}})$. Since A_{I} has full column rank, this implies that $x'_{\mathsf{I}} = x_{o\mathsf{I}}$, and so $x' = x$.

Hence, if we can construct a λ satisfying (3.2.18)–(3.2.19), then any alternative feasible solution x' has larger ℓ^1 norm than x_o. Let us try to produce such a λ. The first equation (3.2.18) above is an underdetermined linear system of equations, with k equations and $m > k$ unknowns λ. Let us write down one particular solution to this system of equations:

$$\hat{\lambda}_{\ell 2} = A_{\mathsf{I}} (A_{\mathsf{I}}^* A_{\mathsf{I}})^{-1} \sigma. \tag{3.2.22}$$

By construction, $A_{\mathsf{I}}^* \hat{\lambda}_{\ell 2} = \sigma$. We are just left to verify (3.2.19), by calculating

$$\left\| A_{\mathsf{I}^c}^* \hat{\lambda}_{\ell 2} \right\|_\infty = \left\| A_{\mathsf{I}^c}^* A_{\mathsf{I}} (A_{\mathsf{I}}^* A_{\mathsf{I}})^{-1} \sigma \right\|_\infty. \tag{3.2.23}$$

Consider a single element of this vector, which has the form (for some $j \in \mathsf{I}^c$) of

$$|a_j^* A_{\mathsf{I}} (A_{\mathsf{I}}^* A_{\mathsf{I}})^{-1} \sigma| \le \underbrace{\left\| A_{\mathsf{I}}^* a_j \right\|_2}_{\le \sqrt{k}\mu} \underbrace{\left\| (A_{\mathsf{I}}^* A_{\mathsf{I}})^{-1} \right\|_{2,2}}_{< \frac{1}{1 - k\mu(A)}} \underbrace{\| \sigma \|_2}_{= \sqrt{k}} \tag{3.2.24}$$

$$< \frac{k\mu(A)}{1 - k\mu(A)} \tag{3.2.25}$$

$$\underset{\text{provided } k\mu(A) \le 1/2.}{\le} 1 . \tag{3.2.26}$$

In (3.2.25), we have used that for any invertible M, $\left\| M^{-1} \right\| = 1/\sigma_{\min}(M)$ and our previous calculation that $\sigma_{\min}(A_{\mathsf{I}}^* A_{\mathsf{I}}) \ge 1 - k\mu(A)$ to bound $\left\| (A_{\mathsf{I}}^* A_{\mathsf{I}})^{-1} \right\|_{2,2}$. This calculation shows that under our assumptions, condition (3.2.19) is verified. □

3.2.3 Constructing an Incoherent Matrix

In Theorem 3.3, we have shown that if $\|x_o\|_0 \le 1/2\mu(A)$, x_o is correctly recovered by ℓ_1 minimization. Many extensions and variants of this result are known. According to this result, matrices with smaller coherence admit better bounds.

Historically, results of this nature were first proved for special A, which consisted of a concatenation of two orthonormal bases:

$$A = \left[\Phi \mid \Psi \right], \tag{3.2.27}$$

with $\Phi = [\phi_1 \mid \cdots \mid \phi_n] \in \mathsf{O}(n)$ and $\Psi = [\psi_1 \mid \cdots \mid \psi_n] \in \mathsf{O}(n)$. For instance, Φ can be the classic Fourier transform bases and Ψ certain wavelet transform bases. In this case, it is possible to prove a sharper bound based on the cross-coherence:

$$\max_{ij} \left| \left\langle \phi_i, \psi_j \right\rangle \right|. \tag{3.2.28}$$

Another case which is of great interest is when the matrix A has the form $A = \Phi_{\mathsf{I}}^* \Psi$, where $\mathsf{I} \subset [n]$, and $\Phi_{\mathsf{I}} \in \mathbb{R}^{n \times |\mathsf{I}|}$ is a submatrix of an orthogonal base. For example, in the MRI problem in the previous chapter, $\boldsymbol{\Phi}$ would correspond to the Fourier transform, while $\boldsymbol{\Psi}$ was the basis of sparsity (e.g., wavelets).

As it turns out, incoherence is a generic property for almost all matrices. So the easiest way to build a matrix $\boldsymbol{A}$ with small $\mu(\boldsymbol{A})$ is simply to choose the matrix at random. The following theorem makes this precise:

THEOREM 3.5. *Let $\boldsymbol{A} = [\boldsymbol{a}_1 \mid \cdots \mid \boldsymbol{a}_n]$ with columns $\boldsymbol{a}_i \sim \mathrm{uni}(\mathbb{S}^{m-1})$ chosen independently according to the uniform distribution on the sphere. Then with probability at least 3/4,*

$$\mu(\boldsymbol{A}) \le C\sqrt{\frac{\log n}{m}}, \tag{3.2.29}$$

where $C > 0$ is a numerical constant.

This result is essentially just a calculation. The main tool needed is the following result, which observes that a Lipschitz function on the sphere concentrates sharply about its median:

THEOREM 3.6. (Spherical measure concentration) *Let $\boldsymbol{u} \sim \mathrm{uni}(\mathbb{S}^{m-1})$ be distributed according to the uniform distribution on the sphere. Let $f : \mathbb{S}^{m-1} \to \mathbb{R}$ be a 1-Lipschitz function.*

$$\forall \boldsymbol{u}, \boldsymbol{u}', \quad \left| f(\boldsymbol{u}) - f(\boldsymbol{u}') \right| \le 1 \cdot \left\| \boldsymbol{u} - \boldsymbol{u}' \right\|_2, \tag{3.2.30}$$

and let med(f) *denote any median of the random variable $Z = f(\boldsymbol{u})$. Then*

$$\mathbb{P}\left[\, f(\boldsymbol{u}) > \mathrm{med}(f) + t \,\right] \le 2 \exp\left(-\frac{mt^2}{2} \right), \tag{3.2.31}$$

$$\mathbb{P}\left[\, f(\boldsymbol{u}) < \mathrm{med}(f) - t \,\right] \le 2 \exp\left(-\frac{mt^2}{2} \right). \tag{3.2.32}$$

This result is the precise reason behind the counterintuitive example about the sphere shown in Figure 1.10 of the Introduction chapter. We have laid out some basic facts in measure concentration and their proofs in Appendix E. For a more detailed introduction to measure concentration, the reader may refer to [Led01, Mat02]. For now, we will take this result for granted and use it to prove our Theorem 3.5.

Proof of theorem 3.5 For any fixed $\boldsymbol{v} \in \mathbb{S}^{m-1}$, we have

$$\left| |\boldsymbol{v}^* \boldsymbol{a}| - |\boldsymbol{v}^* \boldsymbol{a}'| \right| \le \left| \boldsymbol{v}^* (\boldsymbol{a} - \boldsymbol{a}') \right| \le \left\| \boldsymbol{a} - \boldsymbol{a}' \right\|_2. \tag{3.2.33}$$

So, the function $f(\boldsymbol{a}) = |\boldsymbol{v}^* \boldsymbol{a}|$ is 1-Lipschitz. A quick calculation shows that for $\boldsymbol{a} \sim \mathrm{uni}(\mathbb{S}^{m-1})$, we have

$$\mathbb{E}\left[(\boldsymbol{v}^* \boldsymbol{a})^2 \right] = \frac{1}{m}. \tag{3.2.34}$$

As x^2 is convex, $\mathbb{E}\left[|\boldsymbol{v}^* \boldsymbol{a}| \right]^2 \le \mathbb{E}\left[(\boldsymbol{v}^* \boldsymbol{a})^2 \right]$. So, we have $\mathbb{E}\left[|\boldsymbol{v}^* \boldsymbol{a}| \right] \le 1/\sqrt{m}$.

Applying the Markov inequality $\mathbb{P}[X \geq a] \leq \mathbb{E}[X]/a$ to f with $a = \mathrm{med}(f)$, then any median of f satisfies

$$\mathrm{med}(f) \leq 2\mathbb{E}[f] \leq \frac{2}{\sqrt{m}}. \tag{3.2.35}$$

Finally applying the measure concentration fact from Theorem 3.6, we have

$$\mathbb{P}\left[|\boldsymbol{v}^* \boldsymbol{a}| > \frac{2+t}{\sqrt{m}} \right] \leq 2\exp\left(-\frac{t^2}{2}\right). \tag{3.2.36}$$

Since this holds for every fixed $\boldsymbol{v}$, it also holds if $\boldsymbol{v}$ is an independent random vector uniformly distributed on $\mathbb{S}^{m-1}$. So,

$$\mathbb{P}\left[|\boldsymbol{a}_i^* \boldsymbol{a}_j| > \frac{2+t}{\sqrt{m}} \right] \leq 2\exp\left(-\frac{t^2}{2}\right). \tag{3.2.37}$$

Summing the failure probability over all $n(n-1)/2$ pairs of distinct $(\boldsymbol{a}_i, \boldsymbol{a}_j)$, we have an upper (union) bound on the probability of all failure events:

$$\mathbb{P}\left[\exists\,(i,j)\ :\ |\boldsymbol{a}_i^* \boldsymbol{a}_j| > \frac{2+t}{\sqrt{m}} \right] \leq n(n-1)\exp\left(-\frac{t^2}{2}\right). \tag{3.2.38}$$

Setting $t = 2\sqrt{\log 2n}$, the above probability is less than $1/4$ and we obtain the result. □

There are several points about Theorem 3.5 that are worth remarking on here. First, there is nothing particularly special about the success probability 3/4. By a slightly different choice of t (which affects the constant C), one can make the success probability arbitrarily close to 1. Second, there is nothing particularly special about the uniform distribution on $\mathbb{S}^{m-1}$ – many distributions will produce similar results, although this one is especially convenient to analyze.

Figure 3.7 plots the average mutual coherence of matrices sampled according to Theorem 3.5, for various values of n and $m = n/8$. The observations seem to agree with the predictions of the theorem: the average observed mutual coherence is very close to $1.75\sqrt{\log(n)/m}$.

3.2.4 Limitations of Incoherence

Theorem 3.3 gives a quantitative tradeoff between niceness of $\boldsymbol{A}$ and sparsity of $\boldsymbol{x}_o$, which asserts that when $\boldsymbol{x}_o$ is sparse enough, $\|\boldsymbol{x}_o\|_0 \leq 1/2\mu(\boldsymbol{A})$, then $\boldsymbol{x}_o$ is the unique optimal solution to the ℓ^1 minimization problem. This gives a sufficient condition for the ℓ^1 minimization to be correct.

But how sharp is this result? According to Theorem 3.5, a random matrix $\boldsymbol{A} \in \mathbb{R}^{m\times n}$ with high probability has its coherence bounded from above as $\mu(\boldsymbol{A}) \leq C\sqrt{\log(n)/m}$. So, for a "generic" $\boldsymbol{A}$, the above recovery guarantee implies correct recovery of $\boldsymbol{x}_o$ with $O(\sqrt{m/\log n})$ nonzeros. If we turn this around, and think of

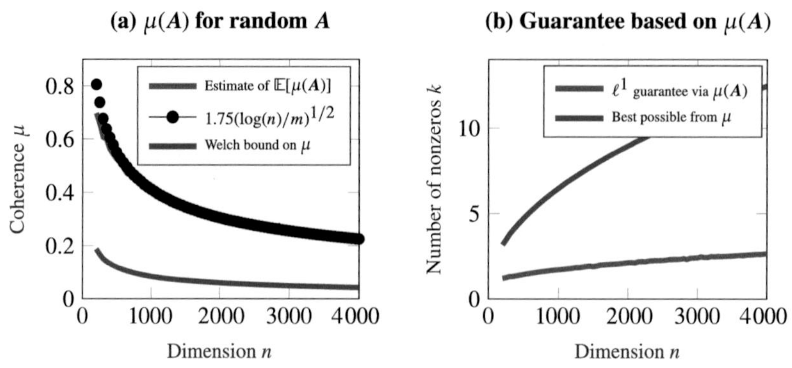

Figure 3.7 How does coherence decay with dimension? (a) Average mutual coherence across 50 trials, for A with columns $a_i \sim_{\text{iid}} \text{uniform}(\mathbb{S}^{m-1})$, for various values of n and $m = n/8$. The black curve, given for reference, is $1.75\sqrt{\log(n)/m}$. The blue curve is the Welch lower bound $\mu_{\min}$ on the smallest achievable mutual coherence for an $m \times n$ matrix (see Theorem 3.7). (b) Average number of nonzeros k which we can guarantee to reconstruct using the observed $\mu(A)$ and Theorem 3.3 (red). The blue curve bounds the best possible number of nonzero entries using Theorem 3.3, for *any* matrix A of size $m \times n$, using the Welch bound.

the matrix multiplication $x \mapsto Ax$ as a sampling procedure, then for appropriately distributed random A, we can recover k-sparse x_o from

$$m \geq C' k^2 \log n \tag{3.2.39}$$

observations. When k is small, this is substantially better than simply sampling all n entries of x. On the other hand, the measurement burden $m = \Omega(k^2)$ seems a little too high – to specify a k-sparse x, we only need to specify its k nonzero entries, … and yet the theory demands k^2 samples!

One might naturally guess that the choice of A as a random matrix was a poor one – perhaps some delicate deterministic construction can yield a better performance guarantee, by making $\mu(A)$ smaller. How small can the coherence $\mu(A)$ be? We already noted that if A is a square matrix with orthogonal columns, $\mu(A) = 0$. However, if we fix m and allow the number of columns, n, to grow, we are forced to pack more and more vectors a_j into a compact set $\mathbb{S}^{m-1}$. As we increase n, the minimum achievable coherence μ increases.

As it turns out in this case, no matter what we do, we cannot construct a matrix whose coherence is significantly smaller than a randomly chosen one: the coherence of the random matrix A is within $C \log n$ of optimal. The following theorem makes this precise:

THEOREM 3.7. (Welch bound) *For any matrix $A = [a_1 \mid \cdots \mid a_n] \in \mathbb{R}^{m \times n}$, $m \leq n$, suppose that the columns a_i have unit ℓ^2 norm. Then*

$$\mu(A) = \max_{i \neq j} \left|\langle a_i, a_j \rangle\right| \geq \sqrt{\frac{n-m}{m(n-1)}}. \tag{3.2.40}$$

Proof Let $G = A^*A \in \mathbb{R}^{n\times n}$, and let $\lambda_1 \geq \cdots \geq \lambda_m \geq 0$ denote its nonzero eigenvalues.[3] Notice that

$$\sum_{i=1}^{m} \lambda_i(G) = \text{trace}\,(G) = \sum_{i=1}^{n} \|a_i\|_2^2 = n. \tag{3.2.41}$$

Using this fact, we obtain that

$$\frac{n^2}{m} \leq \frac{n^2}{m} + \sum_{i=1}^{m} \left(\lambda_i(G) - \frac{n}{m}\right)^2 \tag{3.2.42}$$

$$= \frac{n^2}{m} + \sum_{i=1}^{m} \left\{\lambda_i^2(G) + \frac{n^2}{m^2} - 2\frac{n}{m}\lambda_i(G)\right\} \tag{3.2.43}$$

$$= \sum_{i=1}^{m} \lambda_i^2(G) \;=\; \|G\|_F^2 \tag{3.2.44}$$

$$= \sum_{i,j} \left|a_i^* a_j\right|^2 \;=\; n + \sum_{i\neq j} \left|a_i^* a_j\right|^2 \tag{3.2.45}$$

$$\leq n + n(n-1)\left(\max_{i\neq j} \left|a_i^* a_j\right|\right)^2. \tag{3.2.46}$$

Simplifying, we obtain the desired result.

In the above sequence of inequalities, we have used in (3.2.44) the fact that for any symmetric matrix G, $\|G\|_F^2 = \sum_i \lambda_i(G)^2$, which follows from the eigenvector decomposition $G = V\Lambda V^*$ and the fact that for any matrix M and orthogonal matrices P, Q of appropriate size, $\|M\|_F = \|PMQ\|_F$. □

The important thing to notice here is that if we take n proportional to m, i.e., $n = \beta m$ for some $\beta > 1$, then the bound says that for *any* $m \times n$ matrix A,

$$\mu(A) \geq \Omega\left(\frac{1}{\sqrt{m}}\right). \tag{3.2.47}$$

Hence, in the best possible case, Theorem 3.3 guarantees we can recover x_o with about $\sqrt{m}$ nonzero entries. Or equivalently, no matter how well we choose A, to guarantee success Theorem 3.3 would demand

$$m \geq C'' k^2 \tag{3.2.48}$$

samples to reconstruct a k-sparse vector, which is only $\log n$ factor better than the previous bound (3.2.39) for a randomly chosen A.

Does this behavior reflect a fundamental limitation of the ℓ^1 relaxation? Or is our analysis loose? It turns out that for generic matrices, the situation is much better than the bounds (3.2.39)–(3.2.48) seem to suggest. Again, the easiest way to see this is to do an experiment! We can try solving problems with constant aspect ratio (say, $m = n/2$), and n growing. Try to set $k = \|x_o\|_0$ proportional to m – say, $k = m/4$ (a much better scaling than $k \sim \sqrt{m}$!). Now, try different aspect ratios $m = \alpha n$ and

[3] Because rank $(G) \leq m$, it has at most m nonzero eigenvalues.

sparsity ratios $k = \beta m$. We leave this as an exercise to the reader. You may notice something intriguing:

In a proportional growth setting $m \propto n$, $k \propto m$, ℓ^1 minimization succeeds with very high probability whenever the constants of proportionality n/m and k/m are small enough.

This is a very important observation, since it implies the following.

- **More error correction:** *we can correct constant fractions of errors, using an efficient algorithm.*
- **Better compressive sampling:** *we can sense sparse vectors using a number of measurements that is proportional to the intrinsic "information content" of the signal – the number of nonzero entries.*

However, to have a theory that can explain such observation, we will need a more refined measure of the goodness of $\boldsymbol{A}$ than the (rather crude) coherence or incoherence. In addition, we are going to need to sharpen our theoretical tools too.

3.3 Towards Stronger Correctness Results

3.3.1 The Restricted Isometry Property (RIP)

In the previous section, we saw that the ℓ^1 minimization problem

$$\begin{array}{ll} \min & \|\boldsymbol{x}\|_1 \\ \text{subject to} & \boldsymbol{A}\boldsymbol{x} = \boldsymbol{y} \end{array} \tag{3.3.1}$$

correctly recovers a sparse $\boldsymbol{x}_o$ from observation $\boldsymbol{y} = \boldsymbol{A}\boldsymbol{x}_o$, provided two conditions are in force:

- $\boldsymbol{x}_o$ **is structured**: $k = \|\boldsymbol{x}_o\|_0 \ll n$.
- $\boldsymbol{A}$ **is "nice"**: its coherence $\mu(\boldsymbol{A})$ is small.

The intuition provided by incoherence is qualitatively very suggestive, but it does not provide a quantitative explanation for the good behavior we have seen in our experiments so far. How can we strengthen the condition? Suppose that $\boldsymbol{A}$ has unit-norm columns. Then it is easy to calculate that for every two-column submatrix $\boldsymbol{A}_{\mathsf{I}} = [\boldsymbol{a}_i \mid \boldsymbol{a}_j] \in \mathbb{R}^{m \times 2}$,

$$\boldsymbol{A}_{\mathsf{I}}^* \boldsymbol{A}_{\mathsf{I}} = \begin{bmatrix} 1 & \boldsymbol{a}_i^* \boldsymbol{a}_j \\ \boldsymbol{a}_j^* \boldsymbol{a}_i & 1 \end{bmatrix}. \tag{3.3.2}$$

Exercise 3.6 asks you to show that since $|\boldsymbol{a}_i^* \boldsymbol{a}_j| \le \mu(\boldsymbol{A})$, this matrix is well conditioned:

$$1 - \mu(\boldsymbol{A}) \le \sigma_{\min}(\boldsymbol{A}_{\mathsf{I}}^* \boldsymbol{A}_{\mathsf{I}}) \le \sigma_{\max}(\boldsymbol{A}_{\mathsf{I}}^* \boldsymbol{A}_{\mathsf{I}}) \le 1 + \mu(\boldsymbol{A}). \tag{3.3.3}$$

This property holds simultaneously for every two-column submatrix A_{I}. So, the property that the columns of A are well spread implies that *the column submatrices of A are well conditioned.*

We can generalize both properties by taking the set I to be larger than 2. Indeed, we can demand that all k-column submatrices of A are well conditioned: for every $\mathsf{I} \subset \{1, \dots, n\}$ of size k, we have

$$1 - k\mu(A) \le \sigma_{\min}(A_{\mathsf{I}}^* A_{\mathsf{I}}) \le \sigma_{\max}(A_{\mathsf{I}}^* A_{\mathsf{I}}) \le 1 + k\mu(A), \quad \forall \mathsf{I} \text{ of size} \le k. \tag{3.3.4}$$

This controls the Kruskal rank: if $1-k\mu(A) > 0$, then $\operatorname{krank}(A) \ge k$. This implies that an incoherent matrix with small μ tends to have large Kruskal rank. Hence according to Theorem 2.6, any sufficiently sparse x_o is *the sparsest* solution to the observation equation $Ax = y$.

In (3.3.4), we saw that the coherence $\mu(A)$ controls the conditioning of the column submatrices A_{I} – if $\mu(A)$ is small, every submatrix spanned by just a few columns of A is well conditioned:

$$1 - \delta \le \sigma_{\min}(A_{\mathsf{I}}^* A_{\mathsf{I}}) \le \sigma_{\max}(A_{\mathsf{I}}^* A_{\mathsf{I}}) \le 1 + \delta, \tag{3.3.5}$$

with δ small. This turned out to be critical in our proof of Theorem 3.3. In fact, we will see that for certain well-structured matrices A, including random matrices, the bounds in (3.3.5) hold with δ far smaller than would be predicted by (3.3.4) using only the coherence.[4] They also hold for far larger $k = |\mathsf{I}|$ than might have been predicted from coherence alone. We will see that this leads (via different and slightly more complicated arguments) to substantially tighter guarantees for the performance of both ℓ^0 and ℓ^1 minimization.

The bounds in (3.3.5) hold uniformly over sets I of size k if and only if

$$\forall\, x \; k\text{-sparse}, \quad (1 - \delta)\, \|x\|_2^2 \le \|Ax\|_2^2 \le (1 + \delta)\, \|x\|_2^2. \tag{3.3.6}$$

That is to say, the mapping $x \mapsto Ax$ approximately preserves the norm of sparse vectors x. Informally, we call such a mapping a *restricted isometry*: it is (nearly) an isometry,[5] *if* we restrict our attention to the sparse vectors x.

DEFINITION 3.8. (Restricted isometry property [CT05]) *The matrix A satisfies the* restricted isometry property (RIP) *of* order k, *with constant $\delta \in [0, 1)$, if*

$$\forall\, x \; k\text{-sparse}, \quad (1 - \delta)\, \|x\|_2^2 \le \|Ax\|_2^2 \le (1 + \delta)\, \|x\|_2^2. \tag{3.3.7}$$

The order-k restricted isometry constant $\delta_k(A)$ *is the smallest number δ such that the above inequality holds.*

[4] For example, if A_{I} is a large $m \times k$ ($k < m$) matrix with entries independent $\mathcal{N}(0, 1/m)$, $\sigma_{min}(A_{\mathsf{I}}^* A_{\mathsf{I}}) \approx (\sqrt{1} - \sqrt{k/m})^2 \ge 1 - 2\sqrt{k/m}$, and $\sigma_{max}(A_{\mathsf{I}}^* A_{\mathsf{I}}) \approx (\sqrt{1} + \sqrt{k/m})^2 \le 1 + 3\sqrt{k/m}$. You can check these values numerically; the aforementioned bounds can be made into rigorous statements using tools for Gaussian processes.

[5] An isometry is a mapping that preserves the norm of every vector.

Whenever $\delta_k(\boldsymbol{A}) < 1$, every k-column submatrix has full column rank k. This implies that ℓ^0 recovery succeeds under RIP:

THEOREM 3.9. (ℓ^0 recovery under RIP [CRT06a, Can08]) *Suppose that $\boldsymbol{y} = \boldsymbol{A}\boldsymbol{x}_o$, with $k = \|\boldsymbol{x}_o\|_0$. If $\delta_{2k}(\boldsymbol{A}) < 1$, then $\boldsymbol{x}_o$ is the unique optimal solution to*

$$\begin{array}{ll} \min & \|\boldsymbol{x}\|_0 \\ \text{subject to} & \boldsymbol{A}\boldsymbol{x} = \boldsymbol{y}. \end{array} \tag{3.3.8}$$

Proof Suppose on the contrary that there exists $\boldsymbol{x}' \neq \boldsymbol{x}_o$ with $\|\boldsymbol{x}'\|_0 \leq k$. Then $\boldsymbol{x}_o - \boldsymbol{x}' \in \text{null}(\boldsymbol{A})$, and $\|\boldsymbol{x}_o - \boldsymbol{x}'\|_0 \leq 2k$. This implies that $\delta_{2k}(\boldsymbol{A}) \geq 1$, contradicting our assumption. □

So, provided the RIP constant of order $2k$ is bounded away from one, ℓ^0 minimization successfully recovers $\boldsymbol{x}_o$. If we tighten our demand to $\delta_{2k}(\boldsymbol{A}) < \sqrt{2} - 1$, ℓ^1 minimization succeeds as well:

THEOREM 3.10. (ℓ^1 recovery under RIP) *Suppose that $\boldsymbol{y} = \boldsymbol{A}\boldsymbol{x}_o$, with $k = \|\boldsymbol{x}_o\|_0$. If $\delta_{2k}(\boldsymbol{A}) < \sqrt{2} - 1$, then $\boldsymbol{x}_o$ is the unique optimal solution to*

$$\begin{array}{ll} \min & \|\boldsymbol{x}\|_1 \\ \text{subject to} & \boldsymbol{A}\boldsymbol{x} = \boldsymbol{y}. \end{array} \tag{3.3.9}$$

The significance of this result comes from the fact that for "generic" matrices, the condition $\delta_{2k}(\boldsymbol{A}) < \sqrt{2} - 1$ holds even when k is nearly proportional to m:

THEOREM 3.11. (RIP of gaussian matrices [CRT06a, BDDW08]) *There exists a numerical constant $C > 0$ such that if $\boldsymbol{A} \in \mathbb{R}^{m \times n}$ is a random matrix with entries independent $\mathcal{N}(0, 1/m)$ random variables, with high probability, $\delta_k(\boldsymbol{A}) < \delta$, provided*

$$m \geq C k \log(n/k)/\delta^2. \tag{3.3.10}$$

This implies that recovery of k-sparse $\boldsymbol{x}$ is possible from about $m \geq Ck\log(n/k)$ random measurements. This is a substantial improvement over our previous estimate of $m \sim k^2$. In particular, it allows (k, m, n) to scale proportionally [Don06b, CT05]. This improvement has stimulated a lot of work on efficient sensing and sampling schemes in various application domains.

3.3.2 Restricted Strong Convexity Condition

We have stated the above two theorems without proof. We will prove Theorem 3.10 in several stages. In this section, we introduce two intermediate properties of the sensing matrix $\boldsymbol{A}$, which turn out to be very useful in their own right. In the next section, we prove Theorem 3.10 by proving that when $\delta_{2k}(\boldsymbol{A}) < \sqrt{2} - 1$, these intermediate properties are satisfied, and hence ℓ^1 minimization succeeds.

As above, suppose that $\boldsymbol{y} = \boldsymbol{A}\boldsymbol{x}_o$, for some $\|\boldsymbol{x}_o\|_0 \leq k$. We hope that under certain conditions, $\boldsymbol{x}_o$ is the unique optimal solution to the ℓ^1 minimization program

$$\begin{array}{ll} \min & \|\boldsymbol{x}\|_1 \\ \text{subject to} & \boldsymbol{A}\boldsymbol{x} = \boldsymbol{y}. \end{array} \tag{3.3.11}$$

Let $\boldsymbol{x}'$ be any feasible point, i.e., any point satisfying $\boldsymbol{A}\boldsymbol{x}' = \boldsymbol{y}$. Because $\boldsymbol{A}\boldsymbol{x}_o = \boldsymbol{y}$ as well, *the difference* $\boldsymbol{h} = \boldsymbol{x}' - \boldsymbol{x}_o$ *belongs to the null space* null($\boldsymbol{A}$).

Let I denote the support of $\boldsymbol{x}_o$, and I^c its complement. Then

$$\|\boldsymbol{x}'\|_1 = \|\boldsymbol{x}_o + \boldsymbol{h}\|_1 \tag{3.3.12}$$

$$\geq \|\boldsymbol{x}_o\|_1 - \|\boldsymbol{h}_\mathsf{I}\|_1 + \|\boldsymbol{h}_{\mathsf{I}^c}\|_1. \tag{3.3.13}$$

Hence, if $\|\boldsymbol{h}_{\mathsf{I}^c}\|_1 > \|\boldsymbol{h}_\mathsf{I}\|_1$, $\boldsymbol{x}'$ has strictly larger objective function than $\boldsymbol{x}_o$ and so $\boldsymbol{x}'$ is not optimal. Conversely, if the null space of $\boldsymbol{A}$ contains no vectors $\boldsymbol{h} \neq \boldsymbol{0}$ for which $\|\boldsymbol{h}_\mathsf{I}\|_1 \geq \|\boldsymbol{h}_{\mathsf{I}^c}\|_1$, then $\boldsymbol{x}_o$ must be the unique optimal solution to (3.3.11).

It is helpful to ask what if this were not true. What happens if the optimal solution to the above program, say $\hat{\boldsymbol{x}}_{\ell^1}$, was not $\boldsymbol{x}_o$? Under what conditions could their difference $\boldsymbol{h} \doteq \hat{\boldsymbol{x}}_{\ell^1} - \boldsymbol{x}_o$ be nonzero? Recall that I is the support of $\boldsymbol{x}_o$ and I^c its complement.

Since $\hat{\boldsymbol{x}}_{\ell^1}$ is the optimal solution to the above program, we must have

$$\begin{aligned} 0 &\geq \|\hat{\boldsymbol{x}}_{\ell^1}\|_1 - \|\boldsymbol{x}_o\|_1 \\ &= \|\boldsymbol{x}_o + \boldsymbol{h}\|_1 - \|\boldsymbol{x}_o\|_1 \\ &\geq \|\boldsymbol{x}_o\|_1 - \|\boldsymbol{h}_\mathsf{I}\|_1 + \|\boldsymbol{h}_{\mathsf{I}^c}\|_1 - \|\boldsymbol{x}_o\|_1 \\ &= -\|\boldsymbol{h}_\mathsf{I}\|_1 + \|\boldsymbol{h}_{\mathsf{I}^c}\|_1. \end{aligned} \tag{3.3.14}$$

That is, we have

$$\|\boldsymbol{h}_{\mathsf{I}^c}\|_1 \leq \|\boldsymbol{h}_\mathsf{I}\|_1. \tag{3.3.15}$$

Meanwhile, since $\boldsymbol{y} = \boldsymbol{A}\boldsymbol{x}_o = \boldsymbol{A}\hat{\boldsymbol{x}}_{\ell^1}$, we also have

$$\boldsymbol{A}\boldsymbol{h} = \boldsymbol{0}. \tag{3.3.16}$$

In other words, in order for the ℓ^1 program to admit a better solution $\hat{\boldsymbol{x}}_{\ell^1}$ than the original sparse solution $\boldsymbol{x}_o$, we must have the above two conditions (3.3.15) and (3.3.16) hold simultaneously. Therefore, in order to show that $\boldsymbol{x}_o$ is the unique optimal solution for the ℓ^1 program, we only have to show that these conditions cannot all be true for any such $\boldsymbol{h}$.

Null Space Property

The above discussion suggests that the null space of $\boldsymbol{A}$ is very important for understanding when we can recover $\boldsymbol{x}_o$. Previous ℓ^0 recovery results all come by showing that the null space does not contain sparse vectors. The condition that, for every nonzero $\boldsymbol{h} \in$ null($\boldsymbol{A}$), $\|\boldsymbol{h}_\mathsf{I}\|_1 < \|\boldsymbol{h}_{\mathsf{I}^c}\|_1$ can be interpreted as saying that the null space does not contain any vector that is concentrated on the (small) set of coordinates I. This is sufficient for ℓ^1 minimization to recover $\boldsymbol{x}_o$ with support I. If we want to guarantee recovery of *any* k-sparse $\boldsymbol{x}_o$, we can ask that, for every set I of k coordinates and every nonzero null vector $\boldsymbol{h}$, $\|\boldsymbol{h}_{\mathsf{I}}\|_1 < \|\boldsymbol{h}_{\mathsf{I}^c}\|_1$:

DEFINITION 3.12. (Null space property) *The matrix* $\boldsymbol{A}$ *satisfies the* null space property *of order k if for every* $\boldsymbol{h} \in \operatorname{null}(\boldsymbol{A}) \setminus \{\boldsymbol{0}\}$ *and every* I *of size at most k,*

$$\|\boldsymbol{h}_{\mathsf{I}}\|_1 < \|\boldsymbol{h}_{\mathsf{I}^c}\|_1 . \tag{3.3.17}$$

This can be interpreted as saying that the null space does not contain any near-sparse vectors, where sparsity is measured via the ℓ^1 norm. If $\boldsymbol{A}$ satisfies the null space property, then ℓ^1 succeeds in recovering any k-sparse $\boldsymbol{x}_o$:

LEMMA 3.13. *Suppose that* $\boldsymbol{A}$ *satisfies the null space property of order k. Then for any* $\boldsymbol{y} = \boldsymbol{A}\boldsymbol{x}_o$, *with* $\|\boldsymbol{x}_o\|_0 \le k$, $\boldsymbol{x}_o$ *is the unique optimal solution to the* ℓ^1 *problem*

$$\begin{array}{ll} \min & \|\boldsymbol{x}\|_1 \\ \text{subject to} & \boldsymbol{A}\boldsymbol{x} = \boldsymbol{y}. \end{array} \tag{3.3.18}$$

Proof Let $\boldsymbol{y} = \boldsymbol{A}\boldsymbol{x}_o$, with $\|\boldsymbol{x}_o\|_0 \le k$, and let $\mathsf{I} = \operatorname{supp}(\boldsymbol{x}_o)$. Let $\hat{\boldsymbol{x}}_{\ell^1}$ be the optimal solution, so $\boldsymbol{h} = \hat{\boldsymbol{x}}_{\ell^1} - \boldsymbol{x}_o \in \operatorname{null}(\boldsymbol{A})$. If $\boldsymbol{h} \neq \boldsymbol{0}$, then $\left\|\hat{\boldsymbol{x}}_{\ell^1}\right\|_1 = \|\boldsymbol{x}_o + \boldsymbol{h}\|_1 \ge \|\boldsymbol{x}_o\|_1 - \|\boldsymbol{h}_{\mathsf{I}}\|_1 + \|\boldsymbol{h}_{\mathsf{I}^c}\|_1 > \|\boldsymbol{x}_o\|_1$, contradicting the optimality of $\hat{\boldsymbol{x}}_{\ell^1}$. □

In the viewpoint of the coefficient-space picture for ℓ^1 minimization introduced in Section 3.2.2, the null space condition asserts that when $\operatorname{null}(\boldsymbol{A})$ is translated to any k-sparse point $\boldsymbol{x}_o$ on the boundary of the ℓ^1 ball B_1, the translate $\boldsymbol{x}_o + \operatorname{null}(\boldsymbol{A})$ does not intersect the interior of B_1. Figure 3.8 visualizes this condition for the special case in which $n = 3$, and $\operatorname{null}(\boldsymbol{A})$ is one-dimensional. In the literature, the null space property has been used to establish various sufficient conditions for the success of ℓ^1 minimization for sparse recovery. In fact, Theorem 3.10 can be proved by showing that the RIP condition on the matrix $\boldsymbol{A}$ implies the null space property.

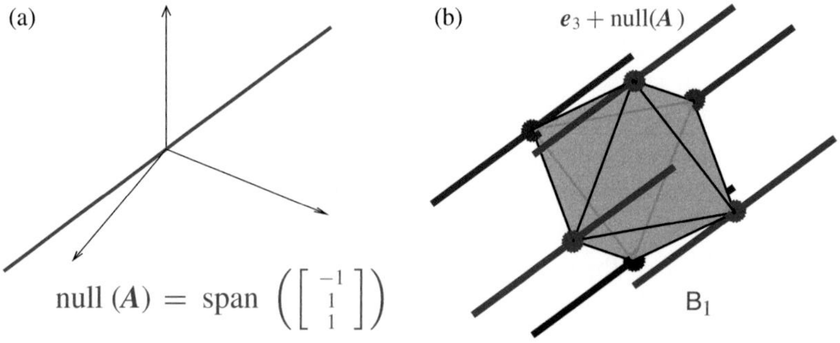

Figure 3.8 Visualizing the null space property in three dimensions. (a) The sensing matrix $\begin{bmatrix} 1 & 1 & 0 \\ 0 & 1 & -1 \end{bmatrix}$ has null space spanned by $[-1, 1, 1]^*$. This matrix satisfies the null space property of order $k = 1$. (b) Geometrically this implies that any translate $\pm\boldsymbol{e}_j + \operatorname{null}(\boldsymbol{A})$ to a vertex of the ℓ^1 ball B_1 intersects B_1 only at the vertex $\pm\boldsymbol{e}_j$.

Restricted Strong Convexity Condition

Alternatively and equivalently, we can study the success of ℓ^1 minimization by considering possible perturbations $\boldsymbol{h}$ that could reduce the value of the objective function. According to condition (3.3.15), they must satisfy

$$\|\boldsymbol{h}_{\mathsf{I}^c}\|_1 \leq \|\boldsymbol{h}_{\mathsf{I}}\|_1 . \tag{3.3.19}$$

To ensure the original k-sparse $\boldsymbol{x}_o$ is the unique optimal solution, we can require that for any nonzero perturbation $\boldsymbol{h}$ satisfying (3.3.19), $\boldsymbol{A}\boldsymbol{h} \neq \mathbf{0}$:

$$\|\boldsymbol{A}\boldsymbol{h}\|_2^2 > 0. \tag{3.3.20}$$

Since the set $\mathsf{S} = \bigcup_{\mathsf{I}}\{\boldsymbol{h} : \|\boldsymbol{h}_{\mathsf{I}^c}\|_1 \leq \|\boldsymbol{h}_{\mathsf{I}}\|_1, \|\boldsymbol{h}\|_2^2 = 1\}$ is compact, $\|\boldsymbol{A}\boldsymbol{h}\|_2^2$ must attain its minimum $\mu > 0$. The above condition is therefore equivalent to

$$\|\boldsymbol{A}\boldsymbol{h}\|_2^2 \geq \mu\|\boldsymbol{h}\|_2^2, \quad \forall\, \boldsymbol{h} \;\; \|\boldsymbol{h}_{\mathsf{I}^c}\|_1 \leq \|\boldsymbol{h}_{\mathsf{I}}\|_1 \tag{3.3.21}$$

for some $\mu > 0$.

If we consider the quadratic loss, $L(\boldsymbol{x}) = \frac{1}{2}\|\boldsymbol{y} - \boldsymbol{A}\boldsymbol{x}\|_2^2$, the second derivative in the $\boldsymbol{h}$ direction is $\boldsymbol{h}^* \nabla^2 L(\boldsymbol{x})\boldsymbol{h} = \|\boldsymbol{A}\boldsymbol{h}\|_2^2 > 0$. The above condition can be interpreted as saying that the function $L(\boldsymbol{x})$ is *strongly convex* when restricted to directions $\boldsymbol{h}$ satisfying (3.3.19) – see Figure 3.9 for a visualization of this interpretation. We term this *(uniform) restricted strong convexity*:

DEFINITION 3.14. (Restricted strong convexity) *The matrix* $\boldsymbol{A}$ *satisfies the* restricted strong convexity *(RSC) condition of order k, with parameters* $\mu > 0$, $\alpha \geq 1$, *if for every* I *of size at most k and for all nonzero* $\boldsymbol{h}$ *satisfying* $\|\boldsymbol{h}_{\mathsf{I}^c}\|_1 \leq \alpha\|\boldsymbol{h}_{\mathsf{I}}\|_1$,

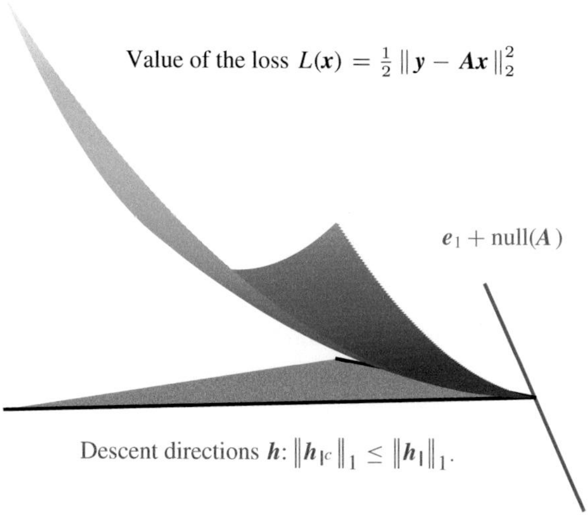

Figure 3.9 Restricted strong convexity implies that the loss $L(\boldsymbol{x})$ exhibits positive curvature along the potential **descent directions** $\boldsymbol{h}$ satisfying $\|\boldsymbol{h}_{\mathsf{I}^c}\|_1 \leq \|\boldsymbol{h}_{\mathsf{I}}\|_1$. Here, $\boldsymbol{x}_o = \boldsymbol{e}_1$. Red: the **feasible set** of $\boldsymbol{x}$ that satisfy $\boldsymbol{A}\boldsymbol{x} = \boldsymbol{y}$. Under RSC, the loss is strictly positive at any point $\boldsymbol{x}$ whose ℓ^1 norm is smaller than $\|\boldsymbol{x}_o\|_1$.

$$\|\boldsymbol{A}\boldsymbol{h}\|_2^2 \geq \mu\|\boldsymbol{h}\|_2^2. \tag{3.3.22}$$

In this definition, we have generalized the condition (3.3.19) to consider instead $\|\boldsymbol{h}_{\mathsf{I}^c}\|_1 \leq \alpha\,\|\boldsymbol{h}_{\mathsf{I}}\|_1$. This generalization will be used in an essential way later when we study sparse recovery from noisy measurements. For now, we note that for noiseless measurements $\boldsymbol{y} = \boldsymbol{A}\boldsymbol{x}_o$, restricted strong convexity indeed implies that ℓ^1 minimization succeeds:

LEMMA 3.15. *Suppose that $\boldsymbol{A}$ satisfies the restricted strong convexity condition of order k with constant $\alpha \geq 1$, for some $\mu > 0$. Then for any $\boldsymbol{y} = \boldsymbol{A}\boldsymbol{x}_o$, with $\|\boldsymbol{x}_o\|_0 \leq k$, $\boldsymbol{x}_o$ is the unique optimal solution to the ℓ^1 problem:*

$$\begin{array}{ll} \min & \|\boldsymbol{x}\|_1 \\ \text{subject to} & \boldsymbol{A}\boldsymbol{x} = \boldsymbol{y}. \end{array} \tag{3.3.23}$$

Proof We leave it as an exercise for the reader to prove this result by verifying that restricted strong convexity implies the null space property. □

3.3.3 Success of ℓ^1 Minimization under RIP

In this section we prove Theorem 3.10. Earlier, in Section 3.2.2, we followed a fairly simple path to prove Theorem 3.3: write down an optimality condition, and then construct a dual certificate using a bit of cleverness. This approach can be used to prove a variant of Theorem 3.10 [CT05]. However, the argument is more delicate than before.

So here, to prove Theorem 3.10, we will take a slightly different path, which utilizes properties of "good" sensing matrices $\boldsymbol{A}$ that we have introduced in the previous section. As we have discussed there, to prove that RIP implies correct recovery, it suffices to show that RIP implies the restricted strong convexity (RSC) condition. Our proof here follows close to that of [CRT06b, Can08].[6] In doing so, we will use the following property of the restricted isometry constants:

LEMMA 3.16. *If $\boldsymbol{x}$, $\boldsymbol{z}$ are vectors with disjoint support, and $|\mathrm{supp}(\boldsymbol{x})| + |\mathrm{supp}(\boldsymbol{z})| \leq k$, then*

$$|\langle \boldsymbol{A}\boldsymbol{x}, \boldsymbol{A}\boldsymbol{z}\rangle| \leq \delta_k(\boldsymbol{A})\,\|\boldsymbol{x}\|_2\,\|\boldsymbol{z}\|_2\,. \tag{3.3.24}$$

Proof Because the expression is invariant to scaling $\boldsymbol{x}$ and $\boldsymbol{z}$, we lose no generality in assuming that $\|\boldsymbol{x}\|_2 = \|\boldsymbol{z}\|_2 = 1$. Notice that

$$\|\boldsymbol{p}+\boldsymbol{q}\|_2^2 = \|\boldsymbol{p}\|_2^2 + \|\boldsymbol{q}\|_2^2 + 2\,\langle \boldsymbol{p}, \boldsymbol{q}\rangle\,, \tag{3.3.25}$$

$$\|\boldsymbol{p}-\boldsymbol{q}\|_2^2 = \|\boldsymbol{p}\|_2^2 + \|\boldsymbol{q}\|_2^2 - 2\,\langle \boldsymbol{p}, \boldsymbol{q}\rangle\,. \tag{3.3.26}$$

[6] We have modified the original proof that shows RIP implies the null space property to RSC.

Hence,

$$|\langle \boldsymbol{Ax}, \boldsymbol{Az}\rangle| \le \frac{1}{4}\left|\|\boldsymbol{Ax}+\boldsymbol{Az}\|_2^2 - \|\boldsymbol{Ax}-\boldsymbol{Az}\|_2^2\right| \tag{3.3.27}$$

$$\le \frac{1}{4}\left|(1+\delta_k)\,\|\boldsymbol{x}+\boldsymbol{z}\|_2^2 - (1-\delta_k)\,\|\boldsymbol{x}-\boldsymbol{z}\|_2^2\right|. \tag{3.3.28}$$

Because $\boldsymbol{x}$ and $\boldsymbol{z}$ have disjoint support, $\|\boldsymbol{x}+\boldsymbol{z}\|_2^2 = \|\boldsymbol{x}-\boldsymbol{z}\|_2^2 = 2$, and the result follows. □

We are now ready to prove the following theorem.

THEOREM 3.17. (RIP implies RSC) *If a matrix $\boldsymbol{A}$ satisfies RIP with $\delta_{2k}(\boldsymbol{A}) < 1/(1+\alpha\sqrt{2})$, then $\boldsymbol{A}$ satisfies the RSC condition of order k with constant α.*

Proof Let I be any set of size k and let $\boldsymbol{h} \in \mathbb{R}^n$ any vector that satisfies the restriction

$$\|\boldsymbol{h}_{\mathsf{I}^c}\|_1 \le \alpha \cdot \|\boldsymbol{h}_{\mathsf{I}}\|_1. \tag{3.3.29}$$

Form disjoint subsets $\mathsf{J}_1, \mathsf{J}_2, \mathsf{J}_3, \ldots \subseteq \mathsf{I}^c$ as follows:

J_1 indexes the k largest (in magnitude) elements of $\boldsymbol{h}_{\mathsf{I}^c}$,
J_2 indexes the k largest (in magnitude) elements of $\boldsymbol{h}_{(\mathsf{I}\cup\mathsf{J}_1)^c}$,
J_3 indexes the k largest (in magnitude) elements of $\boldsymbol{h}_{(\mathsf{I}\cup\mathsf{J}_1\cup\mathsf{J}_2)^c}$,

$$\vdots$$

Notice that because every entry of J_i is at least as large as every entry of J_{i+1}, the average magnitude of an entry in J_i is at least as large as the largest entry in J_{i+1}:

$$\forall\, i \ge 1, \qquad \left\|\boldsymbol{h}_{\mathsf{J}_{i+1}}\right\|_\infty \le \frac{\left\|\boldsymbol{h}_{\mathsf{J}_i}\right\|_1}{k}. \tag{3.3.30}$$

We also note that for any vector $\boldsymbol{z}$ with $\|\boldsymbol{z}\|_0 \le k$, $\|\boldsymbol{z}\|_1 \le \sqrt{k}\,\|\boldsymbol{z}\|_2$ and $\|\boldsymbol{z}\|_2 \le \sqrt{k}\,\|\boldsymbol{z}\|_\infty$.

Using the RIP with the $2k$-sparse vector $\boldsymbol{h}_{\mathsf{I}\cup\mathsf{J}_1}$ and the fact

$$\boldsymbol{Ah}_{\mathsf{I}} + \boldsymbol{Ah}_{\mathsf{J}_1} = \boldsymbol{Ah} - \boldsymbol{Ah}_{\mathsf{J}_2} - \boldsymbol{Ah}_{\mathsf{J}_3} - \ldots, \tag{3.3.31}$$

we have that

$$\begin{aligned}
(1-\delta_{2k})\left\|\boldsymbol{h}_{\mathsf{I}\cup\mathsf{J}_1}\right\|_2^2 &\le \left\|\boldsymbol{Ah}_{\mathsf{I}\cup\mathsf{J}_1}\right\|_2^2 \\
&= \left\langle \boldsymbol{Ah}_{\mathsf{I}} + \boldsymbol{Ah}_{\mathsf{J}_1}, -\boldsymbol{Ah}_{\mathsf{J}_2} - \boldsymbol{Ah}_{\mathsf{J}_3} - \cdots\right\rangle + \left\langle \boldsymbol{Ah}_{\mathsf{I}} + \boldsymbol{Ah}_{\mathsf{J}_1}, \boldsymbol{Ah}\right\rangle \\
&\le \sum_{j=2}^{\infty}\left(\left|\left\langle \boldsymbol{Ah}_{\mathsf{I}}, \boldsymbol{Ah}_{\mathsf{J}_j}\right\rangle\right| + \left|\left\langle \boldsymbol{Ah}_{\mathsf{J}_1}, \boldsymbol{Ah}_{\mathsf{J}_j}\right\rangle\right|\right) + \|\boldsymbol{Ah}_{\mathsf{I}\cup\mathsf{J}_1}\|_2\|\boldsymbol{Ah}\|_2 \\
&\le \delta_{2k}(\|\boldsymbol{h}_{\mathsf{I}}\|_2 + \left\|\boldsymbol{h}_{\mathsf{J}_1}\right\|_2)\sum_{j=2}^{\infty}\left\|\boldsymbol{h}_{\mathsf{J}_j}\right\|_2 + (1+\delta_{2k})^{1/2}\|\boldsymbol{h}_{\mathsf{I}\cup\mathsf{J}_1}\|_2\|\boldsymbol{Ah}\|_2
\end{aligned}$$

$$
\begin{aligned}
&\le \delta_{2k}\sqrt{2}\,\|\boldsymbol{h}_{\mathsf{I}\cup\mathsf{J}_1}\|_2 \sum_{j=2}^{\infty} \left\|\boldsymbol{h}_{\mathsf{J}_j}\right\|_2 + (1+\delta_{2k})^{1/2}\|\boldsymbol{h}_{\mathsf{I}\cup\mathsf{J}_1}\|_2\|\boldsymbol{A}\boldsymbol{h}\|_2 \\
&\le \delta_{2k}\sqrt{2}\,\|\boldsymbol{h}_{\mathsf{I}\cup\mathsf{J}_1}\|_2 \sum_{j=2}^{\infty} \left\|\boldsymbol{h}_{\mathsf{J}_j}\right\|_\infty \sqrt{k} + (1+\delta_{2k})^{1/2}\|\boldsymbol{h}_{\mathsf{I}\cup\mathsf{J}_1}\|_2\|\boldsymbol{A}\boldsymbol{h}\|_2 \\
&\le \delta_{2k}\sqrt{2}\,\|\boldsymbol{h}_{\mathsf{I}\cup\mathsf{J}_1}\|_2 \sum_{j=1}^{\infty} \left\|\boldsymbol{h}_{\mathsf{J}_j}\right\|_1 /\sqrt{k} + (1+\delta_{2k})^{1/2}\|\boldsymbol{h}_{\mathsf{I}\cup\mathsf{J}_1}\|_2\|\boldsymbol{A}\boldsymbol{h}\|_2 \\
&= \delta_{2k}\sqrt{2}\,\|\boldsymbol{h}_{\mathsf{I}\cup\mathsf{J}_1}\|_2 \|\boldsymbol{h}_{\mathsf{I}^c}\|_1 /\sqrt{k} + (1+\delta_{2k})^{1/2}\|\boldsymbol{h}_{\mathsf{I}\cup\mathsf{J}_1}\|_2\|\boldsymbol{A}\boldsymbol{h}\|_2. \qquad (3.3.32)
\end{aligned}
$$

After dividing through by $\|\boldsymbol{h}_{\mathsf{I}\cup\mathsf{J}_1}\|_2$, we have

$$(1-\delta_{2k})\|\boldsymbol{h}_{\mathsf{I}\cup\mathsf{J}_1}\|_2 \le \delta_{2k}\sqrt{2}\,\|\boldsymbol{h}_{\mathsf{I}^c}\|_1/\sqrt{k} + (1+\delta_{2k})^{1/2}\,\|\boldsymbol{A}\boldsymbol{h}\|_2. \qquad (3.3.33)$$

Since $\boldsymbol{h}$ satisfies the restricted cone condition, we have

$$\|\boldsymbol{h}_{\mathsf{I}^c}\|_1 \le \alpha\|\boldsymbol{h}_{\mathsf{I}}\|_1 \le \alpha\sqrt{k}\|\boldsymbol{h}_{\mathsf{I}}\|_2 \le \alpha\sqrt{k}\|\boldsymbol{h}_{\mathsf{I}\cup\mathsf{J}_1}\|_2. \qquad (3.3.34)$$

Substituting this into the previous inequality, we obtain

$$(1-\delta_{2k})\|\boldsymbol{h}_{\mathsf{I}\cup\mathsf{J}_1}\|_2 \le \alpha\delta_{2k}\sqrt{2}\,\|\boldsymbol{h}_{\mathsf{I}\cup\mathsf{J}_1}\|_2 + (1+\delta_{2k})^{1/2}\,\|\boldsymbol{A}\boldsymbol{h}\|_2. \qquad (3.3.35)$$

This gives

$$\|\boldsymbol{A}\boldsymbol{h}\|_2 \ge \frac{1-\delta_{2k}(1+\alpha\sqrt{2})}{(1+\delta_{2k})^{1/2}}\,\|\boldsymbol{h}_{\mathsf{I}\cup\mathsf{J}_1}\|_2. \qquad (3.3.36)$$

Since the i-th element of $\boldsymbol{h}_{(\mathsf{I}\cup\mathsf{J}_1)^c}$ is no larger than the mean of the first i elements of $\boldsymbol{h}_{\mathsf{I}^c}$, we have

$$|\boldsymbol{h}_{(\mathsf{I}\cup\mathsf{J}_1)^c}|_{(i)} \le \|\boldsymbol{h}_{\mathsf{I}^c}\|_1/i. \qquad (3.3.37)$$

Combining with the restriction (3.3.29), we have

$$
\begin{aligned}
\|\boldsymbol{h}_{(\mathsf{I}\cup\mathsf{J}_1)^c}\|_2^2 &\le \|\boldsymbol{h}_{\mathsf{I}^c}\|_1^2 \sum_{i=k+1}^{\infty} \frac{1}{i^2} \qquad (3.3.38)\\
&\le \frac{\|\boldsymbol{h}_{\mathsf{I}^c}\|_1^2}{k} \le \frac{\alpha^2\|\boldsymbol{h}_{\mathsf{I}}\|_1^2}{k} \qquad (3.3.39)\\
&\le \alpha^2\|\boldsymbol{h}_{\mathsf{I}}\|_2^2 \le \alpha^2\|\boldsymbol{h}_{\mathsf{I}\cup\mathsf{J}_1}\|_2^2. \qquad (3.3.40)
\end{aligned}
$$

So we have

$$\|\boldsymbol{h}\|_2^2 \le (1+\alpha^2)\|\boldsymbol{h}_{\mathsf{I}\cup\mathsf{J}_1}\|_2^2. \qquad (3.3.41)$$

Combining this with the previous condition on $\|\boldsymbol{A}\boldsymbol{h}\|_2$, we get

$$\|\boldsymbol{A}\boldsymbol{h}\|_2 \ge \frac{1-\delta_{2k}(1+\alpha\sqrt{2})}{(1+\delta_{2k})^{1/2}\sqrt{1+\alpha^2}}\,\|\boldsymbol{h}\|_2. \qquad (3.3.42)$$

So as long as $\delta_{2k} < 1/(1+\alpha\sqrt{2})$, $\boldsymbol{A}$ satisfies the RSC condition of order k with the constant

$$\mu = \frac{\left(1-\delta_{2k}(1+\alpha\sqrt{2})\right)^2}{(1+\delta_{2k})(1+\alpha^2)}, \tag{3.3.43}$$

as claimed. □

Theorem 3.10 then becomes a corollary to this theorem for the case $\alpha = 1$ since the restriction set we need to consider is $\|\boldsymbol{h}_{\mathsf{I}^c}\|_1 \le \|\boldsymbol{h}_{\mathsf{I}}\|_1$ for the ℓ^1 minimization in Theorem 3.10 and that gives the RIP constant $\delta_{2k} = 1/(1+\sqrt{2}) = \sqrt{2}-1$.

3.4 Matrices with Restricted Isometry Property

The RIP gives a useful tool for analyzing the performance of sparse recovery with random matrices $\boldsymbol{A}$. Below, we will prove the probabilistic result, Theorem 3.11, which asserts that Gaussian random matrix $\boldsymbol{A}$ has RIP when $m > Ck\log(n/k)$. We will make heavy use of the following simple inequality:

LEMMA 3.18. *Let $\boldsymbol{g} = [g_1, \dots, g_m]^* \in \mathbb{R}^m$ be an m-dimensional random vector whose entries are i.i.d. $\mathcal{N}(0, 1/m)$. Then for any $t \in [0, 1]$,*

$$\mathbb{P}\left[\left|\|\boldsymbol{g}\|_2^2 - 1\right| > t\right] \le 2\exp\left(-\frac{t^2 m}{8}\right). \tag{3.4.1}$$

This result can be obtained via the Cramer–Chernoff exponential moment method (in a similar fashion to the Hoeffding inequality). See Appendix E for more information.

3.4.1 The Johnson–Lindenstrauss Lemma

Before proving Theorem 3.11, we will first state and prove a simpler result, as an illustration of the basic approach we will take to this result, and which is very useful in its own right:

THEOREM 3.19. (Johnson–Lindenstrauss lemma) *Let $\boldsymbol{v}_1, \dots, \boldsymbol{v}_n \in \mathbb{R}^D$ for some D. Let $\boldsymbol{A} \in \mathbb{R}^{m\times D}$ be a random matrix whose entries are independent $\mathcal{N}(0, 1/m)$ random variables. Then for any $\varepsilon \in (0, 1)$, with probability at least $1 - 1/n^2$, the following holds:*

$$\forall i \neq j, \quad (1-\varepsilon)\left\|\boldsymbol{v}_i - \boldsymbol{v}_j\right\|_2^2 \le \left\|\boldsymbol{A}\boldsymbol{v}_i - \boldsymbol{A}\boldsymbol{v}_j\right\|_2^2 \le (1+\varepsilon)\left\|\boldsymbol{v}_i - \boldsymbol{v}_j\right\|_2^2, \tag{3.4.2}$$

provided $m > 32\log(n)/\varepsilon^2$.

This result can be thought of as follows: we have a large database $\boldsymbol{v}_1, \dots, \boldsymbol{v}_n$ of very high-dimensional vectors. We would like to embed them in a lower-dimensional space ($m \ll D$) such that the pairwise distances between these vectors are preserved (see Figure 3.10). This is useful, for example, if we think of these as points in a database,

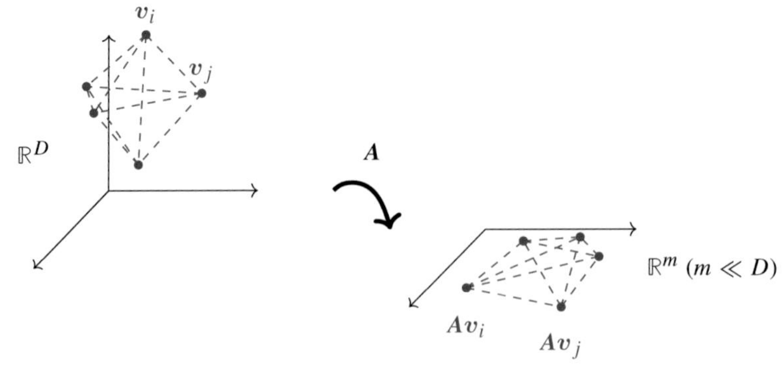

Figure 3.10 The Johnson–Lindenstrauss lemma. Given a fixed collection of points $v_1, \ldots, v_n$ in a high-dimensional space $\mathbb{R}^D$, with high probability a random mapping into $m \sim \log n$ dimensions approximately preserves the distances between all pairs of points.

and we imagine that we would like to be able to query the database to find points that are close to a given input q in norm – a good embedding will reduce both the storage and computation requirements for achieving this. If you think carefully, it should be clear that we can achieve a perfect (norm-preserving) embedding into $m = n$ dimensional space: simply project each point onto the span of the n points v_i.

The surprise in the Johnson–Lindenstrauss lemma is that actually, if we allow some slack ε, the dimension can be much lower – only logarithmic in the number of points, and completely independent of the ambient data dimension D. It should not be too surprising that approaches (loosely) inspired by this result have significant applications in search problems. Interestingly, with some additional clever ideas, it is possible to arrive at algorithms that can find approximate nearest neighbors in a database of points in a search time that depends sublinearly on the size of the dataset.

Proof Set $g_{ij} = A(v_i - v_j)/\|v_i - v_j\|_2$. Notice that for any $v_i \neq v_j$, g_{ij} is distributed as an i.i.d. Gaussian vector, with entries $\mathcal{N}(0, 1/m)$. Applying Lemma 3.18, for each $i \neq j$, we have

$$\mathbb{P}\left[\left|\|g_{ij}\|_2^2 - 1\right| > t\right] \leq 2\exp\left(-t^2 m/8\right). \tag{3.4.3}$$

Summing the probability of failure over all $i \neq j$, and then plugging in $t = \varepsilon$ and $m \geq 32\log(n)/\varepsilon^2$, we get

$$\begin{aligned}\mathbb{P}\left[\exists (i,j) : \left|\|g_{ij}\|_2^2 - 1\right| > t\right] &\leq \frac{n(n-1)}{2} \times 2\exp\left(-t^2 m/8\right) \\ &\leq n^{-2}.\end{aligned} \tag{3.4.4}$$

Whenever $\left|\|g_{ij}\|_2^2 - 1\right| \leq \varepsilon$, we have

$$(1-\varepsilon)\|v_i - v_j\|_2^2 \leq \|Av_i - Av_j\|_2^2 \leq (1+\varepsilon)\|v_i - v_j\|_2^2, \tag{3.4.5}$$

as desired. □

Thus, the fairly powerful embedding result (Theorem 3.19) follows from a fairly straightforward pattern:

- **Discretization**: Argue that if $\boldsymbol{A}$ respects the norms of some finite set of vectors (here $\{\boldsymbol{v}_i - \boldsymbol{v}_j \mid i \neq j\}$), the desired property holds.
- **Tail bound**: Develop an upper bound on the probability that $\boldsymbol{A}$ fails to respect the norm of a single vector (here, this is Lemma 3.18).
- **Union bound**: Sum the failure probabilities over all of the finite set. Choose the embedding dimension m large enough that the total failure probability is small.

EXAMPLE 3.20. (p-Stable distributions [DIIM04]) *From the above theorem, we see that a random Gaussian matrix has the property of preserving ℓ^2 distance between vectors. It turns out that for $p \in (0,2]$, there exist the so-called p-stable distributions such that a random matrix drawn from a p-stable distribution will preserve ℓ^p distance between vectors. For instance, the Cauchy distribution $p(x) = 1/(\pi) \cdot 1/(1+x^2)$ is 1-stable and a random Cauchy matrix preserves ℓ^1 distance. We leave this as an exercise.*

Fast Nearest-Neighbor Methods

The property of distance-preserving (random) projections is the basis for developing most efficient codes and schemes for nearest-neighbor search. The above Johnson–Lindenstrauss lemma works for a set of points of arbitrary configuration in $\mathbb{R}^D$. As it turns out, in many real applications, such as image search [MYW+10, LM16], the data points are reasonably spread in space or have certain additional properties. Under such circumstances, approximate nearest-neighbor search can be made even more memory- and computation-efficient – instead of $O(\log n)$ real numbers, one only needs $O(\log n)$ binary bits! We introduce one such property below as an example since it is related to the property of incoherence studied before.

DEFINITION 3.21. (Weak separability) *We say a set of points $\mathcal{X} = \{\boldsymbol{x}_1, \dots, \boldsymbol{x}_n\}$ in $\mathbb{R}^D$ is (Δ, l)-weakly separable if for any query point $\boldsymbol{q} \in \mathbb{R}^D$, we have*

$$|\{i \mid \angle(\boldsymbol{q}, \boldsymbol{x}_i) \leq \Delta\}| = O(n^l), \tag{3.4.6}$$

where typically $l \in [0,1)$ is desired to be a small constant.

Although the above definition is defined in terms of arbitrary $\boldsymbol{q} \in \mathbb{R}^D$, the following lemma shows that it is sufficient to check this condition within the dataset $\mathcal{X}$ itself.

LEMMA 3.22. *If for every $\boldsymbol{x}_j \in \mathcal{X}$,*

$$|\{i \mid \angle(\boldsymbol{x}_j, \boldsymbol{x}_i) \leq 2\Delta\}| = O(n^l), \tag{3.4.7}$$

then $\mathcal{X}$ is (Δ, l)-weakly separable.

Proof We leave the proof as an exercise to the reader (see Exercise 3.14). □

Notice that weak separability of the $\boldsymbol{x}_i$ is similar to assuming that these data points (viewed as vectors) are weakly incoherent – the majority of the angles between pairwise points are large.

Algorithm 3.1 Compact code for fast nearest neighbor

Problem: Generate compact binary code for efficient nearest-neighbor search of high-dimensional data points.
Input: $\boldsymbol{x}_1, \dots, \boldsymbol{x}_n \in \mathbb{R}^D$ and $m = O(\log n)$.
Generate a random Gaussian matrix $\boldsymbol{R} \in \mathbb{R}^{m \times D}$ with entries i.i.d. $\mathcal{N}(0,1)$.
for $i = 1, \dots, n$ **do**
  Compute $\boldsymbol{R}\boldsymbol{x}_i$,
  Set $\boldsymbol{y}_i = \sigma(\boldsymbol{R}\boldsymbol{x}_i)$ where $\sigma(\cdot)$ is the entry-wise binary thresholding.
end for
Output: $\boldsymbol{y}_1, \dots, \boldsymbol{y}_n \in \{0,1\}^m$.

EXAMPLE 3.23. (Efficient c-approximate nearest neighbor [MYW+10]) *Given a set of data points $\mathcal{X} = \{\boldsymbol{x}_1, \dots, \boldsymbol{x}_n\}$ in $\mathbb{R}^D$ and a constant $c > 1$, the c-approximate nearest-neighbor (c-NN) problem is: for any query point $\boldsymbol{q} \in \mathbb{R}^D$, find $\boldsymbol{x}_\star$ such that*

$$\|\boldsymbol{q} - \boldsymbol{x}_\star\|_2 \le c \cdot \min_{\boldsymbol{x} \in \mathcal{X}} \|\boldsymbol{q} - \boldsymbol{x}\|_2.$$

As it turns out, for any (Δ, l)-weakly separable set $\mathcal{X}$, with the random binary code generated by Algorithm 3.1, with probability $1 - \delta$, the c-NN problem can be solved with the number of binary bits m chosen in the order

$$m = O(\log n) \quad (bits).$$

For any query point $\boldsymbol{q}$, we may first compute its binary code with the same projection as in Algorithm 3.1, i.e., $\boldsymbol{y}_{\boldsymbol{q}} = \sigma(\boldsymbol{R}\boldsymbol{q})$ where $\sigma(\cdot)$ is the binary thresholding function: $\sigma(x) = 1$ for $x > 0$ and $\sigma(x) = 0$ otherwise. Then we find a subset $\tilde{\mathcal{X}}_{\boldsymbol{q}}$ of points of size $O(n^l)$ which have the shortest Hamming distances to $\boldsymbol{y}_{\boldsymbol{q}}$ in $\mathcal{X}$. One can show that

$$\boldsymbol{x}_\star = \arg\min_{\boldsymbol{x} \in \tilde{\mathcal{X}}_{\boldsymbol{q}}} \|\boldsymbol{q} - \boldsymbol{x}\|_2$$

gives the correct solution to the c-NN problem. We leave the proof for the correctness and efficiency of this simple scheme as an exercise for the reader; see Exercise 3.15.

3.4.2 RIP of Gaussian Random Matrices

To prove Theorem 3.11, we follow exactly the same pattern as we did for Johnson–Lindenstrauss. However, we will need to work a little bit harder in the discretization stage, since unlike the Johnson–Lindenstrauss lemma, which was a statement about n (or $n(n-1)/2$) vectors, the RIP is a statement about an infinite family of vectors – all of the sparse vectors.

Discretization
Let

$$\Sigma_k = \{\boldsymbol{x} \mid \|\boldsymbol{x}\|_0 \le k, \ \|\boldsymbol{x}\|_2 = 1\}. \tag{3.4.8}$$

Notice that $\delta_k(\boldsymbol{A}) \le \delta$ if and only if

$$\sup_{\boldsymbol{x}\in\Sigma_k} \left| \|\boldsymbol{A}\boldsymbol{x}\|_2^2 - 1 \right| \le \delta. \tag{3.4.9}$$

This is equivalent to

$$\sup_{\boldsymbol{x}\in\Sigma_k} \left| \langle \boldsymbol{A}^*\boldsymbol{A}\boldsymbol{x}, \boldsymbol{x} \rangle - 1 \right| \le \delta. \tag{3.4.10}$$

LEMMA 3.24. (Discretization) *Suppose we have a set* $\bar{\mathsf{N}} \subseteq \Sigma_k$ *with the following property: for all* $\boldsymbol{x} \in \Sigma_k$, *there exists* $\bar{\boldsymbol{x}} \in \bar{\mathsf{N}}$ *such that*

- $|\text{supp}(\bar{\boldsymbol{x}}) \cup \text{supp}(\boldsymbol{x})| \le k$,
- $\|\boldsymbol{x} - \bar{\boldsymbol{x}}\|_2 \le \varepsilon$.

Set

$$\delta_{\bar{\mathsf{N}}} = \max_{\bar{\boldsymbol{x}}\in\bar{\mathsf{N}}} \left| \|\boldsymbol{A}\bar{\boldsymbol{x}}\|_2^2 - 1 \right|. \tag{3.4.11}$$

Then

$$\delta_k(\boldsymbol{A}) \le \frac{\delta_{\bar{\mathsf{N}}} + 2\varepsilon}{1 - 2\varepsilon}. \tag{3.4.12}$$

So, provided ε is small, not much changes if we restrict our attention to the finite set $\bar{\mathsf{N}}$ (see Figure 3.11). The proof of this result uses the fact that if $\boldsymbol{x}$ and $\boldsymbol{z}$ are k-sparse vectors,

$$\langle \boldsymbol{A}\boldsymbol{x}, \boldsymbol{A}\boldsymbol{z} \rangle \le \sqrt{\|\boldsymbol{A}\boldsymbol{x}\|_2^2 \, \|\boldsymbol{A}\boldsymbol{z}\|_2^2} \le (1 + \delta_k(\boldsymbol{A})) \, \|\boldsymbol{x}\|_2 \, \|\boldsymbol{z}\|_2 . \tag{3.4.13}$$

Proof Take any $\boldsymbol{x} \in \Sigma_k$ and choose $\bar{\boldsymbol{x}} \in \bar{\mathsf{N}}$ such that $\|\boldsymbol{x} - \bar{\boldsymbol{x}}\|_0 \le k$ and $\|\boldsymbol{x} - \bar{\boldsymbol{x}}\|_2 \le \varepsilon$. We have

$$\left| \|\boldsymbol{A}\boldsymbol{x}\|_2^2 - 1 \right| = |\langle \boldsymbol{A}\boldsymbol{x}, \boldsymbol{A}\boldsymbol{x} \rangle - 1| \tag{3.4.14}$$

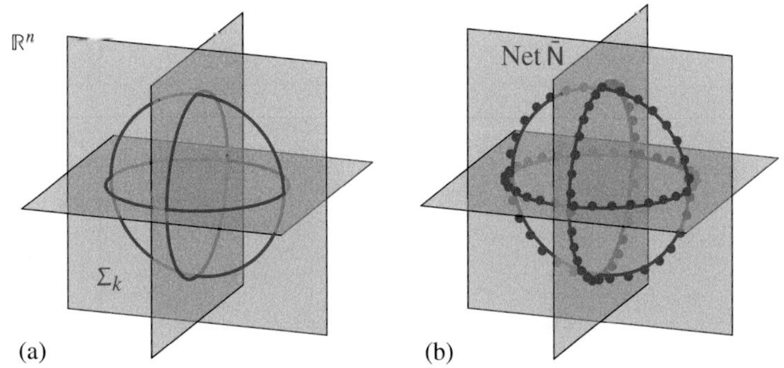

(a) (b)

Figure 3.11 The set Σ_k of unit norm sparse vectors. (a) Visualization of the set $\Sigma_k = \{\boldsymbol{x} \mid \|\boldsymbol{x}\|_0 \le k, \ \|\boldsymbol{x}\|_2 = 1\}$ of unit-norm sparse vectors. Here, $k = 2$ and $n = 3$. (b) An ε-net $\bar{\mathsf{N}}$ for this set.

$$= |\langle \boldsymbol{A}\boldsymbol{x}, \boldsymbol{A}\boldsymbol{x}\rangle - \langle \boldsymbol{A}\bar{\boldsymbol{x}}, \boldsymbol{A}\bar{\boldsymbol{x}}\rangle + \langle \boldsymbol{A}\bar{\boldsymbol{x}}, \boldsymbol{A}\bar{\boldsymbol{x}}\rangle - 1| \tag{3.4.15}$$

$$\leq |\langle \boldsymbol{A}\boldsymbol{x}, \boldsymbol{A}\boldsymbol{x}\rangle - \langle \boldsymbol{A}\bar{\boldsymbol{x}}, \boldsymbol{A}\bar{\boldsymbol{x}}\rangle| + \delta_{\bar{\mathsf{N}}} \tag{3.4.16}$$

$$= |\langle \boldsymbol{A}\boldsymbol{x}, \boldsymbol{A}(\boldsymbol{x} - \bar{\boldsymbol{x}})\rangle - \langle \boldsymbol{A}\bar{\boldsymbol{x}}, \boldsymbol{A}(\bar{\boldsymbol{x}} - \boldsymbol{x})\rangle| + \delta_{\bar{\mathsf{N}}} \tag{3.4.17}$$

$$\leq 2\,(1 + \delta_k(\boldsymbol{A}))\,\varepsilon + \delta_{\bar{\mathsf{N}}}. \tag{3.4.18}$$

Since this inequality holds for all $\boldsymbol{x} \in \Sigma_k$, we obtain that

$$\delta_k(\boldsymbol{A}) \leq 2\,(1 + \delta_k(\boldsymbol{A}))\,\varepsilon + \delta_{\bar{\mathsf{N}}}, \tag{3.4.19}$$

from which the target inequality follows. □

The next task is to construct a set $\bar{\mathsf{N}}$ which has the desired good properties. We call a set N *an ε-net* for a given set S if

$$\forall \boldsymbol{x} \in \mathsf{S}, \quad \exists \bar{\boldsymbol{x}} \in \mathsf{N} \quad \text{such that} \quad \|\boldsymbol{x} - \bar{\boldsymbol{x}}\|_2 \leq \varepsilon. \tag{3.4.20}$$

Let

$$\mathsf{B}(\boldsymbol{x}, r) = \left\{ \boldsymbol{z} \in \mathbb{R}^d \mid \|\boldsymbol{z} - \boldsymbol{x}\|_2 \leq r \right\} \tag{3.4.21}$$

denote the ℓ^2 ball of center $\boldsymbol{x}$ and radius r, in $\mathbb{R}^d$. The following clever argument shows that there exists an ε-net for the ℓ^2 ball $\mathsf{B}(\mathbf{0}, 1)$ of size at most $(3/\varepsilon)^d$. It uses the fact that if $\mathsf{S} \subset \mathbb{R}^d$ is a set, and

$$\alpha\mathsf{S} = \left\{ \alpha \boldsymbol{s} \mid \boldsymbol{s} \in \mathsf{S} \right\} \tag{3.4.22}$$

denotes its α dilation, then

$$\text{vol}(\alpha\mathsf{S}) \leq \alpha^d \text{vol}(\mathsf{S}). \tag{3.4.23}$$

See Figure 3.12 for a visualization of this.

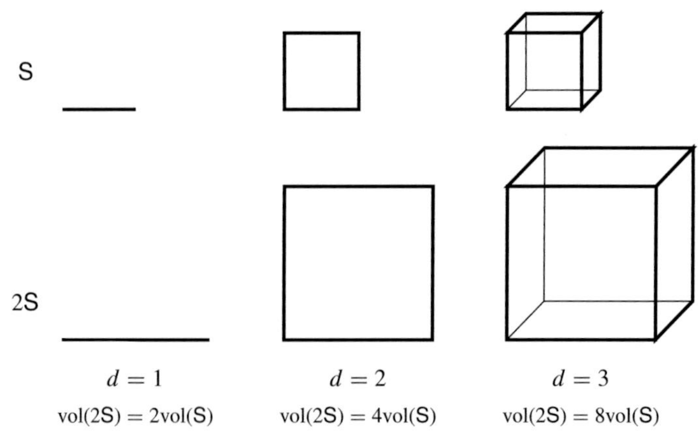

Figure 3.12 Volumes scale as α^d.

LEMMA 3.25. (ε-Nets for the unit ball) *There exists an ε-net for the unit ball* $\mathsf{B}(0,1) \subset \mathbb{R}^d$ *of size at most* $(3/\varepsilon)^d$.

Proof Call a set M ε-separated if every pair of distinct points in M has distance at least ε. Let $\mathsf{N} \subset \mathsf{B}(\mathbf{0},1)$ be a *maximal* ε-separated set. Here, maximal means that it is not contained in any larger ε-separated set.

We claim that N is an ε-net for $\mathsf{B}(\mathbf{0},1)$. Indeed, if it is not an ε-net, then there exists some point $\boldsymbol{x} \in \mathsf{B}(\mathbf{0},1)$ with distance greater than ε to each element of N. Adding $\boldsymbol{x}$ to N, we obtain a larger ε-separated set, contradicting maximality of N.

Since N is ε-separated, the balls $\mathsf{B}(\boldsymbol{x},\varepsilon/2)$ and $\mathsf{B}(\boldsymbol{x}',\varepsilon/2)$ are disjoint, for any pair of distinct elements $\boldsymbol{x} \neq \boldsymbol{x}' \in \mathsf{N}$. Moreover, the union of these balls is contained in $\mathsf{B}(\mathbf{0},1+\varepsilon/2)$. Thus,

$$|\mathsf{N}| \operatorname{vol}(\mathsf{B}(\mathbf{0},\varepsilon/2)) \le \operatorname{vol}(\mathsf{B}(\mathbf{0},1+\varepsilon/2)). \tag{3.4.24}$$

Hence,

$$\begin{aligned} |\mathsf{N}| &\le \frac{\operatorname{vol}(\mathsf{B}(\mathbf{0},1+\varepsilon/2))}{\operatorname{vol}(\mathsf{B}(\mathbf{0},\varepsilon/2))} && (3.4.25)\\ &= \left(\frac{1+\varepsilon/2}{\varepsilon/2}\right)^d = (1+2/\varepsilon)^d && (3.4.26)\\ &\le (3/\varepsilon)^d && (3.4.27) \end{aligned}$$

as desired. Figure 3.13 visualizes the geometry of this argument. □

To construct our target set $\bar{\mathsf{N}}$, we simply consider each support pattern I of size $|\mathsf{I}| = k$ individually. There are $\binom{n}{k}$ such patterns. For each pattern, we use the previous lemma to build an ε-net N for the unit ball of vectors of ℓ^2 norm at most one, whose support is contained in I. Each of these nets has size at most $(3/\varepsilon)^k$. So, finally, we obtain:

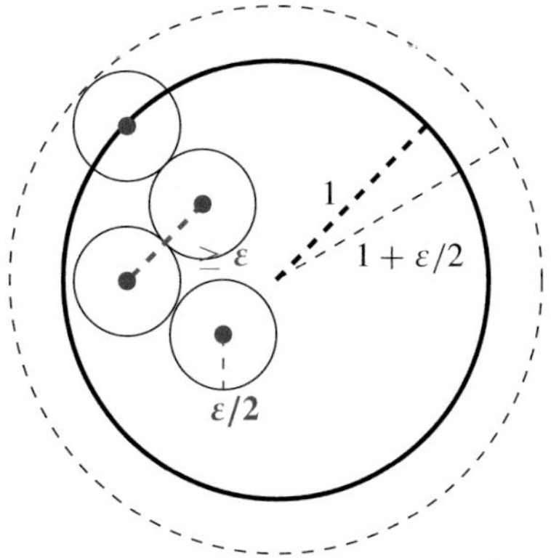

Figure 3.13 Volume calculation for an ε net. An ε-separated set. The interiors of $\varepsilon/2$ balls around the points do not intersect. The union of the $\varepsilon/2$ balls is contained in a $(1+\varepsilon/2)$ ball.

LEMMA 3.26. *There exists an ε-net $\bar{\mathsf{N}}$ for Σ_k satisfying the two properties required in Lemma 3.24, with*

$$\left|\bar{\mathsf{N}}\right| \le \exp\Big(k\log(3/\varepsilon) + k\log(n/k) + k\Big). \tag{3.4.28}$$

Proof The construction follows the above discussion. Using Stirling's formula,[7] we can estimate

$$\left|\bar{\mathsf{N}}\right| \le (3/\varepsilon)^k \binom{n}{k} \tag{3.4.29}$$

$$\le (3/\varepsilon)^k \left(\frac{ne}{k}\right)^k \tag{3.4.30}$$

as desired. □

Union Bound

Proof of theorem 3.11 For each $\boldsymbol{x} \in \bar{\mathsf{N}}$, $\boldsymbol{A}\boldsymbol{x}$ is a random vector with entries independent $\mathcal{N}(0, 1/m)$. We have

$$\mathbb{P}\left[\left|\|\boldsymbol{A}\boldsymbol{x}\|_2^2 - 1\right| > t\right] \le 2\exp(-mt^2/8). \tag{3.4.31}$$

Hence, summing over all elements of $\bar{\mathsf{N}}$, we have

$$\mathbb{P}\left[\delta_{\bar{\mathsf{N}}} > t\right] \le 2\left|\bar{\mathsf{N}}\right| \exp\left(-mt^2/8\right) \tag{3.4.32}$$

$$\le 2\exp\left(-\frac{mt^2}{8} + k\log\left(\frac{n}{k}\right) + k(\log\left(\frac{3}{\varepsilon}\right) + k)\right). \tag{3.4.33}$$

On the complement of the event $\delta_{\bar{\mathsf{N}}} > t$, we have

$$\delta_k(\boldsymbol{A}) < \frac{2\varepsilon + t}{1 - 2\varepsilon}. \tag{3.4.34}$$

Setting $\varepsilon = \delta/8$, $t = \delta/4$, and ensuring that $m \ge Ck\log(n/k)/\delta^2$ for a sufficiently large numerical constant C, large numerical constant C, we obtain the result. □

In the above derivation, especially from equation (3.4.33), we see that a slightly more tight bound for m is of the form

$$m \ge 128k\log(n/k)/\delta^2 + (\log(24/\delta) + 1)k/\delta^2 \doteq C_1 k\log(n/k) + C_2 k.$$

However, for a small δ, the constants C_1 and C_2 can be rather large. Although qualitatively this bound is in the right form, it does not reflect exactly when ℓ^1 minimization works. In the work of [RV08], a much tighter bound for m is given as

$$m \ge 8k\log(n/k) + 12k.$$

This is one of the best known bounds given through the RIP properties of Gaussian matrices. Nevertheless, as we will see later, using more advanced tools, ultimately we will be able to derive for Gaussian matrices a precise condition that characterizes the

[7] Stirling's formula gives the bounds for factorials: $\sqrt{2\pi k}\big(k/e\big)^k \le k! \le e\sqrt{k}\big(k/e\big)^k$.

"phase transition" behavior for the success of ℓ^1 minimization that we can observe through simulations.

3.4.3 RIP of Non-Gaussian Matrices

In many applications of interest, the matrix $\boldsymbol{A}$ cannot be assumed to be i.i.d Gaussian. Perhaps surprisingly, often the theory developed for the Gaussian model is predictive of the behavior of ℓ^1 minimization in other models. However, it is still desirable to have a precise understanding (and corresponding mathematical guarantees) to describe what happens when the model is not so homogeneous.

Random Submatrices of a Unitary Matrix

One model that occurs quite often posits that we generate $\boldsymbol{A}$ by randomly sampling some rows of an orthogonal matrix (in the real case) or a unitary matrix (in the complex case). Actually, we have already seen such a model in our brief discussion of MRI applications. There, we generated $\boldsymbol{A}$ as a row submatrix of $\boldsymbol{F\Psi}$, where $\boldsymbol{F}$ was the DFT matrix, and $\boldsymbol{\Psi} \in \mathbb{C}^{n\times n}$ was a matrix whose columns formed an orthonormal wavelet basis for $\mathbb{C}^{n\times n}$. Since both $\boldsymbol{F}$ and $\boldsymbol{\Psi}$ were unitary, their product is unitary. In the work [CRT06a], it has been shown that for a given k-sparse vector $\boldsymbol{x} \in \mathbb{R}^n$, if $\boldsymbol{A}$ randomly takes $m = O\big(k\log(n)\big)$ rows of a unitary matrix, then with high probability the ℓ^1 minimization $\min \|\boldsymbol{x}\|_1$ such that $\boldsymbol{y} = \boldsymbol{Ax}$ recovers the sparse vector. However, this result does not imply that with the same $\boldsymbol{A}$, the ℓ^1 minimization succeeds for all k-sparse vectors.[8]

The following theorem, according to [RV08], shows that if we sample a random row submatrix from a unitary matrix, it also has RIP with high probability, provided enough rows are chosen. We know that for a matrix satisfying the RIP condition, it is guaranteed that the associated ℓ^1 minimization succeeds for all k-sparse vectors.

THEOREM 3.27. *Let $\boldsymbol{U} \in \mathbb{C}^{n\times n}$ be unitary ($\boldsymbol{U}^*\boldsymbol{U} = \boldsymbol{I}$) and Ω be a random subset of m elements from $\{1,\dots,n\}$. Suppose that*

$$\|\boldsymbol{U}\|_\infty \le \zeta/\sqrt{n}. \tag{3.4.35}$$

If

$$m \ge \frac{C\zeta^2}{\delta^2} k \log^4(n), \tag{3.4.36}$$

then with high probability, $\boldsymbol{A} = \sqrt{n/m}\,\boldsymbol{U}_{\Omega,\bullet}$ satisfies the RIP of order k, with constant $\delta_k(\boldsymbol{A}) \le \delta$.

[8] To see the difference, one can recall in the Johnson–Lindenstrauss lemma, the task is not just to show that given any pair of points, with high probability there exists a projection that approximately preserves the distance. We need to use the union bound to show that with high probability there exists a projection that approximately preserves the distance between all pairs simultaneously.

For simplicity, here we do not give a proof of this theorem and interested readers may refer to the work of [RV08].

In our context, there are two very salient points about this result. The first is the dependence on $\|\boldsymbol{U}\|_\infty$. It is worth noting that for any unitary matrix $\boldsymbol{U}$, $\|\boldsymbol{U}\|_\infty \geq 1/\sqrt{n}$. So, the parameter ζ measures how much we lose with respect to this optimal bound. The bound is clearly achievable in some cases – the DFT matrix $\boldsymbol{F}$ has $\|\boldsymbol{F}\|_\infty = 1/\sqrt{n}$, which follows directly from its definition (A.7.13) in Appendix A. If we are willing to interpret the result a bit, the idea that $\boldsymbol{U}$ should have uniformly bounded elements leads to a very nice intuition about sampling. Namely, if we wish to reconstruct an element that is sparse in some basis $\boldsymbol{\Psi}$, and we can take whatever linear samples $\langle \boldsymbol{f}_i, \boldsymbol{y} \rangle$ we want, we should take samples that are as *incoherent* with the basis of sparsity as possible, in the sense that

$$\left\langle \boldsymbol{f}_i, \boldsymbol{\psi}_j \right\rangle \tag{3.4.37}$$

is uniformly small. This is in contrast to our usual intuition from signal processing, which might suggest that some sort of matched filter would be the best here. The challenge is that there are actually an exponentially large number of potential support patterns for $\boldsymbol{x}$, and hence an exponentially large number of signals to match. If, instead, we let each (incoherent) measurement collect information across all of the basis elements, we can then, using efficient computation, decide which elements of $\boldsymbol{\Psi}$ are active.

The second salient point is that the number of measurements, $k \log^4(n)$, is visually similar to the $k \log(n/k)$ that we saw for the Gaussian ensemble. It is currently conjectured that here $k \log n$ measurements suffice. It is currently an open problem to show this; it is considered hard, and known to connect to a number of interesting questions in probability and functional analysis. In fact, in [RV08] a more precise expression is given as: $m = O\big(k \log(n) \log^2(k) \log(k \log n)\big)$. This bound, against the conjectured optimal bound, is within a $\log\log(n)$ factor for n and within a $\log^3(k)$ factor for k.

Random Convolutions

Another model that occurs quite frequently in engineering practice involves sampling the convolution of the input signal $\boldsymbol{x}$ with some filter $\boldsymbol{r}$. Formally, we can imagine that

$$\boldsymbol{y} = \mathcal{P}_\Omega[\boldsymbol{r} * \boldsymbol{x}] = \boldsymbol{A}\boldsymbol{x}, \tag{3.4.38}$$

where $\boldsymbol{x} \in \mathbb{C}^n$, $\boldsymbol{r} \in \mathbb{C}^n$, and $\Omega \subseteq [n]$ is our collection of sampling locations. Here, $*$ denotes circular convolution:

$$(\boldsymbol{r} * \boldsymbol{x})_i = \sum_{j=0}^{n-1} x_j r_{i+n-j \bmod n}. \tag{3.4.39}$$

This leads to a highly structured linear operator on $\boldsymbol{x}$ since we can represent the convolution in a circulant form as

$$\boldsymbol{r} * \boldsymbol{x} = \begin{bmatrix} r_0 & r_{n-1} & \cdots & r_2 & r_1 \\ r_1 & r_0 & r_{n-1} & & r_2 \\ \vdots & r_1 & r_0 & \ddots & \vdots \\ r_{n-2} & & \ddots & \ddots & r_{n-1} \\ r_{n-1} & r_{n-2} & \cdots & r_1 & r_0 \end{bmatrix} \boldsymbol{x} \doteq \boldsymbol{R}\boldsymbol{x}. \tag{3.4.40}$$

Such a matrix $\boldsymbol{R}$ is called a *circulant matrix*. One may see Appendix A for more nice properties of this type of matrix. In particular, any circulant matrix can be diagonalized by the discrete Fourier transform: $\boldsymbol{R} = \boldsymbol{F}\boldsymbol{D}\boldsymbol{F}^*$ for some diagonal matrix $\boldsymbol{D}$ (see Theorem A.32 of Appendix A). Here, we can view the sampling matrix $\boldsymbol{A}$ as taking a subset of rows of the circulant matrix $\boldsymbol{R}$, that is $\boldsymbol{A} = \boldsymbol{R}_{\Omega,\bullet}$.

The filter $\boldsymbol{r}$ can be rather general as well. For instance, it could be as simple as a random Rademacher vector, i.e., a random vector with independent entries distributed according to $\mathbb{P}(r_i = \pm 1) = 0.5$, or it could be a random vector with independent zero-mean, sub-Gaussian random variables of variance one. The exact randomness of $\boldsymbol{r}$ is not critical.

For this model, the work of [KMR14] has shown that essentially the following statement is true:

THEOREM 3.28. *Let $\Omega \subseteq \{1, \ldots, n\}$ be any fixed subset of size $|\Omega| = m$. Then if*

$$m \geq \frac{Ck \log^2(k) \log^2(n)}{\delta^2}, \tag{3.4.41}$$

then with high probability, $\boldsymbol{A}$ has RIP of order k with $\delta_k(\boldsymbol{A}) \leq \delta$.

Notice that the above statement is rather strong in the following sense: firstly, it states that even for a highly structured sampling matrix (a circulant matrix versus a random Gaussian matrix studied in the previous section), we only lose a small factor of $\log^2(k)\log(n)$ in the required number of samples. Secondly, it claims that any subset of rows of $\boldsymbol{R}$ has the RIP property, not just a random subset with high probability. Third, the RIP property ensures recoverability of any k-sparse vectors $\boldsymbol{x}$ uniformly not just for a fixed k-sparse vector. It has been shown in [Rau09] that, if one relaxes the uniform recoverability requirement, considering only a fixed k-sparse vector, it can be recovered via ℓ^1 minimization from a partial random circulant matrix with $m \geq Ck\log^2(n)$ measurements. This bound is slightly better than the one given in the theorem, but it is not uniform for all k-sparse vectors.

3.5 Noisy Observations or Approximate Sparsity

Thus far, we have been very idealistic in our model. We have assumed that the target $\boldsymbol{x}_o$ is perfectly sparse, and that there is no noise in the measurements, so $\boldsymbol{y} = \boldsymbol{A}\boldsymbol{x}_o$ exactly.

These assumptions are clearly violated in many practical applications. In practice, the observation $\boldsymbol{y}$ is usually perturbed by some amount of noise $\boldsymbol{z}$, which we assume to be small:

$$\boldsymbol{y} = \boldsymbol{A}\boldsymbol{x}_o + \boldsymbol{z}, \qquad \|\boldsymbol{z}\|_2 \leq \varepsilon. \tag{3.5.1}$$

In other practical scenarios, the ground-truth signal $\boldsymbol{x}_o$ may not be perfectly sparse and may be only approximately so.

This motivates two natural questions. First, on the practical side, is it possible to modify our approaches to be stable under noise or for imperfect sparse signals? Second, what should we expect of their performance? Do the conditions and guarantees we introduced in previous sections remain meaningful?

To clearly state our assumptions and goals, we can consider the following three scenarios (or some combination of them):

- **Deterministic (worst-case) noise**: $\boldsymbol{z}$ is bounded: $\|\boldsymbol{z}\|_2 \leq \varepsilon$, and ε is known.
- **Stochastic noise**: entries of $\boldsymbol{z} \sim_{\text{iid}} \mathcal{N}(0, \sigma^2/m)$. Notice that under this random model, a typical noise vector $\boldsymbol{z}$ is of norm $\|\boldsymbol{z}\|_2 \approx \sigma$.[9] Gaussian noise is a very natural assumption; the results obtained here also extend to other noise models.
- **Inexact sparsity**: $\boldsymbol{x}_o$ is not perfectly sparse. Technically speaking, this is not noise, but rather a violation of our sparse modeling assumption. In this scenario, it may be meaningful to assume that $\boldsymbol{x}_o$ is *close* to a k-sparse vector. We can formalize this by letting $[\boldsymbol{x}_o]_k$ denote a best k-term approximation to $\boldsymbol{x}_o$:

$$[\boldsymbol{x}_o]_k \in \arg\min_{\|\boldsymbol{z}\|_0 \leq k} \|\boldsymbol{x}_o - \boldsymbol{z}\|_2^2. \tag{3.5.2}$$

  This just keeps the k largest elements of $\boldsymbol{x}_o$. Then $\boldsymbol{x}_o$ is said to be "approximately sparse" if $\|\boldsymbol{x}_o - [\boldsymbol{x}_o]_k\|$ is small.

In all of these scenarios, we might hope to still "recover" a sparse estimate $\hat{\boldsymbol{x}}$ of $\boldsymbol{x}_o$ in some sense. There are (perhaps) three natural senses to consider.

- **Estimation**: Is $\left\|\hat{\boldsymbol{x}} - \boldsymbol{x}_o\right\|_2$ small?
- **Prediction**: Is $\boldsymbol{A}\hat{\boldsymbol{x}} \approx \boldsymbol{A}\boldsymbol{x}_o$?
- **Support recovery**: Is $\operatorname{supp}(\hat{\boldsymbol{x}}) = \operatorname{supp}(\boldsymbol{x}_o)$?

For engineering practice, we often care about either estimating the signal $\boldsymbol{x}_o$ (for sensing problems) or recovering its support $\operatorname{supp}(\boldsymbol{x}_o)$ (for recognition problems). Nevertheless, statisticians sometimes also care about the prediction error $\boldsymbol{A}(\hat{\boldsymbol{x}} - \boldsymbol{x}_o)$.

In the following subsections, we discuss results on stable estimation under (i) deterministic noise, (ii) stochastic noise, and (iii) deterministic noise *and* inexact sparsity. Results on support recovery are discussed briefly in Section 3.6 and in the Notes section of this chapter.

[9] We scale the variance of the normal distribution by $1/m$ on purpose, so that σ is directly comparable to ε in the deterministic noise case.

3.5.1 Stable Recovery of Sparse Signals

In the ideal sensing model, the observation equation $\boldsymbol{y} = \boldsymbol{A}\boldsymbol{x}_o$ holds exactly for a sparse signal $\boldsymbol{x}_o$. In this subsection, we consider a more practical situation in which the observation $\boldsymbol{y}$ is perturbed by some amount of noise. For simplicity, we still assume the signal $\boldsymbol{x}_o$ is perfectly sparse. We can model the noise as an additive error $\boldsymbol{z}$, which we will assume to have a small magnitude:[10]

$$\boldsymbol{y} = \boldsymbol{A}\boldsymbol{x}_o + \boldsymbol{z}, \qquad \|\boldsymbol{z}\|_2 \leq \varepsilon. \tag{3.5.3}$$

To recover a sparse solution from the above observation, we may extend ℓ^1 minimization to this new setting and solve

$$\begin{array}{ll} \min & \|\boldsymbol{x}\|_1 \\ \text{subject to} & \|\boldsymbol{y} - \boldsymbol{A}\boldsymbol{x}\|_2 \leq \varepsilon. \end{array} \tag{3.5.4}$$

In words, this program asks us to (try to) find the sparsest $\boldsymbol{x}$ that agrees with the observation up to the noise level. Almost equally popular is the Lagrangian relaxation of this problem, which introduces a penalty parameter $\lambda \geq 0$, and solves the unconstrained optimization problem[11]

$$\min \ \lambda \|\boldsymbol{x}\|_1 + \tfrac{1}{2} \|\boldsymbol{y} - \boldsymbol{A}\boldsymbol{x}\|_2^2. \tag{3.5.5}$$

The optimization (3.5.4) is almost uniformly referred to as "basis pursuit denoising" (BPDN) [CDS01], while the problem (3.5.5) is almost uniformly referred to as the "Lasso (least absolute shrinkage and selection operator)" [Tib96]. These two problems are completely equivalent, in the sense that there is a calibration $\lambda \leftrightarrow \varepsilon$ such that if $\boldsymbol{x}$ is a solution to the Lasso problem for some choice of λ, then there exists an ε such that $\boldsymbol{x}$ is also a solution to the BPDN problem with parameter ε, and conversely, whenever $\boldsymbol{x}$ is a solution to BPDN with parameter ε, there exists a corresponding λ such that $\boldsymbol{x}$ also solves the Lasso problem with parameter λ. So, from a theoretical perspective, these two problems are completely equivalent.

On the other hand, from a practical perspective, they may be quite different, since the calibration $\lambda \leftrightarrow \varepsilon$ depends on the problem data $(\boldsymbol{y}, \boldsymbol{A})$, and no explicit form is known. In some situations, it may be easier to tune λ than ε, or vice versa. In particular, in situations in which the norm of the noise is known or can be estimated, the BPDN formulation may be more attractive, since its parameter can be set to be the noise level.[12] The optimal choice of the regularization parameter λ (or ε) is a surprisingly tricky issue in practice. In general, we have to either use generic statistical

[10] This is similar to the setting in conventional signal processing problems where we typically assume the signal-to-noise ratio (SNR) is large.

[11] One may compare this with the ridge regression that regularizes the ℓ^2 norm of $\boldsymbol{x}$, which we have introduced in Exercise 1.8 of Chapter 1.

[12] Historically, the Lasso is preferred by statisticians, and BPDN by engineers, although, confusingly, in the original papers the names Lasso and BPDN are used to refer not to these problems, but to rather different equivalent problems!

rules such as cross-validation, or resort to theoretical analysis to get some insight into what scalings make sense.

Despite their conceptual equivalence, these problems may require rather different optimization techniques. In Chapter 8, we will discuss in more detail about how to solve both (and many related problems!).

Deterministic Noise

To account for measurement noise, we can simply solve one of (3.5.4) or (3.5.5). Both are convex problems. Any global minimizer gives an estimate $\hat{\boldsymbol{x}}$. Unlike the previous two sections, under noise we cannot expect $\hat{\boldsymbol{x}} = \boldsymbol{x}_o$ exactly. However, we *can* hope that if the noise level ε is small, the estimation error $\left\|\hat{\boldsymbol{x}} - \boldsymbol{x}_o\right\|_2$ will also be small.

How well do we expect to do? Imagine that we somehow knew the support I of $\boldsymbol{x}_o$. In this situation, we could form another estimate $\hat{\boldsymbol{x}}'$, by setting

$$\begin{cases} \hat{\boldsymbol{x}}'(\mathsf{I}) = (\boldsymbol{A}_{\mathsf{I}}^* \boldsymbol{A}_{\mathsf{I}})^{-1} \boldsymbol{A}_{\mathsf{I}}^* \boldsymbol{y}, \\ \hat{\boldsymbol{x}}'(\mathsf{I}^c) = \mathbf{0}. \end{cases} \tag{3.5.6}$$

This is just the least-squares estimate, restricted to the set I. It is not difficult to argue that it is optimal, in the sense that it minimizes over all estimators the worst error $\left\|\hat{\boldsymbol{x}} - \boldsymbol{x}_o\right\|_2$ over all $\boldsymbol{x}_o$ supported on I and $\boldsymbol{z}$ of norm at most ε. This "oracle" estimator produces an estimate $\hat{\boldsymbol{x}}'$ that satisfies

$$\left\|\hat{\boldsymbol{x}}' - \boldsymbol{x}_o\right\|_2 \le \frac{\varepsilon}{\sigma_{\min}(\boldsymbol{A}_{\mathsf{I}})}, \tag{3.5.7}$$

and this bound can be tight.

So, the best we can possibly hope for in general is

$$\left\|\hat{\boldsymbol{x}} - \boldsymbol{x}_o\right\|_2 \sim c\varepsilon,$$

with $c = \sigma_{\min}(\boldsymbol{A}_{\mathsf{I}})^{-1}$. As above, if we restrict ourselves to efficient algorithms, this is too much to hope for in general. However, can we still hope that under the same hypotheses as above,

$$\left\|\hat{\boldsymbol{x}} - \boldsymbol{x}_o\right\|_2 \le C\varepsilon? \tag{3.5.8}$$

That is to say, the solution is at least *stable*: the error in estimating $\boldsymbol{x}$ is proportional to the size ε of the perturbation, even though the constant might not be as small as when we know the oracle of the correct support of $\boldsymbol{x}_o$.

The theorem below, which is similar to that in [CRT06b],[13] makes this precise:

THEOREM 3.29. (Stable sparse recovery via BPDN) *Suppose that* $\boldsymbol{y} = \boldsymbol{A}\boldsymbol{x}_o + \boldsymbol{z}$, *with* $\|\boldsymbol{z}\|_2 \le \varepsilon$, *and let* $k = \|\boldsymbol{x}_o\|_0$. *If* $\delta_{2k}(\boldsymbol{A}) < \sqrt{2} - 1$, *then any solution* $\hat{\boldsymbol{x}}$ *to the optimization problem*

$$\begin{array}{ll} \min & \|\boldsymbol{x}\|_1 \\ \text{subject to} & \|\boldsymbol{y} - \boldsymbol{A}\boldsymbol{x}\|_2 \le \varepsilon \end{array} \tag{3.5.9}$$

[13] The condition on RIP constant in [CRT06b] was $\delta_{4k}(\boldsymbol{A}) < 1/4$, which is more restrictive than the one shown here.

satisfies

$$\left\| \hat{\boldsymbol{x}} - \boldsymbol{x}_o \right\|_2 \le C\varepsilon. \tag{3.5.10}$$

Here, C is a constant which depends only on $\delta_{2k}(\boldsymbol{A})$ (and not on the noise level ε).

Proof From our assumptions, $\|\boldsymbol{y} - \boldsymbol{A}\boldsymbol{x}_o\|_2 = \|\boldsymbol{z}\|_2 \le \varepsilon$. Since $\hat{\boldsymbol{x}}$ is feasible, we have $\left\| \boldsymbol{y} - \boldsymbol{A}\hat{\boldsymbol{x}} \right\|_2 \le \varepsilon$ as well. Using the triangle inequality,

$$\begin{aligned} \left\| \boldsymbol{A}(\hat{\boldsymbol{x}} - \boldsymbol{x}_o) \right\|_2 &= \left\| (\boldsymbol{y} - \boldsymbol{A}\hat{\boldsymbol{x}}) - (\boldsymbol{y} - \boldsymbol{A}\boldsymbol{x}_o) \right\|_2 \\ &\le \left\| \boldsymbol{y} - \boldsymbol{A}\hat{\boldsymbol{x}} \right\|_2 + \|\boldsymbol{y} - \boldsymbol{A}\boldsymbol{x}_o\|_2 \\ &\le 2\varepsilon. \end{aligned}$$

Letting $\boldsymbol{h} = \hat{\boldsymbol{x}} - \boldsymbol{x}_o$, we have $\|\boldsymbol{A}\boldsymbol{h}\|_2 \le 2\varepsilon$. Geometrically, this means that the perturbation $\boldsymbol{h}$ must be close to the null space of $\boldsymbol{A}$.

Because $\boldsymbol{x}_o$ is feasible for the optimization problem, and $\hat{\boldsymbol{x}}$ is optimal, $\hat{\boldsymbol{x}}$ must have a lower objective function value than $\boldsymbol{x}_o$:

$$\left\| \hat{\boldsymbol{x}} \right\|_1 \le \|\boldsymbol{x}_o\|_1. \tag{3.5.11}$$

Let I denote the support of $\boldsymbol{x}_o$. We have

$$\begin{aligned} \|\boldsymbol{x}_o\|_1 &\ge \|\boldsymbol{x}_o + \boldsymbol{h}\|_1 \\ &\ge \|\boldsymbol{x}_o\|_1 - \|\boldsymbol{h}_{\mathsf{I}}\|_1 + \|\boldsymbol{h}_{\mathsf{I}^c}\|_1, \end{aligned}$$

and so

$$\|\boldsymbol{h}_{\mathsf{I}^c}\|_1 \le \|\boldsymbol{h}_{\mathsf{I}}\|_1. \tag{3.5.12}$$

Geometrically, this means that $\hat{\boldsymbol{x}}$ lives in an ℓ^1 ball of radius $\|\boldsymbol{x}_o\|_1$, centered at the origin. Locally, this set looks like a convex cone (the "descent cone" of the ℓ^1 norm), hence the constraint $\|\boldsymbol{h}_{\mathsf{I}^c}\|_1 \le \|\boldsymbol{h}_{\mathsf{I}}\|_1$ is also known as a "cone constraint." It describes the set of all possible perturbations of $\hat{\boldsymbol{x}}$ from $\boldsymbol{x}_o$ that would decrease the value of the objective function. The geometric intuition behind the two constraints on the perturbation $\boldsymbol{h}$ is shown in Figure 3.14.

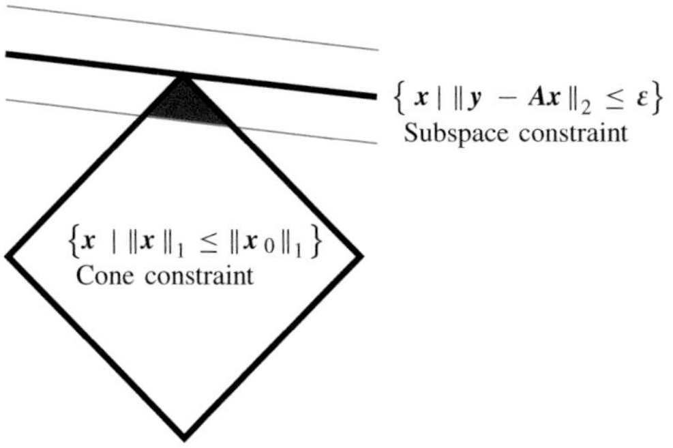

Figure 3.14 Geometry of the proof of Theorem 3.29.

Note that the matrix $\boldsymbol{A}$ satisfies RIP. According to Theorem 3.17, we know that if $\delta_{2k} < \sqrt{2} - 1$, $\boldsymbol{A}$ satisfies the restricted strong convexity property with constant $\alpha = 1$ (which is the case for the restriction condition (3.5.12) on $\boldsymbol{h}$ above). Therefore, we have

$$\|\boldsymbol{A}\boldsymbol{h}\|_2^2 \geq \mu \|\boldsymbol{h}\|_2^2 \tag{3.5.13}$$

for some $\mu > 0$. Combining this with $\|\boldsymbol{A}\boldsymbol{h}\|_2 \leq 2\varepsilon$, we have

$$\|\hat{\boldsymbol{x}} - \boldsymbol{x}_o\|_2 = \|\boldsymbol{h}\|_2 \leq \frac{2}{\sqrt{\mu}}\varepsilon. \tag{3.5.14}$$

Choosing $C = 2/\sqrt{\mu}$ completes the proof. □

Notice that in the above proof, the constant C can be rather large if μ is very small. According to the proof of Theorem 3.17, we know

$$\sqrt{\mu} = \frac{1 - \delta_{2k}(1 + \sqrt{2})}{\sqrt{2(1 + \delta_{2k})}}.$$

The quantity μ becomes small if δ_{2k} is close to $\sqrt{2} - 1$. Therefore, if we do not want the constant C in Theorem 3.29 to be too large, we need to ensure that δ_{2k} is significantly smaller than $\sqrt{2} - 1$. However, no matter how small δ_{2k} is, we always have $\sqrt{\mu} < 1/\sqrt{2}$. Hence, based on this proof, the smallest that the constant C can be in the theorem is $2\sqrt{2}$.

Random Noise

Above, we have shown that for any additive noise $\boldsymbol{z}$ in the observation $\boldsymbol{y} = \boldsymbol{A}\boldsymbol{x}_o + \boldsymbol{z}$, we can estimate $\boldsymbol{x}_o$ with an error of size controlled by $C\,\|\boldsymbol{z}\|_2$ for some constant C. Based on our discussion before Theorem 3.29, this error bound is already close to the best possible.

For random noise, we might hope that if $m \gg k$, most of the energy of $\boldsymbol{z}$ would "miss" the k-dimensional subspace range$(\boldsymbol{A}_\mathsf{I})$. If so, the accuracy in the estimated $\hat{\boldsymbol{x}}$ can improve as m grows. More precisely, the coefficient C in the error bound $C\,\|\boldsymbol{z}\|_2$ decreases as m increases. This turns out to be the case. For simplicity, we here state a theorem for random $\boldsymbol{A}$.[14] More precisely, we assume that the measurement model

$$\boldsymbol{y} = \boldsymbol{A}\boldsymbol{x}_o + \boldsymbol{z}, \tag{3.5.15}$$

where $\boldsymbol{y} \in \mathbb{R}^m$, $\boldsymbol{x}_o$ is k-sparse, and the matrix $\boldsymbol{A} \sim_{\text{iid}} \mathcal{N}(0, 1/m)$ and $\boldsymbol{z} \sim_{\text{iid}} \mathcal{N}(0, \sigma^2/m)$. Notice that in the study of the deterministic case, we have assumed the measurement matrix $\boldsymbol{A}$ is a matrix that satisfies RIP conditions. Hence the norm of the columns of $\boldsymbol{A}$ there is typically normalized to one. Here the scaling factor $1/m$ in the variance is to ensure the columns of $\boldsymbol{A}$ are typically of length one and the noise vector is of length σ, so that the model and the results will be directly comparable to those for the deterministic case.[15]

[14] An analogous result holds for $\boldsymbol{A}$ satisfying the RIP.

[15] The variance σ replaces the role of ε in Theorem 3.29.

As we have discussed earlier, with noisy measurements, we could find an estimate $\hat{\boldsymbol{x}}$ of $\boldsymbol{x}_o$ that strikes a balance between sparsity and minimizing the error. In particular, we would like to solve the following Lasso program for $\hat{\boldsymbol{x}}$:

$$\hat{\boldsymbol{x}} = \arg\min_{\boldsymbol{x}} \tfrac{1}{2} \|\boldsymbol{y} - \boldsymbol{A}\boldsymbol{x}\|_2^2 + \lambda_m \|\boldsymbol{x}\|_1 . \tag{3.5.16}$$

As usual, for convenience, we let $\mathsf{I} = \operatorname{supp}(\boldsymbol{x}_o)$, let I^c denote its complement, and $\boldsymbol{h} = \hat{\boldsymbol{x}} - \boldsymbol{x}_o \in \mathbb{R}^n$ the difference between the estimate and the ground truth. We also define $L(\boldsymbol{x}) = \frac{1}{2}\|\boldsymbol{y} - \boldsymbol{A}\boldsymbol{x}\|_2^2$. Notice that $\nabla L(\boldsymbol{x}) = -\boldsymbol{A}^*(\boldsymbol{y} - \boldsymbol{A}\boldsymbol{x})$ and in particular $\nabla L(\boldsymbol{x}_o) = -\boldsymbol{A}^*(\boldsymbol{y} - \boldsymbol{A}\boldsymbol{x}_o) = -\boldsymbol{A}^*\boldsymbol{z}$ according to (3.5.15).

We want to know how small the difference $\|\boldsymbol{h}\| = \|\hat{\boldsymbol{x}} - \boldsymbol{x}_o\|$ is for a given λ_m. First we show that for a properly chosen λ_m, the difference vector $\boldsymbol{h}$ is highly *restricted* in the way that $\|\boldsymbol{h}_{\mathsf{I}^c}\|_1 \le \alpha\|\boldsymbol{h}_{\mathsf{I}}\|_1$ for some constant α, i.e., the error of the support I of $\boldsymbol{x}_o$ is controlled by that on I.[16] More precisely, we have the following lemma.

LEMMA 3.30. *For the optimization problem* (3.5.16), *if we choose the regularization parameter* $\lambda_m \ge c \cdot 2\sigma\sqrt{\log(n)/m}$, *then with high probability,* $\boldsymbol{h} = \hat{\boldsymbol{x}} - \boldsymbol{x}_o$ *satisfies the cone condition:*

$$\|\boldsymbol{h}_{\mathsf{I}^c}\|_1 \le \frac{c+1}{c-1} \cdot \|\boldsymbol{h}_{\mathsf{I}}\|_1, \tag{3.5.17}$$

where I *is the support of the sparse* $\boldsymbol{x}_o$.

Proof Note that the difference between $\hat{\boldsymbol{x}}$ and $\boldsymbol{x}_o$ is related to the difference between the values of the objective function in (3.5.16). Since $\hat{\boldsymbol{x}}$ minimizes the objective function, we have

$$\begin{aligned} 0 &\ge L(\hat{\boldsymbol{x}}) + \lambda_m\|\hat{\boldsymbol{x}}\|_1 - L(\boldsymbol{x}_o) - \lambda_m\|\boldsymbol{x}_o\|_1 \\ &\ge \langle \nabla L(\boldsymbol{x}_o), \hat{\boldsymbol{x}} - \boldsymbol{x}_o\rangle + \lambda_m(\|\hat{\boldsymbol{x}}\|_1 - \|\boldsymbol{x}_o\|_1) \\ &\ge -|\langle \boldsymbol{A}^*\boldsymbol{z}, \boldsymbol{h}\rangle| + \lambda_m(\|\hat{\boldsymbol{x}}\|_1 - \|\boldsymbol{x}_o\|_1) \\ &\ge -\|\boldsymbol{A}^*\boldsymbol{z}\|_\infty\|\boldsymbol{h}\|_1 + \lambda_m(\|\hat{\boldsymbol{x}}\|_1 - \|\boldsymbol{x}_o\|_1), \end{aligned} \tag{3.5.18}$$

where in the second inequality we used the fact that $L(\boldsymbol{x})$ is a convex function. It remains to be seen how the two terms in the last inequality interact. Obviously we need to have a good idea about the value of $\|\boldsymbol{A}^*\boldsymbol{z}\|_\infty$. This is where we need to resort to results about measure concentration of high-dimensional statistics.

Notice that the column $\boldsymbol{a}_i$ of $\boldsymbol{A}$ is typically of norm $\|\boldsymbol{a}_i\|_2 \approx 1$. Hence here we may assume the columns of $\boldsymbol{A}$ are all normalized to one. Therefore $\boldsymbol{a}_i^*\boldsymbol{z}$ is a Gaussian random variable of variance σ^2/m. We have

$$\mathbb{P}\left[|\boldsymbol{a}_i^*\boldsymbol{z}| \ge t\right] \le 2\exp\left(-\frac{mt^2}{2\sigma^2}\right). \tag{3.5.19}$$

[16] Notice that a similar restriction on $\boldsymbol{h}$ was derived in (3.5.12). There the constant is $\alpha = 1$ and as we will soon see, here the constant needs to be 3.

By union bound on the n columns, we have

$$\mathbb{P}\left[\|\boldsymbol{A}^*\boldsymbol{z}\|_\infty \geq t\right] \leq 2\exp\left(-\frac{mt^2}{2\sigma^2} + \log n\right). \tag{3.5.20}$$

As we may see, as long as we choose t^2 to be on the order of $C\sigma^2\log(n)/m$ for a large enough constant C, the exponent will be negative and the event $\|\boldsymbol{A}^*\boldsymbol{z}\|_\infty \geq t$ will be of low probability. In particular we may choose $t^2 = 4\sigma^2\log(n)/m$, and we know that with high probability at least $1 - cn^{-1}$, we have

$$\|\boldsymbol{A}^*\boldsymbol{z}\|_\infty \leq 2\sigma\sqrt{\frac{\log n}{m}}.$$

So to make the two terms in (3.5.18) comparable in scale, it is natural to choose λ_m of the scale $\sigma\sqrt{\log(n)/m}$. In particular, we choose $\lambda_m \geq c \cdot 2\sigma\sqrt{\log(n)/m}$ for some $c > 0$. Then from the last inequality of (3.5.18), we have

$$\begin{aligned} 0 &\geq -\|\boldsymbol{A}^*\boldsymbol{z}\|_\infty\|\boldsymbol{h}\|_1 + \lambda_m(\|\hat{\boldsymbol{x}}\|_1 - \|\boldsymbol{x}_o\|_1) \\ &\geq -\frac{\lambda_m}{c}\|\boldsymbol{h}\|_1 + \lambda_m(\|\hat{\boldsymbol{x}}\|_1 - \|\boldsymbol{x}_o\|_1) \\ &\geq -\frac{\lambda_m}{c}\|\boldsymbol{h}_\mathsf{I}\|_1 - \frac{\lambda_m}{c}\|\boldsymbol{h}_{\mathsf{I}^c}\|_1 + \lambda_m\|\boldsymbol{h}_{\mathsf{I}^c}\|_1 - \lambda_m\|\boldsymbol{h}_\mathsf{I}\|_1 \\ &= \lambda_m\left(\left(1 - \frac{1}{c}\right)\|\boldsymbol{h}_{\mathsf{I}^c}\|_1 - \left(1 + \frac{1}{c}\right)\|\boldsymbol{h}_\mathsf{I}\|_1\right), \end{aligned} \tag{3.5.21}$$

where in the second to last inequality we used the fact that $\boldsymbol{x}_o$ is zero on I^c and $\|\hat{\boldsymbol{x}}_\mathsf{I}\|_1 - \|\boldsymbol{x}_{o\mathsf{I}}\|_1 \geq -\|\boldsymbol{h}_\mathsf{I}\|_1$. Therefore we have

$$\|\boldsymbol{h}_{\mathsf{I}^c}\|_1 \leq \frac{c+1}{c-1} \cdot \|\boldsymbol{h}_\mathsf{I}\|_1. \tag{3.5.22}$$

Notice that if we choose c to be large, $(c+1)/(c-1)$ can be arbitrarily close to 1. □

As we have discussed in the deterministic case, since $\|\boldsymbol{A}(\hat{\boldsymbol{x}} - \boldsymbol{x}_o)\|_2 \leq \|\boldsymbol{y} - \boldsymbol{A}\hat{\boldsymbol{x}}\|_2 + \|\boldsymbol{y} - \boldsymbol{A}\boldsymbol{x}_o\|_2$, it suggests that $\|\boldsymbol{A}\boldsymbol{h}\|_2$ is typically very small and of the scale $C\sigma$. If the norm $\|\boldsymbol{A}\boldsymbol{h}\|_2$ upper-bounds the norm $\|\boldsymbol{h}\|_2$, then the estimate is stable. Of course, this cannot be true for any $\boldsymbol{h} \in \mathbb{R}^n$ since the matrix $\boldsymbol{A}$ is typically severely under determined and for any $\boldsymbol{h}$ in the null space of $\boldsymbol{A}$, the norm $\|\boldsymbol{A}\boldsymbol{h}\|$ is zero but the norm $\|\boldsymbol{h}\|$ can be arbitrarily large.

Nevertheless, due to the above lemma, we could hope that for $\boldsymbol{h}$ that satisfies the cone restriction $\|\boldsymbol{h}_{\mathsf{I}^c}\|_1 \leq \alpha\|\boldsymbol{h}_\mathsf{I}\|_1$ for $\alpha = (c+1)/(c-1)$, $\|\boldsymbol{A}\boldsymbol{h}\|_2$ controls $\|\boldsymbol{h}\|_2$. Due to Theorem 3.11, we know that with high probability, $\boldsymbol{A}$ as a random Gaussian matrix satisfies RIP. Then Theorem 3.17 ensures that when $\boldsymbol{h}$ is restricted in such a cone, $\|\boldsymbol{A}\boldsymbol{h}\|_2$ controls the norm $\|\boldsymbol{h}\|_2$. This leads to the following theorem.[17]

THEOREM 3.31. (Stable sparse recovery via lasso) *Suppose that* $\boldsymbol{A} \sim_{\text{iid}} \mathcal{N}(0, 1/m)$, *and* $\boldsymbol{y} = \boldsymbol{A}\boldsymbol{x}_o + \boldsymbol{z}$, *with* $\boldsymbol{x}_o$ *k-sparse and* $\boldsymbol{z} \sim_{\text{iid}} \mathcal{N}(0, \sigma^2/m)$. *Solve the Lasso*

[17] This result and its proof essentially follow that of [CT07] and [BRT09].

$$\min \ \tfrac{1}{2}\left\| \boldsymbol{y} - \boldsymbol{A}\boldsymbol{x} \right\|_2^2 + \lambda_m \left\| \boldsymbol{x} \right\|_1, \tag{3.5.23}$$

with regularization parameter $\lambda_m = c \cdot 2\sigma\sqrt{\log(n)/m}$ *for a large enough* c*. Then with high probability,*

$$\left\| \hat{\boldsymbol{x}} - \boldsymbol{x}_o \right\|_2 \le C'\sigma\sqrt{\frac{k\log n}{m}}. \tag{3.5.24}$$

Generally, we are interested in the regime $m \ge k\log n$, because this is when the measurement matrix $\boldsymbol{A}$ satisfies RIP (due to Theorem 3.11). The above theorem indicates that in this case, we actually do much better under random noise than deterministic noise: the estimation error in the random case can be the noise norm σ scaled by a diminishing factor[18] whereas in the deterministic case the error is the noise norm ε scaled by a constant factor (see Theorem 3.29 for comparison).

Proof With $L(\boldsymbol{x}) = \frac{1}{2}\left\| \boldsymbol{y} - \boldsymbol{A}\boldsymbol{x} \right\|_2^2$, we have

$$L(\hat{\boldsymbol{x}}) = L(\boldsymbol{x}_o) + \langle \nabla L(\boldsymbol{x}_o), \hat{\boldsymbol{x}} - \boldsymbol{x}_o \rangle + \tfrac{1}{2}\| \boldsymbol{A}(\hat{\boldsymbol{x}} - \boldsymbol{x}_o)\|_2^2.$$

We now use this equality to better estimate the difference between the values of the objective function at $\hat{\boldsymbol{x}}$ and at $\boldsymbol{x}_o$ than that done in (3.5.18):

$$\begin{aligned} 0 &\ge L(\hat{\boldsymbol{x}}) + \lambda_m \|\hat{\boldsymbol{x}}\|_1 - L(\boldsymbol{x}_o) - \lambda_m \|\boldsymbol{x}_o\|_1 \\ &\ge \frac{1}{2}\|\boldsymbol{A}(\hat{\boldsymbol{x}} - \boldsymbol{x}_o)\|_2^2 + \langle \nabla L(\boldsymbol{x}_o), \hat{\boldsymbol{x}} - \boldsymbol{x}_o \rangle + \lambda_m(\|\hat{\boldsymbol{x}}\|_1 - \|\boldsymbol{x}_o\|_1) \\ &\ge \frac{1}{2}\|\boldsymbol{A}\boldsymbol{h}\|_2^2 + \lambda_m\left(\left(1 - \frac{1}{c}\right)\|\boldsymbol{h}_{\mathsf{I}^c}\|_1 - \left(1 + \frac{1}{c}\right)\|\boldsymbol{h}_{\mathsf{I}}\|_1\right), \end{aligned} \tag{3.5.25}$$

where the last inequality follows exactly the same derivation that we have done in (3.5.18) and (3.5.21) for other terms without the term $\frac{1}{2}\|\boldsymbol{A}(\hat{\boldsymbol{x}} - \boldsymbol{x}_o)\|_2^2 = \frac{1}{2}\|\boldsymbol{A}\boldsymbol{h}\|_2^2$.

From the last inequality we have

$$\frac{1}{2}\|\boldsymbol{A}\boldsymbol{h}\|_2^2 \le \lambda_m\left(1 + \frac{1}{c}\right)\|\boldsymbol{h}_{\mathsf{I}}\|_1,$$

according to Theorem 3.11 and Theorem 3.17, with high probability; so the random Gaussian matrix $\boldsymbol{A}$ satisfies the restricted strong convexity property, we have $\|\boldsymbol{A}\boldsymbol{h}\|_2^2 \ge \mu\|\boldsymbol{h}\|_2^2$ for some constant μ.[19] Also from the relationship between 1-norm and 2-norm, we have $\|\boldsymbol{h}_{\mathsf{I}}\|_1 \le \sqrt{k}\|\boldsymbol{h}_{\mathsf{I}}\|_2 \le \sqrt{k}\|\boldsymbol{h}\|_2$. Finally, with the choice $\lambda_m = c \cdot 2\sigma\sqrt{\log(n)/m}$, the above inequality leads to

$$\frac{\mu}{2}\|\boldsymbol{h}\|_2^2 \le 2(c+1)\sigma\sqrt{\frac{k\log n}{m}}\|\boldsymbol{h}\|_2 \quad \Rightarrow \quad \|\boldsymbol{h}\|_2 \le C'\sigma\sqrt{\frac{k\log n}{m}}$$

for some constant $C' = 4(c+1)/\mu \in \mathbb{R}_+$. □

The error bound given in the above theorem is actually nearly optimal as it is close to the best error that one can achieve by considering all possible estimators:

[18] As $\sqrt{k\log(n)/m}$ can be chosen to be arbitrarily small.

[19] Notice that μ depends on the RIP constant $\delta_{2k}(\boldsymbol{A})$ and the constant $C = (c+1)/(c-1)$ of the cone restriction.

THEOREM 3.32. ([CD13]) *Suppose that we will observe* $\boldsymbol{y} = \boldsymbol{A}\boldsymbol{x} + \boldsymbol{z}$. *Set*

$$M^\star(\boldsymbol{A}) = \inf_{\hat{\boldsymbol{x}}} \sup_{\|\boldsymbol{x}\|_0 \le k} \mathbb{E} \left\| \hat{\boldsymbol{x}}(\boldsymbol{y}) - \boldsymbol{x} \right\|_2^2. \tag{3.5.26}$$

Then for any $\boldsymbol{A}$ *with* $\left\| \boldsymbol{e}_i^* \boldsymbol{A} \right\|_2 \le \sqrt{n}$ *for each* i, *we have*

$$M^\star(\boldsymbol{A}) \ge C\sigma^2 \frac{k \log(n/k)}{m}. \tag{3.5.27}$$

The proof of this theorem is beyond the scope of this book; we refer interested readers to the original paper for a proof. According to Theorem 3.31, the error bound $\left\| \hat{\boldsymbol{x}} - \boldsymbol{x}_o \right\|_2^2 \sim O(\sigma^2 k \log(n)/m)$ achieved by Lasso is within a difference of $O(\sigma^2 k \log(k)/m)$ from the best achievable bound above. When $m \gg k$, such a difference is negligible.

3.5.2 Recovery of Inexact Sparse Signals

In all the above analysis, we have assumed that in the observation model $\boldsymbol{y} = \boldsymbol{A}\boldsymbol{x}_o + \boldsymbol{z}$, the signal $\boldsymbol{x}_o$ is perfectly k-sparse. In many cases, $\boldsymbol{x}_o$ might not be so sparse and even all entries could be nonzero. Then a question naturally arises: for $\boldsymbol{x}_o$ that is close to a k-sparse signal, can we still expect good recovery performance in some sense?

Let $[\boldsymbol{x}_o]_k$ be the best k-sparse signal that approximates $\boldsymbol{x}_o$. Then we can rewrite the observation model as

$$\boldsymbol{y} = \boldsymbol{A}[\boldsymbol{x}_o]_k + \boldsymbol{A}(\boldsymbol{x}_o - [\boldsymbol{x}_o]_k) + \boldsymbol{z}.$$

Strictly speaking the term $\boldsymbol{w} = \boldsymbol{A}(\boldsymbol{x}_o - [\boldsymbol{x}_o]_k)$ is not noise. It is more of a deviation from our idealistic sparse signal assumption. But we may view it as introducing a deterministic error to the observation. Hence, if the norm of $\boldsymbol{w}$ is small, we should expect to obtain an estimate $\hat{\boldsymbol{x}}$ whose error from $\boldsymbol{x}_o$ is proportional to this norm.

The following is a typical result on estimation with inexact sparsity, which also allows deterministic noise.[20]

THEOREM 3.33. ([CRT06b]) *Let* $\boldsymbol{y} = \boldsymbol{A}\boldsymbol{x}_o + \boldsymbol{z}$, *with* $\|\boldsymbol{z}\|_2 \le \varepsilon$. *Let* $\hat{\boldsymbol{x}}$ *solve the basis pursuit denoising problem*

$$\begin{array}{ll} \min & \|\boldsymbol{x}\|_1 \\ \text{subject to} & \|\boldsymbol{y} - \boldsymbol{A}\boldsymbol{x}\|_2 \le \varepsilon. \end{array} \tag{3.5.28}$$

Then for any k *such that* $\delta_{2k}(\boldsymbol{A}) < \sqrt{2} - 1$,

$$\left\| \hat{\boldsymbol{x}} - \boldsymbol{x}_o \right\|_2 \le C \frac{\|\boldsymbol{x}_o - [\boldsymbol{x}_o]_k\|_1}{\sqrt{k}} + C'\varepsilon \tag{3.5.29}$$

for some constants C *and* C' *which only depend on* $\delta_{2k}(\boldsymbol{A})$.

[20] In fact, similar statements hold for random noise. The proof requires slight modification to that of Theorem 3.31. We leave the details to the reader as an exercise.

How should we interpret this result? One way of reading it is to say that if we are working in a regime where noise-free sparse recovery would have succeeded ($\delta_{2k}(\boldsymbol{A}) < \sqrt{2} - 1$), then even if our modeling assumptions are violated (due to the introduction of noise and inexact sparsity), we can still *stably* estimate $\boldsymbol{x}_o$. Moreover, the error in our estimate is proportional to the degree to which our assumptions are violated and proportional to the noise level. When the original signal $\boldsymbol{x}_o$ is indeed k-sparse, we have $\boldsymbol{x}_o - [\boldsymbol{x}_o]_k = \boldsymbol{0}$ and the above result reduces to the deterministic noise case, i.e., Theorem 3.29.

Proof As usual, we denote $\boldsymbol{h} = \hat{\boldsymbol{x}} - \boldsymbol{x}_o$. We also denote the support of $[\boldsymbol{x}_o]_k$ as I so that we have $[\boldsymbol{x}_o]_k = \boldsymbol{x}_{o\mathsf{I}}$. From our assumptions, $\|\boldsymbol{y} - \boldsymbol{A}\boldsymbol{x}_o\|_2 = \|\boldsymbol{z}\|_2 \le \varepsilon$. Since $\hat{\boldsymbol{x}}$ is feasible, we have $\left\|\boldsymbol{y} - \boldsymbol{A}\hat{\boldsymbol{x}}\right\|_2 \le \varepsilon$ as well. Using the triangle inequality,

$$\|\boldsymbol{A}\boldsymbol{h}\|_2 = \left\|\boldsymbol{A}(\hat{\boldsymbol{x}} - \boldsymbol{x}_o)\right\|_2 \le 2\varepsilon.$$

Therefore, in the inexact sparse case, the prediction error $\|\boldsymbol{A}\boldsymbol{h}\|_2$ is again bounded by the noise level.

Since $\hat{\boldsymbol{x}}$ minimizes the objective function, we have

$$\begin{aligned} 0 &\le \|\boldsymbol{x}_o\|_1 - \left\|\hat{\boldsymbol{x}}\right\|_1 \\ &= \|\boldsymbol{x}_o\|_1 - \|\boldsymbol{x}_{o\mathsf{I}} + \boldsymbol{h}_{\mathsf{I}}\|_1 - \|\boldsymbol{x}_{o\mathsf{I}^c} + \boldsymbol{h}_{\mathsf{I}^c}\|_1 \\ &\le \|\boldsymbol{x}_o\|_1 - \|\boldsymbol{x}_{o\mathsf{I}}\|_1 + \|\boldsymbol{h}_{\mathsf{I}}\|_1 + \|\boldsymbol{x}_{o\mathsf{I}^c}\|_1 - \|\boldsymbol{h}_{\mathsf{I}^c}\|_1 . \end{aligned}$$

Thus we have

$$\|\boldsymbol{h}_{\mathsf{I}^c}\|_1 \le \|\boldsymbol{h}_{\mathsf{I}}\|_1 + 2\,\|\boldsymbol{x}_{o\mathsf{I}^c}\|_1 , \tag{3.5.30}$$

where $\boldsymbol{x}_{o\mathsf{I}^c} = \boldsymbol{x}_o - \boldsymbol{x}_{o\mathsf{I}}$. So in the inexact sparse case, the feasible perturbation $\boldsymbol{h}$ no longer satisfies the cone condition as in the exact sparse case (see Theorem 3.29). Therefore, to establish the result of this theorem, we need to modify the proof of Theorem 3.17 to accommodate the extra term $2\,\|\boldsymbol{x}_{o\mathsf{I}^c}\|_1$ in estimating the bounds for $\|\boldsymbol{A}\boldsymbol{h}\|_2$ and $\|\boldsymbol{h}\|_2$.

The proof essentially follows the same steps as in the proof for Theorem 3.17. The only difference is that in places where we used to apply the cone condition $\|\boldsymbol{h}_{\mathsf{I}^c}\|_1 \le \alpha\,\|\boldsymbol{h}_{\mathsf{I}}\|_1$, we now need to replace it with the new condition (3.5.30). Therefore, instead of (3.3.34), the new condition (3.5.30) implies

$$\|\boldsymbol{h}_{\mathsf{I}^c}\|_1 \le \sqrt{k}\,\|\boldsymbol{h}_{\mathsf{I}}\|_2 + 2\,\|\boldsymbol{x}_{o\mathsf{I}^c}\|_1 \le \sqrt{k}\,\left\|\boldsymbol{h}_{\mathsf{I}\cup\mathsf{J}_1}\right\|_2 + 2\,\|\boldsymbol{x}_{o\mathsf{I}^c}\|_1 . \tag{3.5.31}$$

Substituting this into (3.3.33) to establish a bound for $\|\boldsymbol{A}\boldsymbol{h}\|_2$, we obtain

$$(1 - \delta_{2k})\left\|\boldsymbol{h}_{\mathsf{I}\cup\mathsf{J}_1}\right\|_2 \le \sqrt{2}\delta_{2k}\left\|\boldsymbol{h}_{\mathsf{I}\cup\mathsf{J}_1}\right\|_2 + 2\sqrt{2}\delta_{2k}\frac{\|\boldsymbol{x}_{o\mathsf{I}^c}\|_1}{\sqrt{k}} + (1 + \delta_{2k})^{1/2}\,\|\boldsymbol{A}\boldsymbol{h}\|_2 . \tag{3.5.32}$$

This gives

$$\|\boldsymbol{A}\boldsymbol{h}\|_2 \ge \frac{1 - (1 + \sqrt{2})\delta_{2k}}{(1 + \delta_{2k})^{1/2}}\left\|\boldsymbol{h}_{\mathsf{I}\cup\mathsf{J}_1}\right\|_2 - \frac{2\sqrt{2}\delta_{2k}}{(1 + \delta_{2k})^{1/2}}\frac{\|\boldsymbol{x}_{o\mathsf{I}^c}\|_1}{\sqrt{k}}. \tag{3.5.33}$$

Now, to establish a bound for $\|\boldsymbol{h}\|_2$, in (3.3.40) where we have applied the cone condition in the second inequality, we also need to replace the cone condition with the new condition (3.5.30) and that gives

$$\|\boldsymbol{h}_{(\mathsf{I}\cup\mathsf{J}_1)^c}\|_2 \leq \frac{\|\boldsymbol{h}_{\mathsf{I}^c}\|_1}{\sqrt{k}} \leq \frac{\|\boldsymbol{h}_{\mathsf{I}}\|_1 + 2\,\|\boldsymbol{x}_{o\mathsf{I}^c}\|_1}{\sqrt{k}} \tag{3.5.34}$$

$$\leq \|\boldsymbol{h}_{\mathsf{I}}\|_2 + 2\frac{\|\boldsymbol{x}_{o\mathsf{I}^c}\|_1}{\sqrt{k}} \tag{3.5.35}$$

$$\leq \|\boldsymbol{h}_{\mathsf{I}\cup\mathsf{J}_1}\|_2 + 2\frac{\|\boldsymbol{x}_{o\mathsf{I}^c}\|_1}{\sqrt{k}}. \tag{3.5.36}$$

This gives

$$\|\boldsymbol{h}\|_2 \leq \|\boldsymbol{h}_{\mathsf{I}\cup\mathsf{J}_1}\|_2 + \|\boldsymbol{h}_{(\mathsf{I}\cup\mathsf{J}_1)^c}\|_2 \leq 2\|\boldsymbol{h}_{\mathsf{I}\cup\mathsf{J}_1}\|_2 + 2\frac{\|\boldsymbol{x}_{o\mathsf{I}^c}\|_1}{\sqrt{k}}. \tag{3.5.37}$$

Combining this with (3.5.33) and the fact that $\|\boldsymbol{A}\boldsymbol{h}\|_2 \leq 2\varepsilon$, we get

$$\|\boldsymbol{h}\|_2 \leq \left(\frac{2 + 2(\sqrt{2}-1)\delta_{2k}}{1-(1+\sqrt{2})\delta_{2k}}\right)\frac{\|\boldsymbol{x}_{o\mathsf{I}^c}\|_1}{\sqrt{k}} + \left(\frac{4(1+\delta_{2k})^{1/2}}{1-(1+\sqrt{2})\delta_{2k}}\right)\varepsilon, \tag{3.5.38}$$

where we note $\boldsymbol{x}_{o\mathsf{I}^c} = \boldsymbol{x}_o - [\boldsymbol{x}_o]_k$. Therefore, as long as $1-(1+\sqrt{2})\delta_{2k} > 0$ or equivalently $\delta_{2k} < \sqrt{2}-1$, the conclusion of the theorem holds. □

Note that from the above proof, we know that the two constants in Theorem 3.33 can be chosen to be

$$C = \frac{2-2(\sqrt{2}-1)\delta_{2k}}{1-(1+\sqrt{2})\delta_{2k}} \quad \text{and} \quad C' = \frac{4(1+\delta_{2k})}{1-(1+\sqrt{2})\delta_{2k}}. \tag{3.5.39}$$

If δ_{2k} is very small, say approaching to zero, then C approaches to 2 and C' to 4. Those constants give the smallest possible bound for the error $\|\hat{\boldsymbol{x}} - \boldsymbol{x}_o\|_2$ based on this proof.

3.6 Phase Transitions in Sparse Recovery

Above, we showed that sparse vectors $\boldsymbol{x}_o$ can be accurately estimated from linear observations $\boldsymbol{y} = \boldsymbol{A}\boldsymbol{x}_o + \boldsymbol{z}$. One of the surprises was that in the noise-free case ($\boldsymbol{z} = \boldsymbol{0}$), k-sparse vectors could be exactly recovered from just slightly more than k measurements – to be precise, $m \geq Ck\log(n/k)$ measurements, where C is a constant. The key technical tool for doing this was the restricted isometry property (RIP). The RIP and related properties enable simple proofs, with correct orders of growth (i.e., $m \sim k\log(n/k)$), but are not intended to give precise estimates of the constant C.

For some applications, it can be important to know C. In sampling and reconstruction, this tells us precisely how many samples we need to acquire to accurately estimate a sparse signal; in error correction, this tells us precisely how many errors the system can tolerate.

Put another way, we would like to obtain precise relationships between the dimensionality n, the number of measurements m, and the number of nonzero entries k that we can recover. We would like these relationships to be as sharp and explicit as possible. To get some intuition for what to expect, we again resort to numerical simulation. We fix n, and consider different levels of sparsity k, and number of measurements m. For each pair (k, m), we generate a number of random ℓ^1 minimization problems, with noiseless Gaussian measurements $\boldsymbol{y} = \boldsymbol{A}\boldsymbol{x}_o$, and ask *"For what fraction of these problems does ℓ^1 minimization correctly recover $\boldsymbol{x}_o$?"*

Figure 3.15 displays the result as a two-dimensional image. Here, the horizontal axis is the sampling ratio $\delta = m/n$. This ranges from zero on the left (a very short, wide $\boldsymbol{A}$) to one on the right (a nearly square $\boldsymbol{A}$). The vertical axis is the fraction of nonzeros $\eta = k/n$. Again, this ranges from zero at the bottom (very sparse problems)

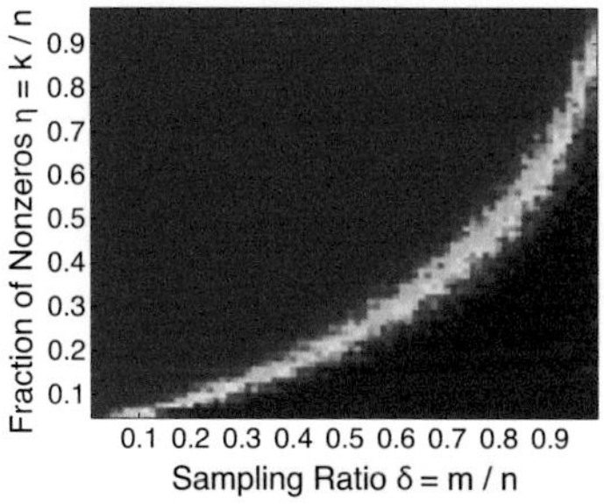

(a) $n = 50$

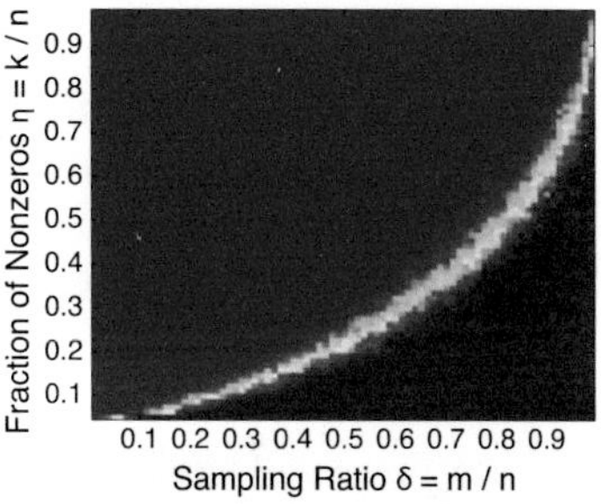

(b) $n = 100$

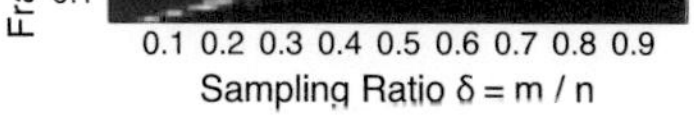

(c) $n = 200$

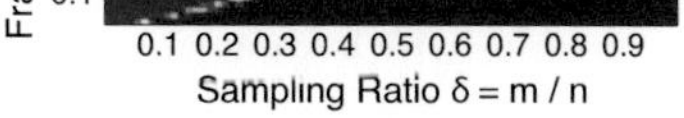

(d) $n = 400$

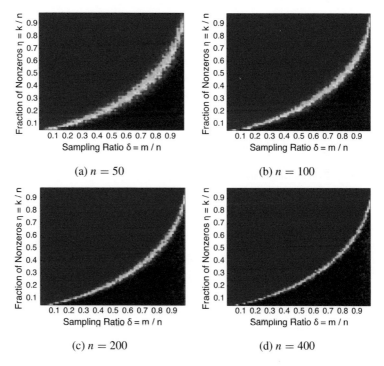

Figure 3.15 Phase transition in sparse recovery with Gaussian matrices. Each panel plots the fraction of correct recoveries using ℓ^1 minimization, over a suite of randomly generated problems. The vertical axis represents the fraction of nonzero entries $\eta = k/n$ in the target vector $\boldsymbol{x}_o$ – the bottom corresponds to very sparse vectors, while the top corresponds to fully dense vectors. The horizontal axis represents the sampling ratio $\delta = m/n$ – the left corresponds to drastically undersampled problems ($m \ll n$), while the right corresponds to almost fully observed problems. For each (η, δ) pair, we generate 200 random problems, which we solve using CVX [GB14]. We declare success if the recovered vector is accurate up to a relative error $\leq 10^{-6}$. Several salient features emerge: first, there is an easy regime (lower right corner) in which ℓ^1 minimization always succeeds. Second, there is a hard regime (upper left corner) in which ℓ^1 minimization always fails. Finally, as n increases, this transition between success and failure becomes increasingly sharp.

to one at the top (denser problems). For each pair (η, δ), we generate 200 random problems. The intensity is the fraction of problems for which ℓ^1 minimization succeeds. The four graphs, from (a) to (d), show the result for $n = 50$, 100, 200, and 400.

Figure 3.15 conveys several important pieces of information. First, as expected, when m is large and k is small (the lower right corner of each graph), ℓ^1 minimization always succeeds. Conversely, when m is small and k is large (the upper left corner of each graph), ℓ^1 minimization always fails. Moreover, as n grows, the transition between success and failure becomes increasingly abrupt. Put another way, for high-dimensional problems, the behavior of ℓ^1 minimization is surprisingly predictable: it either almost always succeeds, or almost always fails. The line demarcating the sharp boundary between success and failure is known as a *phase transition*.

3.6.1 Phase Transitions: Main Conclusions

In this section, we state a result that precisely specifies the location of the phase transition. Namely, we will show that a sharp transition from failure to success occurs when the sampling ratio $\delta = m/n$ exceeds a certain function $\psi(\eta)$ of the sparsity ratio $\eta = k/n$. This result will be sharper than the ones we stated above using incoherence and RIP, in the sense that it identifies the precise number of measurements $m^\star = \psi(k/n)n$ required for success. To obtain such sharp results, we need to make two changes to our setting. First, we will make stronger assumptions on the matrix $\boldsymbol{A}$. Second, we will weaken the goal of our performance guarantee.

Random vs. Deterministic $\boldsymbol{A}$

Thus far, we have focused on deterministic properties of the matrix $\boldsymbol{A}$, such as (in)coherence and the RIP. These properties do not depend on any random model for the matrix $\boldsymbol{A}$, although they are easiest to verify for random $\boldsymbol{A}$. Obtaining sharp estimates on the location of the phase transition requires more sophisticated probabilistic tools, which intrinsically require $\boldsymbol{A}$ to be a random matrix. We will sketch this theory under the assumption that $A_{ij} \sim_{\text{iid}} \mathcal{N}(0, 1/m)$, i.e., $\boldsymbol{A}$ is a standard Gaussian random matrix. We will also briefly describe experiments and theoretical results which show that the results we will obtain for Gaussian $\boldsymbol{A}$ are "universal," in the sense that they precisely describe the behavior of ℓ^1 minimization for a fairly broad family of matrices $\boldsymbol{A}$. Nevertheless, all currently known theory which is sharp enough to precisely characterize the phase transition requires $\boldsymbol{A}$ to be a random matrix.

Recovering a Particular Sparse $\boldsymbol{x}_o$ *vs. Recovering All Sparse* $\boldsymbol{x}_o$

Incoherence and RIP allow one to prove "for all" results, which say that for a given matrix $\boldsymbol{A}$, ℓ^1 minimization recovers *every* sparse $\boldsymbol{x}_o$ from $\boldsymbol{y} = \boldsymbol{A}\boldsymbol{x}_o$. The strongest and most general known results for phase transitions pertain to a slightly weaker statement: for a given, *fixed* $\boldsymbol{x}_o$, with high probability in the random matrix $\boldsymbol{A}$, ℓ^1 minimization recovers that particular $\boldsymbol{x}_o$ from the measurements $\boldsymbol{y} = \boldsymbol{A}\boldsymbol{x}_o$.

A variety of mathematical tools have been brought to bear on the analysis of phase transitions in ℓ^1 minimization.[21] Historically, the phenomenon has been characterized

[21] As well as phase transition phenomena for recovering a broader family of low-dimensional structures, as we will see in Chapter 6.

using several different approaches, by different sets of authors. In the following two sections, we describe briefly two representative approaches, which correspond roughly to the two geometric pictures in Section 3.1, which describe the behavior of ℓ^1 minimization in terms of the space $\mathbb{R}^n$ of coefficient vectors $\boldsymbol{x}$ and the space $\mathbb{R}^m$ of observation vectors $\boldsymbol{y}$. We leave a more general and rigorous theory of the phase transition for a broad family of low-dimensional models to Chapter 6.

3.6.2 Phase Transitions via Coefficient-Space Geometry

Suppose that $\boldsymbol{y} = \boldsymbol{A}\boldsymbol{x}_o$. Recall the geometric picture in Figure 3.16(a), which we introduced in Section 3.1. There, we argued that $\boldsymbol{x}_o$ is the unique optimal solution to the ℓ^1 minimization problem if and only if the affine subspace

$$\boldsymbol{x}_o + \mathrm{null}(\boldsymbol{A}) \tag{3.6.1}$$

of feasible solutions $\boldsymbol{x}$ intersects the scaled ℓ^1 ball

$$\|\boldsymbol{x}_o\|_1 \cdot \mathsf{B}_1 = \{\boldsymbol{x} \mid \|\boldsymbol{x}\|_1 \leq \|\boldsymbol{x}_o\|_1\} \tag{3.6.2}$$

only at $\boldsymbol{x}_o$.

We can express the same geometry more cleanly in terms of the *descent cone*:

$$\mathsf{D} = \{\boldsymbol{v} \mid \|\boldsymbol{x}_o + t\boldsymbol{v}\|_1 \leq \|\boldsymbol{x}_o\|_1 \text{ for some } t > 0\}. \tag{3.6.3}$$

This is the set of directions $\boldsymbol{v}$ for which a small (but nonzero) perturbation of $\boldsymbol{x}_o$ in the $\boldsymbol{v}$ direction does not increase the objective function $\|\cdot\|_1$. The descent cone D is visualized in Figure 3.16(b).

Notice that the perturbation $\boldsymbol{x}_o + t\boldsymbol{v}$ is feasible for $t \neq 0$ if and only if $\boldsymbol{v} \in \mathrm{null}(\boldsymbol{A})$. The feasible perturbations which do not increase the objective function reside in the intersection $\mathsf{D} \cap \mathrm{null}(\boldsymbol{A})$. Because D is a convex cone and $\mathrm{null}(\boldsymbol{A})$ is a subspace, D and $\mathrm{null}(\boldsymbol{A})$ always intersect at $\mathbf{0}$. It is not difficult to see that $\boldsymbol{x}_o$ is the unique optimal

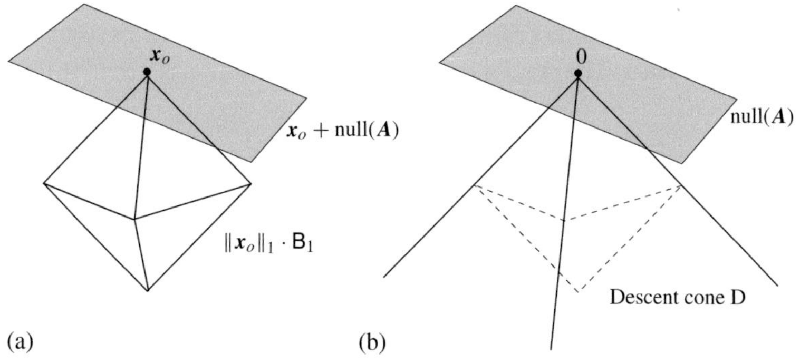

Figure 3.16 Cones and the coefficient-space geometry. ℓ^1 Minimization uniquely recovers $\boldsymbol{x}_o$ if and only if the intersection of the descent cone D with $\mathrm{null}(\boldsymbol{A})$ is $\{\mathbf{0}\}$.

solution to the ℓ^1 problem if and only if $\mathbf{0}$ is the only point of intersection between $\text{null}(\boldsymbol{A})$ and D:

LEMMA 3.34. *Suppose that* $\boldsymbol{y} = \boldsymbol{A}\boldsymbol{x}_o$. *Then* $\boldsymbol{x}_o$ *is the unique optimal solution to the* ℓ^1 *minimization problem*

$$\begin{array}{ll} \min & \|\boldsymbol{x}\|_1 \\ \text{subject to} & \boldsymbol{A}\boldsymbol{x} = \boldsymbol{y} \end{array} \tag{3.6.4}$$

if and only if $\mathsf{D} \cap \text{null}(\boldsymbol{A}) = \{\mathbf{0}\}$.

Proof First, suppose that $\mathsf{D} \cap \text{null}(\boldsymbol{A}) = \{\mathbf{0}\}$. Consider any alternative solution $\boldsymbol{x}'$. Then $\boldsymbol{x}' - \boldsymbol{x}_o \in \text{null}(\boldsymbol{A}) \setminus \{\mathbf{0}\}$. Since $\mathsf{D} \cap \text{null}(\boldsymbol{A}) = \{\mathbf{0}\}$, $\boldsymbol{x}' - \boldsymbol{x}_o \notin \mathsf{D}$, and so $\left\|\boldsymbol{x}'\right\|_1 > \|\boldsymbol{x}_o\|_1$, and $\boldsymbol{x}'$ is not an optimal solution. Since this holds for any feasible $\boldsymbol{x}'$, $\boldsymbol{x}_o$ is the unique optimal solution.

Conversely, suppose $\boldsymbol{x}_o$ is not the unique optimal solution. Then there exists $\boldsymbol{x}' \neq \boldsymbol{x}_o$ with $\left\|\boldsymbol{x}'\right\|_1 \le \|\boldsymbol{x}_o\|_1$. Thus $\boldsymbol{x}' - \boldsymbol{x}_o \in \mathsf{D}$. By feasibility, $\boldsymbol{x}' - \boldsymbol{x}_o \in \text{null}(\boldsymbol{A})$, and so $\mathsf{D} \cap \text{null}(\boldsymbol{A}) \neq \{\mathbf{0}\}$. □

Hence, to study whether ℓ^1 minimization succeeds, we may equivalently study whether the subspace $\text{null}(\boldsymbol{A})$ has nontrivial intersection with the cone D. Because $\boldsymbol{A}$ is a random matrix, $\text{null}(\boldsymbol{A})$ is a random subspace, of dimension $n - m$. If $\boldsymbol{A}$ is Gaussian, then $\text{null}(\boldsymbol{A})$ follows the uniform distribution on the set of subspaces $\mathsf{S} \subset \mathbb{R}^n$ of dimension $n - m$.[22] Clearly, the probability that the random subspace $\text{null}(\boldsymbol{A})$ intersects the descent cone D depends on the properties of D. Intuitively, we would expect intersections to be more likely if D is "big" in some sense.

In Chapter 6, we will generalize the notion of "dimension" to all closed convex cones and show that this dimension precisely characterizes the probability of a convex cone intersecting with a subspace (or another convex cone). The same techniques actually apply to a broad family of norms that promote sparsity or low dimensionality. In particular, we will show that the probability of correct recovery for ℓ^1 minimization undergoes a sharp transition at

$$m^\star = \psi\left(\frac{k}{n}\right) n. \tag{3.6.5}$$

Here, $\psi : [0,1] \to [0,1]$ is a function which takes as input the fraction $\eta = k/n$ of nonzeros, and describes the ratio $m^\star/n$ of number of measurements to the ambient dimension. The precise location ψ of the transition is given by the expression

$$\psi(\eta) = \min_{t \ge 0} \left\{ \eta(1 + t^2) + (1 - \eta)\sqrt{\frac{2}{\pi}} \int_t^\infty (s - t)^2 \exp\left(-\frac{s^2}{2}\right) ds \right\}. \tag{3.6.6}$$

The function ψ is somewhat complicated; in Chapter 6, we will demonstrate how it arises naturally from the geometry of ℓ^1 minimization. While there is no closed-form solution for the minimization over t in this formula, it can be calculated

[22] To be more precise, $\text{null}(\boldsymbol{A})$ is distributed according to the Haar (uniform) measure on the Grassmannian manifold $\mathsf{G}_{n,n-m}$, the set of $(n - m)$-dimensional subspaces in $\mathbb{R}^n$.

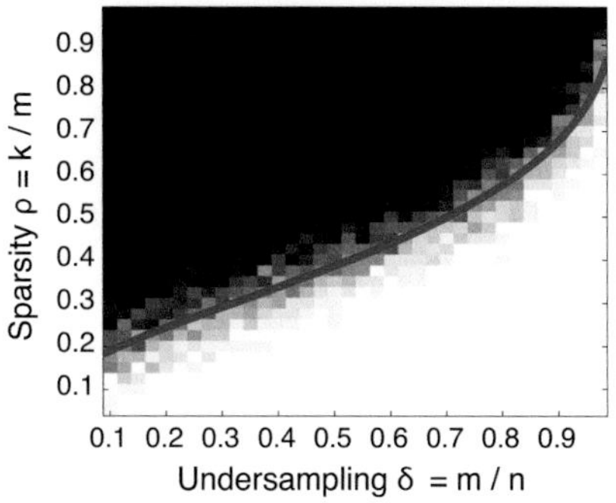

Figure 3.17 Phase transitions: agreement between theory and experiment. Theoretical phase transition predicted by (3.6.5) and (3.6.6), overlaid on fraction of successes in 200 experiments, for varying sparsities $\rho = k/m$ and undersampling $\delta = m/n$.

numerically. Figure 3.17 displays this curve (red) superimposed over the empirical fraction of successes (grayscale) in our experiment. Clearly, there is a very good agreement between this theoretical prediction and our previous experiment: the empirical fraction of successes transitions rapidly from 0 to 1 as m/n exceeds $\psi(k/n)$.[23]

In fact, one can do slightly more: in addition to showing that $\psi(t)$ determines a point of transition between likely success and likely failure, we can give lower bounds on the probability of success (below the phase transition) and failure (above the phase transition) which quantify how sharp the transition is, for finite n. The following theorem makes all of this precise:

THEOREM 3.35. *Let $\boldsymbol{x}_o \in \mathbb{R}^n$ be k-sparse, and suppose that $\boldsymbol{y} = \boldsymbol{A}\boldsymbol{x}_o \in \mathbb{R}^{m\times n}$, with $\boldsymbol{A} \sim_{\text{iid}} \mathcal{N}(0, 1/m)$. Let $m^\star = \psi(k/n)n$, with ψ as in* (3.6.6). *Then*

$$\mathbb{P}\Big[\ell^1 \text{ recovers } \boldsymbol{x}_o\Big] \geq 1 - C\exp\left(-c\frac{(m-m^\star)^2}{n}\right), \qquad m > m^\star,$$

$$\mathbb{P}\Big[\ell^1 \text{ does not recover } \boldsymbol{x}_o\Big] \geq 1 - c'\exp\left(-C'\frac{(m^\star-m)^2}{n}\right), \qquad m < m^\star,$$

where C, c, c', and C' are positive numerical constants.

Again, we leave the proof to Chapter 6 where we study phase transition in a more general setting. This result implies that a sharp transition indeed occurs at $m^\star$ measurements: when $m/n > m^\star/n + C''/\sqrt{n}$, the probability of failure is bounded by a small constant (which can be made arbitrarily small by choosing C'' large). Conversely, when $m/n < m^\star/n - C''/\sqrt{n}$, the probability of success is bounded by a small constant. Hence, the transition region observed in Figure 3.15 has width $O(1/\sqrt{n})$ – in particular, it vanishes as $n \to \infty$.

[23] Figure 3.17 displays the same phase transition as in Figure 3.15 in a different parameterization, in which the vertical axis is $\rho = k/m$ and the horizontal axis is $\delta = m/n$.

3.6.3 Phase Transitions via Observation-Space Geometry

Historically, the first sharp estimates of the location of the phase transition were derived using the "observation-space" geometric picture of ℓ^1 minimization, which we reproduce in Figure 3.4. In this picture, ℓ^1 minimization is visualized through the relationship between two convex polytopes, the unit ℓ^1 ball,

$$\mathsf{B}_1 \doteq \{\boldsymbol{x} \mid \|\boldsymbol{x}\|_1 \le 1\}, \tag{3.6.7}$$

and its projection into $\mathbb{R}^m$,

$$\mathsf{P} \doteq \boldsymbol{A}(\mathsf{B}_1) = \{\boldsymbol{A}\boldsymbol{x} \mid \|\boldsymbol{x}\|_1 \le 1\}. \tag{3.6.8}$$

Namely, ℓ^1 minimization uniquely recovers any $\boldsymbol{x}$ with support I and signs $\boldsymbol{\sigma}$ if and only if

$$\mathsf{F} \doteq \operatorname{conv}(\{\sigma_i \boldsymbol{a}_i \mid i \in \mathsf{I}\}) \tag{3.6.9}$$

forms a face of the polytope P. Conversely, if F intersects the interior of P, then ℓ^1 minimization does not recover $\boldsymbol{x}_o$ with support I and signs $\boldsymbol{\sigma}$.

The first results bounding the phase transition derived from remarkable results in stochastic geometry, which give exact formulas for the expected number of k-dimensional faces of a randomly projected polytope $\mathsf{P} = \boldsymbol{A}(\mathsf{Q})$. This expectation depends on two notions of the "size" of the polytope Q: the *internal angle* and *external angle*.

DEFINITION 3.36. (Internal angle) *The internal angle* $\beta(\mathsf{F},\mathsf{G})$ *of a face* F *of a polytope* G *is the fraction of* $\operatorname{span}(\mathsf{G}-\boldsymbol{x})$ *occupied by* $\mathsf{G}-\boldsymbol{x}$, *where* $\operatorname{span}(\cdot)$ *denotes the linear span, and* $\boldsymbol{x}$ *is any point in* $\operatorname{relint}(\mathsf{F})$, *the relative interior of* F.

The internal angle is visualized for several examples in Figure 3.18. Informally speaking, the internal angle measures the fraction of the space cut out by G, when viewed from F. There is a complementary notion of angle, called the external angle, which captures the fraction of the space cut out by the *normal cone* to G at a point in the relative interior of F:

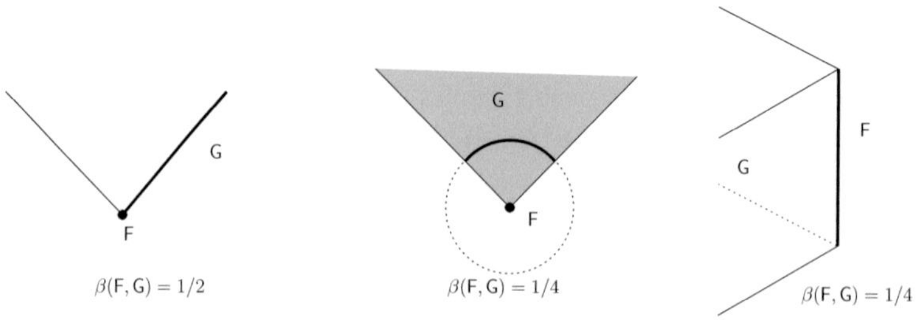

Figure 3.18 Internal angles of convex polytopes. The internal angle $\beta(\mathsf{F},\mathsf{G})$ of a face $\mathsf{F} \subseteq \mathsf{G}$ with respect to another face G containing it is the fraction of the linear span of $\mathsf{G}-\boldsymbol{x}$ occupied by $\mathsf{G}-\boldsymbol{x}$, where $\boldsymbol{x}$ is any point in the relative interior of F.

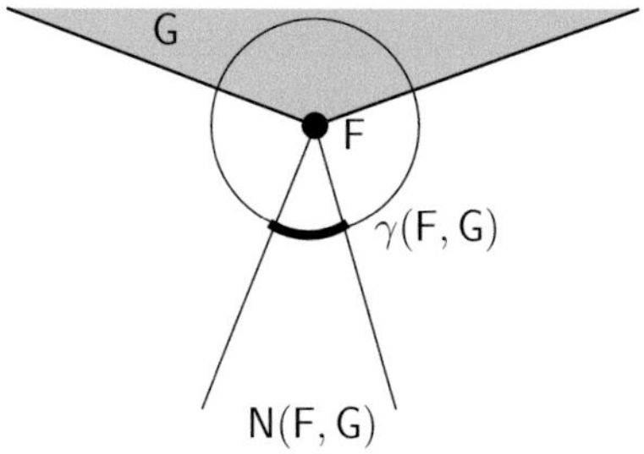

Figure 3.19 External angles of convex polytopes. The external angle $\gamma(\mathsf{F},\mathsf{G})$ of a face $\mathsf{F} \subseteq \mathsf{G}$ with respect to another face G containing it is the fraction of the linear span of $\mathsf{G} - \boldsymbol{x}$ occupied by the normal cone $\mathsf{N}(\mathsf{F},\mathsf{G})$.

DEFINITION 3.37. (External angle) *The external angle* $\gamma(\mathsf{F},\mathsf{G})$ *of a face* $\mathsf{F} \subseteq \mathsf{G}$ *is the fraction of* $\mathrm{span}(\mathsf{G} - \boldsymbol{x})$ *occupied by the normal cone*

$$\mathsf{N}(\mathsf{F},\mathsf{G}) = \left\{ \boldsymbol{v} \in \mathrm{span}(\mathsf{G} - \boldsymbol{x}) \mid \langle \boldsymbol{v} - \boldsymbol{x}, \boldsymbol{x}' - \boldsymbol{x} \rangle \leq 0 \;\forall\, \boldsymbol{x}' \in \mathsf{G} \right\},$$

where $\boldsymbol{x}$ *is any point in* $\mathrm{relint}(\mathsf{F})$.

Figure 3.19 visualizes the external angle. There is an exquisite characterization of the expected number of k-dimensional faces of a random projection of a convex polytope P, in terms of its internal and external angles. Let $f_k(\mathsf{P})$ denote the number of k-dimensional faces of a polytope P, and let F_k denote the collection of such faces. Then for an $m \times n$ Gaussian matrix $\boldsymbol{A}$,

$$\mathbb{E}_{\boldsymbol{A}}[f_k(\boldsymbol{A}\mathsf{P})] = f_k(\mathsf{P}) - \underbrace{2 \sum_{\ell = m+1, m+3, \ldots} \; \sum_{\mathsf{F} \in \mathsf{F}_k(\mathsf{P})} \; \sum_{\mathsf{G} \in \mathsf{F}_\ell(\mathsf{P})} \beta(\mathsf{F},\mathsf{G})\gamma(\mathsf{G},\mathsf{P})}_{\Delta = \text{expected number of faces lost}}.$$

This formula arises out of a line of work in discrete geometry, which aims at understanding the behavior of "typical" point clouds, and studying the simplex method for linear programming for "typical" inputs. One remarkable aspect is that it gives the *exact* value of the expected face count. The connection to ℓ^1 minimization is that ℓ^1 successfully recovers every $(k+1)$-sparse vector $\boldsymbol{x}_o$ from measurements $\boldsymbol{A}\boldsymbol{x}_o$ if and only if $f_k(\boldsymbol{A}(\mathsf{P})) = f_k(\mathsf{P})$. This can be observed from the observation-space geometry described above. This event can be studied through the quantity Δ – the expected number of faces lost. Whenever $\Delta < 1$, there exists an $\boldsymbol{A}$ such that $f_k(\boldsymbol{A}(\mathsf{P})) = f_k(\mathsf{P})$; when Δ is substantially smaller than one, we can use the Markov inequality to argue that the probability that any face is lost in the projection is small.

3.6.4 Phase Transitions in Support Recovery

Thus far, we have focused on the problem of *estimating* a sparse vector $\boldsymbol{x}_o$. We showed that from noisy observations $\boldsymbol{y} = \boldsymbol{A}\boldsymbol{x}_o + \boldsymbol{z}$, convex optimization produces a vector $\hat{\boldsymbol{x}}$ such that $\left\| \hat{\boldsymbol{x}} - \boldsymbol{x}_o \right\|_2$ is small. For many engineering applications, where $\boldsymbol{x}_o$ represents a signal to be sensed or an error to be corrected, this is exactly what we need. However, in some applications, the goal is not so much to estimate $\boldsymbol{x}_o$ as to determine which of the entries of $\boldsymbol{x}_o$ are nonzero. A good example, which we will revisit in later chapters, is in spectrum sensing for wireless communications. Here, the entries of $\boldsymbol{x}_o$ represent frequency bands which might be available for transmission, or which might be occupied. The goal is to know which frequency bands are available, so that we can avoid interfering with other users. In this setting, it is much more important to know which entries of $\boldsymbol{x}_o$ are nonzero than to estimate the particular values.

Support Recovery: Desiderata

In this section, we consider the problem of estimating the signed support

$$\sigma_o = \operatorname{sign}(\boldsymbol{x}_o) \tag{3.6.10}$$

from noisy observations

$$\boldsymbol{y} = \boldsymbol{A}\boldsymbol{x}_o + \boldsymbol{z}. \tag{3.6.11}$$

We will derive theory under the assumptions that the noise $\boldsymbol{z}$ is i.i.d. $\mathcal{N}(0, \sigma^2/m)$. Let $\hat{\boldsymbol{x}}$ solve the Lasso problem

$$\min_{\boldsymbol{x} \in \mathbb{R}^n} \tfrac{1}{2} \|\boldsymbol{y} - \boldsymbol{A}\boldsymbol{x}\|_2^2 + \lambda \|\boldsymbol{x}\|_1 . \tag{3.6.12}$$

We can distinguish between two conclusions.

- **Partial support recovery**: $\operatorname{supp}(\hat{\boldsymbol{x}}) \subseteq \operatorname{supp}(\boldsymbol{x}_o)$. Our estimator exhibits no "false positives": every element of the estimated support is an element of the true support.
- **Signed support recovery**: $\operatorname{sign}(\hat{\boldsymbol{x}}) = \sigma_o$. Our estimator correctly determines the nonzero entries of $\boldsymbol{x}_o$ and their signs.

Signed support recovery is clearly more desirable than partial support recovery. Signed support recovery requires stronger assumptions of the signal $\boldsymbol{x}_o$ than partial support recovery – if the nonzero entries of $\boldsymbol{x}_o$ are too small relative to the noise level σ, no method of any kind will be able to reliably determine the support.

In contrast, partial support recovery can be studied without additional assumptions on the signal $\boldsymbol{x}_o$. We will assume that $\boldsymbol{A} \sim_{\text{iid}} \mathcal{N}(0, 1/m)$. We will first derive a sharp phase transition for partial support recovery, at

$$m_\star = 2k \log(n - k) \tag{3.6.13}$$

measurements. The main result of this section will show that when m significantly exceeds this threshold, partial support recovery obtains with high probability. Moreover, through further analysis, we will show that when m significantly exceeds $m_\star$, *and* all of the nonzero entries of $\boldsymbol{x}_o$ are significantly larger than λ, *signed support recovery* also obtains with high probability. Conversely, if m is significantly smaller than $m_\star$, the probability of signed support recovery is vanishingly small. Thus, $m_\star$ indeed gives a sharp threshold for support recovery. Notice that (3.6.13) grows roughly as $k \log n$, rather than $k \log(n/k)$. So, if m, n, and k grow in fixed ratios, support recovery is unlikely. In this sense, support recovery is a more challenging problem than estimation.

The following theorem makes the above discussion precise:

THEOREM 3.38. (Phase transition in partial support recovery) *Suppose that* $\boldsymbol{A} \in \mathbb{R}^{m \times n}$ *with entries i.i.d.* $\mathcal{N}(0, 1/m)$ *random variables, and let* $\boldsymbol{y} = \boldsymbol{A}\boldsymbol{x}_o + \boldsymbol{z}$, *with* $\boldsymbol{x}_o$ *a* k*-sparse vector and* $\boldsymbol{z} \sim_{\text{iid}} \mathcal{N}\left(0, \sigma^2/m\right)$. *If*

$$m \geq \left(1 + \frac{\sigma^2}{\lambda^2 k} + \varepsilon\right) 2k \log(n - k), \tag{3.6.14}$$

then with probability at least $1 - Cn^{-\varepsilon}$, *any solution* $\hat{\boldsymbol{x}}$ *to the Lasso problem*

$$\min_{\boldsymbol{x} \in \mathbb{R}^n} \tfrac{1}{2} \|\boldsymbol{y} - \boldsymbol{A}\boldsymbol{x}\|_2^2 + \lambda \|\boldsymbol{x}\|_1 \tag{3.6.15}$$

satisfies $\operatorname{supp}(\hat{\boldsymbol{x}}) \subseteq \operatorname{supp}(\boldsymbol{x}_o)$. *Conversely, if*

$$m < \left(1 + \frac{\sigma^2}{\lambda^2 k} - \varepsilon\right) 2k \log(n - k), \tag{3.6.16}$$

then the probability that there exists a solution $\hat{\boldsymbol{x}}$ *of the Lasso which satisfies* $\operatorname{sign}(\hat{\boldsymbol{x}}) = \operatorname{sign}(\boldsymbol{x}_o)$ *is at most* $Cn^{-\varepsilon}$. *Above,* $C > 0$ *is a positive numerical constant.*

Partial vs. (Exact) Signed Support Recovery

The notion of support recovery in Theorem 3.38 is somewhat weak: it only demands that

$$\operatorname{supp}(\hat{\boldsymbol{x}}) \subseteq \operatorname{supp}(\boldsymbol{x}_o). \tag{3.6.17}$$

Put another way, *the support contains no false positives*. In many applications, we would like to *exactly* recover the support – i.e., we would like

$$\operatorname{supp}(\hat{\boldsymbol{x}}) = \operatorname{supp}(\boldsymbol{x}_o). \tag{3.6.18}$$

For this, we need that the nonzero entries of $\boldsymbol{x}_o$ are not too small, so that they do not become "lost" in the noise. Under (3.6.14), it is possible to show that exact support recovery occurs, as long as the smallest nonzero entry of $\boldsymbol{x}_o$ is larger than λ: if

$$\min_{i \in \mathsf{I}} |\boldsymbol{x}_{oi}| \; > \; C\lambda, \tag{3.6.19}$$

then $\operatorname{sign}(\hat{\boldsymbol{x}}) = \boldsymbol{\sigma}_o$ with high probability. In the remainder of this section, we will prove Theorem 3.38. Exercise 3.18 guides the reader through an extension of this argument, which shows that under the same assumptions,

$$\left\|\hat{\boldsymbol{x}} - \boldsymbol{x}_o\right\|_\infty < C\lambda. \tag{3.6.20}$$

When the nonzero entries of $\boldsymbol{x}_o$ have magnitude at least $C\lambda$, this implies that $\operatorname{sign}(\hat{\boldsymbol{x}}) = \boldsymbol{\sigma}_o$, as desired.

Main Ideas of the Proof of Theorem 3.38

The phase transition in Theorem 3.38 has a strikingly simple formula: $m_\star = 2k\log(n-k)$. The proof of this result is similar in spirit to our first proof of the correctness of ℓ^1 minimization, Theorem 3.3, which directly manipulated the optimality conditions for the recovery program.

By differentiating the objective function (3.6.15), we can show that a given vector $\hat{\boldsymbol{x}}$ is optimal if and only if

$$\boldsymbol{A}^*\left(\boldsymbol{y}-\boldsymbol{A}\hat{\boldsymbol{x}}\right) \in \lambda\partial\left\|\cdot\right\|_1(\hat{\boldsymbol{x}}). \tag{3.6.21}$$

Let $\mathsf{J} = \mathrm{supp}(\hat{\boldsymbol{x}})$. Recall that the subdifferential $\partial\left\|\cdot\right\|_1(\hat{\boldsymbol{x}})$ consists of those vectors $\boldsymbol{v} \in \mathbb{R}^n$ such that $\boldsymbol{v}_\mathsf{J} = \mathrm{sign}(\hat{\boldsymbol{x}}_\mathsf{J})$ and $\|\boldsymbol{v}_{\mathsf{J}^c}\|_\infty \le 1$. Hence, the condition (3.6.21) decomposes into two conditions:

$$\boldsymbol{A}_\mathsf{J}^*\left(\boldsymbol{y}-\boldsymbol{A}\hat{\boldsymbol{x}}\right) = \lambda\,\mathrm{sign}(\hat{\boldsymbol{x}}_\mathsf{J}), \tag{3.6.22}$$

$$\left\|\boldsymbol{A}_{\mathsf{J}^c}^*\left(\boldsymbol{y}-\boldsymbol{A}\hat{\boldsymbol{x}}\right)\right\|_\infty \le \lambda. \tag{3.6.23}$$

Much like the proof of Theorem 3.3, we will proceed as follows: we will construct a guess at a solution vector $\boldsymbol{x}_\star$ such that the equality constraints in (3.6.22) are automatically satisfied. We will then be left to check the inequality constraints (3.6.23). In particular, we will construct our guess $\boldsymbol{x}_\star$ at the solution by solving a *restricted* Lasso problem

$$\boldsymbol{x}_\star \in \underset{\mathrm{supp}(\boldsymbol{x})\subseteq\mathsf{I}}{\mathrm{argmin}}\left\{\tfrac{1}{2}\left\|\boldsymbol{A}\boldsymbol{x}-\boldsymbol{y}\right\|_2^2 + \lambda\left\|\boldsymbol{x}\right\|_1\right\}, \tag{3.6.24}$$

where $\mathsf{I} = \mathrm{supp}(\boldsymbol{x}_o)$.

Recall that $\boldsymbol{y} = \boldsymbol{A}\boldsymbol{x}_o + \boldsymbol{z}$. We can write

$$\boldsymbol{r} \doteq \boldsymbol{y} - \boldsymbol{A}\boldsymbol{x}_\star = \boldsymbol{A}_\mathsf{I}(\boldsymbol{x}_{o\mathsf{I}} - \boldsymbol{x}_{\star\mathsf{I}}) + \boldsymbol{z}. \tag{3.6.25}$$

Notice that $\boldsymbol{r}$ depends only on $\boldsymbol{A}_\mathsf{I}$ and $\boldsymbol{z}$; it is probabilistically independent of $\boldsymbol{A}_{\mathsf{I}^c}$. The key work that we will do in proving Theorem 3.38 is to determine whether the ℓ^∞ norm constraint is satisfied on I^c. That is to say, we need to study

$$\left\|\boldsymbol{A}_{\mathsf{I}^c}^*\left(\boldsymbol{y}-\boldsymbol{A}\boldsymbol{x}_\star\right)\right\|_\infty = \left\|\boldsymbol{A}_{\mathsf{I}^c}^*\boldsymbol{r}\right\|_\infty. \tag{3.6.26}$$

The matrix $\boldsymbol{A}_{\mathsf{I}^c}$ is a Gaussian matrix; moreover, it is probabilistically independent of $\boldsymbol{r}$. Conditioned on $\boldsymbol{r}$, $\boldsymbol{A}_{\mathsf{I}^c}^*\boldsymbol{r}$ is distributed as an $(n-k)$-dimensional i.i.d. $\mathcal{N}\left(0, \|\boldsymbol{r}\|_/ 2^2 m\right)$ random vector. We will see that the ℓ^∞ norm of such a vector is sharply concentrated about $\|\boldsymbol{r}\|_2\sqrt{2\log(n-k)/m}$. The following lemma provides the control that we need:

LEMMA 3.39. *Suppose that $\boldsymbol{q} = [q_1, \ldots, q_d]^* \in \mathbb{R}^d$ is a $d \ge 2$ dimensional random vector, whose elements are independent $\mathcal{N}(0,\xi^2)$ random variables. Then, for any $\varepsilon \in [0,1)$,*

$$\mathbb{P}\left[\|\boldsymbol{q}\|_\infty < \xi\sqrt{(2-\varepsilon)\log d}\right] \le \exp\left(-\frac{d^{\varepsilon/2}}{4\sqrt{2\log d}}\right), \tag{3.6.27}$$

$$\mathbb{P}\left[\|\boldsymbol{q}\|_\infty > \xi\sqrt{(2+\varepsilon)\log d}\right] \le 2d^{-\varepsilon/2}. \tag{3.6.28}$$

This lemma can be proved using relatively elementary ideas (the union bound for the upper bound, a direct calculation for the lower bound). Using this lemma, we conclude that, conditioned on $\boldsymbol{r}$ (i.e., with high probability in $\boldsymbol{A}_{\mathsf{I}^c}$), $\left\| \boldsymbol{A}_{\mathsf{I}^c}^* \boldsymbol{r} \right\|_\infty$ is very close to $\|\boldsymbol{r}\|_2 \sqrt{2 \log(n-k)/m}$. To understand whether this quantity is smaller than λ (and hence recovery succeeds) or larger than λ (and hence recovery fails), we will need to study the norm of $\boldsymbol{r}$.

Notice that $\boldsymbol{r} = \boldsymbol{A}_{\mathsf{I}}(\boldsymbol{x}_{o\mathsf{I}} - \boldsymbol{x}_{\star\mathsf{I}}) + \boldsymbol{z}$. To study the size of $\boldsymbol{r}$ it will be important to understand the properties of the random matrix $\boldsymbol{A}_{\mathsf{I}}$ and the random vector $\boldsymbol{z}$. Because $\boldsymbol{A}_{\mathsf{I}} \in \mathbb{R}^{m \times k}$ is a "tall," random matrix, it is well conditioned, in a sense that the following lemma makes precise:

LEMMA 3.40. *Let $\boldsymbol{G} \in \mathbb{R}^{m \times k}$ be a random matrix whose entries are i.i.d. $\mathcal{N}(0, 1/m)$ random variables. Then, with high probability*

$$\left\| \boldsymbol{G}^* \boldsymbol{G} - \boldsymbol{I} \right\|_{\ell^2 \to \ell^2} \le C \sqrt{k/m}. \tag{3.6.29}$$

The proof of this lemma follows similar lines to our proof of the RIP property of Gaussian matrices (discretization, tail bound, union bound). Using this lemma, we can control $\|\boldsymbol{r}\|_2$; combining with the above calculations, we obtain control on $\left\| \boldsymbol{A}_{\mathsf{I}^c}^* \boldsymbol{r} \right\|_\infty$. The prescription for the required number of measurements m follows by demanding that this quantity be smaller than λ. To formally prove Theorem 3.38, we need to do a bit more. First, we need to formally control $\|\boldsymbol{r}\|_2$ and $\left\| \boldsymbol{A}_{\mathsf{I}^c}^* \boldsymbol{r} \right\|_\infty$. This is sufficient to show that our putative solution $\boldsymbol{x}_\star$ is indeed optimal. Second, we need to argue that under the same conditions, *every* solution $\hat{\boldsymbol{x}}$ indeed satisfies $\mathrm{supp}(\hat{\boldsymbol{x}}) \subseteq \mathrm{supp}(\boldsymbol{x}_o)$. This will follow from some auxiliary reasoning about the subdifferential of the ℓ^1 norm. Finally, we obtain the converse portion of Theorem 3.38 by showing that when the number of measurements $m \ll m_\star$, with high probability $\left\| \boldsymbol{A}_{\mathsf{I}^c}^* \boldsymbol{r} \right\|_\infty > \lambda$, and hence no putative solution $\boldsymbol{x}_\star$ with $\mathrm{sign}(\boldsymbol{x}_\star) = \boldsymbol{\sigma}_o$ can be optimal. We carry through all of this reasoning rigorously below.

Proof of theorem 3.38 We proceed as follows.

(i) Sufficient condition for partial support recovery
Let $\mathsf{I} = \mathrm{supp}(\boldsymbol{x}_o)$. We wish to show that every solution $\hat{\boldsymbol{x}}$ to the Lasso problem

$$\min_{\boldsymbol{x} \in \mathbb{R}^n} \varphi(\boldsymbol{x}) \doteq \tfrac{1}{2} \|\boldsymbol{y} - \boldsymbol{A}\boldsymbol{x}\|_2^2 + \lambda \|\boldsymbol{x}\|_1 \tag{3.6.30}$$

satisfies $\mathrm{supp}(\boldsymbol{x}) \subseteq \mathsf{I}$. To do this, we will generate a vector $\boldsymbol{x}_\star$ with $\mathrm{supp}(\boldsymbol{x}_\star) \subseteq \mathsf{I}$, such that the residual

$$\boldsymbol{r} = \boldsymbol{y} - \boldsymbol{A}\boldsymbol{x}_\star \tag{3.6.31}$$

satisfies

$$\boldsymbol{A}^* \boldsymbol{r} \in \lambda \partial \left\| \cdot \right\|_1 (\boldsymbol{x}_\star), \tag{3.6.32}$$

and

$$\left\| \boldsymbol{A}_{\mathsf{I}^c}^* \boldsymbol{r} \right\|_\infty < \lambda. \tag{3.6.33}$$

The first property implies that $\boldsymbol{x}_\star$ is optimal for the Lasso problem, since it implies that

$$\begin{aligned}\mathbf{0} \in \partial\varphi(\boldsymbol{x}_\star) &= \boldsymbol{A}^*(\boldsymbol{A}\boldsymbol{x}_\star - \boldsymbol{y}) + \lambda\partial\left\|\cdot\right\|_1(\boldsymbol{x}_\star)\\ &= -\boldsymbol{r} + \lambda\partial\left\|\cdot\right\|_1(\boldsymbol{x}_\star).\end{aligned} \tag{3.6.34}$$

The property $\left\|\boldsymbol{A}_{\mathsf{I}^c}^*\boldsymbol{r}\right\|_\infty < \lambda$ implies that any other optimal solution *also* has support contained in I. The reason is as follows: let $\lambda' = \lambda - \left\|\boldsymbol{A}_{\mathsf{I}^c}^*\boldsymbol{r}\right\|_\infty > 0$. Then for any vector $\boldsymbol{v}$ supported on I^c, with $\|\boldsymbol{v}\|_\infty < \lambda'$, we have that

$$\boldsymbol{v} \in \partial\varphi_{\text{Lasso}}(\boldsymbol{x}_\star). \tag{3.6.35}$$

For any $\boldsymbol{x}'$ with $\boldsymbol{x}'_{\mathsf{I}^c} \neq \mathbf{0}$, set $\boldsymbol{v} = \lambda' \operatorname{sign}(\boldsymbol{x}'_{\mathsf{I}^c})/2$ and note that by the subgradient inequality,

$$\begin{aligned}\varphi(\boldsymbol{x}') &\geq \varphi(\boldsymbol{x}_\star) + \langle \boldsymbol{x}' - \boldsymbol{x}_\star, \boldsymbol{v}\rangle\\ &= \varphi(\boldsymbol{x}_\star) + \frac{\lambda'}{2}\left\|\boldsymbol{x}'_{\mathsf{I}^c}\right\|_1\\ &> \varphi(\boldsymbol{x}_\star),\end{aligned} \tag{3.6.36}$$

and hence $\boldsymbol{x}'$ is not optimal. Thus, if there exists an $\boldsymbol{x}_\star$ satisfying (3.6.32)–(3.6.33), then every solution $\hat{\boldsymbol{x}}$ to the Lasso problem satisfies $\operatorname{supp}(\hat{\boldsymbol{x}}) \subseteq \operatorname{supp}(\boldsymbol{x}_o)$.

(ii) Constructing the putative solution $\boldsymbol{x}_\star$

Let

$$\boldsymbol{x}_\star \in \arg\min_{\operatorname{supp}(\boldsymbol{x})\subseteq\mathsf{I}} \tfrac{1}{2}\left\|\boldsymbol{y} - \boldsymbol{A}\boldsymbol{x}\right\|_2^2 + \lambda\left\|\boldsymbol{x}\right\|_1. \tag{3.6.37}$$

Let $\mathsf{J} = \operatorname{supp}(\boldsymbol{x}_\star) \subseteq \mathsf{I}$. The Karush–Kuhn–Tucker (KKT) optimality conditions for this problem give that

$$\boldsymbol{A}_{\mathsf{J}}^*(\boldsymbol{y} - \boldsymbol{A}_{\mathsf{I}}\boldsymbol{x}_{\star\mathsf{I}}) = \lambda \operatorname{sign}(\boldsymbol{x}_{\star\mathsf{J}}), \tag{3.6.38}$$

$$\left\|\boldsymbol{A}_{\mathsf{I}\setminus\mathsf{J}}^*(\boldsymbol{y} - \boldsymbol{A}_{\mathsf{I}}\boldsymbol{x}_{\star\mathsf{I}})\right\|_\infty \leq \lambda. \tag{3.6.39}$$

An equivalent way of expressing these conditions is to say that

$$\boldsymbol{A}_{\mathsf{I}}^*(\boldsymbol{y} - \boldsymbol{A}_{\mathsf{I}}\boldsymbol{x}_{\star\mathsf{I}}) = \lambda\boldsymbol{\nu}, \tag{3.6.40}$$

for some $\boldsymbol{\nu} \in \partial\left\|\cdot\right\|_1(\boldsymbol{x}_{\star\mathsf{I}})$.

Because $\boldsymbol{y} = \boldsymbol{A}_{\mathsf{I}}\boldsymbol{x}_{o\mathsf{I}} + \boldsymbol{z}$, we can use (3.6.40) to express the difference $\boldsymbol{x}_{o\mathsf{I}} - \boldsymbol{x}_{\star\mathsf{I}}$ in terms of the subgradient $\boldsymbol{\nu}$ and the noise $\boldsymbol{z}$:

$$\boldsymbol{x}_{o\mathsf{I}} - \boldsymbol{x}_{\star\mathsf{I}} = (\boldsymbol{A}_{\mathsf{I}}^*\boldsymbol{A}_{\mathsf{I}})^{-1}\left(\lambda\boldsymbol{\nu} - \boldsymbol{A}_{\mathsf{I}}^*\boldsymbol{z}\right). \tag{3.6.41}$$

Notice that since $m > k$, with probability one, $\boldsymbol{A}_{\mathsf{I}}^*\boldsymbol{A}_{\mathsf{I}}$ is invertible, and so this expression indeed makes sense.

(iii) Verifying the KKT conditions
We will prove that the restricted solution $\boldsymbol{x}_\star$ is indeed optimal for the full problem (3.6.30). The KKT conditions for *this problem* give that $\boldsymbol{x}_\star$ is optimal if and only if

$$\boldsymbol{A}^* \left(\boldsymbol{y} - \boldsymbol{A}\boldsymbol{x}_\star\right) \in \lambda \partial \left\|\cdot\right\|_1 (\boldsymbol{x}_\star). \tag{3.6.42}$$

Let $\mathsf{J} = \operatorname{supp}(\boldsymbol{x}_\star)$. The above expression can be broken into two parts as

$$\boldsymbol{A}_{\mathsf{J}}^* \left(\boldsymbol{y} - \boldsymbol{A}\boldsymbol{x}_\star\right) = \lambda \operatorname{sign}(\boldsymbol{x}_{\star \mathsf{J}}), \tag{3.6.43}$$

$$\left\|\boldsymbol{A}_{\mathsf{I}\cap\mathsf{J}^c}^* \left(\boldsymbol{y} - \boldsymbol{A}\boldsymbol{x}_\star\right)\right\|_\infty \le \lambda, \tag{3.6.44}$$

$$\left\|\boldsymbol{A}_{\mathsf{I}^c}^* \left(\boldsymbol{y} - \boldsymbol{A}\boldsymbol{x}_\star\right)\right\|_\infty \le \lambda. \tag{3.6.45}$$

Because $\boldsymbol{x}_{\star \mathsf{I}}$ satisfies the restricted KKT conditions, the first two conditions are automatically satisfied; to complete the proof, we establish the stronger version

$$\left\|\boldsymbol{A}_{\mathsf{I}^c}^* \left(\boldsymbol{y} - \boldsymbol{A}\boldsymbol{x}_\star\right)\right\|_\infty < \lambda \tag{3.6.46}$$

of the third – this is the condition (3.6.33) that $\|\boldsymbol{r}\|_\infty < \lambda$. Using (3.6.41), we can express the residual $\boldsymbol{y} - \boldsymbol{A}\boldsymbol{x}_\star$ as

$$\begin{aligned} \boldsymbol{r} &\doteq \boldsymbol{y} - \boldsymbol{A}\boldsymbol{x}_\star \\ &= \left[\boldsymbol{I} - \boldsymbol{A}_{\mathsf{I}}(\boldsymbol{A}_{\mathsf{I}}^*\boldsymbol{A}_{\mathsf{I}})^{-1}\boldsymbol{A}_{\mathsf{I}}^*\right]\boldsymbol{z} + \boldsymbol{A}_{\mathsf{I}}(\boldsymbol{A}_{\mathsf{I}}^*\boldsymbol{A}_{\mathsf{I}})^{-1}\lambda\boldsymbol{v}. \end{aligned} \tag{3.6.47}$$

The two components of $\boldsymbol{r}$ are orthogonal, and so

$$\begin{aligned} \|\boldsymbol{r}\|_2 &= \sqrt{\left\|\left[\boldsymbol{I} - \boldsymbol{A}_{\mathsf{I}}(\boldsymbol{A}_{\mathsf{I}}^*\boldsymbol{A}_{\mathsf{I}})^{-1}\boldsymbol{A}_{\mathsf{I}}^*\right]\boldsymbol{z}\right\|_2^2 + \left\|\boldsymbol{A}_{\mathsf{I}}(\boldsymbol{A}_{\mathsf{I}}^*\boldsymbol{A}_{\mathsf{I}})^{-1}\lambda\boldsymbol{v}\right\|_2^2} \\ &\le \sqrt{\|\boldsymbol{z}\|_2^2 + \lambda^2 \frac{\|\boldsymbol{v}\|_2^2}{\sigma_{\min}(\boldsymbol{A}_{\mathsf{I}}^*\boldsymbol{A}_{\mathsf{I}})}} \\ &\le \sqrt{\sigma^2 + \frac{\lambda^2 k}{1 - Ck/m}} \qquad \text{with high probability} \\ &\le \sqrt{\sigma^2 + \lambda^2 k + C'\lambda^2 k^2/m}. \end{aligned} \tag{3.6.48}$$

Applying the above lemma, with high probability in $\boldsymbol{A}_{\mathsf{I}^c}$,

$$\begin{aligned} \left\|\boldsymbol{A}_{\mathsf{I}^c}^*\boldsymbol{r}\right\|_\infty &< \sqrt{\frac{(2+\varepsilon)\log(n-k)}{m}}\,\|\boldsymbol{r}\|_2 \\ &\le \lambda \left(\frac{2k\log(n-k)\left(1 + \sigma^2/\lambda^2 k + \varepsilon\right)}{m}\right)^{1/2}. \end{aligned} \tag{3.6.49}$$

Under our hypothesis on m, this is strictly smaller than λ, and so indeed (3.6.33) is verified.

(iv) No signed support recovery when $m \ll m_\star$

We next prove that when m is significantly smaller than $2k\log(n-k)$, no vector $\boldsymbol{x}$ satisfying

$$\mathrm{sign}(\boldsymbol{x}) = \mathrm{sign}(\boldsymbol{x}_o) \tag{3.6.50}$$

can be a solution to the Lasso problem. Without loss of generality, we can assume that $m \geq k$.[24] Suppose on the contrary that $\boldsymbol{x}$ was the solution to the Lasso problem. Then $\boldsymbol{x}$ is also the solution to the restricted Lasso problem. Moreover, since $\mathrm{sign}(\boldsymbol{x}_{\mathsf{I}}) = \boldsymbol{\sigma}_{\mathsf{I}}$ has no zero entries, we have

$$\boldsymbol{r} = \left[\boldsymbol{I} - \boldsymbol{A}_{\mathsf{I}}(\boldsymbol{A}_{\mathsf{I}}^*\boldsymbol{A}_{\mathsf{I}})^{-1}\boldsymbol{A}_{\mathsf{I}}^*\right]\boldsymbol{z} + \lambda\boldsymbol{A}_{\mathsf{I}}(\boldsymbol{A}_{\mathsf{I}}^*\boldsymbol{A}_{\mathsf{I}})^{-1}\boldsymbol{\sigma}_{\mathsf{I}}. \tag{3.6.52}$$

With high probability,

$$\left\|\left[\boldsymbol{I} - \boldsymbol{A}_{\mathsf{I}}(\boldsymbol{A}_{\mathsf{I}}^*\boldsymbol{A}_{\mathsf{I}})^{-1}\boldsymbol{A}_{\mathsf{I}}^*\right]\boldsymbol{z}\right\|_2^2 > (1-\varepsilon)(n-k)\sigma^2 \tag{3.6.53}$$

and

$$\left\|\boldsymbol{A}_{\mathsf{I}}(\boldsymbol{A}_{\mathsf{I}}^*\boldsymbol{A}_{\mathsf{I}})^{-1}\lambda\boldsymbol{\sigma}_{\mathsf{I}}\right\|_2^2 > \frac{\lambda^2 k}{1 + Ck/m}, \tag{3.6.54}$$

whence, with high probability,

$$\left\|\boldsymbol{A}_{\mathsf{I}^c}^*\boldsymbol{r}\right\|_\infty > \sqrt{\frac{(2-\varepsilon)\log(n-k)}{m}}\,\|\boldsymbol{r}\|_2 \tag{3.6.55}$$

and

$$\|\boldsymbol{r}\|_2 \geq \sqrt{\sigma^2(1 - ck/m) + \lambda^2 k(1 - c'k/m)}. \tag{3.6.56}$$

Combining, we obtain

$$\begin{aligned} \left\|\boldsymbol{A}_{\mathsf{I}^c}^*\boldsymbol{r}\right\|_\infty &> \lambda\sqrt{\frac{(2-\varepsilon)k\log(n-k)\left(1 + \sigma^2/\lambda^2 k + \varepsilon\right)}{m}} \\ &\geq \lambda. \end{aligned} \tag{3.6.57}$$

Hence, the putative solution $\boldsymbol{x}$ *is not* optimal for the full Lasso problem, with high probability in the matrix $\boldsymbol{A}$ and the noise $\boldsymbol{z}$. The above argument depends on $\boldsymbol{x}$ only through its sign and support pattern, and so on the same (large probability) bad event, *every* $\boldsymbol{x}$ having this sign and support pattern is suboptimal for the full Lasso problem. □

[24] If on the contrary, $m < k$, then the KKT conditions for the restricted problem become

$$\underbrace{\boldsymbol{A}_{\mathsf{I}}^*\boldsymbol{A}_{\mathsf{I}}}_{\text{rank deficient}} \quad \boldsymbol{x}_{\mathsf{I}} = \boldsymbol{A}_{\mathsf{I}}^*\boldsymbol{y} - \lambda\boldsymbol{\sigma}_{\mathsf{I}}. \tag{3.6.51}$$

This equation admits a solution if and only if $\boldsymbol{\sigma}_{\mathsf{I}} \in \mathrm{range}(\boldsymbol{A}_{\mathsf{I}}^*)$. Because $\boldsymbol{A}_{\mathsf{I}}^*$ is a tall Gaussian matrix, the probability that its range contains the fixed vector $\boldsymbol{\sigma}_{\mathsf{I}}$ is zero. So, when $m < k$, the probability that the Lasso problem admits a solution $\hat{\boldsymbol{x}}$ with $\mathrm{sign}(\hat{\boldsymbol{x}}) = \boldsymbol{\sigma}_o$ is zero.

3.7 Summary

In this chapter, we have provided a rather extensive and thorough study of conditions under which we can expect the ℓ^1 minimization

$$\min \|\boldsymbol{x}\|_1 \quad \text{subject to} \quad \boldsymbol{y} = \boldsymbol{A}\boldsymbol{x}$$

to recover a k-sparse vector $\boldsymbol{x}_o \in \mathbb{R}^n$ from the observation $\boldsymbol{y} = \boldsymbol{A}\boldsymbol{x}_o \in \mathbb{R}^m$. Such conditions are developed through three different perspectives that give increasingly sharper characterization about the conditions.

Mutual Coherence

The first approach is based on the notion of *mutual coherence* $\mu(\boldsymbol{A})$ of the measurement matrix $\boldsymbol{A}$, given in Definition 3.2.1. Theorem 3.3 shows that the ℓ^1 minimization finds the correct solution $\boldsymbol{x}_o$ if $k \le 1/2\mu(\boldsymbol{A})$. Based on an upper bound of $\mu(\boldsymbol{A})$ for a random matrix, Theorem 3.5, and a lower bound for an arbitrary matrix, Theorem 3.7, mutual coherence in general ensures that ℓ^1 minimization succeeds when

$$m = O(k^2).$$

Restricted Isometry Property

The *restricted isometric* measure $\delta_k(\boldsymbol{A})$ of a matrix $\boldsymbol{A}$, given in Definition 3.8, provides a more refined characterization of the incoherence property of the measurement $\boldsymbol{A}$, by restricting the notion of isometry to the k-dimensional structures of interest. Theorem 3.10 and Theorem 3.11 show that with high probability the ℓ^1 minimization can succeed in recovering a k-sparse vector from a generic $m \times n$ matrix $\boldsymbol{A}$ with

$$m = O\big(k \log(n/k)\big).$$

In the proportional growth model when $k \propto n$, this means the number of random measurements needed is $m = O(k)$.

Sharp Phase Transition

While the above two approaches give qualitative bounds on the number of random measurements needed for ℓ^1 to succeed, Section 3.6 gives a precise characterization of the sharp *phase transition behavior* for success or failure of ℓ^1 minimization around a critical number of measures

$$m^\star = \psi\Big(\frac{k}{n}\Big)n.$$

An explicit expression (3.6.6) for the function ψ can be derived from the statistical relationships between high-dimensional convex cones and subspaces, as we will study systematically in Chapter 6.

Sensitivity Analysis

The results given in Section 3.5 show that under similar conditions, ℓ^1 minimization, with slight modification, can recover a sufficiently accurate estimate $\hat{\boldsymbol{x}}$ of $\boldsymbol{x}_o$ when there is noise in the measurement $\boldsymbol{y} = \boldsymbol{A}\boldsymbol{x}_o + \boldsymbol{z}$ or the signal $\boldsymbol{x}_o$ is only approximately sparse. These results ensure that ℓ^1 minimization is not sensitive to the modeling assumption that the ground-truth vector $\boldsymbol{x}_o$ needs to be perfectly sparse. Theorem 3.38 shows that when the measurements are noisy, phase transition also occurs when we only care about recovering the correct sign and support of $\boldsymbol{x}_o$.

3.8 Notes

As we have mentioned before, historically ℓ^1 minimization was suggested to be beneficial as early as in the work of Boscovitch [Bos50] and later Laplace [Lap74]. To our knowledge, the first result that offers a guarantee for exact recovery of sparse signals via ℓ^1 minimization was obtained by Logan [Log65]. The advancement in computational power in recent years has made it possible to harness the tremendous benefits of ℓ^1 minimization in high-dimensional spaces, which has led to the revived interests in analyzing its sample and computational complexity more precisely.

Analyses of sparse recovery based on mutual coherence/incoherence are due to [GN03, DE03]. The proof approach described here is due to [Fuc04]. The stronger guarantee of ℓ^1 minimization via the notion of restricted isometry property (RIP) is due to the seminal work [CT05]. Our proof here follows closely that of [CRT06b, Can08]. The analysis of phase transitions via observation-space geometry was developed in a series of work [Don05, DT09, DT10]. The approach to phase transitions via coefficient-space geometry follows mainly the work of [ALMT14]. We will give a more detailed account of this approach in Chapter 6 where we justify why phase transitions occur for the recovery of a broad family of low-dimensional models. The analysis of phase transitions in support recovery is due to [Wai09b].

3.9 Exercises

3.1. (Projection of polytopes) *Notice that in* $\mathbb{R}^3$, *when we project an* ℓ^1 *ball* B_1 *to* $\mathbb{R}^2$, *in general all the vertices (1-faces) will be preserved. Does this generalize to higher-dimensional spaces? That is, if we project an* ℓ^1 *ball in* $\mathbb{R}^n$ *to* $\mathbb{R}^{n-1}$, *can we expect all* $(n-2)$*-faces be preserved by a generic projection? You may run some simulations and argue if your hypothesis is true or false.*

3.2. (Mutual coherence) *Compute by hand the mutual coherence of the matrix in Exercise 2.5. Then, program an algorithm that calculates the mutual coherence of a matrix. Generate an* $n \times n$ *discrete Fourier transform matrix* $\boldsymbol{F}$ *for a very large* n. *Randomly select half of its rows and compute its mutual coherence.*

3.3. (Comparisons between norms) *Show that for all* $\boldsymbol{x} \in \mathbb{R}^n$, *we have the following relationships among the three norms* $\|\cdot\|_1$, $\|\cdot\|_2$, *and* $\|\cdot\|_\infty$:

(a) $\|\boldsymbol{x}\|_2 \le \|\boldsymbol{x}\|_1 \le \sqrt{n}\,\|\boldsymbol{x}\|_2$,

(b) $\|\boldsymbol{x}\|_\infty \le \|\boldsymbol{x}\|_2 \le \sqrt{n}\,\|\boldsymbol{x}\|_\infty$,
(c) $\|\boldsymbol{x}\|_\infty \le \|\boldsymbol{x}\|_1 \le n\,\|\boldsymbol{x}\|_\infty$.

3.4. (Singular values of matrices) *Show that given a positive definite matrix* $\boldsymbol{S} \in \mathbb{R}^{n\times n}$*:*

(a) $\sigma_{\max}(\boldsymbol{S}^{-1}) = \sigma_{\min}(\boldsymbol{S})^{-1}$,
(b) *trace*$(\boldsymbol{S}) = \sum_{i=1}^n \sigma_i(\boldsymbol{S})$,
(c) $\|\boldsymbol{S}\|_F = \sqrt{\sum_{i=1}^n \sigma_i^2(\boldsymbol{S})}$.

3.5. *Given a matrix* $\boldsymbol{A} \in \mathbb{R}^{m\times n}$*:*

(a) *What is the relationship between singular values of a matrix* $\mathbf{A}$ *and* $\mathbf{A}^*\boldsymbol{A}$*?*
(b) *What is the comparison between the spectral norm* $\|\boldsymbol{A}\|$ *and the Frobenius norm of* $\|\boldsymbol{A}\|_F$*?*

3.6. *Prove the inequalities in* (3.2.3).

3.7. (Constrained optimization) *Consider the program:*

$$\min_{\boldsymbol{x}} f(\boldsymbol{x}) \quad \textit{subject to} \quad \boldsymbol{h}(\boldsymbol{x}) = \mathbf{0},$$

where $f(\cdot) \in \mathbb{R}$ *and* $\boldsymbol{h}(\cdot) \in \mathbb{R}^m$ *are all* C^1*-differentiable. Show that if* $\boldsymbol{x}_\star$ *is an optimal solution, we must have*

$$\nabla f(\boldsymbol{x}_\star) = \frac{\partial \boldsymbol{h}(\boldsymbol{x}_\star)}{\partial \boldsymbol{x}} \boldsymbol{\lambda}$$

for $\boldsymbol{\lambda} \in \mathbb{R}^m$*, where* $\partial \boldsymbol{h}(\boldsymbol{x}_\star)/\partial \boldsymbol{x}$ *is the Jacobian of* $\boldsymbol{h}(\cdot)$ *at* $\boldsymbol{x}_\star$*. Notice that in our context:*

(a) *The constraint is* $\boldsymbol{h}(\boldsymbol{x}) = \boldsymbol{A}\boldsymbol{x} - \boldsymbol{y}$*. What is its Jacobian, and what have the above conditions become?*
(b) *The function* $f(\cdot)$ *is not necessarily differentiable at* $\boldsymbol{x}_\star$*. Discuss how the above condition needs to be changed?*

A less relevant but otherwise useful question for bonus points: What if the constraints are replaced with inequalities $\boldsymbol{h}(\boldsymbol{x}) > \mathbf{0}$*?*

3.8. *Prove equation (3.2.34).*

3.9. *In this exercise, use the sphere measure concentration Theorem 3.6 to prove a fact mentioned in the Introduction chapter, equation (1.3.5): in* $\mathbb{R}^m$ *when the dimension m is high, a randomly chosen unit vector* $\boldsymbol{v} \in \mathbb{S}^{m-1}$ *is with high probability highly incoherent (nearly orthogonal) to any of the standard base vectors* $\boldsymbol{e}_i, i = 1, \dots, m$*. More precisely, given any small* $\varepsilon > 0$*, we have*

$$|\langle \boldsymbol{e}_i, \boldsymbol{v}\rangle| \le \varepsilon, \quad \forall\, i = 1, \dots, m,$$

with high probability as m is large enough. Hint: the proof should be very similar to, actually simpler than, the proof for Theorem 3.5. You only need to apply the measure concentration result to the functions $|\langle \boldsymbol{e}_i, \boldsymbol{v}\rangle|$ *and characterize the union bound for the failure probability of all m functions.*

3.10. (ℓ^1 minimization experiments) *Program an algorithm to solve the ℓ^1 minimization problem.*

(a) Set $m = n/2$ and set $k = \|x_o\|_0$ proportional to m – say, $k = m/4$. Then, try different aspect ratios $m = \alpha n$ and sparsity ratios $k = \beta m$.
(b) Validate the phase transition in Figure 3.15.

3.11. *Let A be a large $m \times n$ matrix with $m = n/4$. You are told that any submatrix A_I with $|\mathsf{I}| = k < m$ columns of A satisfies*

$$\forall\, x \in \mathbb{R}^k, \quad (1-\delta)\,\|x\|_2^2 \le \|A_\mathsf{I} x\|_2^2 \le (1+\delta)\,\|x\|_2^2$$

with $\delta \le 3\sqrt{k/m}$. Use this fact and Theorem 3.10 to give your best estimate of k as a fraction of n such that ℓ^1 minimization succeeds for all k-sparse vectors.

3.12. *Prove Lemma 3.15.*

3.13. (Johnson–Lindenstrauss) *Program an algorithm to validate the Johnson–Lindenstrauss lemma.*

3.14. *Prove Lemma 3.22.*

3.15. (Compact projection) *In this exercise, we use the properties of random projection to develop a simple but efficient algorithm for computing approximate nearest neighbors for a high-dimensional dataset. In particular, prove that the scheme described in Example 3.23 is correct and most efficient. Show that:*

(a) With the random binary code generated by Algorithm 3.1, with probability $1-\delta$, the c-NN problem can be solved on any (Δ, l)-weakly separable set $\mathcal{X}$ with the number of binary bits m chosen to be on the order

$$m = O\left(\frac{\log(2/\delta) + \log n}{(1-1/c)^2\Delta}\right).$$

(b) The correct solution to the c-NN problem is given by

$$x_\star = \arg\min_{x \in \tilde{\mathcal{X}}} \|x - q\|_2,$$

where $\tilde{\mathcal{X}}$ is the subset of points of size $O(n^l)$ in $\mathcal{X}$ which have the shortest Hamming distances to $y_q = \sigma(Rq)$.

(c) With the above results, show that the c-NN problem can be solved with the following complexity:[25]
- *Code construction $O(Dn\log n)$;*
- *Computation per query $O(n + Dn^l)$;*
- *Index space $O(n)$.*

[25] Note that, here, one can adopt the standard $(\log n)$-RAM computational model, in which arithmetic operations with $\log n$ bits can be performed in $O(1)$ time.

3.16. *Given a matrix* $\boldsymbol{A}$ *of full column rank, show that*

$$\|(\boldsymbol{A}^*\boldsymbol{A})^{-1}\boldsymbol{A}^*\boldsymbol{z}\|_2 \le \frac{1}{\sigma_{\min}(\boldsymbol{A})}\|\boldsymbol{z}\|_2.$$

3.17. (Restricted isometry property) *Program an algorithm that calculates the order-k RIP constant of a matrix:*

```
delta = rip(A, k).
```

Generate an $n \times n$ *discrete Fourier transform matrix* $\boldsymbol{F}$. *Randomly select half of its rows and compute its RIP constant. How large n can your algorithm go? Compare that with the case with mutual coherence.*

3.18. *Under the same assumption as Theorem 3.38, sketch a proof of signed support recovery in the sense of equation (3.6.20).*

4 Convex Methods for Low-Rank Matrix Recovery

"Mathematics is the art of giving the same name to different things."
– Henri Poincaré, *L'avenir des mathématiques, 1905*

In this chapter, we will branch out from sparse signals to a broader class of models: the low-rank matrices. Similar to the problem of recovering sparse signals, we consider how to recover a matrix $\boldsymbol{X} \in \mathbb{R}^{n_1 \times n_2}$ from linear measurements $\boldsymbol{y} = \mathcal{A}[\boldsymbol{X}] \in \mathbb{R}^m$. This problem can be phrased as searching for a solution $\boldsymbol{X}$ to a linear system of equations:

$$\mathcal{A}\Big[\underbrace{\boldsymbol{X}}_{\text{unknown}}\Big] = \underbrace{\boldsymbol{y}}_{\text{observation}} \tag{4.0.1}$$

Here, $\mathcal{A} : \mathbb{R}^{n_1 \times n_2} \to \mathbb{R}^m$ is a linear map.

We will see that much of the mathematical structure in the sparse vector recovery problem carries over in a very natural way to this more general setting. In particular, in many interesting instances, we need to recover $\boldsymbol{X}$ from far fewer measurements than the number of entries in the matrix, i.e., $m \ll n_1 \times n_2$. Unless we can leverage some additional prior information about $\boldsymbol{X}$, the problem of recovering $\boldsymbol{X}$ from the linear measurements $\boldsymbol{y}$ is ill posed.

We will consider applications in which we can leverage the following powerful piece of structural information: the target matrix $\boldsymbol{X}$ is *low-rank* or approximately so. Recall that the rank of a matrix $\boldsymbol{X}$ is the dimension of the linear subspace $\text{col}(\boldsymbol{X})$ spanned by the columns of $\boldsymbol{X}$. If $\boldsymbol{X} = [\boldsymbol{x}_1 \mid \cdots \mid \boldsymbol{x}_{n_2}] \in \mathbb{R}^{n_1 \times n_2}$ is a data matrix whose columns are n_1-dimensional vectors, then $\text{rank}(\boldsymbol{X}) = r \ll n_1$ if and only if the columns of $\boldsymbol{X}$ lie on an r-dimensional linear subspace of the data space $\mathbb{R}^{n_1}$ – see Figure 4.1 for an illustration. Low-rank matrix recovery problems arise in a broad range of application areas. We sketch a few of these below.

4.1 Motivating Examples of Low-Rank Modeling

4.1.1 3D Shape from Photometric Measurements

As mentioned in the introduction, there are many situations in which low-rank data models arise due to the physical processes that generate the data. If the generative

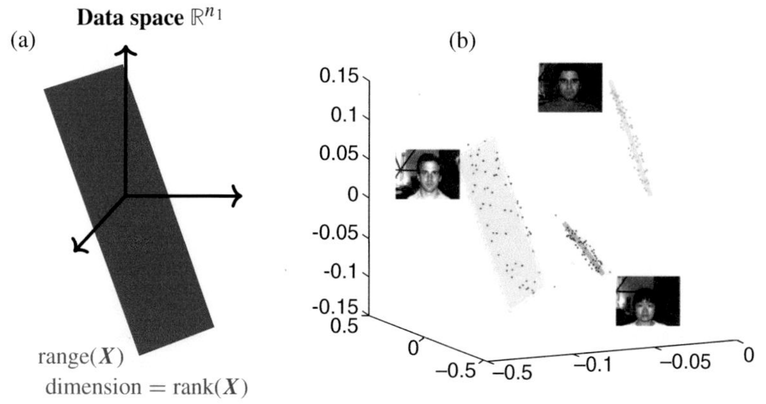

Figure 4.1 Low-rank data matrices. (a) If matrix $\boldsymbol{X}$ with columns $\boldsymbol{x}_1, \dots, \boldsymbol{x}_{n_2}$ has rank r, its columns lie on an r-dimensional subspace range($\boldsymbol{X}$). Many naturally occurring data matrices approximately satisfy this property. (b) Low-dimensional approximations to images of faces under different lighting conditions.

process has limited degrees of freedom, the data we observe would intrinsically be low-dimensional, regardless of the dimension of the ambient space in which such data are observed or measured. For example, in computer vision, low-rank models arise in a number of problems in reconstructing the three-dimensional shape of a scene from two-dimensional images.[1] In *photometric stereo* [Woo80], we obtain images $\boldsymbol{y}_1, \dots, \boldsymbol{y}_{n_2} \in \mathbb{R}^{n_1}$ of an object, say a face, illuminated by different distant point light sources. Write $\boldsymbol{Y} = [\boldsymbol{y}_1 \mid \cdots \mid \boldsymbol{y}_{n_2}] \in \mathbb{R}^{n_1 \times n_2}$. Let $\boldsymbol{l}_1, \dots, \boldsymbol{l}_{n_2} \in \mathbb{S}^2$ denote the directions of these light sources. The *Lambertian model* for reflectance models the reflected light intensity as

$$Y_{ij} = \alpha_i [\langle \boldsymbol{v}_i, \boldsymbol{l}_j \rangle]_+,$$

where $\boldsymbol{v}_i \in \mathbb{S}^2$ is the surface normal at the i-th pixel, α_i is a nonnegative scalar known as the *albedo*, and $[\cdot]_+$ takes the positive part of its argument. This model is appropriate for matte objects. See Figure 4.2 for a visualization of this model.

Under this model, if we let

$$\boldsymbol{N} = \begin{bmatrix} \alpha_1 \boldsymbol{v}_1^* \\ \vdots \\ \alpha_m \boldsymbol{v}_m^* \end{bmatrix} \in \mathbb{R}^{n_1 \times 3} \quad \text{and} \quad \boldsymbol{L} = \begin{bmatrix} \boldsymbol{l}_1 \mid \cdots \mid \boldsymbol{l}_{n_2} \end{bmatrix} \in \mathbb{R}^{3 \times n_2},$$

then we have

$$\boldsymbol{Y} = \mathcal{P}_\Omega[\boldsymbol{N}\boldsymbol{L}],$$

[1] Do not confuse the dimension of the measurements, in this case, the number of pixels, with the physical dimension of the image array, which is two.

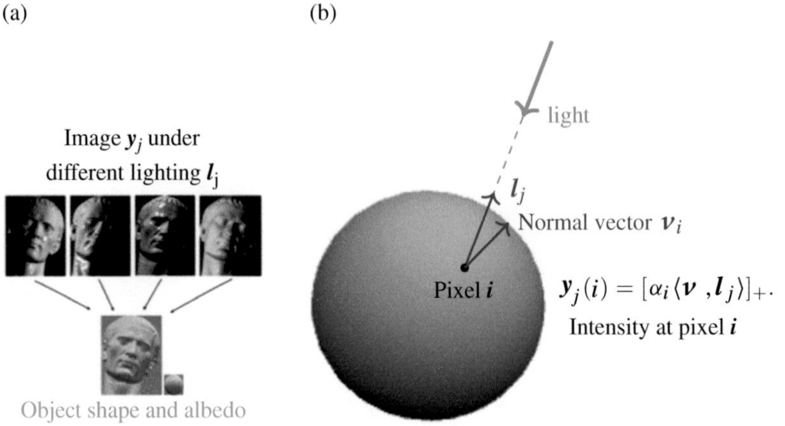

Figure 4.2 Photometric Stereo as Low-rank Matrix Recovery. (a) Photometric stereo seeks to recover object shape from images taken under different illuminations. (b) Under a diffuse reflective (Lambertian) model, this leads directly to a low-rank recovery problem.

where

$$\Omega = \{(i, j) \mid \langle \nu_i, l_j \rangle \geq 0\}.$$

If we can recover the low-rank matrix $X = NL$ (of maximum rank 3), we can then recover information about the shape and reflectance of the object. Again, a useful heuristic is to look for a solution of minimum rank consistent with the observations [WGS+10]:

$$\begin{array}{ll} \min & \operatorname{rank}(X) \\ \text{subject to} & \mathcal{P}_\Omega[X] = Y. \end{array} \tag{4.1.1}$$

The reader can obtain an open-source implementation of this example from `https://github.com/yasumat/RobustPhotometricStereo`. More detailed discussion will be covered in Chapter 14.

4.1.2 Recommendation Systems

In this example, imagine that we have n_2 products of interest, and n_1 users. Users consume products and rate them based on the quality of their experience. Our goal is to use the information of all the users' ratings to predict which products will appeal to a given user. Formally, our object of interest is a large, unknown matrix

$$X \in \mathbb{R}^{n_1 \times n_2},$$

whose (i, j) entry contains user i's degree of preference for item j. If we let

$$\Omega \doteq \Big\{(i, j) \mid \text{user } i \text{ has rated product } j\Big\},$$

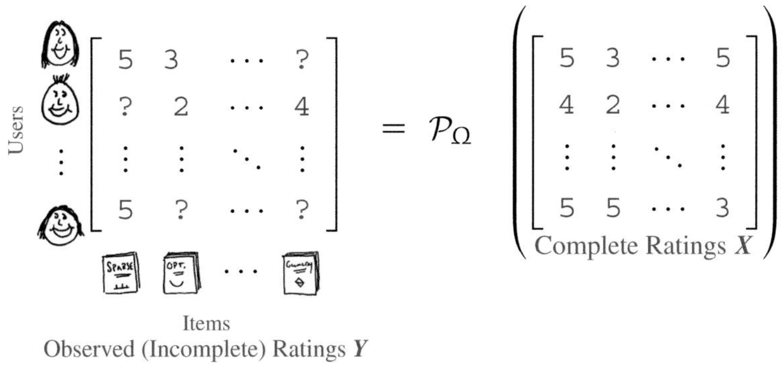

Figure 4.3 Collaborative Filtering as Low-rank Matrix Completion. Consider a universe of n_1 users and n_2 items. Users experience items, and then rate their experience. Our observation $\boldsymbol{Y}$ consists of those ratings that users have provided: Y_{ij} is user i's rating of item j. We wish to predict users' ratings of items that they have not yet rated. This can be viewed as attempting to recover a large matrix $\boldsymbol{X}$ from a subset $\boldsymbol{Y} = \mathcal{P}_\Omega[\boldsymbol{X}]$ of its entries.

then we observe

$$\underset{\text{observed ratings}}{\boldsymbol{Y}} = \mathcal{P}_\Omega\Big[\underset{\text{complete ratings}}{\boldsymbol{X}}\Big].$$

Here, $\mathcal{P}_\Omega$ is the projection operator onto the subset Ω:

$$\mathcal{P}_\Omega[\boldsymbol{X}](i,j) = \begin{cases} X_{ij} & (i,j) \in \Omega, \\ 0 & \text{else.} \end{cases}$$

See Figure 4.3 for a schematic representation of this scenario.

Our goal is to fill in the missing entries of $\boldsymbol{X}$. This problem is encountered in online recommendation systems – the most famous recent instance being the "Netflix Prize" competition conducted between 2006 and 2009. See the Wikipedia page `https://en.wikipedia.org/wiki/Netflix_Prize` for details. Obviously, with no additional assumptions, the problem of filling in the missing entries of $\boldsymbol{X}$ is ill posed. One popular assumption is that the ratings of distinct users (or distinct products) are correlated, and hence the target matrix $\boldsymbol{X}$ is low-rank, or approximately so. The relevant mathematical problem then becomes filling in the missing entries of a low-rank matrix, or, somewhat equivalently, looking for the matrix $\boldsymbol{X}$ of minimum rank that is consistent with our given observations:

$$\begin{array}{ll} \min & \operatorname{rank}(\boldsymbol{X}) \\ \text{subject to} & \mathcal{P}_\Omega[\boldsymbol{X}] = \boldsymbol{Y}. \end{array} \tag{4.1.2}$$

This problem is often referred to as *matrix completion* [CR09].

4.1.3 Euclidean Distance Matrix Embedding

This useful problem can be stated as follows: assume that we have n points $\boldsymbol{X} = [\boldsymbol{x}_1 \mid \cdots \mid \boldsymbol{x}_n]$ living in $\mathbb{R}^d$. We can define a matrix $\boldsymbol{D}$ via

$$D_{ij} = d^2(\boldsymbol{x}_i, \boldsymbol{x}_j) = \|\boldsymbol{x}_i - \boldsymbol{x}_j\|_2^2.$$

Here $\boldsymbol{D}$ is known as a *Euclidean distance matrix*. Now imagine the following scenario: rather than observing the $\boldsymbol{x}_i$ themselves, we instead see their pairwise distances $d(\boldsymbol{x}_i, \boldsymbol{x}_j)$. How can we tell if these distances were generated by some configuration of points living in $\mathbb{R}^d$? A necessary and sufficient condition is given by the following classical result:

THEOREM 4.1. (Schoenberg theorem) $\boldsymbol{D} \in \mathbb{R}^{n\times n}$ *is a Euclidean distance matrix for some set of n points in* $\mathbb{R}^d$ *if and only if the following conditions hold:*

- $\boldsymbol{D}$ *is symmetric.*
- $D_{ii} = 0$ *for all* $i \in \{1, \ldots, n\}$.
- $\boldsymbol{\Phi D \Phi}^* \preceq \mathbf{0}$, *where* $\boldsymbol{\Phi} = \boldsymbol{I} - (1/n)\mathbf{1}\mathbf{1}^*$ *is the centering matrix (here* $\mathbf{1} \in \mathbb{R}^n$ *is the vector whose entries are all ones).*
- $\operatorname{rank}(\boldsymbol{\Phi D \Phi}^*) \le d$.

We leave the proof of this theorem as an exercise to the reader. See Exercise 4.1.

Now imagine we only know D_{ij} for some subset $\Omega \subset \{1, \ldots, n\} \times \{1, \ldots, n\}$, i.e., we observe $\boldsymbol{Y} = \mathcal{P}_\Omega[\boldsymbol{D}]$. We can cast the problem of looking for a Euclidean distance matrix that agrees with our observations as a *rank minimization problem*:

$$\begin{array}{ll} \min & \operatorname{rank}(\boldsymbol{\Phi D \Phi}^*) \\ \text{subject to} & \boldsymbol{\Phi D \Phi}^* \preceq \mathbf{0}, \;\; \boldsymbol{D} = \boldsymbol{D}^*, \;\; \mathcal{P}_\Omega[\boldsymbol{D}] = \boldsymbol{Y}, \;\; \forall\, i \; D_{ii} = 0. \end{array} \tag{4.1.3}$$

4.1.4 Latent Semantic Analysis

Low-dimensional models are very popular in document analysis. Consider an idealized problem in search or document retrieval. The system has access to n_2 documents (say, news articles), each of which is viewed as a collection of words in a dictionary of size n_1. For the j-th document, we compute a histogram of word occurrences, giving an n_1-dimensional vector $\boldsymbol{y}_j$ whose i-th entry is the fraction of occurrences of word i in document j. Set

$$\underset{\text{word occurrences}}{\boldsymbol{Y}} = \text{words}\underbrace{\left[\, \boldsymbol{y}_1 \mid \cdots \mid \boldsymbol{y}_{n_2} \,\right]}_{\text{documents}}.$$

We model these observations as follows. We imagine that there exists a set of "topics" $\boldsymbol{t}_1, \ldots, \boldsymbol{t}_r$. Each topic is a probability distribution on $\{1, 2, \ldots, n_1\}$. We may imagine that the $\boldsymbol{t}_l$ corresponds loosely to our informal notion of what a topic is – say, architecture or New York city. An article on architecture in New York would involve multiple topics. We model this as a mixture distribution, writing

$$\underbrace{\boldsymbol{p}_j}_{\text{word distribution for document } j} = \sum_{l=1}^{r} \underbrace{\boldsymbol{t}_l}_{\text{topic}} \underbrace{\alpha_{l,j}}_{\text{abundance}},$$

where $\alpha_{1,j} + \alpha_{2,j} + \cdots + \alpha_{r,j} = 1$. We imagine that $\boldsymbol{y}_j$ is generated by sampling words independently at random from the mixture distribution $\boldsymbol{p}_j$ and computing a histogram.[2] If the number of words sampled is large, we can imagine $\boldsymbol{y}_j \approx \boldsymbol{p}_j$. So, if we write $\boldsymbol{T} = [\boldsymbol{t}_1, \ldots, \boldsymbol{t}_r]$ and $\boldsymbol{A} = [\boldsymbol{\alpha}_1, \ldots, \boldsymbol{\alpha}_n]$, then we have

$$\underbrace{\boldsymbol{Y}}_{\text{word occurrences}} \approx \underbrace{\boldsymbol{T}}_{\text{topics}} \underbrace{\boldsymbol{A}}_{\text{abundances}}. \tag{4.1.4}$$

Notice that $\operatorname{rank}(\boldsymbol{T}\boldsymbol{A}) \le r$: *the rank is bounded by the number of topics. Latent semantic analysis* computes a best low-rank approximation to $\boldsymbol{Y}$ and then uses it for search and indexing [DFL+88, DDF+90]. There are several advanced extensions to the basic latent semantic indexing (LSI) model, such as probabilistic LSI (pLSI) [Hof99, Hof04], latent Dirichlet allocation (LDA) [BNJ03], and a joint topic–document model (via a low-rank and sparse matrix) [MZWM10].

Many additional examples arise, for example in solving positioning problems, problems in system identification, quantum state tomography, image and video alignment, etc. We will survey more of these in the coming application chapters.

4.2 Representing Low-Rank Matrix via SVD

In all of the applications described above, our goal is to recover an unknown $\boldsymbol{X}$ whose columns live on an r-dimensional linear subspace of the data space $\mathbb{R}^{n_1}$. This subspace can be characterized via the *singular value decomposition* (SVD) of $\boldsymbol{X}$ (see Appendix A.8 for a more detailed review):

THEOREM 4.2. (Compact SVD) *Let $\boldsymbol{X} \in \mathbb{R}^{n_1 \times n_2}$ be a matrix, and $r = \operatorname{rank}(\boldsymbol{X})$. Then there exist $\boldsymbol{\Sigma} = \operatorname{diag}(\sigma_1, \ldots, \sigma_r)$ with numbers $\sigma_1 \ge \sigma_2 \ge \cdots \ge \sigma_r > 0$ and matrices $\boldsymbol{U} \in \mathbb{R}^{n_1 \times r}$ and $\boldsymbol{V} \in \mathbb{R}^{n_2 \times r}$, such that $\boldsymbol{U}^*\boldsymbol{U} = \boldsymbol{I}$, $\boldsymbol{V}^*\boldsymbol{V} = \boldsymbol{I}$, and*

$$\boldsymbol{X} = \boldsymbol{U}\boldsymbol{\Sigma}\boldsymbol{V}^* = \sum_{i=1}^{r} \sigma_i \boldsymbol{u}_i \boldsymbol{v}_i^*. \tag{4.2.1}$$

Exercise 4.2 gives a guided proof of this result. This construction turns out to be a very versatile tool both for theory and for numerical computation. The *full* singular value decomposition extends the matrices $\boldsymbol{U}$ and $\boldsymbol{V}$ to complete orthonormal bases for $\mathbb{R}^{n_1}$ and $\mathbb{R}^{n_2}$, respectively, by adding bases for the left and right null spaces of $\boldsymbol{X}$:

THEOREM 4.3. (SVD) *Let $\boldsymbol{X} \in \mathbb{R}^{n_1 \times n_2}$ be a matrix. Then there exist orthogonal matrices $\boldsymbol{U} \in \mathsf{O}(n_1)$ and $\boldsymbol{V} \in \mathsf{O}(n_2)$, and numbers*

$$\sigma_1 \ge \sigma_2 \ge \cdots \ge \sigma_{\min\{n_1,n_2\}}$$

[2] In practice, researchers have observed that more complicated methods of constructing $\boldsymbol{Y}$ (say, using the term frequency–inverse document frequency (TF–IDF) weighting) improves performance compared to just using the histogram.

such that if we let $\mathbf{\Sigma} \in \mathbb{R}^{n_1 \times n_2}$ *with* $\Sigma_{ii} = \sigma_i$ *and* $\Sigma_{ij} = 0$ *for* $i \neq j$, *then*

$$\boldsymbol{X} = \boldsymbol{U}\mathbf{\Sigma}\boldsymbol{V}^*. \tag{4.2.2}$$

FACT 4.4. (Properties of the SVD) *We note the following properties of the construction in Theorem 4.2:*

- *The left singular vectors* $\boldsymbol{u}_i$ *are the eigenvectors of* $\boldsymbol{X}\boldsymbol{X}^*$ *(check this!).*
- *The right singular vectors* $\boldsymbol{v}_i$ *are the eigenvectors of* $\boldsymbol{X}^*\boldsymbol{X}$.
- *The nonzero singular values* σ_i *are the positive square roots of the positive eigenvalues* λ_i *of* $\boldsymbol{X}^*\boldsymbol{X}$.
- *The nonzero singular values* σ_i *are also the positive square roots of the positive eigenvalues* λ_i *of* $\boldsymbol{X}\boldsymbol{X}^*$.

Notice that since $\boldsymbol{U}$ and $\boldsymbol{V}$ are nonsingular, the $\operatorname{rank}(\boldsymbol{X}) = \operatorname{rank}(\mathbf{\Sigma})$. Since $\mathbf{\Sigma}$ is diagonal, this quantity is especially simple – it is simply the number of nonzero entries σ_i! Here, and below, we will let $\boldsymbol{\sigma}(\boldsymbol{X}) = (\sigma_1, \ldots, \sigma_{\min\{n_1,n_2\}}) \in \mathbb{R}^{\min\{n_1,n_2\}}$ denote the vector of singular values of $\boldsymbol{X}$. Then, in the language that we have been developing thus far,

$$\operatorname{rank}(\boldsymbol{X}) = \|\boldsymbol{\sigma}(\boldsymbol{X})\|_0 . \tag{4.2.3}$$

Hence any problem that minimizes the rank of an unknown matrix $\boldsymbol{X}$ is essentially minimizing the number of nonzero singular values of $\boldsymbol{X}$ – the "sparsity" of singular values, subject to data constraints.

4.2.1 Singular Vectors via Nonconvex Optimization

The SVD can be computed in time $O(\max\{n_1,n_2\}\min\{n_1,n_2\}^2)$. The first r singular value/vector triples can be computed in time $O(n_1 n_2 r)$. Hence, the problem of finding a linear subspace that best fits a given set of data can be solved in polynomial time. On the surface this is quite remarkable – the problem of computing singular vectors is nonconvex. We briefly describe why this nonconvex problem can be solved globally in an efficient manner.

We give a brief indication of *why* it is possible to efficiently compute singular vectors of a matrix $\boldsymbol{X}$. Consider the matrix $\mathbf{\Gamma} \doteq \boldsymbol{X}\boldsymbol{X}^*$. Let $\mathbf{\Gamma} = \boldsymbol{U}\mathbf{\Lambda}\boldsymbol{U}^*$ be the eigenvalue decomposition of $\mathbf{\Gamma}$ and $\mathbf{\Lambda} = \operatorname{diag}(\lambda_1, \ldots, \lambda_{n_1})$ be the eigenvalues. It is obvious that the left singular vectors $\boldsymbol{u}_i$ of $\boldsymbol{X}$ are the eigenvectors of $\mathbf{\Gamma}$. Because our goal in this paragraph is merely to convey intuition, we make the simplifying assumption that $\mathbf{\Gamma}$ has no repeated eigenvalues and λ_1 is the largest. We show how to use nonconvex optimization to compute the leading eigenvector $\boldsymbol{u}_1$ – see Exercise 4.5 for extensions to repeated leading eigenvectors.

Consider the optimization problem

$$\begin{aligned} \min \quad & \varphi(\boldsymbol{q}) \equiv -\tfrac{1}{2}\boldsymbol{q}^*\mathbf{\Gamma}\boldsymbol{q} \\ \text{subject to} \quad & \|\boldsymbol{q}\|_2^2 = 1. \end{aligned} \tag{4.2.4}$$

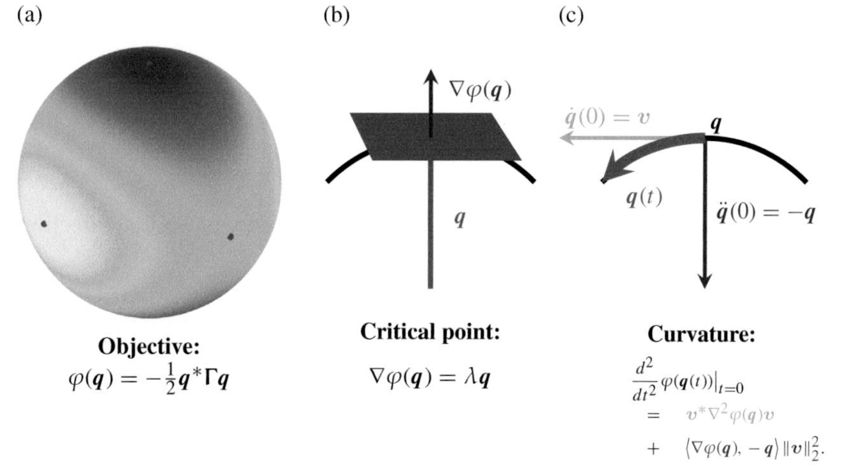

Figure 4.4 Eigenvector Computation as Nonconvex Optimization over the Sphere.
(a) We plot $\varphi(\boldsymbol{q}) = -\frac{1}{2}\boldsymbol{q}^*\boldsymbol{\Gamma}\boldsymbol{q}$ over the sphere, for one particular $\boldsymbol{\Gamma}$. Red dots represent the eigenvectors of $\boldsymbol{\Gamma}$. (b) Critical points are points $\boldsymbol{q}$ for which $\nabla\varphi(\boldsymbol{q})$ is proportional to $\boldsymbol{q}$. Every critical point is an eigenvector of $\boldsymbol{\Gamma}$; the only local minimizers are eigenvectors that correspond to the largest eigenvalue $\lambda_1(\boldsymbol{\Gamma})$. (c) The curvature of φ over the sphere comes from both the curvature $\nabla^2\varphi$ of φ and the curvature of the sphere.

The gradient and Hessian of the function $\varphi(\boldsymbol{q})$ are

$$\nabla\varphi(\boldsymbol{q}) = -\boldsymbol{\Gamma}\boldsymbol{q} \quad \text{and} \quad \nabla^2\varphi(\boldsymbol{q}) = -\boldsymbol{\Gamma}, \tag{4.2.5}$$

respectively. A point $\boldsymbol{q}$ is a *critical point* of the function φ over the sphere,

$$\mathbb{S}^{n-1} = \left\{\boldsymbol{q} \mid \|\boldsymbol{q}\|_2^2 = 1\right\},$$

if there is no direction $\boldsymbol{v} \perp \boldsymbol{q}$ (i.e., no direction that is tangent to the sphere at $\boldsymbol{q}$) along which the function decreases. Equivalently, $\boldsymbol{q}$ is a critical point of φ over the sphere if and only if the gradient is proportional to $\boldsymbol{q}$:

$$\nabla\varphi(\boldsymbol{q}) \propto \boldsymbol{q}. \tag{4.2.6}$$

Figure 4.4 visualizes this condition. Using our expression for $\nabla\varphi$, this is true if and only if $\boldsymbol{\Gamma}\boldsymbol{q} = \lambda\boldsymbol{q}$ for some λ: *the critical points of φ over $\mathbb{S}^{n-1}$ are precisely the eigenvectors $\pm\boldsymbol{u}_i$ of $\boldsymbol{\Gamma}$.*

Which critical points $\pm\boldsymbol{u}_i$ are actual local or global minimizers (instead of saddle points)? To answer this question, we need to study the curvature of the function $\varphi(\boldsymbol{q})$ around a critical point $\bar{\boldsymbol{q}}$. In Euclidean space, the correct tool for studying curvature is the Hessian, as is justified by the second-order Taylor expansion of the function along the curve $\boldsymbol{x}(t) = \boldsymbol{x} + t\boldsymbol{v}$:

$$f(\boldsymbol{x} + t\boldsymbol{v}) = f(\boldsymbol{x}) + \underbrace{t\,\langle\nabla f(\boldsymbol{x}), \boldsymbol{v}\rangle}_{=\,0 \text{ at any critical point}} + \tfrac{1}{2}t^2\boldsymbol{v}^*\nabla^2 f(\boldsymbol{x})\boldsymbol{v} + o(t^2).$$

In Euclidean space, a critical point $\bar{\boldsymbol{x}}$ is a local minimizer if $\nabla^2 f(\bar{\boldsymbol{x}}) \succ \mathbf{0}$. Conversely, if $\nabla^2 f(\bar{\boldsymbol{x}})$ has a negative eigenvalue, the point is not a local minimizer.

Over the sphere, we can perform a similar Taylor expansion, but we need to replace the straight line $\boldsymbol{x}(t) = \boldsymbol{x} + t\boldsymbol{v}$ with a great circle[3]

$$\boldsymbol{q}(t) = \boldsymbol{q}\cos(t) + \boldsymbol{v}\sin(t), \tag{4.2.7}$$

where $\boldsymbol{v} \perp \boldsymbol{q}$ and $\|\boldsymbol{v}\|_2 = 1$. Calculus shows that the second directional derivative of $\varphi(\boldsymbol{q}(t))$ is given by

$$\frac{d^2}{dt^2}\varphi(\boldsymbol{q}(t))\bigg|_{t=0} = \underbrace{\boldsymbol{v}^*\nabla^2\varphi(\boldsymbol{q})\boldsymbol{v}}_{\text{curvature of }\varphi} - \underbrace{\left\langle \nabla\varphi(\boldsymbol{q}), \boldsymbol{q}\right\rangle \boldsymbol{v}^*\boldsymbol{v}}_{\text{curvature of the sphere}}. \tag{4.2.8}$$

This formula contains two terms, which combine the usual Hessian of φ (accounting for the curvature of φ) and a second correction term involving $-\left\langle \nabla\varphi(\boldsymbol{q}), \boldsymbol{q}\right\rangle$ which accounts for the fact that the curve $\boldsymbol{q}(t)$ curves in the $-\boldsymbol{q}$ direction in order to stay on the sphere.

Note that $\nabla^2\varphi(\boldsymbol{q}) = -\boldsymbol{\Gamma}$. So we have $\left\langle \nabla\varphi(\boldsymbol{u}_i), \boldsymbol{u}_i\right\rangle = -\boldsymbol{u}_i^*\boldsymbol{\Gamma}\boldsymbol{u}_i = -\lambda_i$, and we observe that at a critical point $\bar{\boldsymbol{q}} = \pm\boldsymbol{u}_i$, the second derivative in the $\boldsymbol{v}$ direction is

$$\frac{d^2}{dt^2}\varphi(\boldsymbol{q}(t))\bigg|_{t=0} = \boldsymbol{v}^*\Big(-\boldsymbol{\Gamma} + \lambda_i \boldsymbol{I}\Big)\boldsymbol{v}. \tag{4.2.9}$$

The eigenvalues of the operator $-\boldsymbol{\Gamma} + \lambda_i$ take the form $-\lambda_j + \lambda_i$; there is a strictly negative eigenvalue if $\boldsymbol{u}_i$ is an eigenvector that does not correspond to the largest eigenvalue λ_1. So $\pm\boldsymbol{u}_1$ are the only local minimizers of φ. All other critical points have a direction of strict negative curvature. This benign geometry implies that a simple projected gradient method converges to a global optimizer from almost any initialization. This phenomenon turns out to be rather representative of optimization problems associated with learning low-dimensional models for high-dimensional data; we will return more formally to study them in Chapter 7.

For computing the leading eigenvalue and eigenvector, we can do more than employing the generic gradient descent. Exercise 4.6 gives a more specific algorithm, the *power iteration* method, which is much faster and more commonly used. In Section 9.3.2 of Chapter 9, we will give a precise characterization of the computational complexity of this method as well as its more efficient variant.[4] For now, we take these observations as an intuitive indication of why the SVD is amenable to efficient computation.

Implications and History

Whichever rationale we adopt, the fact that the SVD can be both optimal (in a precisely defined and often quite relevant sense) and efficient (at least for moderate problems) makes it a very useful element in the numerical computing toolbox. The canonical

[3] Curves of this form are *geodesics* on $\mathbb{S}^{n-1}$.

[4] The Lanczos method for computing the leading eigenvalue and eigenvector.

example application of the SVD is *principal component analysis* (PCA). Outlined in the 1901 and 1933 papers by Pearson and Hotelling [Pea01, Hot33], respectively, PCA finds a best-fitting low-dimensional subspace, which can be computed via the SVD, as suggested by Theorem 4.5 below. Remarkably, Pearson's 1901 paper asserts that PCA is "well-suited to numerical computation" – meaning hand calculations!

4.2.2 Best Low-Rank Matrix Approximation

We are interested in recovering a low-rank matrix that is consistent with certain linear observations. Because the rank has a similar characteristics to the ℓ^0 norm, one should expect that these problems would be computationally intractable in general, as in the case with recovering a sparse solution (see Theorem 2.8).

Remarkably, there *are* however a few special instances of rank minimization that we *can* solve efficiently, with virtually no assumptions on the input. The most important is the *best rank-r approximation* problem, in which we try to approximate an arbitrary input matrix $\boldsymbol{Y}$ with a matrix $\boldsymbol{X}$ of rank at most r such that the approximation error $\|\boldsymbol{X} - \boldsymbol{Y}\|_F$ is as small as possible. The optimal solution to this problem can be obtained by simply retaining the first r leading singular values/vectors of $\boldsymbol{Y}$:

THEOREM 4.5. (Best low-rank approximation) *Let $\boldsymbol{Y} \in \mathbb{R}^{n_1 \times n_2}$, and consider the following optimization problem:*

$$\begin{array}{ll} \min & \|\boldsymbol{X} - \boldsymbol{Y}\|_F \\ \text{subject to} & \operatorname{rank}(\boldsymbol{X}) \leq r. \end{array} \tag{4.2.10}$$

Every optimal solution $\hat{\boldsymbol{X}}$ to the above problem has the form $\hat{\boldsymbol{X}} = \sum_{i=1}^{r} \sigma_i \boldsymbol{u}_i \boldsymbol{v}_i^*$, where $\boldsymbol{Y} = \sum_{i=1}^{\min(n_1,n_2)} \sigma_i \boldsymbol{u}_i \boldsymbol{v}_i^*$ is a (full) singular value decomposition of $\boldsymbol{Y}$.

In fact, the same solution (truncating the SVD) also solves the low-rank approximation problem when the error is measured in the operator norm, or any other orthogonal-invariant matrix norm (see Appendix A). Please see Exercise 4.3 for guidance on how to prove Theorem 4.5.

The problem (4.2.10) can be turned around and cast as one of minimizing the rank of the unknown matrix, subject to a data fidelity constraint:

$$\begin{array}{ll} \min & \operatorname{rank}(\boldsymbol{X}) \\ \text{subject to} & \|\boldsymbol{X} - \boldsymbol{Y}\|_F \leq \varepsilon. \end{array} \tag{4.2.11}$$

This is an example of a *matrix rank minimization* problem – we seek a matrix of minimum rank that is consistent with some given observations. Because of its very special nature, this particular rank minimization can be solved optimally via the SVD. We leave the solution to this problem as an exercise to the reader (see Exercise 4.4).[5]

[5] Hint: You may first try to guess what the optimal solution is and then show its optimality.

4.3 Recovering a Low-Rank Matrix

4.3.1 General Rank Minimization Problems

In the previous section, we saw that for certain very specific rank minimization problems, globally optimal solutions could be obtained using efficient algorithms based on the singular value decomposition. However, all of the applications discussed above (and many others!) force us to attempt to minimize the rank of $\boldsymbol{X}$ over much more complicated sets. One model example problem is the *affine rank minimization* problem [FHB04]:

$$\begin{array}{ll} \min & \operatorname{rank}(\boldsymbol{X}) \\ \text{subject to} & \mathcal{A}[\boldsymbol{X}] = \boldsymbol{y}. \end{array} \tag{4.3.1}$$

Here $\boldsymbol{y} \in \mathbb{R}^m$ is an observation, and $\mathcal{A} : \mathbb{R}^{n_1 \times n_2} \to \mathbb{R}^m$ is a linear map. When $m \ll n_1 n_2$, the linear system of equations $\mathcal{A}[\boldsymbol{X}] = \boldsymbol{y}$ is underdetermined. The notion of a linear map $\mathcal{A}$ from $n_1 \times n_2$ matrices to m-dimensional vectors may seem somewhat abstract. Any linear map of this form can be represented using the matrix inner product[6]

$$\mathcal{A}[\boldsymbol{X}] = (\langle \boldsymbol{A}_1, \boldsymbol{X} \rangle, \ldots, \langle \boldsymbol{A}_m, \boldsymbol{X} \rangle). \tag{4.3.2}$$

Here, the set of matrices $\boldsymbol{A}_1, \ldots, \boldsymbol{A}_m \in \mathbb{R}^{n_1 \times n_2}$ define our "measurements" $\boldsymbol{y}$, through their inner products with the unknown matrix $\boldsymbol{X}$.[7]

A mathematically simple and natural assumption on these "measurement" matrices is that they are i.i.d. Gaussian matrices. Such an assumption will allow us to understand the conditions under which one could expect to recover a low-rank matrix with generic measurements. Hence, our first attempt to understand the low-rank recovery problem will rely on such a simplifying assumption. However, in many practical problems of interest, the operator $\mathcal{A}$ has particular structures that make it behave differently. As a concrete example, in the matrix completion problems discussed above, we would have $m = |\Omega|$, and $\boldsymbol{A}_l = \boldsymbol{e}_{i_l} \boldsymbol{e}_{j_l}^*$, with $\Omega = \{(i_1, j_1), \ldots, (i_m, j_m)\}$. We will also thoroughly analyze this important special case and provide conditions under which the recovery can be successful.

Connection to ℓ^0, NP-hardness

To make the connection to sparse recovery explicit, using the observation that $\operatorname{rank}(\boldsymbol{X}) = \|\sigma(\boldsymbol{X})\|_0$, we can rewrite the affine rank minimization problem as

$$\begin{array}{ll} \min & \|\sigma(\boldsymbol{X})\|_0 \\ \text{subject to} & \mathcal{A}[\boldsymbol{X}] = \boldsymbol{y}. \end{array} \tag{4.3.3}$$

[6] Recall that the standard inner product between matrices $\boldsymbol{P}, \boldsymbol{Q} \in \mathbb{R}^{n_1 \times n_2}$ is defined by $\langle \boldsymbol{P}, \boldsymbol{Q} \rangle = \sum_{ij} P_{ij} Q_{ij} = \operatorname{trace}[\boldsymbol{Q}^* \boldsymbol{P}]$.

[7] You can think of the measurements $\boldsymbol{A}_i$ as analogous to the *rows* $\boldsymbol{a}_i^*$ of the matrix $\boldsymbol{A}$ in the equation $\boldsymbol{y} = \boldsymbol{A}\boldsymbol{x}$ studied in Chapters 2 and 3.

Moreover, *if* X is a diagonal matrix, then $\text{rank}(X) = \|X\|_0$. So, every ℓ^0 minimization problem can be converted into a rank minimization problem with a diagonal constraint. This means that in the worst case, the rank minimization problem is at least as hard as the ℓ^0 minimization problem: it is NP-hard (as shown in Theorem 2.8).

As was the case for ℓ^0 minimization, we could simply give up here in searching for tractable algorithms. However, given the close analogy between rank minimization and ℓ^0 minimization, we might hope that there could be some fairly broad subclass of "nice enough" instances that we *can* solve efficiently.

4.3.2 Convex Relaxation of Rank Minimization

The close analogy to ℓ^0 minimization suggests a natural strategy. Replace the rank, which is the ℓ^0 norm $\boldsymbol{\sigma}(X)$, with the ℓ^1 norm of $\boldsymbol{\sigma}(X)$:

$$\|\boldsymbol{\sigma}(X)\|_1 = \sum_i \sigma_i(X). \tag{4.3.4}$$

We call this function the *nuclear norm* of X, and reserve the special notation

$$\|X\|_* = \sum_i \sigma_i(X). \tag{4.3.5}$$

When X is a symmetric positive semidefinite matrix, X has real nonnegative eigenvalues, and $\sigma_i(X) = \lambda_i(X)$. Since $\sum_i \lambda_i(X) = \text{trace}(X)$, in the special case when X is semidefinite, $\|X\|_* = \text{trace}[X]$. For this reason, the nuclear norm is sometimes also referred to as the *trace norm*. Other names in various literature include the *Schatten* 1*-norm* and *Ky Fan k-norm*.[8]

When X is not a semidefinite matrix, the function $\|X\|_*$ depends on the entries in a very complicated way. The results below give a couple of equivalent characterizations of the nuclear norm, which will be useful later in this book when we deal with certain nonconvex formulations of rank minimization (in Chapter 7).

PROPOSITION 4.6. (Variational forms of nuclear norm) *The nuclear norm of a matrix* $\|X\|_*$ *is equivalent to the following variational forms:*

(a) $\|X\|_* = \min_{U,V} \frac{1}{2}(\|U\|_F^2 + \|V\|_F^2)$, *such that* $X = UV^*$.
(b) $\|X\|_* = \min_{U,V} \|U\|_F \|V\|_F$, *such that* $X = UV^*$.
(c) $\|X\|_* = \min_{U,V} \sum_k \|u_k\|_2 \|v_k\|_2$, *such that* $X = UV^* \doteq \sum_k u_k v_k^*$.

This proposition can be proved by showing that the global minimum of each of these problems is reached when $U_\star = U_o\sqrt{\Sigma_o}$ and $V_\star = V_o\sqrt{\Sigma_o}$, where $X = U_o \Sigma_o V_o^*$ is any singular value decomposition of X. This can be readily shown, by noting that each of the objective functions is invariant to orthogonal transformations, reducing to the case when X is a diagonal matrix, and carefully examining this special case. We leave the details as an exercise for the reader.

[8] For $p \in [1, \infty]$, the Schatten p-norm of a matrix is $\|X\|_{S_p} = \|\sigma(X)\|_p$. The Ky Fan k-norm is $\|X\|_{KF_k} = \sum_{i=1}^k \sigma_i(X)$. Both of these functions are examples of *orthogonal invariant matrix norms*: see Appendix A.9 for more details.

Notice that in the above variational forms, there is *no* restriction on the dimensions of the two factors $\boldsymbol{U}$ and $\boldsymbol{V}$ as long as the equality $\boldsymbol{X} = \boldsymbol{U}\boldsymbol{V}^*$ holds. Hence choosing $\boldsymbol{U}$ and $\boldsymbol{V}$ to be matrices of larger sizes does not affect the minimization. These forms will become very useful when we consider alternative ways to minimize the nuclear norm for promoting the low-rank property, as we will examine later in Chapter 7.

Despite the above characterization, it remains not obvious at all that the sum of singular values is a norm, or even is indeed a convex function of the matrix. To allay any suspicion, we give a quick proof that $\|\cdot\|_*$ is indeed a norm:

THEOREM 4.7. *For $\boldsymbol{M} \in \mathbb{R}^{n_1 \times n_2}$, let $\|\boldsymbol{M}\|_* = \sum_{i=1}^{\min\{n_1,n_2\}} \sigma_i(\boldsymbol{M})$. Then $\|\cdot\|_*$ is a norm. Moreover, the nuclear norm and the ℓ^2 operator norm (or the spectral norm) are* dual norms*:*

$$\|\boldsymbol{M}\|_* = \sup_{\|\boldsymbol{N}\| \le 1} \langle \boldsymbol{M}, \boldsymbol{N} \rangle \quad \textit{and} \quad \|\boldsymbol{M}\| = \sup_{\|\boldsymbol{N}\|_* \le 1} \langle \boldsymbol{M}, \boldsymbol{N} \rangle . \tag{4.3.6}$$

Proof We begin by proving the first equality in (4.3.6). Let

$$\boldsymbol{M} = \boldsymbol{U}\boldsymbol{\Sigma}\boldsymbol{V}^* \tag{4.3.7}$$

be a full singular value decomposition of $\boldsymbol{M}$, with $\boldsymbol{U} \in \mathsf{O}(n_1)$, $\boldsymbol{V} \in \mathsf{O}(n_2)$, and $\boldsymbol{\Sigma} \in \mathbb{R}^{n_1 \times n_2}$, and note that

$$\begin{aligned}
\sup_{\|\boldsymbol{N}\| \le 1} \langle \boldsymbol{N}, \boldsymbol{M} \rangle &= \sup_{\|\boldsymbol{N}\| \le 1} \left\langle \boldsymbol{N}, \boldsymbol{U}\boldsymbol{\Sigma}\boldsymbol{V}^* \right\rangle \\
&= \sup_{\|\boldsymbol{N}\| \le 1} \left\langle \boldsymbol{U}^*\boldsymbol{N}\boldsymbol{V}, \begin{bmatrix} \sigma_1 & & \\ & \ddots & \\ & & \sigma_{n_2} \\ 0 & 0 & 0 \\ & \vdots & \end{bmatrix} \right\rangle \\
&\ge \sum_{i=1}^{n_2} \sigma_i,
\end{aligned} \tag{4.3.8}$$

where the last line follows by making a particular choice

$$\boldsymbol{N} = \boldsymbol{U} \begin{bmatrix} 1 & & \\ & \ddots & \\ & & 1 \\ 0 & 0 & 0 \\ & \vdots & \end{bmatrix} \boldsymbol{V}^*. \tag{4.3.9}$$

So, $\sup_{\boldsymbol{N}} \langle \boldsymbol{N}, \boldsymbol{M} \rangle \ge \|\boldsymbol{M}\|_*$.

For the opposite direction, notice that if matrix $N \in \mathbb{R}^{n_1 \times n_2}$ satisfies $\|N\| \leq 1$, then $\bar{N} \doteq U^* N V$ has columns of ℓ^2 norm at most one. Thus, for each i, $\bar{N}_{ii} \leq 1$, and

$$\langle N, M \rangle = \langle \bar{N}, \Sigma \rangle = \sum_{i=1}^{n_2} \bar{N}_{ii} \sigma_i \leq \sum_i \sigma_i = \|M\|_* . \tag{4.3.10}$$

This establishes the result.

For the second equality in (4.3.6), notice that for any nonzero M,

$$\langle M, N \rangle = \|M\| \left\langle \frac{M}{\|M\|}, N \right\rangle \leq \|M\| \, \|N\|_* . \tag{4.3.11}$$

Hence, $\sup_{\|N\|_* \leq 1} \langle M, N \rangle \leq \|M\|$. To show that this inequality is actually an equality, let us take $N = u_1 v_1^*$, and notice that $\|N\|_* = 1$ and $\langle M, N \rangle = u_1^* M v_1 = \sigma_1(M) = \|M\|$. This completes the proof of (4.3.6).

To see that $\|\cdot\|_*$ is indeed a norm, we just use (4.3.6) to verify that the three axioms of a norm are satisfied. Since the singular values are nonnegative, and $\sigma_1(M) = 0$ if and only if $M = \mathbf{0}$, it is immediate that $\|M\|_* \geq 0$ with equality iff $M = \mathbf{0}$. For nonnegative homogeneity, notice that for $t \in \mathbb{R}_+$,

$$\|tM\|_* = \sup_{\|N\| \leq 1} \langle tM, N \rangle = t \sup_{\|N\| \leq 1} \langle M, N \rangle = t \, \|M\|_* . \tag{4.3.12}$$

Finally, for the triangle inequality, consider two matrices M and M', and notice that

$$\begin{aligned} \left\|M + M'\right\|_* &= \sup_{\|\tilde{N}\| \leq 1} \left\langle M + M', \tilde{N} \right\rangle \\ &\leq \sup_{\|N\| \leq 1} \langle M, N \rangle \quad + \quad \sup_{\|N'\| \leq 1} \left\langle M', N' \right\rangle \\ &= \|M\|_* + \left\|M'\right\|_* , \end{aligned} \tag{4.3.13}$$

verifying the triangle inequality. This shows that $\|\cdot\|_*$ is indeed a norm. □

The above proof highlights a useful fact about $\|\cdot\|_*$: it is the dual norm of the operator norm $\|X\| = \sigma_1(X)$. The fact that $\|\cdot\|_*$ is the dual norm of $\|\cdot\|$ explains the $*$ notation – this symbol is often used for duality.

Because $\|\cdot\|_*$ is a norm, it is convex. Hence, a natural convex replacement for the rank minimization problem is the *nuclear norm minimization* problem

$$\begin{array}{ll} \min & \|X\|_* \\ \text{subject to} & \mathcal{A}[X] = y. \end{array} \tag{4.3.14}$$

This problem is convex, and moreover is efficiently solvable. In Chapter 8, we will see how to use the special structure of this problem to give practical, efficient algorithms which work well at moderate scales.

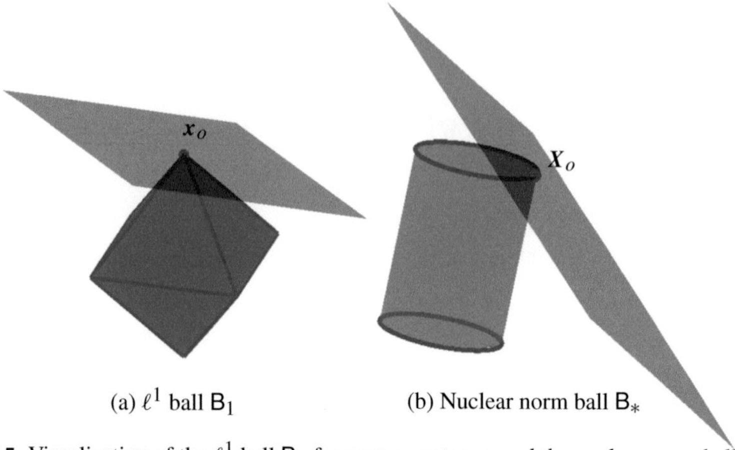

(a) ℓ^1 ball B_1 (b) Nuclear norm ball B_*

Figure 4.5 Visualization of the ℓ^1 ball B_1 for sparse vectors $\boldsymbol{x}$ and the nuclear norm ball B_* for symmetric 2×2 matrices. The red affine subspace represents the solution space to the equation $\boldsymbol{A}\boldsymbol{x} = \boldsymbol{A}\boldsymbol{x}_o$ for vectors (a) and the equation $\mathcal{A}[\boldsymbol{X}] = \mathcal{A}[\boldsymbol{X}_o]$ for matrices (b). The target low-rank matrix $\boldsymbol{X}_o$ is the unique minimum nuclear norm solution to this equation if and only if the solution space only intersects B_* at $\boldsymbol{X}_o$.

EXAMPLE 4.8. (Nuclear norm ball) *To visualize the nuclear norm, let us consider the set of* 2×2 *symmetric matrices, parameterized as*

$$\boldsymbol{M} = \begin{bmatrix} x & y \\ y & z \end{bmatrix} \in \mathbb{R}^{2\times 2}. \tag{4.3.15}$$

We leave as an exercise for the reader to find out the conditions on the three coordinates $(x, y, z) \in \mathbb{R}^3$ *such that* $\|\boldsymbol{M}\|_* = 1$. *Let* $\mathsf{B}_* = \{\boldsymbol{M} \mid \|\boldsymbol{M}\|_* \leq 1\}$ *be the unit ball defined by the nuclear norm. If we visualize such points in* $\mathbb{R}^3$, *the nuclear norm ball looks like a cylinder shown in Figure 4.5. The two circles at either end of the cylinder correspond to matrices of rank 1, which has a high chance to meet the affine subspace containing all solutions satisfying* $\mathcal{A}[\boldsymbol{X}] = \boldsymbol{y}$.

4.3.3 Nuclear Norm as a Convex Envelope of Rank

From the analogy to ℓ^0/ℓ^1 minimization, we might guess that the nuclear norm is a good convex surrogate for the rank, over some appropriate set. Recall that we have proved in Theorem 2.11 that the ℓ^1 norm was the convex envelope of the ℓ^0 norm over the ℓ^∞ ball. Since for a matrix $\boldsymbol{X}$, $\|\sigma(\boldsymbol{X})\|_\infty = \sigma_1(\boldsymbol{X}) = \|\boldsymbol{X}\|$, you might guess the following relationship:

THEOREM 4.9. $\|\boldsymbol{M}\|_*$ *is the convex envelope of* $\operatorname{rank}(\boldsymbol{M})$ *over*

$$\mathsf{B}_{op} \doteq \{\boldsymbol{M} \mid \|\boldsymbol{M}\| \leq 1\}. \tag{4.3.16}$$

Proof We prove that any convex function $f(\cdot)$ which satisfies

$$f(\boldsymbol{M}) \leq \operatorname{rank}(\boldsymbol{M}) \tag{4.3.17}$$

for all $\boldsymbol{M} \in \mathsf{B}_{op}$ is dominated by the nuclear norm: $f(\boldsymbol{M}) \leq \|\boldsymbol{M}\|_*$.

Write the SVD $\boldsymbol{M} = \boldsymbol{U\Sigma V}^*$. Notice that

$$\boldsymbol{\Sigma} \in \operatorname{conv}\left\{\operatorname{diag}(\boldsymbol{w}) \mid \boldsymbol{w} \in \{0,1\}^{\min\{n_1,n_2\}}\right\}, \tag{4.3.18}$$

and for any $\boldsymbol{w} \in \{0,1\}^{\min\{n_1,n_2\}}$,

$$\left\|\boldsymbol{U}\operatorname{diag}(\boldsymbol{w})\boldsymbol{V}^*\right\|_* = \sum_i w_i = \operatorname{rank}(\boldsymbol{U}\operatorname{diag}(\boldsymbol{w})\boldsymbol{V}^*). \tag{4.3.19}$$

Writing

$$\boldsymbol{\Sigma} = \sum_i \lambda_i \operatorname{diag}(\boldsymbol{w}_i) \tag{4.3.20}$$

with $\boldsymbol{w}_i \in \{0,1\}^{\min\{n_1,n_2\}}$ with $\lambda_i \geq 0$ and $\sum_i \lambda_i = 1$, and applying Jensen's inequality, we obtain

$$\begin{aligned}
f(\boldsymbol{M}) &= f\left(\boldsymbol{U}\sum_i \lambda_i \operatorname{diag}(\boldsymbol{w}_i)\boldsymbol{V}^*\right) &(4.3.21)\\
&\leq \sum_i \lambda_i f\left(\boldsymbol{U}\operatorname{diag}(\boldsymbol{w}_i)\boldsymbol{V}^*\right) &(4.3.22)\\
&\leq \sum_i \lambda_i \operatorname{rank}\left(\boldsymbol{U}\operatorname{diag}(\boldsymbol{w}_i)\boldsymbol{V}^*\right) &(4.3.23)\\
&= \sum_i \lambda_i \|\boldsymbol{w}_i\|_1 &(4.3.24)\\
&= \left\|\boldsymbol{U}\sum_i \lambda_i \operatorname{diag}(\boldsymbol{w}_i)\boldsymbol{V}^*\right\|_* &(4.3.25)\\
&= \|\boldsymbol{M}\|_* &(4.3.26)
\end{aligned}$$

as desired. □

Note that this proof essentially mirrored our argument for ℓ^1 and ℓ^∞. This is not a coincidence!

4.3.4 Success of Nuclear Norm under Rank-RIP

For now, assuming that we can solve nuclear norm minimization problems efficiently (say, with algorithms given in Chapter 8), we turn our attention to whether nuclear norm minimization actually gives the correct answers. Namely, if we know that $\boldsymbol{y} = \mathcal{A}[\boldsymbol{X}_o]$, with $r = \operatorname{rank}(\boldsymbol{X}_o) \ll n$, is it true that $\boldsymbol{X}_o$ is the unique optimal solution to the nuclear norm minimization problem (4.3.14)? What we can say depends strongly on what we know about the operator $\mathcal{A}$.

By analogy to the *sparse* recovery problem, we can ask if it is enough for $\mathcal{A}$ to preserve the geometry of a small set of structured objects – here, the low-rank matrices. Formally, we can define a *rank-restricted isometry property*, under which for every rank-r $\boldsymbol{X}$, $\|\mathcal{A}[\boldsymbol{X}]\|_2 \approx \|\boldsymbol{X}\|_F$.

DEFINITION 4.10. (Rank-Restricted isometry property [RFP10]) *The operator $\mathcal{A}$ has the rank-restricted isometry property of rank r with constant δ, if for all the $\boldsymbol{X}$ that satisfy* $\operatorname{rank}(\boldsymbol{X}) \leq r$, *we have*

$$(1-\delta)\|\boldsymbol{X}\|_F^2 \leq \|\mathcal{A}[\boldsymbol{X}]\|_2^2 \leq (1+\delta)\|\boldsymbol{X}\|_F^2. \tag{4.3.27}$$

The rank-r restricted isometry constant $\delta_r(\mathcal{A})$ is the smallest δ such that the above property holds.

As with the RIP for sparse vectors, the rank-RIP implies uniqueness of structured (low-rank) solutions:

THEOREM 4.11. *If $\boldsymbol{y} = \mathcal{A}[\boldsymbol{X}_o]$, with $r = \operatorname{rank}(\boldsymbol{X}_o)$ and $\delta_{2r}(\mathcal{A}) < 1$, then $\boldsymbol{X}_o$ is the unique optimal solution to the rank minimization problem*

$$\begin{array}{ll} \min & \operatorname{rank}(\boldsymbol{X}) \\ \text{subject to} & \mathcal{A}[\boldsymbol{X}] = \boldsymbol{y}. \end{array} \tag{4.3.28}$$

We leave the proof of this claim as an exercise for the reader (see Exercise 4.14). The key property is the subadditivity of the matrix rank, namely,

$$\operatorname{rank}(\boldsymbol{X} + \boldsymbol{X}') \leq \operatorname{rank}(\boldsymbol{X}) + \operatorname{rank}(\boldsymbol{X}'). \tag{4.3.29}$$

Moreover, like the RIP for sparse vectors, when the rank-RIP holds with sufficiently small constant δ, we can conclude that nuclear norm minimization will recover the desired low-rank solution:

THEOREM 4.12. (Nuclear norm minimization [RFP10]) *Suppose that $\boldsymbol{y} = \mathcal{A}[\boldsymbol{X}_o]$ with* $\operatorname{rank}(\boldsymbol{X}_o) \leq r$, *and that $\delta_{4r}(\mathcal{A}) \leq \sqrt{2} - 1$. Then $\boldsymbol{X}_o$ is the unique optimal solution to the nuclear norm minimization problem*

$$\begin{array}{ll} \min & \|\boldsymbol{X}\|_* \\ \text{subject to} & \mathcal{A}[\boldsymbol{X}] = \boldsymbol{y}. \end{array} \tag{4.3.30}$$

There is nothing special here about the numbers $4r$ and $\sqrt{2} - 1$. The interesting part is the qualitative statement: if $\mathcal{A}$ respects the geometry of low-rank matrices in a sufficiently strong sense, then nuclear norm minimization succeeds. The proof is analogous to the proof we gave in the previous chapter for the success of ℓ^1 minimization for recovering sparse signals. However, to extend the proof techniques from ℓ^1 to nuclear norm, we need to generalize a few concepts from vectors to matrices.

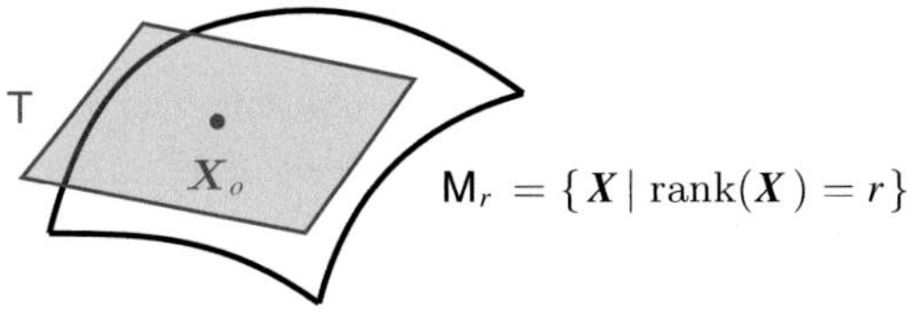

Figure 4.6 "Support" of a Low-rank Matrix X_o. Consider a rank-r matrix X_o with compact singular value decomposition $X_o = U\Sigma V^*$. The subspace $\mathsf{T} = \{UR^* + QV^*\}$ can be interpreted as the *tangent space* to the collection M_r of rank-r matrices at X_o.

"Support" and "Signs" of a Low-Rank Matrix

Let $X_o = U\Sigma V^*$ denote the compact SVD of the true solution X_o. Let

$$\mathsf{T} \doteq \left\{UR^* + QV^* \mid R \in \mathbb{R}^{n_2 \times r},\ Q \in \mathbb{R}^{n_1 \times r}\right\} \subseteq \mathbb{R}^{n_1 \times n_2}. \tag{4.3.31}$$

Notice that T is a linear subspace. In the analogy between ℓ^1 minimization and nuclear norm minimization, the subspace T plays the role of the "support" of X_o. Geometrically, T represents the *tangent space* to the set of rank-r matrices at X_o – see Figure 4.6 and Exercise 4.11. The subspace T is generated by matrices UR^* whose column space is contained in $\operatorname{col}(X_o)$ and matrices QV^* whose row space is contained in $\operatorname{row}(X_o)$. Notice that elements in T have rank no more than $2r$. Meanwhile the matrix UV^* plays the role of the "signs" of X_o since $UV^* \in \mathsf{T}$ and

$$\left\langle X_o, UV^*\right\rangle = \|X_o\|_* . \tag{4.3.32}$$

The orthogonal complement of T is

$$\mathsf{T}^\perp \doteq \{M \mid \operatorname{col}(M) \perp \operatorname{col}(X), \operatorname{row}(M) \perp \operatorname{row}(X)\} . \tag{4.3.33}$$

Let $P_U = UU^*$ and $P_V = VV^*$ be the orthogonal projections onto the column space and row space of X_o, respectively. Then the orthogonal projections onto these subspaces are given by[9]

$$\mathcal{P}_{\mathsf{T}}[M] = P_U M + M P_V - P_U M P_V \tag{4.3.34}$$

and

$$\mathcal{P}_{\mathsf{T}^\perp}[M] = (I - P_U)M(I - P_V). \tag{4.3.35}$$

Notice that because the orthogonal projections $P_{U^\perp} = I - P_U$ and $P_{V^\perp} = I - P_V$ have norm at most one, $\mathcal{P}_{\mathsf{T}^\perp}$ does not increase the operator norm:

$$\left\|\mathcal{P}_{\mathsf{T}^\perp}[M]\right\| \le \|M\| . \tag{4.3.36}$$

[9] Equations (4.3.34) and (4.3.35) can be derived from the condition that at $\mathcal{P}_{\mathsf{T}}[M]$, the error $M - \mathcal{P}_{\mathsf{T}}[M]$ is orthogonal to T.

Feasible Cone Restriction

Note that any matrix $\boldsymbol{M} \in \mathsf{T}^{\perp}$ has columns that are orthogonal to the columns of $\boldsymbol{U}$ and rows that are orthogonal to the rows of $\boldsymbol{V}^*$. This implies that

$$\left\|\boldsymbol{M}+\boldsymbol{U}\boldsymbol{V}^*\right\| = \max\left\{\|\boldsymbol{M}\|, \left\|\boldsymbol{U}\boldsymbol{V}^*\right\|\right\} = \max\left\{\|\boldsymbol{M}\|, 1\right\}. \tag{4.3.37}$$

So, for any matrix $\boldsymbol{X}$,

$$\|\boldsymbol{X}\|_* = \sup_{\|\boldsymbol{Q}\|\le 1} \langle \boldsymbol{X}, \boldsymbol{Q}\rangle \tag{4.3.38}$$

$$\ge \sup_{\|\boldsymbol{M}\|\le 1} \left\langle \boldsymbol{X}, \boldsymbol{U}\boldsymbol{V}^* + \mathcal{P}_{\mathsf{T}^{\perp}}[\boldsymbol{M}]\right\rangle \tag{4.3.39}$$

$$= \left\langle \boldsymbol{X}, \boldsymbol{U}\boldsymbol{V}^*\right\rangle + \sup_{\|\boldsymbol{M}\|\le 1} \left\langle \mathcal{P}_{\mathsf{T}^{\perp}}[\boldsymbol{X}], \boldsymbol{M}\right\rangle \tag{4.3.40}$$

$$= \left\langle \boldsymbol{X}, \boldsymbol{U}\boldsymbol{V}^*\right\rangle + \left\|\mathcal{P}_{\mathsf{T}^{\perp}}[\boldsymbol{X}]\right\|_*. \tag{4.3.41}$$

Let $\hat{\boldsymbol{X}}$ be any optimal solution to our problem (4.3.30). It can be written as $\hat{\boldsymbol{X}} = \boldsymbol{X}_o + \boldsymbol{H}$, with $\boldsymbol{H} = \hat{\boldsymbol{X}} - \boldsymbol{X}_o \in \operatorname{null}(\mathcal{A})$. From the above calculation, we have

$$\|\boldsymbol{X}_o + \boldsymbol{H}\|_* \ge \left\langle \boldsymbol{X}_o + \boldsymbol{H}, \boldsymbol{U}\boldsymbol{V}^*\right\rangle + \left\|\mathcal{P}_{\mathsf{T}^{\perp}}[\hat{\boldsymbol{X}}]\right\|_* \tag{4.3.42}$$

$$= \|\boldsymbol{X}_o\|_* + \left\langle \boldsymbol{H}, \boldsymbol{U}\boldsymbol{V}^*\right\rangle + \left\|\mathcal{P}_{\mathsf{T}^{\perp}}[\boldsymbol{H}]\right\|_* \tag{4.3.43}$$

$$\ge \|\boldsymbol{X}_o\|_* - \|\mathcal{P}_{\mathsf{T}}[\boldsymbol{H}]\|_* + \left\|\mathcal{P}_{\mathsf{T}^{\perp}}[\boldsymbol{H}]\right\|_*. \tag{4.3.44}$$

So, if a better solution than $\boldsymbol{X}_o$ exists, the feasible perturbation $\boldsymbol{H}$ must satisfy the following cone restriction:

$$\left\|\mathcal{P}_{\mathsf{T}^{\perp}}[\boldsymbol{H}]\right\|_* \le \|\mathcal{P}_{\mathsf{T}}[\boldsymbol{H}]\|_*. \tag{4.3.45}$$

Matrix Restricted Strong Convexity Property

As in the proof of ℓ^1 success, we want to show that feasible perturbations $\boldsymbol{H} \in \operatorname{null}(\mathcal{A})$ must have $\left\|\mathcal{P}_{\mathsf{T}^{\perp}}[\boldsymbol{H}]\right\|_* > \|\mathcal{P}_{\mathsf{T}}[\boldsymbol{H}]\|_*$. This is true if the operator $\mathcal{A}$ satisfies the following (uniform) matrix *restricted strong convexity* (RSC) property:

DEFINITION 4.13. (Matrix restricted strong convexity) *The linear operator $\mathcal{A}$ satisfies the matrix* restricted strong convexity *(RSC) condition of rank r with constant α if for the support T of every matrix of rank r and for all nonzero $\boldsymbol{H}$ satisfying*

$$\left\|\mathcal{P}_{\mathsf{T}^{\perp}}[\boldsymbol{H}]\right\|_* \le \alpha \cdot \|\mathcal{P}_{\mathsf{T}}[\boldsymbol{H}]\|_*, \tag{4.3.46}$$

with some constant $\alpha \ge 1$, we have

$$\|\mathcal{A}[\boldsymbol{H}]\|_2^2 > \mu \cdot \|\boldsymbol{H}\|_F^2 \tag{4.3.47}$$

for some constant $\mu > 0$.

The following theorem says that if $\mathcal{A}$ satisfies the rank-RIP, then it satisfies the matrix RSC:

THEOREM 4.14. (Rank-RIP implies matrix RSC) *If a linear operator $\mathcal{A}$ satisfies rank-RIP with $\delta_{4r} < 1/(1+\alpha\sqrt{2})$, then $\mathcal{A}$ satisfies the matrix-RSC condition of rank r with constant α.*

Both the statement and proof of Theorem 4.14 parallel Theorem 3.17 for the ℓ^1 norm. Theorem 4.14 involves δ_{4r}, as opposed to δ_{2k} for k-sparse vectors. The bigger constant in $4r = r + 3r$ reflects the need to account for all three components of the singular value decomposition in the proof.

Proof Using the parallelogram identity, similar to Lemma 3.16, it is not difficult to show that for any $\boldsymbol{Z}, \boldsymbol{Z}'$ such that $\boldsymbol{Z} \perp \boldsymbol{Z}'$, and $\operatorname{rank}(\boldsymbol{Z}) + \operatorname{rank}(\boldsymbol{Z}') \le 4r$,

$$\left|\left\langle \mathcal{A}[\boldsymbol{Z}], \mathcal{A}[\boldsymbol{Z}'] \right\rangle\right| \le \delta_{4r}(\mathcal{A}) \left\|\boldsymbol{Z}\right\|_F \left\|\boldsymbol{Z}'\right\|_F. \tag{4.3.48}$$

Let T denote the support subspace for some matrix of rank r. Take any $\boldsymbol{H}$ that satisfies the cone restriction $\left\|\mathcal{P}_{\mathsf{T}^\perp}[\boldsymbol{Z}]\right\|_* \le \alpha \cdot \|\mathcal{P}_{\mathsf{T}}[\boldsymbol{Z}]\|_*$, and write

$$\boldsymbol{H} = \mathcal{P}_{\mathsf{T}}[\boldsymbol{H}] + \mathcal{P}_{\mathsf{T}^\perp}[\boldsymbol{H}]. \tag{4.3.49}$$

Let $\boldsymbol{H}_{\mathsf{T}}$ denote $\mathcal{P}_{\mathsf{T}}[\boldsymbol{H}]$. For the second term, $\mathcal{P}_{\mathsf{T}^\perp}[\boldsymbol{H}]$, write its compact singular value decomposition

$$\mathcal{P}_{\mathsf{T}^\perp}[\boldsymbol{H}] = \sum_i \eta_i \boldsymbol{\phi}_i \boldsymbol{\zeta}_i^*, \tag{4.3.50}$$

where $\boldsymbol{\phi}_1, \boldsymbol{\phi}_2, \ldots$ are the left singular vectors, $\boldsymbol{\zeta}_1, \boldsymbol{\zeta}_2, \ldots$ the right singular vectors, and $\eta_1 \ge \eta_2 \ge \cdots > 0$ the singular values. From the variational characterization of the singular vectors, each $\boldsymbol{\phi}_i$ is orthogonal to the columns of $\boldsymbol{U}$, and each $\boldsymbol{\zeta}_i$ is orthogonal to the columns of $\boldsymbol{V}$. So, if we partition $\mathcal{P}_{\mathsf{T}^\perp}[\boldsymbol{H}]$ as

$$\mathcal{P}_{\mathsf{T}^\perp}[\boldsymbol{H}] = \underbrace{\sum_{i=1}^{r} \eta_i \boldsymbol{\phi}_i \boldsymbol{\zeta}_i^*}_{\doteq \boldsymbol{\Phi}_1} + \underbrace{\sum_{i=r+1}^{2r} \eta_i \boldsymbol{\phi}_i \boldsymbol{\zeta}_i^*}_{\doteq \boldsymbol{\Phi}_2} + \cdots, \tag{4.3.51}$$

we have $\boldsymbol{\Phi}_i \perp \boldsymbol{\Phi}_j$ for $i \ne j$, $\boldsymbol{\Phi}_i \perp \boldsymbol{H}_{\mathsf{T}}$ for every T.

Since the singular values η_i are nonincreasing, the largest singular value of the $(i+1)$-th block is bounded by the average of the singular values in the i-th block:

$$\forall\, i \ge 1, \quad \|\boldsymbol{\Phi}_{i+1}\| \le \frac{\|\boldsymbol{\Phi}_i\|_*}{r}. \tag{4.3.52}$$

So, noting that as an element in T, we have $\operatorname{rank}(\boldsymbol{H}_{\mathsf{T}}) \le 2r$ and so $\operatorname{rank}(\boldsymbol{H}_{\mathsf{T}} + \boldsymbol{\Phi}_1) \le 3r$. Notice that

$$\mathcal{A}[\boldsymbol{H}_{\mathsf{T}}] + \mathcal{A}[\boldsymbol{\Phi}_1] = \mathcal{A}[\boldsymbol{H}] - \mathcal{A}[\boldsymbol{\Phi}_2] - \mathcal{A}[\boldsymbol{\Phi}_3] - \cdots. \tag{4.3.53}$$

Then, very similar to the derivation of inequalities (3.3.32) in Theorem 3.17, and by applying the rank-RIP to matrices of rank bounded by at most $4r$, we have

$$\begin{aligned}
&(1-\delta_{4r})\,\|\boldsymbol{H}_{\mathsf{T}}+\boldsymbol{\Phi}_1\|_F^2 \\
&\le \langle \mathcal{A}[\boldsymbol{H}_{\mathsf{T}}+\boldsymbol{\Phi}_1], \mathcal{A}[\boldsymbol{H}_{\mathsf{T}}+\boldsymbol{\Phi}_1]\rangle \\
&= \langle \mathcal{A}[\boldsymbol{H}_{\mathsf{T}}+\boldsymbol{\Phi}_1], \mathcal{A}[\boldsymbol{H}]-\mathcal{A}[\boldsymbol{\Phi}_2]-\mathcal{A}[\boldsymbol{\Phi}_3]-\cdots\rangle \\
&\le \sum_{j\ge 2} \left|\langle \mathcal{A}[\boldsymbol{H}_{\mathsf{T}}], \mathcal{A}[\boldsymbol{\Phi}_j]\rangle\right| + \left|\langle \mathcal{A}[\boldsymbol{\Phi}_1], \mathcal{A}[\boldsymbol{\Phi}_j]\rangle\right| + \langle \mathcal{A}[\boldsymbol{H}_{\mathsf{T}}+\boldsymbol{\Phi}_1], \mathcal{A}[\boldsymbol{H}]\rangle \\
&\le \delta_{4r}\left(\|\boldsymbol{H}_{\mathsf{T}}\|_F+\|\boldsymbol{\Phi}_1\|_F\right)\sum_{j\ge 2}\left\|\boldsymbol{\Phi}_j\right\|_F + \|\mathcal{A}[\boldsymbol{H}_{\mathsf{T}}+\boldsymbol{\Phi}_1]\|_2\,\|\mathcal{A}[\boldsymbol{H}]\|_2 \\
&\le \delta_{4r}\sqrt{2}\,\|\boldsymbol{H}_{\mathsf{T}}+\boldsymbol{\Phi}_1\|_F\sum_{j\ge 2}\left\|\boldsymbol{\Phi}_j\right\|_F + (1+\delta_{4r})\,\|\boldsymbol{H}_{\mathsf{T}}+\boldsymbol{\Phi}_1\|_F\,\|\mathcal{A}[\boldsymbol{H}]\|_2 \\
&\le \delta_{4r}\sqrt{2}\,\|\boldsymbol{H}_{\mathsf{T}}+\boldsymbol{\Phi}_1\|_F\,\frac{\left\|\mathcal{P}_{\mathsf{T}^\perp}[\boldsymbol{H}]\right\|_*}{\sqrt{r}} + (1+\delta_{4r})\,\|\boldsymbol{H}_{\mathsf{T}}+\boldsymbol{\Phi}_1\|_F\,\|\mathcal{A}[\boldsymbol{H}]\|_2\,.
\end{aligned}$$

Note that $\boldsymbol{H}$ is restricted by the cone condition (4.3.46), which leads to

$$\left\|\mathcal{P}_{\mathsf{T}^\perp}[\boldsymbol{H}]\right\|_* \le \alpha\,\|\boldsymbol{H}_{\mathsf{T}}\|_* \le \alpha\sqrt{r}\,\|\boldsymbol{H}_{\mathsf{T}}\|_F \le \alpha\sqrt{r}\,\|\boldsymbol{H}_{\mathsf{T}}+\boldsymbol{\Phi}_1\|_F\,. \tag{4.3.54}$$

Combining this with the previous inequality, we obtain

$$\|\mathcal{A}[\boldsymbol{H}]\|_2 \ge \frac{1-\delta_{4r}(1+\alpha\sqrt{2})}{1+\delta_{4r}}\,\|\boldsymbol{H}_{\mathsf{T}}+\boldsymbol{\Phi}_1\|_F\,. \tag{4.3.55}$$

Since the singular values η_i are nonincreasing, the i-th singular value in $\boldsymbol{\Phi}_2+\boldsymbol{\Phi}_3+\cdots$ is no larger than the mean of the first i singular values in $\mathcal{P}_{\mathsf{T}^\perp}[\boldsymbol{H}]$. So we have

$$\forall\, i\ge r+1, \quad \eta_i \le \left\|\mathcal{P}_{\mathsf{T}^\perp}[\boldsymbol{H}]\right\|_*/i. \tag{4.3.56}$$

This leads to

$$\|\boldsymbol{\Phi}_2+\boldsymbol{\Phi}_3+\cdots\|_F^2 = \sum_{i=r+1}^{\infty}\eta_i^2 \tag{4.3.57}$$

$$\le \left\|\mathcal{P}_{\mathsf{T}^\perp}[\boldsymbol{H}]\right\|_*^2\sum_{i=r+1}^{\infty}\frac{1}{i^2} \tag{4.3.58}$$

$$\le \frac{\left\|\mathcal{P}_{\mathsf{T}^\perp}[\boldsymbol{H}]\right\|_*^2}{r} \le \frac{\alpha^2\,\|\boldsymbol{H}_{\mathsf{T}}\|_*^2}{r} \tag{4.3.59}$$

$$\le \alpha^2\,\|\boldsymbol{H}_{\mathsf{T}}\|_F^2 \le \alpha^2\,\|\boldsymbol{H}_{\mathsf{T}}+\boldsymbol{\Phi}_1\|_F^2\,. \tag{4.3.60}$$

Since $\boldsymbol{\Phi}_i$ with $i\ge 2$ are orthogonal to $\boldsymbol{H}_{\mathsf{T}}+\boldsymbol{\Phi}_1$, this gives us

$$\|\boldsymbol{H}\|_F^2 \le (1+\alpha^2)\,\|\boldsymbol{H}_{\mathsf{T}}+\boldsymbol{\Phi}_1\|_F^2\,. \tag{4.3.61}$$

Combining this with the previous bound (4.3.55) on $\|\mathcal{A}[\boldsymbol{H}]\|_2$, we obtain

$$\|\mathcal{A}[\boldsymbol{H}]\|_2 \geq \frac{1-\delta_{4r}(1+\alpha\sqrt{2})}{(1+\delta_{4r})\sqrt{1+\alpha^2}} \|\boldsymbol{H}\|_F . \tag{4.3.62}$$

This concludes the proof. □

Note that for the nuclear norm minimization problem, the feasible perturbation $\boldsymbol{H}$ satisfies the cone restriction (4.3.45). Thus Theorem 4.12 is essentially a corollary to Theorem 4.14 with constant $\alpha = 1$ for the cone restriction.

4.3.5 Rank-RIP of Random Measurements

Theorem 4.12 indicates that the rank-RIP implies a very strong conclusion: nuclear norm minimization exactly recovers low-rank matrices. Moreover the recovery is *uniform* in the sense that a single set of measurements $\mathcal{A}$ suffices to recover any sufficiently low-rank matrix $\boldsymbol{X}_o$. The remaining question is what measurement operators satisfy the rank-RIP?

Random Gaussian Measurements

A simple and natural choice is to consider the random Gaussian measurements:

$$\mathcal{A}[\boldsymbol{X}] = (\langle \boldsymbol{A}_1, \boldsymbol{X}\rangle, \ldots, \langle \boldsymbol{A}_m, \boldsymbol{X}\rangle), \tag{4.3.63}$$

where the entries of the matrices $\boldsymbol{A}_1, \ldots, \boldsymbol{A}_m \in \mathbb{R}^{n_1 \times n_2}$ are all i.i.d. Gaussian $\mathcal{N}(0, 1/m)$. This is equivalent to viewing $\mathcal{A}$ as an $m \times n_1 n_2$ matrix with entries $\mathcal{A}_{ij}$ sampled i.i.d. $\mathcal{N}(0, 1/m)$. We demonstrate that such random maps satisfy the rank-RIP with high probability, using ideas and techniques similar to the proof of the (regular) RIP of random Gaussian matrices in Section 3.4.2:

THEOREM 4.15. (Rank-RIP of gaussian measurements) *If the measurement operator $\mathcal{A}$ is a random Gaussian map with entries i.i.d. $\mathcal{N}(0, 1/m)$, then $\mathcal{A}$ satisfies the rank-RIP with constant $\delta_r(\mathcal{A}) \leq \delta$ with high probability, provided $m \geq Cr(n_1 + n_2) \times \delta^{-2} \log \delta^{-1}$, where $C > 0$ is a numerical constant.*

Proof Let

$$\mathsf{S}_r \doteq \{\boldsymbol{X} \mid \operatorname{rank}(\boldsymbol{X}) \leq r,\ \|\boldsymbol{X}\|_F = 1\}.$$

Notice that $\delta_r(\mathcal{A}) \leq \delta$ if and only if

$$\sup_{\boldsymbol{X} \in \mathsf{S}_r} \mid \langle \mathcal{A}[\boldsymbol{X}], \mathcal{A}[\boldsymbol{X}]\rangle - 1 \mid \leq \delta. \tag{4.3.64}$$

We complete the rest of the proof in three steps.

1. Constructing a covering ε-net for S_r

Notice that for any rank-r matrix $\boldsymbol{X} \in \mathbb{R}^{n_1 \times n_2}$, it can be represented by its SVD: $\boldsymbol{X} = \boldsymbol{U}\boldsymbol{\Sigma}\boldsymbol{V}^*$. So to construct a covering of all rank-r matrices, we can try to construct a covering for each of the terms $\boldsymbol{U}, \boldsymbol{V}$, and $\boldsymbol{\Sigma}$, respectively.

LEMMA 4.16. *There is a covering* ε*-net* N_U *for the* $\mathsf{H} = \{\boldsymbol{U} \in \mathbb{R}^{n_1 \times r} \mid \boldsymbol{U}^*\boldsymbol{U} = \boldsymbol{I}\}$ *in operator norm, i.e.,*

$$\forall\, \boldsymbol{U} \in \mathsf{H},\ \exists\, \boldsymbol{U}' \in \mathsf{N}_U \quad \textit{satisfying} \quad \|\boldsymbol{U} - \boldsymbol{U}'\| \le \varepsilon, \tag{4.3.65}$$

of size $|\mathsf{N}_U| \le (6/\varepsilon)^{n_1 r}$.

Proof Let N' be an $\varepsilon/2$-net for $\{\boldsymbol{U} \in \mathbb{R}^{n_1 \times r} \mid \|\boldsymbol{U}\| \le 1\}$ of size $|\mathsf{N}'| \le (6/\varepsilon)^{n_1 r}$. The existence of such a net follows immediately from the volumetric argument used in the proof of Lemma 3.25. Let

$$\mathsf{Q} \doteq \{\boldsymbol{U}' \in \mathsf{N}' \mid \exists\, \boldsymbol{U} \in \mathsf{H} \text{ with } \|\boldsymbol{U} - \boldsymbol{U}'\| \le \varepsilon/2\}.$$

For each $\boldsymbol{U}' \in \mathsf{Q}$, let $\hat{\boldsymbol{U}}(\boldsymbol{U}')$ be the nearest element of H. Set $\mathsf{N}_U = \{\hat{\boldsymbol{U}}(\boldsymbol{U}') \mid \boldsymbol{U}' \in \mathsf{Q}\} \subseteq \mathsf{H}$. By the triangle inequality, N_U is an ε-net for H. □

Similarly, one can construct an ε-net N_V for $\mathsf{H}' = \{\boldsymbol{V} \in \mathbb{R}^{n_2 \times r} \mid \boldsymbol{V}^*\boldsymbol{V} = \boldsymbol{I}\}$ of size $|\mathsf{N}_V| \le (6/\varepsilon)^{n_2 r}$. With this lemma, we have the following result.

LEMMA 4.17. *There is a covering* ε*-net* N_r *for the set* S_r*, of size* $|\mathsf{N}_r| \le \exp\big((n_1 + n_2) r \log(18/\varepsilon) + r\log(9/\varepsilon)\big)$.

Proof Choose $\varepsilon/3$-nets N_U and N_V that cover H and H', respectively, in operator norm. According to the above lemma, the sizes of the nets can be less than $(18/\varepsilon)^{n_1 r}$ and $(18/\varepsilon)^{n_2 r}$, respectively. Form a covering $\varepsilon/3$-net N_Σ for

$$\mathsf{D} \doteq \{\boldsymbol{\Sigma} \in \mathbb{R}^{r \times r} \mid \boldsymbol{\Sigma} \text{ diagonal}, \|\boldsymbol{\Sigma}\|_F = 1\},$$

in Frobenius norm. According to Lemma 3.25, the size of the net can be less than $|\mathsf{N}_\Sigma| \le (9/\varepsilon)^r$.

Now consider the following net for the whole set S_r:

$$\mathsf{N}_r \doteq \{\boldsymbol{U}\boldsymbol{\Sigma}\boldsymbol{V}^* \mid \boldsymbol{U} \in \mathsf{N}_U, \boldsymbol{\Sigma} \in \mathsf{N}_\Sigma, \boldsymbol{V} \in \mathsf{N}_V\}.$$

Its size is bounded by the product of all three nets, hence the expression in the lemma. Now we only have to show that this is indeed a covering ε-net for S_r. For any given $\boldsymbol{X} = \boldsymbol{U}\boldsymbol{\Sigma}\boldsymbol{V}^*$, we can find $\hat{\boldsymbol{X}} = \hat{\boldsymbol{U}}\hat{\boldsymbol{\Sigma}}\hat{\boldsymbol{V}}^* \in \mathsf{N}_r$ with $\|\boldsymbol{U} - \hat{\boldsymbol{U}}\| \le \varepsilon/3$, $\|\boldsymbol{V} - \hat{\boldsymbol{V}}\| \le \varepsilon/3$, and $\|\boldsymbol{\Sigma} - \hat{\boldsymbol{\Sigma}}\|_F \le \varepsilon/3$.

The triangle inequality gives

$$\begin{aligned} \|\boldsymbol{X} - \hat{\boldsymbol{X}}\|_F &\le \|\boldsymbol{U} - \hat{\boldsymbol{U}}\|\|\boldsymbol{\Sigma}\boldsymbol{V}^*\|_F + \|\hat{\boldsymbol{U}}\|\|\boldsymbol{\Sigma} - \hat{\boldsymbol{\Sigma}}\|_F\|\boldsymbol{V}^*\| + \|\hat{\boldsymbol{U}}\hat{\boldsymbol{\Sigma}}\|_F\|\boldsymbol{V}^* - \hat{\boldsymbol{V}}^*\| \\ &\le \varepsilon, \end{aligned}$$

where we have used that each of the approximation errors is bounded by $\varepsilon/3$, $\|\hat{\boldsymbol{U}}\| = \|\boldsymbol{V}\| = 1$, and $\|\boldsymbol{\Sigma}\boldsymbol{V}^*\|_F = \|\hat{\boldsymbol{U}}\hat{\boldsymbol{\Sigma}}\|_F = 1$. □

2. Discretization

As in the ℓ^1 case for sparse signals in Section 3.4.2, the goal of discretization is trying to show that if $\mathcal{A}$ is restricted isometric on the finite set of (discrete) points in the covering net N_r with a constant δ_{N_r}, so is $\mathcal{A}$ on the whole set S_r, with a constant δ_r possibly slightly larger than δ_{N_r}.

Now consider a point $\boldsymbol{X}$ in S_r and its closest point $\hat{\boldsymbol{X}}$ in N_r. Thus, we have $\|\boldsymbol{X} - \hat{\boldsymbol{X}}\|_F \le \varepsilon$. Also we have[10]

$$
\begin{aligned}
&|\langle \mathcal{A}[\boldsymbol{X}], \mathcal{A}[\boldsymbol{X}]\rangle - \langle \mathcal{A}[\hat{\boldsymbol{X}}], \mathcal{A}[\hat{\boldsymbol{X}}]\rangle| \\
&\quad = |\langle \mathcal{A}[\boldsymbol{X}], \mathcal{A}[\boldsymbol{X} - \hat{\boldsymbol{X}}\boldsymbol{P}_V]\rangle + \langle \mathcal{A}[\boldsymbol{X} - \boldsymbol{P}_{\hat{U}}\boldsymbol{X}], \mathcal{A}[\hat{\boldsymbol{X}}\boldsymbol{P}_V]\rangle \\
&\qquad + \langle \mathcal{A}[\boldsymbol{P}_{\hat{U}}\boldsymbol{X} - \hat{\boldsymbol{X}}], \mathcal{A}[\hat{\boldsymbol{X}}\boldsymbol{P}_V]\rangle + \langle \mathcal{A}[\hat{\boldsymbol{X}}], \mathcal{A}[\hat{\boldsymbol{X}}\boldsymbol{P}_V - \hat{\boldsymbol{X}}]\rangle|.
\end{aligned}
$$

To bound the first term in the above expression, notice that

$$
\|\boldsymbol{X} - \hat{\boldsymbol{X}}\boldsymbol{P}_V\|_F = \|(\boldsymbol{X} - \hat{\boldsymbol{X}})\boldsymbol{P}_V\|_F \le \|\boldsymbol{X} - \hat{\boldsymbol{X}}\|_F \le \varepsilon.
$$

Also, $\boldsymbol{X} - \hat{\boldsymbol{X}}\boldsymbol{P}_V$ is of rank r. So we have

$$
|\langle \mathcal{A}[\boldsymbol{X}], \mathcal{A}[\boldsymbol{X} - \hat{\boldsymbol{X}}\boldsymbol{P}_V]\rangle| \le (1 + \delta_r(\mathcal{A}))\varepsilon.
$$

For the second term, since $\boldsymbol{P}_{\hat{U}}$ is an orthogonal projection onto the space of matrices whose columns are the same as $\hat{\boldsymbol{X}}$, we have

$$
\|\boldsymbol{X} - \boldsymbol{P}_{\hat{U}}\boldsymbol{X}\|_F \le \|\boldsymbol{X} - \hat{\boldsymbol{X}}\|_F \le \varepsilon.
$$

Also, since $\boldsymbol{X}$ and $\boldsymbol{P}_{\hat{U}}\boldsymbol{X}$ have the same row space, so $\boldsymbol{X} - \boldsymbol{P}_{\hat{U}}\boldsymbol{X}$ is of rank r or less. Therefore, we also have

$$
|\langle \mathcal{A}[\boldsymbol{X} - \boldsymbol{P}_{\hat{U}}\boldsymbol{X}], \mathcal{A}[\hat{\boldsymbol{X}}\boldsymbol{P}_V]\rangle| \le (1 + \delta_r(\mathcal{A}))\varepsilon.
$$

Similarly for the third and fourth terms, each is bounded by the same bound. Therefore, we get

$$
|\langle \mathcal{A}[\boldsymbol{X}], \mathcal{A}[\boldsymbol{X}]\rangle - \langle \mathcal{A}[\hat{\boldsymbol{X}}], \mathcal{A}[\hat{\boldsymbol{X}}]\rangle| \le 4(1 + \delta_r(\mathcal{A}))\varepsilon.
$$

From this we have

$$
\delta_r(\mathcal{A}) - \delta_{\mathsf{N}_r} \le 4(1 + \delta_r(\mathcal{A}))\varepsilon. \tag{4.3.66}
$$

This gives

$$
\delta_r(\mathcal{A}) \le \frac{4\varepsilon + \delta_{\mathsf{N}_r}}{1 - 4\varepsilon}. \tag{4.3.67}
$$

3. Union bound

For each $\boldsymbol{X} \in \mathsf{N}_r$, $\mathcal{A}[\boldsymbol{X}] \in \mathbb{R}^m$ is a random vector with entries independent $\mathcal{N}(0, 1/m)$. We have

$$
\mathbb{P}\left[\left|\|\mathcal{A}[\boldsymbol{X}]\|_2^2 - 1\right| > t\right] \le 2\exp(-mt^2/8). \tag{4.3.68}
$$

[10] Notice that here the derivation is more subtle than the ℓ^1 case because $\boldsymbol{X} - \hat{\boldsymbol{X}}$ is not necessarily of rank r.

Hence, summing the probabilities over all elements of N_r, we have

$$\mathbb{P}\left[\delta_{\mathsf{N}_r} > t\right] \le 2\,|\mathsf{N}_r|\exp\left(-mt^2/8\right)$$
$$= 2\exp\left(-\frac{mt^2}{8} + (n_1+n_2)r\log(18/\varepsilon) + r\log(9/\varepsilon)\right).$$

If we choose $\varepsilon = c \cdot \delta$ and $t = c \cdot \delta$ for some small constant c and ensure $m \ge Cr(n_1+n_2)\delta^{-2}\log\delta^{-1}$ for some large enough C, the above failure probability is bounded by $2\exp(-c'm\delta^2)$. On the complement of this "failure" event, $\delta_{\mathsf{N}_r} \le c{\cdot}\delta$, and due to (4.3.67) we have $\delta_r(\mathcal{A}) \le \delta$. This concludes the proof of Theorem 4.15. □

The number of measurements $m = O(r(n_1+n_2))$ required is nearly optimal, since an $n_1 \times n_2$ rank-r matrix has $r(n_1+n_2-r)$ degrees of freedom. Of course, the big O notation hides a numerical constant. Like the ℓ^1 minimization for sparse recovery, when the dimension is high, nuclear norm minimization exhibits a phase transition between success and failure. Identifying this transition yields more precise estimates of the number m of measurements required to reconstruct a low-rank matrix. We discuss this issue in more detail below.

Random Submatrix of a Unitary Basis

Although random Gaussian measurements have very nice properties such as (rank) RIP, the lack of structure in such measurements makes it rather expensive to generate, store, and apply such operators in practice. Hence it is natural to ask if there exist other more structured measurements that have similarly good RIP properties. In Section 3.4.3, we saw that given any unitary matrix that is incoherent from sparse signals, then a randomly selected subset of its rows will satisfy the RIP with high probability. An important special case that has been widely used in practice for compressive sensing is a randomly chosen submatrix of the discrete Fourier transform basis. It is then natural to ask what are the Fourier-type bases for matrices.

In the case of sparse recovery, we start with a unitary basis $\boldsymbol{U} \in \mathbb{C}^{n\times n}$ and show that if the rows $\{\boldsymbol{u}_i\}_{i=1}^n$ of the basis incoherent with sparse signals:

$$\forall\, i, \quad \|\boldsymbol{u}_i\|_\infty = \sup_{\boldsymbol{x}:\|\boldsymbol{x}\|_2=1,\,\|\boldsymbol{x}\|_0=1} \langle \boldsymbol{u}_i, \boldsymbol{x}\rangle \le \zeta/\sqrt{n}$$

for some constant ζ, then a randomly selected (sufficient) number of rows of $\boldsymbol{U}$ will satisfy RIP.

To simplify the discussion of matrices, we will assume $n_1 = n_2 = n$ for the rest of this subsection; a similar approach applies when $n_1 \ne n_2$. Let us assume $\{\boldsymbol{U}_1, \boldsymbol{U}_2, \ldots, \boldsymbol{U}_{n^2}\} \subset \mathbb{C}^{n\times n}$ form a unitary basis for the matrix space $\mathbb{C}^{n\times n}$. Similarly we want each of the matrices $\boldsymbol{U}_i$ to be incoherent with low-rank matrices. Note that for any $\boldsymbol{X} \in \mathbb{C}^{n\times n}$,

$$\|\boldsymbol{U}_i\| = \sup_{\boldsymbol{X}:\|\boldsymbol{X}\|_2=1,\,\mathrm{rank}(\boldsymbol{X})=1} \langle \boldsymbol{U}_i, \boldsymbol{X}\rangle. \tag{4.3.69}$$

Hence in order for each $\boldsymbol{U}_i$ to be incoherent with low-rank matrices, we could require

$$\forall\, i, \quad \|\boldsymbol{U}_i\| \leq \zeta/\sqrt{n}. \tag{4.3.70}$$

Then to construct the measurement operator $\mathcal{A}$, we randomly select a subset of m bases from $\{\boldsymbol{U}_1, \boldsymbol{U}_2, \ldots, \boldsymbol{U}_{n^2}\}$ and properly scale them as[11]

$$\mathcal{A}: \quad \boldsymbol{A}_i = \frac{n}{\sqrt{m}} \boldsymbol{U}_i, \quad i = 1, \ldots, m. \tag{4.3.71}$$

Then one should expect that when m is large enough, with high probability, the so-defined $\mathcal{A}$ satisfies the rank-RIP. The following theorem makes this precise:

THEOREM 4.18. *Let us assume* $\{\boldsymbol{U}_1, \boldsymbol{U}_2, \ldots, \boldsymbol{U}_{n^2}\} \subset \mathbb{C}^{n\times n}$ *is a unitary basis for the matrix space* $\mathbb{C}^{n\times n}$ *and with* $\|\boldsymbol{U}_i\| \leq \zeta/\sqrt{n}$ *for some constant* ζ. *Let* $\mathcal{A}$ *be defined as per* (4.3.71). *Then if*

$$m \geq C\zeta^2 \cdot rn \log^6 n, \tag{4.3.72}$$

then with high probability, $\mathcal{A}$ *satisfies the rank-RIP over the set of all rank-r matrices.*

The proof of this theorem is out of the scope of this book and interested readers may refer to the work of [Liu11].

According to this statement, from an incoherent unitary basis, with high probability we could find a (compressive) sensing operator $\mathcal{A}$ such that it is rank-RIP. Hence with this operator, one can recover all rank-r matrices via the nuclear norm minimization. The remaining question is what type of structured bases (of the matrix space) are rank-incoherent as per (4.3.70)? To this end, one should seek a matrix analog to the Fourier basis.

In the case of MRI imaging, we have seen that measurements that one can physically take are essentially the Fourier coefficients of the brain image. As it turns out, the matrix analog to Fourier basis also has a natural origin from physics. In quantum-state tomography, a system of k qubits is of dimension $n = 2^k$. The quantum state of such a system is described by a density matrix $\boldsymbol{X}_o \in \mathbb{C}^{n\times n}$ which is positive semidefinite with trace 1. When the state is early pure, $\boldsymbol{X}_o$ is a very low-rank matrix with rank $(\boldsymbol{X}_o) = r \ll n$.

One problem in quantum physics is how to recover the quantum state $\boldsymbol{X}_o$ of a system from linear measurements. As it turns out, a set of experimentally feasible measurements are given by the so-called *Pauli observables*. Each Pauli measurement is given by the inner product of $\boldsymbol{X}_o$ with matrices of the form $\boldsymbol{P}_1 \otimes \cdots \otimes \boldsymbol{P}_k$ where $\otimes$ is the tensor (Kronecker) product and each $\boldsymbol{P}_i = (1/\sqrt{2})\sigma$, where σ is a 2×2 matrix chosen from the following four possibilities:

$$\sigma_1 = \begin{bmatrix} 1 & 0 \\ 0 & 1 \end{bmatrix}, \quad \sigma_2 = \begin{bmatrix} 0 & 1 \\ 1 & 0 \end{bmatrix}, \quad \sigma_3 = \begin{bmatrix} 0 & -i \\ i & 0 \end{bmatrix}, \quad \sigma_4 = \begin{bmatrix} 1 & 0 \\ 0 & -1 \end{bmatrix}.$$

[11] The scaling is to ensure that the "column" of $\mathcal{A}$ be of unit norm.

It is easy to see that there are a total of 4^k possible choices for the tensor product, denoted as $\{\boldsymbol{U}_i\}_{i=1}^{4^k}$ and they together form an orthonormal basis for the matrix space $\mathbb{C}^{n\times n}$ where $n = 2^k$.

One can show that for each basis $\boldsymbol{U}_i = \boldsymbol{P}_1 \otimes \cdots \otimes \boldsymbol{P}_k$, its operator norm is bounded as $\|\boldsymbol{U}_i\| \leq 1/\sqrt{n}$ hence incoherent with low-rank matrices. Then according to Theorem 4.18, a randomly selected $m \geq Crn \log^6 n$ rows of the Pauli bases will satisfy the rank-RIP property with high probability. Hence, such a sensing operator will be able to uniformly recover all pure quantum states less than rank r.

4.3.6 Noise, Inexact Low Rank, and Phase Transition

Above, we established that, under fairly broad conditions, nuclear norm minimization correctly recovers a low-rank matrix $\boldsymbol{X}_o$ from ideal measurements $\boldsymbol{y} = \mathcal{A}[\boldsymbol{X}_o]$. In practice, the measurements can be corrupted by noise or measurement errors. In some cases, $\boldsymbol{X}_o$ may not be exactly low-rank. It is desirable to understand whether nuclear norm minimization still gives reasonably good estimates of $\boldsymbol{X}_o$ in these situations.

In Section 3.5, we established that ℓ^1 minimization accurately estimates sparse signals under deterministic noise, random noise, and even inexact sparsity. As we will see in this section, essentially the same analysis and results generalize to the case of nuclear norm minimization for recovering low-rank matrices.

Deterministic Noise

Here we still assume the matrix $\boldsymbol{X}_o$ is perfectly low-rank, but the measurement $\boldsymbol{y}$ is corrupted by small additive noise:

$$\boldsymbol{y} = \mathcal{A}[\boldsymbol{X}_o] + \boldsymbol{z}, \qquad \|\boldsymbol{z}\|_2 \leq \varepsilon. \tag{4.3.73}$$

Similar to Theorem 3.29, for recovering low-rank matrices with (deterministic) noise, we have the following result.

THEOREM 4.19. (Stable low-rank recovery via BPDN) *Suppose that* $\boldsymbol{y} = \mathcal{A}[\boldsymbol{X}_o] + \boldsymbol{z}$, *with* $\|\boldsymbol{z}\|_2 \leq \varepsilon$, *and let* $\operatorname{rank}(\boldsymbol{X}_o) = r$. *If* $\delta_{4r}(\mathcal{A}) < \sqrt{2} - 1$, *then any solution* $\hat{\boldsymbol{X}}$ *to the optimization problem*

$$\begin{array}{ll} \min & \|\boldsymbol{X}\|_* \\ \text{subject to} & \|\mathcal{A}[\boldsymbol{X}] - \boldsymbol{y}\|_2 \leq \varepsilon \end{array} \tag{4.3.74}$$

satisfies

$$\left\| \hat{\boldsymbol{X}} - \boldsymbol{X}_o \right\|_F \leq C\varepsilon. \tag{4.3.75}$$

Here, C is a numerical constant.

Proof The proof of this theorem parallels that for Theorem 3.29 and we leave the details for the reader as an exercise (see Exercise 4.17). □

Random Noise

Now let us consider the case when the noise in the above measurement model (4.3.73) is random (Gaussian):

$$y = \mathcal{A}[X_o] + z, \tag{4.3.76}$$

where entries of z are random i.i.d. Gaussian $\mathcal{N}(0, \sigma^2/m)$. Then we have the following theorem that parallels Theorem 3.31 for the ℓ^1 case.

THEOREM 4.20. (Stable Low-rank recovery via lasso) *Suppose that* $\mathcal{A} \sim_{\text{iid}} \mathcal{N}(0, 1/m)$, *and* $y = \mathcal{A}[X_o] + z$, *with* X_o *of rank* r *and* $z \sim_{\text{iid}} \mathcal{N}(0, \sigma^2/m)$. *Solve the matrix Lasso*

$$\min \ \tfrac{1}{2} \|y - \mathcal{A}[X]\|_2^2 + \lambda_m \|X\|_*, \tag{4.3.77}$$

with regularization parameter $\lambda_m = c \cdot 2\sigma\sqrt{(n_1 + n_2)/m}$ *for a large enough* c. *Then with high probability,*

$$\left\| \hat{X} - X_o \right\|_F \le C'\sigma\sqrt{\frac{r(n_1 + n_2)}{m}}. \tag{4.3.78}$$

Notice that, in contrast to deterministic noise, random noise leads to a much more favorable scaling $\sqrt{r(n_1 + n_2)/m}$ in the estimation error: to see this, notice that in a typical compressive sensing setting (as suggested by Theorem 4.15), the sampling dimension m needs to be at least $C \cdot r(n_1 + n_2)$ for some large constant C. Hence the scaling factor is proportional to $1/\sqrt{C}$ and it becomes small when C is large.

Proof The overall proof strategy is quite similar to that of Theorem 3.31 for the stability of Lasso estimate. We will lay out the key places that are different from the ℓ^1 case and leave the details to the reader as an exercise.

In the proof of Lemma 3.30, we see that in order to establish the cone condition for the Lasso-type minimization, one of the key steps is to bound $|\langle A^* z, h \rangle|$ via

$$|\langle A^* z, h \rangle| \le \left\| A^* z \right\|_\infty \|h\|_1 .$$

Following similar arguments, in the matrix Lasso case here, we need to bound $|\langle \mathcal{A}^* z, H \rangle|$ instead as

$$|\langle \mathcal{A}^* z, H \rangle| \le \left\| \mathcal{A}^* z \right\| \|H\|_*,$$

where $\|\mathcal{A}^* z\|$ is the operator norm (largest singular value) of the matrix $\mathcal{A}^* z = \sum_{i=1}^m z_i A_i$. To this end, we need to provide a tight bound for the operator norm of $\mathcal{A}^* z$.

Notice that

$$M \doteq \left\| \sum_{i=1}^m z_i A_i \right\| = \sup_{u \in \mathbb{S}^{n_1 - 1}, v \in \mathbb{S}^{n_2 - 1}} u^* \sum_{i=1}^m z_i A_i v \tag{4.3.79}$$

$$= \sup_{u \in \mathbb{S}^{n_1 - 1}, v \in \mathbb{S}^{n_2 - 1}} \langle z, \mathcal{A}[uv^*] \rangle. \tag{4.3.80}$$

The $\boldsymbol{u}_\star$ and $\boldsymbol{v}_\star$ that achieve the maximum value in (4.3.80) depend on z and $\mathcal{A}$. So in order to eliminate this dependence and provide a bound for $\left\|\sum_{i=1}^m z_i \boldsymbol{A}_i\right\|$, we cover the two spheres $\mathbb{S}^{n_1-1}$ and $\mathbb{S}^{n_2-1}$ with two ε-nets N_1 and N_2, respectively. According to Lemma 3.25, the sizes of the nets can be less than $(3/\varepsilon)^{n_1}$ and $(3/\varepsilon)^{n_2}$, respectively.

Let us denote

$$M_{\mathsf{N}} \doteq \sup_{\boldsymbol{u}\in\mathsf{N}_1,\, \boldsymbol{v}\in\mathsf{N}_2} \boldsymbol{u}^* \sum_{i=1}^m z_i \boldsymbol{A}_i \boldsymbol{v},$$

then it is easy to show that[12]

$$M \leq \frac{M_{\mathsf{N}}}{1-2\varepsilon}. \tag{4.3.81}$$

Notice that given any $\boldsymbol{u} \in \mathsf{N}_1, \boldsymbol{v} \in \mathsf{N}_2$, $\langle z, \mathcal{A}[\boldsymbol{u}\boldsymbol{v}^*]\rangle$ is a Gaussian variable of distribution $\mathcal{N}(0, \|\mathcal{A}[\boldsymbol{u}\boldsymbol{v}^*]\|_2^2(\sigma^2/m))$. Since $\mathcal{A}$ is rank-RIP and $\boldsymbol{u}\boldsymbol{v}^*$ is a rank-1 matrix of unit Frobenius norm, we have

$$\left\|\mathcal{A}[\boldsymbol{u}\boldsymbol{v}^*]\right\|_2^2 \leq (1+\delta) \leq 2. \tag{4.3.82}$$

Thus, we have

$$\mathbb{P}\left[\left|\boldsymbol{u}^* \sum_{i=1}^m z_i \boldsymbol{A}_i \boldsymbol{v}\right| > t\right] \leq 2\exp\left(-\frac{mt^2}{4\sigma^2}\right). \tag{4.3.83}$$

Apply the union bound on all possible pairs of $(\boldsymbol{u}, \boldsymbol{v})$ from the two nets and choose $t = \alpha\sigma\sqrt{n_1+n_2/m}$ for some large enough α, then we have $M_{\mathsf{N}} > t$ with diminishing probability as n_1 or n_2 becomes large. Therefore, we have

$$M = \left\|\sum_{i=1}^m z_i \boldsymbol{A}_i\right\| \leq \beta\sigma\sqrt{\frac{n_1+n_2}{m}} \tag{4.3.84}$$

for some constant β with high probability.

Now, similar to the proof of Lemma 3.30, if we choose λ_m to be on the order of $O\left(\sigma\sqrt{n_1+n_2/m}\right)$, then the feasible perturbation $\boldsymbol{H}$ satisfies the cone restriction. Since $\mathcal{A}$ is rank-RIP, it implies that $\mathcal{A}$ satisfies the matrix restricted strong convexity (RSC) property. That leads to the bound on the estimation error:

$$\|\boldsymbol{H}\|_F = \left\|\hat{\boldsymbol{X}} - \boldsymbol{X}_o\right\|_F \leq C'\sigma\sqrt{\frac{r(n_1+n_2)}{m}}. \tag{4.3.85}$$

The details of the proof for this follow essentially the same steps as those in the proof of Theorem 3.31 for the ℓ^1 case. We leave those to the reader as an exercise (see Exercise 4.19.) □

The error bound given in the above theorem can actually be shown to be nearly optimal as it is close to the best error that can be achieved by any estimator over all rank-r matrices. The following theorem, due to [CP11] makes this precise:

[12] We leave the details of proving this inequality to the reader as an exercise.

THEOREM 4.21. *Suppose that $\mathcal{A} \sim_{\text{iid}} \mathcal{N}(0, 1/m)$ and we observe $\boldsymbol{y} = \mathcal{A}[\boldsymbol{X}_o] + \boldsymbol{z}$ where entries of $\boldsymbol{z}$ are i.i.d. $\mathcal{N}(0, \sigma^2/m)$ random variables. Set*

$$M^\star(\mathcal{A}) = \inf_{\hat{\boldsymbol{X}}(\boldsymbol{y})} \sup_{\operatorname{rank}(\boldsymbol{X}) \le r} \mathbb{E} \left\| \hat{\boldsymbol{X}}(\boldsymbol{y}) - \boldsymbol{X} \right\|_F^2. \tag{4.3.86}$$

Then we have

$$M^\star(\mathcal{A}) \ge c\sigma^2 \frac{rn}{m}, \tag{4.3.87}$$

for $n = \max\{n_1, n_2\}$, where $c > 0$ is a numerical constant.

The proof of this theorem is beyond the scope of this book; we refer interested readers to [CP11] for a proof. According to Theorem 4.20, the worst error of the matrix Lasso matches the best achievable by any estimator, up to constants.

Inexact Low-Rank Matrices

In the case when $\boldsymbol{X}_o$ is not exactly low-rank, let $[\boldsymbol{X}_o]_r$ be the best rank-r approximation of $\boldsymbol{X}_o$. We can rewrite the observation model

$$\boldsymbol{y} = \mathcal{A}[\boldsymbol{X}_o] + \boldsymbol{z}, \quad \|\boldsymbol{z}\|_2 \le \varepsilon \tag{4.3.88}$$

as:

$$\boldsymbol{y} = \mathcal{A}\left[[\boldsymbol{X}_o]_r\right] + \mathcal{A}\left[\boldsymbol{X}_o - [\boldsymbol{X}_o]_r\right] + \boldsymbol{z}, \quad \|\boldsymbol{z}\|_2 \le \varepsilon.$$

THEOREM 4.22. (Inexact low-rank recovery) *Let $\boldsymbol{y} = \mathcal{A}[\boldsymbol{X}_o] + \boldsymbol{z}$, with $\|\boldsymbol{z}\|_2 \le \varepsilon$. Let $\hat{\boldsymbol{X}}$ solve the denoising problem*

$$\begin{array}{ll} \min & \|\boldsymbol{X}\|_* \\ \text{subject to} & \|\boldsymbol{y} - \mathcal{A}[\boldsymbol{X}]\|_2 \le \varepsilon. \end{array} \tag{4.3.89}$$

Then for any r such that $\delta_{4r}(\boldsymbol{A}) < \sqrt{2} - 1$,

$$\left\| \hat{\boldsymbol{X}} - \boldsymbol{X}_o \right\|_2 \le C \frac{\|\boldsymbol{X}_o - [\boldsymbol{X}_o]_r\|_*}{\sqrt{r}} + C'\varepsilon \tag{4.3.90}$$

for some constants C and C'.

Proof The proof of this theorem parallels that for Theorem 3.33 for the inexact sparse recovery problem. We here only set up some analogous concepts and key ideas that allow us to extend that proof to the matrix case here. But we leave details of the proof as an exercise for the reader.

Let $\boldsymbol{X}_o = \boldsymbol{U}\boldsymbol{\Sigma}\boldsymbol{V}^*$ denote the compact SVD of the true solution $\boldsymbol{X}_o$. Then its best rank-r approximation is $[\boldsymbol{X}_o]_r = \boldsymbol{U}_r\boldsymbol{\Sigma}_r\boldsymbol{V}_r^*$. Now let

$$\mathsf{T} \doteq \left\{ \boldsymbol{U}_r\boldsymbol{R}^* + \boldsymbol{Q}\boldsymbol{V}_r^* \mid \boldsymbol{R} \in \mathbb{R}^{n_2 \times r},\ \boldsymbol{Q} \in \mathbb{R}^{n_1 \times r} \right\} \subseteq \mathbb{R}^{n_1 \times n_2}. \tag{4.3.91}$$

Show that in the inexact low-rank case, instead of the cone restriction (4.3.45), we have the following restriction for the feasible perturbation $\boldsymbol{H} = \hat{\boldsymbol{X}} - \boldsymbol{X}_o$:

$$\left\| \mathcal{P}_{\mathsf{T}^\perp}[\boldsymbol{H}] \right\|_* \le \|\mathcal{P}_{\mathsf{T}}[\boldsymbol{H}]\|_* + 2 \left\| \mathcal{P}_{\mathsf{T}^\perp}[\boldsymbol{X}_o] \right\|_*. \tag{4.3.92}$$

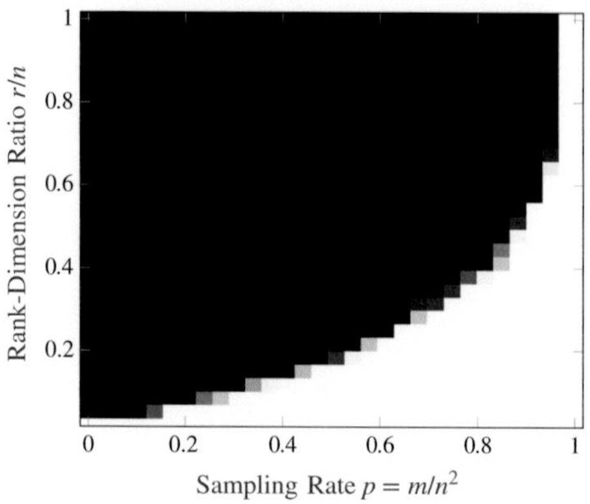

Figure 4.7 Phase Transitions in Low-rank Matrix Recovery. We plot the probability of successfully recovering an $n \times n$ low-rank matrix $\boldsymbol{X}_o$ from Gaussian measurements. Horizontal axis: sampling rate $p = m/n^2$. Vertical axis rank-dimension ratio r/n. The success of nuclear norm minimization exhibits a very sharp transition from success to failure.

Notice that $\mathcal{P}_{\mathsf{T}^\perp}[\boldsymbol{X}_o] = \boldsymbol{X}_o - [\boldsymbol{X}_o]_r$. Then, similar to the proof of Theorem 3.33, simply carry the extra term $2\left\|\mathcal{P}_{\mathsf{T}^\perp}[\boldsymbol{X}_o]\right\|_*$ at the places in the proof of Theorem 4.14 where the cone restriction is applied. One can reach the conclusion of the theorem. We leave details of the proof as an exercise for the reader (see Exercise 4.18). □

Phase Transition in Low-Rank Matrix Recovery

Thus far, we have seen strong parallels between sparse vector recovery using ℓ^1 norm minimization and low-rank matrix recovery using nuclear norm minimization. In both cases, we saw how an appropriate notion of restricted isometry property could be used to guarantee exact recovery from a near-minimal number of random measurements – about $k \log(n/k)$ for k-sparse vectors, and about nr for rank-r matrices. However, just like in the sparse vector case, this tool does not yield sharp constants.

In fact, there is a phase transition phenomenon for low-rank recovery, which mirrors that for sparse recovery: as the dimension grows, the transition between success and failure in low-rank recovery becomes increasingly sharp. Figure 4.7 illustrates this.

Just as we did for sparse recovery, we can use the "coefficient-space" geometry of the low-rank recovery problem to derive very sharp estimates of this transition. This geometry is phrased in terms of the descent cone D of the nuclear norm at the target solution $\boldsymbol{X}_o$:

$$\mathsf{D} \doteq \{\boldsymbol{H} \mid \|\boldsymbol{X}_o + \boldsymbol{H}\|_* \leq \|\boldsymbol{X}_o\|_*\}. \tag{4.3.93}$$

As for sparse recovery, $\boldsymbol{X}_o$ is the unique optimal solution to the nuclear norm minimization problem if and only if $\mathsf{D} \cap \text{null}(\mathcal{A}) = \{\mathbf{0}\}$. Hence, quantifying the probability of success under a random linear projection becomes equivalent to quantifying the probability that the two convex cones D and $\text{null}(\mathcal{A})$ have only trivial intersection. Deploying Theorem 6.14, we find that there is a sharp transition between success and failure around

$$m^\star \sim \delta(\mathsf{D}), \tag{4.3.94}$$

the statistical dimension of the descent cone. Moreover, the theorem tells us that the width of the transition region is roughly $O(\sqrt{n_1 n_2})$. The *location* of the transition region can be characterized using the same machinery that we deployed in Section 3.6 to estimate the statistical dimension of the descent cone of the ℓ^1 norm. This machinery involves estimating the expected squared distance of a random vector (here, random matrix) to the polar cone, which is spanned by the subdifferential of the nuclear norm. For convenience, for a matrix $\boldsymbol{M}$ with singular value decomposition $\boldsymbol{M} = \boldsymbol{U}\boldsymbol{\Sigma}\boldsymbol{V}^*$, let us define the *singular value thresholding operator* as

$$\mathcal{D}_\tau[\boldsymbol{M}] \doteq \boldsymbol{U}\mathcal{S}_\tau[\boldsymbol{\Sigma}]\boldsymbol{V}^*, \tag{4.3.95}$$

where $\mathcal{S}_\tau[\cdot]$ is the entry-wise *soft-thresholding* operator,

$$\forall \boldsymbol{X}, \quad \mathcal{S}_\tau[\boldsymbol{X}] = \operatorname{sign}(\boldsymbol{X}) \circ (|\boldsymbol{X}| - \tau)_+,$$

where $\circ$ is the entry-wise (Hadamard) product of two matrices. An intermediate result produced by these calculations is as follows:

THEOREM 4.23. (Phase Transition in Low-rank Recovery) *Let* D *denote the descent cone of the nuclear norm at any matrix* $\boldsymbol{X}_o \in \mathbb{R}^{n_1 \times n_2}$ *of rank* r. *Let* $\boldsymbol{G}$ *be an* $(n_1 - r) \times (n_2 - r)$ *matrix with entries i.i.d.* $\mathcal{N}(0,1)$. *Set*

$$\psi(n_1, n_2, r) = \inf_{\tau \geq 0} \left\{ r(n_1 + n_2 - r + \tau^2) + \mathbb{E}_{\boldsymbol{G}}\left[\|\mathcal{D}_\tau[\boldsymbol{G}]\|_F^2 \right] \right\}. \tag{4.3.96}$$

Then

$$\psi(n_1, n_2, r) - 2\sqrt{n_2/r} \leq \delta(\mathsf{D}) \leq \psi(n_1, n_2, r). \tag{4.3.97}$$

This theorem identifies a sharp transition in low-rank recovery. It is possible to use asymptotic results on the limiting distribution of the singular values of a random matrix to give a formula for $\psi(n_1, n_2, r)/(n_1 n_2)$, which is valid when $n_1 \to \infty$, $n_1/n_2 \to \alpha \in (0, \infty)$, and $r/n_1 \to \rho \in (0,1)$. In the exercises, we guide the interested reader through this derivation. Here, we merely display the result of this calculation in Figure 4.7, and note the excellent agreement between this theoretical prediction and numerical experiment: *for the idealized setting of "generic" measurements, we have a very precise prediction of the phase transition!*

4.4 Low-Rank Matrix Completion

We have seen how concepts from sparse recovery transpose directly to the low-rank recovery problem. The concept of sparsity had a natural analog in the concept of rank deficiency. The ℓ^1 minimization problem for sparse recovery had a natural analog in the nuclear norm minimization problem for low-rank recovery. Moreover, these convex relaxations succeed under analogous conditions involving restricted isometry properties of the observation operator.

However, in many of the most interesting applications of nuclear norm minimization, the RIP does not hold! In the introduction to this chapter, we sketched applications to recommendation systems, in which we had access to *a subset* of the entries of a low-rank user–item matrix. We also sketched problems in reconstructing 3D shape, in which we observed *a subset* of the pixels of the rank-3 matrix $\boldsymbol{NL}$. Finally, we sketched a problem in Euclidean embedding, in which we observe *a subset* of the distances between some objects of interest. In all of these problems, the object of interest is a low-rank matrix $\boldsymbol{X}_o \in \mathbb{R}^{n\times n}$; the observation selects a subset $\Omega \subset [n]\times[n]$ of the entries of $\boldsymbol{X}_o$. The *matrix completion* problem asks us to fill in the missing entries:

PROBLEM 4.24. (Matrix completion) *Let $\boldsymbol{X}_o \in \mathbb{R}^{n\times n}$ be a low-rank matrix. Suppose we are given $\boldsymbol{Y} = \mathcal{P}_\Omega[\boldsymbol{X}_o]$, where $\Omega \subseteq [n] \times [n]$. Fill in the missing entries of $\boldsymbol{X}_o$.*

In matrix completion, the observation operator $\mathcal{A} = \mathcal{P}_\Omega$ is the restriction onto some small subset $\Omega \subseteq [n]\times[n]$ of the entries. In this situation, if $(i, j) \notin \Omega$, $\mathcal{P}_\Omega[\boldsymbol{E}_{ij}] = \mathbf{0}$, where $\boldsymbol{E}_{ij}$ denotes the matrix with all zeros except for the (i, j)-th entry being 1. That is to say, if Ω is a strict subset of $[n] \times [n]$, then $\mathcal{P}_\Omega$ has matrices of rank 1 in its null space! So, the rank-RIP cannot hold for any positive rank r with any nontrivial $\delta < 1$.

At a more basic level, the example of $\boldsymbol{X}_o = \boldsymbol{E}_{ij}$ suggests that there are some (very sparse) matrices that are impossible to complete from only a few entries. This is in contrast to our discussion of low-rank matrix recovery thus far, in which the only factor that dictates the ease or difficulty of recovering a target $\boldsymbol{X}_o$ is the complexity $\operatorname{rank}(\boldsymbol{X}_o)$. Nevertheless, our development thus far suggests that even for the more challenging problem of matrix completion, there may be some class of *well-structured* matrices $\boldsymbol{X}_o$ of interest for applications, which *can* be efficiently completed from just a few entries. In this section, we will see that this is indeed the case.

4.4.1 Nuclear Norm Minimization for Matrix Completion

In light of our previous study of matrix recovery, a natural approach to completing a low-rank matrix from a small subset $\boldsymbol{Y} = \mathcal{P}_\Omega[\boldsymbol{X}_o]$ of its entries is to look for the matrix $\boldsymbol{X}$ of minimum nuclear norm that agrees with the observation:

$$\begin{array}{ll} \min & \|\boldsymbol{X}\|_* \\ \text{subject to} & \mathcal{P}_\Omega[\boldsymbol{X}] = \boldsymbol{Y}. \end{array} \tag{4.4.1}$$

This is a special instance of the general nuclear norm minimization problem (4.3.14), with observation operator $\mathcal{A} = \mathcal{P}_\Omega$. As such, it is a semidefinite program, and can be solved with high accuracy in polynomial time. In practice, though, it is more important to have methods that scale to large problem instances. In the next section, we sketch one approach to achieving this, using Lagrange multiplier techniques. This approach has pedagogical value: it introduces several objects that will be used for analyzing when we can solve matrix completion problems efficiently. It also yields reasonably scalable algorithms. For practical matrix completion at the scale of $n \sim 10^6$

and beyond, even more scalable methods are needed; we discuss these issues in Chapters 8 and 9.

4.4.2 Algorithm via Augmented Lagrange Multiplier

There are two basic challenges in solving problem (4.4.1) at large scale. The first arises from the nonsmoothness of the nuclear norm $\|\cdot\|_*$; the second is due to the need to satisfy the constraint $\mathcal{P}_\Omega[\boldsymbol{X}] = \boldsymbol{Y}$ exactly.[13] The fundamental technology for handling constraints in optimization is Lagrange duality.

The basic object is the *Lagrangian*, which introduces a matrix $\boldsymbol{\Lambda}$ of Lagrange multipliers for the constraint $\mathcal{P}_\Omega[\boldsymbol{X}] = \boldsymbol{Y}$. The Lagrangian for (4.4.1) is

$$\mathcal{L}(\boldsymbol{X}, \boldsymbol{\Lambda}) = \|\boldsymbol{X}\|_* + \langle \boldsymbol{\Lambda}, \boldsymbol{Y} - \mathcal{P}_\Omega[\boldsymbol{X}] \rangle . \tag{4.4.2}$$

As introduced in the Appendix C, the optimal $\boldsymbol{X}_\star$ solution is characterized as a *saddle point* of the Lagrangian which is *minimized* with respect to $\boldsymbol{X}$, and maximized with respect to $\boldsymbol{\Lambda}$. A basic approach to solving a constrained problem such as (4.4.1) is to seek such a saddle point. In practice, more robustly convergent algorithms can be derived by instead working with the *augmented* Lagrangian

$$\mathcal{L}_\mu(\boldsymbol{X}, \boldsymbol{\Lambda}) = \|\boldsymbol{X}\|_* + \langle \boldsymbol{\Lambda}, \boldsymbol{Y} - \mathcal{P}_\Omega[\boldsymbol{X}] \rangle + (\mu/2) \|\boldsymbol{Y} - \mathcal{P}_\Omega[\boldsymbol{X}]\|_F^2 , \tag{4.4.3}$$

which encourages satisfaction of the constraint by adding an additional quadratic penalty term $(\mu/2) \|\boldsymbol{Y} - \mathcal{P}_\Omega[\boldsymbol{X}]\|_F^2$. A more general introduction to the augmented Lagrangian method (ALM) is given in Section 8.4 of Chapter 8.

The augmented Lagrangian method seeks a saddle point of $\mathcal{L}_\mu$ by alternating between minimizing with respect to the "primal variables" $\boldsymbol{X}$ and taking one step of gradient ascent to increase $\mathcal{L}_\mu$ using the "dual variables" $\boldsymbol{\Lambda}$:

$$\boldsymbol{X}_{k+1} \in \arg\min_{\boldsymbol{X}} \mathcal{L}_\mu(\boldsymbol{X}, \boldsymbol{\Lambda}_k), \tag{4.4.4}$$

$$\boldsymbol{\Lambda}_{k+1} = \boldsymbol{\Lambda}_k + \mu \mathcal{P}_\Omega\big[\boldsymbol{Y} - \boldsymbol{X}_{k+1}\big]. \tag{4.4.5}$$

Here, $\mathcal{P}_\Omega\big[\boldsymbol{Y} - \boldsymbol{X}_{k+1}\big] = \nabla_{\boldsymbol{\Lambda}} \mathcal{L}_\mu(\boldsymbol{X}_{k+1}, \boldsymbol{\Lambda})$. The ALM algorithm makes a very special choice of the step size (μ) for updating $\boldsymbol{\Lambda}$. This choice is important in general: it ensures that $\boldsymbol{\Lambda}$ stays dual feasible, an issue that we will explain in more depth in Section 8.4 of Chapter 8.

Under very general conditions, the iteration (4.4.4)–(4.4.5) converges to a primal–dual optimal pair $(\boldsymbol{X}_\star, \boldsymbol{\Lambda}_\star)$, and hence yields a solution to (4.4.1). While this algorithm appears simple, some caution is necessary: the first step is itself a nontrivial optimization problem! This subproblem has a characteristic form, which we encountered in our study of sparse recovery in noise: the objective function is a sum of a smooth convex term $f(\boldsymbol{X})$, and a nonsmooth convex function $g(\boldsymbol{X}) = \|\boldsymbol{X}\|_*$,

[13] In practice, when observations are noisy, exactly satisfying $\mathcal{P}_\Omega[\boldsymbol{X}] - \boldsymbol{Y}$ is neither necessary nor desirable. We study the noisy matrix completion in Section 4.4.5, and develop dedicated algorithms for it in Chapter 8.

$$\min_{\boldsymbol{X}} \underbrace{\|\boldsymbol{X}\|_*}_{g(\boldsymbol{X})\text{ convex}} + \underbrace{\langle \boldsymbol{\Lambda}, \boldsymbol{Y} - \mathcal{P}_\Omega[\boldsymbol{X}]\rangle + (\mu/2)\|\boldsymbol{Y} - \mathcal{P}_\Omega[\boldsymbol{X}]\|_F^2}_{f(\boldsymbol{X})\ \text{smooth, convex}}. \tag{4.4.6}$$

Here,

$$\nabla f(\boldsymbol{X}) = -\mathcal{P}_\Omega[\boldsymbol{\Lambda}] + \mu\mathcal{P}_\Omega[\boldsymbol{X} - \boldsymbol{Y}]. \tag{4.4.7}$$

This is μ-Lipschitz, in the sense that for any pair of matrices $\boldsymbol{X}$ and $\boldsymbol{X}'$,

$$\left\|\nabla f(\boldsymbol{X}) - \nabla f(\boldsymbol{X}')\right\|_F \le \mu \left\|\boldsymbol{X} - \boldsymbol{X}'\right\|_F. \tag{4.4.8}$$

This class of problem is amenable to the *proximal gradient method.*

The general proximal gradient iteration applies to objectives of the form $F(\boldsymbol{X}) = g(\boldsymbol{X}) + f(\boldsymbol{X})$, where g is convex, and f is convex, smooth, and has L-Lipschitz gradient. See Section 8.2 of Chapter 8. Here we have the Lipschitz constant $L = \mu$. So the iteration takes the form

$$\boldsymbol{X}_{k+1} = \arg\min_{\boldsymbol{X}} \left\{ g(\boldsymbol{X}) + (\mu/2)\left\|\boldsymbol{X} - \left(\boldsymbol{X}_k - (1/\mu)\nabla f(\boldsymbol{X}_k)\right)\right\|_F^2 \right\}. \tag{4.4.9}$$

In particular, it requires us to solve a sequence of "proximal problems"

$$\min_{\boldsymbol{X}} \left\{ g(\boldsymbol{X}) + (\mu/2)\|\boldsymbol{X} - \boldsymbol{M}\|_F^2 \right\}, \tag{4.4.10}$$

for particular choices of the matrix $\boldsymbol{M}$. When g is the nuclear norm, this problem can be solved in closed form from the SVD of $\boldsymbol{M}$. Recall from (4.3.95), for a matrix $\boldsymbol{M}$ with the singular value decomposition $\boldsymbol{M} = \boldsymbol{U}\boldsymbol{\Sigma}\boldsymbol{V}^*$, that its singular value thresholding operator is defined to be

$$\mathcal{D}_\tau[\boldsymbol{M}] = \boldsymbol{U}\mathcal{S}_\tau\left[\boldsymbol{\Sigma}\right]\boldsymbol{V}^*,$$

where $\mathcal{S}_\tau[\boldsymbol{X}] = \operatorname{sign}(\boldsymbol{X}) \circ (|\boldsymbol{X}| - \tau)_+$ is the soft-thresholding operator.

THEOREM 4.25. *The unique solution $\boldsymbol{X}_\star$ to the program*

$$\min_{\boldsymbol{X}} \left\{ \|\boldsymbol{X}\|_* + (\mu/2)\|\boldsymbol{X} - \boldsymbol{M}\|_F^2 \right\} \tag{4.4.11}$$

is given by

$$\boldsymbol{X}_\star = \mathcal{D}_{\mu^{-1}}[\boldsymbol{M}]. \tag{4.4.12}$$

The proof of this result follows from Exercise 4.13. The resulting procedures are stated as Algorithms 4.1 and 4.2. Here, for simplicity, we have neglected important issues such as the choice of stopping conditions, and the effect of inexact solution to subproblem (4.4.4) on the convergence of the basic ALM iteration in Algorithm 4.1.

To understand when the convex program (4.4.1) and the above algorithm correctly recover a matrix $\boldsymbol{X} = \boldsymbol{X}_o$ from a part of its entries, we vary the rank r of the matrix $\boldsymbol{X}_o$ as a fraction of the dimension n and a fraction $p \in (0, 1)$ of (randomly chosen) observed entries. In other words, p is the probability that an entry is given.

Algorithm 4.1 Matrix completion by ALM

1: **initialize:** $X_0 = \Lambda_0 = 0, \mu > 0$.
2: **while** not converged **do**
3: compute $X_{k+1} \in \arg\min_X \mathcal{L}_\mu(X, \Lambda_k)$ (say by Algorithm 4.2);
4: compute $\Lambda_{k+1} = \Lambda_k + \mu(Y - \mathcal{P}_\Omega[X_{k+1}])$.
5: **end while**

Algorithm 4.2 Proximal gradient for augmented Lagrangian

1: **initialize:** X_0 starts with the X_k from the outer loop of Algorithm 4.1.
2: **while** not converged **do**
3: compute

$$\begin{aligned} X_{\ell+1} &= \operatorname{prox}_{g/\mu}\left(X_\ell - \mu^{-1}\nabla f(X_\ell)\right) \\ &= \mathcal{D}_{\mu^{-1}}\left[\mathcal{P}_{\Omega^c}[X_\ell] + Y + \mu^{-1}\mathcal{P}_\Omega[\Lambda_k]\right]. \end{aligned}$$

4: **end while**

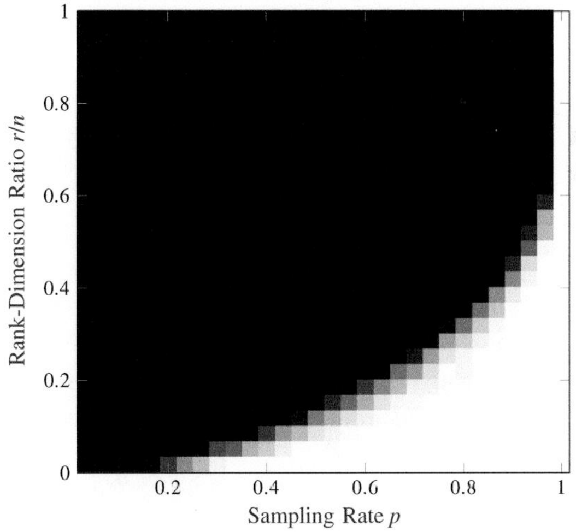

Figure 4.8 Matrix Completion for Varying Rank and Sampling Rate. Fraction of correct recoveries across 50 trials, as a function of the rank-dimension ratio r/n (vertical axis) and fraction p of observed entries (horizontal axis). Here, $n = 60$. In all cases, $X_o = AB^*$ is a product of two independent $n \times r$ i.i.d. $\mathcal{N}(0, 1/n)$ matrices. Trials are considered successful if $\|\hat{X} - X_o\|_F / \|X_o\|_F < 10^{-3}$.

Figure 4.8 shows the simulation results of using the above algorithm to recover a random low-rank matrix X_o under different settings.

We may draw a few observations from the above simulations: (1) the convex program (4.4.1) and the above algorithm indeed succeed under a surprisingly wide range of conditions, as long as the rank of the matrix is relatively low and a fraction of the entries are observed; (2) the success and failure of the convex program (4.4.1) exhibit a sharp phase transition phenomenon.

4.4.3 When Does Nuclear Norm Minimization Succeed?

The above simulations encourage us to understand the conditions under which the nuclear norm minimization program (4.4.1) is guaranteed to succeed for matrix completion.[14] It may be easier to first think about when it fails. It may fail if (i) $\boldsymbol{X}_o$ is *sparse* (as in the example of $\boldsymbol{E}_{ij}$), or (ii) the sampling pattern Ω is chosen adversarially (e.g., if we miss an entire row or column of $\boldsymbol{X}_o$). Below, we will state a theorem that makes this intuition precise – namely, if $\boldsymbol{X}_o$ is low-rank, and not too "spiky," and Ω is chosen at random, then nuclear norm minimization succeeds with high probability. Below we make these assumptions precise.

Incoherent Low-Rank Matrices

Although our intuition is that $\boldsymbol{X}_o$ itself should not be too "sparse," for technical reasons it will be necessary to enforce this condition on the singular vectors of $\boldsymbol{X}_o$, rather than on $\boldsymbol{X}_o$ itself. Let $\boldsymbol{X}_o = \boldsymbol{U}\boldsymbol{\Sigma}\boldsymbol{V}^*$ be the (reduced) singular value decomposition of $\boldsymbol{X}_o$. We say that $\boldsymbol{X}_o$ is ν-*incoherent* if the following hold:

$$\forall i \in [n], \quad \|\boldsymbol{e}_i^*\boldsymbol{U}\|_2^2 \le \nu r/n, \tag{4.4.13}$$

$$\forall j \in [n], \quad \|\boldsymbol{e}_j^*\boldsymbol{V}\|_2^2 \le \nu r/n. \tag{4.4.14}$$

These two conditions control the "spikiness" of the singular vectors of $\boldsymbol{X}_o$. To understand them better, note that $\boldsymbol{U}$ is an $n \times r$ matrix whose columns have unit ℓ^2 norm. Hence, $\sum_i \|\boldsymbol{e}_i^*\boldsymbol{U}\|_2^2 = \|\boldsymbol{U}\|_F^2 = r$. There are n rows, and so at least one of them must have ℓ^2 norm at least as large as the average, r/n. Hence, for any matrix $\boldsymbol{U}$ with unit norm columns, $\max_i \|\boldsymbol{e}_i^*\boldsymbol{U}\|_2^2 \ge r/n$. The *incoherence parameter* ν quantifies how much we lose with respect to this optimal bound. So, if ν is small, the singular vectors are, in a sense, spread around. To give a sense of scale, notice that it is always true that

$$1 \le \nu \le n/r. \tag{4.4.15}$$

If $\boldsymbol{U}$ and $\boldsymbol{V}$ are chosen uniformly at random (say by orthogonalizing the columns of a Gaussian matrix), then with high probability ν is bounded by $C\log(n)$. However, the definition does not require $\boldsymbol{U}$ and $\boldsymbol{V}$ to be random.

One important implication of this definition for matrix completion is that *when ν is small, there are no sparse matrices close to the tangent space* T. Indeed, let $\boldsymbol{E}_{ij} = \boldsymbol{e}_i\boldsymbol{e}_j^*$ denote the one-sparse matrix whose nonzero element occurs in entry (i, j). Then, using the expression (4.3.34) for the projection operator $\mathcal{P}_{\mathsf{T}}$ onto the tangent space T, we have that

[14] Or ultimately, if possible, to precisely characterize the phase transition behavior we have observed through experiments.

$$\begin{aligned}\left\|\mathcal{P}_{\mathsf{T}}[\boldsymbol{E}_{ij}]\right\|_F^2 &= \left\|\boldsymbol{U}\boldsymbol{U}^*\boldsymbol{E}_{ij}\right\|_F^2 + \left\|(\boldsymbol{I}-\boldsymbol{U}\boldsymbol{U}^*)\boldsymbol{E}_{ij}\boldsymbol{V}\boldsymbol{V}^*\right\|_F^2 \\ &\le \left\|\boldsymbol{U}^*\boldsymbol{e}_i\right\|_2^2 + \left\|\boldsymbol{e}_j^*\boldsymbol{V}\right\|_2^2 \\ &\le \frac{2\nu r}{n}. \end{aligned} \tag{4.4.16}$$

This indicates that no standard basis matrix $\boldsymbol{E}_{ij}$ is too close to the subspace T. Strangely enough, this implies the standard basis $\{\boldsymbol{E}_{ij}\}$ is a good choice for reconstructing elements from T. This is similar in spirit to our observations on incoherent operator bases: if no $\boldsymbol{E}_{ij}$ is too close to T, information about any particular element $\boldsymbol{X}_o \in \mathsf{T}$ must be spread across many different $\boldsymbol{E}_{ij}$. It will only take a few of these projections to be able to reconstruct $\boldsymbol{X}_o$. Note, however, a crucial difference between this notion of incoherence and our previous notions for matrix and vector recovery: here, the subspace T depends on $\boldsymbol{X}_o$ itself. The discussion in this section suggests that random sampling will be effective for reconstructing the particular matrix $\boldsymbol{X}_o$. We make this intuition formal below.

Exact Matrix Completion from Random Samples

We assume that each entry (i, j) belongs to the set Ω independently with probability p. We call this a *Bernoulli* sampling model, since the indicators $\mathbb{1}_{(i,j)\in\Omega}$ are independent $\mathrm{Ber}(p)$ random variables. Under this model, the expected number of observed entries is

$$m = \mathbb{E}\left[\,|\Omega|\,\right] = pn^2. \tag{4.4.17}$$

Under this model, nuclear norm minimization succeeds even when the number m of observations is close to the number of intrinsic degrees of freedom in the rank-r matrix $\boldsymbol{X}_o$. The following theorem makes this precise:

THEOREM 4.26. (Matrix completion via nuclear norm minimization) *Let $\boldsymbol{X}_o \in \mathbb{R}^{n\times n}$ be a rank-r matrix with incoherence parameter ν. Suppose that we observe $\boldsymbol{Y} = \mathcal{P}_\Omega[\boldsymbol{X}_o]$, with Ω sampled according to the Bernoulli model with probability*

$$p \ge C_1 \frac{\nu r \log^2(n)}{n}. \tag{4.4.18}$$

Then with probability at least $1 - C_2 n^{-c_3}$, $\boldsymbol{X}_o$ is the unique optimal solution to

$$\text{minimize} \quad \|\boldsymbol{X}\|_* \quad \text{subject to} \quad \mathcal{P}_\Omega[\boldsymbol{X}] = \boldsymbol{Y}. \tag{4.4.19}$$

There are several things to notice about the above theorem. First, the expected number of measurements is

$$m = pn^2 = C_1 \nu n r \log^2(n). \tag{4.4.20}$$

Since a rank-r matrix has $O(nr)$ degrees of freedom, the oversampling factor is only about $C\nu \log^2(n)$ – the number of samples we must see is nearly minimal.[15] Second, the number of samples required scales with the coherence of the matrix $\boldsymbol{X}_o$. So, if we want to recover a very coherent (think, "nearly sparse") $\boldsymbol{X}_o$, we will simply need more observations. Finally, the probability of success is in all the possible choices of the observed subset but is only for a given low-rank matrix $\boldsymbol{X}_o$. This is in contrast with the probability of success in the generic case studied in the previous sections, where an incoherent sampling operator is good for recovering the set of all matrices of rank less than r.

Of course, the precise conditions of the above theorem can only be interpreted as an idealized mathematical abstraction of real matrix completion or collaborative filtering problems. In particular, in real problems there may be noise in the observation, and, more importantly the observations may not be uniformly distributed.

4.4.4 Proving Correctness of Nuclear Norm Minimization

In this section, we prove Theorem 4.26. This section can be skipped for first time readers who are not theory-oriented or are not strongly interested in the techniques needed for a rigorous proof of the theorem.

Our approach is analogous to our proof that ℓ^1 recovers sparse vectors under incoherence (in Section 3.2.2) – we simply write down the optimality conditions and try to show that they are satisfied! Carrying this program through will be trickier, though.

To get started, we need an optimality condition for the nuclear norm minimization problem (4.4.19). As mentioned in the previous section, the Lagrangian associated with the matrix completion problem (4.4.19) is

$$\mathcal{L}(\boldsymbol{X},\boldsymbol{\Lambda}) = \|\boldsymbol{X}\|_* + \langle \boldsymbol{\Lambda}, \boldsymbol{Y} - \mathcal{P}_\Omega[\boldsymbol{X}] \rangle, \tag{4.4.21}$$

and the KKT conditions for the desired optimal $\boldsymbol{X}_o$ are such that there exist Lagrange multipliers $\boldsymbol{\Lambda}$ that satisfy

$$\mathcal{P}_\Omega^c[\boldsymbol{\Lambda}] = 0, \quad \boldsymbol{\Lambda} \in \partial \|\cdot\|_* (\boldsymbol{X}_o). \tag{4.4.22}$$

Similar to the ℓ^1 case in Section 3.2.2, such $\boldsymbol{\Lambda}$, if they can be found, are called a *dual certificate* that certifies the optimality of the ground truth $\boldsymbol{X}_o$.

Subdifferential of the Nuclear Norm

Similar to the case with ℓ^1 norm minimization, the above conditions suggest we need an expression for the subdifferential of the nuclear norm. The following lemma provides one:

[15] According to Theorem 1.7 of [CT09], if the sampling probability $p < \nu r \log(2n)/2n$, there will be infinitely many matrices of rank at most r that satisfy the incoherence condition and all have the same entries on Ω.

LEMMA 4.27. *Let $X \in \mathbb{R}^{n\times n}$ have compact singular value decomposition $X = U\Sigma V^*$. The subdifferential of the nuclear norm at X is given by*

$$\partial \|\cdot\|_* (X) = \left\{ Z \mid \mathcal{P}_{\mathsf{T}}[Z] = UV^*, \ \left\|\mathcal{P}_{\mathsf{T}^\perp}[Z]\right\| \le 1 \right\}. \tag{4.4.23}$$

Proof Consider any Z satisfying $\mathcal{P}_{\mathsf{T}}[Z] = UV^*$, and $\left\|\mathcal{P}_{\mathsf{T}^\perp}[Z]\right\| \le 1$. Notice that $\|Z\| = 1$. Since $X \in \mathsf{T}$,

$$\langle X, Z\rangle = \left\langle X, UV^*\right\rangle = \left\langle U^* X V, I\right\rangle = \langle \Sigma, I\rangle = \|X\|_*. \tag{4.4.24}$$

For every X',

$$\|X\|_* + \left\langle Z, X' - X\right\rangle = \left\langle Z, X'\right\rangle \le \|Z\| \left\|X'\right\|_* = \|X'\|_*. \tag{4.4.25}$$

Thus Z is a subgradient of the nuclear norm at X: $Z \in \partial\|\cdot\|_*(X)$. To complete the proof, we need to show that every element $Z \in \partial\|\cdot\|_*(X)$ satisfies $\mathcal{P}_{\mathsf{T}}[Z] = UV^*$ and $\|\mathcal{P}_{\mathsf{T}^\perp}[Z]\| \le 1$. We leave the converse as an exercise (see Exercise 4.20). □

If we compare to the expression for the subdifferential of the ℓ^1 norm, here, the subspace T plays the role of the *support* of the matrix, while the matrix UV^* is playing the role of the *signs*. Indeed, in this language, $\partial \|\cdot\|_*$ consists of those Z that are equal to the "sign" UV^* on the support T, and whose dual norm $\|\cdot\|$ is bounded by one on the orthogonal complement $\mathsf{T}^\perp$ of the support.

Optimality Conditions

Once we have the subdifferential in hand, we can fairly immediately write down an optimality condition for the convex program of interest. Indeed, consider the optimization problem

$$\begin{array}{ll} \min & \|X\|_* \\ \text{subject to} & \mathcal{P}_\Omega[X] = \mathcal{P}_\Omega[X_o]. \end{array} \tag{4.4.26}$$

Any feasible X can be written as $X_o + H$, where $H \in \text{null}(\mathcal{P}_\Omega)$, i.e., H is supported on the set Ω^c of entries that we do not observe. Similar to the ℓ^1 case in Section 3.2.2, if we can find a dual certificate Λ such that it satisfies (the KKT condition)

(i) Λ is supported on Ω and
(ii) $\Lambda \in \partial \|\cdot\|_* (X_o)$, i.e., $\mathcal{P}_{\mathsf{T}}[\Lambda] = UV^*$ and $\left\|\mathcal{P}_{\mathsf{T}^\perp}[\Lambda]\right\| \le 1$,

then we have

$$\|X_o + H\|_* \ge \|X_o\|_* + \langle \Lambda, H\rangle = \|X_o\|_*, \tag{4.4.27}$$

where the final equality holds because Λ is supported on Ω and H is supported on Ω^c. In addition, if we further have $\|\mathcal{P}_{\Omega^c}\mathcal{P}_{\mathsf{T}}\| < 1$ and $\left\|\mathcal{P}_{\mathsf{T}^\perp}[\Lambda]\right\| < 1$, then one can show that X_o is the *unique* optimal solution. The proof is similar to that in the ℓ^1 case (see the proof of Theorem 3.3) and we leave it to the reader as an exercise (see Exercise 4.16).

A natural idea for constructing $\boldsymbol{\Lambda}$ might be to simply follow the program that has worked before (in the ℓ^1 minimization case) and look for a matrix $\boldsymbol{\Lambda}$ of smallest 2-norm that satisfies the equality constraints

$$\mathcal{P}_{\Omega^c}[\boldsymbol{\Lambda}] = \mathbf{0}, \quad \mathcal{P}_{\mathsf{T}}[\boldsymbol{\Lambda}] = \boldsymbol{U}\boldsymbol{V}^*, \tag{4.4.28}$$

and then hope to check that it satisfies the inequality constraints

$$\left\| \mathcal{P}_{\mathsf{T}^\perp}[\boldsymbol{\Lambda}] \right\| \le 1.$$

For example, we could take $\boldsymbol{\Lambda} = \mathcal{P}_\Omega[\boldsymbol{G}]$, with $\boldsymbol{G} = (\mathcal{P}_{\mathsf{T}}\mathcal{P}_\Omega)^\dagger[\boldsymbol{U}\boldsymbol{V}^*]$, where $(\cdot)^\dagger$ denotes the pseudo-inverse. We are then left to check that

$$\left\| \mathcal{P}_{\mathsf{T}^\perp}\mathcal{P}_\Omega(\mathcal{P}_{\mathsf{T}}\mathcal{P}_\Omega)^\dagger[\boldsymbol{U}\boldsymbol{V}^*] \right\| \tag{4.4.29}$$

is small. This is a random matrix, but it is an exceedingly complicated one. It actually *is* possible to analyze its norm, but the analysis is quite intricate. The challenge arises because the thing that is random here is the support Ω. It is repeated in several places, creating probabilistic dependences, which complicates the analysis.

Relaxed Optimality Conditions

As it is difficult to directly find a dual certificate satisfying the KKT conditions exactly, we might want to relax these conditions and see if we could still find another certificate for the optimality. The following proposition suggests that we can ensure the optimality of $\boldsymbol{X}_o$ with an alternative set of (relaxed) conditions:

PROPOSITION 4.28. (KKT conditions – approximate version) *The matrix $\boldsymbol{X}_o$ is the unique optimal solution to the nuclear minimization problem* (4.4.19) *if the following set of conditions hold.*

1 *The operator norm of the operator $p^{-1}\mathcal{P}_{\mathsf{T}}\mathcal{P}_\Omega\mathcal{P}_{\mathsf{T}} - \mathcal{P}_{\mathsf{T}}$ is small:*

$$\left\| p^{-1}\mathcal{P}_{\mathsf{T}}\mathcal{P}_\Omega\mathcal{P}_{\mathsf{T}} - \mathcal{P}_{\mathsf{T}} \right\| \le \tfrac{1}{2}.$$

2 *There exists a dual certificate $\boldsymbol{\Lambda} \in \mathbb{R}^{n\times n}$ that satisfies $\mathcal{P}_\Omega[\boldsymbol{\Lambda}] = \boldsymbol{\Lambda}$ and*
   (a) $\left\| \mathcal{P}_{\mathsf{T}^\perp}[\boldsymbol{\Lambda}] \right\| \le 1/2$;
   (b) $\left\| \mathcal{P}_{\mathsf{T}}[\boldsymbol{\Lambda}] - \boldsymbol{U}\boldsymbol{V}^* \right\|_F \le 1/(4n)$.

Conditions 2(a) and 2(b) above trade off between the degree of satisfaction of the equality constraint $\mathcal{P}_{\mathsf{T}}[\boldsymbol{\Lambda}] = \boldsymbol{U}\boldsymbol{V}^*$ and the inequality constraint for the dual norm $\left\| \mathcal{P}_{\mathsf{T}^\perp}\boldsymbol{\Lambda} \right\| \le 1$ in the original KKT conditions. This is possible under the additional assumption that $\left\| p^{-1}\mathcal{P}_{\mathsf{T}}\mathcal{P}_\Omega\mathcal{P}_{\mathsf{T}} - \mathcal{P}_{\mathsf{T}} \right\|$ is not too large. This assumption is satisfied whenever the sampling map $p^{-1}\mathcal{P}_\Omega$ nearly preserves the length of all elements $\boldsymbol{X} \in \mathsf{T}$ – in other words, restricted on T the operator $p^{-1}\mathcal{P}_\Omega$ is nearly *isometric*. It can be considered a strengthening of the condition that $\mathsf{T} \cap \Omega^\perp = \{\mathbf{0}\}$, which was needed for unique optimality.

To prove Proposition 4.28, we will need another lemma. This says that provided $\mathcal{P}_\Omega$ acts nicely on matrices from T, every feasible perturbation $\boldsymbol{H}$ (i.e., $\boldsymbol{H}$ such that $\mathcal{P}_\Omega[\boldsymbol{H}] = \mathbf{0}$) must have a nonnegligible component along $\mathsf{T}^\perp$:

LEMMA 4.29. *Suppose that the operator $\mathcal{P}_\Omega$ satisfies*

$$\left\| \mathcal{P}_\mathsf{T} - p^{-1}\mathcal{P}_\mathsf{T}\mathcal{P}_\Omega\mathcal{P}_\mathsf{T} \right\| \le \frac{1}{2}. \tag{4.4.30}$$

Then for any $\boldsymbol{H}$ satisfying $\mathcal{P}_\Omega[\boldsymbol{H}] = \boldsymbol{0}$, we have

$$\left\| \mathcal{P}_{\mathsf{T}^\perp}[\boldsymbol{H}] \right\|_F \ge \sqrt{\frac{p}{2}} \left\| \mathcal{P}_\mathsf{T}[\boldsymbol{H}] \right\|_F. \tag{4.4.31}$$

Proof We have

$$\begin{aligned}
\langle \mathcal{P}_\Omega\mathcal{P}_\mathsf{T}[\boldsymbol{H}], \mathcal{P}_\Omega\mathcal{P}_\mathsf{T}[\boldsymbol{H}] \rangle &= \langle \mathcal{P}_\mathsf{T}[\boldsymbol{H}], \mathcal{P}_\Omega\mathcal{P}_\mathsf{T}[\boldsymbol{H}] \rangle \\
&= p\langle \mathcal{P}_\mathsf{T}[\boldsymbol{H}], p^{-1}\mathcal{P}_\Omega\mathcal{P}_\mathsf{T}[\boldsymbol{H}] \rangle \\
&= p\langle \mathcal{P}_\mathsf{T}[\boldsymbol{H}], \mathcal{P}_\mathsf{T} p^{-1}\mathcal{P}_\Omega\mathcal{P}_\mathsf{T}\mathcal{P}_\mathsf{T}[\boldsymbol{H}] \rangle \\
&\ge p\Big(1 - \left\| \mathcal{P}_\mathsf{T} - \mathcal{P}_\mathsf{T} p^{-1}\mathcal{P}_\Omega\mathcal{P}_\mathsf{T} \right\| \Big) \left\| \mathcal{P}_\mathsf{T}[\boldsymbol{H}] \right\|_F^2 \\
&\ge \frac{p}{2} \left\| \mathcal{P}_\mathsf{T}[\boldsymbol{H}] \right\|_F^2.
\end{aligned} \tag{4.4.32}$$

Then from $\mathcal{P}_\Omega\mathcal{P}_\mathsf{T}[\boldsymbol{H}] + \mathcal{P}_\Omega\mathcal{P}_{\mathsf{T}^\perp}[\boldsymbol{H}] = \mathcal{P}_\Omega[\boldsymbol{H}] = \boldsymbol{0}$, we have

$$\begin{aligned}
0 &= \left\| \mathcal{P}_\Omega\mathcal{P}_\mathsf{T}[\boldsymbol{H}] + \mathcal{P}_\Omega\mathcal{P}_{\mathsf{T}^\perp}[\boldsymbol{H}] \right\|_F \\
&\ge \left\| \mathcal{P}_\Omega\mathcal{P}_\mathsf{T}[\boldsymbol{H}] \right\|_F - \left\| \mathcal{P}_\Omega\mathcal{P}_{\mathsf{T}^\perp}[\boldsymbol{H}] \right\|_F \\
&\ge \sqrt{\frac{p}{2}} \left\| \mathcal{P}_\mathsf{T}[\boldsymbol{H}] \right\|_F - \left\| \mathcal{P}_{\mathsf{T}^\perp}[\boldsymbol{H}] \right\|_F,
\end{aligned} \tag{4.4.33}$$

giving the conclusion. □

We are now ready to prove the optimality of $\boldsymbol{X}_o$ under the conditions given by Proposition 4.28.

Proof of proposition 4.28 We want to show that under the above conditions, for any feasible perturbation $\boldsymbol{H} \neq \boldsymbol{0}$ and $\boldsymbol{X} = \boldsymbol{X}_o + \boldsymbol{H}$, we have $\|\boldsymbol{X}\|_* > \|\boldsymbol{X}_o\|_*$. Let $\mathcal{P}_{\mathsf{T}^\perp}[\boldsymbol{H}] = \bar{\boldsymbol{U}}\bar{\boldsymbol{\Sigma}}\bar{\boldsymbol{V}}^*$. Then we have $\bar{\boldsymbol{U}}\bar{\boldsymbol{V}}^* \in \mathsf{T}^\perp$ and $\left\| \bar{\boldsymbol{U}}\bar{\boldsymbol{V}}^* \right\| \le 1$. Therefore, we have $\boldsymbol{U}\boldsymbol{V}^* + \bar{\boldsymbol{U}}\bar{\boldsymbol{V}}^* \in \partial \left\| \cdot \right\|_* (\boldsymbol{X}_o)$ is a subgradient of the nuclear norm at $\boldsymbol{X}_o$.

Also, we have $\langle \bar{\boldsymbol{U}}\bar{\boldsymbol{V}}^*, \mathcal{P}_{\mathsf{T}^\perp}[\boldsymbol{H}] \rangle = \left\| \mathcal{P}_{\mathsf{T}^\perp}[\boldsymbol{H}] \right\|_*$ and $\langle \boldsymbol{\Lambda}, \boldsymbol{H} \rangle = 0$ and apply them to the following inequalities:

$$\begin{aligned}
\|\boldsymbol{X}_o + \boldsymbol{H}\|_* &\ge \|\boldsymbol{X}_o\|_* + \langle \boldsymbol{U}\boldsymbol{V}^* + \bar{\boldsymbol{U}}\bar{\boldsymbol{V}}^*, \boldsymbol{H} \rangle, \\
&= \|\boldsymbol{X}_o\|_* + \langle \boldsymbol{U}\boldsymbol{V}^* + \bar{\boldsymbol{U}}\bar{\boldsymbol{V}}^* - \boldsymbol{\Lambda}, \boldsymbol{H} \rangle, \\
&= \|\boldsymbol{X}_o\|_* + \langle \boldsymbol{U}\boldsymbol{V}^* - \mathcal{P}_\mathsf{T}[\boldsymbol{\Lambda}], \boldsymbol{H} \rangle + \langle \bar{\boldsymbol{U}}\bar{\boldsymbol{V}}^* - \mathcal{P}_{\mathsf{T}^\perp}[\boldsymbol{\Lambda}], \boldsymbol{H} \rangle,
\end{aligned}$$

$$\geq \|X_o\|_* - \frac{1}{4n} \|\mathcal{P}_{\mathsf{T}}[H]\|_F + \frac{1}{2} \left\|\mathcal{P}_{\mathsf{T}^\perp}[H]\right\|_*,$$

$$\geq \|X_o\|_* + \underbrace{\left(\frac{1}{2} - \frac{1}{4n}\sqrt{\frac{2}{p}}\right)}_{>0, \text{ since } p > n^{-2}.} \left\|\mathcal{P}_{\mathsf{T}^\perp}[H]\right\|_F. \tag{4.4.34}$$

In the final inequality, we have invoked Lemma 4.29.

Hence, for feasible perturbations H, $\|X_o + H\|_* \geq \|X_o\|_*$, with equality if and only if $\mathcal{P}_{\mathsf{T}^\perp}[H] = \mathbf{0}$. But via Lemma 4.29, $\mathcal{P}_{\mathsf{T}^\perp}[H] = \mathbf{0} \implies H = \mathbf{0}$. Thus, for any nonzero feasible perturbation H, $\|X_o + H\|_* > \|X_o\|_*$, establishing the desired condition. □

The Optimality Condition is Satisfied with High Probability

To complete the proof, we simply need to show that the optimality condition can be satisfied with high probability. To do this, we need to verify two claims: First, that with high probability the sampling operator Ω acts nicely on T, in the sense that $\left\|p^{-1}\mathcal{P}_{\mathsf{T}}\mathcal{P}_{\Omega}\mathcal{P}_{\mathsf{T}} - \mathcal{P}_{\mathsf{T}}\right\|$ is small. We then need to show that with high probability we can construct the desired dual certificate Λ.

1. The sampling operator acts nicely on T

We next prove that the sampling operator $\mathcal{P}_{\Omega}$ preserves some part of every element of T, in the sense that $\left\|p^{-1}\mathcal{P}_{\mathsf{T}}\mathcal{P}_{\Omega}\mathcal{P}_{\mathsf{T}} - \mathcal{P}_{\mathsf{T}}\right\|$ is small. This phenomenon is a consequence of the incoherence of the matrix X_o and the uniform random model on Ω. The proof of the following lemma uses the matrix (operator) Bernstein inequality to show this rigorously.

LEMMA 4.30. *Let* $\mathcal{P}_{\Omega} : \mathbb{R}^{n\times n} \to \mathbb{R}^{n\times n}$ *denote the operator*

$$\mathcal{P}_{\Omega}[X] = \sum_{ij} X_{ij} \mathbb{1}_{(i,j)\in\Omega} E_{ij} \tag{4.4.35}$$

with $\mathbb{1}_{(i,j)\in\Omega}$ *independent Bernoulli random variables with probability p. Fix any* ε *with* $c(\sqrt{\log n})/n \leq \varepsilon \leq 1$. *There is a numerical constant C such that if* $p > C(\nu r \log n)/(\varepsilon^2 n)$, *then with high probability,*

$$\left\|\mathcal{P}_{\mathsf{T}} - p^{-1}\mathcal{P}_{\mathsf{T}}\mathcal{P}_{\Omega}\mathcal{P}_{\mathsf{T}}\right\| \leq \varepsilon. \tag{4.4.36}$$

Proof We apply the matrix Bernstein inequality in Theorem E.8 to bound the norm of

$$\mathcal{P}_{\mathsf{T}} - p^{-1}\mathcal{P}_{\mathsf{T}}\mathcal{P}_{\Omega}\mathcal{P}_{\mathsf{T}} = \sum_{ij} \underbrace{\mathcal{P}_{\mathsf{T}}\left(\frac{\mathcal{I}}{n^2} - p^{-1}\mathbb{1}_{(i,j)\in\Omega} E_{ij}\left\langle E_{ij}, \cdot\right\rangle\right)\mathcal{P}_{\mathsf{T}}}_{\doteq \mathcal{W}_{ij}}.$$

Here, $\mathcal{W}_{ij} : \mathbb{R}^{n\times n} \to \mathbb{R}^{n\times n}$ are independent random linear maps, and $\mathbb{E}\left[\sum_{ij}\mathcal{W}_{ij}\right] = 0$. The matrix Bernstein inequality requires (i) an almost sure bound R on $\max_{ij}\|\mathcal{W}_{ij}\|$, and (ii) control of the "variance"

$$\sum_{ij} \mathbb{E}\left[\mathcal{W}_{ij}^* \mathcal{W}_{ij}\right]. \tag{4.4.37}$$

We provide these as follows.
(i) Almost sure control of the summands:

$$\begin{aligned}
\left\| \mathcal{W}_{ij} \right\| &\le \max\left\{ \left\| n^{-2} \mathcal{P}_{\mathsf{T}} \right\|, \left\| p^{-1} \mathcal{P}_{\mathsf{T}}[\boldsymbol{E}_{ij}] \langle \mathcal{P}_{\mathsf{T}}[\boldsymbol{E}_{ij}], \cdot \rangle \right\| \right\}, \quad \text{almost surely} \\
&= \max\left\{ n^{-2}, p^{-1} \left\| \mathcal{P}_{\mathsf{T}}[\boldsymbol{E}_{ij}] \right\|_F^2 \right\} \\
&\le \max\left\{ n^{-2}, \frac{2\nu r}{np} \right\} \\
&\le \max\left\{ \frac{1}{n^2}, \frac{2\varepsilon^2}{C \log n} \right\} \\
&= \frac{2\varepsilon^2}{C \log n}.
\end{aligned} \tag{4.4.38}$$

We may take $R = 2\varepsilon^2/(C \log n)$.
(ii) Control of the "operator variance." Note that

$$\begin{aligned}
\sum_{ij} \mathbb{E}\left[\mathcal{W}_{ij}^* \mathcal{W}_{ij}\right] &= \sum_{ij} \mathbb{E}\Big[\frac{1}{n^4} \mathcal{P}_{\mathsf{T}} - \frac{2p^{-1}}{n^2} \mathbb{1}_{(i,j) \in \Omega} \mathcal{P}_{\mathsf{T}} \boldsymbol{E}_{ij} \langle \boldsymbol{E}_{ij}, \cdot \rangle \mathcal{P}_{\mathsf{T}} \\
&\qquad + \mathbb{1}_{(i,j)\in\Omega}\, p^{-2} \mathcal{P}_{\mathsf{T}} \boldsymbol{E}_{ij} \left\| \mathcal{P}_{\mathsf{T}} \boldsymbol{E}_{ij} \right\|_F^2 \langle \boldsymbol{E}_{ij}, \cdot \rangle \mathcal{P}_{\mathsf{T}} \Big] \\
&\preceq p^{-1} \sum_{ij} \mathcal{P}_{\mathsf{T}} \boldsymbol{E}_{ij} \left\| \mathcal{P}_{\mathsf{T}} \boldsymbol{E}_{ij} \right\|_F^2 \langle \boldsymbol{E}_{ij}, \cdot \rangle \mathcal{P}_{\mathsf{T}} \\
&\preceq p^{-1} \frac{2\nu r}{n} \sum_{ij} \mathcal{P}_{\mathsf{T}} \boldsymbol{E}_{ij} \langle \boldsymbol{E}_{ij}, \cdot \rangle \mathcal{P}_{\mathsf{T}} \\
&\preceq \frac{2\varepsilon^2}{C \log n} \mathcal{P}_{\mathsf{T}}.
\end{aligned} \tag{4.4.39}$$

The operator $\sum_{ij} \mathbb{E}\left[\mathcal{W}_{ij}^* \mathcal{W}_{ij}\right]$ is self-adjoint and positive semidefinite. The above calculation therefore implies that

$$\begin{aligned}
\sigma^2 &= \max\left\{ \left\| \sum_{ij} \mathbb{E}\left[\mathcal{W}_{ij}^* \mathcal{W}_{ij}\right] \right\|, \left\| \sum_{ij} \mathbb{E}\left[\mathcal{W}_{ij} \mathcal{W}_{ij}^*\right] \right\| \right\} \\
&\le \frac{2\varepsilon^2}{C \log n}.
\end{aligned} \tag{4.4.40}$$

Using these calculations, we obtain a bound

$$\mathbb{P}\left[\left\| \sum_{ij} \mathcal{W}_{ij} \right\| > t \right] \le 2n \exp\left(\frac{-t^2/2}{2\varepsilon^2/(C \log n) + t 2\varepsilon^2/(3C \log n)} \right). \tag{4.4.41}$$

The probability of failure for $t = \varepsilon$ is bounded by $n^{-\rho}$; the exponent ρ can be made as large as desired by choosing C appropriately. □

Choosing $\varepsilon = 1/2$ in the statement of the above lemma, we obtain the desired condition needed for Lemma 4.29.

2. Construction of a dual certificate by the golfing scheme

From the above discussion, in order to prove Theorem 4.26, we only have to show that under the conditions of the theorem, we can find a dual certificate that satisfies the two conditions 2(a) and 2(b) of Proposition 4.28. In this section, we show how to construct such a dual certificate, $\boldsymbol{\Lambda}$. In the next chapter, we will reuse this construction to analyze the related problem of *robust matrix recovery*, in which a fraction of the entries of a low-rank matrix have been corrupted. For this purpose, we give a complete summary of the properties of our construction in the following proposition. Here, properties (a) and (b) are essential for matrix completion; property (c) will be used in the following chapters for robust matrix recovery.

PROPOSITION 4.31. (Dual certificate for low-rank recovery) *Let $\boldsymbol{X}_o \in \mathbb{R}^{n\times n}$ be a rank-r matrix, with coherence ν. Let $\boldsymbol{U}, \boldsymbol{V} \in \mathbb{R}^{n\times r}$ be matrices whose columns are leading left and right singular vectors of $\boldsymbol{X}_o$. Let*

$$\mathsf{T} = \left\{ \boldsymbol{U}\boldsymbol{X}^* + \boldsymbol{Y}\boldsymbol{V}^* \mid \boldsymbol{X}, \boldsymbol{Y} \in \mathbb{R}^{n\times r} \right\}. \tag{4.4.42}$$

Then if $\Omega \sim$ Ber(p), with

$$p > C_0 \frac{\nu r \log^2 n}{n}, \tag{4.4.43}$$

there exists a matrix $\boldsymbol{\Lambda}$ supported on Ω, satisfying

(a) $\left\| \mathcal{P}_{\mathsf{T}}[\boldsymbol{\Lambda}] - \boldsymbol{U}\boldsymbol{V}^* \right\|_F \le 1/(4n)$,
(b) $\left\| \mathcal{P}_{\mathsf{T}^\perp}[\boldsymbol{\Lambda}] \right\| \le 1/4$,
(c) $\|\boldsymbol{\Lambda}\|_\infty < C_1 \log(n)/p \times \left\| \boldsymbol{U}\boldsymbol{V}^* \right\|_\infty$,

with high probability. Here, C_1 is a positive numerical constant.

We prove this proposition using an iterative construction. Let

$$\Omega_1, \dots, \Omega_k \tag{4.4.44}$$

be *independent* random subsets, chosen according to the Bernoulli model with parameter q. Set

$$\Omega = \bigcup_{i=1}^{k} \Omega_i. \tag{4.4.45}$$

Then Ω is *also* a Bernoulli subset, with parameter

$$p = 1 - (1 - q)^k. \tag{4.4.46}$$

The parameter p is the probability that a given entry is in *at least one* of the subsets Ω_i. Hence, $p \le kq$. The argument that we develop below will lead us to choose $k = C_g \log(n)$, with C_g a constant. Because k is not too large, this implies that the parameter q is also not too small:

$$q \ge \frac{p}{k} = \frac{C_0}{C_g}\frac{\nu r \log n}{n}. \tag{4.4.47}$$

Provided C_0 is large enough compared to C_g, the subsets Ω_i *all* satisfy the conditions of Lemma 4.30, and so with high probability

$$\left\| \mathcal{P}_{\mathsf{T}} - q^{-1}\mathcal{P}_{\mathsf{T}}\mathcal{P}_{\Omega_j}\mathcal{P}_{\mathsf{T}} \right\| \le \tfrac{1}{2}, \quad j = 1, \dots, k. \tag{4.4.48}$$

We will construct a sequence of matrices $\boldsymbol{\Lambda}_0, \boldsymbol{\Lambda}_1, \dots, \boldsymbol{\Lambda}_k$, in which each $\boldsymbol{\Lambda}_j$ depends only on $\Omega_1, \dots, \Omega_j$. We let $\boldsymbol{\Lambda}_0 = \mathbf{0}$. And let

$$\boldsymbol{E}_j = \mathcal{P}_{\mathsf{T}}[\boldsymbol{\Lambda}_j] - \boldsymbol{U}\boldsymbol{V}^*. \tag{4.4.49}$$

Since our goal is to obtain $\boldsymbol{\Lambda}$ such that $\mathcal{P}_{\mathsf{T}}[\boldsymbol{\Lambda}] \approx \boldsymbol{U}\boldsymbol{V}^*$, $\boldsymbol{E}_j$ should be considered the *error* at iteration j. To get our next $\boldsymbol{\Lambda}$, we simply try to correct the error:

$$\boldsymbol{\Lambda}_j = \boldsymbol{\Lambda}_{j-1} - \left(q^{-1}\mathcal{P}_{\Omega_j}\right)[\boldsymbol{E}_{j-1}]. \tag{4.4.50}$$

This construction is known as the *golfing scheme*, as it tries to reach the goal by reducing error step by step.

There are several things worth noting about this construction. First, it produces $\boldsymbol{\Lambda}_j$ supported only on $\Omega_1 \cup \dots \cup \Omega_j$. Thus, as desired, $\boldsymbol{\Lambda}_k$ is supported on Ω. Second, because $\boldsymbol{U}\boldsymbol{V}^* \in \mathsf{T}$, $\boldsymbol{E}_j \in \mathsf{T}$ for each j. This means that

$$\begin{aligned}
\boldsymbol{E}_j &= \mathcal{P}_{\mathsf{T}}[\boldsymbol{\Lambda}_j] - \boldsymbol{U}\boldsymbol{V}^* \\
&= \mathcal{P}_{\mathsf{T}}[\boldsymbol{\Lambda}_{j-1}] - \boldsymbol{U}\boldsymbol{V}^* - q^{-1}\mathcal{P}_{\mathsf{T}}\mathcal{P}_{\Omega_j}[\boldsymbol{E}_{j-1}] \\
&= \boldsymbol{E}_j - q^{-1}\mathcal{P}_{\mathsf{T}}\mathcal{P}_{\Omega_j}[\boldsymbol{E}_{j-1}] \\
&= (\mathcal{P}_{\mathsf{T}} - q^{-1}\mathcal{P}_{\mathsf{T}}\mathcal{P}_{\Omega_j}\mathcal{P}_{\mathsf{T}})[\boldsymbol{E}_{j-1}].
\end{aligned}$$

Since $\mathbb{E}\left[q^{-1}\mathcal{P}_{\Omega_j}\right] = \mathcal{I}$, in expectation, this iterative process drives the error to zero: $\mathbb{E}[\boldsymbol{E}_j] = \mathbf{0}$.

As it turns out, due to the fact that $\left\| \mathcal{P}_{\mathsf{T}} - q^{-1}\mathcal{P}_{\mathsf{T}}\mathcal{P}_{\Omega_j}\mathcal{P}_{\mathsf{T}} \right\| \le \frac{1}{2}$, after k steps, the error reduces to

$$\left\| \mathcal{P}_{\mathsf{T}}[\boldsymbol{\Lambda}_k] - \boldsymbol{U}\boldsymbol{V}^* \right\|_F = \|\boldsymbol{E}_k\|_F \le 2^{-k}\,\|\boldsymbol{E}_0\|_F \tag{4.4.51}$$

with high probability.

So, based on the golfing scheme, to achieve the desired accuracy as suggested by the above lemma, we want $2^{-k}\,\|\boldsymbol{E}_0\|_F = 2^{-k}\sqrt{r} \le 1/(4n)$. Since $r < n$, we only need to have $2^{-k} \sim O(1/n^2)$, that is, to choose $k = C_g \log(n)$ for some large enough constant C_g, say $C_g = 20$. Therefore, under these conditions, the dual certificate constructed after k iterations $\boldsymbol{\Lambda}_k$ satisfies condition 2(b) of Proposition 4.28:

$$\left\| \mathcal{P}_{\mathsf{T}}[\boldsymbol{\Lambda}_k] - \boldsymbol{U}\boldsymbol{V}^* \right\|_F \leq \frac{1}{4n}. \tag{4.4.52}$$

Finally, to satisfy condition 2(a) of Proposition 4.28, we need to show that the operator norm of the random matrix $\mathcal{P}_{\mathsf{T}^\perp}[\boldsymbol{\Lambda}_k]$ is bounded as

$$\left\| \mathcal{P}_{\mathsf{T}^\perp}[\boldsymbol{\Lambda}_k] \right\| \leq 1/4.$$

Notice that from the construction of $\boldsymbol{\Lambda}_k$, we have

$$\boldsymbol{\Lambda}_k = \sum_{j=1}^{k} -q^{-1}\mathcal{P}_{\Omega_j}[\boldsymbol{E}_{j-1}],$$

$$\boldsymbol{E}_j = (\mathcal{P}_{\mathsf{T}} - \mathcal{P}_{\mathsf{T}} q^{-1}\mathcal{P}_{\Omega_j}\mathcal{P}_{\mathsf{T}})[\boldsymbol{E}_{j-1}], \quad \text{with } \boldsymbol{E}_0 = -\boldsymbol{U}\boldsymbol{V}^*.$$

The matrix of interest can be expressed as

$$\mathcal{P}_{\mathsf{T}^\perp}[\boldsymbol{\Lambda}_k] = \sum_{j=1}^{k} -q^{-1}\mathcal{P}_{\mathsf{T}^\perp}\mathcal{P}_{\Omega_j}[\boldsymbol{E}_{j-1}] = \sum_{j=1}^{k} \mathcal{P}_{\mathsf{T}^\perp}(\mathcal{P}_{\mathsf{T}} - q^{-1}\mathcal{P}_{\Omega_j}\mathcal{P}_{\mathsf{T}})[\boldsymbol{E}_{j-1}], \tag{4.4.53}$$

where the second identity is due to $\mathcal{P}_{\mathsf{T}^\perp}\mathcal{P}_{\mathsf{T}} = 0$ and $\mathcal{P}_{\mathsf{T}}[\boldsymbol{E}_j] = \boldsymbol{E}_j$.

Since we are interested in bounding the norm of $\mathcal{P}_{\mathsf{T}^\perp}[\boldsymbol{\Lambda}_k]$, it would help if we know good bounds on various norms of $\mathcal{P}_{\Omega_j}$ and its interaction with the operator $\mathcal{P}_{\mathsf{T}}$ or $\mathcal{P}_{\mathsf{T}^\perp}$. Notice that each $\mathcal{P}_{\Omega_j}$ is a summation of independent random operators. A very powerful tool we can use to bound the norm of summation of random matrices (or operators) is the so-called matrix Bernstein inequality introduced in the Appendix E, which we have used once before in Lemma 4.30.

To bound the norm of $\mathcal{P}_{\mathsf{T}^\perp}[\boldsymbol{\Lambda}_k]$, we need good bounds on three additional operators similar to that in Lemma 4.30. The proofs of these bounds[16] are all similar to that of Lemma 4.30 by utilizing the matrix Bernstein inequality. We hence leave their derivations as exercises for the reader to get familiar with the matrix Bernstein inequality.

We phrase these bounds in terms of

$$\|\boldsymbol{Z}\|_\infty = \max_{ij} |Z_{ij}|, \tag{4.4.54}$$

and the maximum of the largest ℓ^2 norm of a row and the largest ℓ^2 norm of a column, which we denote by $\|\cdot\|_{rc}$:

$$\|\boldsymbol{Z}\|_{rc} = \max\left\{ \max_i \left\|\boldsymbol{e}_i^*\boldsymbol{Z}\right\|_2, \ \max_j \left\|\boldsymbol{Z}\boldsymbol{e}_j\right\|_2 \right\}. \tag{4.4.55}$$

LEMMA 4.32. *Let* $\boldsymbol{Z}$ *be any fixed* $n \times n$ *matrix, and* Ω *a* Ber(q) *subset, with*

$$q > C_0 \frac{\nu r \log n}{n}. \tag{4.4.56}$$

[16] Following the work of [CJSC13].

Then with high probability

$$\left\| \left(q^{-1}\mathcal{P}_\Omega - \mathcal{I}\right)[\boldsymbol{Z}]\right\| \le C\left(\frac{n}{C_0 \nu r}\|\boldsymbol{Z}\|_\infty + \sqrt{\frac{n}{C_0 \nu r}}\|\boldsymbol{Z}\|_{rc}\right), \tag{4.4.57}$$

where C is a numerical constant.

Proof Exercise 4.23. □

LEMMA 4.33. *Let $\boldsymbol{Z}$ be any fixed $n \times n$ matrix. There exists a numerical constant C_0 such that if Ω is a* Ber(q) *subset with*

$$q > C_0 \frac{\nu r \log n}{n}, \tag{4.4.58}$$

then with high probability

$$\left\|(q^{-1}\mathcal{P}_\mathsf{T}\mathcal{P}_\Omega - \mathcal{P}_\mathsf{T})[\boldsymbol{Z}]\right\|_{rc} \le \frac{1}{2}\left(\sqrt{\frac{n}{\nu r}}\|\boldsymbol{Z}\|_\infty + \|\boldsymbol{Z}\|_{rc}\right). \tag{4.4.59}$$

Proof Exercise 4.24. □

LEMMA 4.34. *Suppose $\boldsymbol{Z}$ is a fixed $n \times n$ matrix in* T. *There exists a constant C_0 such that if Ω is a* Ber(q) *subset with*

$$q > C_0 \frac{\nu r \log n}{n}, \tag{4.4.60}$$

then with high probability we have

$$\left\|(\mathcal{P}_\mathsf{T} - q^{-1}\mathcal{P}_\mathsf{T}\mathcal{P}_\Omega\mathcal{P}_\mathsf{T})[\boldsymbol{Z}]\right\|_\infty \le \tfrac{1}{2}\|\boldsymbol{Z}\|_\infty. \tag{4.4.61}$$

Proof Exercise 4.25. □

With these three lemmas in hand, we are now ready to show that the spectral norm of $\mathcal{P}_{\mathsf{T}^\perp}[\boldsymbol{\Lambda}_k]$ is very small, and in particular can be bounded as $\|\mathcal{P}_{\mathsf{T}^\perp}[\boldsymbol{\Lambda}_k]\| \le 1/4$:

Proof of proposition 4.31 From the golfing construction, $\mathcal{P}_{\mathsf{T}^\perp}[\boldsymbol{\Lambda}_k]$ can be expressed as the series given in (4.4.53). Hence we have

$$\begin{aligned}
\|\mathcal{P}_{\mathsf{T}^\perp}[\boldsymbol{\Lambda}_k]\| &\le \sum_{j=1}^{k}\left\|\mathcal{P}_{\mathsf{T}^\perp}(\mathcal{P}_\mathsf{T} - q^{-1}\mathcal{P}_{\Omega_j}\mathcal{P}_\mathsf{T})[\boldsymbol{E}_{j-1}]\right\| \\
&\le \sum_{j=1}^{k}\left\|(\mathcal{P}_\mathsf{T} - q^{-1}\mathcal{P}_{\Omega_j}\mathcal{P}_\mathsf{T})[\boldsymbol{E}_{j-1}]\right\| \\
&= \sum_{j=1}^{k}\left\|(\mathcal{I} - q^{-1}\mathcal{P}_{\Omega_j})[\boldsymbol{E}_{j-1}]\right\|.
\end{aligned} \tag{4.4.62}$$

Notice that in the construction of the golfing scheme, we have ensured that each subset Ω_j is sampled according to the Bernoulli model, with parameter $q > C_0(\nu r \log n)/n$ for some large enough C_0. This means each of the k subsets

Ω_j satisfies the conditions of the above lemmas. We first apply Lemma 4.32 to the right-hand side of the last inequality and obtain (assuming $C_0 > 1$):

$$\|\mathcal{P}_{\mathsf{T}^\perp}[\boldsymbol{\Lambda}_k]\| \le \frac{C}{\sqrt{C_0}} \sum_{j=1}^{k} \left(\frac{n}{\nu r} \left\| \boldsymbol{E}_{j-1} \right\|_\infty + \sqrt{\frac{n}{\nu r}} \left\| \boldsymbol{E}_{j-1} \right\|_{rc} \right). \tag{4.4.63}$$

To bound $\left\| \boldsymbol{E}_{j-1} \right\|_\infty$ we apply Lemma 4.34 and obtain

$$\begin{aligned} \left\| \boldsymbol{E}_{j-1} \right\|_\infty &= \left\| (\mathcal{P}_\mathsf{T} - (1/q)\mathcal{P}_\mathsf{T}\mathcal{P}_{\Omega_{j-1}}\mathcal{P}_\mathsf{T}) \cdots (\mathcal{P}_\mathsf{T} - (1/q)\mathcal{P}_\mathsf{T}\mathcal{P}_{\Omega_1}\mathcal{P}_\mathsf{T})[\boldsymbol{E}_0] \right\|_\infty \\ &\le \left(\frac{1}{2} \right)^{j-1} \left\| \boldsymbol{U}\boldsymbol{V}^* \right\|_\infty . \end{aligned} \tag{4.4.64}$$

Using this together with the fact that $\boldsymbol{\Lambda}_k = -\sum_j q^{-1} \mathcal{P}_{\Omega_j}[\boldsymbol{E}_{j-1}]$, we obtain

$$\|\boldsymbol{\Lambda}_k\|_\infty \le q^{-1} \sum_j \left\| \boldsymbol{E}_{j-1} \right\|_\infty \tag{4.4.65}$$

$$\le 2q^{-1} \left\| \boldsymbol{U}\boldsymbol{V}^* \right\|_\infty . \tag{4.4.66}$$

Since $q > p/C_q \log n$, this establishes property (c) of Proposition 4.31 for $\boldsymbol{\Lambda}_k$.

To bound $\left\| \boldsymbol{E}_{j-1} \right\|_{rc}$ we apply Lemma 4.33 and obtain

$$\begin{aligned} \left\| \boldsymbol{E}_{j-1} \right\|_{rc} &= \left\| (\mathcal{P}_\mathsf{T} - (1/q)\mathcal{P}_\mathsf{T}\mathcal{P}_{\Omega_{j-1}}\mathcal{P}_\mathsf{T})[\boldsymbol{E}_{j-2}] \right\|_{rc} \\ &\le \frac{1}{2}\sqrt{\frac{n}{\nu r}} \left\| \boldsymbol{E}_{j-2} \right\|_\infty + \frac{1}{2} \left\| \boldsymbol{E}_{j-1} \right\|_{rc} . \end{aligned} \tag{4.4.67}$$

Combine the above two inequalities and apply them recursively to $j-1, j-2, \ldots, 0$ and we obtain

$$\left\| \boldsymbol{E}_{j-1} \right\|_{rc} \le j \left(\frac{1}{2} \right)^{j-1} \sqrt{\frac{n}{\nu r}} \left\| \boldsymbol{U}\boldsymbol{V}^* \right\|_\infty + \left(\frac{1}{2} \right)^{j-1} \left\| \boldsymbol{U}\boldsymbol{V}^* \right\|_{rc} . \tag{4.4.68}$$

Substitute the bounds (4.4.64) and (4.4.68) to the right-hand side of (4.4.63) and we obtain

$$\begin{aligned} \|\mathcal{P}_{\mathsf{T}^\perp}[\boldsymbol{\Lambda}_k]\| &\le \frac{C}{\sqrt{C_0}} \frac{n}{\nu r} \left\| \boldsymbol{U}\boldsymbol{V}^* \right\|_\infty \sum_{j=1}^{k} (j+1) \left(\frac{1}{2} \right)^{j-1} \\ &\quad + \frac{C}{\sqrt{C_0}} \sqrt{\frac{n}{\nu r}} \left\| \boldsymbol{U}\boldsymbol{V}^* \right\|_{rc} \sum_{j=1}^{k} \left(\frac{1}{2} \right)^{j-1} \\ &\le \frac{6C}{\sqrt{C_0}} \frac{n}{\nu r} \left\| \boldsymbol{U}\boldsymbol{V}^* \right\|_\infty + \frac{2C}{\sqrt{C_0}} \sqrt{\frac{n}{\nu r}} \left\| \boldsymbol{U}\boldsymbol{V}^* \right\|_{rc} . \end{aligned} \tag{4.4.69}$$

As the matrix $\boldsymbol{X}_o$ satisfies the incoherence conditions (4.4.13) and (4.4.14), we have

$$\left\|\boldsymbol{U}\boldsymbol{V}^*\right\|_\infty \leq \max_{i,j}\left\{\left\|\boldsymbol{U}^*\boldsymbol{e}_i\right\|_2 \times \left\|\boldsymbol{V}^*\boldsymbol{e}_j\right\|_2\right\} \leq \frac{\nu r}{n},$$

$$\left\|\boldsymbol{U}\boldsymbol{V}^*\right\|_{rc} \leq \max\left\{\max_i \left\|\boldsymbol{e}_i^*\boldsymbol{U}\boldsymbol{V}^*\right\|_2, \max_j \left\|\boldsymbol{U}\boldsymbol{V}^*\boldsymbol{e}_j\right\|_2\right\} \leq \sqrt{\frac{\nu r}{n}}.$$

Therefore,

$$\|\mathcal{P}_{\mathsf{T}^\perp}[\boldsymbol{\Lambda}_k]\| \leq \frac{6C}{\sqrt{C_0}} + \frac{2C}{\sqrt{C_0}} \leq \frac{1}{4} \tag{4.4.70}$$

for large enough C_0. This establishes property (b) of Proposition 4.31 for $\mathcal{P}_{\mathsf{T}^\perp}[\boldsymbol{\Lambda}_k]$. □

The above derivations and results show that the relaxed KKT conditions in Proposition 4.28 can be satisfied with high probability, proving Theorem 4.26.

4.4.5 Stable Matrix Completion with Noise

So far in the matrix completion problem, we have assumed that the observed entries are precise. In real-world matrix completion problems, the observed entries are often corrupted with some noise:

$$Y_{ij} = [\boldsymbol{X}_o]_{ij} + Z_{ij}, \quad (i,j) \in \Omega, \tag{4.4.71}$$

where Z_{ij} can be some small noise. Or equivalently, we can write

$$\mathcal{P}_\Omega[\boldsymbol{Y}] = \mathcal{P}_\Omega[\boldsymbol{X}_o] + \mathcal{P}_\Omega[\boldsymbol{Z}], \tag{4.4.72}$$

where $\boldsymbol{Z}$ is an $n \times n$ matrix of noise. We may assume that the overall noise level is small, $\|\mathcal{P}_\Omega[\boldsymbol{Z}]\|_F < \varepsilon$. As in the stable matrix recovery case, we could expect to recover a low-rank matrix close to $\boldsymbol{X}_o$ via solving the following convex program:

$$\begin{array}{ll} \min & \|\boldsymbol{X}\|_* \\ \text{subjcct to} & \|\mathcal{P}_\Omega[\boldsymbol{X}] - \mathcal{P}_\Omega[\boldsymbol{Y}]\|_F < \varepsilon. \end{array} \tag{4.4.73}$$

The following theorem states that under the same conditions of Theorem 4.26 when the nuclear norm minimization recovers the correct low-rank matrix from noiseless measurements, the above program gives a stable estimate $\hat{\boldsymbol{X}}$ of the true low-rank matrix $\boldsymbol{X}_o$:

THEOREM 4.35. (Stable matrix completion) *Let $\boldsymbol{X}_o \in \mathbb{R}^{n\times n}$ be a rank-r, ν-incoherent matrix. Suppose that we observe $\mathcal{P}_\Omega[\boldsymbol{Y}] = \mathcal{P}_\Omega[\boldsymbol{X}_o] + \mathcal{P}_\Omega[\boldsymbol{Z}]$, where Ω is a subset of $[n] \times [n]$. If Ω is uniformly sampled from subsets of size*

$$m \geq C_1 \nu n r \log^2(n), \tag{4.4.74}$$

then with high probability, the optimal solution $\hat{X}$ *to the convex program* (4.4.73) *satisfies*

$$\|\hat{X} - X_o\|_F \leq c\frac{n\sqrt{n}\log(n)}{\sqrt{m}}\varepsilon \leq c'\frac{n}{\sqrt{r}}\varepsilon \tag{4.4.75}$$

for some constant $c > 0$.

Proof Similar to the proof of Theorem 4.26 in the noiseless case which has the same incoherence condition on X_o and the sampling condition, we know that the sampling operator $\mathcal{P}_\Omega$ and the dual certificate Λ_k constructed via the golfing scheme satisfies the properties in Proposition 4.28. All we need to show here is that these properties also imply the conclusion of this theorem for the case with noisy measurements.

Let $H = \hat{X} - X_o$. Notice that we can split H into two parts, $H = \mathcal{P}_\Omega[H] + \mathcal{P}_{\Omega^c}[H]$. For the first part, we have

$$\begin{aligned}\|\mathcal{P}_\Omega[H]\|_F &= \|\mathcal{P}_\Omega[\hat{X} - X_o]\|_F \\ &\leq \|\mathcal{P}_\Omega[\hat{X} - Y]\|_F + \|\mathcal{P}_\Omega[Y - X_o]\|_F \\ &\leq 2\varepsilon. \end{aligned} \tag{4.4.76}$$

Notice that the second part $\mathcal{P}_{\Omega^c}[H]$ is a feasible perturbation to the noiseless matrix completion problem. From the proof of Proposition 4.28 and in particular (4.4.34), we have

$$\|X_o + \mathcal{P}_{\Omega^c}[H]\|_* \geq \|X_o\|_* + \left(\frac{1}{2} - \frac{1}{4C_2\sqrt{nr}}\right)\left\|\mathcal{P}_{\mathsf{T}^\perp}[\mathcal{P}_{\Omega^c}[H]]\right\|_F, \tag{4.4.77}$$

and based on triangle inequality, we also have

$$\|\hat{X}\|_* = \|X_o + H\|_* \geq \|X_o + \mathcal{P}_{\Omega^c}[H]\|_* - \|\mathcal{P}_\Omega[H]\|_*. \tag{4.4.78}$$

Since $\|\hat{X}\|_* \leq \|X_o\|_*$, we have

$$\|\mathcal{P}_\Omega[H]\|_* \geq \left(\frac{1}{2} - \frac{1}{4C_2\sqrt{nr}}\right)\left\|\mathcal{P}_{\mathsf{T}^\perp}[\mathcal{P}_{\Omega^c}[H]]\right\|_F. \tag{4.4.79}$$

This leads to

$$\left\|\mathcal{P}_{\mathsf{T}^\perp}[\mathcal{P}_{\Omega^c}[H]]\right\|_F \leq 4\,\|\mathcal{P}_\Omega[H]\|_* \leq 4\sqrt{n}\,\|\mathcal{P}_\Omega[H]\|_F \leq 4\sqrt{n}\varepsilon. \tag{4.4.80}$$

Since $\mathcal{P}_{\Omega^c}[H] = \mathcal{P}_{\mathsf{T}^\perp}[\mathcal{P}_{\Omega^c}[H]] + \mathcal{P}_{\mathsf{T}}[\mathcal{P}_{\Omega^c}[H]]$, we remain to bound the term $\mathcal{P}_{\mathsf{T}}[\mathcal{P}_{\Omega^c}[H]]$. Applying the proof of Lemma 4.29 to $\mathcal{P}_{\Omega^c}[H]$, we have

$$\left\|\mathcal{P}_{\mathsf{T}^\perp}[\mathcal{P}_{\Omega^c}[H]]\right\|_F \geq C_1\frac{\sqrt{m}}{n\log(n)}\|\mathcal{P}_{\mathsf{T}}[\mathcal{P}_{\Omega^c}[H]]\|_F$$

for some large enough C_1. Therefore, we have

$$\|\mathcal{P}_{\mathsf{T}}[\mathcal{P}_{\Omega^c}[\boldsymbol{H}]]\|_F \leq \frac{n\log(n)}{C_1\sqrt{m}} \left\|\mathcal{P}_{\mathsf{T}^\perp}[\mathcal{P}_{\Omega^c}[\boldsymbol{H}]]\right\|_F \leq c\frac{n\sqrt{n}\log(n)}{\sqrt{m}}\varepsilon. \tag{4.4.81}$$

This bound dominates the bounds of all the other terms, leading to the conclusion of the theorem. □

4.5 Summary

In this chapter, we have studied the problem of recovering a low-rank matrix from a number of m linear observations much fewer than its number of entries:

$$\boldsymbol{y} = \mathcal{A}[\boldsymbol{X}] \quad \in \mathbb{R}^m,$$

where $\mathcal{A}$ is a linear operator typically *incoherent* to the low-rank structure in $\boldsymbol{X} \in \mathbb{R}^{n\times n}$. This problem arises in a range of applications. It generalizes the problem of recovering a sparse vector. We described a convex relaxation of the low-rank recovery problem, in which we minimize the nuclear norm, which is the sum (ℓ^1 norm) of the singular values of a matrix. We proved that, similar to the ℓ^1 minimization for recovering sparse vectors, if the measurements satisfy the *restricted isometry property* for low-rank matrices, then with a nearly minimum number of linear measurements on the order of

$$m = O(nr),$$

the convex program associated with nuclear norm minimization recovers all rank-r matrices correctly with high probability.

We have also studied a specific matrix completion problem with a more structured measurement model, in which we observe only a small subset of the entries of a low-rank matrix:

$$\boldsymbol{Y} = \mathcal{P}_\Omega[\boldsymbol{X}],$$

where $\mathcal{P}_\Omega$ samples a subset of entries of $\boldsymbol{X} \in \mathbb{R}^{n\times n}$ in the support set Ω, with $|\Omega| = m < n^2$. This matrix completion problem captures the special structure of some of the most important practical low-rank recovery applications, such as in the recommendation problem. It is mathematically more challenging, because certain sparse low-rank matrices cannot be completed without seeing almost all of their entries. Nevertheless, we observe that for low-rank matrices *incoherent* to this measurement model, i.e., matrices whose singular vectors are not so concentrated on any coordinates, nuclear norm minimization succeeds with high probability with nearly minimum number of measurements on the order of

$$m = O(nr\log^2 n).$$

Almost parallel to the development for the recovery of sparse vectors, we have shown that these theoretical results and algorithms can be extended to cope with nuisance factors, such as measurement noise. The resulting algorithms are stable to small noise in the measurements. Moreover, in the next chapter we will see how to combine these ideas with those from sparse recovery to generate even richer classes of models and more robust algorithms.

4.6 Notes

As we have discussed in the beginning of this chapter, rank minimization problems arise in a very broad range of engineering fields and applications. Arguably optimization issues associated with rank minimization have been studied most extensively and systematically in control [MP97] and identification [FHB01, FHB04] of dynamical systems. The fact that the nuclear norm is the convex envelope of the rank over the operator norm ball is due to [FHB01], leading to a convex formulation of the rank minimization problem. The extension of the restricted isometric property (RIP) to the matrix case is due to [RFP10] and it has helped characterize conditions under which the convex formulation succeeds, similar to the theory for sparse vectors studied in the previous chapter.

For the matrix completion problem, the golfing scheme is due to Gross [Gro10]. Variants of Theorem 4.26 have been established by Gross [Gro10] and Recht [Rec11]; both include the extra assumption that $\left\|\boldsymbol{U}\boldsymbol{V}^*\right\|_\infty$ is small. The form stated here (without this assumption) is due to Chen [Che13]. It is easy to see that with little modification, the proofs and results established for matrix completion with respect to the standard basis can be generalized to any orthonormal (matrix) basis $\{\boldsymbol{B}_i\}_{i=1}^{n^2}$ as long as it is incoherent (inner product being small) with low-rank matrices. Since we have $|\langle \boldsymbol{B}_i, \boldsymbol{X}\rangle| \leq \|\boldsymbol{B}_i\| \, \|\boldsymbol{X}\|_*$, for the basis to be incoherent with the low-rank matrix $\boldsymbol{X}$, we usually desire the base matrix $\boldsymbol{B}_i$ to have small operator norm. Fourier or Pauli bases are both such bases.

For the noisy matrix completion problem, the result in Theorem 4.35 is essentially attributed to the work of [CP10] but here the statement and proof are adapted to the weaker notion of incoherence required in the previous section. As result, we need an extra term of $\log(n)$ for the error bound, compared to that of [CP10].

Many methods have been developed in the literature that may sacrifice recoverability for computational efficiency or for measurement efficiency. To push for extreme scalability, the convex formulation that computes with the full $n \times n$ matrix might become unaffordable. In such cases, people start to investigate direct nonconvex formulations such as

$$\min_{\boldsymbol{U},\boldsymbol{V}} \|\boldsymbol{Y} - \mathcal{P}_\Omega[\boldsymbol{U}\boldsymbol{V}^*]\|_2^2,$$

where $\boldsymbol{U}, \boldsymbol{V} \in \mathbb{R}^{n\times r}$ are rank-r matrices. Somewhat surprisingly, despite its nonconvex nature, we will see in Chapter 7 that under fairly broad conditions, one can still find its optimal (and correct) low-rank solution using simple algorithms such as gradient descent.

4.7 Exercises

4.1. (Proof of schoenberg's theorem) *In this exercise, we invite the interested reader to prove Schoenberg's Euclidean embedding theorem (Theorem 4.1). Let $\boldsymbol{D}$ be a Euclidean distance matrix for some point set $\boldsymbol{X} = [\boldsymbol{x}_1, \ldots, \boldsymbol{x}_n] \in \mathbb{R}^{d \times n}$, i.e., $D_{ij} = \|\boldsymbol{x}_i\|_2^2 + \|\boldsymbol{x}_j\|_2^2 - 2\langle \boldsymbol{x}_i, \boldsymbol{x}_j \rangle$. Let $\mathbf{1} \in \mathbb{R}^n$ denote the vector of all ones, and $\boldsymbol{\Phi} = \boldsymbol{I} - (1/n)\mathbf{1}\mathbf{1}^*$. Using that $\boldsymbol{\Phi}\mathbf{1} = \mathbf{0}$, argue that $\boldsymbol{\Phi}\boldsymbol{D}\boldsymbol{\Phi}^*$ satisfies the conditions of Schoenberg's theorem, i.e., it is negative semidefinite and has rank at most d.*

For the converse, let $\boldsymbol{D}$ be a symmetric matrix with zero diagonal, and suppose that $\boldsymbol{\Phi}\boldsymbol{D}\boldsymbol{\Phi}^*$ is negative semidefinite and has rank at most d. Argue that there exists some matrix $\boldsymbol{X} \in \mathbb{R}^{d \times n}$ for which $D_{ij} = \|\boldsymbol{x}_i - \boldsymbol{x}_j\|_2^2$.

4.2. (Derivation of the SVD) *Let $\boldsymbol{X} \in \mathbb{R}^{n_1 \times n_2}$ be a matrix of rank r. Argue that there exist matrices $\boldsymbol{U} \in \mathbb{R}^{n_1 \times r}$ and $\boldsymbol{V} \in \mathbb{R}^{n_2 \times r}$, with orthonormal columns, and a diagonal matrix $\boldsymbol{\Sigma} = \operatorname{diag}(\sigma_1, \ldots, \sigma_r) \in \mathbb{R}^{r \times r}$, with $\sigma_1 \geq \cdots \geq \sigma_r > 0$, such that*

$$\boldsymbol{X} = \boldsymbol{U}\boldsymbol{\Sigma}\boldsymbol{V}^*. \tag{4.7.1}$$

Hint: What is the relationship between the singular values σ_i and singular vectors $\boldsymbol{v}_i$ and the eigenvalues/eigenvectors of the matrix $\boldsymbol{X}^*\boldsymbol{X}$?

4.3. (Best rank-r approximation) *We prove Theorem 4.5. First, consider the special case in which $\boldsymbol{Y} = \boldsymbol{\Sigma} = \operatorname{diag}(\sigma_1, \ldots, \sigma_n)$ with $\sigma_1 > \sigma_2 > \cdots > \sigma_n$. An arbitrary rank-$r$ matrix $\boldsymbol{X}$ can be expressed as $\boldsymbol{X} = \boldsymbol{F}\boldsymbol{G}^*$ with $\boldsymbol{F} \in \mathbb{R}^{n_1 \times r}$, $\boldsymbol{F}^*\boldsymbol{F} = \boldsymbol{I}$, and $\boldsymbol{G} \in \mathbb{R}^{n_2 \times r}$.*

1. *Argue that for any fixed $\boldsymbol{F}$, the solution to the optimization problem*

$$\min_{\boldsymbol{G} \in \mathbb{R}^{n_2 \times r}} \|\boldsymbol{F}\boldsymbol{G}^* - \boldsymbol{\Sigma}\|_F^2 \tag{4.7.2}$$

is given by $\hat{\boldsymbol{G}} = \boldsymbol{\Sigma}^*\boldsymbol{F}$, and the optimal cost is

$$\left\|(\boldsymbol{I} - \boldsymbol{F}\boldsymbol{F}^*)\boldsymbol{\Sigma}\right\|_F^2. \tag{4.7.3}$$

2. *Let $\boldsymbol{P} = \boldsymbol{I} - \boldsymbol{F}\boldsymbol{F}^*$, and write $\nu_i = \|\boldsymbol{P}\boldsymbol{e}_i\|_2^2$. Argue that $\sum_{i=1}^{n} \nu_i = n_1 - r$ and $\nu_i \in [0, 1]$. Conclude that*

$$\|\boldsymbol{P}\boldsymbol{\Sigma}\|_F^2 = \sum_{i=1}^{n_1} \sigma_i^2 \nu_i \geq \sum_{i=r+1}^{n_1} \sigma_i^2, \tag{4.7.4}$$

with equality if and only if $\nu_1 = \nu_2 = \cdots = \nu_r = 0$ and $\nu_{r+1} = \cdots = \nu_n$. Conclude that Theorem 4.5 holds in the special case $\boldsymbol{Y} = \boldsymbol{\Sigma}$.

3. *Extend your argument to the situation in which the σ_i are not distinct (i.e., $\sigma_i = \sigma_{i+1}$ for some i).*
4. *Extend your argument to any $\boldsymbol{Y} \in \mathbb{R}^{n \times n}$. Hint: Use the fact that the Frobenius norm $\|\boldsymbol{M}\|_F$ is unchanged by orthogonal transformations of the rows and columns: $\|\boldsymbol{M}\|_F = \|\boldsymbol{R}\boldsymbol{M}\boldsymbol{S}\|_F$ for any orthogonal matrices $\boldsymbol{R}$ and $\boldsymbol{S}$.*

4.4. (Minimal rank approximation) *We consider a variant of Theorem 4.5 in which we are given a data matrix $\boldsymbol{Y}$ and we want to find a matrix $\boldsymbol{X}$ of minimum rank that approximates $\boldsymbol{Y}$ up to some given fidelity:*

$$\begin{array}{ll} \min & \operatorname{rank}(\boldsymbol{X}), \\ \text{subject to} & \|\boldsymbol{X}-\boldsymbol{Y}\|_F \le \varepsilon. \end{array} \tag{4.7.5}$$

Give an expression for the optimal solution(s) to this problem, in terms of the SVD of $\boldsymbol{Y}$. Prove that your expression is correct.

4.5. (Multiple and repeated eigenvalues) *Consider the eigenvector problem*

$$\min \quad -\tfrac{1}{2}\boldsymbol{q}^*\boldsymbol{\Gamma}\boldsymbol{q} \quad \textit{subject to} \quad \|\boldsymbol{q}\|_2^2 = 1, \tag{4.7.6}$$

where $\boldsymbol{\Gamma}$ is a symmetric matrix. In the text, we argued that when the eigenvalues of $\boldsymbol{\Gamma}$ are distinct, every local minimizer of this problem is global.

(a) Argue that even when $\boldsymbol{\Gamma}$ has repeated eigenvalues, every local minimum of this problem is global.
(b) Now suppose we wish to find multiple eigenvector/eigenvalue pairs. Consider the optimization problem over the Stiefel manifold:

$$\begin{array}{ll} \min & -\tfrac{1}{2}\boldsymbol{Q}^*\boldsymbol{\Gamma}\boldsymbol{Q} \\ \text{subject to} & \boldsymbol{Q} \in \mathsf{St}(n,p) \doteq \left\{\boldsymbol{Q} \in \mathbb{R}^{n\times p} \mid \boldsymbol{Q}^*\boldsymbol{Q} = \boldsymbol{I}\right\}. \end{array} \tag{4.7.7}$$

Argue that every local minimizer of this problem has the form

$$\boldsymbol{Q} = \left[\boldsymbol{u}_1, \ldots, \boldsymbol{u}_p\right]\boldsymbol{\Pi}, \tag{4.7.8}$$

where $\boldsymbol{u}_1, \ldots, \boldsymbol{u}_p$ are eigenvectors of $\boldsymbol{\Gamma}$ associated with the p largest eigenvalues, and $\boldsymbol{\Pi}$ is a permutation matrix.

4.6. (The power method) *In this exercise, we derive how to compute eigenvectors (and hence singular vectors) using the power method. Let $\boldsymbol{\Gamma} \in \mathbb{R}^{n\times n}$ be a symmetric positive semidefinite matrix. Let $\boldsymbol{q}_0$ be a random vector that is uniformly distributed on the sphere $\mathbb{S}^{n-1}$ (we can generate such a random vector by taking an n-dimensional i.i.d. $\mathcal{N}(0,1)$ vector and then normalizing it to have unit ℓ^2 norm). Generate a sequence of vectors $\boldsymbol{q}_1, \boldsymbol{q}_2, \ldots$ via the iteration*

$$\boldsymbol{q}_{k+1} = \frac{\boldsymbol{\Gamma}\boldsymbol{q}_k}{\left\|\boldsymbol{\Gamma}\boldsymbol{q}_k\right\|_2}. \tag{4.7.9}$$

This iteration is called the power method.

Suppose that there is a gap between the first and second eigenvalues of $\boldsymbol{\Gamma}$: $\lambda_1(\boldsymbol{\Gamma}) > \lambda_2(\boldsymbol{\Gamma})$.

(a) What does $\boldsymbol{q}_k$ converge to? Hint: Write $\boldsymbol{\Gamma} = \boldsymbol{V}\boldsymbol{\Lambda}\boldsymbol{V}^*$ in terms of its eigenvectors/values. How does $\boldsymbol{V}^*\boldsymbol{q}_k$ evolve?
(b) Obtain a bound on the error $\|\boldsymbol{q}_k - \boldsymbol{q}_\infty\|_2$ in terms of the spectral gap $(\lambda_1 - \lambda_2)/\lambda_1$.
(c) Your bound in (b) should suggest that as long as there is a gap between λ_1 and λ_2, the power method converges rapidly. How does the method behave if $\lambda_1 = \lambda_2$?

(d) *How can we use the power method to compute the singular values of a matrix* $\boldsymbol{X} \in \mathbb{R}^{n_1 \times n_2}$*?*

4.7. (Variational forms of nuclear norm) *Prove the statements of Proposition 4.6.*

4.8. (Convex envelope property via the bidual) *In Theorem 4.9, we proved that the nuclear norm* $\|\boldsymbol{X}\|_*$ *is the convex envelope of* $\operatorname{rank}(\boldsymbol{X})$ *over the operator norm ball* $\mathsf{B}_{\mathrm{op}} = \{\boldsymbol{X} \mid \|\boldsymbol{X}\| \le 1\}$. *Here, we give an alternative derivation of this result, using the fact that the* biconjugate *of a function over a set* B *is the convex envelope. Let* $f(\boldsymbol{X}) = \operatorname{rank}(\boldsymbol{X})$ *denote the rank function.*

(a) *Prove that the Fenchel* dual

$$f^*(\boldsymbol{Y}) = \sup_{\boldsymbol{X} \in \mathsf{B}} \{\langle \boldsymbol{X}, \boldsymbol{Y} \rangle - f(\boldsymbol{X})\}$$

can be expressed as

$$f^*(\boldsymbol{Y}) = \|\mathcal{D}_1[\boldsymbol{Y}]\|_*,$$

where $\mathcal{D}_\tau[\boldsymbol{M}]$ *is the singular value thresholding operator, given by* $\mathcal{D}_\tau[\boldsymbol{M}] = \boldsymbol{U}\mathcal{S}_\tau[\boldsymbol{S}]\boldsymbol{V}^*$ *for any singular value decomposition* $\boldsymbol{M} = \boldsymbol{U}\boldsymbol{S}\boldsymbol{V}^*$ *of* $\boldsymbol{M}$.

(b) *Prove that the dual of* f^*,

$$f^{**}(\boldsymbol{X}) = \sup_{\boldsymbol{Y}} \langle \boldsymbol{X}, \boldsymbol{Y} \rangle - f^*(\boldsymbol{Y}),$$

satisfies

$$f^{**}(\boldsymbol{X}) = \|\boldsymbol{X}\|_*.$$

(c) *Use Proposition B.14 of Appendix B to conclude that* $\|\cdot\|_*$ *is the convex envelope of* $\operatorname{rank}(\cdot)$ *over* B.

4.9. (Nuclear norm of submatrices) *Let* $\boldsymbol{M}_1, \boldsymbol{M}_2 \in \mathbb{R}^{n \times m}$ *be two matrices, and* $\boldsymbol{M} = [\boldsymbol{M}_1, \boldsymbol{M}_2]$ *be their concatenation. Show that:*

(a) $\|\boldsymbol{M}\|_* \le \|\boldsymbol{M}_1\|_* + \|\boldsymbol{M}_2\|_*$.

(b) $\|\boldsymbol{M}\|_* = \|\boldsymbol{M}_1\|_* + \|\boldsymbol{M}_2\|_*$ *if* $\boldsymbol{M}_1^*\boldsymbol{M}_2 = \boldsymbol{0}$ *(that is, the spans of* $\boldsymbol{M}_1, \boldsymbol{M}_2$ *are orthogonal).*

4.10. (Convexifying low-rank approximation) *Consider the following optimization problem:*

$$\begin{array}{ll} \min & \|\boldsymbol{\Pi}\boldsymbol{Y}\|_F^2 \\ \text{subject to} & \boldsymbol{0} \preceq \boldsymbol{\Pi} \preceq \boldsymbol{I}, \ \operatorname{trace}[\boldsymbol{\Pi}] = m - r. \end{array} \tag{4.7.10}$$

Prove that if $\sigma_r(\boldsymbol{Y}) > \sigma_{r+1}(\boldsymbol{Y})$*, this problem has a unique optimal solution* $\boldsymbol{\Pi}_\star$*, which is the orthoprojector onto the linear span of the* $n_1 - r$ *trailing singular vectors* $\boldsymbol{u}_{r+1}, \boldsymbol{u}_{r+2}, \ldots, \boldsymbol{u}_{n_1}$. *The matrix* $(\boldsymbol{I} - \boldsymbol{\Pi}_\star)\boldsymbol{Y}$ *is the best rank-r approximation to* $\boldsymbol{Y}$.

4.11. (Tangent Space to the Rank-r Matrices) *Consider a matrix $\boldsymbol{X}_o$ of rank r with compact singular value decomposition $\boldsymbol{X}_o = \boldsymbol{U}\boldsymbol{\Sigma}\boldsymbol{V}^*$. Argue that the* tangent space *to the collection $\mathsf{M}_r = \{\boldsymbol{X} \mid \operatorname{rank}(\boldsymbol{X}) = r\}$ at $\boldsymbol{X}_o$ is given by $\mathsf{T} = \{\boldsymbol{U}\boldsymbol{R}^* + \boldsymbol{Q}\boldsymbol{V}^*\}$. Hint: Consider generating a nearby low-rank matrix by writing $\boldsymbol{X}' = (\boldsymbol{U} + \boldsymbol{\Delta}_U)(\boldsymbol{\Sigma} + \boldsymbol{\Delta}_\Sigma)(\boldsymbol{V} + \boldsymbol{\Delta}_V)^*$.*

4.12. (Quadratic measurements) *Consider a target vector $\boldsymbol{x}_o \in \mathbb{R}^{n\times n}$. In many applications, the observation can be modeled as a* quadratic *function of the vector $\boldsymbol{x}_o$. In notation, we see the squares*

$$y_1 = \langle \boldsymbol{a}_1, \boldsymbol{x}_o \rangle^2, \quad y_2 = \langle \boldsymbol{a}_2, \boldsymbol{x}_o \rangle^2, \quad \ldots, \quad y_m = \langle \boldsymbol{a}_m, \boldsymbol{x}_o \rangle^2$$

of the projections of $\boldsymbol{x}_o$ onto vectors $\boldsymbol{a}_1, \ldots, \boldsymbol{a}_m$. Notice that from this observation, it is only possible to reconstruct $\boldsymbol{x}_o$ up to a sign ambiguity: $-\boldsymbol{x}_o$ produces exactly the same observation.

(a) Consider the quadratic problem

$$\min_{\boldsymbol{x}} \sum_{i=1}^{n} \left(y_i - \langle \boldsymbol{a}_i, \boldsymbol{x} \rangle^2 \right)^2 . \tag{4.7.11}$$

Is this problem convex in $\boldsymbol{x}$?

(b) Convert this to a convex problem, by replacing the vector valued variable $\boldsymbol{x}$ with a matrix-valued variable $\boldsymbol{X} = \boldsymbol{x}\boldsymbol{x}^*$: convert the problem to

$$\min_{\boldsymbol{X}} \sum_{i=1}^{n} (y_i - \langle \boldsymbol{A}_i, \boldsymbol{X} \rangle)^2 . \tag{4.7.12}$$

How should we choose the matrices $\boldsymbol{A}_1, \ldots, \boldsymbol{A}_m$? Show that if $m < n^2$, $\boldsymbol{X}_o = \boldsymbol{x}_o\boldsymbol{x}_o^*$ is not *the unique optimal solution to this problem. How can we use the fact that* $\operatorname{rank}(\boldsymbol{X}_o) = 1$ *to improve this?*

(c) In the absence of noise, we can attempt to solve for $\boldsymbol{X}_o$ by solving the convex program

$$\min \|\boldsymbol{X}\|_* \quad \text{such that} \quad \mathcal{A}[\boldsymbol{X}] = \boldsymbol{y}. \tag{4.7.13}$$

Implement this optimization using a custom algorithm or CVX. Does it typically recover $\boldsymbol{X}_o$?

(d) Does the operator $\mathcal{A}$ satisfy the rank-RIP?

4.13. (Proof of theorem 4.25) *We prove Theorem 4.25. The goal here is to show that the solution to*

$$\min_{\boldsymbol{X}} \|\boldsymbol{X}\|_* + \tfrac{1}{2} \|\boldsymbol{X} - \boldsymbol{M}\|_F^2 \tag{4.7.14}$$

is given by $\mathcal{D}_1[\boldsymbol{M}]$.

(a) Argue that Problem (4.7.14) is strongly convex, and hence has a unique optimal solution.

(b) Show that a solution $\boldsymbol{X}_\star$ is optimal if and only if $\boldsymbol{X}_\star \in \boldsymbol{M} - \partial \|\cdot\|_* (\boldsymbol{X}_\star)$.

(c) Using the condition from (b), show that if $\boldsymbol{M}$ is diagonal, i.e., $M_{ij} = 0$ for $i \neq j$, then $\mathcal{S}_1[\boldsymbol{M}]$ is the unique optimal solution to (4.7.14).

(d) Use the SVD to argue that, in general, $\mathcal{D}_1[\boldsymbol{M}]$ is the unique optimal solution to (4.7.14).

4.14. *Prove Theorem 4.11.*

4.15. (Uniform matrix completion) *Let Ω be a strict subset of $[n] \times [n]$. Show that there exist two matrices $\boldsymbol{X}_o$ and $\boldsymbol{X}_o'$ of rank 1 such that $\mathcal{P}_\Omega[\boldsymbol{X}_o] = \mathcal{P}_\Omega[\boldsymbol{X}_o']$.* The implication of this is that it is not possible to reconstruct *all* low-rank matrices from the same observation Ω.

4.16. (Unique optimality for matrix completion) *Consider the optimization problem*

$$\begin{array}{ll} \min & \|\boldsymbol{X}\|_* \\ \text{subject to} & \mathcal{P}_\Omega[\boldsymbol{X}] = \mathcal{P}_\Omega[\boldsymbol{X}_o]. \end{array} \tag{4.7.15}$$

Suppose that $\|\mathcal{P}_{\Omega^c}\mathcal{P}_\mathsf{T}\| < 1$. Assume that we can find some $\boldsymbol{\Lambda}$ such that

(a) $\boldsymbol{\Lambda}$ is supported on Ω and
(b) $\boldsymbol{\Lambda} \in \partial \|\cdot\|_* (\boldsymbol{X}_o)$, i.e., $\mathcal{P}_\mathsf{T}[\boldsymbol{\Lambda}] = \boldsymbol{U}\boldsymbol{V}^*$ and $\left\|\mathcal{P}_{\mathsf{T}^\perp}[\boldsymbol{\Lambda}]\right\| < 1$.

Show that $\boldsymbol{X}_o$ is the unique optimal solution to the optimization problem.

4.17. *Prove Theorem 4.19.*

4.18. *Fill in the detailed steps of the proof for Theorem 4.22.*

4.19. *Derive detailed steps that prove the error bound* (4.3.85) *in the proof of Theorem 4.20.*

4.20. *Show that in Lemma 4.27, any subdifferential of nuclear norm must be of the form given in* (4.4.23).

4.21. *Let $\mathcal{R}_\Omega[\boldsymbol{X}_o] = \sum_{\ell=1}^q [\boldsymbol{X}_o]_{i_\ell, j_\ell} \boldsymbol{e}_{i_\ell} \boldsymbol{e}_{j_\ell}^*$ with each (i_ℓ, j_ℓ) chosen i.i.d. at random from the uniform distribution on $[n] \times [n]$. Use the matrix Bernstein inequality to show that if $q > C\nu n r \log n$ for sufficiently large C, we have*

$$\left\| \mathcal{P}_{\mathsf{T}^\perp} \frac{n^2}{q} \mathcal{R}_\Omega \mathcal{P}_\mathsf{T} \right\| \le t \tag{4.7.16}$$

for any arbitrarily small constant t with high probability. Hint: this is similar to the proof of Lemma 4.30.

4.22. *For the dual certificate $\boldsymbol{\Lambda}$ constructed from the golfing scheme, use the fact in Exercise 4.21 and the fact that*

$$\left\| \frac{n^2}{q} \mathcal{P}_{\mathsf{T}^\perp} \mathcal{R}_{\Omega_j} [\boldsymbol{E}_j] \right\|_F \le \left\| \frac{n^2}{q} \mathcal{P}_{\mathsf{T}^\perp} \mathcal{R}_{\Omega_j} \mathcal{P}_\mathsf{T} \right\| \|\boldsymbol{E}_j\|_F$$

to show that if

$$m \geq Cvnr^2 \log^2 n$$

for a large enough constant C, we have $\left\| \mathcal{P}_{\mathsf{T}^\perp}[\mathbf{\Lambda}] \right\| \leq 1/2$ with high probability.

4.23. *Prove Lemma 4.32. Hint: write*

$$(q^{-1}\mathcal{P}_\Omega - \mathcal{I})[\mathbf{Z}] = \sum_{ij} \underbrace{Z_{ij} \left(q^{-1} \mathbb{1}_{ij \in \Omega} - 1 \right) \boldsymbol{E}_{ij}}_{\doteq \mathbf{W}_{ij}},$$

and apply the operator Bernstein inequality, controlling the operator norm of $\mathbf{W}_{ij}$ in terms of $\|\mathbf{Z}\|_\infty$ and controlling the matrix variance in terms of $\|\mathbf{Z}\|_{rc}$.

4.24. *Prove Lemma 4.33. Use the matrix Bernstein inequality to obtain a bound on the probability that the ℓ-th row $\|\boldsymbol{e}_\ell^* \left(q^{-1}\mathcal{P}_\mathsf{T}\mathcal{P}_\Omega - \mathcal{P}_\mathsf{T}\right)[\mathbf{Z}]\|$ is large, repeat for each column, and then sum the failure probabilities over all rows and columns to obtain a bound on the probability that the $\| \cdot \|_{rc}$ is large. Hint: apply the matrix Bernstein inequality to the random vector*

$$\boldsymbol{e}_\ell^* \left(q^{-1}\mathcal{P}_\mathsf{T}\mathcal{P}_\Omega - \mathcal{P}_\mathsf{T} \right)[\mathbf{Z}] = \sum_{ij} \underbrace{Z_{ij}(q^{-1}\mathbb{1}_{ij\in\Omega} - 1)\boldsymbol{e}_\ell^* \mathcal{P}_\mathsf{T}[\boldsymbol{E}_{ij}]}_{\doteq \boldsymbol{w}_{ij}}.$$

4.25. *Prove Lemma 4.34. Apply the standard Bernstein inequality to bound the probability that the k,l entry of $(\mathcal{P}_\mathsf{T} - q^{-1}\mathcal{P}_\mathsf{T}\mathcal{P}_\Omega\mathcal{P}_\mathsf{T})[\mathbf{Z}]$ is large, and then sum this probability over all entries k,l to bound the probability that the ℓ^∞ norm is large. For the k,l entry, work with the sum of independent random variables*

$$\begin{aligned} \left[\left(\mathcal{P}_\mathsf{T} - q^{-1}\mathcal{P}_\mathsf{T}\mathcal{P}_\Omega\mathcal{P}_\mathsf{T} \right)[\mathbf{Z}] \right]_{kl} &= Z_{kl} - [q^{-1}\mathcal{P}_\mathsf{T}\mathcal{P}_\Omega[\mathbf{Z}]_{kl}] \\ &= \sum_{ij} \underbrace{n^{-2} Z_{kl} - q^{-1}\mathbb{1}_{ij\in\Omega} \left\langle \mathcal{P}_\mathsf{T}[\boldsymbol{E}_{kl}], \mathcal{P}_\mathsf{T}[\boldsymbol{E}_{ij}] \right\rangle Z_{ij}}_{\doteq w_{ij}}. \end{aligned}$$

5 Decomposing Low-Rank and Sparse Matrices

"The whole is greater than the sum of the parts."

– Aristotle, *Metaphysics*

In the previous chapters, we have studied how either a sparse vector or a low-rank matrix can be recovered from compressive or incomplete measurements. In this chapter, we will show that it is also possible to simultaneously recover a sparse signal and a low-rank signal from their superposition (mixture) or from highly compressive measurements of their superposition (mixture). This combination of rank and sparsity gives rise to a broader class of models that can be used to model richer structures underlying high-dimensional data, as we will see in examples in this chapter and later application chapters. Nevertheless, we are also faced with new technical challenges about whether and how such structures can be recovered correctly and effectively, from few observations.

5.1 Robust PCA and Motivating Examples

5.1.1 Problem Formulation

In this chapter, we study variants of the following problem. We are given a large data matrix $\boldsymbol{Y} \in \mathbb{R}^{n_1 \times n_2}$ which is a superposition of two matrices,

$$\boldsymbol{Y} = \boldsymbol{L}_o + \boldsymbol{S}_o, \tag{5.1.1}$$

where $\boldsymbol{L}_o \in \mathbb{R}^{n_1 \times n_2}$ is a low-rank matrix and $\boldsymbol{S}_o \in \mathbb{R}^{n_1 \times n_2}$ is a sparse matrix. Neither $\boldsymbol{L}_o$ nor $\boldsymbol{S}_o$ is known ahead of time. Can we hope to efficiently recover both $\boldsymbol{L}_o$ and $\boldsymbol{S}_o$?

This problem resembles another classical low-rank matrix recovery problem in which the observed data matrix $\boldsymbol{Y} \in \mathbb{R}^{n_1 \times n_2}$ is a superposition of two matrices,

$$\boldsymbol{Y} = \boldsymbol{L}_o + \boldsymbol{Z}_o, \tag{5.1.2}$$

where as before $\boldsymbol{L}_o \in \mathbb{R}^{n_1 \times n_2}$ is a low-rank matrix but here $\boldsymbol{Z}_o \in \mathbb{R}^{n_1 \times n_2}$ is assumed to be a small, but dense, perturbation matrix. For example, $\boldsymbol{Z}_o$ could be a Gaussian random matrix with small standard deviation. In other words, one wants to recover a low-rank matrix $\boldsymbol{L}_o$ (or the low-dimensional subspace spanned by the columns of $\boldsymbol{L}_o$)

from noisy measurements. The classical *principal component analysis* (PCA) [Jol86] seeks the best rank-r estimate of $\boldsymbol{L}_o$ by solving

$$\min_{\boldsymbol{L}} \|\boldsymbol{Y} - \boldsymbol{L}\|_F \quad \text{subject to} \quad \operatorname{rank}(\boldsymbol{L}) \leq r. \tag{5.1.3}$$

This problem is also known as the best rank-r approximation problem. As we have seen in Section 4.2.2, it can be solved very efficiently via the *singular value decomposition* (SVD): if $\boldsymbol{Y} = \boldsymbol{U}\boldsymbol{\Sigma}\boldsymbol{V}^*$ is the SVD of the matrix $\boldsymbol{Y}$, the optimal rank-r approximation to $\boldsymbol{Y}$ is

$$\hat{\boldsymbol{L}} = \boldsymbol{U}\boldsymbol{\Sigma}_r\boldsymbol{V}^*,$$

where $\boldsymbol{\Sigma}_r$ keeps only the first r leading singular values of the diagonal matrix $\boldsymbol{\Sigma}$. This solution enjoys a number of optimality properties when the perturbation in matrix $\boldsymbol{Z}_o$ is small or i.i.d. Gaussian [Jol02].

However, in the new measurement model (5.1.1), the perturbation term $\boldsymbol{S}_o$ can have elements with arbitrary magnitude and hence its ℓ^2 norm can be unbounded. In a sense, the measurement we observe,

$$\boldsymbol{Y} = \boldsymbol{L}_o + \boldsymbol{S}_o,$$

is a corrupted version of the low-rank matrix $\boldsymbol{L}_o$ – entries of $\boldsymbol{Y}$ where $\boldsymbol{S}_o$ is nonzero carry no information about $\boldsymbol{L}_o$. Figure 5.1 visualizes an instance of this model. The problem of recovering the matrix $\boldsymbol{L}_o$ (and the associated low-dimensional subspace) from such highly corrupted measurements can be considered a form of *robust principal component analysis* (RPCA), as opposed to the classical PCA, which is only stable to small noise or perturbation.

In this chapter, we use $\mathfrak{S}$ and $\boldsymbol{\Sigma}_o$ to denote the support and signs of the sparse matrix $\boldsymbol{S}_o$, respectively:

$$\mathfrak{S} \doteq \operatorname{supp}(\boldsymbol{S}_o) \quad \subseteq [n_1] \times [n_2], \tag{5.1.4}$$
$$\boldsymbol{\Sigma}_o \doteq \operatorname{sign}(\boldsymbol{S}_o) \quad \in \{-1, 0, 1\}^{n_1 \times n_2}. \tag{5.1.5}$$

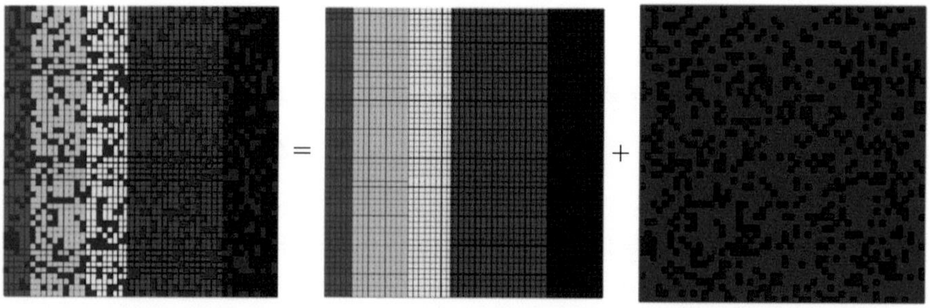

Figure 5.1 Superposition of a low-rank matrix $\boldsymbol{L}_o$ and a sparse matrix $\boldsymbol{S}_o$.

We note that if we somehow knew the support $\mathfrak{S}$ of S_o, we could potentially recover L_o by solving a matrix completion problem (as in the previous chapter) using $\mathcal{P}_\Omega[L_o]$ with $\Omega = \mathfrak{S}^c$. But in the problems described above, both L_o and S_o are unknown.

5.1.2 Matrix Rigidity and Planted Clique

Using this connection to matrix completion, one can show that the robust PCA problem is NP-hard in general. The hardness can also be shown directly via a connection to the concept of *matrix rigidity*. We say a matrix $M \in \mathbb{R}^{n\times n}$ is *rigid* if it is far from a low-rank matrix in Hamming distance. Or more formally,

DEFINITION 5.1. (Matrix rigidity) *The* rigidity *of a matrix* M *(relative to rank-r matrices) is defined to be*

$$R_M(r) \doteq \min\{\|S\|_0 : \operatorname{rank}(M+S) \le r\}, \tag{5.1.6}$$

the smallest number of entries that need to be modified in order to change M *to a rank-r matrix.*

Matrix rigidity is an important concept in computational complexity theory: it has been shown by [Val77] that matrix rigidity gives a lower bound on the circuit complexity for computing the linear transform Mx. Matrix rigidity is also related to the notion of communication complexity [Wun12]. Nevertheless, computing matrix rigidity is in general NP-hard [MS07], and so it is hard to decompose a general matrix

$$M = L + S$$

into a low-rank and sparse one. Exercise 5.2 studies the hardness of matrix rigidity and guides the interested reader through this connection.

The hardness of the robust PCA problem can also be established through its connection to the *planted clique* problem [AB09].

DEFINITION 5.2. (Planted clique problem) *Given a graph* $\mathcal{G}$ *with n nodes, randomly connect each pair of nodes with probability 1/2. Then select any* n_o *nodes and make them a clique – a fully connected subgraph. The goal is to find this hidden clique from the graph* $\mathcal{G}$.

It is known that with high probability the largest clique of the randomly generated graph (with 1/2 connectivity) is $2\log_2 n$. Hence, theoretically, if

$$n_o > 2\log_2 n,$$

we should be able to identify such a planted clique and distinguish the graph from the randomly generated one. It is also known that if

$$n_o = \Omega(\sqrt{n}),$$

it is possible to efficiently identify the planted clique [Kuč95, AKS98] using spectral methods. The interesting and difficult part of this problem is for

$$2 \log_2 n < n_o < \sqrt{n}.$$

There is a working conjecture about the complexity of this problem:[1]

> **Conjecture:** For all $\varepsilon > 0$, if $n_o < n^{0.5-\varepsilon}$, then there is *no* tractable algorithm that can find the hidden clique from $\mathcal{G}$ with high probability.

In our context, if we consider the adjacency matrix $\boldsymbol{A}$ of the graph $\mathcal{G}$, then we have

$$\boldsymbol{A} = \boldsymbol{L}_o + \boldsymbol{S}_o,$$

where $\boldsymbol{L}_o$ is a rank-1 matrix with an $n_o \times n_o$ block of all ones, and $\boldsymbol{S}_o$ is a relatively sparse matrix with around $(n^2 - n_o^2)/2$ nonzero entries. Hence, given the difficulty of the planted clique problem, we should not expect that there exists an efficient algorithm to decompose the matrix $\boldsymbol{A}$ correctly to a rank-1 matrix $\boldsymbol{L}_o$ and a sparse $\boldsymbol{S}_o$ when $n_o < n^{0.5-\varepsilon}$. We leave more detailed study of the planted clique problem as exercises, which will help the reader understand better the working conditions of the method proposed in this chapter.

For our purposes here, however, we simply note that the situation for robust PCA is analogous to that for low-rank recovery and for sparse recovery: *we should not expect to find an efficient algorithm which works for every problem instance.* Instead, the instances $\boldsymbol{Y}$ that are of practical interest are relatively "soft": they can be made significantly low-rank by correcting a small number of entries, as we will see in a number of important applications discussed below.

5.1.3 Applications of Robust PCA

Many important practical applications confront us with instances of the problem (5.1.1). We here give a few representative examples inspired by some contemporary challenges in data science. Notice that depending on the applications, either the low-rank component or the sparse component could be the object of interest.

Video Surveillance

Given a sequence of surveillance video frames, we often need to identify activities that stand out from the background. If we stack the video frames as columns of a matrix $\boldsymbol{Y}$, then the low-rank component $\boldsymbol{L}_o$ represents the stationary background and the sparse component $\boldsymbol{S}_o$ captures the moving objects in the foreground. However, since each image frame may have thousands or millions of pixels and each video fragment may contain hundreds or thousands of frames, it would be only possible to decompose $\boldsymbol{Y}$ this way if we have a truly scalable solution to this problem. The method developed

[1] For more evidence on the complexity of the planted clique problem around $n_o = \Theta(\sqrt{n})$, one may refer to the work of [GZ19]. The more recent work of [BB20] has further revealed the important role of the planted clique problem in characterizing computational hardness taxonomy among various statistical inference problems regarding low-dimensional models in high-dimensional spaces.

in this chapter will enable us to achieve this goal, as we will later see in an example shown in Figure 5.3.

Face Recognition

As we learned in Section 4.1.1, images of a convex, Lambertian surface under varying illuminations span a low-dimensional subspace [BJ03]. That is, if we stack face images of a person as column vectors of a matrix, then this matrix is (approximately) a low-rank matrix $\boldsymbol{L}_o$. This fact has been a major reason why low-dimensional models are effective for imagery data. In particular, images of a human's face can be well approximated by a low-dimensional subspace. Being able to correctly retrieve this subspace is crucial in many applications such as face recognition and alignment. However, realistic face images often suffer from self-shadowing, specularities, or saturation in brightness (as we have seen in images in Figure 4.2(a)), which make this a difficult task and subsequently compromise the recognition performance. A more careful study shows that the face images are better modeled by a low-rank matrix $\boldsymbol{L}_o$ superposed with a sparse matrix $\boldsymbol{S}_o$ which models such imperfection [ZMKW13]. To be able to recover both components from occluded images will allow us to repair such images for better recognition, as we will soon see in an example in Figure 5.4.

Latent Semantic Indexing

Web search engines often need to analyze and index the content of an enormous corpus of documents. A popular scheme is the *latent semantic indexing* (LSI), [DFL$^+$88, PTRV98] which we have discussed in the preceding chapter, Section 4.1.4. Recall that the basic idea is to gather a document-versus-term matrix $\boldsymbol{Y}$ whose entries typically encode the relevance of a term (or a word) to a document such as the frequency with which it appears in the document (e.g., term frequency–inverse document frequency, also known as TF-IDF). PCA (or SVD) has traditionally been used to decompose the matrix as a low-rank part plus a residual, which is not necessarily sparse (as we would like). If we were able to decompose $\boldsymbol{Y}$ as a sum of a low-rank component $\boldsymbol{L}_o$ and a sparse component $\boldsymbol{S}_o$, then $\boldsymbol{L}_o$ could capture a few topic models of all the documents while $\boldsymbol{S}_o$ captures the few keywords that best distinguish each document from others. See [MZWM10] for more details about such a *joint topic–document model* (via a superposition of a low-rank and sparse matrix).

Ranking and Collaborative Filtering

As we have seen in Section 4.1.2, anticipating user preferences has been an important problem in online commerce and advertisement. Companies now routinely collect user rankings for various products, e.g., movies, books, games, or web tools, among which the Netflix Prize for movie ranking is the best known example. The problem posed in the Netflix Prize is to use very sparse and incomplete rankings provided by the users on some of the products to predict the preference of any given user on any products, also known as collaborative filtering [Hof04]. In the previous chapter, this problem has been cast as a problem completing a low-rank matrix, say $\boldsymbol{L}_o$. However, in reality, as the data collection process often lacks control or is sometimes even *ad hoc*, a small portion of the available rankings could be rather random and even tampered with by malicious users or competitors. We may model those entries as a sparse matrix $\boldsymbol{S}_o$. The recommendation problem now becomes more challenging since we need to simultaneously complete a low-rank matrix $\boldsymbol{L}_o$ and correct these (sparse) errors $\boldsymbol{S}_o$. That is, we need to infer the low-rank matrix $\boldsymbol{L}_o$ from a set of incomplete and corrupted entries, a problem that methods introduced in the previous chapter are inadequate to solve.

Community Discovery and Data Clustering

With the increasing popularity of social networks, one important task is to discover hidden patterns and structures in such networks. We model a social network as a graph $\mathcal{G}$, with a node representing a person and an edge representing friendship. Then the adjacency matrix of the graph is a symmetric matrix $\boldsymbol{A}$ with $a_{ij} = a_{ji} = 1$ if and only if i and j are friends, and 0 otherwise. A "community" in the network is a subgroup of nodes that have much higher density of connectivity among themselves than with others. Such a group of nodes is also known as a "cluster," as shown in Figure 5.2. Note that each cluster can be approximately modeled as a fully connected subgraph, also known as a "clique." Each clique corresponds to a rank-1 submatrix with all ones. Hence, for a graph that consists of multiple communities, the adjacent matrix $\boldsymbol{A}$ will be of the form

$$\boldsymbol{A} = \boldsymbol{L}_o + \boldsymbol{S}_o,$$

where $\boldsymbol{L}_o$ is a low-rank matrix consisting of several blocks of rank-1 submatrices with all ones, and $\boldsymbol{S}_o$ is a sparse matrix that corresponds to the remaining few spurious or missing connections. This can be viewed as an extended (more challenging) version of the "planted clique" problem discussed earlier as here we allow multiple cliques in the graph. In data science and engineering, many tasks that try to cluster data into multiple subgroups, segments, subsystems, or subspaces can be reduced to a problem of this nature [VMS16].

All the applications that we have listed above require solving the problem of decomposing a low-rank and sparse matrix possibly of very high dimension,

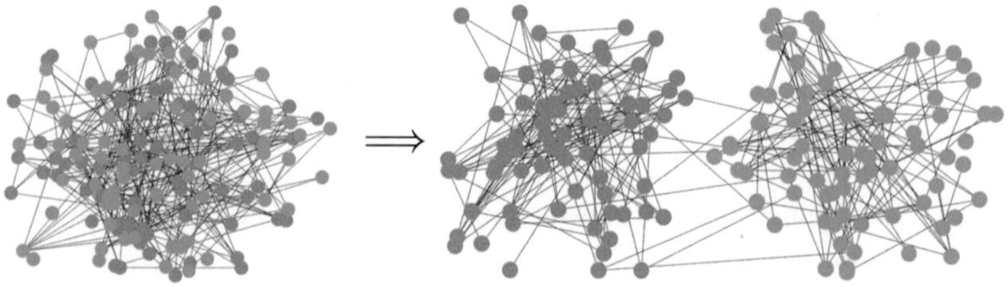

Figure 5.2 A graph with two densely connected clusters, which can be used to model two tight communities in a social network. Image reprinted with permission from Professor Yuxin Chen of Princeton University.

under various conditions. As it turns out, mathematically, this class of problems is rather fundamental to machine learning and system theory. They are actually the underlying problem for correctly and robustly learning graphical models and identifying dynamical systems, as discussed in Chapter 1, the Introduction of this book.

5.2 Robust PCA via Principal Component Pursuit

In each of the above problems, the dataset $\boldsymbol{Y}$ can be modeled as a superposition of a low-rank matrix and a sparse matrix:

$$\boldsymbol{Y} = \boldsymbol{L}_o + \boldsymbol{S}_o. \tag{5.2.1}$$

We would like to simultaneously find the low-rank $\boldsymbol{L}_o$ and the sparse $\boldsymbol{S}_o$ from the given $\boldsymbol{Y}$. For the majority of this chapter, we will simplify notation by assuming $\boldsymbol{Y} \in \mathbb{R}^{n \times n}$ is a square matrix. Extensions of both the theory and algorithms to the nonsquare case $\boldsymbol{Y} \in \mathbb{R}^{n_1 \times n_2}$ are for the most part straightforward, some of which will be discussed in Section 5.3 or left to the reader as exercises.

5.2.1 Convex Relaxation for Sparse Low-Rank Separation

Like sparse vector recovery in Chapter 3 and low-rank matrix recovery in Chapter 4, we *might* expect to find efficient algorithms that solve for such well-structured instances. Based on our knowledge from previous chapters, we should have a very clear idea of how to approach this! A natural idea is to solve a problem with two matrix-valued variables of optimization, $\boldsymbol{L}$ and $\boldsymbol{S}$, in which we try to make the nuclear norm of $\boldsymbol{L}$ small and the ℓ^1 norm of $\boldsymbol{S}$ small:

$$\begin{array}{ll} \text{minimize} & \|\boldsymbol{L}\|_* + \lambda \|\boldsymbol{S}\|_1 \\ \text{subject to} & \boldsymbol{L} + \boldsymbol{S} = \boldsymbol{Y}. \end{array} \tag{5.2.2}$$

Here, $\lambda > 0$ is a positive weight parameter. The linear equality constraint $\boldsymbol{L} + \boldsymbol{S} = \boldsymbol{Y}$ is convex; moreover, since a sum of two convex functions is convex, the objective is also convex. This is a convex program, which we refer to as *principal component pursuit* (PCP).

The relative ease with which we derived this convex relaxation highlights a conceptual advantage of "convex modeling": because convex sets and functions can be combined in nontrivial ways to form new convex sets and functions, it is often straightforward to extend the models to handle new situations of practical interest. Indeed, although it should be straightforward to write down the optimization problem (5.2.2), this opens the door to many new applications, including those listed in the previous section.

Nevertheless, two crucial questions remain. First, since most of these applications involve large datasets, we will need both efficient and scalable algorithms for solving the problem (5.2.2). Second, to deploy the algorithms with confidence, we will need to understand if and when they correctly recover the target low-rank and sparse components L_o and S_o. We will address these questions in Sections 5.2.2 and 5.3, respectively. We will then close the chapter by addressing several additional extensions to problems with both corruptions *and* missing data, which further highlight the flexibility of the framework and allow us to model additional nuisance factors in practical applications.

5.2.2 Solving PCP via Alternating Directions Method

The PCP problem can be solved to very high accuracy in polynomial time using semidefinite programming (SDP). Classical polynomial-time algorithms for SDP are based on interior point methods [GB14], which converge to highly accurate solutions in very few steps, but have a high per-step cost ($O(n^6)$ for a problem involving $n \times n$ matrices). This complexity limits such methods to be practical only for small problems, say with $n < 100$. However, for most aforementioned applications of PCP/RPCA, n can be very large. In such situations, a more appropriate goal is to achieve moderate accuracy with algorithms that are both scalable and efficient. In this section, we sketch one way of achieving this, using the technology of Lagrange duality – in particular, the *alternating directions method of multipliers* (ADMM), which will be studied in more details for general cases in Chapter 8.

The main challenge in efficiently solving the PCP problem is coping with the constraint $L + S = Y$. As in the previous chapter on matrix completion, we use the machinery of Lagrange duality. Here, the *Lagrangian* is

$$\mathcal{L}(L, S, \Lambda) \doteq \|L\|_* + \lambda \|S\|_1 + \langle \Lambda, L + S - Y \rangle, \tag{5.2.3}$$

which is used for characterizing optimality conditions of the constrained program. To derive a practical algorithm, as we will introduce formally in Chapter 8, Section 8.4, it is better to work with the *augmented* Lagrangian:[2]

$$\mathcal{L}_\mu(L, S, \Lambda) \doteq \|L\|_* + \lambda\|S\|_1 + \langle \Lambda, L + S - Y \rangle + \frac{\mu}{2}\|L + S - Y\|_F^2. \tag{5.2.4}$$

A generic Lagrange multiplier algorithm, like the one we derived for matrix completion, would solve PCP by repeatedly setting

$$(L_{k+1}, S_{k+1}) = \arg\min_{L,S} \mathcal{L}_\mu(L, S, \Lambda_k), \tag{5.2.5}$$

and then updating the Lagrange multipliers (here as a matrix)

$$\Lambda_{k+1} = \Lambda_k + \mu(L_{k+1} + S_{k+1} - Y). \tag{5.2.6}$$

Notice that at each iteration, we need to solve a convex program (5.2.5) with both L and S as unknowns. Although this is a convex program, it can be very inefficient to solve with generic algorithms such as subgradient descent. We can avoid doing that by

[2] One may also refer to the classic book [Ber82] for a systematic exposition of the augmented Lagrangian method.

Algorithm 5.1 Principal component pursuit by ADMM

1: **Initialize:** $S_0 = \Lambda_0 = 0, \mu > 0$.
2: **while** not converged **do**
3: Compute $L_{k+1} = \mathcal{D}_{1/\mu}(Y - S_k - \mu^{-1}\Lambda_k)$;
4: Compute $S_{k+1} = \mathcal{S}_{\lambda/\mu}(Y - L_{k+1} - \mu^{-1}\Lambda_k)$;
5: Compute $\Lambda_{k+1} = \Lambda_k + \mu(L_{k+1} + S_{k+1} - Y)$;
6: **end while**
7: **Output:** $L_\star \leftarrow L_k; S_\star \leftarrow S_k$.

recognizing that the two subproblems, $\min_L \mathcal{L}_\mu(L, S, \Lambda)$ and $\min_S \mathcal{L}_\mu(L, S, \Lambda)$, both have very simple and efficient solutions.

Let $\mathcal{S}_\tau : \mathbb{R} \to \mathbb{R}$ denote the shrinkage operator

$$\mathcal{S}_\tau[x] = \operatorname{sgn}(x)\max(|x| - \tau, 0),$$

and extend it to matrices by applying it to each element. It is easy to show that

$$\arg\min_S \mathcal{L}_\mu(L, S, \Lambda) = \mathcal{S}_{\lambda/\mu}(Y - L - \mu^{-1}\Lambda). \tag{5.2.7}$$

Similarly, for matrices M, let $\mathcal{D}_\tau(M)$ denote the singular value thresholding operator given by $\mathcal{D}_\tau(M) = U\mathcal{S}_\tau(\Sigma)V^*$, where $M = U\Sigma V^*$ is any singular value decomposition. It is not difficult to show that

$$\arg\min_L \mathcal{L}_\mu(L, S, \Lambda) = \mathcal{D}_{1/\mu}(Y - S - \mu^{-1}\Lambda). \tag{5.2.8}$$

Thus, a more practical strategy is to first minimize $\mathcal{L}_\mu$ with respect to L (fixing S), then minimize $\mathcal{L}_\mu$ with respect to S (fixing L), and then finally update the Lagrange multiplier matrix Λ based on the residual $L + S - Y$ according to (5.2.6). We summarize this strategy as Algorithm 5.1.

As it turns out, the above alternating strategy is a special case of a more general class of augmented Lagrange multiplier methods known as *alternating directions* methods of multipliers (ADMM). We will formally introduce ADMM in Section 8.5 of Chapter 8 and study its convergence and other matters. Algorithm 5.1 performs excellently on a wide range of instances: as we will see below, relatively small numbers of iterations suffice to achieve good relative accuracy. The dominant cost of each iteration is computing L_{k+1} via singular value thresholding. This requires us to compute those singular vectors of $Y - S_k + \mu^{-1}\Lambda_k$ whose corresponding singular values exceed the the threshold $1/\mu$. Empirically, we have observed that the number of such large singular values is often bounded by $\operatorname{rank}(L_o)$, allowing the next iterate to be computed efficiently via a partial SVD.[3]

[3] Further performance gains might be possible by replacing this partial SVD with an approximate SVD, as suggested in [GM09] for nuclear norm minimization.

Very similar ideas can be used to develop simple and effective augmented Lagrange multiplier algorithms for the robust matrix completion problem (5.6.1) to be introduced in Section 5.6, with similarly good performance.

5.2.3 Numerical Simulations and Experiments of PCP

In this section, we perform numerical simulations and experiments of Algorithm 5.1 for PCP and illustrate several of its many applications in image and video analysis. We first investigate its ability to correctly recover matrices of various rank from errors of various density. We then sketch applications in background modeling from video and removing shadows and specularities from face images.

One important implementation detail in PCP is the choice of λ. As we will see in the next section, theoretical analysis to justify the effectiveness of PCP suggests one natural choice,

$$\lambda = 1/\sqrt{\max(n_1, n_2)},$$

which will be used throughout this section. For practical problems, however, it is often possible to improve performance by choosing λ according to prior knowledge about the solution. For example, if we know that $\boldsymbol{S}$ is very sparse, increasing λ will allow us to recover matrices $\boldsymbol{L}$ of larger rank. For practical problems, we recommend $\lambda = 1/\sqrt{\max(n_1, n_2)}$ as a good rule of thumb, which can then be adjusted slightly to obtain possibly better results.

I. Simulation: exact recovery from varying fractions of error

We first verify how the algorithm does on recovering randomly generated instances, under favorable conditions (i.e., rank of $\boldsymbol{L}$ is very low and $\boldsymbol{S}$ is rather sparse). We consider square matrices of varying dimension $n = 500, \ldots, 3000$. We generate a rank-r matrix $\boldsymbol{L}_o$ as a product $\boldsymbol{L}_o = \boldsymbol{U}\boldsymbol{V}^*$ where $\boldsymbol{U}$ and $\boldsymbol{V}$ are $n \times r$ matrices with entries independently sampled from a $\mathcal{N}(0, 1/n)$ distribution. $\boldsymbol{S}_o$ is generated by choosing a support set $\mathfrak{S}$ of size k uniformly at random, and setting $\boldsymbol{S}_o = \mathcal{P}_{\mathfrak{S}}[\boldsymbol{E}]$, where $\boldsymbol{E}$ is a matrix with independent Bernoulli ± 1 entries.

Table 5.1 reports the results for a challenging scenario: $\operatorname{rank}(\boldsymbol{L}_o) = 0.05 \times n$ and $k = 0.10n^2$. In all cases, we set $\lambda = 1/\sqrt{n}$. Notice that in all cases, solving the convex PCP gives a result $(\hat{\boldsymbol{L}}, \hat{\boldsymbol{S}})$ with the correct rank and sparsity. Moreover, the relative error $\|\hat{\boldsymbol{L}} - \boldsymbol{L}_o\|_F / \|\boldsymbol{L}_o\|_F$ is small, less than 10^{-5} in all examples considered.[4]

The last two columns of Table 5.1 give the number of partial singular value decompositions computed in the course of the optimization (# SVD) as well as the total computation time.[5] As we see from Algorithm 5.1, the dominant cost in solving the convex program comes from computing one partial SVD per iteration. Strikingly, in Table 5.1,

[4] We measure relative error in terms of $\boldsymbol{L}$ only, since we usually view the sparse and low-rank decomposition as recovering a low-rank matrix $\boldsymbol{L}_o$ from gross errors. $\boldsymbol{S}_o$ is of course also well recovered: in this example, the relative error in $\boldsymbol{S}$ is actually smaller than that in $\boldsymbol{L}$.

[5] This experiment was performed in MATLAB on a Mac Pro with dual quad-core 2.66 GHz Intel Xenon processors and 16 GB RAM.

Table 5.1. Correct Recovery for Random Problems of Varying Sizes. Here, $\boldsymbol{L}_o = \boldsymbol{U}\boldsymbol{V}^* \in \mathbb{R}^{n\times n}$ with $\boldsymbol{U}, \boldsymbol{V} \in \mathbb{R}^{n\times r}$; $\boldsymbol{U}, \boldsymbol{V}$ have entries sampled from i.i.d. $\mathcal{N}(0,1/n)$. $\boldsymbol{S}_o \in \{-1;0;1\}^{n\times n}$ has support chosen uniformly at random and independent random signs; $\|\boldsymbol{S}_o\|_0$ is the number of nonzero entries in $\boldsymbol{S}_o$. In all cases, the rank of $\boldsymbol{L}_o$ and ℓ^0 norm of $\boldsymbol{S}_o$ are correctly estimated. Moreover, the number of partial singular value decompositions (# SVD) required to solve PCP is almost constant.

Dim. n	rank($\boldsymbol{L}_o$)	$\|\boldsymbol{S}_o\|_0$	rank($\hat{\boldsymbol{L}}$)	$\|\hat{\boldsymbol{S}}\|_0$	$\frac{\|\hat{\boldsymbol{L}}-\boldsymbol{L}_o\|_F}{\|\boldsymbol{L}_o\|_F}$	# SVD	time(s)
500	25	25 000	25	25 000	1.2×10^{-6}	17	4.0
1000	50	100 000	50	100 000	2.4×10^{-6}	16	13.7
2000	100	400 000	100	400 000	2.4×10^{-6}	16	64.5
3000	150	900 000	150	900 000	2.5×10^{-6}	16	191.0

the number of SVD computations is nearly constant regardless of dimension, and in all cases less than 17, suggesting that the ADMM algorithm gives a reasonably practical solver for PCP.

II. Experiment: background modeling from surveillance video
Video is a natural candidate for low-rank modeling, due to the correlation between frames. One of the most basic algorithmic tasks in video surveillance is to estimate a good model for the background variations in a scene. This task is complicated by the presence of foreground objects: in busy scenes, every frame may contain some anomaly. Moreover, the background model needs to be flexible enough to accommodate changes in the scene, for example due to varying illumination. In such situations, it is natural to model the background variations as approximately low rank. Foreground objects, such as cars or pedestrians, generally occupy only a fraction of the image pixels and hence can be treated as sparse errors.

We investigate whether the convex PCP program can separate these sparse errors from the low-rank background. Here, it is important to note that the error support may not be well modeled as Bernoulli: errors tend to be spatially coherent, and more complicated models such as Markov random fields may be more appropriate [CSD+09, ZWMM09]. Hence, our theorems do not necessarily guarantee the algorithm will succeed with high probability. Nevertheless, as we will see, PCP still gives visually appealing solutions to this practical low-rank and sparse separation problem, without using any additional information about the spatial structure of the error.

We consider two example videos introduced in [LHGT04]. The first is a sequence of 200 grayscale frames taken in an airport. This video has a relatively static background, but significant foreground variations. The frames have resolution 176×144; we stack each frame as a column of our matrix $\boldsymbol{Y} \in \mathbb{R}^{25\,344\times 200}$. We decompose $\boldsymbol{Y}$ into a low-rank term and a sparse term by solving the convex PCP problem (5.2.2) with $\lambda = 1/\sqrt{n_1}$. Figure 5.3(a) shows three frames from the video; (b) and (c) show the corresponding columns of the low-rank matrix $\hat{\boldsymbol{L}}$ and sparse matrix $\hat{\boldsymbol{S}}$ (its absolute

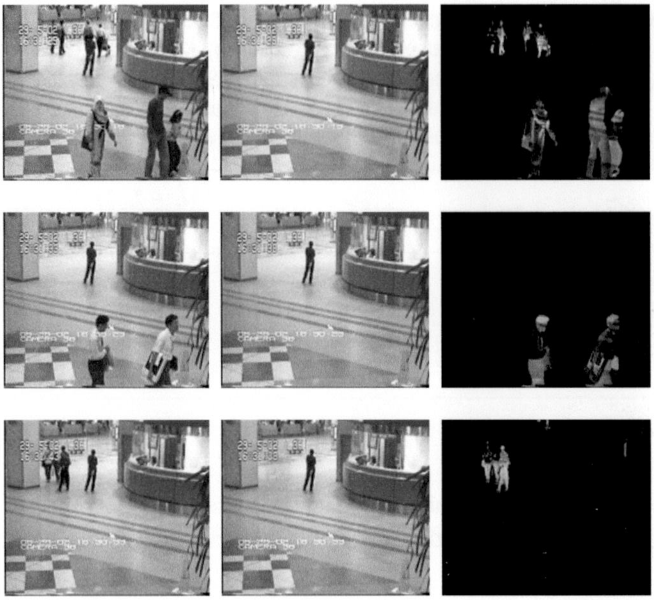

(a) Original frames (b) Low-rank $\hat{L}$ (c) Sparse $\hat{S}$

Figure 5.3 Background modeling from video. Three frames from a 200 frame video sequence taken in an airport [LHGT04]. (a) Frames of original video Y. (b) Low-rank $\hat{L}$ and (c) sparse components $\hat{S}$ obtained by PCP.

value is shown here). Notice that $\hat{L}$ correctly recovers the background, while $\hat{S}$ correctly identifies the moving pedestrians. One person appearing in the images in $\hat{L}$ does not move throughout the video, hence it was (correctly) modeled as part of the static background.

We have noticed that the number of iterations for the real data is typically higher than that of the simulations with random matrices given in Table 5.1. The reason for this discrepancy might be that the structures of real data could slightly deviate from the idealistic low-rank and sparse model. Nevertheless, it is important to realize that practical applications such as video surveillance often provide additional information about the signals of interest, e.g., the support of the sparse foreground is spatially piecewise contiguous and temporally continuous among frames. Or they even impose additional requirements, e.g., the recovered background needs to be nonnegative etc. We note that the simplicity of our objective and solution suggests that one can easily incorporate additional constraints and more accurate models of the signals so as to obtain much more efficient and accurate solutions.

III. Experiment: removing imperfections from face images

Face recognition is another problem domain in computer vision where low-dimensional linear models have received a great deal of attention. This is mostly due to the work of Basri and Jacobs, who showed that for convex, Lambertian objects, images taken

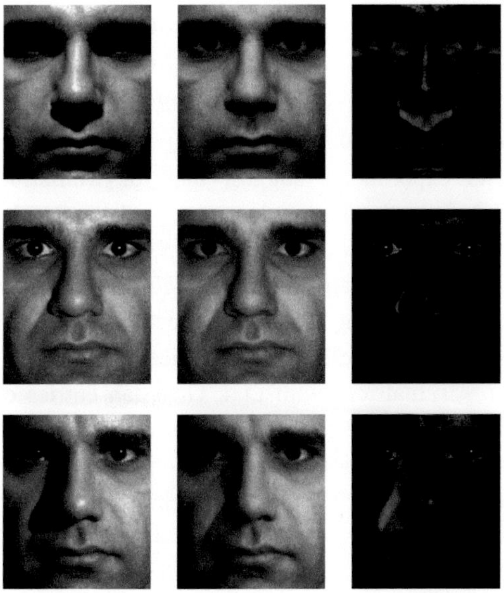

Figure 5.4 Removing shadows, specularities, and saturations from face images. (a) Cropped and aligned images of a person's face under different illuminations from the Extended Yale Face Database B [GBK01]. The size of each image is 192×168 pixels, a total of 58 different illuminations per person. (b) Low-rank approximation $\hat{\boldsymbol{L}}$ recovered by convex programming. (c) Sparse error $\hat{\boldsymbol{S}}$ corresponding to specularities in the eyes, shadows around the nose region, or brightness saturations on the face. Notice in the bottom left that the sparse term also compensates for errors in image acquisition.

under distant illumination lie approximately in a nine-dimensional linear subspace known as the *harmonic plane* [BJ03]. However, since faces are neither perfectly convex nor Lambertian, real face images often violate this low-rank model, in part due to cast shadows and specularities. These errors may be large in magnitude but sparse in the spatial domain. It is reasonable to believe that if we have enough images of the same face, PCP will be able to remove these errors. As with the previous example, some caveats apply: the theoretical result suggests the performance should be good, but does not guarantee it, since again the error support may not follow a Bernoulli model. Nevertheless, as we will see, the results are visually striking.

Figure 5.4 shows face images of one subject taken from the Extended Yale Face Database B [GBK01]. Here, each image has resolution 192×168; and there are a total of 58 illuminations per subject, which we stack as columns of our matrix $\boldsymbol{Y} \in \mathbb{R}^{32\,256 \times 58}$. We again solve PCP with $\lambda = 1/\sqrt{n_1}$.

Figure 5.4 plots the low-rank term $\hat{\boldsymbol{L}}$ and the magnitude of the sparse term $\hat{\boldsymbol{S}}$ obtained as the solution to the convex program. The sparse term $\hat{\boldsymbol{S}}$ compensates for cast shadows and specular regions. In one example (bottom row of Figure 5.4(a)), this term also compensates for errors in image acquisition. These results may be useful for conditioning the training data for face recognition, as well as face alignment and tracking under illumination variations.

IV. Simulation: phase transition in rank and sparsity

The above simulations and experiments suggest that for well-structured problem instances (datasets that indeed admit a low-rank and sparse decomposition $\boldsymbol{Y} = \boldsymbol{L}_o + \boldsymbol{S}_o$), PCP accurately recovers both $\boldsymbol{L}_o$ and $\boldsymbol{S}_o$. With this as motivation, we next systematically investigate the ability of the algorithm to recover matrices of varying rank from errors of varying sparsity. We consider square matrices of dimension $n_1 = n_2 = 400$. We generate low-rank matrices $\boldsymbol{L}_o = \boldsymbol{U}\boldsymbol{V}^*$ with $\boldsymbol{U}$ and $\boldsymbol{V}$ independently chosen $n \times r$ matrices with i.i.d. Gaussian entries of mean zero and variance $1/n$. For our first experiment, we assume a Bernoulli model for the support of the sparse term $\boldsymbol{S}_o$, with random signs: each entry of $\boldsymbol{S}_o$ takes on value 0 with probability $1 - \rho_s$, and values ± 1 each with probability $\rho_s/2$. For each (r, ρ_s) pair, we generate 10 random problem instances, each of which is solved via the ADMM Algorithm 5.1. We declare a trial to be successful if the recovered $\hat{\boldsymbol{L}}$ satisfies $\|\hat{\boldsymbol{L}} - \boldsymbol{L}_o\|_F / \|\boldsymbol{L}_o\|_F \leq 10^{-3}$.

Figure 5.5(a) plots the fraction of correct recoveries in grayscale for each pair (r, ρ_s). Notice that there is a large white region in which the recovery is exact. This inspires us to characterize the working conditions of the algorithm in more precise terms in the next section. The simulation already highlights an interesting aspect of PCP: the recovery is correct even though in some cases $\|\boldsymbol{S}_o\|_F \gg \|\boldsymbol{L}_o\|_F$ (e.g., for $r/n = \rho_s$, $\|\boldsymbol{S}_o\|_F$ is $\sqrt{n} = 20$ times larger!). As we shall see in the next section, this is to be expected from the analysis (see Lemma 5.4): the optimal solution to PCP is unique and correct only depending on the signs and support of $\boldsymbol{S}_o$ and the orientation of the singular spaces of $\boldsymbol{L}_o$.

Finally, inspired by the connection between matrix completion and robust PCA, we compare the breakdown point of PCP for the low-rank and sparse separation problem to the breakdown behavior of the nuclear norm heuristic for matrix completion (studied in the previous chapter). By comparing the two heuristics, we can begin to answer the question: *how much is gained by knowing the location $\mathfrak{S}$ of the corrupted entries*? Here, we again generate $\boldsymbol{L}_o$ as a product of Gaussian matrices. However, we now provide the algorithm with only an incomplete subset $\boldsymbol{M} = \mathcal{P}_{\mathfrak{S}^c}[\boldsymbol{L}_o]$ of its entries. Each (i, j) may be included in $\mathfrak{S}$ independently with probability $1 - \rho_s$, so rather than a probability of error, here, ρ_s stands for the probability that an entry is omitted.

We solve the nuclear norm minimization problem

$$\text{minimize} \quad \|\boldsymbol{L}\|_* \quad \text{subject to} \quad \mathcal{P}_{\mathfrak{S}^c}[\boldsymbol{L}] = \mathcal{P}_{\mathfrak{S}^c}[\boldsymbol{M}]$$

using an augmented Lagrange multiplier algorithm very similar to the one discussed in the above section. We again declare $\boldsymbol{L}_o$ to be successfully recovered if $\|\hat{\boldsymbol{L}} - \boldsymbol{L}_o\|_F / \|\boldsymbol{L}_o\|_F < 10^{-3}$. Figure 5.5(b) plots the fraction of correct recoveries for varying r and ρ_s. Notice that nuclear norm minimization successfully recovers $\boldsymbol{L}_o$

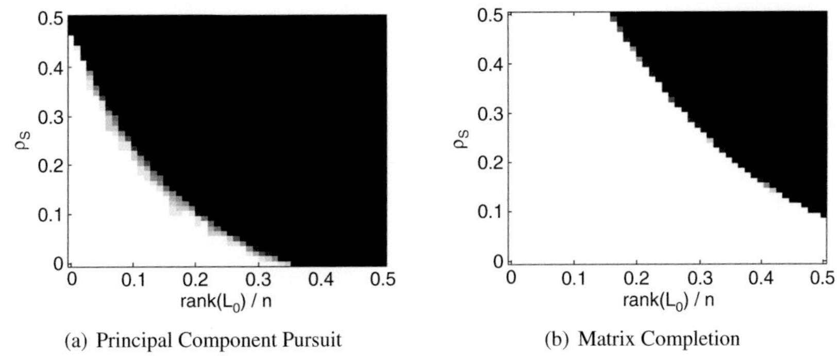

Figure 5.5 Correct Recovery for Varying Rank and Sparse Corruptions (a) or Missing Entries (b). Fraction of correct recoveries across 10 trials, as a function of rank($\boldsymbol{L}_o$) (x-axis) and sparsity of $\boldsymbol{S}_o$ (y-axis). Here, $n_1 = n_2 = 400$. In all cases, $\boldsymbol{L}_o$ is a product of independent $n \times r$ i.i.d. $\mathcal{N}(0, 1/n)$ matrices. Trials are considered successful if $\|\hat{\boldsymbol{L}} - \boldsymbol{L}_o\|_F / \|\boldsymbol{L}_o\|_F < 10^{-3}$. (a) Low-rank and sparse decomposition, in which the signs of the sparse matrix $\boldsymbol{\Sigma}_o = \text{sign}(\boldsymbol{S}_o)$ are random. (b) Matrix completion. For matrix completion, ρ_s is the probability that an entry is omitted from the observation.

over a wider range of (r, ρ_s). The difference between breakdown points can be viewed as the price of not knowing ahead of time which entries are unreliable.

5.3 Identifiability and Exact Recovery

Simulations and real examples of the previous section reveal a similar phenomenon of RPCA to that of matrix completion: when the solution is sufficiently structured (i.e., sufficiently low-rank and sparse), the convex relaxation (and the associated algorithm) succeeds. Our next goal will be to understand this phenomenon at a more mathematical level and to provide a theory that delineates when the convex optimization PCP solves the RPCA problem correctly.

5.3.1 Identifiability Conditions

At first sight, the RPCA problem (5.1.1) of separating a matrix into a low-rank one and a sparse one may seem impossible to solve. In general, there is not enough information to perfectly disentangle the low-rank and the sparse components since the number of unknowns to infer $\boldsymbol{L}_o \in \mathbb{R}^{n \times n}$ and $\boldsymbol{S}_o \in \mathbb{R}^{n \times n}$ is twice as many as the observations given in $\boldsymbol{Y} \in \mathbb{R}^{n \times n}$. Clearly, we will need both $\boldsymbol{L}_o$ and $\boldsymbol{S}_o$ to be well structured, in the sense that $\boldsymbol{L}_o$ is sufficiently low-rank, and $\boldsymbol{S}_o$ is sufficiently sparse.

However, identifiability issues arise even for very structured examples. For instance, suppose the matrix $\boldsymbol{Y}$ is equal to $\boldsymbol{e}_1\boldsymbol{e}_1^*$ (this matrix has a one in the top left corner and zeros everywhere else). Then since $\boldsymbol{Y}$ is both sparse and low-rank, how can we decide whether it is low-rank or sparse? To make the problem meaningful, we need to impose that the low-rank component $\boldsymbol{L}_o$ is *not* sparse so it can be differentiated from $\boldsymbol{S}_o$.[6]

Incoherence Conditions on $\boldsymbol{L}_o$

In the matrix completion problem of the previous chapter (Section 4.4), we have introduced the notion of ν-incoherence to ensure that a low-rank matrix is not too sparse. Let us write the singular value decomposition of $\boldsymbol{L}_o \in \mathbb{R}^{n\times n}$ as

$$\boldsymbol{L}_o = \boldsymbol{U}\boldsymbol{\Sigma}\boldsymbol{V}^* = \sum_{i=1}^{r} \sigma_i \boldsymbol{u}_i \boldsymbol{v}_i^*,$$

where r is the rank of the matrix, $\sigma_1, \ldots, \sigma_r$ are the positive singular values, and $\boldsymbol{U} = [\boldsymbol{u}_1, \ldots, \boldsymbol{u}_r]$, $\boldsymbol{V} = [\boldsymbol{v}_1, \ldots, \boldsymbol{v}_r]$ are the matrices of left and right singular vectors. Then according to (4.4.13) and (4.4.14), $\boldsymbol{L}_o$ is ν-incoherent:

$$\max_i \|\boldsymbol{e}_i^* \boldsymbol{U}\|_2^2 \le \frac{\nu r}{n}, \quad \max_j \|\boldsymbol{e}_j^* \boldsymbol{V}\|_2^2 \le \frac{\nu r}{n}. \tag{5.3.1}$$

For technical reasons that we will see later in our derivation, in low-rank and sparse separation we need a stronger notion of incoherence than the one that sufficed for matrix completion. In addition to the above two incoherence conditions, we further require:

$$\|\boldsymbol{U}\boldsymbol{V}^*\|_\infty \le \frac{\sqrt{\nu r}}{n}. \tag{5.3.2}$$

Here and below, $\|\boldsymbol{M}\|_\infty = \max_{i,j} |\boldsymbol{M}_{ij}|$, i.e., is the ℓ^∞ norm of $\boldsymbol{M}$ viewed as a long vector. This incoherence condition asserts that for small values of ν, the singular vectors are reasonably spread out. As it turns out, the above condition is not just needed for technical reasons, its necessity can also be justified from the complexity conjecture regarding the planted clique problem, as one can see through Exercises 5.4 and 5.5.

Regardless, one can show that the above incoherence conditions are not atypical, in that they hold with high probability for low-rank matrices that are generated with random orthogonal factors $\boldsymbol{U}$ and $\boldsymbol{V}$.

Randomness of $\boldsymbol{S}_o$

Another identifiability issue arises if the sparse matrix has low rank. This will occur if, say, all the nonzero entries of $\boldsymbol{S}_o$ occur in a column or in a few columns. Suppose, for instance, that the first column of $\boldsymbol{S}_o$ is the opposite of that of $\boldsymbol{L}_o$, and that all the other columns of $\boldsymbol{S}_o$ vanish. Then it is clear that we would not be able to recover $\boldsymbol{L}_o$ and $\boldsymbol{S}_o$ by any method whatsoever since $\boldsymbol{Y} = \boldsymbol{L}_o + \boldsymbol{S}_o$ would have a column space equal to or included in that of $\boldsymbol{L}_o$. To avoid such meaningless situations, we may assume that the sparsity pattern of the sparse component $\boldsymbol{S}_o$ is selected independently and identically according to a Bernoulli distribution

[6] In Chapter 15, we will study the case when a matrix is simultaneously low-rank and sparse, when the goal is to recover it as a whole instead of separating low-rank and sparse components.

$$\mathfrak{S} \sim \mathrm{Ber}(\rho_s).$$

Under this model, the expected number of nonzero entries in $\boldsymbol{S}_o$ is $\mathbb{E}\,[|\mathfrak{S}|] = \rho_s \cdot n^2$.

Uniqueness

The incoherence conditions are sufficient to ensure that we will not confuse the low-rank matrix $\boldsymbol{L}_o$ with the sparse matrix $\boldsymbol{S}_o$. However, they do not yet give a tractable algorithm for recovering them from the sum $\boldsymbol{L}_o + \boldsymbol{S}_o$. One natural approach is to seek a pair $(\boldsymbol{L}^*, \boldsymbol{S}^*)$ that is in some sense the *simplest.* In our context, we would desire $\boldsymbol{L}^*$ to have the lowest possible rank and $\boldsymbol{S}^*$ the sparsest. Or more precisely, we wish to minimize a certain measure of "simplicity" or "compactness" that encourages a decomposition such that $\boldsymbol{L}$ is low-rank and $\boldsymbol{S}$ is sparse. Thus, if the ground truth is such that the rank of $\boldsymbol{L}_o$ is low enough and $\boldsymbol{S}_o$ is sparse enough, then they will be the only optimal solution that minimizes such a measure. In this section, we will try to show that, for a properly chosen $\lambda \in \mathbb{R}_+$,

$$\|\boldsymbol{L}\|_* + \lambda\|\boldsymbol{S}\|_1$$

is precisely such a measure of model simplicity.

Similar to the case with recovering a sparse vector (Chapter 3) or with recovering a low-rank matrix (Chapter 4), could we expect that under reasonable conditions, the above convex program PCP can actually recover the correct low-rank $\boldsymbol{L}_o$ and sparse $\boldsymbol{S}_o$?

In fact, under the minimal conditions discussed in the identifiability section above, the solution to the convex PCP program exactly recovers the low-rank and sparse components, provided that the rank of $\boldsymbol{L}_o$ is not too large and $\boldsymbol{S}_o$ is reasonably sparse. To be more precise, the following statement is true:

THEOREM 5.3. (Principal component pursuit) *Suppose $\boldsymbol{L}_o$ is $n \times n$ and obeys* (5.3.1)–(5.3.2). *Suppose that the support $\mathfrak{S}$ of $\boldsymbol{S}_o$ follows the Bernoulli model with parameter $\rho < \rho_s$, and that the signs of the nonzero entries of $\boldsymbol{S}_o$ are chosen independently from the uniform distribution on $\{\pm 1\}$. Then, there is a numerical constant C such that with probability at least $1 - Cn^{-10}$ (over the choice of signs and support of $\boldsymbol{S}_o$), PCP* (5.2.2) *with $\lambda = 1/\sqrt{n}$ is* exact, *i.e., $\hat{\boldsymbol{L}} = \boldsymbol{L}_o$ and $\hat{\boldsymbol{S}} = \boldsymbol{S}_o$, provided that*

$$\operatorname{rank}(\boldsymbol{L}_o) \le C_r \frac{n}{\nu \log^2 n}. \tag{5.3.3}$$

Above, C_r and ρ_s are positive numerical constants.

5.3.2 Correctness of Principal Component Pursuit

In this section, we prove Theorem 5.3. This section can be skipped for first-time readers who are not theory oriented or are not strongly interested in the techniques needed for a rigorous proof of the theorem.

Dual Certificates for Optimality

As for each optimization problem we have encountered thus far, we begin by writing down an optimality condition. To prove that the target pair $(\boldsymbol{L}_o, \boldsymbol{S}_o)$ is the unique optimal solution to the convex program, we then must prove that under our assumptions, this condition is satisfied with high probability.

The key tool for obtaining optimality conditions is the KKT conditions of convex optimization; these conditions are naturally phrased in terms of the subdifferential of the objective function. Recall the subdifferential of the ℓ^1 norm

$$\partial \left\|\cdot\right\|_1 (\boldsymbol{S}_o) = \{\boldsymbol{\Sigma}_o + \boldsymbol{F} \mid \mathcal{P}_{\mathsf{\Omega}}[\boldsymbol{F}] = \boldsymbol{0},\ \ \|\boldsymbol{F}\|_\infty \le 1\}, \tag{5.3.4}$$

and the nuclear norm

$$\partial \left\|\cdot\right\|_* (\boldsymbol{L}_o) = \left\{\boldsymbol{U}\boldsymbol{V}^* + \boldsymbol{W} \mid \mathcal{P}_{\mathsf{T}}[\boldsymbol{W}] = \boldsymbol{0},\ \ \|\boldsymbol{W}\| \le 1\right\}. \tag{5.3.5}$$

Here, $\boldsymbol{U}$ and $\boldsymbol{V}$ are matrices of left and right singular vectors of $\boldsymbol{L}_o$, corresponding to nonzero singular values, and

$$\mathsf{T} \doteq \left\{\boldsymbol{U}\boldsymbol{R}^* + \boldsymbol{Q}\boldsymbol{V}^* \mid \boldsymbol{R}, \boldsymbol{Q} \in \mathbb{R}^{n\times r}\right\}$$

is the tangent space to the variety of rank r matrices at $\boldsymbol{L}_o$.

To the optimization problem

$$\min_{\boldsymbol{L},\boldsymbol{S}} \|\boldsymbol{L}\|_* + \lambda \|\boldsymbol{S}\|_1 \quad \text{subject to} \quad \boldsymbol{L} + \boldsymbol{S} = \boldsymbol{Y}, \tag{5.3.6}$$

associate a matrix $\boldsymbol{\Lambda} \in \mathbb{R}^{n\times n}$ of Lagrange multipliers, and the Lagrangian

$$\mathcal{L}(\boldsymbol{L}, \boldsymbol{S}, \boldsymbol{\Lambda}) = \|\boldsymbol{L}\|_* + \lambda \|\boldsymbol{S}\|_1 + \langle \boldsymbol{\Lambda}, \boldsymbol{Y} - \boldsymbol{L} - \boldsymbol{S}\rangle. \tag{5.3.7}$$

The KKT conditions imply that $(\boldsymbol{L}_\star, \boldsymbol{S}_\star)$ are optimal if there exists $\boldsymbol{\Lambda}$ such that $\boldsymbol{0} \in \partial_{\boldsymbol{L}}\mathcal{L}(\boldsymbol{L}, \boldsymbol{S}, \boldsymbol{\Lambda})$ *and* $\boldsymbol{0} \in \partial_{\boldsymbol{S}}\mathcal{L}(\boldsymbol{L}, \boldsymbol{S}, \boldsymbol{\Lambda})$. Thus,

$$\boldsymbol{\Lambda} \in \partial \left\|\cdot\right\|_* (\boldsymbol{L}_\star) \quad \text{and} \quad \boldsymbol{\Lambda} \in \lambda\partial \left\|\cdot\right\|_1 (\boldsymbol{S}_\star). \tag{5.3.8}$$

To show optimality, *it is enough to find a matrix* $\boldsymbol{\Lambda}$ *that is in both the subdifferential of the nuclear norm, and the subdifferential of the* ℓ^1 *norm, at the same time.*

From the KKT Conditions to Usable Optimality Conditions

Although the KKT conditions are a useful guide, the form that we have derived is neither strong enough nor robust enough for our purposes. We need to strengthen them to guarantee *unique* optimality, so that we can eventually ensure that the true pair $(\boldsymbol{L}_o, \boldsymbol{S}_o)$ is the only solution to the PCP problem. Moreover, as in matrix completion, it will be easier to demonstrate that a modified condition is satisfied, in which we merely guarantee that there exists $\boldsymbol{\Lambda}$ which is *close to* the two subdifferentials, rather than lying exactly within them.

We introduce a simple condition for the pair $(\boldsymbol{L}_o, \boldsymbol{S}_o)$ to be the unique optimal solution to PCP. These conditions, given in the following lemma, are stated in terms of a dual vector, the existence of which certifies optimality.

LEMMA 5.4. (Unique optimality) *Assume that* $\|\mathcal{P}_{\mathsf{S}}\mathcal{P}_{\mathsf{T}}\| < 1$ *or equivalently* $\mathsf{S} \cap \mathsf{T} = \{\mathbf{0}\}$. *Then* $(\boldsymbol{L}_o, \boldsymbol{S}_o)$ *is the unique optimal solution to the PCP problem if there exists* $\boldsymbol{\Lambda}$ *such that*

$$\text{[subdifferential of } \|\cdot\|_*\text{]:} \quad \mathcal{P}_{\mathsf{T}}[\boldsymbol{\Lambda}] = \boldsymbol{U}\boldsymbol{V}^*, \quad \left\|\mathcal{P}_{\mathsf{T}^\perp}[\boldsymbol{\Lambda}]\right\| < 1, \tag{5.3.9}$$

and

$$\text{[subdifferential of } \lambda\,\|\cdot\|_1\text{]:} \quad \mathcal{P}_{\mathsf{S}}[\boldsymbol{\Lambda}] = \lambda\boldsymbol{\Sigma}_o, \quad \|\mathcal{P}_{\mathsf{S}^c}[\boldsymbol{\Lambda}]\|_\infty < \lambda. \tag{5.3.10}$$

There are two aspects of this lemma which deserve comment. First, compared to the KKT condition, it has the extra requirement that $\|\mathcal{P}_{\mathsf{S}}\mathcal{P}_{\mathsf{T}}\| < 1$. This condition means that the subspace of matrices supported on S does not intersect the tangent space T to the low-rank matrices at $\boldsymbol{L}_o$. Second, compared to the KKT condition, which just requires that $\boldsymbol{\Lambda}$ lie in the subdifferentials of $\|\cdot\|_*$ and $\lambda\,\|\cdot\|_1$, this condition requires that $\boldsymbol{\Lambda}$ lie within the *relative interiors* of these two sets, by requiring $\left\|\mathcal{P}_{\mathsf{T}^\perp}[\boldsymbol{\Lambda}]\right\|$ to be strictly less than one and $\|\mathcal{P}_{\mathsf{S}^c}[\boldsymbol{\Lambda}]\|_\infty$ to be strictly less than λ. Under these stronger conditions, we can guarantee that $(\boldsymbol{L}_o, \boldsymbol{S}_o)$ is the *unique* optimal solution to the PCP problem.

Proof We consider a feasible perturbation $(\boldsymbol{L}_o + \boldsymbol{H}, \boldsymbol{S}_o - \boldsymbol{H})$ and show that the objective increases whenever $\boldsymbol{H} \neq \mathbf{0}$, hence proving that $(\boldsymbol{L}_o, \boldsymbol{S}_o)$ is the unique optimal solution. To do this, let $\mathcal{P}_{\mathsf{T}^\perp}[\boldsymbol{H}] = \bar{\boldsymbol{U}}\bar{\boldsymbol{\Sigma}}\bar{\boldsymbol{V}}^*$ denote the reduced singular value decomposition of $\mathcal{P}_{\mathsf{T}^\perp}[\boldsymbol{H}]$. Set $\boldsymbol{W} \doteq \bar{\boldsymbol{U}}\bar{\boldsymbol{V}}^* \in \mathsf{T}^\perp$, and notice that

$$\langle \boldsymbol{W}, \boldsymbol{H}\rangle = \left\langle \boldsymbol{W}, \mathcal{P}_{\mathsf{T}^\perp}[\boldsymbol{H}]\right\rangle = \left\|\mathcal{P}_{\mathsf{T}^\perp}[\boldsymbol{H}]\right\|_*. \tag{5.3.11}$$

Note further that $\boldsymbol{U}\boldsymbol{V}^* + \boldsymbol{W} \in \partial\,\|\cdot\|_*\,(\boldsymbol{L}_o)$.

Similarly, set $\boldsymbol{F} \doteq -\mathrm{sign}(\mathcal{P}_{\mathsf{S}^c}[\boldsymbol{H}])$, notice that $\lambda(\boldsymbol{\Sigma}_o + \boldsymbol{F}) \in \partial\lambda\,\|\cdot\|_1\,(\boldsymbol{S}_o)$, and that $-\lambda\,\langle \boldsymbol{F}, \boldsymbol{H}\rangle = \lambda\,\|\mathcal{P}_{\mathsf{S}^c}[\boldsymbol{H}]\|_1$.

Using the subgradient inequality for both $\|\cdot\|_*$ and $\lambda\,\|\cdot\|_1$, we obtain that

$$\begin{aligned}
&\|\boldsymbol{L}_o + \boldsymbol{H}\|_* + \lambda\|\boldsymbol{S}_o - \boldsymbol{H}\|_1 \\
&\quad\geq \|\boldsymbol{L}_o\|_* + \lambda\|\boldsymbol{S}_o\|_1 + \langle \boldsymbol{U}\boldsymbol{V}^* + \boldsymbol{W}, \boldsymbol{H}\rangle - \lambda\langle \boldsymbol{\Sigma}_o + \boldsymbol{F}, \boldsymbol{H}\rangle \\
&\quad= \|\boldsymbol{L}_o\|_* + \lambda\|\boldsymbol{S}_o\|_1 + \|\mathcal{P}_{\mathsf{T}^\perp}[\boldsymbol{H}]\|_* + \lambda\|\mathcal{P}_{\mathsf{S}^c}[\boldsymbol{H}]\|_1 + \langle \boldsymbol{U}\boldsymbol{V}^* - \lambda\boldsymbol{\Sigma}_o, \boldsymbol{H}\rangle, \\
&\quad= \|\boldsymbol{L}_o\|_* + \lambda\|\boldsymbol{S}_o\|_1 + \|\mathcal{P}_{\mathsf{T}^\perp}[\boldsymbol{H}]\|_* + \lambda\|\mathcal{P}_{\mathsf{S}^c}[\boldsymbol{H}]\|_1 + \langle \mathcal{P}_{\mathsf{T}}[\boldsymbol{\Lambda}] - \lambda\mathcal{P}_{\mathsf{S}}[\boldsymbol{\Lambda}], \boldsymbol{H}\rangle \\
&\quad= \|\boldsymbol{L}_o\|_* + \lambda\|\boldsymbol{S}_o\|_1 + \|\mathcal{P}_{\mathsf{T}^\perp}[\boldsymbol{H}]\|_* + \lambda\|\mathcal{P}_{\mathsf{S}^c}[\boldsymbol{H}]\|_1 + \langle \mathcal{P}_{\mathsf{T}^\perp}[\boldsymbol{\Lambda}] - \lambda\mathcal{P}_{\mathsf{S}^c}[\boldsymbol{\Lambda}], \boldsymbol{H}\rangle \\
&\quad\geq \|\boldsymbol{L}_o\|_* + \lambda\|\boldsymbol{S}_o\|_1 + \|\mathcal{P}_{\mathsf{T}^\perp}[\boldsymbol{H}]\|_* + \lambda\|\mathcal{P}_{\mathsf{S}^c}[\boldsymbol{H}]\|_1 \\
&\qquad - \left\|\mathcal{P}_{\mathsf{T}^\perp}[\boldsymbol{\Lambda}]\right\|\left\|\mathcal{P}_{\mathsf{T}^\perp}[\boldsymbol{H}]\right\|_* - \lambda\,\|\mathcal{P}_{\mathsf{S}^c}[\boldsymbol{\Lambda}]\|_\infty\,\|\mathcal{P}_{\mathsf{S}^c}[\boldsymbol{H}]\|_1 \\
&\quad\geq \|\boldsymbol{L}_o\|_* + \lambda\,\|\boldsymbol{S}_o\|_1 + (1-\beta)\left\{\left\|\mathcal{P}_{\mathsf{T}^\perp}[\boldsymbol{H}]\right\|_* + \lambda\,\|\mathcal{P}_{\mathsf{S}^c}[\boldsymbol{H}]\|_1\right\},
\end{aligned}$$

where $\beta = \max\left\{\left\|\mathcal{P}_{\mathsf{T}^\perp}[\boldsymbol{\Lambda}]\right\|, \lambda^{-1}\,\|\mathcal{P}_{\mathsf{S}^c}[\boldsymbol{\Lambda}]\|_\infty\right\} < 1$. Since by assumption, $\mathsf{S} \cap \mathsf{T} = \{\mathbf{0}\}$, we have $\|\mathcal{P}_{\mathsf{T}^\perp}[\boldsymbol{H}]\|_* + \lambda\|\mathcal{P}_{\mathsf{S}^c}[\boldsymbol{H}]\|_1 > 0$ unless $\boldsymbol{H} = \mathbf{0}$. □

This lemma gives a sufficient condition for $(\boldsymbol{L}_o, \boldsymbol{S}_o)$ to be the *unique* optimal solution. It is still challenging to work with, because it demands that $\boldsymbol{\Lambda}$ is an element of both $\partial\,\|\cdot\|_*\,(\boldsymbol{L}_o)$ and $\partial\lambda\,\|\cdot\|_1\,(\boldsymbol{S}_o)$. This forces $\boldsymbol{\Lambda}$ to exactly satisfy the equalities

$\mathcal{P}_{\mathsf{T}}[\mathbf{\Lambda}] = \boldsymbol{U}\boldsymbol{V}^*$ and $\mathcal{P}_{\mathfrak{S}}[\mathbf{\Lambda}] = \lambda \mathbf{\Sigma}_o$. As we did for matrix completion, it will be helpful to state a modified optimality condition, which accepts $\mathbf{\Lambda}$ that satisfied these equalities *approximately*. We state this new condition as follows:

LEMMA 5.5. *Assume* $\|\mathcal{P}_{\mathfrak{S}}\mathcal{P}_{\mathsf{T}}\| \le 1/2$ *and* $\lambda < 1$. *Then with the same notation,* $(\boldsymbol{L}_o, \boldsymbol{S}_o)$ *is the unique solution if there exists* $\mathbf{\Lambda}$ *such that*

$$\text{[approx. subgradient of } \|\cdot\|_*\text{]:} \quad \left\|\mathcal{P}_{\mathsf{T}}[\mathbf{\Lambda}] - \boldsymbol{U}\boldsymbol{V}^*\right\|_F \le \lambda/8, \quad \left\|\mathcal{P}_{\mathsf{T}^\perp}[\mathbf{\Lambda}]\right\| < 1/2, \tag{5.3.12}$$

and

$$\text{[approx. subgradient of } \lambda\,\|\cdot\|_1\text{]:} \quad \|\mathcal{P}_{\mathfrak{S}}[\mathbf{\Lambda}] - \lambda\mathbf{\Sigma}_o\|_F \le \lambda/8, \quad \|\mathcal{P}_{\mathfrak{S}^c}[\mathbf{\Lambda}]\|_\infty < \lambda/2. \tag{5.3.13}$$

Proof Consider any nonzero $\boldsymbol{H} \in \mathbb{R}^{n\times n}$. We demonstrate that in a particular sense, $\boldsymbol{H}$ cannot be simultaneously concentrated on T and $\mathfrak{S}$. Observe that

$$\begin{aligned}\|\mathcal{P}_{\mathfrak{S}}[\boldsymbol{H}]\|_F &\le \|\mathcal{P}_{\mathfrak{S}}\mathcal{P}_{\mathsf{T}}[\boldsymbol{H}]\|_F + \|\mathcal{P}_{\mathfrak{S}}\mathcal{P}_{\mathsf{T}^\perp}[\boldsymbol{H}]\|_F \\ &< \tfrac{1}{2}\|\boldsymbol{H}\|_F + \|\mathcal{P}_{\mathsf{T}^\perp}[\boldsymbol{H}]\|_F \\ &\le \tfrac{1}{2}\|\mathcal{P}_{\mathfrak{S}}[\boldsymbol{H}]\|_F + \tfrac{1}{2}\|\mathcal{P}_{\mathfrak{S}^c}[\boldsymbol{H}]\|_F + \|\mathcal{P}_{\mathsf{T}^\perp}[\boldsymbol{H}]\|_F,\end{aligned}$$

and, therefore,

$$\|\mathcal{P}_{\mathfrak{S}}[\boldsymbol{H}]\|_F \le \|\mathcal{P}_{\mathfrak{S}^c}[\boldsymbol{H}]\|_F + 2\|\mathcal{P}_{\mathsf{T}^\perp}[\boldsymbol{H}]\|_F.$$

Symmetric reasoning establishes that

$$\|\mathcal{P}_{\mathsf{T}}[\boldsymbol{H}]\|_F \le \left\|\mathcal{P}_{\mathsf{T}^\perp}[\boldsymbol{H}]\right\|_F + 2\,\|\mathcal{P}_{\mathfrak{S}^c}[\boldsymbol{H}]\|_F\,. \tag{5.3.14}$$

With these observations in hand, we proceed in a similar spirit to the proof of Lemma 5.4. Notice that

$$\begin{aligned}\boldsymbol{U}\boldsymbol{V}^* &= \mathcal{P}_{\mathsf{T}}[\mathbf{\Lambda}] + \left(\boldsymbol{U}\boldsymbol{V}^* - \mathcal{P}_{\mathsf{T}}[\mathbf{\Lambda}]\right) \\ &= \mathbf{\Lambda} - \mathcal{P}_{\mathsf{T}^\perp}[\mathbf{\Lambda}] + \left(\boldsymbol{U}\boldsymbol{V}^* - \mathcal{P}_{\mathsf{T}}[\mathbf{\Lambda}]\right), \end{aligned} \tag{5.3.15}$$

$$\begin{aligned}\lambda\mathbf{\Sigma}_o &= \mathcal{P}_{\mathfrak{S}}[\mathbf{\Lambda}] + (\lambda\mathbf{\Sigma}_o - \mathcal{P}_{\mathfrak{S}}[\mathbf{\Lambda}]) \\ &= \mathbf{\Lambda} - \mathcal{P}_{\mathfrak{S}^c}[\mathbf{\Lambda}] + (\lambda\mathbf{\Sigma}_o - \mathcal{P}_{\mathfrak{S}}[\mathbf{\Lambda}]), \end{aligned} \tag{5.3.16}$$

and so

$$\boldsymbol{U}\boldsymbol{V}^* - \lambda\mathbf{\Sigma}_o = -\mathcal{P}_{\mathsf{T}^\perp}[\mathbf{\Lambda}] + \mathcal{P}_{\mathfrak{S}^c}[\mathbf{\Lambda}] + \left(\boldsymbol{U}\boldsymbol{V}^* - \mathcal{P}_{\mathsf{T}}[\mathbf{\Lambda}]\right) + (\lambda\mathbf{\Sigma}_o - \mathcal{P}_{\mathfrak{S}}[\mathbf{\Lambda}])\,.$$

Following the proof of Lemma 5.4, we have

$$\begin{aligned}
&\|\boldsymbol{L}_o + \boldsymbol{H}\|_* + \lambda \|\boldsymbol{S}_o - \boldsymbol{H}\|_1 \\
&\geq \|\boldsymbol{L}_o\|_* + \lambda \|\boldsymbol{S}_o\|_1 + \left\|\mathcal{P}_{\mathsf{T}^\perp}[\boldsymbol{H}]\right\|_* + \lambda \|\mathcal{P}_{\mathfrak{S}^c}[\boldsymbol{H}]\|_1 + \left\langle \boldsymbol{U}\boldsymbol{V}^* - \lambda \boldsymbol{\Sigma}_o, \boldsymbol{H}\right\rangle \\
&\geq \|\boldsymbol{L}_o\|_* + \lambda \|\boldsymbol{S}_o\|_1 + \tfrac{1}{2}\left(\|\mathcal{P}_{\mathsf{T}^\perp}[\boldsymbol{H}]\|_* + \lambda \|\mathcal{P}_{\mathfrak{S}^c}[\boldsymbol{H}]\|_1\right) \\
&\quad - \tfrac{\lambda}{8} \|\mathcal{P}_{\mathsf{T}}[\boldsymbol{H}]\|_F - \tfrac{\lambda}{8} \|\mathcal{P}_{\mathfrak{S}}[\boldsymbol{H}]\|_F \\
&\geq \|\boldsymbol{L}_o\|_* + \lambda \|\boldsymbol{S}_o\|_1 + \underbrace{\left(\tfrac{1}{2} - \tfrac{\lambda}{8} - \tfrac{\lambda}{4}\right)}_{\geq 1/8} \left\|\mathcal{P}_{\mathsf{T}^\perp}[\boldsymbol{H}]\right\|_* + \underbrace{\left(\tfrac{\lambda}{2} - \tfrac{\lambda}{4} - \tfrac{\lambda}{8}\right)}_{\geq \lambda/8} \|\mathcal{P}_{\mathfrak{S}^c}[\boldsymbol{H}]\|_1 \\
&> \|\boldsymbol{L}_o\|_* + \lambda \|\boldsymbol{S}_o\|_1 ,
\end{aligned} \tag{5.3.17}$$

where the final (strict) inequality holds because $\boldsymbol{H} \neq \boldsymbol{0}$ and $\mathfrak{S} \cap \mathsf{T} = \{\boldsymbol{0}\}$. □

Showing that the Optimality Conditions Can be Satisfied

We next show that under our conditions, with high probability the conditions of Lemma 5.5 can be satisfied. To do this, we have to show two things:

1 $\|\mathcal{P}_{\mathfrak{S}}\mathcal{P}_{\mathsf{T}}\| < 1/2$;

2 existence of a near dual certificate $\boldsymbol{\Lambda}$ as in Lemma 5.5.

Let $\Omega = \mathfrak{S}^c$. These are the *clean* entries. Notice that if $\mathfrak{S} \sim \mathrm{Ber}(\rho_s)$, then $\Omega \sim \mathrm{Ber}(1 - \rho_s)$. We are going to show 1 and 2 by building on machinery developed in Chapter 4 for *matrix completion*. In particular, in that chapter we showed that if

$$\rho_{\text{clean}} = 1 - \rho_s > C_0 \frac{\nu r \log n}{n}, \tag{5.3.18}$$

and with high probability

$$\left\|\mathcal{P}_{\mathsf{T}} - \rho_{\text{clean}}^{-1} \mathcal{P}_{\mathsf{T}} \mathcal{P}_{\mathfrak{S}^c} \mathcal{P}_{\mathsf{T}}\right\| < \tfrac{1}{8}. \tag{5.3.19}$$

Under this condition,

$$\begin{aligned}
\|\mathcal{P}_{\mathsf{T}}\mathcal{P}_{\mathfrak{S}}\mathcal{P}_{\mathsf{T}}\| &= \|\mathcal{P}_{\mathsf{T}} - \mathcal{P}_{\mathsf{T}}\mathcal{P}_{\mathfrak{S}^c}\mathcal{P}_{\mathsf{T}}\| \\
&\leq \left\|\rho_{\text{clean}}\mathcal{P}_{\mathsf{T}} - \mathcal{P}_{\mathsf{T}}\mathcal{P}_{\mathfrak{S}^c}\mathcal{P}_{\mathsf{T}}\right\| + \left\|(1 - \rho_{\text{clean}})\mathcal{P}_{\mathsf{T}}\right\| \\
&= \rho_{\text{clean}} \left\|\mathcal{P}_{\mathsf{T}} - \rho_{\text{clean}}^{-1}\mathcal{P}_{\mathsf{T}}\mathcal{P}_{\mathfrak{S}^c}\mathcal{P}_{\mathsf{T}}\right\| + 1 - \rho_{\text{clean}} \\
&\leq \frac{\rho_{\text{clean}}}{8} + 1 - \rho_{\text{clean}} \\
&< \tfrac{1}{4},
\end{aligned} \tag{5.3.20}$$

provided $\rho_{\text{clean}} > \frac{6}{7}$. This implies that

$$\|\mathcal{P}_{\mathfrak{S}}\mathcal{P}_{\mathsf{T}}\| = \|\mathcal{P}_{\mathsf{T}}\mathcal{P}_{\mathfrak{S}}\mathcal{P}_{\mathsf{T}}\|^{1/2} \leq \tfrac{1}{2}. \tag{5.3.21}$$

This establishes statement 1. By exactly the same reasoning, for any constant $\sigma > 0$, there exists a constant $\rho_{\text{clean},\star}(\sigma) < 1$ such that if $\rho_{\text{clean}} > \rho_{\text{clean},\star}$, then with high probability $\|\mathcal{P}_{\mathfrak{S}}\mathcal{P}_{\mathsf{T}}\| < \sigma$.

Constructing the Certificate $\boldsymbol{\Lambda}$

To show that $(\boldsymbol{L}_o, \boldsymbol{S}_o)$ is the unique optimal solution, we further need to establish statement 2. That is, there exists a matrix $\boldsymbol{\Lambda}$ that is simultaneously close to the subdifferential $\partial \|\cdot\|_* (\boldsymbol{L}_o)$ and the subdifferential $\partial\lambda \|\cdot\|_1 (\boldsymbol{S}_o)$ as in Lemma 5.5.

In the previous paragraph, we saw that the clean entries $\Omega = \mathfrak{S}^c$ are distributed as a Bernoulli subset, with parameter

$$\rho_{\text{clean}} \doteq 1 - \rho_s. \tag{5.3.22}$$

This is exactly the same model of randomness as in our analysis of matrix completion! We use this fact as a starting point for our construction. Proposition 4.31 implies that as long as the rank of $\boldsymbol{L}_o$ is not too large, i.e.,

$$r < \frac{\rho_{\text{clean}} n}{C_0 \nu \log^2 n}, \tag{5.3.23}$$

with high probability there exists a matrix $\boldsymbol{\Lambda}_L$ supported only on the clean set Ω satisfying:

1 $\left\|\mathcal{P}_{\mathsf{T}}[\boldsymbol{\Lambda}_L] - \boldsymbol{U}\boldsymbol{V}^*\right\|_F \le 1/(4n)$,

2 $\left\|\mathcal{P}_{\mathsf{T}^\perp}[\boldsymbol{\Lambda}_L]\right\| \le 1/4$,

3 $\|\boldsymbol{\Lambda}_L\|_\infty < \frac{C \log n}{\rho_{\text{clean}}} \left\|\boldsymbol{U}\boldsymbol{V}^*\right\|_\infty$.

This certificate $\boldsymbol{\Lambda}_L$ lies close enough to the subdifferential of the nuclear norm. Furthermore, let us further verify that it satisfies the condition $\|\mathcal{P}_{\mathfrak{S}^c}[\boldsymbol{\Lambda}_L]\|_\infty < \lambda/2$ in Lemma 5.5. This is because $\boldsymbol{U}\boldsymbol{V}^*$ is ν-incoherent: from (5.3.2), $\|\boldsymbol{U}\boldsymbol{V}^*\|_\infty \le \sqrt{\nu r}/n$ and with the assumption on the rank r of the matrix $\boldsymbol{L}_o$, we have

$$\|\boldsymbol{\Lambda}_L\|_\infty < \frac{C \log n}{\rho_{\text{clean}}} \frac{\sqrt{\nu r}}{n} \le \frac{C}{\sqrt{C_0 \rho_{\text{clean}} \nu}} \frac{1}{\sqrt{n}} = \frac{C}{\sqrt{\rho_{\text{clean}} C_0 \nu}} \lambda. \tag{5.3.24}$$

By properly choosing the constants C_0 and C we can ensure that the coefficient $C/\sqrt{\rho_{\text{clean}} C_0 \nu} < 1/4$.

But $\boldsymbol{\Lambda}_L$ is not yet close to the subdifferential of the ℓ^1 norm – in particular, elements of the subdifferential of the ℓ^1 norm should satisfy $\mathcal{P}_{\mathfrak{S}}[\boldsymbol{\Lambda}] = \lambda \boldsymbol{\Sigma}_o$, but $\mathcal{P}_{\mathfrak{S}}[\boldsymbol{\Lambda}_L] = \boldsymbol{0}$. To correct this, we choose

$$\boldsymbol{\Lambda} = \boldsymbol{\Lambda}_L + \boldsymbol{\Lambda}_S,$$

where the second element $\boldsymbol{\Lambda}_S$ satisfies $\mathcal{P}_{\mathfrak{S}}[\boldsymbol{\Lambda}_S] = \lambda \boldsymbol{\Sigma}_o$. We need to show that we can choose $\boldsymbol{\Lambda}_S$ such that this combined certificate $\boldsymbol{\Lambda}$ remains close to the subdifferential of the nuclear norm at $\boldsymbol{L}_o$, and is also close to the subdifferential of $\lambda \|\cdot\|_1$ at $\boldsymbol{S}_o$. The following lemma shows that this is possible:

LEMMA 5.6. *Under the conditions of Theorem 5.3, with high probability, there exists* $\boldsymbol{\Lambda}_S$ *such that:*

(i) $\mathcal{P}_{\mathsf{G}}[\boldsymbol{\Lambda}_S] = \lambda \boldsymbol{\Sigma}_o$,
(ii) $\|\mathcal{P}_{\mathsf{G}^c}[\boldsymbol{\Lambda}_S]\|_\infty < \lambda/4$,
(iii) $\mathcal{P}_{\mathsf{T}}[\boldsymbol{\Lambda}_S] = \mathbf{0}$,
(iv) $\left\|\mathcal{P}_{\mathsf{T}^\perp}[\boldsymbol{\Lambda}_S]\right\| < 1/4$.

Under the assumptions of Theorem 5.3, we have in total for $\boldsymbol{\Lambda} = \boldsymbol{\Lambda}_L + \boldsymbol{\Lambda}_S$:

$$\left\|\mathcal{P}_{\mathsf{T}}[\boldsymbol{\Lambda}] - \boldsymbol{U}\boldsymbol{V}^*\right\|_F = \left\|\mathcal{P}_{\mathsf{T}}[\boldsymbol{\Lambda}_L] - \boldsymbol{U}\boldsymbol{V}^*\right\|_F \le \frac{1}{4n}, \tag{5.3.25}$$

$$\left\|\mathcal{P}_{\mathsf{T}^\perp}[\boldsymbol{\Lambda}]\right\| \le \left\|\mathcal{P}_{\mathsf{T}^\perp}[\boldsymbol{\Lambda}_L]\right\|_1 + \left\|\mathcal{P}_{\mathsf{T}^\perp}[\boldsymbol{\Lambda}_S]\right\| \le \frac{1}{2}, \tag{5.3.26}$$

$$\mathcal{P}_{\mathsf{G}}[\boldsymbol{\Lambda}] = \mathcal{P}_{\mathsf{G}}[\boldsymbol{\Lambda}_S] = \lambda \boldsymbol{\Sigma}_o, \tag{5.3.27}$$

$$\begin{aligned} \|\mathcal{P}_{\mathsf{G}^c}[\boldsymbol{\Lambda}]\|_\infty &\le \|\mathcal{P}_{\mathsf{G}^c}[\boldsymbol{\Lambda}_L]\|_\infty + \|\mathcal{P}_{\mathsf{G}^c}[\boldsymbol{\Lambda}_S]\|_\infty \\ &\le \|\boldsymbol{\Lambda}_L\|_\infty + \frac{\lambda}{4} \\ &\le \frac{\lambda}{4} + \frac{\lambda}{4} = \frac{\lambda}{2}, \end{aligned} \tag{5.3.28}$$

where in the final inequality we have used the inequality (5.3.24). So with the so-constructed $\boldsymbol{\Lambda}_S$ and $\boldsymbol{\Lambda}_L$, the combined

$$\boldsymbol{\Lambda} = \boldsymbol{\Lambda}_L + \boldsymbol{\Lambda}_S$$

satisfies all conditions of Lemma 5.5 under the assumptions of Theorem 5.3. So if we could prove Lemma 5.6, Theorem 5.3 would follow.

Constructing the Dual Certificate $\boldsymbol{\Lambda}_S$ *Using Least Squares*

To finish our proof, we need to verify Lemma 5.6, by showing that we can indeed construct $\boldsymbol{\Lambda}_S$ that satisfies the requisite properties. To do this, we resort to a strategy that has proved useful at several points over the past few chapters: the method of least squares (minimum energy). Namely, we choose $\boldsymbol{\Lambda}_S$ to satisfy the constraints $\mathcal{P}_{\mathsf{G}}[\boldsymbol{\Lambda}_S] = \lambda \boldsymbol{\Sigma}_o$ and $\mathcal{P}_{\mathsf{T}}[\boldsymbol{\Lambda}_S] = \mathbf{0}$, but have the smallest possible energy: formally,

$$\boldsymbol{\Lambda}_S = \arg\min_{\tilde{\boldsymbol{\Lambda}}} \left\|\tilde{\boldsymbol{\Lambda}}\right\|_F^2 \quad \text{subject to} \quad \mathcal{P}_{\mathsf{G}}[\tilde{\boldsymbol{\Lambda}}] = \lambda \boldsymbol{\Sigma}_o,\ \mathcal{P}_{\mathsf{T}}[\tilde{\boldsymbol{\Lambda}}] = \mathbf{0}. \tag{5.3.29}$$

This optimization problem is feasible, provided $\mathsf{G} \cap \mathsf{T} = \{\mathbf{0}\}$. The constraints ensure that $\boldsymbol{\Lambda}_S$ satisfies criteria (i) and (iii) of Lemma 5.6 automatically.

To check that criteria (ii) and (iv) are satisfied, i.e., that $\mathcal{P}_{\mathsf{G}^c}[\boldsymbol{\Lambda}_S]$ has small ℓ^∞ norm and $\mathcal{P}_{\mathsf{T}^\perp}[\boldsymbol{\Lambda}_S]$ has small operator norm, we utilize the scalar and operator Bernstein's inequalities, respectively. These calculations are facilitated by the existence of a closed-form solution to (5.3.29):

$$\boldsymbol{\Lambda}_S = \lambda \mathcal{P}_{\mathsf{T}^\perp} \sum_{k=0}^{\infty} (\mathcal{P}_{\mathsf{G}} \mathcal{P}_{\mathsf{T}} \mathcal{P}_{\mathsf{G}})^k \, [\boldsymbol{\Sigma}_o]. \tag{5.3.30}$$

Exercise 5.13 asks you to check that this construction indeed satisfies the constraints, and that it is indeed the solution to the energy minimization problem (5.3.29).

Proof of lemma 5.6 Let $\mathcal{E}$ be the event that $\|\mathcal{P}_{\mathsf{T}}\mathcal{P}_{\mathfrak{S}}\| \le \sigma$. This holds with high probability in the support set $\mathfrak{S}$. Notice that on the event $\mathcal{E}$,

$$\sum_{k=0}^{\infty} \left\| (\mathcal{P}_{\mathsf{S}}\mathcal{P}_{\mathsf{T}}\mathcal{P}_{\mathsf{S}})^k \right\| \le \sum_{k=0}^{\infty} \sigma^{2k} = \frac{1}{1-\sigma^{2k}} < \infty. \tag{5.3.31}$$

So, on $\mathcal{E}$, the summation in (5.3.30) converges, and

$$\mathbf{\Lambda}_S = \lambda \mathcal{P}_{\mathsf{T}^\perp} \sum_{k=0}^{\infty} (\mathcal{P}_{\mathfrak{S}}\mathcal{P}_{\mathsf{T}}\mathcal{P}_{\mathfrak{S}})^k \left[\mathbf{\Sigma}_o\right] \tag{5.3.32}$$

is well defined. Property (iii), which states that $\mathcal{P}_{\mathsf{T}}[\mathbf{\Lambda}_S] = \mathbf{0}$, follows immediately, since $\mathcal{P}_{\mathsf{T}}\mathcal{P}_{\mathsf{T}^\perp} = 0$. Property (i), which states that $\mathcal{P}_{\mathfrak{S}}[\mathbf{\Lambda}_S] = \lambda \mathbf{\Sigma}_o$, is a consequence of the construction of $\mathbf{\Lambda}_S$ as the solution to a least-squares problem (5.3.30). To verify this property, we can note that

$$\begin{aligned} \mathcal{P}_{\mathfrak{S}}[\mathbf{\Lambda}_S] &= \lambda \sum_{k=0}^{\infty} (\mathcal{P}_{\mathfrak{S}}\mathcal{P}_{\mathsf{T}}\mathcal{P}_{\mathfrak{S}})^k \left[\mathbf{\Sigma}_o\right] - \lambda \sum_{k=1}^{\infty} (\mathcal{P}_{\mathfrak{S}}\mathcal{P}_{\mathsf{T}}\mathcal{P}_{\mathfrak{S}})^k \left[\mathbf{\Sigma}_o\right] \\ &= \lambda \mathbf{\Sigma}_o, \end{aligned} \tag{5.3.33}$$

as desired. Properties (iv) and (ii) state that $\mathbf{\Lambda}_S$ is small, in two appropriate senses. These require a bit more work.

Verifying (iv). Write

$$\mathbf{\Lambda}_S = \underbrace{\lambda \mathcal{P}_{\mathsf{T}^\perp}[\mathbf{\Sigma}_o]}_{\mathbf{\Lambda}_S^{(1)}} + \underbrace{\lambda \mathcal{P}_{\mathsf{T}^\perp} \sum_{k=1}^{\infty} (\mathcal{P}_{\mathfrak{S}}\mathcal{P}_{\mathsf{T}}\mathcal{P}_{\mathfrak{S}})^k [\mathbf{\Sigma}_o]}_{\mathbf{\Lambda}_S^{(2)}}. \tag{5.3.34}$$

For the second term, we introduce the more concise notation

$$\mathcal{R} = \mathcal{P}_{\mathsf{T}^\perp} \sum_{k=1}^{\infty} (\mathcal{P}_{\mathfrak{S}}\mathcal{P}_{\mathsf{T}}\mathcal{P}_{\mathfrak{S}})^k, \tag{5.3.35}$$

so that

$$\mathbf{\Lambda}_S^{(2)} = \lambda \mathcal{R}[\mathbf{\Sigma}_o]. \tag{5.3.36}$$

Notice that

$$\|\mathcal{R}\| \le \frac{\sigma^2}{1-\sigma^2}. \tag{5.3.37}$$

The norm of $\mathbf{\Lambda}_S^{(1)}$ can be controlled by noting that

$$\left\| \mathbf{\Lambda}_S^{(1)} \right\| = \lambda \left\| \mathcal{P}_{\mathsf{T}^\perp}[\mathbf{\Sigma}_o] \right\| \le \lambda \left\| \mathbf{\Sigma}_o \right\|. \tag{5.3.38}$$

With high probability,

$$\|\boldsymbol{\Sigma}_o\| \le C\sqrt{\rho m}, \tag{5.3.39}$$

whence for $\rho < \rho_\star$ a small constant, $\left\|\boldsymbol{\Lambda}_S^{(1)}\right\| \le \frac{1}{16}$. To control the norm of $\boldsymbol{\Lambda}_S^{(2)}$, let N be a $\frac{1}{2}$ net for $\mathbb{S}^{n-1}$. By Lemma 3.25, such a net exists, with size $|\mathsf{N}| \le 6^n$. Moreover,

$$\begin{aligned}
\left\|\boldsymbol{\Lambda}_S^{(2)}\right\| &= \sup_{\boldsymbol{u},\boldsymbol{v}\in\mathbb{S}^{n-1}} \boldsymbol{u}^*\boldsymbol{\Lambda}_S^{(2)}\boldsymbol{v} \\
&\le 4 \max_{\boldsymbol{u},\boldsymbol{v}\in\mathsf{N}} \boldsymbol{u}^*\boldsymbol{\Lambda}_S^{(2)}\boldsymbol{v} \\
&= 4 \max_{\boldsymbol{u},\boldsymbol{v}\in\mathsf{N}} \left\langle \boldsymbol{u}\boldsymbol{v}^*, \lambda\mathcal{R}\left[\boldsymbol{\Sigma}_o\right]\right\rangle \\
&= 4 \max_{\boldsymbol{u},\boldsymbol{v}\in\mathsf{N}} \left\langle \lambda\mathcal{R}[\boldsymbol{u}\boldsymbol{v}^*], \boldsymbol{\Sigma}_o\right\rangle \\
&= 4 \max_{\boldsymbol{u},\boldsymbol{v}\in\mathsf{N}} \left\langle \boldsymbol{X}_{\boldsymbol{u},\boldsymbol{v}}, \boldsymbol{\Sigma}_o\right\rangle.
\end{aligned} \tag{5.3.40}$$

Conditioned on the support $\mathfrak{S}$ of the sparse error term, we can observe that the random variable $\left\langle \boldsymbol{X}_{\boldsymbol{u},\boldsymbol{v}}, \boldsymbol{\Sigma}_o\right\rangle$ is a linear combination of Rademacher (±1) random variables. Hoeffding's inequality gives

$$\mathbb{P}\left[\left\langle \boldsymbol{X}_{\boldsymbol{u},\boldsymbol{v}}, \boldsymbol{\Sigma}_o\right\rangle > t \mid \mathfrak{S}\right] \le \exp\left(-\frac{t^2}{2\left\|\boldsymbol{X}_{\boldsymbol{u},\boldsymbol{v}}\right\|_F^2}\right). \tag{5.3.41}$$

On $\mathcal{E}$, using the bound (5.3.37), we can control the norm of $\boldsymbol{X}_{\boldsymbol{u},\boldsymbol{v}}$, via

$$\left\|\boldsymbol{X}_{\boldsymbol{u},\boldsymbol{v}}\right\|_F \le \frac{\lambda\sigma^2}{1-\sigma^2}. \tag{5.3.42}$$

So, for each $\boldsymbol{u},\boldsymbol{v}$,

$$\mathbb{P}\left[\left\langle \boldsymbol{X}_{\boldsymbol{u},\boldsymbol{v}}, \boldsymbol{\Sigma}_o\right\rangle > t \mid \mathcal{E}\right] \le \exp\left(-\frac{t^2}{2\left\|\boldsymbol{X}_{\boldsymbol{u},\boldsymbol{v}}\right\|_F^2}\right). \tag{5.3.43}$$

Hence,

$$\begin{aligned}
\mathbb{P}\left[\left\|\boldsymbol{\Lambda}_S^{(2)}\right\| > t\right] &\le \mathbb{P}\left[\max_{\boldsymbol{u},\boldsymbol{v}\in\mathsf{N}} \left\langle \boldsymbol{X}_{\boldsymbol{u},\boldsymbol{v}}, \boldsymbol{\Sigma}_o\right\rangle > t/4\right] \\
&\le \mathbb{P}\left[\max_{\boldsymbol{u},\boldsymbol{v}\in\mathsf{N}} \left\langle \boldsymbol{X}_{\boldsymbol{u},\boldsymbol{v}}, \boldsymbol{\Sigma}_o\right\rangle > t/4 \mid \mathcal{E}\right] + \mathbb{P}\left[\mathcal{E}^c\right] \\
&\le |\mathsf{N}|^2 \times \max_{\boldsymbol{u},\boldsymbol{v}\in\mathsf{N}} \mathbb{P}\left[\left\langle \boldsymbol{X}_{\boldsymbol{u},\boldsymbol{v}}, \boldsymbol{\Sigma}_o\right\rangle > t/4 \mid \mathcal{E}\right] + \mathbb{P}\left[\mathcal{E}^c\right] \\
&\le 6^{2n} \times \exp\left(-\frac{t^2(1-\sigma^2)^2}{2\lambda^2\sigma^4}\right) + \mathbb{P}\left[\mathcal{E}^c\right].
\end{aligned} \tag{5.3.44}$$

Setting $t = \frac{1}{8}$, and ensuring that σ is appropriately small, we obtain that with high probability $\left\|\boldsymbol{\Lambda}_S^{(2)}\right\| \le \frac{1}{8}$; combining with our bound on $\left\|\boldsymbol{\Lambda}_S^{(1)}\right\|$, we obtain that $\|\boldsymbol{\Lambda}_S\| < \frac{1}{4}$ with high probability, as desired.

Verifying (ii). We finish by verifying that with high probability, $\|\mathcal{P}_{\mathfrak{S}^c}[\boldsymbol{\Lambda}_S]\|_\infty < \lambda/4$. For this, notice that

$$\begin{aligned}
\mathcal{P}_{\mathfrak{S}^c}[\boldsymbol{\Lambda}_S] &= \lambda \mathcal{P}_{\mathfrak{S}^c}\mathcal{P}_{\mathsf{T}^\perp} \sum_{k=0}^{\infty} (\mathcal{P}_{\mathfrak{S}}\mathcal{P}_{\mathsf{T}}\mathcal{P}_{\mathfrak{S}})^k [\boldsymbol{\Sigma}_o] \\
&= \lambda \mathcal{P}_{\mathfrak{S}^c}\mathcal{P}_{\mathsf{T}}\mathcal{P}_{\mathfrak{S}} \sum_{k=0}^{\infty} (\mathcal{P}_{\mathfrak{S}}\mathcal{P}_{\mathsf{T}}\mathcal{P}_{\mathfrak{S}})^k [\boldsymbol{\Sigma}_o] \\
&\doteq \lambda \mathcal{H}[\boldsymbol{\Sigma}_o].
\end{aligned} \tag{5.3.45}$$

On $\mathcal{E}$, for any $(i,j) \in \mathfrak{S}^c$, we have

$$\begin{aligned}
\left\| \mathcal{H}^*[\boldsymbol{e}_i\boldsymbol{e}_j^*] \right\|_F &= \left\| \left[\sum_{k=0}^{\infty} (\mathcal{P}_{\mathfrak{S}}\mathcal{P}_{\mathsf{T}}\mathcal{P}_{\mathfrak{S}})^k \right] \mathcal{P}_{\mathfrak{S}}\mathcal{P}_{\mathsf{T}}[\boldsymbol{e}_i\boldsymbol{e}_j^*] \right\|_F \\
&\le \left\| \left[\sum_{k=0}^{\infty} (\mathcal{P}_{\mathfrak{S}}\mathcal{P}_{\mathsf{T}}\mathcal{P}_{\mathfrak{S}})^k \right] \mathcal{P}_{\mathfrak{S}}\mathcal{P}_{\mathsf{T}} \right\| \left\| \mathcal{P}_{\mathsf{T}}[\boldsymbol{e}_i\boldsymbol{e}_j^*] \right\|_F \\
&\le \frac{\sigma}{1-\sigma^2} \times \sqrt{\frac{2\nu r}{n}} \\
&\le C\sqrt{\log n}.
\end{aligned} \tag{5.3.46}$$

Notice that

$$\|\mathcal{P}_{\mathfrak{S}^c}[\boldsymbol{\Lambda}_S]\|_\infty = \lambda \max_{i,j} \left| \boldsymbol{e}_i^* \mathcal{H}[\boldsymbol{\Sigma}_o]\boldsymbol{e}_j \right| = \lambda \max_{i,j} \left| \left\langle \mathcal{H}[\boldsymbol{e}_i\boldsymbol{e}_j^*], \boldsymbol{\Sigma}_o \right\rangle \right|. \tag{5.3.47}$$

Write

$$Y_{ij} = \left\langle \mathcal{H}[\boldsymbol{e}_i\boldsymbol{e}_j^*], \boldsymbol{\Sigma}_o \right\rangle \quad \in \mathbb{R}. \tag{5.3.48}$$

Using Hoeffding's inequality again, we have

$$\mathbb{P}\Big[|Y_{ij}| > t \ \mid \ \mathfrak{S} \Big] \le 2\exp\left(-\frac{t^2}{2\left\| \mathcal{H}[\boldsymbol{e}_i\boldsymbol{e}_j^*] \right\|_F^2} \right). \tag{5.3.49}$$

Hence,

$$\mathbb{P}\Big[|Y_{ij}| > t \ \mid \ \mathcal{E} \Big] \le 2n^{-12}. \tag{5.3.50}$$

We have

$$\begin{aligned}
\mathbb{P}\Big[\|\mathcal{P}_{\mathfrak{S}^c}[\boldsymbol{\Lambda}_S]\|_\infty \ge \lambda/4 \Big] &\le \mathbb{P}\Big[\max_{i,j} |Y_{ij}| > \tfrac{1}{4} \Big] \\
&\le \mathbb{P}\Big[\max_{i,j} |Y_{ij}| > \tfrac{1}{4} \ \mid \ \mathcal{E} \Big] + \mathbb{P}\Big[\ \mathcal{E}^c \ \Big] \\
&\le \sum_{i,j} \mathbb{P}\Big[|Y_{ij}| > \tfrac{1}{4} \ \mid \ \mathcal{E} \Big] + \mathbb{P}\Big[\ \mathcal{E}^c \ \Big]
\end{aligned}$$

$$\leq n^2 \times 2n^{-12} + \mathbb{P}\left[\mathcal{E}^c\right]$$
$$\leq 2n^{-10} + \mathbb{P}\left[\mathcal{E}^c\right]. \tag{5.3.51}$$

This completes the proof. □

5.3.3 Some Extensions to the Main Result

Several refinements or extensions to Theorem 5.3 are possible. We describe these here, and leave their proofs as exercises.

Nonsquare Matrices

In the general rectangular case where $\boldsymbol{L}_o$ is $n_1 \times n_2$, let $n_{(1)} \doteq \max\{n_1, n_2\}$. Then PCP with $\lambda = 1/\sqrt{n_{(1)}}$ succeeds with probability at least $1 - cn_{(1)}^{-10}$, provided that $\text{rank}(\boldsymbol{L}_o) \leq \rho_r n_{(2)} \nu^{-1} (\log n_{(1)})^{-2}$ and $m \leq \rho_s n_1 n_2$. A rather remarkable fact is that there is no tuning parameter in solving the PCP program. Under the assumption of the theorem, solving

$$\min_{\boldsymbol{L},\boldsymbol{S}} \|\boldsymbol{L}\|_* + \frac{1}{\sqrt{n_{(1)}}}\|\boldsymbol{S}\|_1 \quad \text{subject to} \quad \boldsymbol{Y} = \boldsymbol{L} + \boldsymbol{S}$$

always returns the correct answer. This is surprising because one might have expected that one would have to choose the right scalar λ to balance the two terms in $\|\boldsymbol{L}\|_* + \lambda\|\boldsymbol{S}\|_1$ appropriately (perhaps depending on their relative size). This is, however, clearly not the case. In this sense, the choice $\lambda = 1/\sqrt{n_{(1)}}$ is universal. Further, it is not so clear *a priori* why $\lambda = 1/\sqrt{n_{(1)}}$ is a correct choice no matter what $\boldsymbol{L}_o$ and $\boldsymbol{S}_o$ are. It is the mathematical analysis which reveals the correctness of this value. In fact, the proof of the theorem gives a range of correct values, and we have selected arguably the simplest one in that range.

Dense Error Correction

In the above Theorem 5.3, one may wonder how large the fraction of nonzero entries in $\boldsymbol{S}_o$, namely ρ_s, can be in practice. The result will not be very useful if ρ_s has to be extremely small. As it turns out, in most cases, ρ_s can be rather significant, and in some extreme cases, $\boldsymbol{S}_o$ does not even have to be sparse at all!

To be more precise, under the same assumptions of Theorem 5.3, one can rigorously prove the following: for any $\rho_s < 1$, as n becomes large,[7] principal component pursuit (5.2.2) exactly recovers $(\boldsymbol{L}_o, \boldsymbol{S}_o)$ with high probability,[8] provided

$$\lambda = C_1 \left(4\sqrt{1-\rho_s} + \frac{9}{4}\right)^{-1} \sqrt{\frac{1-\rho_s}{\rho_s n}}, \quad r < \frac{C_2 n}{\nu \log^2 n}, \tag{5.3.52}$$

where $0 < C_1 \leq 4/5$ and $C_2 > 0$ are certain constants. In other words, provided the rank of a matrix is of the order of $n/(\nu \log^2 n)$, if we can choose a λ that is

[7] For ρ_s closer to one, the dimension n must be larger; formally, $n > n_0(\rho_s)$.

[8] By "high probability," we mean with probability at least $1 - cn^{-\beta}$ for some fixed $\beta > 0$.

dependent on ρ_s, PCP recovers the low-rank matrix exactly even when an arbitrarily large fraction of its entries are corrupted by errors of arbitrary magnitudes and the locations of the uncorrupted entries are unknown!

Furthermore, by slightly modifying the proof for the above statement, one can show that the exact recovery will be guaranteed with high probability if the rank r and the parameter λ are chosen as follows instead:

$$\lambda = \frac{1}{\sqrt{n \log n}}, \quad r < \frac{C_2 n}{\nu \log^3 n}. \tag{5.3.53}$$

That is, if there is reason to believe the rank of the matrix $\boldsymbol{L}_o$ is more restricted (say, in practice, fixed), we only have to set $\lambda = 1/\sqrt{n \log n}$, which does not depend on any knowledge in the fraction of errors ρ_s. With such settings, PCP would succeed in finding the correct solution. As we will see in Section 5.6, a similar choice of λ works for recovering a low-rank matrix with both missing and corrupted entries.

In this book, we chose not to provide detailed proof to these extensions as their proof strategy and techniques are very similar to the proof of Theorem 5.3. Nevertheless, interested readers might resort to the work [GWL+10, CJSC13] for more details.

Derandomization of Error Signs

In the above Theorem 5.3, both the support and signs of the error term $\boldsymbol{S}_o$ are assumed to be random. In practice, such random models might be considered as less practical as many practical sparse signals might not be entirely random. As it turns out, the randomness assumption on the signs of $\boldsymbol{S}_o$ is not crucial for the conclusion of the theorem.

More precisely, one can prove that: suppose $\boldsymbol{L}_o$ obeys the conditions of Theorem 5.3 and that the locations of the nonzero entries of $\boldsymbol{S}_o$ follow the Bernoulli model with parameter ρ_s, and the signs of $\boldsymbol{S}_o$ are i.i.d. ± 1 (independent from the locations). Then if the PCP solution is exact with high probability, then it is also exact with at least the same probability for the model in which the signs (and values) of $\boldsymbol{S}_o$ are fixed and the locations are sampled from the Bernoulli model with parameter $\frac{1}{2}\rho_s$.

That is, we may consider $\boldsymbol{S}_o$ comes from an *arbitrary prefixed* matrix $\boldsymbol{S}$ as

$$\boldsymbol{S}_o = \mathcal{P}_{\mathfrak{S}}[\boldsymbol{S}],$$

where $\mathfrak{S}$ is sampled from a Bernoulli model with parameter $\frac{1}{2}\rho_s$. Then the PCP recovers the correct $\boldsymbol{L}_o$ and $\boldsymbol{S}_o$ with high probability too. In other words, to remove the randomness in the signs, we lose half of the density in the error term $\boldsymbol{S}_o$. Note that the values and signs of the fixed matrix $\boldsymbol{S}$ can even be chosen to be the most "adversarial": $\boldsymbol{S} = \boldsymbol{L}_o$!

What about the randomness in the locations $\mathfrak{S}$? Can we remove it too without significantly reducing the strength of the conclusion? As we have discussed earlier in this section, the randomness of the support of $\boldsymbol{S}_o$ is to ensure identifiability. If the support of $\boldsymbol{S}_o$ is not sufficiently random in both columns and rows, say it concentrates on a certain row or column, then it might easily become impossible to recover the corresponding row or column of L_o. One may refer to [CSPW09] for conditions under which PCP succeeds with deterministic models for the support of S_o.

Sparse Outlier Pursuit

In many applications, the corruptions might concentrate on a small number of columns of the low-rank matrix L_o, instead of individual entries. In other words, the data matrix is of the form

$$Y = L_o + O_o,$$

where O_o is a matrix with a sparse number of nonzero columns. The corresponding columns can be viewed as "outliers" which have little to do with the low-rank matrix L_o. This problem is also known as robust PCA with sparse (column-wise) outliers [XCS12]. In this case, one may consider a norm that promotes column-wise sparsity: the sum of ℓ^2 norms of all columns, also known as the $(2, 1)$-norm:

$$\|O\|_{2,1} = \sum_{i}^{n_2} \|O_i\|_2, \tag{5.3.54}$$

where $O_i \in \mathbb{R}^{n_1}$ are the columns of the matrix $O \in \mathbb{R}^{n_1 \times n_2}$. So to decompose the matrix Y, one may consider the following convex program known as "outlier pursuit":

$$\min_{L, S} \|L\|_* + \lambda \|O\|_{2,1} \quad \text{subject to} \quad L + O = Y. \tag{5.3.55}$$

Like the PCP for sparse corruptions, the above program can recover the correct low-rank and the column-sparse components under fairly broad conditions,[9] as detailed in the work of [XCS12].

5.4 Stable Principal Component Pursuit with Noise

The PCP model and result (Theorem 5.3) is limited to situations in which the low-rank component is exactly low-rank and the sparse component is exactly sparse. However, in real-world applications the observations are often perturbed by noise, which may be stochastic or deterministic, affecting every entry of the data matrix. For example, in face recognition that we mentioned earlier, the human face is not a strictly convex and Lambertian surface, hence the low-rank model (due to photometric properties) is only approximately low-rank. In ranking and collaborative filtering, users' ratings could be noisy because of the lack of control in the data collection process. Therefore, for the PCP method to be applicable to a wider range of real-world problems, we need to examine if it can handle small entry-wise (dense) noise.

In the presence of noise, the new measurement model becomes

$$Y = L_o + S_o + Z_o, \tag{5.4.1}$$

[9] The columns of the low-rank matrix L_o satisfy certain incoherent conditions, and the fraction of outliers is bounded accordingly.

where $\boldsymbol{Z}_o$ is a small error term that could affect the value of each entry of the matrix. However, all we assume about $\boldsymbol{Z}_o$ here is that $\|\boldsymbol{Z}_o\|_F \leq \varepsilon$ for some $\varepsilon > 0$.

To recover the unknown matrices $\boldsymbol{L}_o$ and $\boldsymbol{S}_o$, one may consider solving the following optimization problem, as a relaxed version to PCP (5.2.2):

$$\min_{\boldsymbol{L},\boldsymbol{S}} \|\boldsymbol{L}\|_* + \lambda\|\boldsymbol{S}\|_1 \quad \text{subject to} \quad \|\boldsymbol{Y} - \boldsymbol{L} - \boldsymbol{S}\|_F \leq \varepsilon, \tag{5.4.2}$$

where we choose $\lambda = 1/\sqrt{n}$. Note that with this choice, we typically have $\lambda < 1/2$ for large n. Our main result is that under the same conditions as PCP, the above convex program gives a stable estimate of $\boldsymbol{L}_o$ and $\boldsymbol{S}_o$:

THEOREM 5.7. (Stability of PCP to bounded noise) *We make the same assumptions as in Theorem 5.3, that is,* $\boldsymbol{L}_o$ *obeys the incoherence conditions and the support of* $\boldsymbol{S}_o$ *is uniformly distributed of size* m. *Then if* $\boldsymbol{L}_o$ *and* $\boldsymbol{S}_o$ *satisfy*

$$\operatorname{rank}(\boldsymbol{L}_o) \leq \frac{\rho_r n}{\nu \log^2 n} \quad \textit{and} \quad m \leq \rho_s n^2, \tag{5.4.3}$$

with $\rho_r, \rho_s > 0$ *being sufficiently small numerical constants, with high probability in the support of* $\boldsymbol{S}_o$, *for any* $\boldsymbol{Z}_o$ *with* $\|\boldsymbol{Z}_o\|_F \leq \varepsilon$, *the solution* $(\hat{\boldsymbol{L}}, \hat{\boldsymbol{S}})$ *to the convex program* (5.4.2) *satisfies*

$$\|\hat{\boldsymbol{L}} - \boldsymbol{L}_o\|_F^2 + \|\hat{\boldsymbol{S}} - \boldsymbol{S}_o\|_F^2 \leq C\varepsilon^2, \tag{5.4.4}$$

where the constant $C = \left(16\sqrt{5n} + \sqrt{2}\right)^2$.

Here, we would like to point out two ways to view the significance of this result. To some extent, the model (5.4.2) unifies the classical PCA and the robust PCA by considering both gross sparse errors and small entry-wise noise in the measurements. So on the one hand, the above theorem says that the low-rank and sparse decomposition via PCP is stable in the presence of small entry-wise noise, hence making PCP more widely applicable to practical problems where the low-rank structure is not exact. On the other hand, the theorem convincingly justifies that the classical PCA can now be made robust to sparse gross corruptions via a certain convex program. Since this convex program can be solved very efficiently via algorithms similar to Algorithm 5.1, at a cost not so much higher than the classical PCA, this model and result can be applied to many practical problems where both small noise and gross corruption are present simultaneously.

Before we set out to prove the above result, let us first introduce some new notation. For any matrix pair $\boldsymbol{X} = (\boldsymbol{L}, \boldsymbol{S})$ let

$$\|\boldsymbol{X}\|_F \doteq \left(\|\boldsymbol{L}\|_F^2 + \|\boldsymbol{S}\|_F^2\right)^{1/2}, \quad \|\boldsymbol{X}\|_\diamond = \|\boldsymbol{L}\|_* + \lambda\|\boldsymbol{S}\|_1.$$

Define a projection operator

$$\mathcal{P}_{\mathsf{T}} \times \mathcal{P}_{\mathfrak{S}} : (\boldsymbol{L}, \boldsymbol{S}) \mapsto (\mathcal{P}_{\mathsf{T}}[\boldsymbol{L}], \mathcal{P}_{\mathfrak{S}}[\boldsymbol{S}]).$$

Also we define the subspaces $\Gamma \doteq \{(\boldsymbol{Q}, \boldsymbol{Q}) \mid \boldsymbol{Q} \in \mathbb{R}^{n\times n}\}$ and $\Gamma^\perp \doteq \{(\boldsymbol{Q}, -\boldsymbol{Q}) \mid \boldsymbol{Q} \in \mathbb{R}^{n\times n}\}$, and let $\mathcal{P}_\Gamma$ and $\mathcal{P}_{\Gamma^\perp}$ denote their respective projection operators.

LEMMA 5.8. *Suppose that* $\|\mathcal{P}_{\mathsf{T}}\mathcal{P}_{\mathfrak{S}}\| \le 1/2$. *Then for any pair* $\boldsymbol{X} = (\boldsymbol{L}, \boldsymbol{S})$, $\|\mathcal{P}_{\Gamma}(\mathcal{P}_{\mathsf{T}} \times \mathcal{P}_{\mathfrak{S}})[\boldsymbol{X}]\|_F^2 \ge \frac{1}{4}\|(\mathcal{P}_{\mathsf{T}} \times \mathcal{P}_{\mathfrak{S}})[\boldsymbol{X}]\|_F^2$.

Proof For any matrix pair $\boldsymbol{X}' = (\boldsymbol{L}', \boldsymbol{S}')$,

$$\mathcal{P}_{\Gamma}[\boldsymbol{X}'] = \left(\frac{\boldsymbol{L}' + \boldsymbol{S}'}{2}, \frac{\boldsymbol{L}' + \boldsymbol{S}'}{2}\right)$$

and so $\|\mathcal{P}_{\Gamma}[\boldsymbol{X}']\|_F^2 = \frac{1}{2}\|\boldsymbol{L}' + \boldsymbol{S}'\|_F^2$. So,

$$\begin{aligned}\|\mathcal{P}_{\Gamma}(\mathcal{P}_{\mathsf{T}} \times \mathcal{P}_{\mathfrak{S}})[\boldsymbol{X}]\|_F^2 &= \tfrac{1}{2}\|\mathcal{P}_{\mathsf{T}}[\boldsymbol{L}] + \mathcal{P}_{\mathfrak{S}}[\boldsymbol{S}]\|_F^2 \\ &= \tfrac{1}{2}\left(\|\mathcal{P}_{\mathsf{T}}[\boldsymbol{L}]\|_F^2 + \|\mathcal{P}_{\mathfrak{S}}[\boldsymbol{S}]\|_F^2 + 2\langle \mathcal{P}_{\mathsf{T}}[\boldsymbol{L}], \mathcal{P}_{\mathfrak{S}}[\boldsymbol{S}]\rangle\right).\end{aligned}$$

Now,

$$\begin{aligned}\langle \mathcal{P}_{\mathsf{T}}[\boldsymbol{L}], \mathcal{P}_{\mathfrak{S}}[\boldsymbol{S}]\rangle &= \langle \mathcal{P}_{\mathsf{T}}[\boldsymbol{L}], (\mathcal{P}_{\mathsf{T}}\mathcal{P}_{\mathfrak{S}})\mathcal{P}_{\mathfrak{S}}[\boldsymbol{S}]\rangle \\ &\ge -\|\mathcal{P}_{\mathsf{T}}\mathcal{P}_{\mathfrak{S}}\|\|\mathcal{P}_{\mathsf{T}}[\boldsymbol{L}]\|_F\|\mathcal{P}_{\mathfrak{S}}[\boldsymbol{S}]\|_F.\end{aligned}$$

Since $\|\mathcal{P}_{\mathsf{T}}\mathcal{P}_{\mathfrak{S}}\| \le 1/2$,

$$\begin{aligned}\|\mathcal{P}_{\Gamma}(\mathcal{P}_{\mathsf{T}} \times \mathcal{P}_{\mathfrak{S}})[\boldsymbol{X}]\|_F^2 &\ge \tfrac{1}{2}\left(\|\mathcal{P}_{\mathsf{T}}[\boldsymbol{L}]\|_F^2 + \|\mathcal{P}_{\mathfrak{S}}[\boldsymbol{S}]\|_F^2 - \|\mathcal{P}_{\mathsf{T}}[\boldsymbol{L}]\|_F\|\mathcal{P}_{\mathfrak{S}}[\boldsymbol{S}]\|_F\right) \\ &\ge \tfrac{1}{4}\left(\|\mathcal{P}_{\mathsf{T}}[\boldsymbol{L}]\|_F^2 + \|\mathcal{P}_{\mathfrak{S}}[\boldsymbol{S}]\|_F^2\right) = \tfrac{1}{4}\|(\mathcal{P}_{\mathsf{T}} \times \mathcal{P}_{\mathfrak{S}})[\boldsymbol{X}]\|_F^2,\end{aligned}$$

where we have used that for any a, b, $a^2 + b^2 - ab \ge (a^2 + b^2)/2$. □

Proof of theorem 5.7 The proof for the noisy case largely relies on the method and results we have developed before for proving the noiseless case of PCP. From the proof of Theorem 5.3, we know that, with high probability, there exists a dual certificate $\boldsymbol{\Lambda}$ satisfying the conditions in Lemma (5.5):

$$\begin{cases} \left\|\mathcal{P}_{\mathsf{T}}[\boldsymbol{\Lambda}] - \boldsymbol{U}\boldsymbol{V}^*\right\|_F \le \lambda/8, & \left\|\mathcal{P}_{\mathsf{T}^\perp}[\boldsymbol{\Lambda}]\right\| < 1/2, \\ \|\mathcal{P}_{\mathfrak{S}}[\boldsymbol{\Lambda}] - \lambda\boldsymbol{\Sigma}_o\|_F \le \lambda/8, & \|\mathcal{P}_{\mathfrak{S}^c}[\boldsymbol{\Lambda}]\|_\infty < \lambda/2. \end{cases} \tag{5.4.5}$$

Our proof uses two crucial properties of $\hat{\boldsymbol{X}} = (\hat{\boldsymbol{L}}, \hat{\boldsymbol{S}})$. First, since $\boldsymbol{X}_o$ is also a feasible solution to (5.4.2), we have $\|\hat{\boldsymbol{X}}\|_\diamond \le \|\boldsymbol{X}_o\|_\diamond$. Second, we use the triangle inequality to get

$$\begin{aligned}\|\hat{\boldsymbol{L}} + \hat{\boldsymbol{S}} - \boldsymbol{L}_o - \boldsymbol{S}_o\|_F &\le \|\hat{\boldsymbol{L}} + \hat{\boldsymbol{S}} - \boldsymbol{Y}\|_F + \|\boldsymbol{L}_o + \boldsymbol{S}_o - \boldsymbol{Y}\|_F \\ &\le 2\varepsilon.\end{aligned} \tag{5.4.6}$$

Furthermore, set $\hat{\boldsymbol{X}} = \boldsymbol{X}_o + \boldsymbol{H}$, where $\boldsymbol{H} = (\boldsymbol{H}_L, \boldsymbol{H}_S)$. We want to bound the norm of the perturbation $\|\boldsymbol{H}\|_F^2 = \|\boldsymbol{H}_L\|_F^2 + \|\boldsymbol{H}_S\|_F^2$. Notice that unlike the noise-free case, here $\boldsymbol{H}_L + \boldsymbol{H}_S$ is not necessarily equal to zero. So in order to leverage results from the noise-free case, we decompose the perturbation into the two orthogonal components in Γ and $\Gamma^\perp$, respectively: $\boldsymbol{H}^\Gamma = \mathcal{P}_\Gamma[\boldsymbol{H}]$ and $\boldsymbol{H}^{\Gamma^\perp} = \mathcal{P}_{\Gamma^\perp}[\boldsymbol{H}]$. Then $\|\boldsymbol{H}\|_F^2$ can be expanded as

$$\|H\|_F^2 = \|H^{\Gamma}\|_F^2 + \|H^{\Gamma^\perp}\|_F^2$$
$$= \|H^{\Gamma}\|_F^2 + \|(\mathcal{P}_{\mathsf{T}} \times \mathcal{P}_{\Omega})[H^{\Gamma^\perp}]\|_F^2 + \|(\mathcal{P}_{\mathsf{T}^\perp} \times \mathcal{P}_{\mathfrak{S}^c})[H^{\Gamma^\perp}]\|_F^2. \quad (5.4.7)$$

Since (5.4.6) gives us

$$\|H^{\Gamma}\|_F = \left(\|(H_L + H_S)/2\|_F^2 + \|(H_L + H_S)/2\|_F^2\right)^{1/2} \le \sqrt{2}/2 \times 2\varepsilon = \sqrt{2}\varepsilon, \quad (5.4.8)$$

it suffices to bound the second and third terms on the right-hand side of (5.4.7).

(a) Bound the third term of (5.4.7). Let Λ be a dual certificate satisfying (5.4.5). Then we have

$$\|X_o + H\|_\diamond \ge \|X_o + H^{\Gamma^\perp}\|_\diamond - \|H^{\Gamma}\|_\diamond. \quad (5.4.9)$$

Since $H_L^{\Gamma^\perp} + H_S^{\Gamma^\perp} = 0$, following the proof of Lemma 5.5, we have

$$\|X_o + H^{\Gamma^\perp}\|_\diamond \ge \|X_o\|_\diamond + (1/8)\|\mathcal{P}_{\mathsf{T}^\perp}[H_L^{\Gamma^\perp}] + (\lambda/8)\|_*\|\mathcal{P}_{\mathfrak{S}^c}[H_S^{\Gamma^\perp}]\|_1$$
$$\ge \|X_o\|_\diamond + \frac{1}{8}\left(\|\mathcal{P}_{\mathsf{T}^\perp}[H_L^{\Gamma^\perp}]\|_* + \lambda\|\mathcal{P}_{\mathfrak{S}^c}[H_S^{\Gamma^\perp}]\|_1\right),$$

which implies that

$$\|\mathcal{P}_{\mathsf{T}^\perp}[H_L^{\Gamma^\perp}]\|_* + \lambda\|\mathcal{P}_{\mathfrak{S}^c}[H_S^{\Gamma^\perp}]\|_1 \le 8\|H^{\Gamma}\|_\diamond. \quad (5.4.10)$$

For any matrix $Y \in \mathbb{R}^{n\times n}$, we have the following inequalities:

$$\|Y\|_F \le \|Y\|_* \le \sqrt{n}\|Y\|_F, \qquad \frac{1}{\sqrt{n}}\|Y\|_F \le \lambda\|Y\|_1 \le \sqrt{n}\|Y\|_F,$$

where we assume $\lambda = 1/\sqrt{n}$. Therefore

$$\|(\mathcal{P}_{\mathsf{T}^\perp} \times \mathcal{P}_{\mathfrak{S}^c})[H^{\Gamma^\perp}]\|_F$$
$$\le \|\mathcal{P}_{\mathsf{T}^\perp}[H_L^{\Gamma^\perp}]\|_F + \|\mathcal{P}_{\mathfrak{S}^c}[H_S^{\Gamma^\perp}]\|_F$$
$$\le \|\mathcal{P}_{\mathsf{T}^\perp}[H_L^{\Gamma^\perp}]\|_* + \lambda\sqrt{n}\|\mathcal{P}_{\mathfrak{S}^c}[H_S^{\Gamma^\perp}]\|_1$$
$$\le 8\sqrt{n}\|H^{\Gamma}\|_\diamond = 8\sqrt{n}\left(\|H_L^{\Gamma}\|_* + \lambda\|H_S^{\Gamma}\|_1\right)$$
$$\le 8n(\|H_L^{\Gamma}\|_F + \|H_S^{\Gamma}\|_F) \le 8\sqrt{2}n\|H^{\Gamma}\|_F \le 16n\varepsilon, \quad (5.4.11)$$

where the last equation uses the fact that $H_L^{\Gamma} = H_S^{\Gamma}$.

(b) Bound the second term of (5.4.7). By Lemma 5.8,

$$\|\mathcal{P}_{\Gamma}(\mathcal{P}_{\mathsf{T}} \times \mathcal{P}_{\mathfrak{S}})[H^{\Gamma^\perp}]\|_F^2 \ge \frac{1}{4}\|(\mathcal{P}_{\mathsf{T}} \times \mathcal{P}_{\mathfrak{S}})[H^{\Gamma^\perp}]\|_F^2.$$

But since $\mathcal{P}_{\Gamma}[H^{\Gamma^\perp}] = \mathbf{0} = \mathcal{P}_{\Gamma}[\mathcal{P}_{\mathsf{T}} \times \mathcal{P}_{\mathfrak{S}})[H^{\Gamma^\perp}] + \mathcal{P}_{\Gamma}[\mathcal{P}_{\mathsf{T}^\perp} \times \mathcal{P}_{\mathfrak{S}^c})[H^{\Gamma^\perp}]$, we have

$$\|\mathcal{P}_{\Gamma}(\mathcal{P}_{\mathsf{T}} \times \mathcal{P}_{\mathfrak{S}})[H^{\Gamma^\perp}]\|_F = \|\mathcal{P}_{\Gamma}(\mathcal{P}_{\mathsf{T}^\perp} \times \mathcal{P}_{\mathfrak{S}^c})[H^{\Gamma^\perp}]\|_F$$
$$\le \|(\mathcal{P}_{\mathsf{T}^\perp} \times \mathcal{P}_{\mathfrak{S}^c})[H^{\Gamma^\perp}]\|_F.$$

Combining the previous two inequalities, we have

$$\|(\mathcal{P}_{\mathsf{T}} \times \mathcal{P}_{\mathfrak{S}})[\boldsymbol{H}^{\Gamma^{\perp}}]\|_F^2 \leq 4\|(\mathcal{P}_{\mathsf{T}^{\perp}} \times \mathcal{P}_{\mathfrak{S}^c})[\boldsymbol{H}^{\Gamma^{\perp}}]\|_F^2,$$

which, together with (5.4.11), gives us the desired result,

$$\|\boldsymbol{H}^{\Gamma^{\perp}}\|_F^2 \leq 5\|(\mathcal{P}_{\mathsf{T}^{\perp}} \times \mathcal{P}_{\mathfrak{S}^c})[\boldsymbol{H}^{\Gamma^{\perp}}]\|_F^2 \leq 5 \times 16^2 n^2 \varepsilon^2. \tag{5.4.12}$$

Combining this bound with (5.4.8), we obtain the conclusion for Theorem 5.7. □

Notice that in the statement of Theorem 5.7, the constant C still depends on the dimension n, which arguably could still be removed or reduced. Indeed, with a slightly stronger condition, say the magnitude of the low-rank component $\boldsymbol{L}_o$ is bounded, one could obtain better estimates by solving a Lasso-type program:

$$\min_{\boldsymbol{L},\boldsymbol{S}} \|\boldsymbol{L}\|_* + \lambda \|\boldsymbol{S}\|_1 + \tfrac{\mu}{2} \|\boldsymbol{L} + \boldsymbol{S} - \boldsymbol{Y}\|_F^2 \quad \text{subject to} \quad \|\boldsymbol{L}\|_\infty < \alpha. \tag{5.4.13}$$

With properly chosen weights λ and μ, the bound on the estimation error incurred by the noise can be significantly improved, compared to that in Theorem 5.7. The analysis and result are similar to those for stable sparse recovery (Theorem 3.31) and stable low-rank recovery (Theorem 4.20) where the noise is assumed to be random (Gaussian). For detailed analysis of the error bound for this program, we refer the reader to the work of [ANW12]. The same analysis also applies to the stable version of the outlier pursuit program (5.3.55):

$$\min_{\boldsymbol{L},\boldsymbol{O}} \|\boldsymbol{L}\|_* + \lambda \|\boldsymbol{O}\|_{2,1} + \tfrac{\mu}{2} \|\boldsymbol{L} + \boldsymbol{O} - \boldsymbol{Y}\|_F^2 \quad \text{subject to} \quad \|\boldsymbol{L}\|_\infty < \alpha. \tag{5.4.14}$$

5.5 Compressive Principal Component Pursuit

From the above sections, we saw that under fairly broad conditions, via convex optimization, a low-rank matrix $\boldsymbol{L}_o$ and the sparse matrix $\boldsymbol{S}_o$ can be recovered correctly if we observe fully their superposition $\boldsymbol{Y} = \boldsymbol{L}_o + \boldsymbol{S}_o$. This is possible because the pair $(\boldsymbol{L}_o, \boldsymbol{S}_o)$ have far fewer degrees of freedom than the number of observations n^2. Since this target is so low-dimensional, it is natural to wonder whether it would be possible to recover it from an even smaller set of general linear measurements $\boldsymbol{Y}$. That is, are we are able to perform "compressive sensing" of a low-rank structure and a sparse model superimposed together. Mathematically, we assume the observations have the form

$$\boldsymbol{Y} \doteq \mathcal{P}_{\mathsf{Q}}[\boldsymbol{L}_o + \boldsymbol{S}_o], \tag{5.5.1}$$

where $\mathsf{Q} \subseteq \mathbb{R}^{n_1 \times n_2}$ is a linear subspace, and $\mathcal{P}_{\mathsf{Q}}$ denotes the projection operator onto that subspace. In fact, this problem may arise whenever we observe a "deformed" version of a certain 2D array $\boldsymbol{M}$, say $\boldsymbol{M} \circ \tau = \boldsymbol{L}_o + \boldsymbol{S}_o$, where τ is a certain domain deformation. One natural approach to recover the deformation τ and the low-rank and sparse components is to linearize the above equation with respect to τ and obtain the differential of the above equation at a given τ_o:

$$\boldsymbol{M} \circ \tau_o + \boldsymbol{J} \circ d\tau \approx \boldsymbol{L}_o + \boldsymbol{S}_o,$$

where $\boldsymbol{J}$ is the Jacobian matrix and $d\tau$ is the infinitesimal deformation. To eliminate the unknown $d\tau$, let Q be the left kernel of the Jacobian $\boldsymbol{J}$, i.e., Q is a subspace spanned by all matrices $\mathsf{Q} \doteq \{\boldsymbol{Q} \mid \langle \boldsymbol{Q}, \boldsymbol{J} \rangle = 0\}$. So we have

$$\boldsymbol{Y} \doteq \mathcal{P}_{\mathsf{Q}}[\boldsymbol{M} \circ \tau_o] = \mathcal{P}_{\mathsf{Q}}[\boldsymbol{L}_o + \boldsymbol{S}_o].$$

Can we simultaneously recover the low-rank and sparse components correctly from highly compressive measurements via the natural convex program

$$\min \quad \|\boldsymbol{L}\|_* + \lambda \|\boldsymbol{S}\|_1 \quad \text{subject to} \quad \mathcal{P}_{\mathsf{Q}}[\boldsymbol{L} + \boldsymbol{S}] = \boldsymbol{Y}\ ? \tag{5.5.2}$$

We call this convex program *compressive principal component pursuit*, or shortly *CPCP*. In this section, we study when this program can correctly recover $\boldsymbol{L}_o$ and $\boldsymbol{S}_o$. As before, throughout this section, we assume the low-rank matrix $\boldsymbol{L}_o$ is ν-incoherent and the support of the sparse component $\boldsymbol{S}_o$, say $\mathfrak{S}$, is (Bernoulli) random.

To recover both $\boldsymbol{L}_o$ and $\boldsymbol{S}_o$ correctly, we must require measurements Q to be incoherent with *both* the low-rank and the sparse component. To ensure the incoherence property, we may assume that Q is a randomly chosen subspace in the matrix space $\mathbb{R}^{n_1 \times n_2}$.

More precisely, suppose the dimension of the subspace Q is q, and we assume Q is distributed according to the Haar measure on the Grassmannian $\mathbb{G}(\mathbb{R}^{m \times n}, q)$. On a more intuitive level, this means that Q is equal in distribution to the linear span of a collection of q independent i.i.d. $\mathcal{N}(0, 1)$ matrices. In notation more familiar from compressive sensing, we may let $\boldsymbol{Q}_1, \ldots, \boldsymbol{Q}_q$ denote such a set of matrices, and define an operator $\mathcal{Q} : \mathbb{R}^{n_1 \times n_2} \to \mathbb{R}^q$ via

$$\mathcal{Q}[\boldsymbol{M}] \;=\; \big(\langle \boldsymbol{Q}_1, \boldsymbol{M} \rangle, \ldots, \langle \boldsymbol{Q}_q, \boldsymbol{M} \rangle\big)^* \;\in\; \mathbb{R}^q. \tag{5.5.3}$$

Our analysis also pertains to the equivalent convex program:

$$\min \quad \|\boldsymbol{L}\|_* + \lambda\, \|\boldsymbol{S}\|_1 \quad \text{subject to} \quad \mathcal{Q}[\boldsymbol{L} + \boldsymbol{S}] = \mathcal{Q}[\boldsymbol{L}_o + \boldsymbol{S}_o]. \tag{5.5.4}$$

Since $\mathcal{Q}$ has full rank q almost surely, (5.5.4) and (5.5.2) are completely equivalent.

With these assumptions, the following theorem gives a tight bound on the number of (random) measurements required to correctly recover the pair $(\boldsymbol{L}_o, \boldsymbol{S}_o)$ from $\mathcal{P}_{\mathsf{Q}}[\boldsymbol{L}_o + \boldsymbol{S}_o]$ via CPCP:

THEOREM 5.9. (Compressive PCP) *Let $\boldsymbol{L}_o, \boldsymbol{S}_o \in \mathbb{R}^{n_1 \times n_2}$, with $n_1 \geq n_2$, and suppose that $\boldsymbol{L}_o \neq \boldsymbol{0}$ is a rank-r, ν-incoherent matrix with*

$$r \leq \frac{c_r n_2}{\nu \log^2 n_1}, \tag{5.5.5}$$

and $\operatorname{sign}(\boldsymbol{S}_o)$ *is i.i.d. Bernoulli–Rademacher with nonzero probability* $\rho < c_\rho$. *Let* $\mathsf{Q} \subset \mathbb{R}^{n_1 \times n_2}$ *be a random subspace of dimension*

$$\dim(\mathsf{Q}) \geq C_{\mathsf{Q}} \cdot (\rho n_1 n_2 + n_1 r) \cdot \log^2 n_1 \tag{5.5.6}$$

distributed according to the Haar measure, probabilistically independent of $\operatorname{sign}(\boldsymbol{S}_o)$. *Then with probability at least* $1 - C n_1^{-9}$ *in* $(\operatorname{sign}(\boldsymbol{S}_o), \mathsf{Q})$, *the solution to*

$$\min \quad \|\boldsymbol{L}\|_* + \lambda \|\boldsymbol{S}\|_1 \quad \text{subject to} \quad \mathcal{P}_{\mathsf{Q}}[\boldsymbol{L} + \boldsymbol{S}] = \mathcal{P}_{\mathsf{Q}}[\boldsymbol{L}_o + \boldsymbol{S}_o] \tag{5.5.7}$$

with $\lambda = 1/\sqrt{n_1}$ *is unique, and equal to* $(\boldsymbol{L}_o, \boldsymbol{S}_o)$. *Above,* $c_r, c_\rho, C_{\mathsf{Q}}$, *and* C *are positive numerical constants.*

Here, the magnitudes of the nonzeros in $\boldsymbol{S}_o$ are arbitrary, and no randomness is assumed in $\boldsymbol{L}_o$. The randomness in this result occurs in the sign and support pattern of $\boldsymbol{S}_o$ and in the measurements Q. The bounds on r and ρ essentially match those of PCP for the fully observed case, possibly with different constants. So, again, r and $\|\boldsymbol{S}_o\|_0$ can be rather large. On the other hand, when these quantities are small, the bound on $\dim(\mathsf{Q})$ ensures that the number of measurements needed for accurate recovery is also commensurately small. In fact, this result can be obtained via general arguments that can also be applied to other compressive sensing and decomposition problems of a family of low-dimensional structures in high-dimensional space (as we will introduce in the next chapter). Since the approach and techniques of the proof are rather similar to that for the PCP, we here do not elaborate and instead point interested readers to [WGMM13] for a complete proof.

5.6 Matrix Completion with Corrupted Entries

We have seen that the main result on PCP (Theorem 5.3) asserts that it is possible to recover a low-rank matrix even though a significant fraction of its entries are corrupted. Furthermore, the above section reveals that both the low-rank and sparse components can be recovered even if only a small number of general linear measurements of the corrupted matrix $\boldsymbol{Y}$ are given.

In many applications, however, the (linear) measurements of the corrupted matrix available to us are not general and have very peculiar structures. For instance, we only get to see a small fraction of the entries of $\boldsymbol{Y}$, and the remainder of the entries may be missing. For instance, in the case of taking face images under different illuminations, we can use random corruptions to model pixels associated with surfaces that violate the Lambertian property (such as specular surfaces); and we may assume the intensities of pixels which are blocked from light sources (in the shadow areas) are missing. Hence the data (matrix) have both corrupted and missing entries. Can we still expect to recover the low-rank matrix? As the observations are no longer general (e.g., they are not incoherent with the sparse term $\boldsymbol{S}_o$), results from the above section do not directly apply to the situations here. This section addresses this problem.

To be precise, as before, we assume $\boldsymbol{Y} = \boldsymbol{L}_o + \boldsymbol{S}_o$ is a low-rank matrix $\boldsymbol{L}_o$ corrupted by a sparse matrix $\boldsymbol{S}_o$ whose support $\mathfrak{S}$ is distributed as $\mathfrak{S} \sim \text{Ber}(\rho_s)$ for some small constant $\rho_s < 1$.

We further assume we only observe a small fraction ρ_o of the entries of $\boldsymbol{Y}$. Let O be a support distributed as $\mathsf{O} \sim \text{Ber}(\rho_o)$, where O stands for "observed" entries. We may assume $\mathfrak{S}$ and O are independent Bernoulli variables.

Let $\mathcal{P}_{\mathsf{O}}$ be the orthogonal projection onto the linear space of matrices supported on $\mathsf{O} \subset [n_1] \times [n_2]$,

$$\mathcal{P}_{\mathsf{O}}[\boldsymbol{X}] = \begin{cases} X_{ij}, & (i, j) \in \mathsf{O}, \\ 0, & (i, j) \notin \mathsf{O}. \end{cases}$$

Then imagine we only have available those entries of $\boldsymbol{L}_o + \boldsymbol{S}_o$ such that $(i, j) \in \mathsf{O} \subset [n_1] \times [n_2]$, which we conveniently write as

$$\mathcal{P}_O[\boldsymbol{Y}] = \mathcal{P}_{\mathsf{O}}[\boldsymbol{L}_o + \boldsymbol{S}_o] = \mathcal{P}_{\mathsf{O}}[\boldsymbol{L}_o] + \boldsymbol{S}'_o.$$

This models the following problem: we wish to recover $\boldsymbol{L}_o$ but only see a few entries about $\boldsymbol{L}_o$, and among those a fraction happen to be corrupted, and we of course do not know which ones. As is easily seen, this is an extension to the matrix completion problem of the previous chapter, which seeks to recover $\boldsymbol{L}_o$ from undersampled but otherwise perfect data $\mathcal{P}_{\mathsf{O}}[\boldsymbol{L}_o]$; and this is also an extension to the RPCA problem as there we only see a small fraction of the corrupted matrix $\boldsymbol{Y}$.

We propose recovering $\boldsymbol{L}_o$ (and $\boldsymbol{S}'_o$) by solving the following problem:

$$\begin{array}{ll} \text{minimize} & \|\boldsymbol{L}\|_* + \lambda \|\boldsymbol{S}\|_1 \\ \text{subject to} & \mathcal{P}_{\mathsf{O}}[\boldsymbol{L} + \boldsymbol{S}] = \mathcal{P}_{\mathsf{O}}[\boldsymbol{Y}]. \end{array} \tag{5.6.1}$$

In words, among all decompositions matching the available data, principal component pursuit finds the one that minimizes the weighted combination of the nuclear norm and of the ℓ^1 norm. Our observation is that under some conditions, this simple approach recovers the low-rank component exactly. In fact, the techniques developed here establish this result:

THEOREM 5.10. (Matrix completion with corruptions) *Suppose $\boldsymbol{L}_o$ is $n \times n$, and obeys the conditions* (5.3.1)–(5.3.2). *Suppose $\rho_0 > C_0(\nu r \log^2 n)/n$ and $\rho_s \le C_s$, and let $\lambda = 1/\sqrt{\rho_0 n \log n}$. Then the optimal solution to the convex program* (5.6.1) *is exactly $\boldsymbol{L}_o$ and $\boldsymbol{S}'_o$ with probability at least $1 - Cn^{-3}$ for some constant C, provided the constant C_0 is large enough and C_s is small enough.*

In short, perfect recovery from incomplete and corrupted entries is possible by convex optimization. The approach and techniques of the proof are similar to that of the PCP; we refer interested readers for a complete and rigorous proof to the work of [Li13].

On the one hand, this result extends the RPCA result in the following way: if all the entries are available, i.e., $\rho_0 = 1$, the above theorem guarantees perfect recovery as long as $1 > C_0(\nu r \log^2 n)/n$ or $r < C_0^{-1} n \nu^{-1} (\log n)^{-2}$ for small enough C_0^{-1}, which is exactly Theorem 5.3. The choice of λ here reduces to the case $\lambda = 1/\sqrt{n \log n}$ for dense error correction discussed in Section 5.3.3. On the other hand, this result extends the matrix completion results developed in the previous chapter too. Indeed, if $\rho_s = 0$, we have a pure matrix completion problem from about ρ_0 fraction of entries, and the above theorem guarantees perfect recovery as long as $\rho_0 > C_0(\nu r \log^2 n)/n$ for large enough C_0, which is exactly Theorem 4.26.

We remark that the recovery is exact, however, via a different algorithm. To be sure, in matrix completion one typically minimizes the nuclear norm $\|\boldsymbol{L}\|_*$ subject to the constraint $\mathcal{P}_{\mathsf{O}}[\boldsymbol{L}] = \mathcal{P}_{\mathsf{O}}[\boldsymbol{L}_o]$. Here, our program would solve

$$\begin{array}{ll} \text{minimize} & \|\boldsymbol{L}\|_* + \lambda \|\boldsymbol{S}\|_1 \\ \text{subject to} & \mathcal{P}_{\mathsf{O}}[\boldsymbol{L} + \boldsymbol{S}] = \mathcal{P}_{\mathsf{O}}[\boldsymbol{L}_o], \end{array} \tag{5.6.2}$$

and return $\hat{\boldsymbol{L}} = \boldsymbol{L}_o$, $\hat{\boldsymbol{S}} = \boldsymbol{0}$! In this context, Theorem 5.10 implies that matrix completion is robust vis-à-vis gross errors.

5.7 Summary

In this chapter we have studied the problem of simultaneously recovering a low-rank matrix $\boldsymbol{L}_o$ and a sparse matrix $\boldsymbol{S}_o$ from their superposition:

$$\boldsymbol{Y} = \boldsymbol{L}_o + \boldsymbol{S}_o \quad \in \mathbb{R}^{n \times n}.$$

This problem can be viewed as a *robust principal component analysis* (RPCA) problem – how to robustly estimate a low-dimensional subspace while being robust to gross (random) corruptions in the data. We have learned that under certain benign *incoherence* conditions between $\boldsymbol{L}_o$ and $\boldsymbol{S}_o$, the two matrices can be correctly recovered with high probability from minimizing a weighted sum of the nuclear norm of $\boldsymbol{L}_o$ and ℓ^1 norm of $\boldsymbol{S}_o$, also known as *principal component pursuit* (PCP),

$$\begin{array}{ll} \text{minimize} & \|\boldsymbol{L}\|_* + \dfrac{1}{\sqrt{n}} \|\boldsymbol{S}\|_1 \\ \text{subject to} & \boldsymbol{L} + \boldsymbol{S} = \boldsymbol{Y}, \end{array}$$

as long as the following conditions are satisfied:

$$|\boldsymbol{S}_o| \le \rho_s n^2, \quad \operatorname{rank}(\boldsymbol{L}_o) = O(n \log^{-2} n),$$

where $\rho_s > 0$ is some constant factor.

We have also studied how the basic PCP program naturally extends to several important variants of the RPCA problem, including when there is additive (Gaussian) noise $\boldsymbol{Z}_o$, with randomly projected measurements on a subspace Q, and when only entries in a subset O are observed:

$$\boldsymbol{Y} = \boldsymbol{L}_o + \boldsymbol{S}_o + \boldsymbol{Z}_o, \quad \mathcal{P}_{\mathsf{Q}}[\boldsymbol{Y}] = \mathcal{P}_{\mathsf{Q}}[\boldsymbol{L}_o + \boldsymbol{S}_o], \quad \mathcal{P}_{\mathsf{O}}[\boldsymbol{Y}] = \mathcal{P}_{\mathsf{O}}[\boldsymbol{L}_o + \boldsymbol{S}_o],$$

respectively.

Table 5.2. Comparison between sparse vectors and low-rank matrices.

Sparse versus low-rank	Sparse vector	Low-rank matrix
Low dimensionality of	individual signal $\boldsymbol{x}$	a set of signals $\boldsymbol{X}$
Low-dimensional measure	ℓ^0 norm $\|\boldsymbol{x}\|_0$	rank $(\boldsymbol{X})$
Convex surrogate	ℓ^1 norm $\|\boldsymbol{x}\|_1$	nuclear norm $\|\boldsymbol{X}\|_*$
Compressive sensing	$\boldsymbol{y} = \boldsymbol{A}\boldsymbol{x}$	$\boldsymbol{Y} = \mathcal{A}(\boldsymbol{X})$
Stable recovery	$\boldsymbol{y} = \boldsymbol{A}\boldsymbol{x} + \boldsymbol{z}$	$\boldsymbol{Y} = \mathcal{A}(\boldsymbol{X}) + \boldsymbol{Z}$
Error correction	$\boldsymbol{y} = \boldsymbol{A}\boldsymbol{x} + \boldsymbol{e}$	$\boldsymbol{Y} = \mathcal{A}(\boldsymbol{X}) + \boldsymbol{E}$
Recovery of mixed structures	$\mathcal{P}_{\mathsf{Q}}[\boldsymbol{Y}] = \mathcal{P}_{\mathsf{Q}}[\boldsymbol{L}_o + \boldsymbol{S}_o] + \boldsymbol{Z}$	

As we have seen from Chapter 2 to Chapter 4, we have developed in parallel the basic theory and algorithms for recovering sparse signals or low-rank matrices, via convex optimization. In this chapter, we also see how these two low-dimensional models can be combined together to model more sophisticated structures in the data. Table 5.2 summarizes the similarity of these two most basic low-dimensional models studied so far. In the next chapter, we will see how the same ideas generalize to a broader family of low-dimensional models.

5.8 Notes

Second-Order Convex Methods

For small problem sizes, the above principal component pursuit program can be solved using off-the-shelf tools such as interior point methods [GB14]. This method was initially suggested for rank minimization in [FHB04, RFP10] and for low-rank and sparse decomposition [CSPW09]. However, despite their superior convergence rates, interior point methods are typically limited to small-size problems, say $n < 100$, due to the $O(n^6)$ complexity of computing a step direction.

First-Order Convex Methods

The limited scalability of interior point methods has inspired a recent flurry of work on first-order methods. Exploiting an analogy with iterative thresholding algorithms for ℓ^1 minimization [HYZ08, YOGD08], the work of [CCS08] has developed an algorithm that performs nuclear norm minimization by repeatedly shrinking the *singular values* of an appropriate matrix, essentially reducing the complexity of each iteration to the cost of an SVD. However, for our low-rank and sparse decomposition problem, this form of iterative thresholding converges slowly, requiring up to 10^4 iterations. [GM09] suggests to improve convergence using continuation techniques, and has demonstrated how Bregman iterations [YOGD08] can be applied to nuclear norm minimization.

Accelerated Methods

The convergence of iterative thresholding can be significantly improved using ideas from Nesterov's accelerated first-order algorithm for smooth minimization [Nes83], which was extended to nonsmooth functions in [Nes05, Nes07], and later successfully applied to ℓ^1 minimization by [BT09, BBC09]. Based on [BT09], [TY09] have developed a proximal gradient algorithm for matrix completion which they have named as *accelerated proximal gradient (APG)*. Around the same time, a very similar APG algorithm was suggested for low-rank and sparse decomposition in [LGW+09]. In theory, these algorithms inherit the optimal $O(1/k^2)$ convergence rate of the accelerated methods. Empirical evidence suggests that these algorithms can solve the convex PCP problem at least 50 times faster than straightforward iterative thresholding (see [LGW+09]).

Augmented Lagrange Multiplier Methods

However, despite their good convergence guarantees, the practical performance of APG depends strongly on the design of a good continuation scheme. Generic continuation does not guarantee good accuracy and convergence across a wide range of problem settings.[10] In this chapter, we have instead chosen to solve the convex PCP problem (5.2.2) using an augmented Lagrange multiplier (ALM) algorithm introduced in [LCWM09, YY09]. In our experience, ALM achieves much higher accuracy than APG, in fewer iterations. It works stably across a wide range of problem settings with no tuning of parameters. Moreover we observe an appealing (empirical) property: the rank of the iterates often remains bounded by rank($\boldsymbol{L}_o$) throughout the optimization, allowing them to be computed efficiently. APG, on the other hand, does not have this property.

A systematic development of all these convex optimization methods for recovering both sparse and low-rank models will be given in Chapter 8. We will also study natural nonconvex formulations of the low-rank and sparse recovery problems in Chapter 7 and develop efficient algorithms for the nonconvex programs in Chapter 9.

5.9 Exercises

5.1. (RPCA as an underdetermined linear inverse problem) *Consider the space* V *of pairs* $(\boldsymbol{L}, \boldsymbol{S}) \in \mathbb{R}^{n\times n} \times \mathbb{R}^{n\times n}$. *This is a vector space over* $\mathbb{R}$. *Consider the function*

$$\|\cdot\|_{\diamond} : \mathsf{V} \to \mathbb{R} \tag{5.9.1}$$

via

$$\|(\boldsymbol{L}, \boldsymbol{S})\|_{\diamond} = \|\boldsymbol{L}\|_* + \lambda \|\boldsymbol{S}\|_1 . \tag{5.9.2}$$

Show that $\|\cdot\|_{\diamond}$ *is a norm on* V, *by showing that it satisfies the axioms of a norm. For* $\boldsymbol{x} = (\boldsymbol{L}, \boldsymbol{S})$ *in* V, *let* $\mathcal{A}[\boldsymbol{x}] = \boldsymbol{L} + \boldsymbol{S}$. *Interpret the PCP problem as*

$$\min \|\boldsymbol{x}\|_{\diamond} \quad \text{subject to} \quad \mathcal{A}[\boldsymbol{x}] = \boldsymbol{Y}. \tag{5.9.3}$$

[10] In our experience, the optimal choice may depend on the relative magnitudes of the $\boldsymbol{L}$ and $\boldsymbol{S}$ terms and the sparsity of $\boldsymbol{S}$.

5.2. (Matrix rigidity) *Give an example of "rigid" matrices in terms of Definition 5.1 and give some examples of "soft" matrices. Can you identify the main difference between rigid and soft matrices? Propose an algorithm that can compute the rigidity of any given matrix. Discuss the worst computational complexity of the proposed algorithm.*

5.3. (Find maximum low-rank matrix) *Given an $n \times n$ matrix $\boldsymbol{M}$, design an algorithm that finds the largest submatrix $\boldsymbol{S}$ such that*

$$\operatorname{rank}(\boldsymbol{S}) \leq r$$

for some given small rank r. Discuss the complexity of your algorithm.

5.4. (Planted clique via RPCA) *In the* planted clique *problem (see Definition 5.2), we are given a large graph $\mathcal{G}$ of n nodes. Now suppose it has a largest clique of size n_o. Consider the adjacent matrix $\boldsymbol{A}$ of the graph $\mathcal{G}$. Then we have*

$$\boldsymbol{A} = \boldsymbol{L}_o + \boldsymbol{S}_o,$$

where $\boldsymbol{L}_o$ is an $n_o \times n_o$ rank-1 matrix whose entries are all ones, and $\boldsymbol{S}_o$ is a matrix with at least half its entries zeros. Determine (i) $\operatorname{rank}(\boldsymbol{L}_o)$*, (ii) $\nu(\boldsymbol{L}_o)$ according to* (5.3.1)*, and (iii) $\nu_\infty(\boldsymbol{L}_o)$ according to* (5.3.2)*. How big does the clique* C *need to be for PCP to succeed?*

5.5. (Lower bounds from planted clique) *Show the necessity of the condition* (5.3.2) *based on the hardness conjecture of finding the largest clique in a graph.*

5.6. (Finding planted cliques) *Develop an experiment to test how the PCP algorithm works on the planted clique problem. Is the working range consistent with the hardness conjecture?*

5.7. (Low-rank representation*) *low-rank representation (LRR) [LLY+13] is an extension of RPCA. It aims to solve the problem of clustering a set of n data points in $\mathbb{R}^m$: $\boldsymbol{X} = [\boldsymbol{x}_1, \ldots, \boldsymbol{x}_n]$ that are drawn from a union of multiple low-dimensional subspaces, with potential noise and corruption. The key idea is to find a self-expressive representation for $\boldsymbol{X} = \boldsymbol{X}\boldsymbol{Z}$. But to avoid using each point $\boldsymbol{x}_i$ to represent itself, we enforce points from the same subspace to form a "cluster." In other words, the coefficient $\boldsymbol{Z}$ is preferably a low-rank matrix, as we have discussed in the community discovery problem. To account for possible sparse corruptions or outliers (points sampled outside of these subspaces), we solve $\boldsymbol{X} = \boldsymbol{X}\boldsymbol{Z} + \boldsymbol{E}$ with $\boldsymbol{E}$ being sparse or column-sparse. This leads to the following program:*

$$\min_{\boldsymbol{Z}, \boldsymbol{E}} \|\boldsymbol{Z}\|_* + \lambda \|\boldsymbol{E}\|_{2,1} \quad \text{subject to} \quad \boldsymbol{X} = \boldsymbol{X}\boldsymbol{Z} + \boldsymbol{E}.$$

Program a MATLAB function for LRR and use it for clustering a set of frontal face images from several people, say using the Yale Face Dataset [Ext].

5.8. (Background subtraction*) *Code a MATLAB program that utilizes robust PCA to separate the foreground images and background images in video sequences captured by stationary cameras.*

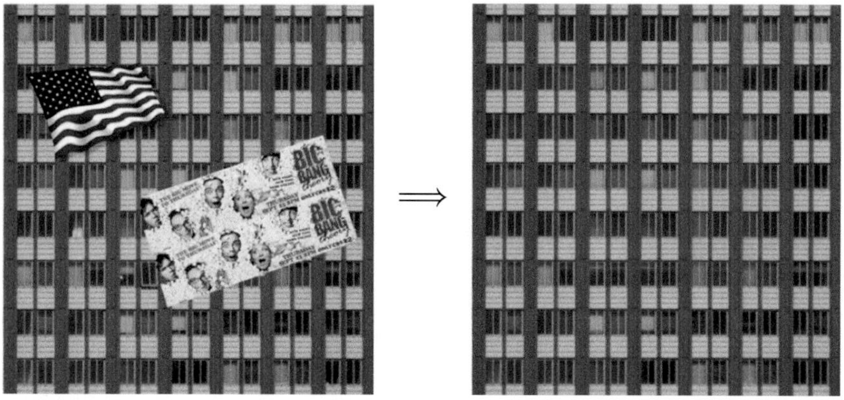

Figure 5.6 Write a program to take an input as the image on the left with occlusion and output a clean image on the right. Note that the image on the right is indeed a recovered image from the left by a program like PCP.

5.9. (Robust texture inpainting*) *Code a MATLAB program that utilizes robust PCA to perform texture inpainting to compensate corrupted texture images without knowing the location of the corrupted pixels:*

```
(I_hat, E) = robust_inpainting(I),
```

where `I` *is the input texture image,* `I_hat` *is the recovered texture image, and* `E` *is the detected corruption in the same image space. See Figure 5.6 as an example. To test how good your algorithm is, try different types and sizes of occlusion on the input images. Try any ideas that may further improve the performance of your algorithm, say by taking into account additional structures of the possible occlusion, in addition to being sparse.*

5.10. (A monotonicity property of PCP) *Call* $\boldsymbol{S}'$ *a* trimmed version *of* $\boldsymbol{S}$ *if* $\operatorname{supp}(\boldsymbol{S}') \subset \operatorname{supp}(\boldsymbol{S})$ *and* $\boldsymbol{S}'_{ij} = \boldsymbol{S}_{ij}$ *whenever* $\boldsymbol{S}'_{ij} \neq 0$. *Prove that whenever* $(\boldsymbol{L}_o, \boldsymbol{S}_o)$ *is the unique optimal solution to the PCP problem with data* $\boldsymbol{Y}_o = \boldsymbol{L}_o + \boldsymbol{S}_o$, $(\boldsymbol{L}_o, \boldsymbol{S}')$ *is the unique optimal solution to the PCP problem with data* $\boldsymbol{Y}' = \boldsymbol{L}_o + \boldsymbol{S}'$.

5.11. (Derandomizing the signs) *In this exercise, we "derandomize" the signs in the RPCA problem, using the elimination property from Exercise 5.10. Suppose that for a given* $\boldsymbol{L}_o$, *RPCA succeeds with high probability when* $\operatorname{sign}(\boldsymbol{S}_o)$ *is a* $\operatorname{Ber}(\rho_s)$ *Rademacher matrix. Prove that with at least the same probability, RPCA succeeds when* $\mathfrak{S} \sim_{\text{iid}} \operatorname{Ber}(\rho_s/2)$, *and* $\operatorname{sign}(\boldsymbol{S}_o) = \mathcal{P}_{\mathfrak{S}}[\bar{\boldsymbol{\Sigma}}]$ *for some fixed matrix of signs* $\bar{\boldsymbol{\Sigma}} \in \{\pm 1\}^{n \times n}$.

5.12. *Show that for two projection operators* $\mathcal{P}_{\mathfrak{S}}$ *and* $\mathcal{P}_{\mathsf{T}}$, *we have:*

$$\|\mathcal{P}_{\mathfrak{S}} \mathcal{P}_{\mathsf{T}}\| = \|\mathcal{P}_{\mathsf{T}} \mathcal{P}_{\mathfrak{S}} \mathcal{P}_{\mathsf{T}}\|^{1/2}. \tag{5.9.4}$$

5.13. (Least squares for dual certificates) *To prove Theorem 5.3, in Lemma 5.6 we used the method of least squares (minimum energy) to construct a dual certificate* $\boldsymbol{\Lambda}_S$ *satisfying* $\mathcal{P}_{\mathsf{S}}[\boldsymbol{\Lambda}_S] = \lambda \boldsymbol{\Sigma}_o$ *and* $\mathcal{P}_{\mathsf{T}}[\boldsymbol{\Lambda}_S] = \mathbf{0}$. *We asserted that whenever* $\|\mathcal{P}_{\mathsf{S}}\mathcal{P}_{\mathsf{T}}\| < 1$, *the solution to the problem* (5.3.29),

$$\min \left\|\tilde{\boldsymbol{\Lambda}}\right\|_F^2 \quad \textit{subject to} \quad \mathcal{P}_{\mathsf{S}}[\tilde{\boldsymbol{\Lambda}}] = \lambda \boldsymbol{\Sigma}_o, \quad \mathcal{P}_{\mathsf{T}}[\tilde{\boldsymbol{\Lambda}}] = \mathbf{0}, \tag{5.9.5}$$

is given in closed form by the Neumann series (5.3.30)*:*

$$\boldsymbol{\Lambda}_S = \lambda \mathcal{P}_{\mathsf{T}^\perp} \sum_{k=0}^{\infty} (\mathcal{P}_{\mathsf{S}}\mathcal{P}_{\mathsf{T}}\mathcal{P}_{\mathsf{S}})^k [\boldsymbol{\Sigma}_o]. \tag{5.9.6}$$

Show that (i) when $\|\mathcal{P}_{\mathsf{S}}\mathcal{P}_{\mathsf{T}}\| < 1$, *the infinite summation in* (5.9.6) *converges, and (ii)* $\boldsymbol{\Lambda}_S$ *solves* (5.9.5).

5.14. (Dense errors with random signs) *Prove that with an appropriate choice of* λ, *PCP can handle any constant fraction* $\rho_s < 1$ *of errors.*

6 Recovering General Low-Dimensional Models

"An idea which can be used once is a trick. If one can use it more than once it becomes a method."

– George Pólya and Gábor Szegö, *Problems and Theorems in, Analysis I*

In the first five chapters of this book, we introduced two main families of low-dimensional models for high-dimensional data: sparse models and low-rank models. In Chapter 5, we saw how we could combine these basic models to accommodate data matrices that are superpositions of sparse and low-rank matrices. This generalization allowed us to model richer classes of data, including data containing erroneous observations. In this chapter, we further generalize these basic models to a situation in which the object of interest consists of a superposition of a few elements from some set of "atoms" (Section 6.1). This construction is general enough to include all of the models discussed so far, as well as several other models of practical importance. With this general idea in mind, we then discuss unified approaches to studying the power of low-dimensional signal models for estimation, measured in terms of the number of measurements needed for exact recovery or recovery with sparse errors (Section 6.2). These analyses generalize and unify the ideas developed over the earlier chapters, and offer definitive results on the power of convex relaxation. Finally, in Section 6.3, we discuss limitations of convex relaxation, which in some situations will force us to consider nonconvex alternatives, to be studied in later chapters.

6.1 Concise Signal Models

We have considered two models of low-dimensional signal structure. A *sparse vector* $\boldsymbol{x} \in \mathbb{R}^n$ is a superposition of a few coordinate basis vectors:

$$\boldsymbol{x} = \sum_{i \in \mathsf{I} \subset [n]} x_i \boldsymbol{e}_i. \tag{6.1.1}$$

A *low-rank matrix* $\boldsymbol{X} \in \mathbb{R}^{n \times n}$ is a superposition of just a few rank-1 matrices $\boldsymbol{u}_i \boldsymbol{v}_i^*$:

$$\boldsymbol{X} = \sum_{i=1}^{r} \sigma_i \boldsymbol{u}_i \boldsymbol{v}_i^*, \quad r < n. \tag{6.1.2}$$

The standard basis vectors form the elementary components for constructing sparse vectors. The rank-1 matrices form the elementary components for constructing low-rank matrices.

6.1.1 Atomic Sets and Examples

These are two specific examples of a more general situation, in which the signal $\boldsymbol{x}$ of interest can be expressed as a superposition of a few elementary components, selected from some set $\mathcal{D}$:

$$\boldsymbol{x} = \sum_i \alpha_i \boldsymbol{d}_i, \quad \boldsymbol{d}_i \in \mathcal{D}. \tag{6.1.3}$$

For sparse vectors, we can take

$$\mathcal{D} = \mathcal{D}_{\text{sparse}} \equiv \{\pm \boldsymbol{e}_i \mid i = 1, \ldots, n\}. \tag{6.1.4}$$

For low-rank matrices, we can take

$$\mathcal{D} = \mathcal{D}_{\text{low-rank}} \equiv \left\{\boldsymbol{u}\boldsymbol{v}^* \mid \|\boldsymbol{u}\|_2 = \|\boldsymbol{v}\|_2 = 1\right\}. \tag{6.1.5}$$

The set $\mathcal{D}$ is sometimes referred to as an *atomic set* – it consists of a collection of elementary components ("atoms") from which the structured signal of interest can be constructed. In the literature, such an atomic set is often called a "dictionary," hence the capital letter $\mathcal{D}$. Here, for simplicity, we assume the dictionary $\mathcal{D}$ is already known or given in advance. In Chapter 7, we will study how to learn the dictionary from data when it is not known ahead of time.

There are at least two reasons to consider the general notion of an atomic set. The first is that it gives a unified way of thinking about the models that we have already studied. The second is that it allows us to model other structures of practical interest. We describe a few examples below; Exercises 6.1 and 6.2 develop several others.

Column-Sparse Matrices

In Chapter 5, we described how to estimate an underlying low-rank matrix $\boldsymbol{L}$ even in the presence of grossly corrupted *observations* (or entries), which we modeled using a sparse matrix $\boldsymbol{S}$. In statistical applications, a different type of corruption can occur: some *data samples* (or vectors) may be outliers. Hence, some columns of the data matrix $\boldsymbol{Y}$ may be entirely corrupted. We can model this situation as

$$\boldsymbol{Y} = \boldsymbol{L} + \boldsymbol{C}, \tag{6.1.6}$$

where $\boldsymbol{C} = \left[\boldsymbol{c}_1 \mid \boldsymbol{c}_2 \mid \cdots \mid \boldsymbol{c}_{n_2}\right]$ is a matrix whose column $\boldsymbol{c}_i$ is nonzero if and only if the i-th sample $\boldsymbol{y}_i$ is an outlier (e.g., see the work [XCS12]).

In this situation, we can write

$$\mathcal{D} = \mathcal{D}_{\text{column-sparse}} \equiv \left\{\boldsymbol{u}\boldsymbol{e}_i^* \mid \boldsymbol{u} \in \mathbb{R}^n,\ \|\boldsymbol{u}\|_2 = 1, i \in \{1, \ldots, n_2\}\right\}. \tag{6.1.7}$$

If $\mathsf{I} \subseteq [n]$ is the set of indices of outliers, we can write

$$C = \sum_{i \in \mathsf{I}} \alpha_i D_i, \tag{6.1.8}$$

with

$$D_i = \frac{c_i}{\|c_i\|_2} e_i^* \in \mathcal{D} \quad \text{and} \quad \alpha_i = \|c_i\|_2 .$$

Spatially Continuous Sparse Patterns

Besides column-wise sparsity, for matrices $X \in \mathbb{R}^{n_1 \times n_2}$, we may consider atoms of the more general form X_I with support $\mathsf{I} \subset [n_1] \times [n_2]$ and $\|X_\mathsf{I}\|_p = 1$ for some norm $\|\cdot\|_p$. Popular choices of the norm include $p = 2$ or $p = \infty$. In theory, we may choose any set of supports

$$\mathcal{G} \doteq \{\mathsf{I}_i, i = 1, \ldots, N\}$$

for the atomic set. For instance, if $\mathcal{G}$ consists of supports representing columns of the matrix and $p = 2$, it recovers the above column-sparse atomic set. But if we view a matrix as a 2D grid of pixels for an image, we may select an atomic set that promotes spatial continuity of the image:

$$\mathcal{D}_{\text{spatial continuous}} \equiv \left\{ X_\mathsf{I} \mid X_\mathsf{I} \in \mathbb{R}^{n_1 \times n_2}, \|X_\mathsf{I}\|_p = 1, \mathsf{I} \in \mathcal{G} \right\}, \tag{6.1.9}$$

with $\mathcal{G}$ containing supports that are spatially adjacent. One such choice consists of all 8×8, 4×4, 2×2, and 1×1 subgrids. As shown in Figure 6.1, these support sets form a natural tree structure with 8×8 patches as root nodes, denoted as $\mathcal{G}^0$, and then branches into groups of smaller patches, with $\mathcal{G}^i$ indicating patches after i partitions. This choice of atomic set promotes sparse patterns that are spatially continuous in terms of the grid topology. For instance, in applications to robust face recognition [JCM12], such a choice of atomic set was used to model spatially continuous occlusions, say due to wearing sunglasses or a mask.

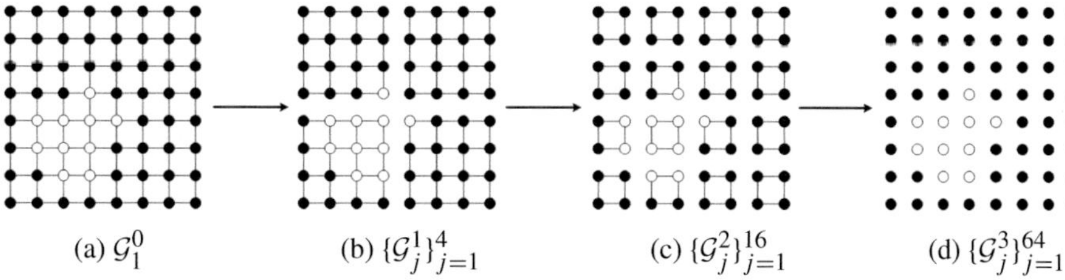

Figure 6.1 Illustration of a four-level hierarchical tree group structure defined on a 2D grid of pixels of an image. Each circle represents a pixel, and connected circles represent a node/group in the tree. An 8×8 group in (a) is divided into four subgroups in (b) according to spatial continuity, and each subgroup can be viewed as a child node of (a). The similar relation goes from (b) to (c), and from (c) to (d). Black circles represent a pixel with zero value and white circles are nonzero.

Simultaneously Sparse and Low-Rank Matrices
Another important low-dimensional model for matrices is the simultaneously sparse and low-rank matrices. These matrices arise naturally in applications in which we wish to find a low-rank approximation to a data matrix which uses only a few features (sparse PCA), or when we want to find small but densely connected communities in a large graph (community detection). They also arise naturally in modeling imagery data such as regular textures (see Chapter 15), videos, and hyperspectral images, which exhibit both low rank *and* sparsity. For example, videos may be low-rank along the time axis; since each frame of the video is also a natural image, individual frames should be sparse in an appropriate basis.

We can idealize this situation a bit by considering matrices $\boldsymbol{X} \in \mathbb{R}^{n \times n}$ whose nonzero entries are populated on a single block of size $k \times k$ (so $\|\boldsymbol{X}\|_0 \leq k^2 \ll n^2$) *and* whose rank is substantially smaller than k. Such matrices can be constructed using the atomic set

$$\mathcal{D} = \mathcal{D}_{\text{sparse and low-rank}} \equiv \left\{ \boldsymbol{u}\boldsymbol{v}^* \mid \|\boldsymbol{u}\|_2 = \|\boldsymbol{v}\|_2 = 1, \ \|\boldsymbol{u}\|_0 \leq k, \|\boldsymbol{v}\|_0 \leq k \right\}. \tag{6.1.10}$$

This class of models is of fundamental importance for both theory and applications. Under the hardness of planted clique (see Section 5.1.2), this class of models is hard. To the best of our knowledge, there is no computationally tractable tight convex relaxation to this class of models, as we will discuss further in Section 6.3.

Low-Rank Tensors
Another important example of a low-dimensional model which does not admit efficient algorithms is high-order tensors. The rank($\mathcal{X}$) of a tensor $\mathcal{X} \in \mathbb{R}^{n_1 \times n_2 \times \cdots \times n_K}$ is the smallest number r of components in an expression

$$\mathcal{X} = \sum_{i=1}^{r} \boldsymbol{u}_i \otimes \boldsymbol{v}_i \otimes \cdots \otimes \boldsymbol{w}_i. \tag{6.1.11}$$

This is known as the Candecomp-Parafac (CP) rank. There are several different notions of tensor rank, which may be appropriate in different situations [KB09].

A *low-rank* tensor $\mathcal{X}$ can be expressed as a superposition of just a few elements from the atomic set

$$\mathcal{D} = \mathcal{D}_{\text{low-rank tensor}} \equiv \{ \boldsymbol{u} \otimes \boldsymbol{v} \otimes \cdots \otimes \boldsymbol{w} \mid \|\boldsymbol{u}\|_2 = \|\boldsymbol{v}\|_2 = \|\boldsymbol{w}\|_2 = 1 \}. \tag{6.1.12}$$

Notice that, when the order of the tensor is $K = 2$, this generalizes the atomic set for low-rank matrices which we discussed above.

This class of models is very important for applications. However, there is an important distinction from the matrix case: for tensors of order $K \geq 3$, problems such as computing the rank or finding a decomposition of the form (6.1.11) are NP-hard [HL13]. The low-rank tensors are our first example of a low-dimensional signal model which *does not* admit tight efficient algorithms! We will discuss this matter further in Section 6.3.

Sinusoids with Continuous Frequency

In applications such as RF communications and line spectrum estimation in scientific imaging, we encounter signals which have relatively narrow support in the Fourier domain. The *multitone* signals are a useful idealization of this situation: a multitone signal is a superposition of a few complex exponentials,

$$x = \sum_i \alpha_i \xi(\omega_i, \phi_i) \in \mathbb{C}^N, \tag{6.1.13}$$

where

$$\xi(\omega, \phi)[n] = \exp\left(2\pi \mathrm{i}\left(\omega n + \phi\right)\right). \tag{6.1.14}$$

For such multitone signals, we can take

$$\mathcal{D} = \left\{\xi(\omega, \phi) \mid \omega \in [0,1],\ \phi \in [0,1]\right\}. \tag{6.1.15}$$

The model (6.1.14) is a sparse model, but the atomic set (dictionary) is continuous! Surprisingly (and unlike our previous two examples) in many situations, it *is* possible to compute efficiently with such a continuous dictionary. The advantage of this formulation is that it avoids artifacts associated with discretizing the set of frequencies.

6.1.2 Atomic Norm Minimization for Structured Signals

In the previous section, we saw how to use the notion of an atomic set to capture various types of low-dimensional signal structure. The value of these low-dimensional signal models is that they can render ill-posed inverse problems well-posed: instead of requiring a number of observations which is proportional to the ambient dimension n, we may hope to recover the signal x from a number of measurements which is instead determined by the number of intrinsic degrees of freedom. For example, suppose that $x = \sum_{i=1}^k \alpha_i d_i$ is a superposition of $k < n$ elements from $\mathcal{D}$, and that we observe $y = \mathcal{A}[x]$, where $\mathcal{A} : \mathbb{R}^n \to \mathbb{R}^m$ is a linear map. How can we use the knowledge that x is simple to recover it?

Recall that to recover a sparse vector, we minimize the ℓ^1 norm of the coefficients α_i in an expression $x = \sum_i \alpha_i d_i$ of x with respect to $\mathcal{D}_{\text{sparse}}$. To recover a low-rank matrix, we minimize the nuclear norm of X – also the sum of the coefficients α_i in an expression $X = \sum_i \alpha_i d_i$ with respect to $\mathcal{D}_{\text{low-rank}}$. In both cases, *to recover a signal which consists of a superposition of a few elements from an atomic set, we minimize the sum of the coefficients in an expression of* x *as a superposition of elements from that set.* This principle immediately generalizes to other atomic sets. To this end, we define a function $\|\cdot\|_{\mathcal{D}}$ called the *atomic gauge*, which measures the minimum of the sum of the coefficients α_i, over all ways of expressing x as a superposition of elements from $\mathcal{D}$:

DEFINITION 6.1. (Atomic gauge) *The* atomic gauge *associated with the set $\mathcal{D}$ is the function*

$$\|\boldsymbol{x}\|_{\mathcal{D}} \doteq \inf\left\{\sum_{i=1}^{k}\alpha_i \;\middle|\; \alpha_1,\dots,\alpha_k \geq 0 \textit{ and } \exists \boldsymbol{d}_1,\dots,\boldsymbol{d}_k \in \mathcal{D} \textit{ s.t. } \sum_i \alpha_i \boldsymbol{d}_i = \boldsymbol{x}\right\}. \tag{6.1.16}$$

The notion of atomic gauge is general enough to include all of the convex relaxations that we have studied so far:

EXAMPLE 6.2. (Examples of atomic gauges) *The following are examples of atomic gauges.*

- Sparse vectors: $\|\boldsymbol{x}\|_{\mathcal{D}_{\text{sparse}}} = \|\boldsymbol{x}\|_1$.
- Low-rank matrices: $\|\boldsymbol{X}\|_{\mathcal{D}_{\text{low-rank}}} = \|\boldsymbol{X}\|_*$.
- Column-sparse matrices: $\|\boldsymbol{X}\|_{\mathcal{D}_{\text{column-sparse}}} = \sum_i \|\boldsymbol{x}_i\|_2$.

From these examples, we can see that the atomic gauge is often actually a norm. In fact, this is true whenever the atomic set $\mathcal{D}$ is symmetric:

LEMMA 6.3. (Atomic gauges and norms) *For* any *set $\mathcal{D}$, $\|\cdot\|_{\mathcal{D}}$ is a convex function. Moreover, if $\mathcal{D}$ is a symmetric set whose convex hull contains an open ball about $\mathbf{0}$, i.e., $\boldsymbol{d} \in \mathcal{D} \implies -\boldsymbol{d} \in \mathcal{D}$, and $\mathbf{0} \in$ int(conv[$\mathcal{D}$]),[1] then $\|\cdot\|_{\mathcal{D}}$ is a norm.*

Proof Convexity follows from the definition: consider any $\boldsymbol{x}$, $\boldsymbol{x}'$, and any $\lambda \in [0,1]$. For any $\varepsilon > 0$, let

$$\boldsymbol{x} = \sum_{i=1}^{r}\alpha_i \boldsymbol{d}_i \quad \text{and} \quad \boldsymbol{x}' = \sum_{i=1}^{r'}\alpha_i' \boldsymbol{d}_i' \tag{6.1.17}$$

be such that

$$\sum_{i=1}^{r}\alpha_i \leq \|\boldsymbol{x}\|_{\mathcal{D}} + \varepsilon \quad \text{and} \quad \sum_{i=1}^{r'}\alpha_i' \leq \|\boldsymbol{x}'\|_{\mathcal{D}} + \varepsilon. \tag{6.1.18}$$

Then noting that

$$\lambda\boldsymbol{x} + (1-\lambda)\boldsymbol{x}' = \sum_{i=1}^{r}\lambda\alpha_i\boldsymbol{d}_i + \sum_{i=1}^{r'}(1-\lambda)\alpha_i'\boldsymbol{d}_i', \tag{6.1.19}$$

we have that

$$\left\|\lambda\boldsymbol{x} + (1-\lambda)\boldsymbol{x}'\right\|_{\mathcal{D}} \leq \sum_{i=1}^{r}\lambda\alpha_i + \sum_{j=1}^{r'}(1-\lambda)\alpha_i' \tag{6.1.20}$$

$$\leq \lambda\|\boldsymbol{x}\|_{\mathcal{D}} + (1-\lambda)\left\|\boldsymbol{x}'\right\|_{\mathcal{D}} + \varepsilon. \tag{6.1.21}$$

[1] Here conv[$\mathcal{D}$] is the convex hull spanned by $\mathcal{D}$, and int($\cdot$) is the (open) interior of a set.

Since $\varepsilon > 0$ can be made arbitrarily small,

$$\left\| \lambda \boldsymbol{x} + (1-\lambda)\boldsymbol{x}' \right\|_{\mathcal{D}} \le \lambda \left\| \boldsymbol{x} \right\|_{\mathcal{D}} + (1-\lambda) \left\| \boldsymbol{x}' \right\|_{\mathcal{D}}. \tag{6.1.22}$$

It is similarly immediate from the definition that $\|\boldsymbol{x}\|_{\mathcal{D}}$ is positively homogeneous: for $\alpha > 0$

$$\|\alpha \boldsymbol{x}\|_{\mathcal{D}} = \alpha \|\boldsymbol{x}\|_{\mathcal{D}}. \tag{6.1.23}$$

Symmetry of $\mathcal{D}$ implies that $\|-\boldsymbol{x}\|_{\mathcal{D}} = \|\boldsymbol{x}\|_{\mathcal{D}}$; combining with positive homogeneity, we obtain that for every $\alpha \in \mathbb{R}$

$$\|\alpha \boldsymbol{x}\|_{\mathcal{D}} = |\alpha| \, \|\boldsymbol{x}\|_{\mathcal{D}}. \tag{6.1.24}$$

Finally, if $\mathrm{conv}(\mathcal{D})$ contains an open ball about $\mathbf{0}$, i.e., there exists $\varepsilon > 0$ such that $\mathsf{B}(\mathbf{0}, \varepsilon) \subseteq \mathrm{conv}(\mathcal{D})$, then $\|\boldsymbol{x}\|_{\mathcal{D}}$ is finite valued for every $\boldsymbol{x}$, i.e., $\|\boldsymbol{x}\|_{\mathcal{D}} \le \|\boldsymbol{x}\|_{\ell^2} / \varepsilon$. This, together with the previous considerations, implies that $\|\cdot\|_{\mathcal{D}}$ is a norm. $\square$

The atomic gauge allows us to define a general class of convex problems for recovering a structured signal $\boldsymbol{x}_o$ from underdetermined and/or noisy observations. For example, for recovering $\boldsymbol{x}_o$ from noise-free measurements $\boldsymbol{y} = \mathcal{A}[\boldsymbol{x}_o]$, we can try to minimize the atomic norm $\|\boldsymbol{x}\|_{\mathcal{D}}$ of $\boldsymbol{x}$ subject to the measurement constraint:

$$\min_{\boldsymbol{x}} \|\boldsymbol{x}\|_{\mathcal{D}} \quad \text{subject to} \quad \mathcal{A}[\boldsymbol{x}] = \boldsymbol{y}. \tag{6.1.25}$$

In the presence of noise, we can instead solve an optimization problem which balances between fidelity to the observed data and model simplicity, measured by the atomic gauge:

$$\min_{\boldsymbol{x}} \tfrac{1}{2} \|\mathcal{A}[\boldsymbol{x}] - \boldsymbol{y}\|_2^2 + \lambda \|\boldsymbol{x}\|_{\mathcal{D}}. \tag{6.1.26}$$

This is a convex optimization problem, which generalizes the Lasso problem studied in Chapter 3, as well as the nuclear norm minimization problems studied in Chapter 4 for low-rank recovery.

For some choices of $\mathcal{D}$, these problems admit very efficient algorithms – important examples include $\mathcal{D}_{\text{sparse}}$, $\mathcal{D}_{\text{low-rank}}$, $\mathcal{D}_{\text{column-sparse}}$, and $\mathcal{D}_{\text{sinusoids}}$. For other choices of $\mathcal{D}$, they may be intractable – examples include $\mathcal{D}_{\text{low-rank tensor}}$ and $\mathcal{D}_{\text{sparse and low-rank}}$. The key property that distinguishes the examples for which the convex problems (6.1.25)–(6.1.26) are tractable is whether the simpler problem

$$\min_{\boldsymbol{x}} \; \|\boldsymbol{x}\|_{\mathcal{D}} + \tfrac{1}{2} \|\boldsymbol{x} - \boldsymbol{z}\|_2^2 \tag{6.1.27}$$

admits an efficient solution. This simpler problem, called the *proximal problem* associated with the gauge $\|\cdot\|_{\mathcal{D}}$, will form the basis for efficient and scalable algorithms, which we will study in more depth in Chapter 8.

Other Approaches to Structured Sparsity

The atomic norm is based on a *synthesis* model, in which the target signal $\boldsymbol{x}$ is constructed as a sparse superposition of atoms. A dual approach to deriving optimization problems for recovering structured sparse signals is based on *analysis* models, which ask certain projections of the signal $\boldsymbol{x}$ to be zero. We illustrate this approach through the notion of *group sparsity* for vectors in $\mathbb{R}^n$. Given a collection of supports $\mathcal{G} \subseteq 2^{[n]}$ of the indices $\{1, \ldots, n\}$, we can write

$$\|\boldsymbol{x}\|_{\mathcal{G}} = \sum_{\mathsf{I} \in \mathcal{G}} \|\boldsymbol{x}_{\mathsf{I}}\|_2. \tag{6.1.28}$$

As long as $\bigcup_{I \in \mathcal{G}} I = \{1, \ldots, n\}$, this is a norm. Minimizing (6.1.28) encourages as many of the $\boldsymbol{x}_{\mathsf{I}}$ to be zero as possible.

How does this construction relate to the atomic norm model described above? *When the groups* $\mathsf{I} \in \mathcal{G}$ *do not overlap*, they are equivalent. Writing

$$\mathcal{D}_{\text{group}} \equiv \{\boldsymbol{x}_{\mathsf{I}} \mid \mathsf{I} \in \mathcal{G}, \|\boldsymbol{x}_{\mathsf{I}}\|_2 = 1\}, \tag{6.1.29}$$

we have

$$\|\boldsymbol{x}\|_{\mathcal{D}_{\text{group}}} = \|\boldsymbol{x}\|_{\mathcal{G}}. \tag{6.1.30}$$

However, when the groups $\mathsf{I} \in \mathcal{G}$ do overlap, the atomic norm and the group sparsity norm (6.1.28) differ, and optimizing them produces subtly different effects. For concreteness, consider $\boldsymbol{x} \in \mathbb{R}^3$. Let us consider two different groups of supports:

$$\mathcal{G}_1 = \{\{1,2\},\{3\}\}, \quad \mathcal{G}_2 = \{\{1,2,3\},\{1,2\},\{1\},\{2\},\{3\}\}. \tag{6.1.31}$$

Notice that supports in $\mathcal{G}_1$ do not overlap but those in $\mathcal{G}_2$ do. These groups give two corresponding group sparsity norms:

$$\|\boldsymbol{x}\|_{\mathcal{G}_1} = \|\boldsymbol{x}_{\{1,2\}}\|_2 + |\boldsymbol{x}_3|, \quad \|\boldsymbol{x}\|_{\mathcal{G}_2} = \|\boldsymbol{x}_{\{1,2,3\}}\|_2 + \|\boldsymbol{x}_{\{1,2\}}\|_2 + |\boldsymbol{x}_1| + |\boldsymbol{x}_2| + |\boldsymbol{x}_3|.$$

Figure 6.2 shows the norm ball defined by the norms associated with these groups. In the latter situation, the group sparse norm differs from the atomic norm: minimizing the atomic norm encourages the signal to be expressible as just a few atoms, whereas minimizing the group sparse norm encourages many of the $\boldsymbol{x}_{\mathsf{I}}$ to be zero. There is a vast literature that studies group sparsity-inducing norms for structured signals. The

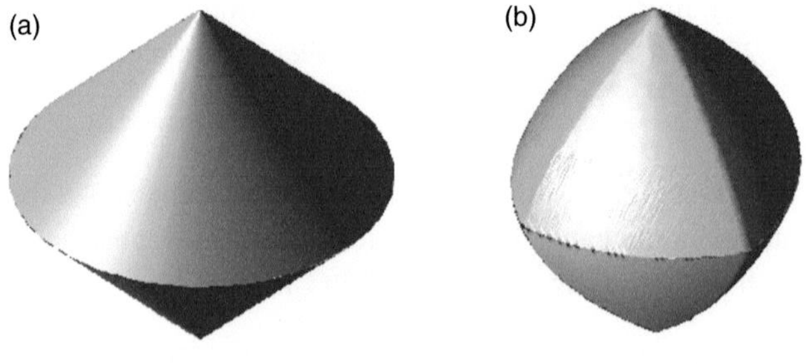

Figure 6.2 (a) A nonoverlapping group sparsity norm-1 ball in three-dimensional space: $\|\boldsymbol{x}\|_{\mathcal{G}_1}$. (b) A structured sparsity norm-1 ball with overlapping subsets in three-dimensional space: $\|\boldsymbol{x}\|_{\mathcal{G}_2}$. Singular points appearing on these balls characterize the sparsity-inducing behavior of the associated norms.

manuscript of Bach et al. [BJMO12] gives a systematic introduction to these norms and their associated optimization algorithms.

6.2 Geometry, Measure Concentration, and Phase Transition

In Chapter 3 and Chapter 4, we have characterized conditions for $\mathcal{D}_{\text{sparse}}$ and $\mathcal{D}_{\text{low-rank}}$ under which the program (6.1.25) can recover the correct solution $\boldsymbol{x}_o$. We would like to know for a more general atomic set $\mathcal{D}$ whether the program (6.1.25) also succeeds under broad conditions. Furthermore, as we have alluded to earlier in these chapters, there seems to be a sharp *phase transition* between the success and failure of the program (6.1.25). This section provides a rigorous explication of the phase transition phenomenon in a general setting, using tools from high-dimensional statistics and geometry of convex cones.

6.2.1 Success Condition as Two Nonintersecting Cones

Geometry of ℓ^1 Norm Minimization

Let us first draw inspiration from the familiar case of ℓ^1 norm to make general conclusions about atomic minimization. Suppose that $\boldsymbol{y} = \boldsymbol{A}\boldsymbol{x}_o$ for a k-sparse vector $\boldsymbol{x}_o$. Recall the geometric picture of the ℓ^1 ball in Figure 6.3(a), which we introduced in Section 3.1 and in Section 3.6.2. There, we argued that $\boldsymbol{x}_o$ is the unique optimal solution to the ℓ^1 minimization problem

$$\min_{\boldsymbol{x}} \|\boldsymbol{x}\|_1 \quad \text{subject to} \quad \boldsymbol{A}\boldsymbol{x} = \boldsymbol{y} \tag{6.2.1}$$

if and only if the affine subspace $\boldsymbol{x}_o + \text{null}(\boldsymbol{A})$ of feasible solutions $\boldsymbol{x}$ intersects the scaled ℓ^1 ball

$$\mathsf{B}_1 = \{\boldsymbol{x} \mid \|\boldsymbol{x}\|_1 \leq \|\boldsymbol{x}_o\|_1\} \tag{6.2.2}$$

only at $\boldsymbol{x}_o$, as illustrated in Figure 6.3(a).

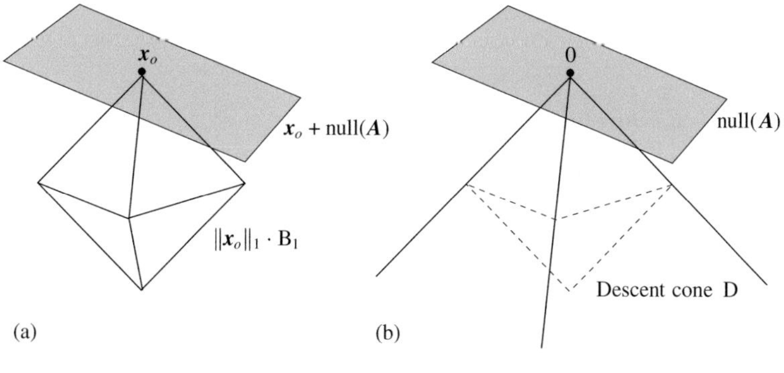

Figure 6.3 Cones and the Coefficient Space Geometry. ℓ^1 minimization uniquely recovers $\boldsymbol{x}_o$ if and only if the intersection of the descent cone D with null$(\boldsymbol{A})$ is $\{\boldsymbol{0}\}$.

We can express the same geometry more cleanly in terms of the *descent cone*:

$$\mathsf{D} \doteq \{ \boldsymbol{v} \mid \|\boldsymbol{x}_o + t\boldsymbol{v}\|_1 \le \|\boldsymbol{x}_o\|_1 \text{ for some } t > 0 \}. \tag{6.2.3}$$

This is the set of directions $\boldsymbol{v}$ for which a small (but nonzero) perturbation of $\boldsymbol{x}_o$ in the $\boldsymbol{v}$ direction does not increase the objective function $\|\cdot\|_1$. The descent cone D is visualized in Figure 6.3(b).

Notice that the perturbation $\boldsymbol{x}_o + t\boldsymbol{v}$ is a feasible solution for $t \ne 0$ if and only if $\boldsymbol{v} \in \text{null}(\boldsymbol{A})$. The feasible perturbations which do not increase the objective function reside in the intersection $\mathsf{D} \cap \text{null}(\boldsymbol{A})$. Because D is a convex cone and $\text{null}(\boldsymbol{A})$ is a subspace (a special convex cone), D and $\text{null}(\boldsymbol{A})$ always intersect at $\boldsymbol{0}$. It is not difficult to see that $\boldsymbol{x}_o$ is the unique optimal solution to the ℓ^1 problem if and only if $\boldsymbol{0}$ is the only point of intersection between $\text{null}(\boldsymbol{A})$ and D. This was proved in Lemma 3.34.

Hence, to study whether ℓ^1 minimization succeeds, we may equivalently check that the subspace $\text{null}(\boldsymbol{A})$ does not have nontrivial intersection with the cone D. Because $\boldsymbol{A}$ is a random matrix, $\text{null}(\boldsymbol{A})$ is a random subspace, of dimension $n - m$. If $\boldsymbol{A}$ is Gaussian, then $\text{null}(\boldsymbol{A})$ follows the uniform distribution on the set of subspaces $\mathsf{S} \subset \mathbb{R}^n$ of dimension $n - m$.[2] Clearly, the probability that the random subspace $\text{null}(\boldsymbol{A})$ intersects the descent cone D depends on the properties of D. Intuitively, we would expect intersections to be more likely if D is "big" in some sense.

REMARK 6.4. *Notice that the probability of success mentioned above is for a given* fixed *$\boldsymbol{x}_o$ with respect to a randomly chosen $\boldsymbol{A}$. As we have discussed in Section 3.6.1, this is a weaker notion of success guarantee than the case with incoherence and RIP that we studied in Chapter 3, which states that for a* fixed *matrix $\boldsymbol{A}$, the ℓ^1 minimization* (6.2.1) *succeeds for* all *sufficiently sparse $\boldsymbol{x}_o$ with high probability.*

The General Case with the Atomic Norm

For a general atomic norm $\|\cdot\|_{\mathcal{D}}$, the condition for the program (6.1.25) to succeed is very similar to the program (6.2.1) for the ℓ^1 norm. We only need to replace the descent cone of the ℓ^1 norm with the descent cone associated with the atomic norm,

$$\mathsf{C} \doteq \{ \boldsymbol{v} \mid \|\boldsymbol{x}_o + t\boldsymbol{v}\|_{\mathcal{D}} \le \|\boldsymbol{x}_o\|_{\mathcal{D}} \text{ for some } t > 0 \}, \tag{6.2.4}$$

and replace the null space of $\boldsymbol{A}$ with the null space of $\mathcal{A}$,

$$\mathsf{S} \doteq \text{null}(\mathcal{A}).$$

Then, similar to Lemma (3.34), we have:

PROPOSITION 6.5. *Suppose that $\boldsymbol{y} = \mathcal{A}(\boldsymbol{x}_o)$. Then $\boldsymbol{x}_o$ is the unique optimal solution to the atomic norm minimization problem if and only if $\mathsf{C} \cap \mathsf{S} = \{\boldsymbol{0}\}$.*

For a given atomic norm, the descent cone C is fixed. The measurement operator $\mathcal{A}$ is typically a random operator. Its null space $\mathsf{S} = \text{null}(\mathcal{A})$ is a random subspace. Hence, to characterize the probability of success of the program (6.1.25), the problem

[2] To be more precise, $\text{null}(\boldsymbol{A})$ is distributed according to the Haar measure on the Grassmannian $\mathsf{G}_{n,m-n}$.

reduces to characterizing the probability of a random linear subspace S intersecting a given convex cone C.

6.2.2 Intrinsic Volumes and Kinematic Formula

How can we calculate the probability of one random linear subspace S intersecting a convex cone C? Moreover, what does the probability depend on? To get intuition for what to expect in the general case, let us start with the simplest case when the convex cone C itself is a linear subspace S'.

Example: Two Intersecting Subspaces

When does a randomly chosen subspace S intersect another subspace S'? From elementary geometry, we know that if the sum of the dimensions $\dim(\mathsf{S}) + \dim(\mathsf{S}')$ is greater than the ambient dimension n, then S and S' necessarily have a nontrivial intersection. Conversely, if $\dim(\mathsf{S}) + \dim(\mathsf{S}') \leq n$, the probability that S intersects S' nontrivially is zero:

PROPOSITION 6.6. (Intersection of two linear subspaces) *Let S' be any linear subspace of $\mathbb{R}^n$, and let S be a uniform random subspace. Then*

$$\mathbb{P}\left[\mathsf{S} \cap \mathsf{S}' = \{\mathbf{0}\}\right] = 0, \quad \dim(\mathsf{S}) + \dim(\mathsf{S}') > n; \tag{6.2.5}$$

$$\mathbb{P}\left[\mathsf{S} \cap \mathsf{S}' = \{\mathbf{0}\}\right] = 1, \quad \dim(\mathsf{S}) + \dim(\mathsf{S}') \leq n. \tag{6.2.6}$$

Figure 6.4 illustrates two examples of how two subspaces in $\mathbb{R}^3$ intersect in general. From the example of two intersecting subspaces, we see that the probability of whether or not they intersect only at the origin $\mathbf{0}$ depends only on the sum of their dimensions.

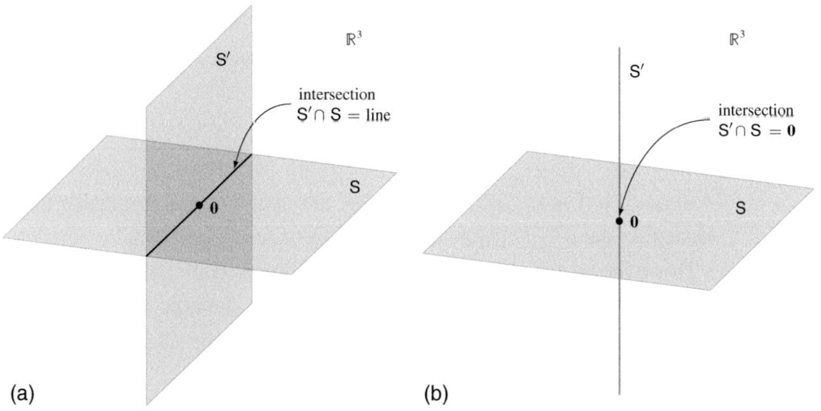

Figure 6.4 (a) Intersection of two generic 2D planes in $\mathbb{R}^3$ contains a line. (b) Intersection of a 2D plane and a 1D line, in general position, is only the origin $\mathbf{0}$.

Intrinsic Volumes

In our case, however, we are dealing with the intersection of a linear subspace and a convex cone. Or in more general cases that we will see later, we need to study the intersection of two convex cones.[3] Hence, it is natural to ask whether the notion of "dimension" for subspaces can be generalized to convex cones? If so, we may expect to characterize the probability for two convex cones to intersect in a similar way as Proposition 6.6 for linear subspaces. We next develop a more generalized way to measure the "dimension" or "size" of a given convex cone. In mathematics, such topics are studied in the field of conic integral geometry [SW08, Ame11].[4]

EXAMPLE 6.7. (Equivalent definitions of dimension for subspaces) *Again, let us first draw some ideas from the special case of a linear subspace. Notice that the dimension, say d, of a linear subspace S can also be equivalently computed as the average (squared) length of a random (Gaussian) vector, say $\boldsymbol{g} \sim \mathcal{N}(\mathbf{0}, \boldsymbol{I})$, projected onto the subspace:*

$$d = \dim(\mathsf{S}) = \mathbb{E}_{\boldsymbol{g}}\left[\|\mathcal{P}_{\mathsf{S}}[\boldsymbol{g}]\|_2^2\right], \tag{6.2.7}$$

where $\mathcal{P}_{\mathsf{S}}[\boldsymbol{g}]$ is the unique nearest vector to $\boldsymbol{g}$ in S,

$$\mathcal{P}_{\mathsf{S}}[\boldsymbol{g}] \doteq \arg\min_{\boldsymbol{x} \in \mathsf{S}} \|\boldsymbol{x} - \boldsymbol{g}\|_2^2. \tag{6.2.8}$$

We may also take the random vector $\boldsymbol{g}$ as uniformly distributed on the unit sphere $\mathbb{S}^{n-1}$. In this case we have

$$d = \dim(\mathsf{S}) = n \cdot \mathbb{E}_{\boldsymbol{g}}\left[\|\mathcal{P}_{\mathsf{S}}[\boldsymbol{g}]\|_2^2\right], \quad \boldsymbol{g} \sim \text{uniform}(\mathbb{S}^{n-1}). \tag{6.2.9}$$

We leave this as an exercise for the reader.

As it turns out, projecting a (random) vector is precisely the right way to measure the "size" of a convex cone. Like a subspace, for a closed convex cone $\mathsf{C} \subseteq \mathbb{R}^n$ and a vector $\boldsymbol{z}$, there is a unique nearest vector to $\boldsymbol{z}$ in C, denoted $\mathcal{P}_{\mathsf{C}}[\boldsymbol{z}]$:

$$\mathcal{P}_{\mathsf{C}}[\boldsymbol{z}] \doteq \arg\min_{\boldsymbol{x} \in \mathsf{C}} \|\boldsymbol{x} - \boldsymbol{z}\|_2^2. \tag{6.2.10}$$

Figure 6.5 shows the projections $\mathcal{P}_{\mathsf{C}_i}[\boldsymbol{z}]$ of a vector $\boldsymbol{z}$ onto two convex cones C_1 and C_2. Notice that it is always true that

$$\|\mathcal{P}_{\mathsf{C}}[\boldsymbol{z}]\|_2 \leq \|\boldsymbol{z}\|_2. \tag{6.2.11}$$

Moreover, in Figure 6.5, the norm of the projection is larger for the wider C_i. Thus, we could take $\|\mathcal{P}_{\mathsf{C}}[\boldsymbol{z}]\|_2^2$ as an indication of the "size" of C.

However, unlike a linear subspace, a convex cone, like the descent cone of the ℓ^1 norm, may consist of many faces of different dimensions. In particular, the descent cone of the ℓ^1 norm is a special case of an important family of convex cones known

[3] For instance, for the problem of decomposing sparse and low-rank matrices, we need to study the intersection of the descent cone of the ℓ^1 norm and that of the nuclear norm.

[4] For a more thorough survey of the history of spherical or conic integral geometry, one may refer to [ALMT13].

as polyhedral cones. Each polyhedral cone is the intersection of a finite number of half spaces. Given a polyhedral cone in $\mathbb{R}^n$, in theory, it could have faces in dimension $k = 0, 1, \ldots, n$. We may consider the projection of a standard normal random vector $\boldsymbol{g}$ onto faces of a particular dimension k.

DEFINITION 6.8. (Intrinsic volume) *If* C *is a polyhedral cone in* $\mathbb{R}^n$*, then the kth intrinsic volume* $v_k(\mathsf{C})$ *is defined to be*

$$v_k(\mathsf{C}) \doteq \mathbb{P}\left[\mathcal{P}_{\mathsf{C}}[\boldsymbol{g}] \in a\ k\text{-}dim\ face\ of\ \mathsf{C}\right], \quad k = 0, 1, \ldots, n, \tag{6.2.12}$$

where $\boldsymbol{g} \sim \mathcal{N}(\mathbf{0}, \boldsymbol{I})$.

According to the definition, the intrinsic volumes are actually a probability distribution on $\{0, 1, \ldots, n\}$. Hence we have $v_k(\mathsf{C}) \geq 0$ for all $k = 0, 1, \ldots, n$ and

$$\sum_{k=0}^{n} v_k(\mathsf{C}) = 1. \tag{6.2.13}$$

The intrinsic volumes have many interesting properties that have been systematically developed in conic integral geometry.

EXAMPLE 6.9. (Intrinsic volumes of a linear subspace) *If* C *is a d-dimensional linear subspace* S*, then we have*

$$v_k(\mathsf{S}) = \begin{cases} 1 & d = k, \\ 0 & else. \end{cases}$$

We leave this as an exercise for the reader.

EXAMPLE 6.10. (Intrinsic volumes of a cone in $\mathbb{R}^2$) *Consider a convex cone* C *in* $\mathbb{R}^2$ *similar to the ones illustrated in Figure 6.5. Denote the angle of the cone as* α*. Then it is easy to show that*

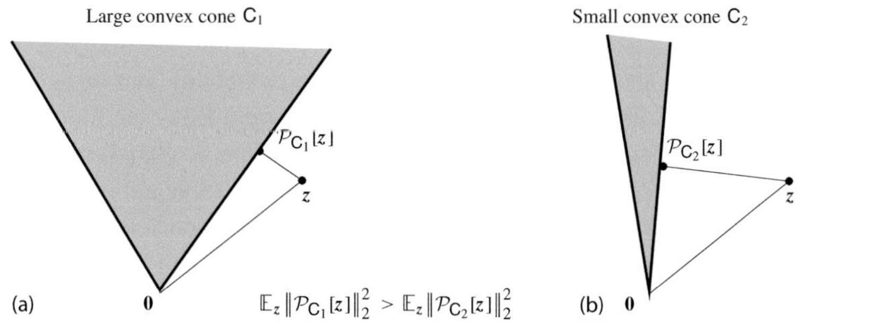

Figure 6.5 Projections onto a Closed Convex Cone. For a closed convex cone C, $\mathcal{P}_{\mathsf{C}}[z]$ is the nearest point to z in C. Notice that in this case, the projection of z onto the larger cone C_1 has greater norm than the projection of z onto the smaller cone C_2: $\|\mathcal{P}_{\mathsf{C}_1}[z]\|_2^2 > \|\mathcal{P}_{\mathsf{C}_2}[z]\|_2^2$. We can measure the "size" of a convex cone C by averaging $\|\mathcal{P}_{\mathsf{C}}[z]\|_2^2$ over all directions z; this average is known as the *statistical dimension* of the cone, denoted $\delta(\mathsf{C})$.

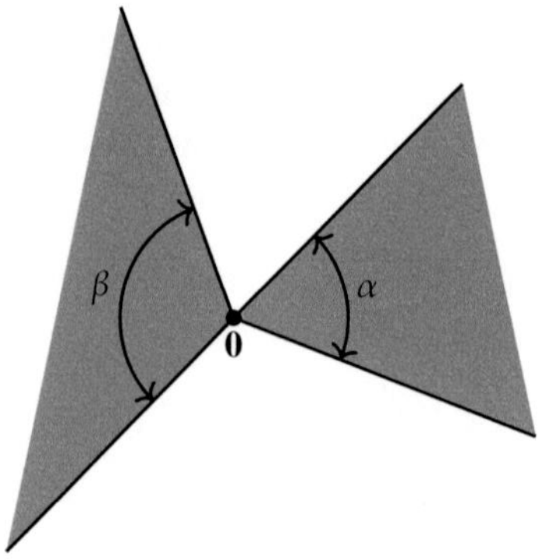

Figure 6.6 The probability of two planar cones intersecting is the sum of their angles (as fraction of 2π).

$$v_2(\mathsf{C}) = \alpha/2\pi, \quad v_1(\mathsf{C}) = 1/2, \quad \textit{and} \quad v_0(\mathsf{C}) = (\pi - \alpha)/2\pi.$$

We leave the proof as an exercise for the reader.

Conic Kinematic Formula

As usual, let us start with a simple example.

EXAMPLE 6.11. (Two cones in $\mathbb{R}^2$) *We have two convex cones C_1 and C_2 in $\mathbb{R}^2$, with angles α and β, respectively. Let C_1 be fixed and rotate C_2 by a rotation $\boldsymbol{R}$ uniformly chosen from $\mathbb{S}^1$. Then the two cones C_1 and $\boldsymbol{R}(\mathsf{C}_2)$ will always have nontrivial overlap (besides at the origin $\mathbf{0}$) if and only if $\alpha + \beta > 2\pi$. If $\alpha + \beta \leq 2\pi$, the probability that they have nontrivial intersection is precisely $(\alpha + \beta)/2\pi = v_2(\mathsf{C}_1) + v_2(\mathsf{C}_2)$, as shown in Figure 6.6. Or equivalently, we have*

$$\mathbb{P}[\mathsf{C}_1 \cap \boldsymbol{R}(\mathsf{C}_2) \neq \{\mathbf{0}\}] = \min\left\{1, v_2(\mathsf{C}_1) + v_2(\mathsf{C}_2\right\}. \tag{6.2.14}$$

We leave the verification as an exercise for the reader.

The above example suggests that the probability that two convex cones intersect nontrivially depends on their intrinsic volumes. However, for convex cones in a high-dimensional space, the situation can be much more complicated than in the 2D space. Surprisingly, as one of the main results in conic integral geometry, the probability of two convex cones intersecting can be precisely characterized in terms of their intrinsic volumes. This is known as the *kinematic formula*.

PROPOSITION 6.12. (The kinematic formula for two convex cones) *Consider two convex (polyhedral) cones C_1 and C_2 in $\mathbb{R}^n$. Let $\boldsymbol{A} \in \mathbb{R}^{n \times n}$ be a random matrix uniformly distributed in the orthogonal group $\mathsf{O}(n, \mathbb{R})$. Then we have*

$$\mathbb{P}[\mathsf{C}_1 \cap \boldsymbol{A}(\mathsf{C}_2) \neq \{\mathbf{0}\}] = \sum_{i=0}^{n} (1 + (-1)^{i+1}) \sum_{j=i}^{n} v_i(\mathsf{C}_1) v_{d+i-j}(\mathsf{C}_2), \tag{6.2.15}$$

where $\boldsymbol{A}(\mathsf{C}_2)$ is a cone obtained by applying the random orthogonal matrix $\boldsymbol{A}$ to all of the elements of C_2.

One may check that equation (6.2.14) for two convex cones in $\mathbb{R}^2$ is a special case of this formula. Interested readers may refer to [SW08] for a proof of this formula.

Despite its rigor and elegance, the kinematic formula is challenging to directly use, since the intrinsic volumes $v_k(\mathsf{C})$ are typically not computable except for very simple cones. For the descent cones of most atomic norms, explicit expressions for their intrinsic volumes are not known (and also difficult to compute numerically). Without such expressions, how can we assess the probability $\mathbb{P}[\mathsf{C}_1 \cap \boldsymbol{A}(\mathsf{C}_2) \neq \{\mathbf{0}\}]$? This is where measure concentration in high-dimensional spaces comes to help: one can use the fact that $\mathcal{P}_{\mathsf{C}}[\boldsymbol{g}]$ is a function of many independent random variables to argue that the intrinsic volumes concentrate, giving simple but accurate bounds on the probability of intersection (6.2.15).

6.2.3 Statistical Dimension and Phase Transition

As we have seen earlier in the case of a subspace (6.2.7), averaging the projection of a random vector $\boldsymbol{g}$ onto the subspace gives an equivalent way of measuring the dimension of the subspace. This concept has led to the notion of the intrinsic volumes for a convex cone, which give the probability v_k that the random vector is projected onto the interior of a k-dimensional face. It is then natural to wonder if the average of the projection over the entire cone or all faces gives an equivalent measure of "dimension" of the cone. This leads to the notion of *statistical dimension* of a convex cone.

Statistical Dimension and Approximate Kinematic Formula

DEFINITION 6.13. (Statistical dimension) *Given C is a closed convex cone in $\mathbb{R}^n$, then its statistical dimension, denoted as $\delta(\mathsf{C})$, is given by*

$$\delta(\mathsf{C}) \doteq \mathbb{E}_{\boldsymbol{g}}\left[\|\mathcal{P}_{\mathsf{C}}[\boldsymbol{g}]\|_2^2\right], \tag{6.2.16}$$

where $\boldsymbol{g} \sim \mathcal{N}(\mathbf{0}, \boldsymbol{I})$.

To see the connection with the intrinsic volumes defined above, we may consider computing the overall expectation through the conditional expectation of $\boldsymbol{g}$ projected on k-dimensional faces, denoted as S_k. We know from (6.2.7) that this expectation is exactly the dimension of the subspace k. Therefore, conceptually, we have

$$\mathbb{E}_{\boldsymbol{g}}\left[\|\mathcal{P}_{\mathsf{C}}[\boldsymbol{g}]\|_2^2\right] = \sum_{k=0}^{n} k \cdot v_k(\mathsf{C}). \tag{6.2.17}$$

The right-hand side is often taken as an alternative definition of the statistical dimension of a convex cone.[5]

[5] A formal proof can be obtained using the *spherical Steiner formula* [SW08]. Interested readers may refer to [ALMT14] for a detailed derivation.

To a great extent, the statistical dimension is the natural generalization of the notion of "dimension" of subspaces to convex cones. It is easy to show that it has the following nice properties:

1 For a linear subspace S, we have

$$\delta(\mathsf{S}) = \dim(\mathsf{S}).$$

2 It is invariant under orthogonal transformation:

$$\delta(\mathsf{C}) = \delta(\boldsymbol{A}(\mathsf{C}))$$

for all orthogonal matrices $\boldsymbol{A}$ in the orthogonal group $\mathsf{O}(n, \mathbb{R})$.

3 The sum of the statistical dimension of a cone C and that of its orthogonal complement, also known as the polar cone C^o,[6] equals the dimension of the ambient space:

$$\delta(\mathsf{C}) + \delta(\mathsf{C}^o) = n.$$

4 For the direct product of two closed convex cones C_1 and C_2, we have

$$\delta(\mathsf{C}_1 \times \mathsf{C}_2) = \delta(\mathsf{C}_1) + \delta(\mathsf{C}_2).$$

We leave the proof of these properties to the reader as exercises, as well as a few other useful properties and facts.

Phase Transition of Atomic Norm Minimization

As we have seen in Proposition 6.6 for linear subspaces, the sum of the statistical dimensions precisely controls whether two subspaces S and S' have nontrivial intersection: once $\delta(\mathsf{S}) + \delta(\mathsf{S}') > n$, the probability of nontrivial intersection goes from zero to one. For general convex cones, there is a similar phenomenon: if S is a random subspace of $\mathbb{R}^n$, and C a closed convex cone, then we have

$$\begin{aligned} \delta(\mathsf{S}) + \delta(\mathsf{C}) \gg n &\implies \mathsf{S} \cap \mathsf{C} \neq \{\mathbf{0}\} \text{ with high probability;} \\ \delta(\mathsf{S}) + \delta(\mathsf{C}) \ll n &\implies \mathsf{S} \cap \mathsf{C} = \{\mathbf{0}\} \text{ with high probability.} \end{aligned}$$

The following theorem makes this precise:

THEOREM 6.14. *Let C denote any closed convex cone in $\mathbb{R}^n$, and let S be a uniformly distributed random subspace of dimension $\delta(\mathsf{S})$. Then*

$$\mathbb{P}\left[\mathsf{S} \cap \mathsf{C} = \{\mathbf{0}\}\right] \leq C \exp\left(-c\frac{(n - \delta(\mathsf{S}) - \delta(\mathsf{C}))^2}{n}\right), \quad \delta(\mathsf{S}) + \delta(\mathsf{C}) \geq n,$$

$$\mathbb{P}\left[\mathsf{S} \cap \mathsf{C} = \{\mathbf{0}\}\right] \geq 1 - C \exp\left(-c\frac{(\delta(\mathsf{S}) + \delta(\mathsf{C}) - n)^2}{n}\right), \quad \delta(\mathsf{S}) + \delta(\mathsf{C}) \leq n,$$

for some constants $C, c > 0$.

[6] The polar cone C^o is defined to be $\mathsf{C}^o = \{\boldsymbol{y} \in \mathbb{R}^n : \langle \boldsymbol{y}, \boldsymbol{x} \rangle \leq 0, \forall\, \boldsymbol{x} \in \mathsf{C}\}$.

The above equations are also known as the *approximate kinematic formula* which captures the essential behavior of the kinematic formula (6.2.15) in a high-dimensional space due to measure concentration. This theorem is a special case of a somewhat more general result controlling the probability that two randomly oriented convex cones intersect (that we will elaborate later). The proof relies on technical results in spherical integral geometry. We refer the interested reader to Theorem 1 of [ALMT14], its proof, and references therein.

Theorem 6.14 then implies our main claim about the phase transition in atomic norm minimization (6.1.25). In our situation, the cone C of interest is the descent cone D of the atomic norm $\|\cdot\|_{\mathcal{D}}$ at $\boldsymbol{x}_o$. We wish to know whether $\mathsf{S} = \mathrm{null}(\mathcal{A})$ has nontrivial intersection with C. The dimension of S is $n - m$, and so the above heuristics become

$$\begin{aligned} \text{FAILURE:}\quad \delta(\mathsf{D}) \gg m &\implies \mathrm{null}(\mathcal{A}) \cap \mathsf{D} \neq \{\mathbf{0}\} \text{ with high probability;} \\ \text{SUCCESS:}\quad \delta(\mathsf{D}) \ll m &\implies \mathrm{null}(\mathcal{A}) \cap \mathsf{D} = \{\mathbf{0}\} \text{ with high probability.} \end{aligned}$$

In the first case, the atomic norm minimization (6.1.25) fails to recover $\boldsymbol{x}_o$; in the second case it succeeds. Using Theorem 6.14 to make this precise, we obtain:

COROLLARY 6.15. (Phase transition for atomic norm minimization) *Let $\mathcal{A} \in \mathbb{R}^{m\times n}$ be (the matrix representation of) a random linear operator, and suppose that $\boldsymbol{y} = \mathcal{A}(\boldsymbol{x}_o)$. Let D denote the descent cone of the atomic norm $\|\cdot\|_{\mathcal{D}}$ at $\boldsymbol{x}_o$. Then*

$$\mathbb{P}\left[\,(6.1.25) \textit{ uniquely recovers } \boldsymbol{x}_o\,\right] \le C \exp\left(-c\frac{(\delta(\mathsf{D}) - m)^2}{n}\right), \quad m \le \delta(\mathsf{D});$$

$$\mathbb{P}\left[\,(6.1.25) \textit{ uniquely recovers } \boldsymbol{x}_o\,\right] \ge 1 - C \exp\left(-c\frac{(m - \delta(\mathsf{D}))^2}{n}\right), \quad m \ge \delta(\mathsf{D}).$$

Thus, when the number of (random) measurements m is substantially smaller than $\delta(\mathsf{D})$, recovery fails with high probability; when m is substantially larger than $\delta(\mathsf{D})$, recovery succeeds with high probability. To a great extent, the above theorem explains the phase transition phenomena, around $\delta(\mathsf{D})$, that we have observed in Chapter 3 for sparse vector recovery and in Chapter 4 for low-rank matrix recovery.

6.2.4 Statistical Dimension of Descent Cone of the ℓ^1 Norm

According to the above corollary, the success of the atomic norm minimization (6.1.25) depends on whether the number of independent measurements exceeds the statistical dimension $\delta(\mathsf{D})$ of the descent cone of the atomic norm. Hence, it is extremely important to be able to accurately estimate $\delta(\mathsf{D})$. In this section, we give a detailed derivation of the statistical dimension of the descent cones of the ℓ^1 norm. One may derive in a similar way an expression for the descent cone of the nuclear norm, which we state (without proof) in Theorem 4.23 in Chapter 4. Interested readers may find details for the nuclear norm in [ALMT14].

In Chapter 3, we have given an expression for the phase transition of ℓ^1 norm minimization in Theorem 3.35. We here give a detailed calculation and show that the statistical dimension $\delta(\mathsf{D})$ of the descent cone D is very close to $n\psi(k/n)$, where the function $\psi(\cdot)$ is defined in (3.6.6). We state this result as a lemma below:

LEMMA 6.16. *Let* D *be the descent cone of the* ℓ^1 *norm at any* $\boldsymbol{x}_o \in \mathbb{R}^n$ *satisfying* $\|\boldsymbol{x}_o\|_0 = k$. *Then*

$$n\psi\left(\frac{k}{n}\right) - 4\sqrt{n/k} \leq \delta(\mathsf{D}) \leq n\psi\left(\frac{k}{n}\right). \tag{6.2.18}$$

Proof For this, we will need two basic facts about projections onto convex cones. The first is the generalized Pythagorean formula, which implies that for a closed convex cone D with polar cone

$$\mathsf{D}^\circ = \{\boldsymbol{v} \mid \langle \boldsymbol{v}, \boldsymbol{x}\rangle \leq 0 \; \forall\, \boldsymbol{x} \in \mathsf{D}\}, \tag{6.2.19}$$

for any $z \in \mathbb{R}^n$,

$$\|\mathcal{P}_{\mathsf{D}} z\|_2^2 = \|z - \mathcal{P}_{\mathsf{D}^\circ} z\|_2^2 = \operatorname{dist}^2(z, \mathsf{D}^\circ). \tag{6.2.20}$$

This allows us to replace the norm of the projection of z onto D with the distance of z to the polar cone D°. The second fact is that the polar of the descent cone is the conic hull of the subdifferential

$$\mathsf{S} \doteq \partial \left\|\cdot\right\|_1(\boldsymbol{x}_o) = \{\boldsymbol{v} \mid \boldsymbol{v}_{\mathsf{I}} = \operatorname{sign}(\boldsymbol{x}_{o\mathsf{I}}),\; \|\boldsymbol{v}_{\mathsf{I}^c}\|_\infty \leq 1\}. \tag{6.2.21}$$

Namely,

$$\begin{aligned} \mathsf{D}^\circ &= \operatorname{cone}(\mathsf{S}) = \bigcup_{t\geq 0} t\,\mathsf{S} \\ &= \{t\boldsymbol{v} \mid t \geq 0,\; \boldsymbol{v}_{\mathsf{I}} = \boldsymbol{\sigma}_{\mathsf{I}},\; \|\boldsymbol{v}_{\mathsf{I}^c}\|_\infty \leq 1\}, \end{aligned} \tag{6.2.22}$$

where $\boldsymbol{\sigma}_{\mathsf{I}}$ is a shorthand for $\operatorname{sign}(\boldsymbol{x}_{o\mathsf{I}})$. For any vector z, the nearest vector $\hat{z} \in t\mathsf{S}$ satisfies

$$\hat{z}_i = \begin{cases} t\operatorname{sign}(z_i) & i \in \mathsf{I}, \\ z_i & i \in \mathsf{I}^c,\; |z_i| \leq t, \\ t\operatorname{sign}(z_i) & i \in \mathsf{I}^c,\; |z_i| > t, \end{cases} \tag{6.2.23}$$

and the distance is given by

$$\begin{aligned} \operatorname{dist}^2(z, t\mathsf{S}) &= \left\|z - \hat{z}\right\|_2^2 \\ &= \|z_{\mathsf{I}} - t\boldsymbol{\sigma}_{\mathsf{I}}\|_2^2 + \sum_{j\in\mathsf{I}^c} \max\left\{|z_j| - t, 0\right\}^2. \end{aligned} \tag{6.2.24}$$

Hence, for any vector z,

$$\begin{aligned} \operatorname{dist}^2(z, \mathsf{D}^\circ) &= \min_{t\geq 0} \operatorname{dist}^2(z, t\mathsf{S}) \\ &= \min_{t\geq 0} \left\{ \|z_{\mathsf{I}} - t\boldsymbol{\sigma}_{\mathsf{I}}\|_2^2 + \sum_{j\in\mathsf{I}^c} \max\left\{|z_j| - t, 0\right\}^2 \right\}. \end{aligned} \tag{6.2.25}$$

Using these facts, we calculate

$$\begin{aligned}
\delta(\mathsf{D}) &= \mathbb{E}_{g\sim\mathcal{N}(\mathbf{0},\boldsymbol{I})}\left[\|\mathcal{P}_{\mathsf{D}}\boldsymbol{g}\|_2^2\right] \\
&= \mathbb{E}_{g\sim\mathcal{N}(\mathbf{0},\boldsymbol{I})}\left[\operatorname{dist}^2(\boldsymbol{g},\mathsf{D}^\circ)\right] \\
&= \mathbb{E}_{\boldsymbol{g}}\left[\min_{t\geq 0}\operatorname{dist}^2\left(\boldsymbol{g},t\,\mathsf{S}\right)\right] \\
&\leq \min_{t\geq 0}\ \mathbb{E}_{\boldsymbol{g}}\left[\operatorname{dist}^2\left(\boldsymbol{g},t\,\mathsf{S}\right)\right] \\
&= \min_{t\geq 0}\ \mathbb{E}_{\boldsymbol{g}}\left[\ \left\|\boldsymbol{g}_{\mathsf{I}}-t\sigma_{\mathsf{I}}\right\|_2^2+\sum_{j\in\mathsf{I}^c}\max\left\{|g_j|-t,0\right\}^2\right] \\
&= \min_{t\geq 0}\left\{|\mathsf{I}|(1+t^2)+2|\mathsf{I}^c|\int_{s=t}^{\infty}(s-t)^2\varphi(s)ds\right\} \\
&= n\,\psi(k/n),
\end{aligned} \tag{6.2.26}$$

where $\varphi(s)=(1/\sqrt{2\pi})e^{-s^2/2}$ is the Gaussian density and $\psi(\cdot)$ is defined in (3.6.6). Thus, we have established $n\psi(k/n)$ as an upper bound on the statistical dimension; and hence $m^\star = n\psi(k/n)$ as a lower bound on the phase transition.

To finish, we show that this upper bound on $\delta(\mathsf{D})$ is tight, by establishing a (nearly) matching lower bound. Let $\hat{t}$ minimize $\mathbb{E}_{\boldsymbol{g}}\left[\operatorname{dist}^2(\boldsymbol{g},t\mathsf{S})\right]$. Then

$$0=\frac{d}{dt}\mathbb{E}_{\boldsymbol{g}}\left[\operatorname{dist}^2(\boldsymbol{g},t\mathsf{S})\right]\Big|_{t=\hat{t}}=\mathbb{E}_{\boldsymbol{g}}\left[\frac{d}{dt}\operatorname{dist}^2(\boldsymbol{g},t\mathsf{S})\Big|_{t=\hat{t}}\right]. \tag{6.2.27}$$

Let $t_{\boldsymbol{g}}$ minimize $\operatorname{dist}^2(\boldsymbol{g},t\mathsf{S})$ with respect to t. By convexity of this function in t,

$$\operatorname{dist}^2(\boldsymbol{g},t_{\boldsymbol{g}}\mathsf{S})\geq\operatorname{dist}^2(\boldsymbol{g},\hat{t}\mathsf{S})+\left(t_{\boldsymbol{g}}-\hat{t}\right)\frac{d}{dt}\operatorname{dist}^2(\boldsymbol{g},t\mathsf{S})\Big|_{t=\hat{t}}. \tag{6.2.28}$$

Notice that by (6.2.27),

$$0=\hat{t}\,\mathbb{E}_{\boldsymbol{g}}\left[\frac{d}{dt}\operatorname{dist}^2(\boldsymbol{g},t\mathsf{S})\Big|_{t=\hat{t}}\right]=\mathbb{E}\left[t_{\boldsymbol{g}}\right]\mathbb{E}_{\boldsymbol{g}}\left[\frac{d}{dt}\operatorname{dist}^2(\boldsymbol{g},t\mathsf{S})\Big|_{t=\hat{t}}\right], \tag{6.2.29}$$

and so

$$\begin{aligned}
\mathbb{E}_{\boldsymbol{g}}\left[\min_t\operatorname{dist}^2(\boldsymbol{g},t\mathsf{S})\right] &= \mathbb{E}_{\boldsymbol{g}}\left[\operatorname{dist}^2(\boldsymbol{g},t_{\boldsymbol{g}}\mathsf{S})\right] \\
&\geq \mathbb{E}_{\boldsymbol{g}}\left[\operatorname{dist}^2(\boldsymbol{g},\hat{t}\mathsf{S})\right]+\mathbb{E}_{\boldsymbol{g}}\left[\left(t_{\boldsymbol{g}}-\mathbb{E}_{\boldsymbol{g}}\left[t_{\boldsymbol{g}}\right]\right)\frac{d}{dt}\operatorname{dist}^2(\boldsymbol{g},t\mathsf{S})\Big|_{t=\hat{t}}\right], \\
&\geq \mathbb{E}_{\boldsymbol{g}}\left[\operatorname{dist}^2(\boldsymbol{g},\hat{t}\mathsf{S})\right]-\operatorname{var}(t_{\boldsymbol{g}})^{1/2}\operatorname{var}\left(\frac{d}{dt}\operatorname{dist}^2(\boldsymbol{g},t\mathsf{S})\Big|_{t=\hat{t}}\right)^{1/2}.
\end{aligned} \tag{6.2.30}$$

In the last line we have used the Cauchy–Schwarz inequality for random variables.

To conclude, we bound the variance of the two terms. For t_g, let $\boldsymbol{v}_g \in \mathsf{S}$ be such that $t_g \boldsymbol{v}_g$ is the nearest element to $\boldsymbol{g}$ in D°. Notice that

$$\left\|\boldsymbol{g} - \boldsymbol{g}'\right\|_2 \geq \left\|t_g \boldsymbol{v}_g - t_{g'} \boldsymbol{v}_{g'}\right\|_2 \geq \left\|t_g \sigma_{\mathsf{I}} - t_{g'} \sigma_{\mathsf{I}}\right\|_2 = |t_g - t_{g'}|\sqrt{k}, \tag{6.2.31}$$

whence t_g is a $1/\sqrt{k}$-Lipschitz function of $\boldsymbol{g}$. By the Gaussian Poincaré inequality,[7] its variance is bounded as $\operatorname{var}(t_g) \leq 1/k$.

Meanwhile, by Danskin's theorem,

$$\frac{d}{dt}\operatorname{dist}^2(\boldsymbol{g}, t\mathsf{S}) = \frac{d}{dt}\left\|\boldsymbol{g} - t\boldsymbol{v}_g\right\|_2^2 = 2\boldsymbol{v}_g^*\left(t\boldsymbol{v}_g - \boldsymbol{g}\right). \tag{6.2.32}$$

Note that because $t\boldsymbol{v}_g$ is the projection of $\boldsymbol{g}$ onto the convex set D°, for any other $\boldsymbol{v} \in \mathsf{S}$,

$$(t\boldsymbol{v}_g - t\boldsymbol{v})^*(t\boldsymbol{v}_g - \boldsymbol{g}) \leq 0, \tag{6.2.33}$$

whence

$$\boldsymbol{v}_g^*(t\boldsymbol{v}_g - \boldsymbol{g}) \leq \boldsymbol{v}_{g'}^*(t\boldsymbol{v}_g - \boldsymbol{g}), \tag{6.2.34}$$

and

$$\begin{aligned}
\frac{d}{dt}\operatorname{dist}^2(\boldsymbol{g}, t\mathsf{S}) - \frac{d}{dt}\operatorname{dist}^2(\boldsymbol{g}', t\mathsf{S}) &= 2\boldsymbol{v}_g^*(t\boldsymbol{v}_g - \boldsymbol{g}) - 2\boldsymbol{v}_{g'}^*(t\boldsymbol{v}_{g'} - \boldsymbol{g}') \\
&\leq 2\boldsymbol{v}_{g'}^*(t\boldsymbol{v}_g - \boldsymbol{g}) - 2\boldsymbol{v}_{g'}^*(t\boldsymbol{v}_{g'} - \boldsymbol{g}') \\
&\leq 2\left\|\boldsymbol{v}_{g'}\right\|_2\left(\left\|t\boldsymbol{v}_g - t\boldsymbol{v}_{g'}\right\|_2 + \left\|\boldsymbol{g} - \boldsymbol{g}'\right\|_2\right) \\
&\leq 4\left\|\boldsymbol{v}_{g'}\right\|_2\left\|\boldsymbol{g} - \boldsymbol{g}'\right\|_2 \\
&\leq 4\sqrt{n}\left\|\boldsymbol{g} - \boldsymbol{g}'\right\|_2.
\end{aligned} \tag{6.2.35}$$

By the same reasoning,

$$\begin{aligned}
\frac{d}{dt}\operatorname{dist}^2(\boldsymbol{g}, t\mathsf{S}) - \frac{d}{dt}\operatorname{dist}^2(\boldsymbol{g}', t\mathsf{S}) &\geq 2\boldsymbol{v}_g^*\left(t\boldsymbol{v}_g - \boldsymbol{g} - t\boldsymbol{v}_{g'} + \boldsymbol{g}'\right) \\
&\geq -4\sqrt{n}\left\|\boldsymbol{g} - \boldsymbol{g}'\right\|_2,
\end{aligned} \tag{6.2.36}$$

whence

$$\left|\frac{d}{dt}\operatorname{dist}^2(\boldsymbol{g}, t\mathsf{S}) - \frac{d}{dt}\operatorname{dist}^2(\boldsymbol{g}', t\mathsf{S})\right| \leq 4\sqrt{n}\left\|\boldsymbol{g} - \boldsymbol{g}'\right\|_2, \tag{6.2.37}$$

and $\frac{d}{dt}\operatorname{dist}^2(\boldsymbol{g}, t\mathsf{S})$ is $4\sqrt{n}$-Lipschitz. By the Gaussian Poincaré inequality,

$$\operatorname{var}\left(\left.\frac{d}{dt}\operatorname{dist}^2(\boldsymbol{g}, t\mathsf{S})\right|_{t=\hat{t}}\right) \leq 4\sqrt{n}, \tag{6.2.38}$$

and so

$$\mathbb{E}_{\boldsymbol{g}}\left[\min_t \operatorname{dist}^2(\boldsymbol{g}, t\mathsf{S})\right] \geq \min_t \mathbb{E}_{\boldsymbol{g}}\left[\operatorname{dist}^2(\boldsymbol{g}, t\mathsf{S})\right] - 4\sqrt{n/k}. \tag{6.2.39}$$

[7] Which states that if f is an L-Lipschitz function and $\boldsymbol{g}$ a Gaussian vector, then $\operatorname{var}(f(\boldsymbol{g})) \leq L^2$.

Thus,

$$n\psi(k/n) - 4\sqrt{n/k} \le \delta(\mathsf{D}) \le n\psi(k/n). \tag{6.2.40}$$

Combining this bound with the above results proves that the phase transition occurs within $O(\sqrt{n})$ of $m^\star = n\psi(k/n)$. □

6.2.5 Phase Transition in Decomposing Structured Signals

Examples of Decomposing Structured Signals

In the robust face recognition problem that we have seen in Chapter 2 and will later study in Chapter 13, we want to solve a problem of recovering a sparse $\boldsymbol{x}_o$ and a sparse error $\boldsymbol{e}_o$ from the mixed measurements

$$\boldsymbol{y} = \boldsymbol{A}\boldsymbol{x}_o + \boldsymbol{e}_o, \tag{6.2.41}$$

where $\boldsymbol{A}$ is a known matrix, drawn from a certain random distribution. This problem can be viewed as a special case of the so-called *morphological component analysis* [SDC03, SED05, ESQD05].

In the robust principal component analysis (RPCA) problem that we have studied in Chapter 5, we want to recover a low-rank matrix $\boldsymbol{L}_o$ and a sparse matrix $\boldsymbol{S}_o$ from their sum:

$$\boldsymbol{Y} = \boldsymbol{L}_o + \boldsymbol{S}_o. \tag{6.2.42}$$

Or in the compressive principal component pursuit, we want to recover the low-rank and sparse matrices from a random projection of their sum:

$$\boldsymbol{Y} \doteq \mathcal{P}_{\mathsf{Q}}[\boldsymbol{L}_o + \boldsymbol{S}_o], \tag{6.2.43}$$

where $\mathsf{Q} \subseteq \mathbb{R}^{n_1 \times n_2}$ is a random linear subspace and $\mathcal{P}_{\mathsf{Q}}$ denotes the projection operator onto that subspace.

Incoherence through Randomness

As we have seen in developing solutions to the above problems, we often require the two mixed structured signals to be "incoherent" with each other. Otherwise the decomposition itself is not well defined and solutions will not be unique. Hence to understand the underlying geometric reason when such decompositions are possible and the solution is unique, a simple but illuminating model is to assume that, when we mix two structured signals, say $\boldsymbol{x}_o$ and $\boldsymbol{s}_o$, together, one signal is in a random position with respect to the other:

$$\boldsymbol{y} = \mathcal{A}(\boldsymbol{x}_o) + \boldsymbol{z}_o, \tag{6.2.44}$$

where $\mathcal{A}$ is a random orthogonal transformation in the space of $\boldsymbol{x}_o$. The random operator $\mathcal{A}$ ensures that $\boldsymbol{x}_o$ is in general position to $\boldsymbol{z}_o$, hence the two components $\mathcal{A}(\boldsymbol{x}_o)$ and $\boldsymbol{z}_o$ are incoherent with each other.

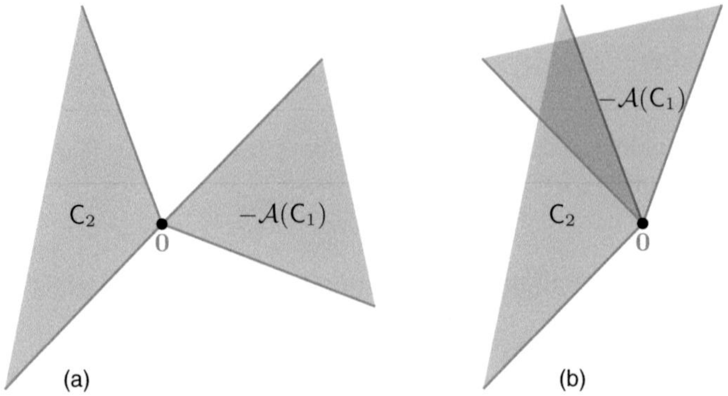

Figure 6.7 The success of the program (6.2.45) depends on whether the random cone $-\mathcal{A}(\mathsf{C}_1)$ intersects with the fixed cone C_2. (a) If the intersection is trivial, then the decomposition problem succeeds. (b) If the intersection is not trivial, then the decomposition problem fails.

Decomposition through Atomic Norm Minimization

Now assume $\boldsymbol{x}_o$ is a low-dimensional structured signal associated with an atomic set $\mathcal{D}_1$, and $\boldsymbol{z}_o$ with $\mathcal{D}_2$. As we have seen in the face recognition and the robust PCA cases, a natural convex program to recover $\boldsymbol{x}_o$ and $\boldsymbol{z}_o$ is

$$\min_{\boldsymbol{x},\boldsymbol{z}} \|\boldsymbol{x}\|_{\mathcal{D}_1} \quad \text{subject to} \quad \|\boldsymbol{z}\|_{\mathcal{D}_2} \le \|\boldsymbol{z}_o\|_{\mathcal{D}_2},\ \boldsymbol{y} = \mathcal{A}(\boldsymbol{x}) + \boldsymbol{z}, \tag{6.2.45}$$

where $\|\cdot\|_{\mathcal{D}_1}$ and $\|\cdot\|_{\mathcal{D}_2}$ are the atomic norms associated with $\mathcal{D}_1$ and $\mathcal{D}_2$, respectively.[8]

Now let $\mathsf{C}_1(\boldsymbol{x}_o)$ be the descent cone of the atomic norm $\|\cdot\|_{\mathcal{D}_1}$ at $\boldsymbol{x}_o$ and $\mathsf{C}_2(\boldsymbol{z}_o)$ the cone for $\|\cdot\|_{\mathcal{D}_2}$ at $\boldsymbol{z}_o$. Suppose $(\boldsymbol{x}_o, \boldsymbol{z}_o)$ is not the (unique) optimal solution to the above program and

$$(\boldsymbol{x}_o + \Delta\boldsymbol{x}, \boldsymbol{z}_o + \Delta\boldsymbol{z})$$

is an optimal solution. Then we must have $\Delta\boldsymbol{x}$ is in the descent cone $\mathsf{C}_1(\boldsymbol{x}_o)$ and $\Delta\boldsymbol{z}$ is in the descent cone $\mathsf{C}_2(\boldsymbol{z}_o)$. Furthermore, from the constraint $\boldsymbol{y} = \mathcal{A}(\boldsymbol{x}) + \boldsymbol{z}$ we have

$$-\mathcal{A}(\Delta\boldsymbol{x}) = \Delta\boldsymbol{z}.$$

In other words, $\Delta\boldsymbol{z}$ must be in the intersection of the cone $\mathsf{C}_2(\boldsymbol{z}_o)$ and $-\mathcal{A}(\mathsf{C}_1(\boldsymbol{x}_o))$:

$$\mathbf{0} \neq \Delta\boldsymbol{z} \in \mathsf{C}_2(\boldsymbol{z}_o) \cap -\mathcal{A}(\mathsf{C}_1(\boldsymbol{x}_o)),$$

as illustrated in Figure 6.7(b). For $(\boldsymbol{x}_o, \boldsymbol{z}_o)$ to be the only optimal solution to the program (6.2.45), we must have the intersection of the two cones to be trivial – it only contains the origin $\mathbf{0}$, as illustrated in Figure 6.7(a).

[8] The optimization problem (6.2.45) is equivalent to the problem

$$\min_{\boldsymbol{x},\boldsymbol{z}} \|\boldsymbol{x}\|_{\mathcal{D}_1} + \lambda\|\boldsymbol{z}\|_{\mathcal{D}_2} \quad \text{subject to} \quad \boldsymbol{y} = \mathcal{A}(\boldsymbol{x}) + \boldsymbol{z},$$

under an appropriate (instance-specific) choice of $\lambda > 0$. This form may be more familiar from our discussion of face recognition and robust PCA. In this section, we study the constrained form (6.2.45), which is slightly more convenient for geometric analysis.

Phase Transition for Decomposition

As we have alluded to earlier, in a high-dimensional space $\mathbb{R}^n$, we anticipate the probability of two cones intersecting transitions sharply around

$$\delta(\mathsf{C}_1(\boldsymbol{x}_o)) + \delta(\mathsf{C}_2(\boldsymbol{z}_o)) = n.$$

In other words,

$$\delta(\mathsf{C}_1) + \delta(\mathsf{C}_2) \gg n \implies \mathsf{C}_1 \cap \mathsf{C}_2 \neq \{\mathbf{0}\} \text{ with high probability;}$$
$$\delta(\mathsf{C}_1) + \delta(\mathsf{C}_2) \ll n \implies \mathsf{C}_1 \cap \mathsf{C}_2 = \{\mathbf{0}\} \text{ with high probability.}$$

The following theorem makes this precise:

THEOREM 6.17. *Let C_1 and C_2 be two closed convex cones in $\mathbb{R}^n$, and let $\mathcal{A}$ be a random orthogonal matrix uniformly distributed in the orthogonal group. Then*

$$\mathbb{P}\left[-\mathcal{A}(\mathsf{C}_1) \cap \mathsf{C}_2 = \{\mathbf{0}\}\right] \leq C \exp\left(-c\frac{(n - \delta(\mathsf{C}_1) - \delta(\mathsf{C}_2))^2}{n}\right), \quad \delta(\mathsf{C}_1) + \delta(\mathsf{C}_2) \geq n,$$

$$\mathbb{P}\left[-\mathcal{A}(\mathsf{C}_1) \cap \mathsf{C}_2 = \{\mathbf{0}\}\right] \geq 1 - C \exp\left(-c\frac{(\delta(\mathsf{C}_1) + \delta(\mathsf{C}_2) - n)^2}{n}\right), \quad \delta(\mathsf{C}_1) + \delta(\mathsf{C}_2) \leq n,$$

for some constant $C, c > 0$.

The above bounds can be considered an *approximate kinematic formula* which captures the essential behavior of the kinematic formula (6.2.15) in a high-dimensional space due to measure concentration [ALMT14]. This is a more general statement than Theorem 6.14 where one of the two cones is a subspace.

6.3 Limitations of Convex Relaxation

Our story up to this point has been one of success. The development up to this point has demonstrated general ways of constructing regularizers that encode various structural assumptions about the signals we are interested in computing with. For sparse vectors, low-rank matrices, and several other structures discussed in Section 6.1, these regularizers have turned out to be computationally tractable, and to yield statistical performance which is nearly the best possible under their assumptions. In a sense, it is surprising that we do not have to pay a stronger statistical price for effective and efficient algorithms. Nevertheless, one should not expect convex relaxation to work equally effectively for *all* challenging problems. Below we discuss a few scenarios in which convex relaxation becomes limited or even may fail to work.

6.3.1 Suboptimality of Convex Relaxation for Multiple Structures

In Section 6.1.1 we have discussed that in some problems such as sparse PCA, we would like to recover a matrix $\boldsymbol{X}$ that is simultaneously sparse and low-rank.

In fact, such problems arise naturally in practical applications such as structured texture inpainting or repairing that we will study in great detail in Chapter 15; see Section 15.3. The images of regular patterns shown in Figure 15.4, if viewed as matrices, are both low-rank and sparse in the Fourier or wavelet domain.

A sparse and low-rank matrix is a special case of a signal that has multiple structures. It seems that one natural convex relaxation to promote multiple structures is to use a weighted sum of their corresponding atomic norms. For instance, we may minimize

$$\lambda_1 \|\boldsymbol{X}\|_1 + \lambda_2 \|\boldsymbol{X}\|_* \tag{6.3.1}$$

to promote the recovered matrix to be *both* sparse and low-rank.[9] This is exactly what we will be practicing in Chapter 15 for regular texture repairing, and indeed, empirically, the combined regularization does work better than using only one.

However, the above combined convex regularization is not optimal in terms of statistical efficiency. To see this, let us consider the simple problem of estimating a sparse and low-rank matrix $\boldsymbol{X}_o \in \mathbb{R}^{n \times n}$ from noisy measurements:

$$\boldsymbol{Y} = \boldsymbol{X}_o + \boldsymbol{Z} \ \in \mathbb{R}^{n \times n}, \tag{6.3.2}$$

where $\boldsymbol{Z} \in \mathbb{R}^{n \times n}$ is a matrix whose entries are i.i.d. Gaussian noise. Hence using the above combined regularization, one may use the following convex program to estimate $\boldsymbol{X}_o$:

$$\hat{\boldsymbol{X}}(\boldsymbol{Y}) = \arg\min_{\boldsymbol{X}} \frac{1}{2} \|\boldsymbol{Y} - \boldsymbol{X}\|_F^2 + \lambda_1 \|\boldsymbol{X}\|_1 + \lambda_2 \|\boldsymbol{X}\|_*. \tag{6.3.3}$$

To evaluate the goodness of the estimate $\hat{\boldsymbol{X}}(\boldsymbol{Y})$, we measure the mean square error (MSE) with respect to the ground truth:

$$\text{MSE} \doteq \mathbb{E}[\|\hat{\boldsymbol{X}}(\boldsymbol{Y}) - \boldsymbol{X}_o\|_F^2]. \tag{6.3.4}$$

Suppose the ground truth $\boldsymbol{X}_o$ is a $k \times k$ sparse matrix and of rank less than r. It has been shown in [OJFH13] that the above convex program (6.3.3) leads to a mean square error bounded from below as

$$\text{MSE} \geq c \cdot \min\{k^2, n\}$$

for some $c > 0$. Nevertheless, as shown in [OJFH13], it is actually relatively easy to solve a *nonconvex* program to obtain an estimate with much lower MSE:

$$\text{MSE} \leq C \cdot k$$

for some $C > 0$. Unlike the case with a single low-dimensional structure, the convex relaxation gives an estimate that is suboptimal in terms of statistical accuracy. This suboptimality can also be felt in the number of (noiseless) random measurements required to reconstruct $\boldsymbol{X}_o$: minimizing any combination of the ℓ^1 norm and

9 Asking $\boldsymbol{X}$ to be *simultaneously* low-rank and sparse is quite different from asking it to be *decomposable* as a sum of low-rank and sparse, $\boldsymbol{X} = \boldsymbol{L} + \boldsymbol{S}$. The latter problem, studied in Chapter 5, does admit convex relaxations, which succeed when $\boldsymbol{L}$ and $\boldsymbol{S}$ are sufficiently structured and incoherent.

nuclear norm requires at least $c \min\{k^2, n\,\mathrm{rank}(\boldsymbol{X}_o)\}$ measurements, even if $\boldsymbol{X}_o$ has only $O(k\,\mathrm{rank}(\boldsymbol{X}_o))$ degrees of freedom [OJF+15]. This can be explained in terms of the statistical dimension of the descent cone associated with a combined convex regularization such as (6.3.1), as we will describe in the next section.

6.3.2 Intractable Convex Relaxation for High-Order Tensors

Section 6.1 also gave the first hint that a tight correspondence between the statistical and computational limits might not obtain for certain types of low-dimensional structures. For example, for recovering a high-order low-rank tensor $\mathcal{X}_o$ of the form (6.1.11), the atomic norm associated with the set (6.1.12) (as a natural generalization of the nuclear norm) has excellent statistical performance, but is computationally intractable.

In practice, people often seek a computationally tractable alternative to approximately promote low rank for high-order tensors. One popular choice is to convert a high-order tensor to matrix forms and consider the so-called Tucker rank [Tuc66, KB09]. Given a K-order tensor $\mathcal{X} \in \mathbb{R}^{n_1 \times \cdots \times n_K}$, for each of its modes $i = 1, \ldots, K$, we construct the matrix $\mathcal{X}_{(i)} \in \mathbb{R}^{n_i \times \prod_{j \neq i} n_j}$ by concatenating all the mode-i fibers of $\mathcal{X}$ as columns of $\mathcal{X}_{(i)}$. Then the so-called Tucker rank is defined as

$$\mathrm{rank}_{tc}(\mathcal{X}) \doteq \left(\mathrm{rank}\left(\mathcal{X}_{(1)}\right), \mathrm{rank}\left(\mathcal{X}_{(2)}\right), \ldots, \mathrm{rank}\left(\mathcal{X}_{(K)}\right)\right). \tag{6.3.5}$$

Hence, to recover a tensor $\mathcal{X}_o$ of low (Tucker) rank, say from random measurements $\mathcal{Y} = \mathcal{A}(\mathcal{X}_o)$, we may impose that the ranks of all K unfolded matrices $\mathcal{X}_{(i)}$ be low. A natural convex regularization is to minimize a weighted sum of nuclear norms of all the K matrices:

$$\min_{\mathcal{X}} \sum_{i=1}^{K} \lambda_i \|\mathcal{X}_{(i)}\|_* \quad \text{subject to} \quad \mathcal{Y} = \mathcal{A}(\mathcal{X}), \tag{6.3.6}$$

where $\lambda_i \geq 0$ are chosen weights. Notice that this convex regularization is of the same nature as that (6.3.1) for a sparse and low-rank matrix. Each term $\lambda_i \|\mathcal{X}_{(i)}\|_*$ imposes some additional structure on the same high-order tensor $\mathcal{X}$. In practice, however, one may choose to use any subset of the K matrices, as we will see in an example with camera calibration from multiple images in Chapter 15.

We may understand the role of composing multiple norms from the perspective of statistical dimension. That is, we want to know, by superposing multiple norms, how the statistical dimension of the descent cone of the composite norm changes. To this end, let us consider the general problem of recovering a high-dimensional signal $\boldsymbol{x}_o \in \mathbb{R}^n$ that has K low-dimensional structures simultaneously. Let $\|\cdot\|_{(i)}$ be the (atomic) norm associated with the i-th structure, $i = 1, \ldots, K$. Then, given random measurements $\boldsymbol{y} = \mathcal{A}(\boldsymbol{x}_o)$, we may try to recover $\boldsymbol{x}_o$ by minimizing the composite norm:

$$\min_{\boldsymbol{x}} \|\boldsymbol{x}\|_{com} \doteq \sum_{i=1}^{K} \lambda_i \|\boldsymbol{x}\|_{(i)} \quad \text{subject to} \quad \boldsymbol{y} = \mathcal{A}(\boldsymbol{x}). \tag{6.3.7}$$

Analysis of [MHWG13] has shown that the statistical dimension of the descent cone of the composite norm $\|\cdot\|_{com}$ is actually dominated by the largest among all cones for the norms $\lambda_i\|\cdot\|_{(i)}$. So adding more penalty terms gives diminishing return in terms of improving statistical efficiency. In particular, [MHWG13] have shown that, using the composite nuclear norm in (6.3.6) to solve for a (Tucker) rank-r tensor uniquely, the number of measurements needed is essentially $O(rn^{K-1})$; with better arrangement of the unfolded matrices, one can reduce the number of measurements to $O(r^{K/2}n^{K/2})$, whereas a certain nonconvex (potentially intractable) formulation needs only $O(r^K + nrK)$ measurements. There are good reasons to believe that, in order to bridge the gap, we may have to deal with the nonconvex nature of high-order tensor estimation directly.

6.3.3 Lack of Convex Relaxation for Bilinear Problems

So far, we have mainly considered the problem of recovering a low-dimensional signal $\boldsymbol{x}_o$ from a set of (random or incoherent) measurements $\boldsymbol{y} = \boldsymbol{A}\boldsymbol{x}_o$ where the measurement operator/matrix $\boldsymbol{A}$ is known. However, in many practical applications, we do not know the matrix $\boldsymbol{A}$.

For instance, consider $\boldsymbol{A} \in \mathbb{R}^{n\times n}$ is some (invertible) transformation on some sparse signals, and we have observed many samples of such signals:

$$\boldsymbol{y}_i = \boldsymbol{A}\boldsymbol{x}_i \in \mathbb{R}^n, \quad i = 1, 2, \ldots, m.$$

If we do not know the transformation $\boldsymbol{A}$ in advance, we want to recover the transformation so that $\boldsymbol{x}_i = \boldsymbol{A}^{-1}\boldsymbol{y}_i$ will be maximally sparse. In other words, if we stack $\boldsymbol{y}_i$ as columns of a matrix $\boldsymbol{Y} = [\boldsymbol{y}_1, \ldots, \boldsymbol{y}_m] \in \mathbb{R}^{n\times m}$ and similarly $\boldsymbol{X} = [\boldsymbol{x}_1, \ldots, \boldsymbol{x}_m] \in \mathbb{R}^{n\times m}$, we want to decompose $\boldsymbol{Y}$ into

$$\boldsymbol{Y} = \boldsymbol{A}\boldsymbol{X} \in \mathbb{R}^{n\times m},$$

such that $\boldsymbol{X}$ is the sparsest. This is a special matrix factorization problem, also known as the *dictionary learning* problem, with $\boldsymbol{A}$ being the (complete) sparsifying dictionary to be identified. In applications such as scientific imaging, the matrix $\boldsymbol{A}$ may even have additional structures such as being a convolution. Just like many other structured matrix factorization problems, there is no nontrivial convex relaxation to these nonlinear problems. For these problems, we are often forced to deal with their nonlinear and nonconvex nature directly. Nevertheless, as we will see in Section 7.3.2 of Chapter 7, such a nonconvex problem has extremely nice structures and properties. Such nice properties make the seemingly challenging nonconvex problem amenable to extremely efficient optimization algorithms (as we will see in Section 9.6.2 of Chapter 9).

6.3.4 Nonlinear Low-Dimensional Structures

All the low-dimensional models (sparse, low-rank) that we have studied so far assume the low-dimensional structures of the data are piecewise or locally linear – hence they can be represented as a linear superposition of a few atoms. As we will see in many of the application chapters, for most real-world data, nonlinearity can easily come from the measurement process or certain nonlinear deformations of the otherwise structured data (say, image rectification in Chapter 15). As a result, the intrinsic structures of such data are still very low-dimensional, but they are *not necessarily linear*. The support of their distribution may become *nonlinear submanifolds*, instead of linear subspaces! For instance, in speech recognition or object recognition in images, the information we care about is *invariant* to a certain group of transformations: shifting, translation, scaling, or rotation of the signals (say, image rectification in Chapter 15 or classification in Chapter 16). Mathematically speaking, we care about the (low-dimensional) structures of equivalent classes of the signals under such transformations. Such structures are known to be highly nonlinear and complicated [WDCB05].

Hence, to make the fundamental models, concepts, and methods developed in this book truly applicable and useful for real-world data and problems, we often need to learn such a nonlinear transform of the data:

$$f(\boldsymbol{x}) : \boldsymbol{x} \mapsto z, \quad f \in \mathcal{F} \tag{6.3.8}$$

in some family of functions $\mathcal{F}$.[10] After the transformation, we expect the intrinsic structures of $z = f(\boldsymbol{x})$ to become low-dimensional linear subspaces (as in sparse and low-rank models), which are easier to interpret and use. As we will see in the application chapters, the principles and computational tools developed in this book can be readily extended to undo such nonlinear mappings and reveal the low-dimensional structures of real-world data in terms of the canonical (linear) models that we are familiar with.

6.3.5 Return of Nonconvex Formulation and Optimization

The above difficulties with convex relaxation have compelled people to reexamine these more challenging problems in their natural nonconvex setting. Somewhat surprisingly, even in the nonconvex setting, the low-dimensional structures of the signals have played a crucial role in making such nonconvex problems amenable to efficient and effective solutions. These nonconvex programs are very different from generic nonconvex problems that are known to suffer from local minima and slow convergence. Instead, they have surprisingly good geometric and statistical properties which, if properly leveraged, give rise to simple, efficient algorithms. We will reveal properties of these nonconvex problems in Chapter 7 and develop scalable algorithms to solve them with (optimal) convergence and complexity guarantees in Chapter 9.

[10] Typically, we assume f is a smooth or at least continuous mapping, which can be parameterized as polynomials (see Chapter 15) or as deep networks (see Chapter 16).

To apply the fundamental theory and models of this book to real-world problems, in the last Chapter 16, we will touch upon the very important and challenging issue with real-world data: the intrinsic low-dimensional structures of the data can be highly nonlinear and multimodal. The modern practice of machine learning, especially deep learning, is precisely aiming to learn a nonlinear mapping that leads to a certain optimal (linear) representation of the data. We will see how the concepts and principles developed in this book for low-dimensional models play a fundamental role in rigorously interpreting and potentially improving the design of deep networks.

6.4 Notes

As mentioned in Chapter 3, the phase transition phenomenon associated with the ℓ^1 norm minimization was studied in the observation space by Tanner and Donoho from the perspective of random projection of high-dimensional polytopes [Don05, DT09, DT10]. Later studies focused on analyzing in the coefficient space as this approach applies to more general low-dimensional structures [Sto09, OH10, CRPW12, ALMT14]. The upper bound on the statistical dimension of the descent cone of the ℓ^1 norm is due to Stojnic [Sto09], which derives empirically sharp guarantees for recovery by ℓ^1 minimization. The proof of the corresponding lower bound follows Amelunxen et al. [ALMT14], as does our use of the term "statistical dimension" and much of the exposition in this chapter.

The study of low-dimensional structures through convex relaxation has been generalized through the introduction of atomic norm [BTR12] and linear inverse problems via convex optimization [CRPW12]. These earlier works have led to the unified framework based on statistical dimension of the descent cones [ALMT14], presented in this chapter. Statistical analysis of the recovery and decomposition problems under noisy measurements has also been systematically developed in a series of work from Wainwright and colleagues [Wai09a, ANW12].

Limitations of convex relaxation for certain low-dimensional structures have been revealed through the work of [OJFH13, OJF$^+$15] for sparse low-rank matrices and later [MHWG13] for high-order tensors. In subsequent years, nonconvex formulations have received tremendous attention, as surveyed in the recent papers [SQW15, JK17, CLC19, Sun19a]. In the next Chapter 7, we will give a more detailed account for the key rationale behind the nonconvex approach, and try to elucidate why and when a nonconvex program is expected to work well. In Chapter 9, we systematically introduce effective and efficient optimization algorithms for solving this class of nonconvex problems in high-dimensional spaces.

6.5 Exercises

6.1. (Nonnegative sparse vectors and low-rank matrices) *Consider the* nonnegative *sparse vectors. Identify an atomic set* $\mathcal{D}_{\text{nonnegative sparse}}$ *such that a vector* $\boldsymbol{x}$ *is a nonnegative and k-sparse if and only if it is a nonnegative combination of k elements of* $\mathcal{D}_{\text{nonnegative sparse}}$.

Now consider low-rank matrices with nonnegative factors, i.e., matrices that can be expressed as

$$\boldsymbol{X} = \sum_{i=1}^{r} \boldsymbol{a}_i \boldsymbol{b}_i^*, \tag{6.5.1}$$

with $\boldsymbol{a}_i$ *and* $\boldsymbol{b}_i$ *element-wise nonnegative. Identify an atomic set* $\mathcal{D}_{\text{nonnegative low-rank}}$ *such that a matrix* $\boldsymbol{X}$ *is of the form* (6.5.1) *if and only if it can be expressed as a nonnegative linear combination of r elements of* $\mathcal{D}_{\text{nonnegative low-rank}}$. *Can you guess which of the atomic norms* $\|\cdot\|_{\mathcal{D}_{\text{nonnegative sparse}}}$ *and* $\|\cdot\|_{\mathcal{D}_{\text{nonnegative low-rank}}}$ *leads to tractable optimization problems?*

6.2. (The k-support norm) *Consider the atomic set defined as*

$$\mathcal{D}_k = \{\boldsymbol{x} \in \mathbb{R}^n \mid \|\boldsymbol{x}\|_0 \le k, \|\boldsymbol{x}\|_2 = 1\}. \tag{6.5.2}$$

Show that the atomic norm given by the gauge function of this set is the so-called k-support norm:

$$\|\boldsymbol{x}\|_k^{sp} = \min \left\{ \sum_{\mathsf{I} \in \mathcal{G}_k} \|\boldsymbol{v}_{\mathsf{I}}\|_2 \ \ s.t. \ \sum_{\mathsf{I} \in \mathcal{G}_k} \boldsymbol{v}_{\mathsf{I}} = \boldsymbol{x} \right\}. \tag{6.5.3}$$

This gives an alternative convex regularizer for recovering sparse vectors.

6.3. *Consider an atomic set for* $\mathbb{R}^2$*:*

$$\mathcal{D} = \{\boldsymbol{x}_1 \in \mathbb{S}^1, \boldsymbol{x}_2 = [\pm 1, 0]^*\}. \tag{6.5.4}$$

What is the associated atomic (gauge) norm $\|\boldsymbol{x}\|_{\mathcal{D}}$ *for an* $\boldsymbol{x} \in \mathbb{R}^2$*? From this example, what can you say about a group atomic set* (6.1.29) *that has two supports* $\mathsf{I}' \subset \mathsf{I}$*?*

6.4. *Prove that the definitions of the dimension of a linear subspace are equivalent in Example 6.7.*

6.5. *Compute the intrinsic volumes of a d-dimensional subspace in* $\mathbb{R}^n$ *according to the Definition 6.8 for convex cones.*

6.6. *Compute the intrinsic volumes of a cone in* $\mathbb{R}^2$ *described in Example 6.10.*

6.7. *Derive the kinematic formula for two cones in* $\mathbb{R}^2$ *described in Example 6.11.*

6.8. *Prove the following properties of the statistical dimension of close convex clones:*

(a) The sum of the statistical dimension of a cone $\mathsf{C} \subset \mathbb{R}^n$ *and that of its polar cone* $\mathsf{C}^o \subset \mathbb{R}^n$ *satisfies*

$$\delta(\mathsf{C}) + \delta(\mathsf{C}^o) = n.$$

(b) For the direct product of two closed convex cones C_1 *and* C_2*, we have*

$$\delta(\mathsf{C}_1 \times \mathsf{C}_2) = \delta(\mathsf{C}_1) + \delta(\mathsf{C}_2).$$

6.9. *In the derivation of* (6.2.26)*, first, show that for* $\boldsymbol{g} \sim \mathcal{N}(\mathbf{0}, \boldsymbol{I})$*, we have*

$$\mathbb{E}_{\boldsymbol{g}}\left[\left\|\boldsymbol{g}_{\mathsf{I}} - t\boldsymbol{\sigma}_{\mathsf{I}}\right\|_2^2\right] = |\mathsf{I}|(1+t^2).$$

Second, discuss how you can solve the following minimization problem:

$$\psi(\eta) = \min_{t \geq 0}\left\{\eta(1+t^2) + 2(1-\eta)\int_{s=t}^{\infty}(s-t)^2\varphi(s)ds\right\}.$$

7 Nonconvex Methods for Low-Dimensional Models

"The mathematical sciences particularly exhibit order, symmetry, and limitations; and these are the greatest forms of the beautiful."

– Aristotle, *Metaphysica*

7.1 Introduction

As engineering and the sciences become increasingly data- and computation-driven, the role of optimization has expanded to touch almost every stage of the data analysis pipeline, from the signal and data acquisition to modeling, analysis, and prediction. While the challenges in computing with physical data are many and varied, basic recurring issues arise from *nonlinearities* at different stages of this pipeline:

- *Nonlinear measurements* are ubiquitous in imaging, optics, and astronomy. A canonical example are magnitude measurements, which arise when, due to physical limitations, it is easy to measure the (Fourier) modulus of a complex signal, but hard to measure the phase. For example, we might measure the Fourier magnitude of a complex signal $\boldsymbol{x} \in \mathbb{C}^n$ [Pat34, Pat44, SEC$^+$15, JEH17]:[1]

$$\underset{\textbf{observation}}{\boldsymbol{y}} = \left| \mathcal{F}\left(\underset{\textbf{unknown signal}}{\boldsymbol{x}} \right) \right| \in \mathbb{R}^m. \tag{7.1.1}$$

  Here, $\boldsymbol{x}$ represents a signal or image of interest, and the goal is to reconstruct $\boldsymbol{x}$ from the *nonlinear* measurements $\boldsymbol{y}$. This is sometimes called a *Fourier phase retrieval* problem.
- *Nonlinear models* are often well suited to express the variability of real datasets. For example, observations in microscopy, neuroscience, and astronomy can often be approximated as sparse superpositions of basic motifs.[2] We can cast the problem of finding these motifs as one of seeking a representation of the form

$$\underset{\textbf{data}}{\boldsymbol{Y}} = \underset{\textbf{motifs}}{\boldsymbol{A}} \; \underset{\textbf{sparse coefficients}}{\boldsymbol{X}}. \tag{7.1.2}$$

[1] In contrast, in the MRI example of Section 2.1 of Chapter 2, we studied a much simplified linear model in which we assume to have the full complex measurements of the Fourier transform of a brain image. In reality that is not the case.

[2] Mathematically, one may view such motifs as the atoms of a dictionary that we have studied in the previous chapter.

Here, the columns of $\boldsymbol{Y} \in \mathbb{R}^{m \times p}$ are observed data vectors, the columns of $\boldsymbol{A} \in \mathbb{R}^{m \times n}$ are basic motifs, and $\boldsymbol{X} \in \mathbb{R}^{n \times p}$ is a sparse matrix of coefficients that expresses each observed data point as a superposition of motifs. This is sometimes called a *sparse dictionary model*. A typical goal is to infer both $\boldsymbol{A}$ and $\boldsymbol{X}$ from observed data. Because both $\boldsymbol{A}$ and $\boldsymbol{X}$ are unknown, this model should be considered nonlinear (strictly, bilinear). Natural images may have even more variability, which is better modeled by hierarchical models (convolutional neural networks) with more complicated nonlinearities [LB95a, GPAM$^+$14, GBC16].

7.1.1 Nonlinearity, Symmetry, and Nonconvexity

In the two examples described above, nonlinearities are not just a nuisance: they are part of the structure of the problems we face. They have strong implications on the sense in which we can hope to solve these problems, and, as we will see in this chapter, on our ability to efficiently compute solutions.

Notice that both models exhibit certain *symmetries*. The model $\boldsymbol{y} = |\mathcal{F}(\boldsymbol{x})|$ in (7.1.1) exhibits a *phase symmetry*: both $\boldsymbol{x}$ and $\boldsymbol{x}e^{i\phi}$ (for any $\phi \in [0, 2\pi)$) produce the same observation $\boldsymbol{y}$. The sparse dictionary model $\boldsymbol{Y} = \boldsymbol{A}\boldsymbol{X}$ in (7.1.2) exhibits a *permutation symmetry*: for any signed permutation $\boldsymbol{\Pi}$, $(\boldsymbol{A}, \boldsymbol{X})$ and $(\boldsymbol{A}\boldsymbol{\Pi}, \boldsymbol{\Pi}^*\boldsymbol{X})$ produce the same observation $\boldsymbol{Y}$.[3] In either case, we can only hope to recover the physical ground truth up to these basic symmetries.

Nonconvex Programs from Symmetry

A typical computational approach to find the correct solution is to formulate an optimization problem

$$\min_{z} \varphi(z), \tag{7.1.3}$$

and attempt to solve it with iterative methods such as gradient descent [Cau47].[4] Here, z represents the signal or model to be recovered – for example, in phase retrieval, $z = \boldsymbol{x}$, while in dictionary learning the optimization variable z is the pair $(\boldsymbol{A}, \boldsymbol{X})$. Typically, $\varphi(\cdot)$ measures quality of fit to observed data and the extent to which the solution satisfies assumptions such as sparsity. As we shall see, most natural choices of φ inherit the symmetries of the data generation model: e.g., for phase recovery, we have

$$\varphi(e^{i\theta}\boldsymbol{x}) = \varphi(\boldsymbol{x}), \quad \forall\, \theta \in [0, 2\pi) = \mathbb{S}^1,$$

while for dictionary learning,

$$\varphi((\boldsymbol{A}, \boldsymbol{X})) = \varphi((\boldsymbol{A}\boldsymbol{\Pi}, \boldsymbol{\Pi}^*\boldsymbol{X})), \quad \forall\, \boldsymbol{\Pi} \in \mathsf{SP}(n),$$

[3] Here, and below, the notation $\boldsymbol{M}^*$ denotes the complex conjugate transpose of a matrix $\boldsymbol{M}$. If $\boldsymbol{M}$ is real-valued, this is simply the matrix transpose.

[4] We will give a full exposition of optimization methods in the next part of the book, in particular Chapter 9 for nonconvex programs. In this chapter, we focus on characterizing geometric properties of the optimization problems and their algorithmic implications.

where $\mathsf{SP}(n)$ indicates the group of signed permutations. As we see, *symmetries of the observation models become symmetries in the objective function of the associated optimization problems.*

If we are judicious in our choice of $\varphi(\cdot)$, we can hope that the true $\boldsymbol{x}$ is a (near) global minimizer; our task becomes one of solving the optimization problem (7.1.3) to global optimality. In contrast to certain applications of optimization (e.g., in finance, logistics, etc.), we care not just about decreasing the objective function, but also about obtaining the physical ground truth. As such, we are forced to care about ensuring not just that our algorithms converge, but also that they converge to global minimizers.

In applied optimization, a time-honored approach to guaranteeing global optimality is to seek formulations that are *convex*. The global minimizers of a convex function form a convex set. Moreover, every local minimizer (indeed, every critical point) of a convex function is global. As a result, many convex problems can be efficiently solved to global optimality by local methods. This makes the area of convex analysis and optimization a model for how geometric understanding can support practical computation, as we have practiced extensively for sparse and low-rank models in the previous chapters.

Unfortunately, as alluded to above, the symmetric programs we encounter in statistics, signal processing, and related areas are typically nonconvex [SQW15, JK17, CLC19, Sun19a], and they do not admit any obvious or meaningful convex relaxation. So we need to look for other geometric principles that will enable us to guarantee high-quality (preferably globally optimal) solutions. Indeed, these problems exhibit multiple global minimizers, which may be disjoint (due to permutation symmetry) or may reside on a continuous nonconvex set (due to rotation or phase symmetry). Any optimization formulation that inherits these symmetries will be most likely nonconvex.[5]

Worst-Case Obstructions to Nonconvex Optimization

This observation might suggest a certain pessimism: *nonconvex optimization is impossible in general.* There are simple classes of nonconvex problems (e.g., in polynomial optimization) that are already *NP-hard.* At a more intuitive level, there are two geometric obstructions to solving nonconvex problems globally. First, nonconvex problems can exhibit *spurious local minimizers*, i.e., local minimizers that are not global. Local descent methods can get trapped; finding the global optimum is hard in general. Perhaps surprisingly, even finding a *local* minimizer can be NP-hard in general [MK87, Nes00]. Figure 7.1(b) illustrates one of the challenges: it is possible to construct objective functions that are so flat that it is impossible to efficiently determine a direction of descent.

[5] **Disclaimer**: Not *every* symmetric problem is nonconvex. Indeed, the objective function $\varphi(z) = \frac{1}{2}\|z\|_2^2$ is rotationally symmetric, $\varphi(\boldsymbol{R}z) = \varphi(z)$ for all $\boldsymbol{R} \in \mathsf{O}(n)$, $z \in \mathbb{R}^n$, and convex. It is easy to construct additional examples of this type. However, the symmetric problems encountered in statistics, signal processing, and related areas are typically nonconvex; moreover, their nonconvexity can be directly attributed to symmetry.

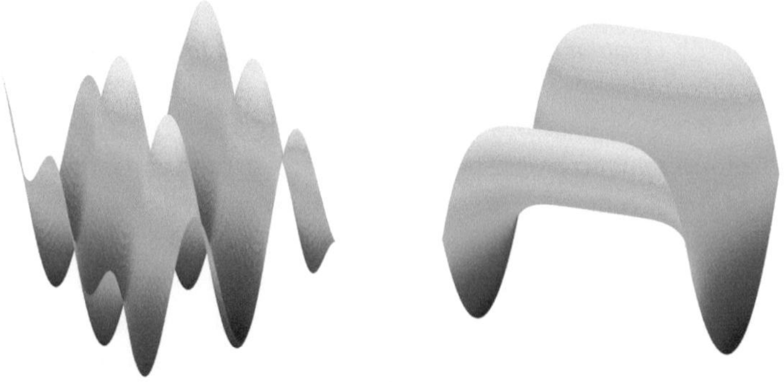

(a) Spurious local minimizers **(b) Flat saddle points**

Figure 7.1 Two Geometric Obstructions to Nonconvex Optimization. Descent methods can become trapped near local minimizers (a) or stagnate near flat saddle points (b).

Of course, it is possible to find global optima under minimal assumptions by exhaustively exploring the space of optimization, e.g., by discretization of the space [EMS18] or by random search [Haj90, BLO05]. The worst-case obstructions described above still rear their heads, in the form of search times that are exponential in dimension. Such a brute-force approach is only applicable to problems in which the dimension of the search space is not so high.

Calculus and the Local Geometry of Optimization

Because of these worst-case obstructions, the classical literature on efficient nonconvex optimization[6] has focused on guaranteeing

1 convergence to some critical point ($\bar{z}$ such that $\nabla\varphi(\bar{z}) = \mathbf{0}$), or
2 convergence to some local minimizer, for functions φ which are not too flat.

The curvature of a smooth function $\varphi(\cdot)$ around a critical point $\bar{z}$ can be studied through the Hessian $\nabla^2\varphi(\bar{z})$. If $\nabla^2\varphi(\bar{z})$ is nonsingular, the signs of its eigenvalues completely determine whether $\bar{z}$ is a minimizer, maximizer, or saddle point – see Figure 7.2(b). In particular, if $\bar{z}$ is a saddle point or a maximizer, there is a direction of negative curvature – a direction along which the second derivative is negative. This information can be used to escape saddles and converge to a local minimizer, either explicitly (using the Hessian) or implicitly (using gradient information to approximate the negative curvature direction).

In Chapter 9, we will introduce a variety of iterative methods that trade off in various ways between the amount of computation used to determine a good direction of negative curvature at a given iteration and the number of iterations required to converge [Gol80, CGT00, NP06, LSJR16, JNJ18, LPP$^+$19]. However, the high-level

[6] We will systematically study representative algorithms for nonconvex optimization in Chapter 9 and characterize what kind of guarantees they can provide and the associated computational complexity.

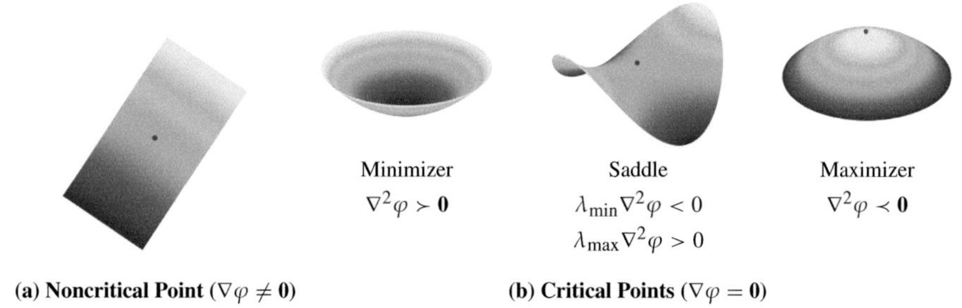

Figure 7.2 Calculus and the *Local* Geometry of Optimization. The *gradient* $\nabla\varphi$ captures the slope of the function φ. At *critical points* $\bar{z}$, $\nabla\varphi(\bar{z}) = \mathbf{0}$. The type of critical point (minimizer, maximizer, saddle) can often be determined from the curvature of φ at $\bar{z}$, which is captured by the *Hessian* $\nabla^2\varphi(\bar{z})$.

message of these methods is consistent: if all critical points are nondegenerate,[7] we can escape them and efficiently converge to a local minimizer. In fact, slightly less is required: it is enough that every nonminimizing critical point have a direction of strict negative curvature[8] [JGN+17, JNJ18, LPP+17, LSJR16].

Results of this nature control the worst-case behavior of methods over very broad classes of problems. In such a general setting, it is not possible to provide strong guarantees on *what* local minimizer methods converge to, and whether that minimizer is global. Nevertheless, it is difficult to overstate the impact of this kind of thinking for stimulating the development of useful methods and elucidating their properties. Moreover, methods developed to guarantee good worst-case performance often outperform their worst-case guarantees on practical problem instances – witness longstanding "folk theorems" on the ease of optimizing neural networks [CHM+14, Kaw16, SJL18, AZLS19, DLL+19, Sun19b], solving problems in quantum mechanics [KKP+18, STDV18, HLWY19], or clustering separated data [QZC19, KQC+19, QZC20, WYD20]. Delineating problem classes that capture the difficulty (or ease!) of naturally occurring optimization problems is a pressing challenge for the mathematics of data science [SQW15, JK17, CLC19, Sun19a].

7.1.2 Symmetry and the Global Geometry of Optimization

The goal of this chapter is to illustrate a particular family of nonconvex problems associated with low-dimensional models which, under surprisingly mild conditions, can be solved globally with efficient methods. This family includes a number of contemporary problems in signal processing, data analysis, and related fields [SQW15,

[7] In the language of differential topology, if the function φ is Morse [Mil63, Bot82].

[8] In the recent literature, this is called a "strict saddle" property [GHJY15, SQW15]. Concrete rates of convergence are typically stated in terms of quantitative versions of this property, which explicitly control the size of the gradient and the smallest eigenvalue of the Hessian uniformly over the domain of optimization.

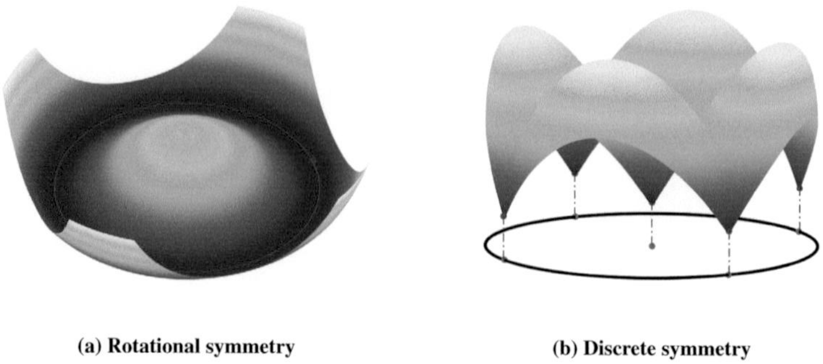

Figure 7.3 Symmetry and the *Global* Geometry of Optimization. Model problems with continuous (a) and discrete (b) symmetry. For these particular problems, and others we will study, every local minimizer is global.

JK17, CLC19, Sun19a]. The most important high-level property of these problems is that they are all *symmetric* – in slightly more formal language:

DEFINITION 7.1. (Symmetric function) *Let* $\mathbb{G}$ *be a group acting on* $\mathbb{R}^n$. *A function* $\varphi : \mathbb{R}^n \to \mathbb{R}^{n'}$ *is* $\mathbb{G}$*-symmetric if for all* $\mathfrak{z} \in \mathbb{R}^n$, $\mathfrak{g} \in \mathbb{G}$, $\varphi(\mathfrak{g} \circ \mathfrak{z}) = \varphi(\mathfrak{z})$.

As argued above, symmetry forces us to grapple with properties of nonconvex functions. On the other hand, the particular symmetric nonconvex functions encountered in practice are often quite benign. Figure 7.3 shows two examples – one with rotational symmetry ($\mathbb{G}$ an orthogonal group) and one with discrete symmetry ($\mathbb{G}$ a discrete group, such as the signed permutations). We will develop these examples in more mathematical detail below. For now, we simply observe that these two instances do not exhibit spurious local minimizers or flat saddles. The absence of these worst-case obstructions can be attributed to symmetry. In slogan form, we shall see that:

Slogan 1: *the (only!) local minimizers are symmetric versions of the ground truth.*
Slogan 2: *a local critical point has negative curvature in directions that break symmetry.*

When these two slogans are in force, efficient (local) methods produce global minimizers. Moreover, symmetry constrains the global layout of the critical points, leading to additional structure that facilitates efficient optimization. We will show examples where the saddle points of symmetric problems "cascade," with negative curvature directions feeding into negative curvature directions, a property which appears to prevent first-order methods from stagnating [GBW19].

Before we embark, a few disclaimers are in order. First, slogans 1 and 2 are only slogans. As we will see, they have been established rigorously for specific problems under specific (restrictive) technical hypotheses. We hope to convey a sense of the beauty and robustness of certain observed phenomena in optimization, while also making clear that the existing mathematics supporting these claims is, in places, lacking uniformity and simplicity. There is a need for more unified analysis and better technical tools. We highlight some potential avenues for this in Section 7.4. The

Nonconvex Problems with Rotational Symmetries

(a) Eigenspace Computation

*Compute the principal subspace
of a symmetric matrix*

$\min_{X^*X=I} -\frac{1}{2}\text{trace}\left[X^*AX\right]$

Symmetry: $X \mapsto XR$

$\mathbb{G} = \mathsf{O}(r)$

(b) Generalized Phase Retrieval

*Recover a complex vector x_o from
magnitude measurements $y = |Ax_o|$*

$\min_x \frac{1}{2}\||y^2 - |Ax|^2\|_2^2$

Symmetry: $x \mapsto xe^{i\phi}$

$\mathbb{G} = \mathsf{S}^1 \cong \mathsf{O}(2)$

(c) Matrix Recovery

*Recover a low-rank matrix $X = UV^*$
from incomplete/corrupted observations*

$\min_{U,V} \mathcal{L}(Y - \mathcal{A}[UV^*]) + \rho(U,V)$

Symmetry: $(U,V) \mapsto (U\Gamma, V\Gamma^{-*})$

$\mathbb{G} = \mathsf{GL}(r)$ or $\mathbb{G} = \mathsf{O}(r)$

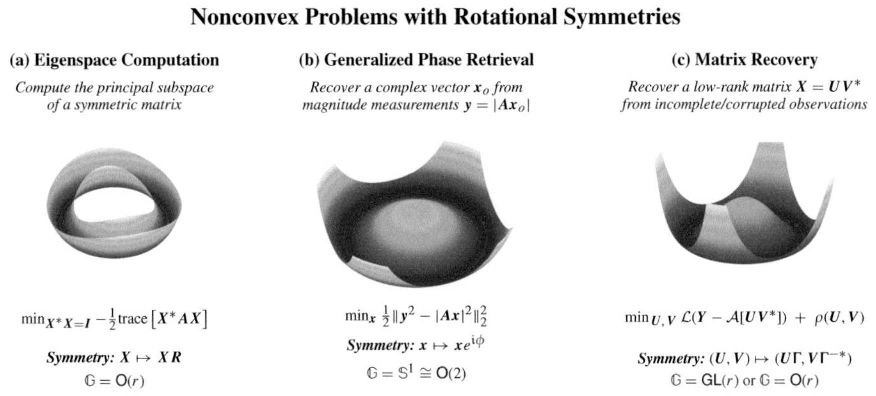

Figure 7.4 Three examples of nonconvex optimization problems with rotational symmetries (Section 7.2). Each of these three tasks can be reduced to optimization problems in various ways; for each, we give a representative formulation and discuss its symmetries.

second, more fundamental, disclaimer is that not all symmetric problems have benign global geometry. It is easy to construct counterexamples. Nevertheless, as we will see, symmetry provides a lens through which one can understand the geometric properties that enable efficient optimization for our particular family of problems. Moreover, when we study these problems through their symmetries, common structures and common intuitions emerge: problems with similar symmetries exhibit similar geometric properties and behaviors.

7.1.3   A Taxonomy of Symmetric Nonconvex Problems

In this chapter, we identify two families of symmetric nonconvex problems, which exhibit similar geometric characteristics.

- The first family of problems exhibit continuous *rotational symmetries*: the group $\mathbb{G}$ is $\mathsf{O}(n)$ or $\mathsf{SO}(n)$. The phase retrieval problem described above is a canonical example; Figure 7.4 illustrates this family.
- The second family of problems exhibit *discrete symmetries*: signed permutations $\mathsf{SP}(n)$, signed shifts $\mathbb{Z}_n \times \{\pm1\}$, or products of these. The dictionary learning problem discussed above is a canonical example; Figure 7.5 shows several others.

In the remainder of this chapter, we explore the geometry of these two families of problems in more depth. Section 7.2 studies problems with rotational symmetries, beginning with a very simple model problem in which the goal is to recover a single complex scalar from magnitude measurements. The analysis helps extract conclusions that carry over to more complicated measurement models for phase recovery [CESV13, CLS15b, SEC+15, SQW18, FS20] and related problems in low-rank matrix factorization and recovery [GLM16, GJZ17, CLC19].

Nonconvex Problems with Discrete Symmetries

(a) Eigenvector Computation

Maximize a quadratic form over the sphere

$$\max\nolimits_{x \in \mathbb{S}^{n-1}} \tfrac{1}{2} x^* A x$$

Symmetry: $x \mapsto -x$
$\mathbb{G} = \{\pm 1\}$

(b) Dictionary Learning

Approximate a given matrix Y as $Y = AX$, with X sparse

$$\min\nolimits_{A \in \mathcal{A}, X} \tfrac{1}{2} \|Y - AX\|_F^2 + \lambda \|X\|_1$$

Symmetry: $(A, X) \mapsto (A\Gamma, X\Gamma^*)$
$\mathbb{G} = \mathsf{SP}(n)$

(c) Tensor Decomposition

Determine components a_i of an orthogonal decomposable tensor $T = \sum_i a_i \otimes a_i \otimes a_i \otimes a_i$

$$\max\nolimits_{X \in \mathsf{O}(n)} \sum_i T(x_i, x_i, x_i, x_i)$$

Symmetry: $X \mapsto X\Gamma$
$\mathbb{G} = \mathsf{P}(n)$

(d) Short-and-Sparse Deconvolution

Recover a short a and a sparse x from their convolution $y = a \circledast x$

$$\min\nolimits_{a, x} \tfrac{1}{2} \|y - a \circledast x\|_2^2 + \lambda \|x\|_1$$

Symmetry: $(a, x) \mapsto (\alpha s_\tau[a], \alpha^{-1} s_{-\tau}[x])$
$\mathbb{G} = \mathbb{Z}_n \times \mathbb{R}_*$ or $\mathbb{G} = \mathbb{Z}_n \times \{\pm 1\}$

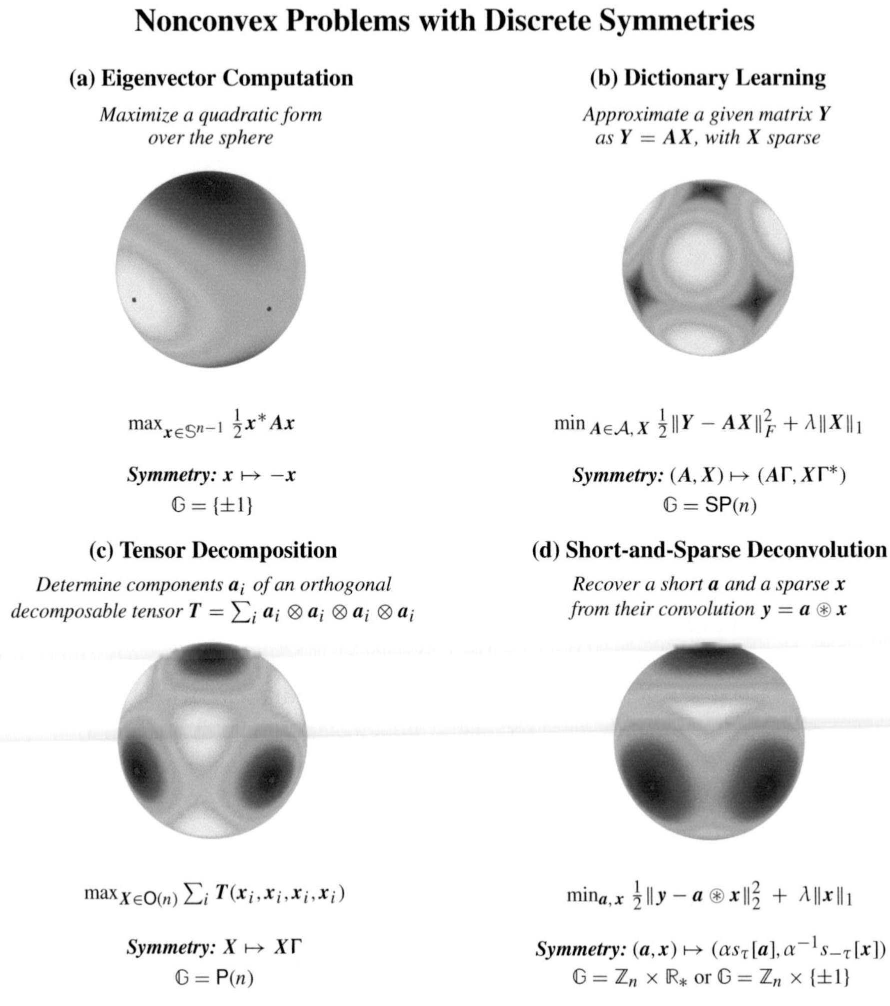

Figure 7.5 Four examples of problems with discrete symmetries. We discuss this family of problems in more detail in Section 7.3.

Section 7.3 studies problems with discrete symmetries, starting again from another simple model problem and extracting conclusions that carry over to problems such as dictionary learning [SQW17a, SQW17b, GBW19, QZL+19], blind deconvolution [LS17, ZKW18, KZLW19, LQK+19, LB18, QLZ19], and tensor decomposition [GHJY15, GM17].

As mentioned above, this area is rich with open problems; we highlight a few of these in Section 7.4. These open problems span both geometry and algorithms. Nevertheless, our main focus throughout this survey is geometric: we will concentrate on the connection between symmetry and geometry. As described above, these geometric analyses have strong implications: in many cases, they guarantee that problems can be solved globally in polynomial time. In order to keep the development focused on geometric intuitions, we will only treat computational issues at a high level.

We recommend the survey paper [CLC19] for a more detailed exposition of issues at the interface of statistics and computation, for problems with rotational symmetry. Section 7.4 also briefly discusses similar considerations for problems exhibiting discrete symmetries, where we refer readers to the paper [QZL$^+$20b] for more computational and application aspects on these problems.

7.2 Nonconvex Problems with Rotational Symmetries

In this section, we study the first main class of problems in our taxonomy of symmetric nonconvex problems: problems with continuous *rotational symmetry*. This class includes important model problems in phase recovery [SEC$^+$15, FS20] and low-rank estimation [CLC19]. We begin by developing a few basic intuitions through a toy phase retrieval problem; we then show how these intuitions help to explain the geometry of a range of problems from imaging to machine learning.

7.2.1 Minimal Example: Phase Retrieval with One Unknown

We first consider a model problem, in which our goal is to recover a single complex scalar $x_o \in \mathbb{C}$ from m magnitude measurements

$$y_1 = |a_1 x_o|, \; \ldots, \; y_m = |a_m x_o|, \tag{7.2.1}$$

where $a_1, \ldots, a_m \in \mathbb{C}$ are known complex scalars. Collecting our observations y_i into a single vector $\boldsymbol{y} \in \mathbb{R}^m$ and collecting the a_i into a single vector $\boldsymbol{a} \in \mathbb{C}^m$, we can express this measurement model more compactly as

$$\boldsymbol{y} = |\boldsymbol{a} x_o|. \tag{7.2.2}$$

Our goal is to determine x_o, up to a phase. This is a heavily simplified (indeed, trivialized!) version of the *generalized phase retrieval* problem [CSV13, CLS15b, SQW18], which we will describe in more detail in Section 7.2.2. Here our goal is simply to understand the consequences of the phase symmetry of the measurement model (7.2.2) for optimization. To this end, we study a model optimization problem,

$$\min \; \varphi(x) \doteq \tfrac{1}{4} \| \boldsymbol{y}^2 - |\boldsymbol{a} x|^2 \|_2^2, \tag{7.2.3}$$

which minimizes the sum of squared differences between the squared magnitudes of $\boldsymbol{a}x$ and those of $\boldsymbol{a}x_o$. Note that

$$\varphi(x) = \tfrac{1}{4} \|\boldsymbol{a}\|_4^4 \left(|x|^2 - |x_o|^2 \right)^2. \tag{7.2.4}$$

This is a function of a complex scalar $x = x_r + \mathfrak{i} x_i$. We can study its geometry by identifying x with a two-dimensional real vector $\bar{\boldsymbol{x}} = (x_r, x_i)$. The slope and curvature of the function $\varphi(\bar{\boldsymbol{x}})$ are captured by the gradient and Hessian,

$$\nabla \varphi(\bar{\boldsymbol{x}}) = \|\boldsymbol{a}\|_4^4 \left(|x|^2 - |x_o|^2 \right) \begin{bmatrix} x_r \\ x_i \end{bmatrix}, \tag{7.2.5}$$

$$\nabla^2 \varphi(\bar{\boldsymbol{x}}) = \|\boldsymbol{a}\|_4^4 \left(\left(|x|^2 - |x_o|^2 \right) \boldsymbol{I} + 2 \bar{\boldsymbol{x}} \bar{\boldsymbol{x}}^* \right). \tag{7.2.6}$$

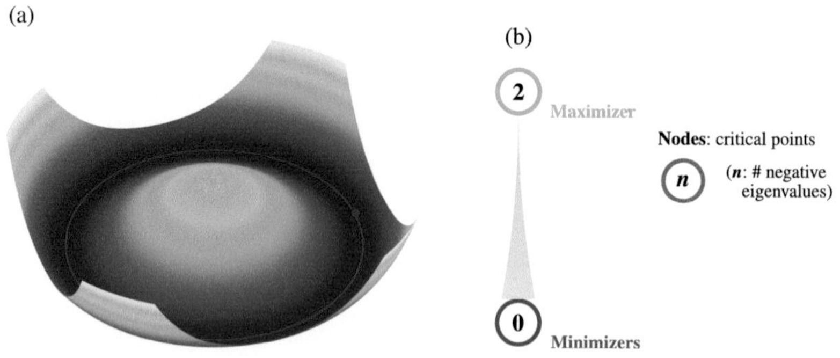

Figure 7.6 Phase Retrieval with a Single Unknown. (a) We plot the objective function $\varphi(x)$ for phase retrieval with a single complex unknown. All local minimizers (red) are symmetric copies $x_o e^{\mathrm{i}\phi}$ of the ground truth $x_o \in \mathbb{C}$. There is also a local maximizer (green) at $x = 0$; at this point, φ exhibits negative curvature in directions that break symmetry. (b) Critical points arranged according to objective function φ, labeled according to their index (number of negative eigenvalues).

Figure 7.6 visualizes the objective $\varphi(\cdot)$ and its critical points. By setting $\nabla\varphi = 0$, and inspecting the Hessian, we obtain that there exist two families of critical points: global minimizers at $x = x_o e^{\mathrm{i}\phi}$, and a global maximizer at $x = 0$. We notice that:

- *Symmetric copies of the ground truth are minimizers.* The points $x_o e^{\mathrm{i}\phi}$ are the only local minimizers. In problems with phase ambiguities, we expect a circle $\mathsf{O}(2) \cong \mathbb{S}^1$ of minimizers. In addition, the Hessian is positive semidefinite, but rank-deficient at the global minimizers: the zero curvature direction (along which the objective φ is flat) is precisely the direction that is tangent to the set of equivalent solutions $g \circ \boldsymbol{x}_\star$ at $\boldsymbol{x}_\star$ with $g \in \mathbb{S}^1$. Normal to this set, the objective function exhibits positive curvature – a form of restricted strong convexity.
- *Negative curvature in symmetry-breaking directions.* There is a local maximizer at $x = 0$, which is equidistant from the target solutions $\{x_o e^{\mathrm{i}\phi}\}$. At this point $\nabla^2\varphi \prec \mathbf{0}$; there is negative curvature in every direction, and movement in any direction breaks symmetry.

7.2.2 Generalized Phase Retrieval

The univariate phase retrieval problem is an extreme idealization of a basic problem in imaging: recovering a signal from phaseless measurements [CESV13, SEC+15]. This problem arises in many application areas, including electron microscopy [MIJ+02], diffraction and array imaging [BDP+07, CMP10], acoustics [BCE06, Bal10], quantum mechanics [Cor06, Rei65], and quantum information [HMW13], where the goal is to image complex molecular structures. Illuminating a sample with coherent light produces a diffraction pattern, which is approximately the Fourier transform of the sample's density. If we could measure this diffraction pattern, we could recover an image of the sample with atomic resolution, simply by inverting the Fourier transform. However, there is a wrinkle: typically, the magnitude of the Fourier transform is much easier to measure than the phase – the magnitude can be measured by aggregating energy over time, whereas measuring the phase of a high-frequency signal requires the detector to be sensitive to very rapid changes. The Fourier phase retrieval problem asks us to reconstruct a complex signal from magnitude measurements only:

$$\text{find} \quad \boldsymbol{x} \quad \text{such that} \quad |\mathcal{F}[\boldsymbol{x}]| = \boldsymbol{y}.$$

This problem is widespread in scientific imaging [Mil90, Rob93, Wal63, DF87]. It is also challenging: it is ill-posed in one dimension, and in higher dimensions even the most effective numerical methods remain sensitive to initialization and tuning [Fie13]. We refer readers to recent survey papers [SEC$^+$15, JEH15, FS20] for more details. We would like to emphasize here that one main reason for this difficulty resides in the symmetries of the measurement operator $|\mathcal{F}[\cdot]|$: in addition to phase symmetry, the mapping $\boldsymbol{x} \mapsto |\mathcal{F}[\boldsymbol{x}]|$ is invariant under shifts and conjugate reversal of the signal $\boldsymbol{x}$. We will discuss more challenges and open problems around Fourier measurements in later sections.

In recent years, the applied mathematics community has investigated variants of the above problem in which the Fourier transform $\mathcal{F}$ is replaced by a more general linear operator $\mathcal{A}(\cdot)$ [CSV13, CESV13, CLS15a]. A "generic" map $\boldsymbol{x} \mapsto |\mathcal{A}[\boldsymbol{x}]|$ has simpler symmetries – typically only a phase symmetry, $|\mathcal{A}[\boldsymbol{x}e^{\mathrm{i}\phi}]| = |\mathcal{A}[\boldsymbol{x}]|$. This makes generic phase recovery problems easier to study and easier to solve. While the Fourier model is more widely applicable to physical imaging, the generic phase retrieval model does capture aspects of certain less conventional imaging setups, including ptychography [YDZ$^+$15, JEH16, Pfe18] (i.e., $\mathcal{A}(\cdot)$ is the short-time Fourier transform), coded illuminations [TW15, KBRW19], and coded diffraction patterns [CLS15b]. A model m-dimensional version of the generalized phase retrieval problem can be formulated as follows:

$$\text{find} \quad \boldsymbol{x} \in \mathbb{C}^n \quad \text{such that} \quad |\boldsymbol{A}\boldsymbol{x}| = \boldsymbol{y}, \tag{7.2.7}$$

where $\boldsymbol{A} \in \mathbb{C}^{m \times n}$ is a matrix which represents the measurement process.

As in univariate phase retrieval, we can attempt to recover $\boldsymbol{x}_o$ by minimizing the misfit to the observed data, e.g., by solving

$$\min_{\boldsymbol{x} \in \mathbb{C}^n} \varphi(\boldsymbol{x}) \equiv \frac{1}{4m} \sum_{k=1}^{m} \left(y_k^2 - \left| \boldsymbol{a}_k^* \boldsymbol{x} \right|^2 \right)^2, \tag{7.2.8}$$

where $\boldsymbol{a}_1, \ldots, \boldsymbol{a}_m \in \mathbb{C}^n$ are the rows of $\boldsymbol{A}$. We saw above that the univariate version of this function has a very simple landscape, which is dictated almost entirely by phase symmetry, and that it has no spurious local minimizers. *Should we expect similar behavior in this higher-dimensional setting?*

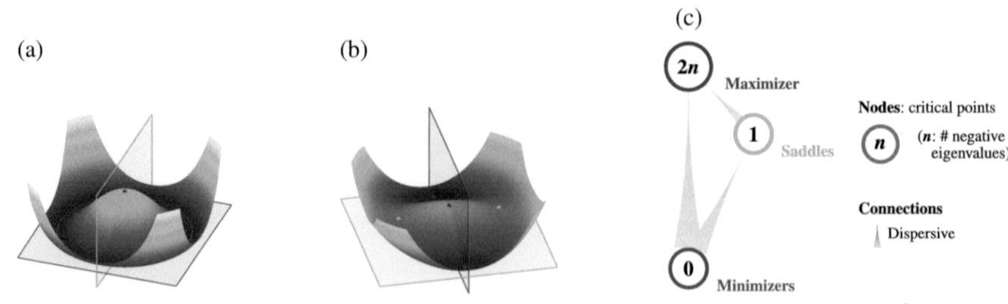

Figure 7.7 Generalized Phase Retrieval. We plot two slices of the landscape of the generalized phase retrieval problem with Gaussian measurements. (a) Slice containing symmetric copies of the ground truth $\boldsymbol{x}_o e^{\mathrm{i}\phi}$. (b) Slice containing minimizers $\boldsymbol{x}_o$, $-\boldsymbol{x}_o$, and one orthogonal direction. Notice that at both the maximizer and saddle points, there is negative curvature in the direction that breaks symmetry between $\boldsymbol{x}_o$ and $-\boldsymbol{x}_o$. (c) Critical points arranged according to objective $\mathbb{E}[\varphi]$, labeled with their indices (number of negative eigenvalues). Connections between critical points are "dispersive": downstream negative curvature directions are the image of upstream negative curvature directions under gradient flow.

Geometry of Generalized Phase Retrieval

One way of generating intuition is to assume that the sampling vectors $\boldsymbol{a}_i$ are chosen at random, and analyze $\varphi(\boldsymbol{x})$ using tools from statistics. Figure 7.7 visualizes $\varphi(\boldsymbol{x})$ when the $\boldsymbol{a}_k$ are Gaussian vectors[9] and m is large. As $m \to \infty$, $\varphi(\boldsymbol{x})$ converges to its expectation $\mathbb{E}[\varphi]$, which can be calculated in closed form. In Figure 7.7(a), we can see the characteristic phase symmetry, identical to our univariate example above. However, this problem is higher-dimensional. Figure 7.7(b) plots the objective over a two-dimensional slice containing the ground truth and an orthogonal direction. We observe the following:

- *Symmetric copies of the ground truth are minimizers.* All the local minimizers are on the circle of points $\boldsymbol{x}_o e^{\mathrm{i}\phi}$, which corresponds to the ground truth up to the (rotational) phase symmetry. Problems with higher-dimensional symmetries will have larger sets of minimizers – e.g., $\mathsf{O}(r)$ symmetry leads to a manifold of minimizers that is isometric to $\mathsf{O}(r)$.
- *Negative curvature in symmetry-breaking directions.* In higher-dimensional examples, we encounter a variety of local maximizers, saddle points, etc. Nevertheless, these critical points occur near balanced superpositions of equivalent solutions, and exhibit negative curvature in directions $\pm\boldsymbol{x}_o$, which breaks symmetry.
- *Cascade of saddle points.* As shown schematically in Figure 7.7, the critical points can be graded based on the number of negative eigenvalues of the Hessian:[10] critical points with higher objective have more negative eigenvalues. Moreover, the objective has a "dispersive" property: upstream negative curvature discourages stagnation near the stable manifold of downstream critical points.

9 Formally, $\boldsymbol{a}_k$ are independent random vectors, with $\boldsymbol{a}_k = \boldsymbol{a}_k^r + \mathrm{i}\boldsymbol{a}_k^i$ with $\boldsymbol{a}_k^r$ and $\boldsymbol{a}_k^i$ independent i.i.d. $\mathcal{N}(0, \frac{1}{2})$.

10 In differential geometry, or more specifically in the Morse theory [Mil63, Bot82], the number of negative eigenvalues is also known as *the index* of the critical point.

Practical Variations and Extensions

The exposition in the previous section is still quite idealized: the measurements are Gaussian, and we have infinitely many of them. Moreover, we have assumed a particular objective $\varphi(\boldsymbol{x})$, which is not widely used in practice. Fortunately, the qualitative conclusions of the previous subsection carry over to more structured and challenging settings for generalized phase retrieval.[11] We briefly describe these extensions, while noting technical caveats and open problems.

Practical Sample Complexity

Phase retrieval is a sensing problem; measurements cost resources. It is important to minimize the number of measurements m required to accurately reconstruct $\boldsymbol{x}$. Under the Gaussian model, the particular loss function $\varphi(\cdot)$ in (7.2.8) is a sum of independent heavy-tailed random variables. Relatively straightforward considerations show that when $m \gtrsim n^2$, gradients and Hessians concentrate uniformly about their expectations, and the objective has no spurious local minimizers. This number of samples is clearly suboptimal – n^2 measurements to recover about n complex numbers. The challenge is that the objective function (7.2.8) contains fourth moments of Gaussian variables, and is therefore somewhat heavy-tailed. Using arguments that are tailored to this situation, the required number of samples can be improved to $m \gtrsim n \log^3 n$ [SQW18]. Moreover, modifying the objective (7.2.8) to remove large terms (*à la* robust statistics) can improve this to essentially optimal ($m \gtrsim n$) [CC17].[12]

Different Objective Functions

The "squares of the squares" formulation in (7.2.8) is smooth and hence simple to analyze, but is typically not preferred in practice, especially when observations are noisy. Alternatives include $\varphi(\boldsymbol{x}) = \sum_i \left| y_i^2 - |\boldsymbol{a}_i^* \boldsymbol{x}|^2 \right|$ [WGE17], $\varphi(\boldsymbol{x}) = \sum_i \left| y_i - |\boldsymbol{a}_i^* \boldsymbol{x}| \right|^2$ [DDP17], and maximum likelihood formulations that model (Poisson) noise in the observations y_i [CC17]. Although these formulations differ in details, the major features of the objective landscape are independent of the choice of φ. For Gaussian $\boldsymbol{a}_i$, the expectation $\mathbb{E}[\varphi]$ has no spurious minimizers; moreover, all objectives have a minimizer at zero and a family of saddle points orthogonal to $\boldsymbol{x}_o$. On the other hand, proving (or disproving) that these objectives have benign global geometry for small m is an open problem. Existing small-sample analyses [CC17, WGE17, DDP17] control the behavior of the objective in a neighborhood of $\boldsymbol{x}_o e^{\mathrm{i}\phi}$, and initialize in this neighborhood using statistical properties of the measurement model.

[11] But *not* to the Fourier model, which has different symmetries. We discuss challenges and open problems around Fourier measurements in Section 7.3 and Section 7.4.

[12] Other approaches to producing analyses with small-sample complexity include restricting the analysis to a small neighborhood of the ground truth, and initializing in this neighborhood using spectral methods that leverage the statistics of the measurement model [CLS15b, WdM15], or forgoing uniform geometric analysis and directly reasoning about trajectories of randomly initialized gradient descent [MWCC18].

Structured Measurements

Geometric intuitions for Gaussian $\boldsymbol{A}$ carry over to several models that are more closely connected with imaging practice. Examples include convolutional models, in which we observe the modulus of the convolution $\boldsymbol{y} = |\boldsymbol{a} \circledast \boldsymbol{x}|$ of the unknown signal $\boldsymbol{x}$ with a known sequence $\boldsymbol{a}$ [QZEW17], and coded diffraction patterns, in which we make multiple observations $\boldsymbol{y}_l = |\mathcal{F}[\boldsymbol{d}_l \odot \boldsymbol{x}]|$, where $\odot$ denotes an element-wise product [CLS15a]. If the filter $\boldsymbol{a}$ or the masks $\boldsymbol{d}_l$ are chosen at random from appropriate distributions, these structured measurements yield the same asymptotic objective function $\mathbb{E}[\varphi]$. In particular, in the large-sample limit ($\boldsymbol{a}$ being long in the convolutional model, or many diffraction patterns in the coded diffraction model), these measurements still lead to optimization problems with no spurious local minimizers. Similar to the situation with nonsmooth objective functions, the best known theoretical sample complexities are obtained by initializing near the ground truth, using statistical properties of $\boldsymbol{A}$. Globally analyzing structured measurements in the small-sample regime is a challenging open problem.

The above discussion only scratches the surface of the growing literature on generalized phase retrieval; we refer readers to [SEC$^+$15, JEH15, FS20] for a more comprehensive survey on recent developments. The main purpose of this chapter is to reveal that the unifying thread through all of these models, objectives, and problems is the simple model geometry in Figure 7.7. In the next section, we will see a similar phenomenon with low-rank matrices: a model geometry from matrix factorization recurs across a sequence of increasingly challenging matrix recovery problems.

7.2.3 Low-Rank Matrix Recovery

As we have discussed and studied in great detail in Chapter 4, the problem of recovering a low-rank matrix from incomplete and unreliable observations finds broad applications in robust statistics, recommender systems, data compression, computer vision, and so on [DR16]. In matrix recovery problems, the goal is to estimate a matrix $\boldsymbol{X}_o \in \mathbb{R}^{n_1 \times n_2}$ from incomplete or noisy observations. Typically, this problem is ill-posed without some assumptions on the matrix $\boldsymbol{X}_o$. In many applications, $\boldsymbol{X}_o$ can be assumed to be *low-rank*, or approximately so:

$$r = \operatorname{rank}(\boldsymbol{X}_o) \ll \min\{n_1, n_2\}. \tag{7.2.9}$$

Any rank-r matrix can be expressed as a product of a tall $n_1 \times r$ matrix and a wide $r \times n_2$ matrix:

$$\boldsymbol{X}_o = \boldsymbol{U}\boldsymbol{V}^*, \quad \boldsymbol{U} \in \mathbb{R}^{n_1 \times r}, \boldsymbol{V} \in \mathbb{R}^{n_2 \times r}. \tag{7.2.10}$$

A very popular strategy for recovering $\boldsymbol{X}_o$ is to start with some objective function $\psi(\boldsymbol{X})$ that enforces consistency with observed data, and then parameterize $\boldsymbol{X}$ in terms of the factors $\boldsymbol{U}$ and $\boldsymbol{V}$ [BM03], yielding the optimization problem

$$\min_{\boldsymbol{U}, \boldsymbol{V}} \varphi(\boldsymbol{U}, \boldsymbol{V}) \equiv \psi(\boldsymbol{U}\boldsymbol{V}^*). \tag{7.2.11}$$

Symmetries of Low-Rank Models

Formulations like (7.2.11) are almost always nonconvex, due to symmetries of the factorization (7.2.10). Indeed, for any invertible $r \times r$ matrix Γ,

$$\boldsymbol{U}\boldsymbol{V}^* = \boldsymbol{U}\Gamma\Gamma^{-1}\boldsymbol{V}^* = (\boldsymbol{U}\Gamma)\left(\boldsymbol{V}\Gamma^{-*}\right)^*. \tag{7.2.12}$$

Because of this ambiguity, the problem (7.2.11) always possesses a *general linear* (invertible matrix) symmetry:

$$(\boldsymbol{U}, \boldsymbol{V}) \equiv (\boldsymbol{U}\Gamma, \boldsymbol{V}\Gamma^{-*}), \quad \forall\, \Gamma \in \mathsf{GL}(r). \tag{7.2.13}$$

Because a general linear matrix Γ can have a determinant arbitrarily close to zero, and hence be arbitrarily ill-conditioned, the equivalence class of solutions $(\boldsymbol{U}, \boldsymbol{V})$ has somewhat complicated geometry, as a subset of $\mathbb{R}^{n_1 \times r} \times \mathbb{R}^{n_2 \times r}$.[13] Fortunately, it is not difficult to reduce this general linear symmetry to a simpler and better-conditioned orthogonal symmetry $\mathsf{O}(r)$, either by using information about the target $\boldsymbol{X}_o$, or by adding additional penalty terms to (7.2.11).

Rotational Symmetries for Symmetric $\boldsymbol{X}_o$

If the target solution $\boldsymbol{X}_o$ is *symmetric and positive semidefinite*, then it admits factorization of the form $\boldsymbol{X}_o = \boldsymbol{U}_o\boldsymbol{U}_o^*$, and so we can take $\boldsymbol{U} = \boldsymbol{V}$. This gives a slightly simpler problem

$$\min_{\boldsymbol{U}} \; \varphi(\boldsymbol{U}) \equiv \psi(\boldsymbol{U}\boldsymbol{U}^*), \tag{7.2.14}$$

with a smaller symmetry group. For any $\Gamma \in \mathsf{O}(r)$, $\boldsymbol{U}\boldsymbol{U}^* = \boldsymbol{U}\Gamma\Gamma^*\boldsymbol{U}^* = (\boldsymbol{U}\Gamma)(\boldsymbol{U}\Gamma)^*$, and so the problem (7.2.14) exhibits an orthogonal symmetry $\varphi(\boldsymbol{U}) \equiv \varphi(\boldsymbol{U}\Gamma)$, for all $\Gamma \in \mathsf{O}(r)$.

Rotational Symmetries for General $\boldsymbol{X}_o$ via Penalization

For general (nonsymmetric) matrices $\boldsymbol{X}$, it is possible to introduce additional penalties to (7.2.11) in such a way that the general linear symmetry reduces to an orthogonal symmetry. At a high level, the idea is to add a penalty $\rho(\boldsymbol{U}, \boldsymbol{V})$ that enforces $\boldsymbol{U}^*\boldsymbol{U} \approx \boldsymbol{V}^*\boldsymbol{V}$; this prevents $\boldsymbol{U}$ and $\boldsymbol{V}$ from having vastly different scales.[14] The penalty ρ can be chosen to be $\mathsf{O}(r)$-symmetric, such that the combined problem

$$\min_{\boldsymbol{U}, \boldsymbol{V}} \; \varphi(\boldsymbol{U}, \boldsymbol{V}) \equiv \phi(\boldsymbol{U}, \boldsymbol{V}) + \rho(\boldsymbol{U}, \boldsymbol{V}) \tag{7.2.15}$$

possesses an $\mathsf{O}(r)$ symmetry: $\varphi(\boldsymbol{U}, \boldsymbol{V}) \equiv \varphi(\boldsymbol{U}\Gamma, \boldsymbol{V}\Gamma)$, for all $\Gamma \in \mathsf{O}(r)$.

Model Problems and the Matrix Recovery Zoo

There are many variants of matrix recovery, which are motivated by different applications and impose different assumptions on the observations and the noise [DR16, GJZ17, CLC19]. Although these problems have their own technical challenges, they

[13] For example, it is neither closed nor bounded.

[14] For example, $\rho(\boldsymbol{U}, \boldsymbol{V}) = \frac{1}{2}\|\boldsymbol{U}^*\boldsymbol{U} - \boldsymbol{V}^*\boldsymbol{V}\|_F$ accomplishes this.

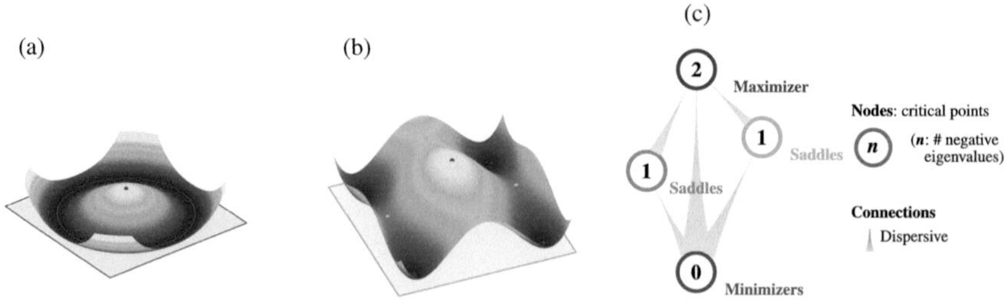

Figure 7.8 Geometry of Matrix Factorization. Geometry of a model problem in which the target $\boldsymbol{X}_o$ is a symmetric matrix of rank 2, with eigenvalues $\frac{3}{4}$ and $\frac{1}{2}$. (a) Plot of the objective φ over a slice of the domain containing all optimal solutions. (b) Two families of saddle points, corresponding to rank-1 approximations. (c) Objective value φ versus index for the four families of critical points in this problem. Again, the critical points are *graded*, in the sense that φ decreases with decreasing index, and the paths between them are dispersive, in the sense that downstream negative curvature directions are the image of upstream negative curvature directions under gradient flow.

have certain qualitative features in common. At a slogan level, "matrix *recovery* problems act like matrix *factorization* problems" [GJZ17]. In the next section, we will begin by describing in detail the geometry of matrix factorization, and then describe how these intuitions carry over to matrix recovery from incomplete or unreliable observations.

Geometry of Matrix Factorization

Our first model problem starts with a complete, noise-free observation $\boldsymbol{Y} = \boldsymbol{X}_o$ of a symmetric, positive semidefinite matrix $\boldsymbol{X}_o \in \mathbb{R}^{n \times n}$ of rank $r < n$, and attempts to factor it as $\boldsymbol{X}_o = \boldsymbol{U}\boldsymbol{U}^*$ by minimizing the misfit to the observed data [LLA+19]:

$$\min_{\boldsymbol{U} \in \mathbb{R}^{n \times r}} \varphi(\boldsymbol{U}) \doteq \frac{1}{4} \left\| \boldsymbol{Y} - \boldsymbol{U}\boldsymbol{U}^* \right\|_F^2. \tag{7.2.16}$$

This is a nonconvex optimization problem, with orthogonal symmetry $\varphi(\boldsymbol{U}) \equiv \varphi(\boldsymbol{U}\boldsymbol{\Gamma})$. Figure 7.8 visualizes the objective landscape for this problem. It turns out that the critical points of φ are dictated by the eigenvalue decomposition of the symmetric matrix $\boldsymbol{X}_o$ – *every critical point $\boldsymbol{U}$ is generated by selecting and appropriately scaling a subset of the eigenvectors of $\boldsymbol{X}_o$, and then applying a right rotation $\boldsymbol{U} \mapsto \boldsymbol{U}\boldsymbol{R}$*. At a slogan level, critical points correspond to "under factorizations" of the ground truth. Inspecting the Hessian, we find that:

- *Symmetric copies of the ground truth are minimizers.* Local minimizers are the critical points which select all of the top r eigenvectors, which correspond to the ground truth up to rotation symmetry.
- *Negative curvature in symmetry-breaking directions.* At a saddle point, there is strict negative curvature in any direction which increases the number of top eigenvectors that participate.

- *Cascade of saddle points.* Saddle points are critical points selecting subsets of the top r eigenvectors. These saddle points can be graded based on number of selected eigenvectors.[15]

Figure 7.8(b) visualizes these effects.

This model geometry carries over to nonsymmetric matrices. For example, considering a penalized low-rank estimation problem

$$\min_{U \in \mathbb{R}^{n_1 \times r}, V \in \mathbb{R}^{n_2 \times r}} \quad \varphi(U, V) \doteq \frac{1}{4} \left\| Y - U V^* \right\|_F^2 + \rho(U, V), \tag{7.2.17}$$

we obtain a problem with $\mathsf{O}(r)$ symmetry. Critical points are generated by appropriately scaling subsets of the *singular* vectors of Y. We leave the details to the reader as an exercise.

From Factorization to Matrix Recovery and Completion

We next describe how precise geometric analyses of matrix factorization extend to the more realistic problem of recovering a low-rank matrix from incomplete and unreliable observations, which we have studied in Chapter 4 via convex optimization. As we shall see, with their natural nonconvex formulations, the matrix recovery problems often retain important qualitative features of matrix factorization. We will illustrate this phenomenon through several instances of a model recovery problem, in which we observe m linear functions of an unknown matrix $X_o \in \mathbb{R}^{n_1 \times n_2}$:

$$y_i = \langle A_i, X_o \rangle, \quad 1 \le i \le m, \tag{7.2.18}$$

and the goal is to recover X_o. This model is flexible enough to represent matrix completion from missing entries [CR09], as well as more exotic sensing problems [RFP10, DR16]. We can write this observation model more compactly by defining a linear operator $\mathcal{A} : \mathbb{R}^{n_1 \times n_2} \to \mathbb{R}^m$ with $\mathcal{A}(X) := [\langle A_i, X \rangle]_{1 \le i \le m}$. In this notation,

$$y = \mathcal{A}(X). \tag{7.2.19}$$

If $m < n_1 n_2$, the number of observations is smaller than the number of unknowns, and the recovery problem is ill-posed. Fortunately, the matrices encountered in applications have low-complexity structures; for instance, they are usually low-rank or approximately so. As above, a rank-r X_o admits a factorization $X_o = U_o V_o^*$, so that we can enforce this low-rank structure by directly recovering the factors $U \in \mathbb{R}^{n_1 \times r}$ and $V \in \mathbb{R}^{n_2 \times r}$, up to symmetry.[16] A natural approach is to minimize the misfit to the observed data:

[15] A natural descent algorithm only visits at most r saddle points whose trajectory depends on the containment of the active eigenvectors at those saddle points.

[16] For simplicity, we here and below assume the rank r is known. As it turns out this is not so crucial: when r is not known, one may simply over-parameterize the matrix with larger factors $U \in \mathbb{R}^{n_1 \times n}$ and $V \in \mathbb{R}^{n_2 \times n}$ where n can be much larger than the true r. Then one can show that gradient descent algorithms in general converge to the correct low-rank solution. We leave the details as exercises for the reader.

$$\begin{aligned}\min_{U,V} \varphi(U,V) &\doteq \frac{1}{4m}\sum_{i=1}^{m}\left(y_i - \langle A_i, UV^*\rangle\right)^2 + \rho(U,V)\\ &= \frac{1}{4m}\left\|y - \mathcal{A}(UV^*)\right\|_F^2 + \rho(U,V),\end{aligned} \tag{7.2.20}$$

where as above ρ is a regularizer that encourages the factors to be balanced.

Matrix Sensing

If $\mathcal{A} = \mathcal{I}$ is the identity operator, (7.2.20) is simply the factorization problem. In this special situation, the measurement operator $\mathcal{A}$ *exactly* preserves the geometry of *all* $n_1 \times n_2$ matrices, in the sense that $\|\mathcal{A}[X]\|_F = \|X\|_F$ for all X. When the number of measurements is small ($m < n_1 n_2$), this is impossible. Fortunately, (7.2.20) still "behaves like factorization," and hence can be used to recover X_o, as long as $\mathcal{A}$ *approximately* preserves the geometry of the *low-rank* matrices – a much lower-dimensional set [PKCS16, BNS16, ZLTW18, LZT18, LLA+19].[17] When this approximation is sufficiently accurate, there is a bijection between the critical points of the sensing problem (7.2.20) and those of factorization, which preserves the index (number of negative eigenvalues). Under this condition, every local minimum of the sensing problem is global [BNS16].

Matrix Completion

The most practical and important instance of the general sensing model (7.2.20) is the *matrix completion* problem [CR09], in which the goal is to recover a low-rank matrix from a subset of $m < n_1 n_2$ entries, supported on, say, Ω. This model problem arises, for example, in collaborative filtering [RS05, Kor09], where the goal is to predict users' preferences for various products based on a few observed preferences. Variants of this problem also appear in sensor networks (determining positions of sensors from a few distance measurements) [BLWY06, SY07], imaging (recovering shape from illumination[18]) [WGS+10, ZYZY14], and the geosciences [YMO13, KDSA+15], just to name a few.

We have studied the matrix completion problem in great detail in Chapter 4 via the convex approach. Here, for its natural nonconvex formulation,

$$\min \frac{1}{4m}\left\|y - \mathcal{P}_\Omega(UV^*)\right\|_F^2 + \rho(U,V), \tag{7.2.21}$$

matrix completion also inherits the geometry of matrix factorization, with several technical caveats, which are consequences of the fact that it is challenging to recover X_o that are concentrated on a small number of entries: if we fail to sample these important entries, we will fail to recover X_o. This basic issue affects both the well-posedness of the matrix completion problem and our ability to solve it globally using nonconvex optimization. Local optimization methods could potentially become trapped in the

[17] This intuition can be formalized through the *rank restricted isometry property* (rank RIP) [RFP10, DR16], which we have also studied in Chapter 4.

[18] We will feature this particular application thoroughly in Chapter 14.

region of the space in which $\boldsymbol{U}\boldsymbol{V}^*$ is nearly sparse, since the measurements do not effectively sense such matrices. One simple fix is to add an additional regularizer on the rows $\boldsymbol{u}_i$ and $\boldsymbol{v}_i$ of the factors, which encourages them to have small norm. This forces the energy of $\boldsymbol{U}\boldsymbol{V}^*$ to be spread across many entries.[19] Ge et al. [GLM16] proved that the resulting problem has benign global geometry whenever we observe a sufficiently large random subset Ω and the target matrix $\boldsymbol{X}_o$ is not too concentrated on a few entries, in a precise technical sense.[20]

Robust Matrix Recovery

Many data analysis problems confront the analyst with datasets that are not only incomplete, but also corrupted. Robust matrix recovery is the problem of estimating a low-rank matrix $\boldsymbol{X}_o$ from such an unreliable observation (as we have seen in Chapter 5). Different models of corruption may be applicable in different application scenarios. For example, in imaging and vision, individual features (entries of the matrix) may be corrupted, e.g., due to occlusion [CLMW11, PGW+12]. This can be modeled as a sparse error: $\boldsymbol{Y} = \boldsymbol{X}_o + \boldsymbol{S}_o$, with both $\boldsymbol{X}_o = \boldsymbol{U}_o\boldsymbol{V}_o^*$ *and* $\boldsymbol{S}_o$ unknown. We may start from the natural formulation

$$\min_{\boldsymbol{U},\boldsymbol{V},\boldsymbol{S}} \tfrac{1}{2}\|\boldsymbol{U}\boldsymbol{V}^* + \boldsymbol{S} - \boldsymbol{Y}\|_F^2 + g_s(\boldsymbol{S}) + \rho_r(\boldsymbol{U},\boldsymbol{V}), \tag{7.2.22}$$

where $g_s(\boldsymbol{S})$ is a regularizer that encourages $\boldsymbol{S}$ to be sparse. Partially minimizing with respect to $\boldsymbol{S}$, we obtain

$$\min_{\boldsymbol{U},\boldsymbol{V}} \psi(\boldsymbol{U}\boldsymbol{V}^* - \boldsymbol{Y}) + \rho_r(\boldsymbol{U},\boldsymbol{V}), \tag{7.2.23}$$

where $\psi(\cdot)$ is a new function that measures data fidelity. For example, if g_s is a weighted ℓ^1 penalty $\lambda\|\cdot\|_1$, then ψ entry-wise is of the form

$$h_\lambda(u) \doteq \min_x \tfrac{1}{2}(u-x)^2 + \lambda|x|.$$

One can show that the so-defined h_λ is given by the so-called *Huber function* [Hub92]:

$$h_\lambda(u) = \begin{cases} \lambda|u| - \lambda^2/2 & |u| > \lambda, \\ u^2/2 & |u| \le \lambda. \end{cases} \tag{7.2.24}$$

We leave the verification as an exercise for the reader.

The problem (7.2.23) is again a matrix factorization problem, but with a different loss $\psi(\boldsymbol{U}\boldsymbol{V}^* - \boldsymbol{Y})$. While there are a number of open issues around the global (and even local! [LZSV20, CCD+19]) geometry of this problem, known results again suggest that for certain choices of g_s and ρ_r it indeed inherits the geometry of factorization [CLC19]. Similar to matrix completion, technical issues arise due to the possibility

[19] In detail, one can add a penalty $\rho_{\mathrm{mc}}(\boldsymbol{U},\boldsymbol{V}) = \lambda_1 \sum_{i=1}^{n_1} \left(\|\boldsymbol{e}_i^*\boldsymbol{U}\| - \alpha_1\right)_+^4 + \lambda_2 \sum_{j=1}^{n_2} \left(\|\boldsymbol{e}_j^*\boldsymbol{V}\| - \alpha_2\right)_+^4$ to (7.2.20).

[20] Formally, $\boldsymbol{X}_o$ is μ-incoherent, in the sense that for its compact SVD $\boldsymbol{X}_o = \boldsymbol{U}_o\boldsymbol{\Sigma}_o\boldsymbol{V}_o^*$, we have $\|\boldsymbol{e}_i^*\boldsymbol{U}_o\|_2 \le \sqrt{\mu r/n_1}$ and $\|\boldsymbol{e}_j^*\boldsymbol{V}_o\|_2 \le \sqrt{\mu r/n_2}$.

of encountering low-rank matrices $\boldsymbol{U}\boldsymbol{V}^*$ that are themselves sparse. If the regularizer ρ_r is chosen to discourage such solutions, it is possible to prove that the resulting objective function has no spurious local minimizers, and negative curvature at every nonminimizing critical point.

Equation (7.2.22) is just one model for matrix recovery from unreliable observations. Versions in which entire columns of $\boldsymbol{Y}$ are corrupted are also of interest for robust statistical estimation (see, e.g., [XCS10]), where they model outlying data vectors. Certain variants of this problem also inherit the geometry of factorization – local minimizers are global, saddle points are generated by partial factorizations of the ground-truth, and exhibit negative curvature in directions that introduce additional ground truth factors [LM18]. It is also possible to formulate this version of the robust matrix recovery problem as one of finding a hyperplane that contains the majority of the data points. This dual viewpoint leads to nonconvex problems with a sign symmetry, which again have benign geometry under certain conditions on the input data [TV18, ZWR$^+$18].

7.2.4 Other Nonconvex Problems with Rotational Symmetry

Other Low-Rank Recovery Problems

There are a number of nonlinear inverse problems that can be converted to rank-1 recovery problems, and hence inherit the good geometry of low-rank recovery. Examples include subspace deconvolution [ARR14, LLB16, LS17], phase synchronization [Bou16, LXB18, MMMO17, ZB18], community detection [BBV16], amongst others.

Deep and Linear Neural Networks

Most neural network learning problems are nonconvex. Neural network problems arising in practical deep learning typically exhibit complicated symmetries, which include compositions of permutations. For example, for a fully connected network, if we arbitrarily permute the order of the nodes in each intermediate layer, the network can represent the same function. *Linear* neural networks, whose predictions

$$\boldsymbol{y} \approx f(\boldsymbol{x}) = \boldsymbol{W}^L \boldsymbol{W}^{L-1} \cdots \boldsymbol{W}^0 \boldsymbol{x}$$

are a *linear* function of the input $\boldsymbol{x}$, have attracted attention as a more approachable object of theoretical investigation. This model exhibits rotational symmetries at each layer. Using similar considerations to those described above, [Kaw16] and related work prove that every local minimum is global. As with matrix factorization, critical points of natural optimization models correspond to "under factorizations." However, in contrast to matrix factorization, this problem does possess "flat" saddle points at which the Hessian has no negative eigenvalues – this is the result of the compound effect of symmetries at multiple layers. We will study more general and practical deep networks in Chapter 16. In particular, we will see how certain (symmetric) structural regularization, such as orthogonality for each layer $\boldsymbol{W}$, would be crucial for ensuring good performance of deep networks in practice.

7.3 Nonconvex Problems with Discrete Symmetries

In this section, we study nonconvex problems with discrete symmetry groups $\mathbb{G}$. Canonical examples include sparse dictionary learning (signed permutation symmetry) [SQW17a, SQW17b, QZL+19, ZYL+20], sparse blind deconvolution (signed shift symmetry) [ZLK+17, ZKW18, KZLW19, LQK+19, QLZ19, LB18], tensor decomposition [GHJY15, GM17], and clustering (permutation symmetry). Problems of this type are not easily amenable to convexification; understanding nonconvex optimization landscapes becomes critical. Design choices, such as the choice of objective function and constraints, also seem to play a critical role: many of the examples we review below are formulated as constrained optimization problems over compact manifolds such as spheres or orthogonal groups.[21] We again begin by studying a very simple model problem: *dictionary learning with one-sparse data*. We extract several key intuitions for problems with discrete symmetries, and then examine how these intuitions carry over to less idealized (and more useful!) problem settings.

7.3.1 Minimal Example: Dictionary Learning with One-Sparsity

We introduce some basic intuitions through a model problem, which is a highly idealized version of *dictionary learning*. In this model problem, we observe a matrix $\boldsymbol{Y}$ which is the product of an orthogonal matrix $\boldsymbol{A}_o \in \mathsf{O}(m)$ (called a dictionary) and a matrix $\boldsymbol{X}_o \in \mathbb{R}^{m\times n}$ whose columns are one-sparse, i.e., each column of $\boldsymbol{X}_o$ has one nonzero entry:

$$\underbrace{\boldsymbol{Y}}_{\textbf{data}} = \underbrace{\boldsymbol{A}_o}_{\textbf{orthogonal dictionary}} \underbrace{\boldsymbol{X}_o}_{\textbf{one-sparse coefficients}}. \tag{7.3.1}$$

This observation model exhibits a *signed permutation symmetry* ($\mathbb{G} = \mathsf{SP}(n)$): for a given pair $(\boldsymbol{A}_o, \boldsymbol{X}_o)$, and any $\boldsymbol{\Gamma} \in \mathsf{SP}(n)$, the pair $(\boldsymbol{A}_o\boldsymbol{\Gamma}, \boldsymbol{\Gamma}^*\boldsymbol{X}_o)$ also reproduces $\boldsymbol{Y}$. The goal is to recover $\boldsymbol{A}_o$ and $\boldsymbol{X}_o$, up to this symmetry.

A natural approach for recovering $\boldsymbol{A}_o$ is to search for an orthogonal matrix $\boldsymbol{A}$ such that $\boldsymbol{A}^*\boldsymbol{Y}$ is *as sparse as possible*:

$$\min\ h(\boldsymbol{A}^*\boldsymbol{Y}) \quad \text{such that} \quad \boldsymbol{A} \in \mathsf{O}(m), \tag{7.3.2}$$

where $h(\boldsymbol{X}) = \sum_{ij} h(\boldsymbol{X}_{ij})$ is a function that promotes sparsity. There are many possible choices for h [ZYL+20, LCD+19, SXZ+20] (and we will explore some in the exercises); for concreteness, here we take h to be the Huber function

$$h_\lambda(u) = \begin{cases} \lambda|u| - \lambda^2/2 & |u| > \lambda, \\ u^2/2 & |u| \le \lambda. \end{cases} \tag{7.3.3}$$

This can be viewed as a differentiable surrogate for the sparsity-promoting ℓ^1 norm.

[21] Optimization algorithms that exploit structures of such manifolds will be studied in Section 9.6 of Chapter 9.

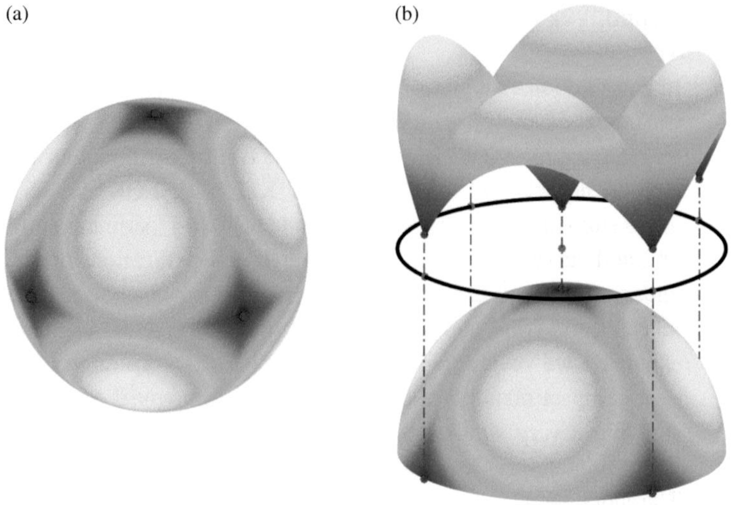

Figure 7.9 A Model Problem with Discrete Symmetry. The Huber function $h_\lambda(\boldsymbol{u})$ is a differentiable approximation to the ℓ^1 norm. Minimizing h_λ encourages sparsity. (a) This shows $h_\lambda(\boldsymbol{u})$ as a function on the sphere $\mathbb{S}^2$. Local minimizers (red) are signed standard basis vectors $\pm\boldsymbol{e}_i$. These are the maximally sparse vectors on $\mathbb{S}^2$. (b) Graph of h_λ; notice the strong negative curvature at points that are not sparse.

In (7.3.2), we solve for the entire dictionary $\boldsymbol{A} = [\boldsymbol{a}_1, \dots, \boldsymbol{a}_m]$ at once. An even simpler model problem can be formulated by instead solving for the columns $\boldsymbol{a}_i$ one at a time:

$$\min\ h_\lambda(\boldsymbol{a}^*\boldsymbol{Y}) \quad \text{such that} \quad \boldsymbol{a} \in \mathbb{S}^{m-1}. \tag{7.3.4}$$

Here, the goal is to recover a signed column $\pm\boldsymbol{a}_i$ of the dictionary $\boldsymbol{A}$.[22] This problem asks us to minimize an ℓ^1-like function over the sphere.[23]

To further simplify matters, we assume that the true dictionary $\boldsymbol{A}_o$ is the identity matrix. This does not change our geometric conclusions – changing to another $\boldsymbol{A}_o$ simply rotates the objective function. Similarly, since in this model problem each column of $\boldsymbol{X}_o$ has one nonzero entry, we lose little generality in taking $\boldsymbol{X}_o = \boldsymbol{I}$. With these idealizations, the problem simply becomes one of minimizing a sparsity surrogate over the sphere:

$$\min\ \varphi(\boldsymbol{a}) \equiv h_\lambda(\boldsymbol{a}) \quad \text{such that} \quad \boldsymbol{a} \in \mathbb{S}^{m-1}. \tag{7.3.5}$$

Here, recovering a signed column of the true dictionary $\boldsymbol{A}_o = \boldsymbol{I}$ corresponds to recovering one of the signed standard basis vectors $\pm\boldsymbol{e}_1, \dots, \pm\boldsymbol{e}_m$ in this model problem.

[22] The entire dictionary can be recovered by solving a sequence of problems of this type; see [SWW12, SQW17a, SQW17b].

[23] The problem (7.3.4) can also be interpreted geometrically as searching for a sparse vector in the linear subspace row($\boldsymbol{Y}$); see also [QSW14, QZL+20b].

Geometry of the Model Problem

The one-sparse dictionary learning model problem also exhibits a signed permutation symmetry: for any $\Gamma \in \mathsf{SP}(m)$, $\varphi(\Gamma \boldsymbol{a}) = \varphi(\boldsymbol{a})$. The set of target solutions $\pm \boldsymbol{e}_1, \ldots, \pm \boldsymbol{e}_m$ is also symmetric. Figure 7.9 plots the objective function, and these target solutions, in a three-dimensional example. Clearly, in this example, these target solutions are the only local minimizers.

To study this phenomenon more formally, we need to understand the slope (gradient) and curvature (Hessian) of φ as functions over the sphere $\mathbb{S}^{m-1}$. Recall that we encountered an optimization problem over the sphere in Section 4.2.1 of Chapter 4 when we characterized the computation of singular value decomposition (SVD). The sphere is a smooth manifold; its tangent space at a point $\boldsymbol{a}$ can be identified with $\boldsymbol{a}^{\perp}$:

$$T_{\boldsymbol{a}}\mathbb{S}^{m-1} = \left\{ \boldsymbol{\delta} \mid \boldsymbol{a}^*\boldsymbol{\delta} = 0 \right\}.$$

The orthogonal projector onto the tangent space is simply given by $\boldsymbol{P}_{\boldsymbol{a}^{\perp}} = \boldsymbol{I} - \boldsymbol{a}\boldsymbol{a}^*$. The slope of φ over the sphere (formally, the Riemannian gradient) is simply the component of the standard gradient that is tangent to the sphere:

$$\operatorname{grad}[\varphi](\boldsymbol{a}) = \boldsymbol{P}_{\boldsymbol{a}^{\perp}} \nabla \varphi(\boldsymbol{a}). \tag{7.3.6}$$

The curvature of φ over the sphere is slightly more complicated. For a direction $\boldsymbol{\delta} \in T_{\boldsymbol{a}}\mathbb{S}^{m-1}$, the second derivative of φ along the geodesic curve (great circle)[24]

$$\gamma(t) = \exp_{\boldsymbol{a}}(t\boldsymbol{\delta}) = \boldsymbol{a}\cos(t) + \boldsymbol{\delta}\sin(t),$$

is given by $\boldsymbol{\delta}^*\operatorname{Hess}[\varphi](\boldsymbol{a})\boldsymbol{\delta}$, where $\operatorname{Hess}[\varphi]$ is the *Riemannian Hessian*[25]

$$\operatorname{Hess}[\varphi](\boldsymbol{a}) = \boldsymbol{P}_{\boldsymbol{a}^{\perp}} \Big(\underbrace{\nabla^2 \varphi(\boldsymbol{a})}_{\textbf{curvature of } \varphi} - \underbrace{\langle \nabla \varphi(\boldsymbol{a}), \boldsymbol{a} \rangle \boldsymbol{I}}_{\textbf{curvature of the sphere}} \Big) \boldsymbol{P}_{\boldsymbol{a}^{\perp}}. \tag{7.3.7}$$

This expression contains two terms. The first is the standard (Euclidean) Hessian $\nabla^2\varphi$, which accounts for the curvature of the objective function φ. The second term accounts for the curvature of the sphere itself. Analogous to the case in Euclidean space, critical points are characterized by $\operatorname{grad}[\varphi](\boldsymbol{a}) = \mathbf{0}$; curvature can be studied through $\operatorname{Hess}[\varphi](\boldsymbol{a})$.[26]

To study the critical points, we begin by calculating the Euclidean gradient of φ given in (7.3.5):

$$\nabla \varphi(\boldsymbol{a}) = \lambda \operatorname{sign}(\boldsymbol{a}) \odot \mathbb{1}_{|\boldsymbol{a}|>\lambda} + \boldsymbol{a} \odot \mathbb{1}_{|\boldsymbol{a}|\leq\lambda}, \tag{7.3.8}$$

[24] Here $\exp(\cdot)$ represents the exponential map from a tangent vector, here $\boldsymbol{\delta}$, to a geodesic curve on a manifold, here the great circle on the sphere.

[25] This expression can be derived in a simple way by letting $\|\boldsymbol{\delta}\| = 1$, and calculating

$$\left.\frac{d^2}{dt^2}\right|_{t=0} \varphi\Big(\boldsymbol{a}\cos t + \boldsymbol{\delta}\sin t\Big).$$

We leave this as an exercise for the reader.

[26] For a more general reference to extending the notion of gradient and Hessian to optimization on manifolds, we refer readers to [AMS09].

where $\odot$ denotes element-wise multiplication. Using this expression, we can show that the Riemannian gradient vanishes ($\mathrm{grad}[\varphi](\boldsymbol{a}) = \mathbf{0}$) if and only if $\nabla\varphi(\boldsymbol{a}) \propto \boldsymbol{a}$ (here, $\propto$ denotes proportionality, i.e., there exists an s such that $\nabla\varphi(\boldsymbol{a}) = s\boldsymbol{a}$). This occurs whenever

$$\boldsymbol{a} \propto \mathrm{sign}(\boldsymbol{a}). \tag{7.3.9}$$

We can therefore index critical points by the support I and sign pattern $\boldsymbol{\sigma}$ of $\boldsymbol{a}$, writing $\boldsymbol{a}_{\mathsf{I},\sigma}$. To understand which critical points are minimizers or saddles, we can study the Hessian $\mathrm{Hess}[\varphi](\boldsymbol{a})$. The Euclidean Hessian is $\nabla^2\varphi(\boldsymbol{a}) = \mathbb{1}_{|\boldsymbol{a}|\le\lambda}$; its Riemannian counterpart is

$$\mathrm{Hess}[\varphi](\boldsymbol{a}_{\mathsf{I},\sigma}) = \boldsymbol{P}_{\boldsymbol{a}_{\mathsf{I},\sigma}^{\perp}} \left(\boldsymbol{P}_{|\boldsymbol{a}_{\mathsf{I},\sigma}|\le\lambda} - \lambda|\mathsf{I}|\boldsymbol{I}\right) \boldsymbol{P}_{\boldsymbol{a}_{\mathsf{I},\sigma}^{\perp}}. \tag{7.3.10}$$

At critical points $\boldsymbol{a}_{\mathsf{I},\sigma}$ the Hessian exhibits $|\mathsf{I}| - 1$ negative eigenvalues, and $m - |\mathsf{I}|$ positive eigenvalues. Based on these calculations, we obtain the following conclusions about the geometry of φ:

- *Symmetric copies of the ground truth are minimizers.* Local minimizers are the signed standard basis vectors $\boldsymbol{a} = \pm\boldsymbol{e}_i$ with the positive Riemannian Hessian; the objective function is strongly convex in the vicinity of local minimizers.
- *Negative curvature in symmetry-breaking directions.* Saddle points are balanced superpositions of target solutions: $\boldsymbol{a}_{\mathsf{I},\sigma} = (1/\sqrt{|\mathsf{I}|})\sum_{i\in\mathsf{I}}\sigma_i\boldsymbol{e}_i$ for $\mathsf{I} \subseteq \{1,\dots,m\}$ and signs $\sigma_i \in \{\pm 1\}$. There is negative curvature in directions $\boldsymbol{\delta} \in \mathrm{span}(\{\boldsymbol{e}_i \mid i \in \mathsf{I}\})$ that break the balance between target solutions.
- *Cascade of saddle points.* Saddle points are graded: points $\boldsymbol{a}_{\mathsf{I},\sigma}$ with larger objective value have more directions of negative curvature. Moreover, similar to the examples discussed in the last section, the objective function exhibits a "dispersive" structure: downstream negative curvature directions are the image of upstream negative curvature directions under gradient flow. This means that negative curvature upstream helps to prevent local gradient descent methods from stagnating near downstream saddle points.

The above phenomena are exactly opposite to the worst-case scenarios in which gradient descent may take exponential time to escape saddle points. For instance, the work [DJL+17] has constructed the so-called "octopus" function whose upstream unstable manifold is channeled into stable manifolds of downstream saddle points. As we see here, natural nonconvex programs associated with low-dimensional structures are far from such worst-case scenarios. In the following subsections, we will see how these basic phenomena recur in more practical nonconvex problems with discrete symmetries, including general dictionary learning (Section 7.3.2), blind deconvolution (Section 7.3.3), and others.

7.3.2 Dictionary Learning

The one-sparse dictionary learning problem is an extreme simplification of the basic modern data processing problem: seeking a concise representation of data. The goal of dictionary learning is to produce a sparse model for an observed dataset $Y = [y_1, \dots, y_p] \in \mathbb{R}^{m \times p}$. Namely, we seek matrices $A_o \in \mathbb{R}^{m \times n}$ and $X_o \in \mathbb{R}^{n \times p}$ such that

$$Y \approx \underbrace{A_o}_{\textbf{dictionary}} \underbrace{X_o}_{\textbf{sparse coefficients}}, \tag{7.3.11}$$

with X_o as sparse as possible. Sparsity is desirable for data compression, and to facilitate tasks such as sensing, denoising, super-resolution, etc. [WMM+10, Ela10].

In the representation (7.3.11), the data points y_j are approximated as superpositions $y_j \approx A_o x_{oj}$ of a few columns of the matrix $A_o = [a_{01}, \dots, a_{0n}]$. This matrix is sometimes called a *dictionary*. Clearly, the size of the dictionary, n, has an impact on the accuracy, sparsity, and utility of this data representation. The appropriate dictionary size depends on application: for learning from a single image, a complete $(n = m)$ dictionary may suffice, whereas for learning from larger collections of images, an overcomplete $(n > m)$ dictionary may be more appropriate [MKD06, EA06, YWHM10]. Below, we discuss how our basic intuitions from the orthogonal, one-sparse case carry over to each of these more realistic model problems.

Complete Dictionary Learning

Let us first consider the complete case $n = m$, in which $A_o \in \mathbb{R}^{n \times n}$ is a square invertible matrix. There are two basic issues in moving from the one-sparse dictionary learning problem to more general complete dictionary learning problems. First, the target dictionary A_o may not be orthogonal. Second, the columns of the coefficient matrix X_o are generally not one-sparse. For theoretical purposes, both of these issues can be addressed using probabilistic properties of X_o. First, using the statistics of $Y = A_o X_o$ it is possible to reduce the problem of learning a general invertible $A_o \in \mathsf{GL}(n)$ to one of learning an orthogonal matrix $\bar{A} = \left(A_o A_o^*\right)^{-1/2} A_o$. Concretely, if X_o is a sparse random matrix with independent symmetric entries, then

$$\bar{Y} = \left(Y Y^*\right)^{-1/2} Y \propto \bar{A} X_o$$

satisfies a sparse model with orthogonal dictionary $\bar{A} \in \mathsf{O}(n)$.

Similar to our discussion above, one can recover the columns of A by solving the optimization problem for a sparsity-promoting function h:

$$\min \ \varphi(a) \equiv h\left(a^* \bar{Y}\right) \quad \text{such that} \quad a \in \mathbb{S}^{n-1}. \tag{7.3.12}$$

This is essentially to find a sparse vector $a^* \bar{Y}$ in the row space of X_o. If we repeat this process m times, we in principle can recover all the n sparse rows of X_o. Although the columns of X_o are not one-sparse, when the number of samples is large, this objective function retains all of the qualitative properties observed in the one-sparse problem, including local minimizers near symmetric solutions and saddle points near balanced superpositions of symmetric solutions, with negative curvature in symmetry-breaking directions. The proofs of these properties rely heavily on probabilistic reasoning: one argues that the "population" objective function $\mathbb{E}[\varphi]$ has benign structure, and then argues that when the number p of samples is large, the gradients and Hessians of φ

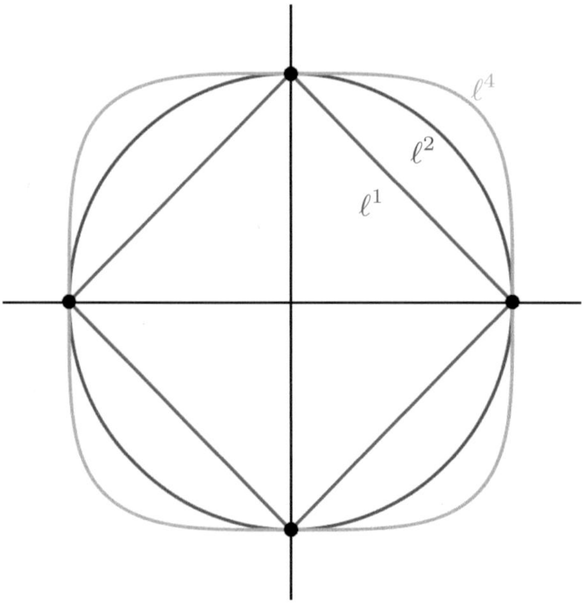

Figure 7.10 Illustration of the ℓ^1 ball, ℓ^2 ball, and ℓ^4 ball in $\mathbb{R}^2$.

are uniformly close to those of $\mathbb{E}[\varphi]$, and hence φ has the same benign properties [SQW17a, SQW17b].

In early chapters, we have studied the ℓ^1 norm extensively as it is the (unique) convex envelope of the sparse ℓ^0 norm. Nevertheless, once we consider nonconvex surrogates, there are many more choices of sparsity-promoting functions. Some can be extremely effective when the optimization domain is confined to a structured space such as the sphere. For example, it is easy to show that the maximizers of the ℓ^4 norm of a vector $\boldsymbol{x} \in \mathbb{R}^n$ over the sphere $\mathbb{S}^{n-1}$ are equivalent to minimizers of the ℓ^0norm over the sphere:

$$argmax_{\boldsymbol{x}\in\mathbb{S}^{n-1}} \|\boldsymbol{x}\|_4 = argmin_{\boldsymbol{x}\in\mathbb{S}^{n-1}} \|\boldsymbol{x}\|_0 . \tag{7.3.13}$$

Figure 7.10 illustrates the relationships of the ℓ^1, ℓ^2, and ℓ^4 balls. Notice that for points on the sphere (the ℓ^2 ball), points that minimize the ℓ^1 norm coincide with those that maximize the ℓ^4 norm.

Hence given $\bar{\boldsymbol{Y}}$, in order to find the orthogonal dictionary $\bar{\boldsymbol{A}}$, we may consider solving the following (nonconvex) ℓ^4 norm maximization problem over the orthogonal group $\mathsf{O}(n)$:

$$\max \ \|\boldsymbol{A}^*\bar{\boldsymbol{Y}}\|_4^4 \quad \text{subject to} \quad \boldsymbol{A}^* \in \mathsf{O}(n). \tag{7.3.14}$$

It has been shown that with sufficient samples, say p the order of $O(n^2 \log n)$, the global maximizers of the above program are the correct dictionary [ZYL+20]. The overall landscape is rather benign and leads to a very efficient power-iteration-like algorithm [ZYL+20, ZMZM20].[27] We will leave the algorithmic details as an exercise for the reader and study it more in Chapter 9.

Overcomplete Dictionary Learning

In practice, *overcomplete* dictionaries, in which the number of dictionary atoms n is larger than the signal dimension m, are often favored compared to complete dictionaries. Overcomplete dictionaries have greater expressive power, yielding sparser coefficient matrices $\boldsymbol{X}$. Our current theoretical understanding of the objective landscape associated with overcomplete dictionary learning is still developing. One suggestive result shows that when the dictionary is moderately overcomplete ($n \leq 3m$), under appropriate technical hypotheses, a formulation based on maximizing the ℓ^4 norm exhibits benign global geometry [QZL+19]: again, every local minimizer is global and saddle points exhibit strict negative curvature.[28] These results suggest that overcomplete dictionary learning problems can exhibit benign global geometry; there are a number of open questions around

1 the degree of overcompleteness n/m that this structure can tolerate and
2 the extent to which similar properties hold in more conventional *synthesis* dictionary learning formulations, in which one optimizes over both $\boldsymbol{A}$ and $\boldsymbol{X}$ simultaneously.

7.3.3 Sparse Blind Deconvolution

Convolutional models arise in a wide range of problems in imaging and data analysis. The most basic convolutional data model expresses an observation $\boldsymbol{y}$ as the convolution of two signals $\boldsymbol{a}_o$ and $\boldsymbol{x}_o$. *Blind deconvolution* aims to recover $\boldsymbol{a}_o$ and $\boldsymbol{x}_o$ from the observation $\boldsymbol{y} = \boldsymbol{a}_o \circledast \boldsymbol{x}_o$, up to certain intrinsic symmetries that we describe below. This problem is ill-posed in general – there are infinitely many $(\boldsymbol{a}_o, \boldsymbol{x}_o)$ that convolve to produce $\boldsymbol{y}$. To make progress, some low-dimensional priors about $\boldsymbol{a}_o$ and $\boldsymbol{x}_o$ are essential. Different priors yield different nonconvex optimization problems; in this section, we will focus on several variants of blind deconvolution with sparsity priors on $\boldsymbol{x}_o$, and then briefly mention other popular variants of blind deconvolution.

[27] The algorithm has been shown to converge superlinearly locally and overwhelming empirical evidence shows that it always converges to the globally optimal solution. However, a rigorous proof of its global optimality remains an open problem [ZYL+20]. The authors of the book are offering a thousand dollars for anyone who can provide such a proof.

[28] When the dictionary is overcomplete, dictionary atoms $\boldsymbol{a}_i$ are correlated and $\boldsymbol{a}^*\bar{\boldsymbol{Y}}$ is no longer sparse, even if $\boldsymbol{a}$ is chosen as one of the atoms $\boldsymbol{a}_i$. Rather, at $\boldsymbol{a} = \boldsymbol{a}_i$, $\boldsymbol{a}^*\bar{\boldsymbol{Y}}$ is *spiky*, with a few large entries amongst many small ones. ℓ^4 maximization is well suited to encouraging this kind of spikiness. The most widely used practical dictionary learning algorithms are based on synthesis sparsity. Understanding the global geometry of this kind of formulation remains an important open problem.

Short and Sparse (SaS) Blind Deconvolution

Analyzing signals comprising repeated motifs is a common task in areas such as neuroscience, materials science, astronomy, and natural and scientific imaging [SPM02, PSG$^+$16, CSL$^+$20, LQK$^+$19]. Such signals can be modeled as the *convolution* of a short motif $\boldsymbol{a}_o$ and a sparse coefficient signal $\boldsymbol{x}_o$, which encodes where the motif occurs in time/space. Mathematically, the observation $\boldsymbol{y} \in \mathbb{R}^m$ is the windowed[29] convolution of the short $\boldsymbol{a}_o$, which is supported on k ($k \ll m$) consecutive entries and the sparse $\boldsymbol{x}_o$:

$$\boldsymbol{y} = \mathcal{P}_m \left[\boldsymbol{a}_o \circledast \boldsymbol{x}_o \right]. \tag{7.3.15}$$

Here, $\circledast$ denotes linear convolution and $\mathcal{P}_m(\cdot)$ retains the entries supported on indices $0, \ldots, m-1$.

The inverse problem of recovering $\boldsymbol{a}_o$ and $\boldsymbol{x}_o$ from $\boldsymbol{y}$ is called *short and sparse* blind deconvolution (SaS-BD) [ZLK$^+$17, ZKW18, KZLW19]. The linear convolution $\circledast$ exhibits a *signed shift symmetry*:

$$\boldsymbol{a}_o \circledast \boldsymbol{x}_o = \alpha s_\tau[\boldsymbol{a}_o] \circledast \alpha^{-1} s_{-\tau}[\boldsymbol{x}_o]. \tag{7.3.16}$$

Here α is some nonzero scalar and $s_\tau[\boldsymbol{v}]$ denotes a shift of vector $\boldsymbol{v}$ by τ entries, i.e., $s_\tau[\boldsymbol{v}](i) = \boldsymbol{v}(i - \tau)$. As with the other nonconvex problems we have studied up to this point, we should expect this symmetry to play a critical role in shaping the landscape of optimization – in particular, we would expect the *global* minimizers to be symmetric copies of the ground truth.[30]

Symmetry Breaking?

However, there is a wrinkle: in order to obtain a finite-dimensional optimization problem, one typically constrains the length-k signal $\boldsymbol{a}_o$ to be supported on $\{0, \ldots, k-1\}$. This constraint appears to remove the shift symmetry: now only a scaled version $(\alpha \boldsymbol{a}_o, \alpha^{-1}\boldsymbol{x}_o)$ of the truth exactly reproduces the observation. Perhaps surprisingly, even with this constraint, symmetry *still* shapes the landscape of optimization. However, instead of dictating the global minimizers, in constrained formulations, symmetry dictates the *local* minimizers. The reason is simple: a shift of $\boldsymbol{a}_o$ by τ samples is not supported on $\{0, \ldots, k-1\}$, and hence is not feasible. However, its truncation to $\{0, \ldots, k-1\}$ *is* feasible, and still approximates $\boldsymbol{y}$:

$$\boldsymbol{y} \approx \mathcal{P}_k \left[s_\tau[\boldsymbol{a}_o] \right] \circledast s_{-\tau}[\boldsymbol{x}_o]. \tag{7.3.17}$$

Because this approximation is not perfect, truncated shifts are not global minimizers. However, they are very close to *local* minimizers [ZLK$^+$17, ZKW18]. These points have suboptimal objective value and do not exactly reproduce $(\boldsymbol{a}_o, \boldsymbol{x}_o)$. Despite this,

[29] Rather than having complete access to the convolved signal (which could be infinitely long), we observe m consecutive entries of it.

[30] Notice that the scale and shift symmetries are intrinsic to the convolution operator in (7.3.15). Although we focus on *sparse* deconvolution, these symmetries will persist in deconvolution with any shift-invariant structural model for $\boldsymbol{a}_o$ and $\boldsymbol{x}_o$. Moreover, as we will see below, they persist even in the presence of artificial symmetry-breaking mechanisms, in the sense that they still dictate the local minimizers.

the optimization landscape is still sufficiently benign[31] that it is possible to exactly recover $(\boldsymbol{a}_o, \boldsymbol{x}_o)$ with efficient methods – one can, for example, first find a local minimizer that is close to a truncated shift of $\boldsymbol{a}_o$, and then refine it to exactly recover $\boldsymbol{a}_o$.

This problem illustrates how hard it is to avoid symmetry in studying deconvolution problems: even with an explicit symmetry-breaking constraint, symmetry still shapes the landscape of optimization! The main motivation for studying this more complicated deconvolution model is its applicability (as we will see in Chapter 12 for an application in scientific imaging). Giving formulations that better respect the symmetry structure, and hence have no spurious local minimizers, remains an important open problem.

Multi-Channel Sparse (MCS) Blind Deconvolution

The problem of *multi-channel sparse blind deconvolution* assumes access to multiple observations $\boldsymbol{y}_i = \boldsymbol{a}_o \circledast \boldsymbol{x}_i \in \mathbb{R}^k$ generated from circular convolution (also denoted by $\circledast$) of $\boldsymbol{a}_o \in \mathbb{R}^k$ and distinct sparse signals $\boldsymbol{x}_i$ [LB18, QLZ19, QZL+19, SC19]. Here, shift symmetry becomes a *cyclic* shift symmetry: there exist k equivalent solutions corresponding to k different cyclic shifts. The resulting optimization landscape exhibits similar characteristics to that of complete dictionary learning, described in Section 7.3.1 and Figure 7.9. In particular, any local minimizer is a scaled cyclic shift of the ground truth [LB18, QLZ19, SC19].

Geometry of Sparse Blind Deconvolution

Despite the technical difference of the convolution operator in MCS and SaS blind deconvolution problems, their optimization landscapes share the following key phenomena:

- *Symmetric copies of the ground truth are minimizers.* In the above two variants of sparse blind deconvolution problems, the local minimizers are either a cyclic shifted or shifted truncation of the ground truth under conditions. Both can be viewed as a result of the inherent shift symmetry.
- *Negative curvature in symmetry-breaking directions.* Near saddle points, there is negative curvature in the direction of any particular (truncated) shifted copy of the ground truth, and the objective value decreases by moving towards this symmetry-breaking direction.
- *Cascade of saddle points.* The saddle points are approximately balanced superpositions of several shifts of the ground truth. The more shifts participate, the larger the objective value and the more negative eigenvalues the Hessian exhibits.

Other Blind Deconvolution Variants

Subspace blind deconvolution is another widely studied variant of blind deconvolution that leverages a low-dimensional model for the pair $(\boldsymbol{a}_o, \boldsymbol{x}_o)$. In this variant, $\boldsymbol{a}_o$ and $\boldsymbol{x}_o$ are assumed to lie on known low-dimensional subspaces [ARR14]. This problem can

[31] In particular, there is negative curvature in symmetry-breaking directions.

be cast as a rank-1 matrix recovery problem, which exhibits a similar geometry to the problems studied in Section 7.2.

Convolutional dictionary learning extends the basic convolution model by allowing for multiple basic motifs $\boldsymbol{a}_1, \dots, \boldsymbol{a}_N$ [GCW18]. More precisely, we observe one or more signals of the form $\boldsymbol{y} = \sum_{i=1}^{N} \boldsymbol{a}_i \circledast \boldsymbol{x}_i$, and the goal is to recover all the $\boldsymbol{a}_i$ and $\boldsymbol{x}_i$. In addition to the symmetries inherited from the convolution operator, this problem processes an additional *permutation symmetry*: permuting the index i does not change the approximation to $\boldsymbol{y}$. Despite this additional complexity, empirically local minimizers remain symmetric copies of the ground truth [ZLK$^+$17, LQK$^+$19]; under certain technical hypotheses, one can prove that natural first-order algorithms always recover one such symmetric copy [QZL$^+$19].

In fact, one may model natural images to be (sparsely) generated by such a convolutional dictionary. In some applications, it may not be necessary to recover the dictionary $\{\boldsymbol{a}_i\}$ and sparse codes $\{\boldsymbol{x}_i\}$ precisely. For example, we only want to classify similar images into the same category. But the assumption of such a model is crucial for obtaining an (approximately) correct solution, say via a deep network. We will discuss the connection of this type of model to deep (convolutional) networks in Chapter 16.

7.3.4 Other Nonconvex Problems with Discrete Symmetry

Symmetric Tensor Decomposition

Tensors can be regarded as a high-dimensional generalization of matrices. Tensor decomposition problems find many applications in statistics, data science, and machine learning [KB09, AGH$^+$14, SDLF$^+$17, JGKA19]. Although we can usually generalize algebraic notions from matrices to tensors, their counterparts in tensors are often not as well behaved or easy to compute [KB09]. In fact, many natural tensor problems are NP-hard in the worst case [HL13].

Nonetheless, recent results suggest that certain appealing special cases of tensor decomposition are tractable [AGH$^+$14, GHJY15, JGKA19]. This is especially true for orthogonal tensor decomposition, where the task is to decompose a p-th-order symmetric tensor into these orthogonal components. More specifically, an orthogonal tensor $\mathcal{T}$ can be represented in the following form:

$$\mathcal{T} = \sum_{k=1}^{r} \boldsymbol{a}_k^{\otimes p}, \quad r \le n, \tag{7.3.18}$$

with $\{\boldsymbol{a}_k\}_{k=1}^{r}$ a collection of orthogonal vectors, and $\boldsymbol{a}^{\otimes p}$ denotes the p-way outer product of a vector $\boldsymbol{a}$. The orthogonal tensor decomposition shares many similarities with the other nonconvex problems with discrete symmetry discussed above:

- The problem exhibits a *signed permutation symmetry* which is similar to dictionary learning: given $\mathcal{T}$ we can only hope to recover the orthogonal components $\{\boldsymbol{a}_k\}_{k=1}^{r}$ up to order permutation.

- When p is even order, as shown in Figure 7.5, a natural nonconvex formulation

$$\min_{\boldsymbol{x} \in \mathbb{S}^{n-1}} -\mathcal{T}(\boldsymbol{x}, \dots, \boldsymbol{x}) = -\left\| \boldsymbol{A}^* \boldsymbol{x} \right\|_p^p \quad \text{with} \quad \boldsymbol{A} = \begin{bmatrix} \boldsymbol{a}_1 & \cdots & \boldsymbol{a}_r \end{bmatrix} \tag{7.3.19}$$

  manifests a similar optimization landscape, for which every local minimizer is close to one of the signed orthogonal components and other critical points exhibit strict negative curvature.

These results have inspired further endeavors beyond orthogonal tensors [QZL+19, SBRL19, GM17]. One particular case of interest is decomposing a symmetric tensor $\mathcal{T}$ in (7.3.18) with $r > n$ and nonorthogonal $\{\boldsymbol{a}_k\}_{k=1}^r$, which is often referred to as *overcomplete* tensor decomposition. In particular, when $p = 4$, $r \in O(n^{1.5})$, and $\{\boldsymbol{a}_k\}_{k=1}^r$ are i.i.d. Gaussian, [GM17] show that (7.3.19) has no bad local minimizer over a level set whose measure geometrically shrinks with respect to the problem dimension; for $p = 4$, $r < 3n$, and incoherent $\{\boldsymbol{a}_k\}_{k=1}^r$, [QZL+19] presented a global analysis for overcomplete tensor decomposition, disclosing its connection to overcomplete dictionary learning. Nonetheless, these results are still far from providing a complete understanding of overcomplete tensor decomposition. One interesting question that remains largely open is when bad local minimizers exist for large rank $r \gg n$ in the nonorthogonal case.

Clustering

Clustering is arguably the most fundamental problem in unsupervised learning. This problem possesses a *permutation symmetry*: one can generate equivalent clusters by permuting the indices for cluster centers. Popular nonconvex algorithms include the Lloyd algorithm and variants of expectation maximization. Despite the broad applications and empirical success of these methods, few theoretical guarantees have been obtained until recently. The problem of demixing two balanced, identical data clusters manifests global convergence to (a symmetric copy of) the ground truth [BWY17, XHM16, DTZ16, QZC19, KQC+19]. We see similar geometric properties hold here: *symmetric copies of the ground truth are minimizers* and *saddle points exhibit directions of strict negative curvature*. Moreover, the saddle points are also located at balanced superpositions of local minimizers. Sometimes, these saddle points may contain redundant cluster estimates. In this case, the redundant cluster estimates can be interpreted as an under parameterized solution (with a smaller k specified).

However, in general clustering problems with more than two clusters, local minimizers provably exist [DS07, JZB+16]. When the clusters are sufficiently separated, these local minimizers possess characteristic structures [QZC20]: they correspond to imbalanced segmentations of the data, in which a subset of the true clusters are optimally under segmented and another subset is optimally over segmented.

Deep Neural Networks

Deep neural networks have more complicated symmetry groups than the problems described above. For example, natural objective functions associated with fitting a fully connected neural network are invariant under simultaneous permutations of the features at *each* layer. We currently lack tools for reasoning about the global geometry of such problems. However, progress has been made on certain special cases: for example, certain problems associated with fitting shallow networks share similar geometry to tensor decomposition [JSA15, MM18]. With varying technical assumptions, all local solutions have been shown to be global in a single-layer neural network [HV17, FJZT17, GLM17, GMOV18, SJL18]. However, general deep nonlinear neural networks can exhibit flat saddles and spurious local minimizers [SS17, VBGS17]. We refer interested readers to [Sun19b] for more comprehensive developments on optimization theory and algorithms of deep learning.

In Chapter 16, we will study deep learning from the perspective of learning discriminative low-dimensional representations. We will see how data clustering and representation learning can be naturally unified in a nonconvex objective function that inherits the rich symmetric structures of both deep networks and data clustering.

Fourier Phase Retrieval

The problem of *Fourier* phase retrieval is crucial to scientific imaging. In this problem, the goal is to recover $\boldsymbol{x}_o$ from observation $\boldsymbol{y} = |\mathcal{F}(\boldsymbol{x}_o)|$. Apart from the rotational (phase) symmetry, the problem of Fourier phase retrieval manifests two additional symmetries:[32] *(cyclic) shift symmetry* $|\mathcal{F}(\boldsymbol{x})| = |\mathcal{F}(s_\tau[\boldsymbol{x}])|$ and *conjugate inversion symmetry* $|\mathcal{F}(\boldsymbol{x})| = \left|\mathcal{F}(\check{\boldsymbol{x}})\right|$, where $\check{\boldsymbol{x}}(n) = \bar{\boldsymbol{x}}(-n)$ [BDE17]. This complicated symmetry structure is reflected in a complicated optimization landscape, which is challenging to study analytically. Many basic problems in the algorithmic theory of Fourier phase retrieval remain open.

7.4 Notes and Open Problems

In this chapter, we have reviewed recent advances in provable nonconvex methods for signal processing and machine learning, through the lens of symmetry. It is an exciting time to work on both the theory and practice of nonconvex optimization. For complementary perspectives on the area, we refer interested readers to other recent review papers [JK17, Sun19a, CLC19, QZL$^+$20b]. In the following, we close by discussing several methodological points and general directions for future work.

Convexification

In the past decades, convex relaxation has been demonstrated to be a powerful tool for solving nonconvex problems such as sparse recovery (Chapters 2 and 3), low-rank matrix completion (Chapters 4 and 5), and even more general atomic structures (Chapter 6). For these problems, convex relaxation achieves near-optimal sample complexity. Which nonconvex problems are amenable to convex relaxation? There are general results that suggest that *unimodal* functions (i.e., functions with one local

[32] When $\boldsymbol{x}$ is one-dimensional, the problem becomes even more pessimistic – there exist multiple one-dimensional signals with the same Fourier magnitude, but not related by an obvious symmetry.

minimizer) on convex sets can be convexified, by endowing the space with an appropriate geometry [RC93].[33] The symmetric problems encountered in this survey are not unimodal. The degree to which they are amenable to convex relaxation varies substantially:

- *Problems with rotational symmetry.* Many problems with rotational symmetry *can* be convexified by lifting to a higher-dimensional space [CR09, CLMW11, CSV13], e.g., by replacing the factor $\boldsymbol{U}$ with a matrix-valued variable $\boldsymbol{X} = \boldsymbol{U}\boldsymbol{U}^*$. This collapses the $\mathsf{O}(r)$ symmetry; the resulting problems can often be converted to semidefinite programs and solved globally. Typically, nonconvex formulations are still preferred in practice, due to their scalability to large datasets. Section 7.2 and the references therein describe alternative geometric principles that help to explain the success of these methods.
- *Problems with discrete symmetry.* Most of the discrete symmetric problems described in Section 7.3 do not admit simple convex relaxations. For example, complete dictionary learning can be reduced to a sequence of linear programs [SWW12], but only in the highly sparse case, in which the target sparse representation has $O(\sqrt{n})$ nonzero entries per length-n data vector. These limitations are attributable in part to the more complicated discrete symmetry structure. Natural ideas, such as taking a quotient by the symmetry group, encounter obstacles at both the conceptual and implementation levels. One general methodology which *does* meet with success in this setting is sum-of-squares relaxation, which for variants of dictionary learning and tensor decomposition leads to quasi-polynomial- or even polynomial-time algorithms [BKS15].

Efficient First-Order Algorithms

In this chapter, we have described families of symmetric nonconvex optimization problems with benign global geometry: local minimizers are global and saddle points exhibit strict negative curvature. Although we have not emphasized algorithmic aspects of these problems, this geometric structure *does* have strong implications for computation – for a variety of methods the key is leveraging negative curvature to efficiently obtain minimizers. We will provide a systematic introduction to nonconvex optimization algorithms and their convergence and complexity properties in Chapter 9.

One class of methods explicitly models negative curvature, e.g., using a second-order approximation to the objective function. Methods in this class include trust region methods [CGT00], cubic regularization [NP06], and curvilinear search [Gol80]. These methods can be challenging to scale to very large problems, since they typically require computation and storage of the Hessian. It is also possible to leverage negative curvature using more scalable first-order methods such as gradient

[33] These are existence results; their direct implications for efficient computation are limited, since they apply to NP-hard problems. It is also worth noting that many of our discrete symmetric problems in Section 7.3 are formulated over compact manifolds such as $\mathbb{S}^{n-1}$; the only continuous geodesically convex function on a compact Riemannian manifold is a constant [BO69, Yau74].

descent. In the vicinity of a saddle point, the gradient method essentially performs a power iteration which moves in directions of negative curvature. Although this scheme *can* stagnate at or near saddle points, it is possible to guarantee efficient escape by perturbing the iterates with an appropriate amount of random noise [GHJY15, JGN$^+$17, JNJ18, CB19, SFF19].

The methods described above are efficient across the broad class of *strict saddle functions* [GHJY15, SQW15], i.e., functions whose saddle points all have directions of strict negative curvature. This is a worst-case performance guarantee. Perhaps surprisingly, the most widely used first-order method, gradient descent, is not efficient for worst-case strict saddle functions: although randomly initialized gradient descent *does* obtain a minimizer with probability one [LSJR16, LPP$^+$19], for certain functions it can take time exponential in dimension [DJL$^+$17]. These challenging functions have a large number of saddle points, which are conspicuously arranged such that upstream negative curvature directions align with *positive* curvature directions for downstream saddle points.

This worst-case behavior is in some sense the opposite of what is observed in the type of highly symmetric functions studied here: functions encountered in generalized phase retrieval [CCFM18], dictionary learning [GBW19], deconvolution[QLZ19, SC19], etc., exhibit a global negative curvature structure, in which upstream negative curvature directions align with *negative* curvature directions of downstream saddle points. In this situation, *randomly initialized gradient descent is efficient.* This points to another gap between naturally occurring nonconvex optimization problems and their worst-case counterparts. There is substantial room for future work in this direction.

Disciplined Formulations and Analysis

Our understanding of nonconvex optimization is still far from satisfactory – analyses are delicate, case-by-case, and pertain to problems with elementary symmetry (e.g., rotation or permutation) and simple constraints (e.g., the sphere or simple homogeneous spaces).

- *A unified theory.* Analogous to the study of convex functions [BV04], there is a pressing need for simpler analytic tools, to identify and generalize benign properties for new nonconvex problems, despite some recent endeavors [QZL$^+$19, LCD$^+$19] of identifying general conditions and operations preserving benign geometric structures. Unlike the convex case in which convex surrogates are typically unique, one can have multiple nonconvex surrogates for the same problem. For instance, to promote low-rankedness of a matrix, one could choose to use the log det function [FHB03], random dropout in training deep neural networks [SHK$^+$14], or over parameterization with matrix products (see the exercises). Nevertheless, as we will see, those surrogates are fundamentally related to the convex surrogates (such as the nuclear norm) and yet offer other benefits such as simpler implementation or a broader range of working conditions.
- *Complicated symmetries and constraints.* Practical nonconvex problems often involve *multiple symmetries* (e.g., Fourier phase retrieval and deep neural networks)

and/or *complicated manifolds* (e.g., Stiefel manifolds [HLWY19]). We need better technical tools to understand the impact of compound symmetries (especially compound discrete symmetries) on the optimization landscape, despite some steps in this direction [LCD+19, HLWY19, ZYL+20]. More interesting and challenging phenomena arise when the symmetry of the problem and manifold/group structure of the domain are intertwined. For instance, in dictionary learning via ℓ^4 maximization, we have both the signed permutation symmetry $\mathsf{SP}(n)$ and the orthogonal group $\mathsf{O}(n)$. In Section 9.6 of Chapter 9, we will see that power-iteration or fixed-point-type algorithms are very natural and effective in exploiting such manifold structures. However, unified analyses and understandings for broader problem classes are still lacking.

- *Nonsmoothness.* In many scenarios we encounter nonconvex problems with *nonsmooth* functions [DDMP18, DD18, LZSV20, LCD+19, BJS19, ZWR+18, CDDD19, CCD+19], for better promoting solution sparsity or robustness. As we will see in Chapter 8, in the convex setting, nonsmoothness usually can be dealt with very effectively. However, in the nonconvex setting, most of our current analysis is local [CDDD19, LCD+19], and (subgradient) optimization [LCD+19, BJS19, ZWR+18] could be slow to converge. Attempts to obtain global analyses and fast optimization methods might benefit from more sophisticated tools from variational analysis [RW09] and development of efficient second-order or higher-order methods [DR19].

7.5 Exercises

7.1. *In this section, we study how to derive the Huber function given in* (7.2.24). *First, find a closed-form solution to the problem:*

$$x_\star(u) = \arg\min_x \tfrac{1}{2}(u - x)^2 + \lambda |x|.$$

Then, show that the function

$$h_\lambda(u) \doteq \min_x \tfrac{1}{2}(u - x)^2 + \lambda |x| = \tfrac{1}{2}(u - x_\star)^2 + \lambda |x_\star|$$

has the same form as the Huber function (7.2.24).

7.2. (Complete dictionary learning via ℓ^4 norm maximization) *In this exercise, we derive and practice an algorithm to solve the ℓ^4 norm maximization problem* (7.3.14) *for complete dictionary learning.*

(a) Derive the gradient $\varphi(\boldsymbol{A}^*) = \|\boldsymbol{A}^*\bar{\boldsymbol{Y}}\|_4^4$ with respect to $\boldsymbol{A}^*$.

(b) Derive a projected gradient ascent algorithm for maximizing $\varphi(\boldsymbol{A}^*)$:

$$\boldsymbol{A}_{k+1}^* = \mathcal{P}_{\mathsf{O}(n)}[\boldsymbol{A}_k^* + \gamma \cdot \nabla\varphi(\boldsymbol{A}_k^*)].$$

(c) *Conduct a simulation of the algorithm and play with different step sizes γ of the gradient ascent. What happens if you make the step size infinite? That is,*

$$A_{k+1}^* = \mathcal{P}_{\mathsf{O}(n)}[\nabla\varphi(A_k^*)].$$

7.3. (Sparsity regularization via over-parameterization and gradient descent) *Given a vector $\boldsymbol{y} \in \mathbb{R}^m$ and a matrix $\boldsymbol{A} \in \mathbb{R}^{m\times n}$, consider the optimization problem*

$$\min_{\{\boldsymbol{u},\boldsymbol{v}\}\subseteq\mathbb{R}^m} f(\boldsymbol{u},\boldsymbol{v}) \doteq \frac{1}{4}\|\boldsymbol{y} - \boldsymbol{A}(\boldsymbol{u}\odot\boldsymbol{u} - \boldsymbol{v}\odot\boldsymbol{v})\|_2^2, \tag{7.5.1}$$

where $\odot$ denotes the Hadamard (i.e., entry-wise) product between two vectors. Let $(\boldsymbol{u}_t(\gamma), \boldsymbol{v}_t(\gamma))$ be given by the gradient flow dynamics (i.e., gradient descent with infinitesimally small step size) of (7.5.1)*:*

$$\begin{cases} \dot{\boldsymbol{u}}_t(\gamma) = -\nabla f\left(\boldsymbol{u}_t(\gamma), \boldsymbol{v}_t(\gamma)\right) = -\left(\boldsymbol{A}^*\boldsymbol{r}_t(\gamma)\right)\odot\boldsymbol{u}_t(\gamma), \\ \dot{\boldsymbol{v}}_t(\gamma) = -\nabla f\left(\boldsymbol{u}_t(\gamma), \boldsymbol{v}_t(\gamma)\right) = \left(\boldsymbol{A}^*\boldsymbol{r}_t(\gamma)\right)\odot\boldsymbol{v}_t(\gamma), \end{cases} \tag{7.5.2}$$

with the initial condition $\boldsymbol{u}_o(\gamma) = \boldsymbol{v}_o(\gamma) = \gamma\cdot\mathbf{1}$ (i.e., a vector with all entries being γ), and $\boldsymbol{r}_t(\gamma) \doteq \boldsymbol{A}\left(\boldsymbol{u}_t(\gamma)\odot\boldsymbol{u}_t(\gamma) - \boldsymbol{v}_t(\gamma)\odot\boldsymbol{v}_t(\gamma)\right) - \boldsymbol{y}$. Let

$$\boldsymbol{x}_t(\gamma) = \boldsymbol{u}_t(\gamma)\odot\boldsymbol{u}_t(\gamma) - \boldsymbol{v}_t(\gamma)\odot\boldsymbol{v}_t(\gamma), \tag{7.5.3}$$

and assume that the following conditions hold:

- *the limit $\boldsymbol{x}_\infty(\gamma) := \lim_{t\to\infty}\boldsymbol{x}_t(\gamma)$ exists and satisfies $\boldsymbol{A}\boldsymbol{x}_\infty(\gamma) = \boldsymbol{y}$ for all γ;*
- *the limit $\boldsymbol{x}_\infty := \lim_{\gamma\to 0}\boldsymbol{x}_\infty(\gamma)$ exists.*

Then, show that $\boldsymbol{x}_\infty$ is a global solution to the following optimization problem:

$$\min_{\boldsymbol{x}} \|\boldsymbol{x}\|_1 \quad \text{subject to} \quad \boldsymbol{A}\boldsymbol{x} = \boldsymbol{y}. \tag{7.5.4}$$

Hint: Note that from Chapter 3, the conclusion holds if and only if there exists a $\boldsymbol{\lambda}\in\mathbb{R}^m$, a dual certificate, such that the condition $\boldsymbol{A}^\top\boldsymbol{\lambda}\in\partial\|\boldsymbol{x}_\infty\|_1$ holds. Then, show that

$$\boldsymbol{\lambda} = \lim_{\gamma\to 0}\frac{-\lim_{t\to\infty}\int_0^t \boldsymbol{r}_\tau(\gamma)d\tau}{\log(1/\gamma)}$$

provides such a dual certificate.

Conceptually, this phenomenon is the same as the one we have seen in Exercise 2.10 of Chapter 2: the gradient descent with proper initialization introduces implicit bias on which solution (among all infinitely many optimal solutions) it eventually converges to.

7.4. (Low-rank regularization via the $\log\det(\cdot)$ function) *When a matrix $\boldsymbol{X}\in\mathbb{R}^{n\times n}$ is symmetric and positive semidefinite, the nuclear norm $\|\boldsymbol{X}\|_*$ is the same as its trace* *of the matrix. In this exercise, we study the connection of the convex nuclear norm (or the trace norm) with another popular nonconvex surrogate for* rank $(\boldsymbol{X})$.[34]

$$\min_{\boldsymbol{X}\in\mathsf{C}} f(\boldsymbol{X}) \doteq \log\det(\boldsymbol{X}+\delta\boldsymbol{I}), \tag{7.5.5}$$

where $\delta > 0$ *is a small regularization constant and* $\boldsymbol{X}$ *belongs to some constraint set* C. *To see how this objective is related to the trace norm:*

(a) *First, show that* $\nabla_{\boldsymbol{X}} f(\boldsymbol{X}) = (\boldsymbol{X}+\delta\boldsymbol{I})^{-1}$.
(b) *Second, the first-order expansion of* $f(\boldsymbol{X})$ *around a point* $\boldsymbol{X}_k$ *is given by:*

$$f(\boldsymbol{X}) \approx f(\boldsymbol{X}_k) + \operatorname{trace}\left((\boldsymbol{X}_k+\delta\boldsymbol{I})^{-1}(\boldsymbol{X}-\boldsymbol{X}_k)\right) + o(\|\boldsymbol{X}-\boldsymbol{X}_k\|).$$

Then to minimize $f(\boldsymbol{X})$, *we can use a greedy descent algorithm with the iteration*

$$\boldsymbol{X}_{k+1} = \arg\min_{\boldsymbol{X}\in\mathsf{C}} \operatorname{trace}\left((\boldsymbol{X}_k+\delta\boldsymbol{I})^{-1}\boldsymbol{X}\right). \tag{7.5.6}$$

Notice that when $\boldsymbol{X}_k$ *is initialized around* $\boldsymbol{X}_o = \boldsymbol{I}$, *then the above iteration becomes minimizing the trace norm* $\boldsymbol{X}_{k+1} = \arg\min_{\boldsymbol{X}\in\mathsf{C}} \operatorname{trace}(\boldsymbol{X})$.

7.5. (Low-rank regularization through matrix product) *Given a matrix* $\boldsymbol{Y}\in\mathbb{R}^{m\times n}$, *we may consider computing a low-rank approximation to it through the proximal operator of the nuclear norm:*

$$\min_{\boldsymbol{X}} \|\boldsymbol{Y}-\boldsymbol{X}\|_2^2 + \lambda\|\boldsymbol{X}\|_*.$$

Use Proposition 4.6 to show that if we parameterize $\boldsymbol{X}$ *as matrix product,* $\boldsymbol{X} = \boldsymbol{U}\boldsymbol{V}^* \doteq \sum_k \boldsymbol{u}_k\boldsymbol{v}_k^*$, *then the above convex program is equivalent to the following nonconvex program:*

$$\min_{\boldsymbol{U},\boldsymbol{V}} \|\boldsymbol{Y}-\boldsymbol{U}\boldsymbol{V}^*\|_2^2 + \lambda\sum_k \|\boldsymbol{u}_k\|_2\|\boldsymbol{v}_k\|_2. \tag{7.5.7}$$

7.6. (Stochastic matrix factorization) *Consider approximating a given matrix* $\boldsymbol{Y}\in\mathbb{R}^{m\times n}$ *by a random superposition of a set of rank-1 factors:*

$$\boldsymbol{Y} \approx \frac{1}{\theta}\sum_{k=1}^{d} r_k\boldsymbol{u}_k\boldsymbol{v}_k^*,$$

where $r_k \sim \operatorname{Ber}(\theta)$ *are i.i.d. Bernoulli variables, and* $\boldsymbol{u}_k$ *are columns from a matrix* $\boldsymbol{U}\in\mathbb{R}^{m\times d}$, *similarly for* $\boldsymbol{v}_k$. *The goal is to minimize the expected error*

$$\mathbb{E}\left\|\boldsymbol{Y} - \frac{1}{\theta}\boldsymbol{U}\operatorname{diag}(\boldsymbol{r})\boldsymbol{V}^*\right\|_F^2,$$

[34] For example, the $\log\det(\cdot)$ function arises in the context of lossy data compression [MDHW07] as a good measure of the binary coding length for encoded data that span a low-dimensional subspace. As we will see in Chapter 16, this nonconvex measure plays a crucial role in a principled approach to derive and interpret modern deep neural networks. In that context, the convex nuclear norm becomes inadequate.

with respect to $\boldsymbol{r}$*, the vector of all the d Bernoulli variables. Show that*

$$\mathbb{E}\left\|\boldsymbol{Y} - \frac{1}{\theta}\boldsymbol{U}\operatorname{diag}(\boldsymbol{r})\boldsymbol{V}^*\right\|_F^2 = \left\|\boldsymbol{Y} - \boldsymbol{U}\boldsymbol{V}^*\right\|_F^2 + \frac{1-\theta}{\theta}\sum_{k=1}^{d}\|\boldsymbol{u}_k\|_2^2\|\boldsymbol{v}_k\|_2^2. \tag{7.5.8}$$

Notice that the second term is very similar to that in the previous exercise, except for the square. The stochastic factorization can be used to model the so-called "dropout" techniques used in training deep neural networks, introduced by [SHK+14].

7.7. *Consider the factorization of a matrix* $\boldsymbol{X} = \boldsymbol{U}\boldsymbol{V}^* \doteq \sum_{k=1}^d \boldsymbol{u}_k\boldsymbol{v}_k^*$ *and the associated quantity:*

$$\rho(\boldsymbol{U},\boldsymbol{V}) \doteq \sum_{k=1}^{d}\|\boldsymbol{u}_k\|_2^2\|\boldsymbol{v}_k\|_2^2.$$

Show that if we may allow the factor to be of arbitrarily large size, that is, d can be arbitrarily large, then we have

$$\inf_{d,\, \boldsymbol{X}=\boldsymbol{U}\boldsymbol{V}^*} \rho(\boldsymbol{U},\boldsymbol{V}) = 0.$$

This property shows that the second term in the previous exercise prefers redundant factorization if we allow d to be free.

7.8. (Dropout as low-rank regularization) *Now in the stochastic matrix factorization exercise above, consider that the sampling probability* θ *of the Bernoulli random variables is a function of the number d of columns in* $\boldsymbol{U}$ *and* $\boldsymbol{V}$*: for a given p,* $0 < p < 1$,

$$\theta(d) = \frac{p}{d-(d-1)p}. \tag{7.5.9}$$

Then show that

$$\inf_{d,\, \boldsymbol{X}=\boldsymbol{U}\boldsymbol{V}^*} \frac{1-\theta(d)}{\theta(d)}\sum_{k=1}^{d}\|\boldsymbol{u}_k\|_2^2\|\boldsymbol{v}_k\|_2^2 = \frac{1-p}{p}\|\boldsymbol{X}\|_*^2. \tag{7.5.10}$$

Conclude that with the above choice of sampling rate, the above dropout technique is equivalent to:

$$\min_{d,\boldsymbol{U},\boldsymbol{V}} \mathbb{E}\left\|\boldsymbol{Y} - \frac{1}{\theta(d)}\boldsymbol{U}\operatorname{diag}(\boldsymbol{r})\boldsymbol{V}^*\right\|_F^2 = \min_{\boldsymbol{X}} \|\boldsymbol{Y}-\boldsymbol{X}\|_2^2 + \frac{1-p}{p}\|\boldsymbol{X}\|_*^2. \tag{7.5.11}$$

7.9. (Nuclear norm squared as a regularizer) *The above exercise shows that the dropout technique used in deep learning is essentially equivalent to regularizing parameters of two adjacent layers through a nuclear norm squared penalty. Given a matrix* $\boldsymbol{Y}$ *with singular value decomposition* $\boldsymbol{Y} = \boldsymbol{U}\boldsymbol{\Sigma}\boldsymbol{V}^*$*, show that the optimal solution to the program*

$$\min_{\boldsymbol{X}} \|\boldsymbol{Y}-\boldsymbol{X}\|_2^2 + \lambda\|\boldsymbol{X}\|_*^2$$

is of the form $X_\star = U\mathcal{S}_\mu(\Sigma)V^*$, *where* $\mathcal{S}_\mu$ *is a shrinkage operator with a certain threshold depending on both* λ *and* Σ. *This concludes that stochastic matrix factorization (also known as dropout in deep learning) is essentially imposing low-rank regularization on the resulting matrix.*

7.10. (Low-rank regularization through over-parameterization and implicit bias) *In this exercise, we reconsider the* affine rank minimization *problem studied in Chapter 4:*

$$\min_{X} \operatorname{rank}(X) \quad \textit{subject to} \quad \mathcal{A}[X] = y. \tag{7.5.12}$$

Here $y = \mathcal{A}[X_o] \in \mathbb{R}^m$ *is the observation, and we consider the special case that* $X \in \mathbb{R}^{n \times n}$ *is a symmetric matrix and* $\mathcal{A}$ *is a linear map:* $\mathbb{R}^{n\times n} \to \mathbb{R}^m$. *Hence each measurement is of the form* $y_i = \langle A_i, X\rangle$ *for some matrix* $A_i \in \mathbb{R}^{n\times n}$; *see also* (4.3.2). *For simplicity, we here further assume the measurement matrices* A_i *are commutable, i.e.,* $A_i A_j = A_j A_i$ *for all* i, j.

To recover the low-rank solution X_o, *we over parameterize* X *as* $X = UU^*$ *with* $U \in \mathbb{R}^{n\times n}$ *and consider solving the following nonconvex program:*

$$\min_{U} f(U) \doteq \|\mathcal{A}[UU^*] - y\|_2^2. \tag{7.5.13}$$

Obviously the above program does not have a unique solution as X *is over parameterized by* U. *We are interested in how we can still recover the correct solution* X_o *by taking a special optimization strategy. Let us construct* $U(t)$ *as the solution to the gradient flow of* $f(U)$:

$$\dot{U}(t) = -\nabla f(U(t)) = -\mathcal{A}^*[\mathcal{A}[U(t)U^*(t)] - y]U(t), \tag{7.5.14}$$

where $\mathcal{A}^*$ *is the adjoint of the linear map* $\mathcal{A}$. *Let* $e(t) \doteq \mathcal{A}[U(t)U^*(t)] - y \in \mathbb{R}^m$.

(a) *Show that, under the above flow of* $U(t)$, $X(t) = U(t)U^*(t)$ *satisfies the following differential equation:*

$$\dot{X}(t) = -\mathcal{A}^*[e(t)]X(t) - X(t)\mathcal{A}^*[e(t)]. \tag{7.5.15}$$

(b) *Starting from* $X(0) = X_o$, *derive the solution to* $X(t)$ *for the special case of* $m = 1$.

(c) *Assume the following limits exist:*[35]

$$X_\infty(X_o) = \lim_{t\to\infty} X(t) \quad \textit{and} \quad \hat{X} = \lim_{\varepsilon\to 0} X_\infty(\varepsilon X_o).$$

Show that $\hat{X}$ *is the optimal solution to the following (familiar) program:*

$$\min_{X} \|X\|_* \quad \textit{subject to} \quad \mathcal{A}[X] = y, \tag{7.5.16}$$

where here $\mathcal{A}[X] = \langle A_1, X\rangle$ *since* $m = 1$.

[35] We leave the conditions under which such limits exist for students as extra bonus questions.

(d) *Now generalize this to the case of m measurements: show that* $\hat{\mathbf{X}}$ *is the optimal solution to the above convex program as long as* $\mathbf{A}_i$, $i = 1, \ldots, m$, *are commutable.*

One may view this as an extension of the over parameterization for sparsity in Exercise 7.3 to the case for low-rank matrices.

Part II

Computation for Large-Scale Problems

8 Convex Optimization for Structured Signal Recovery

"In our opinion, convex optimization is a natural next topic after advanced linear algebra (topics like least-squares, singular values), and linear programming."
– Stephen Boyd and Lieven Vandenberghe, *Convex Optimization*

In the previous theoretical Part I of the book, we showed that under fairly broad conditions on the number of measurements needed, many important classes of structured signals can be recovered via computationally tractable optimization problems, such as ℓ^1 minimization for recovering sparse signals and nuclear norm minimization for recovering low-rank matrices. As we will see in Part III of this book, many of these structures are essential for modeling the high-dimensional data that arise in a wide variety of applications. Hence, from a practical perspective, it is important that we develop efficient and scalable algorithms for these classes of optimization problems. We take on this task in the coming two chapters.

In this chapter, we mainly focus on the *convex approach* for structured signal recovery (and leave nonconvex optimization to the next Chapter 9). There are two compelling reasons to study the convex approach first. First, the previous chapters have established very precise conditions under which convex programs give correct solutions to the recovery problems. Second, as we will see through this chapter, the class of convex programs we are dealing with have unique properties that lend themselves to faster and more scalable solutions than generic convex programs. Although we will primarily use ℓ^1 norm or nuclear norm minimization as working examples, the techniques that we introduce are fairly general, extending to a much broader class of convex programs with similar structure.

This chapter (or book) is not intended to give a comprehensive introduction to convex analysis and optimization, for which there are already excellent references such as [BV04, BNO03, Nes18]. Instead, this chapter will focus mainly on showing how one can exploit special structures of the problems so as to develop more efficient and scalable algorithms than generic convex optimization methods. To make the book self-contained, we briefly survey related concepts and properties of convex functions as well as generic optimization methods in Appendices B–D.

8.1 Challenges and Opportunities

In this chapter, we will describe a few basic ideas which go a long way towards achieving the development of efficient and scalable algorithms, by leveraging special properties of the particular convex optimization problems that arise in structured signal recovery. Our discussion will center around four model problems: basis pursuit (i.e., equality constrained ℓ^1 minimization), its regularized version (basis pursuit denoising), principal component pursuit, and its regularized version. We recap these four optimization problems below.

Recall the problem of recovering a sparse vector $\boldsymbol{x}_o \in \mathbb{R}^n$ from observations $\boldsymbol{y} = \boldsymbol{A}\boldsymbol{x}_o \in \mathbb{R}^m$ via a convex program, also known as *basis pursuit* (BP):

$$\begin{array}{ll} \min_{\boldsymbol{x}} & \|\boldsymbol{x}\|_1 \\ \text{subject to} & \boldsymbol{A}\boldsymbol{x} = \boldsymbol{y}. \end{array} \tag{8.1.1}$$

A variant of the problem considers the noisy case, in which the observations $\boldsymbol{y}$ are contaminated by moderate Gaussian noise $\boldsymbol{y} = \boldsymbol{A}\boldsymbol{x}_o + \boldsymbol{z}$, also known as the *Lasso*:

$$\min_{\boldsymbol{x}} \frac{1}{2}\|\boldsymbol{y} - \boldsymbol{A}\boldsymbol{x}\|_2^2 + \lambda\|\boldsymbol{x}\|_1, \tag{8.1.2}$$

where λ is a scalar weight parameter.

In robust PCA, the goal is to recover a low-rank matrix $\boldsymbol{L}_o$ from sparsely corrupted observations $\boldsymbol{Y} = \boldsymbol{L}_o + \boldsymbol{S}_o \in \mathbb{R}^{m \times n}$. A natural approach suggested in earlier chapters is to solve the so-called *principal component pursuit* (PCP) program:

$$\begin{array}{ll} \min_{\boldsymbol{L},\boldsymbol{S}} & \|\boldsymbol{L}\|_* + \lambda\,\|\boldsymbol{S}\|_1 \\ \text{subject to} & \boldsymbol{L} + \boldsymbol{S} = \boldsymbol{Y}, \end{array} \tag{8.1.3}$$

where $\lambda > 0$ is a scalar weight. Again, if the data are noisy we could also consider solving a stable version of the PCP program:

$$\min_{\boldsymbol{L},\boldsymbol{S}} \|\boldsymbol{L}\|_* + \lambda\,\|\boldsymbol{S}\|_1 + \frac{\mu}{2}\,\|\boldsymbol{Y} - \boldsymbol{L} - \boldsymbol{S}\|_F^2, \tag{8.1.4}$$

to produce stable estimates $\hat{\boldsymbol{L}}$ and $\hat{\boldsymbol{S}}$, where $\lambda, \mu > 0$ are two scalar weights.

Challenge of Scale

When the dimension of the problem is not so high, one could simply apply classical second-order convex optimization algorithms, such as the interior point methods (see, e.g., [BV04]), to solve the above convex programs. These powerful methods, under favorable conditions such as for smooth strongly convex functions, need only very few iterations to converge to a highly accurate solution: $O(\log(1/\varepsilon))$, where ε is the target accuracy. However, for problems in n variables, each iteration requires the solution to a system of linear equations of size $n \times n$, incurring a typical per-iteration cost of $O(n^3)$. For applications in modern signal processing, the number of variables n can be quite high – in the case of image processing, it is typically of the same magnitude as the number of pixels, easily in the range of millions. For such problems, the cost of a single iteration is prohibitively large. As a result, we will need to consider simple alternatives with cheaper iterations.

EXAMPLE 8.1. (Solving large-scale BP problems via interior point methods) *Just to motivate yourself from a practical perspective, construct a simulation to plot the average run time of BP on CVX from 100 to 1000 dimensions. See how a generic convex optimization solver (that is mainly based on the second-order, interior point method) scales for this class of optimization problems.*

Difficulty with Nonsmoothness

The large scale of the problems forces us to consider simple, scalable algorithms that use only first-order information about the objective function. The prototypical first-order method is *gradient descent*. However, one technical difficulty arises though, as the objective functions may contain nonsmooth terms that are not differentiable. For instance, the ℓ^1 norm $\|\boldsymbol{x}\|_1$ in the basis pursuit denoising (BPDN) problem does not have a gradient in the normal sense. In such cases, the simplest solution is to employ a generic subgradient method, as we did in Chapter 2. Although the subgradient method has very simple and efficient iterations, its rate of convergence is very poor, typically $O(1/\sqrt{k})$.[1] That means it usually takes many (thousands of) iterations for the algorithm to converge to the optimal solution. In this chapter, we will show how to exploit some important properties of structured signal recovery. Such properties allow us to develop gradient descent algorithms as if the objective is smooth, the so-called proximal gradient (PG) method (Section 8.2). The same properties also allow us to utilize acceleration techniques that were designed for smooth functions and lead to much more scalable and fast-converging algorithms, with convergence rates much better than the generic situation (Scction 8.3).

Enforcing Equality Constraints

To solve the basis pursuit problem (8.1.1), we need to ensure that the final solution $\boldsymbol{x}$ satisfies the equality constraint $\boldsymbol{y} = \boldsymbol{A}\boldsymbol{x}$ exactly. A naive way to enforce the equality constraint is to incorporate it as a penalty term and minimize: $\min_{\boldsymbol{x}} \|\boldsymbol{x}\|_1 + (\mu/2)\|\boldsymbol{y} - \boldsymbol{A}\boldsymbol{x}\|_2^2$. This is a similar optimization problem to the BPDN except that we need to solve a series of problems of this type for an increasing sequence of $\mu_i \to \infty$ so as to enforce the equality constraint in the end. However, as the weight μ_i increases, the corresponding BPDN problem becomes increasingly ill-conditioned and hence algorithms converge slower. In Section 8.4, we will see how to employ the *augmented Lagrange multiplier* (ALM) technique to alleviate this difficulty.

Exploiting Separable Structures

Often the structured signal that we are recovering is a superposition of multiple structured terms. This is the case for the principal component pursuit (PCP) program that we have mentioned earlier:

$$\min_{\boldsymbol{L},\boldsymbol{S}} \|\boldsymbol{L}\|_* + \lambda\|\boldsymbol{S}\|_1 \quad \text{subject to} \quad \boldsymbol{Y} = \boldsymbol{L} + \boldsymbol{S}. \tag{8.1.5}$$

[1] See [Nem95, Nem07] for a characterization of typical subgradient methods.

As we will show in Section 8.5, such separable structures of the objective function can be naturally exploited through methods such as the *alternating direction of multipliers method* (ADMM). We end up with more simple and efficient algorithms for solving this class of convex programs as ADMM converts the global optimization to several subproblems of much smaller dimension.

Finally, in Section 8.6, we will study how to exploit additional structures either in the objective function or in the constraint set to further improve the scalability of the optimization algorithms against the problem dimension or the sample size.

8.2 Proximal Gradient Methods

As one can see, the optimization problems we are dealing with can be reduced to solve the structured convex minimization problems with objective functions of the form

$$F(\boldsymbol{x}) \doteq f(\boldsymbol{x}) + g(\boldsymbol{x}), \tag{8.2.1}$$

where $f(\boldsymbol{x})$ is a smooth convex term and $g(\boldsymbol{x})$ is a convex but nonsmooth term. For instance, in the Lasso problem (8.1.2), we could set $f(\boldsymbol{x}) \doteq \frac{1}{2}\|\boldsymbol{y} - \boldsymbol{A}\boldsymbol{x}\|_2^2$ and $g(\boldsymbol{x}) \doteq \lambda\|\boldsymbol{x}\|_1$ with $\lambda > 0$. We want to develop both scalable and efficient algorithms for this type of problem.

Since the composite objective function $F(\boldsymbol{x})$ is not differentiable, generic gradient algorithms do not apply. The first recourse in this situation is to replace the gradient with a *subgradient*, yielding the simple subgradient method with the iteration:

$$\boldsymbol{x}_{k+1} = \boldsymbol{x}_k - \gamma_k \boldsymbol{g}_k, \quad \boldsymbol{g}_k \in \partial F(\boldsymbol{x}_k). \tag{8.2.2}$$

The main disadvantage to this approach is its relatively poor convergence rate.[2] Let $\boldsymbol{x}_\star$ be the (global) minimizer of $F(\boldsymbol{x})$. In general, the convergence rate of the subgradient method for nonsmooth objective functions, in terms of function value $F(\boldsymbol{x}_k) - F(\boldsymbol{x}_\star)$, is (see [Nes03])

$$O(1/\sqrt{k}). \tag{8.2.3}$$

The constants in the big-O notation depend on various properties of the problem. The important point is that for even a moderate target accuracy

$$F(\boldsymbol{x}_k) - F(\boldsymbol{x}_\star) \le \varepsilon,$$

we will have to set $k = O(\varepsilon^{-2})$ very large.

8.2.1 Convergence of Gradient Descent

We can compare the behavior of the subgradient method with the behavior of the simple *gradient descent* method for minimizing a smooth function. Consider, briefly, the simpler problem

[2] Also, the step size γ_k can be challenging to set.

$$\min_{\boldsymbol{x}} \quad f(\boldsymbol{x}), \tag{8.2.4}$$

with f convex and differentiable. The gradient descent iteration for this problem is

$$\boldsymbol{x}_{k+1} = \boldsymbol{x}_k - \gamma_k \nabla f(\boldsymbol{x}_k). \tag{8.2.5}$$

This iteration comes from a first-order approximation to f at $\boldsymbol{x} = \boldsymbol{x}_k$:

$$f(\boldsymbol{x}') \geq f(\boldsymbol{x}) + \left\langle \nabla f(\boldsymbol{x}), \boldsymbol{x}' - \boldsymbol{x} \right\rangle. \tag{8.2.6}$$

Because f is convex, this first-order approximation provides a global lower bound on f. Nevertheless, we expect this lower bound to be more accurate in a neighborhood of $\boldsymbol{x}$. The size of this neighborhood depends substantially on the properties of f. For example, if f is relatively smooth, and its gradient does not vary much from point to point, we might imagine that the first-order approximation at $\boldsymbol{x}$ would be accurate over a relatively large region. To make this more formal, we say that a differentiable function $f(\boldsymbol{x})$ has *L-Lipschitz continuous gradients* if

$$\|\nabla f(\boldsymbol{x}') - \nabla f(\boldsymbol{x})\|_2 \leq L \|\boldsymbol{x}' - \boldsymbol{x}\|_2, \quad \forall\, \boldsymbol{x}', \boldsymbol{x} \in \mathbb{R}^n \tag{8.2.7}$$

for some $L > 0$. The quantity L is known as the *Lipschitz constant* of ∇f.

When the Lipschitz condition holds, a bit of calculus shows that we can complement the linear lower bound (8.2.6) with a corresponding quadratic upper bound:

LEMMA 8.2. *Suppose that f is differentiable, and ∇f is L-Lipschitz. Then for every $\boldsymbol{x}, \boldsymbol{x}' \in \mathbb{R}^n$,*

$$f(\boldsymbol{x}') \leq f(\boldsymbol{x}) + \left\langle \nabla f(\boldsymbol{x}), \boldsymbol{x}' - \boldsymbol{x} \right\rangle + \frac{L}{2} \left\| \boldsymbol{x}' - \boldsymbol{x} \right\|_2^2. \tag{8.2.8}$$

Proof We calculate:

$$\begin{aligned}
f(\boldsymbol{x}') &= f(\boldsymbol{x} + t(\boldsymbol{x}' - \boldsymbol{x}))|_{t=1} \\
&= f(\boldsymbol{x}) + \int_{t=0}^{1} \frac{d}{dt} f(\boldsymbol{x} + t(\boldsymbol{x}' - \boldsymbol{x}))\, dt \\
&= f(\boldsymbol{x}) + \int_{t=0}^{1} \left\langle \nabla f(\boldsymbol{x} + t(\boldsymbol{x}' - \boldsymbol{x})), \boldsymbol{x}' - \boldsymbol{x} \right\rangle dt \\
&= f(\boldsymbol{x}) + \left\langle \nabla f(\boldsymbol{x}), \boldsymbol{x}' - \boldsymbol{x} \right\rangle \\
&\quad + \int_{t=0}^{1} \left\langle \nabla f(\boldsymbol{x} + t(\boldsymbol{x}' - \boldsymbol{x})) - \nabla f(\boldsymbol{x}), \boldsymbol{x}' - \boldsymbol{x} \right\rangle dt \\
&\leq f(\boldsymbol{x}) + \left\langle \nabla f(\boldsymbol{x}), \boldsymbol{x}' - \boldsymbol{x} \right\rangle \\
&\quad + \int_{t=0}^{1} \|\nabla f(\boldsymbol{x} + t(\boldsymbol{x}' - \boldsymbol{x})) - \nabla f(\boldsymbol{x})\|_2 \|\boldsymbol{x}' - \boldsymbol{x}\|_2\, dt \\
&\leq f(\boldsymbol{x}) + \left\langle \nabla f(\boldsymbol{x}), \boldsymbol{x}' - \boldsymbol{x} \right\rangle + \int_{t=0}^{1} tL \left\| \boldsymbol{x}' - \boldsymbol{x} \right\|_2^2 dt \\
&= f(\boldsymbol{x}) + \left\langle \nabla f(\boldsymbol{x}), \boldsymbol{x}' - \boldsymbol{x} \right\rangle + \frac{L}{2} \left\| \boldsymbol{x}' - \boldsymbol{x} \right\|_2^2,
\end{aligned} \tag{8.2.9}$$

giving the claim. □

Thus, when ∇f is Lipschitz, we have a matching quadratic upper bound,

$$f(\boldsymbol{x}') \le \hat{f}(\boldsymbol{x}',\boldsymbol{x}) \doteq f(\boldsymbol{x}) + \langle \nabla f(\boldsymbol{x}), \boldsymbol{x}' - \boldsymbol{x} \rangle + \frac{L}{2} \left\| \boldsymbol{x}' - \boldsymbol{x} \right\|_2^2 \tag{8.2.10}$$

$$= \frac{L}{2} \left\| \boldsymbol{x}' - \left(\boldsymbol{x} - \frac{1}{L} \nabla f(\boldsymbol{x}) \right) \right\|_2^2 + h(\boldsymbol{x}), \tag{8.2.11}$$

for some function $h(\boldsymbol{x})$ that does not depend on $\boldsymbol{x}'$. This upper bound agrees with f at the point $\boldsymbol{x}$ at which it is formed: $f(\boldsymbol{x}) = \hat{f}(\boldsymbol{x},\boldsymbol{x})$. Suppose that we minimize this upper bound, with respect to $\boldsymbol{x}'$. By inspecting the second identity above, the minimizer has a very familiar form:

$$\arg\min_{\boldsymbol{x}'} \hat{f}(\boldsymbol{x}',\boldsymbol{x}) = \boldsymbol{x} - \frac{1}{L} \nabla f(\boldsymbol{x}). \tag{8.2.12}$$

This is simply a gradient descent step, taken from $\boldsymbol{x}$, with a special choice of step size $\gamma = 1/L$. Moreover, because $\hat{f}(\boldsymbol{x},\boldsymbol{x}) = f(\boldsymbol{x})$, this minimization does not increase the objective function: if $\boldsymbol{x}'_\star \in \arg\min_{\boldsymbol{x}'} \hat{f}(\boldsymbol{x}',\boldsymbol{x})$, then

$$f(\boldsymbol{x}'_\star) \le \hat{f}(\boldsymbol{x}'_\star,\boldsymbol{x}) \le \hat{f}(\boldsymbol{x},\boldsymbol{x}) = f(\boldsymbol{x}). \tag{8.2.13}$$

Thus, if we apply the gradient descent method with step size $1/L$, we are guaranteed to produce a monotone sequence of function values $f(\boldsymbol{x}_k)$. Furthermore, we can show convergence[3] to the optimal function value at a rate of $O(1/k)$:

$$f(\boldsymbol{x}_k) - f(\boldsymbol{x}_\star) \le \frac{L \left\| \boldsymbol{x}_0 - \boldsymbol{x}_\star \right\|_2^2}{2k} = O(1/k). \tag{8.2.14}$$

This is still not a particularly fast rate of convergence, but it is much better than the $O(1/\sqrt{k})$ rate of convergence experienced by the subgradient algorithm on nonsmooth functions.

8.2.2 From Gradient to Proximal Gradient

Can we draw inspiration from the gradient method to produce a more efficient algorithm for minimizing the composite function $F(\boldsymbol{x}) = f(\boldsymbol{x}) + g(\boldsymbol{x})$, with f differentiable? Again, the gradient method does not directly apply, since F is nondifferentiable. Nevertheless, if the gradient ∇f of the smooth term is Lipschitz, we can still make a simpler upper bound to F, by upper-bounding f, say around the current iterate $\boldsymbol{x}_k$, by a quadratic and leaving the nonsmooth term g intact:

$$\hat{F}(\boldsymbol{x},\boldsymbol{x}_k) = f(\boldsymbol{x}_k) + \langle \nabla f(\boldsymbol{x}_k), \boldsymbol{x} - \boldsymbol{x}_k \rangle + \frac{L}{2} \left\| \boldsymbol{x} - \boldsymbol{x}_k \right\|_2^2 + g(\boldsymbol{x}). \tag{8.2.15}$$

Since above repeatedly minimizing $\hat{f}$ of (8.2.10) produced the gradient method, resulting in a better convergence rate, let us try minimizing the upper bound $\hat{F}$ around $\boldsymbol{x}_k$:

$$\boldsymbol{x}_{k+1} = \arg\min_{\boldsymbol{x}} \hat{F}(\boldsymbol{x},\boldsymbol{x}_k). \tag{8.2.16}$$

[3] We will not prove (8.2.14) here, since we will obtain a more general result below which implies it.

For commonly encountered g, this minimization often takes on a very simple form. Completing the square in (8.2.15), we obtain that

$$\hat{F}(\boldsymbol{x},\boldsymbol{x}_k) = \frac{L}{2}\left\|\boldsymbol{x} - \left(\boldsymbol{x}_k - \frac{1}{L}\nabla f(\boldsymbol{x}_k)\right)\right\|_2^2 + g(\boldsymbol{x}) + h(\boldsymbol{x}_k), \tag{8.2.17}$$

where $h(\boldsymbol{x}_k)$ is a term that depends only on $\boldsymbol{x}_k$.

Hence, the iteration (8.2.16) becomes

$$\begin{aligned} \boldsymbol{x}_{k+1} &= \arg\min_{\boldsymbol{x}} \frac{L}{2}\left\|\boldsymbol{x} - \left(\boldsymbol{x}_k - \frac{1}{L}\nabla f(\boldsymbol{x}_k)\right)\right\|_2^2 + g(\boldsymbol{x}) \\ &= \arg\min_{\boldsymbol{x}} g(\boldsymbol{x}) + \frac{L}{2}\|\boldsymbol{x} - \boldsymbol{w}_k\|_2^2, \end{aligned} \tag{8.2.18}$$

where for convenience we define $\boldsymbol{w}_k \doteq \boldsymbol{x}_k - (1/L)\nabla f(\boldsymbol{x}_k)$. Thus, at each step of the iteration (8.2.16), we have to minimize the function g plus a separable quadratic $(L/2)\|\boldsymbol{x} - \boldsymbol{w}_k\|_2^2$. In a sense, this problem asks us to make g as small as possible, while not straying too far from the point $\boldsymbol{w}_k$. Because $\|\cdot\|_2^2$ is strongly convex, this problem always has a unique solution. So, the sequence $\boldsymbol{x}_k$ defined recursively by (8.2.16) is well defined.

In fact, the operation of minimizing a convex function g plus a separable quadratic $\|\boldsymbol{x} - \boldsymbol{w}_k\|_2^2$ recurs so frequently in convex analysis and optimization that it has its own name. This is known as the *proximal operator* for the convex function $g(\boldsymbol{x})$:

DEFINITION 8.3. (Proximal operator) *The proximal operator of a convex function g is*

$$\operatorname{prox}_g[\boldsymbol{w}] \doteq \arg\min_{\boldsymbol{x}} \left\{ g(\boldsymbol{x}) + \frac{1}{2}\|\boldsymbol{x} - \boldsymbol{w}\|_2^2 \right\}. \tag{8.2.19}$$

In this language, iteration (8.2.16) can be written as

$$\boldsymbol{x}_{k+1} = \operatorname{prox}_{g/L}[\boldsymbol{w}_k]. \tag{8.2.20}$$

Fortunately, many of the convex functions (or norms) that we encounter in structured signal recovery have either closed-form proximal operators or proximal operators that can be computed very efficiently via numerical means. We give a few examples below:

PROPOSITION 8.4. *Proximal operators for the indicator function, ℓ^1 norm, and nuclear norm are given by the following:*

1 *Let $g(\boldsymbol{x}) = I_{\mathcal{D}}$ be the indicator function for a closed convex set $\mathcal{D}$, namely, $I_{\mathcal{D}}(\boldsymbol{x}) = 0, \boldsymbol{x} \in \mathcal{D}$, otherwise $I_{\mathcal{D}}(\boldsymbol{x}) = \infty$. Then* $\operatorname{prox}_g[\boldsymbol{w}]$ *is the projection operator:*

$$\operatorname{prox}_g[\boldsymbol{w}] = \arg\min_{\boldsymbol{x}\in\mathcal{D}} \|\boldsymbol{x} - \boldsymbol{w}\|_2^2 = \mathcal{P}_{\mathcal{D}}[\boldsymbol{w}].$$

2 *Let $g(\boldsymbol{x}) = \lambda\|\boldsymbol{x}\|_1$ be the ℓ^1 norm. Then* $\operatorname{prox}_g[\boldsymbol{w}]$ *is the* soft-thresholding *function applied element-wise:*

$$(\operatorname{prox}_g[\boldsymbol{w}])_i = \operatorname{soft}(w_i, \lambda) \doteq \operatorname{sign}(w_i)\max(|w_i| - \lambda, 0).$$

3 *Let* $g(\boldsymbol{X}) = \lambda\|\boldsymbol{X}\|_*$ *be the matrix nuclear norm. Then* $\text{prox}_g[\boldsymbol{W}]$ *is the* singular value soft-thresholding *function:*

$$\text{prox}_g[\boldsymbol{W}] = \boldsymbol{U}\text{soft}(\boldsymbol{\Sigma}, \lambda)\boldsymbol{V}^*,$$

where $(\boldsymbol{U}, \boldsymbol{\Sigma}, \boldsymbol{V})$ *are the singular value decomposition (SVD) of* $\boldsymbol{W}$*. In other words,* $\text{prox}_g[\boldsymbol{W}]$ *applies component-wise soft thresholding on the singular values of* $\boldsymbol{W}$.

Proof We prove the second assertion and leave the rest to the reader as exercises. The objective function reaches a minimum when the subdifferential of $\lambda\|\boldsymbol{x}\|_1 + \frac{1}{2}\|\boldsymbol{x} - \boldsymbol{w}\|_2^2$ contains zero,

$$0 \in (\boldsymbol{x} - \boldsymbol{w}) + \lambda\partial\|\boldsymbol{x}\|_1 = \begin{cases} x_i - w_i + \lambda, & x_i > 0, \\ -w_i + \lambda[-1, 1], & x_i = 0 \ , \\ x_i - w_i - \lambda, & x_i < 0, \end{cases} \quad i = 1, \ldots, n.$$

Therefore, the solution to this optimality condition is the soft-thresholding function applied element-wise:

$$x_{i\star} = \text{soft}(w_i, \lambda) \doteq \text{sign}\,(w_i)\max(|w_i| - \lambda, 0), \quad i = 1, \ldots, n.$$

See Figure 8.1(a) for an illustration of the soft-thresholding function. We leave the first and third assertions as exercises for the reader. Hint: for the first, use the definition; for the third, use the subdifferential of $\|\cdot\|_*$. □

EXAMPLE 8.5. (Proximal operators for powers of nuclear norm) *In problems such as high-order low-rank tensor completion [ZZWM14] or stochastic matrix factorization [CMH+17] (also known as "dropout" in deep learning; see Exercise 7.8 of Chapter 7), we may need to find the proximal operator for a given matrix* $\boldsymbol{W}$*,*

$$\text{prox}_g[\boldsymbol{W}] \doteq \arg\min_{\boldsymbol{X}} \left\{ g(\boldsymbol{X}) + \frac{1}{2}\|\boldsymbol{X} - \boldsymbol{W}\|_F^2 \right\}, \tag{8.2.21}$$

for $g(\boldsymbol{X})$ *as certain powers of the nuclear norm or its exponential,*[4] *say*

$$g(\boldsymbol{X}) = \lambda\|\boldsymbol{X}\|_*^2 \quad or \quad g(\boldsymbol{X}) = \lambda e^{\|\boldsymbol{X}\|_*}. \tag{8.2.22}$$

For each of these two cases, one can show that the proximal operator takes the form

$$\text{prox}_g[\boldsymbol{W}] = \boldsymbol{U}\text{soft}(\boldsymbol{\Sigma}, \tau)\boldsymbol{V}^*,$$

where τ *is a certain threshold that depends on* λ *and the singular values of* $\boldsymbol{W}$. *See Figure 8.1(b) for an illustration of the soft-thresholding function on the singular values. In fact, this is true if* $g(\boldsymbol{X}) = f(\|\boldsymbol{X}\|_*)$ *for any monotonic convex function* f. *The only question is whether the associated threshold* τ *can be solved in closed form or efficiently computed numerically. We explore some of these extensions in*

[4] The reader may refer to [ZM20] for the more general case.

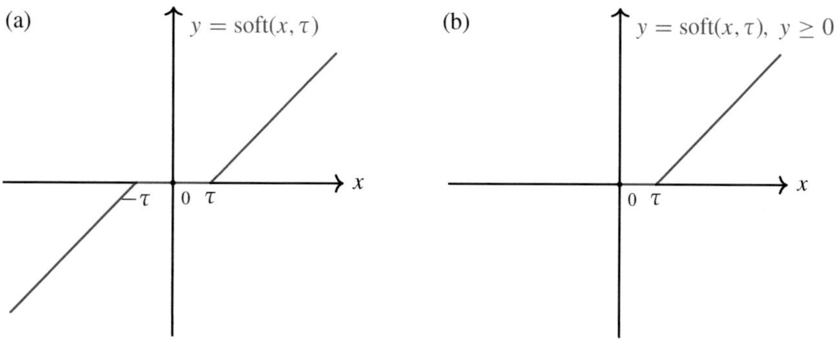

Figure 8.1 Illustrations of soft-thresholding (or shrinkage) operators associated with proximal operators of the ℓ^1 norm (a) and the nuclear norm (b), respectively. Note that singular values are always nonnegative. Typically the threshold $\tau \geq 0$ is a small value.

the exercises (see Exercise 8.4). The reader may further explore whether the same property holds for any unitary invariant matrix norm (introduced in Appendix A.9).

Thus, for the problems of our interest, we can compute the proximal operator efficiently. In this setting, it provides an alternative replacement for the gradient step. Unlike the subgradient method, this *proximal gradient* algorithm enjoys a convergence rate of $O(1/k)$ – exactly the same as if the nonsmooth term was not present! More formally:

THEOREM 8.6. (Convergence of proximal gradient) *Let $F(\boldsymbol{x}) = f(\boldsymbol{x}) + g(\boldsymbol{x})$, where f is a convex, differentiable function with L-Lipschitz continuous gradients, and g a convex function. Consider the following iterative update scheme:*

$$\boldsymbol{w}_k \leftarrow \boldsymbol{x}_k - \frac{1}{L}\nabla f(\boldsymbol{x}_k), \quad \boldsymbol{x}_{k+1} \leftarrow \operatorname{prox}_{g/L}[\boldsymbol{w}_k].$$

Assume $F(\boldsymbol{x})$ has a minimum at $\boldsymbol{x}_\star$. Then for any $k \geq 1$,

$$F(\boldsymbol{x}_k) - F(\boldsymbol{x}_\star) \leq \frac{L\|\boldsymbol{x}_0 - \boldsymbol{x}_\star\|_2^2}{2k}.$$

We will give a detailed proof of this theorem in Section 8.2.4. Thus, for a composite nonsmooth convex function, under certain conditions, we can still obtain an efficient "gradient descent"-like algorithm that has the same convergence rate $O(1/k)$ as that for a smooth function. As long as the nonsmooth part has an easy-to-solve proximal operator, the proximal gradient algorithm has very cheap iterations. Hence it is typically much more scalable than second-order methods. We summarize properties of the iterative process that we have derived so far for minimizing the convex composite problem in Figure 8.2, which is also known as the *proximal gradient* method.

Proximal Gradient (PG)

Problem Class:

$$\min_{x} F(x) = f(x) + g(x)$$

$f, g : \mathbb{R}^n \to \mathbb{R}$ are convex, ∇f L-Lipschitz and g (may be) nonsmooth.

Basic Iteration: set $x_0 \in \mathbb{R}^n$.
Repeat:

$$w_k \leftarrow x_k - \frac{1}{L}\nabla f(x_k),$$

$$x_{k+1} \leftarrow \mathrm{prox}_{g/L}[w_k].$$

Convergence Guarantee:

$F(x_k) - F(x_\star)$ converges at a rate of $O(1/k)$.

Figure 8.2 An overview of the proximal gradient method.

Algorithm 8.1 Proximal Gradient (PG) for Lasso

1: **Problem:** $\min_x \frac{1}{2}\|y - Ax\|_2^2 + \lambda\|x\|_1$, given $y \in \mathbb{R}^m$, $A \in \mathbb{R}^{m\times n}$.
2: **Input:** $x_0 \in \mathbb{R}^n$ and $L \geq \lambda_{\max}(A^*A)$.
3: **for** $(k = 0, 1, 2, \ldots, K-1)$ **do**
4: $\quad w_k \leftarrow x_k - (1/L)A^*(Ax_k - y)$.
5: $\quad x_{k+1} \leftarrow \mathrm{soft}(w_k, \lambda/L)$.
6: **end for**
7: **Output:** $x_\star \leftarrow x_K$.

8.2.3 Proximal Gradient for the Lasso and Stable PCP

For the rest of the section, we will see how to apply the proximal gradient algorithm to several important cases of structured signal recovery problems that we have encountered.

Proximal Gradient for the Lasso

As the first instance, the Lasso problem (8.1.2) obviously falls into the class of problems that can be addressed by the proximal gradient method. We can view g to be the ℓ^1 norm function $\lambda\|x\|_1$ whose proximal operator is given in Proposition 8.4; f is simply the quadratic data term $\frac{1}{2}\|y - Ax\|_2^2$ whose gradient is clearly Lipschitz: the Lipschitz constant L can be the largest eigenvalue of the matrix A^*A, which can be computed in advance.

The resulting proximal gradient descent algorithm for Lasso is sometimes referred to as the *iterative soft-thresholding algorithm* (ISTA), which is summarized in Algorithm 8.1. In terms of computational complexity, the main cost is calculating

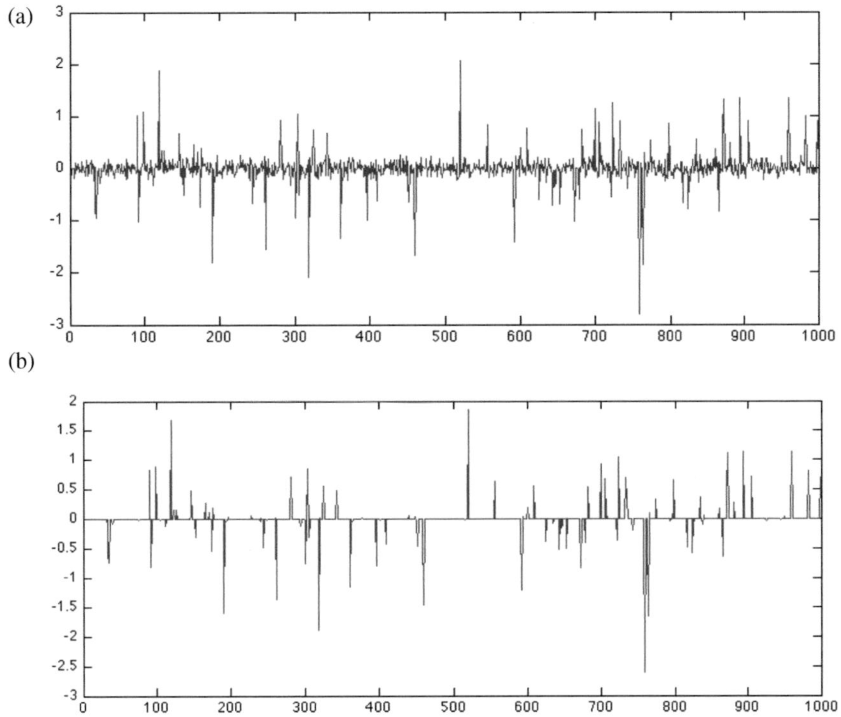

Figure 8.3 (a) A sparse signal $\boldsymbol{x}$ perturbed by small Gaussian noise $\boldsymbol{n}$. (b) The output from a properly chosen soft-thresholding function soft($\boldsymbol{w}, \lambda$).

the gradient $\nabla f(\boldsymbol{x}) = \boldsymbol{A}^*\boldsymbol{A}\boldsymbol{x} - \boldsymbol{A}^*\boldsymbol{y}$ in the inner loop, which in general takes time $O(mn)$.

EXAMPLE 8.7. *We randomly generate a sparse signal $\boldsymbol{x} \in \mathbb{R}^{1000}$ and then add a small Gaussian noise $\boldsymbol{n}$ to all of its coefficients, as shown in Figure 8.3(a). With the added Gaussian noise, the signal $\boldsymbol{w} = \boldsymbol{x} + \boldsymbol{n}$ is not sparse anymore. Then we may try to recover $\boldsymbol{x}$ from $\boldsymbol{w}$ by solving the following problem: $\min_{\boldsymbol{x}} \lambda \|\boldsymbol{x}\|_1 + \frac{1}{2}\|\boldsymbol{w} - \boldsymbol{x}\|_2^2$, where λ is proportional to the noise level. We know the solution to this problem is simply the soft thresholding $\hat{\boldsymbol{x}} = \mathrm{soft}(\boldsymbol{w}, \lambda)$. The result is shown in Figure 8.3(b). We see that the operator successfully removes most of the noise in $\boldsymbol{w}$ and returns a sparse estimate for $\boldsymbol{x}$.*

Proximal Gradient for Stable PCP

According to Proposition 8.4, the nuclear norm $\|\boldsymbol{X}\|_*$ also has a simple proximal operator. Hence we could apply the proximal gradient algorithm to solve low-rank matrix recovery problems. For instance, the stable principal component pursuit (PCP) program is also amenable to the proximal gradient method:

$$\min_{\boldsymbol{L}, \boldsymbol{S}} \|\boldsymbol{L}\|_* + \lambda \|\boldsymbol{S}\|_1 + \frac{\mu}{2}\|\boldsymbol{Y} - \boldsymbol{L} - \boldsymbol{S}\|_F^2. \tag{8.2.23}$$

Notice that, however, for this problem the nonsmooth term $g(\boldsymbol{L}, \boldsymbol{S}) = \|\boldsymbol{L}\|_* + \lambda\|\boldsymbol{S}\|_1$ now contains two nonsmooth functions $\|\boldsymbol{L}\|_*$ and $\lambda\|\boldsymbol{S}\|_1$, each having a simple proximal operator.

We leave as an exercise for the reader to prove the following simple fact about the proximal operator of a separable convex function, which comes in handy for this problem: let $\boldsymbol{x} = [\boldsymbol{x}_1; \boldsymbol{x}_2]$ and $g(\boldsymbol{x}) = g_1(\boldsymbol{x}_1) + g_2(\boldsymbol{x}_2)$ be a separable function. Then

$$\operatorname{prox}_g[\boldsymbol{w}] = \left(\operatorname{prox}_{g_1}[\boldsymbol{w}_1], \operatorname{prox}_{g_2}[\boldsymbol{w}_2]\right),$$

where $\boldsymbol{w}_1$ and $\boldsymbol{w}_2$ in $\boldsymbol{w} = [\boldsymbol{w}_1; \boldsymbol{w}_2]$ correspond to the variables $\boldsymbol{x}_1$ and $\boldsymbol{x}_2$ in $\boldsymbol{x}$, respectively.

Hence, the proximal operator for $g(\boldsymbol{L}, \boldsymbol{S})$ can be computed separately from the proximal operators for the ℓ^1 norm for $\boldsymbol{S}$ and nuclear norm for $\boldsymbol{L}$, respectively. The rest of the proximal gradient algorithm for the stable principal component pursuit program then is easy to derive (and we leave this as an exercise for the reader; see Exercise 8.6). We summarize the overall algorithm below for clarity.

Algorithm 8.2 Proximal Gradient for Stable Principal Component Pursuit

Problem: $\min_{\boldsymbol{L},\boldsymbol{S}} \|\boldsymbol{L}\|_* + \lambda\|\boldsymbol{S}\|_1 + (\mu/2)\|\boldsymbol{Y} - \boldsymbol{L} - \boldsymbol{S}\|_F^2$, given $\boldsymbol{Y}, \lambda, \mu > 0$.
Input: $\boldsymbol{L}_0 \in \mathbb{R}^{m\times n}$, $\boldsymbol{S}_0 \in \mathbb{R}^{m\times n}$.
for $(k = 0, 1, 2, \ldots, K-1)$ **do**
  $\boldsymbol{W}_k \leftarrow \boldsymbol{Y} - \boldsymbol{S}_k$ and compute $\boldsymbol{W}_k = \boldsymbol{U}_k \boldsymbol{\Sigma}_k \boldsymbol{V}_k^*$.
  $\boldsymbol{L}_{k+1} \leftarrow \boldsymbol{U}_k \operatorname{soft}(\boldsymbol{\Sigma}_k, 1/\mu)\boldsymbol{V}_k^*$.
  $\boldsymbol{S}_{k+1} \leftarrow \operatorname{soft}((\boldsymbol{Y} - \boldsymbol{L}_k), \lambda/\mu)$.
end for
Output: $\boldsymbol{L}_\star \leftarrow \boldsymbol{L}_K; \boldsymbol{S}_\star \leftarrow \boldsymbol{S}_K$.

8.2.4 Convergence of Proximal Gradient

In this subsection, we prove Theorem 8.6. We find it convenient to do this in two steps. In the first step, we provide an analysis of a simpler algorithm, known as the *proximal point algorithm*, which only consists of repeated application of the proximal operator. This algorithm is of independent interest, and we will reuse its analysis when we encounter augmented Lagrangian techniques.

PROPOSITION 8.8. (Convergence of proximal point algorithm) *Let $g : \mathbb{R}^n \to \mathbb{R}$ be a convex function, and $\boldsymbol{x}_\star$ a minimizer of g. Let $\boldsymbol{x}_0 \in \mathbb{R}^n$ be arbitrary, and consider the iteration*

$$\boldsymbol{x}_{k+1} = \operatorname{prox}_{\gamma_k g}[\boldsymbol{x}_k], \tag{8.2.24}$$

with $\gamma_k \in \mathbb{R}_+$. Then

$$g(\boldsymbol{x}_{k+1}) - g(\boldsymbol{x}_\star) \leq \frac{\|\boldsymbol{x}_0 - \boldsymbol{x}_\star\|_2^2}{2\sum_{i=0}^k \gamma_i}. \tag{8.2.25}$$

Moreover, if $\sum_{i=0}^\infty \gamma_i = +\infty$, then $\boldsymbol{x}_k \to \boldsymbol{x}_\star$, a minimizer of g.

Proof By construction,

$$\mathbf{0} \in \gamma_k \partial g(\boldsymbol{x}_{k+1}) + \boldsymbol{x}_{k+1} - \boldsymbol{x}_k. \tag{8.2.26}$$

Equivalently, $\boldsymbol{x}_k - \boldsymbol{x}_{k+1} \in \gamma_k \partial g(\boldsymbol{x}_{k+1})$. Using the convexity of $g(\boldsymbol{x})$, we have that

$$\langle \boldsymbol{x}_k - \boldsymbol{x}_{k+1}, \boldsymbol{x}_k - \boldsymbol{x}_{k+1} \rangle \le \gamma_k \left(g(\boldsymbol{x}_k) - g(\boldsymbol{x}_{k+1}) \right). \tag{8.2.27}$$

Since the left-hand side is nonnegative, $g(\boldsymbol{x}_k) \ge g(\boldsymbol{x}_{k+1})$. So, the objective function value is nonincreasing.

Using the subgradient inequality again, we have that

$$\langle \boldsymbol{x}_\star - \boldsymbol{x}_{k+1}, \boldsymbol{x}_k - \boldsymbol{x}_{k+1} \rangle \le \gamma_k \left(g(\boldsymbol{x}_\star) - g(\boldsymbol{x}_{k+1}) \right). \tag{8.2.28}$$

Let us use this fact to bound the distance of $\boldsymbol{x}_{k+1}$ to the optimum. Notice that

$$\begin{aligned}
\|\boldsymbol{x}_{k+1} - \boldsymbol{x}_\star\|_2^2 &= \|\boldsymbol{x}_k - \boldsymbol{x}_\star + \boldsymbol{x}_{k+1} - \boldsymbol{x}_k\|_2^2 \\
&= \|\boldsymbol{x}_k - \boldsymbol{x}_\star\|_2^2 + 2 \langle \boldsymbol{x}_k - \boldsymbol{x}_\star, \boldsymbol{x}_{k+1} - \boldsymbol{x}_k \rangle + \|\boldsymbol{x}_{k+1} - \boldsymbol{x}_k\|_2^2 \\
&= \|\boldsymbol{x}_k - \boldsymbol{x}_\star\|_2^2 - \|\boldsymbol{x}_{k+1} - \boldsymbol{x}_k\|_2^2 + 2 \langle \boldsymbol{x}_{k+1} - \boldsymbol{x}_\star, \boldsymbol{x}_{k+1} - \boldsymbol{x}_k \rangle \\
&\le \|\boldsymbol{x}_k - \boldsymbol{x}_\star\|_2^2 + 2 \langle \boldsymbol{x}_{k+1} - \boldsymbol{x}_\star, \boldsymbol{x}_{k+1} - \boldsymbol{x}_k \rangle \\
&\le \|\boldsymbol{x}_k - \boldsymbol{x}_\star\|_2^2 + 2\gamma_k \left(g(\boldsymbol{x}_\star) - g(\boldsymbol{x}_{k+1}) \right).
\end{aligned} \tag{8.2.29}$$

Since $g(\boldsymbol{x}_{k+1}) \ge g(\boldsymbol{x}_\star)$, the distance of $\boldsymbol{x}_k$ to $\boldsymbol{x}_\star$ also does not increase. In fact, we can say slightly more. Summing the relationship (8.2.29), we obtain

$$\sum_{i=0}^{k} 2\gamma_i \left(g(\boldsymbol{x}_{i+1}) - g(\boldsymbol{x}_\star) \right) \le \|\boldsymbol{x}_0 - \boldsymbol{x}_\star\|_2^2. \tag{8.2.30}$$

Since $g(\boldsymbol{x}_i)$ is nonincreasing, this implies that

$$2 \left(\sum_{i=0}^{k} \gamma_i \right) \left(g(\boldsymbol{x}_{k+1}) - g(\boldsymbol{x}_\star) \right) \le \|\boldsymbol{x}_0 - \boldsymbol{x}_\star\|_2^2. \tag{8.2.31}$$

This gives convergence in function values, as in (8.2.25).

Since $\|\boldsymbol{x}_k - \boldsymbol{x}_\star\|_2$ is nonincreasing, the sequence $\boldsymbol{x}_k$ is bounded, and hence has a cluster point $\bar{\boldsymbol{x}}$. Since $g(\boldsymbol{x}_k) \searrow g(\boldsymbol{x}_\star)$, $g(\bar{\boldsymbol{x}}) = g(\boldsymbol{x}_\star)$, and hence $\bar{\boldsymbol{x}}$ is optimal. Applying inequality (8.2.29) with $\boldsymbol{x}_\star$ replaced by $\bar{\boldsymbol{x}}$, we obtain that $\|\boldsymbol{x}_k - \bar{\boldsymbol{x}}\|_2$ is also nonincreasing, whence the cluster point $\bar{\boldsymbol{x}}$ is a limit of the sequence $\{\boldsymbol{x}_k\}$. □

The key idea in the above proof is to use the optimality condition (8.2.26) for the proximal operator, together with the subgradient inequality to relate the suboptimality $g(\boldsymbol{x}_{k+1}) - g(\boldsymbol{x}_\star)$ in objective function to the distance to the feasible set. To prove Theorem 8.6, we follow a very similar program.

Proof of theorem 8.6 Notice that, by construction, there exists $\gamma \in \partial g(\boldsymbol{x}_{k+1})$ such that

$$\nabla f(\boldsymbol{x}_k) + L(\boldsymbol{x}_{k+1} - \boldsymbol{x}_k) + \gamma = \mathbf{0}. \tag{8.2.32}$$

The subgradient and gradient inequalities for the convex functions f and g give that for any $\boldsymbol{x}$,

$$f(\boldsymbol{x}) \geq f(\boldsymbol{x}_k) + \langle \boldsymbol{x} - \boldsymbol{x}_k, \nabla f(\boldsymbol{x}_k)\rangle, \tag{8.2.33}$$

$$g(\boldsymbol{x}) \geq g(\boldsymbol{x}_{k+1}) + \langle \boldsymbol{x} - \boldsymbol{x}_{k+1}, \gamma\rangle, \tag{8.2.34}$$

whence

$$F(\boldsymbol{x}) \geq f(\boldsymbol{x}_k) + g(\boldsymbol{x}_{k+1}) + \langle \boldsymbol{x} - \boldsymbol{x}_k, \nabla f(\boldsymbol{x}_k)\rangle + \langle \boldsymbol{x} - \boldsymbol{x}_{k+1}, \gamma\rangle. \tag{8.2.35}$$

Recall the definition of an upper bound $\hat{F}$ of F defined in (8.2.15). So, we have

$$\begin{aligned} F(\boldsymbol{x}) - F(\boldsymbol{x}_{k+1}) &\geq F(\boldsymbol{x}) - \hat{F}(\boldsymbol{x}_{k+1}, \boldsymbol{x}_k) \\ &\geq f(\boldsymbol{x}_k) + g(\boldsymbol{x}_{k+1}) + \langle \boldsymbol{x} - \boldsymbol{x}_k, \nabla f(\boldsymbol{x}_k)\rangle \\ &\quad + \langle \boldsymbol{x} - \boldsymbol{x}_{k+1}, \gamma\rangle - \hat{F}(\boldsymbol{x}_{k+1}, \boldsymbol{x}_k) \\ &= -\frac{L}{2}\|\boldsymbol{x}_{k+1} - \boldsymbol{x}_k\|_2^2 + \langle \boldsymbol{x} - \boldsymbol{x}_{k+1}, \nabla f(\boldsymbol{x}_k) + \gamma\rangle \\ &= -\frac{L}{2}\|\boldsymbol{x}_{k+1} - \boldsymbol{x}_k\|_2^2 + L\langle \boldsymbol{x} - \boldsymbol{x}_{k+1}, \boldsymbol{x}_k - \boldsymbol{x}_{k+1}\rangle \\ &= \frac{L}{2}\|\boldsymbol{x} - \boldsymbol{x}_{k+1}\|_2^2 - \frac{L}{2}\|\boldsymbol{x} - \boldsymbol{x}_k\|_2^2. \end{aligned} \tag{8.2.36}$$

Evaluating this expression at $\boldsymbol{x} = \boldsymbol{x}_\star$, we see that $\|\boldsymbol{x}_k - \boldsymbol{x}_\star\|_2$ is nonincreasing. Moreover, rearranging the relationship and summing from 0 to $k-1$, we obtain that

$$\sum_{i=0}^{k-1} \{F(\boldsymbol{x}_{i+1}) - F(\boldsymbol{x}_\star)\} \leq \frac{L}{2}\|\boldsymbol{x}_0 - \boldsymbol{x}_\star\|_2^2. \tag{8.2.37}$$

Evaluating (8.2.36) at $\boldsymbol{x} = \boldsymbol{x}_k$, we obtain

$$F(\boldsymbol{x}_k) - F(\boldsymbol{x}_{k+1}) \geq \frac{L}{2}\|\boldsymbol{x}_k - \boldsymbol{x}_{k+1}\|_2^2. \tag{8.2.38}$$

Hence, (8.2.37) implies that

$$k\{F(\boldsymbol{x}_k) - F(\boldsymbol{x}_\star)\} \leq \frac{L}{2}\|\boldsymbol{x}_0 - \boldsymbol{x}_\star\|_2^2. \tag{8.2.39}$$

Rearranging, we get the desired conclusion. □

8.3 Accelerated Proximal Gradient Methods

In the previous section, we have seen that by exploiting the fact that if the nonsmooth part of a convex function has an easily computable proximal operator, we are able to extend the gradient descent algorithm for smooth functions to the special class of composite objective functions that we encounter in structured signal recovery. The resulting algorithm enjoys the same $O(1/k)$ convergence rate as in the smooth case. Recognizing the special structure in our problem of interest yields a significantly more accurate and efficient algorithm.

8.3.1 Acceleration via Nesterov's Method

With the taste of victory still on our lips, we might naturally ask whether further improvements are still possible – is our proximal gradient algorithm optimal for this class of functions? For the question to be meaningful, we need to restrict our attention to methods with efficient iterations, such as gradient-like methods. For example, we could restrict our attention to *first-order methods*, which base their future actions on the past iterates $\boldsymbol{x}_0, \ldots, \boldsymbol{x}_k$, objective values at these iterates, and the gradients $\nabla f(\boldsymbol{x}_0), \ldots, \nabla f(\boldsymbol{x}_k)$. The corresponding question for *smooth functions* was studied in great depth in the late 1970s and early 1980s by Russian optimization theorists, including Polyak, Nesterov, Nemirovski, and Yudin.[5]

They asked the very natural question: *for minimizing a smooth function f, is the gradient method optimal amongst first-order methods?* Again, to study this problem one needs a model for computation. They considered a *black box* model, in which the algorithm produces a sequence of iterates $\boldsymbol{x}_0, \ldots, \boldsymbol{x}_k$. At each iteration, the algorithm is provided with the value $f(\boldsymbol{x}_i)$ and the gradient $\nabla f(\boldsymbol{x}_i)$. It produces the next iterate as a function of the history of iterates, gradients, and function values up to this time:

$$\boldsymbol{x}_{k+1} = \varphi_k\big(\boldsymbol{x}_0, \ldots, \boldsymbol{x}_k, f(\boldsymbol{x}_0), \ldots, f(\boldsymbol{x}_k), \nabla f(\boldsymbol{x}_0), \ldots, \nabla f(\boldsymbol{x}_k)\big). \tag{8.3.1}$$

With this model in mind, one can begin to study algorithms from a worst-case perspective. To do so, we fix a class of functions $\mathcal{F}$, and ask how well the algorithm does on the "worst function" from this class:

$$\sup_{f \in \mathcal{F},\, \boldsymbol{x}_0} \left\{ f(\boldsymbol{x}_k) - \inf_{\boldsymbol{x}} f(\boldsymbol{x}) \right\}. \tag{8.3.2}$$

One can study various classes of functions $\mathcal{F}$. However, for our purposes, one interesting class is the convex differentiable functions $f : \mathsf{B}(0,r) \to \mathbb{R}$, defined on a ball of radius r, with L-Lipschitz gradients:

$$\mathcal{F}_{L,r} \doteq \left\{ f : \mathsf{B}(0,r) \to \mathbb{R} \mid \left\| \nabla f(\boldsymbol{x}) - \nabla f(\boldsymbol{x}') \right\|_2 \le L \left\| \boldsymbol{x} - \boldsymbol{x}' \right\|_2 \;\; \forall \boldsymbol{x}, \boldsymbol{x}' \in \mathsf{B}(0,r) \right\}. \tag{8.3.3}$$

The gradient method achieves a rate of $O(1/k)$ over this class:

$$\sup_{f \in \mathcal{F}_{L,r},\, \boldsymbol{x}_0} \left\{ f(\boldsymbol{x}_k) - \inf_{\boldsymbol{x}} f(\boldsymbol{x}) \right\} \le \frac{CLr^2}{k}, \tag{8.3.4}$$

[5] For a more comprehensive introduction to this circle of ideas, see [Nes03] or [Nem95].

where $C > 0$ is a constant. However, the best lower bound that anyone could prove was of much lower order:

$$\sup_{f \in \mathcal{F}_{L,r},\, \boldsymbol{x}_0} \left\{ f(\boldsymbol{x}_k) - \inf_{\boldsymbol{x}} f(\boldsymbol{x}) \right\} \geq \frac{cLr^2}{k^2}, \tag{8.3.5}$$

where $c > 0$ is some constant. Was this merely a gap in the theory? Or might there actually exist a "faster" gradient method than gradient descent itself?

In 1983, Yurii Nesterov closed this gap, to remarkable effect [Nes83]. He demonstrated a relatively simple first-order method, which achieved the optimal rate of convergence, $O(1/k^2)$. The analysis of this algorithm is straightforward to read – the 1983 paper is only five pages! However, it is not straightforward to build intuition into *how* the method achieves this rate. To gain some loose appreciation for what is going on, we start from a simpler idea.

Let us first consider the gradient descent method for a smooth function with Lipschitz gradients. At each iteration, the update simply follows the direction of the gradient:

$$\boldsymbol{x}_{k+1} = \boldsymbol{x}_k - \alpha \nabla f(\boldsymbol{x}_k),$$

where a good choice of α for an L-Lipschitz function is $1/L$. The negative gradient $-\nabla f(\boldsymbol{x}_k)$ indicates the direction in which the function drops its value the fastest. Instead of updating along this most greedy direction at the current estimate $\boldsymbol{x}_k$, a slightly more conservative strategy is to update by keeping some momentum from the previous update direction: $\boldsymbol{x}_k - \boldsymbol{x}_{k-1}$. That leads to an update rule that is known as the *heavy ball method* [Pol64]:

$$\boldsymbol{x}_{k+1} = \boldsymbol{x}_k - \alpha \nabla f(\boldsymbol{x}_k) + \beta \big(\boldsymbol{x}_k - \boldsymbol{x}_{k-1}\big). \tag{8.3.6}$$

For properly chosen parameters, the heavy ball method can reduce oscillations in the trajectories and leads to faster convergence.

Like the heavy ball method, Nesterov's acceleration method uses a momentum step. It introduces an auxiliary point $\boldsymbol{p}_{k+1}$ of the form similar to that in the heavy ball method:

$$\boldsymbol{p}_{k+1} \doteq \boldsymbol{x}_k + \beta_{k+1} \big(\boldsymbol{x}_k - \boldsymbol{x}_{k-1}\big).$$

At each iteration, we move to this new point, and then descend from it:

$$\boldsymbol{x}_{k+1} = \boldsymbol{p}_{k+1} - \alpha \nabla f(\boldsymbol{p}_{k+1}). \tag{8.3.7}$$

The weights $\alpha = 1/L$ and $\{\beta_{k+1}\}$ are carefully chosen to achieve the optimal convergence rate:

$$t_1 = 1, \quad t_{k+1} = \frac{1 + \sqrt{1 + 4t_k^2}}{2}, \quad \beta_{k+1} = \frac{t_k - 1}{t_{k+1}}. \tag{8.3.8}$$

These particular values come from the convergence analysis. One can rigorously show that with this update scheme, the resulting algorithm achieves the theoretically optimal convergence rate $O(1/k^2)$ for the class of smooth functions with Lipschitz gradient.

Accelerating the Proximal Gradient Method

As we have seen in the previous section, convex programs that arise in the context of structured signal recovery are often of the composite form $F(\boldsymbol{x}) = f(\boldsymbol{x}) + g(\boldsymbol{x})$, where f is a smooth term whose gradient is L-Lipschitz and $g(\boldsymbol{x})$ is convex but not necessarily smooth. In the proximal gradient method introduced in the previous section, we have seen that at the k-th iteration, the value of the objective function $F(\boldsymbol{x})$ can be upper-bounded by

$$\begin{aligned}\hat{F}(\boldsymbol{x},\boldsymbol{x}_k) &\doteq f(\boldsymbol{x}_k) + \langle \nabla f(\boldsymbol{x}_k), \boldsymbol{x} - \boldsymbol{x}_k\rangle + (L/2)\|\boldsymbol{x} - \boldsymbol{x}_k\|_2^2 + g(\boldsymbol{x})\\ &\doteq (L/2)\|\boldsymbol{x} - \boldsymbol{w}_k\|_2^2 + g(\boldsymbol{x}) + \text{terms that do not depend on } \boldsymbol{x},\end{aligned}$$

where $\boldsymbol{w}_k = \boldsymbol{x}_k - (1/L)\nabla f(\boldsymbol{x}_k)$. As we have seen in the previous section, the gradient descent algorithm for the smooth part $f(\boldsymbol{x})$ corresponds to directly minimizing its quadratic approximation of $f(\boldsymbol{x})$ at $\boldsymbol{x}_k$.

In this language, if $g \equiv 0$, Nesterov's method corresponds to: *extrapolating* to find the point $\boldsymbol{p}_{k+1}$ based on the past two iterates, and then *minimizing* a quadratic upper bound $\hat{f}$ to f, taken at the new point $\boldsymbol{p}_{k+1}$, by taking a gradient step. Let us attempt to do the same thing for our composite function $\hat{F}$. Set

$$\boldsymbol{p}_{k+1} = \boldsymbol{x}_k + \beta_{k+1}\big(\boldsymbol{x}_k - \boldsymbol{x}_{k-1}\big), \tag{8.3.9}$$

instead of the current estimate $\boldsymbol{x}_k$. Then minimize $\hat{F}(\boldsymbol{x}, \boldsymbol{p}_{k+1})$ to obtain the next iterate $\boldsymbol{x}_{k+1}$:

$$\boldsymbol{x}_{k+1} = \operatorname{prox}_{g/L}\left[\boldsymbol{p}_{k+1} - \frac{1}{L}\nabla f(\boldsymbol{p}_{k+1})\right]. \tag{8.3.10}$$

We summarize this scheme in Figure 8.4. Theorem 8.9 establishes that, with this simple modification to the proximal gradient method, the resulting new algorithm achieves the theoretically optimal convergence rate $O(1/k^2)$ for this class of methods, despite the presence of a nonsmooth term in the objective function.

THEOREM 8.9. (Convergence of accelerated proximal gradient) *Let the sequence* $\{\boldsymbol{x}_k\}$ *be generated by the above accelerated proximal gradient scheme for the convex composite function* $F(\boldsymbol{x}) = f(\boldsymbol{x}) + g(\boldsymbol{x})$*, where the gradient of* f *is* L*-Lipschitz. Let* $\boldsymbol{x}_\star$ *be a minimizer of* $F(\boldsymbol{x})$*. Then for any* $k \geq 1$*,*

$$F(\boldsymbol{x}_k) - F(\boldsymbol{x}_\star) \leq \frac{2L\|\boldsymbol{x}_0 - \boldsymbol{x}_\star\|_2^2}{(k+1)^2}.$$

Accelerated Proximal Gradient (APG)

Problem Class:

$$\min_{\boldsymbol{x}} F(\boldsymbol{x}) = f(\boldsymbol{x}) + g(\boldsymbol{x})$$

$f, g : \mathbb{R}^n \to \mathbb{R}$ are convex, ∇f L-Lipschitz and g nonsmooth.

Basic Iteration: set $\boldsymbol{x}_0 \in \mathbb{R}^n$, $\boldsymbol{p}_1 = \boldsymbol{x}_1 \leftarrow \boldsymbol{x}_0$, and $t_1 \leftarrow 1$.
Repeat for $k = 1, 2, \ldots, K$:

$$t_{k+1} \leftarrow \frac{1 + \sqrt{1 + 4t_k{}^2}}{2}, \quad \beta_{k+1} \leftarrow \frac{t_k - 1}{t_{k+1}}.$$

$$\boldsymbol{p}_{k+1} \leftarrow \boldsymbol{x}_k + \beta_{k+1}\big(\boldsymbol{x}_k - \boldsymbol{x}_{k-1}\big).$$

$$\boldsymbol{x}_{k+1} \leftarrow \operatorname{prox}_{g/L}\Big[\boldsymbol{p}_{k+1} - \frac{1}{L}\nabla f(\boldsymbol{p}_{k+1})\Big].$$

Convergence Guarantee:

$F(\boldsymbol{x}_k) - F(\boldsymbol{x}_\star)$ converges at a rate of $O(1/k^2)$.

Figure 8.4 An overview of the accelerated proximal gradient method.

Algorithm 8.3 Accelerated Proximal Gradient (APG) for BPDN

- **Problem:** $\min_{\boldsymbol{x}} \frac{1}{2}\|\boldsymbol{y} - \boldsymbol{A}\boldsymbol{x}\|_2^2 + \lambda\|\boldsymbol{x}\|_1$, given $\boldsymbol{y} \in \mathbb{R}^m$, $\boldsymbol{A} \in \mathbb{R}^{m \times n}$.
- **Input:** $\boldsymbol{x}_0 \in \mathbb{R}^n$, $\boldsymbol{p}_1 = \boldsymbol{x}_1 \leftarrow \boldsymbol{x}_0$, and $t_1 \leftarrow 1$, and $L \geq \lambda_{\max}(\boldsymbol{A}^*\boldsymbol{A})$.
- **for** $(k = 1, 2, \ldots, K-1)$ **do**
  - $t_{k+1} \leftarrow \dfrac{1 + \sqrt{1 + 4t_k^2}}{2}; \; \beta_{k+1} \leftarrow \dfrac{t_k - 1}{t_{k+1}}.$
  - $\boldsymbol{p}_{k+1} \leftarrow \boldsymbol{x}_k + \beta_{k+1}(\boldsymbol{x}_k - \boldsymbol{x}_{k-1}).$
  - $\boldsymbol{w}_{k+1} \leftarrow \boldsymbol{p}_{k+1} - (1/L)\boldsymbol{A}^*(\boldsymbol{A}\boldsymbol{p}_{k+1} - \boldsymbol{y}).$
  - $\boldsymbol{x}_{k+1} \leftarrow \operatorname{soft}(\boldsymbol{w}_{k+1}, \lambda/L).$
- **end for**
- **Output:** $\boldsymbol{x}_\star \leftarrow \boldsymbol{x}_K$.

8.3.2 APG for Basis Pursuit Denoising

Applying the APG algorithm in Figure 8.4 to the basis pursuit denoising problem (8.1.2), we obtain Algorithm 8.3. This algorithm is also known as the fast iterative shrinkage-thresholding algorithm (FISTA), coined by Beck and Teboulle [BT09].

8.3.3 APG for Stable Principal Component Pursuit

Similarly we could apply the APG algorithm in Figure 8.4 to solve the stable principal component pursuit (PCP) problem (8.2.23). Again, notice that the APG scheme respects the natural separable structure of the objective function.

Algorithm 8.4 Accelerated Proximal Gradient (APG) for Stable PCP

Problem: $\min_{L,S} \|L\|_* + \lambda\|S\|_1 + (\mu/2)\|Y - L - S\|_F^2$, given $Y, \lambda, \mu > 0$.
Input: $L_0 \in \mathbb{R}^{m\times n}$, $S_0 \in \mathbb{R}^{m\times n}$, $P_1^S = S_1 \leftarrow S_0$, $P_1^L = L_1 \leftarrow L_0$, $t_1 \leftarrow 1$.
for ($k = 1, 2, \ldots, K-1$) **do**
  $t_{k+1} \leftarrow \dfrac{1+\sqrt{1+4t_k^2}}{2}$, $\beta_{k+1} \leftarrow \dfrac{t_k - 1}{t_{k+1}}$.
  $P_{k+1}^L \leftarrow L_k + \beta_{k+1}\big(L_k - L_{k-1}\big)$.
  $P_{k+1}^S \leftarrow S_k + \beta_{k+1}\big(S_k - S_{k-1}\big)$.
  $W_{k+1} \leftarrow Y - P_{k+1}^S$ and compute the SVD: $W_{k+1} = U_{k+1}\Sigma_{k+1}V_{k+1}^*$.
  $L_{k+1} \leftarrow U_{k+1}\mathrm{soft}(\Sigma_{k+1}, 1/\mu)V_{k+1}^*$.
  $S_{k+1} \leftarrow \mathrm{soft}((Y - P_{k+1}^L), \lambda/\mu)$.
end for
Output: $L_\star \leftarrow L_K$; $S_\star \leftarrow S_K$.

8.3.4 Convergence of APG

Our convergence analysis follows, almost verbatim, Beck and Teboulle [BT09]. Let $\varphi(\boldsymbol{y})$ denote the operator that takes a step in the direction of the gradient of f at $\boldsymbol{y}$, and then applies the proximal operator of g/L:

$$\varphi(\boldsymbol{y}) = \mathrm{prox}_{g/L}\left[\boldsymbol{y} - \frac{1}{L}\nabla f(\boldsymbol{y})\right]. \tag{8.3.11}$$

In this language, the accelerated proximal gradient iteration is

$$\boldsymbol{x}_{k+1} = \varphi(\boldsymbol{p}_{k+1}). \tag{8.3.12}$$

The following lemma allows us to compare the value of $F(\boldsymbol{x})$ at any point $\boldsymbol{x}$ to the value at $\varphi(\boldsymbol{p})$ for an arbitrary point $\boldsymbol{p}$:

LEMMA 8.10. *For every* $\boldsymbol{x}, \boldsymbol{p} \in \mathbb{R}^n$,

$$F(\boldsymbol{x}) - F(\varphi(\boldsymbol{p})) \geq \frac{L}{2}\left\|\varphi(\boldsymbol{p}) - \boldsymbol{p}\right\|_2^2 + L\big\langle \boldsymbol{p} - \boldsymbol{x}, \varphi(\boldsymbol{p}) - \boldsymbol{p}\big\rangle. \tag{8.3.13}$$

Proof For it, we note that from the optimality condition for the proximal problem, $\boldsymbol{z} = \varphi(\boldsymbol{p})$ if and only if there exists $\boldsymbol{\gamma} \in \partial g(\boldsymbol{z})$ such that

$$\boldsymbol{\gamma} + L(\boldsymbol{z} - \boldsymbol{p}) + \nabla f(\boldsymbol{p}) = \boldsymbol{0}. \tag{8.3.14}$$

Using the subgradient inequalities for f and g, we obtain that

$$f(\boldsymbol{x}) \geq f(\boldsymbol{p}) + \langle \boldsymbol{x} - \boldsymbol{p}, \nabla f(\boldsymbol{p})\rangle, \tag{8.3.15}$$

$$g(\boldsymbol{x}) \geq g(\varphi(\boldsymbol{p})) + \big\langle \boldsymbol{x} - \varphi(\boldsymbol{p}), \boldsymbol{\gamma}\big\rangle. \tag{8.3.16}$$

Hence,

$$\begin{aligned} F(\boldsymbol{x}) - F(\varphi(\boldsymbol{p})) &\geq f(\boldsymbol{p}) + g(\varphi(\boldsymbol{p})) + \langle \boldsymbol{x} - \boldsymbol{p}, \nabla f(\boldsymbol{p}) \rangle \\ &\quad + \langle \boldsymbol{x} - \varphi(\boldsymbol{p}), \boldsymbol{\gamma} \rangle - F(\varphi(\boldsymbol{p})) \\ &\geq f(\boldsymbol{p}) + g(\varphi(\boldsymbol{p})) + \langle \boldsymbol{x} - \boldsymbol{p}, \nabla f(\boldsymbol{p}) \rangle \\ &\quad + \langle \boldsymbol{x} - \varphi(\boldsymbol{p}), \boldsymbol{\gamma} \rangle - \hat{F}(\varphi(\boldsymbol{p}), \boldsymbol{p}) \\ &= -\frac{L}{2} \left\| \varphi(\boldsymbol{p}) - \boldsymbol{p} \right\|_2^2 + \langle \boldsymbol{x} - \varphi(\boldsymbol{p}), \nabla f(\boldsymbol{p}) + \boldsymbol{\gamma} \rangle \\ &= -\frac{L}{2} \left\| \varphi(\boldsymbol{p}) - \boldsymbol{p} \right\|_2^2 + L \langle \boldsymbol{x} - \varphi(\boldsymbol{p}), \boldsymbol{p} - \varphi(\boldsymbol{p}) \rangle \\ &= \frac{L}{2} \left\| \varphi(\boldsymbol{p}) - \boldsymbol{p} \right\|_2^2 + L \langle \boldsymbol{p} - \boldsymbol{x}, \varphi(\boldsymbol{p}) - \boldsymbol{p} \rangle, \end{aligned} \tag{8.3.17}$$

as desired. □

Using Lemma 8.10, we obtain a relationship between the suboptimality in function values and the distance of an interpolated point to the optimum:

LEMMA 8.11. *Let $\{(\boldsymbol{x}_k, \boldsymbol{p}_k)\}$ be the sequence generated by the proximal gradient method. Set*

$$v_k = F(\boldsymbol{x}_k) - F(\boldsymbol{x}_\star) \tag{8.3.18}$$

and

$$\boldsymbol{u}_k = t_k \boldsymbol{x}_k - (t_k - 1)\boldsymbol{x}_{k-1} - \boldsymbol{x}_\star. \tag{8.3.19}$$

Then

$$\frac{2}{L} t_k^2 v_k - \frac{2}{L} t_{k+1}^2 v_{k+1} \geq \|\boldsymbol{u}_{k+1}\|_2^2 - \|\boldsymbol{u}_k\|_2^2. \tag{8.3.20}$$

Proof Let us apply the previous lemma with $\boldsymbol{x} = \boldsymbol{x}_k$ and $\boldsymbol{p} = \boldsymbol{p}_{k+1}$. This gives

$$\frac{2}{L}(v_k - v_{k+1}) \geq \left\| \boldsymbol{x}_{k+1} - \boldsymbol{p}_{k+1} \right\|_2^2 + 2\langle \boldsymbol{p}_{k+1} - \boldsymbol{x}_k, \boldsymbol{x}_{k+1} - \boldsymbol{p}_{k+1} \rangle. \tag{8.3.21}$$

Applying the lemma with $\boldsymbol{x} = \boldsymbol{x}_\star$ and $\boldsymbol{p} = \boldsymbol{p}_{k+1}$, we get

$$-\frac{2}{L} v_{k+1} \geq \left\| \boldsymbol{x}_{k+1} - \boldsymbol{p}_{k+1} \right\|_2^2 + 2\langle \boldsymbol{p}_{k+1} - \boldsymbol{x}_\star, \boldsymbol{x}_{k+1} - \boldsymbol{p}_{k+1} \rangle. \tag{8.3.22}$$

Multiplying the first inequality by $t_{k+1} - 1$ and adding that to the second inequality, we get

$$\begin{aligned} &\frac{2}{L}\left((t_{k+1} - 1)v_k - t_{k+1} v_{k+1}\right) \\ &\geq t_{k+1} \left\| \boldsymbol{x}_{k+1} - \boldsymbol{p}_{k+1} \right\|_2^2 + 2\langle \boldsymbol{x}_{k+1} - \boldsymbol{p}_{k+1}, t_{k+1}\boldsymbol{p}_{k+1} - (t_{k+1} - 1)\boldsymbol{x}_k - \boldsymbol{x}_\star \rangle. \end{aligned}$$

Multiplying both sides by t_{k+1}, and using that $t_k^2 = t_{k+1}(t_{k+1} - 1)$, we get

$$\begin{aligned}
&\frac{2}{L}\left(t_k^2 v_k - t_{k+1}^2 v_{k+1}\right)\\
&\geq \left\| t_{k+1}\left(\boldsymbol{x}_{k+1} - \boldsymbol{p}_{k+1}\right)\right\|_2^2 + 2t_{k+1}\left\langle \boldsymbol{x}_{k+1} - \boldsymbol{p}_{k+1}, t_{k+1}\boldsymbol{p}_{k+1} - (t_{k+1}-1)\boldsymbol{x}_k - \boldsymbol{x}_\star\right\rangle\\
&= \| t_{k+1}\boldsymbol{x}_{k+1} - (t_{k+1}-1)\boldsymbol{x}_k - \boldsymbol{x}_\star\|_2^2 - \left\| t_{k+1}\boldsymbol{p}_{k+1} - (t_{k+1}-1)\boldsymbol{x}_k - \boldsymbol{x}_\star\right\|_2^2\\
&= \|\boldsymbol{u}_{k+1}\|_2^2 - \|\boldsymbol{u}_k\|_2^2,
\end{aligned}$$

where the last equality follows from plugging in

$$\boldsymbol{p}_{k+1} = \boldsymbol{x}_k + \frac{t_k - 1}{t_{k+1}}(\boldsymbol{x}_k - \boldsymbol{x}_{k-1}),$$

as per the APG algorithm. □

To prove the desired result, we note two simple facts, and then perform a calculation. First:

LEMMA 8.12. *Let $\{(a_k, b_k)\}$ be sequences of positive real numbers satisfying*

$$a_k - a_{k+1} \geq b_{k+1} - b_k \quad \forall\, k, a_1 + b_1 \leq c. \tag{8.3.23}$$

Then $a_k \leq c$ for every k.

Second:

LEMMA 8.13. *The sequence $\{t_k\}$ generated by the accelerated proximal gradient method satisfies*

$$t_k \geq \frac{k+1}{2} \quad \forall\, k \geq 1. \tag{8.3.24}$$

With these facts in mind, we prove Theorem 8.9.

Proof of theorem 8.9 Define

$$a_k \doteq \frac{2}{L} t_k^2 v_k, \quad b_k \doteq \|\boldsymbol{u}_k\|_2^2, \quad c \doteq \|\boldsymbol{x}_0 - \boldsymbol{x}_\star\|_2^2. \tag{8.3.25}$$

By Lemma 8.11, for every k,

$$a_k - a_{k+1} \geq b_{k+1} - b_k, \tag{8.3.26}$$

so, provided $a_1 + b_1 \leq c$, we obtain that $a_k \leq c$ for every k, whence

$$\frac{2}{L} t_k^2 v_k \leq \|\boldsymbol{x}_0 - \boldsymbol{x}_\star\|_2^2. \tag{8.3.27}$$

Since $t_k \geq (k+1)/2$, this gives

$$F(\boldsymbol{x}_k) - F(\boldsymbol{x}_\star) \leq \frac{2L\,\|\boldsymbol{x}_0 - \boldsymbol{x}_\star\|_2^2}{(k+1)^2}. \tag{8.3.28}$$

So, it just remains to check that $a_1 + b_1 \le c$. Since $t_1 = 1$, $a_1 = (2/L)v_1$, while $b_1 = \|\boldsymbol{x}_1 - \boldsymbol{x}_\star\|_2^2$. In Lemma 8.10, set $\boldsymbol{x} = \boldsymbol{x}_\star$, $\boldsymbol{p} = \boldsymbol{p}_1$, to obtain

$$F(\boldsymbol{x}_\star) - F(\boldsymbol{x}_1) \ge \frac{L}{2}\left\|\boldsymbol{x}_1 - \boldsymbol{p}_1\right\|_2^2 + L\left\langle \boldsymbol{p}_1 - \boldsymbol{x}_\star, \boldsymbol{x}_1 - \boldsymbol{p}_1\right\rangle \tag{8.3.29}$$

$$= \frac{L}{2}\left(\|\boldsymbol{x}_1 - \boldsymbol{x}_\star\|_2^2 - \left\|\boldsymbol{p}_1 - \boldsymbol{x}_\star\right\|_2^2\right). \tag{8.3.30}$$

Since $\left\|\boldsymbol{p}_1 - \boldsymbol{x}_\star\right\|_2^2 = \|\boldsymbol{x}_0 - \boldsymbol{x}_\star\|_2^2$, this gives the result. □

8.3.5 Further Developments on Acceleration

Acceleration is a surprising phenomenon for gradient-based (hence first-order) optimization methods. The previous subsection merely introduced the very basic concept and technique of acceleration, probably just enough for practitioners to apply such methods to the low-dimensional model estimation problems. As noted before, our derivation relies on techniques of Beck and Teboulle [BT09], also known as *momentum analysis*. This is actually different from the original construction by Nesterov based on *estimation sequences*. For a more detailed description of the origin of acceleration techniques, one may refer to the classic book "*Introductory Lectures on Convex Programming: A Basic Course*" by Nesterov [Nes13].

Nesterov's original construction by estimation sequence is often viewed as an algebra trick and thus is difficult to comprehend. Considering the great significance and impact of acceleration methods in modern large-scale optimization problems (that arise in compressive sensing and machine learning), it is of interest to explain the acceleration phenomenon in a more intuitive way so that one could potentially design acceleration methods in a more principled way or for broader classes of problems. To this end, there has been an increasing interest to explain acceleration from the perspective of *continuous dynamics*.

It is widely known that (nonaccelerated) gradient descent can be viewed as discretization of a first-order ordinary differential equation (ODE) associated with the gradient flow. Recently, the work of [SBC14] (and many subsequent works [KBB16, KBB15, WWJ16], etc.) have shown that Nesterov's accelerated gradient descent can be explained as the discretization of a second-order ODE. A similar idea of speeding up iterative methods via discretizing a second-order ODE can be traced back to the work of Polyak [Pol64] in the 1960s. Because of the simplicity of continuous-time dynamics, such a point of view provides a good explanation of the inner mechanism of acceleration. However, to obtain actual iterative algorithms, such a formulation requires proper discretization, which is often not a trivial problem.

Meanwhile, the recent work on the "*approximate duality gap technique*" (ADGT) [DO19] provides a new framework that revisits Nesterov's original estimation sequence construction from a continuous-time perspective. Within this framework, in continuous time, the estimation sequence can be viewed as a way to construct more precise lower and upper bounds for the difference between the optimal value and the current value by exploiting the convexity of the objective function; while in discrete time, the upper bound constructed by ADGT will incur a discretization error, which then can be canceled out by exploiting the smoothness property of the objective function (e.g., by gradient descent). As the duality gap becomes more precise, the optimal accelerated convergence rate can be guaranteed.

These recent developments have enriched our understanding of Nesterov's acceleration method. Nevertheless, as we have noted before, as far as first-order methods are concerned, the Nesterov construction has reached the optimal iteration complexity $O(1/k^2)$ for this class of methods. To achieve better iteration complexity, one must resort to high-order information. Somewhat surprisingly, the ADGT framework does allow us to further generalize acceleration techniques to *high-order* settings and leads to accelerated algorithms that can achieve the optimal iteration complexity [SJM19].

8.4 Augmented Lagrange Multipliers

So far, we have described how to solve certain classes of *unconstrained* convex optimization problems arising in structured signal recovery. However, in some scenarios – e.g., if the noise level is low, or if the target solution $\boldsymbol{x}$ is known ahead of time to possess additional application-specific structure – it may be desirable to exactly enforce equality constraints such as in the exact BP program (8.1.1) or the PCP (8.1.5).

In this section, we describe a framework for solving *equality constrained* problems of the form

$$\begin{array}{ll} \min_{\boldsymbol{x}} & g(\boldsymbol{x}) \\ \text{subject to} & \boldsymbol{A}\boldsymbol{x} = \boldsymbol{y}, \end{array} \tag{8.4.1}$$

where $g : \mathbb{R}^n \to \mathbb{R}$ is a convex function, $\boldsymbol{A} \in \mathbb{R}^{m\times n}$ is a matrix, and $\boldsymbol{y} \in \text{range}(\boldsymbol{A})$ (so that the problem is feasible). One very intuitive approach to producing an approximate solution to (8.4.1) is to simply replace the equality constraint $\boldsymbol{A}\boldsymbol{x} = \boldsymbol{y}$ with a penalty function $f(\boldsymbol{x}) = \frac{1}{2}\|\boldsymbol{A}\boldsymbol{x} - \boldsymbol{y}\|_2^2$, and solve the unconstrained problem

$$\min_{\boldsymbol{x}} \; g(\boldsymbol{x}) + \frac{\mu}{2}\|\boldsymbol{A}\boldsymbol{x} - \boldsymbol{y}\|_2^2 \tag{8.4.2}$$

for a very large value of μ. As μ increases to $+\infty$, the solution set of this problem approaches the solution set of the equality constrained problem (8.4.1). This is known as the *penalty method* in the optimization literature, and has a long history, with many variants. Its main advantage is that it leaves us with a simpler unconstrained problem, to which we can directly apply scalable first-order methods such as the proximal gradient methods of the previous two sections.

However, there is a serious drawback to this approach. For first-order methods such as PG and APG, the rate of convergence is dictated by how quickly the gradient $\nabla(\mu f) = \mu \boldsymbol{A}^*(\boldsymbol{A}\boldsymbol{x} - \boldsymbol{y})$ can change from point to point, which is measured through the Lipschitz constant

$$L_{\nabla \mu f} = \mu \left\| A \right\|_2^2 .$$

This increases linearly with μ: *the larger μ is, the harder the unconstrained problem* (8.4.2) *is to solve!* One practical approach to mitigating this effect is to solve a sequence of unconstrained problems, with increasing μ, and use the solution to each as an initial guess for the next. This *continuation* technique is often valuable in practice. Nevertheless, it suffers from the same drawback: as μ increases, accurate solutions become increasingly difficult to obtain.

Lagrange duality gives a more principled mechanism for studying and solving the constrained problem (8.4.1) via solving unconstrained problems. In particular, it will give us a mechanism for exactly solving the constrained problem (8.4.1) by solving a sequence of unconstrained problems *whose difficulty does not increase*. The central object in Lagrange duality is the Lagrangian

$$\mathcal{L}(\boldsymbol{x}, \boldsymbol{\lambda}) \doteq g(\boldsymbol{x}) + \langle \boldsymbol{\lambda}, \boldsymbol{A}\boldsymbol{x} - \boldsymbol{y} \rangle , \tag{8.4.3}$$

where $\boldsymbol{\lambda} \in \mathbb{R}^m$ is a vector of *Lagrange multipliers* corresponding to the equality constraint $\boldsymbol{A}\boldsymbol{x} = \boldsymbol{y}$. In particular, we can characterize optimal solutions $(\boldsymbol{x}, \boldsymbol{\lambda})$ as saddle points of the Lagrangian:

$$\sup_{\boldsymbol{\lambda}} \inf_{\boldsymbol{x}} \mathcal{L}(\boldsymbol{x}, \boldsymbol{\lambda}) = \sup_{\boldsymbol{\lambda}} \inf_{\boldsymbol{x}} \; g(\boldsymbol{x}) + \langle \boldsymbol{\lambda}, \boldsymbol{A}\boldsymbol{x} - \boldsymbol{y} \rangle . \tag{8.4.4}$$

If we define the dual function

$$d(\boldsymbol{\lambda}) \doteq \inf_{\boldsymbol{x}} \; g(\boldsymbol{x}) + \langle \boldsymbol{\lambda}, \boldsymbol{A}\boldsymbol{x} - \boldsymbol{y} \rangle , \tag{8.4.5}$$

then the saddle point characterization of optimal solutions suggests a natural computational approach to finding $(\boldsymbol{x}, \boldsymbol{\lambda})$:

$$\boldsymbol{x}_{k+1} = \arg\min_{\boldsymbol{x}} \; \mathcal{L}(\boldsymbol{x}, \boldsymbol{\lambda}_k), \tag{8.4.6}$$

$$\boldsymbol{\lambda}_{k+1} = \boldsymbol{\lambda}_k + t_{k+1}(\boldsymbol{A}\boldsymbol{x}_{k+1} - \boldsymbol{y}). \tag{8.4.7}$$

It is not difficult to show that $\boldsymbol{A}\boldsymbol{x}_{k+1} - \boldsymbol{y}$ is a subgradient[6] of the dual function $d(\boldsymbol{\lambda})$. This iteration corresponds to a subgradient ascent algorithm for maximizing the dual function, and hence is called *dual ascent*. In (8.4.7), t_{k+1} is the step size. For certain problem classes, dual ascent yields efficient, convergent algorithms, which produce an optimal primal–dual pair $(\boldsymbol{x}_\star, \boldsymbol{\lambda}_\star)$. However, for problems arising in structured signal recovery, the straightforward iteration (8.4.6)–(8.4.7) may fail:

EXAMPLE 8.14. *Show that*

$$\inf_{\boldsymbol{x}} \; \|\boldsymbol{x}\|_1 + \langle \boldsymbol{\lambda}, \boldsymbol{A}\boldsymbol{x} - \boldsymbol{y} \rangle = \begin{cases} -\infty & \left\| \boldsymbol{A}^* \boldsymbol{\lambda} \right\|_\infty > 1, \\ -\langle \boldsymbol{\lambda}, \boldsymbol{y} \rangle & \left\| \boldsymbol{A}^* \boldsymbol{\lambda} \right\|_\infty \le 1. \end{cases} \tag{8.4.8}$$

So, for basis pursuit, if the dual ascent step (8.4.7) *happens to produce a $\boldsymbol{\lambda}$ such that $\left\| \boldsymbol{A}^* \boldsymbol{\lambda} \right\|_\infty > 1$, the algorithm will break down. Notice, in particular, that when*

[6] Strictly, a *supergradient* since the dual $d(\boldsymbol{\lambda})$ is concave.

$\|A^*\lambda\|_\infty > 1$, we can produce arbitrarily large (in magnitude) negative values of $\mathcal{L}(x, \lambda)$ by choosing x far away from the feasible set $\{x \mid Ax = y\}$.

This bad behavior occurs more generally. Thus, for structured signal recovery, the classical Lagrangian is sufficient for characterizing optimality conditions, but it does not penalize the equality $Ax = y$ strongly enough for (8.4.6)–(8.4.7) to lead to a useful algorithm. A natural remedy is to *augment* the Lagrangian with an extra penalty term, by introducing the function

$$\mathcal{L}_\mu(x, \lambda) \doteq g(x) + \langle \lambda, Ax - y \rangle + \frac{\mu}{2} \|Ax - y\|_2^2. \tag{8.4.9}$$

This function is known as the *augmented Lagrangian* [Hes69, Roc73, Pow69]. As before, $\mu > 0$ is a penalty parameter. The augmented Lagrangian can be regarded as the Lagrangian for the constrained problem

$$\begin{array}{ll} \min & g(x) + (\mu/2)\|Ax - y\|_2^2 \\ \text{subject to} & Ax = y. \end{array} \tag{8.4.10}$$

Since the penalty term $\|y - Ax\|_2^2$ is zero for all feasible x, the optimal solutions of this problem coincide with the optimal solutions of the original problem (8.4.1).

Despite this formal equivalence, augmentation has dramatic consequences for numerical optimization. In particular, it can render the dual ascent iteration provably convergent, under very weak assumptions on the objective function g. To achieve this, we apply dual ascent to the regularized problem (8.4.10), and make a very particular choice of step size, $t_{k+1} = \mu$, yielding the iteration

$$x_{k+1} \in \arg\min_x \ \mathcal{L}_\mu(x, \lambda_k), \tag{8.4.11}$$

$$\lambda_{k+1} = \lambda_k + \mu\,(Ax_{k+1} - y). \tag{8.4.12}$$

This iteration, with the particular choice $t_{k+1} = \mu$, is known as the *method of multipliers*. The update step (8.4.11) for x is a convex optimization problem itself and can typically be solved via the proximal gradient methods introduced in the previous sections.

REMARK 8.15. *The choice $t_{k+1} = \mu$ is important, because it allows us to avoid the breakdown described in Example 8.14. To see this, since x_{k+1} minimizes the convex function $\mathcal{L}_\mu$,*

$$\begin{aligned} \mathbf{0} &\in \partial \mathcal{L}_\mu(x_{k+1}, \lambda_k), \\ &= \partial g(x_{k+1}) + A^*\lambda_k + \mu A^*(Ax_{k+1} - y), \\ &= \partial g(x_{k+1}) + A^*\lambda_{k+1}, \\ &= \partial \mathcal{L}(x_{k+1}, \lambda_{k+1}). \end{aligned}$$

Thus, x_{k+1} minimizes the unaugmented Lagrangian $\mathcal{L}(x, \lambda_{k+1})$ with $\lambda = \lambda_{k+1}$ fixed. This means that $d(\lambda_{k+1}) > -\infty$, and λ_{k+1} is dual feasible *for the original problem. In particular, $\mathcal{L}(x, \lambda_{k+1})$ is bounded below. Because λ_{k+1} is always dual feasible, the bad behavior in Example 8.14 cannot occur.*

Augmented Lagrange Multiplier (ALM)

Problem Class:

$$\begin{array}{ll} \min_{x} & g(x) \\ \text{subject to} & Ax = y. \end{array}$$

$g : \mathbb{R}^n \to \mathbb{R}$ convex, $y \in \text{range}(A)$.

Basic Iteration: set

$$\mathcal{L}_\mu(x, \Lambda) = g(x) + \langle \Lambda, Ax - y \rangle + \frac{\mu}{2} \|Ax - y\|_2^2 .$$

Repeat:

$$x_{k+1} \in \arg\min_x \; \mathcal{L}_\mu(x, \Lambda_k),$$

$$\Lambda_{k+1} = \Lambda_k + \mu\,(Ax_{k+1} - y).$$

Convergence Guarantee:

If g is coercive, every limit point of $\{x_k\}$ is optimal.

Figure 8.5 An overview of the augmented Lagrangian method of multipliers.

Under appropriate assumptions on g, the iterates x_k produced by this modified algorithm converge to an optimal solution $x_\star$ to the constrained problem (8.4.1). We state a slightly more general result that allows the penalty parameters μ to vary from iteration to iteration, as long as they remain bounded away from zero:

THEOREM 8.16. (Convergence of augmented lagrangian) *Let $g : \mathbb{R}^n \to \mathbb{R}$ be a convex, coercive function,*[7] *$A \in \mathbb{R}^{m \times n}$ an arbitrary matrix, and $y \in$ range(A). Then the problem*

$$\begin{array}{ll} \min_{x} & g(x) \\ \text{subject to} & Ax = y, \end{array} \tag{8.4.13}$$

has at least one optimal solution. Moreover, the ALM iteration

$$x_{k+1} \in \arg\min_x \; \mathcal{L}_{\mu_k}(x, \Lambda_k), \tag{8.4.14}$$

$$\Lambda_{k+1} = \Lambda_k + \mu_k\,(Ax_{k+1} - y), \tag{8.4.15}$$

with sequence $\{\mu_k\}$ bounded away from zero produces a sequence $\{\Lambda_k\}$ that converges to a dual optimal solution at the rate $O(1/k)$. Moreover, every limit point of the sequence $\{x_k\}$ is optimal for (8.4.13).

Figure 8.5 summarizes our general observations on the ALM method up to this point.

REMARK 8.17. (More general convergence theorems) *The statement of Theorem 8.16 represents a deliberate tradeoff between simplicity and generality. With somewhat*

[7] A function $g(x)$ is said to be coercive if $\lim_{\|x\| \to \infty} g(x) = +\infty$.

more technical analysis, it is possible to show convergence of ALM for much more general classes of g. The most practically important extension allows g to be an extended real-valued function (a function from $\mathbb{R}^n$ to $\mathbb{R} \cup \{+\infty\}$). For example, if we wish to optimize a real-valued convex function g_0 over the set of $\boldsymbol{x}$ that satisfy the equality constraint $\boldsymbol{A}\boldsymbol{x} = \boldsymbol{y}$, and *reside in some additional (nonempty closed, convex) constraint set* C,

$$\begin{array}{ll} \min_{\boldsymbol{x}} & g_0(\boldsymbol{x}) \\ \text{subject to} & \boldsymbol{A}\boldsymbol{x} = \boldsymbol{y}, \ \boldsymbol{x} \in \mathsf{C}, \end{array} \tag{8.4.16}$$

we can apply ALM to the problem

$$\begin{array}{ll} \min_{\boldsymbol{x}} & g(\boldsymbol{x}) \doteq g_0(\boldsymbol{x}) + I_{\boldsymbol{x} \in \mathsf{C}} \\ \text{subject to} & \boldsymbol{A}\boldsymbol{x} = \boldsymbol{y}, \end{array} \tag{8.4.17}$$

where $I_{\boldsymbol{x} \in \mathsf{C}}$ is the indicator function for C:

$$I_{\boldsymbol{x} \in \mathsf{C}} = \begin{cases} 0 & \boldsymbol{x} \in \mathsf{C}, \\ +\infty & \boldsymbol{x} \notin \mathsf{C}. \end{cases} \tag{8.4.18}$$

The survey of Eckstein [Eck12] and the monograph of Bertsekas [Ber82] are good introductory points for the more general theory, which enables such modifications.

Implementation Considerations

The most important practical consideration is how to choose the sequence of penalty parameters $\{\mu_k\}$. As discussed above, this choice induces a tradeoff between the cost of solving subproblems and the overall number of outer iterations – larger μ leaves us with fewer outer iterations, but harder subproblems. A typical strategy is to increase μ geometrically, up to some prefixed ceiling:

$$\mu_k = \min\left\{\beta \mu_k, \mu_{\max}\right\},$$

where $\beta \approx 1.25$ is typical. The ceiling $\mu_{\max}$ is strongly problem-dependent; choosing it "optimally" is something of a black art.

Our description and analysis of ALM assume that each of the subproblems is solved exactly. However, practically speaking, it may not be necessary to obtain high-accuracy solutions to the subproblems, especially in the early iterations. This can be justified theoretically. The choice of iterative method for solving the unconstrained subproblems is largely problem-dependent. However, because the penalty term is quadratic, for many problems of interest in this book, the subproblems have composite form, and the APG algorithm applies.

In using APG (or any other iterative solver) to solve the unconstrained subproblems, it is highly advisable to use the previous iterate $\boldsymbol{x}_k$ as an initialization to solve for the subsequent iterate $\boldsymbol{x}_{k+1}$. While the subproblems are convex, and the global optimality

---

Algorithm 8.5 Augmented Lagrange Multiplier (ALM) for BP

Problem: $\min_{\boldsymbol{x}} \|\boldsymbol{x}\|_1$ subject to $\boldsymbol{y} = \boldsymbol{A}\boldsymbol{x}$, given $\boldsymbol{y} \in \mathbb{R}^m$ and $\boldsymbol{A} \in \mathbb{R}^{m\times n}$.
Input: $\boldsymbol{x}_0 \in \mathbb{R}^n$, $\boldsymbol{\lambda}_0 \in \mathbb{R}^m$, and $\beta > 1$.
for $(k = 0, 1, 2, \ldots, K-1)$ **do**
  $\boldsymbol{x}_{k+1} \leftarrow \arg\min \mathcal{L}_{\mu_k}(\boldsymbol{x}, \boldsymbol{\lambda}_k)$ using APG.
  $\boldsymbol{\lambda}_{k+1} \leftarrow \boldsymbol{\lambda}_k + \mu_k(\boldsymbol{A}\boldsymbol{x}_{k+1} - \boldsymbol{y})$.
  $\mu_{k+1} \leftarrow \min\left\{\beta\mu_k, \mu_{\max}\right\}$.
end for
Output: $\boldsymbol{x}_\star \leftarrow \boldsymbol{x}_K$.

---

of iterative algorithms does not depend on initialization, choosing an appropriate initializer can drastically reduce the overall number of iterations.

8.4.1 ALM for Basis Pursuit

We may apply ALM to the exact BP problem (8.1.1), which we summarize as Algorithm 8.5. This algorithm was introduced by [YOGD08], where it was interpreted as a *Bregman iteration*.

8.4.2 ALM for Principal Component Pursuit

In Chapter 4, Section 4.4, we have presented an important application of the ALM algorithm, to solve the low-rank matrix completion (MC) problem (Algorithm 4.1).

We here (and in the section below) discuss how to extend it to the more challenging low-rank and sparse matrix decomposition problem studied in Chapter 5. We recall that principal component pursuit (PCP) (5.2.2) proposed in Chapter 5 solves the following program:

$$\min_{\boldsymbol{L},\boldsymbol{S}} \|\boldsymbol{L}\|_* + \lambda\|\boldsymbol{S}\|_1 \quad \text{subject to} \quad \boldsymbol{L} + \boldsymbol{S} = \boldsymbol{Y}. \tag{8.4.19}$$

First, we rewrite the above program as a standard ALM objective function:

$$\mathcal{L}_\mu(\boldsymbol{L}, \boldsymbol{S}, \boldsymbol{\Lambda}) \doteq \|\boldsymbol{L}\|_* + \lambda\|\boldsymbol{S}\|_1 + \langle \boldsymbol{\Lambda}, \boldsymbol{L} + \boldsymbol{S} - \boldsymbol{Y}\rangle + \frac{\mu}{2}\|\boldsymbol{L} + \boldsymbol{S} - \boldsymbol{Y}\|_F^2,$$

where $\mathcal{L}_\mu(\cdot)$ consists of a Lagrangian term with a Lagrange multiplier matrix $\boldsymbol{\Lambda}$ of the same size as $\boldsymbol{Y}$ and an augmented quadratic term that encourages the equality condition $\boldsymbol{L}+\boldsymbol{S} = \boldsymbol{Y}$. The ALM algorithm for this problem is summarized in Algorithm 8.6. However, in step 4 of the algorithm, one is required to solve $\min_{\boldsymbol{L},\boldsymbol{S}} \mathcal{L}_{\mu_k}(\boldsymbol{L}, \boldsymbol{S}, \boldsymbol{\Lambda}_k)$. Unfortunately, there is no closed-form solution for the proximal operator for the nuclear norm and ℓ^1 norm combined. We will address this difficulty in the next section with an alternating direction method.

Algorithm 8.6 Augmented Lagrange Multiplier (ALM) for PCP

1: **Problem:** $\min_{L,S} \|L\|_* + \lambda\|S\|_1$ subject to $L + S = Y$, given Y and $\lambda > 0$.
2: **Input:** $L_0, S_0, \Lambda_0 \in \mathbb{R}^{m\times n}$ and $\beta > 1$.
3: **for** $(k = 0, 1, 2, \ldots, K-1)$ **do**
4: $\{L_{k+1}, S_{k+1}\} \leftarrow \arg\min \mathcal{L}_{\mu_k}(L, S, \Lambda_k)$ using APG.
5: $\Lambda_{k+1} \leftarrow \Lambda_k + \mu_k(L_{k+1} + S_{k+1} - Y)$.
6: $\mu_{k+1} \leftarrow \min\{\beta\mu_k, \mu_{\max}\}$.
7: **end for**
8: **Output:** $L_\star \leftarrow L_K, S_\star \leftarrow S_K$.

8.4.3 Convergence of ALM

In this subsection, we prove Theorem 8.16. The proof will actually reveal another interpretation of the method of augmented Lagrangian, as an application of the proximal point algorithm to the dual problem.

Proof Let $d(\boldsymbol{\lambda})$ denote the dual function

$$d(\boldsymbol{\lambda}) = \inf_{\boldsymbol{x}} g(\boldsymbol{x}) + \langle \boldsymbol{\lambda}, \boldsymbol{A}\boldsymbol{x} - \boldsymbol{y}\rangle . \tag{8.4.20}$$

The dual function is concave, and so its negative

$$q(\boldsymbol{\lambda}) = -d(\boldsymbol{\lambda}) \tag{8.4.21}$$

is convex.

Note that for any $\boldsymbol{\lambda}$,

$$\begin{aligned} d(\boldsymbol{\lambda}) &\le g(\boldsymbol{x}_{k+1}) + \langle \boldsymbol{\lambda}, \boldsymbol{A}\boldsymbol{x}_{k+1} - \boldsymbol{y}\rangle \\ &= g(\boldsymbol{x}_{k+1}) + \langle \boldsymbol{\lambda}_{k+1}, \boldsymbol{A}\boldsymbol{x}_{k+1} - \boldsymbol{y}\rangle + \langle \boldsymbol{\lambda} - \boldsymbol{\lambda}_{k+1}, \boldsymbol{A}\boldsymbol{x}_{k+1} - \boldsymbol{y}\rangle . \end{aligned} \tag{8.4.22}$$

Now recall from Remark 8.15 that the augmented Lagrangian method ensures that $\boldsymbol{x}_{k+1}$ minimizes the unaugmented Lagrangian $g(\boldsymbol{x}) + \langle \boldsymbol{\lambda}, \boldsymbol{A}\boldsymbol{x} - \boldsymbol{y}\rangle$ with $\boldsymbol{\lambda} = \boldsymbol{\lambda}_{k+1}$ fixed. Hence, by definition of the function $d(\boldsymbol{\lambda})$, we have $d(\boldsymbol{\lambda}_{k+1}) = g(\boldsymbol{x}_{k+1}) + \langle \boldsymbol{\lambda}_{k+1}, \boldsymbol{A}\boldsymbol{x}_{k+1} - \boldsymbol{y}\rangle$. Applying this to the above inequality, we obtain

$$d(\boldsymbol{\lambda}) \le d(\boldsymbol{\lambda}_{k+1}) + \langle \boldsymbol{\lambda} - \boldsymbol{\lambda}_{k+1}, \boldsymbol{A}\boldsymbol{x}_{k+1} - \boldsymbol{y}\rangle . \tag{8.4.23}$$

As $q(\boldsymbol{\lambda}) = -d(\boldsymbol{\lambda})$, we have

$$q(\boldsymbol{\lambda}) \ge q(\boldsymbol{\lambda}_{k+1}) + \langle \boldsymbol{\lambda} - \boldsymbol{\lambda}_{k+1}, \boldsymbol{y} - \boldsymbol{A}\boldsymbol{x}_{k+1}\rangle . \tag{8.4.24}$$

Hence $\boldsymbol{y} - \boldsymbol{A}\boldsymbol{x}_{k+1}$ is in the subgradient of $q(\cdot)$ at $\boldsymbol{\lambda}_{k+1}$, and

$$\boldsymbol{\lambda}_k - \boldsymbol{\lambda}_{k+1} = \mu_k(\boldsymbol{y} - \boldsymbol{A}\boldsymbol{x}_{k+1}) \in \mu_k \partial q(\boldsymbol{\lambda}_{k+1}), \tag{8.4.25}$$

and so

$$\boldsymbol{\lambda}_{k+1} = \operatorname{prox}_{\mu_k q}[\boldsymbol{\lambda}_k]. \tag{8.4.26}$$

Thus, dual ascent corresponds to the proximal point iteration applied to $q(\cdot)$. Under our assumptions, the dual optimal value $\sup_{\boldsymbol{\lambda}} d(\boldsymbol{\lambda}) > -\infty$ is finite, hence a dual optimal solution $\bar{\boldsymbol{\lambda}}$ exists. Proposition 8.8 then implies that $\boldsymbol{\lambda}_k \to \boldsymbol{\lambda}_\star$, where $\boldsymbol{\lambda}_\star$ is some dual optimal point. This and the fact that μ_k is bounded away from zero give that

$$\|\boldsymbol{A}\boldsymbol{x}_k - \boldsymbol{y}\|_2 = \frac{\|\boldsymbol{\lambda}_k - \boldsymbol{\lambda}_{k-1}\|_2}{\mu_k} \to 0, \tag{8.4.27}$$

and so the sequence $\{\boldsymbol{x}_k\}$ approaches the feasible set. The sequence $\{\boldsymbol{\lambda}_k\}$ inherits the same convergence rate as the proximal gradient method. Hence according to Proposition 8.8, the rate of convergence is at least $O(1/k)$, say $\mu_k > \mu_o$ for some $\mu_o > 0$.

From the coercivity of g, there exists at least one primal optimal solution $\boldsymbol{x}_\star$. By optimality of $\boldsymbol{x}_{k+1}$, we have

$$g(\boldsymbol{x}_{k+1}) + \langle \boldsymbol{\lambda}_k, \boldsymbol{A}\boldsymbol{x}_{k+1} - \boldsymbol{y}\rangle + \frac{\mu}{2}\|\boldsymbol{A}\boldsymbol{x}_{k+1} - \boldsymbol{y}\|_2^2 \le g(\boldsymbol{x}_\star). \tag{8.4.28}$$

For any cluster point $\bar{\boldsymbol{x}}$, continuity of g and $\boldsymbol{A}\boldsymbol{x}_k - \boldsymbol{y} \to \boldsymbol{0}$ imply that $g(\bar{\boldsymbol{x}}) \le g(\boldsymbol{x}_\star)$, whence $g(\bar{\boldsymbol{x}}) = g(\boldsymbol{x}_\star)$. Hence, every cluster point is optimal. □

8.5 Alternating Direction Method of Multipliers

The previous section showed how the augmented Lagrangian method (ALM) could be used to solve equality constrained convex optimization problems, by reducing them to a sequence of unconstrained subproblems. These subproblems may still be challenging optimization problems if we need to minimize against all the variables simultaneously, as in step 4 of Algorithm 8.6. In many situations, though, it is possible to exploit special separable structures of the objective function and to alleviate the difficulty by reducing the overall optimization to multiple subproblems of smaller sizes, as the following example shows.

EXAMPLE 8.18. (Principal component pursuit) *We solve*

$$\begin{array}{ll} \min_{\boldsymbol{L},\boldsymbol{S}} & \|\boldsymbol{L}\|_* + \lambda\,\|\boldsymbol{S}\|_1 \\ \text{subject to} & \boldsymbol{L} + \boldsymbol{S} = \boldsymbol{Y}. \end{array} \tag{8.5.1}$$

The objective function is separable *into two terms,* $\|\cdot\|_*$ *and* $\|\cdot\|_1$*, each of which has an efficient proximal operator.*

In this section, we study a family of augmented Lagrangian algorithms that can exploit this special, separable structure. We begin by treating a generic problem of the form

$$\begin{array}{ll} \min_{\boldsymbol{x},\boldsymbol{z}} & g(\boldsymbol{x}) + h(\boldsymbol{z}) \\ \text{subject to} & \boldsymbol{A}\boldsymbol{x} + \boldsymbol{B}\boldsymbol{z} = \boldsymbol{y}, \end{array} \tag{8.5.2}$$

where g and h are convex functions, $\boldsymbol{A}$ and $\boldsymbol{B}$ are matrices, and $\boldsymbol{y} \in \operatorname{range}([\boldsymbol{A} \mid \boldsymbol{B}])$. The Lagrangian $\mathcal{L}(\boldsymbol{x}, \boldsymbol{z}, \boldsymbol{\lambda})$ associated with this problem simply is

$$\mathcal{L}(\boldsymbol{x}, \boldsymbol{z}, \boldsymbol{\lambda}) = g(\boldsymbol{x}) + h(\boldsymbol{z}) + \langle \boldsymbol{\lambda}, \boldsymbol{A}\boldsymbol{x} + \boldsymbol{B}\boldsymbol{z} - \boldsymbol{y} \rangle . \tag{8.5.3}$$

As in the previous section, we form the augmented Lagrangian $\mathcal{L}_\mu(\boldsymbol{x}, \boldsymbol{z}, \boldsymbol{\lambda})$ associated with this problem:

$$\mathcal{L}_\mu(\boldsymbol{x}, \boldsymbol{z}, \boldsymbol{\lambda}) = g(\boldsymbol{x}) + h(\boldsymbol{z}) + \langle \boldsymbol{\lambda}, \boldsymbol{A}\boldsymbol{x} + \boldsymbol{B}\boldsymbol{z} - \boldsymbol{y} \rangle + \frac{\mu}{2} \|\boldsymbol{A}\boldsymbol{x} + \boldsymbol{B}\boldsymbol{z} - \boldsymbol{y}\|_2^2 . \tag{8.5.4}$$

In many applications, including the examples listed above, it is easy to minimize $\mathcal{L}_\mu$ with respect to $\boldsymbol{x}$, when $\boldsymbol{\lambda}$ and $\boldsymbol{z}$ are fixed, and also easy to minimize it with respect to $\boldsymbol{z}$ when $\boldsymbol{\lambda}$ and $\boldsymbol{x}$ are fixed. This suggests a simple, alternating iteration:

$$\boldsymbol{z}_{k+1} \in \arg\min_{\boldsymbol{z}} \mathcal{L}_\mu(\boldsymbol{x}_k, \boldsymbol{z}, \boldsymbol{\lambda}_k), \tag{8.5.5}$$

$$\boldsymbol{x}_{k+1} \in \arg\min_{\boldsymbol{x}} \mathcal{L}_\mu(\boldsymbol{x}, \boldsymbol{z}_{k+1}, \boldsymbol{\lambda}_k), \tag{8.5.6}$$

$$\boldsymbol{\lambda}_{k+1} = \boldsymbol{\lambda}_k + \mu \left(\boldsymbol{A}\boldsymbol{x}_{k+1} + \boldsymbol{B}\boldsymbol{z}_{k+1} - \boldsymbol{y} \right) . \tag{8.5.7}$$

This is known as the *alternating directions method of multipliers* (ADMM). In the numerical analysis literature, this style of updating is referred to as a *Gauss–Seidel iteration*. We recommend [BPC$^+$11] for a friendly introduction to these methods, as well as useful recommendations on stopping criteria, parameter setting, etc.

8.5.1 ADMM for Principal Component Pursuit

When applied to the principal component pursuit program (8.4.19), the ADMM iteration takes on a particularly simple form. Here, the two groups of variables are the unknown low-rank matrix $\boldsymbol{L}$ and the unknown sparse error $\boldsymbol{S}$. The augmented Lagrangian is

$$\mathcal{L}_\mu(\boldsymbol{L}, \boldsymbol{S}, \boldsymbol{\Lambda}) = \|\boldsymbol{L}\|_* + \lambda \|\boldsymbol{S}\|_1 + \langle \boldsymbol{\Lambda}, \boldsymbol{L} + \boldsymbol{S} - \boldsymbol{Y} \rangle + \frac{\mu}{2} \|\boldsymbol{L} + \boldsymbol{S} - \boldsymbol{Y}\|_F^2 . \tag{8.5.8}$$

The ADMM iteration sequentially updates $\boldsymbol{L}$, then $\boldsymbol{S}$, then $\boldsymbol{\Lambda}$. Each of these updates has a very simple familiar form. For example,

$$\begin{aligned}
\boldsymbol{L}_{k+1} &= \arg\min_{\boldsymbol{L}} \mathcal{L}_\mu(\boldsymbol{L}, \boldsymbol{S}_k, \boldsymbol{\Lambda}_k) \\
&= \arg\min_{\boldsymbol{L}} \|\boldsymbol{L}\|_* + \langle \boldsymbol{\Lambda}_k, \boldsymbol{L} + \boldsymbol{S}_k - \boldsymbol{Y} \rangle + \frac{\mu}{2} \|\boldsymbol{L} + \boldsymbol{S}_k - \boldsymbol{Y}\|_F^2 \\
&= \arg\min_{\boldsymbol{L}} \|\boldsymbol{L}\|_* + \frac{\mu}{2} \left\| \boldsymbol{L} + \boldsymbol{S}_k - \boldsymbol{Y} + \mu^{-1}\boldsymbol{\Lambda}_k \right\|_F^2 + \varphi(\boldsymbol{S}_k, \boldsymbol{\Lambda}_k) \\
&= \operatorname{prox}_{\mu^{-1}\|\cdot\|_*} \left[\boldsymbol{Y} - \boldsymbol{S}_k - \mu^{-1}\boldsymbol{\Lambda}_k \right] .
\end{aligned} \tag{8.5.9}$$

Thus, the update step for the low-rank term can be evaluated simply by computing the proximal operator for the nuclear norm.

Algorithm 8.7 ADMM for Principal Component Pursuit

1: **Problem:** $\min_{L,S} \|L\|_* + \lambda\|S\|_1 + \langle \Lambda, L + S - Y\rangle + (\mu/2)\|L + S - Y\|_F^2$, given $Y, \lambda, \mu > 0$.
2: **Input:** $L_0, S_0, \Lambda_0 \in \mathbb{R}^{m\times n}$.
3: **for** $(k = 0, 1, 2, \dots, K-1)$ **do**
4: $\quad L_{k+1} \leftarrow \mathrm{prox}_{\mu^{-1}\|\cdot\|_*}\left[Y - S_k - \mu^{-1}\Lambda_k\right]$.
5: $\quad S_{k+1} \leftarrow \mathrm{prox}_{\lambda\mu^{-1}\|\cdot\|_1}\left[Y - L_{k+1} - \mu^{-1}\Lambda_k\right]$.
6: $\quad \Lambda_{k+1} \leftarrow \Lambda_k + \mu(L_{k+1} + S_{k+1} - Y)$.
7: **end for**
8: **Output:** $L_\star \leftarrow L_K; S_\star \leftarrow S_K$.

A similar simple rule can be derived for the sparse term:

$$\begin{aligned} S_{k+1} &= \arg\min_S \mathcal{L}_\mu(L_{k+1}, S, \Lambda_k) \\ &= \arg\min_S \lambda\,\|S\|_1 + \langle \Lambda_k, L_{k+1} + S - Y\rangle + \frac{\mu}{2}\,\|L_{k+1} + S - Y\|_F^2 \\ &= \arg\min_S \lambda\,\|S\|_1 + \frac{\mu}{2}\left\|S + L_{k+1} - Y + \mu^{-1}\Lambda_k\right\|_F^2 + \varphi(L_{k+1}, \Lambda_k) \\ &= \mathrm{prox}_{\lambda\mu^{-1}\|\cdot\|_1}\left[Y - L_{k+1} - \mu^{-1}\Lambda_k\right]. \end{aligned} \tag{8.5.10}$$

Combining these two observations, we obtain a simple, lightweight algorithm for solving the principal component pursuit program.

8.5.2 Monotone Operators

There has been a rich history and literature on characterizing the convergence and convergence rates of the ADMM algorithm under various conditions [DY16]. The ADMM can be naturally viewed as an approximation to the classical ALM method studied in the previous section. In the case when the objective function is separable, one uses a single pass of "Gauss–Seidel" block minimization to substitute for full minimization of the augmented Lagrangian in each iteration (8.4.11). However, as pointed out in [Eck12], this interpretation does not seem to lead to any known convergence proof for the ADMM.

In the remainder of this section, we give a rigorous proof for the convergence of the ADMM algorithm from the perspective of *monotone operators*, following the work of [HY12, GHY14, Xu17]. As we will see, this approach leads to an alternative proof for the convergence (and convergence rate) of the ALM that is different from the one given in the previous Section 8.4.3. To a large extent, this new approach gives a truly unified convergence analysis for both ALM and ADMM. Many of the concepts and techniques to be introduced are very useful in their own right. But for readers who are not immediately concerned with convergence guarantees, they may skip the rest of the section without loss of continuity.

Monotonicity

A *relation* $\mathcal{R}$ on $\mathbb{R}^n$ is defined to be a subset of $\mathbb{R}^n \times \mathbb{R}^n$. Typically, we may view $\mathcal{R}$ as a set-valued mapping. If there exists $\boldsymbol{x} \in \mathbb{R}^n$, $\mathcal{R}(\boldsymbol{x})$ is a singleton or empty, $\mathcal{R}$ is then a function in the conventional sense. Operations such as inverse, composition, scalar multiplication, and addition can be defined as natural extensions to those for functions.

DEFINITION 8.19. (Monotone relation) *A relation $\mathcal{F}$ on $\mathbb{R}^n$ is monotone if*

$$(\boldsymbol{u} - \boldsymbol{v})^*(\boldsymbol{x} - \boldsymbol{y}) \geq 0 \quad \forall (\boldsymbol{x}, \boldsymbol{u}), (\boldsymbol{y}, \boldsymbol{v}) \in \mathcal{F}. \tag{8.5.11}$$

Moreover, $\mathcal{F}$ is maximal monotone if there is no other monotone relation that properly contains it.

From this definition, we leave as Exercise 8.14 for the reader to show that, given two monotone relations $\mathcal{F}_1$ and $\mathcal{F}_2$, their sum $\mathcal{F}_1 + \mathcal{F}_2$ is also monotone.

LEMMA 8.20. (Monotonicity of subgradient) *Given a convex function $f(\boldsymbol{x}) : \mathbb{R}^n \to \mathbb{R} \cup \{\infty\}$, we have $\mathcal{F}(\boldsymbol{x}) = \partial f(\boldsymbol{x})$ is monotone. That is, for any $\boldsymbol{x}, \boldsymbol{x}', \boldsymbol{v}, \boldsymbol{v}' \in \mathbb{R}^n$ such that $\boldsymbol{v} \in \partial f(\boldsymbol{x})$ and $\boldsymbol{v}' \in \partial f(\boldsymbol{x}')$, we have*

$$\langle \boldsymbol{x} - \boldsymbol{x}', \boldsymbol{v} - \boldsymbol{v}' \rangle \geq 0. \tag{8.5.12}$$

Proof From the definition of subgradient, we have

$$f(\boldsymbol{x}') \geq f(\boldsymbol{x}) + \langle \boldsymbol{v}, \boldsymbol{x}' - \boldsymbol{x} \rangle, \quad f(\boldsymbol{x}) \geq f(\boldsymbol{x}') + \langle \boldsymbol{v}', \boldsymbol{x} - \boldsymbol{x}' \rangle. \tag{8.5.13}$$

Adding these two inequalities together we obtain

$$f(\boldsymbol{x}) + f(\boldsymbol{x}') \geq f(\boldsymbol{x}) + f(\boldsymbol{x}') + \langle \boldsymbol{v} - \boldsymbol{v}', \boldsymbol{x}' - \boldsymbol{x} \rangle. \tag{8.5.14}$$

Canceling $f(\boldsymbol{x}) + f(\boldsymbol{x}')$ from both sides obtains the desired result. □

Now consider linear equality constrained convex problems of the form

$$\begin{array}{ll} \min & g(\boldsymbol{x}) \\ \text{subject to} & \boldsymbol{A}\boldsymbol{x} = \boldsymbol{y}, \end{array} \tag{8.5.15}$$

where $g : \mathbb{R}^n \to \mathbb{R}$ is a convex function, $\boldsymbol{A} \in \mathbb{R}^{m \times n}$ is a matrix, and $\boldsymbol{y} \in \text{range}(\boldsymbol{A})$. The associated Lagrangian is

$$\mathcal{L}(\boldsymbol{x}, \boldsymbol{\lambda}) \doteq g(\boldsymbol{x}) + \langle \boldsymbol{\lambda}, \boldsymbol{A}\boldsymbol{x} - \boldsymbol{y} \rangle, \tag{8.5.16}$$

where $\boldsymbol{\lambda} \in \mathbb{R}^m$. Now consider the relation defined on $\mathbb{R}^n \times \mathbb{R}^m$ by the KKT operator:

$$\mathcal{F}(\boldsymbol{x}, \boldsymbol{\lambda}) = \begin{bmatrix} \partial_{\boldsymbol{x}} \mathcal{L}(\boldsymbol{x}, \boldsymbol{\lambda}) \\ -\partial_{\boldsymbol{\lambda}} \mathcal{L}(\boldsymbol{x}, \boldsymbol{\lambda}) \end{bmatrix} = \begin{bmatrix} \partial g(\boldsymbol{x}) + \boldsymbol{A}^* \boldsymbol{\lambda} \\ \boldsymbol{y} - \boldsymbol{A}\boldsymbol{x} \end{bmatrix}. \tag{8.5.17}$$

LEMMA 8.21. (Monotonicity of the KKT operator) *The KKT operator associated with the linear equality constrained convex optimization problem* (8.5.15) *gives a monotone relation.*

Proof We leave the proof to the reader as part of Exercise 8.14. □

Mixed Variational Inequality (MVI)
To simplify notation, let us define $\boldsymbol{w} = \binom{\boldsymbol{x}}{\boldsymbol{\lambda}} \in \mathbb{R}^n \times \mathbb{R}^m$. Then we have:

LEMMA 8.22. *The linear equality constrained optimization problem* (8.5.15) *is equivalent to the problem of solving the mixed variational inequality (MVI): finding* $\boldsymbol{w}_\star \in \mathbb{R}^n \times \mathbb{R}^m$ *such that for all* $\boldsymbol{w}$

$$g(\boldsymbol{x}) - g(\boldsymbol{x}_\star) + (\boldsymbol{w} - \boldsymbol{w}_\star)^* \mathcal{F}(\boldsymbol{w}_\star) \geq 0, \tag{8.5.18}$$

where $\mathcal{F}$ *is a monotone operator:*

$$\mathcal{F}(\boldsymbol{w}) = \mathcal{F}(\boldsymbol{x}, \boldsymbol{\lambda}) = \begin{bmatrix} \boldsymbol{A}^*\boldsymbol{\lambda} \\ \boldsymbol{y} - \boldsymbol{A}\boldsymbol{x} \end{bmatrix} = \begin{bmatrix} 0 & \boldsymbol{A}^* \\ -\boldsymbol{A} & 0 \end{bmatrix} \begin{bmatrix} \boldsymbol{x} \\ \boldsymbol{\lambda} \end{bmatrix} + \begin{bmatrix} \boldsymbol{0} \\ \boldsymbol{y} \end{bmatrix}. \tag{8.5.19}$$

Proof The Lagrangian of (8.5.15) is

$$\mathcal{L}(\boldsymbol{x}, \boldsymbol{\lambda}) \doteq g(\boldsymbol{x}) + \langle \boldsymbol{\lambda}, \boldsymbol{A}\boldsymbol{x} - \boldsymbol{y} \rangle . \tag{8.5.20}$$

It is equivalent to finding a pair $(\boldsymbol{x}_\star, \boldsymbol{\lambda}_\star)$ such that

$$(\boldsymbol{x}_\star, \boldsymbol{\lambda}_\star) = \underset{\boldsymbol{x} \in \mathbb{R}^n}{argmin} \, \underset{\boldsymbol{\lambda} \in \mathbb{R}^m}{argmax} \, \mathcal{L}(\boldsymbol{x}, \boldsymbol{\lambda}), \tag{8.5.21}$$

which is a saddle point of $\mathcal{L}(\boldsymbol{x}, \boldsymbol{\lambda})$ and thus satisfies: for all $\boldsymbol{x} \in \mathbb{R}^n, \boldsymbol{\lambda} \in \mathbb{R}^m$,

$$\mathcal{L}(\boldsymbol{x}_\star, \boldsymbol{\lambda}) \leq \mathcal{L}(\boldsymbol{x}_\star, \boldsymbol{\lambda}_\star) \leq \mathcal{L}(\boldsymbol{x}, \boldsymbol{\lambda}_\star). \tag{8.5.22}$$

This is equivalent to: for all $\boldsymbol{x} \in \mathbb{R}^n, \boldsymbol{\lambda} \in \mathbb{R}^m$,

$$\langle \boldsymbol{\lambda} - \boldsymbol{\lambda}_\star, \boldsymbol{y} - \boldsymbol{A}\boldsymbol{x}_\star \rangle \geq 0, \tag{8.5.23}$$

$$g(\boldsymbol{x}) - g(\boldsymbol{x}_\star) + \langle \boldsymbol{\lambda}_\star, \boldsymbol{A}\boldsymbol{x} - \boldsymbol{A}\boldsymbol{x}_\star \rangle \geq 0. \tag{8.5.24}$$

By the definition of $\mathcal{F}(\boldsymbol{w}_\star)$, on the one hand, summing (8.5.23) and (8.5.24), we obtain (8.5.18). On the other hand, in (8.5.18), by setting $\boldsymbol{x} = \boldsymbol{x}^*$, we obtain (8.5.23); by setting $\boldsymbol{\lambda} = \boldsymbol{\lambda}_\star$, we obtain (8.5.24). Therefore (8.5.23) and (8.5.24) are equivalent to (8.5.18). □

The above lemma establishes a fundamental connection between constrained convex optimization (8.5.15) and mixed variational inequality (MVI) of the type (8.5.18). As it turns out, it is much easier to characterize the convergence of such algorithms, including ALM and ADMM, using MVI. As we will soon see, their iterations can all be interpreted as solving the associated mixed variational inequality approximately. MVIs also arise in a variety of other settings; hence it is of independent value to understand their properties and how to solve them.

To this end, let us consider the general mixed variational inequality problem.

PROBLEM 8.23. (Mixed variational inequality problem) *Find* $\boldsymbol{w}_\star = (\boldsymbol{x}_\star, \boldsymbol{\lambda}_\star)$ *such that in a certain closed convex set* $\Omega \subseteq \mathbb{R}^{n \times m}$, *we have*

$$\forall\, \boldsymbol{w} \in \Omega, \quad \theta(\boldsymbol{u}) - \theta(\boldsymbol{u}_\star) + (\boldsymbol{w} - \boldsymbol{w}_\star)^* \mathcal{F}(\boldsymbol{w}_\star) \geq 0, \tag{8.5.25}$$

where $\mathcal{F}$ *is monotone,* $\boldsymbol{u}$ *is a subvector of* $\boldsymbol{w}$, *and* $\theta(\boldsymbol{u})$ *is a general convex function in* $\boldsymbol{u}$.

It is easy to show that (8.5.25) is equivalent to the following condition:

$$\forall\, \boldsymbol{w} \in \Omega, \quad \theta(\boldsymbol{u}) - \theta(\boldsymbol{u}_\star) + (\boldsymbol{w} - \boldsymbol{w}_\star)^* \mathcal{F}(\boldsymbol{w}) \geq 0. \tag{8.5.26}$$

We leave the proof as an exercise for the reader, and others may find one in [HY12, Theorem 2.1].

To find a solution to (8.5.26), a natural approach is to find an approximate solution $\tilde{\boldsymbol{w}}$ that is an ε-accurate solution. Or more precisely, for all $\boldsymbol{w} \in \Omega$,

$$\theta(\boldsymbol{u}) - \theta(\tilde{\boldsymbol{u}}) + (\boldsymbol{w} - \tilde{\boldsymbol{w}})^* \mathcal{F}(\boldsymbol{w}) \geq -\varepsilon, \tag{8.5.27}$$

or equivalently,

$$\theta(\tilde{\boldsymbol{u}}) - \theta(\boldsymbol{u}) + (\tilde{\boldsymbol{w}} - \boldsymbol{w})^* \mathcal{F}(\boldsymbol{w}) \leq \varepsilon. \tag{8.5.28}$$

To find an ε-accurate solution $\tilde{\boldsymbol{w}}$ for (8.5.28), a popular method is the following *proximal point algorithm* (PPA): in the k-th iteration ($k \geq 1$), generating the new iterate $\boldsymbol{w}_{k+1} \in \Omega$ such that

$$\theta(\boldsymbol{u}) - \theta(\boldsymbol{u}_{k+1}) + (\boldsymbol{w} - \boldsymbol{w}_{k+1})^* (\mathcal{F}(\boldsymbol{w}_{k+1}) + \boldsymbol{Q}(\boldsymbol{w}_{k+1} - \boldsymbol{w}_k)) \geq 0, \tag{8.5.29}$$

where $\boldsymbol{Q}$ is symmetric and positive semidefinite. This objective is intended to emulate the proximal method that we have introduced earlier: while in each iteration we try to achieve the objective, say (8.5.27), but we do not want to deviate from the previous $\boldsymbol{w}_k$ too much. If we are able to find such an iterate $\boldsymbol{w}_{k+1}$, then we have the following nice convergence result for the PPA:

THEOREM 8.24. (Convergence of the proximal point algorithm) *For all integers* $k \geq 1$, *define* $\tilde{\boldsymbol{w}}_k \doteq (1/k) \sum_{i=1}^{k} \boldsymbol{w}_i$, *where* $\boldsymbol{w}_i$ *is generated by* (8.5.29). *Then we have* $\tilde{\boldsymbol{w}}_k \in \Omega$ *and for all* $\boldsymbol{w} \in \Omega$,

$$\sum_{i=1}^{k} \big(\theta(\boldsymbol{u}_i) - \theta(\boldsymbol{u}) + (\boldsymbol{w}_i - \boldsymbol{w})^* \mathcal{F}(\boldsymbol{w}_i)\big) \leq \frac{1}{2} \|\boldsymbol{w} - \boldsymbol{w}_0\|_{\boldsymbol{Q}}^2 \tag{8.5.30}$$

and

$$\theta(\tilde{\boldsymbol{u}}_k) - \theta(\boldsymbol{u}) + (\tilde{\boldsymbol{w}}_k - \boldsymbol{w})^* \mathcal{F}(\boldsymbol{w}) \leq \frac{1}{2k} \|\boldsymbol{w} - \boldsymbol{w}_0\|_{\boldsymbol{Q}}^2, \tag{8.5.31}$$

where $\tilde{\boldsymbol{u}}_k$ *(respectively* $\boldsymbol{u}$*) is the corresponding subvector of* $\tilde{\boldsymbol{w}}_k$ *(respectively* $\boldsymbol{w}$*).*

Proof By (8.5.29), we have

$$\theta(\boldsymbol{u}) - \theta(\boldsymbol{u}_{k+1}) + (\boldsymbol{w} - \boldsymbol{w}_{k+1})^* \mathcal{F}(\boldsymbol{w}_{k+1}) \geq (\boldsymbol{w} - \boldsymbol{w}_{k+1})^* \boldsymbol{Q}(\boldsymbol{w}_k - \boldsymbol{w}_{k+1}). \tag{8.5.32}$$

Meanwhile, we have the following relation:

$$\begin{aligned}(\boldsymbol{w} - \boldsymbol{w}_{k+1})^* \boldsymbol{Q}(\boldsymbol{w}_k - \boldsymbol{w}_{k+1}) &= \frac{1}{2}\big(\|\boldsymbol{w} - \boldsymbol{w}_{k+1}\|_{\boldsymbol{Q}}^2 - \|\boldsymbol{w} - \boldsymbol{w}_k\|_{\boldsymbol{Q}}^2\big) + \frac{1}{2}\|\boldsymbol{w}_k - \boldsymbol{w}_{k+1}\|_{\boldsymbol{Q}}^2 \\ &\geq \frac{1}{2}(\|\boldsymbol{w} - \boldsymbol{w}_{k+1}\|_{\boldsymbol{Q}}^2 - \|\boldsymbol{w} - \boldsymbol{w}_k\|_{\boldsymbol{Q}}^2).\end{aligned} \tag{8.5.33}$$

By combining (8.5.32) and (8.5.33), we have

$$\theta(\boldsymbol{u}) - \theta(\boldsymbol{u}_{k+1}) + (\boldsymbol{w} - \boldsymbol{w}_{k+1})^* \mathcal{F}(\boldsymbol{w}) \geq \frac{1}{2}\left(\|\boldsymbol{w} - \boldsymbol{w}_{k+1}\|_{\boldsymbol{Q}}^2 - \|\boldsymbol{w} - \boldsymbol{w}_k\|_{\boldsymbol{Q}}^2\right). \quad (8.5.34)$$

Summing (8.5.34) over $i = 1, 2, \ldots, k$, we have

$$k\left(\left(\theta(\boldsymbol{u}) - \sum_{i=1}^{k} \frac{1}{k}\theta(\boldsymbol{u}_i) + \left(\boldsymbol{w} - \sum_{i=1}^{k}\frac{1}{k}\boldsymbol{w}_i\right)^* \mathcal{F}(\boldsymbol{w})\right)\right)$$
$$\geq \frac{1}{2}(\|\boldsymbol{w} - \boldsymbol{w}_k\|_{\boldsymbol{Q}}^2 - \|\boldsymbol{w} - \boldsymbol{w}_0\|_{\boldsymbol{Q}}^2) \geq -\frac{1}{2}\|\boldsymbol{w} - \boldsymbol{w}_0\|_{\boldsymbol{Q}}^2. \quad (8.5.35)$$

By the convexity of $\theta(\boldsymbol{u})$, we have

$$\theta\left(\sum_{i=1}^{k}\frac{1}{k}\boldsymbol{u}_i\right) \leq \sum_{i=1}^{k}\frac{1}{k}\theta(\boldsymbol{u}_i). \quad (8.5.36)$$

Combining (8.5.35) and (8.5.36) leads to the statement of the theorem. □

Notice the theorem implies that the convergence rate of PPA is at least $O(1/k)$.

0.5.3 Convergence of ALM and ADMM

Reducing ALM and ADMM to PPA

Now let us use the above result to show the convergence (and convergence rate) of the ALM algorithm that we have previously studied in Section 8.4.3.

THEOREM 8.25. (Reducing ALM to PPA) *The update rule of ALM in* (8.4.11) *and* (8.4.12) *reduces to the following PPA problem: in the k-th iteration, finding a* $\boldsymbol{w}_{k+1} \doteq (\boldsymbol{x}_{k+1}, \boldsymbol{\lambda}_{k+1})$ *such that, for all* $\boldsymbol{w} \in \mathbb{R}^n \times \mathbb{R}^m$,

$$g(\boldsymbol{x}) - g(\boldsymbol{x}_{k+1}) + (\boldsymbol{w} - \boldsymbol{w}_{k+1})^*\left(\mathcal{F}(\boldsymbol{w}_{k+1}) + \boldsymbol{Q}(\boldsymbol{w}_{k+1} - \boldsymbol{w}_k)\right) \geq 0, \quad (8.5.37)$$

where

$$\mathcal{F}(\boldsymbol{w}) \doteq \begin{bmatrix} \boldsymbol{A}^*\boldsymbol{\lambda} \\ \boldsymbol{y} - \boldsymbol{A}\boldsymbol{x} \end{bmatrix} \quad \textit{and} \quad \boldsymbol{Q} \doteq \begin{bmatrix} \boldsymbol{0} & \boldsymbol{0} \\ \boldsymbol{0} & (1/\mu)\boldsymbol{I}_m \end{bmatrix}. \quad (8.5.38)$$

Proof By the optimality condition (8.4.11), we have: for all $\boldsymbol{x} \in \mathbb{R}^n$,

$$g(\boldsymbol{x}) - g(\boldsymbol{x}_{k+1}) + \langle \boldsymbol{x} - \boldsymbol{x}_{k+1}, \boldsymbol{A}^*\boldsymbol{\lambda}_k + \mu\boldsymbol{A}^*(\boldsymbol{A}\boldsymbol{x}_{k+1} - \boldsymbol{y})\rangle \geq 0. \quad (8.5.39)$$

By (8.4.12), (8.5.39) is equivalent to: for all $\boldsymbol{x} \in \mathbb{R}^n$,

$$g(\boldsymbol{x}) - g(\boldsymbol{x}_{k+1}) + \langle \boldsymbol{x} - \boldsymbol{x}_{k+1}, \boldsymbol{A}^*\boldsymbol{\lambda}_{k+1}\rangle \geq 0. \quad (8.5.40)$$

The update rule for λ (8.4.12) itself is also equivalent to: for all $\boldsymbol{\lambda} \in \mathbb{R}^m$,

$$\left\langle \boldsymbol{\lambda} - \boldsymbol{\lambda}_{k+1}, (\boldsymbol{y} - \boldsymbol{A}\boldsymbol{x}_{k+1}) + \frac{1}{\mu}(\boldsymbol{\lambda}_{k+1} - \boldsymbol{\lambda}_k)\right\rangle = 0. \quad (8.5.41)$$

Then by the definition of $\mathcal{F}(\boldsymbol{w}_{k+1})$ and $\boldsymbol{Q}$ in (8.5.38), combining (8.5.40) and (8.5.41), this gives (8.5.37). □

This theorem gives another proof for the convergence of the ALM based on PPA, which is different from the proximal-gradient-based proof given in Section 8.4.3. According to Theorem 8.24, the convergence rate of ALM is at least $O(1/k)$, the same as the previous proof. The reason for going through this new approach is that this leads to a unified proof for the convergence for the ADMM algorithm, at least its symmetric version below.

Now let us consider the ADMM method for the problem (8.5.2). Recall that the associate augmented Lagrangian is

$$\mathcal{L}_\mu(\boldsymbol{x}, \boldsymbol{z}, \boldsymbol{\lambda}) \doteq g(\boldsymbol{x}) + h(\boldsymbol{z}) + \langle \boldsymbol{\lambda}, \boldsymbol{A}\boldsymbol{x} + \boldsymbol{B}\boldsymbol{z} - \boldsymbol{y}\rangle + \frac{\mu}{2}\|\boldsymbol{A}\boldsymbol{x} + \boldsymbol{B}\boldsymbol{z} - \boldsymbol{y}\|_2^2.$$

Then in the k-th iteration, consider the following ADMM update rules:[8]

$$\boldsymbol{x}_{k+1} = \operatorname*{argmin}_{\boldsymbol{x}} \mathcal{L}_\mu(\boldsymbol{x}, \boldsymbol{z}_k, \boldsymbol{\lambda}_k), \tag{8.5.42}$$

$$\boldsymbol{\lambda}_{k+1} = \boldsymbol{\lambda}_k + \mu(\boldsymbol{A}\boldsymbol{x}_{k+1} + \boldsymbol{B}\boldsymbol{z}_k - \boldsymbol{y}), \tag{8.5.43}$$

$$\boldsymbol{z}_{k+1} = \operatorname*{argmin}_{\boldsymbol{z}} \mathcal{L}_\mu(\boldsymbol{x}_{k+1}, \boldsymbol{z}, \boldsymbol{\lambda}_{k+1}). \tag{8.5.44}$$

THEOREM 8.26. (Reducing ADMM to PPA) *The update rules of ADMM in* (8.5.42) *to* (8.5.44) *can be reduced to the following PPA problem: in the k-th iteration, finding a $\boldsymbol{w}_{k+1} \doteq (\boldsymbol{x}_{k+1}, \boldsymbol{z}_{k+1}, \boldsymbol{\lambda}_{k+1})$ such that, for all $\boldsymbol{w}$,*

$$\begin{aligned}&(g(\boldsymbol{x}) + h(\boldsymbol{z})) - (g(\boldsymbol{x}_{k+1}) + h(\boldsymbol{z}_{k+1}))\\ &\quad + (\boldsymbol{w} - \boldsymbol{w}_{k+1})^*\big(\mathcal{F}(\boldsymbol{w}_{k+1}) + \boldsymbol{Q}(\boldsymbol{w}_{k+1} - \boldsymbol{w}_k)\big) \geq 0,\end{aligned} \tag{8.5.45}$$

where

$$\mathcal{F}(\boldsymbol{w}) \doteq \begin{bmatrix} \boldsymbol{A}^*\boldsymbol{\lambda} \\ \boldsymbol{B}^*\boldsymbol{\lambda} \\ \boldsymbol{y} - \boldsymbol{A}\boldsymbol{x} - \boldsymbol{B}\boldsymbol{z} \end{bmatrix} \quad \text{and} \quad \boldsymbol{Q} \doteq \begin{bmatrix} \mathbf{0} & \mathbf{0} & \mathbf{0} \\ \mathbf{0} & \mu\boldsymbol{B}^*\boldsymbol{B} & -\boldsymbol{B}^* \\ \mathbf{0} & -\boldsymbol{B} & (1/\mu)\boldsymbol{I}_m \end{bmatrix} \succeq 0. \tag{8.5.46}$$

Proof By the optimality condition (8.5.42), we have: for all $\boldsymbol{x}$,

$$g(\boldsymbol{x}) - g(\boldsymbol{x}_{k+1}) + \langle \boldsymbol{x} - \boldsymbol{x}_{k+1}, \boldsymbol{A}^*\boldsymbol{\lambda}_k + \mu\boldsymbol{A}^*(\boldsymbol{A}\boldsymbol{x}_{k+1} + \boldsymbol{B}\boldsymbol{z}_k - \boldsymbol{y})\rangle \geq 0.$$

By (8.5.43), (8.5.47) is equivalent to: for all $\boldsymbol{x}$

$$g(\boldsymbol{x}) - g(\boldsymbol{x}_{k+1}) + \langle \boldsymbol{x} - \boldsymbol{x}_{k+1}, \boldsymbol{A}^*\boldsymbol{\lambda}_{k+1}\rangle \geq 0. \tag{8.5.47}$$

The update rule (8.5.43) is also equivalent to: for all $\boldsymbol{\lambda}$

$$\left\langle \boldsymbol{\lambda} - \boldsymbol{\lambda}_{k+1}, (\boldsymbol{y} - \boldsymbol{A}\boldsymbol{x}_{k+1} - \boldsymbol{B}\boldsymbol{z}_{k+1}) + \boldsymbol{B}(\boldsymbol{z}_{k+1} - \boldsymbol{z}_k) + \frac{1}{\mu}(\boldsymbol{\lambda}_{k+1} - \boldsymbol{\lambda}_k)\right\rangle = 0. \tag{8.5.48}$$

By the optimality condition of (8.5.44), we have: for all $\boldsymbol{z}$,

$$h(\boldsymbol{z}) - h(\boldsymbol{z}_{k+1}) + \langle \boldsymbol{z} - \boldsymbol{z}_{k+1}, \boldsymbol{B}^*\boldsymbol{\lambda}_{k+1} + \mu\boldsymbol{B}^*(\boldsymbol{A}\boldsymbol{x}_{k+1} + \boldsymbol{B}\boldsymbol{z}_{k+1} - \boldsymbol{y})\rangle \geq 0.$$

[8] Notice that these update rules are in slightly different order than those in (8.5.5)–(8.5.7). The rules here are also known as a *symmetric* version of ADMM. The proof of convergence for the symmetric version is relatively simpler. The proof for the conventional ADMM rules can follow a similar strategy but the analysis is a little more involved.

This is equivalent to: for all z,

$$h(z) - h(z_{k+1}) + \langle z - z_{k+1}, \boldsymbol{B}^*\boldsymbol{\lambda}_{k+1} + \boldsymbol{B}^*(\boldsymbol{\lambda}_{k+1} - \boldsymbol{\lambda}_k) + \mu \boldsymbol{B}^*\boldsymbol{B}(z_{k+1} - z_k)\rangle \\ \geq 0. \tag{8.5.49}$$

Then with the definition of $\mathcal{F}(\boldsymbol{w}_{k+1})$ and $\boldsymbol{Q}$ in (8.5.46), by combining (8.5.47), (8.5.48), and (8.5.49), we obtain (8.5.45). □

This theorem implies that ADMM can be reduced to PPA; hence it inherits the $O(1/k)$ convergence rate established earlier for PPA.

Convergence of ALM and ADMM

Notice that the convergence in terms of PPA only guarantees the sum of objective function value and the constraint, i.e., left-hand side of (8.5.31), converges.[9] As it turns out, in our context, the constraints are mostly linear equalities. By exploiting the nice properties of such constraints, it is possible to ensure that the objective function value and the constraint accuracy converge separately [Xu17]. This only requires minor modification to the above proofs.

THEOREM 8.27. (Convergence of ALM) *Assume* $(\boldsymbol{x}_\star, \boldsymbol{\lambda}_\star)$ *is the optimal solution of* (8.4.9). *Then the update rules of ALM in* (8.4.11) *and* (8.4.12) *have the following guarantee that letting* $\tilde{\boldsymbol{x}}_k \doteq (1/k)\sum_{i=1}^{k} \boldsymbol{x}_i$ *and given* $\rho > \|\boldsymbol{\lambda}_\star\|_2$, *we have*

$$\|\boldsymbol{A}\tilde{\boldsymbol{x}}_k - \boldsymbol{y}\|_2 \leq \frac{1}{2(\rho - \|\boldsymbol{\lambda}_*\|_2)k}\|\boldsymbol{w} - \boldsymbol{w}_0\|_{\boldsymbol{Q}}^2 \tag{8.5.50}$$

and

$$-\frac{\|\boldsymbol{\lambda}_\star\|_2}{2(\rho - \|\boldsymbol{\lambda}_\star\|_2)k}\|\boldsymbol{w} - \boldsymbol{w}_0\|_{\boldsymbol{Q}}^2 \leq g(\tilde{\boldsymbol{x}}_k) - g(\boldsymbol{x}_\star) \leq \frac{1}{2k}\|\boldsymbol{w} - \boldsymbol{w}_0\|_{\boldsymbol{Q}}^2, \tag{8.5.51}$$

with

$$\boldsymbol{w} \doteq \begin{bmatrix} \boldsymbol{x}_\star \\ \frac{\rho(\boldsymbol{A}\tilde{\boldsymbol{x}}_k - \boldsymbol{y})}{\|\boldsymbol{A}\tilde{\boldsymbol{x}}_k - \boldsymbol{y}\|_2} \end{bmatrix}, \boldsymbol{w}_0 \doteq \begin{bmatrix} \boldsymbol{x}_0 \\ \boldsymbol{\lambda}_0 \end{bmatrix}.$$

Proof For ALM, let

$$\boldsymbol{w} \doteq \begin{bmatrix} \boldsymbol{x}_\star \\ \boldsymbol{\lambda} \end{bmatrix},$$

where $\boldsymbol{x}_\star$ is the global minimum with $\boldsymbol{A}\boldsymbol{x}_\star = \boldsymbol{y}$ and $\boldsymbol{\lambda} \in \mathbb{R}^m$ is to be determined. Then for the $\mathcal{F}(\boldsymbol{w})$ defined in (8.5.38), we have

$$\begin{aligned} &(\boldsymbol{w} - \boldsymbol{w}_{k+1})^*\mathcal{F}(\boldsymbol{w}_{k+1}) \\ &= \langle \boldsymbol{x}_\star - \boldsymbol{x}_{k+1}, \boldsymbol{A}^*\boldsymbol{\lambda}_{k+1}\rangle + \langle \boldsymbol{\lambda} - \boldsymbol{\lambda}_{k+1}, \boldsymbol{y} - \boldsymbol{A}\boldsymbol{x}_{k+1}\rangle \\ &= \langle \boldsymbol{\lambda}_{k+1}, \boldsymbol{A}\boldsymbol{x}_\star - \boldsymbol{y}\rangle + \langle \boldsymbol{\lambda}, \boldsymbol{y} - \boldsymbol{A}\boldsymbol{x}_{k+1}\rangle \\ &= \langle \boldsymbol{\lambda}, \boldsymbol{y} - \boldsymbol{A}\boldsymbol{x}_{k+1}\rangle, \end{aligned} \tag{8.5.52}$$

which is a linear function with respect to $\boldsymbol{x}_{k+1}$.

[9] So, rigorously speaking, there is no guarantee that each of the terms would necessarily converge separately.

Then combining (8.5.30) of Theorem 8.24 and Theorem 8.25, we have

$$\sum_{i=1}^{k} \big(g(\boldsymbol{x}_i) - g(\boldsymbol{x}) + (\boldsymbol{w}_i - \boldsymbol{w})^* \mathcal{F}(\boldsymbol{w}_i)\big) \le \frac{1}{2}\|\boldsymbol{w} - \boldsymbol{w}_0\|_{\boldsymbol{Q}}^2. \tag{8.5.53}$$

So by our setting of $\boldsymbol{w}$, applying the convexity of $g(\boldsymbol{x})$, and combining (8.5.52) and (8.5.53), it follows that

$$\begin{aligned} &k(g(\tilde{\boldsymbol{x}}_k) - g(\boldsymbol{x}_\star) + \langle \boldsymbol{\lambda}, \boldsymbol{A}\tilde{\boldsymbol{x}}_k - \boldsymbol{y}\rangle) \\ &\quad \le \sum_{i=1}^{k} \big(g(\boldsymbol{x}_i) - g(\boldsymbol{x}) + (\boldsymbol{w}_i - \boldsymbol{w})^* \mathcal{F}(\boldsymbol{w}_i)\big) \\ &\quad \le \frac{1}{2}\|\boldsymbol{w} - \boldsymbol{w}_0\|_{\boldsymbol{Q}}^2, \end{aligned} \tag{8.5.54}$$

where $\tilde{\boldsymbol{x}}_k \doteq (1/k)\sum_{i=1}^{k} \boldsymbol{x}_i$. By setting

$$\boldsymbol{\lambda} \doteq \frac{\rho(\boldsymbol{A}\tilde{\boldsymbol{x}}_k - \boldsymbol{y})}{\|\boldsymbol{A}\tilde{\boldsymbol{x}}_k - \boldsymbol{y}\|_2}$$

with $\rho > 0$ to be determined, we have

$$g(\tilde{\boldsymbol{x}}_k) - g(\boldsymbol{x}_\star) + \rho\|\boldsymbol{A}\tilde{\boldsymbol{x}}_k - \boldsymbol{y}\|_2 \le \frac{1}{2k}\|\boldsymbol{w} - \boldsymbol{w}_0\|_{\boldsymbol{Q}}^2. \tag{8.5.55}$$

Assume that $(\boldsymbol{x}_\star, \boldsymbol{\lambda}_\star)$ is the optimal solution of (8.4.9), then by the KKT condition we have: for all $\boldsymbol{x}$,

$$g(\boldsymbol{x}) - g(\boldsymbol{x}_\star) - \langle \boldsymbol{\lambda}_\star, \boldsymbol{A}\boldsymbol{x} - \boldsymbol{y}\rangle \ge 0. \tag{8.5.56}$$

So we have

$$g(\tilde{\boldsymbol{x}}_k) - g(\boldsymbol{x}_\star) \ge -\|\boldsymbol{\lambda}_\star\|_2\|\boldsymbol{A}\tilde{\boldsymbol{x}}_k - \boldsymbol{y}\|_2. \tag{8.5.57}$$

By combining (8.5.55) and (8.5.57), with the setting $\rho > \|\boldsymbol{\lambda}_\star\|_2$, we have

$$\|\boldsymbol{A}\tilde{\boldsymbol{x}}_k - \boldsymbol{y}\|_2 \le \frac{1}{2(\rho - \|\boldsymbol{\lambda}_*\|_2)k}\|\boldsymbol{w} - \boldsymbol{w}_0\|_{\boldsymbol{Q}}^2 \tag{8.5.58}$$

and

$$-\frac{\|\boldsymbol{\lambda}_\star\|_2}{2(\rho - \|\boldsymbol{\lambda}_\star\|_2)k}\|\boldsymbol{w} - \boldsymbol{w}_0\|_{\boldsymbol{Q}}^2 \le g(\tilde{\boldsymbol{x}}_k) - g(\boldsymbol{x}_\star) \le \frac{1}{2k}\|\boldsymbol{w} - \boldsymbol{w}_0\|_{\boldsymbol{Q}}^2. \tag{8.5.59}$$

□

THEOREM 8.28. (Convergence of ADMM) *Assume* $(\boldsymbol{x}_\star, \boldsymbol{\lambda}_\star)$ *is the optimal solution of* (8.5.4). *Then the update rules of ADMM* (8.5.42) *to* (8.5.44) *have the following guarantee that letting* $\tilde{\boldsymbol{x}}_k = (1/k)\sum_{i=1}^{k} \boldsymbol{x}_i$ *and given* $\rho > \|\boldsymbol{\lambda}_\star\|_2$, *we have*

$$\|\boldsymbol{A}\tilde{\boldsymbol{x}}_k - \boldsymbol{y}\|_2 \le \frac{1}{2(\rho - \|\boldsymbol{\lambda}_\star\|_2)k}\|\boldsymbol{w} - \boldsymbol{w}_0\|_{\boldsymbol{Q}}^2 \tag{8.5.60}$$

and

$$-\frac{\|\boldsymbol{\lambda}_\star\|_2}{2(\rho-\|\boldsymbol{\lambda}_\star\|_2)k}\|\boldsymbol{w}-\boldsymbol{w}_0\|_{\boldsymbol{Q}}^2 \le g(\tilde{\boldsymbol{x}}_k)+h(\tilde{\boldsymbol{z}}_k)-(g(\boldsymbol{x}_\star)+h(\boldsymbol{z}_\star)) \le \frac{1}{2k}\|\boldsymbol{w}-\boldsymbol{w}_0\|_{\boldsymbol{Q}}^2,$$

with

$$\boldsymbol{w}=\begin{bmatrix}\boldsymbol{x}_\star\\ \boldsymbol{z}_\star\\ \frac{\rho(\boldsymbol{A}\tilde{\boldsymbol{x}}_k+\boldsymbol{B}\tilde{\boldsymbol{z}}_k-\boldsymbol{y})}{\|\boldsymbol{A}\tilde{\boldsymbol{x}}_k+\boldsymbol{B}\tilde{\boldsymbol{z}}_k-\boldsymbol{y}\|_2}\end{bmatrix},\quad \boldsymbol{w}_0=\begin{bmatrix}\boldsymbol{x}_0\\ \boldsymbol{z}_0\\ \boldsymbol{\lambda}_0\end{bmatrix}.$$

Proof For ADMM, by setting

$$\boldsymbol{w}\doteq\begin{bmatrix}\boldsymbol{x}_\star\\ \boldsymbol{z}_\star\\ \boldsymbol{\lambda}\end{bmatrix},$$

where $(\boldsymbol{x}_\star,\boldsymbol{z}_\star)$ is the global minimum of the equality constrained convex problem that satisfies $\boldsymbol{A}\boldsymbol{x}_\star+\boldsymbol{B}\boldsymbol{z}_\star-\boldsymbol{y}=\boldsymbol{0}$ and $\boldsymbol{\lambda}\in\mathbb{R}^m$ is to be determined, we have

$$\begin{aligned}
&(\boldsymbol{w}-\boldsymbol{w}_{k+1})^*\mathcal{F}(\boldsymbol{w}_{k+1})\\
&\quad=\langle\boldsymbol{x}_\star-\boldsymbol{x}_{k+1},\boldsymbol{A}^*\boldsymbol{\lambda}_{k+1}\rangle+\langle\boldsymbol{z}_\star-\boldsymbol{z}_{k+1},\boldsymbol{B}^*\boldsymbol{\lambda}_{k+1}\rangle+\langle\boldsymbol{\lambda}-\boldsymbol{\lambda}_{k+1},\boldsymbol{y}-\boldsymbol{A}\boldsymbol{x}_{k+1}-\boldsymbol{B}\boldsymbol{z}_{k+1}\rangle\\
&\quad=\langle\boldsymbol{\lambda}_{k+1},\boldsymbol{A}\boldsymbol{x}_\star+\boldsymbol{B}\boldsymbol{z}_\star-\boldsymbol{y}\rangle+\langle\boldsymbol{\lambda},\boldsymbol{y}-\boldsymbol{A}\boldsymbol{x}_{k+1}-\boldsymbol{B}\boldsymbol{z}_{k+1}\rangle\\
&\quad=\langle\boldsymbol{\lambda},\boldsymbol{y}-\boldsymbol{A}\boldsymbol{x}_{k+1}-\boldsymbol{B}\boldsymbol{z}_{k+1}\rangle,
\end{aligned}\tag{8.5.61}$$

which is a linear function with respect to $\boldsymbol{x}_{k+1}$ and $\boldsymbol{z}_{k+1}$.

Then combining (8.5.30) of Theorem 8.24 and Theorem 8.26, we have

$$\sum_{i=1}^{k}\left(g(\boldsymbol{x}_i)+h(\boldsymbol{z}_i)-(g(\boldsymbol{x}_\star)+h(\boldsymbol{x}_\star))+(\boldsymbol{w}_i-\boldsymbol{w})^*\mathcal{F}(\boldsymbol{w}_i)\right)\le\frac{1}{2}\|\boldsymbol{w}-\boldsymbol{w}_0\|_{\boldsymbol{Q}}^2.\tag{8.5.62}$$

So applying the convexity of $g(\boldsymbol{x})$ and $h(\boldsymbol{z})$, and combining (8.5.61) and (8.5.62), it follows that

$$\begin{aligned}
&k(g(\tilde{\boldsymbol{x}}_k)+h(\tilde{\boldsymbol{z}}_k)-(g(\boldsymbol{x}_\star)+h(\boldsymbol{z}_\star))+\langle\boldsymbol{\lambda},\boldsymbol{A}\tilde{\boldsymbol{x}}_k+\boldsymbol{B}\tilde{\boldsymbol{z}}_k-\boldsymbol{y}\rangle)\\
&\quad\le\sum_{i=1}^{k}\left(g(\boldsymbol{x}_i)-g(\boldsymbol{x}_\star)+h(\boldsymbol{x}_i)-h(\boldsymbol{x}_\star)+(\boldsymbol{w}_i-\boldsymbol{w})^*\mathcal{F}(\boldsymbol{w}_i)\right)\\
&\quad\le\frac{1}{2}\|\boldsymbol{w}-\boldsymbol{w}_0\|_{\boldsymbol{Q}}^2,
\end{aligned}\tag{8.5.63}$$

where $\tilde{\boldsymbol{x}}_k\doteq(1/k)\sum_{i=1}^k\boldsymbol{x}_i$. By setting

$$\boldsymbol{\lambda}\doteq\frac{\rho(\boldsymbol{A}\tilde{\boldsymbol{x}}_k+\boldsymbol{B}\tilde{\boldsymbol{z}}_k-\boldsymbol{y})}{\|\boldsymbol{A}\tilde{\boldsymbol{x}}_k+\boldsymbol{B}\tilde{\boldsymbol{z}}_k-\boldsymbol{y}\|_2}$$

with $\rho > 0$ to be determined, we have

$$(g(\tilde{\boldsymbol{x}}_k) + h(\tilde{z}_k)) - (g(\boldsymbol{x}_\star) + h(z_\star)) + \rho\|\boldsymbol{y} - \boldsymbol{A}\tilde{\boldsymbol{x}}_k - \boldsymbol{B}\tilde{z}_k\|_2 \le \frac{1}{2k}\|\boldsymbol{w} - \boldsymbol{w}_0\|_{\boldsymbol{Q}}^2. \tag{8.5.64}$$

Assume that $(\boldsymbol{x}_\star, z_\star, \boldsymbol{\Lambda}_\star)$ is the optimal solution of (8.5.4), then by the KKT condition, we have: for all $\boldsymbol{x}, z$,

$$g(\boldsymbol{x}) + h(z) - (g(\boldsymbol{x}_\star) + h(z_\star)) - \langle \boldsymbol{\Lambda}_\star, \boldsymbol{A}\boldsymbol{x} + \boldsymbol{B}z - \boldsymbol{y}\rangle \ge 0. \tag{8.5.65}$$

So we have

$$g(\tilde{\boldsymbol{x}}_k) + h(\tilde{z}_k) - (g(\boldsymbol{x}_\star) + h(z_\star)) \ge -\|\boldsymbol{\Lambda}_\star\|_2\|\boldsymbol{A}\tilde{\boldsymbol{x}}_k + \boldsymbol{B}\tilde{z}_k - \boldsymbol{y}\|_2. \tag{8.5.66}$$

By combining (8.5.64) and (8.5.66), with the setting $\rho > \|\boldsymbol{\Lambda}_\star\|_2$, we have

$$\|\boldsymbol{A}\tilde{\boldsymbol{x}}_k + \boldsymbol{B}\tilde{z}_k - \boldsymbol{y}\|_2 \le \frac{1}{2(\rho - \|\boldsymbol{\Lambda}_\star\|_2)k}\|\boldsymbol{w} - \boldsymbol{w}_0\|_{\boldsymbol{Q}}^2$$

and

$$-\frac{\|\boldsymbol{\Lambda}_\star\|_2}{2(\rho - \|\boldsymbol{\Lambda}_\star\|_2)k}\|\boldsymbol{w} - \boldsymbol{w}_0\|_{\boldsymbol{Q}}^2 \le g(\tilde{\boldsymbol{x}}_k) + h(\tilde{z}_k) - (g(\boldsymbol{x}_\star) + h(z_\star)) \le \frac{1}{2k}\|\boldsymbol{w} - \boldsymbol{w}_0\|_{\boldsymbol{Q}}^2.$$

□

The above convergence rate $O(1/k)$ is actually optimal for first-order methods, according to [OX18]. However, when the linear constraint $\boldsymbol{A}\boldsymbol{x} = \boldsymbol{y}$ satisfies certain special properties, one may a achieve convergence rate faster than $O(1/k)$, as we will discuss more in the Notes section.

Alternating among Multiple Separable Terms

Finally, we want to point out that, more generally, separable structures also arise in many large-scale learning problems, where the goal is to fit a parametric model to a collection of observation vectors $\boldsymbol{y}_1, \ldots, \boldsymbol{y}_p$. Typically, we are provided with a *loss* $L(\boldsymbol{y}, \boldsymbol{x})$, which could be, for example, the log likelihood of observation $\boldsymbol{y}$ given parameters $\boldsymbol{x}$ or the logistic loss in training a classifier with a deep network. Our goal is to minimize $\sum_i L(\boldsymbol{y}_i, \boldsymbol{x})$ over $\boldsymbol{x}$.

In very large-scale applications, it may be prohibitively expensive to store the $\boldsymbol{y}_i$ centrally, or to transmit them during the operation of an iterative algorithm. Rather, we can assume that they are stored in a distributed fashion, in N locations: the j-th location stores $\{\boldsymbol{y}_i, i \in \mathsf{I}_j\}$. The loss on this subset is $f_j(\boldsymbol{x}) = \sum_{i \in \mathsf{I}_j} L(\boldsymbol{y}_i, \boldsymbol{x})$. Our overall goal is then to solve

$$\min_{\boldsymbol{x}} \sum_{j=1}^{N} f_j(\boldsymbol{x}). \tag{8.5.67}$$

Again, this objective function appears to separate into independent terms. To exploit this structure, we can introduce N additional parameter vectors $\boldsymbol{x}_j$, which are constrained to coincide with $\boldsymbol{x}$:

$$\begin{array}{ll} \min_{\{\boldsymbol{x}_j\}} & \sum_{j=1}^N f_j(\boldsymbol{x}_j) \\ \text{subject to} & \boldsymbol{x}_j = \boldsymbol{x}, \quad j = 1, \dots, N. \end{array} \tag{8.5.68}$$

It is common practice that people apply similar alternating schemes to optimize this class of problems. But the convergence and complexity analysis for ADMM with multiple terms are much more difficult, as we will discuss more in the Notes.

8.6 Leveraging Problem Structures for Better Scalability

In the previous sections, we showed how the special structure of optimization problems arising in sparse and low-dimensional data analysis can be leveraged to obtain efficient and scalable algorithms. One key piece of structure was the existence of an easy-to-compute proximal operator. For example, for nuclear norm minimization we showed that at a point $\boldsymbol{Z} = \boldsymbol{U}\boldsymbol{\Sigma}\boldsymbol{V}^*$,

$$\operatorname{prox}_{\lambda\|\cdot\|_*}[\boldsymbol{Z}] = \boldsymbol{U}\operatorname{soft}(\boldsymbol{\Sigma}, \lambda)\boldsymbol{V}^*, \tag{8.6.1}$$

where $\operatorname{soft}(\cdot, \lambda)$ is the soft-thresholding operator on the singular values. Using the proximal operator, we obtain proximal gradient methods that enjoy the same convergence rate as if the objective was smooth, even though it is nonsmooth. Each iteration consists of simple linear operations, followed by the application of $\operatorname{prox}_{\lambda\|\cdot\|_*}[\cdot]$. Each iteration can be computed in time polynomial in the size of the target matrix: the proximal operator can be computed in time $O(n_1 n_2 \max\{n_1, n_2\})$ in the worst case. This is sufficient for moderate-sized datasets where n_1 and n_2 are each in the thousands.

Nevertheless, many problems in data science, scientific imaging, and machine learning require even more scalable solutions. The Frank–Wolfe method and stochastic gradient descent (SGD) are two such methods. The two methods exploit two complementary types of structures that are common in high-dimensional optimization problems on large-scale datasets. The Frank–Wolfe method exploits structures in the constraints or in the data (e.g., the atomic structures) so as to *reduce the dependence of an algorithm's complexity on the dimension* n, typically from linear to sublinear. Roughly speaking, SGD exploits finite-sum structure in the objective function, say a sum of errors or losses for a large number of samples. By leveraging gradients computed from small random batches of samples instead of the full set, SGD can *reduce the dependence of an algorithm's complexity on the sample size* m, again from linear to sublinear. In this section, we illustrate basic ideas behind both methods and illustrate their connections to our problems.

8.6.1 Frank–Wolfe for Structured Constraint Set

In this section, we introduce a classical method from optimization, known as the *Frank–Wolfe* or *conditional gradient* algorithm, which is scalable enough to solve extremely large sparse and low-rank recovery problems. The key property of this method is that in each iteration, it solves a subproblem which is simpler and easier to compute than the proximal operator.

In its classical form, the Frank–Wolfe algorithm, originally proposed in [FW56], applies to the problem of optimizing a smooth, convex function over a *compact* convex set:

$$\begin{array}{ll} \min_{\boldsymbol{x}} & f(\boldsymbol{x}) \\ \text{subject to} & \boldsymbol{x} \in \mathsf{C}. \end{array} \tag{8.6.2}$$

Here, the objective function f is assumed to be a convex,[10] differentiable function whose gradient $\nabla f(\boldsymbol{x})$ is L-Lipschitz. The constraint set C is assumed to be a compact (hence closed and bounded) convex set with a diameter

$$\operatorname{diam}(\mathsf{C}) \doteq \max \left\{ \left\| \boldsymbol{x} - \boldsymbol{x}' \right\|_2 \mid \boldsymbol{x}, \boldsymbol{x}' \in \mathsf{C} \right\}. \tag{8.6.3}$$

Constrained Formulations of Sparse and Low-Rank Recovery

Many of the sparse and low-rank recovery problems that we have considered thus far can be reformulated in terms of (8.6.2). For example, for sparse recovery, we can choose $\mathsf{C} = \{\boldsymbol{x} \mid \|\boldsymbol{x}\|_1 \le \tau\}$ to be an ℓ^1 ball, and solve

$$\begin{array}{ll} \min_{\boldsymbol{x}} & \frac{1}{2}\|\boldsymbol{A}\boldsymbol{x} - \boldsymbol{y}\|_2^2 \\ \text{subject to} & \|\boldsymbol{x}\|_1 \le \tau. \end{array} \tag{8.6.4}$$

Similarly, for low-rank matrix completion, we can choose C to be a nuclear norm ball and solve

$$\begin{array}{ll} \min_{\boldsymbol{X}} & \frac{1}{2}\|\mathcal{P}_\Omega[\boldsymbol{X}] - \boldsymbol{Y}\|_F^2 \\ \text{subject to} & \|\boldsymbol{X}\|_* \le \tau. \end{array} \tag{8.6.5}$$

Exercises 8.10 and 8.11 explore further reformulations of unconstrained sparse and low-rank optimization in the form (8.6.2).

Similar to the other methods we have discussed thus far, Frank–Wolfe is an iterative method, which generates a sequence of iterates $\boldsymbol{x}_0, \boldsymbol{x}_1, \ldots, \boldsymbol{x}_k, \ldots$ as follows. At each iteration, we generate a new point $\boldsymbol{v}_k$ by solving a constrained optimization problem

$$\boldsymbol{v}_k \in \arg\min_{\boldsymbol{v} \in \mathsf{C}} \ \langle \boldsymbol{v}, \nabla f(\boldsymbol{x}_k) \rangle. \tag{8.6.6}$$

We then set

$$\boldsymbol{x}_{k+1} = (1 - \gamma_k)\boldsymbol{x}_k + \gamma_k \boldsymbol{v}_k \in \mathsf{C}, \tag{8.6.7}$$

[10] The Frank–Wolfe algorithm can also work when $f(\boldsymbol{x})$ is nonconvex. One can show that it also converges but has a convergence rate $O(1/\sqrt{k})$ [LJ16].

Frank–Wolfe Method (FW)

Problem Class:

$$\begin{array}{ll} \min_{x} & f(x) \\ \text{subject to} & x \in \mathsf{C}. \end{array}$$

$f : \mathbb{R}^n \to \mathbb{R}$ convex, differentiable, $\nabla f(x)$ L-Lipschitz.
C a compact convex set.

Basic Iteration: Repeat

$$v_k \in \arg\min_{v \in \mathsf{C}} \langle v, \nabla f(x_k) \rangle,$$

$$x_{k+1} = x_k + \gamma_k (v_k - x_k),$$

with $\gamma_k = \dfrac{2}{k+2}$.

Convergence Guarantee:

$$f(x_k) - f(x_\star) \leq \frac{2L \operatorname{diam}^2(\mathsf{C})}{k+2}.$$

Figure 8.6 An overview of the Frank–Wolfe method.

where $\gamma_k \in (0, 1)$ is a specially chosen step size. Figure 8.6 summarizes the properties of this method.

Interpretation as Minimizing a First-Order Approximation

The Frank–Wolfe method can be interpreted as follows. At a given point x_k, we form a first-order approximation to the objective function f:

$$f(v) \approx \hat{f}(v, x_k) \doteq f(x_k) + \langle v - x_k, \nabla f(x_k) \rangle. \tag{8.6.8}$$

We minimize the approximation $\hat{f}(v, x_k)$ over $v \in \mathsf{C}$ to produce v_k. We then take a step in the direction $w_k = v_k - x_k$:

$$x_{k+1} = x_k + \gamma_k w_k. \tag{8.6.9}$$

Computing the Step Direction

The crucial subproblem in the Frank–Wolfe method involves minimizing a linear function over a compact convex set C:

$$\min_{v \in \mathsf{C}} \langle v, \nabla f(x) \rangle. \tag{8.6.10}$$

Depending on the constraint set C, this could itself be a challenging (or even intractable!) optimization problem. Fortunately, for the problems of interest in this book, this subproblem can be solved in an efficient and scalable manner. We give two examples below:

EXAMPLE 8.29. (Frank–Wolfe subproblem over an ℓ^1 ball) *Given a vector* $\boldsymbol{g}$*, consider the problem*

$$\min_{\boldsymbol{v}} \langle \boldsymbol{v}, \boldsymbol{g} \rangle \quad \textit{subject to} \quad \|\boldsymbol{v}\|_1 \leq \tau. \tag{8.6.11}$$

Let i *be any index for which* $\boldsymbol{g}_i = \|\boldsymbol{g}\|_\infty$ *and* $\sigma_i = \operatorname{sign}(\boldsymbol{g}_i)$*. Then* (8.6.11) *has a solution*

$$\boldsymbol{v}_\star = -\tau \sigma_i \boldsymbol{e}_i, \tag{8.6.12}$$

where $\boldsymbol{e}_i$ *is the* i*-th standard basis vector. The solution* $\boldsymbol{v}_\star$ *can be computed in linear time, simply by finding the largest magnitude entry of* $\boldsymbol{g}$.

EXAMPLE 8.30. (Frank–Wolfe subproblem of a nuclear norm ball) *Given a matrix* $\boldsymbol{G}$*, consider the problem*

$$\min_{\boldsymbol{V}} \langle \boldsymbol{V}, \boldsymbol{G} \rangle \quad \textit{subject to} \quad \|\boldsymbol{V}\|_* \leq \tau. \tag{8.6.13}$$

Let $\boldsymbol{G} = \boldsymbol{U}\boldsymbol{\Sigma}\boldsymbol{V}^* = \sum_{i=1}^{n_1} \boldsymbol{u}_i \sigma_i \boldsymbol{v}_i$ *denote the singular value decomposition of* $\boldsymbol{G}$*. Then* (8.6.13) *has an optimal solution*

$$\boldsymbol{V}_\star = -\tau \boldsymbol{u}_1 \boldsymbol{v}_1^*. \tag{8.6.14}$$

This optimal solution can be computed in time $O(n_1 n_2)$ *by computing (only) the leading singular vector pair* $(\boldsymbol{u}_1, \boldsymbol{v}_1)$ *of* $\boldsymbol{G}$*; see Section 4.2.1 of Chapter 4 for details.*

The latter example illustrates the special virtue of the Frank–Wolfe method in nuclear norm minimization: the key subproblem only requires us to compute *one* singular value/vector triple. For a problem involving $n_1 \times n_2$ matrices, this can be done in time $O(n_1 n_2)$ – a dramatic improvement over proximal gradient methods, which require a full singular value decomposition in each iteration.

This scalability comes at a price, though. Compared to accelerated proximal gradient methods, which converge at a rate of $O(1/k^2)$ in function values, the Frank–Wolfe method only achieves a rate of $O(1/k)$.[11] The following theorem gives a precise bound on the worst-case rate of convergence for Frank–Wolfe over the class of convex functions with Lipschitz gradient.

THEOREM 8.31. (Convergence of Frank–Wolfe) *Let* $\boldsymbol{x}_0, \boldsymbol{x}_1, \ldots$ *denote the sequence of iterates generated by the Frank–Wolfe method, with step size* $\gamma_k = 2/(k+2)$*. Then*

$$f(\boldsymbol{x}_k) - f(\boldsymbol{x}_\star) \leq \frac{2L \operatorname{diam}^2(\mathsf{C})}{k+2}. \tag{8.6.15}$$

[11] When the function is nonconvex, the worst convergence rate reduces to $O(1/\sqrt{k})$ [LJ16].

Proof For ease of notation, write $d = \text{diam}(\mathsf{C})^2$, $\boldsymbol{x} = \boldsymbol{x}_k$, $\boldsymbol{x}^+ = \boldsymbol{x}_{k+1}$, $\gamma = \gamma_k$, and $\boldsymbol{v} = \boldsymbol{v}_k$. Note that

$$\boldsymbol{x}^+ - \boldsymbol{x} = \gamma\,(\boldsymbol{v} - \boldsymbol{x})\,. \tag{8.6.16}$$

Because $\nabla f(\boldsymbol{x})$ is L-Lipschitz, we can use the upper bound (8.2.8) to obtain

$$\begin{aligned} f(\boldsymbol{x}^+) &\le f(\boldsymbol{x}) + \left\langle \nabla f(\boldsymbol{x}), \boldsymbol{x}^+ - \boldsymbol{x} \right\rangle + \frac{L}{2}\left\| \boldsymbol{x}^+ - \boldsymbol{x} \right\|_2^2 \\ &\le f(\boldsymbol{x}) + \gamma\,\langle \nabla f(\boldsymbol{x}), \boldsymbol{v} - \boldsymbol{x}\rangle + \frac{\gamma^2 L}{2}\left\| \boldsymbol{v} - \boldsymbol{x} \right\|_2^2 \\ &\le f(\boldsymbol{x}) + \gamma\,\langle \nabla f(\boldsymbol{x}), \boldsymbol{v} - \boldsymbol{x}\rangle + \frac{\gamma^2 L}{2} d^2. \end{aligned} \tag{8.6.17}$$

Meanwhile, by convexity,

$$\begin{aligned} f(\boldsymbol{x}_\star) &\ge f(\boldsymbol{x}) + \langle \nabla f(\boldsymbol{x}), \boldsymbol{x}_\star - \boldsymbol{x}\rangle \\ &\ge f(\boldsymbol{x}) + \langle \nabla f(\boldsymbol{x}), \boldsymbol{v} - \boldsymbol{x}\rangle\,, \end{aligned} \tag{8.6.18}$$

where the final line follows because $\boldsymbol{v}$ is chosen to minimize $\langle \nabla f(\boldsymbol{x}), \boldsymbol{v}\rangle$. Combining these two inequalities, we find that

$$\langle \nabla f(\boldsymbol{x}), \boldsymbol{v} - \boldsymbol{x}\rangle \le -\Big(f(\boldsymbol{x}) - f(\boldsymbol{x}_\star) \Big), \tag{8.6.19}$$

whence, plugging into (8.6.17) and subtracting $f(\boldsymbol{x}_\star)$ from both sides, we obtain

$$f(\boldsymbol{x}^+) - f(\boldsymbol{x}_\star) \le \big(1 - \gamma\big)\Big(f(\boldsymbol{x}) - f(\boldsymbol{x}_\star) \Big) + \frac{\gamma^2}{2} L d^2. \tag{8.6.20}$$

We use this basic relationship together with an inductive argument to bound the rate of convergence of the Frank–Wolfe method. Let ε_k denote the suboptimality (in function values) at iteration k:

$$\varepsilon_k = f(\boldsymbol{x}_k) - f(\boldsymbol{x}_\star). \tag{8.6.21}$$

Set $\gamma_k = 2/(k+2)$, so $\gamma_0 = 1$. Applying (8.6.20), we find that

$$\varepsilon_1 \le \tfrac{1}{2} L d^2. \tag{8.6.22}$$

Suppose now that for $\ell = 1, \ldots, k$, $\varepsilon_\ell \le (2/(\ell+2)) L d^2$. Applying (8.6.20) again, we find that

$$\begin{aligned} \varepsilon_{k+1} &\le \frac{k}{k+2}\varepsilon_k + \frac{2}{(k+2)^2} L d^2 \\ &\le \frac{k+1}{(k+2)^2} \times 2Ld^2 \\ &\le \frac{2Ld^2}{(k+1)+2}. \end{aligned} \tag{8.6.23}$$

Hence, the relationship $\varepsilon_\ell \le (2/(\ell+2)) L d^2$ holds for all iterations ℓ, as claimed. □

8.6.2 Frank–Wolfe for Stable Matrix Completion

In the context of nuclear norm minimization, the above result can be viewed as follows: Frank–Wolfe allows us to derive methods that produce moderate-quality solutions to extremely large problems, for which methods with better worst-case rates simply take too long to compute even a single iteration. To be more specific, in this section we illustrate the general Frank–Wolfe method for the particular problem of recovering a low-rank matrix from incomplete and noisy observations:

$$\boldsymbol{Y} = \mathcal{P}_\Omega[\boldsymbol{X}_o + \boldsymbol{Z}], \tag{8.6.24}$$

where $\boldsymbol{X}_o \in \mathbb{R}^{n_1 \times n_2}$ has low rank, $\boldsymbol{Z} \in \mathbb{R}^{n_1 \times n_2}$ is a matrix of small, dense noise, and $\Omega \subseteq [n_1] \times [n_2]$ is the set of observed entries. One approach to approximately recovering $\boldsymbol{X}_o$ is to minimize the reconstruction error over the set of all matrices of small nuclear norm:

$$\begin{array}{ll} \min & f(\boldsymbol{X}) \equiv \frac{1}{2}\|\mathcal{P}_\Omega[\boldsymbol{X}] - \boldsymbol{Y}\|_F^2 \\ \text{subject to} & \|\boldsymbol{X}\|_* \le \tau. \end{array} \tag{8.6.25}$$

Here, the constraint $\|\boldsymbol{X}\|_* \le \tau$ encourages $\boldsymbol{X}$ to have low rank. The constraint set $\mathsf{C} = \{\boldsymbol{X} \mid \|\boldsymbol{X}\|_* \le \tau\}$ is closed and bounded. Moreover, the gradient

$$\nabla f(\boldsymbol{X}) = \mathcal{P}_\Omega[\boldsymbol{X} - \boldsymbol{Y}] \tag{8.6.26}$$

is 1-Lipschitz, and so the Frank–Wolfe method indeed applies to this problem.

The key step in the Frank–Wolfe method is to minimize a linear function $\langle \boldsymbol{V}, \nabla f(\boldsymbol{X})\rangle$ over the constraint set C. As described above, this problem can be solved in closed form: if

$$\nabla f(\boldsymbol{X}) = \sum_{i=1}^{n_1} \boldsymbol{u}_i \sigma_i \boldsymbol{v}_i^* \tag{8.6.27}$$

is the singular value decomposition of ∇f, then

$$-\tau \boldsymbol{u}_1 \boldsymbol{v}_1^* \in \arg\min_{\boldsymbol{V} \in \mathsf{C}} \langle \boldsymbol{V}, \nabla f(\boldsymbol{X})\rangle . \tag{8.6.28}$$

The leading singular value/vectors can be extracted from the matrix $\nabla f(\boldsymbol{X})$ efficiently, without computing the entire SVD (8.6.27). Typically, this is done using the power method, which was described in some detail in Chapter 4 and Exercise 4.6.[12] To cleanly describe the method, we simply let

$$(\boldsymbol{u}_1, \sigma_1, \boldsymbol{v}_1) \doteq \operatorname{LeadSV}(\boldsymbol{G}) \tag{8.6.29}$$

denote the operation which extracts a leading singular value/vector triple from a matrix $\boldsymbol{G}$. Using this notation, the complete Frank–Wolfe algorithm for stable matrix completion is described in Algorithm 8.8.

[12] Or by the more efficient Lanczos method to be introduced in Section 9.3.2 of the next chapter.

Algorithm 8.8 Frank–Wolfe for Stable Matrix Completion

Problem: given $\boldsymbol{Y} \in \mathbb{R}^{n_1 \times n_2}$ and $\Omega \subseteq [n_1] \times [n_2]$,

$$\min_{\boldsymbol{X}} \tfrac{1}{2} \|\mathcal{P}_\Omega[\boldsymbol{X}] - \boldsymbol{Y}\|_F^2 \quad \text{subject to} \quad \|\boldsymbol{X}\|_* \le \tau.$$

Input: $\boldsymbol{X}_0 \in \mathbb{R}^{n_1 \times n_2}$ satisfying $\|\boldsymbol{X}_0\|_* \le \tau$.
for $(k = 0, 1, 2, \dots, K-1)$ **do**
  $(\boldsymbol{u}_1, \sigma_1, \boldsymbol{v}_1) \leftarrow \text{LeadSV}\,(\mathcal{P}_\Omega\,[\boldsymbol{X}_k - \boldsymbol{Y}])$.
  $\boldsymbol{V}_k \leftarrow -\tau \boldsymbol{u}_1 \boldsymbol{v}_1^*$.
  $\boldsymbol{X}_{k+1} \leftarrow \dfrac{k}{k+2}\boldsymbol{X}_k + \dfrac{2}{k+2}\boldsymbol{V}_k$.
end for
Output: $\boldsymbol{X}_\star \leftarrow \boldsymbol{X}_K$.

The Frank–Wolfe method requires only a single singular value/vector triple at each iteration. Moreover, since $\boldsymbol{V}_k = -\tau \boldsymbol{u}_1 \boldsymbol{v}_1^*$ has rank 1, the rank of $\boldsymbol{X}_k$ increases by at most one at each iteration. In this sense, Frank–Wolfe can be viewed as a *greedy method*. It constructs a low-rank matrix $\boldsymbol{X}_\star$ by adding on one (optimally chosen) rank-1 factor at a time.

8.6.3 Connection to Greedy Methods for Sparsity

In sparse and low-rank approximation, *greedy methods* are sometimes favored for their simplicity and scalability. For sparse approximation, the Frank–Wolfe method gives one such greedy algorithm. Consider the problem

$$\begin{array}{ll} \min_{\boldsymbol{x}} & f(\boldsymbol{x}) \equiv \tfrac{1}{2}\|\boldsymbol{A}\boldsymbol{x} - \boldsymbol{y}\|_2^2 \\ \text{subject to} & \|\boldsymbol{x}\|_1 \le \tau. \end{array} \tag{8.6.30}$$

Notice that

$$\nabla f(\boldsymbol{x}) = \boldsymbol{A}^*(\boldsymbol{A}\boldsymbol{x} - \boldsymbol{y}). \tag{8.6.31}$$

The Frank–Wolfe subproblem

$$\min_{\boldsymbol{v}} \langle \boldsymbol{v}, \nabla f(\boldsymbol{x}) \rangle \quad \text{subject to} \quad \|\boldsymbol{v}\|_1 \le \tau \tag{8.6.32}$$

has an especially simple solution: letting i be the index of the largest-magnitude entry of ∇f, and σ its sign,

$$\boldsymbol{v}_\star = -\tau\sigma\boldsymbol{e}_i. \tag{8.6.33}$$

Algorithm 8.9 describes in detail the Frank–Wolfe method for problem (8.6.30). At each iteration, it increases the number of nonzero entries in the vector $\boldsymbol{x}$ by at most one, by adding on a multiple of $\boldsymbol{e}_{i_k}$. Let

$$\mathsf{I}_k = \{i_1, \dots, i_{k-1}\} = \operatorname{supp}(\boldsymbol{x}_k) \tag{8.6.34}$$

Algorithm 8.9 Frank–Wolfe for Noisy Sparse Recovery

Problem: given $\boldsymbol{y} \in \mathbb{R}^m$, $\boldsymbol{A} \in \mathbb{R}^{m \times n}$,

$$\min_{\boldsymbol{x}} \tfrac{1}{2} \|\boldsymbol{A}\boldsymbol{x} - \boldsymbol{y}\|_2^2 \quad \text{subject to} \quad \|\boldsymbol{x}\|_1 \leq \tau.$$

Input: $\boldsymbol{x}_0 \in \mathbb{R}^n$ satisfying $\|\boldsymbol{x}_0\|_1 \leq \tau$.
for $(k = 0, 1, 2, \ldots, K-1)$ **do**
  $\boldsymbol{r}_k \leftarrow \boldsymbol{A}\boldsymbol{x}_k - \boldsymbol{y}$.
  $i_k \leftarrow \arg\max_i \left|\boldsymbol{a}_i^* \boldsymbol{r}_k\right|$.
  $\sigma \leftarrow \operatorname{sign}\left(\boldsymbol{a}_{i_k}^* \boldsymbol{r}_k\right)$.
  $\boldsymbol{v}_k \leftarrow -\tau\sigma\boldsymbol{e}_{i_k}$.
  $\boldsymbol{x}_{k+1} \leftarrow \dfrac{k}{k+2}\boldsymbol{x}_k + \dfrac{2}{k+2}\boldsymbol{v}_k$.
end for
Output: $\boldsymbol{x}_\star \leftarrow \boldsymbol{x}_K$.

denote the collection of indices that have been chosen up to time k. We generate I_{k+1} from I_k by introducing a (potentially) new index

$$\mathsf{I}_{k+1} = \mathsf{I}_k \cup \{i_k\}. \tag{8.6.35}$$

This new index is chosen according to the largest-magnitude entry in the gradient ∇f. Write

$$\boldsymbol{A} = [\boldsymbol{a}_1 \mid \cdots \mid \boldsymbol{a}_n] \tag{8.6.36}$$

for the columns of $\boldsymbol{A}$, and let

$$\boldsymbol{r}_k = \boldsymbol{A}\boldsymbol{x}_k - \boldsymbol{y} \tag{8.6.37}$$

denote the measurement residual at point $\boldsymbol{x}_k$. Since $\nabla f(\boldsymbol{x}_k) = \boldsymbol{A}^* \boldsymbol{r}_k$, the Frank–Wolfe method chooses the index i_k corresponding to the column $\boldsymbol{a}_{i_k}$ that is most correlated with the residual $\boldsymbol{r}_k$.

Matching Pursuit

A number of classical *greedy methods* for sparse approximation have this basic structure. A canonical example is the *matching pursuit* algorithm [MZ93]. This algorithm generates a sequence of iterates $\boldsymbol{x}_0 = \boldsymbol{0}, \boldsymbol{x}_1, \boldsymbol{x}_2, \ldots$, by repeatedly choosing a column $\boldsymbol{a}_{i_k}$ of $\boldsymbol{A}$ that is most correlated with the residual $\boldsymbol{r}_k$. Similar to Frank–Wolfe, matching pursuit[13] sets

$$i_k = \arg\max_i \left| \left[\nabla f(\boldsymbol{x}_k)\right]_i \right| = \arg\max_i \left|\boldsymbol{a}_i^* \boldsymbol{r}_k\right|. \tag{8.6.38}$$

[13] Despite the strong parallels to the Frank–Wolfe method, matching pursuit was motivated independently from a rather different perspective for solving a more specific class of signal processing tasks [MZ93].

Algorithm 8.10 Matching Pursuit for Sparse Approximation

Problem: find a sparse $\boldsymbol{x}$ such that $f(\boldsymbol{x}) \equiv \frac{1}{2} \|\boldsymbol{A}\boldsymbol{x} - \boldsymbol{y}\|_2^2$ is small.
$\boldsymbol{x}_0 \leftarrow \boldsymbol{0}$.
for $(k = 0, 1, 2, \ldots, K-1)$ **do**
  $\boldsymbol{r}_k \leftarrow \boldsymbol{A}\boldsymbol{x}_k - \boldsymbol{y}$.
  $i_k \leftarrow \arg\max_i \left|\boldsymbol{a}_i^* \boldsymbol{r}_k\right|$.
  $t_k \leftarrow -\dfrac{\left\langle \boldsymbol{a}_{i_k}, \boldsymbol{r}_k \right\rangle}{\left\|\boldsymbol{a}_{i_k}\right\|_2^2}$.
  $\boldsymbol{x}_{k+1} \leftarrow \boldsymbol{x}_k + t_k \boldsymbol{e}_{i_k}$.
end for
Output: $\boldsymbol{x}_\star \leftarrow \boldsymbol{x}_K$.

However, rather than stepping a predetermined length in the $\boldsymbol{e}_{i_k}$ direction, matching pursuit chooses the step size t_k by solving a one-dimensional minimization problem:

$$t_k = \arg\min_t f\left(\boldsymbol{x}_k + t\boldsymbol{e}_{i_k}\right) = -\frac{\left\langle \boldsymbol{a}_{i_k}, \boldsymbol{r}_k \right\rangle}{\left\|\boldsymbol{a}_{i_k}\right\|_2^2}. \tag{8.6.39}$$

This can be viewed as a form of *exact line search* and typically leads to more rapid convergence in practice. The overall matching pursuit algorithm is specified as Algorithm 8.10.

Orthogonal Matching Pursuit

Matching pursuit achieves better convergence by choosing the step size t_k in an optimal manner. Since

$$\boldsymbol{x}_{k+1} = \boldsymbol{x}_k + t_k \boldsymbol{e}_{i_k}, \tag{8.6.40}$$

this is equivalent to making an optimal choice of the i_k-th entry in $\boldsymbol{x}_{k+1}$, while leaving all of the other entries fixed. It is possible to further improve the rate of convergence of this approach by choosing *all* of the nonzero entries of $\boldsymbol{x}_{k+1}$ optimally (rather than just the i_k-th entry). In notation, let $\mathsf{I}_k = \{i_1, i_2, \ldots, i_{k-1}\}$ denote the collection of indices that have been chosen up to step k. The *orthogonal matching pursuit* method [PRK93, TG07] selects an index i_k that maximizes the correlation $|\boldsymbol{a}_i^* \boldsymbol{r}_k|$ of a column of $\boldsymbol{A}$ with the residual $\boldsymbol{r}_k = \boldsymbol{A}\boldsymbol{x}_k - \boldsymbol{y}$. It sets $\mathsf{I}_{k+1} = \mathsf{I}_k \cup \{i_k\}$, and then updates all of the nonzero entries in $\boldsymbol{x}$ by setting

$$\boldsymbol{x}_{k+1} = \arg\min_{\boldsymbol{x}} \ \tfrac{1}{2} \|\boldsymbol{A}\boldsymbol{x} - \boldsymbol{y}\|_2^2 \quad \text{subject to} \quad \operatorname{supp}(\boldsymbol{x}) \subseteq \mathsf{I}_{k+1}. \tag{8.6.41}$$

This problem can be solved in closed form:

$$\left[\boldsymbol{x}_{k+1}\right]_{\mathsf{I}_{k+1}} = \left(\boldsymbol{A}_{\mathsf{I}_{k+1}}^* \boldsymbol{A}_{\mathsf{I}_{k+1}}\right)^{-1} \boldsymbol{A}_{\mathsf{I}_{k+1}}^* \boldsymbol{y}, \tag{8.6.42}$$

$$\left[\boldsymbol{x}_{k+1}\right]_{\mathsf{I}_{k+1}^c} = \boldsymbol{0}. \tag{8.6.43}$$

Algorithm 8.11 Orthogonal Matching Pursuit for Sparse Approximation

Problem: find a sparse $\boldsymbol{x}$ such that $f(\boldsymbol{x}) \equiv \frac{1}{2}\|\boldsymbol{A}\boldsymbol{x} - \boldsymbol{y}\|_2^2$ is small.
$\boldsymbol{x}_0 \leftarrow \boldsymbol{0}$, $\mathsf{I}_0 \leftarrow \varnothing$.
for $(k = 0, 1, 2, \ldots, K-1)$ **do**
    $\boldsymbol{r}_k \leftarrow \boldsymbol{A}\boldsymbol{x}_k - \boldsymbol{y}$.
    $i_k \leftarrow \arg\max_i \left|\boldsymbol{a}_i^* \boldsymbol{r}_k\right|$.
    $\mathsf{I}_{k+1} \leftarrow \mathsf{I}_k \cup \{i_k\}$.
    $\left[\boldsymbol{x}_{k+1}\right]_{\mathsf{I}_{k+1}} \leftarrow \left(\boldsymbol{A}_{\mathsf{I}_{k+1}}^* \boldsymbol{A}_{\mathsf{I}_{k+1}}\right)^{-1} \boldsymbol{A}_{\mathsf{I}_{k+1}}^* \boldsymbol{y}$.
    $\left[\boldsymbol{x}_{k+1}\right]_{\mathsf{I}_{k+1}^c} \leftarrow \boldsymbol{0}$.
end for
Output: $\boldsymbol{x}_\star \leftarrow \boldsymbol{x}_K$.

The name *orthogonal* matching pursuit comes from the observation that the residual

$$\boldsymbol{r}_{k+1} = \boldsymbol{A}\boldsymbol{x}_{k+1} - \boldsymbol{y} = \left(\boldsymbol{A}_{\mathsf{I}_{k+1}}\left(\boldsymbol{A}_{\mathsf{I}_{k+1}}^* \boldsymbol{A}_{\mathsf{I}_{k+1}}\right)^{-1} \boldsymbol{A}_{\mathsf{I}_{k+1}}^* - \boldsymbol{I}\right)\boldsymbol{y} \tag{8.6.44}$$

is orthogonal to the range, $\operatorname{range}\left(\boldsymbol{A}_{\mathsf{I}_{k+1}}\right)$, of the dictionary columns selected through the first $k+1$ iterations.

The overall orthogonal matching pursuit (OMP) algorithm is given as Algorithm 8.11. This method is sometimes favored by practitioners due to its simplicity, and the fact that it maintains an explicit *active set* I_k. The latter property is useful for problems in which the support of the sparse solution $\boldsymbol{x}_\star$ is the object of interest.[14]

Although OMP has many variants and extensions, it was originally derived for the specific problem of finding sparse near-solutions to a linear system of equations $\boldsymbol{A}\boldsymbol{x} = \boldsymbol{y}$. Like ℓ^1 minimization, OMP is guaranteed to succeed whenever $\boldsymbol{y}$ is generated from some sufficiently sparse $\boldsymbol{x}_o$ and the columns of $\boldsymbol{A}$ are sufficiently spread in the high-dimensional space $\mathbb{R}^m$. In particular:

THEOREM 8.32. (Convergence of orthogonal matching pursuit) *Suppose that* $\boldsymbol{y} = \boldsymbol{A}\boldsymbol{x}_o$, *with*

$$k = \|\boldsymbol{x}_o\|_0 \leq \frac{1}{2\mu(\boldsymbol{A})}. \tag{8.6.45}$$

Then after k *iterations, the OMP algorithm terminates with* $\boldsymbol{x}_k = \boldsymbol{x}_o$ *and* $\mathsf{I}_k = \operatorname{supp}(\boldsymbol{x}_o)$.

Exercise 8.12 guides the reader through a proof of Theorem 8.32. The key message of the proof is that under the conditions of the theorem, at each iteration ℓ the algorithm selects an index i_ℓ that belongs to the true support set $\operatorname{supp}(\boldsymbol{x}_o)$.

14 For example, in the RF spectrum sensing discussed in Chapter 11, the goal is to determine which bands of the RF spectrum are occupied, in order to avoid interference. The specific energy levels within these bands are of secondary importance.

The form of Theorem 8.32 can be directly compared to that of Theorem 3.3 of Chapter 3. These results imply that *both* OMP and ℓ^1 minimization recover $\boldsymbol{x}_o$ whenever $\|\boldsymbol{x}_o\|_0 \leq 1/2\mu(\boldsymbol{A})$. Hence, at an intuitive level, both methods succeed whenever the target solution is sparse and the matrix $\boldsymbol{A}$ is "nice."

However, as shown in Chapter 3, the incoherence condition requires $\boldsymbol{x}_o$ to be extremely sparse. ℓ^1 minimization also recovers denser $\boldsymbol{x}_o$ under the stronger condition that $\boldsymbol{A}$ satisfies the restricted isometry property (RIP) $\delta(\boldsymbol{A}) < c$. While various improved analyses of OMP are available, the RIP is not sufficient for OMP to succeed. In this sense, convex relaxation achieves a better uniform guarantee. However, OMP can be modified to also guarantee sparse recovery under the RIP. The key ideas are to allow the algorithm to *remove* elements from the active set I_k at each iteration, and to add multiple elements. The resulting method, called compressed sampling matching pursuit (COSAMP) [NT09] is described in more detail in Exercise 8.13. The large and varied literature on greedy algorithms also includes greedy methods for more general problems such as low-rank recovery, as we will give more references in the final Notes section.

8.6.4 Stochastic Gradient Descent for Finite Sum

The type of optimization we often encounter is of the type

$$F(\boldsymbol{x}) = f(\boldsymbol{x}) + g(\boldsymbol{x}), \quad \boldsymbol{x} \in \mathbb{R}^n, \tag{8.6.46}$$

where $f(\boldsymbol{x})$ is typically the measurement error term, also known as the "data" term, say $\|\boldsymbol{y} - \boldsymbol{A}\boldsymbol{x}\|_2^2$, and $g(\boldsymbol{x})$ is typically a regularization for promoting certain low-dimensional structure on the solution $\boldsymbol{x}$, also known as the "model" term, say the ℓ^1 norm $\|\boldsymbol{x}\|_1$ for a vector or the nuclear norm for a matrix. As we have seen in the previous section, to strive for better scalability, the Frank–Wolfe method exploits the (compositional) structure in the term $g(\boldsymbol{x})$, by restricting the search for good descent direction to a small set of coordinates or directions. See Section D.4 of Appendix B for a more explicit scheme, known as *block coordinate descent*, to exploit such structures. Such schemes typically allow us to reduce the dependence of algorithmic complexity on the dimension n, from $O(n)$ to sublinear in n, say[15]

$$O(n) \rightarrow O(n^{1/2}).$$

A remaining question is whether there are good structures in the data term $f(\boldsymbol{x})$ that can be exploited too for better scalability. Indeed, in many problems that arise in compressive sensing or machine learning, the data term is typically a *finite sum* of (statistically independent) terms, say measurement errors. That is, $f(\boldsymbol{x})$ is typically of the form

$$f(\boldsymbol{x}) = \frac{1}{m}\sum_{i=1}^{m} h_i(\boldsymbol{x}), \quad \boldsymbol{x} \in \mathbb{R}^n, \tag{8.6.47}$$

[15] For example, in the case of recovering an $n_1 \times n_2$ low-rank matrix, the Frank–Wolfe method reduces the dependence from $O(n_1 \times n_2)$ to $O(n_1 + n_2)$.

where each $h_i(\boldsymbol{x})$ is an independent sample of the function $f(\boldsymbol{x})$ hence $\mathbb{E}[h_i(\boldsymbol{x})] = f(\boldsymbol{x})$. For example, for m measurements of a sparse vector $\boldsymbol{x}$, $\boldsymbol{y} = \boldsymbol{A}\boldsymbol{x} \in \mathbb{R}^m$, we can write the data fitting term as

$$\frac{1}{m}\|\boldsymbol{y} - \boldsymbol{A}\boldsymbol{x}\|_2^2 = \frac{1}{m}\sum_{i=1}^{m}(y_i - \boldsymbol{a}_i^*\boldsymbol{x})^2, \tag{8.6.48}$$

where $\boldsymbol{a}_i^*$ is the i-th row of $\boldsymbol{A}$. This is also the case in many machine learning problems, where the total loss to minimize is a sum of logistic or ℓ^p losses for a large set of training samples.

Notice that, when the number of samples m is very large, even the gradient descent algorithm can be very expensive: to evaluate the gradient of $f(\boldsymbol{x})$, the complexity is typically linear in the number of samples, i.e., of the order $O(m)$. To further reduce the complexity's dependence on m, one key idea is to use the so-called *stochastic gradient descent (SGD)* method [RM51, Bot10]. That is, at each iteration k, instead of using all the m samples to compute the full gradient $\nabla f(\boldsymbol{x})$, we compute the gradient approximately with a random batch of samples $B_k \subset [m]$ of a fixed size $b \ll m$:

$$f_k(\boldsymbol{x}) \doteq \frac{1}{b}\sum_{i\in B_k} h_i(\boldsymbol{x}), \quad \nabla f_k(\boldsymbol{x}) \doteq \frac{1}{b}\sum_{i\in B_k} \nabla h_i(\boldsymbol{x}). \tag{8.6.49}$$

We then use this approximate gradient to replace the full gradient in the descent scheme, leading to the stochastic gradient descent (SGD) scheme:

$$\boldsymbol{x}_{k+1} = \boldsymbol{x}_k - \gamma_k \nabla f_k(\boldsymbol{x}_k). \tag{8.6.50}$$

This reduces the computational cost of each iteration to be $O(n)$. Following our proofs for the gradient descent, using the fact $\mathbb{E}[\nabla f_k(\boldsymbol{x})] = \nabla f(\boldsymbol{x})$, it is easy to show that the expected value of the objective function $\mathbb{E}[f(\boldsymbol{x}_k)]$ converges using the stochastic gradient descent scheme.

However, despite high scalability, SGD has poor convergence rate due to a constant variance of the stochastic gradient $\mathbb{E}[\|\nabla f_k(\boldsymbol{x}) - \nabla f(\boldsymbol{x})\|] > 0$. To improve the convergence behavior of SGD, several methods of *variance reduced* SGD have been developed in the past decade or so [JZ13, DBLJ14, LMH15, AZ17]. In such *variance reduction* methods, instead of directly using $\nabla f_k(\boldsymbol{x})$, one computes a full gradient $\nabla f(\tilde{\boldsymbol{x}})$ at an anchor point $\tilde{\boldsymbol{x}}$ beforehand. Then one uses the following variance reduced gradient,

$$\tilde{\nabla} f_k(\boldsymbol{x}) \doteq \nabla f_k(\boldsymbol{x}) - \nabla f_k(\tilde{\boldsymbol{x}}) + \nabla f(\tilde{\boldsymbol{x}}), \tag{8.6.51}$$

as a proxy for the full gradient $\nabla f(\boldsymbol{x})$ during each iteration,

$$\boldsymbol{x}_{k+1} = \boldsymbol{x}_k - \gamma_k \tilde{\nabla} f_k(\boldsymbol{x}_k). \tag{8.6.52}$$

As a result, the amortized per-iteration cost is still the same as for SGD. However, the variance reduced gradient (8.6.51) is unbiased and can reduce the variance from

$\mathbb{E}[\|\nabla f_k(\boldsymbol{x}) - \nabla f(\boldsymbol{x})\|]$ to $\mathbb{E}[\|\nabla f_k(\boldsymbol{x}) - \nabla f_k(\tilde{\boldsymbol{x}})\|]$. In theory, the variance $\mathbb{E}[\|\nabla f_k(\boldsymbol{x}) - \nabla f_k(\tilde{\boldsymbol{x}})\|]$ can vanish asymptotically, thus the convergence rate of SGD can be substantially improved.

Roughly speaking, these methods can reduce the variance of stochastic gradient by exploiting the structure of the finite sum. With variance reduction, they have the same per-iteration cost with SGD in the amortized sense whereas they can achieve better total complexity than the gradient descent method in terms of dependence on the number of samples, typically from $O(m)$ to sublinear in m, say

$$O(m) \rightarrow O(m^{1/2}).$$

All of these methods can work with the Nesterov acceleration schemes introduced in earlier sections and can be extended to the nonsmooth setting for structured signal recovery [DBLJ14, XZ14, AZ17]. More specifically, to achieve a prescribed accuracy in the objective function, say $|f(\boldsymbol{x}_k) - f(\boldsymbol{x}_\star)| \leq \varepsilon$, instead of the generic rate $O(\varepsilon^{-2})$ of stochastic gradient descent for general convex functions, one can achieve the accelerated rate of

$$O(\varepsilon^{-2}) \rightarrow O(\varepsilon^{-1/2}).$$

The recent work [SJM20b], which combines the variance reduction and acceleration methods, has achieved an overall computational complexity that practically meets the theoretical lower bound for this class of finite-sum problems. In addition, the variance reduced SGD can also be used in conjunction with the Frank–Wolfe method to simultaneously exploit the finite-sum structure and low-dimensional structure for even better scalability; e.g., see the work [HL16].

8.7 Notes

Greedy Algorithms

The name *basis pursuit* was first suggested by Chen and Donoho in their early work on recovering sparse representation [Che95, CDS01]. Many greedy algorithms such as matching pursuit (MP) [MZ93] were first used to solve the associated optimization problems, for an incoherent measurement matrix. The original idea of orthogonal matching pursuit (OMP) can be traced to the work [PRK93] on wavelets in the early 1990s and was later reintroduced by [TG07] to the problem of compressed sensing with random measurements. The OMP algorithm was later improved by [NT09] as the (compressed sampling matching pursuit) COSAMP algorithm, which works for measurement matrices with the RIP property. As we have seen in this chapter, these greedy algorithms bear great resemblance to the Franke–Wolfe algorithm [FW56] developed in the 1950s.

Convex Optimization Approach

An almost parallel line of study strives to develop efficient algorithms based on convex optimization. The study of the proximal operator for various convex functions can be traced to the work of Moreau in the 1960s [Mor62]. The iterative shrinkage-thresholding algorithm (ISTA), with its early roots tracing back to [Tib96], has been studied under different names, such as forward–backward splitting [CW05], thresholded Landweber [DDM04], and separable approximation (SpaRSA) [WNF08]. The fast iterative shrinkage-thresholding algorithm (FISTA), based on Nesterov's acceleration technique [Nes83], was introduced later by [BT09].

Large-Scale Algorithmic Implementations

The methods featured in this chapter aim to elucidate the main ideas and techniques for solving the BP-type (8.1.1) or Lasso-type (8.1.2) programs. The algorithms given here can already solve problems of moderate size efficiently. Nevertheless, for very large-scale problems, say with $\boldsymbol{x}$ being hundreds of millions in dimension, one should resort to more scalable approaches. For example, one can screen the variables in $\boldsymbol{x}$ so that we do not have to work with all variables at once. For instance, for the Lasso-type (or any ℓ^1 regularized convex) problems, more careful studies of the primal–dual variables lead to efficient screening rules [TBF$^+$12, GVR12]. Based on different screening strategies, one can subsequently develop more scalable greedy algorithms, including sequential screening methods [WZL$^+$14] or dynamical screening methods [NFGS15]. Another related strategy is to maintain and update a relatively small working or active set according to some violation rules [JG15]. This has also led to some of the more recent scalable algorithms such as the BLITZ [JG15] and CELER [MSG18].

Convergence of ALM and ADMM

The convergence of ALM- and ADMM-type algorithms has been long studied (see, e.g., [Hes69, Roc73, Pow69] for ALM and [LM79, KM89] for ADMM). Like the ALM method, the most natural approach is to recognize ADMM as some known algorithm applied to the dual. In fact, ADMM turns out to be equivalent to Douglas–Rachford splitting applied to the dual. For more details on this, see [EB92, CW05]. We recommend [Eck12] for a tutorial introduction to a more formal convergence analysis of ADMM. For more recent analysis of a generalized version of ADMM including their convergence rates, we recommend the work of [DY16]. ADMM has also been widely applied to problems when the number of terms is more than three [BPC$^+$11]. The convergence analysis of ADMM with more than three terms is much more difficult and it has been shown to diverge in many cases.

The proof given in this book follows the framework of [HY12] which was applied to the linear equality case by [Xu17]. We have seen that *monotone operators* play a powerful role in providing unified convergence analysis for both ALM and ADMM. In fact, monotone operators not only help with the convergence analysis. They may also lead to rather unified methods of algorithm design for convex optimization, by interpreting the optimal solution as the fixed point to certain contracting mappings associated with the monotone operators of the Lagrangian. The reader may refer to the recent manuscript [RB16] for a more systematic survey on this method.

Exploit Structures in Data Measurements

In this chapter, the algorithms developed typically treat the data fitting term for the measurement $\boldsymbol{y} = \boldsymbol{A}\boldsymbol{x}$ as a general smooth convex function. The convergence rates of all the algorithms are characterized under this (somewhat unnecessarily) general assumption. For instance, the rate $O(1/k)$ for ALM and ADMM, proven in Theorems 8.27 and 8.28, is actually optimal for this class of problems for first-order methods, according to [Nes03, Nem04, OX18]. However, in the compressed sensing setting, the data matrix is often a random measurement matrix and thus is full-rank and well conditioned. This property induces implicit *strong convexity* in the data-fitting term. Recent work [SJM20a] has shown that, somewhat surprisingly, for this class of problems, the bound $O(1/k)$ for ALM-like algorithms can be broken and one can obtain accelerated algorithms that achieve an improved convergence rate of $O(1/k^2 \log k)$.

Exploit Structures in Sparsity-Promoting Norms

In this chapter, we have mainly used the model problems of recovering sparse signals and/or low-rank matrices to introduce key algorithmic ideas that lead to provably efficient and effective algorithms for convex optimization. We only customize all the general algorithms to the ℓ^1 norm and the nuclear norm. As we have alluded to in Chapter 6, there are many other norms that promote a broader family of low-dimensional structures. In particular, the so-called *group sparsity* norms can be used to promote various sparse patterns in signals and images. One may develop efficient optimization algorithms that are specially tailored to such norms. Interested readers may refer to the manuscript [BJMO12] on this topic.

8.8 Exercises

8.1. (Proximal operators) *Prove the first and the third assertions of Proposition 8.4.*

8.2. (Average proximal operator) *Given multiple matrices* $\{\boldsymbol{W}_i \in \mathbb{R}^{m\times n}\}_{i=1}^k$, *show that we have:*

$$\operatorname{soft}\left(\frac{1}{k}\sum_{i=1}^{k}\boldsymbol{W}_i, \frac{\lambda}{k}\right) = \arg\min_{\boldsymbol{X}} \|\boldsymbol{X}\|_* + \frac{1}{2}\sum_{i=1}^{k}\|\boldsymbol{X}-\boldsymbol{W}_i\|_F^2. \tag{8.8.1}$$

This can be viewed as the proximal to find a low-rank matrix such that the averaged squared Frobenius norms to multiple matrices are small.

8.3. (Hybrid singular value thresholding) *Consider a matrix* $\boldsymbol{W}$ *of rank* r *and with singular values* $\{\sigma_i\}_{i=1}^r$ *in descending order. Let* $h : \mathbb{R} \to \mathbb{R}_+$ *be an increasing function and* $h(0) \le 1$.

(a) *Show that, given any* $\lambda \in (0, \sigma_1)$, *there exists a unique integer* $j \in [1, r]$ *such that the solution* t_j *to the equation*

$$h\left(\sum_{i=1}^{j} \sigma_i - j t_j\right) = \frac{t_j}{\lambda}$$

satisfies the condition:

$$\sigma_{j+1} \leq t_j < \sigma_j.$$

(b) *Design an algorithm that can compute this unique j and t_j efficiently. Notice that the worst you can do is to do a sequential search for all j.*

Denote this unique solution as $t_j^*(\lambda)$, and this gives a so-called hybrid thresholding operator *on the matrix $\boldsymbol{W}$ with singular value decomposition $\boldsymbol{U\Sigma V}^*$:*

$$\mathcal{H}(\boldsymbol{W}, \lambda) = \boldsymbol{U}\mathrm{soft}\big(\boldsymbol{\Sigma}, t_j^*(\lambda)\big)\boldsymbol{V}^*. \tag{8.8.2}$$

8.4. (Proximal operator for function of nuclear norm) *Let $f : \mathbb{R} \to \mathbb{R}$ be any convex and differentiable function with an increasing derivative $f'(x)$ and $f'(0) \leq 1$. Then given any matrix $\boldsymbol{W} \in \mathbb{R}^{m \times n}$ and a $\lambda > 0$, we have*

$$\mathcal{H}(\boldsymbol{W}, \lambda) = \arg\min_{\boldsymbol{X}} \lambda f(\|\boldsymbol{X}\|_*) + \frac{1}{2}\|\boldsymbol{X} - \boldsymbol{W}\|_F^2, \tag{8.8.3}$$

where $\mathcal{H}(\boldsymbol{W}, \lambda)$ is the hybrid thresholding operator defined in the previous exercise. Notice that the squared nuclear norm $\|\boldsymbol{X}\|_*^2$ or exponential $e^{\|\boldsymbol{X}\|_*}$ discussed in Example 8.5 are all special cases of the above result.

8.5. *Given multiple matrices $\{\boldsymbol{W}_i \in \mathbb{R}^{m \times n}\}_{i=1}^k$, consider a function f of the same property as in the previous exercise. Show that*

$$\mathcal{H}\left(\frac{1}{k}\sum_{i=1}^{k} \boldsymbol{W}_i, \frac{\lambda}{k}\right) = \arg\min_{\boldsymbol{X}} \lambda f(\|\boldsymbol{X}\|_*) + \frac{1}{2}\sum_{i=1}^{k} \|\boldsymbol{X} - \boldsymbol{W}_i\|_F^2. \tag{8.8.4}$$

8.6. (Iterative soft-thresholding algorithm for PCP) *Regarding solving the stable principal component pursuit program using proximal gradient descent:*

(a) *Apply the proximal gradient method to the PCP program. Based on separability of the two nonsmooth terms in the objective function, write down the corresponding proximal operators and the associated $\boldsymbol{w}_1$ and $\boldsymbol{w}_2$. Justify the updates for $\boldsymbol{L}_{k+1}$ and $\boldsymbol{S}_{k+1}$ in Algorithm 8.2.*

(b) *Code a MATLAB function that implements the iterative soft-thresholding algorithm (Algorithm 8.2) for PCP, and demonstrate it on synthetic problem instances in which the data are superpositions of low-rank and sparse matrices.*

8.7. (Lasso and elastic net) *Use the PG and APG methods to solve the following two problems:*

(a) *Suppose the observation $\boldsymbol{y} = \boldsymbol{A}\boldsymbol{x}_o + \boldsymbol{n}$, where $\boldsymbol{x}_o$ is sparse and n is some noise. Given $\boldsymbol{y}$ and $\boldsymbol{A}$, we would like to solve the* Lasso *problem of the form*

$$\min_{\boldsymbol{x}} \underbrace{\frac{1}{2}\|\boldsymbol{y} - \boldsymbol{A}\boldsymbol{x}\|_2^2}_{f(\boldsymbol{x})} + \underbrace{\lambda \|\boldsymbol{x}\|_1}_{g(\boldsymbol{x})}$$

to approximately recover the sparse vector $\boldsymbol{x}_o$. *For the PG and APG with a constant step size, compute the step size based on the Lipschitz constant of* ∇f. *Report your chosen step size for the proximal gradient in analytic form (i.e., with respect to the derived Lipschitz constant). For each method implemented, report the number of iterations needed for convergence, the norm difference with respect to the ground truth, a plot of objective value convergence in log scale, and the run time.*

(b) Furthermore, consider the following elastic net *problem:*

$$\min_{\boldsymbol{x}} \underbrace{\frac{1}{2}\|\boldsymbol{y} - \boldsymbol{A}\boldsymbol{x}\|_2^2 + \mu \|\boldsymbol{x}\|_2^2}_{f(\boldsymbol{x})} + \underbrace{\lambda \|\boldsymbol{x}\|_1}_{g(\boldsymbol{x})},$$

where f *is* μ*-strongly convex for* $\mu > 0$. *Use PG and APG to solve the problem and conduct similar reports to those for the previous part (a).*

8.8. (Implementation; augmented lagrange multiplier algorithm for PCP) *Derive an algorithm for the (equality constrained) principal component pursuit problem:*

$$\min_{\boldsymbol{L},\boldsymbol{S}} \|\boldsymbol{L}\|_* + \lambda\|\boldsymbol{S}\|_1 \quad \textit{subject to} \quad \boldsymbol{L} + \boldsymbol{S} = \boldsymbol{Y}. \tag{8.8.5}$$

This algorithm will solve a sequence of unconstrained problems; sketch how these problems can be solved using (accelerated) proximal gradient. Which solver do you expect to be more efficient, the one you've derived in this exercise, or a solver based on the alternating directions method of multipliers, which alternates between $\boldsymbol{L}$ *and* $\boldsymbol{S}$*?*

8.9. (Data self-expressive representation) *In many data processing problems such as subspace clustering [VMS16], the inter-relationships among all the data are best revealed through using data to represent (or regress) themselves. More precisely, given a set of data points* $\boldsymbol{X} = [\boldsymbol{x}_1, \boldsymbol{x}_2, \ldots, \boldsymbol{x}_m] \in \mathbb{R}^{n\times m}$, *we try to represent every data point as the (sparse) linear combination of other data points as:*

$$\boldsymbol{X} = \boldsymbol{X}\boldsymbol{C}, \tag{8.8.6}$$

where $\boldsymbol{C} \in \mathbb{R}^{m\times m}$ *is a matrix of coefficients. Since we do not want the pathological solution where every point is represented by itself, we can enforce the diagonal entries of* $\boldsymbol{C}$ *to be zero:* $\mathrm{diag}(\boldsymbol{C}) = \boldsymbol{0}$. *In addition, we would like to represent each point with the fewest points, hence we prefer the sparse solution for* $\boldsymbol{C}$. *This is particularly the case when the data lie on low-dimensional structures such as a union of subspaces, or approximately so for submanifolds. This entails us to solve the following program:*

$$\min \|\boldsymbol{C}\|_1 \quad \textit{subject to} \quad \boldsymbol{X} = \boldsymbol{X}\boldsymbol{C},\ \mathrm{diag}(\boldsymbol{C}) = \boldsymbol{0}. \tag{8.8.7}$$

Use the techniques provided in this chapter and write an algorithm to solve this problem.

One may also interpret the data points as nodes of a graph and the coefficient matrix $\boldsymbol{C}$ *as a matrix of the "state transition" probability. In this case, if the data form certain "clusters" or "communities," we may expect the matrix* $\boldsymbol{C}$ *to be low-rank [LLY+13]. Replace the* ℓ^1 *norm in the above problem and write an algorithm to solve the following program:*

$$\min \|\boldsymbol{C}\|_* \quad \textit{subject to} \quad \boldsymbol{X} = \boldsymbol{X}\boldsymbol{C},\ \operatorname{diag}(\boldsymbol{C}) = \boldsymbol{0}. \tag{8.8.8}$$

8.10. (Unconstrained problems via Frank–Wolfe) *Consider an unconstrained optimization problem of the form*

$$\min_{\boldsymbol{x}} f(\boldsymbol{x}) + g(\boldsymbol{x}), \tag{8.8.9}$$

with f *differentiable with Lipschitz continuous gradient. Derive a Frank–Wolfe like method for this problem by instead solving*

$$\min_{\boldsymbol{x},t} f(\boldsymbol{x}) + t \quad \textit{subject to} \quad g(\boldsymbol{x}) \le t,\ t \le t_0, \tag{8.8.10}$$

where t_0 *is an upper bound on* $g(\boldsymbol{x}_\star)$ *at any optimal solution* $\boldsymbol{x}_\star$ *(you may assume that* t_0 *is provided by the user).*

8.11. (Sparse and low-rank via Frank–Wolfe) *Consider the constrained problem*

$$\min f(\boldsymbol{L}, \boldsymbol{S}) \equiv \tfrac{1}{2}\|\boldsymbol{Y} - \boldsymbol{L} - \boldsymbol{S}\|_F^2 \quad \textit{subject to} \quad \|\boldsymbol{L}\|_* \le \tau_L,\ \|\boldsymbol{S}\|_1 \le \tau_S. \tag{8.8.11}$$

Derive a Frank–Wolfe algorithm for solving this problem. By how much can the rank of $\boldsymbol{L}$ *increase at each iteration? By how much can the number of nonzeros in* $\boldsymbol{S}$ *increase at each iteration?*

Suppose we modify the algorithm by, after each Frank–Wolfe iteration, taking a projected gradient step

$$\boldsymbol{S}^+ = \mathcal{P}_{\|\boldsymbol{S}\|_1 \le \tau_S}\left[\boldsymbol{S} - (1/L)\nabla_{\boldsymbol{S}} f(\boldsymbol{L}, \boldsymbol{S})\right], \tag{8.8.12}$$

where L *is a Lipschitz constant of the gradient of* f. *What are some potential advantages of this hybrid method, in terms of the number of iterations required to converge?*

8.12. (Sparse recovery by orthogonal matching pursuit) *The goal of this exercise is to prove Theorem 8.32, which shows that OMP correctly recovers any target sparse solution* $\boldsymbol{x}_o$ *with* $k = \|\boldsymbol{x}_o\|_0 \le 1/2\mu(\boldsymbol{A})$. *Let* $\mathsf{I} = \operatorname{supp}(\boldsymbol{x}_o)$.

(a) OMP selects a true support index in the first iteration. *Let* $i_{\max}$ *index a maximum-magnitude entry of* $\boldsymbol{x}_o$, *i.e.,* $\boldsymbol{x}_o(i_{\max}) = \|\boldsymbol{x}_o\|_\infty$. *Using the incoherence of* $\boldsymbol{A}$, *argue that*

$$\left|\boldsymbol{a}_{i_{\max}}^* \boldsymbol{r}_0\right| \ge \left|\boldsymbol{a}_j^* \boldsymbol{r}_0\right| \quad \forall\, j \in \mathsf{I}^c. \tag{8.8.13}$$

(b) Argue by induction that OMP selects some $i_\ell \in \mathsf{I}$ *for every iteration* $\ell = 0, \dots, k-1$.

(c) Using the fact that $\boldsymbol{r}_\ell \perp \operatorname{span}\left(\boldsymbol{A}_{\mathsf{I}_\ell}\right)$, *argue that OMP selects a* new *index* $i_\ell \in \mathsf{I}$ *at each iteration* $\ell = 0, \dots, k-1$. *Conclude that OMP terminates with* $\boldsymbol{x}_k = \boldsymbol{x}_o$ *and* $\mathsf{I}_k = \mathsf{I}$, *as claimed.*

8.13. (Greedy methods that succeed under RIP) *The compressive sampling matching pursuit (COSAMP) algorithm modifies OMP by adding and subtracting multiple indices from the active set* I_ℓ *at each iteration* ℓ. *This algorithm takes as input a target number of nonzero entries,* s, *and modifies OMP as follows:*

- *At iteration* ℓ, *let* $\mathsf{I}_{1/2}$ *be the support of the* $2s$ *largest entries of* $\boldsymbol{u}_\ell = \boldsymbol{A}^* \boldsymbol{r}_\ell$.
- *Let* $\mathsf{I}_{\ell+1/2} = \mathsf{I}_\ell \cup \mathsf{I}_{1/2}$
- *Solve for* $\boldsymbol{x}_{\ell+1/2}$ *by least squares on the support* $\mathsf{I}_{\ell+1/2}$.
- *Then let* $\boldsymbol{x}_{\ell+1}$ *be* $\boldsymbol{x}_{\ell+1/2}$ *pruned to its* s *largest entries.*

Implement the COSAMP algorithm, and compare its breakdown in terms of sparsity level to OMP.

8.14. (Monotone relation) *Show the following properties for monotone relations:*

(a) Given two monotone relations $\mathcal{F}_1$ *and* $\mathcal{F}_2$, *their sum* $\mathcal{F}_1 + \mathcal{F}_2$ *is also monotone.*
(b) An affine function $\mathcal{F}(\boldsymbol{x}) = \boldsymbol{A}\boldsymbol{x} + \boldsymbol{b}$ *is monotone if and only if* $\boldsymbol{A} + \boldsymbol{A}^* \succeq 0$.
(c) Prove the monotonicity of the KKT operator of equality constrained convex optimization, that is, Lemma 8.21.

8.15. (ADMM for basis pursuit) *One way of solving the basis pursuit problem*

$$\min \|\boldsymbol{x}\|_1 \quad \textit{subject to} \quad \boldsymbol{A}\boldsymbol{x} = \boldsymbol{y} \tag{8.8.14}$$

is to introduce an auxiliary variable z, *and solve the problem*

$$\min \|\boldsymbol{x}\|_1 \quad \textit{subject to} \quad \boldsymbol{A}\boldsymbol{z} = \boldsymbol{y},\ \boldsymbol{x} = \boldsymbol{z}. \tag{8.8.15}$$

Derive an algorithm for this problem, by applying the alternating directions method of multipliers *(ADMM). Implement your algorithm in a language of your choice, and investigate both its convergence speed and ability to reconstruct a target signal* $\boldsymbol{x}_o$ *using synthetic problem instances.*

8.16. (Dual of principal component pursuit) *Show that the dual program to the PCP program is*

$$\max_{\boldsymbol{\Lambda}} \operatorname{trace}\left(\boldsymbol{Y}^* \boldsymbol{\Lambda}\right) \quad \textit{subject to} \quad J(\boldsymbol{\Lambda}) \le 1,$$

where $\boldsymbol{\Lambda}$ *is the matrix of Lagrange multipliers for the equality constraint* $\boldsymbol{Y} = \boldsymbol{L} + \boldsymbol{S}$, *and* $J(\boldsymbol{\Lambda}) = \max(\|\boldsymbol{\Lambda}\|_2, \lambda^{-1}\|\boldsymbol{\Lambda}\|_\infty)$.

9 Nonconvex Optimization for High-Dimensional Problems

"Premature optimization is the root of all evil."

– Donald Ervin Knuth, *The Art of Computer Programming*

The previous chapter and this chapter are due in no small part to contributions from Dr. Chaobing Song.

In Chapter 8, we introduced optimization techniques that efficiently solve many convex optimization problems that arise in recovering structured signals from incomplete or corrupted measurements, using *known* low-dimensional models. In contrast, as we saw in Chapter 7, problems associated with *learning* low-dimensional models from sample data are often nonconvex: either they do not have tractable convex relaxations or the nonconvex formulation is preferred due to physical or computational constraints (such as limited memory). In this chapter, we introduce optimization algorithms for nonconvex programs.

This chapter is not intended to give a complete exposition of nonconvex optimization, which has a long history and a vast literature. We will rather provide an overview of the most fundamental ideas and representative methods, with any eye towards (i) how problems leverage negative curvature to guarantee local (and sometimes global) optimality, and (ii) how to characterize more precisely the computational complexity of different algorithms in order to achieve the optimal efficiency. Unlike previous chapters, some methods will be presented without detailed proofs, but with pointers to relevant references where appropriate.[1]

As mentioned in the previous chapter, one major difference between nonconvex and convex problems is that nonconvex objective functions may exhibit spurious critical points[2] other than the (desired, global) minimizers. These can include spurious local minimizers, local maximizers, and various types of saddle points, etc. Generally speaking, for nonconvex optimization we need to give up on the ambition of guaranteeing global optimality across broad classes of problems, and content ourselves to develop methods which guarantee to produce local optima in general,

[1] Indeed, in some situations the best known guarantees of worst-case performance have lengthy and technical proofs. For a more comprehensive exposition of basic techniques for *nonlinear optimization*, one may refer to classic textbooks such as [Ber03].

[2] Points $\boldsymbol{x}_\star$ whose gradient vanishes: $\nabla f(\boldsymbol{x}_\star) = \mathbf{0}$.

and global optima for specially structured problems such as those described in Chapter 7. The key to both of these goals is leveraging *negative curvature* of the objective function. In Chapter 7, problem symmetries induced negative curvature in symmetry-breaking directions, in some situations leading to nonconvex functions with benign global geometry. Identifying directions of negative curvature allowed us to prove that some such functions have no spurious local minimizers. Here, we will use negative curvature in a different, algorithmic way: to build methods that escape saddle points and converge to minimizers.

We will explore a variety of means to accomplish this, which require different types of local information about the objective function, from both the gradient and the full Hessian matrix (Section 9.2) or the gradient alone (Sections 9.3–9.5). At the technical level, we will reveal clearly that useful negative curvature information in the Hessian can be efficiently computed or approximated from a sequence of gradient evaluations, either explicitly (Sections 9.3 and 9.4) or implicitly with noise (Section 9.5).

Recall that in Section 8.3.1 of Chapter 8, we have discussed whether a long history of states and gradients may help improve the convergence of first-order methods. Nesterov's method has shown that in the convex case two previous states and one gradient per iteration are sufficient to achieve the optimal rate of convergence. We will see in this chapter that in the nonconvex case a longer sequence of gradient evaluations is needed to achieve another objective: escaping unstable saddle points. Roughly speaking, how efficiently and accurately one can use gradients to estimate the direction of negative curvature is the key to achieve different, and eventually optimal, tradeoffs between per-iteration cost and rate of convergence. This is reflected through the improved sophistication in algorithm design and analysis from Section 9.3, to Section 9.4, and to Section 9.5.

Last but not least, in our context, many nonconvex problems arise due to the fact that the optimization is constrained over a nonlinear submanifold. The submanifold typically has very good geometric structures. We will discuss in Section 9.6 how to exploit such structures to develop more efficient algorithms.

9.1 Challenges and Opportunities

In this chapter, we focus on the problem of minimizing a function $f(\boldsymbol{x})$,

$$\min_{\boldsymbol{x}} f(\boldsymbol{x}), \quad \boldsymbol{x} \in \mathbb{R}^n, \tag{9.1.1}$$

which we assume to be twice continuously differentiable.[3] We know that at any local minimizer $\boldsymbol{x}_\star$, the gradient vanishes:

$$\nabla f(\boldsymbol{x}_\star) = \mathbf{0},$$

[3] For simplicity, we focus on smooth, unconstrained optimization problems. Generally speaking, like the convex case in Chapter 8, constrained problems can be dealt with using the Lagrange multiplier method and in our context most nonsmooth objectives admit efficient proximal operators. We defer discussions of nonsmoothness and constraints to the Notes section, as well as the exercises at the end of this chapter.

i.e., $\boldsymbol{x}_\star$ is a critical point. In Section 9.1.1, we review what is arguably the simplest and most widely used optimization method: *gradient descent*. We will see that, in general, gradient methods guarantee convergence to a critical point. For *convex* f, this suffices to solve the problem in a very strong sense: for convex f, every critical point is a global minimizer. In contrast, *nonconvex* f can exhibit other types of critical points, including local minimizers, local maximizers, and saddle points. Hence, convergence to a critical point is not sufficient even to guarantee local optimality: to achieve this, we must somehow use information about the curvature of the objective function.[4] We therefore next review a classical approach to leveraging curvature information to rapidly minimize *convex* functions f, *Newton's method*, and, with these two methods as motivating background, embark on a tour of approaches to using (negative) curvature information to locally minimize *nonconvex* f.

9.1.1 Finding Critical Points via Gradient Descent

Perhaps the simplest and most widely used optimization method is *gradient descent*,[5] which generates a sequence of iterates

$$\boldsymbol{x}_{k+1} = \boldsymbol{x}_k - \gamma_k \nabla f(\boldsymbol{x}_k) \tag{9.1.2}$$

by repeatedly stepping in the direction of the negative gradient of the function f. Because this method only requires one to compute the gradient of the objective function f at each iteration, it is often quite scalable. The choice of $-\nabla f$ as a descent direction makes intuitive sense, since this is the direction of steepest descent of the object function f. Indeed, ∇f is the slope of a first-order approximation to f at the given point $\boldsymbol{x}_k$:

$$f(\boldsymbol{y}) \approx f(\boldsymbol{x}_k) + \langle \nabla f(\boldsymbol{x}_k), \boldsymbol{y} - \boldsymbol{x}_k \rangle . \tag{9.1.3}$$

In (9.1.2), $\gamma_k > 0$ is a step size, which can be chosen adaptively from iteration to iteration, or can be set ahead of time based on knowledge of the objective function f. In particular, suppose that gradient ∇f is Lipschitz continuous:

$$\forall\, \boldsymbol{x}, \boldsymbol{y} \quad \|\nabla f(\boldsymbol{y}) - \nabla f(\boldsymbol{x})\|_2 \le L_1 \|\boldsymbol{y} - \boldsymbol{x}\|_2 \tag{9.1.4}$$

for some $L_1 > 0$.[6] In this setting, one can augment the *local* approximation (9.1.3) to produce a *global upper bound*:

[4] Strictly speaking, many of the methods we describe guarantee convergence not to a local minimizer, but to a second-order stationary point, i.e., a point satisfying $\nabla f(\boldsymbol{x}) = \mathbf{0}$ and $\nabla^2 f(\boldsymbol{x}) \succeq \mathbf{0}$. For "generic" (i.e., Morse) f, every such point is a local minimizer; this is also the case for the functions studied in Chapter 7. However, it is possible to construct objectives f with second-order stationary points that are not minimizers; take, for example, $f(x) = -x^4$.

[5] Like most natural ideas, gradient methods have a rich history, having been (re)discovered many times. The first formal exposition is believed to have been given by Augustin Cauchy in 1847, in the context of finding numerical solutions to equations [Cau47].

[6] Or equivalently, as f is twice differentiable, the absolute values of eigenvalues of the Hessian $\nabla^2 f(\boldsymbol{x}) \in \mathbb{R}^{n \times n}$ are uniformly bounded by L_1.

$$f(\boldsymbol{y}) \le f(\boldsymbol{x}_k) + \langle \nabla f(\boldsymbol{x}_k), \boldsymbol{y} - \boldsymbol{x}_k \rangle + \frac{L_1}{2} \|\boldsymbol{y} - \boldsymbol{x}_k\|_2^2. \tag{9.1.5}$$

As we showed in Chapter 8, the upper bound on the right-hand side is minimized at $\boldsymbol{y}_\star = \boldsymbol{x}_k - (1/L_1)\nabla f(\boldsymbol{x}_k)$, i.e., taking on a gradient step is equivalent to minimizing a quadratic upper bound on the objective function f.

This observation suggests choosing $\gamma_k = 1/L_1$. This step size guarantees that (i) the gradient method is a *descent* method, i.e., the objective function does not increase from iteration to iteration, and (ii) that the iterates $\boldsymbol{x}_k$ converge to a critical point $\boldsymbol{x}_\star$, satisfying $\nabla f(\boldsymbol{x}_\star) = \mathbf{0}$. Intuitively, we might expect to converge to a critical point $\boldsymbol{x}_\star$ that is a local minimizer. Although this is often the case in practice, in general all one can guarantee is convergence to *some* critical point, which could be a maximizer or a saddle point. Indeed, if $\boldsymbol{x}_k$ happens to be a saddle point and so $\nabla f(\boldsymbol{x}_k) = \mathbf{0}$, the iteration (9.1.2) will never leave $\boldsymbol{x}_k$.

In Chapter 8, we obtained useful intuition (and good methods!) by not only proving that methods converge, but also assessing *how rapidly* they converge, and seeking methods whose convergence rate is the best possible. In the nonconvex setting, it does not make sense to measure the progress of gradient descent in terms of function values, because it may not converge to a global minimizer. Instead, one typically measures how close $\boldsymbol{x}_k$ is to being a critical point through the norm of the gradient $\|\nabla f(\boldsymbol{x}_k)\|_2$. In this setting, one can show:

PROPOSITION 9.1. (Convergence rate of gradient descent for nonconvex functions) *Suppose that $f(\boldsymbol{x})$ is a (possibly nonconvex) differentiable function with ∇f Lipschitz continuous with constant L_1. The gradient descent scheme* (9.1.2) *with the step size $\gamma_k = 1/L_1$ converges to a critical point $\boldsymbol{x}_\star$. Furthermore, the gradient norm at the best iterate* $\min_{0 \le i \le k-1} \|\nabla f(\boldsymbol{x}_i)\|$ *goes to zero at the rate $O(1/\sqrt{k})$.*

Proof For all $k \ge 1$, the gradient descent iteration $\boldsymbol{x}_k = \boldsymbol{x}_{k-1} - (1/L_1)\nabla f(\boldsymbol{x}_{k-1})$ is equivalent to

$$\boldsymbol{x}_k := \arg\min_{\boldsymbol{x}} \left\{ f(\boldsymbol{x}_{k-1}) + \langle \nabla f(\boldsymbol{x}_{k-1}), \boldsymbol{x} - \boldsymbol{x}_{k-1} \rangle + \frac{L_1}{2} \|\boldsymbol{x} - \boldsymbol{x}_{k-1}\|_2^2 \right\}.$$

Also note that, according to Lemma 8.2, Lipschitz continuity (9.1.4) is equivalent to: for all $\boldsymbol{x}, \boldsymbol{y}$,

$$f(\boldsymbol{y}) \le f(\boldsymbol{x}) + \langle \nabla f(\boldsymbol{x}), \boldsymbol{y} - \boldsymbol{x} \rangle + \frac{L_1}{2} \|\boldsymbol{y} - \boldsymbol{x}\|_2^2. \tag{9.1.6}$$

It follows that

$$\begin{aligned} f(\boldsymbol{x}_k) &\le f(\boldsymbol{x}_{k-1}) + \langle \nabla f(\boldsymbol{x}_{k-1}), \boldsymbol{x}_k - \boldsymbol{x}_{k-1} \rangle + \frac{L_1}{2} \|\boldsymbol{x}_k - \boldsymbol{x}_{k-1}\|_2^2 \\ &\le f(\boldsymbol{x}_{k-1}) - \frac{1}{2L_1} \|\nabla f(\boldsymbol{x}_{k-1})\|_2^2. \end{aligned} \tag{9.1.7}$$

Hence the value of the objective function decreases with the iteration. Telescoping (9.1.7), we obtain

$$f(\boldsymbol{x}_k) \le f(\boldsymbol{x}_0) - \frac{1}{2L_1} \sum_{i=0}^{k-1} \|\nabla f(\boldsymbol{x}_i)\|_2^2.$$

This gives

$$\frac{k}{2L_1} \min_{i \in \{0,1,\ldots,k-1\}} \|\nabla f(\boldsymbol{x}_i)\|_2^2 \le \sum_{i=0}^{k-1} \frac{1}{2L_1} \|\nabla f(\boldsymbol{x}_i)\|_2^2 \le f(\boldsymbol{x}_0) - f(\boldsymbol{x}_k).$$

With respect to the critical point $\boldsymbol{x}_\star$ to which the sequence converges, we have $f(\boldsymbol{x}_0) - f(\boldsymbol{x}_k) \le f(\boldsymbol{x}_0) - f(\boldsymbol{x}_\star)$. So we have

$$\min_{i \in \{0,1,\ldots,k-1\}} \|\nabla f(\boldsymbol{x}_i)\|_2 \le \sqrt{\frac{2L_1(f(\boldsymbol{x}_0) - f(\boldsymbol{x}_\star))}{k}}. \tag{9.1.8}$$

□

We note several key differences from the analyses of gradient and proximal gradient methods in Chapter 8. First, and most importantly, in the nonconvex setting we only guarantee convergence to a (first-order) critical point – which may not be a minimizer. Second, in contrast to the convex setting, here, the gradient method is essentially optimal amongst first-order methods. In Chapter 8, we were able to improve the behavior of (proximal) gradient descent, by comparing its rate of convergence to the best achievable rate of convergence for first-order methods, i.e., methods assuming access to only the *first-order oracle*:

$$\text{the gradient } \nabla f(\boldsymbol{x}) \text{ of the function } f(\boldsymbol{x}), \tag{9.1.9}$$

at each iteration. The convergence rate in Proposition 9.1 can be interpreted as saying that to achieve $\|\nabla f\| \le \varepsilon_g$, we require $O(\varepsilon_g^{-2})$ iterations. This turns out to be the best (worst-case) rate that first-order methods can achieve for the class of functions f with Lipschitz gradients: in contrast to the convex case, introducing momentum or other forms of acceleration does not improve the worst-case performance.

However, if we assume a little more about the objective function, namely that the Hessian is also Lipschitz, the picture changes dramatically. In this setting, it is possible to obtain information about the curvature of the objective function by comparing gradients at nearby points: the second derivative $\nabla^2 f(\boldsymbol{x})\boldsymbol{\delta}$ in the $\boldsymbol{\delta}$ direction satisfies $\nabla^2 f(\boldsymbol{x})\boldsymbol{\delta} \approx \nabla f(\boldsymbol{x} + \boldsymbol{\delta}) - \nabla f(\boldsymbol{x})$. We will see that by using this information, it is possible to fundamentally improve the convergence rate of gradient descent *and* to enable it to escape (nondegenerate) saddle points and maximizers. This highlights the importance of curvature information in nonconvex optimization. In the coming sections, we will first review efforts to explicitly leverage curvature information through the Hessian $\nabla^2 f(\boldsymbol{x})$, before describing lighter-weight methods that leverage curvature using gradients only.

9.1.2 Finding Critical Points via Newton's Method

The simplest and most natural approach to incorporating curvature information into iterative methods is to replace the first-order approximation (9.1.3) with a second-order approximation. Suppose that the Hessian $\nabla^2 f(\boldsymbol{x})$ is Lipschitz:

$$\forall\, \boldsymbol{x}, \boldsymbol{y} \quad \|\nabla^2 f(\boldsymbol{y}) - \nabla^2 f(\boldsymbol{x})\| \le L_2 \|\boldsymbol{y} - \boldsymbol{x}\|_2, \tag{9.1.10}$$

where $\|\cdot\|$ denotes the spectral norm of a matrix. Then in the vicinity of a point $\boldsymbol{x}$, we can accurately approximate $f(\boldsymbol{y})$ with the Taylor expansion

$$f(\boldsymbol{y}) \approx \hat{f}(\boldsymbol{y}, \boldsymbol{x}) \doteq f(\boldsymbol{x}) + \langle \nabla f(\boldsymbol{x}), \boldsymbol{y} - \boldsymbol{x} \rangle + \tfrac{1}{2}(\boldsymbol{y} - \boldsymbol{x})^* \nabla^2 f(\boldsymbol{x})(\boldsymbol{y} - \boldsymbol{x}). \tag{9.1.11}$$

This approximation $\hat{f}$ has the same slope and curvature as f at $\boldsymbol{y} = \boldsymbol{x}$. When f is a strongly convex function, the eigenvalues of $\nabla^2 f$ are all positive and the approximation is also strongly convex. In this setting, the approximation $\hat{f}$ has a unique minimizer:

$$\boldsymbol{y}_\star = \arg\min_{\boldsymbol{y}} \hat{f}(\boldsymbol{y}, \boldsymbol{x}) = \boldsymbol{x} - \left[\nabla^2 f(\boldsymbol{x})\right]^{-1} \nabla f(\boldsymbol{x}). \tag{9.1.12}$$

The expression on the right-hand side can be obtained simply by setting the derivative $\nabla_{\boldsymbol{y}} \hat{f}(\boldsymbol{y}, \boldsymbol{x}) = \boldsymbol{0}$ and solving for $\boldsymbol{y}$. This suggests the following iterative approach to minimizing f: starting from an initial point $\boldsymbol{x}_0$, we generate a sequence of iterates $\boldsymbol{x}_k$ by setting

$$\boldsymbol{x}_{k+1} = \boldsymbol{x}_k - \left[\nabla^2 f(\boldsymbol{x}_k)\right]^{-1} \nabla f(\boldsymbol{x}_k). \tag{9.1.13}$$

This is known as *Newton iteration*, and is closely related to the Newton–Raphson method for finding roots of polynomials. Indeed, searching for a critical point of a smooth function f is equivalent to looking for a solution (root) of the equation $\nabla f(\boldsymbol{x}) = \boldsymbol{0}$.[7] Newton's method clearly belongs to the class of methods which assume access to *the second-order oracle*:

$$\text{the gradient } \nabla f(\boldsymbol{x}) \text{ and the Hessian } \nabla^2 f(\boldsymbol{x}). \tag{9.1.14}$$

Typically, this makes the iterations of Newton's method much more expensive than those of gradient descent: generally, one needs to compute and store the full $n \times n$ Hessian matrix $\nabla^2 f(\boldsymbol{x}_k)$ and its inverse. The benefit of this per-iteration complexity is a drastic reduction in the number of iterations required to converge to an accurate solution. Consider, for example, a strongly convex objective function f (i.e., an f which satisfies $\nabla^2 f(\boldsymbol{x}) \succeq \lambda \boldsymbol{I}$ for all $\boldsymbol{x}$), with Lipschitz Hessian. Because f is strongly convex, it has a unique minimizer $\boldsymbol{x}_\star$. We will show that the iterates produced by Newton's method satisfy

[7] Like gradient descent, Newton's method (or the Newton–Raphson method) has a long history. It can be interpreted as a method for solving the critical point equation $\nabla f(\boldsymbol{x}_\star) = \boldsymbol{0}$, i.e., finding "roots" of $\nabla f(\boldsymbol{x})$. The Newton–Raphson method was originally introduced in the late 1680s by Isaac Newton and Joseph Raphson for finding roots of polynomials, and generalized to find critical points of smooth functions by Thomas Simpson in 1750 [Sim50].

$$\|x_{k+1} - x_\star\|_2 \le \frac{L_2}{2\lambda}\|x_k - x_\star\|_2^2. \tag{9.1.15}$$

This means that as long as x_0 is close to $x_\star$ (say, $\|x_0 - x_\star\| < 2\lambda/L_2$), the iterates x_k converge to $x_\star$ extraordinarily rapidly:

$$\|x_k - x_\star\|_2 \le \left(\frac{L_2}{2\lambda}\right)^{2^{k+1}} \|x_0 - x_\star\|_2^{2^k}. \tag{9.1.16}$$

In optimization, this is referred to as *superlinear* convergence: $\log \|x_k - x_\star\|_2$ diminishes faster than any linear function of k. Slightly more formally:

PROPOSITION 9.2. (Convergence rate of newton's method) *Let $f(x)$ be strongly convex, with $\lambda_{\min}(\nabla^2 f(x)) \ge \lambda > 0$ for all x, and assume that $\nabla^2 f$ is Lipschitz continuous with constant L_2, and let $x_\star$ be the (unique) minimizer of f over $\mathbb{R}^n$. Assuming $\|x_0 - x_\star\| < 2\lambda/L_2$, the iterates x_k converge to $x_\star$, with quadratic rate* (9.1.16).

Proof Using the Taylor expansion of the gradient $\nabla f(x)$ around the critical point $x_\star$ and the mean value theorem, we have

$$\|\nabla f(x_\star) - [\nabla f(x_k) + \nabla^2 f(x_k)(x_\star - x_k)]\|_2 \le \frac{L_2}{2}\|x_\star - x_k\|_2^2.$$

With $x_{k+1} = x_k - \left[\nabla^2 f(x_k)\right]^{-1} \nabla f(x_k)$, this gives

$$\|\nabla^2 f(x_k)(x_\star - x_{k+1})\|_2 \le \frac{L_2}{2}\|x_\star - x_k\|_2^2.$$

The operator norm of the Hessian inverse $\left[\nabla^2 f(x)\right]^{-1}$ is bounded uniformly from above, by $\lambda^{-1} < \infty$. Combining this with the above inequality, we obtain

$$\|x_\star - x_{k+1}\|_2 \le \frac{L_2}{2\lambda}\|x_\star - x_k\|_2^2.$$

□

Despite its fast rate of convergence for strongly convex problems, there are several limitations that render Newton's method inapplicable in our setting of high-dimensional, nonconvex optimization. First, Newton's method requires us to compute $\left[\nabla^2 f(x)\right]^{-1} \nabla f(x)$. Simply storing the $n \times n$ Hessian matrix is infeasible when n is large. Typical approaches to solving the Newton system require $O(n^3)$ arithmetic operations, making even a single step of Newton's method computationally prohibitive when n is large. These limitations are why, in Chapter 8, we focused on convex optimization methods with cheaper iterations.

Second, and more fundamentally, in the nonconvex setting, we have no control over what kind of critical point the iterates x_k converge to! Close inspection shows that the argument of Proposition 9.2 works just as well to prove convergence to a maximizer, with essentially the same quadratic rate. There is a simple reason why Newton's method cannot distinguish between minimizers, maximizers, and saddles. In the nonconvex setting, solving $\nabla_y \hat{f}(y, x) = \mathbf{0}$ does not necessarily yield a minimizer of the quadratic approximation $\hat{f}$ – rather, it asks for a *critical point* of this approximation, which, depending on the signs of the eigenvalues of $\nabla^2 f(x)$, could be a minimizer, maximizer, or saddle point. Hence, in the nonconvex setting, the classical Newton's method can be interpreted not as repeatedly *minimizing* approximations to the objective, but as repeatedly finding critical points of approximations to the objective. Exercise 9.1 guides the reader through examples showing that Newton's method may converge to minimizers, maximizers, and saddle points.

Clearly, if our goal is to leverage negative curvature to *minimize* nonconvex functions, some modifications to Newton's method are required. In the subsequent sections, we will show how to modify Newton's method to escape saddle points and obtain minimizers (strictly speaking, to obtain second-order critical points satisfying $\nabla f(\boldsymbol{x}_\star) = \mathbf{0}$ and $\nabla^2 f(\boldsymbol{x}_\star) \succeq \mathbf{0}$). We will then show how to reduce the per-iteration complexity by leveraging negative curvature without the full Hessian, or even using only gradient information, yielding methods that are applicable to high-dimensional problems. Finally, similar to our development of proximal and accelerated proximal gradient methods in Chapter 8, we will show how to carefully combine gradient and curvature information to obtain first-order methods that achieve the best known rate of convergence.

9.2 Cubic Regularization of Newton's Method

As we saw in the previous section, when applied to strongly convex problems, Newton's method converges extremely rapidly. In comparison to the gradient method, it better leverages positive curvature of the objective function. However, when applied to *nonconvex* problems, it does not distinguish between minimizers, maximizers, and saddle points. In particular, it is incapable of leveraging *negative curvature* to escape saddle points. To develop second-order methods that make better use of negative curvature, a natural idea is to build a local model of the objective function which contains both first- and second-order information, i.e., to write

$$f(\boldsymbol{y}) \approx f(\boldsymbol{x}) + \langle \nabla f(\boldsymbol{x}), \boldsymbol{y} - \boldsymbol{x} \rangle + \tfrac{1}{2}(\boldsymbol{y} - \boldsymbol{x})^* \nabla^2 f(\boldsymbol{x})(\boldsymbol{y} - \boldsymbol{x}), \tag{9.2.1}$$

and to determine a step direction by *minimizing* this model. This is in contrast to Newton's method, which only seeks a critical point of this approximation.

Here, a comparison with our development of gradient methods in Chapter 8 is instructive. There, we motivated gradient and proximal gradient methods from a first-order approximation to the objective function,

$$f(\boldsymbol{y}) \approx f(\boldsymbol{x}) + \langle \nabla f(\boldsymbol{x}), \boldsymbol{y} - \boldsymbol{x} \rangle . \tag{9.2.2}$$

In contrast, the second-order approximation in (9.2.1) retains information about the curvature of f, through the Hessian $\nabla^2 f$. In particular, f has directions of negative curvature at $\boldsymbol{x}$ if and only if the smallest eigenvalue $\lambda_{\min}(\nabla^2 f)$ is negative. In particular, any eigenvector corresponding to this smallest eigenvalue gives a direction of negative curvature.

9.2.1 Convergence to Second-Order Stationary Points

How can we use the model (9.2.1) to reduce the objective function f? In our study of gradient and proximal gradient methods, we found it useful to augment the *local* approximation in (9.2.2) to produce a *global* upper bound on $f(\boldsymbol{y})$. Minimizing this global upper bound produced a new point $\boldsymbol{x}^+$ with $f(\boldsymbol{x}^+) \le f(\boldsymbol{x})$, i.e., it guarantees descent in the objective value f. Here, we proceed in the same spirit. Suppose that the Hessian $\nabla^2 f$ is Lipschitz, i.e.,

$$\forall\, \boldsymbol{x}, \boldsymbol{y} \quad \|\nabla^2 f(\boldsymbol{y}) - \nabla^2 f(\boldsymbol{x})\| \le L_2 \|\boldsymbol{y} - \boldsymbol{x}\|_2, \tag{9.2.3}$$

for some $L_2 > 0$. Here $\|\cdot\|$ denotes the spectral norm of a matrix. In this setting, we have that, for all $\boldsymbol{x}, \boldsymbol{y}$,

$$\begin{aligned} f(\boldsymbol{y}) &\le \hat{f}(\boldsymbol{y}, \boldsymbol{x}) \\ &\doteq f(\boldsymbol{x}) + \langle \nabla f(\boldsymbol{x}), \boldsymbol{y} - \boldsymbol{x} \rangle + \frac{1}{2}(\boldsymbol{y} - \boldsymbol{x})^* \nabla^2 f(\boldsymbol{x})(\boldsymbol{y} - \boldsymbol{x}) + \frac{L_2}{6} \|\boldsymbol{y} - \boldsymbol{x}\|_2^3. \end{aligned} \tag{9.2.4}$$

The right-hand side is a global upper bound on $f(\boldsymbol{y})$, which has the same value, slope, and curvature at $\boldsymbol{x}$. Similar to our discussion of gradient descent in Chapter 8 and Section 9.1.1, given an iterate $\boldsymbol{x}_k$, we can produce the next iterate $\boldsymbol{x}_{k+1}$ by minimizing this upper bound:

$$\boldsymbol{x}_{k+1} = \arg\min_{\boldsymbol{y}} \hat{f}(\boldsymbol{y}, \boldsymbol{x}_k). \tag{9.2.5}$$

The resulting method is known as the *cubic regularized Newton's method*, and is described in Figure 9.1.

In contrast to gradient descent, the problem of minimizing the approximation $\hat{f}$ in (9.2.5) is itself in general a nonconvex problem – we intentionally choose an approximation that retains negative curvature information! Perhaps surprisingly, this particular nonconvex problem *can* be solved efficiently: it can be reduced to solving a one-dimensional convex optimization problem [NP06]. We guide the reader through a derivation of this subproblem in Exercise 9.3, and describe more scalable alternatives in the next section, after discussing convergence issues.

REMARK 9.3. (The trust region method) *The cubic regularized Newton's method is not the only way of using the second-order approximation* (9.2.1) *to solve nonconvex optimization problems. One important (and historically earlier) alternative is the* trust region method. *Rather than building a global upper bound to* $f(\boldsymbol{y})$, *the trust region method chooses a step direction by minimizing the approximation* (9.2.1) *over a small neighborhood of the point* $\boldsymbol{x}$, *where the approximation is known to be accurate:*

$$\boldsymbol{x}_{k+1} = \arg\min_{\|\boldsymbol{y} - \boldsymbol{x}_k\|_2 \le \delta_k} \; f(\boldsymbol{x}_k) + \langle \nabla f(\boldsymbol{x}_k), \boldsymbol{y} - \boldsymbol{x}_k \rangle + \tfrac{1}{2}(\boldsymbol{y} - \boldsymbol{x}_k)^* \nabla^2 f(\boldsymbol{x}_k)(\boldsymbol{y} - \boldsymbol{x}_k). \tag{9.2.6}$$

Like the cubic Newton subproblem, this subproblem can be solved efficiently; like cubic Newton, the resulting method is able to leverage negative curvature, as captured by the Hessian $\nabla^2 f$. *The main difference is simply the use of the constraint*

Cubic Regularized Newton's Method

Problem Class:

$$\min_{x} f(x), \quad x \in \mathbb{R}^n,$$

where $f : \mathbb{R}^n \to \mathbb{R}$ is nonconvex, and is twice continuously differentiable, with both gradient and Hessian Lipschitz continuous. We have access to the second-order oracle: $\nabla f(x) \in \mathbb{R}^n$ and $\nabla^2 f(x) \in \mathbb{R}^{n \times n}$.

Setup: Let $\hat{f}(y, x)$ be defined similarly as in (9.2.4):

$$\hat{f}(y,x) \doteq \langle \nabla f(x), y - x \rangle + \frac{1}{2}(y - x)^* \nabla^2 f(x)(y - x) + \frac{L_2}{6} \|y - x\|_2^3 .$$

Initialization: Set $x_0 \in \mathbb{R}^n$,

Iteration: For $k = 0, 1, 2, \dots$

$$x_{k+1} = \arg\min_{y} \hat{f}(y, x_k).$$

Convergence Guarantee: x_k converges with $\lim_{k\to\infty} \mu(x_k) = 0$.

Figure 9.1 An overview of the Cubic Regularization of Newton's Method.

$\|y - x_k\|_2 \le \delta_k$ *instead of the cubic penalty* $\|y - x_k\|_2^3$. *We guide the interested reader through the development of the trust region method and the solution of the trust region subproblem in Exercise 9.2.*

We next show that the iterates produced by the cubic regularized Newton's method converge to a point $x_\star$ that satisfies

$$\nabla f(x_\star) = \mathbf{0}, \quad \nabla^2 f(x_\star) \succeq \mathbf{0}, \tag{9.2.7}$$

i.e., a second-order stationary solution. We will measure our progress in terms of the quantity

$$\mu(x) \doteq \max \left\{ \sqrt{\frac{1}{L_2} \|\nabla f(x)\|_2}, \; -\frac{2}{3L_2} \lambda_{\min}\left(\nabla^2 f(x)\right) \right\}, \tag{9.2.8}$$

where $\lambda_{\min}$ is the smallest eigenvalue of the Hessian $\nabla^2 f(x)$, which we desire to be nonnegative. If $\mu(x) \to 0$, x_k converges to a solution $x_\star$ that satisfies (9.2.7). The following theorem shows that this indeed occurs, and controls the rate at which $\mu(x_k)$ approaches zero:

THEOREM 9.4. (Convergence rate of cubic newton's method) *Suppose* $f(x)$ *is bounded from below. Then the sequence* $\{x_k\}$ *generated by the cubic regularized Newton step* (9.2.5) *converges to a nonempty set of limit points* $X_\star$. *Let* $x_\star \in X_\star$. *Then we further have* $\lim_{k\to\infty} \mu(x_k) = 0$ *and for any* $k \ge 1$, *we have*

$$\min_{1\le i\le k} \mu(\boldsymbol{x}_i) \le C\left(\frac{f(\boldsymbol{x}_0)-f(\boldsymbol{x}_\star)}{k\cdot L_2}\right)^{1/3} \tag{9.2.9}$$

for some constant $C > 0$.

Sketch of proof Since $\boldsymbol{x}_k$ is the minimizer of $\hat{f}(\boldsymbol{y},\boldsymbol{x}_{k-1})$ as defined in (9.2.4), it satisfies the first-order optimality condition:

$$\nabla f(\boldsymbol{x}_{k-1}) + \nabla^2 f(\boldsymbol{x}_{k-1})(\boldsymbol{x}_k-\boldsymbol{x}_{k-1}) + \frac{L_2}{2}\|\boldsymbol{x}_k-\boldsymbol{x}_{k-1}\|_2(\boldsymbol{x}_k-\boldsymbol{x}_{k-1}) = \mathbf{0}. \tag{9.2.10}$$

In addition, from the derivation of the global minimizer for (9.2.5), one can also show that $\boldsymbol{x}_k$ satisfies the condition (see Proposition 1 of [NP06]):

$$\nabla^2 f(\boldsymbol{x}_{k-1}) + \frac{L_2}{2}\|\boldsymbol{x}_k-\boldsymbol{x}_{k-1}\|_2 \boldsymbol{I} \succeq \mathbf{0}. \tag{9.2.11}$$

Since $\hat{f}(\boldsymbol{y},\boldsymbol{x}_k)$ defined in (9.2.4) is an upper bound of $f(\boldsymbol{y})$, at iterate $\boldsymbol{x}_k$ we have

$$\begin{aligned}
f(\boldsymbol{x}_k) &\le f(\boldsymbol{x}_{k-1}) + \langle \nabla f(\boldsymbol{x}_{k-1}), \boldsymbol{x}_k-\boldsymbol{x}_{k-1}\rangle \\
&\quad + \frac{1}{2}\langle \nabla^2 f(\boldsymbol{x}_{k-1})(\boldsymbol{x}_k-\boldsymbol{x}_{k-1}), \boldsymbol{x}_k-\boldsymbol{x}_{k-1}\rangle + \frac{L_2}{6}\|\boldsymbol{x}_k-\boldsymbol{x}_{k-1}\|_2^3 \\
&= f(\boldsymbol{x}_{k-1}) + \langle \nabla f(\boldsymbol{x}_{k-1}), \boldsymbol{x}_k-\boldsymbol{x}_{k-1}\rangle \\
&\quad + \langle \nabla^2 f(\boldsymbol{x}_{k-1})(\boldsymbol{x}_k-\boldsymbol{x}_{k-1}), \boldsymbol{x}_k-\boldsymbol{x}_{k-1}\rangle \\
&\quad - \frac{1}{2}\langle \nabla^2 f(\boldsymbol{x}_{k-1})(\boldsymbol{x}_k-\boldsymbol{x}_{k-1}), \boldsymbol{x}_k-\boldsymbol{x}_{k-1}\rangle + \frac{L_2}{6}\|\boldsymbol{x}_k-\boldsymbol{x}_{k-1}\|_2^3 \\
&= f(\boldsymbol{x}_{k-1}) - \frac{L_2}{2}\|\boldsymbol{x}_k-\boldsymbol{x}_{k-1}\|_2^3 \\
&\quad - \frac{1}{2}\langle \nabla^2 f(\boldsymbol{x}_{k-1})(\boldsymbol{x}_k-\boldsymbol{x}_{k-1}), \boldsymbol{x}_k-\boldsymbol{x}_{k-1}\rangle + \frac{L_2}{6}\|\boldsymbol{x}_k-\boldsymbol{x}_{k-1}\|_2^3 \\
&\le f(\boldsymbol{x}_{k-1}) - \frac{L_2}{12}\|\boldsymbol{x}_k-\boldsymbol{x}_{k-1}\|_2^3,
\end{aligned} \tag{9.2.12}$$

where from the second equality to the third is by the first-order optimality condition (9.2.10), and the last inequality is by applying the second optimality condition (9.2.11). The last inequality (9.2.12) indicates that the cubic regularized Newton's method is indeed a descent method.

Telescoping (9.2.12), we have

$$f(\boldsymbol{x}_k) \le f(\boldsymbol{x}_0) - \frac{L_2}{12}\sum_{i=1}^{k}\|\boldsymbol{x}_i-\boldsymbol{x}_{i-1}\|_2^3.$$

So we have

$$\frac{L_2 k}{12}\min_{i\in[k]}\|\boldsymbol{x}_i-\boldsymbol{x}_{i-1}\|_2^3 \le \frac{L_2}{12}\sum_{l=1}^{k}\|\boldsymbol{x}_i-\boldsymbol{x}_{i-1}\|_2^3 \le f(\boldsymbol{x}_0)-f(\boldsymbol{x}_k) \le f(\boldsymbol{x}_0)-f(\boldsymbol{x}_\star),$$

where $\boldsymbol{x}_\star$ is a minimizer to which the sequence converges. So we have

$$\min_{i\in[k]} \|\boldsymbol{x}_i - \boldsymbol{x}_{i-1}\|_2 \le \left(\frac{12(f(\boldsymbol{x}_0) - f(\boldsymbol{x}_\star))}{L_2 k}\right)^{1/3}.$$

Now to ensure the convergence rate, we need to determine the relationship between $\nabla f(\boldsymbol{x}_k)$, $\nabla^2 f(\boldsymbol{x}_k)$, and $\|\boldsymbol{x}_k - \boldsymbol{x}_{k-1}\|_2$.

First, note that through Taylor expansion and the mean value theorem, the Lipschitz Hessian condition implies that, for all $\boldsymbol{x}, \boldsymbol{y}$,

$$\|\nabla f(\boldsymbol{y}) - (\nabla f(\boldsymbol{x}) + \nabla^2 f(\boldsymbol{x})(\boldsymbol{y} - \boldsymbol{x}))\|_2 \le \frac{L_2}{2}\|\boldsymbol{y} - \boldsymbol{x}\|_2^2. \tag{9.2.13}$$

Combining with (9.2.10), we have

$$\begin{aligned}\|\nabla f(\boldsymbol{x}_k)\|_2 &= \|\nabla f(\boldsymbol{x}_k) - (\nabla f(\boldsymbol{x}_{k-1}) + \nabla^2 f(\boldsymbol{x}_{k-1})(\boldsymbol{x}_k - \boldsymbol{x}_{k-1}))\\ &\quad + (\nabla f(\boldsymbol{x}_{k-1}) + \nabla^2 f(\boldsymbol{x}_{k-1})(\boldsymbol{x}_k - \boldsymbol{x}_{k-1}))\|_2\\ &\le \|\nabla f(\boldsymbol{x}_k) - (\nabla f(\boldsymbol{x}_{k-1}) + \nabla^2 f(\boldsymbol{x}_{k-1})(\boldsymbol{x}_k - \boldsymbol{x}_{k-1}))\|_2\\ &\quad + \|\nabla f(\boldsymbol{x}_{k-1}) + \nabla^2 f(\boldsymbol{x}_{k-1})(\boldsymbol{x}_k - \boldsymbol{x}_{k-1})\|_2\\ &\le L_2\|\boldsymbol{x}_k - \boldsymbol{x}_{k-1}\|_2^2. \end{aligned}\tag{9.2.14}$$

Second, by (9.1.10) and (9.2.11), we have

$$\nabla^2 f(\boldsymbol{x}_k) \succeq \nabla^2 f(\boldsymbol{x}_{k-1}) - L_2\|\boldsymbol{x}_k - \boldsymbol{x}_{k-1}\|_2\boldsymbol{I} \succeq -\frac{3L_2}{2}\|\boldsymbol{x}_k - \boldsymbol{x}_{k-1}\|_2\boldsymbol{I}.$$

Therefore we have[8]

$$\|\nabla f(\boldsymbol{x}_k)\|_2 \le L_2\left(\frac{12(f(\boldsymbol{x}_0) - f(\boldsymbol{x}_\star))}{L_2 k}\right)^{2/3}, \tag{9.2.15}$$

$$-\lambda_{\min}(\nabla^2 f(\boldsymbol{x}_k)) \le \frac{3L_2}{2}\left(\frac{12(f(\boldsymbol{x}_0) - f(\boldsymbol{x}_\star))}{L_2 k}\right)^{1/3}. \tag{9.2.16}$$

By definition of $\mu(\boldsymbol{x})$, we have that $\mu(\boldsymbol{x}_k) \le (12(f(\boldsymbol{x}_0) - f(\boldsymbol{x}_\star))/L_2 k)^{1/3}$ converges as $k \to \infty$. □

The fact that $\mu(\boldsymbol{x}_k) \to 0$ implies that the cubic regularized Newton iteration (9.2.5) indeed converges asymptotically to stationary limit points with $\nabla f(\boldsymbol{x}_\star) = \boldsymbol{0}$ and $\nabla^2 f(\boldsymbol{x}_\star) \succeq \boldsymbol{0}$. Furthermore, the bound (9.2.9) on μ implies that with a finite number of k iterations,

$$\min_{1\le i\le k} \|\nabla f(\boldsymbol{x}_i)\|_2 \le O(k^{-2/3}),$$

which, as expected, is improved over the bound $O(k^{-1/2})$ for first-order (accelerated) gradient descent (see Proposition 9.1), and is tight for methods with access to the second-order oracle (9.1.14).

[8] Strictly speaking, we here should consider the iterate that achieves $\min_{i\in[k]} \|\boldsymbol{x}_i - \boldsymbol{x}_{i-1}\|_2$. We here use the last iterate $\boldsymbol{x}_k$ for simplicity.

9.2.2 More Scalable Solution to the Subproblem

The subproblem (9.2.5) in the cubic regularized Newton's method essentially aims to minimize the following function:

$$\min_{w} \psi(w) \doteq \langle \nabla f(x), w \rangle + \frac{1}{2} w^* \nabla^2 f(x) w + \frac{L_2}{6} \|w\|_2^3. \tag{9.2.17}$$

Although this subproblem can be reduced to a one-dimensional convex program [NP06], that solution assumes knowing the Hessian inverse or its factorization, which can be costly when the dimension n is very large.

To obtain a more scalable implementation, one may choose to minimize the nonconvex function $\psi(w)$ using gradient-descent-type methods. Notice that the gradient is of the form

$$\nabla \psi(w) = \nabla f(x) + \nabla^2 f(x) w + \nabla \frac{L_2}{6} \|w\|_2^3, \tag{9.2.18}$$

and only the second term $\nabla^2 f(x) w$ involves the Hessian. Nevertheless, it is required only in the form of a "Hessian-vector product"[9] between the Hessian $\nabla^2 f(x)$ and the vector w. One can approximate such a Hessian-vector product by

$$\nabla^2 f(x) w \approx \frac{\nabla f(x + tw) - \nabla f(x)}{t} \tag{9.2.19}$$

for a small $t > 0$. So we only need one additional evaluation of the gradient $\nabla f(x + tw)$ to obtain the gradient of $\nabla \psi(w)$.

It has been shown that gradient descent (with noise[10]) can efficiently find the global minimizer of $\psi(w)$ within ε accuracy[11] in $O(\varepsilon^{-1} \log(1/\varepsilon))$ steps in the worst case. Moreover, when ε is small enough, the algorithm converges to an ε-accurate solution with a linear rate in $O(\log(1/\varepsilon))$ steps [CD16, CD19].

9.3 Gradient and Negative Curvature Descent

As we have alluded to in the preceding section, to escape from unstable critical points, it is not necessary to compute the full Hessian matrix $\nabla^2 f(x)$ at each iteration, or to have to find the precise minimizer of the proxy function in the cubic Newton's method. It often suffices if we can find just a direction that sufficiently reduces the objective function. This could help alleviate the computational burden of second-order methods associated with computing the full Hessian and its inverse.[12] Hence in this section, we study methods that assume access to the *negative curvature oracle*:

[9] The role of such a Hessian–vector product will become clear when we study how to efficiently compute the direction of negative curvature for $f(x)$ for descending purpose in Section 9.3.2 as well as in Section 9.5.3.

[10] Noise is needed to help escape spurious critical points in some hard cases. We will reveal the role of noise clearly in Section 9.5.

[11] Here, if w_o is the global minimizer of $\psi(w)$, an ε-accurate solution $w_\star$ is such that $\psi(w_\star) \leq \psi(w_o) + \varepsilon$.

[12] Which becomes prohibitive when the dimension of the problem is extremely high.

$$\text{the gradient } \nabla f(\boldsymbol{x}) \text{ and a negative eigenvector } \boldsymbol{e} \text{ of } \nabla^2 f(\boldsymbol{x}). \tag{9.3.1}$$

For many practical problems, it is cheaper to obtain such a direction $\boldsymbol{e}$ of negative curvature than to compute the full Hessian. In some problems, the complexity of obtaining $\boldsymbol{e}$ can even be on par with evaluating the gradient $\nabla f(\boldsymbol{x})$.[13] Even if the negative curvature direction $\boldsymbol{e}$ must be computed numerically, one can resort to efficient methods that we will soon introduce in Section 9.3.2. For now, we assume we have this information at each iterate.

9.3.1 Hybrid Gradient and Negative Curvature Descent

To be consistent with the gradient descent and Newton's method, we here assume that both gradient and Hessian are Lipschitz continuous:

$$\|\nabla f(\boldsymbol{y}) - \nabla f(\boldsymbol{x})\|_2 \le L_1 \|\boldsymbol{y} - \boldsymbol{x}\|_2, \quad \|\nabla^2 f(\boldsymbol{y}) - \nabla^2 f(\boldsymbol{x})\| \le L_2 \|\boldsymbol{y} - \boldsymbol{x}\|_2.$$

One should notice one common idea in the design of all the above optimization algorithms: given a prescribed precision ε, the function value is expected to decrease by ε per iteration,

$$f(\boldsymbol{x}_k) - f(\boldsymbol{x}_{k-1}) \le -\varepsilon,$$

unless the first-order and second-order derivatives have met the conditions of convergence.

From Proposition 9.1, we know that when we conduct gradient descent, we should expect the norm of the gradient $\nabla f(\boldsymbol{x}_k)$ to descend according to (9.1.8):

$$\|\nabla f(\boldsymbol{x}_k)\|_2 \le O\left(\frac{L_1(f(\boldsymbol{x}_0) - f(\boldsymbol{x}_\star))}{k}\right)^{1/2} = O\big((L_1\varepsilon)^{1/2}\big). \tag{9.3.2}$$

According to Theorem 9.4, if we use the second-order descent method, the smallest eigenvalue of Hessian $\nabla^2 f(\boldsymbol{x}_k)$ should decay with the number of iterations k as (9.2.16):

$$-\lambda_{\min}\big(\nabla^2 f(\boldsymbol{x}_k)\big) \le O\left(\frac{L_2^2(f(\boldsymbol{x}_0) - f(\boldsymbol{x}_\star))}{k}\right)^{1/3} = O\big((L_2^2\varepsilon)^{1/3}\big). \tag{9.3.3}$$

These conditions naturally suggest a simple descent strategy that alternates between gradient descent and negative curvature descent:

- When the gradient has not reached the desired precision according to (9.3.2), we keep conducting gradient descent.
- Whenever condition (9.3.2) is reached, we conduct the negative curvature search if the smallest eigenvalue of the Hessian has not reached the desired bound (9.3.3).

We summarize this hybrid descent scheme as an algorithm in Figure 9.2. Note that with this scheme, one does not have to compute the negative curvature direction

[13] Say, problems in which we may have analytic expressions for evaluating $\boldsymbol{e}$.

Hybrid Gradient and Negative Curvature Descent

Problem Class:

$$\min_{\boldsymbol{x}} f(\boldsymbol{x}), \quad \boldsymbol{x} \in \mathbb{R}^n,$$

where $f : \mathbb{R}^n \to \mathbb{R}$ is twice continuously differentiable, with Lipschitz continuous gradient and Hessian. Have access to the oracle: the gradient $\nabla f(\boldsymbol{x})$ and the smallest eigenvalue–vector pair $(\lambda_{\min}, \boldsymbol{e})$ of the Hessian $\nabla^2 f(\boldsymbol{x})$.

Setup: prescribed accuracy $\varepsilon > 0$, $\varepsilon_g = (2L_1\varepsilon)^{1/2}$, and $\varepsilon_H = \left(1.5L_2^2\varepsilon\right)^{1/3}$.

Initialization: Set $\boldsymbol{x}_0 \in \mathbb{R}^n$,

For $k = 0, 1, 2, \ldots$

1 Compute the gradient $\nabla f(\boldsymbol{x}_k)$.
2 **if** $\|\nabla f(\boldsymbol{x}_k)\|_2 \geq \varepsilon_g$, **then** conduct gradient descent:

$$\boldsymbol{x}_{k+1} = \boldsymbol{x}_k - \frac{1}{L_1}\nabla f(\boldsymbol{x}_k); \tag{9.3.4}$$

3 **else** compute the smallest eigenvalue λ_k and eigenvector $\boldsymbol{e}_k$ of $\nabla^2 f(\boldsymbol{x}_k)$, and choose its direction such that $\langle \nabla f(\boldsymbol{x}_k), \boldsymbol{e}_k\rangle \leq 0$.
4 **if** $-\lambda_k \geq \varepsilon_H$, **then** conduct negative curvature descent:

$$\boldsymbol{x}_{k+1} = \boldsymbol{x}_k + \frac{2\lambda_k}{L_2}\boldsymbol{e}_k; \tag{9.3.5}$$

5 **else end for** and **return** $\boldsymbol{x}_\star = \boldsymbol{x}_k$.

Convergence guarantee: $\|\nabla f(\boldsymbol{x}_\star)\|_2 \leq \varepsilon_g$, $-\lambda_{\min}\left(\nabla^2 f(\boldsymbol{x}_\star)\right) \leq \varepsilon_H$.

Figure 9.2 An overview of the hybrid gradient and negative curvature descent.

unless it is needed. Then the following theorem states that the algorithm converges to the prescribed precision with the constants specified in the algorithm.

THEOREM 9.5. (Convergence of hybrid gradient and negative curvature descent) *The gradient and negative curvature descent algorithm in Figure 9.2 converges to a second-order stationary point $\boldsymbol{x}_\star$ with the desired precision ε in no more than $k = (f(\boldsymbol{x}_0) - f(\boldsymbol{x}_\star))/\varepsilon$ iterations.*

Proof If $\|\nabla f(\boldsymbol{x}_k)\|_2 \geq \varepsilon_g = (2L_1\varepsilon)^{1/2}$, the algorithm conducts gradient descent: $\boldsymbol{x}_{k+1} = \boldsymbol{x}_k - (1/L_1)\nabla f(\boldsymbol{x}_k)$. Then following the same arguments as in Proposition 9.1, in particular equation (9.1.7), we have

$$\begin{aligned} f(\boldsymbol{x}_{k+1}) &\leq f(\boldsymbol{x}_k) + \langle \nabla f(\boldsymbol{x}_k), \boldsymbol{x}_{k+1} - \boldsymbol{x}_k\rangle + \frac{L_1}{2}\|\boldsymbol{x}_{k+1} - \boldsymbol{x}_k\|_2^2 \\ &\leq f(\boldsymbol{x}_k) - \frac{1}{2L_1}\|\nabla f(\boldsymbol{x}_k)\|_2^2 \\ &\leq f(\boldsymbol{x}_k) - \varepsilon. \end{aligned} \tag{9.3.6}$$

Otherwise, if $-\lambda_k \geq \varepsilon_H = \left(3L_2^2\varepsilon/2\right)^{1/3}$, then the algorithm conducts negative curvature descent: $\boldsymbol{x}_{k+1} = \boldsymbol{x}_k + (2\lambda_k/L_2)\boldsymbol{e}_k$. Since $\boldsymbol{e}_k$ is the eigenvector, we have $\nabla^2 f(\boldsymbol{x}_k)(\boldsymbol{x}_{k+1} - \boldsymbol{x}_k) = \lambda_k(\boldsymbol{x}_{k+1} - \boldsymbol{x}_k)$. Therefore, we have

$$
\begin{aligned}
f(\boldsymbol{x}_{k+1}) &\leq f(\boldsymbol{x}_k) + \langle \nabla f(\boldsymbol{x}_k), \boldsymbol{x}_{k+1} - \boldsymbol{x}_k \rangle \\
&\quad + \frac{1}{2}\langle \nabla^2 f(\boldsymbol{x}_k)(\boldsymbol{x}_{k+1} - \boldsymbol{x}_k), \boldsymbol{x}_{k+1} - \boldsymbol{x}_k \rangle + \frac{L_2}{6}\|\boldsymbol{x}_{k+1} - \boldsymbol{x}_k\|_2^3 \\
&\leq f(\boldsymbol{x}_k) + \frac{1}{2}\langle \nabla^2 f(\boldsymbol{x}_k)(\boldsymbol{x}_{k+1} - \boldsymbol{x}_k), \boldsymbol{x}_{k+1} - \boldsymbol{x}_k \rangle + \frac{L_2}{6}\|\boldsymbol{x}_{k+1} - \boldsymbol{x}_k\|_2^3 \\
&\leq f(\boldsymbol{x}_k) + \frac{1}{2}\lambda_k\left(\frac{2\lambda_k}{L_2}\right)^2 + \frac{L_2}{6}\left(\frac{2|\lambda_k|}{L_2}\right)^3 = f(\boldsymbol{x}_k) - \frac{2|\lambda_k|^3}{3L_2^2} \\
&\leq f(\boldsymbol{x}_k) - \frac{2\varepsilon_H^3}{3L_2^2} &(9.3.7)\\
&\leq f(\boldsymbol{x}_k) - \varepsilon. &(9.3.8)
\end{aligned}
$$

So in each iteration, the function value will decrease by ε. To attain ε, the number of gradient descents and negative curvature descents will be bounded by

$$
\frac{f(\boldsymbol{x}_0) - f(\boldsymbol{x}_\star)}{\varepsilon}. \tag{9.3.9}
$$

That is to say, we need at most $k \leq (f(\boldsymbol{x}_0) - f(\boldsymbol{x}_\star))/\varepsilon$ iterations to attain

$$
\|\nabla f(\boldsymbol{x}_\star)\|_2 \leq \varepsilon_g, \quad \nabla^2 f(\boldsymbol{x}_\star) \succeq -\varepsilon_H \boldsymbol{I}. \tag{9.3.10}
$$

□

REMARK 9.6. (Curvilinear search) *The idea of mixing gradient descent with negative curvature descent can be traced back to the* curvilinear search method *[Gol80]. At each iterate $\boldsymbol{x}_k$, the curvilinear search suggests searching for the next iterate along a curve:*

$$
\boldsymbol{x}(\alpha) = \boldsymbol{x}_k + \alpha \boldsymbol{s}_k + \alpha^2 \boldsymbol{d}_k, \quad \alpha \in (0,1), \tag{9.3.11}
$$

where $\boldsymbol{s}_k$ is typically the negative gradient, say $-\nabla f(\boldsymbol{x})$, and $\boldsymbol{d}_k$ is a direction of negative curvature, say the negative eigenvector $\boldsymbol{e}$. The motivation behind such a scheme is rather intuitive: when the gradient is large, we only need to take a small step (i.e., α is small) along the negative gradient for an adequate descent; when the gradient is small, it is safe to follow more towards a direction of negative curvature and we need to take a larger step (i.e., α is large) to ensure an adequate descent. One can show under certain conditions that such a scheme asymptotically converges to a stable critical point. However, the precise convergence rate is not so easy to characterize.

9.3.2 Computing Negative Curvature via the Lanczos Method

In the above scheme, we need the direction of (the most) negative curvature $\boldsymbol{e}$, which is associated with the smallest eigenvalue of the Hessian. To characterize the precise computational complexity of the scheme, we here show that such a direction can be efficiently computed by evaluating gradients only, using the Hessian-vector product-type operations. The mechanism involved is also known as the *power iteration* or a more advanced variation as the *Lanczos method*.

Around the neighborhood of a given point $\boldsymbol{x}$, consider the second-order approximation to the function $f(\boldsymbol{x}+\boldsymbol{w})$:

$$\phi(\boldsymbol{w}) \doteq f(\boldsymbol{x}) + \langle \nabla f(\boldsymbol{x}), \boldsymbol{w}\rangle + \frac{1}{2}\boldsymbol{w}^* \nabla^2 f(\boldsymbol{x})\boldsymbol{w}. \tag{9.3.12}$$

In general, the negative gradient $-\nabla f(\boldsymbol{x})$ indicates the steepest descent direction. However, if $\boldsymbol{x}$ is near a critical point, we have $\nabla f(\boldsymbol{x}) \approx \boldsymbol{0}$ hence $\langle \nabla f(\boldsymbol{x}), \boldsymbol{w}\rangle \approx 0$. In this case, the approximate steepest descending direction $\boldsymbol{d}$ for $f(\boldsymbol{x})$ is the solution to

$$\boldsymbol{d} = \operatorname*{argmin}_{\boldsymbol{w}} \frac{1}{2}\boldsymbol{w}^* \nabla^2 f(\boldsymbol{x})\boldsymbol{w} \quad \text{subject to} \quad \|\boldsymbol{w}\|_2 = 1. \tag{9.3.13}$$

Then $\boldsymbol{d}$ is the eigenvector $\boldsymbol{e} \in \mathbb{R}^n$ associated with the smallest (negative) eigenvalue $\lambda_{\min}$ of the Hessian. To simplify notation, here we define $\boldsymbol{H} \doteq \nabla^2 f(\boldsymbol{x})$. So we have

$$\boldsymbol{H}\boldsymbol{e} = \lambda_{\min}(\boldsymbol{H})\boldsymbol{e}.$$

Geometrically, this is the direction in which the surface of $f(\boldsymbol{x})$ has the most negative curvature. Note that $\boldsymbol{d}$ can have two choices: $\boldsymbol{d} = \pm\boldsymbol{e}$. If $\boldsymbol{x}$ is not precisely a critical point, i.e., $\nabla f(\boldsymbol{x})$ is not zero, we usually choose $\boldsymbol{d}$ to align with the descent direction:

$$\langle \nabla f(\boldsymbol{x}), \boldsymbol{d}\rangle \le 0. \tag{9.3.14}$$

Recall that we have analyzed the problem (4.2.4) of computing the largest eigenvalue and eigenvector of a matrix in Chapter 4. Here we are interested in the smallest (likely negative) eigenvalue and the associated eigenvector. Notice that the Lipschitz condition (9.1.4) implies that L_1 is an upper bound of the largest eigenvalue $\max_i |\lambda_i|$ of $\boldsymbol{H}$. Hence, if we define a new matrix

$$\boldsymbol{A} \doteq \boldsymbol{I} - L_1^{-1}\boldsymbol{H} \succ \boldsymbol{0},$$

then the largest eigenvalue and eigenvector of $\boldsymbol{A}$ are

$$\lambda_{\max}(\boldsymbol{A}) = 1 - \lambda_{\min}(\boldsymbol{H})/L_1 > 0 \quad \text{and} \quad \boldsymbol{A}\boldsymbol{e} = \lambda_{\max}(\boldsymbol{A})\boldsymbol{e}.$$

This eigenvector $\boldsymbol{e}$ is exactly the most negative curvature direction of the Hessian:

$$\boldsymbol{H}\boldsymbol{e} = \lambda_{\min}(\boldsymbol{H})\boldsymbol{e}.$$

The analysis of singular vectors given in Section 4.2.1 of Chapter 4 suggests that computing the largest eigenvalue/eigenvector can be rather efficient, say using the power iteration method in Exercise 4.6 – we will give a more general account of power iteration methods later in Section 9.6. In light of designing scalable optimization algorithms, we here give a more precise account of its complexity subject to a prescribed accuracy.

Power Iteration and Lanczos Method

The power iteration and Lanczos method [KW92] are two popular methods to compute the leading eigenvalue and eigenvector of a matrix $\boldsymbol{A} \in \mathbb{R}^{n \times n}$. They both rely on computing a series of matrix–vector products of $\boldsymbol{A}$ with a random vector $\boldsymbol{b} \in \mathbb{R}^n$, known as the *Krylov information*:

$$\boldsymbol{K} \doteq \left[\boldsymbol{b}, \boldsymbol{A}\boldsymbol{b}, \boldsymbol{A}^2\boldsymbol{b}, \ldots, \boldsymbol{A}^k\boldsymbol{b}\right]. \tag{9.3.15}$$

Notice that in our context, the matrix–vector product $\boldsymbol{A}\boldsymbol{b}$ depends only on the Hessian-vector product $\boldsymbol{H}\boldsymbol{b}$, which in turn can be approximated from the difference of two gradients:

$$\boldsymbol{A}\boldsymbol{b} = \left[\boldsymbol{I} - L_1^{-1}\boldsymbol{H}\right]\boldsymbol{b} \approx \boldsymbol{b} - (tL_1)^{-1}\left(\nabla f(\boldsymbol{x} + t\boldsymbol{b}) - \nabla f(\boldsymbol{x})\right), \tag{9.3.16}$$

for some small $t > 0$. This can be done recursively for all the products $\boldsymbol{A}^i\boldsymbol{b}$ in $\boldsymbol{K}$, for $i = 1, \ldots, k$.

Then, based on the Krylov information, the power iteration and Lanczos method estimate the largest eigenvalue $\lambda_{\max}(\boldsymbol{A})$ respectively as:

$$\text{power iteration} \quad \hat{\lambda}_{k+1} = \frac{\langle \boldsymbol{A}\boldsymbol{x}, \boldsymbol{x}\rangle}{\langle \boldsymbol{x}, \boldsymbol{x}\rangle}, \quad \boldsymbol{x} = \boldsymbol{A}^n\boldsymbol{b}, \tag{9.3.17}$$

$$\text{Lanczos method} \quad \hat{\lambda}_{k+1} = \max_{\boldsymbol{x}} \frac{\langle \boldsymbol{A}\boldsymbol{x}, \boldsymbol{x}\rangle}{\langle \boldsymbol{x}, \boldsymbol{x}\rangle}, \quad \boldsymbol{x} \in \operatorname{span}(\boldsymbol{K}), \tag{9.3.18}$$

for $k = 0, 1, \ldots$. In our context, we are interested in precisely how many iterations (hence number of gradient evaluations) are needed in order to obtain an estimate within a prescribed accuracy $\varepsilon > 0$:

$$\left|\frac{\hat{\lambda} - \lambda_{\max}(\boldsymbol{A})}{\lambda_{\max}(\boldsymbol{A})}\right| \le \varepsilon. \tag{9.3.19}$$

Of course, it is easy to see that this cannot always be achieved for all matrices $\boldsymbol{A}$ if the vector $\boldsymbol{b}$ is fixed. One only has to consider the special case (of zero probability though) when $\boldsymbol{b}$ is perpendicular to the leading eigenvector: $\boldsymbol{b} \perp \boldsymbol{e}$. We leave this as an exercise for the reader.

Random Initialization

Nevertheless, one can expect this to work with high probability for a *randomly chosen* $\boldsymbol{b}$. The usage of randomness here is to help avoid zero-measure pathological (or hard) cases mentioned above. In the next section, we will utilize randomness in a similar spirit – adding some random noise to gradient descent can help escape spurious critical points. From a random initialization, we can also precisely characterize how quickly the iteration reaches the desired accuracy.

THEOREM 9.7. (Convergence rates of power iteration and lanczos method) *Let $\boldsymbol{b}$ be chosen randomly from a uniform distribution on the sphere $\mathbb{S}^{n-1}$. Then we have:*

$$\textit{power iteration}\ \mathbb{E}_{\boldsymbol{b}}\left[\left|\frac{\hat{\lambda}_{k+1}(\boldsymbol{b}) - \lambda_{\max}(\boldsymbol{A})}{\lambda_{\max}(\boldsymbol{A})}\right|\right] \leq c_1 \log(n)/k, \tag{9.3.20}$$

$$\textit{Lanczos method}\ \mathbb{E}_{\boldsymbol{b}}\left[\left|\frac{\hat{\lambda}_{k+1}(\boldsymbol{b}) - \lambda_{\max}(\boldsymbol{A})}{\lambda_{\max}(\boldsymbol{A})}\right|\right] \leq c_2 (\log(n)/k)^2, \tag{9.3.21}$$

for some small constants $c_1, c_2 > 0$.

That is, the expected error in the estimated largest eigenvalue converges to zero at the rate of $O(\log(n)/k)$ and $O((\log(n)/k)^2)$ for the power iteration and Lanczos method, respectively. Or equivalently, to reach a prescribed accuracy ε as in (9.3.19), the number of iterations needed is $O(\log(n)/\varepsilon)$ and $O(\log(n)/\sqrt{\varepsilon})$, respectively. One may refer to [KW92] for a detailed proof of the theorem above.

Approximate Least Eigenvalue and Eigenvector

The above theorem immediately leads to a result that is very useful in our setting [RW18].

COROLLARY 9.8. *Let $\boldsymbol{H}$ be a symmetric matrix satisfying $\|\boldsymbol{H}\| \leq L_1$ for some $L_1 > 0$. Suppose that the Lanczos procedure is applied to find the largest eigenvalue of $L_1\boldsymbol{I} - \boldsymbol{H}$ starting from a random vector uniformly distributed over the unit sphere. Then, for any $\varepsilon_\lambda > 0$ and $\delta \in (0,1)$, there is a probability at least $1 - \delta$ that the procedure outputs a unit vector $\boldsymbol{e}'$ such that*

$$(\boldsymbol{e}')^* \boldsymbol{H} \boldsymbol{e}' \leq \lambda_{\min}(\boldsymbol{H}) + \varepsilon_\lambda \tag{9.3.22}$$

in at most

$$\min\left\{n, \frac{\log(n/\delta^2)}{2\sqrt{2}}\sqrt{\frac{L_1}{\varepsilon_\lambda}}\right\} \tag{9.3.23}$$

iterations. The procedure obtains a unit vector $\boldsymbol{e}$ such that $\boldsymbol{e}^* \boldsymbol{H} \boldsymbol{e} = \lambda_{\min}(\boldsymbol{H})$ after at most n iterations.

9.3.3 Overall Complexity in First-Order Oracle

Now we know we can use the power iteration or Lanczos method to compute the direction of negative curvature. This essentially reduces the computation to a series of Hessian vector product operations that involve evaluating gradients (9.3.16). If we use the first-order oracle, evaluating a gradient, as the basic unit for measuring the complexity of an algorithm, then how can we measure or estimate the complexity of the proposed algorithm precisely?

Notice from the proof of Theorem 9.5 that, at each negative curvature descent step, the function value decreases by about $O(\varepsilon_H^3)$. The Lanczos process above can estimate the least eigenvalue up to the precision $O(\varepsilon_H)$ for about $O(\varepsilon_H^{-1/2})$ iterations (or Hessian vector products). Hence per gradient evaluation, we can achieve a descent of $O(\varepsilon_H^{7/2})$. For this to be on par with the pure gradient descent, that is, an ε descent per gradient, we could set $\varepsilon = O(\varepsilon_H^{7/2})$ or $\varepsilon_H = O(\varepsilon^{2/7})$. Then the overall complexity in terms of the number of gradient evaluations can be bounded as $O(\varepsilon^{-1})$ or $O(\varepsilon_g^{-2})$. That is, the above hybrid scheme has the same computational complexity in terms of first-order oracle as the gradient descent scheme, introduced in the beginning of the chapter (see Proposition 9.1). However, it guarantees to converge to a second-order stationary point.

To see this more rigorously, we can modify the hybrid gradient and negative curvature algorithm in Figure 9.2 as follows. Whenever the gradient is below ε_g, we use the Lanczos method to compute an inexact unit eigenvector $\boldsymbol{e}_k'$ such that (with probability $1-\delta$)

$$\langle \boldsymbol{e}_k', \nabla f(\boldsymbol{x}_k)\rangle \le 0, \quad \lambda_k' \le \lambda_{\min}\left(\nabla^2 f(\boldsymbol{x}_k)\right) + \frac{\varepsilon_H}{2}, \tag{9.3.24}$$

where $\lambda_k' := (\boldsymbol{e}_k')^* \nabla^2 f(\boldsymbol{x}_k)\boldsymbol{e}_k'$. We know from Corollary 9.8 that this requires $O(\varepsilon_H^{-1/2})$ of Hessian vector product operations or gradient evaluations. With the inexact eigenvector, we conduct negative curvature descent when $\lambda_k' \le -\varepsilon_H/2$:

$$\boldsymbol{x}_{k+1} = \boldsymbol{x}_k + \frac{2\lambda_k'}{L_2}\boldsymbol{e}_k'. \tag{9.3.25}$$

Then, similar to the proof in Theorem 9.5, we have

$$\begin{aligned}
f(\boldsymbol{x}_{k+1}) - f(\boldsymbol{x}_k) &\le \langle \nabla f(\boldsymbol{x}_k), \boldsymbol{x}_{k+1} - \boldsymbol{x}_k\rangle + \frac{1}{2}(\boldsymbol{x}_{k+1} - \boldsymbol{x}_k)^* \nabla^2 f(\boldsymbol{x}_k)(\boldsymbol{x}_{k+1} - \boldsymbol{x}_k) \\
&\quad + \frac{L_2}{6}\|\boldsymbol{x}_{k+1} - \boldsymbol{x}_k\|_2^3 \\
&= \left\langle \nabla f(\boldsymbol{x}_k), \frac{2\lambda_k'}{L_2}\boldsymbol{e}_k' \right\rangle + \frac{1}{2}\left(\frac{2\lambda_k'}{L_2}\boldsymbol{e}_k'\right)^* \nabla^2 f(\boldsymbol{x}_k)\left(\frac{2\lambda_k'}{L_2}\boldsymbol{e}_k'\right) \\
&\quad + \frac{L_2}{6}\left\|\frac{2\lambda_k'}{L_2}\boldsymbol{e}_k'\right\|_2^3 \\
&\le \frac{1}{2}\left(\frac{2\lambda_k'}{L_2}\boldsymbol{e}_k'\right)^* \nabla^2 f(\boldsymbol{x}_k)\left(\frac{2\lambda_k'}{L_2}\boldsymbol{e}_k'\right) + \frac{L_2}{6}\left\|\frac{2\lambda_k'}{L_2}\boldsymbol{e}_k'\right\|_2^3 \\
&= \frac{2(\lambda_k')^3}{L_2^2} + \frac{4|\lambda_k'|^3}{3L_2^2} = \frac{2(\lambda_k')^3}{3L_2^2} \\
&\le -\frac{\varepsilon_H^3}{12L_2^2}.
\end{aligned} \tag{9.3.26}$$

Therefore, the total descent is $(1/12L_2^2)\varepsilon_H^3$ for $O(\varepsilon_H^{-1/2})$ gradient evaluations. The average descent per gradient is $O(\varepsilon_H^{7/2})$. With the choice $\varepsilon_H = O(\varepsilon^{2/7})$, the per gradient evaluation will incur a descent of $O(\varepsilon)$. Hence, the number of iterations is

$k \le O(\varepsilon^{-1})$. With the same choice of $\varepsilon_g = O(\varepsilon^{1/2})$, the overall computational complexity of the inexact negative curvature descent in terms of the first-order oracle is[14]

$$k \le O(\varepsilon_g^{-2}),$$

and the scheme guarantees to converge to a critical point $\boldsymbol{x}_\star$ that satisfies

$$\|\nabla f(\boldsymbol{x}_\star)\|_2 \le O(\varepsilon^{1/2}), \quad -\lambda_{\min}(\nabla^2 f(\boldsymbol{x}_\star)) \le O(\varepsilon^{2/7}). \tag{9.3.27}$$

9.4 Negative Curvature and Newton Descent

As we have seen in the cubic regularized Newton's method in Section 9.2, if we have access to the second-order oracle (the gradient and Hessian), the best rate of convergence that can be achieved is $O(\varepsilon_g^{-1.5})$. However, if we have access only to the gradient, then for functions with Lipschitz gradient and Hessian, the lower bound of first-order methods can be relaxed to $\Omega(\varepsilon_g^{-12/7})$ [CDHS17], while the best known achievable upper bound is $O(\varepsilon_g^{-7/4})$.

We notice that the above hybrid gradient and negative curvature descent converges at the rate $O(\varepsilon_g^{-2})$ and does not yet achieve the best known complexity result. The main problem is with the step of gradient descent: to achieve the prescribed descent ε per gradient step, it requires that the gradient is at least on the order of $O(\varepsilon^{1/2})$, disregarding any second-order information. When the gradient is not as large, to achieve the same amount of descent, one must leverage second-order information about the Hessian as we did in the above Newton-type methods.

In this section, we show that a slightly more careful use of the negative curvature information (computed from gradients) can indeed lead to algorithms that reach the best known complexity bound. For readers who are not interested in such a theoretical guarantee, they may skip this section without loss of continuity.

9.4.1 Curvature Guided Newton Descent

In the preceding algorithm, the negative curvature descent step offers useful second-order information about the function that probably can be utilized by the gradient step, a key observation by [RW18]. This suggests that we could reverse the order of the two steps: we first evaluate the smallest eigenvalue $\lambda_{\min}$ of the Hessian $\nabla^2 f(\boldsymbol{x})$. Based on its value, we decide to conduct either a negative curvature descent or a more effective descent based on the gradient $\nabla f(\boldsymbol{x})$.

Notice that for the latter choice, with the second-order information about the negative curvature, we can conduct a more effective regularized Newton-type descent:

$$\boldsymbol{s}_k = \operatorname*{argmin}_{\boldsymbol{s}} \langle \nabla f(\boldsymbol{x}_k), \boldsymbol{s}\rangle + \frac{1}{2}\boldsymbol{s}^* \nabla^2 f(\boldsymbol{x}_k)\boldsymbol{s} + \frac{\lambda}{2}\|\boldsymbol{s}\|_2^2 \tag{9.4.1}$$

[14] Up to some log factor in n.

with $\lambda > \lambda_{\min}$. The choice of the quadratic regularization term $\lambda\|s\|_2^2$ ensures the function is strongly convex in s or, equivalently, $\nabla^2 f(x)+\lambda I \succ 0$ is positive definite. If we directly use the so-computed optimal $s_k = -[\nabla^2 f(x_k) + \lambda I]^{-1}\nabla f(x_k)$ as increment, we arrive at the well-known *Levenberg–Marquardt* method:[15]

$$x_{k+1} = x_k - \left[\nabla^2 f(x_k) + \lambda I\right]^{-1} \nabla f(x_k). \tag{9.4.2}$$

Nevertheless, here, to ensure that the function value decreases by at least the prescribed amount, we should be judicious about the step size γ_k along the direction s_k:[16]

$$x_{k+1} = x_k + \gamma_k s_k. \tag{9.4.3}$$

Figure 9.3 and the following theorem give the proper conditions under which the above hybrid scheme converges to a second-order stationary point.

THEOREM 9.9. (Convergence of hybrid negative curvature and newton descent) *Assume $\{x_k\}$ are generated by the hybrid negative curvature and Newton descent algorithm in Figure 9.3. Then in at most*

$$k \le \frac{f(x_0) - f(x_\star)}{\varepsilon} \tag{9.4.7}$$

iterations, x_k will be an approximate second-order stationary point such that $\|\nabla f(x_k)\|_2 \le \varepsilon_g, \lambda_{\min}(\nabla^2 f(x_k)) \ge -\varepsilon_H$, where

$$\varepsilon_g = 3^{8/3}/2L_2^{1/3}\varepsilon^{2/3}, \quad \varepsilon_H = \left(3L_2^2\varepsilon\right)^{1/3}.$$

Proof If $\lambda_k \le -\varepsilon_H$ or $-\lambda_k \ge \left(3L_2^2\varepsilon\right)^{1/3}$, we conduct negative curvature descent (9.4.4). From the proof of Theorem 9.5, we know that then we have

$$f(x_{k+1}) - f(x_k) \le \frac{2(\lambda_k)^3}{3L_2^2} \le -\frac{2\varepsilon_H^3}{3L_2^2} = -2\varepsilon. \tag{9.4.8}$$

If $\lambda_k > -\varepsilon_H$, then we discuss two cases.

Case 1. If

$$\left(\frac{3\varepsilon_H}{2L_2\|s_k\|_2}\right)^{1/2} \ge 1,$$

that is, $\|s_k\|_2 \le 3\varepsilon_H/2L_2$, we accept the unit step size. By the optimality condition of s_k in (9.4.5), we have

$$\nabla^2 f(x_k)s_k + 2\varepsilon_H s_k + \nabla f(x_k) = \mathbf{0}. \tag{9.4.9}$$

15 We will provide more references to the Levenberg–Marquardt method in the Notes section. A similar update rule can be derived from the perspective of the trust region method, as we will see in Exercise 9.2.

16 In optimization, a good step size is often found through a "line search" step. Nevertheless, when the function Lipschitz constants are given, we can give an explicit expression for the proper step size.

Hybrid Negative Curvature and Newton Descent

Problem Class:

$$\min_{x} f(x), \quad x \in \mathbb{R}^n,$$

where $f : \mathbb{R}^n \to \mathbb{R}$ is twice continuously differentiable, with Lipschitz continuous gradient and Hessian. Have access to the oracle: $\nabla f(x)$ and $\nabla^2 f(x)$.

Setup: given a prescribed accuracy $\varepsilon > 0$, $\varepsilon_g = 3^{8/3} L_2^{1/3} \varepsilon^{2/3}/2$, $\varepsilon_H = \left(3L_2^2 \varepsilon\right)^{1/3}$.

Initialization: Set $x_0 \in \mathbb{R}^n$.

For $k = 0, 1, 2, \ldots$

1 Compute $\nabla f(x_k)$, and the smallest eigenvalue and unit eigenvector pair (λ_k, e_k) of $\nabla^2 f(x_k)$ with $\langle \nabla f(x_k), e_k \rangle \leq 0$.

2 **if** $\lambda_k \leq -\varepsilon_H$, **then** conduct negative curvature descent:

$$x_{k+1} = x_k + \frac{2\lambda_k}{L_2} e_k; \tag{9.4.4}$$

3 **else if** $\|\nabla f(x_k)\|_2 \geq \varepsilon_g$, then solve the convex quadratic problem:

$$s_k = \operatorname*{argmin}_{s} \langle \nabla f(x_k), s \rangle + \frac{1}{2} s^* \nabla^2 f(x_k) s + \varepsilon_H \|s\|_2^2, \tag{9.4.5}$$

$$x_{k+1} = x_k + \gamma_k s_k, \tag{9.4.6}$$

with $\gamma_k = \min\left\{ \left(\frac{3\varepsilon_H}{2L_2 \|s_k\|_2} \right)^{1/2}, 1 \right\}$.

4 **else end for** and **return** $x_\star = x_k$.

Convergence Guarantee: $\|\nabla f(x_\star)\|_2 \leq \varepsilon_g, \; -\lambda_{\min}(\nabla^2 f(x_\star)) \leq \varepsilon_H$.

Figure 9.3 An overview of the hybrid negative curvature and Newton descent.

Then together with the property of Lipschitz Hessian condition (9.2.13), we have

$$\begin{aligned}
\|\nabla f(x_{k+1})\|_2 &= \|\nabla f(x_k + s_k)\| \\
&\leq \|\nabla f(x_k + s_k) - (\nabla f(x_k) + \nabla^2 f(x_k) s_k)\|_2 \\
&\quad + \|\nabla f(x_k) + \nabla^2 f(x_k) s_k\|_2 \\
&\leq \frac{L_2}{2} \|s_k\|_2^2 + \|2\varepsilon_H s_k\|_2 \\
&\leq \frac{L_2}{2} \|s_k\|_2^2 + 2\varepsilon_H \|s_k\|_2 \\
&\leq \left(\frac{9}{8} + 3 \right) \frac{\varepsilon_H^2}{L_2} \leq \frac{9\varepsilon_H^2}{2L_2} \\
&\leq \varepsilon_g.
\end{aligned} \tag{9.4.10}$$

Then, by the property of Lipschitz Hessian condition (9.2.4), we have

$$
\begin{aligned}
f(\boldsymbol{x}_{k+1}) &= f(\boldsymbol{x}_k + \boldsymbol{s}_k) \\
&\leq f(\boldsymbol{x}_k) + \langle \nabla f(\boldsymbol{x}_k), \boldsymbol{s}_k \rangle + \frac{1}{2} \boldsymbol{s}_k^* \nabla^2 f(\boldsymbol{x}_k) \boldsymbol{s}_k + \frac{L_2}{6} \|\boldsymbol{s}_k\|_2^3 \\
&\leq f(\boldsymbol{x}_k) - \frac{1}{2} \boldsymbol{s}_k^* \nabla^2 f(\boldsymbol{x}_k) \boldsymbol{s}_k - 2\varepsilon_H \|\boldsymbol{s}_k\|_2^2 + \frac{L_2}{6} \|\boldsymbol{s}_k\|_2^3 \\
&\leq f(\boldsymbol{x}_k) - \frac{3}{2} \varepsilon_H \|\boldsymbol{s}_k\|_2^2 + \frac{L_2}{6} \|\boldsymbol{s}_k\|_2^3 \\
&\leq f(\boldsymbol{x}_k) - \frac{3}{2} \varepsilon_H \|\boldsymbol{s}_k\|_2^2 + \frac{\varepsilon_H}{4} \|\boldsymbol{s}_k\|_2^2 \\
&\leq f(\boldsymbol{x}_k) - \frac{5}{4} \varepsilon_H \|\boldsymbol{s}_k\|_2^2.
\end{aligned} \tag{9.4.11}
$$

That is, when the step size $\gamma_k = 1$, we have that $\nabla f(\boldsymbol{x}_{k+1})$ is already smaller than ε_g and $f(\boldsymbol{x}_{k+1})$ is smaller than $f(\boldsymbol{x}_k)$. As a result, we must have

$$
\lambda_{\min}(\nabla^2 f(\boldsymbol{x}_{k+1})) < -\varepsilon_H;
$$

otherwise, we have found a desired second-order stationary point. So, for the case of accepting step size 1, before the algorithm stops, the function value will be decreased by at least 2ε in the next iteration by negative curvature descent (9.4.8).

Case 2. If

$$
\left(\frac{3\varepsilon_H}{2L_2 \|\boldsymbol{s}_k\|_2} \right)^{1/2} < 1,
$$

that is, $\|\boldsymbol{s}_k\|_2 > 3\varepsilon_H / 2L_2$. To simplify notation, we let

$$
\alpha = \left(\frac{3\varepsilon_H}{2L_2 \|\boldsymbol{s}_k\|_2} \right)^{1/2} < 1.
$$

Then we have

$$
\begin{aligned}
f(\boldsymbol{x}_{k+1}) &= f(\boldsymbol{x}_k + \alpha \boldsymbol{s}_k) \\
&\leq f(\boldsymbol{x}_k) + \alpha \langle \nabla f(\boldsymbol{x}_k), \boldsymbol{s}_k \rangle + \frac{\alpha^2}{2} \boldsymbol{s}_k^* \nabla^2 f(\boldsymbol{x}_k) \boldsymbol{s}_k + \frac{L_2 \alpha^3}{6} \|\boldsymbol{s}_k\|_2^3 \\
&\leq f(\boldsymbol{x}_k) + \alpha \left(\frac{\alpha}{2} - 1 \right) \boldsymbol{s}_k^* \nabla^2 f(\boldsymbol{x}_k) \boldsymbol{s}_k - 2\alpha \varepsilon_H \|\boldsymbol{s}_k\|_2^2 + \frac{L_2 \alpha^3}{6} \|\boldsymbol{s}_k\|_2^3 \\
&\leq f(\boldsymbol{x}_k) - \alpha \varepsilon_H \left(\frac{\alpha}{2} - 1 \right) \|\boldsymbol{s}_k\|_2^2 - 2\alpha \varepsilon_H \|\boldsymbol{s}_k\|_2^2 + \frac{L_2 \alpha^3}{6} \|\boldsymbol{s}_k\|_2^3 \\
&\leq f(\boldsymbol{x}_k) - \alpha \varepsilon_H \|\boldsymbol{s}_k\|_2^2 + \frac{L_2 \alpha^3}{6} \|\boldsymbol{s}_k\|_2^3
\end{aligned}
$$

$$
\begin{aligned}
&= f(\boldsymbol{x}_k) - \left(\frac{3}{2L_2}\right)^{1/2} (\varepsilon_H \|\boldsymbol{s}_k\|_2)^{3/2} + \frac{(3/2)^{3/2}}{6L_2^{1/2}} (\varepsilon_H \|\boldsymbol{s}_k\|_2)^{3/2} \\
&\leq f(\boldsymbol{x}_k) - \frac{(3/2)^{1/2} 3}{4L_2^{1/2}} (\varepsilon_H \|\boldsymbol{s}_k\|_2)^{3/2} \\
&\leq f(\boldsymbol{x}_k) - \frac{27\varepsilon_H^3}{16L_2^2} \\
&= f(\boldsymbol{x}_k) - 5\varepsilon. \qquad (9.4.12)
\end{aligned}
$$

Combining (9.4.8)–(9.4.12), we know that before finding an approximate second-order stationary point such that $\|\nabla f(\boldsymbol{x}_k)\|_2 \leq \varepsilon_g, \lambda_{\min}(\nabla^2 f(\boldsymbol{x}_k)) \geq -\varepsilon_H$, we can always decrease the function value by at least 2ε in two consecutive iterations. As a result, to find such a point, the total number of iterations will be upper-bounded by $k \leq (f(\boldsymbol{x}_0) - f(\boldsymbol{x}_\star))/\varepsilon$. □

9.4.2 Inexact Negative Curvature and Newton Descent

In the above scheme, we have assumed that we have access to the Hessian and its smallest eigenvalue and eigenvector. However, if we only have access to the gradient and the Hessian–vector product, how costly would it be to compute the eigenvector? How accurately should it be computed so that the resulting scheme achieves the best known complexity (with respect to the first-order oracle)?

In this section, we consider an inexact version of the algorithm in Figure 9.3, which allows us to approximately compute the smallest eigenvalue and eigenvector pair, and approximately solve the convex quadratic problem. By carefully choosing the stopping criterion, the inexact version of the algorithm, shown in Figure 9.4, can maintain the convergence rate of the exact version, differing only in constants. The corresponding convergence result is given in the theorem below.

THEOREM 9.10. *Assume $\{\boldsymbol{x}_k\}$ are generated by the hybrid negative curvature and Newton descent algorithm in Figure 9.4. Then in at most*

$$
k \leq \frac{f(\boldsymbol{x}_0) - f(\boldsymbol{x}_\star)}{\varepsilon} \qquad (9.4.17)
$$

iterations, $\boldsymbol{x}_k$ will be an approximate second-order stationary point such that $\|\nabla f(\boldsymbol{x}_k)\|_2 \leq \varepsilon_g, \lambda_{\min}(\nabla^2 f(\boldsymbol{x}_k)) \geq -\varepsilon_H$, where

$$
\varepsilon_g = (5/L_2)(24L_2^2\varepsilon)^{2/3}, \quad \varepsilon_H = \left(24L_2^2\varepsilon\right)^{1/3}.
$$

Proof If $\lambda_k' \leq -\varepsilon_H/2$, we estimate the amount of descent by the negative curvature descent. This is exactly the same as we have done in (9.3.26). The slight difference here is the choice of ε_H. Hence we have

$$
f(\boldsymbol{x}_{k+1}) - f(\boldsymbol{x}_k) \leq -\frac{\varepsilon_H^3}{12L_2^2} = -2\varepsilon. \qquad (9.4.18)
$$

Inexact Hybrid Negative Curvature and Newton Descent

Problem Class:

$$\min_{\boldsymbol{x}} f(\boldsymbol{x}), \quad \boldsymbol{x} \in \mathbb{R}^n,$$

where $f : \mathbb{R}^n \to \mathbb{R}$ is twice continuously differentiable, with Lipschitz continuous gradient and Hessian. Have access to the oracle: $\nabla f(\boldsymbol{x})$ and the Hessian product $\nabla^2 f(\boldsymbol{x})\boldsymbol{v}$.

Setup: prescribed accuracy $\varepsilon > 0$, $\varepsilon_g = (5/L_2)(24L_2^2\varepsilon)^{2/3}$, $\varepsilon_H = \left(24L_2^2\varepsilon\right)^{1/3}$.

Initialization: Set $\boldsymbol{x}_0 \in \mathbb{R}^n$.

For $k = 0, 1, 2, \ldots$

1 Compute $\nabla f(\boldsymbol{x}_k)$ and an inexact unit eigenvector $\boldsymbol{e}'_k$ such that (with probability $1 - \delta$)

$$\langle \boldsymbol{e}'_k, \nabla f(\boldsymbol{x}_k)\rangle \le 0, \quad \lambda'_k \le \lambda_{\min}\left(\nabla^2 f(\boldsymbol{x}_k)\right) + \frac{\varepsilon_H}{2}, \tag{9.4.13}$$

where $\lambda'_k := (\boldsymbol{e}'_k)^* \nabla^2 f(\boldsymbol{x}_k)\boldsymbol{e}'_k$.

2 **if** $\lambda'_k \le -\varepsilon_H/2$, **then** conduct negative curvature descent:

$$\boldsymbol{x}_{k+1} = \boldsymbol{x}_k + \frac{2\lambda'_k}{L_2}\boldsymbol{e}'_k; \tag{9.4.14}$$

3 **else if** $\|\nabla f(\boldsymbol{x}_k)\|_2 \ge \varepsilon_g$, then find $\boldsymbol{s}_k$ such that

$$\|\nabla^2 f(\boldsymbol{x}_k)\boldsymbol{s}_k + 2\varepsilon_H \boldsymbol{s}_k + \nabla f(\boldsymbol{x}_k)\|_2 \le \frac{1}{2}\varepsilon_H \|\boldsymbol{s}_k\|_2, \tag{9.4.15}$$

$$\boldsymbol{x}_{k+1} = \boldsymbol{x}_k + \gamma_k \boldsymbol{s}_k, \tag{9.4.16}$$

where $\gamma_k = \min\left\{\left(\frac{3\varepsilon_H}{2L_2\|\boldsymbol{s}_k\|_2}\right)^{1/2}, 1\right\}$.

4 **else end for** and **return** $\boldsymbol{x}_\star = \boldsymbol{x}_k$.

Convergence Guarantee: $\|\nabla f(\boldsymbol{x}_\star)\|_2 \le \varepsilon_g, \ -\lambda_{\min}\left(\nabla^2 f(\boldsymbol{x}_\star)\right) \le \varepsilon_H$.

Figure 9.4 Overview of the inexact hybrid negative curvature and Newton descent.

If $\lambda'_k > -\varepsilon_H/2$, then by the conditions of λ'_k, we have

$$-\frac{\varepsilon_H}{2} \le \lambda'_k \le \lambda_{\min}\left(\nabla^2 f(\boldsymbol{x}_k)\right) + \frac{\varepsilon_H}{2}, \tag{9.4.19}$$

i.e., we have $\lambda_{\min}\left(\nabla^2 f(\boldsymbol{x}_k)\right) \ge -\varepsilon_H$. Then we discuss two cases.

Case 1. If

$$\left(\frac{3\varepsilon_H}{2L_2\|\boldsymbol{s}_k\|_2}\right)^{1/2} \ge 1,$$

that is, $\|s_k\|_2 \le 3\varepsilon_H/2L_2$, then we accept the unit step size. Letting

$$\boldsymbol{r}_k := \nabla^2 f(\boldsymbol{x}_k)\boldsymbol{s}_k + 2\varepsilon_H \boldsymbol{s}_k + \nabla f(\boldsymbol{x}_k), \tag{9.4.20}$$

we know $\|\boldsymbol{r}_k\|_2 \le \frac{1}{2}\varepsilon_H \|\boldsymbol{s}_k\|_2$. By the Lipschitz Hessian condition (9.2.13), we have

$$\begin{aligned}
\|\nabla f(\boldsymbol{x}_{k+1})\|_2 &= \|\nabla f(\boldsymbol{x}_k + \boldsymbol{s}_k)\|_2 \\
&\le \|\nabla f(\boldsymbol{x}_k + \boldsymbol{s}_k) - (\nabla f(\boldsymbol{x}_k) + \nabla^2 f(\boldsymbol{x}_k)\boldsymbol{s}_k)\|_2 \\
&\quad + \|\nabla f(\boldsymbol{x}_k) + \nabla^2 f(\boldsymbol{x}_k)\boldsymbol{s}_k\|_2 \\
&\le \frac{L_2}{2}\|\boldsymbol{s}_k\|_2^2 + \|\boldsymbol{r}_k - 2\varepsilon_H \boldsymbol{s}_k\|_2 \\
&\le \frac{L_2}{2}\|\boldsymbol{s}_k\|_2^2 + 2\varepsilon_H\|\boldsymbol{s}_k\|_2 + \|\boldsymbol{r}_k\|_2 \\
&\le \frac{L_2}{2}\|\boldsymbol{s}_k\|_2^2 + 2\varepsilon_H\|\boldsymbol{s}_k\|_2 + \frac{1}{2}\varepsilon_H\|\boldsymbol{s}_k\|_2 \\
&\le \left(\frac{9}{8} + 3 + \frac{3}{4}\right)\frac{\varepsilon_H^2}{L_2} \\
&\le \frac{5\varepsilon_H^2}{L_2} \\
&= \varepsilon_g.
\end{aligned} \tag{9.4.21}$$

Then, by the Hessian Lipschitz condition (9.2.4), we have,

$$\begin{aligned}
f(\boldsymbol{x}_{k+1}) &= f(\boldsymbol{x}_k + \boldsymbol{s}_k) \\
&\le f(\boldsymbol{x}_k) + \langle \nabla f(\boldsymbol{x}_k), \boldsymbol{s}_k\rangle + \frac{1}{2}\boldsymbol{s}_k^*\nabla^2 f(\boldsymbol{x}_k)\boldsymbol{s}_k + \frac{L_2}{6}\|\boldsymbol{s}_k\|_2^3 \\
&= f(\boldsymbol{x}_k) + \langle \boldsymbol{r}_k - (\nabla^2 f(\boldsymbol{x}_k)\boldsymbol{s}_k + 2\varepsilon_H\boldsymbol{s}_k), \boldsymbol{s}_k\rangle \\
&\quad + \frac{1}{2}\boldsymbol{s}_k^*\nabla^2 f(\boldsymbol{x}_k)\boldsymbol{s}_k + \frac{L_2}{6}\|\boldsymbol{s}_k\|_2^3 \\
&\le f(\boldsymbol{x}_k) + \langle \boldsymbol{r}_k, \boldsymbol{s}_k\rangle - \frac{1}{2}\boldsymbol{s}_k^*\nabla^2 f(\boldsymbol{x}_k)\boldsymbol{s}_k - 2\varepsilon_H\|\boldsymbol{s}_k\|_2^2 + \frac{L_2}{6}\|\boldsymbol{s}_k\|_2^3 \\
&\le f(\boldsymbol{x}_k) + \|\boldsymbol{r}_k\|_2\|\boldsymbol{s}_k\|_2 - \frac{1}{2}\boldsymbol{s}_k^*\nabla^2 f(\boldsymbol{x}_k)\boldsymbol{s}_k - 2\varepsilon_H\|\boldsymbol{s}_k\|_2^2 + \frac{L_2}{6}\|\boldsymbol{s}_k\|_2^3 \\
&\le f(\boldsymbol{x}_k) + \frac{1}{2}\varepsilon_H\|\boldsymbol{s}_k\|_2^2 + \frac{1}{2}\varepsilon_H\|\boldsymbol{s}_k\|_2^2 - 2\varepsilon_H\|\boldsymbol{s}_k\|_2^2 + \frac{L_2}{6}\|\boldsymbol{s}_k\|_2^3 \\
&\le f(\boldsymbol{x}_k) - \varepsilon_H\|\boldsymbol{s}_k\|_2^2 + \frac{L_2}{6}\|\boldsymbol{s}_k\|_2^3 \\
&\le f(\boldsymbol{x}_k) - \varepsilon_H\|\boldsymbol{s}_k\|_2^2 + \frac{\varepsilon_H}{4}\|\boldsymbol{s}_k\|_2^2 \\
&\le f(\boldsymbol{x}_k) - \frac{3}{4}\varepsilon_H\|\boldsymbol{s}_k\|_2^2.
\end{aligned} \tag{9.4.22}$$

That is, if we accept the step size $\gamma_k = 1$, then $\nabla f(\boldsymbol{x}_{k+1})$ is already smaller than ε_g and $f(\boldsymbol{x}_{k+1})$ is smaller than $f(\boldsymbol{x}_k)$. As a result, we next should have $\lambda_{\min}(\nabla^2 f(\boldsymbol{x}_{k+1})) < -\varepsilon_H$; otherwise, we have found a desired second-order stationary point. So for the case of accepting step size 1, before the algorithm stops, we must decrease the function value by at least 2ε in the next iteration by the negative curvature descent (9.4.18).

Case 2. If

$$\left(\frac{3\varepsilon_H}{2L_2\|s_k\|_2}\right)^{1/2} < 1,$$

that is, $\|s_k\|_2 > 3\varepsilon_H/2L_2$. For simplicity, we denote

$$\alpha = \left(\frac{3\varepsilon_H}{2L_2\|s_k\|_2}\right)^{1/2} < 1.$$

Then we have

$$\begin{aligned}
f(\boldsymbol{x}_{k+1}) &= f(\boldsymbol{x}_k + \alpha \boldsymbol{s}_k) \\
&\le f(\boldsymbol{x}_k) + \alpha\langle \nabla f(\boldsymbol{x}_k), \boldsymbol{s}_k\rangle + \frac{\alpha^2}{2}\boldsymbol{s}_k^* \nabla^2 f(\boldsymbol{x}_k)\boldsymbol{s}_k + \frac{L_2\alpha^3}{6}\|\boldsymbol{s}_k\|_2^3 \\
&\le f(\boldsymbol{x}_k) + \alpha\|\boldsymbol{r}_k\|_2\|\boldsymbol{s}_k\|_2 + \alpha\left(\frac{\alpha}{2}-1\right)\boldsymbol{s}_k^*\nabla^2 f(\boldsymbol{x}_k)\boldsymbol{s}_k \\
&\quad - 2\alpha\varepsilon_H\|\boldsymbol{s}_k\|_2^2 + \frac{L_2\alpha^3}{6}\|\boldsymbol{s}_k\|_2^3 \\
&\le f(\boldsymbol{x}_k) + \frac{\alpha\varepsilon_H}{2}\|\boldsymbol{s}_k\|_2^2 - \alpha\varepsilon_H\left(\frac{\alpha}{2}-1\right)\|\boldsymbol{s}_k\|_2^2 \\
&\quad - 2\alpha\varepsilon_H\|\boldsymbol{s}_k\|_2^2 + \frac{L_2\alpha^3}{6}\|\boldsymbol{s}_k\|_2^3 \\
&\le f(\boldsymbol{x}_k) - \frac{\alpha\varepsilon_H}{2}\|\boldsymbol{s}_k\|_2^2 + \frac{L_2\alpha^3}{6}\|\boldsymbol{s}_k\|_2^3 \\
&= f(\boldsymbol{x}_k) - \frac{1}{2}\left(\frac{3}{2L_2}\right)^{1/2}(\varepsilon_H\|\boldsymbol{s}_k\|_2)^{3/2} + \frac{(3/2)^{3/2}}{6L_2^{1/2}}(\varepsilon_H\|\boldsymbol{s}_k\|_2)^{3/2} \\
&\le f(\boldsymbol{x}_k) - \frac{(3/2)^{1/2}}{4L_2^{1/2}}(\varepsilon_H\|\boldsymbol{s}_k\|_2)^{3/2} \\
&\le f(\boldsymbol{x}_k) - \frac{9\varepsilon_H^3}{16L_2^2} \\
&\le f(\boldsymbol{x}_k) - \frac{27}{2}\varepsilon.
\end{aligned} \tag{9.4.23}$$

So when using step size less than 1, we can always guarantee sufficient decrease.

Combining (9.4.18)–(9.4.23), we know that before finding an approximate second-order stationary point such that $\|\nabla f(\boldsymbol{x}_k)\|_2 \le \varepsilon_g, \lambda_{\min}\left(\nabla^2 f(\boldsymbol{x}_k)\right) \ge -\varepsilon_H$, we can always decrease the function value by at least 2ε in two consecutive iterations. As a result, to find such a point, the total number of iterations will be upper-bounded by $k \le (f(\boldsymbol{x}_0) - f(\boldsymbol{x}_\star))/\varepsilon$. □

9.4.3 Overall Complexity in First-Order Oracle

Notice that in the inexact scheme above, we need both to approximate the eigenvector e' associated with the smallest eigenvalue (9.4.13) as well as to find an approximate solution s_k to the convex quadratic problem (9.4.1) that satisfies the condition (9.4.15).

Inexact Negative Curvature Descent

As we have characterized before in Section 9.3.3, to compute the smallest eigenvalue and eigenvector up to the prescribed accuracy $\varepsilon_H/2$, the number of Hessian–vector product (or gradient) evaluations is of order $O(\varepsilon_H^{-1/2})$. With the choice $\varepsilon_H = O(\varepsilon^{1/3})$, this is equivalent to $O(\varepsilon^{-1/6})$.[17]

Then, according to the proof of Theorem 9.9, each negative curvature descent is ε. Hence per gradient evaluation, the descent is $O(\varepsilon^{7/6})$. The number of iterations is $k = O(\varepsilon^{-7/6})$.

According to Theorem 9.9, the total number of iterations of the algorithm in Figure 9.4 is $O(\varepsilon^{-1})$, while per iteration we need $O(\varepsilon^{-1/6})$ number of Hessian–vector products to produce the desired inexact solution. So the total number of Hessian–vector products we need in negative curvature descent is $O(\varepsilon^{-7/6})$. Since we have $\varepsilon = O(\varepsilon_g^{3/2})$, this leads to the best known rate $k = O(\varepsilon_g^{-7/4})$.

Inexact Convex Quadratic Program

Now, notice that we also need an approximate solution to the convex quadratic problem (9.4.1). The above rate will hold only if we can solve the problem (9.4.15) with the same complexity in first-order oracle for the Newton descent step. That is, we need to show that the number of Hessian vector products, hence gradient evaluations, needed to solve the quadratic problem approximately is also of order $O(\varepsilon_H^{-1/2})$, i.e., $O(\varepsilon^{-1/6})$.

By the optimality condition of the convex quadratic problem (9.4.5), we have

$$\nabla^2 f(\boldsymbol{x}_k)\boldsymbol{s}_k + 2\varepsilon_H \boldsymbol{s}_k + \nabla f(\boldsymbol{x}_k) = \mathbf{0}. \tag{9.4.24}$$

This is equivalent to

$$(\nabla^2 f(\boldsymbol{x}_k) + 2\varepsilon_H \boldsymbol{I})\boldsymbol{s}_k = -\nabla f(\boldsymbol{x}_k), \tag{9.4.25}$$

which is of the form of a linear system: $\boldsymbol{A}\boldsymbol{s} = \boldsymbol{b}$, with $\boldsymbol{A} = \nabla^2 f(\boldsymbol{x}_k) + 2\varepsilon_H \boldsymbol{I}$ and $\boldsymbol{b} = -\nabla f(\boldsymbol{x}_k)$. Notice that in the above algorithm, when we conduct the Newton descent, we have the condition $\lambda_{\min}(\nabla^2 f(\boldsymbol{x}_k)) \geq -\varepsilon_H$. So for our problem here:

$$\varepsilon_H \boldsymbol{I} \preceq \boldsymbol{A} \preceq (L_1 + 2\varepsilon_H)\boldsymbol{I}.$$

Of course, one could simply compute the inverse of $\boldsymbol{A}$ to solve $\boldsymbol{s} = \boldsymbol{A}^{-1}\boldsymbol{b}$, but the complexity would be very high. To avoid computing the matrix inverse, one could try to solve the program numerically,

$$\min_{\boldsymbol{s}} \|\boldsymbol{A}\boldsymbol{s} - \boldsymbol{b}\|_2^2,$$

[17] Here for simplicity, we have omitted possible log factors in the orders.

using the steepest gradient descent. However, the complexity would not be the best one can do. The classic *conjugate gradient method*, described in equation (A.6.3) in Appendix A, is precisely an accelerated gradient algorithm designed to solve the above quadratic program more efficiently than the steepest descent. The reader may refer to [She94, NW06] for an excellent derivation and justification of this elegant, classical method.

For our interest here, one should notice that, at each iteration i, the conjugate gradient scheme only needs to evaluate the multiplication of $\boldsymbol{A}$ with the current estimate $\boldsymbol{s}_i$ to compute the residual

$$\boldsymbol{r}_{i+1} = \boldsymbol{r}_i - \alpha_i \boldsymbol{A}\boldsymbol{s}_i$$

for the next iteration. For our purpose, we need to characterize the precise number of iterations for the conjugate gradient method to produce an approximate solution that satisfies the following (relative) accuracy:

$$\|\boldsymbol{A}\boldsymbol{s} - \boldsymbol{b}\|_2 \leq \mu \|\boldsymbol{b}\|_2,$$

for some small $\mu > 0$. Then from the property of the conjugate gradient, it is easy to show the following result for our problem.

THEOREM 9.11. (Complexity of approximate conjugate gradient) *To solve* $\boldsymbol{A}\boldsymbol{s} = \boldsymbol{b}$ *with* $\alpha \boldsymbol{I} \preceq \boldsymbol{A} \preceq \beta \boldsymbol{I}$, *the conjugate gradient method computes an* $\boldsymbol{s}'$ *that satisfies* $\|\boldsymbol{A}\boldsymbol{s}' - \boldsymbol{b}\|_2 \leq \mu \|\boldsymbol{b}\|_2$ *for* $\mu \in (0, 1)$ *in at most*

$$\min \left\{ n, \frac{1}{2} \ln \left(\frac{4}{\mu} \left(\frac{\beta}{\alpha} \right)^{3/2} \right) \sqrt{\frac{\beta}{\alpha}} \right\} \tag{9.4.26}$$

iterations.

Interested readers may see [She94, RW18] for a proof. In the setting of our problem (9.4.15), we have $\alpha = \varepsilon_H$, $\mu = \frac{1}{2}\varepsilon_H$, and β is bounded by a constant close to L_1. Therefore, the number of iterations, or matrix–vector products, is of the order $O\big(\varepsilon_H^{-1/2} \log(1/\varepsilon_H)\big)$. If we ignore the log factor, the complexity $\tilde{O}\big(\varepsilon_H^{-1/2}\big)$ is the same as that using the Lanczos method for computing the approximate solution to the smallest eigenvalue.

Putting together the respective complexity of the inexact negative curvature descent and inexact Newton descent, the overall computational complexity in terms of the first-order oracle is (up to some log factors[18])

$$k \leq O\big(\varepsilon_g^{-7/4}\big),$$

and the scheme guarantees to converge to a point $\boldsymbol{x}_\star$ that satisfies

$$\|\nabla f(\boldsymbol{x}_\star)\|_2 \leq O(\varepsilon^{2/3}), \quad -\lambda_{\min}\left(\nabla^2 f(\boldsymbol{x}_\star)\right) \leq O(\varepsilon^{1/3}). \tag{9.4.27}$$

[18] Such as $\log(n)$ in the Lanczos method or $\log(1/\varepsilon_H)$ in the conjugate gradient.

Compared to the vanilla gradient descent scheme introduced in Section 9.1.1, the above method not only has lower complexity in terms of first-order oracle, $O\left(\varepsilon_g^{-7/4}\right)$ versus $O\left(\varepsilon_g^{-2}\right)$, but also converges to a second-order stationary point.

9.5 Gradient Descent with Small Random Noise

As we have mentioned before, when the dimension is very large, it can be very costly to compute second-order information. Hence for scalable implementation in practice, one may be restricted to have access only to the gradient information. However, it is well known that, in the worst case, gradient descent alone can be very ineffective for minimizing nonconvex functions. It can be extremely slow to escape saddle points,[19] unless we utilize schemes introduced in Sections 9.3 and 9.4, which explicitly exploit negative curvature computed from evaluating an extra number of gradients.

Historically, to avoid spurious critical points, people have also found that it is beneficial to introduce some *random noise* in the descent process. Conceptually, the random noise allows the algorithm to search a broader local landscape of the objective function and creates a fair chance to escape from unstable critical points,[20] or even to escape local minima (at least asymptotically, as we will soon see).

This section studies the role of random noise in nonconvex optimization and develops gradient descent-type algorithms with convergence guarantees to global (asymptotically) or local minimizers. In other words, we assume the algorithms only have access to *the noisy gradient oracle*:

$$\text{the gradient } \nabla f(\boldsymbol{x}) \text{ and small random noise } \boldsymbol{n}.$$

We will reveal that gradient descent with random noise is actually *implicitly* computing the second-order information and exploiting the direction of negative curvature to achieve adequate local descent. In particular, for converging to second-order stationary points, the best achievable complexity (in the first-order oracle) is, not surprisingly, the same as the best methods introduced in the previous section.

9.5.1 Diffusion Process and Laplace's Method

To understand the role of random noise, it is clearest to examine the continuous dynamics of the state $\boldsymbol{x}$ under the gradient flow with random noise (e.g., see [Sas83]). Given a nonconvex function $f(\boldsymbol{x})$, consider the following dynamics with noisy gradient flow:

$$\dot{\boldsymbol{x}}(t) = -\frac{1}{2}\nabla f(\boldsymbol{x}(t)) + \sqrt{\lambda}\boldsymbol{n}(t), \tag{9.5.1}$$

[19] Even when the saddle points are not so flat or are nondegenerate [DJL$^+$17].

[20] As we have seen in the power iteration and Lanczos method in Section 9.3.2, random initialization also helps avoid certain (zero-measure) pathological cases with high probability.

where $\lambda > 0$ and $\boldsymbol{n} \in \mathbb{R}^n$ is a white noise process. This is also known as the *diffusion process*, or continuous-time *Langevin dynamics*. It is known from stochastic processes that, given the derivative $\nabla f(\boldsymbol{x})$ grows rapidly enough as $\|\boldsymbol{x}\| \to \infty$,[21] then the probability density of this diffusion process of the state $\boldsymbol{x}$ converges exponentially to a stationary distribution, known as the *Gibbs measure* [PSV77]:

$$p^{\lambda}(\boldsymbol{x}) = C^{\lambda} \exp\left(-\frac{1}{\lambda} f(\boldsymbol{x})\right), \tag{9.5.2}$$

where $C^{\lambda} > 0$ is a normalizing factor such that $\int_{\boldsymbol{x}} p^{\lambda}(\boldsymbol{x}) d\boldsymbol{x} = 1$. We are interested in what the density $p^{\lambda}(\boldsymbol{x})$ converges to, as the variance of the noise λ goes from small to zero.

The Most Basic Case

To this end, we recall a well-known result from calculus:

LEMMA 9.12. (Laplace's method: scalar case) *Suppose $f(x)$ is a twice continuously differentiable function with a unique maximizer x_0 and $f''(x_0) < 0$. Then we have*

$$\lim_{\lambda \to 0} \int e^{(1/\lambda) f(x)} dx = e^{(1/\lambda) f(x_0)} \sqrt{\frac{2\pi\lambda}{-f''(x_0)}} \propto \int e^{(1/\lambda) f(x)} \delta(x - x_0) dx. \tag{9.5.3}$$

Proof We here give a sketch of the proof that illustrates the reason why this is expected. We leave a more rigorous derivation and proof for the multivariate case (below) to the reader as exercises.

Since x_0 is a maximizer, we have $f'(x_0) = 0$. So with Taylor expansion, we may approximate the function up to second order:

$$f(x) \approx f(x_0) + \frac{1}{2} f''(x_0)(x - x_0)^2.$$

Then for the integral we have:

$$\begin{aligned} \int e^{(1/\lambda) f(x)} dx &\approx e^{(1/\lambda) f(x_0)} \int e^{(1/2\lambda) f''(x_0)(x - x_0)^2} dx \\ &= e^{(1/\lambda) f(x_0)} \int e^{-(1/2\lambda)|f''(x_0)|(x - x_0)^2} dx. \end{aligned}$$

Notice that the last integral is exactly a Gaussian integral with variance $\sigma^2 = \lambda / |f''(x_0))$ hence its value is $\sqrt{2\pi\lambda / |f''(x_0)|}$. So we have

$$\int e^{(1/\lambda) f(x)} dx \approx e^{(1/\lambda) f(x_0)} \sqrt{\frac{2\pi\lambda}{-f''(x_0)}}.$$

As $\lambda \to 0$ the approximation becomes exact in the sense that the ratio between the two sides approaches 1. □

[21] For instance, it suffices for the function $f(\boldsymbol{x})$ to grow quadratically as $\|\boldsymbol{x}\| \to \infty$.

Based on this lemma, when λ becomes small, the integral on the left-hand side is well approximated by a point-mass distribution at the global maximizer x_0, and it has nothing to do with any other values (including local maximizers) of $f(x)$.

Multiple Global Optima

As we have seen in Chapter 7, due to discrete symmetry, the objective functions we try to optimize often have multiple global optima, associated with the elements of the symmetry group (see Figure 7.3). It is easy to generalize the above lemma to this case. Suppose $f(x)$ has multiple global maximizers $x_1, \dots, x_N \in \mathbb{R}$. We then have

$$\lim_{\lambda \to 0} \int e^{(1/\lambda) f(x)} dx = \sum_{i=1}^{N} e^{(1/\lambda) f(x_i)} \sqrt{\frac{2\pi\lambda}{-f''(x_i)}}. \tag{9.5.4}$$

We leave the proof as an exercise for the reader; see Exercise 9.6. Notice that the integral above is very similar in style to

$$\int_{\boldsymbol{x}} p^{\lambda}(\boldsymbol{x}) d\boldsymbol{x} \propto \int_{\boldsymbol{x}} \exp\left(-\frac{1}{\lambda} f(\boldsymbol{x})\right) d\boldsymbol{x}$$

as $\lambda \downarrow 0$, except that $-f(\boldsymbol{x})$ here is a multivariate function with possibly multiple global maximizers at $\boldsymbol{x}_\star^1, \dots, \boldsymbol{x}_\star^N$, corresponding to the multiple global minimizers of $f(\boldsymbol{x})$. Then one can show that, in this case, we have the following statement that generalizes the above lemma:

THEOREM 9.13. (Laplace method: multivariate and multiple global minimizers) *Let $f(\boldsymbol{x})$ be a function with at least quadratic growth as $\boldsymbol{x} \to \infty$. Suppose $f(\boldsymbol{x})$ has multiple global minimizers at $\boldsymbol{x}_\star^1, \dots, \boldsymbol{x}_\star^N$ and they are all nondegenerate. Then in the limit $\lambda \downarrow 0$, the density $p^{\lambda}(\boldsymbol{x})$ of the noisy gradient descent dynamics* (9.5.1) *converges to*

$$p^0(\boldsymbol{x}) = \frac{\sum_{i=1}^N a_i \delta(\boldsymbol{x} - \boldsymbol{x}_\star^i)}{\sum_{i=1}^N a_i}, \quad \textit{with} \quad a_i = \det[\boldsymbol{H}(\boldsymbol{x}_\star^i)]^{-1/2}, \tag{9.5.5}$$

where $\boldsymbol{H}(\boldsymbol{x}) = \nabla^2 f(\boldsymbol{x})$ is the Hessian of the function $f(\boldsymbol{x})$.

A Continuous Family of Global Optima

As we have seen in Chapter 7, sometimes a nonconvex function $f(\boldsymbol{x})$ may have a continuous family of global minimizers, say due to rotational symmetry (see Figure 7.3). The above theorem also generalizes naturally to this case. Let us assume that the set of all minimizers makes a continuous submanifold $\mathcal{M}$, and the Hessian of the function is nondegenerate along the directions orthogonal to the submanifold.[22] For simplicity, we still use $\boldsymbol{H}(\boldsymbol{x})$ to denote the Hessian restricted to the orthogonal directions to the submanifold (tangent space) at any global minimizer $\boldsymbol{x} \in \mathcal{M}$. In this case, the Gibbs distribution $p^{\lambda}(\boldsymbol{x})$ converges to a density on $\mathcal{M}$ given by

[22] Such a function is called a Morse–Bott function in differential geometry.

$$p^0(\boldsymbol{x}) = \frac{\det[\boldsymbol{H}(\boldsymbol{x})]^{-1/2}}{\int_{\mathcal{M}} \det[\boldsymbol{H}(\boldsymbol{y})]^{-1/2} d\boldsymbol{y}}, \quad \boldsymbol{x} \in \mathcal{M}, \tag{9.5.6}$$

and $d\boldsymbol{y}$ is the naturally induced metric on $\mathcal{M}$.

A simple proof of Theorem 9.13 for the multivariate case, or the case with multiple global minimizers, or the case with a family of global minimizers, can be found in [Sas83], which is very much in the same spirit as Lemma 9.12 for the scalar case. Only here the second-order derivative is naturally replaced by the determinant of the Hessian. We leave the details to the reader as an exercise; see Exercise 9.6.

The above theorem states an interesting fact: under the noisy gradient flow (9.5.1), as the noise variance λ is gradually reduced to nearly zero, the density of the state converges to a point-mass distribution with support only on the global minimizers of the function $f(\boldsymbol{x})$. Historically, the above phenomenon has motivated optimization methods that leverage random noise for nonconvex optimization, including the well-known *simulated annealing* [KGV83].

Although the above theorem reveals a nice qualitative behavior of noisy gradient descent, it *by no means* suggests that this behavior can be exploited effectively and efficiently for optimization. In fact, in order for the diffusion process to converge to the density with support on the global minimizers, the noise variance λ needs to be reduced to zero *exponentially slowly* in time t [GH86, CHS87]:

$$\lambda = \frac{c}{\log t} \quad \text{for large } t \text{ and } c > 0.$$

9.5.2 Noisy Gradient with Langevin Monte Carlo

Inspired by properties of the above diffusion process, to minimize a function $f(\boldsymbol{x})$, one may consider a discrete approximation to the noisy gradient flow (9.5.1). The resulting discrete process is known as *Langevin Monte Carlo*:

$$\boldsymbol{x}_{k+1} = \boldsymbol{x}_k - \alpha \nabla f(\boldsymbol{x}_k) + \sqrt{2\alpha\lambda}\,\boldsymbol{n}_k, \tag{9.5.7}$$

where $\boldsymbol{n}_k \sim \mathcal{N}(0, \boldsymbol{I})$ is i.i.d. Gaussian noise and $\alpha > 0$ is a step size (correlated with the noise level). It can be shown that if the discretization is done properly, the above discrete Langevin process can asymptotically converge to the same Gibbs stationary distribution as in the continuous case mentioned above [RT96].[23] Algorithms based on the above discrete stochastic process for optimization have been long proposed and studied in the literature of stochastic control and optimization [Kus87, GM90]. Below we try to illustrate the fundamental rationale behind such schemes through analysis of the most basic cases.

[23] A few words of caution though: the relationship between the continuous diffusion (9.5.1) and the discrete approximation (9.5.7) can be subtle. Even if the original diffusion converges, naive discretizations need not do so. Or even if the original diffusion converges exponentially quickly to its stationary distribution, discretized versions need not converge exponentially fast. For details of proper discretizing of the Langevin dynamics, one may refer to [RT96].

To simplify the analysis, as in the previous section, we assume again that $f : \mathbb{R}^n \to \mathbb{R}$ is nonconvex, and is twice continuously differentiable, with Lipschitz continuous gradient $\nabla f(\boldsymbol{x}) \in \mathbb{R}^n$ with Lipschitz constant L_1. Notice that if we choose the step size to be the Lipschitz constant $\alpha = 1/L_1$, then the above scheme becomes

$$\boldsymbol{x}_{k+1} = \boldsymbol{x}_k - \frac{1}{L_1}\nabla f(\boldsymbol{x}_k) + \sqrt{2\lambda/L_1}\boldsymbol{n}_k. \tag{9.5.8}$$

Now let us consider a similar setting as in the negative curvature descent scheme studied in Theorem 9.5, with a prescribed precision $\varepsilon > 0$.[24] Then we have the following statement regarding the above noisy gradient descent scheme:

PROPOSITION 9.14. (Noisy gradient descent) *Considering the above noisy gradient descent scheme* (9.5.8), *if* $\|\nabla f(\boldsymbol{x}_k)\|_2 \geq (2L_1\varepsilon)^{1/2}$, *then we have*

$$\mathbb{E}[f(\boldsymbol{x}_{k+1}) \mid \boldsymbol{x}_k] \leq f(\boldsymbol{x}_k) - \varepsilon + \lambda. \tag{9.5.9}$$

Proof From the Lipschitz condition, we have

$$f(\boldsymbol{x}_{k+1}) \leq f(\boldsymbol{x}_k) + \langle \nabla f(\boldsymbol{x}_k), \boldsymbol{x}_{k+1} - \boldsymbol{x}_k\rangle + \frac{L_1}{2}\|\boldsymbol{x}_{k+1} - \boldsymbol{x}_k\|_2^2.$$

Also from the iteration (9.5.8), we have $\boldsymbol{x}_{k+1} - \boldsymbol{x}_k = -(1/L_1)\nabla f(\boldsymbol{x}_k) + \sqrt{2\lambda/L_1}\boldsymbol{n}_k$. So we have

$$\begin{aligned} f(\boldsymbol{x}_{k+1}) \leq f(\boldsymbol{x}_k) &+ \left\langle \nabla f(\boldsymbol{x}_k), -\frac{1}{L_1}\nabla f(\boldsymbol{x}_k) + \sqrt{2\lambda/L_1}\boldsymbol{n}_k \right\rangle \\ &+ \frac{L_1}{2}\left\| \frac{1}{L_1}\nabla f(\boldsymbol{x}_k) - \sqrt{2\lambda/L_1}\boldsymbol{n}_k \right\|_2^2. \end{aligned}$$

Taking the conditional expectation on both sides, we have

$$\begin{aligned} \mathbb{E}[f(\boldsymbol{x}_{k+1}) \mid \boldsymbol{x}_k] &\leq f(\boldsymbol{x}_k) - \frac{1}{L_1}\|\nabla f(\boldsymbol{x}_k)\|_2^2 + \frac{1}{2L_1}\|\nabla f(\boldsymbol{x}_k)\|_2^2 + \lambda \\ &= f(\boldsymbol{x}_k) - \frac{1}{2L_1}\|\nabla f(\boldsymbol{x}_k)\|_2^2 + \lambda \\ &\leq f(\boldsymbol{x}_k) - \varepsilon + \lambda. \end{aligned}$$

□

This proposition reveals a simple and important relationship between the optimization precision ε and the noise variance λ. It has several implications. On the one hand, it ensures that as long as the gradient is strictly over the threshold $\|\nabla f(\boldsymbol{x}_k)\|_2 > (2L_1\lambda)^{1/2}$, the noisy gradient descent scheme reduces the expected function value per iteration. Or equivalently, as long as we choose the noise level adaptively according to

$$\lambda_k < \frac{1}{2L_1}\|\nabla f(\boldsymbol{x}_k)\|_2^2,$$

the scheme is expected to be descending always. On the other hand, if one uses a fixed noise variance $\lambda > 0$, then whenever the iterates approach a critical point with gradient dropping below the threshold

[24] That is, we desire to eventually achieve $|f(\boldsymbol{x}_{k+1}) - f(\boldsymbol{x}_k)| \leq \varepsilon$.

$$\|\nabla f(\boldsymbol{x}_k)\|_2 < (2L_1\lambda)^{1/2},$$

the random effect starts to take over and to explore if the critical point is stable. This mechanism allows the noisy descent algorithm to escape from unstable critical points such as saddle points, as we will elucidate further below.

9.5.3 Negative Curvature Descent with Random Noise

Despite the asymptotic consistency, there is *no theoretical guarantee* that the Langevin Monte Carlo process (9.5.7) is able to find the global minimum of a general nonconvex function *in polynomial time*. In fact, according to [BEGK11], it takes the Langevin diffusion at least $e^{\Omega(h/\lambda)}$ time to escape any local minima of height $h > 0$. This implies that for functions that contain deep local minima, it is unavoidable for noisy gradient descent to take an *exponentially long* time to escape before finding global ones. Hence, contrary to our earlier hope, it is actually computationally intractable to use this method (alone) to find global minima of general nonconvex functions!

Dynamics of Noisy Gradient Descent around a Strict Saddle Point

It seems that noise is no magical sauce and there is *no free lunch* at all when it comes to solving general nonconvex optimization problems. Then what can noisy gradient descent methods actually end up helping with in practice with nonconvex optimization? As it turns out, random noise helps gradient descent to escape nonstationary critical points, such as saddle points, efficiently.[25] As we have seen in the negative curvature descent methods, any nondegenerate saddle point has a direction with strict negative curvature. Intuitively such a point is very "unstable" (as shown in Figure 7.2), and any random perturbation would drive the state away from it. The only question is how quickly this may take place, say under the noisy gradient descent scheme.

To see this, notice that without loss of generality, we may consider dynamics of the noisy gradient descent around the critical point $\boldsymbol{x} = \boldsymbol{0}$ of the standard quadratic function[26]

$$f(\boldsymbol{x}) = \frac{1}{2}\boldsymbol{x}^*\boldsymbol{H}\boldsymbol{x}$$

for a constant $\boldsymbol{H} \in \mathbb{R}^{n\times n}$, with the smallest eigenvalue $\lambda_{\min} < 0$, and the Lipschitz constant $L_1 = \max_i |\lambda_i(\boldsymbol{H})|$.

PROPOSITION 9.15. (Escaping saddle point via noisy gradient descent) *Consider the noisy gradient descent via the Langevin dynamics* (9.5.8) *for the function* $f(\boldsymbol{x}) = \frac{1}{2}\boldsymbol{x}^*\boldsymbol{H}\boldsymbol{x}$, *starting from* $\boldsymbol{x}_0 \sim \mathcal{N}(\boldsymbol{0}, \sigma^2\boldsymbol{I})$. *Then after*

[25] Hence, this ensures that the process converges at least to local minima, in *polynomial time* [ZLC17].

[26] Since we only care about local behaviors, any nonconvex function is diffeomorphic to this standard form around a nondegenerate critical point $\boldsymbol{x}_\star$ with Hessian $\boldsymbol{H}(\boldsymbol{x}_\star)$.

$$k \geq \frac{\log n - \log(|\lambda_{\min}|/L_1)}{2\log(1 + |\lambda_{\min}|/L_1)} \tag{9.5.10}$$

steps, we have

$$\mathbb{E}[f(\boldsymbol{x}_{k+1}) - f(\boldsymbol{x}_0)] \leq -\lambda. \tag{9.5.11}$$

Proof Notice that for this function, the Lipschitz constant for the gradient L_1 is exactly the spectral norm of the Hessian $\boldsymbol{H}$. So the Langevin dynamics (9.5.8) becomes

$$\begin{aligned}\boldsymbol{x}_{k+1} &= \boldsymbol{x}_k - \frac{1}{L_1}\nabla f(\boldsymbol{x}_k) + \sqrt{2\lambda/L_1}\boldsymbol{n}_k\\ &= (\boldsymbol{I} - L_1^{-1}\boldsymbol{H})\boldsymbol{x}_k + \sqrt{2\lambda/L_1}\boldsymbol{n}_k.\end{aligned}$$

Notice that the matrix $\boldsymbol{A} \doteq \boldsymbol{I} - L_1^{-1}\boldsymbol{H}$ has eigenvalues outside of the unit circle if and only if the Hessian has a negative eigenvalue $\lambda_{\min} < 0$:

$$\lambda_{\max}(\boldsymbol{A}) = 1 - \frac{\lambda_{\min}(\boldsymbol{H})}{L_1} > 1.$$

This defines *an unstable linear dynamic system* with random noise as the input:

$$\boldsymbol{x}_{k+1} = \boldsymbol{A}\boldsymbol{x}_k + b\,\boldsymbol{n}_k, \tag{9.5.12}$$

with $b \doteq \sqrt{2\lambda/L_1}$. Therefore we have

$$\boldsymbol{x}_{k+1} = \boldsymbol{A}^{k+1}\boldsymbol{x}_0 + b\sum_{i=0}^{k}\boldsymbol{A}^{k-i}\boldsymbol{n}_i. \tag{9.5.13}$$

Notice that all the terms $\boldsymbol{A}^{k+1}\boldsymbol{x}_0$ and $\boldsymbol{A}^{k-i}\boldsymbol{n}_i$ on the right-hand side are nothing but powers of the matrix $\boldsymbol{A}$ applied to a (random) vector.

From *the power iteration method* that we have seen in Section 9.3.2, as the power increases, each of these terms converges to the eigenvector of the largest eigenvalue of $\boldsymbol{A}$,[27] or equivalently the eigenvector of the smallest (negative) eigenvalue of $\boldsymbol{H}$. That is exactly the direction of the most negative curvature of $f(\boldsymbol{x})$ that we have computed before in Section 9.3.2. Hence when the gradient is small, the noisy gradient descent implicitly performs negative curvature descent, exactly in the same spirit as the gradient and negative curvature descent algorithm in Figure 9.2.

Now we only have to turn the state evolution (9.5.13) to a bound for the descent of the expected value of the function $f(\boldsymbol{x})$. Let $\{\lambda_j\}_{j=1}^n$ be the n eigenvalues of the Hessian $\boldsymbol{H}$, sorted from the largest to the smallest. Notice that $\boldsymbol{A}$ and $\boldsymbol{H}$ share the same eigenvectors and can be diagonalized by the same orthogonal transform; the corresponding eigenvalues of $\boldsymbol{A}$ are $\{1 - \lambda_j/L_1\}_{j=1}^n$. Since $\boldsymbol{x}_0$ and $\boldsymbol{n}_k$ are all independent zero-mean random variables, we have

[27] We will also characterize the geometry of the landscape of the objective function for power iteration more precisely in Section 9.6.

$$
\begin{aligned}
&\mathbb{E}[f(\boldsymbol{x}_{k+1}) - f(\boldsymbol{x}_0)] \\
&= \mathbb{E}\left[\frac{1}{2}\boldsymbol{x}_{k+1}^* \boldsymbol{H}\boldsymbol{x}_{k+1} - \frac{1}{2}\boldsymbol{x}_0^* \boldsymbol{H}\boldsymbol{x}_0\right] \\
&= \frac{1}{2}\sigma^2 \text{trace}\left(\boldsymbol{A}^{2(k+1)}\boldsymbol{H}\right) + \frac{1}{2}b^2 \sum_{i=0}^{k} \text{trace}\left(\boldsymbol{A}^{2(k-i)}\boldsymbol{H}\right) - \frac{1}{2}\sigma^2 \text{trace}(\boldsymbol{H}).
\end{aligned}
$$

For the first and third terms related to the initial condition $\boldsymbol{x}_0$, we have

$$
\begin{aligned}
&\frac{1}{2}\sigma^2 \text{trace}\left(\boldsymbol{A}^{2(k+1)}\boldsymbol{H}\right) - \frac{1}{2}\sigma^2 \text{trace}(\boldsymbol{H}) \\
&= \frac{1}{2}\sigma^2 \sum_{j=1}^{n} \left[\left(1 - \frac{\lambda_j}{L_1}\right)^{2(k+1)} \lambda_j - \lambda_j\right] \leq 0
\end{aligned}
$$

because $1 - \lambda_j/L_1$ is smaller than 1 when λ_j is positive and larger than 1 when λ_j is negative. So without the random noise, the deterministic part of the system $\boldsymbol{x}_{k+1} = \boldsymbol{A}\boldsymbol{x}_k$ always leads to descending in the objective value regardless of the initial condition!

So we have

$$
\begin{aligned}
\mathbb{E}[f(\boldsymbol{x}_{k+1}) - f(\boldsymbol{x}_0)] &\leq \frac{1}{2}b^2 \sum_{i=0}^{k} \text{trace}\left(\boldsymbol{A}^{2(k-i)}\boldsymbol{H}\right) \\
&= \frac{1}{2}b^2 \sum_{j=1}^{n} \left(\sum_{i=0}^{k} \left(1 - \frac{\lambda_j}{L_1}\right)^{2(k-i)} \lambda_j\right).
\end{aligned}
$$

Notice that we have

$$
\begin{aligned}
&\sum_{i=0}^{k} \left(1 - \frac{\lambda_j}{L_1}\right)^{2(k-i)} \lambda_j \leq L_1, \quad \text{when } \lambda_j > 0, \\
&\sum_{i=0}^{k} \left(1 - \frac{\lambda_j}{L_1}\right)^{2(k-i)} \lambda_j < 0, \quad \text{when } \lambda_j < 0.
\end{aligned}
$$

There are at most $n - 1$ positive eigenvalues. Since $b = \sqrt{2\lambda/L_1}$, we have

$$
\begin{aligned}
\mathbb{E}[f(\boldsymbol{x}_{k+1}) - f(\boldsymbol{x}_0)] &\leq \frac{1}{2}b^2 \left((n-1)L_1 + \lambda_{\min} \sum_{i=0}^{k} \left(1 - \frac{\lambda_{\min}}{L_1}\right)^{2i}\right) \\
&\leq \lambda \left((n-1) + \frac{\lambda_{\min}}{L_1}\left(1 - \frac{\lambda_{\min}}{L_1}\right)^{2k}\right).
\end{aligned}
$$

To have

$$
\frac{\lambda_{\min}}{L_1}\left(1 - \frac{\lambda_{\min}}{L_1}\right)^{2k} \leq -n,
$$

we only need to choose

$$k \geq \frac{\log n - \log(|\lambda_{\min}|/L_1)}{2\log(1 + |\lambda_{\min}|/L_1)}. \tag{9.5.14}$$

With this choice of number of noisy descent iterations around the saddle point, we have

$$\mathbb{E}[f(\boldsymbol{x}_{k+1}) - f(\boldsymbol{x}_0)] \leq -\lambda. \tag{9.5.15}$$

□

In fact, one can see from the above expression for k that the number of iterations needed increases when the ratio $\kappa = L_1/|\lambda_{\min}|$ is large. In this case $\log(1 + |\lambda_{\min}|/L_1) \approx |\lambda_{\min}|/L_1 = \kappa^{-1}$. So from (9.5.14), the number of noisy gradient steps required to achieve the desired descent λ is simplified to:

$$k \geq \frac{\kappa}{2}\log(n).$$

Stopping Criteria

Notice that the above lower bound for the number of noisy descent steps k is monotonic in $|\lambda_{\min}| = -\lambda_{\min}$: the smaller is $|\lambda_{\min}|$, the larger k needs to be. Then without computing and knowing the smallest eigenvalue $\lambda_{\min}$ of the Hessian $\boldsymbol{H}$, *how do we know what k to use and when should we stop, once the curvature becomes nearly nonnegative?* Answers to these questions can be tricky if we do not resort to any explicit process to estimate $\lambda_{\min}$.

From the proof of the above Proposition 9.15, the noisy gradient descent essentially conducts negative curvature descent implicitly through power iteration on noise. If we choose the noise variance λ in the noisy gradient descent to be the same as the prescribed precision ε for the function value (as in Section 9.3.2),

$$\lambda = \varepsilon,$$

then k noisy gradient descent iterations are equivalent to one step of deterministic negative curvature descent (as characterized by Theorem 9.5).

Following the same line of arguments in Theorem 9.5, as long as we have

$$-\lambda_{\min}(\boldsymbol{H}) \geq \varepsilon_H = \left(1.5L_2^2\varepsilon\right)^{1/3},$$

we should expect to achieve a descent amount of $\lambda = \varepsilon$. So using $\varepsilon_H = \left(1.5L_2^2\varepsilon\right)^{1/3}$ as a lower bound[28] for $|\lambda_{\min}|$, we get an estimate of the number of noisy gradient descents needed:

$$k_{\max} \geq \frac{\log n - \log\left(L_1^{-1}\left(1.5L_2^2\varepsilon\right)^{1/3}\right)}{2\log\left(1 + L_1^{-1}\left(1.5L_2^2\varepsilon\right)^{1/3}\right)}. \tag{9.5.16}$$

[28] Notice that for the standard quadratic function $f(\boldsymbol{x}) = \frac{1}{2}\boldsymbol{x}^*\boldsymbol{H}\boldsymbol{x}$, the Lipschitz constant L_2 can be as small as zero. However, for a general function, L_2 can be nonzero and we can choose any nonzero upper bound for this constant.

Hence, if, after $k_{\max}$ noisy gradient descents, the function value drops to less than ε, that indicates the minimum eigenvalue should have reached the desired threshold,

$$-\lambda_{\min}(\boldsymbol{H}) \leq \varepsilon_H = \left(1.5L_2^2\varepsilon\right)^{1/3}, \tag{9.5.17}$$

and the critical point reached is an approximate second-order stationary point.

Hybrid Noisy Gradient Descent

As we have seen from the analysis in Section 9.5.2 and Section 9.5.3, when the gradient is large, it is not so helpful to add noise. Only when the gradient is small enough and we are near a strict saddle point does adding small random noise help escape from it – but with a price about $O(\kappa \log n)$ noisy gradient steps to reach the same amount of descent. So to make the algorithm more efficient, we may modify the basic noisy gradient scheme with a hybrid scheme illustrated in Figure 9.5, in which we choose different descent strategies based on the local landscape. One should

Hybrid Noisy Gradient Descent

Problem Class:

$$\min_{\boldsymbol{x}} f(\boldsymbol{x}), \quad \boldsymbol{x} \in \mathbb{R}^n,$$

where $f : \mathbb{R}^n \to \mathbb{R}$ is nonconvex, and is twice continuously differentiable, with Lipschitz continuous gradient and Hessian with constants L_1 and L_2, respectively. Have access to the oracle: gradient $\nabla f(\boldsymbol{x})$ and random noise $\boldsymbol{n}$.

Setup: given a prescribed accuracy $\varepsilon > 0$, $\varepsilon_g = (2L_1\varepsilon)^{1/2}$ and $\varepsilon_H = \left(1.5L_2^2\varepsilon\right)^{1/3}$.

Initialization: Set $\boldsymbol{x}_0 \in \mathbb{R}^n$.

For $k = 0, 1, 2, \ldots$

1 Compute the gradient $\nabla f(\boldsymbol{x}_k)$.
2 **if** $\|\nabla f(\boldsymbol{x}_k)\|_2 \geq \varepsilon_g$, **then** gradient descent:

$$\boldsymbol{x}_{k+1} = \boldsymbol{x}_k - \frac{1}{L_1}\nabla f(\boldsymbol{x}_k);$$

3 **else** $\boldsymbol{x}_k^0 = \boldsymbol{x}_k$, and negative curvature descent with noisy gradients:
for $i = 0, 1, 2, \ldots, k_{\max}$ as in (9.5.10)

$$\boldsymbol{x}_k^{i+1} = \boldsymbol{x}_k^i - \frac{1}{L_1}\nabla f(\boldsymbol{x}_k^i) + \sqrt{2\varepsilon/L_1}\,\boldsymbol{n}^i,$$

where $\boldsymbol{n}^i \sim \mathcal{N}(0, \boldsymbol{I})$.
end for and set $\boldsymbol{x}_{k+1} = \boldsymbol{x}_k^{i+1}$.

End for when $|f(\boldsymbol{x}_{k+1}) - f(\boldsymbol{x}_k)| \leq \varepsilon$ and return $\boldsymbol{x}_\star = \boldsymbol{x}_k$.

Convergence guarantee: $\|\nabla f(\boldsymbol{x}_\star)\| \leq \varepsilon_g, \; -\lambda_{\min}(\nabla^2 f(\boldsymbol{x}_\star)) \leq \varepsilon_H$.

Figure 9.5 An overview of the hybrid noisy gradient descent method.

notice that this scheme is very similar to the hybrid gradient and negative curvature descent scheme in Figure 9.2. The only difference is that here we replace the negative curvature descent step with a sequence of $O(\kappa \log n)$ random gradient descent steps.

Optimize Overall Complexity

As we have discussed above, around a critical point, to achieve the same amount of descent, say ε, by exploiting negative curvature using noisy gradient descent, it requires evaluating a number $k_{\max}$ of gradients. If we use gradients as the oracle to evaluate overall complexity, the cost of the negative curvature step in the above algorithm will be more than the gradient step. From the analysis above, if we require $\lambda_{\min} \geq -O(\varepsilon^{1/3})$, to achieve ε amount of descent, we need $k_{\max} = O(\varepsilon^{-1/3}\log(n))$. Hence on average, the function value decrease per gradient evaluation is in the order of $O(\varepsilon^{-4/3}\log(n))$. So to guarantee $\|\nabla f(\boldsymbol{x})\| \leq \varepsilon_g = O(\varepsilon^{1/2})$, we need (up to a $\log(n)$ factor) $O(\varepsilon_g^{-8/3})$ number of gradients, which is actually worse than the rate $O(\varepsilon_g^{-2})$ of the gradient descent given in Proposition 9.1.

Since the negative curvature descent is much more costly, we may relax our requirements on the accuracy in the smallest eigenvalue, say from $-\lambda_{\min} \leq \varepsilon_H = O(\varepsilon^{1/3})$ to

$$-\lambda_{\min} \leq \varepsilon_H = O(\varepsilon^{1/4})$$

instead. Then the number of noisy gradient descent becomes

$$k_{\max} = O(\varepsilon^{-1/4}\log(n))$$

and the function value decreases by $O(\varepsilon^{3/4})$. On average, up to a $\log(n)$ factor, the function value decrease per gradient evaluation is $O(\varepsilon)$, the same as a gradient descent step. So to guarantee $\|\nabla f(\boldsymbol{x})\| \leq \varepsilon_g$, the number of total gradient evaluations needed is $O(\varepsilon_g^{-2})$, up to a $\log(n)$ factor.

9.5.4 Complexity of Perturbed Gradient Descent

In the above hybrid descent scheme, for simplicity and clarity of analysis, we have separated the normal gradient descent and noisy gradient descent around critical points. The hybrid scheme achieves a complexity of $O(\varepsilon_g^{-2})$. As we have seen in the previous section, the best complexity we are able to achieve is $O(\varepsilon_g^{-7/4})$. A remaining question is whether it is possible to achieve this rate with a noisy gradient descent scheme.

As we have mentioned before, the simple gradient descent is not the most efficient way to decrease the function value. The Newton descent introduced in Section 9.4.1 is precisely aimed at improving its efficiency. Nevertheless, it requires accessing or approximating the direction of negative curvature. For algorithmic simplicity, one may prefer only to conduct the (noisy) gradient descent. What else can we do to improve the efficiency of (noisy) gradient descent without explicitly computing the second-order information?

Perturbed Accelerated Gradient Descent

Problem Class:

$$\min_{\boldsymbol{x}} f(\boldsymbol{x}), \quad \boldsymbol{x} \in \mathbb{R}^n,$$

where $f : \mathbb{R}^n \to \mathbb{R}$ is nonconvex, and is twice continuously differentiable, with Lipschitz continuous gradient and Hessian with constants L_1 and L_2, respectively. Have access to the oracle: gradient $\nabla f(\boldsymbol{x})$ and random noise $\boldsymbol{n}$.

Setup: given properly chosen parameters $\varepsilon_g, \varepsilon_H, \sigma, s$, and $k_{\min}$.

Initialization: Set the state $\boldsymbol{x}_0 \in \mathbb{R}^n$ and momentum $\boldsymbol{v}_0 = \boldsymbol{0}$.

For $k = 0, 1, 2, \ldots$

1 Compute the gradient $\nabla f(\boldsymbol{x}_k)$.

2 **If** $\|\nabla f(\boldsymbol{x}_k)\|_2 \le \varepsilon_g$ and there is no random perturbation in last $k_{\min}$ steps, **then** randomly perturb the current iterate:

$$\boldsymbol{x}_k \leftarrow \boldsymbol{x}_k + \boldsymbol{n}_k, \quad \boldsymbol{n}_k \sim \mathcal{N}(0, \sigma \boldsymbol{I}).$$

3 Conduct accelerated gradient descent:

$$\begin{cases} \boldsymbol{p}_{k+1} = \boldsymbol{x}_k + \beta \boldsymbol{v}_k, \\ \boldsymbol{x}_{k+1} = \boldsymbol{p}_{k+1} - \alpha \nabla f(\boldsymbol{p}_{k+1}), \\ \boldsymbol{v}_{k+1} = \boldsymbol{x}_{k+1} - \boldsymbol{x}_k. \end{cases} \tag{9.5.18}$$

4 **If**

$$f(\boldsymbol{x}_k) \le f(\boldsymbol{p}_{k+1}) + \langle \nabla(\boldsymbol{p}_{k+1}), \boldsymbol{x}_k - \boldsymbol{p}_{k+1} \rangle - \frac{\varepsilon_H}{2} \|\boldsymbol{x}_k - \boldsymbol{p}_{k+1}\|_2^2,$$

then use $\boldsymbol{v}_k$ to conduct negative curvature exploitation:

- **if** $\|\boldsymbol{v}_k\|_2 \ge s$ then $\boldsymbol{x}_{k+1} = \boldsymbol{x}_k$;
- **else** $\boldsymbol{x}_{k+1} = \boldsymbol{x}_k + \boldsymbol{\delta}$ with $\boldsymbol{\delta} = \pm s \boldsymbol{v}_k / \|\boldsymbol{v}_k\|$ that minimizes $f(\boldsymbol{x}_k + \boldsymbol{\delta})$;
- **reset** $\boldsymbol{v}_{k+1} = \boldsymbol{0}$.

End for.

Figure 9.6 An overview of the perturbed accelerated gradient descent method.

In fact, we have seen such a scheme in the context of convex optimization: *Nesterov's acceleration* (see Section 8.3 of Chapter 8 or Section D.2 of Appendix D). The same acceleration scheme should also work for the nonconvex case (at least locally). Following this line of thought, a randomly *perturbed accelerated gradient descent* (PAGD) scheme has been proposed by [JNJ18], as illustrated in Figure 9.6.

One remarkably insightful and clever idea of this scheme is to directly leverage the momentum from the acceleration scheme, the vector $\boldsymbol{v}_k$ in step 3 of the PAGD algorithm, as a candidate to exploit the negative curvature. This saves the effort to (approximately) compute the negative curvature direction as we have done in the methods introduced earlier. By combining the random perturbation and the acceleration, careful analysis can show that the resulting scheme indeed achieves the best complexity of $O(\varepsilon_g^{-7/4})$ (saving some log factors) [JNJ18].

The reader should be aware that all the complexity guarantees characterized for all methods so far are for the worst case among a broad family of functions considered.[29] As we have seen in Chapter 7, many of the problems that we encounter in low-dimensional structure recovery are much better than the worst case. Even to the opposite, the functions often have additional benign geometric structures. For instance, the objective functions have nondegenerate saddle points, the functions do not have any spurious local minima in conspicuous configurations [DJL$^+$17], the functions are strongly convex around the minima, etc. Hence, it is often observed in practice that even much simplified vanilla versions of the randomly initialized or perturbed gradient descent can be surprisingly efficient and effective (in escaping strict saddles and converging to minimizers), far more than what is characterized for the worst case.

9.6 Leveraging Symmetry Structure: Generalized Power Iteration

This chapter so far has provided a rather systematic and complete characterization of convergence and complexity of first- (and second-) order methods for a very general class of (unconstrained) nonconvex programs. However, the complexities characterized are typically for the worst case (in a broad class of problems considered). In practice, very often the particular optimization problems we encounter for recovering low-dimensional models have special structures which can be exploited for much better computational efficiency. This clearly has been the case for convex optimization as we have seen in Section 8.6 where methods such as Franke–Wolfe and stochastic gradient descent can be utilized to exploit the structures in the constraints and in the objective function, respectively.

In Chapter 7, we have argued that in processing structured data, nonconvexity often arises due to certain structural symmetries in the problems, and the domain spaces are typically compact manifolds that are invariant under the associated symmetry group actions. Such special manifolds are known as *homogeneous spaces* in differential geometry [Lan01]. They include important cases that we have frequently encountered before: high-dimensional spheres, orthogonal groups, and Stiefel manifolds, etc. The nice global geometric structures of these manifolds make them amenable to *global* analysis and computation. In this section, we illustrate several important instances for which we can go beyond the local gradient-descent-type methods, and exploit more global geometric structures for more efficient optimization algorithms.

9.6.1 Power Iteration for Computing Singular Vectors

Consider the problem of computing the leading singular value vector of a matrix $\boldsymbol{Y}$ that we have seen earlier in Chapter 4:

$$\begin{array}{ll} \min & \varphi(\boldsymbol{q}) \equiv -\frac{1}{2}\boldsymbol{q}^*\boldsymbol{\Gamma}\boldsymbol{q} \\ \text{subject to} & \boldsymbol{q}^*\boldsymbol{q} = 1 \ \ (\text{or } \boldsymbol{q} \in \mathbb{S}^{n-1}), \end{array} \tag{9.6.1}$$

[29] Here functions with Lipschitz gradient and Hessian only have strict saddles.

with $\boldsymbol{\Gamma} = \boldsymbol{Y}\boldsymbol{Y}^*$. As we have shown in Section 4.2.1, when φ is viewed as a function on the sphere, its saddle points are associated with the (ordered) eigenvalues λ_i of $\boldsymbol{\Gamma}$ with $\lambda_i > \lambda_{i+1}$, and we have

$$\varphi(\boldsymbol{q}(\lambda_{i+1})) > \varphi(\boldsymbol{q}(\lambda_i)), \quad \text{for } i = 1, \ldots, n.$$

From the second derivative of the objective function (4.2.9), we see that we always have

$$\mathcal{S}^-[\boldsymbol{q}(\lambda_{i+1})] \supset \mathcal{S}^-[\boldsymbol{q}(\lambda_i)], \quad \text{for } i = 1, \ldots, n,$$

where $\mathcal{S}^-$ indicates the unstable submanifold of a critical point. It suggests that unstable submanifolds of upstream saddle points contain the entire unstable submanifolds of the downstream saddle points. Further analysis shows that the direction towards the global minimum has the most negative curvature among all directions. Therefore, we expect most reasonable methods to converge to a global minimizer. For almost all the problems that we have studied in Chapter 7, the landscape of their objective functions has similar global geometric properties. In addition, the objective functions do not have any spurious local minima in conspicuous configurations. There are both theoretical and experimental reasons to expect standard, randomly initialized, gradient descent to converge to a small neighborhood of a global minimizer, in polynomial time.[30]

In fact, for the singular vector problem, the nice global geometry of the objective function φ may enable even more efficient methods than the vanilla gradient descent. For instance, we know, from the Lagrangian formulation of (9.6.1), that the necessary condition of the critical points of φ gives

$$\nabla\varphi(\boldsymbol{q}) = \boldsymbol{\Gamma}\boldsymbol{q} = \lambda\boldsymbol{q}$$

for some λ (the eigenvalues of the matrix $\boldsymbol{\Gamma}$). Hence any critical point, including the optimal solution, is a "fixed point" in the following equation:

$$\boldsymbol{q} = \mathcal{P}_{\mathbb{S}^{n-1}}(\boldsymbol{\Gamma}\boldsymbol{q}) = \frac{\boldsymbol{\Gamma}\boldsymbol{q}}{\|\boldsymbol{\Gamma}\boldsymbol{q}\|_2}, \tag{9.6.2}$$

where $\mathcal{P}_{\mathbb{S}^{n-1}}$ means projection onto the sphere $\mathbb{S}^{n-1}$. If we view

$$g(\cdot) \doteq \mathcal{P}_{\mathbb{S}^{n-1}}[\boldsymbol{\Gamma}(\cdot)] : \mathbb{S}^{n-1} \to \mathbb{S}^{n-1}$$

as a map from $\mathbb{S}^{n-1}$ to $\mathbb{S}^{n-1}$ itself, the map is actually a contraction mapping. That is,

$$d(g(\boldsymbol{q}), g(\boldsymbol{p})) \le \rho \cdot d(\boldsymbol{q}, \boldsymbol{p})$$

for some $0 < \rho < 1$ and $d(\cdot,\cdot)$ a natural distance on the sphere. It is easy to show that here ρ is bounded from above by the ratio $\rho \le \lambda_2/\lambda_1$ where λ_2 is the second largest eigenvalue of $\boldsymbol{\Gamma}$. This leads to another more popular method to compute the eigenvector, known as the *power iteration method* (as we have seen in Exercise 4.6):

[30] This has been proved for specific problems, including dictionary learning [GBW19] and generalized phase retrieval [CCFM18].

$$q_{k+1} = g(q_k) = \frac{\Gamma q_k}{\|\Gamma q_k\|_2} \in \mathbb{S}^{n-1}. \tag{9.6.3}$$

It can be shown that this iteration is much more efficient than the gradient descent method for solving the singular vector problem (9.6.1).[31] The rate of convergence of the iteration is typically *linear*: If $q_\star$ is a fixed point $q_\star = g(q_\star)$, we always have

$$d(q_\star, q_k) \le \rho^k \cdot d(q_\star, q_0).$$

That is, the error decreases geometrically according to the kth power of ρ, hence the name of the method.

9.6.2 Complete Dictionary Learning

In Chapter 7, we have introduced and studied *dictionary learning* as an important example of structured nonconvex problems. Now, consider solving a special case of dictionary learning where the dictionary is complete (i.e., square and invertible). Without loss of generality, we assume the dictionary is orthogonal[32] and we solve the problem via maximizing the ℓ^4 norm: given a data matrix $Y = D_o X_o$ where D_o is orthogonal and X_o is sparse, we try to recover the dictionary from solving the following optimization problem:

$$\begin{array}{ll} \min & \psi(A) \equiv -\frac{1}{4}\|AY\|_4^4 \\ \text{subject to} & A^*A = I \ \ (\text{or } A \in \mathsf{O}(n)). \end{array} \tag{9.6.4}$$

Notice that this is very similar in style to the singular vector problem (9.6.1). Unfortunately, a careful study would show that, unlike the singular vector problem, here ψ is in general *not* a Morse function on $\mathsf{O}(n)$.[33] Hence there is no guarantee that the gradient-flow-type algorithms would be efficient for solving this problem.

But what about the fixed-point approach then? Let us consider the Lagrangian:

$$\mathcal{L}(A, \Lambda) \doteq -\frac{1}{4}\|AY\|_4^4 + \langle \Lambda, A^*A - I \rangle. \tag{9.6.5}$$

This gives the necessary condition $\nabla_A \mathcal{L}(A, \Lambda) = \mathbf{0}$:

$$-\nabla_A \psi(A) = (AY)^{\circ 3} Y^* = AS, \tag{9.6.6}$$

for a symmetric matrix $S = (\Lambda + \Lambda^*)$ (of Lagrange multipliers). Here $(AY)^{\circ 3}$ represents the element-wise cube of the matrix AY. Notice that if A is an orthogonal matrix and S is symmetric, then the projection of AS onto the orthogonal group $\mathsf{O}(n)$ is

$$\mathcal{P}_{\mathsf{O}(n)}[AS] = A.$$

[31] As we have seen, the same scheme arises several times in the earlier sections of this chapter, whenever a direction with negative curvature of the Hessian matrix is concerned.

[32] If the dictionary is not orthogonal, one can always convert the problem to an orthogonal one by a certain normalization process, see [ZYL+20].

[33] One can show that when $n = 6$, there exist critical points whose Hessian has multiple zero eigenvalues.

Then, by projecting both sides of (9.6.6) onto the orthogonal group $\mathsf{O}(n)$, the critical point, including the optimal solutions $\boldsymbol{A}_\star$, should satisfy the following "fixed-point" equation:

$$\boldsymbol{A} = \mathcal{P}_{\mathsf{O}(n)}[(\boldsymbol{A}\boldsymbol{Y})^{\circ 3}\boldsymbol{Y}^*]. \tag{9.6.7}$$

So if we view

$$g(\cdot) \doteq \mathcal{P}_{\mathsf{O}(n)}[((\cdot)\boldsymbol{Y})^{\circ 3}\boldsymbol{Y}^*] : \mathsf{O}(n) \to \mathsf{O}(n)$$

as a map from $\mathsf{O}(n)$ to $\mathsf{O}(n)$ itself, one can show that this map is again a (local) contraction map. This leads to the *matching, stretching, and projection* (MSP) algorithm [ZYL$^+$20] for solving the dictionary learning problem:

$$\boldsymbol{A}_{k+1} = \mathcal{P}_{\mathsf{O}(n)}[(\boldsymbol{A}_k\boldsymbol{Y})^{\circ 3}\boldsymbol{Y}^*]. \tag{9.6.8}$$

Hence, the MSP can be viewed as a power iteration algorithm for solving the above fixed-point problem.

The original Newton's method (9.1.13), introduced earlier in this chapter, is precisely a "fixed-point"-type algorithm for computing the roots of an equation. Only it gives a contraction mapping locally around a critical point – see the proof of Proposition 9.2. The power iteration for computing eigenvectors or for dictionary learning is *unlike* any of the local (first-order or second-order) methods that we have introduced earlier in this chapter. It actually exploits *the global geometry* of the objective function over a nice manifold of the solution space: it has the ability to converge to the globally optimal solution from a random starting point, and enjoys much higher convergence rates. In fact, one can show that the MSP iteration for dictionary learning converges locally with *cubic rate* around the globally optimal solutions [ZYL$^+$20], far more efficient than any first-order or second-order local methods introduced earlier.[34]

9.6.3 Optimization over Stiefel Manifolds

From the previous examples, we could try to generalize the method to a broader set of problems. Consider the problem of minimizing a *concave* function $f(\boldsymbol{X})$ over the so-called *Stiefel manifold*, for $m \le n$:

$$\mathsf{V}_m(\mathbb{R}^n) \doteq \{\boldsymbol{X} \in \mathbb{R}^{n\times m} \mid \boldsymbol{X}^*\boldsymbol{X} = \boldsymbol{I}_{m\times m}\}. \tag{9.6.9}$$

Then for the program

$$\min_{\boldsymbol{X}} f(\boldsymbol{X}) \quad \text{subject to} \quad \boldsymbol{X}^*\boldsymbol{X} = \boldsymbol{I}, \tag{9.6.10}$$

we consider the Lagrangian

$$\mathcal{L}(\boldsymbol{X},\boldsymbol{\Lambda}) \doteq f(\boldsymbol{X}) + \langle \boldsymbol{\Lambda}, \boldsymbol{X}^*\boldsymbol{X} - \boldsymbol{I}\rangle. \tag{9.6.11}$$

[34] However, the global convergence of MSP remains an open problem, despite compelling empirical evidence suggesting that is the case.

The necessary condition for optimality $\nabla_{\boldsymbol{X}} \mathcal{L}(\boldsymbol{X}, \boldsymbol{\Lambda}) = \mathbf{0}$ gives

$$-\nabla f(\boldsymbol{X}) = \boldsymbol{X}\boldsymbol{S}, \tag{9.6.12}$$

for a symmetric matrix $\boldsymbol{S} = (\boldsymbol{\Lambda} + \boldsymbol{\Lambda}^*)$. This gives

$$\nabla f(\boldsymbol{X})^* \nabla f(\boldsymbol{X}) = \boldsymbol{S}^* \boldsymbol{X}^* \boldsymbol{X} \boldsymbol{S} = \boldsymbol{S}^2. \tag{9.6.13}$$

We can solve for $\boldsymbol{S} = [\nabla f(\boldsymbol{X})^* \nabla f(\boldsymbol{X})]^{1/2}$. When $\boldsymbol{S}$ is invertible,[35] the necessary condition (9.6.12) for optimality becomes:

$$\boldsymbol{X} = -\nabla f(\boldsymbol{X})[\nabla f(\boldsymbol{X})^* \nabla f(\boldsymbol{X})]^{-1/2}. \tag{9.6.14}$$

For simplicity, we define

$$g(\boldsymbol{X}) \doteq -\nabla f(\boldsymbol{X})[\nabla f(\boldsymbol{X})^* \nabla f(\boldsymbol{X})]^{-1/2} \tag{9.6.15}$$

as a mapping from $\mathsf{V}_m(\mathbb{R}^n)$ to itself,

$$g(\boldsymbol{X}) : \mathsf{V}_m(\mathbb{R}^n) \to \mathsf{V}_m(\mathbb{R}^n).$$

Hence the optimal solution $\boldsymbol{X}_\star$ can be viewed as the "fixed point" in the equation:

$$\boldsymbol{X} = g(\boldsymbol{X}).$$

To compute the fixed point, we can simply take the iteration

$$\boldsymbol{X}_{k+1} = g(\boldsymbol{X}_k) = -\nabla f(\boldsymbol{X}_k)[\nabla f(\boldsymbol{X}_k)^* \nabla f(\boldsymbol{X}_k)]^{-1/2}. \tag{9.6.16}$$

It is easy to check that the iterations for the singular vector computation and the dictionary learning are precisely special cases of this iteration, with $m = 1$ and $m = n$, respectively.

The above descent scheme is also known as the *generalized power method* [JNRS10] (applied over Stiefel manifolds). With similar techniques as in the gradient descent case (in Section 9.1.1), one can show that when the objective function is concave, the iterative process converges to a first-order critical point at least with the rate $O(1/k)$ (see Exercise 9.8). However, as we see in the cases of singular vector and dictionary learning, when the function $f(\boldsymbol{X})$ has good properties, the actual performance of the above scheme (9.6.16) can be far more efficient than the rate $O(1/k)$ for the worst case, especially when the associated function $g(\boldsymbol{X})$ is a (global or local) contraction mapping.

9.6.4 Fixed Point of a Contraction Mapping

Notice that the power iteration algorithms for all three problems have one thing in common: they all rely on a (local) contraction mapping from a compact manifold to itself. More generally speaking, let $\mathcal{M}$ be a compact smooth manifold with a distance metric $d(\cdot, \cdot)$.

[35] Which is normally the case, as we have seen in the cases with the singular vector and dictionary learning.

DEFINITION 9.16. (Contraction mapping) *A map* $g : \mathcal{M} \to \mathcal{M}$ *is called a contraction mapping on* $\mathcal{M}$ *if there exists* $\rho \in (0, 1)$ *such that*

$$d(g(\boldsymbol{x}), g(\boldsymbol{y})) \leq \rho \cdot d(\boldsymbol{x}, \boldsymbol{y})$$

for all $\boldsymbol{x}, \boldsymbol{y} \in \mathcal{M}$.

The constant ρ can be viewed as the Lipschitz constant for g. For a contraction mapping, we have the following well-known result:

THEOREM 9.17. (Banach–Caccioppoli fixed point) *Let* $(\mathcal{M}, d)$ *be a complete metric space with a contraction mapping* $g : \mathcal{M} \to \mathcal{M}$. *Then* g *has* a unique fixed point $\boldsymbol{x}_\star \in \mathcal{M}$:

$$g(\boldsymbol{x}_\star) = \boldsymbol{x}_\star.$$

In particular, as the previous examples have indicated, the unique fixed point $\boldsymbol{x}_\star$ can be found through the simple power iteration:

$$\boldsymbol{x}_{k+1} \leftarrow g(\boldsymbol{x}_k), \quad k = 0, 1, \ldots,$$

and we have $\boldsymbol{x}_k \to \boldsymbol{x}_\star$ at least geometrically. Notice that the fixed-point scheme does not rely on local information such as gradient, hence it can even escape degenerate critical points. Empirically, we observe that the MSP algorithm works very well for the ℓ^4-based dictionary learning problem, even though the ℓ^4 norm has degenerate critical points on the orthogonal group $\mathsf{O}(n)$. In addition, the contraction factor ρ does not need to be a constant. If it scales with powers of $\|\boldsymbol{x}_{k+1} - \boldsymbol{x}_k\|$, the contraction mapping enjoys higher-than-linear rates of convergence, as in the Newton or the MSP

Fixed Point of a Contraction Mapping

Problem Class:

$$\min_{\boldsymbol{x}} f(\boldsymbol{x}), \quad \boldsymbol{x} \in \mathcal{M}, \text{ with } \mathcal{M} \text{ being a compact manifold.}$$

Critical points of f correspond to the fixed point of a (local) contraction mapping $g(\cdot) : \mathcal{M} \to \mathcal{M}$:

$$g(\boldsymbol{x}) = \boldsymbol{x}.$$

Initialization: Set $\boldsymbol{x}_0 \in \mathbb{R}^n$ randomly (or locally near a critical point).

Iteration: For $k = 0, 1, 2, \ldots, K$,

$$\boldsymbol{x}_{k+1} = g(\boldsymbol{x}_k).$$

Convergence guarantee: $\boldsymbol{x}_k$ converges to a fixed point $\boldsymbol{x}_\star$ at least geometrically fast (i.e., at least linear rate of convergence).

Figure 9.7 An overview of optimization via the fixed point of a contraction mapping.

iteration. We summarize this in Figure 9.7 as a general algorithm of power iteration for solving the fixed point of a contraction mapping.

9.7 Notes

Modifications to Newton's Method

Despite its simplicity and fast convergence, Newton's method (9.1.13) has several known problems. One problem is that for a nonconvex function the Hessian $\nabla^2 f(\boldsymbol{x})$ can sometimes be degenerate (hence not invertible). So the iteration (9.1.13) is not even defined. A popular fix to this problem is to regularize the Hessian with a unit matrix such that $\nabla^2 f(\boldsymbol{x}) + \lambda \boldsymbol{I} \succ \boldsymbol{0}$ is positive definite. The above Newton iteration is then modified to be

$$\boldsymbol{x}_{k+1} = \boldsymbol{x}_k - \left[\nabla^2 f(\boldsymbol{x}_k) + \lambda \boldsymbol{I}\right]^{-1} \nabla f(\boldsymbol{x}_k). \tag{9.7.1}$$

This is known as the popular *Levenberg–Marquardt regularization* [Lev44, Mar63, Mor78]. The above update rule can often be viewed as a mixture of gradient descent and Newton step with the parameter λ weighing between the two. Another, arguably more rigorous, justification of the above form of update is from the perspective of the trust region method [CGT00], which we will study in more details in Exercise 9.2. Due to its flexibility, the Levenberg–Marquardt method has been widely used in practice for solving nonconvex optimization problems, especially nonlinear least-squares-type problems.

Complexity Bounds

For functions with Lipschitz gradient and Hessian, [CDHS17] have derived the lower bound of first-order methods $O(\varepsilon_g^{-12/7})$, while it is believed that the best attainable upper bound is $O(\varepsilon_g^{-7/4})$. [AAZB$^+$16, CDHS18] were among the first to make the attempt to develop algorithms that can achieve the optimal bound. Later the work [RW18, JNJ18] provided simplified approaches to achieve this bound by combining negative curvature and accelerated gradient descent. To a large extent, the methods presented in this chapter are inspired by these works.

Table 9.1 summarizes all the algorithms introduced in this chapter and their respective complexities in terms of associated oracles and convergence guarantees. These complexity bounds are for the worst case in the class of functions considered. If a particular function of interest has better structure or property (which is often the case in our settings), the complexity of even the vanilla gradient descent can be dramatically improved: for instance, if the function is locally strongly convex around a minimizer, the local convergence rate becomes linear $O(\log(1/\varepsilon))$ (see Theorem D.4 of Appendix D).

Notice that these complexities are characterized for functions that have global Lipschitz gradient and Hessian. In practice, this may not be the case and we cannot easily decide on the step size without knowing the Lipschitz constants. So we

Table 9.1. Oracles and complexities (up to log factors) of different optimization methods. "Stat. point" stands for the type of stationary point $\boldsymbol{x}_*$ to which the method guarantees to converge. All complexities are measured in terms of the number of oracles accessed before attaining a prescribed accuracy $\|\nabla f(\boldsymbol{x}_*)\| \le \varepsilon_g$.

Method	Oracle	Stat. point	Complexity
Vanilla gradient descent	first-order	first-order	$O(\varepsilon_g^{-2})$
Cubic Newton, Figure 9.1	second-order	second-order	$O(\varepsilon_g^{-1.5})$
Gradient/negative curvature, Figure 9.2	first-order	second-order	$O(\varepsilon_g^{-2})$
Negative curvature/Newton, Figure 9.4	first-order	second-order	$O(\varepsilon_g^{-1.75})$
Hybrid noisy gradient, Figure 9.5	first-order	second-order	$O(\varepsilon_g^{-2})$
Perturbed accelerated gradient, Figure 9.6	first-order	second-order	$O(\varepsilon_g^{-1.75})$

generally may resort to a local line search scheme to determine the proper step size (see (D.1.2) of Appendix D) and then to establish corresponding convergence and complexity analysis.

Exploiting Geometric Structures
In the last Section 9.6, we have shown a few important instances in which the optimization is over a certain nonlinear manifold. The recent book [Bou20] gives a good introduction to optimization on general smooth manifolds. As we have seen in Chapter 7 and also will in the application chapters, optimization problems that arise in low-dimensional models often have nice global geometric structures such as certain symmetry over a homogeneous space. In such cases, we can develop extremely effective and scalable optimization algorithms, far beyond the local greedy gradient-based schemes. However, unlike the generic first-order or second-order methods summarized in Table 9.1, there is still a lack of systematic analysis of convergence and complexity for such geometric optimization problems. As we have alluded to before in Section 7.4 of Chapter 7, developing scalable algorithms for this class of problems and characterizing conditions under which there is guaranteed (global) convergence and complexity are certainly an important and pressing research topic for the future.

9.8 Exercises

9.1. (Examples for newton's method) *Apply Newton's method around the critical point,* $x = 0$, *of three functions* $f(x) = \frac{1}{2}x^2$, $f(x) = -\frac{1}{2}x^2$, *and* $f(x_1, x_2) = \frac{1}{2}(x_1^2 - x_2^2)$, *and describe what Newton iteration does respectively in these three cases.*

9.2. (Trust region method) *In the Remark 9.3 about the trust region method, we need to find the minimizer to a constrained quadratic program of the form:*

$$\boldsymbol{w}_\star = \arg\min f(\boldsymbol{x}_k) + \langle \nabla f(\boldsymbol{x}_k), \boldsymbol{w}\rangle + \frac{1}{2}\boldsymbol{w}^* \nabla^2 f(\boldsymbol{x}_k)\boldsymbol{w} \quad \text{s.t.} \quad \|\boldsymbol{w}\|_2 \leq \delta_k. \tag{9.8.1}$$

To compute the optimal minimizer $\boldsymbol{w}_\star$, there are essentially three cases depending on the relationships between the gradient ∇f and the Hessian $\nabla^2 f$. Let λ_1 be the smallest eigenvalue of $\nabla^2 f$, and $\boldsymbol{e}_1$ be the associated eigenvector: $\nabla^2 f \boldsymbol{e}_1 = \lambda_1 \boldsymbol{e}_1$. If $\lambda_1 > 0$, the Hessian is positive definite. If $\lambda_1 < 0$, then $\boldsymbol{e}_1$ is the direction in which the surface has the largest negative curvature. We denote the eigen-subspace associated with $\boldsymbol{e}_1$ as

$$\mathsf{S}_1 \doteq \{\alpha \boldsymbol{e}_1, \alpha \in \mathbb{R}\}.$$

(a) Case 1: *When $\nabla^2 f(\boldsymbol{x}_k)$ is positive definite, i.e., $\lambda_1 > 0$, and*

$$\left\| \left[\nabla^2 f(\boldsymbol{x}_k)\right]^{-1} \nabla f \right\|_2 < \delta,$$

show that the optimal solution is given by $\boldsymbol{w}_\star = -\left[\nabla^2 f(\boldsymbol{x}_k)\right]^{-1} \nabla f(\boldsymbol{x}_k)$. Whenever this happens, the trust region Newton descent reduces to a regular Newton descent:

$$\boldsymbol{x}_{k+1} = \boldsymbol{x}_k + \boldsymbol{w}_\star = \boldsymbol{x}_k - \left[\nabla^2 f(\boldsymbol{x}_k)\right]^{-1} \nabla f(\boldsymbol{x}_k). \tag{9.8.2}$$

When the minimizer is not in the interior of the trust region, the problem becomes how to minimize a quadratic function over a sphere $\|\boldsymbol{w}\|_2 = 1$. The situation becomes a little more complicated as we see below.

(b) Case 2: *Show that if the gradient $\nabla f(\boldsymbol{x}_k)$ is not perpendicular to S_1, then the equation*

$$\left\| \left[\nabla^2 f(\boldsymbol{x}_k) + \lambda \boldsymbol{I}\right]^{-1} \nabla f(\boldsymbol{x}_k) \right\|_2^2 = \delta^2 \tag{9.8.3}$$

has a solution $\lambda_\star \geq 0$ in the range $(-\lambda_1, \infty)$ which gives the optimal minimizer $\boldsymbol{w}_\star = -\left[\nabla^2(\boldsymbol{x}_k) + \lambda_\star \boldsymbol{I}\right]^{-1} \nabla f(\boldsymbol{x}_k)$. In fact, here finding the optimal $\lambda_\star$ is itself a one-dimensional nonlinear optimization problem. One can use any optimization method (such as Newton's method) to solve it, and some specific options can be found in [CGT00]. Once the optimal minimizer $\boldsymbol{w}_\star$ is found, the trust region Newton descent in this case is[36]

$$\boldsymbol{x}_{k+1} = \boldsymbol{x}_k + \boldsymbol{w}_\star = \boldsymbol{x}_k - \left[\nabla^2 f(\boldsymbol{x}_k) + \lambda_\star \boldsymbol{I}\right]^{-1} \nabla f(\boldsymbol{x}_k). \tag{9.8.4}$$

Further show that when the gradient ∇f is perpendicular to S_1, i.e., $\nabla f \perp \mathsf{S}_1$, if the equation $\left\| \left[\nabla^2 f(\boldsymbol{x}_k) + \lambda \boldsymbol{I}\right]^{-1} \nabla f \right\|_2^2 = \delta^2$ still has a solution $\lambda_\star \geq 0$ in

[36] Notice that this update rule can be considered as a special case of the popular Levenberg–Marquardt regularization (9.4.2), with λ chosen to be a specific value, according to the second-order local geometry.

the range $(-\lambda_1, \infty)$*, then* $\boldsymbol{w}_\star = -\left[\nabla^2 f(\boldsymbol{x}_k) + \lambda_\star \boldsymbol{I}\right]^{-1} \nabla f$ *again is the desired minimizer.*

(c) Case 3: *The situation becomes a little trickier when* $\nabla f \perp \mathsf{S}_1$ *but the above equation does not have any solution. That is,* $\left\| \left[\nabla^2 f(\boldsymbol{x}_k) + \lambda \boldsymbol{I}\right]^{-1} \nabla f \right\|_2^2 < \delta^2$ *for any* λ *that makes* $\nabla^2 f(\boldsymbol{x}_k) + \lambda \boldsymbol{I}$ *positive definite. Show that this case only happens when* $\lambda_1 \leq 0$*. In this case, let* $\boldsymbol{w}_1$ *be the minimum norm solution to* $\left[\nabla^2 f(\boldsymbol{x}_k) - \lambda_1 \boldsymbol{I}\right] \boldsymbol{w} = -\nabla f$*, i.e.,* $\boldsymbol{w}_1 = -\left[\nabla^2 f(\boldsymbol{x}_k) - \lambda_1 \boldsymbol{I}\right]^{\dagger} \nabla f$*. Then show that the minimizer* $\boldsymbol{w}_\star$ *on the unit sphere is of the form*

$$\boldsymbol{w}_\star = \boldsymbol{w}_1 + \beta \boldsymbol{e}_1 = -\left[\nabla^2 f(\boldsymbol{x}_k) - \lambda_1 \boldsymbol{I}\right]^{\dagger} \nabla f + \beta \boldsymbol{e}_1$$

with β *chosen such that* $\|\boldsymbol{w}_\star\|_2^2 = \delta^2$*. It is easy to see that the so-constructed* $\boldsymbol{w}_\star$ *satisfies the condition for minimizer:*

$$\left[\nabla^2 f(\boldsymbol{x}_k) - \lambda_1 \boldsymbol{I}\right](\boldsymbol{w}_1 + \beta \boldsymbol{e}_1) = \left[\nabla^2 f(\boldsymbol{x}_k) - \lambda_1 \boldsymbol{I}\right] \boldsymbol{w}_1 = -\nabla f.$$

Geometrically, $\boldsymbol{w}_1$ *is the minimizer restricted to the subspace* $\mathsf{S}_1^{\perp}$*. If it is in the interior of the trust region, we then simply add a step along the direction of the largest negative curvature to reach the global minimizer* $\boldsymbol{w}_\star$ *on the boundary. The trust region Newton descent in this case becomes*

$$\boldsymbol{x}_{k+1} = \boldsymbol{x}_k + \boldsymbol{w}_\star = \boldsymbol{x}_k - \left[\nabla^2 f(\boldsymbol{x}_k) + \lambda_\star \boldsymbol{I}\right]^{\dagger} \nabla f(\boldsymbol{x}_k) + \beta \boldsymbol{e}_1. \tag{9.8.5}$$

9.3. (Cubic regularized newton's method) *For the cubic Newton's method studied in Section 9.2,*

(a) *Show that the cubic Newton step* (9.2.5) *reduces to solving a one-dimensional convex optimization problem, similar to the one that we have seen in the trust region method above.*

(b) *Show that the optimal solution to the cubic Newton step satisfies the condition* (9.2.11).

9.4. (Power iteration and lanczos method) *Implement in detail the power iteration and Lanczos method introduced in Section 9.3.2. Generate a real symmetric matrix* $\boldsymbol{A} \in \mathbb{R}^{n \times n}$ *with* $\lambda_{\min}(\boldsymbol{A}) < 0$*, say for* $n = 1000$*. Use the power iteration and the Lanczos method to compute the eigenvector associated with the smallest (negative) eigenvalue. Plot the approximation error versus the number of iterations, and compare the two methods.*

9.5. (Conjugate gradient method) *In this exercise, implement the conjugate gradient method mentioned in Section 9.4.3 to solve the linear equation* $\boldsymbol{A}\boldsymbol{s} = \boldsymbol{b}$*, say for a matrix* $\boldsymbol{A}$ *of size* 1000×1000*. Compare the efficiency with solving the equation by directly computing the inverse of* $\boldsymbol{A}$*, i.e.,* $\boldsymbol{s} = \boldsymbol{A}^{-1}\boldsymbol{b}$*.*

9.6. (Laplace method) *This exercise generalizes the basic ideas of the Laplace method to general cases.*

(a) *Prove the Lemma 9.12 for the case when the function* $f(x), x \in \mathbb{R}$, *has multiple global maximizers.*
(b) *Prove the Theorem 9.13 for the case when the function* $f(\boldsymbol{x}), \boldsymbol{x} \in \mathbb{R}^n$, *has a unique global maximizer.*
(c) *For the case when the function* $f(\boldsymbol{x}), \boldsymbol{x} \in \mathbb{R}^n$, *has a continuous family of global maximizers, show that the Gibbs distribution converges to the density in* (9.5.6).

9.7. (Orthogonal dictionary learning) *Let us consider another formulation for finding an orthogonal dictionary* $\boldsymbol{A}_o$ *up to some signed permutations in one shot. We want to solve*

$$\min_{\boldsymbol{A},\boldsymbol{X}} \frac{1}{2} \|\boldsymbol{Y} - \boldsymbol{A}\boldsymbol{X}\|_F^2 + \mu \|\boldsymbol{X}\|_1 \quad \textit{subject to} \quad \boldsymbol{A} \in \mathsf{O}(n),$$

where $\mathsf{O}(n) = \left\{\boldsymbol{Z} \in \mathbb{R}^{n\times n} \mid \boldsymbol{Z}^*\boldsymbol{Z} = \boldsymbol{I}\right\}$ *is the orthogonal group. Show that the problem can be reduced to*

$$\min_{\boldsymbol{A}} \mathrm{Huber}_\mu \left(\boldsymbol{A}^*\boldsymbol{Y}\right) \quad \textit{subject to} \quad \boldsymbol{A} \in \mathsf{O}(n), \tag{9.8.6}$$

where $\mathrm{Huber}_\mu(\cdot)$ *is the Huber loss, which is the sum of scalar Huber functions, introduced in* (7.2.24), *applied element-wise across all the matrix elements.*

9.8. (Generalized power iteration) *Show that the generalized power iteration* (9.6.16) *is equivalent to the following descent scheme:*

$$\boldsymbol{X}_{k+1} = \operatorname*{argmin}_{\boldsymbol{Y}\in\mathsf{V}_m(\mathbb{R}^n)} f(\boldsymbol{X}_k) + \langle\nabla f(\boldsymbol{X}_k), \boldsymbol{Y} - \boldsymbol{X}_k\rangle. \tag{9.8.7}$$

Use this fact to show that for a concave function, this descent scheme converges to a first-order critical point with a rate at least $O(1/k)$.

Part III

Applications to Real-World Problems

10 Magnetic Resonance Imaging

"If you want to find the secrets of the universe, think in terms of energy, frequency and vibration."

– Nikola Tesla

10.1 Introduction

Magnetic resonance imaging (MRI) is based on the science of nuclear magnetic resonance (NMR). Magnetic resonance states that certain atomic nuclei (such as the protons in water molecules) can absorb and emit radio-frequency energy when placed in an external magnetic field. The emitted energy is proportional to important physical properties of a material such as proton density. Therefore in physics and chemistry, magnetic resonance is an important method for studying structures of chemical substances, and its discoverers were awarded the Nobel Prize in Physics in 1952.

Later, in the 1970s, Paul Lauterbur and Peter Mansfield discovered that by introducing spatial gradients in the magnetic field, it is possible to create two-dimensional images of the structures, now known as magnetic resonance imaging (MRI). MRI soon proved to be extremely useful for medical diagnosis, as it provides an accurate and noninvasive method for imaging internal organs of the human body. Unlike X-rays or computed tomography (CT) scans, MRI does not utilize ionizing radiation, hence is much less harmful. Today, MRI has become a routine medical examination in hospitals worldwide, especially for examining the brain and the spinal cord. For their contributions to MRI, Lauterbur and Mansfield were awarded the Nobel Prize in Physiology or Medicine in 2003.

Nevertheless, MRI machines can be rather expensive, and the acquisition process of MRI is considerably time-consuming, as it needs to densely sample the magnetization responses with many different gradient fields. In order to lower the cost of MRI and improve patient comfort or safety,[1] in recent years, techniques from compressive sensing have proven to be extremely effective in improving the efficiency of MRI [LDSP08], which was briefly highlighted in Chapter 2 as one of the heralding successes.

[1] For young pediatric cancer patients, frequent exposures to strong magnetic fields for long periods of time can be unsafe and even fatal.

In this chapter, we explain in more technical detail why MRI is particularly suitable for techniques of compressive sensing. First, a high-level review of the physics of MRI in Section 10.2 reveals that the MRI imaging process is amenable to compressive sampling, as it naturally takes spatially encoded samples of the image in the frequency domain. Second, medical images of human organs are naturally structured and mostly piecewise smooth. We can verify empirically that such images are highly compressible/sparse in a properly chosen transform domain, and introduce several effective sampling schemes in Section 10.3. Finally, we introduce in Section 10.4 some customized fast algorithms that can efficiently reconstruct the image from such compressive samples with high fidelity, despite imaging noise and other nuisance factors.

10.2 Formation of MR Images

In medical applications, MRI is based on measurements of a radio-frequency (RF) signal, known as the *transverse magnetization*, generated by protons which exist in abundance as the hydrogen nuclei in the molecules of water and fat in human tissues. The signal measured is largely proportional to the density of protons at each spatial location, which indicates the presence or absence of such molecules. This information can then be used by physicians for diagnostic purposes. Here, we give a simplified mathematical model that captures the essence of this process. For a more detailed description of the physical process, one may refer, for example, to [Wri97].

10.2.1 Basic Physics

It is known in quantum physics that each proton spins along an axis that creates an angular momentum. In the absence of any external magnetic field, the angular momenta of the protons are oriented randomly in their neutral state, hence collectively the protons (in the body tissue) do not produce any measurable magnetization. However, when a strong external magnetic field, denoted as $\boldsymbol{B}_0$, is applied to the tissue mass, it polarizes the protons and aligns their spins along the direction of $\boldsymbol{B}_0$ and produces a net magnetization, denoted as $\boldsymbol{M}$. Field $\boldsymbol{B}_0$ is also called the *primary magnetic field*, and its strength typically can range from 1.5 to 3 tesla.[2] An MRI machine usually has three RF coils along the x-, y-, and z-axes, respectively, as shown in Figure 10.1, and can produce a magnetic field in any direction by running electric currents through respective coils.

Following conventional notation in physics, we use $(\boldsymbol{i}, \boldsymbol{j}, \boldsymbol{k})$ to denote the three unit vectors in the x-, y-, z-axes of a (local) Cartesian frame. Without loss of generality, we may assume the direction of the external static magnetic field $\boldsymbol{B}_0$ aligns with the z-axis, that is, $\boldsymbol{B}_0 = B_0\boldsymbol{k}$. In general the magnetization $\boldsymbol{M}$ takes the form

[2] In comparison, the magnitude of the Earth's natural magnetic field only ranges from 25 to 65 microtesla.

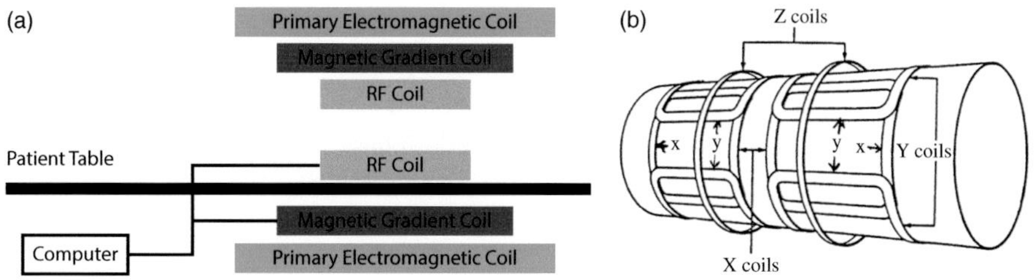

Figure 10.1 (a) Key components of a basic MRI machine. (b) The three-axis gradient coils.

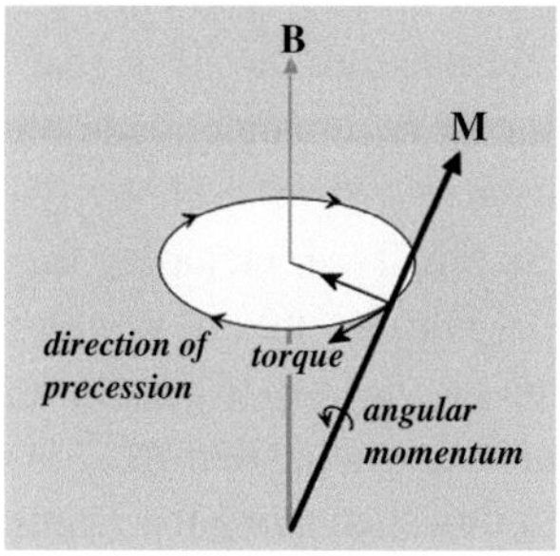

Figure 10.2 The direction of the magnetization $\boldsymbol{M}$ as a vector is precessing in a cone around $\boldsymbol{B}_0$, driven by the torque generated by the cross product $\boldsymbol{M} \times \boldsymbol{B}_0$, in a direction orthogonal to both $\boldsymbol{M}$ and $\boldsymbol{B}_0$. (Image from `https://mri-q.com/bloch-equations.html` and reprinted with permission from Allen D. Elster, MD.)

$\boldsymbol{M} = M_x\boldsymbol{i} + M_y\boldsymbol{j} + M_z\boldsymbol{k}$. If the external magnetic field is static, $\boldsymbol{M}$ will eventually reach an equilibrium magnetization of the form $M_0\boldsymbol{k}$.

Although protons can respond very quickly to the external magnetic field, the polarization itself does not yield any RF signal that can be measured by the machine. The key is that the magnetization $\boldsymbol{M}_{xy} = M_x\boldsymbol{i} + M_y\boldsymbol{j}$ in the *transverse plane* orthogonal to the primary axis undergoes very different dynamics and can be exploited for measurement. This transverse magnetization precesses about $\boldsymbol{B}_0$ according to the so-called *Bloch equation*:

$$\frac{d\boldsymbol{M}_{xy}}{dt} = \gamma \boldsymbol{M}_{xy} \times \boldsymbol{B}_0, \tag{10.2.1}$$

where γ is a physical constant. Figure 10.2 visualizes the precessing of $\boldsymbol{M}_{xy}$ around $\boldsymbol{B}_0$. From this equation, we see that the precession frequency is $\omega_0 = \gamma B_0$, known as the *Larmor frequency*. This rotating magnetic moment radiates an electromagnetic signal which is picked up by the MRI machine.

So in order to produce a precessing magnetization orthogonal to $\boldsymbol{B}_0$, in the second step of MRI imaging, one applies a second time-varying magnetic field $\boldsymbol{B}_1$ in the xy-plane transverse to $\boldsymbol{B}_0 = B_0\boldsymbol{k}$. Typically $\boldsymbol{B}_1$ is chosen to be $\boldsymbol{B}_1 = \cos(\omega_0 t)\boldsymbol{i} + \sin(\omega_0 t)\boldsymbol{j}$ which rotates around $\boldsymbol{B}_0$ at the radian frequency ω_0. This magnetic field excites the protons to a higher energy state.

The excitation stops after a short period, and the protons gradually fall back to their equilibrium state. This relaxation process lasts from milliseconds to several seconds. As the transverse magnetization $\boldsymbol{M}_{xy}$ precesses, it induces an electromagnetic force in the RF coils. The magnitude, phase, and relaxation time of the signal represent different properties of the matter that can be recorded in different types of MR images.

10.2.2 Selective Excitation and Spatial Encoding

One question remains with regard to the imaging process, namely, how does the MRI machine isolate and measure the RF signal from different parts of the body, because if the body is affected by a single static magnetic field, then all the protons will be aligned homogeneously? Several clever (Nobel Prize-worthy clever) techniques are required to address this issue, including the so-called *selective excitation* and *spatial encoding*. The goal is to be able to sample and measure magnetization signals from any spatial location (x, y, z) (up to certain resolution).

As the transverse magnetization $\boldsymbol{M}_{xy}$ is of interest, we may choose to excite the magnetic field in a thin slice along the z-axis, say around z_0. That is, we are interested in the plane (x, y, z_0). The selective excitation can be achieved by first making the Larmor frequency vary linearly in the z-direction with the magnetic field:

$$\boldsymbol{B}_0(z) = \big(B_0 + G_z(z - z_0)\big)\boldsymbol{k}.$$

We then apply an additional RF excitation pulse with energy over a limited range of frequency bandwidth Ω corresponding to the Larmor frequency $\omega_0 = \gamma B_0$ at the slice z_0. Typically, we could choose the pulse to be

$$\boldsymbol{B}_1(t) = \operatorname{sinc}(\Omega t)\big(\cos(\omega_0 t)\boldsymbol{i} + \sin(\omega_0 t)\boldsymbol{j}\big),$$

which has a rectangular (energy) distribution around the frequency ω_0. As a result, only protons around the slice (x, y, z_0) may resonate with the excitation and reach a high magnetization level, say $\boldsymbol{M}_{xy}(x, y) \doteq \boldsymbol{M}_{xy}(x, y, z_0)$. This is why the whole process is called *magnetic resonance imaging*.

The remaining question is how to image magnetization of different spatial locations inside the plane (x, y, z_0). As we see from the above, spatial selectivity (along the z-axis) can be achieved through introducing a spatially varying excitation with a gradient (G_z) in the z-direction. Hence, we could generalize this idea by introducing an additional magnetic field $\boldsymbol{B}$ with a gradient G_x and G_y in the x- and y-directions, respectively. Moreover, we could vary the gradients as functions of time t:

$$\boldsymbol{B} = \big(B_0 + G_x(t)x + G_y(t)y\big)\boldsymbol{k}.$$

After the selective excitation, the magnetic field in the transverse plane (x, y, z_0) is $\boldsymbol{M}_{xy}(x, y)$. Once the slice is subject to the above magnetic field, $\boldsymbol{M}_{xy}$ precesses according to the Bloch equation and we can measure the electromagnetic signal generated by it. Assume that the magnitude $|\boldsymbol{M}_{xy}|$ remains relatively constant during the acquisition period, then from the Bloch equation, we have

$$M_{xy}(x, y, t) = |\boldsymbol{M}_{xy}(x, y)| e^{-\mathrm{i}\omega_0 t} e^{-\mathrm{i}\gamma \int_0^t (G_x(\tau)x + G_y(\tau)y)d\tau},$$

where $\mathrm{i} = \sqrt{-1}$ is the imaginary unit. From this equation, we can ascertain the true reason for introducing a gradient magnetic field: it allows us to manipulate the phase of the transverse magnetic field $\boldsymbol{M}_{xy}$ so as to encode the spatial information about $\boldsymbol{M}_{xy}$ that we needed in the first place.

To see this, note that the actual signal we measure is the collective effect of all $\boldsymbol{M}_{xy}$ in the xy-plane. To simplify the notation, let us define

$$k_x(t) \doteq \gamma \int_0^t G_x(\tau)d\tau, \quad k_y(t) \doteq \gamma \int_0^t G_y(\tau)d\tau.$$

In the MRI literature, the so-defined quantities (k_x, k_y) index a two-dimensional space called *k-space*. We then have the measured signal, say $s(t)$, as

$$s(t) = e^{-\mathrm{i}\omega_0 t} \int_x \int_y |\boldsymbol{M}_{xy}(x, y)| e^{-\mathrm{i}(k_x(t)x + k_y(t)y)} dx dy.$$

Notice that this measured signal $s(t)$, once with the $e^{-\mathrm{i}\omega_0 t}$ component demodulated, is essentially a *2D spatial Fourier transform* of $|\boldsymbol{M}_{xy}(x, y)|$ at the spatial frequency $(k_x(t), k_y(t))$:

$$S(k_x, k_y) = \int_x \int_y |\boldsymbol{M}_{xy}(x, y)| e^{-\mathrm{i}(k_x x + k_y y)} dx dy. \tag{10.2.2}$$

In the MRI literature, this technique is called *spatial frequency encoding*. So, in principle, once we have collected measurements of S at sufficiently many spatial frequencies (k_x, k_y), we could recover $|\boldsymbol{M}_{xy}(x, y)|$ simply from its *inverse Fourier transform*:

$$|\boldsymbol{M}_{xy}(x, y)| \propto \int_{k_x} \int_{k_y} S(k_x, k_y) e^{\mathrm{i}(k_x x + k_y y)} dk_x dk_y, \tag{10.2.3}$$

which can be visualized as a 2D image, say $I(x, y)$, on the xy-plane (at z_0).

10.2.3 Sampling and Reconstruction

We have described above in a nutshell the physical and mathematical models of MR imaging. In short, we see that the value of the measured signal S at any given time t is essentially the 2D Fourier transform of the image of interest $I(x, y)$ (or $|\boldsymbol{M}_{xy}(x, y)|$) at a particular spatial frequency (k_x, k_y). For any given gradient field generated by $(G_x(t), G_y(t))$, if we measure the signal S at a sequence of time $\{t_1, t_2, \ldots\}$, we obtain the samples of the Fourier transform of $I(x, y)$ at different frequencies $\{(k_x(t_1), k_y(t_1)), (k_x(t_2), k_y(t_2)), \ldots\}$ in the transform domain (the k-space).

In practice, we are interested in recovering the image up to certain spatial resolution. That is, instead of a function on a continuous domain (the entire xy-plane), we consider the image $I(x, y)$ is a function on a finite Cartesian grid (say of size

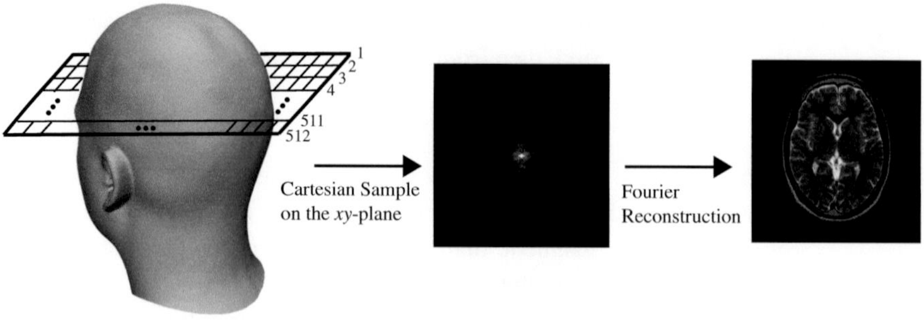

Figure 10.3 A Cartesian sample of the human brain (left) and its reconstructed MRI image (right). The sampling resolution in this example is $m = 512 \times 512$.

$N \times N$). We denote the coordinates of the pixels as a vector $\boldsymbol{v} = (x, y)$. In this case, the measurements can be viewed as the discrete Fourier transform of the image, which lie on a Cartesian grid (of size $N \times N$) in the k-space. We denote the coordinates of the frequencies as a vector $\boldsymbol{u} = (k_x, k_y)$. We collect all measurements as a vector $\boldsymbol{y} \in \mathbb{R}^m$ with $m = N^2$. That is, each entry of $\boldsymbol{y}$ is of the form

$$y_i = \sum_{\boldsymbol{v}} I(\boldsymbol{v}) e^{-\mathrm{i}\boldsymbol{u}_i^* \boldsymbol{v}} \Delta \boldsymbol{v}, \quad i = 1, \ldots, m,$$

where the sum is over the grid and $\Delta \boldsymbol{v}$ is the grid step size. If we also view the image $I(\boldsymbol{v})$ as a vector of dimension m, then we have

$$\boldsymbol{y}(\boldsymbol{u}) = \mathcal{F}[I(\boldsymbol{v})](\boldsymbol{u}), \tag{10.2.4}$$

where $\mathcal{F}$ is an $m \times m$ matrix representing the discrete (2D) Fourier transform. As the matrix $\mathcal{F}$ is invertible, the MR image I can be simply recovered from such Cartesian samples as

$$I(\boldsymbol{v}) = \mathcal{F}^{-1}[\boldsymbol{y}(\boldsymbol{u})](\boldsymbol{v}). \tag{10.2.5}$$

Figure 10.3 shows an example of a recovered MR image from such a Cartesian sampling scheme.

At first sight, sampling the entire Cartesian grid in the transform domain seems natural, and the reconstruction via inverse Fourier transform is straightforward. However, for practical images, it is too redundant to get all the $m = N^2$ samples as illustrated in the example in Figure 10.3. Conventional signal processing techniques have been applied to reduce the number of samples. For instance, if the image largely consists of low-frequency components and has a cutoff bandwidth $f_{\max}$, then we only need to sample the transform domain on a subgrid according to the Nyquist rate

$$f_{\text{Nyquist}} \geq 2 f_{\max}.$$

Nevertheless, the number of samples required by the Nyquist rate is still very large,[3] which makes the conventional MRI imaging process very time-consuming. For the rest of this chapter, we will see that by harnessing additional structures (e.g., sparsity and smoothness) of the MR image, one can significantly reduce the number of samples needed. We will first discuss the sparsity of MR images, and then introduce a few effective compressive sampling schemes. Finally, we will discuss numerical methods for reconstructing MR images from small sets of samples, since, in this under sampled regime we can no longer simply rely on the inverse Fourier transform.

10.3 Sparsity and Compressive Sampling of MR Images

10.3.1 Sparsity of MR Images

In order to improve the sampling efficiency of MR images, we need to leverage additional structure of the target image I. We know from Chapters 2 and 3 that *sparsity* is a very powerful structural assumption, which, when present, can substantially reduce the number of measurements that are required to reconstruct a signal of interest. However, MR images are not sparse – most of the pixels are nonzero! On the other hand, MR images *are* structured: they can be approximated as piecewise smooth functions with relatively few sharp edges. We will see that this type of structure actually leads to a form of sparsity, in an appropriately chosen transform domain.

From signal processing and harmonic analysis, we know that piecewise smooth functions are compressible (nearly sparse) when represented in terms of appropriate basis functions – say, wavelets. There is a deep theory associated with wavelets and related 2D signal representations. Here, we only sketch these constructions at a loose, operational level.

A wavelet transform $\boldsymbol{\Phi}$ maps an $N \times N$ image I to a collection of N^2 coefficients $\boldsymbol{x} = \boldsymbol{\Phi}[I]$. The inverse transform $\boldsymbol{\Psi} = \boldsymbol{\Phi}^{-1}$ maps the coefficients $\boldsymbol{x}$ to an image $I = \boldsymbol{\Psi}[\boldsymbol{x}]$. The inverse mapping can be interpreted as expressing the image as a superposition of basis functions $\psi_1, \ldots, \psi_{N^2}$:

$$I = \boldsymbol{\Psi}[\boldsymbol{x}] = \sum_{i=1}^{N^2} \psi_i x_i. \tag{10.3.1}$$

Figure 10.4 visualizes several of the basis functions associated with a particular two-dimensional wavelet transform.[4]

The coefficients x_i have a very nice interpretation. To transform the image I, we split the image into four bands, which capture vertical and horizontal frequency content at different spatial locations in the image. The low-frequency band, typically labeled LL, contains low-frequency content in both directions, while the

[3] For images with sharp edges and contours, its cutoff bandwidth may be very high.

[4] There are a variety of wavelets, leading to a variety of different transforms. In the experiments in this chapter, we adopt the Daubechies `db4` wavelet. Other choices of separable wavelets lead to different transforms, but their behavior is qualitatively similar.

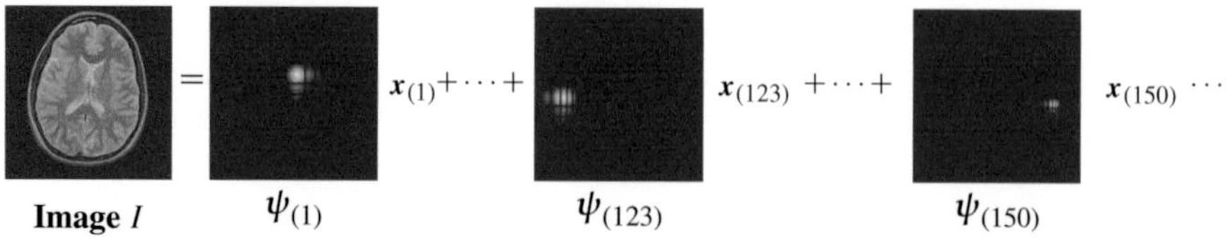

Figure 10.4 Wavelet Representation of an Image. The image I is expressed as a superposition of basis functions ψ_i, with coefficients $\boldsymbol{x}_{(i)}$. In this figure, we order the coefficients by magnitude, in descending order: $\boldsymbol{x}_{(1)}$ is the largest-magnitude coefficient, and $\psi_{(1)}$ its corresponding basis function, $\boldsymbol{x}_{(2)}$ the second largest, and so on. The largest coefficients capture low-frequency structure, as well as high-frequency structure around edges. Notice, for example, that $\psi_{(123)}$ and $\psi_{(155)}$ are located near sharp edges at the left and right side of the brain.

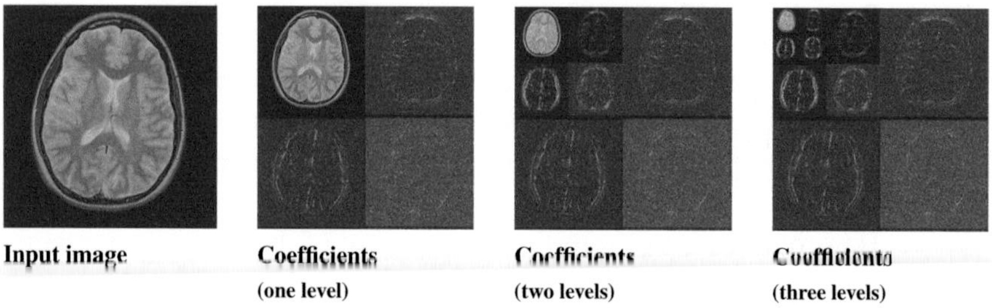

Figure 10.5 Wavelet Coefficients of an Image. From left to right, an original image, and the coefficients of one-level, two-level, and three-level wavelet decompositions using the Daubechies db4 wavelet. The level-one coefficients are organized as LL (upper left), LH (upper right), HL (lower left), and HH (lower right). The detail coefficients (high frequency) are concentrated near sharp edges.

high-frequency band HH contains high-frequency content in both directions. Two other bands HL and LH contain high-frequency content in one direction and low-frequency content in the other direction. Figure 10.5 illustrates this operation. Notice that most of the significant entries occur in the LL band. By repeating this operation on the LL band, we obtain a two-level transform which captures localized frequency content at multiple scales in the image. We can continue in this manner. Figure 10.5 illustrates the three-level to five-level transforms of this image.

MR images tend to be piecewise smooth, with only a few sharp edges. The HL, LH, and HH coefficients concentrate around edges, and so they tend to be quite sparse. Indeed, classical results in harmonic analysis can be paraphrased as arguing that the one-dimensional version of this representation is nearly optimal for representing one-dimensional functions which are piecewise smooth with only a few discontinuities.[5] Figure 10.6 plots the sorted magnitudes of the coefficients $\boldsymbol{x}$, for each level l, from $l = 0$ (the original image) to $l = 3$. Notice that as we increase the number of levels in the transform, the coefficients become increasingly compressible.

Because the wavelet coefficients are nearly sparse, we can accurately approximate the input image using just a few wavelet coefficients. Let $\mathsf{J} = \{i_1, \ldots, i_k\}$ denote the

[5] For piecewise smooth functions on a two-dimensional domain, the situation is more complicated, and there is a large literature of image representations.

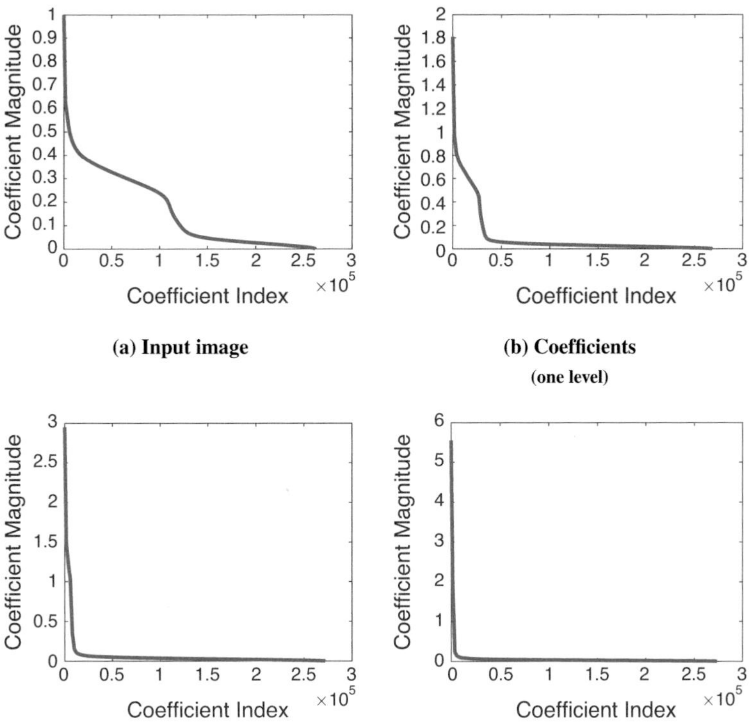

(a) Input image

(b) Coefficients (one level)

(c) Coefficients (two levels)

(d) Coefficients (three levels)

Figure 10.6 Decay of the Wavelet Coefficients. (a) The magnitudes of the image pixel values, plotted in descending order. (b)–(d) The magnitudes of the wavelet coefficients $\boldsymbol{x}$ in descending order, for one-, two-, and three-level wavelet transforms. The wavelet coefficients decay much more rapidly than the original pixel values.

indices of the k largest coefficients x_i (across all scales) in absolute value. We can form the *best k-term approximation*

$$\hat{I} = \sum_{i \in \mathsf{J}} \psi_i x_i, \tag{10.3.2}$$

by retaining only these largest coefficients. Figure 10.7(a) visualizes approximations with the best 1%, 4%, and 7% of the coefficients, respectively. It also visualizes the approximation error $|I - \hat{I}|$. Notice that the approximation errors are almost entirely populated with noise. For comparison, Figure 10.7(b) shows approximations using the best 1%, 4%, and 7% of the original image pixels. The wavelet approximations are dramatically more accurate than pixel approximations.

Of course, there is no reason to believe that wavelet sparsity captures *all* of the structure in an MR image. Other structural assumptions may lead to sparser representations, which can be leveraged to sample even more efficiently. The literature is rich with alternatives, including representations that capture oriented edges, nonlocal representations that capture repeated structure, and learned representations that adapt to the specific classes of images. We will return to this point in Section 10.4, where

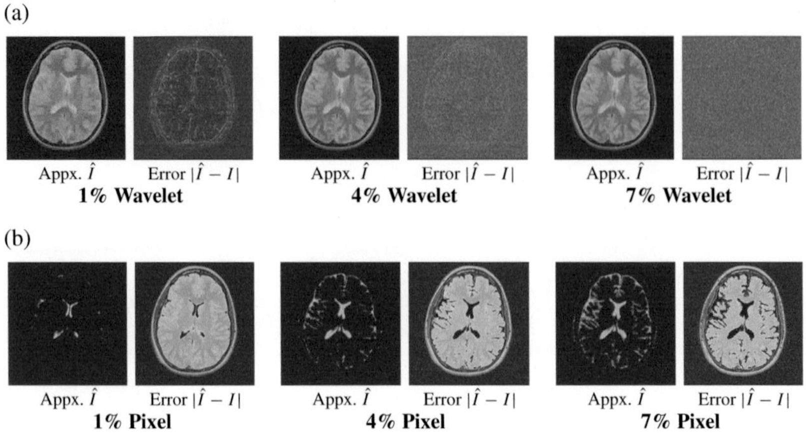

Figure 10.7 Wavelet Reconstructions. (a) Approximations of the brain image using the most significant wavelet coefficients. We plot reconstructions $\hat{I}$ using the largest 1%, 4%, and 7% of the wavelet coefficients, as well as the approximation error $|\hat{I} - I|$. Retaining roughly 7% of the wavelet coefficients captures most of the important structure in the image; what remains is mostly noise. (b) For comparison purposes, we plot reconstructions and errors using the 1%, 4%, and 7% largest image pixels. These approximations are very inaccurate: the image is nearly sparse in the wavelet domain, but not in the original pixel domain.

we sketch one means of further reducing the sampling burden for MRI, by leveraging an additional form of sparsity. For now, we turn to the question of how we can use the knowledge that the wavelet coefficients are sparse to sample more efficiently.

10.3.2 Compressive Sampling of MR Images

Although a wavelet transform is able to sparsify the MR image I, notice that we cannot have access to the wavelet coefficients $\boldsymbol{x}$ unless we have acquired the entire image I (and then apply the transform $\boldsymbol{\Phi}$). Hence in conventional image processing, wavelet transforms have mostly been used in the post-processing of an image after it has been acquired, such as for compression. Now the question is: how can we exploit the fact that the MR image is sufficiently sparse in certain (wavelet) domains so that we can significantly reduce the number of measurements sampled in the acquisition time and still recover the image with good quality?

First we notice that the relationship between the measurements (Fourier coefficients) $\boldsymbol{y} \in \mathbb{C}^{N^2}$ and the (sparse) wavelet coefficients $\boldsymbol{x} \in \mathbb{R}^{N^2}$ is given by

$$\boldsymbol{y} = \mathcal{F}[\boldsymbol{\Psi}\boldsymbol{x}].$$

From the physical model we have described above, we can directly measure any subset of the Fourier coefficients $\boldsymbol{y}$ or any linear superpositions of them. For convenience we denote the image I as a vector $\boldsymbol{z} \doteq I \in \mathbb{R}^{N^2}$:

$$\boldsymbol{z} = \boldsymbol{\Psi}\boldsymbol{x}.$$

Suppose, instead of taking all the N^2 Fourier coefficients, we measure only $m \ll N^2$ samples of (linear superpositions of) the Fourier coefficients. Then the transform from

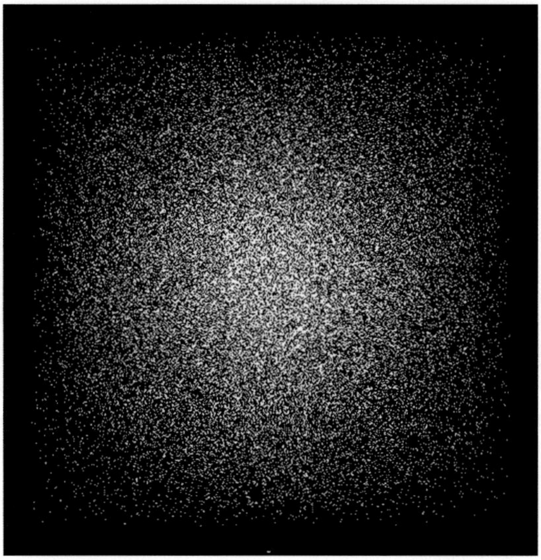

Figure 10.8 A variable density random sampling pattern in the Fourier domain.

z to the m partial measurements y can be represented as an $m \times N^2$ matrix, denoted as $\mathcal{F}_U \in \mathbb{C}^{m \times N^2}$. Hence we have

$$y = \mathcal{F}_U[\Psi x] \doteq Ax, \tag{10.3.3}$$

where we denote $A \doteq \mathcal{F}_U \Psi \in \mathbb{C}^{m \times N^2}$.

As we have learned from early chapters of the book, if the overall sampling matrix A is sufficiently *incoherent*, then in principle we can correctly recover all the sparse (wavelet) coefficients x from significantly fewer m samples. To ensure the matrix A is incoherent, we know from Chapter 3 (Section 3.4.3) that a randomly chosen partial submatrix of the Fourier (or wavelet) transform $\mathcal{F}$ is incoherent. Hence, a conceptually simple compressive sampling scheme is to take some random measurements of the Fourier coefficients y.

However, as we can notice in Figure 10.3, the most significant nonzero Fourier coefficients of a typical MR image are mainly in the low-frequency region, and the coefficients in the high-frequency region are already quite sparse and small. Hence a uniformly random sampling of the Fourier domain is not necessarily the most efficient. A more suitable sampling scheme for so-distributed coefficients is the *variable density random sampling*. It is designed specifically for 2D image objects where most of their energy is concentrated close to the origin of the frequency domain. More specifically, although the locations of the samples are still randomly selected, it progressively gives higher chances for samples in lower frequencies to be selected than in the higher frequencies. Figure 10.8 shows one example of the variable density random sample pattern.

In practice, however, from the physical model of MRI that we have described above, we know that the MRI machine cannot take measurements at totally random locations from time to time. Instead, it produces a sequence of samples of the Fourier

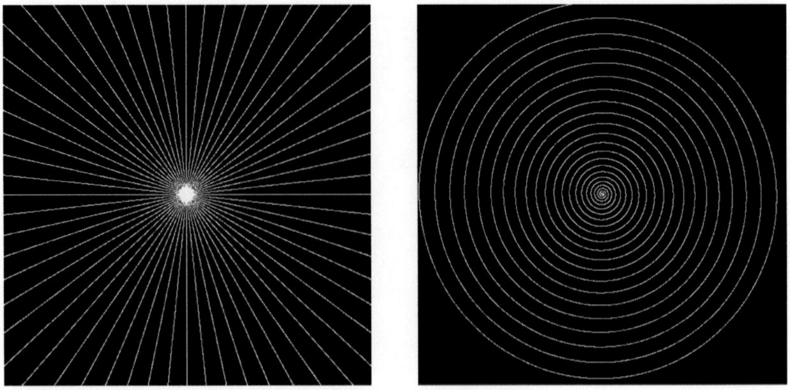

Figure 10.9 Examples of a radial sampling pattern and a spiral pattern.

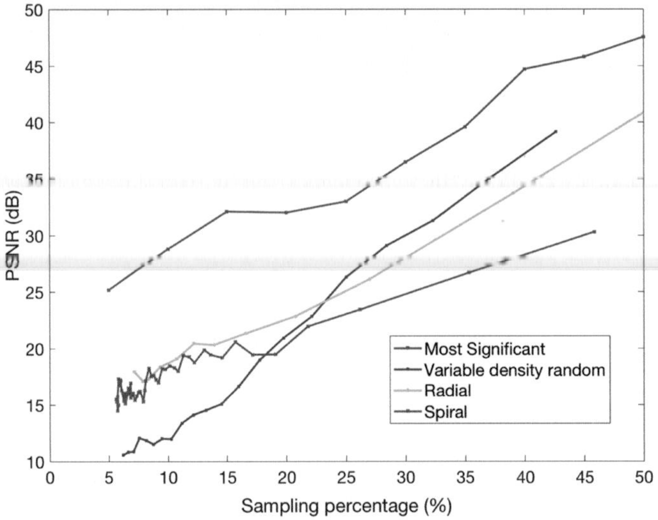

Figure 10.10 The reconstruction quality of the brain image using different subsampling patterns.

coefficients along a continuous trajectory $(k_x(t), k_y(t))$ in the k-space. Hence, the main challenge of compressive MRI is to design both practical and efficient sampling schemes in the Fourier domain for real MR images that are subject to the constraints of the physical process. To this end, some popular subsampling patterns have been proven (empirically) effective for MRI. Examples include a *radial* sampling pattern and a *spiral* pattern as shown in Figure 10.9. Clearly, both patterns are designed to have more coefficients densely sampled close to the origin and sparser coefficients far away from the origin.

To see the effectiveness of different sampling patterns, in Figure 10.10, we plot the peak signal-to-noise ratios (PSNRs) of the reconstructed images against different sample percentages.[6] To establish a baseline, we first calculate the PSNR values when

[6] We will describe details of the reconstruction algorithm in the next section.

the most significant nonzero wavelet coefficients in $\boldsymbol{x}$ are given. The results are shown in the red curve. It clearly outperforms the other subsampling methods that do not have the knowledge of the ground-truth sparse signal $\boldsymbol{x}$. Furthermore, compared to the deterministic radial and spiral patterns, the variable density random sampling initially achieves the worst reconstruction quality when the sampling percentage is low, namely, less than 20%. Then its performance increases significantly when the sampling percentage becomes higher, gradually surpassing the performance of the other subsampling patterns. The reader may refer to [LDSP08] for more discussions about compressive sampling of MRI.

10.4 Algorithms for MR Image Recovery

In this section, we discuss algorithms for reconstructing MR images from the sampled measurements $\boldsymbol{y}$. This is conceptually straightforward: many of the methods described in Chapter 8 can be applied to reconstruct the sparse coefficients $\boldsymbol{x}$ from the measurements $\boldsymbol{y} = \boldsymbol{A}\boldsymbol{x}$. However, there are several practical considerations that demand additional attention. First, MR measurements are subject to various nonidealities, including noise. Second, because it is so important to make the sampling scheme as efficient as possible, it is often helpful to leverage other structural information about the target image, beyond sparsity of its wavelet coefficients $\boldsymbol{x}$.

Measurement Noise

In practice, the measured MR image I can be degraded by thermal noise, so that the measurements $\boldsymbol{y}$ are

$$\boldsymbol{y} = \boldsymbol{A}\boldsymbol{x} + \boldsymbol{n}, \tag{10.4.1}$$

where $\boldsymbol{n}$ is a noise term with bounded norm $\|\boldsymbol{n}\|_2 < \varepsilon$ or assumed to be Gaussian for simplicity. One can accurately estimate the sparse coefficients $\boldsymbol{x}$ by looking for the minimum ℓ^1 norm coefficients that agree with the observations $\boldsymbol{y}$ up to the noise level (see Chapter 3, Section 3.5):

$$\hat{\boldsymbol{x}} = \arg\min_{\boldsymbol{x}} \|\boldsymbol{x}\|_1 \quad \text{subject to} \quad \|\boldsymbol{A}\boldsymbol{x} - \boldsymbol{y}\|_2 \leq \varepsilon. \tag{10.4.2}$$

Once $\boldsymbol{x}$ is recovered from solving this program, we can recover the image as $\hat{\boldsymbol{z}} = \boldsymbol{\Psi}[\hat{\boldsymbol{x}}]$.[7]

Gradient Sparsity

The wavelet representation developed above is well suited for representing piecewise smooth functions with smooth discontinuities. As we can see from the brain image, MR images may exhibit stronger properties than just piecewise smoothness: an image may be approximated as piecewise *constant* [MYZC08]. This means that the image

[7] Here by abuse of notation, we use $\hat{\boldsymbol{z}}$ to denote both the 2D MR image I and its vectorized version as a vector in $\mathbb{R}^{N^2}$, as its meaning is clear from the context.

value is constant away from a few sharp edges. The gradient of such an image is nonzero only at the edges, and hence is sparse.

To be more precise, let ∇_1 and ∇_2 represent finite-difference (differentiation) operators on the first (x) and second (y) coordinates of the image I, respectively. We use $(\nabla z)_i = ((\nabla_1 z)_i, (\nabla_2 z)_i) \in \mathbb{R}^2$ to denote the gradient vector at a pixel i. The ℓ^2 norm $\|(\nabla z)_i\|_2 = \left((\nabla_1 z)_i^2 + (\nabla_2 z)_i^2\right)^{1/2}$ measures the length of this vector.

A piecewise constant image has relatively few pixels at which the gradient is nonzero:

$$\sum_i \mathbb{1}_{\|(\nabla z)_i\|_2 \neq 0} \tag{10.4.3}$$

is small. This can be interpreted as a group sparsity assumption on the gradient vector field – see Chapter 6.

The number of points of nonzero gradient, (10.4.3), is conceptually simple, but is not well suited to efficient computation. Following the intuition for group sparsity in Chapter 6, we can define a convex relaxation of this function, known as the *total variation* of the image z:

$$\|z\|_{\mathrm{TV}} \doteq \sum_i \|(\nabla z)_i\|_2 \,. \tag{10.4.4}$$

This is a convex function of z.[8]

Using this convex function, we can verify experimentally that MR images are well approximated as gradient-sparse. To do this, we take an image z, and compute approximations to it using the proximal operator[9] for the total variation:

$$\hat{z}_\lambda = \operatorname{prox}_{\lambda \mathrm{TV}}(z) \doteq \arg\min_{x} \lambda \, \|x\|_{\mathrm{TV}} + \tfrac{1}{2} \, \|x - z\|_2^2 \,. \tag{10.4.5}$$

For each $\lambda \geq 0$, we have an approximation $\hat{z}_\lambda$, whose gradient is sparse. The parameter λ trades off between gradient sparsity of $\hat{z}$ and fidelity to the original image z. Here, the proximal operator $\operatorname{prox}_{\lambda \mathrm{TV}}(\cdot)$ can be computed using the alternating directions method of multipliers (ADMM); we will describe this in more generality below.

Figure 10.11 shows approximations $\hat{z}_\lambda$ to z, with $\lambda = 0.6, 0.4$, and 0.2. From the figure, we see that the image admits visually plausible approximations with roughly 10% of the nonzero gradient vectors.

Combining Gradient Sparsity and Wavelet Sparsity

To encourage the recovered image to have sparse gradients, we can incorporate the total variation into the above stable sparse recovery program (10.4.2) as an additional regularization term. Notice that $x = \Phi z$ and $Ax = \mathcal{F}_U[z]$. So the resulting program becomes

$$z^* = \arg\min_z \alpha \|\Phi z\|_1 + \beta \|z\|_{\mathrm{TV}} \quad \text{subject to} \quad \|\mathcal{F}_U[z] - y\|_2 < \varepsilon, \tag{10.4.6}$$

[8] Strictly speaking, it is not a norm, because it is not positive definite.

[9] For more details on proximal operators, see Sections 8.1–8.3 of Chapter 8.

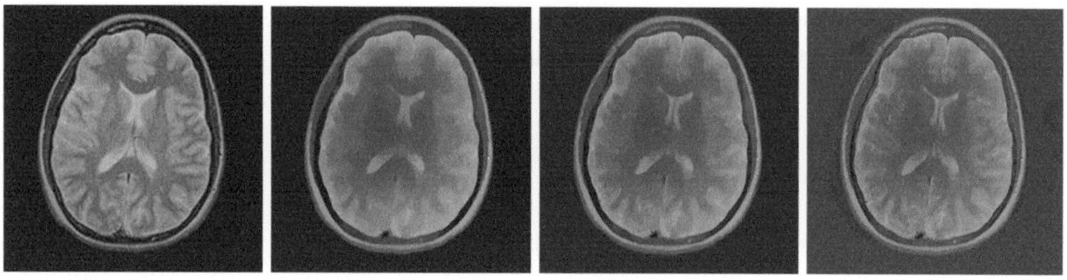

(a) Original (b) $\hat{z}_{0.6}$ (5.8%) (c) $\hat{z}_{0.4}$ (7.1%) (d) $\hat{z}_{0.2}$ (10.5%)

Figure 10.11 Gradient-sparse Approximations. (a) Target MR image z. (b)–(d) Gradient-sparse approximations computed using the proximal operator for the total variation, $\mathrm{prox}_{\lambda \mathrm{TV}}(z)$ for $\lambda = 0.6, 0.4$, and 0.2, respectively. For each approximation, we also display the fraction of pixels at which the gradient is nonzero.

where $\alpha \in \mathbb{R}$ and $\beta \in \mathbb{R}$ are two positive weight parameters. The use of total variation and ℓ^1 norm together for MRI recovery was originally introduced by the work of [LDP07] and [MYZC08].

We can rewrite the above program in an unconstrained form as

$$z^* = \arg\min_{z} \alpha \|\boldsymbol{\Phi} z\|_1 + \beta \sum_i \|(\nabla z)_i\|_2 + \frac{1}{2}\|\mathcal{F}_U[z] - \boldsymbol{y}\|_2^2. \tag{10.4.7}$$

Since every term is a convex function of z, the overall objective function is also convex. Such a program can be efficiently solved by the so-called fixed-point iteration (see [MYZC08] for more details).

Optimization Algorithm

We introduce here a simpler (and arguably faster) algorithm by exploiting the special structure of the program. We observe that the main challenge in solving the above program seems to be that the objective function contains two separate terms, one minimizing the ℓ^1 norm of $\boldsymbol{\Phi} z$ and the other minimizing the sum of ℓ^2 norms of the gradient of z. If we optimize one of the two terms $\|\boldsymbol{\Phi} z\|_1$ and $\|z\|_{\mathrm{TV}}$ while treating the other as constant, each of the two subproblems will be a relatively easy optimization problem. Hence one may utilize the alternating direction minimization method (ADMM) introduced in Chapter 8, Section 8.5, to solve this program. This was first suggested by the work of [YZY10]. We here give a brief description of the algorithm.

The first two terms of (10.4.7) both depend on z. So to utilize ADMM, we need to separate the variables first. To this end, we introduce some auxiliary variables: $\boldsymbol{x} \doteq \boldsymbol{\Phi} z \in \mathbb{R}^{N^2}$ for the (sparse) wavelet coefficients and $\boldsymbol{v}_i \doteq (\nabla z)_i \in \mathbb{R}^2$ with $i = 1, \dots, N^2$ for the (sparse) image gradients. With these auxiliary variables, the program (10.4.7) becomes

$$\begin{aligned} &\min_{z, \boldsymbol{x}, \boldsymbol{v}} \alpha \|\boldsymbol{x}\|_1 + \beta \sum_i \|\boldsymbol{v}_i\|_2 + \tfrac{1}{2}\|\mathcal{F}_U[z] - \boldsymbol{y}\|_2^2 \\ &\text{subject to} \quad \boldsymbol{x} = \boldsymbol{\Phi} z, \quad \boldsymbol{v}_i = (\nabla z)_i \in \mathbb{R}^2 \ \forall\, i. \end{aligned} \tag{10.4.8}$$

Consider the augmented Lagrangian formulation of (10.4.8). We define the two functions associated with these auxiliary variables:

$$g_1(z, \boldsymbol{x}, \boldsymbol{\Lambda}_1) \doteq \alpha \|\boldsymbol{x}\|_1 + \boldsymbol{\Lambda}_1^*(\boldsymbol{x} - \boldsymbol{\Phi} z) + \frac{\mu_1}{2}\|\boldsymbol{x} - \boldsymbol{\Phi} z\|_2^2 \tag{10.4.9}$$

and

$$g_2(z, \boldsymbol{v}_i, (\boldsymbol{\Lambda}_2)_i) \doteq \beta \|\boldsymbol{v}_i\|_2 + (\boldsymbol{\Lambda}_2)_i^*(\boldsymbol{v}_i - (\nabla z)_i) + \frac{\mu_2}{2}\|\boldsymbol{v}_i - (\nabla z)_i\|_2^2. \tag{10.4.10}$$

The augmented Lagrangian function of (10.4.8) is given by

$$\mathcal{L}(z, \boldsymbol{x}, \boldsymbol{v}, \boldsymbol{\Lambda}_1, \boldsymbol{\Lambda}_2) \doteq g_1(z, \boldsymbol{x}, \boldsymbol{\Lambda}_1) + \sum_i g_2(z, \boldsymbol{v}_i, (\boldsymbol{\Lambda}_2)_i) + \frac{1}{2}\|\mathcal{F}_U[z] - \boldsymbol{y}\|_2^2. \tag{10.4.11}$$

Then the above constrained optimization program (10.4.8) is equivalent to the unconstrained one:

$$\min_{z, \boldsymbol{x}, \boldsymbol{v}, \boldsymbol{\Lambda}_1, \boldsymbol{\Lambda}_2} \mathcal{L}(z, \boldsymbol{x}, \boldsymbol{v}, \boldsymbol{\Lambda}_1, \boldsymbol{\Lambda}_2), \tag{10.4.12}$$

which can be optimized iteratively following the alternating direction method:[10]

$$\begin{cases} \boldsymbol{x}^{(k+1)} = \arg\min_{\boldsymbol{x}} g_1\big(z^{(k)}, \boldsymbol{x}, \boldsymbol{\Lambda}_1^{(k)}\big), \\ \boldsymbol{v}_i^{(k+1)} = \arg\min_{\boldsymbol{v}_i} g_2\big(z^{(k)}, \boldsymbol{v}_i, \boldsymbol{\Lambda}_2^{(k)}\big), \\ z^{(k+1)} = \arg\min_z \mathcal{L}\big(z, \boldsymbol{x}^{(k+1)}, \boldsymbol{v}^{(k+1)}, \boldsymbol{\Lambda}_1^{(k)}, \boldsymbol{\Lambda}_2^{(k)}\big), \\ \boldsymbol{\Lambda}_1^{(k+1)} = \boldsymbol{\Lambda}_1^{(k)} + \mu_1\big(\boldsymbol{x}^{(k+1)} - \boldsymbol{\Phi} z^{(k+1)}\big), \\ \boldsymbol{\Lambda}_2^{(k+1)} = \boldsymbol{\Lambda}_2^{(k)} + \mu_2\big(\boldsymbol{v}^{(k+1)} - \nabla z^{(k+1)}\big). \end{cases} \tag{10.4.13}$$

We notice that all terms of the Lagrangian function (10.4.11) are convex functions. Hence all the above subprograms are convex optimizations.

To solve the first subprogram in (10.4.13),

$$\boldsymbol{x}^{(k+1)} = \arg\min_{\boldsymbol{x}} g_1\big(z^{(k)}, \boldsymbol{x}, \boldsymbol{\Lambda}_1^{(k)}\big),$$

although g_1 is nondifferentiable with respect to $\boldsymbol{x}$, it has a closed-form solution in terms of the proximal operator for ℓ^1 norm minimization:

$$\boldsymbol{x}^{(k+1)} = \operatorname{soft}\Big(\boldsymbol{\Phi} z^{(k)} - \boldsymbol{\Lambda}_1^{(k)}/\mu_1, \alpha/\mu_1\Big). \tag{10.4.14}$$

Here, we recall that $\operatorname{soft}(\cdot,\cdot)$ is the soft-thresholding operator

$$\operatorname{soft}(x, \tau) \doteq \max\{|x| - \tau, 0\} \cdot \operatorname{sign}(x), \quad x \in \mathbb{R}, \tag{10.4.15}$$

applied to the vector $\boldsymbol{\Phi} z^{(k)} - \boldsymbol{\Lambda}_1^{(k)}/\mu_1$ entry-wise. We leave the derivation of this as an exercise for the reader.

To solve the second subprogram in (10.4.13),

$$\boldsymbol{v}_i^{(k+1)} = \arg\min_{\boldsymbol{v}_i} g_2\Big(z^{(k)}, \boldsymbol{v}_i, \boldsymbol{\Lambda}_2^{(k)}\Big),$$

[10] Here, different from the notation we have used in the optimization chapters, we will use superscript k to indicate iteration of the algorithm since the subscript i is already used for indexing the pixels.

notice that g_2 is essentially a 2D version of the 1D proximal operator for the ℓ^1 norm:

$$\min_{v} \beta|v| + \frac{\mu}{2}(v-x)^2.$$

It also has a closed-form solution in terms of a 2D version of the soft thresholding:

$$\boldsymbol{v}_i^{(k+1)} = \operatorname{soft}_2\Big(\big(\nabla \boldsymbol{z}^{(k)}\big)_i - \big(\boldsymbol{\Lambda}_2^{(k)}\big)_i/\mu_2,\ \beta/\mu_2\Big), \tag{10.4.16}$$

where $\operatorname{soft}_2(\cdot,\cdot)$ indicates the 2D shrinkage operator

$$\operatorname{soft}_2(\boldsymbol{x},\tau) \doteq \max\{\|\boldsymbol{x}\|_2 - \tau, 0\} \cdot \boldsymbol{x}/\|\boldsymbol{x}\|_2, \quad \boldsymbol{x} \in \mathbb{R}^2. \tag{10.4.17}$$

Again, we leave the derivation of this as an exercise for the reader.

Finally, to solve the third subprogram in (10.4.13),

$$\boldsymbol{z}^{(k+1)} = \arg\min_{\boldsymbol{z}} \mathcal{L}\Big(\boldsymbol{z}, \boldsymbol{x}^{(k+1)}, \boldsymbol{v}^{(k+1)}, \boldsymbol{\Lambda}_1^{(k)}, \boldsymbol{\Lambda}_2^{(k)}\Big),$$

we notice that with $\boldsymbol{x}^{(k+1)}, \boldsymbol{v}^{(k+1)}, \boldsymbol{\Lambda}_1^{(k)}$, and $\boldsymbol{\Lambda}_2^{(k)}$ all being fixed, each term of the Lagrangian function $\mathcal{L}(\cdot)$ is a quadratic function in $\boldsymbol{z}$. As the optimal solution $\boldsymbol{z}^{(k+1)}$ satisfies the condition $\partial\mathcal{L}/\partial\boldsymbol{z}\Big|_{\boldsymbol{z}^{(k+1)}} = 0$, this gives

$$\boldsymbol{M}\boldsymbol{z}^{(k+1)} = \boldsymbol{b} \quad \text{or} \quad \boldsymbol{z}^{(k+1)} = \boldsymbol{M}^{-1}\boldsymbol{b}, \tag{10.4.18}$$

where

$$\begin{aligned} \boldsymbol{M} &= \mathcal{F}_U^*\mathcal{F}_U + \mu_1\boldsymbol{I} + \mu_2\nabla^*\nabla, \\ \boldsymbol{b} &= \mathcal{F}_U^*[\boldsymbol{y}] + \boldsymbol{\Phi}^*\Big(\mu_1\boldsymbol{x}^{(k+1)} + \boldsymbol{\Lambda}_1^{(k)}\Big) + \nabla^*\Big(\mu_2\boldsymbol{v}^{(k+1)} + \boldsymbol{\Lambda}_2^{(k)}\Big). \end{aligned}$$

Here, ∇^* denotes the adjoint of the discrete derivative operator ∇.[11]

One can show that as long as the step sizes μ_1 and μ_2 are chosen to be reasonably small, the above alternating minimization scheme (10.4.13) will always converge to the optimal solution, starting from any initial conditions [YZY10].

10.5 Notes

MRI was one of the early successful applications of compressive sensing and was first convincingly verified through a series of seminal work [LDP07, LDSP08]. Many follow-up works have continued to further improve the efficiency of the associated optimization methods [MYZC08, YZY10] or sampling schemes. Today, compressive sensing has been widely practiced in MRI as well as many other similar medical imaging systems. For interested readers, more extensive resources about compressive sensing MRI can be found at [Lus13].

As we have seen through the physical process of MRI, the full potential of compressive sampling is still somewhat limited by what measurements we can make and at what locations with the MRI machine. The physical restrictions of the machine

[11] This is the linear operator that satisfies $\langle \boldsymbol{g}, \nabla\boldsymbol{z}\rangle = \langle \nabla^*\boldsymbol{g}, \boldsymbol{z}\rangle$ for all $\boldsymbol{g}$ and $\boldsymbol{z}$.

limit what type of sensing matrix $\boldsymbol{A}$ we may construct and hence compromise its incoherent or isometric properties. In many scientific or recreational imaging systems, however, one may have much more freedom in controlling or designing the type of measurements we may acquire, say through the so-called *coded aperture* technique [CF80]. Such methods allow us to design flexible and rich sensing schemes that can acquire the physical signals with different spatial, temporal, and spectral patterns that best match the structures of the signals. One somewhat extreme example along this line of work is the so-called "single-pixel" camera [DDT$^+$08]. The intention is to maximize information captured by every additional measurement in scenarios where measurements are extremely expensive or difficult (say, in some outer space astronomical physical observations).

10.6 Exercises

10.1. (Compressive sensing of Shepp–Logan phantom) *Design and implement a pair of efficient encoder and decoder to encode the Shepp–Logan phantom based on the principles of compressive sensing. To measure the performance of the encoder/decoder pair, plot the PSNR curve with respect to the dimension of the compressed signal.*

10.2. (Sparse gradient approximation with debiasing) *For each $\lambda \geq 0$, equation (10.4.5) computes $\hat{\boldsymbol{z}}_\lambda$ from the proximal operator of the total variation. Based on $\hat{\boldsymbol{z}}_\lambda$, one may further compute the so-called debiased estimate:*

$$\hat{\boldsymbol{z}}_{\lambda,\mathrm{debiased}} = \arg\min_{\boldsymbol{x}} \tfrac{1}{2}\,\|\boldsymbol{x} - \boldsymbol{z}\|_2^2 \quad \textit{subject to} \quad \mathrm{supp}(\|\nabla \boldsymbol{x}\|_2) \subseteq \mathrm{supp}(\|\nabla \hat{\boldsymbol{z}}_\lambda\|_2).$$

Debiasing improves fidelity to the observation $\boldsymbol{z}$, by removing shrinkage effects on the nonzeros. Show that $\hat{\boldsymbol{z}}_{\lambda,\mathrm{debiased}}$ can be computed from $\hat{\boldsymbol{z}}_\lambda$ simply by solving a linear system of equations.

10.3. (Proximal operators) *What is the optimal solution to the following program:*

$$\min_{v} \beta|v| + \frac{\mu}{2}(v - x)^2 \,? \tag{10.6.1}$$

Based on this, prove that:

(a) The optimal solution for $\boldsymbol{x}^{(k+1)}$ in (10.4.13) *is given by* (10.4.14).
(b) The optimal solution for $\boldsymbol{v}_i^{(k+1)}$ in (10.4.13) *is given by* (10.4.16).

10.4. (MRI recovery with anisotropic total variation [WYYZ08, Bir11, BUF07, CAB$^+$16]) *Sometimes, for simplicity, people also consider the anisotropic total variation (ATV) of the image I:*

$$\|\boldsymbol{z}\|_{\mathrm{ATV}} \doteq \sum_i |(\nabla_1 \boldsymbol{z})_i| + |(\nabla_2 \boldsymbol{z})_i|.$$

Notice that this is exactly the ℓ^1 *norm of partial derivatives of the image at all pixels. Hence, minimizing* $\|z\|_{\text{ATV}}$ *would encourage the image to have sparse partial derivatives. Let* ∇ *be the (finite-difference) gradient operator* (∇_1, ∇_2) *on the image* z. *Then we have* $\|z\|_{\text{ATV}} = \|\nabla z\|_1$.

We may consider replacing the TV term in (10.4.7) *with the ATV,* $\|z\|_{\text{TV}} \to \|z\|_{\text{ATV}}$*:*

$$z^* = \arg\min_z \alpha\|\mathbf{\Phi} z\|_1 + \beta\|z\|_{\text{ATV}} + \frac{1}{2}\|\mathcal{F}_U[z] - \boldsymbol{y}\|_2^2. \tag{10.6.2}$$

The goal of this exercise is to see how to derive a simpler algorithm for the ATV regulated problem using the ALM and ADMM method discussed in Section 8.5.

Using the operator ∇*, the above program can be rewritten as:*

$$\begin{aligned} z^* &= \arg\min_z \alpha\|\mathbf{\Phi} z\|_1 + \beta\|\nabla z\|_1 + \frac{1}{2}\|\mathcal{F}_U[z] - \boldsymbol{y}\|_2^2 & (10.6.3)\\ &= \arg\min_z \left\|\begin{pmatrix}\alpha\mathbf{\Phi}\\ \beta\nabla\end{pmatrix} z\right\|_1 + \frac{1}{2}\|\mathcal{F}_U[z] - \boldsymbol{y}\|_2^2. & (10.6.4)\end{aligned}$$

If we denote

$$\boldsymbol{W} \doteq \begin{pmatrix}\alpha\mathbf{\Phi}\\ \beta\nabla\end{pmatrix} \quad \textit{and} \quad \boldsymbol{w} \doteq \boldsymbol{W} z \in \mathbb{C}^{3m},$$

then the above program becomes:

$$z^* = \arg\min_{z,\boldsymbol{w}} \|\boldsymbol{w}\|_1 + \frac{1}{2}\|\mathcal{F}_U[z] - \boldsymbol{y}\|_2^2 \quad \textit{subject to} \quad \boldsymbol{w} = \boldsymbol{W} z. \tag{10.6.5}$$

Then using the augmented Lagrange multiplier method discussed in Chapter 8 for ℓ^1 *minimization,* z^* *can be solved by alternately minimizing* z, $\boldsymbol{w}$*, and a Lagrange multiplier vector* $\boldsymbol{\lambda} \in \mathbb{R}^{3m}$ *in*

$$z^* = \arg\min_{z,\boldsymbol{w},\boldsymbol{\lambda}} \|\boldsymbol{w}\|_1 + \boldsymbol{\lambda}^*(\boldsymbol{w} - \boldsymbol{W} z) + \frac{\mu}{2}\|\boldsymbol{w} - \boldsymbol{W} z\|_2^2 + \frac{1}{2}\|\mathcal{F}_U[z] - \boldsymbol{y}\|_2^2. \tag{10.6.6}$$

We leave as an exercise to the reader to derive a detailed algorithm for (10.6.6).

11 Wideband Spectrum Sensing

"We'll have infinite bandwidth in a decade's time."

– Bill Gates, PC Magazine, October, 1994

In this chapter, we present an application of compressive sensing to a crucial problem in modern wireless (radio) communication: *How can cognitive radios efficiently identify available spectrum?* We will see that this problem can be cast as one of recovering the support of a sparse signal, in the presence of noise. We will see how the methods and algorithms described in this book will allow us to break theoretical limits of conventional approaches, and, once properly implemented in hardware, they can significantly advance the state of the art, by enabling better tradeoffs between energy consumption and scan time. Besides its practical importance, this application is very interesting as it is kind of *dual* to the situation in the magnetic resonance imaging that we studied in the preceding chapter. In MRI, the measurements are the Fourier transform of the image of interest and the sparse patterns are in the image domain; whereas for spectrum sensing, the sparse patterns are in the Fourier domain which we do not measure directly.

11.1 Introduction

11.1.1 Wideband Communications

In modern wireless (radio) communication systems, it is common for a wide radio spectrum range to be shared by many users. A classic protocol for sharing a wide spectrum is to divide the spectrum into multiple narrow bands. Each individual user transmits a narrowband signal within the designated channel band by modulation, typically by multiplying a periodic "carrier signal" with a frequency at the center of the assigned band. To be more precise, let us assume that the entire available spectrum is between $(f_{\min}, f_{\max})$.[1] We denote the bandwidth of the spectrum as $W = f_{\max} - f_{\min}$.

[1] For a real signal, its Fourier transform is symmetric in the frequency domain. So for simplicity, we will only talk about the positive (or upper) range of the spectrum $(f_{\min}, f_{\max})$; the corresponding negative (lower) spectrum $(-f_{\max}, -f_{\min})$ is assumed to be available too by default.

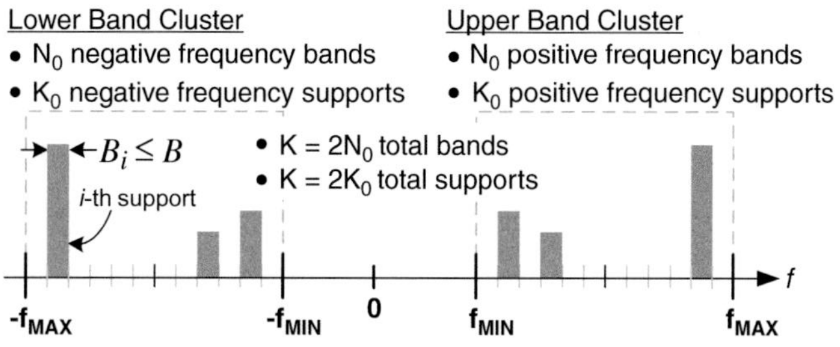

Figure 11.1 A wideband spectrum between $(f_{\min}, f_{\max})$ and $(-f_{\max}, -f_{\min})$ is divided into multiple narrow bands of width B. At any given time a (sparse) number of channels are actively in use.

If the spectrum is divided into N_0 narrow bands, then each individual channel has a resolution bandwidth (RBW) $B = W/N_0$. See Figure 11.1 for an illustration.

11.1.2 Nyquist Sampling and Beyond

To recover the signals at the receiver side, one needs to demodulate the signal from its carrier, sample the signal at a high frequency through an analog-to-digital converter (ADC), and then filter through a low-pass filter. The classic *Nyquist sampling theorem* [OSB99] in digital signal processing stipulates that, to perfectly recover an analog band-limited signal, say $x(t)$, from its discrete (periodic) samples $\{x(nT)\}_{n\in\mathbb{Z}}$, one needs to sample the signal at a frequency $f_s = 1/T$ at least twice the signal's possible bandwidth, known as the Nyquist rate. Hence in the above wideband setting, if a receiver does not know the carrier frequencies of the (active) channels,[2] in order to recover the narrow band signals in every possible channel, one needs to demodulate the signals by sampling at a rate higher than twice the spectrum bandwidth W, that is:

$$f_s \geq 2W.$$

If so, any signal $x(t)$ within this spectrum can be perfectly recovered from its samples $\{x(nT)\}_{n\in\mathbb{Z}}$ via the so-called *cardinal series*:

$$x(t) = \sum_{n\in\mathbb{Z}} x(nT)\text{sinc}(t/T - n),$$

or other similar interpolation schemes [OSB99].

For wideband communication, however, the Nyquist rate $2W$ often exceeds the specifications of typical ADCs by magnitudes. For example, in the year 2012, the US President's Council of Advisors on Science and Technology (PCAST) recommended sharing 1 GHz of federal government spectrum from 2.7 to 3.7 GHz with nongovernmental entities for public use. The Nyquist rate would require an ADC of 2 GHz!

[2] Which is quite common in many applications such as interference detection. However, if the carrier frequency is known, the receiver can simply demodulate the signals at the carrier frequency [Lan67].

Given that the actual bandwidth B of the signals in each channel is rather small[3] compared to the entire spectrum, demodulating at the Nyquist rate for every channel seems rather demanding and likely unnecessary too.

As mobile wireless devices such as cellular phones and personal computers have become ubiquitous in modern-day life, it has become increasingly critical to improve the efficiency of spectrum sharing as well as improve the power efficiency of individual mobile devices. In terms of spectrum usage, modern mobile devices are very different from conventional wireless communication systems such as radio broadcasting. At any given time and place, only a relatively small number of devices/users may be active. Hence such devices do not need designated channels at all times and can share a common spectrum via certain data transmission protocols (such as in WiFi). As Figure 11.1 has illustrated, although the PCAST spectrum can simultaneously support N_0 narrow bands, at any given time or place, only a small number of bands (say K_0) are active and any new user does not know in advance which bands are being occupied. In such new scenarios, compressive sensing is relevant and beneficial: if the support of a signal is *sparse in the spectrum*, the necessary sampling rate for signal recovery can be significantly lower than the Nyquist rate $2W$. For instance, using techniques such as *random demodulation* [Tro10], one only needs a sampling rate at

$$f_s = O(K_0 \log(W/K_0))$$

to stably reconstruct the signal, which is exponentially lower than $2W$. A more practical scheme named *modulated wideband converter* [ME10, ME11] requires only a sampling rate at

$$f_s = 2K_0B,$$

which is usually magnitudes lower than the Nyquist rate when $K_0 \ll N_0$.

11.2 Wideband Interferer Detection

The next-generation 5G technologies like Long-Term Evolution (LTE) aim to utilize under-utilized unlicensed public spectrum (like the PCAST spectrum mentioned above) in addition to designated licensed spectrum. Figure 11.2 shows an example of such a deployment. In order to utilize and share the unlicensed spectrum efficiently with all other possible users, the user terminal needs to sense in real time which channels are occupied by other users (called interferers) so that it can opportunistically use other idle channels for subsequent data transfer. Terminals with such capabilities are called cognitive radio (CR) terminals.

To model the interference, we may assume that the entire spectrum $(f_{\min}, f_{\max})$ is partitioned into N_0 bands. We say a band is occupied (or used) by an interferer

[3] Radio stations are typically assigned a 200 kHz bandwidth. That is more than enough for most audio signals in the 20 kHz to 30 kHz range. For data transmission tasks of mobile devices, the desired bandwidth is typically 20 MHz.

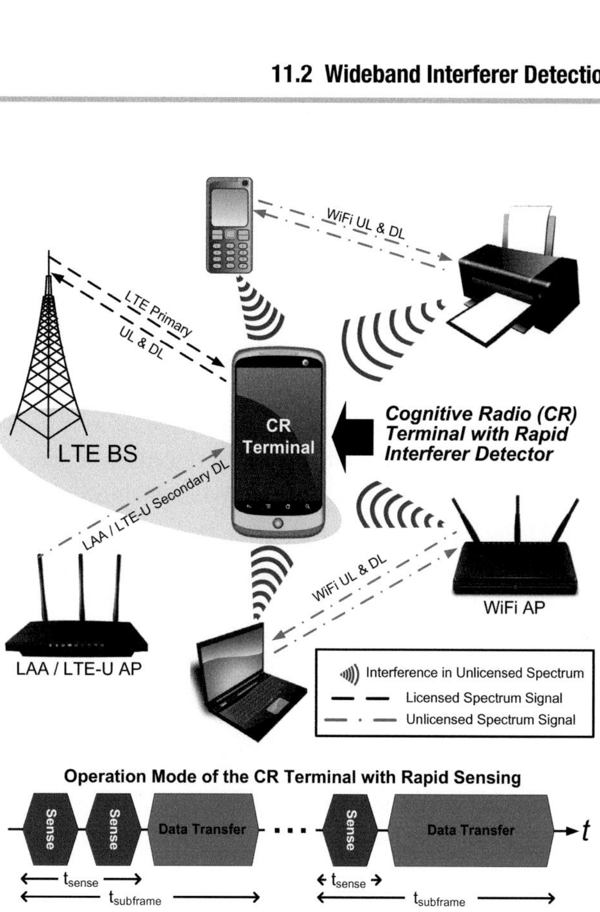

Figure 11.2 Illustration of the deployment of LTE-Unlicensed using cognitive ratio (CR) to detect active interferers.

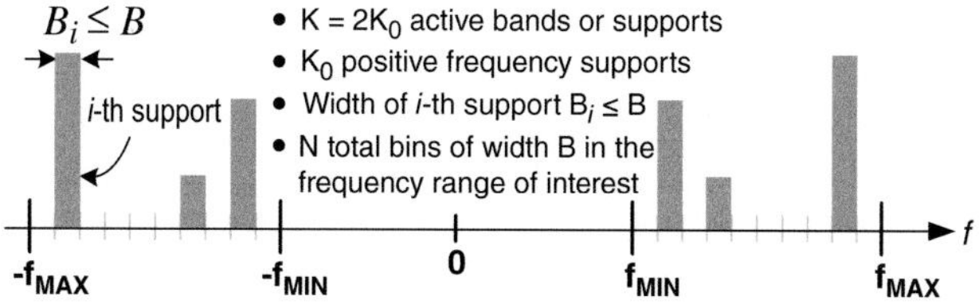

Figure 11.3 At any given time a sparse number of K_0 channels are actively in use.

(or another user) if the energy on that band is above a certain threshold (say above the background radio noise level). At any given time, we assume K_0 out of the N_0 bands are occupied by interferers, as illustrated in Figure 11.3. We call the aggregated signal of all the interferers $x(t)$. The problem of interference detection is to find out the supports of the K_0 bands of $X(f)$, the Fourier transform of $x(t)$.

11.2.1 Conventional Scanning Approaches

Conventionally, there are two straightforward approaches to detect (the support of) the interfering signal $x(t)$ in the frequency domain:

1 *Scan one band at a time:* For each of the N_0 bands, one can first down convert the signal using a local oscillator with frequency f_{lo} at the center of each band

$$f_{lo} = f_{\min} + 0.5B + iB, \quad i = 0, \ldots, N_0 - 1,$$

and then sample the signal at the Nyquist rate for each band,

$$f_s = 2B.$$

This allows one to recover the component of $x(t)$ in each band and determine if that band is occupied. Obviously, one needs to repeat this process N_0 times, once for each band, or one can build a system with N_0 parallel branches, again once for each band.

2 *Recover all bands together:* One can first down convert the signal using a local oscillator with frequency f_{lo} at the center of the entire spectrum,

$$f_{lo} = (f_{\min} + f_{\max})/2,$$

and then sample the signal at the Nyquist rate for the entire spectrum,

$$f_s = 2W = 2(f_{\max} - f_{\min}).$$

This allows one to recover the entire signal $x(t)$ within the spectrum, regardless of which bands have been occupied.

Despite their simplicity, these approaches are costly either in time (e.g., scanning N_0 times), or in hardware complexity (e.g., building N_0 branches), or in energy consumption (e.g., sampling at the high Nyquist rate $2W$).

As an example, Figure 11.4 illustrates applying the above schemes to the PCAST spectrum. For a sweeping spectrum scanner (Figure 11.4(a)), each frequency bin is scanned sequentially by progressively sweeping the local oscillator (LO) driving the downconverter. This architecture requires widely tunable, high-quality RF components that are difficult to implement on a chip. Identifying signals over a 1 GHz span with a 20 MHz RBW requires a long scan time which is proportional to the number of

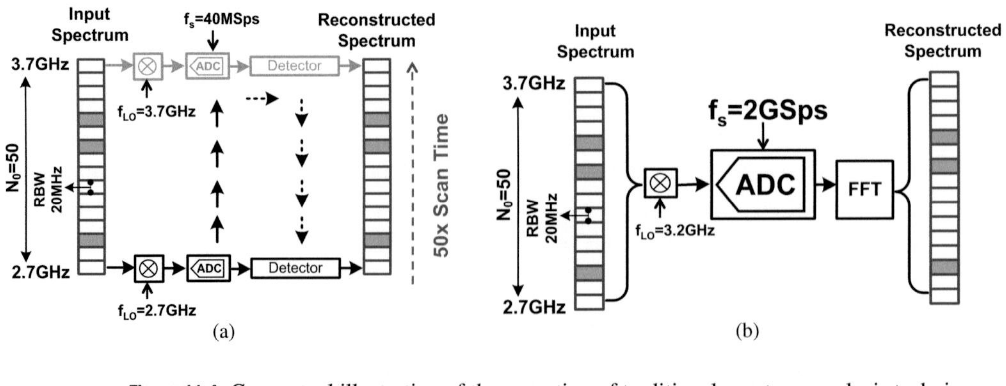

Figure 11.4 Conceptual illustration of the operation of traditional spectrum analysis techniques applied for a 2.7–3.7GHz spectrum analyzer with a 20MHz RBW; the occupied spectrum bins are shaded in green: (a) sweeping spectrum scanner, (b) Nyquist-rate FFT spectrum sensor.

bins $N_0 = 50$. This results in large energy consumption and the risk of missing rapidly changing interferers.

The scan time in sweeping scanners can in principle be reduced by using a multi branch architecture with multiple narrowband scanners operating in parallel. However, the hardware complexity becomes impracticable since each branch requires a separate phase-locked loop (PLL) to generate the LO signal and the 50 PLL frequencies would need to be spaced closely with a distance equal to the 20 MHz RBW.

A Nyquist-rate fast Fourier transform (FFT) spectrum sensor (Figure 11.4(b)) for a 1 GHz bandwidth would require a prohibitively high aggregate analog-to-digital (A/D) conversion rate of 2 GSps after I/Q downconversion. Even though the scan time is reduced, this is a power-hungry approach due to the high sampling rate required for the Nyquist-rate wideband sensing.

How can we do better? As we have mentioned earlier, at any given time, the number of bands used by other users, K_0, is typically sparse with respect to N_0. By exploiting this additional knowledge about the spectrum of the interference $x(t)$, i.e., $X(f)$ being sparse, we can come up with much more efficient solutions than the above approaches using techniques from compressive sensing. It has been well studied in Chapter 3 that one can recover a sparse signal from a small number of random (incoherent) linear measurements. However, here the sparsity is in the frequency domain and we need to know how to effectively and efficiently take random linear measurements of $X(f)$.

11.2.2 Compressive Sensing in the Frequency Domain

To take a random linear measurement of the spectrum $X(f)$, a very clever scheme has been suggested by [ME10] and [HYP$^+$15]: one can first multiply $x(t)$ with a periodic mixing function $p(t)$ say of period T_p. The mixed signal is then truncated with a low-pass filter $h(t)$ with cutoff frequency $1/(2T_s)$ and the filtered signal is then sampled at rate $f_s = 1/T_s$. The hope is that, for properly chosen mixing function $p(t)$, T_p, and T_s, the (discrete-time) Fourier transform of the output sequence, say $y(n)$, would be precisely random linear measurements of the (sparse) spectrum $X(f)$. Below we give a brief sketch of this scheme.

The mixing function $p(t)$, as a T_p-periodic function, can be written as a Fourier expansion:

$$p(t) = \sum_{l=-\infty}^{\infty} c_l e^{\mathrm{i}(2\pi/T_p)lt}, \tag{11.2.1}$$

where $\mathrm{i} = \sqrt{-1}$ is the imaginary unit and c_l is the Fourier coefficient,

$$c_l = \frac{1}{T_p}\int_0^{T_p} p(t)e^{-\mathrm{i}\frac{2\pi}{T_p}lt}\,dt.$$

After $x(t)$ is mixed with $p(t)$, the Fourier transform of the mixed signal $\tilde{x}(t) = x(t)p(t)$ would be

$$\tilde{X}(f) = \sum_{l=-\infty}^{\infty} c_l X(f - lf_p), \tag{11.2.2}$$

where $f_p = 1/T_p$. Since $X(f)$ is band-limited, the above sum will only have finite terms.

If the subsequent filter $h(t)$ is a perfect low-pass filter, only the frequencies in the interval $\left(-\frac{1}{2}f_s, +\frac{1}{2}f_s\right)$ will stay in the sequence $y[n]$. Hence, the discrete-time Fourier transform of $y[n]$ has the expression

$$Y(f) = \sum_{l=-L_0}^{L_0} c_l X(f - lf_p), \quad f \in \left(-\frac{1}{2}f_s, +\frac{1}{2}f_s\right), \tag{11.2.3}$$

where L_0 is large enough to cover the support of $X(f)$.

For simplicity, we may stack all the coefficients c_l into a vector

$$\boldsymbol{c} \doteq [c_{L_0}, \ldots, c_{-L_0}]^*$$

of length $L = 2L_0 + 1$ and $X(f - lf_p)$ into another vector

$$z(f) \doteq [X(f - L_0 f_p), \ldots, X(f + L_0 f_p)]^*. \tag{11.2.4}$$

The vector $z(f)$ is sparse if $X(f)$ is. We can write the above expression as

$$Y(f) = \boldsymbol{c}^* z(f). \tag{11.2.5}$$

The remaining question is how to properly choose the T_p-periodic mixing function $p(t)$ so that the expression in (11.2.3) would be a sufficiently random (or incoherent) measure of nonzero components in $X(f)$. An easy scheme is to make the values of $p(t)$ in each of its period $(0, T_p)$ be a pseudo-random bit sequence (PRBS) of length L:

$$p(t) = \alpha_k, \quad k\frac{T_p}{L} \leq t \leq (k+1)\frac{T_p}{L}, \quad 0 \leq k \leq L-1, \tag{11.2.6}$$

where α_k is a random variable taking binary values in $\{-1, +1\}$ of equal probability. For so-chosen $p(t)$, its Fourier coefficients c_l can be computed as

$$\begin{aligned} c_l &= \frac{1}{T_p}\int_0^{T_p/L} \sum_{k=0}^{L-1} \alpha_k e^{-\mathrm{i}(2\pi/T_p)l(t+kT_p/L)} dt \\ &= \sum_{k=0}^{L-1} \alpha_k e^{-\mathrm{i}(2\pi/L)lk} \frac{1}{T_p}\int_0^{T_p/L} e^{-\mathrm{i}(2\pi/T_p)lt} dt. \end{aligned}$$

Let us define the scalar

$$d_l \doteq \frac{1}{T_p}\int_0^{T_p/L} e^{-\mathrm{i}(2\pi/T_p)lt} dt$$

and let $\boldsymbol{D}$ be the diagonal matrix with d_l on its diagonal. Notice that $\{e^{-\mathrm{i}(2\pi/L)lk}\}$ is exactly the (k,l)-th entry of the discrete Fourier transform (DFT) matrix $\boldsymbol{F}$ of size $L \times L$. So we have

$$\boldsymbol{c}^* = \boldsymbol{a}^* \boldsymbol{F} \boldsymbol{D}, \tag{11.2.7}$$

where $\boldsymbol{a} = [\alpha_0, \alpha_1, \ldots, \alpha_{L-1}]^*$ is the sequence of random bits.

Combining the above equation with the measurement equation (11.2.5), we have

$$Y(f) = \boldsymbol{a}^* \boldsymbol{F} \boldsymbol{D} z(f). \tag{11.2.8}$$

The above equation is obtained from mixing with one signal $p(t)$ from one pseudo-random bit sequence $\boldsymbol{a}$. To recover the sparse vector $z(f)$, we can mix the input $x(t)$ with multiple signals $p_i(t), i = 1, \ldots, m$, each with an independent pseudo-random bit sequence $\boldsymbol{a}_i$. We collect all the measurements $Y_i(f)$ into one vector $\boldsymbol{y}(f) = [Y_1(f), \ldots, Y_m(f)]^*$. Then we have

$$\boldsymbol{y}(f) = \boldsymbol{A} \boldsymbol{F} \boldsymbol{D} z(f), \tag{11.2.9}$$

where $\boldsymbol{A}$ is an $m \times L$ matrix containing all the independent pseudo-random bit sequences $\boldsymbol{a}_i$ as its rows.

Notice that the diagonal operator $\boldsymbol{D}$ does not change the sparsity of $z(f)$ and the DFT matrix $\boldsymbol{F}$ is unitary. As we know from the analysis in Chapter 3, the $m \times L$ measurement matrix $\boldsymbol{A}\boldsymbol{F}$ would be highly incoherent and the so-obtained measurements $\boldsymbol{y}(f)$ would be a set of incoherent measurements of $z(f)$. As long as m is large enough, say in the order $O(K_0 \log(L/K_0))$, we are guaranteed to correctly recover the sparse vector $z(f)$ using the ℓ^1 minimization:

$$\min \|z(f)\|_1 \quad \text{subject to} \quad \boldsymbol{y}(f) = \boldsymbol{A}\boldsymbol{F}\boldsymbol{D} z(f). \tag{11.2.10}$$

In thcory, onc may solve the above ℓ^1 minimization problem to identify the support of the used bands. However, to minimize processing memory and power in hardware implementation, instead of using the generic convex optimization methods introduced in Chapter 8, greedy algorithms such as the orthogonal matching pursuit (OMP) Algorithm 8.11 of Chapter 8 become well suited for our purpose here. The OMP is a simple greedy heuristic for sparse recovery, which forms an estimate of the signal support one element at a time. In each iteration, the algorithm involves a minimal set of columns of the sensing matrix, here the matrix $\boldsymbol{A}\boldsymbol{F}\boldsymbol{D}$. It offers an attractive tradeoff between algorithm simplicity and recovery guarantees [TG07], hence is better suited for low-level hardware implementation than other generic ℓ^1 solvers.

11.3 System Implementation and Performance

The remaining issue is how one can implement the above spectrum sensing scheme with a practical real hardware system design. The resulting system should be able to realize the theoretical benefits of compressive sensing and break a good balance between power consumption, scanning time, and hardware complexity. The goal is to achieve significantly improved performance compared to the conventional approaches mentioned earlier. We here introduce one such system, the so-called quadrature analog to information converter (QAIC) system [HYP+15, YHW+15], for energy-efficient wideband spectrum sensing.

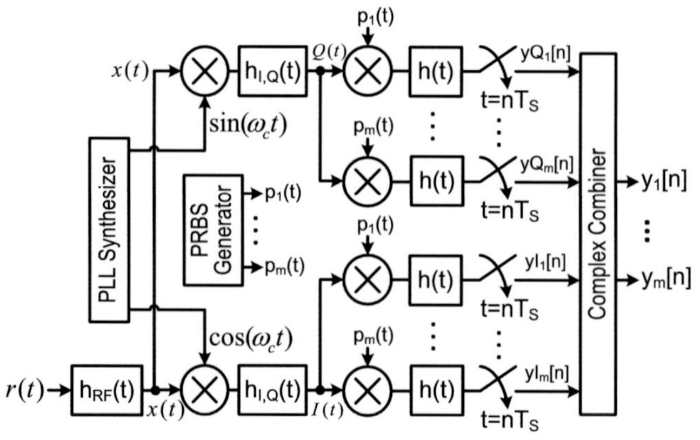

Figure 11.5 System diagram of the quadrature analog to information converter (QAIC).

11.3.1 Quadrature Analog to Information Converter

The QAIC illustrated in Figure 11.5 consists of three major functional blocks – an RF downconverter, I and Q path modulator banks (mixers, filters, and analog-to-digital converters), and a pairwise complex combiner. The input signal $x(t)$ is first downconverted to complex baseband with the in-phase branch I and the quadrature-phase Q. The downconverter outputs $I(t)$ and $Q(t)$ are multiplied by a periodic pseudo-random bit sequence (PRBS) $p_i(t)$, then filtered and sampled at a low rate in the I and Q path modulator banks. The QAIC exploits the compressive spectrum sensing principles discussed above: multiplication by the PRBS aliases the spectrum such that a portion from each band of the downconverter output signals $I(t)$ and $Q(t)$ appears at a low frequency centered around DC. The outputs of the I and Q path modulator banks are pairwise added by the complex combiner to select either the upper $(f_{\min}, f_{\max})$ or lower $(-f_{\max}, -f_{\min})$ band cluster of the input signal $x(t)$. The I and Q modulator banks of the QAIC consist of multiple branches each employing a different PRBS such that in principle a sufficiently large number of band mixtures output $y_1[n] \ldots y_m[n]$ allows us to recover the sparse multiband signal $x(t)$.

For QAIC, the frequency of the downconverter is chosen to be

$$f_c = (f_{\max} + f_{\min})/2$$

and $\omega_c = 2\pi f_c$. This shifts the spectrum of $x(t)$ from $(f_{\min}, f_{\max})^4$ to the base range $\left(-(f_{\max} - f_{\min})/2, +(f_{\max} - f_{\min})/2\right)$, centered around the DC, as shown in Figure 11.6. The low-pass filter $h_{I,Q}(t)$ extracts this baseband with a cutoff frequency

$$f_{I,Q} = (f_{\max} - f_{\min})/2.$$

The I and Q path modulator banks employed by the QAIC together process a complex signal $I(t) + \mathrm{j} \cdot Q(t)$ at baseband. As a result, the QAIC is able to isolate and process either the upper $(f_{\min}, f_{\max})$ or the lower $(-f_{\max}, -f_{\min})$ band cluster of the $x(t)$. The spectrum of the QAIC downconverter complex output configured to retain the upper band cluster of $x(t)$ is shown in Figure 11.6.

[4] Similarly for the lower $(-f_{\max}, -f_{\min})$ band cluster.

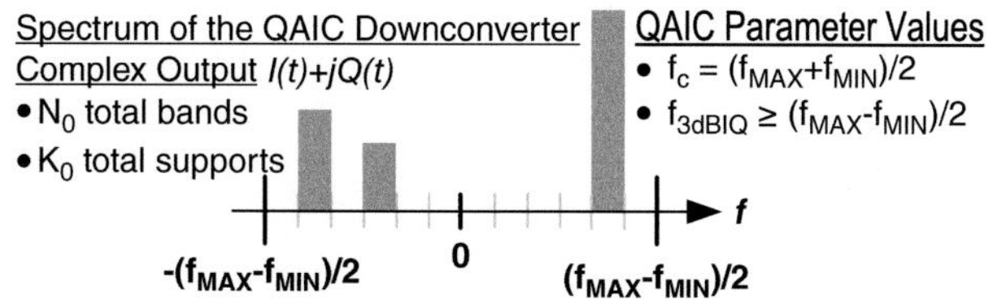

Figure 11.6 QAIC downconverter output at complex baseband.

The span of the QAIC extends from roughly $f_{\min}$ to $f_{\max}$ and QAIC simultaneously observes all bands within this frequency span. Therefore the instantaneous bandwidth of the QAIC is roughly $(f_{\max} - f_{\min})$ Hz, which is partitioned into $N_0 = \lceil (f_{\max} - f_{\min})/B \rceil$ bands with K_0 active bands. With the downconversion, the frequency of the pseudo-random bit sequence f_p can be chosen to be

$$f_p = (f_{\max} - f_{\min})/2.$$

Based on the theory of compressive sensing, the number of measurements we need is $m = C_Q K_0 \log(N_0/K_0)$. Due to the quadrature configuration, the total number of branches is then

$$M = 2m = 2C_Q K_0 \log(N_0/K_0),$$

and the output sampling rate (hence the cutoff frequency of the filter $h(t)$ in Figure 11.5) can be half of the band resolution:

$$f_s = B/2.$$

The number of branches M may be traded (say reduced by an integer factor q) for the branch sampling rate f_s (increased by the same factor q).

11.3.2 A Prototype Circuit Implementation

Based on the above design, a first prototype circuit implementation of the QAIC system for detecting up to three interferers in the 2.7–3.7 GHz PCAST spectrum was introduced by [YHW$^+$15]. The circuit was integrated in a chip implemented with the 65 nm CMOS GP (complementary metal oxide semiconductor general purpose) technology, with an active area of 0.428 mm^2. A photograph of the die of the prototype system is shown in Figure 11.7. In this section we give a brief description of the prototype system.

Figure 11.8 shows the block diagram of the prototype system that employs the QAIC design. The system controller configures the QAIC hardware and software resources according to user-specified system constants and performance targets such as RBW, sensitivity, maximum and minimum frequencies of interest, $f_{\max}$ and $f_{\min}$, etc.

The PCAST spectrum is a 1 GHz spectrum ranging from 2.7 to 3.7 GHz with an RBW of 20 MHz. For the QAIC design, $m = 8$ I/Q branches would be sufficient, which is a total of $M = 16$ physical branches. The length of random sequence is chosen to be

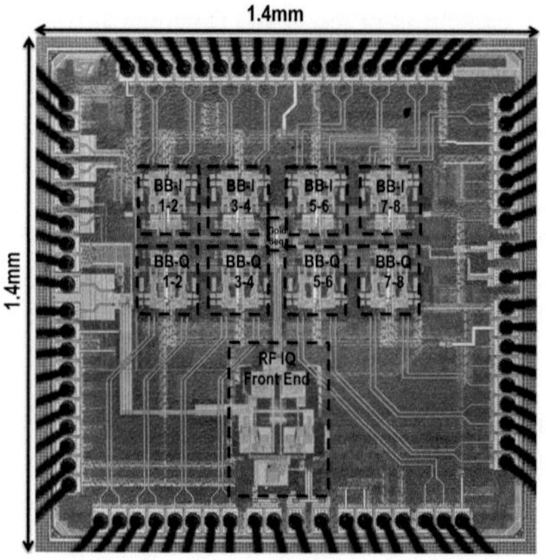

Figure 11.7 Die photograph of the 65 nm QAIC prototype.

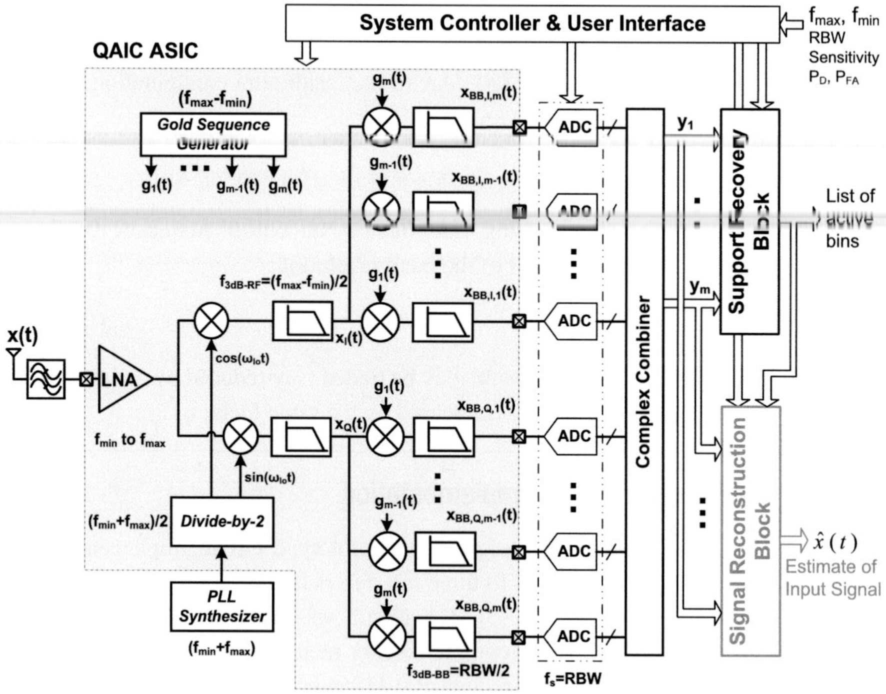

Figure 11.8 Block diagram of the rapid interferer detector based on bandpass compressed sampling with a QAIC.

$L = 63$. More detailed justification of the chosen parameters and other specifications of the system can be found in [YHW+15].

Compared to the conventional approaches mentioned in Section 11.2.1, the QAIC-based spectrum sensor has 50 times faster scan time compared to the sweeping spectrum scanners while it has 6.3 times compression in the aggregate sampling rate (or in the number of branches) compared to multi-branch spectrum sensors and Nyquist-rate FFT spectrum scanners.

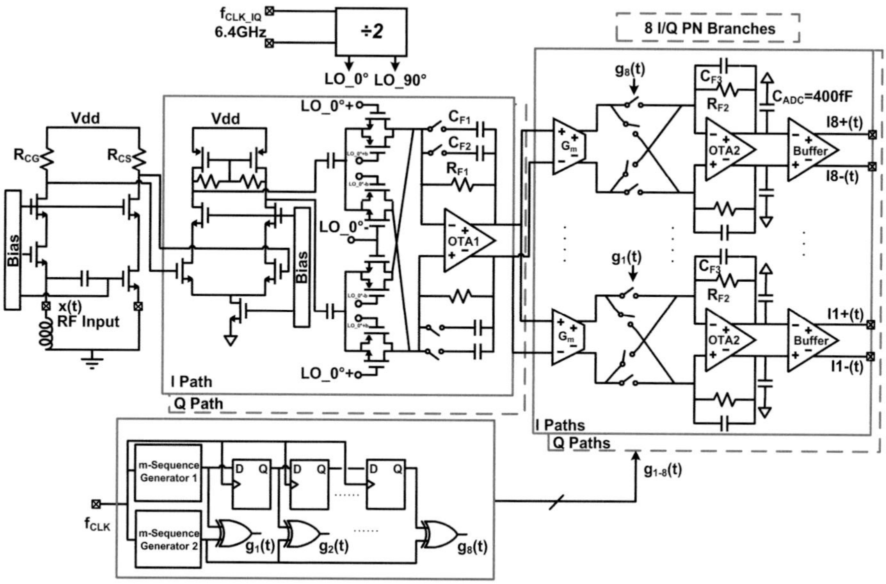

Figure 11.9 Circuit implementation details of the QAIC front end.

Circuit Implementation of the RF Front-End Blocks

The 2.7–3.7 GHz QAIC prototype circuit implementation is shown in Figure 11.9. It implements the functions in the shaded box in the system diagram in Figure 11.8. The chip has been implemented in a 65 nm CMOS GP technology. The QAIC chip uses a wideband noise-canceling low-noise amplifier (LNA) [BKN04, BKLN08]. A wideband noise-canceling LNA is preferred since impedance matching is required for an instantaneous bandwidth of 1 GHz. The post-layout simulated LNA gain for a typical process corner is 15.8 dB to 14.6 dB from 2.7 to 3.7 GHz and the simulated $S_{11} < -10\,\text{dB}$ for a wide bandwidth from 1 to 3.7 GHz for a typical process corner. The measured LNA power consumption is 14 mW from a 1.1 V supply.

The LNA is followed by current-driven passive I/Q mixers and transimpedance amplifiers (TIAs) [MDL$^+$09, BMC$^+$06, Raz98]. The input stage is implemented as a transconductance G_m amplifier operating at an RF frequency range 2.7 to 3.7 GHz followed by four pairs of CMOS transmission gate switches driven by complementary clock phases at 3.2 GHz. An off-chip RF clock fed to the chip is 6.4 GHz, and 3.2 GHz quadrature LO signals with a 50% duty cycle driving the RF I/Q down-converter mixers, $\cos(\omega_{lo}t)$ and $\sin(\omega_{lo}t)$, are generated by the on-chip divide-by-2 circuit that is followed by clock buffers and a nonoverlap generator that is formed by two cross-coupled NAND gates with inverter chains to generate complementary phase clocks for transmission gate type passive mixer switches. The downconverted current signal is converted into a voltage output by a transimpedance amplifier that is configured as an RF I/Q filter. Single-stage operational transconductance amplifier (OTA) topology [Raz01] is chosen for RF I/Q filter design since it was critical to achieve a wide 500 MHz bandwidth while driving the eight I/Q paths and minimizing the power consumption. Measured power consumption of the RF I/Q downconversion stage including the current-driven passive I/Q mixers, TIA-based filters, and I/Q LO generation based on divide-by-2 circuitry is 20.9 mW from a 1.1 V supply.

Positive–Negative (PN) Sequence Generation and Compressed Sensing (CS) Baseband Circuits

The RF TIAs drive eight I/Q paths, each with a current-driven passive mixer and TIA used as a baseband filter loaded with 400 fF emulating the equivalent load of an eight-bit ADC (C_{ADC} in Figure 11.9). Measured power consumption of the eight I/Q PN branches is 38.9 mW from a 1.1 V supply.

The I/Q mixing stages are driven by eight unique gold sequences [PSM82, Gol67] generated on-chip with a gold sequence generator. Gold sequences are preferred because a large set of periodic sequences with good cross-correlation and autocorrelation properties can be generated with less circuitry compared to a shift register

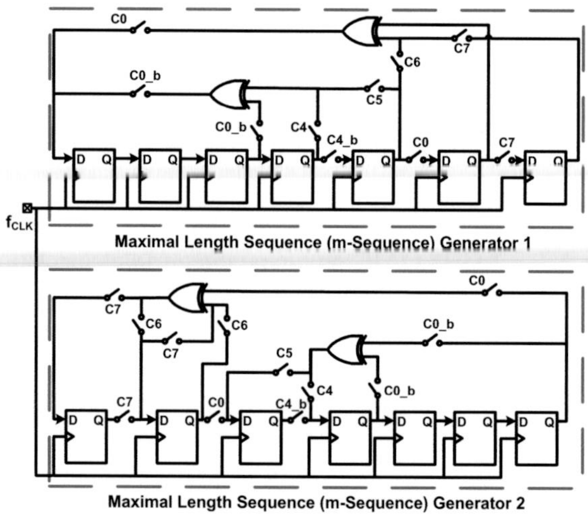

	C0	C0_b	C4	C4_b	C5	C6	C7
L=15	Open	Closed	Closed	Open	Open	Open	Open
L=31	Open	Closed	Open	Closed	Closed	Open	Open
L=63	Closed	Open	Open	Closed	Open	Closed	Open
L=127	Closed	Open	Open	Closed	Open	Open	Closed

(a)

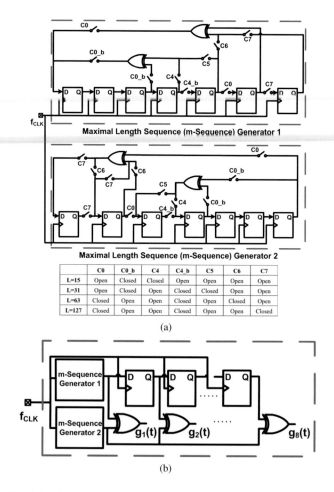

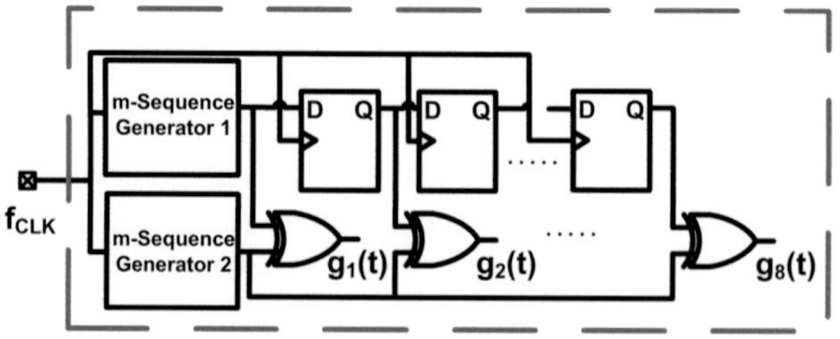

(b)

Figure 11.10 Circuit implementation details of gold sequence generator for eight unique gold sequences with low cross-correlation operating at 1.26 GHz for length 15, 31, 63, and 127. (a) Two unique m-sequence generators based on an LFSR implementation. (b) Eight unique gold sequences generation based on the two unique m-sequences with RBW programmability.

implementation [PSM82]. Gold sequences generated from preferred m-sequence pairs satisfy the following inequalities for cross-correlation, θ [PSM82, Gol67]: $|\theta| \leq t = 2^{(n+2)/2} + 1$, *n even*, and $|\theta| \leq t = 2^{(n+1)/2} + 1$, *n odd*. The on-chip gold sequence generator (Figure 11.10) has various length options of 15, 31, 63, and 127 for programmable RBW options and the switches $C0$, $C0_b$, $C4$, $C4_b$, $C5$, $C6$, and $C7$ are used to control the length of the gold sequences by changing the length of the m-sequences. It generates eight $(2^n - 1)$ long gold sequences by XORing two m-sequences generated by two n-flip-flop linear feedback shift registers (LFSRs). By keeping one m-sequence (Figure 11.10(a)) the same and delaying the other one before the XOR, up to $2^n - 1$ distinct gold sequences (Figure 11.10(b)) can be generated with sufficiently low cross-correlation. Figure 11.11(a) shows the autocorrelation and

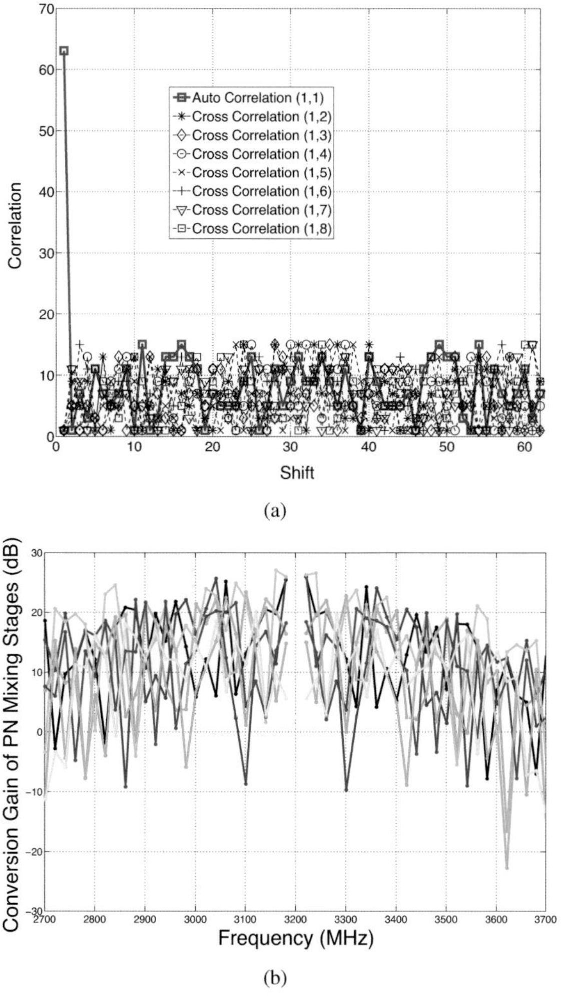

Figure 11.11 Properties of the eight unique gold sequences generated on-chip. (a) Auto-correlation and cross-correlation properties of one of the eight gold sequences is shown for a shift of 63 for a length 63. (b) Input referred conversion gain from 2.7 to 3.7 GHz of the eight PN mixing stages driven by the eight gold sequences for a length of 63, and RBW of 20 MHz.

cross-correlation properties of one of the eight unique gold sequences for a length of 63 which satisfy the sequence requirements (i.e., θ). Figure 11.11(b) shows the measured input referred conversion gain from 2.7 to 3.7 GHz of the eight PN I/Q mixing stages driven by eight unique gold sequences for an RBW of 20 MHz.[5] Measured power consumption of the on-chip gold sequence generator for the nominal length of 63 is 7.04 mW from a 1.1 V supply.

CS Digital Signal Processing

As we have mentioned before, the orthogonal matching pursuit (OMP) Algorithm 8.11 of Chapter 8 is used to identify the input bands that exceed a user-defined threshold. The OMP stopping criterion is derived from the system dimension and a user-defined threshold. This threshold can be set to maximize the detection probability P_D or minimize the false-alarm probability P_{FA}. In this work, the threshold is set close to the QAIC noise floor to maximize P_D performance of the system.

Overall System Performance

The prototype QAIC system front end is implemented in 65 nm CMOS with a size 0.43 mm^2 and consumes 81 mW from a 1.1 V supply. It can detect up to three interferers in a frequency span of 1 GHz ranging from 2.7 to 3.7 GHz (PCAST band) with a resolution bandwidth of 20 MHz in 4.4 μs, 50 times faster than traditional sweeping spectrum scanners. A rapid interferer detector with the bandpass QAIC is two orders of magnitude more energy-efficient than traditional Nyquist rate architectures and one order of magnitude more energy-efficient than previous low-pass CS methods. The aggregate sampling rate of the QAIC interferer detector is compressed by 6.3 compared to traditional Nyquist-rate architectures for the same instantaneous bandwidth.

11.3.3 Recent Developments in Hardware Implementation

Since the first prototype [YHW$^+$15], two new chips have been designed to further improve the system's efficiency and compatibility with other communication hardware systems.

Time-Segmented QAIC

[YHK$^+$16] introduced a new chip design that realizes a rapid interferer sensing solution that employs compressed sampling with a time-segmented quadrature analog-to-information converter (TS-QAIC). TS-QAIC enables system scalability by adaptive thresholding in the information recovery engine and by extending the eight physical I/Q branches of the QAIC to 16 with time segmentation, while limiting the silicon cost and complexity. TS-QAIC can detect up to six interferers (compared to three for QAIC) over a 1 GHz bandwidth between 2.7 and 3.7 GHz in 10.4 μS with only eight I/Q physical branches. The TS-QAIC prototype is implemented in 65 nm CMOS on a 0.517 mm^2 active area and consumes 81.2 mW from a 1.2 V supply.

[5] Some of the implemented gold sequences are balanced while others are unbalanced. Balanced gold sequences have better spectral properties (i.e., are more evenly distributed) [Hol07]. Also eight unique m-sequences that are known to have uniform (evenly distributed) spectrum can be used in future work to overcome the conversion gain fluctuations over frequency.

Direct RF-to-Information Converter

The direct RF-to-information converter (DRF2IC) [HBZ$^+$17] unifies high-sensitivity signal reception, narrowband spectrum sensing, and energy-efficient wideband interferer detection into a rapidly reconfigurable and easily scalable architecture. In reception mode, the DRF2IC RF front-end (RFFE) consumes 46.5 mW and delivers 40 MHz RF bandwidth, 41.5 dB conversion gain, 3.6 dB noise figure (NF), and −2 dBm B1dB (blocker 1-dB compression point). Also, 72 dB out-of-channel blocker rejection is achieved in narrowband sensing mode. In compressed sensing wideband interferer detection mode, 66 dB operational dynamic range, 40 dB instantaneous dynamic range, and 1.43 GHz instantaneous bandwidth are demonstrated, and six interferers scattered over 1.26 GHz are detected in 1.2 μS consuming 58.5 mW.

11.4 Notes

This chapter is based on a series of work [YHW$^+$15, YHK$^+$16, HBZ$^+$17]. Acute readers may already draw some interesting comparisons between the spectrum sensing problem and the MRI problem studied in the previous Chapter 10. For MRI, our direct measurements are the Fourier transform of a signal (the brain image) in the spectral domain and yet the sparse structure of the signal is in a different wavelet domain or is in the spatial characteristics (spatial derivatives) of the signal. In the spectrum sensing problem, our measurements are samples of a temporal signal whose sparse structure is in its spectral domain. Hence in MRI, we need to transform the measurements back to the spatial domain to impose sparsity, whereas in spectrum sensing, we are very much doing the opposite: we need to transform the signal to its spectral domain first in order to discover the sparse structure.

Signal versus Support Recovery

There is also another difference in what we are interested in about the signals. In the MRI problem, we are interested in recovering the signal as accurately as possible, whereas in the spectrum sensing, we are interested in recovering *only the support* of the sparse pattern in the spectral domain, as long as the signal is above a certain confidence threshold on a band of interest. Related theory was characterized in Section 3.6.4 of Chapter 3. This will also be the case for the face *recognition* problem to be studied in Chapter 13 and more general *classification* problems in Chapter 16. The difference in purpose would determine how many resources we should allocate in terms of the number of measurements and the computational complexity. In particular, we can choose different algorithms to achieve different accuracies in the sparse solution recovered. Of course, the choice in algorithms and accuracies also depends on whether the recovery needs to be in real time (for spectrum sensing) or can be done offline (for recovering MRI). The principles and methods introduced in this book, once properly customized for every different application, would enable us to achieve different goals with the minimal measurement and computational resources.

12 Scientific Imaging Problems

"Where the telescope ends, the microscope begins. Which of the two has the grander view?"

– Victor Hugo, *Les Misérables*

12.1 Introduction

In this chapter, we consider a form of low-dimensional structure that arises in many applications in scientific data analysis: we consider datasets consisting of a few basic motifs, repeated at different locations in space and/or time. Figure 12.1 shows three examples of this structure: in neuroscience, in which the motifs represent spike patterns of a neuron [SGHK03, GK12], in image deblurring [CW98, RBZ06, LWDF11], and in microscopy, in which the motifs represent repeated features of interest in a sample [CSL$^+$20]. This is a very simple and fundamental type of low-dimensional structure. However, it raises challenges both for theory and for computation. Typically, both the motifs and their locations are not known ahead of time. As discussed in Chapter 7, this naturally leads to *nonconvex* optimization problems, which can be studied through their symmetries, and solved efficiently using the methods introduced in Chapter 9. In this chapter, we motivate this model in more depth using an example from a particular scientific imaging modality, scanning tunneling microscopy [BR83]. We also emphasize the particular challenges arising in motif finding, which force us to go beyond the simpler theoretical settings of Chapter 7.

12.2 Data Model and Optimization Formulation

In this section, we focus on one particular imaging modality, *scanning tunneling microscopy* (STM), which gives rise to images that consist of repeated motifs. STM produces atomic-resolution images of the quantum electronic structure of the surface of a material [BR83]. In this modality, a conducting tip is rastered across the surface of a sample of interest. A two-dimensional image of the surface can be constructed by recording at each spatial location the tip height needed to maintain a constant current.

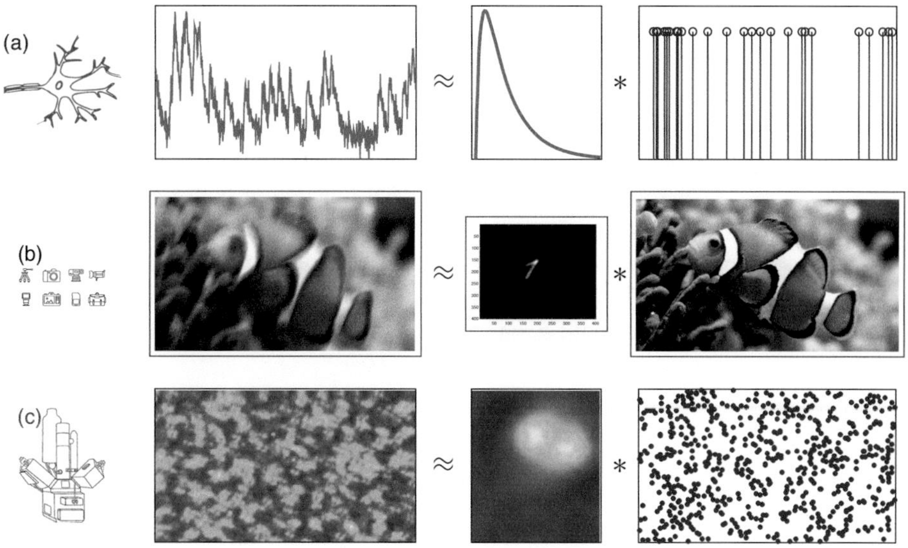

Figure 12.1 Natural Signals with Short-and-Sparse Structures. (a) In calcium imaging, each neuronal spike induces a fluorescence pattern measuring a transient increase in calcium concentration. (b) In photography, photos with sharp edges (sparse in the gradient domain) are often obfuscated by blurring due to shaking the camera. (c) In scanning tunneling microscopy, dopants embedded in some base material produce individual electronic signatures. For each of these cases, the observed signal can be modeled as a convolution between a *short* kernel and a *sparse* activation map.

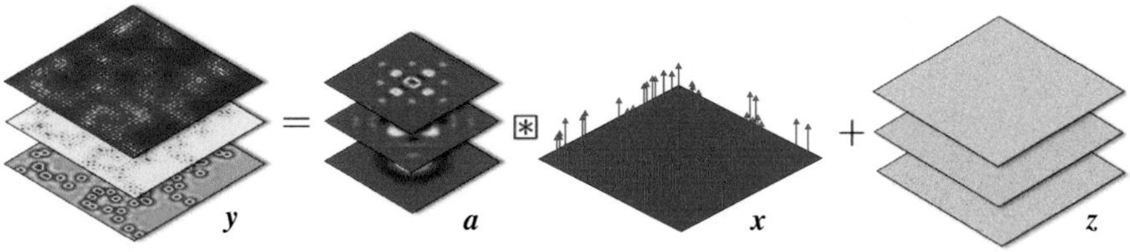

Figure 12.2 Convolutional Data Model for STM. The data $\boldsymbol{y}$ (left) are expressed as a convolution of a basic motif $\boldsymbol{a}$ and a sparse spike train $\boldsymbol{x}$, plus noise $\boldsymbol{z}$. Here, each two-dimensional slice of $\boldsymbol{y}$ is the convolution of the corresponding two-dimensional slice of $\boldsymbol{a}$ and the common sparse signal $\boldsymbol{x}$. The data analysis goal is, given $\boldsymbol{y}$, to determine both the motif $\boldsymbol{a}$ and the sparse spike train $\boldsymbol{x}$, neither of which is known ahead of time.

It is also possible to interrogate the quantum mechanical structure of the material at different energies by operating the device in an open-loop fashion and varying the voltage difference between the tip and surface. This produces a *three-dimensional* observation $\boldsymbol{y} \in \mathbb{R}^{w \times h \times E}$, which we visualize in Figure 12.2 (left).

STM Data Analysis as Finding Repeated Motifs

The broad goal in analyzing STM data is to extract information about the quantum electronic structure of the material; this bears on questions about physical phenomena such as superconductivity. In many concrete instances, this problem boils down to extracting repeated motifs from the observation $\boldsymbol{y}$. Physical properties in the material are strongly influenced by the way in which electrons interact with "defects" in the crystal lattice, which occur at different locations $(i_1, j_1), \ldots, (i_k, j_k)$ in space. The interaction between electrons and a defect produces a characteristic motif $\boldsymbol{a} \in \mathbb{R}^{w \times h \times E}$, which is a three-dimensional function of both spatial location and energy. An example of such a pattern is visualized in Figure 12.2 (middle). Typically, these motifs are spatially localized, i.e., their spatial extent is small relative to the size of the sample. The overall observation $\boldsymbol{y}$ can be modeled as a superposition of translated versions of the motif $\boldsymbol{a}$, one for each of the defect locations (i_ℓ, j_ℓ):

$$\underbrace{\boldsymbol{y}(i,j,e)}_{\textbf{data}} = \sum_{\ell=1}^{k} \underbrace{\boldsymbol{a}(i - i_\ell, j - j_\ell, e)}_{\textbf{translated motif}} + \underbrace{\boldsymbol{z}(i,j,e)}_{\textbf{noise}}. \tag{12.2.1}$$

This expression can be written more concisely as the convolution of $\boldsymbol{a}(\cdot, \cdot, e)$ and a two-dimensional sparse signal $\boldsymbol{x} \in \mathbb{R}^{w \times h}$, which takes on value 1 at locations (i_ℓ, j_ℓ) and 0 elsewhere:

$$\boldsymbol{y}(\cdot, \cdot, e) = \boldsymbol{a}(\cdot, \cdot, e) * \boldsymbol{x} + \boldsymbol{z}(\cdot, \cdot, e). \tag{12.2.2}$$

Combining these equations for all energy levels e, we obtain a model for the dataset as a whole, which we write as

$$\underbrace{\boldsymbol{y}}_{\textbf{data}} = \underbrace{\boldsymbol{a}}_{\textbf{motif}} * \underbrace{\boldsymbol{x}}_{\textbf{sparse spikes}} + \underbrace{\boldsymbol{z}}_{\textbf{noise}}, \tag{12.2.3}$$

where in this expression, each two-dimensional slice of $\boldsymbol{a}$ is convolved with the two-dimensional spike train $\boldsymbol{x}$ to produce one two-dimensional slice of $\boldsymbol{y}$ [CSL+20]. This model is visualized in Figure 12.2.

Sparse Optimization for Motif Finding

Our goal is to recover both the motif $\boldsymbol{a}$ and spike train $\boldsymbol{x}$ from the observation $\boldsymbol{y}$. This is an underdetermined problem; to make progress we need to leverage low-dimensional structure in both $\boldsymbol{a}$ and $\boldsymbol{x}$. We will use the facts that:

1 $\boldsymbol{a}$ is spatially localized, i.e., it is a *short* signal, whose spatial extent is small compared to that of $\boldsymbol{y}$; and

2 $\boldsymbol{x}$ is *sparse*, since it contains only one nonzero entry for each instance of the motif in $\boldsymbol{y}$.

We call this a *short-and-sparse* model, and call the corresponding recovery problem *short-and-sparse deconvolution* (SaSD). This model was studied in the 1990s [Hay94b, LB95b, KH96] and has drawn increased interest in recent years due to improved computation capability and understanding of its geometry [ZLK+17, KZLW19]. This structure is common to many motif finding problems, in microscopy, neuroscience, astronomy, etc. Using ideas from Chapters 2, 3, and 7, we can formulate an optimization problem that attempts to simultaneously recover both $\boldsymbol{a}$ and $\boldsymbol{x}$:

$$\min_{\boldsymbol{a},\boldsymbol{x}} \varphi_{\mathrm{BL}}(\boldsymbol{a},\boldsymbol{x}) \doteq \underbrace{\tfrac{1}{2}\|\boldsymbol{y}-\boldsymbol{a}*\boldsymbol{x}\|_F^2}_{\textbf{data fidelity}} + \underbrace{\lambda\|\boldsymbol{x}\|_1}_{\boldsymbol{x}\textbf{ sparse}} \quad \text{such that} \quad \underbrace{\boldsymbol{a}\in\mathcal{A}.}_{\boldsymbol{a}\textbf{ short}} \tag{12.2.4}$$

Here, the data fidelity term is the sum of the squared differences between $\boldsymbol{a}*\boldsymbol{x}$ and $\boldsymbol{y}$. The regularizer $\|\boldsymbol{x}\|_1$ encourages $\boldsymbol{x}$ to be sparse. This objective function is sometimes referred to as the *bilinear Lasso* (hence, the notation φ_{BL}), since it composes the Lasso objective with the bilinear map $(\boldsymbol{a},\boldsymbol{x}) \mapsto \boldsymbol{a}*\boldsymbol{x}$ [CSL+20, ZLK+17, KZLW19]. The constraint $\boldsymbol{a}\in\mathcal{A}$ asks $\boldsymbol{a}$ to be short. One way of doing this is constraining $\boldsymbol{a}$ to be supported on a relatively small region $\{1,\dots,w\}\times\{1,\dots,h\}\times\{1,\dots,E\}$, with $w \ll W$ and $h \ll H$. There is a further bilinear degree of freedom between $\boldsymbol{a}$ and $\boldsymbol{x}$: for any nonzero λ, $(\lambda\boldsymbol{a})*(\lambda^{-1}\boldsymbol{x}) = \boldsymbol{a}*\boldsymbol{x}$. We eliminate this degree of freedom by constraining $\boldsymbol{a}$ to have unit Frobenius norm, setting

$$\mathcal{A} \doteq \{\boldsymbol{a} \mid \mathrm{supp}(\boldsymbol{a}) \subseteq \{1,\dots,w\}\times\{1,\dots,h\}\times\{1,\dots,E\},\ \|\boldsymbol{a}\|_F = 1\}. \tag{12.2.5}$$

As we will see in the next section, due to the symmetries of the convolution operator $*$, this problem is nonconvex. As with the simpler model problems in Chapter 7, the particular choice $\|\boldsymbol{a}\|_F = 1$ plays an important role in shaping the geometry of this nonconvex problem, by interacting with the objective to create regions of negative curvature.

12.3 Symmetry in Short-and-Sparse Deconvolution

The short-and-sparse model admits a basic shift symmetry, which is inherited from the symmetries of the convolution operator $*$: letting s_τ denote a shift by τ pixels, we have

$$s_\tau[\boldsymbol{a}] * s_{-\tau}[\boldsymbol{x}] = \boldsymbol{a}*\boldsymbol{x}. \tag{12.3.1}$$

In the two-dimensional setting of STM, τ represents a two-dimensional shift in space. In Figure 12.3, we illustrate this symmetry in a one-dimensional setting. The shift symmetry is a form of discrete symmetry, similar to those studied in Chapter 7. Because of this symmetry, natural formulations of short-and-sparse deconvolution admit multiple equivalent solutions, and are nonconvex. Indeed, viewed as a function of the pair $(\boldsymbol{a},\boldsymbol{x})$, the objective (12.2.4) is a nonconvex function; the constraint set is also nonconvex.

Similar to Chapter 7, it is possible to study the geometry of deconvolution problems through their symmetries [ZLK+17, ZKW18, KZLW19]. For example, it is possible to derive simpler approximations $\varphi_{\mathrm{ABL}} \approx \varphi_{\mathrm{BL}}$ to the objective in (12.2.4) that can be studied mathematically. If $\boldsymbol{a}$ is *shift-incoherent*, i.e., for any shift τ $\langle \boldsymbol{a}, s_\tau[\boldsymbol{a}]\rangle \approx 0$, then the loss in (12.2.4) can be approximated as

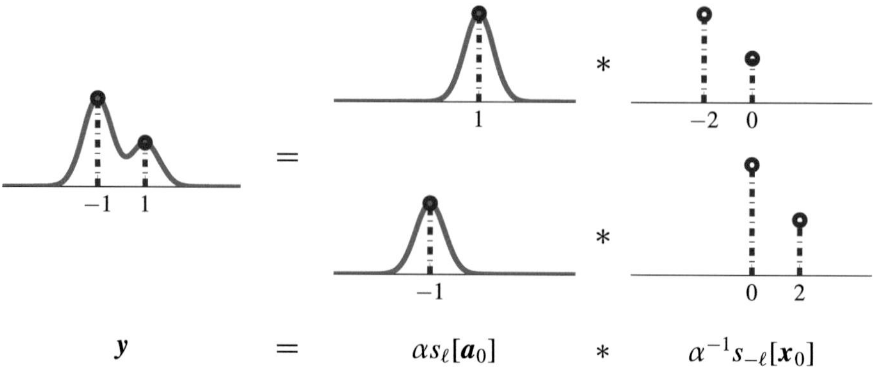

Figure 12.3 Scaling-Shift Symmetry. The SaS convolution model exhibits a scaled shift symmetry: $\alpha s_\ell[\boldsymbol{a}_0]$ and $\alpha^{-1} s_{-\ell}[\boldsymbol{x}_0]$ have the same convolution as $\boldsymbol{a}_0$ and $\boldsymbol{x}_0$. Therefore, the ground truth $(\boldsymbol{a}_0, \boldsymbol{x}_0)$ can only by identified up to some scale and shift ambiguity.

$$\begin{aligned} \tfrac{1}{2}\left\| \boldsymbol{y} - \boldsymbol{a} * \boldsymbol{x} \right\|_F^2 &= \tfrac{1}{2}\|\boldsymbol{y}\|_F^2 + \tfrac{1}{2}\|\boldsymbol{a} * \boldsymbol{x}\|_F^2 - \langle \boldsymbol{y}, \boldsymbol{a} * \boldsymbol{x} \rangle \\ &\approx \tfrac{1}{2}\|\boldsymbol{y}\|_F^2 + \tfrac{1}{2}\|\boldsymbol{x}\|_F^2 - \langle \boldsymbol{y}, \boldsymbol{a} * \boldsymbol{x} \rangle . \end{aligned} \tag{12.3.2}$$

This gives

$$\varphi_{\mathrm{ADL}}(\boldsymbol{a}, \boldsymbol{x}) \doteq \tfrac{1}{2}\|\boldsymbol{y}\|_F^2 + \tfrac{1}{2}\|\boldsymbol{x}\|_F^2 - \langle \boldsymbol{y}, \boldsymbol{a} * \boldsymbol{x} \rangle + \lambda \|\boldsymbol{x}\|_1, \quad \boldsymbol{a} \in \mathsf{A} \tag{12.3.3}$$

Exercise 12.1 explores this approximation in more detail; the key intuition is that this approximation is accurate when the *shift-coherence*

$$\mu_s = \max_{\tau \neq 0} \left| \langle \boldsymbol{a}, s_\tau[\boldsymbol{a}] \rangle \right| \tag{12.3.4}$$

is small. Figure 12.4 visualizes the geometry of this approximation for shift-incoherent problems. As expected, equivalent (symmetric) solutions are local minimizers, and there is negative curvature in symmetry-breaking directions.

The theory points to a key difference between real deconvolution problems and the idealized models studied in Figure 12.4 and Chapter 7. As the motif $\boldsymbol{a}$ becomes more shift-coherent, the problem becomes more challenging, both numerically and theoretically. This can be quantified in terms of a sparsity–coherence tradeoff, illustrated in Figure 12.5. The less coherent $\boldsymbol{a}$ is, the denser $\boldsymbol{x}$ can be. This tradeoff is reminiscent of our discussion of coherence in matrix completion and recovery in Chapters 4 and 5.

This tradeoff points to an important challenge in practical deconvolution problems: deconvolution problems in imaging and the sciences tend to be highly coherent – the motif or blur kernel $\boldsymbol{a}$ is typically spatially smooth. In contrast to orthogonal dictionary learning (Chapter 7) and certain neural network learning problems (Chapter 16), we have to contend directly with highly coherent kernels. Approximations such as (12.3.3) break down, and we have to contend directly with the more complicated geometry of (12.2.4). In the next section, we will describe some algorithmic ideas for coping with high-coherence instances of SaSD.

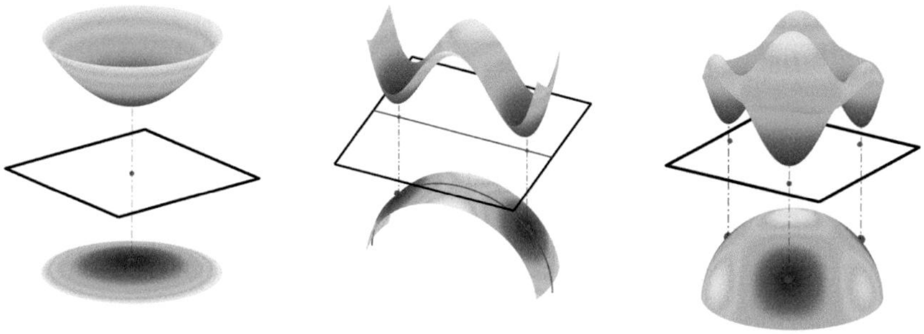

(a) a single shift $s_{\ell_1}[\boldsymbol{a}_0]$ (b) two shifts $s_{\ell_1}[\boldsymbol{a}_0]$, $s_{\ell_2}[\boldsymbol{a}_0]$ (c) multiple shifts

Figure 12.4 Geometry of Approximate Bilinear Lasso Objective $\varphi_{\text{ABL}}(\boldsymbol{a})$ near superpositions of shifts of $\boldsymbol{a}_0$ [KZLW19]. Top: Function values of $\varphi_{\text{ABL}}(\boldsymbol{a})$ visualized as height. Bottom: Heat maps of $\varphi_{\text{ABL}}(\boldsymbol{a})$ on the sphere $\mathbb{S}^{n-1}$. (a) The region near a single shift is strongly convex; (b) the region between two shifts contains a saddle point, with negative curvature pointing towards each shift and positive curvature pointing away; and (c) the region near the span of several shifts of $\boldsymbol{a}_0$.

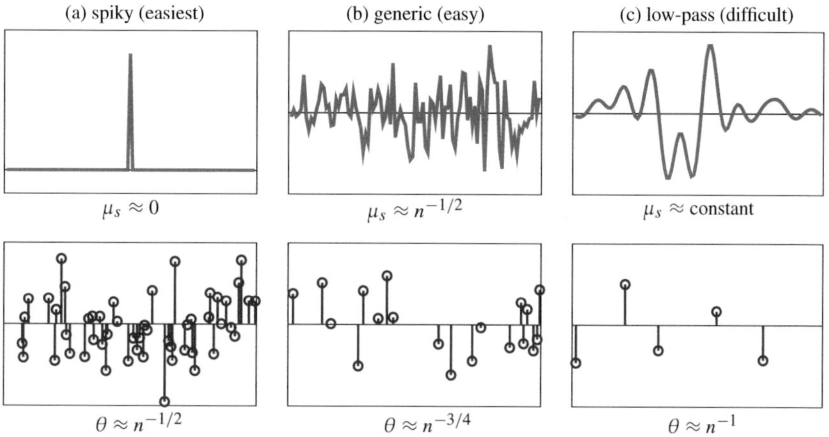

Figure 12.5 Sparsity–Coherence Tradeoff [KZLW19]: examples with varying coherence parameter $\mu_s(\boldsymbol{a}_0)$ and sparsity rate θ (i.e., probability a given entry is nonzero). Smaller shift-coherence $\mu_s(\boldsymbol{a}_0)$ allows SaSD to be solved with higher θ, and vice versa. In order of increasing difficulty: (a) when $\boldsymbol{a}_0$ is a Dirac delta function, $\mu_s(\boldsymbol{a}_0) = 0$; (b) when $\boldsymbol{a}_0$ is sampled from a uniform distribution on the sphere $\mathbb{S}^{n-1}$, its shift-coherence is roughly $\mu_s(\boldsymbol{a}_0) \approx n^{-1/2}$; and (c) when $\boldsymbol{a}_0$ is low-pass, $\mu_s(\boldsymbol{a}_0) \to$ const. as n grows.

12.4 Algorithms for Short-and-Sparse Deconvolution

In this section, we describe practical algorithms for (12.2.4), which leverage ideas from Chapters 8 and 9, to contend with the complicated geometry of practical deconvolution problems. Our problem is a specific instance of the general form

$$\min_{\boldsymbol{a},\boldsymbol{x}} \Psi(\boldsymbol{a},\boldsymbol{x}) = \psi(\boldsymbol{a},\boldsymbol{x}) + \lambda \cdot g(\boldsymbol{x}), \qquad \text{s.t.} \quad \boldsymbol{a} \in \mathcal{M}, \tag{12.4.1}$$

Algorithm 12.1 Alternating Descent Method (ADM)

Input: observation $\boldsymbol{y}$, step sizes t_0 and τ_0; penalty $\lambda > 0$.
Initialize $\boldsymbol{a}_0$ at random on the sphere, $\boldsymbol{x}_0 \leftarrow \boldsymbol{0}_n$, and $k \leftarrow 0$.
while not converged **do**
Fix $\boldsymbol{a}_k$ and take a proximal gradient step on $\boldsymbol{x}$ with step size t_k

$$\boldsymbol{x}_{k+1} \leftarrow \operatorname{prox}_{t_k \lambda g}\left[\boldsymbol{x}_k - t_k \nabla_{\boldsymbol{x}} \psi\left(\boldsymbol{a}_k, \boldsymbol{x}_k\right)\right].$$

Fix $\boldsymbol{x}_{k+1}$ and take a Riemannian gradient step on $\boldsymbol{a}$ with stepsize τ_k

$$\boldsymbol{a}_{k+1} \leftarrow \mathcal{P}_{\mathcal{A}}\left[\boldsymbol{a}_k - \tau_k \nabla_{\boldsymbol{a}} \psi\left(\boldsymbol{a}_k, \boldsymbol{x}_{k+1}\right)\right].$$

Update $k \leftarrow k+1$.
end while
Output: Final iterate $\boldsymbol{a}_\star$, $\boldsymbol{x}_\star$.

where $\psi(\boldsymbol{a},\boldsymbol{x})$ is twice continuously differentiable, $g(\boldsymbol{x})$ is a convex (possibly nonsmooth) sparse promoting penalty, and $\mathcal{M}$ is a smooth Riemannian manifold such as a sphere.

12.4.1 Alternating Descent Method

We begin by introducing a vanilla first-order method for solving (12.4.1) based on an alternating descent method (ADM). The method reduces the objective by alternating between taking descent steps on one variable with the other fixed. The basic algorithm pipeline is summarized in Algorithm 12.1. We provide more detailed explanation for each of the steps below.

*Fix **a** and take a proximal gradient step on **x***

Fix $\boldsymbol{a}$, and consider the marginal function

$$\Psi_{\boldsymbol{a}}(\boldsymbol{x}) = \psi(\boldsymbol{a},\boldsymbol{x}) + \lambda g(\boldsymbol{x}) \tag{12.4.2}$$

as a function of $\boldsymbol{x}$ only. This is a sum of a smooth function ψ which is convex in $\boldsymbol{x}$ and a nonsmooth convex function $g(\boldsymbol{x})$. This form is familiar from our discussion of proximal gradient methods in Chapter 8. We can express the derivative of ψ with respect to $\boldsymbol{x}$ as

$$\nabla_{\boldsymbol{x}} \psi(\boldsymbol{a},\boldsymbol{x}) = \iota_{\boldsymbol{x}}^* \, \check{\boldsymbol{a}} * (\boldsymbol{a} * \boldsymbol{x} - \boldsymbol{y}). \tag{12.4.3}$$

Here, $\iota_{\boldsymbol{x}}^*$ restricts to the interval $\{1,\dots,n\}$, and $\check{\boldsymbol{a}}$ denotes the reversal of the signal $\boldsymbol{a}$. In Exercise 12.3 we verify this formula for the gradient, by verifying that convolution $\check{\boldsymbol{a}} * \cdot$ with the reversal of $\boldsymbol{a}$ is the formal adjoint of the convolution operator $\boldsymbol{x} \mapsto \boldsymbol{a} * \boldsymbol{x}$. For $\boldsymbol{a}$ fixed, the gradient $\nabla_{\boldsymbol{x}} \psi(\boldsymbol{a},\boldsymbol{x})$ is a Lipschitz function of $\boldsymbol{x}$. The Lipschitz constant L

is the norm of the operator $\boldsymbol{x} \mapsto \iota_{\boldsymbol{x}}^* \check{\boldsymbol{a}} * \boldsymbol{a} * \boldsymbol{x}$.[1] Following our discussion in Chapter 8, we can reduce the function $\Psi_{\boldsymbol{a}}(\boldsymbol{x})$ by taking a gradient step and then applying the proximal operator associated with the regularizer λg:

$$\boldsymbol{x}_{k+1} = \operatorname{prox}_{t\lambda g}\left[\boldsymbol{x}_k - t\nabla_{\boldsymbol{x}}\psi(\boldsymbol{a}_k, \boldsymbol{x}_k)\right]. \tag{12.4.4}$$

As long as $t \leq 1/L$, this reduces the objective: $\Psi(\boldsymbol{a}_k, \boldsymbol{x}_{k+1}) \leq \Psi(\boldsymbol{a}_k, \boldsymbol{x})$. The Lipschitz constant L can be estimated from the discrete Fourier transform of $\boldsymbol{a}_k$, or an effective step size can be determined by backtracking (i.e., reducing the step size until a sufficient reduction in objective is observed). Our regularizer g is the ℓ^1 norm; the proximal operator associated with this convex function is simply the soft-thresholding operation,

$$\operatorname{prox}_{\tau\lambda g}(\boldsymbol{x}) = \mathcal{S}_{t\lambda}(\boldsymbol{x}), \tag{12.4.5}$$

where $\mathcal{S}_{t\lambda}(\boldsymbol{x}) = \operatorname{sign}(\boldsymbol{x})\left(|\boldsymbol{x}| - \lambda t\right)_+$ shrinks the entries of the vector $\boldsymbol{x}$ towards zero (see Section 8.2 for more discussion and derivation of this operator).

Fix $\boldsymbol{x}$ *and take a projected gradient step on* $\boldsymbol{a}$

Proceeding in a similar manner, we can calculate the derivative of $\psi(\boldsymbol{a}, \boldsymbol{x})$ with respect to $\boldsymbol{a}$:

$$\nabla_{\boldsymbol{a}}\psi(\boldsymbol{a}, \boldsymbol{x}) = \iota_{\boldsymbol{a}}^* \check{\boldsymbol{x}} * (\boldsymbol{a} * \boldsymbol{x} - \boldsymbol{y}). \tag{12.4.6}$$

Here, again $\iota_{\boldsymbol{a}}^*$ restricts to the allowed support of $\boldsymbol{a}$. Taking a gradient step $\boldsymbol{a} \mapsto \boldsymbol{a} - \tau\nabla_{\boldsymbol{a}}\psi(\boldsymbol{a}, \boldsymbol{x})$ for appropriate step size (chosen smaller than $1/L_{\boldsymbol{a}}$, where $L_{\boldsymbol{a}}$ is the norm of the operator $\boldsymbol{a} \mapsto \iota_{\boldsymbol{a}}^* \check{\boldsymbol{x}} * \boldsymbol{x} * \boldsymbol{a}$ and the Lipschitz constant of $\nabla_{\boldsymbol{a}}\psi$) reduces the objective function Ψ. However, the resulting $\boldsymbol{a}_+$ may not have unit norm, and hence may not reside in the feasible set $\mathcal{A}$. We address this by projecting onto $\mathcal{A}$, simply by scaling $\boldsymbol{a}_+$ to have unit ℓ^2 norm:

$$\boldsymbol{a}_{k+1} = \mathcal{P}_{\mathcal{A}}\left[\boldsymbol{a}_k - \tau_k\nabla_{\boldsymbol{a}}\psi\left(\boldsymbol{a}_k, \boldsymbol{x}_{k+1}\right)\right]. \tag{12.4.7}$$

This projected gradient approach to $\boldsymbol{a}$ update is simple and often quite effective in practice. It is also possible to derive a variety of algorithms through the perspective of Riemannian optimization – viewing the constraint $\|\boldsymbol{a}\|_F = 1$ as forcing $\boldsymbol{a}$ to reside on a particular smooth manifold.

12.4.2 Additional Heuristics for Highly Coherent Problems

Although the bilinear Lasso is able to account for interactions between $\boldsymbol{a}$ and $\boldsymbol{x}$ even when $\boldsymbol{a}$ is highly coherent, the smooth term $\|\boldsymbol{a} * \boldsymbol{x} - \boldsymbol{y}\|_2^2$ nonetheless becomes ill-conditioned as $\mu(\boldsymbol{a})$ increases, leading to slow convergence for practical problem instances. Here we will discuss a number of heuristics which will help to obtain faster algorithmic convergence and produce better solutions in such settings.

[1] Since convolution in time is equivalent to multiplication in frequency, this can be controlled in terms of the largest Fourier coefficient of $\boldsymbol{a}$.

Momentum Acceleration

When $\mu_s(\boldsymbol{a})$ is large, the Hessian of ψ_{BL} becomes ill-conditioned as $\boldsymbol{a}$ converges to single shifts. The objective landscape contains "narrow valleys" in which first-order methods tend to exhibit severe oscillations. For a nonconvex problem such as the bilinear Lasso, iterates of first-order methods could encounter many narrow and flat valleys along the descent trajectory, resulting in slow convergence.

One remedy here is to add *momentum* [Pol64, BT09] to standard first-order iterations, as we have introduced in Appendix D. For example, when updating $\boldsymbol{x}$, we could modify the iterate in (12.4.4) by

$$\boldsymbol{w}_k = \boldsymbol{x}_k + \beta \cdot \underbrace{(\boldsymbol{x}_k - \boldsymbol{x}_{k-1})}_{\text{inertial term}}, \tag{12.4.8}$$

$$\boldsymbol{x}_{k+1} = \operatorname{prox}_{t_k g}\left[\boldsymbol{w}_k - t_k \nabla_{\boldsymbol{x}} \psi\left(\boldsymbol{a}_k, \boldsymbol{w}_k\right)\right]. \tag{12.4.9}$$

Here, the *inertial term* incorporates the momentum from previous iterations, and $\beta \in (0,1)$ controls the inertia.[2] In a similar fashion, we can modify the iterate for updating $\boldsymbol{a}$ in (12.4.7). This algorithm is sometimes referred to as the *inertial alternating descent method* (iADM) [AMS09].[3]

The additional inertial term improves convergence by substantially reducing oscillation effects for ill-conditioned problems. The acceleration of momentum methods for convex problems are well known in practice.[4] Recently, momentum methods have also been proven to improve convergence for nonconvex and nonsmooth problems [PS16, JNJ18].

Homotopy Continuation

It is also possible to improve optimization by modifying the objective Ψ_{BL} directly through the sparsity penalty λ. Variations of this idea appear in both [ZLK+17] and [KZLW19], and can also help to mitigate the effects of large shift-coherence in practical problems.

When solving (12.2.4) in the noise-free case, it is clear that larger choices of λ encourage sparser solutions for $\boldsymbol{x}$. Conversely, smaller choices of λ place local minimizers of the marginal objective $\varphi_{\mathrm{BL}}(\boldsymbol{a}) \doteq \min_{\boldsymbol{x}} \psi_{\mathrm{BL}}(\boldsymbol{a}, \boldsymbol{x})$ closer to signed shifts of $\boldsymbol{a}_0$ by emphasizing reconstruction quality. When $\mu(\boldsymbol{a})$ is large, however, φ_{BL} becomes ill-conditioned as $\lambda \to 0$ due to the poor spectral conditioning of $\boldsymbol{a}_0$, leading to severe flatness near local minimizers or the creation of spurious local minimizers when noise is present. At the expense of precision, larger values of λ limit $\boldsymbol{x}$ to a small set of support patterns and simplify the landscape of φ_{BL}. It is therefore important for both fast convergence and accurate recovery for λ to be chosen appropriately.

When problem parameters – such as noise level or sparsity – are not known *a priori*, a *homotopy continuation method* [HYZ08, WNF09, XZ13] can be used to obtain

[2] Setting $\beta = 0$ here removes momentum and reverts to standard proximal gradient descent.

[3] It modifies iPALM [PS16] to perform updates on $\boldsymbol{a}$ via retraction on the sphere.

[4] In the setting of a strongly convex and smooth function $f(\boldsymbol{z})$, the momentum method improves the iteration complexity from $O(\kappa \log(1/\varepsilon))$ to $O(\sqrt{\kappa} \log(1/\varepsilon))$ with κ being the condition number, while leaving the computational complexity approximately unchanged [Bub15].

a *range* of solutions for SaSD. Using a random initialization as in ADM, a rough estimate $(\hat{\boldsymbol{a}}_1, \hat{\boldsymbol{x}}_1)$ is first obtained by solving (12.2.4) with iADM using a large choice for λ_1; this estimate is refined by gradually decreasing λ_n to produce the *solution path* $\{(\hat{\boldsymbol{a}}_n, \hat{\boldsymbol{x}}_n; \lambda_n)\}$. By ensuring that $\boldsymbol{x}$ remains sparse along the solution path, homotopy provides the objective Ψ_{BL} with (restricted) strong convexity with respect to both $\boldsymbol{a}$ and $\boldsymbol{x}$ throughout optimization [ANW10]; in numerical experiments, this often leads to a linear rate of convergence.

Data-Driven Initialization

The structure of the SaSD problem suggests a means of initializing the motif $\boldsymbol{a}_0$. Our goal is to recover $\boldsymbol{a}$, up to shift symmetry. That is, the goal is to recover a single shift of $\boldsymbol{a}$. The data $\boldsymbol{y}$ is the convolution of $\boldsymbol{a}$ with a sparse signal $\boldsymbol{x}$. This implies that small pieces of $\boldsymbol{y}$ are themselves superpositions of a few shifted copies of $\boldsymbol{a}_0$. This suggests a means of initialization: one selects a small window of the data and then normalizes it to lie on the sphere.

12.4.3 Computational Examples

Figure 12.6 shows an example of motif finding in STM data using the method introduced above, which is featured in the recent work [CSL+20]. The particular dataset consists of measurements across a $100 \times 100\,\mathrm{nm}^2$ area at $E = 41$ different bias voltages. Panels (a)–(d) show the modulus of the two-dimensional Fourier transform of two spatial slices. This relatively noisy product is the basis for conventional data analysis techniques in the area. Panels (e)–(i) present a much cleaner analysis produced by solving a SaSD problem. Panels (f) and (g) show two slices of the motif signature $\boldsymbol{a}_\star$, while panel (e) shows the sparse activation map $\boldsymbol{x}_\star$. The modulus Fourier transforms in panels (h) and (i) are cleaner and easier to interpret than their counterparts in panels (c) and (d).

12.5 Extensions: Multiple Motifs

In many scientific problems, the data consist of superpositions of more than one type of basic motif. For example, in scanning tunneling microscopy, data may contain multiple types of impurities, or multiple states of matter. In neural spike sorting, data may consist of spike patterns from multiple neurons. Many of the algorithmic ideas discussed above extend very naturally to handle data with multiple motifs. One simply introduces variables of optimization $\boldsymbol{a}_1, \dots, \boldsymbol{a}_K$, with corresponding sparse spike trains $\boldsymbol{x}_1, \dots, \boldsymbol{x}_K$, and solves:

$$\min_{\boldsymbol{a}_1,\dots,\boldsymbol{a}_K,\boldsymbol{x}_1,\dots,\boldsymbol{x}_K} \frac{1}{2}\left\| \boldsymbol{y} - \sum_{\ell=1}^{K} \boldsymbol{a}_\ell * \boldsymbol{x}_\ell \right\|_F^2 + \lambda \sum_{\ell=1}^{K} \|\boldsymbol{x}_\ell\|_1$$
$$\text{subject to} \quad \boldsymbol{a}_\ell \in \mathcal{A},\ \ell = 1, \dots, K. \tag{12.5.1}$$

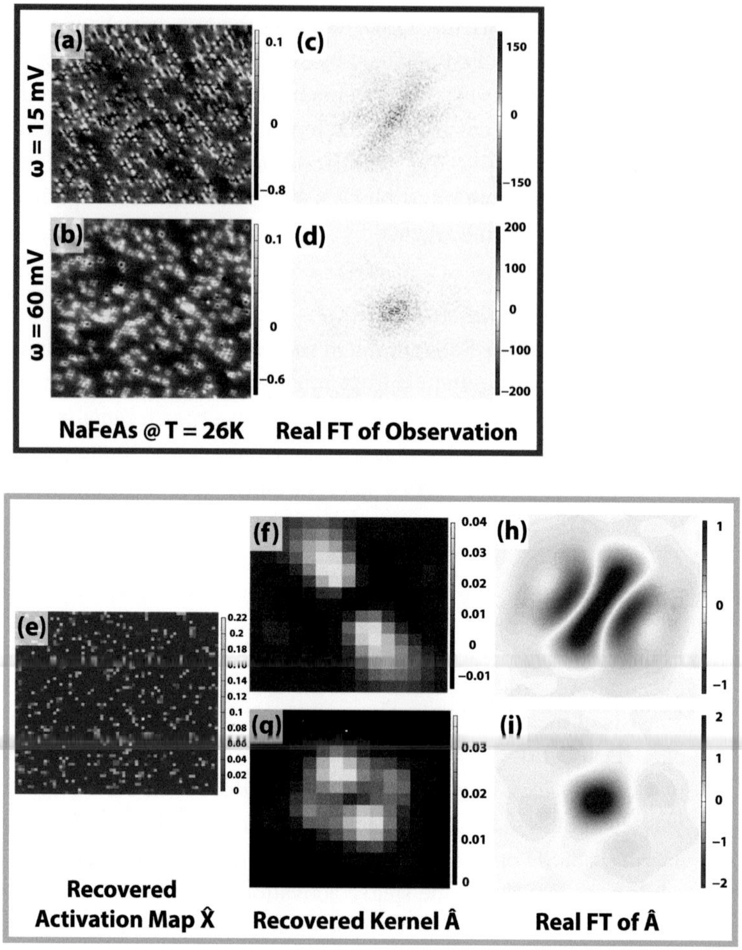

Figure 12.6 Short and Sparse Deconvolution on Real NaFeAs Data. (a)–(d) Two slices of a dataset at different energy levels (a) and (b). One conventional approach to analyzing such data is to visualize the magnitude of the Fourier transform (c) and (d). In dense samples, this produces a "phase noise" which obscures physically meaningful structures. (e)–(i) Deconvolution via the bilinear Lasso. Sparse activation map $\boldsymbol{x}$ (e) and motif $\boldsymbol{a}$ (f) and (g). The Fourier transform (h) and (i) of the motif is clearer and reveals more structure than that of the original data (c) and (d).

This extension is sometimes referred to as multi-channel sparse blind deconvolution [QLZ19] or *convolutional dictionary learning* [QZL$^+$20a]. This problem is again nonconvex. In addition to the shift symmetry described above, this problem exhibits a permutation symmetry: reordering the motifs $\boldsymbol{a}_\ell$ and their corresponding sparsity maps $\boldsymbol{x}_\ell$ does not change the objective. Nevertheless, many of the algorithmic ideas described above generalize naturally to this higher-dimensional problem. Ideas of momentum acceleration, continuation, and reweighting remain essential to obtaining high-quality results on practical data. There are many open theoretical issues associated with deconvolution and convolutional dictionary learning. One avenue to theoretical progress is to solve for the motifs $\boldsymbol{a}_\ell$ one at a time. If the shifts of the $\boldsymbol{a}_\ell$ are mutually incoherent, it is possible to analyze the geometry of the resulting problem and prove that nonconvex methods produce accurate estimates of the ground truth. Interested readers may refer to some of the latest progress on these topics [QLZ19, QZL$^+$20a].

12.6 Exercises

12.1. (Approximate bilinear lasso and incoherent problems) *Consider a length-k signal $\boldsymbol{a} \in \mathbb{R}^k$ of unit ℓ^2 norm. Consider the partial convolution matrix*

$$\boldsymbol{C}_{\boldsymbol{a}} = \begin{bmatrix} \boldsymbol{a} & s_1[\boldsymbol{a}] & s_2[\boldsymbol{a}] & \cdots & s_{k-1}[\boldsymbol{a}] \end{bmatrix}. \tag{12.6.1}$$

Argue that

$$\left\| \boldsymbol{C}_{\boldsymbol{a}}^* \boldsymbol{C}_{\boldsymbol{a}} - \boldsymbol{I} \right\| \le k(k-1)\mu_s(\boldsymbol{a}), \tag{12.6.2}$$

where μ_s is the shift-coherence. For what $\boldsymbol{a}$ is the approximation $\|\boldsymbol{a} * \boldsymbol{x}\|_2^2 \approx \|\boldsymbol{x}\|_2^2$ accurate?

12.2. (Coherence of a gaussian motif) *Consider a Gaussian signal $\boldsymbol{a}$ of length k, with $a_i = \beta \exp(-(i-k)^2/\sigma^2)$, $(i = 1, \dots, k$, where β is chosen to ensure that $\boldsymbol{a}$ has unit ℓ^2 norm. Argue that as $\sigma \to 0$, $\mu_s(\boldsymbol{a})$ approaches 0, while as $\sigma \to \infty$, $\mu_s \to 1 - 1/k$. In the latter (large coherence) setting, the approximation φ_{ABL} is inaccurate.*

12.3. (Gradient of quadratic loss under convolution) *Consider the quadratic loss*

$$\psi(\boldsymbol{a}, \boldsymbol{x}) = \tfrac{1}{2} \|\boldsymbol{a} * \iota \boldsymbol{x} - \boldsymbol{y}\|_2^2. \tag{12.6.3}$$

Show that the gradient of this loss with respect to $\boldsymbol{x}$ is given by

$$\nabla_{\boldsymbol{x}} \psi = \iota^* \left(\boldsymbol{a} * \iota \boldsymbol{x} - \boldsymbol{y} \right). \tag{12.6.4}$$

13 Robust Face Recognition

"Machines take me by surprise with great frequency."
– Alan Turing, *Computing Machinery and Intelligence*

13.1 Introduction

In human perception, the role of sparse representation has been studied extensively. As we have alluded to in the Introduction, Chapter 1, investigators in neuroscience have revealed that in both low-level and mid-level human vision, many neurons in the visual pathway are selective for recognizing a variety of specific stimuli, such as color, texture, orientation, scale, and even view-tuned object images [OF97, Ser06]. Considering these neurons to form an overcomplete dictionary of base signal elements at each visual stage, the firing of the neurons with respect to a given input image is typically highly sparse.

As we discussed in the earlier part of the book, the original goal of sparse representation was not inference nor classification *per se*, but rather representation and compression of signals, potentially using lower sampling rates than the Shannon–Nyquist bound. Therefore, the algorithm performance was measured mainly by the sparsity of the representation and the fidelity to the original signals. Furthermore, individual base elements in the dictionary were not assumed to have any particular semantic meaning – they were typically chosen from standard bases (e.g., Fourier, wavelets, curvelets, Gabor filters, etc.), or learned from data with principal component analysis (PCA) [PMS94, CJG$^+$15], or a deep convolution neural network (as we will detail in Chapter 16), or even generated from random projections [WYG$^+$09, CJG$^+$15]. Nevertheless, the sparsest representation *is* naturally discriminative: amongst all subsets of base vectors, it would select the subset which most compactly expresses the input signal and rejects all other possible but less compact representations.

In this chapter, we exploit the discriminative nature of sparse representation to perform *classification*.[1] Instead of using the generic dictionaries mentioned above, we represent a test sample using a data-driven dictionary, whose base elements are

[1] In Chapter 16, we will revisit the discriminative nature of low-dimensional models, including sparsity, in a broader context of deep networks for classification.

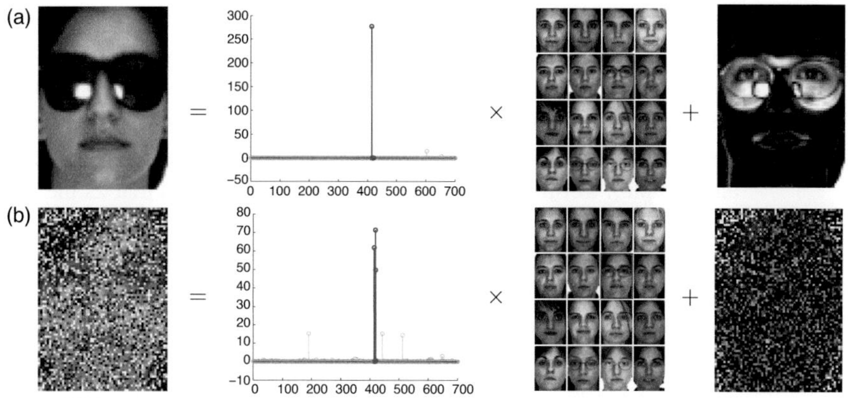

Figure 13.1 An Overview of the Formulation. We represent a test image (left), which is potentially occluded (a) or corrupted (b), as a sparse linear combination of all the training images (middle) plus sparse errors (right) due to occlusion or corruption. Red (darker) coefficients correspond to training images of the correct individual. The algorithm determines the true identity (indicated with a red box at second row and third column) from 700 training images of 100 individuals (seven each) in the standard AR face database [MB98].

the training samples themselves. If sufficient training samples are available from each class, it will be possible to represent the test sample as a linear combination of just those training samples from the same class. This representation is naturally sparse, involving only a small fraction of the overall training database. We will see that in many problems of interest, it is actually the *sparsest* linear representation of the test sample in terms of this dictionary, and can be recovered efficiently via sparse optimization. Seeking the sparsest representation therefore automatically discriminates between the various classes present in the training set. Figure 13.1 illustrates this simple idea using face recognition as an example. Sparse representation also provides a simple yet surprisingly effective means of rejecting invalid test samples not arising from any class in the training database: these samples' sparsest representations tend to involve many dictionary elements, spanning multiple classes.

We will motivate and study this new approach to classification within the context of automatic face recognition. Human faces are arguably the most extensively studied object in image-based recognition. This is partly due to the remarkable face recognition capability of the human visual system [SBOR06], and partly due to numerous important applications for face recognition technology [ZCPR03]. In addition, technical issues associated with face recognition are sufficiently representative of object recognition and even data classification in general. In this chapter, the application of sparse representation and compressed sensing to face recognition yields new insights into compensating gross image error or facial occlusion in the context of face recognition.

It is known that facial occlusion or disguise poses a significant obstacle to robust real-world face recognition [LB00, Mar02, SSL06]. This difficulty is mainly due to the unpredictable nature of the error incurred by occlusion: it may affect any part of the image, and may be arbitrarily large in magnitude. Nevertheless, this error typically corrupts only a fraction of the image pixels, and is therefore sparse in the standard pixel space basis. When the error has such a sparse representation, it can be handled uniformly within the classical sparse representation framework (see Figure 13.1 for an example). Yet in experiments, we further discovered that as the dimension of the problem grows higher, sparsity solvers such as ℓ^1 minimization seem to be able to recover dense error with ease. In this context, the general theory of sparse representation and compressive sensing falls short in explaining the phenomenon of dense error correction with a special kind of dictionary, called the *cross-and-bouquet* model. We will discuss the conditions in which ℓ^1 minimization guarantees to recover dense error approaching 100% under the cross-and-bouquet model.

13.2 Classification Based on Sparse Representation

A basic problem in object recognition is to use labeled training samples from k distinct object classes to correctly determine the class to which a new test sample belongs. We arrange the given n_i training samples from the i-th class as columns of a matrix $A_i = [v_{i,1}, v_{i,2}, \ldots, v_{i,n_i}] \in \mathbb{R}^{m \times n_i}$. In the context of face recognition, we will identify a $w \times h$ grayscale image with the vector $v \in \mathbb{R}^m$ $(m = wh)$ given by stacking its columns. Then the columns of A_i are the training face images of the i-th subject.

An immense variety of statistical models have been proposed for exploiting the structure of the A_i for recognition. One particularly simple and effective approach models the samples from a single class as lying on a linear subspace. Subspace models are flexible enough to capture much of the variation in real datasets. In particular in the context of face recognition, it has been observed that images of a face under varying lighting and with various expressions lie on a special low-dimensional subspace [BHK97, BJ03], often called a *face subspace*. This is the only prior knowledge about the training samples we will be using in proposing a solution using sparse representation.

Given sufficient training samples of the i-th object class, $A_i \in \mathbb{R}^{m \times n_i}$, any new (test) sample $y \in \mathbb{R}^m$ from the same class approximately lies in the linear span of the training samples associated with object i:

$$y = \alpha_{i,1} v_{i,1} + \alpha_{i,2} v_{i,2} + \cdots + \alpha_{i,n_i} v_{i,n_i}, \tag{13.2.1}$$

for some scalars $\alpha_{i,j} \in \mathbb{R}$, $j = 1, 2, \ldots, n_i$.

Since the membership i of the test sample is initially unknown, we define a new matrix A for the entire training set as the concatenation of the $n = n_1 + \cdots + n_k$ training samples from all k object classes:

$$A \doteq [A_1, A_2, \ldots, A_k] = [v_{1,1}, v_{1,2}, \ldots, v_{k,n_k}]. \tag{13.2.2}$$

Then the linear representation of $\boldsymbol{y}$ can be rewritten in terms of all training samples as

$$\boldsymbol{y} = \boldsymbol{A}\boldsymbol{x}_o \quad \in \mathbb{R}^m, \tag{13.2.3}$$

where $\boldsymbol{x}_o = [0, \ldots, 0, \alpha_{i,1}, \alpha_{i,2}, \ldots, \alpha_{i,n_i}, 0, \ldots, 0]^* \in \mathbb{R}^n$ is a coefficient vector whose entries are zero except those associated with the i-th class.[2]

This motivates us to seek the sparsest solution to $\boldsymbol{y} = \boldsymbol{A}\boldsymbol{x}$ via sparse optimization, such as ℓ^1 minimization:

$$\hat{\boldsymbol{x}} = \arg\min \|\boldsymbol{x}\|_1 \quad \text{subject to} \quad \boldsymbol{A}\boldsymbol{x} = \boldsymbol{y}. \tag{13.2.4}$$

Given a new test sample $\boldsymbol{y}$ from one of the classes in the training set, we first compute its sparse representation $\hat{\boldsymbol{x}}$ via (13.2.4). Ideally, the nonzero entries in the estimate $\hat{\boldsymbol{x}}$ will be all associated with the columns of $\boldsymbol{A}$ from a single object class i, and we can easily assign the test sample $\boldsymbol{y}$ to that class. However, noise and modeling error may lead to small nonzero entries associated with multiple object classes (for example, see Figure 13.1(b)). Based on the global, sparse representation, one can design many possible classifiers to resolve this. For instance, we can classify $\boldsymbol{y}$ based on how well the coefficients associated with all the training samples of each object reproduce $\boldsymbol{y}$.

More specifically, for each class i, let $\delta_i(\cdot) : \mathbb{R}^n \to \mathbb{R}^n$ be the characteristic function which selects the coefficients associated with the i-th class. For $\boldsymbol{x} \in \mathbb{R}^n$, $\delta_i(\boldsymbol{x}) \in \mathbb{R}^n$ is a new vector whose only nonzero entries are the entries in $\boldsymbol{x}$ that are associated with class i. Using only the coefficients associated with the i-th class, one can approximate the given test sample $\boldsymbol{y}$ as $\hat{\boldsymbol{y}}_i = \boldsymbol{A}\delta_i(\hat{\boldsymbol{x}})$. We then classify $\boldsymbol{y}$ based on these approximations by assigning it to the object class that minimizes the residual between $\boldsymbol{y}$ and $\hat{\boldsymbol{y}}_i$:

$$\min_i \; r_i(\boldsymbol{y}) \doteq \|\boldsymbol{y} - \hat{\boldsymbol{y}}_i\|_2. \tag{13.2.5}$$

Algorithm 13.1 summarizes the complete recognition procedure, in which for the ℓ^1 minimization problem (13.2.6) in step 3, one can use any of the methods introduced in Chapter 8 to solve. In particular, the augmented Lagrangian multiplier (ALM) method in Section 8.4 is well suited for this constrained optimization problem.

EXAMPLE 13.1. *(ℓ^1 Minimization vs. ℓ^2 Minimization) To illustrate how Algorithm 13.1 works, we randomly select half of the* 2414 *images in the Extended Yale Face Database B [GBK01] as the training set, and the rest for testing. In this example, we subsample the images from the original* 192×168 *to size* 12×10. *The pixel values of the downsampled image are used as 120-D features – stacked as columns of the matrix* $\boldsymbol{A}$ *in the algorithm. Hence matrix* $\boldsymbol{A}$ *has size* 120×1207, *and the system* $\boldsymbol{y} = \boldsymbol{A}\boldsymbol{x}$ *is underdetermined. Figure 13.2(a) illustrates the sparse coefficients recovered by Algorithm 13.1 for a test image from the first subject. The figure*

[2] Notice that in the practice of deep networks for classification (as we will see in Chapter 16), people typically use the network to map a given image, here $\boldsymbol{y}$, to a "one-hot" vector $[0, \ldots, 0, 1, 0 \ldots, 0]^* \in \mathbb{R}^k$ that indicates its class out of k classes. So essentially, the deep network plays the same role as any algorithm that solves the sparse solution $\boldsymbol{x}$ here.

Algorithm 13.1 Sparse Representation-based Classification (SRC)

Input: a matrix of training samples $\boldsymbol{A} = [\boldsymbol{A}_1, \boldsymbol{A}_2, \ldots, \boldsymbol{A}_k] \in \mathbb{R}^{m \times n}$ for k classes, a test sample $\boldsymbol{y} \in \mathbb{R}^m$.

Normalize the columns of $\boldsymbol{A}$ to have unit ℓ^2 norm.

Solve the ℓ^1 minimization problem (13.2.4):

$$\hat{\boldsymbol{x}} = \arg\min_{\boldsymbol{x}} \|\boldsymbol{x}\|_1 \quad \text{subject to} \quad \boldsymbol{A}\boldsymbol{x} = \boldsymbol{y}. \tag{13.2.6}$$

Compute the residuals $r_i(\boldsymbol{y}) = \|\boldsymbol{y} - \boldsymbol{A}\,\delta_i(\hat{\boldsymbol{x}})\|_2$ for $i = 1, \ldots, k$.

Output: identity$(\boldsymbol{y}) = \arg\min_i r_i(\boldsymbol{y})$.

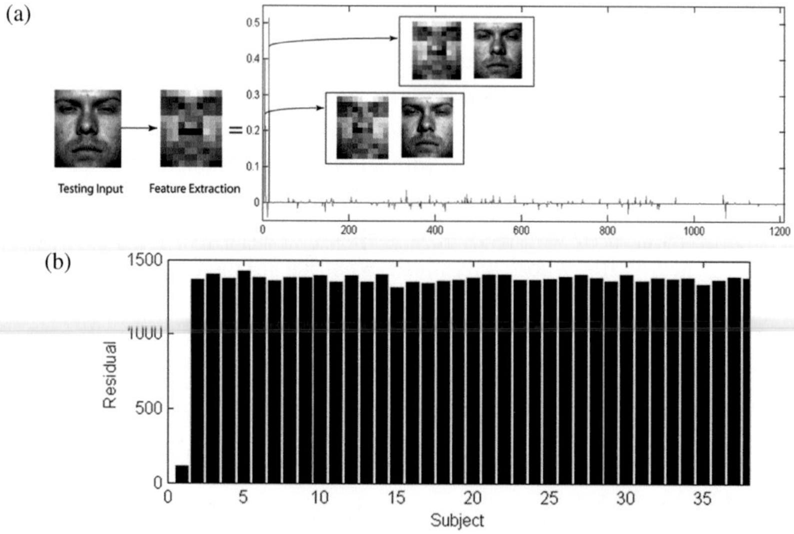

Figure 13.2 A Valid Test Image. (a) Recognition with 12×10 downsampled images as features. The test image $\boldsymbol{y}$ belongs to subject 1. The values of the sparse coefficients recovered from Algorithm 13.1 are plotted on the right together with the two training examples that correspond to the two largest sparse coefficients. (b) The residuals $r_i(\boldsymbol{y})$ of a test image of subject 1 with respect to the projected sparse coefficients $\delta_i(\hat{\boldsymbol{x}})$ by ℓ^1 minimization. The ratio between the two smallest residuals is about 1:8.6.

also shows the features and the original images that correspond to the two largest coefficients. The two largest coefficients are both associated with training samples from subject 1. Figure 13.2(b) shows the residuals with respect to the 38 projected coefficients $\delta_i(\hat{\boldsymbol{x}}_1)$, $i = 1, 2, \ldots, 38$. *With* 12×10 *downsampled images as features, Algorithm 13.1 achieves an overall recognition rate of* 92.1% *across the Extended Yale B database. Whereas the more conventional minimum* ℓ^2 *norm solution to the underdetermined system* $\boldsymbol{y} = \boldsymbol{A}\boldsymbol{x}$ *is typically quite dense, minimizing the* ℓ^1 *norm favors sparse solutions, and provably recovers the sparsest solution when this solution*

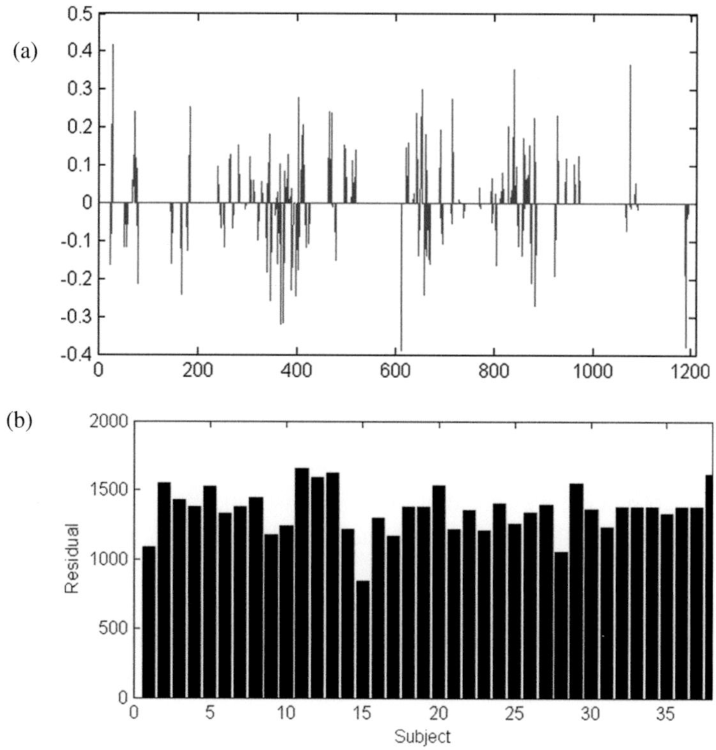

Figure 13.3 Non-sparsity of the ℓ^2 Minimizer. (a) Coefficients from ℓ^2 minimization, using the same test image as Figure 13.2. The recovered solution is not sparse and hence less informative for recognition (large coefficients do not correspond to training images of this test subject). (b) The residuals of the test image from subject 1 with respect to the projection $\delta_i(\hat{\boldsymbol{x}})$ of the coefficients obtained by ℓ^2 minimization. The ratio between the two smallest residuals is about 1:1.3. The smallest residual is not associated with subject 1.

is sufficiently sparse. To illustrate this contrast, Figure 13.3(a) shows the coefficients of the same test image given by the conventional ℓ^2 minimization, and Figure 13.3(b) shows the corresponding residuals with respect to the 38 subjects. The coefficients are much less sparse than those given by ℓ^1 minimization (in Figure 13.2), and the dominant coefficients are not associated with subject 1. As a result, the smallest residual in Figure 13.3 does not correspond to the correct subject.

13.3 Robustness to Occlusion or Corruption

In many real-world scenarios, the test image $\boldsymbol{y}$ could be partially occluded or corrupted. In this case, the linear model (13.2.3) should be modified as

$$\boldsymbol{y} = \boldsymbol{y}_o + \boldsymbol{e}_o = \boldsymbol{A}\boldsymbol{x}_o + \boldsymbol{e}_o, \tag{13.3.1}$$

where $\boldsymbol{e}_o \in \mathbb{R}^m$ is a vector of errors – a fraction, ρ, of its entries are nonzero. The nonzero entries of $\boldsymbol{e}_o$ represent which pixels in $\boldsymbol{y}$ are corrupted or occluded. The locations of corruption can differ for different test images and are not known to the algorithm. The errors may have arbitrary magnitude and therefore cannot be ignored or treated with techniques designed for small noise.

A fundamental principle of coding theory [MS81] is that *redundancy* in the measurement is essential to detecting and correcting gross errors. Redundancy arises in object recognition because the number of image pixels is typically far greater than the number of subjects that have generated the images. In this case, even if a fraction of the pixels are completely corrupted, recognition may still be possible based on the remaining pixels. On the other hand, the traditional feature extraction schemes discussed in the previous section would discard useful information that could help compensate for the occlusion. In this sense, no representation is more redundant, robust, or informative than the original images. Thus, when dealing with occlusion and corruption, we should always work with the highest possible resolution, performing downsampling or feature extraction only if the resolution of the original images is too high to process.

Of course, redundancy would be of no use without efficient computational tools for exploiting the information encoded in the redundant data. The difficulty in directly harnessing the redundancy in corrupted raw images has led researchers to instead focus on *spatial locality* as a guiding principle for robust recognition. Local features computed from only a small fraction of the image pixels are clearly less likely to be corrupted by occlusion than holistic features. In face recognition, methods such as ICA [KCYT05] and LNMF [LHZC01] exploit this observation by adaptively choosing filter bases that are locally concentrated. Local binary patterns [AHP06] and Gabor wavelets [LVB+93] exhibit similar properties, since they are also computed from local image regions. A related approach partitions the image into fixed regions and computes features for each region [PMS94, Mar02]. Notice, though, that projecting onto locally concentrated bases transforms the domain of the occlusion problem, rather than eliminating the occlusion. Errors on the original pixels become errors in the transformed domain, and may even become less local. The role of feature extraction in achieving spatial locality is therefore questionable, since *no bases or features are more spatially localized than the original image pixels themselves.* In fact, the most popular approach to robustifying feature-based methods is based on randomly sampling individual pixels [LB00].

Now, let us show how the sparse representation classification framework can be extended to deal with occlusion. Let us assume that the corrupted pixels are a relatively small portion ρ of the total image pixels. Then the error vector $\boldsymbol{e}_o$, like the vector $\boldsymbol{x}_o$, should be sparse nonzero entries. Since $\boldsymbol{y}_o = \boldsymbol{A}\boldsymbol{x}_o$, we can rewrite (13.3.1) as

$$\boldsymbol{y} = \left[\, \boldsymbol{A},\ \boldsymbol{I} \,\right] \begin{bmatrix} \boldsymbol{x}_o \\ \boldsymbol{e}_o \end{bmatrix} \doteq \boldsymbol{B}\, \boldsymbol{w}_o. \tag{13.3.2}$$

Here, $\boldsymbol{B} = [\boldsymbol{A},\ \boldsymbol{I}] \in \mathbb{R}^{m \times (n+m)}$, so the system $\boldsymbol{y} = \boldsymbol{B}\boldsymbol{w}$ is always underdetermined and does not have a unique solution for $\boldsymbol{w}$. However, in theory, the correct generating

Algorithm 13.2 Robust Sparse Representation-based Classification

1: **Input:** a matrix of training samples $\boldsymbol{A} = [\boldsymbol{A}_1, \boldsymbol{A}_2, \ldots, \boldsymbol{A}_k] \in \mathbb{R}^{m \times n}$ for k classes, a test sample $\boldsymbol{y} \in \mathbb{R}^m$ (and an optional error tolerance $\varepsilon > 0$).
2: Normalize the columns of $\boldsymbol{A}$ to have unit ℓ^2 norm.
3: Solve the ℓ^1 minimization problem:

$$\begin{bmatrix} \hat{\boldsymbol{x}} \\ \hat{\boldsymbol{e}} \end{bmatrix} = \arg\min_{\boldsymbol{x}} \|\boldsymbol{x}\|_1 + \|\boldsymbol{e}\|_1 \quad \text{subject to} \quad [\boldsymbol{A}, \boldsymbol{I}] \begin{bmatrix} \boldsymbol{x} \\ \boldsymbol{e} \end{bmatrix} = \boldsymbol{y}. \tag{13.3.4}$$

4: Compute the residuals $r_i(\boldsymbol{y}) = \|\boldsymbol{y} - \hat{\boldsymbol{e}} - \boldsymbol{A}\, \delta_i(\hat{\boldsymbol{x}})\|_2$ for $i = 1, \ldots, k$.
5: **Output:** identity$(\boldsymbol{y}) = \arg\min_i r_i(\boldsymbol{y})$.

$\boldsymbol{w}_o = [\boldsymbol{x}_o,\ \boldsymbol{e}_o]$ has at most $n_i + \rho m$ nonzeros. We might therefore hope to recover $\boldsymbol{w}_o$ as the sparsest solution to the system $\boldsymbol{y} = \boldsymbol{B}\boldsymbol{w}$. As before, we attempt to recover the sparsest solution $\boldsymbol{w}_o$ via sparse optimization, such as solving the following ℓ^1 minimization problem:

$$\hat{\boldsymbol{w}} = \arg\min \|\boldsymbol{w}\|_1 \quad \text{subject to} \quad \boldsymbol{B}\boldsymbol{w} = \boldsymbol{y}. \tag{13.3.3}$$

Algorithm 13.2 summarizes the complete recognition procedure.

More generally, one can assume that the corrupting error $\boldsymbol{e}_o$ has a sparse representation with respect to some basis $\boldsymbol{A}_e \in \mathbb{R}^{m \times n_e}$. That is, $\boldsymbol{e}_o = \boldsymbol{A}_e \boldsymbol{u}_o$ for some sparse vector $\boldsymbol{u}_o \in \mathbb{R}^m$. Here, we have chosen the special case $\boldsymbol{A}_e = \boldsymbol{I} \in \mathbb{R}^{m \times m}$, as $\boldsymbol{e}_o$ is assumed to be sparse in the natural pixel coordinates. If the error $\boldsymbol{e}_o$ is instead more sparse with respect to another basis, e.g., Fourier or Haar, we can simply redefine the matrix $\boldsymbol{B}$ by appending $\boldsymbol{A}_e$ to $\boldsymbol{A}$ and instead seek the sparsest solution $\boldsymbol{w}_o$ to the equation:

$$\boldsymbol{y} = \boldsymbol{B}\boldsymbol{w} \quad \text{with} \quad \boldsymbol{B} = [\boldsymbol{A},\ \boldsymbol{A}_e] \quad \in \mathbb{R}^{m \times (n+n_e)}. \tag{13.3.5}$$

In this way, the same formulation can handle more general classes of sparse corruption.

Experimental Verification of the Algorithm

We test the robust version of SRC applied to face recognition using the Extended Yale Face Database B [GBK01]. We choose Subsets 1 and 2 (717 images, normal-to-moderate lighting conditions) for training, and Subset 3 (453 images, more extreme lighting conditions) for testing. Without occlusion, this is a relatively easy recognition problem. This choice is deliberate, in order to isolate the effect of occlusion. The images are resized to 96×84 pixels, so in this case $\boldsymbol{B} = [\boldsymbol{A},\ \boldsymbol{I}]$ is an 8064×8761 matrix, a manageable size for most computers.

We then corrupt a percentage of randomly chosen pixels from each of the test images, replacing their values with i.i.d. samples from a uniform distribution. The corrupted pixels are randomly chosen for each test image and the locations are unknown to the algorithm. We vary the percentage of corrupted pixels from 0% to 90%.

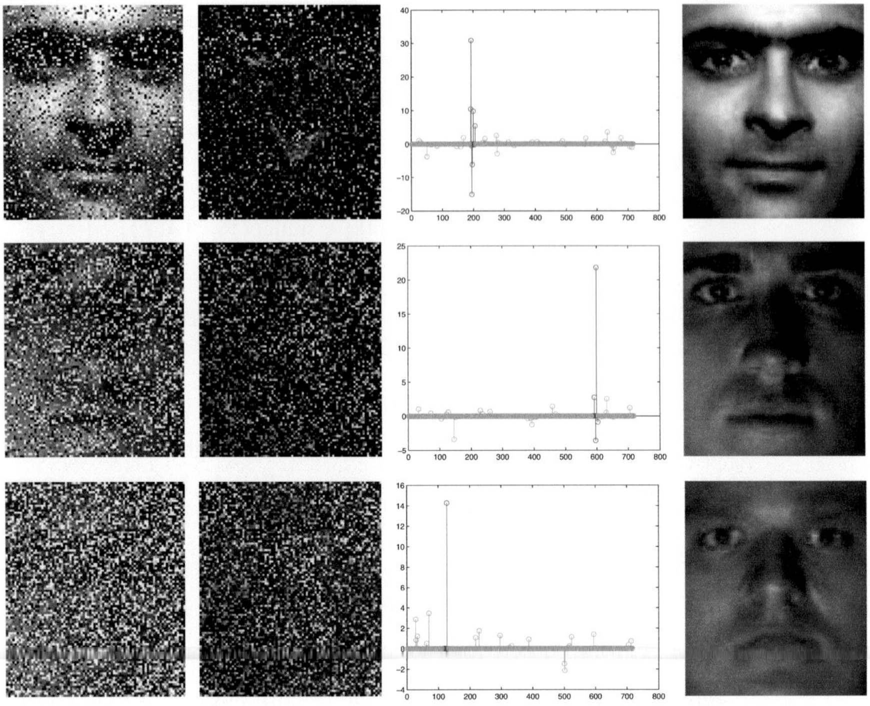

Figure 13.4 Recovered Sparse Representation and Sparse Error under Random Corruption. (a) Test images $\boldsymbol{y}$ from the Extended Yale Face Database B [GBK01], with random corruption. Top row, 30% of pixels are corrupted; middle row, 50% corrupted; bottom row, 70% corrupted. (b) Estimated errors $\hat{\boldsymbol{e}}_1$. (c) Estimated sparse coefficients $\hat{\boldsymbol{x}}_1$. (d) Reconstructed images $\boldsymbol{y}_r$. SRC correctly identifies all three corrupted face images.

Figure 13.4 shows several example test images. To the human eye, beyond 50% corruption, the corrupted images (Figure 13.4(a) second and third rows) are barely recognizable as face images; determining their identity seems out of the question. Yet even in this extreme circumstance, SRC correctly recovers the identity of the subjects.

We quantitatively compare the sparse method to four popular techniques for face recognition in the vision literature. The principal component analysis (PCA) approach of [TP91] is not robust to occlusion. Although there are many variations to make PCA robust to corruption or incomplete data, some of which have been applied to robust face recognition, e.g., [SSL06], here we use the basic PCA to provide a standard baseline for comparison. The remaining three techniques are designed to be more robust to occlusion. Independent component analysis (ICA) architecture I [KCYT05] attempts to express the training set as a linear combination of statistically independent basis images. Local nonnegative matrix factorization (LNMF) [LHZC01] approximates the training set as an additive combination of basis images, computed with a bias towards sparse bases. For PCA, ICA, and LNMF, the number of basis components is chosen to give the best performance over the range $\{100, 200, 300, 400, 500, 600\}$.

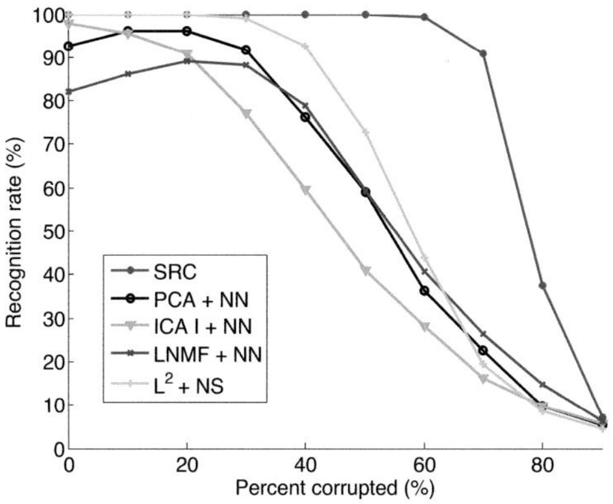

Figure 13.5 Recognition Rates with Random Corruption. The recognition rate across the entire range of corruption for various algorithms. SRC (red curve) significantly outperforms others, performing almost perfectly up to 60% random corruption.

Finally, to demonstrate that the improved robustness is really due to the use of the ℓ^1 norm, we compare to a least-squares technique that first projects the test image onto the subspace spanned by all face images, and then applies the nearest subspace classifier.

Figure 13.5 plots the recognition performance of SRC and five competitors, as a function of the level of corruption. We see that the algorithm dramatically outperforms others. From 0% up to 50% occlusion, SRC correctly classifies all subjects. At 50% corruption, none of the others achieves higher than 73% recognition rate, while the proposed algorithm achieves 100%. Even at 70% occlusion, the recognition rate is still 90.7%. This greatly surpasses the theoretical bound of worst-case corruption (13.3%) that the algorithm is ensured to tolerate. Clearly, the worst-case analysis is too conservative for random corruption.

13.4 Dense Error Correction with the Cross and Bouquet

In this section, we will take a closer look at the sparsity model (13.3.2). Recall, in the classical sparse representation theory, that one of the conditions for the successful recovery of a sparse signal is that the dictionary under which the sparsity is represented must be sufficiently incoherent. However, the dictionary $\boldsymbol{B} = [\boldsymbol{A},\ \boldsymbol{I}] \in \mathbb{R}^{m\times(n+m)}$ is quite special.

In its first part, the matrix $\boldsymbol{A}$ consists of column vectors that represent the pixel values of all face images. As m grows higher, the convex hull spanned by all the face image vectors becomes an extremely tiny portion of the unit sphere in $\mathbb{R}^m$, which means they are highly correlated.[3] As an example, all the face images of the example

[3] Notice that we have encountered a similar issue with coherence with real-world problems in the scientific imaging problems in Chapter 12: the shifted versions of the motif can be coherent. In such cases, certain heuristics can be used to improve the performance, as discussed in Section 12.4.2.

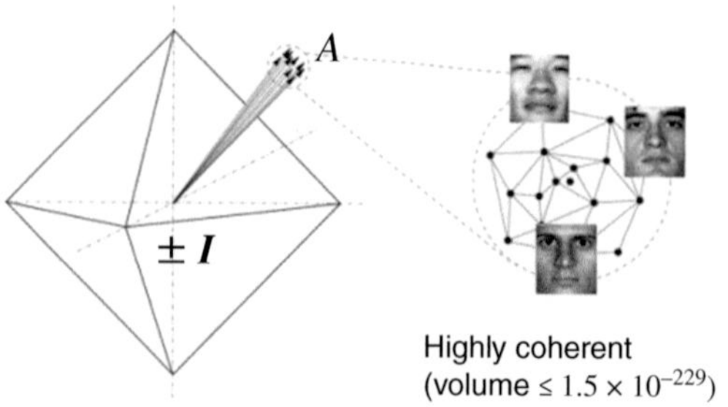

Figure 13.6 The Cross-and-Bouquet Model for Robust Face Recognition. The raw images of human faces expressed as columns of $\boldsymbol{A}$ are clustered with a very tiny variance.

in Figure 13.4 lie in $\mathbb{R}^m$ where $m = 8064$, and calculation shows that all the image vectors are contained within a spherical cap of volume $\leq 1.5 \times 10^{-229}$, as shown in Figure 13.6. These vectors are tightly bundled together as a "bouquet." Hence it is fair to say that identifying a face image within a big pool of candidates is like *finding a needle in a haystack which, in turn, lies on the tip of a needle.*

In the second part of $\boldsymbol{B}$, $\boldsymbol{I}$ is a standard $m \times m$ identity matrix, which is also called a standard pixel basis. Then $\boldsymbol{I}$ and its negative copy $-\boldsymbol{I}$ form a "cross" in $\mathbb{R}^m$, also illustrated in Figure 13.6. We call this type of dictionary a *cross-and-bouquet* (CAB) model. It is important to understand how such special (coherent and incoherent) structures may affect the performance of ℓ^1 minimization in finding the correct (sparse) solution.

The CAB model belongs to a special class of sparse representation problems where the dictionary is a concatenation of two or more subdictionaries. Examples include the merger of wavelet and heavy-side dictionaries [CDS01] and the combination of texture and cartoon dictionaries in morphological component analysis [ESQD05]. However, in contrast to most other examples, not only is the CAB dictionary as a whole inhomogeneous as we discussed above, in fact the ground-truth signal $(\boldsymbol{x}_o, \boldsymbol{e}_o)$ is also very inhomogeneous; namely, the sparsity of $\boldsymbol{x}_o$ is limited by the number of training images per subject for the purpose of recognition, while we would like to handle as dense corruption error $\boldsymbol{e}_o$ as possible, to guarantee good error correction performance. The above experiment is indeed a concrete demonstration that shows sparse optimization such as ℓ^1 minimization seems to be able to recover very dense error $\boldsymbol{e}_o$. This further contradicts our understanding in the classical sparse representation theory, where the corruption error to be recovered is typically assumed to be sparse.

The reason sparse optimization could recover even dense error is mainly due to the special nature of the sparsity of the signal $\boldsymbol{x}_o$, which is called *weak proportional growth*. Again, assume the signal

$$\boldsymbol{w}_o = \boldsymbol{A}\boldsymbol{x}_o + \boldsymbol{e}_o,$$

where $\boldsymbol{e}_o \in \mathbb{R}^m$ is a vector of error of arbitrary magnitude. We also assume the columns of $\boldsymbol{A}$ are i.i.d. samples from a Gaussian distribution: $\boldsymbol{A} = [\boldsymbol{v}_1, \ldots, \boldsymbol{v}_n] \in \mathbb{R}^{m \times n}$, where $\boldsymbol{v}_i \sim_{\text{iid}} \mathcal{N}(\boldsymbol{\mu}, (\nu^2/m)\boldsymbol{I}_m)$, and $\|\boldsymbol{\mu}\|_2 = 1$, $\|\boldsymbol{\mu}\|_\infty \leq C_\mu m^{-1/2}$.

DEFINITION 13.2. (Weak Proportional Growth) *A sequence of signal–error problems* $(\boldsymbol{x}_o, \boldsymbol{e}_o)$ *exhibits weak proportional growth with parameters* $\delta > 0$, $\rho \in (0,1)$, $C_0 > 0$, *and* $\eta_0 > 0$, *denoted as* $WPG_{\delta,\rho,C_0,\eta_0}$, *if as* $m \to \infty$,

$$\frac{n}{m} \to \delta, \qquad \frac{\|\boldsymbol{e}_o\|_0}{m} \to \rho, \quad \|\boldsymbol{x}_o\|_0 \le C_0 m^{1-\eta_0}. \tag{13.4.1}$$

In other words, in the weak proportional growth scenario, $\|\boldsymbol{e}_o\|_0$ grows linearly with respect to m, but $\|\boldsymbol{x}_o\|_0$ is sublinear.

THEOREM 13.3. (Dense error correction with the cross and bouquet) *For any* $\delta > 0$, *there exists* $\nu_0(\delta) > 0$ *such that if* $\nu < \nu_0$ *and* $\rho < 1$, *in* $WPG_{\delta,\rho,C_0,\eta_0}$ *with* $\boldsymbol{A}$ *distributed according to* (13.4.1), *if the error support and the signs of nonzero elements are chosen uniformly at random, then as* $m \to \infty$, *the probability of successfully recovering* $(\boldsymbol{x}_o, \boldsymbol{e}_o)$ *via Algorithm 13.2 approaches one.*

That is, as long as the bouquet is sufficiently tight, under the assumption of weak proportional growth, asymptotically ℓ^1 minimization recovers any nonnegative sparse signal from almost any error with support size less than 100%! A detailed proof of this theorem can be found in [WM10]. Although in general sparse representation problems may not satisfy the weak proportional growth assumption, the assumption is valid in the face recognition example, whereby the number of training samples per subject n_i usually does not grow proportionally with the dimension of the image.

13.5 Notes

Results in this chapter are based on the work [WYG+09], which has provided the earliest evidence that sparse representation can be extremely discriminative and robust for object recognition purposes. As we will reveal in Chapter 16, similar properties of sparse representation have been implicitly exploited by modern deep neural networks for general classification tasks.

Nonuniform Incoherence

The robust face recognition example also provides a good lesson on the practice of principles introduced in this book. Depending on the applications, "incoherence" is not an absolute notion: relative to corruptions and errors, the face images are rather coherent among themselves. That is actually the reason why error correction for face images (together) can be so effective. Nevertheless, the seemingly coherent face images have just enough incoherence to allow correct identification of the input image. Like the spectrum identification problem studied in Chapter 11, here we are only interested in the support of the recovered sparse signals; furthermore, unlike applications where one needs to recover a signal with as many nonzero entries as possible, here the correct solution is preferably the sparser the better. These special conditions significantly relax the incoherence requirement on the sensing matrix (here face images or features). Motivated by these empirical observations, a more rigorous analysis of this type of incoherence was given in the follow-up work [WM10].

Contiguous Occlusion
In this chapter, for corruption or occlusion of the pixels, we only consider their sparse structure as individual pixels. In practice, however, if the corruption is due to real occlusions, the occluded pixels are not entirely random in their locations. Occluded pixels are often spatially contiguous in their locations. Such structures can probably be better captured by the notion of group sparsity mentioned in Section 6.1.1 of Chapter 6. Empirically, it has been verified that if one can explicitly model and harness such structure in occluded pixels, say as a Markov random field, one can achieve an even higher level of robustness to contiguous occlusion for face recognition [ZWMM09]. But to the best of our knowledge, a rigorous analysis and justification remains elusive at this point.

Importance of Alignment
In this chapter, we have assumed the test image and images in the gallery are all well aligned. This is, however, not necessarily the case with real-world face images. As one may see from testing the algorithm, although the scheme is extremely robust to corruption in the pixels, it is rather sensitive to any (small) misalignment in the input face images. This is the case even for the highly engineered and trained modern deep neural networks [AW18, ETT+17], as we will discuss more in Chapter 16. In this situation, we need to consider an extended model of (13.3.1):

$$\boldsymbol{y} \circ \tau = \boldsymbol{A}\boldsymbol{x}_o + \boldsymbol{e}_o,$$

for some unknown deformation τ of the image domain (say translation). Nevertheless, in such cases, one may still exploit sparsity for finding the correct alignment and identification simultaneously, as shown in the work [WWG+09, WWG+12]. In the case where even gallery images (as columns $\{\boldsymbol{v}_i\}$ of the matrix $\boldsymbol{A}$) are not so well aligned themselves, one may have to align them first before applying the scheme here. To align multiple gallery face images together, one may exploit the fact that the images become highly correlated (hence form a low-rank matrix) when they are correctly aligned. That is, the following matrix

$$\boldsymbol{M}(\tau) = [\boldsymbol{v}_1 \circ \tau_1, \boldsymbol{v}_2 \circ \tau_2, \ldots, \boldsymbol{v}_n \circ \tau_n]$$

would have the lowest rank when the correct transformations $\{\tau_i\}$ are found for each of the gallery images $\boldsymbol{v}_i$. Hence the efficient techniques on robust low-rank matrix recovery introduced in this book can be used to automatically align multiple face images, as demonstrated in the work [PGW+12]. We will see how similar robust low-rank techniques can be utilized to correct other common deformations in images in Chapter 15.

13.6 Exercises

13.1. (Robust face recognition*) *Download the Extended Yale B database. Use the cropped face image set in the database to form a gallery set and a query set. Code a* *robust face recognition system and demonstrate its performance in the same setting as discussed in the experiment of this chapter.*

13.2. (Randomfaces) *In the literature, there are facial feature extraction methods that reduce the dimensionality of face images according to some linear transformations. In this exercise, we will implement two well-established methods, and compare their performance in terms of recognition accuracy with the results using random projection in compressive sensing.*

(a) *Code a function that extracts Eigenface features. Demonstrate the recognition accuracy of robust face recognition in Exercise 13.1 in the Eigenface space with respect to different feature dimensions.*
(b) *Code a function that extracts Fisherface features. Demonstrate its recognition accuracy with respect to different feature dimensions.*
(c) *Code a function that extracts lower-dimensional features using random projection. This is called* Randomface *features. Demonstrate its recognition accuracy with respect to different feature dimensions, and compare with those of Eigenface and Fisherface features.*

13.3. (Receiver operating characteristic (ROC)) *In the presence of potential irrelevant test samples, it is important to evaluate the performance of a classifier based not only on the* true positive rate, *but often more importably on the* false positive rate. *The curve that measures the true positive rates under various false positive rates is known as the* receiver operating characteristic *(ROC) curve.*[4]

In this exercise, code a program that plots a representative ROC curve of the robust face recognition algorithm. Exclude half of the subject classes from the gallery set of the Extended Yale B database, and designate them as outlying subjects. Implement the outlier rejection rule based on the sparse coefficient concentration, and plot the ROC curve with respect to different threshold values of the concentration index.

[4] There are different definitions of the ROC curve. There are four basic performance rates: true positive, false positive, true negative, and false negative.

14 Robust Photometric Stereo

"*All the variety, all the charm, all the beauty of life is made up of light and shadow.*"
– Leo Tolstoy, *Anna Karenina*

14.1 Introduction

One of the most fundamental problems in computer vision is to capture the 3D shape of an object or a scene. Most popular 3D shape capturing techniques fall into one of the two categories:

1. The so-called *structure from motion* approach reconstructs the 3D geometry by taking multiple images of an object or a scene from different viewpoints [HZ00, MSKS04]. See Figure 14.1(a) for illustration. The images are usually taken under the same or similar lighting conditions since such methods rely on establishing correspondence of common feature points across all the images.
2. The *active light* approach captures the 3D shape by taking multiple images of the object or a scene under different illumination conditions or patterns, but usually from a fixed viewpoint. Methods such as structured lights, photometric stereo, and shape from shading all belong to this category. See Figure 14.1(b) and (c) for illustration.

One can tell from the setup that these two approaches are rather complementary to each other: one varies the camera viewpoints while fixing the lighting whereas the other varies the lighting conditions with a fixed view. Their results are also complementary to each other: structure from motion techniques typically recover 3D positions of a sparse set of points in the scene that have distinguishable local textures for easy correspondence across views; whereas active lighting techniques usually recover a dense per-pixel geometry (depth or surface normal) of the scene even for nontextured regions.

Both approaches have been developed in computer vision and related fields with a long and rich history, and there has been a vast body of literature associated with each method within both categories. In hindsight, though, it would be illuminating to understand now, from the perspective of high-dimensional data analysis, how 3D

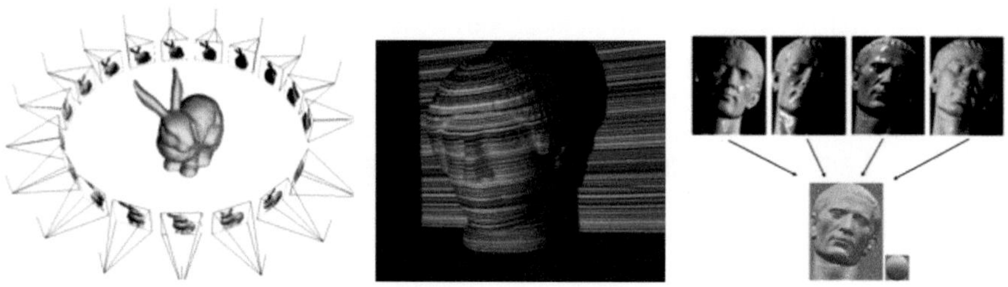

(a) structure from motion (b) structured lights (c) photometric stereo

Figure 14.1 Representative Techniques for Capturing 3D Shapes: (a) structure from motion takes multiple images of an object from different viewpoints to triangulate its shape; (b) structured light methods cast different light patterns onto an object surface to reveal its 3D geometry; and (c) photometric stereo illuminates the object with multiple directional lights to recover its surface normal.

geometric information of the scene is encoded in the vast data measured in both approaches,[1] and why one can efficiently and accurately recover such information from the data.

According to the settings of both approaches, all the images are capturing a common object or a scene. Then, under some reasonable assumptions such as the scene being mostly static and most surfaces having well-conditioned photometric properties, these imagery data should be highly correlated. It has been well studied and understood that in the structure from motion setting, no matter how many corresponding feature points are captured in arbitrarily many views, they form a large measurement matrix, the so-called *multiple-view matrix*, whose rank will always be bounded below *one or two*. Such a low-rank matrix precisely encodes all the camera poses and the depths of all the feature points. Essentially all structure from motion algorithms harness the same low-rank properties to recover the camera poses and depth of feature points. We refer interested readers to [MSKS04] for a full account.

The situation is similar in the active light approach. In this chapter, we will use photometric stereo as an example to show how low-dimensional structures naturally arise from the physical model of the data generation process and how to harness such low-dimensional structures (using tools from this book) to deal with imperfections in the measurement process so as to accurately recover the object's 3D geometry.

14.2 Photometric Stereo via Low-Rank Matrix Recovery

Photometric stereo [Woo80, Sil80] has been a very popular method for 3D shape capture. It estimates surface orientations of the scene from images taken from a fixed viewpoint under multiple directional lights. As we will soon see, photometric stereo

[1] Typically hundreds or thousands of feature points in structure from motion and millions of pixels for the active light methods.

can produce a dense field of surface normals at the level of detail that cannot be achieved by any other feature-based approaches such as structure from motion.

14.2.1 Lambertian Surface under Directional Lights

In the setting for photometric stereo, the relative position of the camera and object is usually fixed. The intrinsic parameters of the camera are usually precalibrated and known. We do not need to know the camera pose (the extrinsic parameters), as all geometric quantities can be expressed with respect to the camera frame.

For simplicity, we assume a static object is illuminated by a single point light source at infinity.[2] The direction of the light source can be represented as a vector $\boldsymbol{l} \in \mathbb{R}^3$ (with respect to the camera frame). If we take multiple, say n, images under n different lighting directions, we denote the directions as vectors $\boldsymbol{l}_1, \ldots, \boldsymbol{l}_n \in \mathbb{R}^3$. The magnitude of the vector $\boldsymbol{l}$ is assigned to be proportional to the power of the light source.

Next, we need to know, under the illumination, how much light is reflected from the surface and then measured by the sensor of the camera. Notice that this could be a very complicated process. For every point on the surface, we need to describe by how much the incoming light energy, known as irradiance in radiometry, in any direction is absorbed and emitted in any other outgoing direction, known as radiance. This relationship fully characterizes the photometric properties of the surface and is formally known as the *bidirectional reflectance distribution function* (BRDF). In general, the BRDFs for different material surfaces can be very different. For example, metal, plastic, and cloth look very different under the same light.

Nevertheless, for the majority of the objects and scenes we encounter in the real world, their surface photometric property can be approximately modeled by a simple reflectance function known as the *Lambertian model*. For an ideal Lambertian surface, when illuminated by a light source, the surface diffuses and reflects the light equally in all directions. The fraction of light reflected only depends on the angle between the incoming light direction and the surface normal. More precisely, for a point p on a Lambertian surface illuminated under a light in direction $\boldsymbol{l}$, if the surface normal vector at p is $\boldsymbol{n} \in \mathbb{R}^3$, then the amount of light radiated from point p in all directions is given by (the radiance R):

$$R \doteq \rho \langle \boldsymbol{n}, \boldsymbol{l} \rangle = \rho \boldsymbol{n}^* \boldsymbol{l} = \rho \cos(\theta) \|\boldsymbol{l}\|_2, \tag{14.2.1}$$

where ρ is the diffuse albedo that models the percentage of light that gets reflected by the surface at point p, $\langle \cdot, \cdot \rangle$ is the inner product, and θ is the angle between the light direction $\boldsymbol{l}$ and surface $\boldsymbol{n}$. See Figure 14.2 for a basic idea. It is easy to see from the model that the brightness of the point p does not depend on the view direction $\boldsymbol{v}$.

The albedo ρ of a purely black surface would be zero, hence photometric stereo does not apply to black surfaces or surfaces with very small albedo. Note that the above expression is only valid when $\boldsymbol{n}$ and $\boldsymbol{l}$ form an acute angle ($\theta < 90°$) since radiance R is nonnegative. That is, the surface needs to face the light source. In the

[2] In practice, we only need the light source to be relatively far from the object.

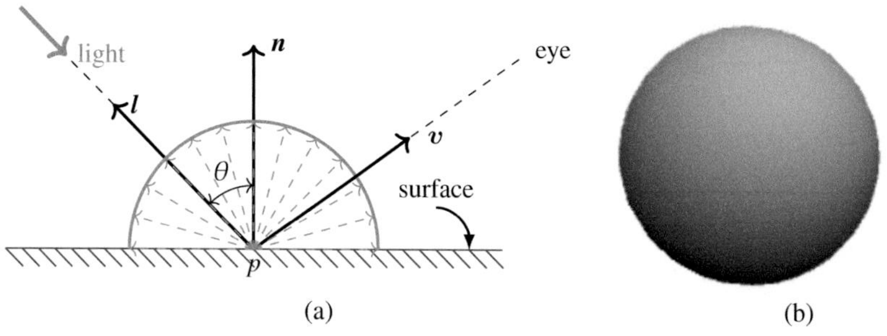

Figure 14.2 Illustration of an Ideal Lambertian Surface Reflectance Model. (a) Incoming light is diffused equally to all directions and the amount of diffused light is proportional to the angle θ between the light direction $\boldsymbol{l}$ and the surface normal $\boldsymbol{n}$. (b) An image of a Lambertian (diffusive) sphere.

case when the surface is facing away from the light source (i.e., $\theta > 90°$), it receives no irradiance, hence $R = 0$. We say such an area is in the shadow. See the bottom of the image of the sphere in Figure 14.2(b).

We further assume that there is no inter-reflection,[3] which is often the case if the object is convex or approximately convex. So the corresponding pixel on the imaging sensor receives only the radiance R contributed from a single point p. If the imaging sensor responds linearly to the radiance, the value of the pixel (x, y) (at the image of the point p) would simply be

$$I(x, y) = R = \rho \boldsymbol{n}^* \boldsymbol{l}. \tag{14.2.2}$$

Let the region of interest be composed of a total of m pixels in each image.[4] We order the pixels with a single index $i \in \{1, \dots, m\}$, and let $I_j(i)$ denote the observed intensity at pixel i in image I_j. With this notation, we have the following relation about the observation $I_j(i)$:

$$I_j(i) = \rho_i \, \boldsymbol{n}_i^* \boldsymbol{l}_j, \tag{14.2.3}$$

where ρ_i is the albedo of the scene at pixel i, $\boldsymbol{n}_i \in \mathbb{R}^3$ is the (unit) surface normal of the scene at pixel i, and $\boldsymbol{l}_j \in \mathbb{R}^3$ represents the light direction vector corresponding to image I_j.[5]

Consider the matrix $\boldsymbol{D} \in \mathbb{R}^{m \times n}$ constructed by stacking all the vectorized images $\text{vec}(I)$ as

$$\boldsymbol{D} \doteq [\text{vec}(I_1) \mid \cdots \mid \text{vec}(I_n)], \tag{14.2.4}$$

[3] Inter-reflection is a phenomenon where light rebounds off surfaces multiple times before reaching the sensor.

[4] Typically, m is much larger than the number of images n.

[5] The convention here is that the lighting direction vectors point from the surface of the object to the light source.

where $\text{vec}(I_j) = [I_j(1), \ldots, I_j(m)]^*$ for $j = 1, \ldots, n$. It follows from (14.2.3) that $\boldsymbol{D}$ can be factorized as follows:

$$\boldsymbol{D} = \boldsymbol{N} \cdot \boldsymbol{L}, \tag{14.2.5}$$

where $\boldsymbol{N} \doteq [\rho_1 \boldsymbol{n}_1 \mid \cdots \mid \rho_m \boldsymbol{n}_m]^* \in \mathbb{R}^{m\times 3}$, and $\boldsymbol{L} \doteq [\,\boldsymbol{l}_1 \mid \cdots \mid \boldsymbol{l}_n\,] \in \mathbb{R}^{3\times n}$. Suppose that the number of images $n \geq 3$. Here $\boldsymbol{N} \cdot \boldsymbol{L}$ is a regular matrix multiplication between $\boldsymbol{N}$ and $\boldsymbol{L}$ and we use a "$\cdot$" to emphasize that its (i, j)-th entry is the inner product between the surface normal $\boldsymbol{n}_i$ and the light direction $\boldsymbol{l}_j$. Then, irrespective of the number of pixels m and the number of images n, the rank of the matrix $\boldsymbol{D}$ is at most

$$\text{rank}\,(\boldsymbol{D}) \leq 3. \tag{14.2.6}$$

14.2.2 Modeling Shadows and Specularities

The low-rank structure of the observation matrix $\boldsymbol{D}$ (14.2.5) is seldom observed with real images. This is due to the presence of shadows and specularities in real images.

Shadows

Shadows arise in real images in two possible ways. As we have discussed before in the Lambertian model, some areas on the object will be entirely dark in the image because they face away from the light source. Such dark pixels in the image are referred to as *attached shadows* [KMK97]. See the image of a sphere in Figure 14.2(b) as an example, where the bottom of the sphere is dark, as that part of the surface is facing away from the light source. In deriving the low-rank model (14.2.5) from (14.2.3), we have implicitly assumed that all pixels of the object are illuminated by the light source in every image. However, that is impossible to achieve in reality: for a generic object (other than a flat surface), almost in every image, there will always be some pixels facing away from the light source and in the shadows. Mathematically, this implies that (14.2.3) should be modified as follows:

$$I_j(i) = \max\left\{\rho_i\, \boldsymbol{n}_i^* \boldsymbol{l}_j, 0\right\}. \tag{14.2.7}$$

Shadows can also occur in images when the shape of the object's surface is not entirely convex: parts of the surface can be occluded from the light source by other parts. Even though the normal vectors at such occluded pixels may form an acute angle with the lighting direction, these pixels appear entirely dark. We refer to such dark pixels as *cast shadows*. See the image of Caesar in Figure 14.5(b) as an example, where, unlike the sphere, the face is not exactly convex and the sporadic shadows around the left side of Caesar's face are cast shadows due to occlusions.

We may pre-detect all the dark shadowed pixels in each image by testing if

$$I_j(i) \approx 0.$$

These pixels are associated with a set of entries $\{(k, j)\}$ in the data matrix $\boldsymbol{D}$ where $\boldsymbol{D}(i, j) \approx 0$. We denote the support of these shadowed entries as Ω^c and all the other valid entries as its complement Ω. With this notation, the valid measurements of the (low-rank) data matrix $\boldsymbol{D}$ are given by

$$\mathcal{P}_{\Omega}[\boldsymbol{D}] = \mathcal{P}_{\Omega}[\boldsymbol{N} \cdot \boldsymbol{L}]. \tag{14.2.8}$$

For the remaining pixels not in the shadows, we have assumed that each pixel measures the radiance directly from each point on the surface. For a nonconvex object like a human face, that is not entirely the case. Light can rebound back and forth between different parts of the surface and create the so-called *inter-reflection*. The radiance that some pixels receive might be compounded by such inter-reflection. Nevertheless, studies have shown that if the object is approximately convex, pixels that are affected by inter-reflection will be relatively few [ZMKW13]. We may model such an effect as a sparse error $\boldsymbol{E}_1$ in the data matrix:

$$\mathcal{P}_{\Omega}[\boldsymbol{D}] = \mathcal{P}_{\Omega}[\boldsymbol{N} \cdot \boldsymbol{L} + \boldsymbol{E}_1]. \tag{14.2.9}$$

Specularities

Specular reflection arises when the object of interest is not perfectly diffusive, i.e., when the surface luminance is not purely isotropic. A mirror is an extreme case which reflects the light with the same angle as the incoming light on the opposite side of the surface normal:

$$\boldsymbol{r} = 2(\boldsymbol{n}^*\boldsymbol{l})\boldsymbol{n} - \boldsymbol{l}.$$

Many real surfaces have both diffusive and reflective characteristics and their reflectance model is a combination of a Lambertian component and a reflective component. The so-called *Phong model* [Pho75] is a correction to the pure Lambertian model with such a reflective component:

$$R = \rho \boldsymbol{n}^*\boldsymbol{l} + k(\boldsymbol{r}^*\boldsymbol{v})^{\alpha}, \tag{14.2.10}$$

where $\boldsymbol{v}$ is the viewing direction (to the sensor), $k \geq 0$ is a weight parameter, and $\alpha > 0$ is an exponent parameter. Figure 14.3 illustrates such a reflectance model.

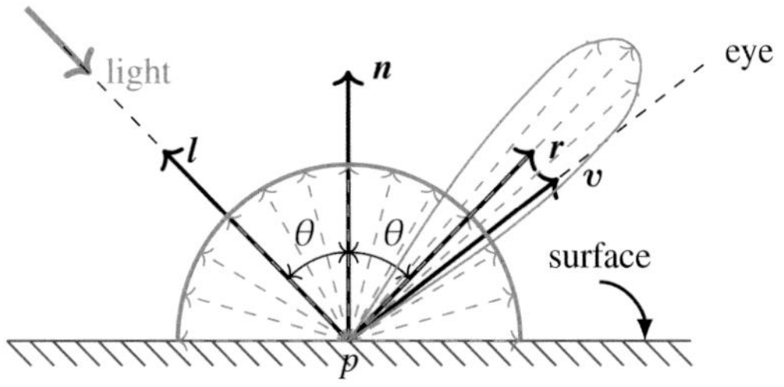

Figure 14.3 A Phong Reflectance Model. Incoming light is diffused equally to all directions and an extra amount of light is reflected close to the direction of reflection $\boldsymbol{r}$, known as a specular lobe.

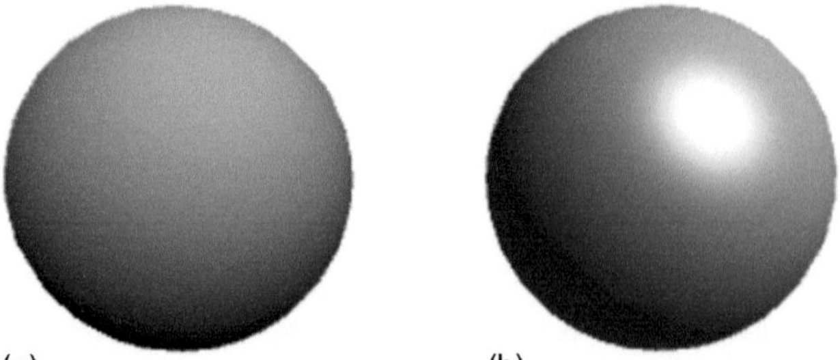

(a) (b)

Figure 14.4 Comparison of (a) a Lambertian (diffusive) sphere and (b) a Phong (specular) sphere under the same (directional) lighting condition.

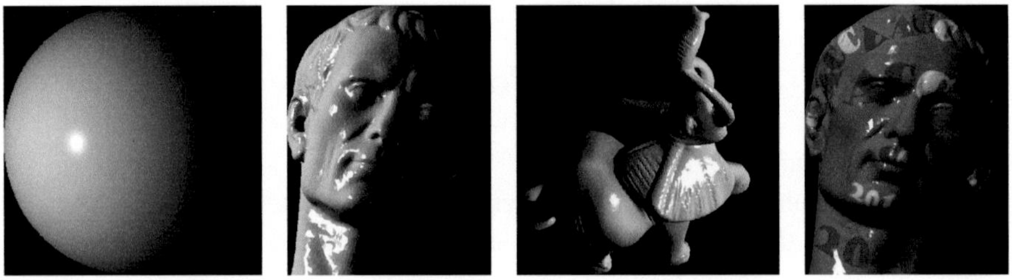

(a) Sphere (b) Caesar (c) Elephant (d) Caesar (with texture)

Figure 14.5 Synthetic image samples used for experiments.

In the computer vision and graphics literature, people have also used other functions to model the reflective component, such as the Cook–Torrance reflectance model [CT81].

In general, for a surface of the Phong model (or of the Cook–Torrance model), the intensity of radiance depends on the viewing direction: part of the light is reflected in a mirror-like fashion that generates a specular lobe when the viewing direction $\boldsymbol{v}$ is close to the reflecting direction $\boldsymbol{r}$. This gives rise to some bright spots or shiny patches on the surface of the object, known as *specularities*. Figure 14.3 illustrates this concept and Figure 14.4 compares the Phong model to the Lambertian model with the images of a sphere.

For most real surfaces, the reflective components are usually benign in the sense that the value of the reflective term is significant only when the view direction is very close to the reflecting direction.[6] The specular lobe is usually very small, and from any given viewing angle, only a small fraction of the surface has the specular effect. See Figure 14.5 for some examples of object surfaces with specular effect.

As the surface normals and the viewing angles are not known *a priori*, we cannot determine which part of the surface is specular. Nevertheless, knowing that specularities are few and sporadic, we may model them as an additional sparse error $\boldsymbol{E}_2$ to the measured data matrix $\boldsymbol{D}$:

[6] In the Phong model, that corresponds to choosing a large exponent α.

$$D = N \cdot L + E_2. \tag{14.2.11}$$

Now, if we combine the sparse errors E_1 due to inter-reflections and E_2 due to specularities and let $E = E_1 + E_2$, then, instead of the ideal low-rank model (14.2.5), a more realistic model for the image measurements should be:

$$\mathcal{P}_\Omega[D] = \mathcal{P}_\Omega[N \cdot L + E], \tag{14.2.12}$$

where Ω marks out pixels in the shadows and the sparse matrix E accounts for corruptions by inter-reflections or specularities.

In order to find out the light directions L and the surface normals N, we need to recover the complete matrix $A = N \cdot L$. Since A is of rank at most 3, the problem becomes a low-rank matrix completion problem subject to sparse errors E. That is, we need to solve the following optimization problem:

$$\min_{A,E} \operatorname{rank}(A) + \gamma \|E\|_0 \quad \text{subject to} \quad \mathcal{P}_\Omega[D] = \mathcal{P}_\Omega[A + E], \tag{14.2.13}$$

where $\|\cdot\|_0$ denotes the ℓ^0 norm (number of nonzero entries in the matrix), and $\gamma > 0$ is a parameter that trades off the rank of the solution A versus the sparsity of the error E.

Let $(A_\star, E_\star)$ be the optimal solution to (14.2.13). If the lighting directions L are given, we can easily recover the matrix N of surface normals from $A_\star$ as

$$N = A_\star L^\dagger, \tag{14.2.14}$$

where $L^\dagger$ denotes the Moore–Penrose pseudo-inverse of L. The surface normals $n_1, \ldots, n_m$ can then be estimated by normalizing each row of N to have unit norm.

14.3 Robust Matrix Completion Algorithm

While (14.2.13) follows from our formulation, it is not tractable since both rank and ℓ^0norm are nonconvex and discontinuous functions. As we have learned from earlier chapters, we can try to solve the convex version of this program:

$$\min_{A,E} \|A\|_* + \lambda \|E\|_1 \quad \text{subject to} \quad \mathcal{P}_\Omega[D] = \mathcal{P}_\Omega[A + E]. \tag{14.3.1}$$

The above problem is almost identical to the PCP program studied in Chapter 5, except that the linear equality constraint is now applied only on the subset Ω of pixels that are not in the shadows. In the rest of this section, we show how the augmented Lagrange multiplier (ALM) method, introduced earlier for matrix completion or matrix recovery in Chapter 5, can be adapted to efficiently solve the problem (14.3.1) that requires simultaneously completing and correcting a low-rank matrix.

Recall that the basic idea of the ALM method, introduced in Section 8.4 of Chapter 8, is to minimize the augmented Lagrangian function instead of the original constrained optimization problem. For our problem (14.3.1), the augmented Lagrangian is given by

$$\mathcal{L}_\mu(\boldsymbol{A},\boldsymbol{E},\boldsymbol{Y}) = \|\boldsymbol{A}\|_* + \lambda\|\boldsymbol{E}\|_1 + \langle \boldsymbol{Y}, \mathcal{P}_\Omega[\boldsymbol{D}-\boldsymbol{A}-\boldsymbol{E}]\rangle + \frac{\mu}{2}\|\mathcal{P}_\Omega[\boldsymbol{D}-\boldsymbol{A}-\boldsymbol{E}]\|_F^2, \tag{14.3.2}$$

where $\boldsymbol{Y} \in \mathbb{R}^{m\times n}$ is a Lagrange multiplier matrix, μ is a positive constant, $\langle\cdot,\cdot\rangle$ denotes the matrix inner product,[7] and $\|\cdot\|_F$ denotes the Frobenius norm. For appropriate choice of the Lagrange multiplier matrix $\boldsymbol{Y}$ and sufficiently large constant μ, it can be shown that the augmented Lagrangian function has the same minimizer as the original constrained optimization problem. The ALM algorithm iteratively estimates both the Lagrange multiplier and the optimal solution. The basic ALM iteration is given by

$$\begin{cases} (\boldsymbol{A}_{k+1},\boldsymbol{E}_{k+1}) = \operatorname{argmin}_{\boldsymbol{A},\boldsymbol{E}} \mathcal{L}_{\mu_k}(\boldsymbol{A},\boldsymbol{E},\boldsymbol{Y}_k), \\ \boldsymbol{Y}_{k+1} \quad = \boldsymbol{Y}_k + \mu_k \mathcal{P}_\Omega[\boldsymbol{D}-\boldsymbol{A}_{k+1}-\boldsymbol{E}_{k+1}], \\ \mu_{k+1} \quad = \rho\cdot\mu_k, \end{cases} \tag{14.3.3}$$

where $\{\mu_k\}$ is a monotonically increasing positive sequence ($\rho > 1$).

We now focus our attention on solving the nontrivial first step of the above iteration. Since it is difficult to minimize $\mathcal{L}_{\mu_k}(\cdot)$ with respect to both $\boldsymbol{A}$ and $\boldsymbol{E}$ simultaneously, we adopt an alternating minimization strategy as follows:

$$\begin{cases} \boldsymbol{E}_{j+1} = \operatorname{argmin}_{\boldsymbol{E}} \lambda\|\boldsymbol{E}\|_1 - \langle \boldsymbol{Y}_k, \mathcal{P}_\Omega[\boldsymbol{E}]\rangle + (\mu_k/2)\|\mathcal{P}_\Omega[\boldsymbol{D}-\boldsymbol{A}_j-\boldsymbol{E}]\|_F^2, \\ \boldsymbol{A}_{j+1} = \operatorname{argmin}_{\boldsymbol{A}} \|\boldsymbol{A}\|_* - \langle \boldsymbol{Y}_k, \mathcal{P}_\Omega[\boldsymbol{A}]\rangle + (\mu_k/2)\|\mathcal{P}_\Omega[\boldsymbol{D}-\boldsymbol{A}-\boldsymbol{E}_{j+1}]\|_F^2. \end{cases} \tag{14.3.4}$$

Without loss of generality, we assume that the $\boldsymbol{Y}_k$ and the $\boldsymbol{E}_k$ (and hence $\boldsymbol{Y}$ and $\boldsymbol{E}$, respectively) have their support in Ω^c. Then, the above minimization problems in (14.3.4) can be solved as described below.

Recall from the proximal gradient method in Chapter 8 that the soft-thresholding (or *shrinkage*) operator for scalars is as follows:

$$\operatorname{soft}(x,\alpha) = \operatorname{sign}(x)\cdot\max\{|x|-\alpha, 0\}, \tag{14.3.5}$$

where $\alpha > 0$.[8] When applied to vectors or matrices, the shrinkage operator acts element-wise. Then, the first step in (14.3.4) has a closed-form solution given by

$$\boldsymbol{E}_{j+1} = \operatorname{soft}\left(\mathcal{P}_\Omega[\boldsymbol{D}] + \frac{1}{\mu_k}\boldsymbol{Y}_k - \mathcal{P}_\Omega[\boldsymbol{A}_j], \frac{\lambda}{\mu_k}\right). \tag{14.3.6}$$

Since it is not possible to express the solution to the second step in (14.3.4) in closed form, we adopt an iterative strategy based on the accelerated proximal gradient (APG) algorithm discussed in Section 8.3 of Chapter 8 to solve it. The iterative procedure is given as:

$$\begin{cases} (\boldsymbol{U}_i,\boldsymbol{\Sigma}_i,\boldsymbol{V}_i) = \operatorname{SVD}\left(1/\mu_k\boldsymbol{Y}_k + \mathcal{P}_\Omega[\boldsymbol{D}] - \boldsymbol{E}_{j+1} + \mathcal{P}_{\Omega^c}[\boldsymbol{Z}_i]\right), \\ \boldsymbol{A}_{i+1} = \boldsymbol{U}_i \operatorname{soft}\left(\boldsymbol{\Sigma}_i, 1/\mu_k\right) \boldsymbol{V}_i^*, \\ \boldsymbol{Z}_{i+1} = \boldsymbol{A}_{i+1} + t_i - 1/t_{i+1}(\boldsymbol{A}_{i+1}-\boldsymbol{A}_i), \end{cases} \tag{14.3.7}$$

7 $\langle \boldsymbol{X},\boldsymbol{Y}\rangle \doteq \operatorname{trace}\left(\boldsymbol{X}^*\boldsymbol{Y}\right)$.

8 If $\alpha = 0$, then the shrinkage operator reduces to the identity operator.

Algorithm 14.1 Matrix Completion and Recovery via ALM

Input: $\boldsymbol{D} \in \mathbb{R}^{m \times n}$, $\Omega \subset \{1,\ldots,m\} \times \{1,\ldots,n\}$, $\lambda > 0$.
Initialize $\boldsymbol{A}_1 \leftarrow 0$, $\boldsymbol{E}_1 \leftarrow 0$, $\boldsymbol{Y}_1 \leftarrow 0$.
while not converged ($k = 1, 2, \ldots$) **do**
  $\boldsymbol{A}_{k,1} = \boldsymbol{A}_k$, $\boldsymbol{E}_{k,1} = \boldsymbol{E}_k$;
  while not converged ($j = 1, 2, \ldots$) **do**
    $\boldsymbol{E}_{k,j+1} = \text{soft}\left(\mathcal{P}_\Omega[\boldsymbol{D}] + 1/\mu_k \boldsymbol{Y}_k - \mathcal{P}_\Omega[\boldsymbol{A}_{k,j}], \lambda/\mu_k\right)$;
    $t_1 = 1$; $\boldsymbol{Z}_1 = \boldsymbol{A}_{k,j}$; $\boldsymbol{A}_{k,j,1} = \boldsymbol{A}_{k,j}$;
    while not converged ($i = 1, 2, \ldots$) **do**
      $(\boldsymbol{U}_i, \boldsymbol{\Sigma}_i, \boldsymbol{V}_i) = \text{SVD}\left(1/\mu_k \boldsymbol{Y}_k + \mathcal{P}_\Omega[\boldsymbol{D}] - \boldsymbol{E}_{k,j+1} + \mathcal{P}_{\Omega^c}[\boldsymbol{Z}_i]\right)$;
      $\boldsymbol{A}_{k,j,i+1} = \boldsymbol{U}_i \, \text{soft}\left(\boldsymbol{\Sigma}_i, 1/\mu_k\right) \boldsymbol{V}_i^*$, $t_{i+1} = 0.5\left(1 + \sqrt{1 + 4t_i^2}\right)$;
      $\boldsymbol{Z}_{i+1} = \boldsymbol{A}_{k,j,i+1} + t_i - 1/t_{i+1}(\boldsymbol{A}_{k,j,i+1} - \boldsymbol{A}_{k,j,i})$, $\boldsymbol{A}_{k,j+1} = \boldsymbol{A}_{k,j,i+1}$;
    end while
    $\boldsymbol{A}_{k+1} = \boldsymbol{A}_{k,j+1}$; $\boldsymbol{E}_{k+1} = \boldsymbol{E}_{k,j+1}$;
  end while
  $\boldsymbol{Y}_{k+1} = \boldsymbol{Y}_k + \mu_k \mathcal{P}_\Omega[\boldsymbol{D} - \boldsymbol{A}_{k+1} - \boldsymbol{E}_{k+1}]$, $\mu_{k+1} = \rho \cdot \mu_k$;
end while
Output: $(\boldsymbol{A}_\star, \boldsymbol{E}_\star) = (\boldsymbol{A}_k, \boldsymbol{E}_k)$.

where SVD$(\cdot)$ denotes the singular value decomposition operator, and $\{t_i\}$ is a positive sequence satisfying $t_1 = 1$ and $t_{i+1} = 0.5\left(1 + \sqrt{1 + 4t_i^2}\right)$. The entire algorithm to solve (14.3.1) has been summarized as Algorithm 14.1.

14.4 Experimental Evaluation

In this section, we verify the effectiveness of the proposed method using both synthetic and real-world images. We compare results of the above robust matrix completion (RMC) method with a simple least-squares (LS) approach, which assumes the ideal diffusive model given by (14.2.5). However, we do not use those pixels that were classified as shadows (the set Ω). Thus, the LS method can be summarized by the following optimization problem:

$$\min_{\boldsymbol{N}} \|\mathcal{P}_\Omega[\boldsymbol{D} - \boldsymbol{N} \cdot \boldsymbol{L}]\|_F. \tag{14.4.1}$$

We first test the algorithms using synthetic images whose ground-truth normal maps are known. In these experiments, we quantitatively verify the correctness of the algorithms by computing the angular errors between the estimated normal map and the ground truth. We then test the algorithms on more challenging real images. Throughout this section, we denote by m the number of pixels in the region of interest in each image, and by n the number of input images (typically, $m \gg n$).

14.4.1 Quantitative Evaluation with Synthetic Images

In this section, we use synthetic images of three different objects (see Figure 14.5(a)–(c)) under different scenarios to evaluate the performance of the algorithms. Since these images are free of any noise, we use a pixel threshold value of zero to detect shadows in the images. Unless otherwise stated, we set $\lambda = 1/\sqrt{m}$ in (14.3.1).

(a) Specular Objects

In this experiment, we generate images of an object under 40 different lighting conditions, where the lighting directions are chosen at random from a hemisphere with the object placed at the center. The images are generated with some specular reflection. For all experiments, we use the Cook–Torrance reflectance model [CT81] to generate images with specularities. Thus, there are two sources of corruption in the images – attached shadows and specularities.

A quantitative evaluation of our method and the least-squares approach is presented in Table 14.1. The estimated normal maps are shown in Figure 14.6(b) and (c).

We use the RGB channel to encode the spatial components (XYZ) of the normal map for display purposes. The error is measured in terms of the angular difference between the ground-truth normal and the estimated normal at each pixel location. The pixel-wise error maps are shown in Figure 14.6(d) and (e). From the mean and the

Table 14.1. Specular Scene Results. Statistics of angle error (in degrees) in the normals for different objects. In each case, 40 images were used. In the rightmost column, we indicate the average percentage of pixels corrupted by attached shadows and specularities in each image.

	Mean error		Max. error		Corrupted pixels (%)	
Object	LS	RMC	LS	RMC	Shadow	Specularity
Sphere	0.99	5.1×10^{-3}	8.1	0.20	18.4	16.1
Caesar	0.96	1.4×10^{-2}	8.0	0.22	20.7	13.6
Elephant	0.96	8.7×10^{-3}	8.0	0.29	18.1	16.5

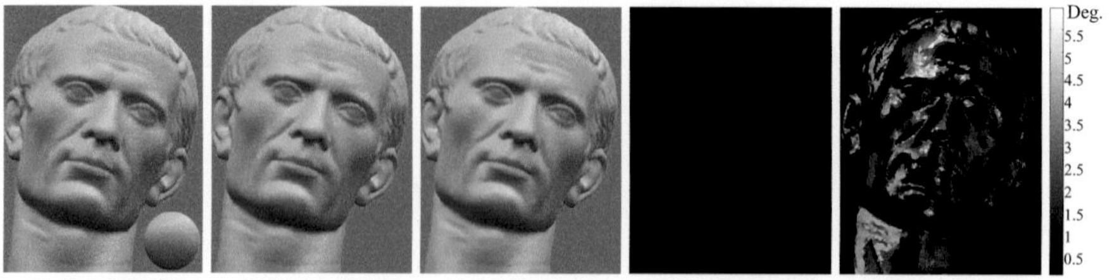

(a) Ground truth (b) Our method (c) Least squares (d) Error map (our method) (e) Error map (LS)

Figure 14.6 Specular Scene Results. Forty different images of Caesar were generated using the Cook–Torrance model for specularities. (a) Ground-truth normal map with reference sphere. (b) and (c) The surface normals recovered by the robust matrix completion (RMC) method and LS, respectively. (d) and (e) The pixel-wise angular error with respect to the ground truth.

maximum angular error (in degrees) in Table 14.1, we see that the RMC method is much more accurate than the LS approach. This is because specularities introduce large-magnitude errors to a small fraction of pixels in each image whose locations are unknown. The LS algorithm is not robust to such corruptions while RMC can correct these errors and recover the underlying rank-3 structure of the matrix. The column on the extreme right of Table 14.1 indicates the average percentage of pixels in each image (averaged over all images) that were corrupted by shadows and specularities, respectively. We note that even when more than 30% of the pixels are corrupted by shadows and specularities, RMC can efficiently retrieve the surface normals.

(b) Textured Objects

We also test the RMC method using a textured scene. Like the traditional photometric stereo approach, the RMC method does not have a dependence on the albedo distribution and works well on such scenes.

We use 40 images of Caesar for this experiment with each image generated under a different lighting condition (see Figure 14.5(d) for example input image). The estimated normal maps as well as the pixel-wise error maps are shown in Figure 14.7. We provide a quantitative comparison in Table 14.2 with respect to the ground-truth normal map. From the mean and maximum angular errors, it is evident that the RMC performs much better than the LS approach in this scenario.

Table 14.2. Textured Scene with Specularity. Statistics of angle errors. We use 40 images under different illuminations.

	Mean error (in degrees)		Max error (in degrees)	
Object	LS	RMC	LS	RMC
Caesar	2.4	0.016	32.2	0.24

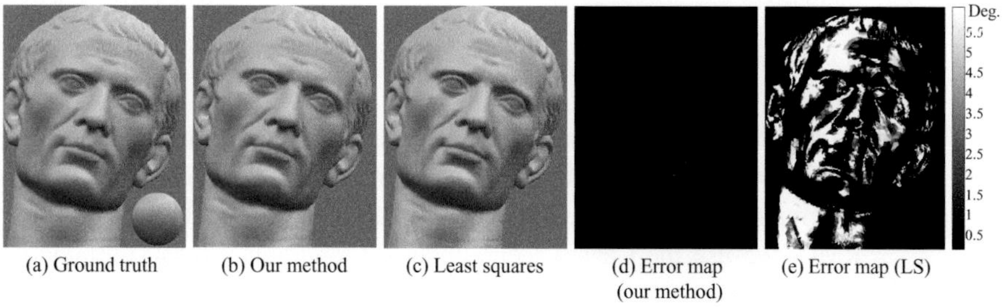

Figure 14.7 Textured Scene with Specularity. Forty different images of Caesar were generated with texture and using the Cook–Torrance model for specularities. (a) Ground-truth normal map with reference sphere. (b) and (c) The surface normals recovered by RMC and LS, respectively. (d) and (e) The pixel-wise angular error with respect to the ground truth.

Table 14.3. Effect of Number of Images. We use synthetic images of Caesar under different lighting conditions. The number of illuminations is varied from 10 to 40. The angle error is measured with respect to the ground-truth normal map. The illuminations are chosen at random, and the error has been averaged over 20 different sets of illumination.

Number of images		10	20	30	40
Mean error	LS	0.52	0.53	0.59	0.57
(in degrees)	RMC	0.23	0.026	0.019	0.013
Max. error	LS	34.5	9.0	7.6	7.0
(in degrees)	RMC	56.6	5.8	0.48	0.37

(c) Effect of the Number of Images

In the above experiments, we have used images of the object under 40 different illuminations. In this experiment, we study the effect of the number of illuminations used. In particular, we would like to find out empirically the minimum number of images required for the RMC method to be effective. For this experiment, we generate images of Caesar using the Cook–Torrance reflectance model, where the lighting directions are generated at random. The mean percentage of specular pixels in the input images is maintained approximately constant at 10%. The angular difference between the estimated normal map and the ground truth is used as a measure of accuracy of the estimate.

The experimental results are given in Table 14.3. We observe that with fewer than 10 input illuminations, the estimates of both algorithms are very inaccurate but RMC is worse than LS. However, when the number of illuminations is larger than 10, we observe that the mean error in the LS estimate becomes higher than that in RMC. Upon increasing the number of images further, the proposed method consistently outperforms the LS approach. If the number of input images is fewer than 20, then the maximum error in the LS estimate is smaller than that of RMC. However, RMC performs much better when more than 30 different illuminations are available. Thus, the proposed technique performs significantly better as the number of input images increases.

(d) Varying Amount of Specularities

From the above experiments, it is clear that the proposed technique is quite robust to specularities in the input images when compared to the LS method. In this experiment, we empirically determine the maximum amount of specularity that can be handled by RMC. We use the Caesar scene under 40 randomly chosen illumination conditions for this experiment. On average, about 20% of the pixels in each image are corrupted by attached shadows. We vary the size of the specular lobe in the input images (as illustrated in Figure 14.8(a)), thereby varying the number of corrupted pixels. We compare the accuracy of RMC against the LS technique using the angular error of the estimates with respect to the ground truth.

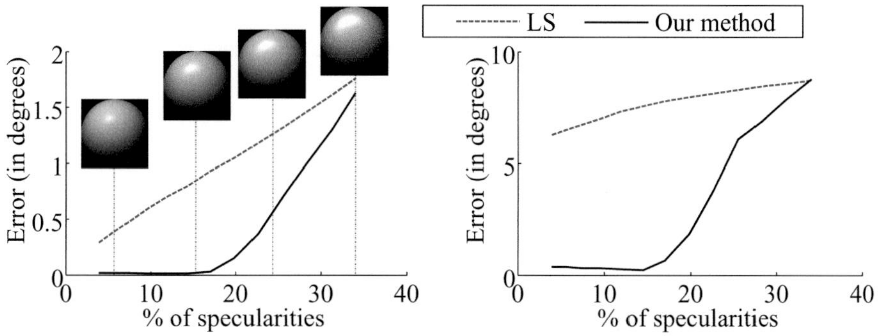

(a) Mean error (b) Maximum error

Figure 14.8 Effect of Increasing Size of Specular Lobes. We use synthetic images of Caesar under 40 randomly chosen lighting conditions. (a) Mean angular error. (b) Maximum angular error with respect to the ground truth. The illuminations are chosen at random, and the error has been averaged over 10 different sets of illumination. Panel (a) contains illustrations of increasing size of specular lobe.

The experimental results are illustrated in Figure 14.8. We observe that RMC is very robust when up to 16% of all pixels in the input images are corrupted by specularities. The LS method, on the other hand, is extremely sensitive to even small amounts of specularities in the input images. The angular error in the estimates of both methods rises as the size of the specular lobe increases.

(e) Enhancing Performance by Tuning λ

We recall that λ is a weighting parameter in our formulation given by (14.3.1). In all the above experiments, we have fixed the value of the parameter $\lambda = 1/\sqrt{m}$, as suggested by the theory in Chapter 5. While this choice promises a certain degree of error correction, it may be possible to correct larger amounts of corruption by choosing λ appropriately, as demonstrated in [GWL$^+$10] for instance. Unfortunately, the best choice of λ depends on the input images, and cannot be determined analytically.

We demonstrate the effect of the weighting parameter λ on a set of 40 images of Caesar used in the previous experiments. In this set of images, approximately 20% of the pixels are corrupted by attached shadows and about 28% by specularities. We choose $\lambda = C/\sqrt{m}$, and vary the value of C. We evaluate the results using angular error with respect to the ground-truth normal map. We observe from Table 14.4 that the choice of C influences the accuracy of the estimated normal map. For real-world applications, where the data is typically noisy, the choice of λ could play an important role in the efficacy of RMC.

(f) Computation

The core computation of RMC is solving a convex program (14.3.1). For the specular Caesar data (Figure 14.5(b)) with 40 images of 450×350 resolution, a single-core MATLAB implementation of RMC takes about 7 minutes on a Macbook Pro with a 2.8 GHz Core 2 Duo processor and 4 GB memory, as against 42 seconds taken by the

Table 14.4. Handling More Specularities by Tuning λ. We use 40 images of Caesar under different lighting conditions with about 28% specularities and 20% shadows, and set $\lambda = C/\sqrt{m}$.

C	1.0	0.8	0.6	0.4
Mean error (in degrees)	1.42	0.78	0.19	0.029
Max. error (in degrees)	8.78	8.15	1.86	0.91

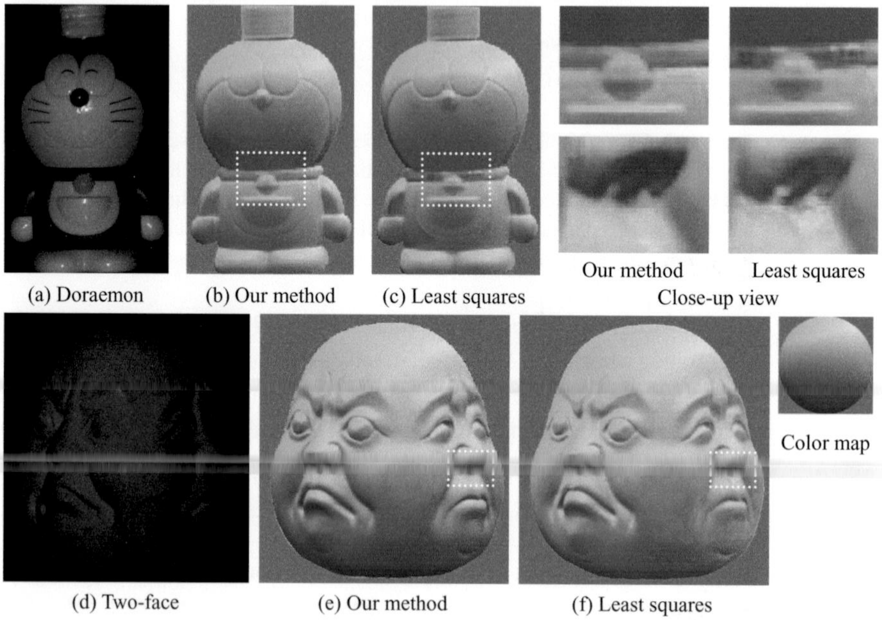

Figure 14.9 Qualitative Comparison on Real Images. We use images of Doraemon and Two-face taken under 40 different lighting conditions to qualitatively evaluate the performance of the RMC method against the LS approach. (a),(d) Sample input images. (b),(e) Normal map estimated by RMC. (c),(f) Normal map estimated by least squares. Close-up views of the dotted rectangular areas are shown on the top right.

LS approach. While RMC is slower than the LS approach, it is much more accurate in a wide variety of scenarios and is more efficient than other methods (e.g., [MHI10]).

14.4.2 Qualitative Evaluation with Real Images

We now test the algorithms on real images. We use a set of 40 images of a toy Doraemon and Two-face taken under different lighting conditions (see Figure 14.9(a) and (d)). A glossy sphere was placed in the scene for light source calibration when capturing the data. We used a Canon 5D camera with the RAW image mode.[9]

[9] We did not apply Gamma correction.

These images present new challenges to RMC. In addition to shadows and specularities, there is potentially additional noise inherent to the acquisition process as well as possible deviations from the idealistic Lambertian model illuminated by distant lights. In this experiment, we use a threshold of 0.01 to detect shadows in images.[10] We also found experimentally that setting $\lambda = 0.3/\sqrt{m}$ works well for these datasets.

Since the ground truth normal map is not available for these scenes, we compare the RMC method and the LS approach by visual inspection of the output normal maps shown in Figure 14.9(b),(c),(e) and (f). We observe that the normal map estimated by RMC appears smoother and hence more realistic. This can be observed particularly around the necklace area in Doraemon and nose area in Two-face (see Figure 14.9) where the LS estimate exhibits some discontinuity in the normal map.

14.5 Notes

Low Dimensionality from Illumination

It is well understood that when a Lambertian surface is illuminated by at least three known lighting directions, the surface orientation at each visible point can be uniquely determined from its intensities. From different perspectives, it has long been shown that if there are no shadows, the appearance of a convex Lambertian scene illuminated from different lighting directions spans a three-dimensional subspace [Sha92] or an illumination cone [BK96]. Basri and Jacobs [BJ03] and Georghiades et al. [GBK01] have further shown that the images of a convex-shaped object with cast shadows can also be well approximated by a low-dimensional linear subspace. The more recent study [ZMKW13] has shown that even for a nonconvex Lambertian object, the images can be well modeled as a low-rank matrix plus some sparse errors. The aforementioned works indicate that there exists a degenerate structure in the appearance of Lambertian surfaces under variation in illumination. This is the key property that all photometric stereo methods harness to determine the surface normals.

Classical Methods for Photometric Stereo

Previously, photometric stereo algorithms for Lambertian surfaces generally find surface normals as the *least-squares* solution to a set of linear equations that relate the observations and known lighting directions, or equivalently, try to identify the low-dimensional subspace using conventional principal component analysis (PCA) [Jol86]. Such a solution is known to be optimal if the measurements are corrupted by only i.i.d. Gaussian noise of small magnitude. Unfortunately, in reality, photometric measurements rarely obey such a simplistic noisy linear model: the intensity values at some pixels can be severely affected by specular reflections (deviation from the basic Lambertian assumption), sensor saturations, or shadowing effects. As a result, the least-squares solution normally ends up with incorrect estimates of surface orientations in practice. To overcome this problem, researchers have explored

[10] All pixels are normalized to have intensity between 0 and 1.

various heuristic approaches to eliminate such deviations by treating the corrupted measurements as outliers, e.g., using the so-called RANSAC scheme [FB81, VHC08], or a median-based approach [MHI10]. To identify the different types of corruptions in images more carefully, Mukaigawa et al. [MMMS01, MIS07] have proposed a method for classifying diffuse, specular, attached, and cast shadow pixels based on RANSAC and outlier elimination.

Low-Rank Matrix Approach

The method presented in this chapter was first introduced through the work [WGS$^+$10]. In contrast to previous robust approaches, this method is computationally more efficient and provides theoretical guarantees for robustness to large errors. More importantly, the method is able to use all the available information simultaneously for obtaining the optimal result, instead of preprocessing measurements which might discard useful information, e.g., by either selecting the best set of illumination directions [VHC08] or using the median estimator [MHI10]. The method in this chapter can also be used to improve virtually any existing photometric stereo method, including uncalibrated photometric stereo [Hay94a], where, traditionally, corruption in the data (e.g., by specularities) is either neglected or ineffectively dealt with by conventional heuristic robust estimation methods.

15 Structured Texture Recovery

> "*What humans do with the language of mathematics is to describe patterns... To grow mathematically children must be exposed to a rich variety of patterns appropriate to their own lives through which they can see variety, regularity, and interconnections.*"
>
> – Lynn Arthur Steen, *The Future of Mathematics Education*

15.1 Introduction

In man-made environments, most objects of interest are rich in regular, repetitive, symmetric structures. Figure 15.1 shows images of some representative structured objects. An image of such an object clearly inherits such regular structures and encodes rich information about the 3D shape, pose, or identity of the object. If we view the image of such an object as a matrix, columns of the matrix will obviously be correlated to one another, hence the rank of the matrix will be very low, or approximately so. For example, for reflectively symmetric objects like a face or a car, the rank of their images will be at most half of the size of the matrices. Besides being symmetric, images of such objects typically have other additional structures (e.g., being piecewise smooth, etc.) which will render the rank of the image even much lower.[1] We generally refer to images (or image regions) associated with such structure objects as "structured textures" to separate them from other random textures.

In this chapter, we will study how the low-dimensional structures of such structured textures may help us to robustly and accurately recover the appearance, pose, and shape of the associated objects in 2D or 3D. This makes structured textures extremely important for many computer vision tasks such as recognition, localization, and reconstruction of objects in man-made environments. From a compressive sensing perspective, we will see in this chapter how to recover a low-rank matrix (that models structured textures) despite significant corruption (due to occlusion) or transformation[2] (due to pose, shape, or camera lens distortion, etc.). To be more precise, we first introduce some notation.

[1] The reader should test the validity of this assumption by computing the actual rank of real images similar to those in Figure 15.1. We leave this as an exercise.

[2] In the 2D domain of the matrix.

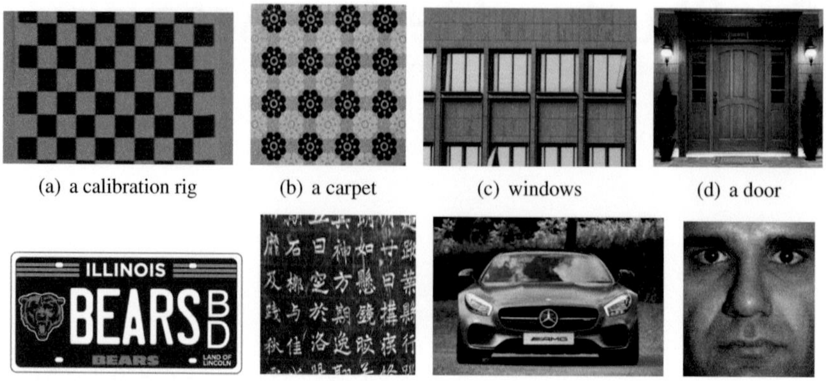

(a) a calibration rig (b) a carpet (c) windows (d) a door

(e) a license plate (f) characters (g) a car (h) a face

Figure 15.1 Representative examples of structured objects. These images viewed as matrices are all (approximately) low-rank matrices. The face image is from the Extended Yale Face Database B [GBK01].

15.2 Low-Rank Textures

Strictly speaking, an image (viewed as a matrix[3]) is a discrete sampling of a continuous texture (function) defined on a 2D domain. Consider a 2D texture as a function $\boldsymbol{I}_o(x, y)$, defined in $\mathbb{R}^2$. We say that $\boldsymbol{I}_o$ is a *low-rank texture* if the family of one-dimensional functions $\{\boldsymbol{I}_o(x, y) \mid y \in \mathbb{R}\}$ spans a finite low-dimensional linear subspace, i.e.,

$$r \doteq \dim(\text{span}\{\boldsymbol{I}_o(x, y) \mid y \in \mathbb{R}\}) \leq k \tag{15.2.1}$$

for some small positive integer k. If r is finite, then we refer to $\boldsymbol{I}_o$ as a rank-r texture. It is easy to see that a rank-1 function $\boldsymbol{I}_o(x, y)$ must be of the form $u(x) \cdot v(y)$ for some functions $u(x)$ and $v(y)$; and in general, a rank-r function $\boldsymbol{I}_o(x, y)$ can be explicitly factorized as the combination of r rank-1 functions:

$$\boldsymbol{I}_o(x, y) \doteq \sum_{i=1}^{r} u_i(x) \cdot v_i(y). \tag{15.2.2}$$

Figure 15.2 shows some ideal low-rank textures: edges and corners were traditionally used in computer vision to characterize local features of an object and they can be viewed as the simplest low-rank textures. An ideal vertical edge (or slope) as shown in Figure 15.2(a) can be considered a rank-1 texture with $u(x) = -\text{sign}(x)$ and $v(y) = 1$. An ideal corner as shown in Figure 15.2(b) is also a rank-1 texture with $u(x) = \text{sign}(x)$ and $v(y) = \text{sign}(y)$.

Thus, in a sense, the notion of low-rank textures unifies many of the conventional local features but goes beyond that: by its definition, it is easy to see that *images*

3 Hence, in this chapter, we will use the bold-face symbol $\boldsymbol{I}$ to denote an image because we will mostly identify the image as a matrix.

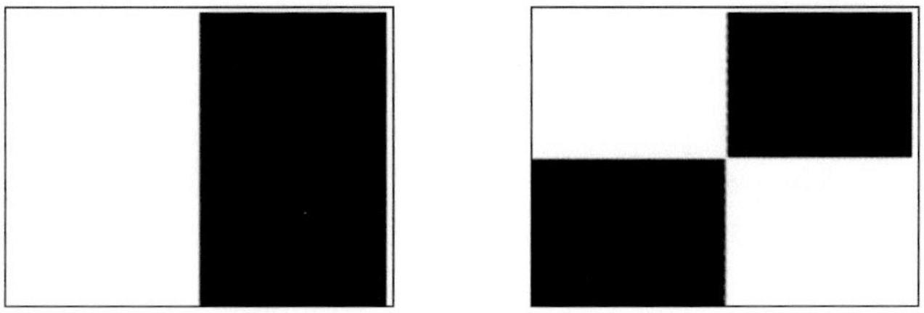

(a) an edge (b) a corner

Figure 15.2 Examples of some ideal low-rank textures: an edge and a corner.

of regular, repetitive, symmetric patterns typically lead to low-rank textures. Low-rank textures of rank higher than 1 would be able to represent a much richer class of structured objects than local edges or corners and they can capture the global characteristics of a structured object.

Given a low-rank texture, obviously its rank is *invariant* under any scaling of the function, as well as scaling or translation in the x and y coordinates. That is, if

$$\boldsymbol{I}(x,y) \doteq \alpha \cdot \boldsymbol{I}_o(ax+t_1, by+t_2)$$

for some constants $\alpha, a, b \in \mathbb{R}_+$ and $t_1, t_2 \in \mathbb{R}$, then $\boldsymbol{I}(x,y)$ and $\boldsymbol{I}_o(x,y)$ have the same rank according to the definition in (15.2.1). For most practical purposes, it suffices to recover any scaled or translated version of the low-rank texture $\boldsymbol{I}_o(x,y)$, as the remaining ambiguity left in the scaling can often be easily resolved in practice by imposing additional constraints on the texture. Hence, in this chapter, unless otherwise stated, we view two low-rank textures to be *equivalent* if they are scaled and translated versions of each other:

$$\boldsymbol{I}_o(x,y) \sim \boldsymbol{I}_o(ax+t_1, by+t_2),$$

for some $a, b, c \in \mathbb{R}_+, t_1$ and $t_2 \in \mathbb{R}$. In homogeneous representation, this equivalence group of transformations consists of all elements of the form:

$$g \in \left\{ \begin{bmatrix} a & 0 & t_1 \\ 0 & b & t_2 \\ 0 & 0 & 1 \end{bmatrix} \in \mathbb{R}^{3\times 3} \,\middle|\, a, b \in \mathbb{R}_+, t_1, t_2 \in \mathbb{R} \right\}. \tag{15.2.3}$$

It is, however, easy to see that the low-rank form (15.2.2) will *not* be preserved under a general linear transform of the domain:

$$\boldsymbol{I}(x,y) \doteq \boldsymbol{I}_o(ax+bx+t_1, cx+dy+t_2) \tag{15.2.4}$$

will have a different (usually much higher) rank than that of $\boldsymbol{I}_o(x,y)$. For instance, if we rotate the edge or the corner in Figure 15.2 by 45°, the resulting image will become full rank (as a matrix). Similarly, the rank will mostly increase under more general nonlinear distortions or transformations of the domain. As we will see in this chapter, this fact is actually rather beneficial: it suggests that *the correct transformation that can undo the distortion would be the one that makes the rank of the texture the lowest.*

In practice, an image of a 2D texture is not a continuous function defined on $\mathbb{R}^2$. We only have its values sampled on a finite discrete grid in $\mathbb{Z}^2$, of size $m \times n$ say. In this case, the 2D texture $\boldsymbol{I}_o(x, y)$ is represented by an $m \times n$ matrix of real numbers. For a low-rank texture, we always assume that the size of the sampling grid is significantly larger than the intrinsic rank of the texture,[4] i.e.,

$$r \ll \min\{m, n\}.$$

It is easy to show that as long as the sampling rate is not one of the aliasing frequencies of the functions $u_i(x)$ or $v_i(x)$ of the continuous $\boldsymbol{I}_o(x, y)$ defined in (15.2.2), the resulting matrix has the same rank as the continuous function.[5] Thus, the 2D texture $\boldsymbol{I}_o(x, y)$ when discretized as a matrix, denoted by $\boldsymbol{I}_o(i, j)$ for convenience, has very low rank relative to its dimensions.

For the remainder of this chapter, for convenience, we will treat the continuous 2D function and its sampled matrix form as the same, with the understanding that whenever we talk about distortion or transformation of a texture or an image, we mean a transformation in the 2D domain of its underlying continuous function. When only an image (a matrix of sampled values) is given, values of the function off the sampling grid can be obtained through any reasonable interpolation schemes.[6]

15.3 Structured Texture Inpainting

In this section, we will see how to automatically repair a structured texture when it is severely corrupted or occluded. From Chapter 4, we know that if a texture $\boldsymbol{I}_o$ is a low-rank matrix, we can recover it even if only a small fraction of its entries (pixels), say with support Ω, are observable. Let Ω be the set of pixels given. The problem to recover the full texture image $\boldsymbol{I}_o$ is simply a low-rank matrix completion problem:

$$\min_{\boldsymbol{L}} \ \text{rank}(\boldsymbol{L}) \quad \text{subject to} \quad \boldsymbol{L}(i, j) = \boldsymbol{I}_o(i, j) \ \forall\, (i, j) \in \Omega. \tag{15.3.1}$$

Although being low-rank is a necessary condition for most regular, structured textures, it is certainly *not sufficient*. Figure 15.3 shows three images that have exactly the same rank. Obviously the first two are more smooth and regular than the third one. As discussed in the preceding section, a rank-r texture is a 2D function $\boldsymbol{I}_o(x, y)$, defined on $\mathbb{R}^2$. Then $\boldsymbol{I}_o(x, y)$ can be factorized as

$$\boldsymbol{I}_o(x, y) = \sum_{i=1}^{r} u_i(x) v_i(y).$$

If $\boldsymbol{I}_o$ represents a more realistic regular or nearly regular pattern, it is typically piecewise smooth. Hence, the functions u_i and v_i are not arbitrary and they may have additional structures. As we have discussed in earlier chapters of the book, piecewise

[4] The scale of the window needs to be large enough to meet this assumption.
[5] In other words, the resolution of the image cannot be too low.
[6] From our experience, the bicubic interpolation is good enough for most purposes.

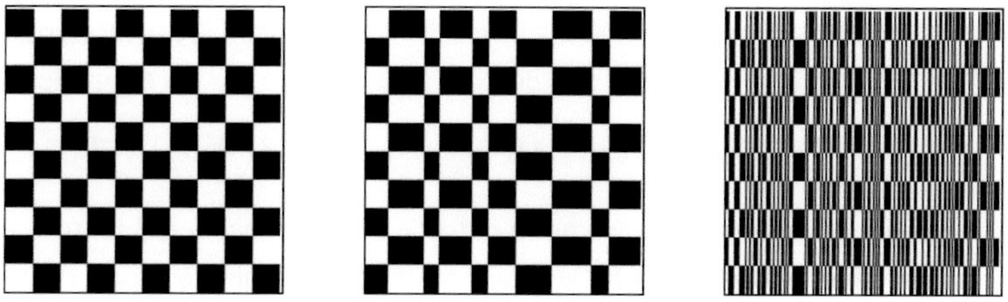

Figure 15.3 Different textural patterns: all three textures have exactly the same rank, but they go from purely regular, to nearly regular, and to almost irregular texture.

smooth functions are typically sparse in a certain transformed domain (say, by a wavelet transform).

So, in the discrete setting, the low-rank matrix $\boldsymbol{I}_o$ can be factorized as

$$\boldsymbol{I}_o = \boldsymbol{U}\boldsymbol{V}^*,$$

where $\boldsymbol{U}$ and $\boldsymbol{V}$ can be represented as

$$\boldsymbol{U} = \boldsymbol{B}_1\boldsymbol{X}_1 \quad \text{and} \quad \boldsymbol{V} = \boldsymbol{B}_2\boldsymbol{X}_2$$

for some pair of bases $(\boldsymbol{B}_1, \boldsymbol{B}_2)$. If the bases are properly chosen, both $\boldsymbol{X}_1$ and $\boldsymbol{X}_2$ will be sufficiently sparse. Or equivalently, if we write

$$\boldsymbol{I}_o = \boldsymbol{B}_1\boldsymbol{X}_1\boldsymbol{X}_2^*\boldsymbol{B}_2^* \doteq \boldsymbol{B}_1\boldsymbol{W}_o\boldsymbol{B}_2^*,$$

then the matrix $\boldsymbol{W}_o \doteq \boldsymbol{X}_1\boldsymbol{X}_2^*$ will be a sparse matrix, which has the same (low) rank as $\boldsymbol{I}_o$.

Hence, if we want the recovered image from a partially observed $\boldsymbol{I}$ (of the ground truth $\boldsymbol{I}_o$) to be both low-rank and sparse (in a certain transformed domain), we could modify the low-rank matrix completion problem (15.3.1) as follows to impose additional spatial structures:

$$\min_{\boldsymbol{L}, \boldsymbol{W}} \operatorname{rank}(\boldsymbol{L}) + \lambda \|\boldsymbol{W}\|_0 \quad \text{s.t.} \quad \mathcal{P}_\Omega[\boldsymbol{L}] = \mathcal{P}_\Omega[\boldsymbol{I}],\ \boldsymbol{L} = \boldsymbol{B}_1\boldsymbol{W}\boldsymbol{B}_2^*, \tag{15.3.2}$$

where $\|\boldsymbol{W}\|_0$ denotes the number of nonzero entries in $\boldsymbol{W}$. That is, we aim to find the ground-truth texture image $\boldsymbol{I}_o$ as the lowest possible rank matrix $\boldsymbol{L}_\star$ and the matrix $\boldsymbol{W}_\star = \boldsymbol{B}_1^*\boldsymbol{L}_\star\boldsymbol{B}_2$ with the fewest possible nonzero entries that agrees with the partial observation $\mathcal{P}_\Omega[\boldsymbol{I}]$. Here, λ is a weighting parameter which trades off the rank and sparsity of the recovered image.

As we have learned from earlier chapters, in the above problem (15.3.2), both the rank function and the ℓ^0norm are difficult to optimize directly. Instead, they can be replaced by their convex surrogates: the matrix nuclear norm $\|\boldsymbol{L}\|_*$ for $\operatorname{rank}(\boldsymbol{L})$ and the ℓ^1norm $\|\boldsymbol{W}\|_1$ for $\|\boldsymbol{W}\|_0$, respectively. Thus, we end up with the following optimization problem:

$$\min_{\boldsymbol{L}, \boldsymbol{W}} \|\boldsymbol{L}\|_* + \lambda \|\boldsymbol{W}\|_1 \quad \text{s.t.} \quad \mathcal{P}_\Omega[\boldsymbol{L}] = \mathcal{P}_\Omega[\boldsymbol{I}],\ \boldsymbol{L} = \boldsymbol{B}_1\boldsymbol{W}\boldsymbol{B}_2^*. \tag{15.3.3}$$

If we further assume that the bases $\boldsymbol{B}_1$ and $\boldsymbol{B}_2$ used are orthonormal, we have $\|\boldsymbol{I}_o\|_* = \|\boldsymbol{B}_1\boldsymbol{W}\boldsymbol{B}_2^*\|_* = \|\boldsymbol{W}\|_*$. The convex program (15.3.3) is equivalent to:

$$\min_{\boldsymbol{W}} \|\boldsymbol{W}\|_* + \lambda\|\boldsymbol{W}\|_1 \quad \text{s.t.} \quad \mathcal{P}_\Omega[\boldsymbol{B}_1\boldsymbol{W}\boldsymbol{B}_2^*] = \mathcal{P}_\Omega[\boldsymbol{I}]. \tag{15.3.4}$$

This formulation allows us to enforce that the recovered texture image be simultaneously low-rank and sparse in a certain transformed domain. As we have discussed in Section 6.3 of Chapter 6, the above convex relaxation is only suboptimal for enforcing simultaneous sparse and low-rank structures on $\boldsymbol{W}_o$. Nevertheless, as we will see, in practice this formulation is sufficient for our purposes of recovering low-rank images.

Notice that entry-wise observation operator $\mathcal{P}_\Omega[\cdot]$ is not incoherent with a sparse matrix. However, here instead of directly sampling $\boldsymbol{W}_o$, the operator samples a transformed version of $\boldsymbol{W}_o$ by the bases $\boldsymbol{B}_1$ and $\boldsymbol{B}_2$. As we will see in experiments, apparently such transforms make the operator $\mathcal{P}_\Omega[\cdot]$ "incoherent" with both the sparse and low-rank structures $\boldsymbol{W}_o$.[7]

Furthermore, notice that the above convex program (15.3.4) is different from the convex program we have encountered before in problems like PCP where the nuclear norm and ℓ^1 norm were for two different matrices. To utilize the same optimization techniques, we only have to introduce an auxiliary variable $\boldsymbol{L}$ to replace $\boldsymbol{W}$ in the low-rank term and render the variables separable:

$$\min_{\boldsymbol{L},\boldsymbol{W}} \|\boldsymbol{L}\|_* + \lambda\|\boldsymbol{W}\|_1 \quad \text{s.t.} \quad \boldsymbol{L} = \boldsymbol{W},\ \mathcal{P}_\Omega[\boldsymbol{B}_1\boldsymbol{W}\boldsymbol{B}_2^*] = \mathcal{P}_\Omega[\boldsymbol{I}]. \tag{15.3.5}$$

The reader may recognize that this program falls into the same class of programs as PCP that we have dealt with in Chapter 5, and they can be solved efficiently by methods such as ALM and ADMM introduced in Chapter 8.[8]

EXAMPLE 15.1. (Texture inpainting) *To demonstrate the importance of enforcing the sparse and low-rank prior together, we here conduct some texture inpainting experiments on real images and compare the solution to the above program with that to the low-rank matrix completion algorithm from Chapter 4.*

Here we choose $\lambda = 0.001$, *and we use the discrete cosine transform (DCT) basis for both* $\boldsymbol{B}_1$ *and* $\boldsymbol{B}_2$.[9] *We test the recovery under three different types of corruptions, i.e., uniform random corruptions, one disk corruption, and random block corruptions, on three representative low-rank textures, i.e., a checkerboard image (typically used in camera calibration) and two real texture images. The checkerboard is of precise rank 2 and the other two are full-rank but approximately low-rank. From the completion results in Figure 15.4, it is clear to see that the recovered results are significantly better by imposing both low-rank and sparse priors than low-rank alone.*

[7] To the best of our knowledge, there is little work that rigorously characterizes conditions on such transforms such that correct recovery of $\boldsymbol{W}_o$ can be guaranteed, despite compelling empirical success.

[8] More detailed implementation of this particular program can be found in [LRZM12].

[9] DCT is the basis used in the JPEG image compression standard. Here the choice of DCT is for simplicity. One may also use a wavelet basis, such as the one used in JPEG2000, to obtain likely better performance.

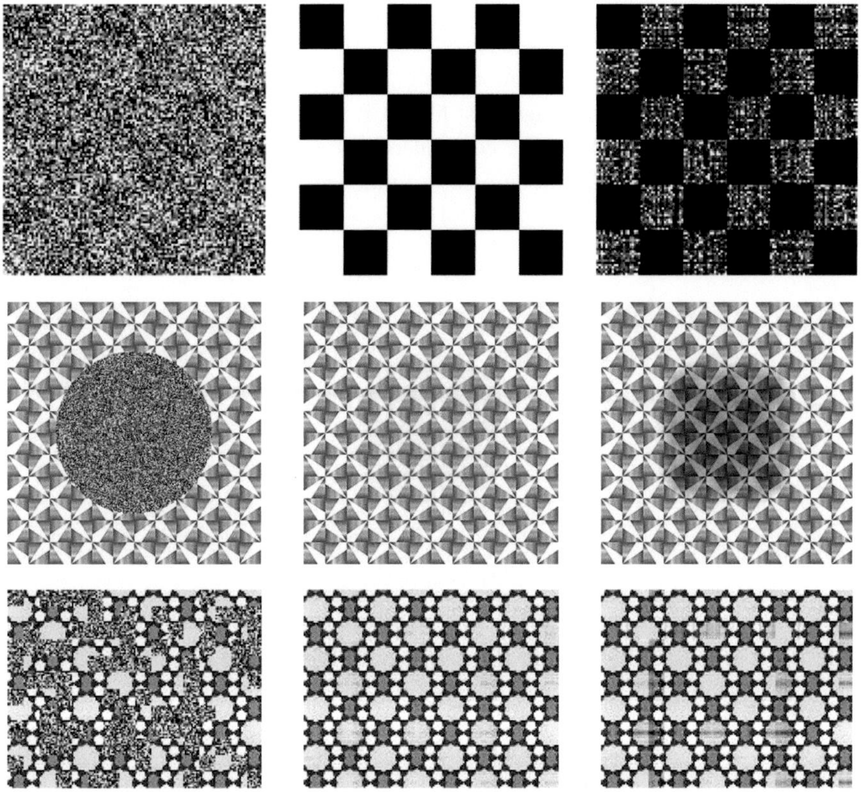

(a) Input image (b) Sparse + low-rank (c) Low-rank only

Figure 15.4 Qualitative comparison of sparse low-rank texture recovery and low-rank completion only. The first row is a checkerboard texture with 91% randomly chosen pixels corrupted (recall Theorem 5.10 of Chapter 5); the second row is a real texture with about 30% pixels occluded by a disk; and the third row is a real texture with about 40% pixels corrupted by random small blocks.

Almost all methods for image inpainting or completion need information about the support Ω of the corrupted regions (e.g., [BSBC00, MES08, FSM09], etc.). This information is usually obtained through being manually marked out by the user or detected by other independent methods. This often severely limits the applicability of all the image completion or inpainting methods.

In many practical scenarios, the information about the support of the corrupted regions might be unknown or only partially known. Hence the pixels in the given region Ω can also contain some corruptions that violate the low-rank and sparse structures. Similar to the robust PCA problem in Chapter 5, we could model such corruptions with unknown support as a sparse error term $\boldsymbol{E}_o$:

$$\boldsymbol{I} = \boldsymbol{I}_o + \boldsymbol{E}_o = \boldsymbol{B}_1 \boldsymbol{W}_o \boldsymbol{B}_2^* + \boldsymbol{E}_o.$$

To recover the image $\boldsymbol{I}_o = \boldsymbol{B}_1 \boldsymbol{W}_o \boldsymbol{B}_2^*$, we now only have to solve the following PCP-like program:

$$\min_{\boldsymbol{W}} \|\boldsymbol{W}\|_* + \lambda\|\boldsymbol{W}\|_1 + \alpha\|\boldsymbol{E}\|_1 \quad \text{s.t.} \quad \mathcal{P}_\Omega[\boldsymbol{B}_1 \boldsymbol{W} \boldsymbol{B}_2^* + \boldsymbol{E}] = \mathcal{P}_\Omega[\boldsymbol{I}]. \tag{15.3.6}$$

Notice that if we know nothing about the corruption areas, we only need to set Ω to be the entire image. Just like PCP, the above convex program will decompose the image into a low-rank component and a sparse one. Of course, the nonzero entries in estimated $\boldsymbol{E}$ can help us to further refine the support Ω. For instance, we could simply set

$$\text{supp}(\boldsymbol{E}) \doteq \{(i, j) \in \Omega, \ |\boldsymbol{E}_{ij}| > \varepsilon\}, \tag{15.3.7}$$

for some threshold $\varepsilon > 0$. Or we could estimate the support of $\boldsymbol{E}$ using a more sophisticated model to encourage additional structures such as spatial continuity [ZWMM09]. Once supp($\boldsymbol{E}$) is known, we can exclude those corrupted entries from Ω (the support of presumably good entries).

We could further iterate between the image completion and support estimation:

$$\begin{aligned} (\boldsymbol{W}_k, \boldsymbol{E}_k) &= \text{argmin}_{\boldsymbol{W},\boldsymbol{E}} \ \|\boldsymbol{W}\|_* + \lambda\|\boldsymbol{W}\|_1 + \alpha\|\boldsymbol{E}\|_1 \\ &\qquad \text{subject to } \mathcal{P}_{\Omega_k}[\boldsymbol{B}_1 \boldsymbol{W} \boldsymbol{B}_2^* + \boldsymbol{E}] = \mathcal{P}_{\Omega_k}[\boldsymbol{I}], \\ \Omega_{k+1} &= \Omega_k \setminus \text{supp}(\boldsymbol{E}_{k+1}), \end{aligned} \tag{15.3.8}$$

where α is a weighting parameter between sparsity and low-rankedness. We could continue the above process till convergence and obtain the repaired image $\boldsymbol{I}_\star = \boldsymbol{B}_1 \boldsymbol{W}_\star \boldsymbol{B}_2^*$. In practice, we notice a good side effect of adding the additional $\boldsymbol{E}$ term; it not only helps estimate the support of the corrupted regions but also helps reduce noise on the repaired texture image $\boldsymbol{I}_\star$.

EXAMPLE 15.2. (Texture recovery) *In this experiment, we conduct some comparison between the above method and some typical image completion methods used in highly engineered commercial systems: Patch Match (PM) used by Adobe Photoshop [BSFG09, BSGF10], and Image Completion with Structure Propagation (SP) developed by Microsoft [SYJS05]. Figure 15.5 shows the results on three different images: a simulated nonuniform low-rank texture, a uniform building facade, and a somewhat less uniform building facade, which correspond to the three rows in Figure 15.5, respectively.*

The other two methods all share the spirit of sample-based texture synthesis: they stitch sampled local patches together to ensure certain global statistical consistency. As these methods rely mostly on local statistics and structures, they tend to work on natural images or random textures too, while our method does not. However, as we see from the results, when applied to completing or repairing regular or nearly regular *low-rank patterns, they often fail to preserve the global regularity accurately. The reason is partially because these methods normally do not or cannot exploit global structural information about the textures.*

Unlike the structured texture recovery method introduced here, these image completion systems typically require the user to mark out rather precisely the to-be-corrected region or regions (as the contours of the regions for Photoshop shown in Figure 15.5), and even to provide additional information about the structures to be recovered (such as suggested lines marked out in the red regions that are required by the SP method).

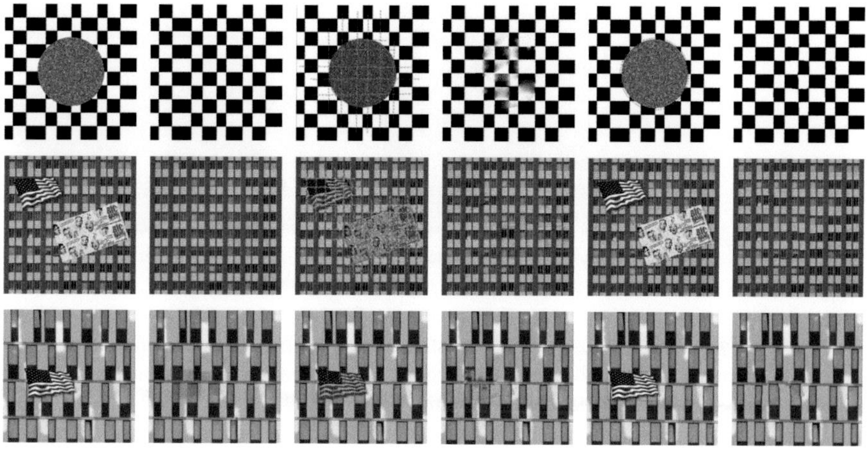

Figure 15.5 Comparison results with Microsoft SP [SYJS05] and Adobe Photoshop [BSFG09]. Columns 1 and 2: inputs and results of the structured texture recovery method. Columns 3 and 4: inputs and results of SP. Columns 5 and 6: inputs and results of Adobe Photoshop.

However, the structured texture recovery method does not need any knowledge about the support of the corrupted regions nor any information about the structure.

15.4 Transform-Invariant Low-Rank Textures

15.4.1 Deformed and Corrupted Low-Rank Textures

Although a structured object that has regular or repetitive 2D or 3D textural patterns in space is often low-rank, its image $\boldsymbol{I}$ under an arbitrary camera viewpoint may exhibit much higher rank compared to its upright frontal view $\boldsymbol{I}_o(x, y)$. An example is illustrated in Figure 15.6. In order to extract the intrinsic low-rank textures from such deformed images, we need to carefully model the effect of deformation and see how to undo it correctly.

Deformed Low-Rank Textures

Suppose a low-rank texture $\boldsymbol{I}_o(x, y)$ lies on a certain surface in the scene. The image $\boldsymbol{I}$ is $\boldsymbol{I}_o$ taken from a certain camera viewpoint. We use τ to denote the transform, where $\tau : \mathbb{R}^2 \to \mathbb{R}^2$ belongs to a certain Lie group $\mathbb{G}$ on $\mathbb{R}^2$ (we here only consider the case where τ is invertible). Hence $\boldsymbol{I} \circ \tau = \boldsymbol{I}_o$ or the image $\boldsymbol{I}$ can be viewed as a transformed version of the original function $\boldsymbol{I}_o(x, y)$:

$$\boldsymbol{I}(x, y) = \boldsymbol{I}_o \circ \tau^{-1}(x, y) = \boldsymbol{I}_o\left(\tau^{-1}(x, y)\right), \quad \tau \in \mathbb{G}.$$

If the texture is on a planar surface in the 3D space, under a typical perspective camera model, one can assume $\mathbb{G}$ to be either the 2D affine group $\mathsf{Aff}(2, \mathbb{R})$, or the homography group $\mathsf{GL}(3, \mathbb{R})$ acting linearly on the image domain. Nevertheless, in principle, the

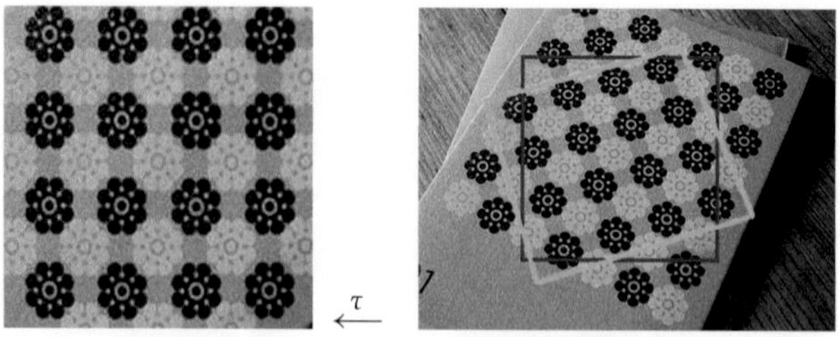

(a) Low-rank texture $\boldsymbol{I}_o$ (b) Its image $\boldsymbol{I}$ under a different viewpoint

Figure 15.6 An example of a transformed low-rank texture. The upright low-rank texture $\boldsymbol{I}_o$ in panel (a) is associated with the region in the green window in panel (b). The matrix $\boldsymbol{I}$ associated with the region in the red window in panel (b) is clearly not low-rank.

formulation also works for more general classes of domain deformations or camera projection models as long as they can be modeled well by a finite-dimensional parametric group [ZMM11, ZLM11]. We will see a few concrete examples soon in Section 15.5.

Corrupted Low-Rank Textures

In addition to domain transformations, the observed image of the texture might be corrupted by pixel noise and occlusion. As before, we can model such nuisance by an error matrix $\boldsymbol{E}_o$ as follows:

$$\boldsymbol{I} = \boldsymbol{I}_o + \boldsymbol{E}_o.$$

As a result, the image $\boldsymbol{I}$ might no longer be a low-rank texture. In the low-rank texture framework, we assume that only a small fraction of the image pixels are corrupted by gross errors. Hence, $\boldsymbol{E}_o$ is generally a sparse matrix.

So the problem we are facing here is this: *given a possibly corrupted and deformed image of a low-rank texture,* $\boldsymbol{I} = (\boldsymbol{I}_o + \boldsymbol{E}_o) \circ \tau^{-1}$, *can we recover both the intrinsic low-rank texture representation* $\boldsymbol{I}_o$ *and the domain transformation* $\tau \in \mathbb{G}$*?*

The answer to this problem is whether we are able to find solutions to the following optimization program:

$$\min_{\boldsymbol{L}, \boldsymbol{E}, \tau} \ \operatorname{rank}(\boldsymbol{L}) + \gamma \|\boldsymbol{E}\|_0 \quad \text{subject to} \quad \boldsymbol{I} \circ \tau = \boldsymbol{L} + \boldsymbol{E}. \tag{15.4.1}$$

That is, we aim to find the upright ground-truth texture $\boldsymbol{I}_o$ as the lowest possible rank $\boldsymbol{L}_\star$ and the error $\boldsymbol{E}_\star$ with the fewest possible nonzero entries that agrees with the observation $\boldsymbol{I}$ up to a domain transformation τ. Here, $\gamma > 0$ is a weighting parameter that trades off the rank of the texture versus the sparsity of the error. For convenience, we refer to the so-rectified solution $\boldsymbol{I}_o$ of the observed tilted pattern $\boldsymbol{I}$ as a *transform-invariant low-rank texture* (TILT), coined by [ZLGM10, ZGLM12].[10]

[10] By a slight abuse of terminology, we also refer to the procedure of solving the optimization problem as TILT.

15.4.2 The TILT Algorithm

As we have studied in previous chapters, the rank function and the ℓ^0norm in the original problem (15.4.1) are extremely difficult to optimize, let alone with an unknown deformation τ. However, under fairly broad conditions, they can be replaced by their convex surrogates: the matrix nuclear norm $\|\boldsymbol{I}_o\|_*$ for rank($\boldsymbol{I}_o$) and the ℓ^1norm $\|\boldsymbol{E}\|_1$ for $\|\boldsymbol{E}\|_0$, respectively. Thus, we end up with the following optimization problem:

$$\min_{\boldsymbol{L},\boldsymbol{E},\tau} \|\boldsymbol{L}\|_* + \lambda\|\boldsymbol{E}\|_1 \quad \text{subject to} \quad \boldsymbol{I} \circ \tau = \boldsymbol{L} + \boldsymbol{E}. \tag{15.4.2}$$

Dealing with Domain Deformation via Linearization

Note that although the objective function in (15.4.2) is convex, the constraint $\boldsymbol{I} \circ \tau = \boldsymbol{L} + \boldsymbol{E}$ is nonlinear in $\tau \in \mathbb{G}$, and hence the overall problem is no longer convex. We have seen a similar problem in Section 5.5. As we have discussed there, we may overcome this difficulty by linearizing the constraint around the current estimate and iterate, which is a typical technique to deal with nonlinearity in mathematical programming [LK81, BM04]. If we approximate the nonlinear constraint up to its first order (with respect to the deformation parameter τ), the constraint for the linearized version of the above program becomes

$$\boldsymbol{I} \circ \tau + \nabla \boldsymbol{I} \cdot d\tau \approx \boldsymbol{L} + \boldsymbol{E}, \tag{15.4.3}$$

where $\nabla \boldsymbol{I}$ is the Jacobian (derivatives of the image with respect to the transformation parameters in τ).[11] The optimization problem in (15.4.2) reduces to

$$\min_{\boldsymbol{L},\boldsymbol{E},d\tau} \|\boldsymbol{L}\|_* + \lambda\|\boldsymbol{E}\|_1 \quad \text{subject to} \quad \boldsymbol{I} \circ \tau + \nabla \boldsymbol{I} \cdot d\tau = \boldsymbol{L} + \boldsymbol{E}. \tag{15.4.4}$$

The linearized problem above is a convex program as the constraint is linear in all unknowns $\boldsymbol{L}, \boldsymbol{E}$, and $d\tau$, hence it is amenable to efficient solution. One may use the algorithms introduced in Chapter 8 to solve the above convex program.

Since the linearization is only a local approximation to the original nonlinear problem, we solve it iteratively in order to converge to a (local) minimum of the original nonconvex problem (15.4.2). The resulting optimization scheme is summarized as Algorithm 15.1.

The iterative linearization scheme outlined above is a common technique in optimization to solve nonlinear problems. It can be shown that this kind of iterative linearization converges quadratically to a local minimum of the original nonlinear problem. A complete proof is out of the scope of this book. We refer the interested reader to [Cro78, JO80] and the references therein.

Solving the Linearized Inner Loop Program

To implement Algorithm 15.1 numerically, the most computationally expensive part is solving the inner loop convex program in step 2. This can be cast as a semidefinite program and solved using conventional algorithms such as interior point methods.

11 Strictly speaking, $\nabla \boldsymbol{I}$ is a 3D tensor: it gives a vector of derivatives at each pixel whose length is the number of parameters in the transformation τ. When we "multiply" $\nabla \boldsymbol{I}$ with another matrix or vector, it contracts in the obvious way which should be clear from the context.

Algorithm 15.1 The TILT Algorithm

Input: Input image $\boldsymbol{I} \in \mathbb{R}^{w \times h}$, initial transformation $\tau \in \mathbb{G}$ (affine or projective), and a weight $\lambda > 0$.
while not converged **do**
Step 1: Normalization and compute Jacobian:

$$\boldsymbol{I} \circ \tau \leftarrow \frac{\boldsymbol{I} \circ \tau}{\|\boldsymbol{I} \circ \tau\|_F}; \quad \nabla \boldsymbol{I} \leftarrow \frac{\partial}{\partial \zeta}\left(\frac{\operatorname{vec}(\boldsymbol{I} \circ \zeta)}{\|\operatorname{vec}(\boldsymbol{I} \circ \zeta)\|_2} \right)\Big|_{\zeta=\tau};$$

Step 2 (inner loop): Solve the linearized problem:

$$\begin{aligned}(\boldsymbol{L}_\star, \boldsymbol{E}_\star, d\tau_\star) \quad \leftarrow \quad & \arg\min_{\boldsymbol{L},\boldsymbol{E},d\tau} \ \|\boldsymbol{L}\|_* + \lambda \|\boldsymbol{E}\|_1 \\ & \text{subject to} \quad \boldsymbol{I} \circ \tau + \nabla \boldsymbol{I} \cdot d\tau = \boldsymbol{L} + \boldsymbol{E};\end{aligned}$$

Step 3: Update the transformation: $\tau \leftarrow \tau + d\tau_\star$;
end while
Output: Converged solution $\boldsymbol{L}_\star$, $\boldsymbol{E}_\star$, $\tau_\star$ to problem (15.4.2).

However, as we discussed in Chapter 8, while interior point methods have excellent convergence properties, they do not scale very well with the problem size. As TILT is a very, very useful tool for computer vision, we here derive in more detail a fast implementation based on the augmented Lagrangian method (ALM) via the *alternating direction method of multipliers* (ADMM), which was also covered in Chapter 8.

First, for the problem given in (15.4.4), its augmented Lagrangian is defined as

$$\begin{aligned}\mathcal{L}_\mu(\boldsymbol{L}, \boldsymbol{E}, d\tau, \boldsymbol{Y}) \doteq \|\boldsymbol{L}\|_* + \lambda\|\boldsymbol{E}\|_1 + \langle \boldsymbol{Y}, \boldsymbol{I} \circ \tau + \nabla \boldsymbol{I} \cdot d\tau - \boldsymbol{L} - \boldsymbol{E} \rangle \\ + \frac{\mu}{2} \|\boldsymbol{I} \circ \tau + \nabla \boldsymbol{I} \cdot d\tau - \boldsymbol{L} - \boldsymbol{E}\|_F^2,\end{aligned} \tag{15.4.5}$$

where $\mu > 0$, $\boldsymbol{Y}$ is a Lagrange multiplier matrix, and $\langle \cdot, \cdot \rangle$ denotes the matrix inner product. To optimize the above augmented Lagrangian, the augmented Lagrangian method requires the following steps to be solved iteratively:

$$\begin{aligned}(\boldsymbol{L}_{k+1}, \boldsymbol{E}_{k+1}, d\tau_{k+1}) &= \arg\min_{\boldsymbol{L},\boldsymbol{E},d\tau} \mathcal{L}_{\mu_k}(\boldsymbol{L}, \boldsymbol{E}, d\tau, \boldsymbol{Y}_k), \\ \boldsymbol{Y}_{k+1} &= \boldsymbol{Y}_k + \mu_k(\boldsymbol{I} \circ \tau + \nabla \boldsymbol{I} \cdot d\tau_{k+1} - \boldsymbol{L}_{k+1} - \boldsymbol{E}_{k+1}).\end{aligned}$$

Throughout the rest of the book, we will always assume that $\mu_k = \rho^k \mu_0$ for some $\mu_0 > 0$ and $\rho > 1$, unless otherwise specified.

We only have to solve the first step of the above iterative scheme. In general, it is computationally expensive to minimize over all the variables $\boldsymbol{L}$, $\boldsymbol{E}$, and $d\tau$ simultaneously. So, we adopt a common strategy to solve it *approximately* by adopting an *alternating minimizing* strategy, i.e., minimizing with respect to $\boldsymbol{L}$, $\boldsymbol{E}$, and $d\tau$ one at a time:

$$\begin{cases} \boldsymbol{L}_{k+1} = \arg\min_{\boldsymbol{L}} \mathcal{L}_{\mu_k}(\boldsymbol{L}, \boldsymbol{E}_k, d\tau_k, \boldsymbol{Y}_k), \\ \boldsymbol{E}_{k+1} = \arg\min_{\boldsymbol{E}} \mathcal{L}_{\mu_k}(\boldsymbol{L}_{k+1}, \boldsymbol{E}, d\tau_k, \boldsymbol{Y}_k), \\ d\tau_{k+1} = \arg\min_{d\tau} \mathcal{L}_{\mu_k}(\boldsymbol{L}_{k+1}, \boldsymbol{E}_{k+1}, d\tau, \boldsymbol{Y}_k). \end{cases} \tag{15.4.6}$$

Algorithm 15.2 Inner Loop of TILT

Input: The current (deformed and normalized) image $\boldsymbol{I} \circ \tau \in \mathbb{R}^{m \times n}$ and its Jacobian $\nabla \boldsymbol{I}$ against current deformation τ (from the outer loop), and $\lambda > 0$.

Initialization: $k = 0, \boldsymbol{Y}_0 = 0, \boldsymbol{E}_0 = 0, d\tau_0 = 0, \mu_0 > 0, \rho > 1$;

while not converged **do**

$(\boldsymbol{U}_k, \boldsymbol{\Sigma}_k, \boldsymbol{V}_k) = \mathrm{SVD}\big(\boldsymbol{I} \circ \tau + \nabla \boldsymbol{I} \cdot d\tau_k - \boldsymbol{E}_k + \mu_k^{-1} \boldsymbol{Y}_k\big)$;

$\boldsymbol{L}_{k+1} = \boldsymbol{U}_k \,\mathrm{soft}(\boldsymbol{\Sigma}_k, \mu_k^{-1}) \boldsymbol{V}_k^*$;

$\boldsymbol{E}_{k+1} = \mathrm{soft}(\boldsymbol{I} \circ \tau + \nabla \boldsymbol{I} \cdot d\tau_k - \boldsymbol{L}_{k+1} + \mu_k^{-1} \boldsymbol{Y}_k, \lambda \mu_k^{-1})$;

$d\tau_{k+1} = (\nabla \boldsymbol{I})^\dagger (-\boldsymbol{I} \circ \tau + \boldsymbol{L}_{k+1} + \boldsymbol{E}_{k+1} - \mu_k^{-1} \boldsymbol{Y}_k)$;

$\boldsymbol{Y}_{k+1} = \boldsymbol{Y}_k + \mu_k (\boldsymbol{I} \circ \tau + \nabla \boldsymbol{I} \cdot d\tau_{k+1} - \boldsymbol{L}_{k+1} - \boldsymbol{E}_{k+1})$;

$\mu_{k+1} = \rho \mu_k$;

end while

Output: Converged solution $(\boldsymbol{L}_\star, \boldsymbol{E}_\star, d\tau_\star)$ to problem (15.4.4).

Due to the special structure of our problem, each of the above optimization problems has a simple closed-form solution, and hence can be solved in a single step. More precisely, recalling the proximal operators for the ℓ^1 norm and the nuclear norm in Chapter 8, the solutions to (15.4.6) can be expressed explicitly using the soft-thresholding operator as follows:

$$\begin{cases} \boldsymbol{L}_{k+1} \leftarrow \boldsymbol{U}_k \,\mathrm{soft}(\boldsymbol{\Sigma}_k, \mu_k^{-1}) \boldsymbol{V}_k^*, \\ \boldsymbol{E}_{k+1} \leftarrow \mathrm{soft}(\boldsymbol{I} \circ \tau + \nabla \boldsymbol{I} \cdot d\tau_k - \boldsymbol{L}_{k+1} + \mu_k^{-1} \boldsymbol{Y}_k, \lambda \mu_k^{-1}), \\ d\tau_{k+1} \leftarrow (\nabla \boldsymbol{I})^\dagger (-\boldsymbol{I} \circ \tau + \boldsymbol{L}_{k+1} + \boldsymbol{E}_{k+1} - \mu_k^{-1} \boldsymbol{Y}_k), \end{cases} \tag{15.4.7}$$

where $\boldsymbol{U}_k \boldsymbol{\Sigma}_k \boldsymbol{V}_k^*$ is the SVD of $\big(\boldsymbol{I} \circ \tau + \nabla \boldsymbol{I} \cdot d\tau_k - \boldsymbol{E}_k + \mu_k^{-1} \boldsymbol{Y}_k\big)$, and $(\nabla \boldsymbol{I})^\dagger$ denotes the Moore–Penrose pseudo-inverse of $\nabla \boldsymbol{I}$.

We summarize the ADMM scheme for solving (15.4.4) as Algorithm 15.2. We note that the operations in each step of the algorithm are very simple, with the SVD computation being the most computationally expensive step.[12]

Connection to Compressive Principal Component Pursuit

Notice that there is another way to view the linearized constraint (15.4.3):

$$\boldsymbol{I} \circ \tau + \nabla \boldsymbol{I} \cdot d\tau = \boldsymbol{L} + \boldsymbol{E}. \tag{15.4.8}$$

Let Q be the left kernel of the Jacobian $\nabla \boldsymbol{I}$, that is, $\mathcal{P}_{\mathsf{Q}}[\nabla \boldsymbol{I}] = 0$. Applying $\mathcal{P}_{\mathsf{Q}}[\cdot]$ to both sides of the equation, we obtain

$$\mathcal{P}_{\mathsf{Q}}[\boldsymbol{I} \circ \tau] = \mathcal{P}_{\mathsf{Q}}[\boldsymbol{L} + \boldsymbol{E}]. \tag{15.4.9}$$

[12] Empirically, we notice that for larger window sizes (over 100×100 pixels), it is much faster to run the partial SVD instead of the full SVD, if the rank of the texture is known to be very low.

Then the program (15.4.4) becomes equivalent to

$$\min_{L,E,d\tau} \|L\|_* + \lambda\|E\|_1 \quad \text{subject to} \quad \mathcal{P}_Q[I \circ \tau] = \mathcal{P}_Q[L + E]. \tag{15.4.10}$$

Notice that this is exactly the compressive principal component pursuit problem (5.5.2) discussed in Chapter 5. However, Theorem 5.9 only provides recovery guarantee for random projection operator $\mathcal{P}_Q[\cdot]$ but the above kernel projection is certainly not random. To the best of our knowledge, there is little work that characterizes how such projection is incoherent with the low-rank and sparse component so that correct recovery is guaranteed. Empirical results below with images show that that is obviously the case for typical types of transformations (e.g., 2D linear or affine transformation groups or 3D curved surfaces). Rigorous theoretical analysis of the interplay of group transformations and low-dimensional structures remains to be established. We will discuss more in the Notes as well as see more interplay between the two in the next chapter.

Now putting it all together, we see that the original problem (15.4.2) is essentially a nonlinear optimization problem that tries to recover both the low-rank texture and its deformation. The TILT Algorithm 15.1 relies on linearizing the nonlinear constraint locally and then iteratively solves the locally linearized version using Algorithm 15.2. Hence, in general, there is no guarantee that the algorithm converges to the globally optimal (usually the correct) solution. As studies in the literature [ZLGM10, ZGLM12] have shown, if the above algorithm is properly implemented, the range of convergence for typical deformations encountered in practice can be surprisingly large. For instance, for a typical checkerboard pattern tilted in front of a camera, the algorithm manages to converge correctly even if the tilting angle is around 50°! For details of implementing the TILT algorithm and a careful quantitative examination of the range of convergence for the TILT algorithm, the reader can refer to [ZLGM10, ZGLM12]. Again, a rigorous characterization of the global landscape of this nonlinear program and justification for the large range of contraction remains wide open.

15.5 Applications of TILT

The above algorithm is derived for τ being an arbitrary (parametric) transform in a prescribed group $\mathbb{G}$. In this section, we show how to apply the above algorithm to several typical types of transformations we often encounter in computer vision applications:

1 The low-rank texture is (approximately) on a planar surface and the camera is an ideal perspective projection. In this case, the deformation τ belongs to the group of general linear transforms on a plane (also known as the homography group in the computer vision literature). The TILT algorithm allows us to recover the precise location and orientation of the plane in 3D relative to the camera.

2 The low-rank texture is on a generalized cylindrical surface. The TILT algorithm would allow us to recover both the 3D shape of the surface as well as its location and orientation relative to the camera.
3 The camera is not projective and its lens has certain nonlinear distortion. The images of a standard calibration rig (a planar checkerboard pattern) would allow us to recover the camera lens distortion.

15.5.1 Rectifying Planar Low-Rank Textures

If a low-rank texture $\boldsymbol{I}_o$ is on a planar surface, then at an arbitrary viewpoint, its image $\boldsymbol{I}$ (under ideal perspective projection) is related to the original (rectified) texture $\boldsymbol{I}_o$ by a homography τ [MSKS04], or formally known as a projective transformation. Figure 15.6 shows one such example. More precisely, let (u, v) be the coordinates of the image $\boldsymbol{I}$, and (x, y) be the coordinates of the original texture $\boldsymbol{I}_o$. Let us represent the two image planes with the homogeneous coordinates $[u, v, 1]^* \in \mathbb{R}^3$ and $[x, y, 1]^* \in \mathbb{R}^3$, respectively. Then the coordinates of a point on $\boldsymbol{I}_o$ and those of its (projective) image on $\boldsymbol{I}$ will be related by

$$\tau(x, y) = \begin{bmatrix} u \\ v \\ 1 \end{bmatrix} \sim \begin{bmatrix} h_{11} & h_{12} & h_{13} \\ h_{21} & h_{22} & h_{23} \\ h_{31} & h_{32} & h_{33} \end{bmatrix} \begin{bmatrix} x \\ y \\ 1 \end{bmatrix}, \tag{15.5.1}$$

where "$\sim$" means equal up to a scale and $\boldsymbol{H} = [h_{ij}] \in \mathbb{R}^{3\times 3}$ is an invertible matrix belonging to the general linear group $\mathsf{GL}(3)$:

$$\mathsf{GL}(3) \doteq \left\{ \boldsymbol{H} \in \mathbb{R}^{3\times 3} \,\middle|\, \det(\boldsymbol{H}) \neq 0 \right\}. \tag{15.5.2}$$

However, there is a little caveat in this formulation. If we allow the transformation τ in the TILT algorithm to be free in the entire group $\mathsf{GL}(3)$, it could lead to a trivial solution in which the algorithm will choose a black region and a τ to blow it up to the size of $\boldsymbol{I}_o$ so that the value of the objective function will be nearly zero. To avoid such degenerate solutions, one way is to fix the scale of the region which we would like to rectify. We may restrict the transform to be in a subgroup of $\mathsf{GL}(3)$ with scale normalized, known as the special linear group:

$$\mathsf{SL}(3) \doteq \left\{ \boldsymbol{H} \in \mathbb{R}^{3\times 3} \,\middle|\, \det(\boldsymbol{H}) = 1 \right\}. \tag{15.5.3}$$

This imposes additional (nonlinear) constraints among the parameters of the transformation.[13] In practical implementation of the TILT algorithm for the projective case, to fix the scale, we may simply specify and fix two diagonal corners of the region we would like to rectify. Interested readers may find more implementation details in [ZGLM12]. Figure 15.7 shows some of the representative results of the

[13] A systematic way to handle any additional constraints on the parameters of the transformation τ is to linearize it and then add the additional linear constraints to the inner loop of the TILT algorithm.

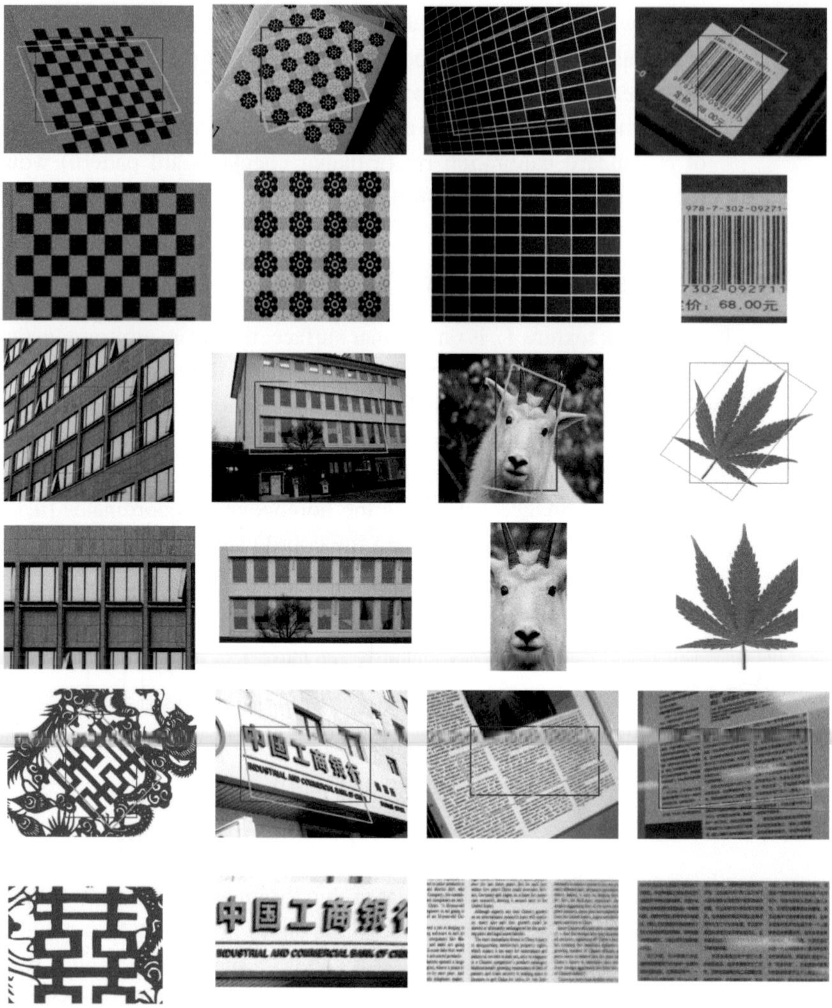

Figure 15.7 Representative Results of TILT on several categories of structured objects: textures with repetitive patterns, building facades, bar codes, characters and texts, bilateral symmetrical objects, etc. In each case, the red window denotes the initial input of the TILT algorithm and the green window denotes the final converged output. The (matrix associated with the) green window is displayed to highlight the recovered low-rank texture.

TILT algorithm applied to low-rank textures on a plane. Notice that the rectification is typically accurate to the pixel level.

15.5.2 Rectifying Generalized Cylindrical Surfaces

In man-made environments, structured objects do not always have planar surfaces. In many cases, the surface can be curved and cannot be approximated by a planar one, as the example in Figure 15.8(a) shows. Clearly, if we approximate the surface by a plane

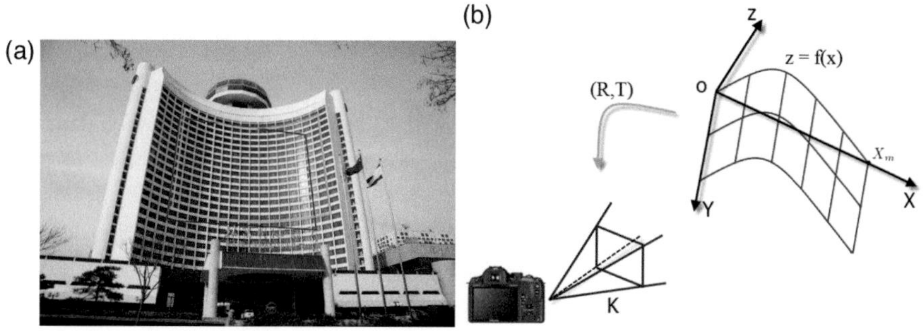

Figure 15.8 (a) An example of a curved building facade. Red window is a planar approximation to the surface; and green window outlines the true low-rank texture of the facade. (b) Generalized cylindrical surface C viewed by a perspective camera $\boldsymbol{K}$.

outlined as the red window (adapted to the orientation of the facade), the texture will not be regular. Instead, the texture enclosed in the green window would be close to an ideal low-rank texture. However, to recover such low-rank texture, it would require us to recover the shape of the surface as well (in addition to the unknown camera projection in the planar case).

In this section, we see how TILT can be extended to rectify and recover low-rank texture on such curved surfaces in 3D space. Let us assume the image $\boldsymbol{I}(u, v)$ is a transformed version of low-rank texture $\boldsymbol{I}_o(x, y)$ wrapped on a curved surface C, as illustrated in Figure 15.8(b).

Presumably there exists a composite map from the intrinsic texture coordinate (x, y) to the image coordinate (u, v) as

$$g(x, y) : (x, y) \mapsto (u, v), \tag{15.5.4}$$

such that $\boldsymbol{I} \circ g = \boldsymbol{I}_o$ in the noise-free case. In this section, we will explain how to parameterize such a transformation g based on a generalized cylindrical surface model for the surface [ZLM11]. The model represents a very important family of 3D shapes, as they describe the majority of curved building facades or deformed texts on curved surfaces. Mathematically, a generalized cylindrical surface can be described as

$$\boldsymbol{c}(s, t) = t\boldsymbol{p} + \boldsymbol{h}(s) \quad \in \mathbb{R}^3, \tag{15.5.5}$$

where $s, t \in \mathbb{R}$, $\boldsymbol{p}, \boldsymbol{h}(s) \in \mathbb{R}^3$, and $\boldsymbol{p} \perp \partial \boldsymbol{h}(s)$.

Without loss of generality, we may choose a 3D coordinate frame (X, Y, Z) for the surface such that the center o is on the surface and the Y-axis aligns with the direction of $\boldsymbol{p}$. If we limit our calculation within a "rectangular" section of the surface whose X-coordinate is in the interval $[0, X_m]$, then the expression of the function $\boldsymbol{h}(\cdot)$ can be simplified and uniquely determined by a scalar function $Z = f(X)$, as shown in Figure 15.8(b).

Without loss of generality, we may choose to parameterize the function $Z = f(X)$ by a polynomial up to degree $d + 2$, where typically $d \leq 4$ for most natural images. So an explicit expression of the surface can be written as

$$Z = f_c(X) \doteq X(X - X_m) \sum_{i=0}^{d} a_i X^i, \tag{15.5.6}$$

where we use $\boldsymbol{c} \doteq \{a_0, a_1, \ldots, a_d\}$ to denote the collection of surface parameters. Further note that when all the a_i are zero, the surface reduces to a planar surface $Z = 0$ in 3D as considered in the previous section.

For any point (x, y) in the rectified and flattened texture coordinates, we need to find its 3D coordinates (X_c, Y_c, Z_c) on the cylindrical surface C. We can calculate the geodesic distance from the origin O to $(X_m, 0, 0)$ on the surface as

$$L_c \doteq \int_0^{X_m} \sqrt{1 + f_c'(X)^2}\, dX. \tag{15.5.7}$$

The following set of equations uniquely determine the wrapping map between (x, y) and (X_c, Y_c, Z_c):

$$\begin{cases} x = \dfrac{X_m}{L_c} \displaystyle\int_0^{X_c} \sqrt{1 + f_c'(X)^2}\, dX, \\ y = Y_c, \\ Z_c = f_c(X_c). \end{cases} \tag{15.5.8}$$

Finally, suppose we are given a perspective camera model with intrinsic parameters[14]

$$\boldsymbol{K} = \begin{bmatrix} f_x & \alpha & o_x \\ 0 & f_y & o_y \\ 0 & 0 & 1 \end{bmatrix} \in \mathbb{R}^{3\times 3},$$

and its relative position with respect to the surface coordinate frame is described by an unknown Euclidean transform $(\boldsymbol{R}, \boldsymbol{T}) \in \mathsf{SE}(3, \mathbb{R})$, where $\boldsymbol{R} \in \mathbb{R}^{3\times 3}$ is a rotation matrix and $\boldsymbol{T} \in \mathbb{R}^3$ is a translation vector. Then a point with 3D coordinates (X_c, Y_c, Z_c) is mapped to the image pixel coordinates (u, v) according to the following relationship:

$$\begin{bmatrix} x_n \\ y_n \end{bmatrix} = \begin{bmatrix} \frac{R_{11}X_c + R_{12}Y_c + R_{13}Z_c + T_1}{R_{31}X_c + R_{32}Y_c + R_{33}Z_c + T_3} \\ \frac{R_{21}X_c + R_{22}Y_c + R_{23}Z_c + T_2}{R_{31}X_c + R_{32}Y_c + R_{33}Z_c + T_3} \end{bmatrix}, \quad \begin{bmatrix} u \\ v \\ 1 \end{bmatrix} = \boldsymbol{K} \begin{bmatrix} x_n \\ y_n \\ 1 \end{bmatrix} = \begin{bmatrix} f_x x_n + \alpha y_n + o_x \\ f_y y_n + o_y \\ 1 \end{bmatrix}. \tag{15.5.9}$$

Therefore the transformation g from the texture coordinates (x, y) to the image coordinates (u, v) is a composition of the following mappings specified above:

$$g : (x, y) \mapsto (X_c, Y_c, Z_c) \mapsto (x_n, y_n) \mapsto (u, v). \tag{15.5.10}$$

The parameters needed to specify g include the parameters for the surface $\boldsymbol{c}$, the camera pose $(\boldsymbol{R}, \boldsymbol{T})$ (and the camera intrinsic parameters $\boldsymbol{K}$ if unknown). Although here the deformation group $\mathbb{G}$ is not explicitly defined, the so-defined mappings g are

[14] Be aware that here f_x and f_y stand for focus lengths and are not to be confused with the curve function f_c above. In practice, the intrinsic parameters can be well approximated from the EXIF information in the image file recorded by modern digital cameras. For more details, please refer to [ZLM11].

all one-to-one and invertible. For our purposes, it suffices if such transformations are defined in a range around the identity mapping.[15]

In order to recover the low-rank component $\boldsymbol{I}_o$ subject to some possible sparse error component $\boldsymbol{E}_o$, we can now solve the following optimization problem:

$$\min_{\boldsymbol{L},\boldsymbol{E},\boldsymbol{c},\boldsymbol{R},\boldsymbol{T}} \|\boldsymbol{L}\|_* + \lambda\|\boldsymbol{E}\|_1 \quad \text{subject to} \quad \boldsymbol{I}\circ g = \boldsymbol{L} + \boldsymbol{E}. \tag{15.5.11}$$

As we have done in the TILT algorithm, this nonlinear problem can be estimated *iteratively* by solving its linearized version as

$$\min_{\boldsymbol{L},\boldsymbol{E},dg} \|\boldsymbol{L}\|_* + \lambda\|\boldsymbol{E}\|_1 \quad \text{subject to} \quad \boldsymbol{I}\circ g + \nabla\boldsymbol{I}_g \cdot dg = \boldsymbol{L} + \boldsymbol{E}, \tag{15.5.12}$$

where $\nabla\boldsymbol{I}_g$ is the Jacobian matrix of the image with respect to both the unknown general cylindrical surface parameters $\boldsymbol{c}$ and the unknown Euclidean transform $(\boldsymbol{R},\boldsymbol{T})$ (and the camera calibration $\boldsymbol{K}$ if unknown too), and dg is the differential of these unknown variables. Notice that the above program is exactly the same as the program that we have solved for the TILT problem in the previous section. The only difference is that the deformation τ (or $d\tau$) is replaced by g (or dg) here. We can use the same Algorithm 15.1 to solve the above program. For a more detailed implementation, please refer to [ZLM11]. Figure 15.9 shows some real examples and results of curved low-rank textures unwrapped and recovered by the TILT Algorithm 15.1 with the transformation g described above.

15.5.3 Calibrating Camera Lens Distortion

In the above planar and curved surface cases, we have always assumed that the image of a low-rank texture is taken by a (calibrated) camera which can be represented by an ideal perspective projection. However, with the proliferation of low-cost cameras, many of the cameras (and their images) that we encounter in practice are not carefully calibrated by the manufacturer; and some cameras are deliberately made with different projection models from the perspective one (in order to maximize the use of the imaging sensors and increase the field of view), such as fisheye cameras or omnidirectional cameras. Figure 15.10(a) shows an example of an image taken by a fisheye camera. Figure 15.10 (b) shows an image of the same building by an ideal perspective camera. Notice that for the latter case, there is no distortion caused by the lens and all straight lines in the scene are straight in the image.

Camera calibration is arguably the most crucial task for any application that requires the computer or machine to perceive and interact with the 3D world through a camera (such as 3D reconstruction, mapping, navigation, and manipulation, etc.). When calibrating a camera (with respect to a certain world coordinate frame), in addition to the aforementioned *lens distortion*, we also need to calibrate the *intrinsic parameters* $\boldsymbol{K}$ for its perspective projection and the *extrinsic parameters* $(\boldsymbol{R},\boldsymbol{T})$ for the camera viewpoint. For conventional calibration methods such as the popular

[15] Strictly speaking, such a set of transformations form a groupoid.

Figure 15.9 Unwrapping low-rank texture on curved surfaces based on a generalized cylindrical surface model. (a) Input image. The red bounding box indicates the manually labeled initial position of the texture region. The green bounding box indicates the recovered texture surface. (b) Unwrapped low-rank texture.

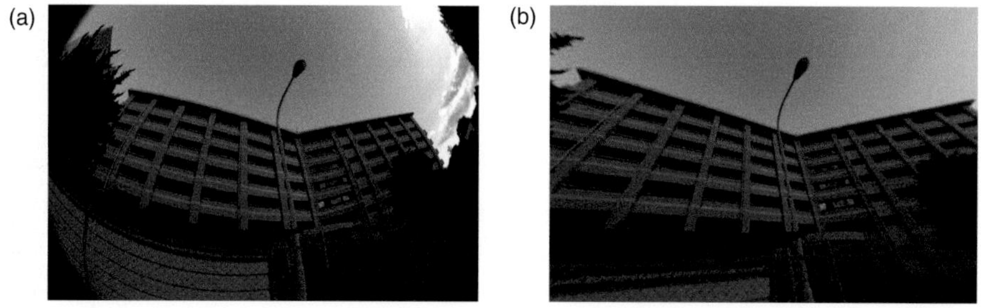

Figure 15.10 (a) Typical image of a fisheye camera. (b) Image of a perspective camera.

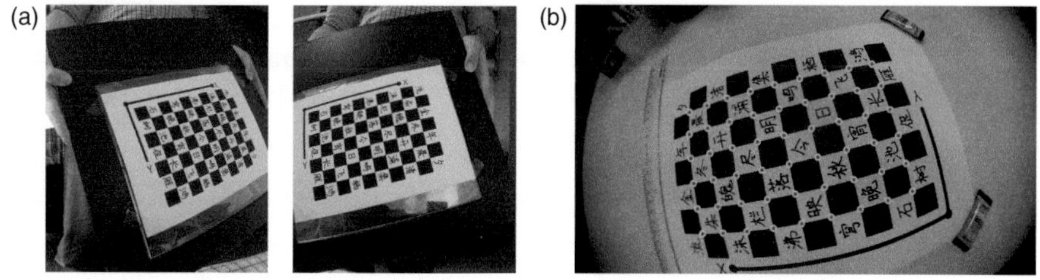

Figure 15.11 (a) Images of a typical calibration rig. (b) Corners need to be marked (or detected) for conventional calibration methods.

toolbox [Bou], one needs to take a few images of a calibration rig (usually a planar checkerboard pattern with known geometry [Zha00]). The corners of the checkerboard then need to be carefully marked out for calibration. Figure 15.11 shows an example.

As we see, the calibration rig is typically a regular pattern, hence is low-rank. The imaging process of an uncalibrated camera is a sequence of mappings that transform the low-rank texture to the image plane. Instead of marking the corners manually, which is tedious and time-consuming,[16] in principle we could utilize the low-rankedness of the calibration pattern and use the TILT algorithm to automatically estimate all unknown parameters associated with the imaging process.

Similar to the previous section, we here give a brief description of the sequence of mappings involved in the imaging process of an uncalibrated camera, which can then be used in customizing the TILT algorithm for calibration purposes. For a more careful and complete description of camera models, the reader may refer to [HZ00, MSKS04].

We first briefly describe the common mathematical model used for camera calibration and introduce the notation used in this book. We use a vector $\boldsymbol{P} = [X_0, Y_0, Z_0]^* \in \mathbb{R}^3$ to denote the 3D coordinates of a point in the world coordinate frame, and use $\boldsymbol{p}_n = [x_n, y_n]^* \in \mathbb{R}^2$ to denote its projection on the canonical image plane in the camera coordinate frame. For convenience, we denote the homogeneous coordinates of a point $\boldsymbol{p}$ as $\tilde{\boldsymbol{p}} = \left[\begin{smallmatrix} \boldsymbol{p} \\ 1 \end{smallmatrix}\right] \in \mathbb{R}^3$.

[16] Automatically detecting the corner features is a seemingly simple task but remains a difficult problem that has not yet been entirely solved under general conditions.

As before, we use $\boldsymbol{R} \in \mathsf{SO}(3)$ and $\boldsymbol{T} \in \mathbb{R}^3$ to denote the rotation and translation from the world coordinate frame to the camera frame – so-called extrinsic parameters.[17] So we have

$$\tilde{\boldsymbol{p}}_n \sim \boldsymbol{R}\boldsymbol{P} + \boldsymbol{T} \quad \in \mathbb{R}^3.$$

If the lens of the camera is distorted, on the image plane, the coordinates of a point $\boldsymbol{p}_n$ may be transformed to a different one, denoted as $\boldsymbol{p}_d = [x_d, y_d]^* \in \mathbb{R}^2$. A very commonly used general mathematical model for this distortion $D(\cdot) : \boldsymbol{p}_n \mapsto \boldsymbol{p}_d$ is given by a polynomial distortion model by neglecting any higher-order terms as below [Bro71]:

$$\begin{cases} r \doteq \sqrt{x_n^2 + y_n^2}, \\ f(r) \doteq 1 + k_c(1)r^2 + k_c(2)r^4 + k_c(5)r^6, \\ \boldsymbol{p}_d = \begin{bmatrix} f(r)x_n + 2k_c(3)x_n y_n + k_c(4)(r^2 + 2x_n^2) \\ f(r)x_n + 2k_c(4)x_n y_n + k_c(3)(r^2 + 2y_n^2) \end{bmatrix}. \end{cases} \tag{15.5.13}$$

Notice that this model has a total of five unknowns $k_c(1), \ldots, k_c(5) \in \mathbb{R}$. If there is no distortion, simply set all $k_c(i)$ to be zero, and then it becomes $\boldsymbol{p}_d = \boldsymbol{p}_n$.

The intrinsic matrix $\boldsymbol{K} \in \mathbb{R}^{3\times 3}$ represents a linear transformation of points on the image plane to their pixel coordinates, denoted as $\boldsymbol{p} = [u, v]^* \in \mathbb{R}^2$. $\boldsymbol{K}$ also has five unknowns; the focal length along x- and y-axes f_x and f_y, skew parameter θ, and coordinates of the principal point (o_x, o_y). In matrix form, it is described as

$$\boldsymbol{K} \doteq \begin{bmatrix} f_x & \theta & o_x \\ 0 & f_y & o_y \\ 0 & 0 & 1 \end{bmatrix} \quad \in \mathbb{R}^{3\times 3}. \tag{15.5.14}$$

With all the notation, the overall imaging process of a point $\boldsymbol{P}$ in the world coordinates to the camera pixel coordinates $\boldsymbol{p}$ by a pinhole camera can be described as

$$\tilde{\boldsymbol{p}} = \boldsymbol{K}\tilde{\boldsymbol{p}}_d = \boldsymbol{K} \circ D(\tilde{\boldsymbol{p}}_n), \quad \lambda\tilde{\boldsymbol{p}}_n = \boldsymbol{R}\boldsymbol{P} + \boldsymbol{T}, \tag{15.5.15}$$

where λ is the depth of the point. If there is no lens distortion ($\tilde{\boldsymbol{p}}_d = \tilde{\boldsymbol{p}}_n$), the above model reduces the typical perspective projection with an uncalibrated camera: $\lambda\tilde{\boldsymbol{p}} = \boldsymbol{K}(\boldsymbol{R}\boldsymbol{P} + \boldsymbol{T})$.

For compact presentation, we will let τ_0 denote the intrinsic parameters and lens distortion parameters all together. When we take multiple, say N, images to calibrate the intrinsic parameters and the lens distortion, we use τ_i $(i = 1, 2, \ldots, N)$ to denote

[17] As in [MSKS04], the rotation $\boldsymbol{R}$ can be parameterized by a vector $\boldsymbol{\omega} = [\omega_1, \omega_2, \omega_3]^* \in \mathbb{R}^3$ using the Rodrigues formula:

$$\boldsymbol{R}(\boldsymbol{\omega}) = \boldsymbol{I} + \sin\|\boldsymbol{\omega}\|\frac{\hat{\boldsymbol{\omega}}}{\|\boldsymbol{\omega}\|} + (1 - \cos\|\boldsymbol{\omega}\|)\frac{\hat{\boldsymbol{\omega}}^2}{\|\boldsymbol{\omega}\|^2},$$

where $\hat{\boldsymbol{\omega}}$ denotes the 3×3 matrix form of the rotation vector $\boldsymbol{\omega}$, defined as $\hat{\boldsymbol{\omega}} = [0, -\omega_3, \omega_2; \omega_3, 0, -\omega_1; -\omega_2, \omega_1, 0] \in \mathbb{R}^{3\times 3}$.

the extrinsic parameters $\boldsymbol{R}_i$ and $\boldsymbol{T}_i$ for the i-th image. By a slight abuse of notation, we will occasionally use τ_0 to represent the combined transformation of $\boldsymbol{K}$ and $D(\cdot)$ acting on the image domain, i.e., $\tau_0(\cdot) = \boldsymbol{K} \circ D(\cdot)$, and use τ_i $(i = 1, 2, \ldots, N)$ to represent the transformations from the world frame to each individual image plane. Using this notation, each image $\boldsymbol{I}_i$ and the calibration rig (low-rank texture) $\boldsymbol{I}_o$ are related by

$$\boldsymbol{I}_i \circ (\tau_0 \circ \tau_i) = \boldsymbol{I}_o + \boldsymbol{E}_i, \quad i = 1, 2, \ldots, N, \tag{15.5.16}$$

where we use a sparse error term $\boldsymbol{E}_i$ to model possible occlusion or corruption introduced in the imaging process.

It seems that we now can use TILT to estimate all the transformation parameters in τ_0 and τ_i without using any marked feature points. However, there is one caveat: as we have discussed in the beginning of the chapter in Section 15.2, there is some ambiguity in the notion of a low-rank texture, in that a scaled or translated version of the same texture would have the same rank. Hence, if we use TILT to each individual image $\boldsymbol{I}_i$, the so-recovered $\hat{\boldsymbol{I}}_o$ might be a scaled or translated version of one another. More precisely, we solve the following robust rank minimization problems individually:

$$\min \|\boldsymbol{L}_i\|_* + \lambda \|\boldsymbol{E}_i\|_1 \quad \text{subject to} \quad \boldsymbol{I}_i \circ (\tau_0 \circ \tau_i) = \boldsymbol{L}_i + \boldsymbol{E}_i, \tag{15.5.17}$$

with $\boldsymbol{L}_i, \boldsymbol{E}_i, \tau_i$, and τ_0 as unknowns. Then we can only expect $\boldsymbol{L}_\star$ to recover the low-rank pattern $\boldsymbol{I}_o$ up to a translation and scaling in each axis, i.e.,

$$\boldsymbol{L}_\star = \boldsymbol{I}_o \circ \tau \quad \text{for some} \quad \tau = \begin{bmatrix} a & 0 & t_1 \\ 0 & b & t_2 \\ 0 & 0 & 1 \end{bmatrix}. \tag{15.5.18}$$

Each of the N programs provides its own estimate of the τ_0 of interest.

There are many possible ways we can use all the N images together and try to estimate a common solution for τ_0 and $\boldsymbol{I}_o$. The most straightforward way is to lump all the objective functions together and enforce that the recovered $\boldsymbol{L}_i$ are all the same. Therefore, the natural optimization problem associated with this problem becomes

$$\begin{aligned} &\min \sum_{i=1}^{N} \|\boldsymbol{L}_i\|_* + \|\boldsymbol{E}_i\|_1 \\ &\text{subject to} \quad \boldsymbol{I}_i \circ (\tau_0 \circ \tau_i) = \boldsymbol{L}_i + \boldsymbol{E}_i, \ \boldsymbol{L}_i = \boldsymbol{L}_j. \end{aligned} \tag{15.5.19}$$

One can use optimization techniques similar to that of TILT to solve the above optimization problem, such as ALM and ADMM. However, having too many constraining terms affects the convergence of such algorithms.

To relax the equality constraints $\boldsymbol{L}_i = \boldsymbol{L}_j$, we may only need to require that they are correlated. So an alternative is to concatenate all the recovered low-rank textures as submatrices of a joint low-rank matrix:

$$L_c \doteq [L_1, L_2, \ldots, L_N], \quad L_r \doteq [L_1^*, L_2^*, \ldots, L_N^*], \quad E \doteq [E_1, E_2, \ldots, E_N].$$

Then we try to simultaneously align the columns and rows of L_i by minimizing the ranks of L_c and L_r:

$$\begin{aligned} &\min \ \|L_c\|_* + \|L_r\|_* + \lambda \|E\|_1 \\ &\text{subject to} \quad I_i \circ (\tau_0 \circ \tau_i) = L_i + E_i, \end{aligned} \tag{15.5.20}$$

with L_i, E_i, τ_0, and τ_i as unknowns. Notice that, by comparing to equation (15.5.19), the new optimization program has just half the number of constraints and hence is easier to solve. In addition, it is insensitive to illumination and contrast change across different images, as it does not require the recovered images L_i to be equal in values.

REMARK 15.3. (High-order low-rank tensors) *In fact, one may view the stack of images $L_c = [L_1, L_2, \ldots, L_N]$ as a three-dimensional tensor. When calibrated correctly, this tensor is supposed to be highly structured: not only is each slice L_i a low-rank matrix, but also all slices are highly correlated. As we have discussed in Section 6.3 of Chapter 6, the above convex relaxation of L_c is only for one Tucker rank of this tensor. Based on our study there, from the compressive sensing perspective this relaxation is not optimal. Nevertheless, here for higher calibration accuracy, we actually desire higher resolution of the images. The computational cost is usually not a main concern as the calibration process is typically done offline.*

It can be shown (see [ZMM11]) that under general conditions, when the number of images $N \geq 5$, then the optimal solution to the above program will be unique and

$$\tau_{0\star} = \tau_0, \quad K_\star = K, \quad R_{i\star} = R_i, \quad i = 1, \ldots, N.$$

In practice, the method actually works with as few as a single ($N = 1$) image (of low-rank texture). To calibrate the camera from a single image, we have to work with fairly strong assumptions, say that the principal point (o_x, o_y) is known (and simply set as the center of the image) and the pixel is square $f_x = f_y$. Then from the image, one can calibrate the focal length as well as eliminating the lens distortion k_c values. Figure 15.12 shows an example with an image given in the standard toolbox. As we see in Figure 15.12(b), the radial distortion is completely removed by the TILT algorithm.

Notice that the low-rank texture-based calibration method does not require precise geometry about the calibration rig. Hence one does not have to use a checkerboard pattern and in principle can utilize any low-rank structures (such as a building facade) for calibration purposes. Figure 15.13 shows two examples of using the TILT algorithm to estimate and correct the radial lens distortion of a fisheye camera (from a single image).

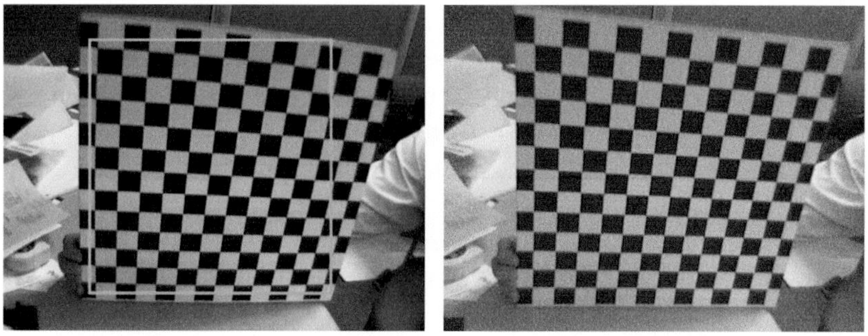

(a) Input image with an initial window (b) Lens distortion removed

Figure 15.12 Calibration from a single image in the toolbox [Bou].

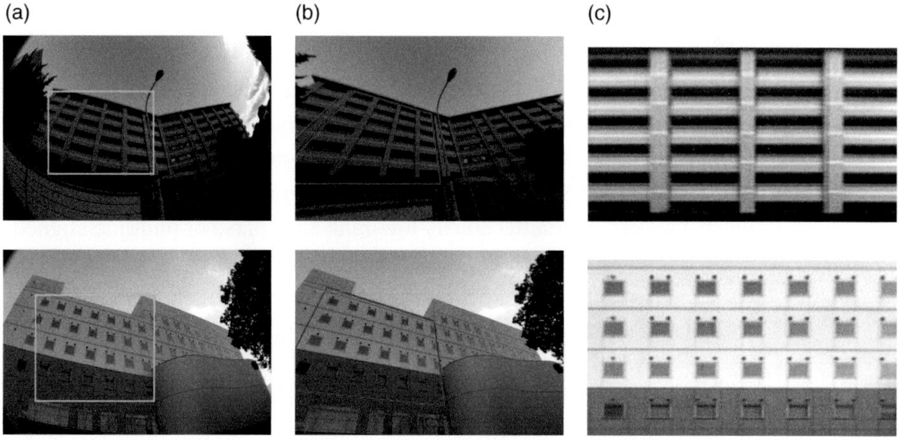

Figure 15.13 Rectifying fisheye images with significant lens distortion: (a) input images with selected initialization windows (green); (b) lens distortion removed images with final converged windows (red); and (c) rectified low-rank textures.

15.6 Notes

The story presented in this chapter follows from the original work of [ZLGM10, ZGLM12] on the TILT method and its extensions to curved surfaces [ZLM11], camera calibration [ZMM11], and texture inpainting [LRZM12]. There are many other extensions for which we give a brief account below.

3D Vision in Structure Scenes

Man-made environments are rich in objects with structured shapes and textures. TILT provides a useful tool to harness one important type of holistic structure in a scene for 3D reconstruction purposes. It enables us to process and extract geometric information that is accurately encoded in large regions of the image, instead of local primitives such as corner-like or edge-like features which are used in conventional 3D reconstruction methods. Successfully harnessing holistic structures seems to be the key to future more accurate and robust 3D reconstruction methods. One may refer to [MZYM11] for some early promising results.

Learning to Detect Structures

Currently, the TILT method requires knowledge of the general location of the structured region in the image. To automatically initialize TILT with a region of interest is essentially a detection or recognition problem. To this end, one can develop effective low-rank texture detectors with learning-based methods, similar to learning to detect other holistic structures such as wireframes [ZQZ$^+$19, ZQM19], vanishing points [ZQHM19], 2D planes [LKG$^+$19], and 3D symmetry [ZLM20].

Alignment of Multiple Correlated Images

In the same spirit of TILT, transformed sparse or low-rank models have also been explored and utilized in the work for sparsity-based robust face alignment and recognition [WWG$^+$09, WWG$^+$12] and for the low-rank-based robust multiple-image alignment method RASL [PGW$^+$12]. As we have discussed in Section 6.3 of Chapter 6, when a matrix is simultaneously low-rank and sparse or multiple aligned images form a three-dimensional tensor, the convex relaxation approach may not be the optimal choice. Hence it would be very interesting to investigate whether certain nonconvex formulations can lead to even better solutions for these tasks.

Extension to Multiple Nonlinear Low-Dimensional Structures

In this chapter, we see how to recover primarily one low-dimensional structure under a certain nonlinear transformation. We see the convex nuclear norm and ℓ^1 norm are rather effective in promoting the desired low-dimensional property in the solution. In the next and final chapter of the book, we will see how to recover a mixture of multiple low-dimensional structures under certain nonlinear transformation. In that more challenging context, we will resort to a more accurate, but nonconvex, measure for compactness: the lossy coding length in terms of the "$\log\det(\cdot)$" function (as we have seen in Exercise 7.4 of Chapter 7).

Low-Dimensional Structures and Group Equivariance and Invariance

From the work of transformed low-dimensional structures, one may observe a common phenomenon: a class of deformations $\mathbb{G}$ can be correctly recovered from a deformed low-dimensional structure as long as the deformations (or their infinitesimal actions) are "incoherent" with the low-dimensional structure. That is, the Jacobian $\nabla_\tau \boldsymbol{I}$ with respect to a deformation $\tau \in \mathbb{G}$ needs to be "incoherent" to the low-dimensional structure of $\boldsymbol{I}$. The precise conditions that would guarantee (at least local) correctness and success of the recovered deformation merit a more thorough examination in the future. Methods like TILT [ZLGM10, ZGLM12], RASL [PGW$^+$12], and face alignment [WWG$^+$12] provide compelling empirical evidence that low-dimensional structures in the data are the key to ensure true "equivariance," with respect to any group of transformations of interest.

In the next chapter, we will encounter yet again another interaction between group invariance and low-dimensional structures. In particular, we will see why sparsity is actually necessary in order to ensure that classification tasks (such as face recognition) can be truly "invariant" to certain group transformations such as translation. Both work in this chapter and that in the next suggest that it is extremely important to understand the relationship (or tradeoff) between low-dimensional structures and group transformations. Our current understanding (and results) remain rather limited and this is definitely a promising new direction for future study.

16 Deep Networks for Classification

"What I cannot create, I do not understand."

– Richard Feynman

16.1 Introduction

In the past decade or so, (deep) neural networks have captured people's imagination through their empirical success in learning problems involving real-world high-dimensional data such as images, speech, and text [LBH15]. Nevertheless, there is quite a bit of mystery as to how deep networks achieve such striking results. Modern deep networks are typically designed through trial and error. Then they are typically trained and deployed as "black boxes" which implement desired input–output relationships, but whose inner workings are unclear. As a consequence, it is not easy to rigorously guarantee the performance of a trained network, such as being truly invariant to transformation [AW18, ETT$^+$17] or not overfitting noisy or arbitrarily assigned class labels [ZBH$^+$17].

In the final chapter of this book, we establish fundamental connections between the practice of deep neural networks and the theory for low-dimensional structures developed in this book. Hence, the mathematical concepts, principles, and methods developed here can help us to understand, interpret, and even improve the practice of deep learning, or learning from high-dimensional data in general. As this is still an active research field, we will provide only an overview of one promising framework, which approaches the *data classification* problem[1] from the perspective of data compression and discriminative representation.

As we have seen in the previous chapter, low-dimensional structures of real-world data often are not linear (low-rank) nor piecewise linear (sparse). The structure can be deformed by certain nonlinear transforms. For a classification task then, the (mixed) data from all classes typically lie on *multiple* nonlinear low-dimensional structures (or distributions), one per class. In this chapter, we will see how a few key ingredients

[1] Image classification is where deep learning demonstrated the initial success that has catalyzed the recent explosion of interest in these models and techniques [KSH12]. Although we will focus on classification only in this chapter, the basic ideas and same principles can be naturally generalized to the case of regression.

that we have introduced and studied in this book, including measures that promote low dimensionality, gradient schemes for optimization, sparsifying dictionaries, and convolutions for shift invariance, can be naturally integrated to learn a discriminative linear representation for such mixed low-dimensional data. Deep networks most naturally arise in this context as an optimization scheme to achieve this objective. In particular, as we will see, they can be constructed as "white boxes" from *first principles*.

In the remainder of this section, we give a brief introduction to deep networks. In Section 16.2, we introduce a measure of low dimensionality, namely coding *rate reduction*, as a principled objective for learning a discriminative and informative representation for classification. In Section 16.3, we show how a basic iterative gradient scheme to optimize this objective naturally leads to a typical deep network, entirely as a "white box." All modern deep networks (for classification) share the same characteristics of their architecture. If we further enforce the classification to be invariant to shift or translation, the network naturally becomes a deep convolutional network. In Section 16.4, we use a basic problem of classifying data lying on one-dimensional (nonlinear) submanifolds to illustrate why a deep network, of tractable size, can provide rigorous guarantees for correct classification under proper conditions. The network's width and depth can be naturally interpreted as statistical and computational resources, respectively, similar to those needed in a compressive sensing scheme for low-dimensional models.

So at high levels, one may view that Section 16.3 justifies the *necessity* of deep network architectures, from the perspective of optimizing a principled objective; while Section 16.4 characterizes *sufficient conditions* on when such a deep network provides tractable guarantees for the given classification task, if additional fine-tuning by back propagation is conducted. Finally in Section 16.5, we lay out some exciting *open problems* that emerge from interpreting deep networks from the perspective of *learning low-dimensional models via iterative optimization.*

16.1.1 Deep Learning in a Nutshell

It is arguably easiest to illustrate deep learning through the task of classification. The typical setting is as follows: We are given labeled samples $\{(\boldsymbol{x}^1, \boldsymbol{y}^1), \dots, (\boldsymbol{x}^m, \boldsymbol{y}^m)\}$, where the $\boldsymbol{x}^i$ are drawn from a mixture of k distributions $\mathcal{D} = \{\mathcal{D}_j\}_{j=1}^k$, and the $\boldsymbol{y}^i$ indicate which mixture component generated each observation $\boldsymbol{x}^i$. Here, we assume that the class labels $\boldsymbol{y}^i \in \mathbb{R}^k$ are encoded in "one-hot" format:[2]

$$\boldsymbol{y}^i = [0, \dots, 0, \underbrace{1}_{j\text{-th entry}}, 0, \dots, 0]^* \quad \in \mathbb{R}^k.$$

[2] In a more general interpretation of the label information, one may use the k-dimensional vector $\boldsymbol{y}^i$ to indicate the probability of a sample $\boldsymbol{x}^i$ belonging to each of the k classes. Hence each entry of $\boldsymbol{y}$ can be a continuous number in $[0, 1]$ and all entries sum to 1. In the case of regression, when one tries to approximate a continuous function (defined on each of the classes), we may also allow the value of the corresponding entry to be a continuous number.

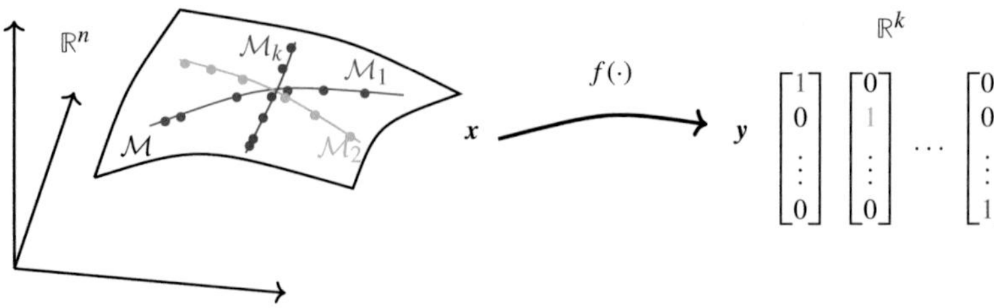

Figure 16.1 Classification as Sparse Representation. High-dimensional data $\boldsymbol{x} \in \mathbb{R}^n$ which lie on a mixture of low-dimensional submanifolds $\mathcal{M}_j$ within a manifold $\mathcal{M}$. Here $\boldsymbol{y}$ is the class label of $\boldsymbol{x}$ represented as a one-hot vector in $\mathbb{R}^k$. The goal is to learn a nonlinear mapping $f(\cdot) : \boldsymbol{x} \mapsto \boldsymbol{y}$.

Notice that although the number of classes k may be large, the vector $\boldsymbol{y}^i$ is always one-sparse.[3] For the task of classification, the goal of (deep) learning is to solve the inverse problem of mapping the input $\boldsymbol{x} \in \mathbb{R}^n$ to its (sparse) label vector $\boldsymbol{y} \in \mathbb{R}^k$.[4] We denote this mapping as $f : \mathbb{R}^n \to \mathbb{R}^k$,

$$f(\cdot) : \boldsymbol{x} \mapsto \boldsymbol{y}.$$

As we will see, when the observations $\boldsymbol{x}^i$ are high-dimensional, this task is greatly facilitated by leveraging low-dimensional structure in the class distributions $\mathcal{D}_1, \ldots, \mathcal{D}_k$. That is, the support of each of the distributions $\mathcal{D}_j$ is on certain low-dimensional submanifolds, denoted as $\mathcal{M}_j$, as illustrated in Figure 16.1.

Extensive empirical studies in recent years have shown that for many practical datasets (images, audios, and natural languages, etc.), the possibly complicated and nonlinear mapping $\boldsymbol{y} = f(\boldsymbol{x})$ can be effectively modeled by a deep network [GBC16].[5] A deep network is a composition of a series of simple maps, called "layers." Each layer, say denoted as $f^\ell(\cdot)$, is composed of a linear transform, represented by a matrix $\boldsymbol{W}_\ell$, followed by a simple (entry-wise) nonlinear activation function $\phi(\cdot)$.[6] More precisely, a network of L layers can be defined recursively as

$$z_{\ell+1} = f^\ell(z_\ell) \doteq \phi(\boldsymbol{W}_\ell z_\ell), \quad \ell = 0, 1, \ldots, L-1, \quad z_0 = \boldsymbol{x}, \tag{16.1.1}$$

where $\{\boldsymbol{W}_\ell\}_{\ell=0}^{L-1}$ are tunable parameters of the network[7] and $\phi(\cdot)$ is the nonlinear activation function.[8] For simplicity, we denote the overall map as $f(\boldsymbol{x}, \boldsymbol{\theta}) : \boldsymbol{x} \mapsto \boldsymbol{y}$

[3] We have seen a similar situation before in which we interpreted class labels as sparse vectors: the robust face recognition problem studied in Chapter 13.

[4] Be aware that in the literature of deep learning, it is customary to use $\boldsymbol{x}$ as the input and $\boldsymbol{y}$ as the output. In compressive sensing, as in the face recognition application of Chapter 13, we instead use $\boldsymbol{x}$ as the sparse signal to be recovered from an input image $\boldsymbol{y}$.

[5] Notice that in the setting of face recognition, such an inverse problem is solved by an iterative algorithm such as the ISTA or FISTA introduced in Chapter 8.

[6] For simplicity, we here ignore for now some other operations between layers such as batch normalization and dropouts, etc., but will discuss their roles later.

[7] There might be additional structures such as convolution in the linear transform $\boldsymbol{W}_\ell$.

[8] Popular choices for $\phi(\cdot)$ include the sigmoid, arctan, and more recently the rectified linear unit (ReLU) function. Sometimes $\phi(\cdot)$ may also contain some tunable parameters.

and use $\boldsymbol{\theta} \in \Theta$ to denote all the network parameters $\{\boldsymbol{W}_\ell\}_{\ell=0}^{L-1}$ and possibly some in the activation function ϕ too:

$$f(\boldsymbol{x}, \boldsymbol{\theta}) \doteq \phi(\boldsymbol{W}_{L-1}\phi(\cdots \phi(\boldsymbol{W}_1\phi(\boldsymbol{W}_0\boldsymbol{x}))\cdots)) \tag{16.1.2}$$

$$= f^{L-1} \circ \cdots \circ f^1 \circ f^0(\boldsymbol{x}). \tag{16.1.3}$$

The goal of tuning the parameters $\boldsymbol{\theta}$ of the network is for the output of this map to best match the class label $\boldsymbol{y}$ for samples $\boldsymbol{x}$ from the distribution $\mathcal{D}$. In machine learning, this is often done by minimizing the *cross-entropy loss*:[9]

$$\min_{\boldsymbol{\theta}\in\Theta} L_{CE}(\boldsymbol{\theta}, \boldsymbol{x}, \boldsymbol{y}) \doteq -\mathbb{E}\big[\langle \boldsymbol{y}, \log[f(\boldsymbol{x}, \boldsymbol{\theta})]\rangle\big]. \tag{16.1.4}$$

Hence, given a large (presumably correctly) labeled dataset $\{(\boldsymbol{x}^i, \boldsymbol{y}^i)\}_{i=1}^m$, one solves the following (nonconvex) program:

$$\min_{\boldsymbol{\theta}\in\Theta} L_{CE}(\boldsymbol{\theta}, \boldsymbol{X}, \boldsymbol{Y}) \doteq -\frac{1}{m}\sum_{i=1}^{m} \langle \boldsymbol{y}^i, \log[f(\boldsymbol{x}^i, \boldsymbol{\theta})]\rangle, \tag{16.1.5}$$

where $\log[\cdot]$ is entry-wise for the vector-valued $f(\boldsymbol{x}, \boldsymbol{\theta}) \in \mathbb{R}^k$. Since this loss function is in the form of a finite sum and the sample size m is very large (e.g., millions), the function is typically optimized by using variants of the stochastic gradient descent method (SGD) introduced in Section 8.6.4 of Chapter 8:

$$\boldsymbol{\theta}_{k+1} = \boldsymbol{\theta}_k - \gamma_k \cdot \left.\frac{\partial L(\boldsymbol{X}^k, \boldsymbol{\theta})}{\partial \boldsymbol{\theta}}\right|_{\boldsymbol{\theta}_k}, \tag{16.1.6}$$

where the gradient $\partial L/\partial \boldsymbol{\theta}\big|_{\boldsymbol{\theta}_k}$ is evaluated approximately using a random batch $\boldsymbol{X}^k \subset \boldsymbol{X}$ of samples at each iteration. Such optimization schemes have been efficiently implemented on many software platforms (e.g., Caffe, PyTorch, and TensorFlow). These numerical tools have significantly boosted the utility and popularity of deep learning.

16.1.2 The Practice of Deep Learning

Above, we have briefly described basic deep network structures and training methods. A vast array of modifications to the basic approach have been proposed, with the goal of improving the ease of training or performance of the learned network. An incomplete list of examples includes:

- choices in loss functions or regularizations on parameters $\boldsymbol{W}_\ell$ [KH92, SZ14];
- different choices in the activation function ϕ (16.1.1) [XWCL15, NIGM18];
- width and depth of the networks [BC14, SLJ+15, LPW+17, DLL+19, AZLS19];
- skip connections across layers $f^\ell(\cdot)$ [SGS15, RFB15, HZRS16];
- normalization of feature $\boldsymbol{z}_\ell$ in each layer [IS15, BKH16, UVL16, WH18, MKKY18];

[9] The cross-entropy loss is convenient for multi-class classification tasks. In practice, for tasks such as functional regression, the typical ℓ^2 loss $\|\boldsymbol{y} - f(\boldsymbol{x}, \boldsymbol{\theta})\|_2^2$ is also commonly used.

- structures (convolutions) in the linear transform $\boldsymbol{W}_\ell$ [LBBH98, KSH12, Cho17];
- downsampling (pooling) and upsampling operations between layers [SMB10];
- initialization of the parameters $\boldsymbol{\theta}$ [LBOM12, GB10, HZRS15, XBSD$^+$18, HXP20];
- choices in the batch size $|\boldsymbol{X}^k|$ (16.1.6) [HHS17, ML18, LSPJ18];
- learning rates γ_k for the SGD algorithm (16.1.6) [LBOM12, LH16, GKXS18];
- random dropout of connections during training [SHK$^+$14, CMH$^+$18];
- early stopping of the training sometimes [GJP95, Pre98, YRC07];
- different optimization algorithms [LNC$^+$11, KB14, Mar14, MG15, BCN18, BJT19].

It can be challenging for practitioners to navigate this somewhat dizzying array of variations over the basic themes of deep learning. One recent trend in industrial practice is to leverage random search to identify architectures or training strategies that give better empirical performance, e.g., Neural Architecture Search (NAS) [ZL17, BGNR17], AutoML [HKV19], and Learning to Learn [ADG$^+$16].

In subsequent sections, we will describe how ideas from low-dimensional data modeling can suggest principled architectures and clarify the roles of various architectural and algorithmic choices. In fact, a number of themes from low-dimensional data modeling recur throughout the deep learning practice:

(i) *Network Architectures from Unrolled Optimization Algorithms.* The widely used ReLU nonlinearity closely resembles the proximal operator for the (nonnegative) ℓ^1 norm. In fact, the proximal gradient algorithms that we introduced in Chapters 8 and 9 can be interpreted as particular neural networks, since they interleave linear operations with nonlinearities [GL10, LCWY19, SPRE18, PRSE18, MLE19]. This connection suggests new network designs from unrolling sparse coding algorithms for solving inverse problems from data with intrinsic *low-dimensional structures* [WLY$^+$15, YSLX16, SLLB17, BJPD17, JMFU17, MJU17, NWMS18, OJM$^+$20]. Some even outperform popular generic networks (e.g., ResNet and U-Net) with much more compact or simpler models [SNT20, LCBD20].

(ii) *Isometry as a Design Principle.* Because network training algorithms propagate information through a large number of layers, it is important that these operations implement near-isometries. This can be achieved by properly initializing the weights [GB10, HZRS15], normalizing the features [IS15], or regularizing the network structure [SGS15, HZRS16], and can suggest modifications to network components such as nonlinearities [QYW$^+$20]. This (empirical) principle suggests analogies to the *restricted isometry property* arising in sparse and low-rank recovery (see Chapters 3 and 4).

(iii) *Explicit or Implicit Regularization.* Certain regularization strategies can be interpreted as encouraging low-dimensional structure in the learned network. A principal example is *dropout* [SHK$^+$14], which has been shown to induce a form of low-rank (nuclear norm) regularization [CMH$^+$18, MAV18, PLVH20] (see the exercises of Chapter 7). *Sparse routing* is also proven to be the key to enhance training and performance of ultra-large-scale models [FZS21].

> Many current mysteries around the generalization of learned networks can be approached from the perspective of implicit regularization induced by particular optimization methods or low-dimensional structures of the data [GLSS18, SHN$^+$18, LMZ18, YZQM20].

In the remainder of this chapter, we will sketch a new approach to deriving neural networks from *first principles* and guaranteeing their performance on data exhibiting low-dimensional structure. The approach will provide some plausible explanations to the above connections. It leverages a connection to lossy data compression, which effectively encourages the network to embed mixed nonlinear data structures onto unions of incoherent linear subspaces.

16.1.3 Challenges with Nonlinearity and Discriminativeness

This chapter entails a significant expansion of scope compared to the first part of this book, which studied the recovery of sparse, low-rank, or atomic structures from linear measurements. These models are, in a sense, piecewise *linear*. For instance, k-sparse vectors in the space $\mathbb{R}^n$ model data that lie on a particular union of k-dimensional linear subspaces, aligned with the standard basis. Our discussion of dictionary learning in Chapters 6 and 7 shows how to extend these models to unions of subspaces that are not aligned with the standard basis (and not known ahead of time). Nevertheless, real-world high-dimensional data, such as images, often exhibit nonlinear structure, due to nonlinear nuisance factors such as deformation. We have seen many examples of this in the application to *structured texture recovery* in Chapter 15.

In general, the distribution $\mathcal{D} = \{\mathcal{D}_j\}_{j=1}^k$ of a real (mixed) dataset, say in a typical setting for classification or clustering, is more likely to have its support on a mixture of low-dimensional *nonlinear* submanifolds $\{\mathcal{M}_j\}_{j=1}^k$, as illustrated on the left of Figure 16.2. Hence, for the models and methods of this book to be applicable to real-world classification tasks, we have to overcome at least two major challenges:

- *From Nonlinear to Linear:* How to learn from the data a nonlinear (feature) mapping, say $f(\cdot, \boldsymbol{\theta}) : \boldsymbol{x} \mapsto \boldsymbol{z}$, such that we can first transform $\boldsymbol{x}$ on nonlinear submanifolds to $\boldsymbol{z}$ with linear structures, such as (a union of) low-dimensional subspaces.[10]
- *From Separable to Discriminative:* How to transform the resulting (separable) linear subspaces to be highly discriminative ones, i.e., in positions such that the subspaces are highly incoherent (preferably orthogonal) to one another, as illustrated on the right of Figure 16.2.

Such a discriminative linear representation $\boldsymbol{z}$ can easily facilitate subsequent tasks. Its linear nature makes linear interpolation or extrapolation of the features $\boldsymbol{z}$ (in each

[10] Such a linear representation is highly desirable for many practical purposes. For instance, a linear superposition of features in the same subspace could be interpreted as a new instance in the same class. There is evidence that a linear subspace is the kind of representation preferred by nature too, say for object recognition [CT17].

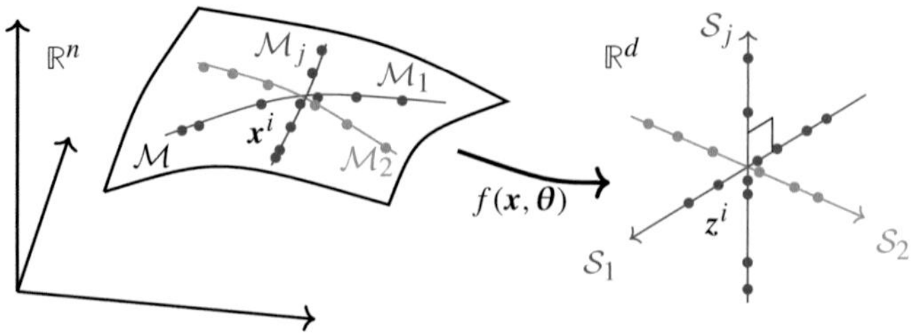

Figure 16.2 A mixed distribution $\mathcal{D} = \{\mathcal{D}_j\}$ of high-dimensional data $\boldsymbol{x} \in \mathbb{R}^n$ is supported on a manifold $\mathcal{M}$ which can be a mixture of multiple low-dimensional submanifolds $\{\mathcal{M}_j\}$. We want to learn a map $f(\boldsymbol{x}, \boldsymbol{\theta})$ such that $\boldsymbol{z}^i = f(\boldsymbol{x}^i, \boldsymbol{\theta})$ are on a union of low-dimensional subspaces $\{\mathcal{S}_j\}$.

subspace) meaningful, and its discriminative nature makes prediction of the class label $\boldsymbol{y}$ easy, say by training a (linear) classifier $h(\boldsymbol{z})$:[11]

$$\boldsymbol{x} \xrightarrow{\; f(\boldsymbol{x}, \boldsymbol{\theta}) \;} \boldsymbol{z}(\boldsymbol{\theta}) \xrightarrow{\; h(\boldsymbol{z}) \;} \boldsymbol{y}. \tag{16.1.7}$$

Notice that both challenges require us to perform *nonlinear* transformations of the data or features. Acute readers may have guessed it: the role of a deep network is precisely to model and perform such a nonlinear transformation! Now the remaining difficult questions are *why* such a nonlinear map should be represented by a composition of many simple layers, and *what* structures and properties the layers and operators need to have in order to efficiently realize such a map? Which parts of the network need to be learned and trained, and which can be determined in advance? In the end, how do we evaluate the optimality of the resulting network? To provide answers to these fundamental questions, we need a principled approach.

16.2 Desiderata for Learning Discriminative Representation

Whether the given data $\boldsymbol{X}$ of a mixed distribution $\mathcal{D}$ can be effectively classified depends on how separable (or discriminative) the component distributions $\mathcal{D}_j$ are (or can be made). One good working assumption is that the distribution of each class has relatively *low-dimensional* intrinsic structures.[12] Hence we may assume the distribution $\mathcal{D}_j$ of each class has a support on a low-dimensional submanifold, say $\mathcal{M}_j$ with dimension $d_j \ll n$, and the distribution $\mathcal{D}$ of $\boldsymbol{x}$ is supported on the mixture

[11] Intuitively speaking, the more incoherent the subspaces are, the larger the margin, hence more generalizable the classifier would be.

[12] There are many reasons why this assumption is plausible: (1) high-dimensional data are highly redundant; (2) data that belong to the same class should be similar and correlated to each other; and (3) typically we only care about equivalent structures of $\boldsymbol{x}$ that are invariant to certain classes of transformations, as we will see in the next section.

of those submanifolds, $\mathcal{M} = \bigcup_{j=1}^{k} \mathcal{M}_j$, in the high-dimensional ambient space $\mathbb{R}^n$, as illustrated on the left of Figure 16.2.

With the manifold assumption in mind, we want to learn a smooth mapping $z = f(\boldsymbol{x}, \boldsymbol{\theta})$ that maps each of the submanifolds $\mathcal{M}_j \subset \mathbb{R}^n$ to a *linear* subspace $\mathcal{S}_j \subset \mathbb{R}^d$ (see the right of Figure 16.2). For the resulting features to be easy to classify or cluster, we require the learned representation to have the following properties.

1 *Between-Class Discriminative:* Features of samples from different classes or clusters should belong to different linear subspaces that are highly *incoherent* or uncorrelated.
2 *Within-Class Compressible:* Features of samples from the same class or cluster should be *compressible* in the sense that they belong to a relatively low-dimensional linear subspace.
3 *Maximally Informative Representation:* The dimension (or variance) of features for each class or cluster should be *as large as possible* as long as they stay incoherent from those of the other classes.

Notice that, although the intrinsic structures of each class or cluster may be low-dimensional, they are by no means simply linear in their original form (as we will elaborate on more in Section 16.4). The more ideal case when the data $\boldsymbol{X}$ lie on multiple linear subspaces has been systematically studied as *generalized principal component analysis* (GPCA) [VMS16]. Here the subspaces $\{\mathcal{S}_j\}$ obtained after the nonlinear mapping $f(\cdot)$ can be viewed as *nonlinear generalized principal components* for the original (mixed) data $\boldsymbol{X}$. If the resulting optimal subspaces are orthogonal (or statistically independent), they can also be viewed as *nonlinear independent components* of the data.

16.2.1 Measure of Compactness for a Representation

Although the above properties are all highly desirable for the learned representation z, they are by no means easy to achieve. Recent work [PHD20] shows that the representations learned via the popular cross-entropy loss (16.1.5) expose a *neural collapsing* phenomenon, where within-class variability and structural information are completely suppressed and ignored, as we will also see in the experiments. So are the properties listed above compatible so that we can expect to achieve them all at once? More specifically, is it possible to find a *simple but principled* objective that can promote all these desired properties for the resulting representations?[13]

The key to these questions is to find a principled "measure of compactness" for the distribution of a random variable z or from its finite samples $\boldsymbol{Z}$. Such a measure should directly and accurately characterize intrinsic geometric or statistical properties of the distribution, in terms of its intrinsic dimension or volume. Unlike cross-entropy

[13] In a similar spirit to the ℓ^1 norm promoting sparsity and the nuclear norm $\|\cdot\|_*$ promoting low-rankedness.

(16.1.4), such a measure should not depend explicitly on class labels so that it can work uniformly in all supervised, semi-supervised, self-supervised, and unsupervised settings.

Low-Dimensional Degenerate Distributions

In information theory [CT91], the notion of entropy $H(z)$ is designed to be such a measure.[14] However, entropy is not well defined for continuous random variables with degenerate distributions.[15] This is unfortunately the case here. To alleviate this difficulty, another related concept in information theory, more specifically in lossy data compression, that measures the "compactness" of a random distribution is the so-called *rate distortion* [CT91]: given a random variable z and a prescribed precision $\varepsilon > 0$, the rate distortion $R(z, \varepsilon)$ is the minimal number of binary bits needed to encode z such that the expected decoding error is less than ε. That is, say in terms of the ℓ^2 norm, we have

$$\mathbb{E}[\|z - \hat{z}\|_2] \leq \varepsilon$$

for the decoded $\hat{z}$.

Nonasymptotic Rate Distortion for Finite Samples

When evaluating the lossy coding rate R, one practical difficulty is that we normally do not know the distribution of z. Instead, we have a finite number of samples as learned representations where $z^i = f(x^i, \theta) \in \mathbb{R}^d, i = 1, \ldots, m$, for the given data samples $X = [x^1, \ldots, x^m]$. Fortunately, from the perspective of lossy data compression, Ma et al. [MDHW07, VMS16] have provided a precise estimate on the number of binary bits needed to encode finite samples from a subspace-like distribution. In order to encode the learned representation $Z = [z^1, \ldots, z^m]$ up to a precision ε, the total number of bits needed is given by the following expression:[16]

$$\mathcal{L}(Z, \varepsilon) \doteq \left(\frac{m+d}{2}\right) \log\det\left(I + \frac{d}{m\varepsilon^2} ZZ^*\right). \tag{16.2.1}$$

See Figure 16.3 for an illustration. Therefore, the compactness of learned features *as a whole* can be measured in terms of the average coding length per sample (as the sample size m is large), also known as the *coding rate* subject to the distortion ε:

$$R(Z, \varepsilon) \doteq \frac{1}{2} \log\det\left(I + \frac{d}{m\varepsilon^2} ZZ^*\right). \tag{16.2.2}$$

As we have seen in Exercise 7.4 of Chapter 7, the $\log\det(\cdot)$ function is a smooth but nonconvex surrogate for promoting low dimensionality of the representation Z. We will soon discuss why here we need the more accurate nonconvex surrogate for low dimensionality rather than the convex nuclear norm $\|\cdot\|_*$. In addition, the particular

[14] Given the probability density $p(z)$ of a random variable, $H(z) \doteq -\int p(z) \log p(z)\, dz$.

[15] The same difficulty arises with evaluating mutual information $I(x, z)$ for degenerate distributions.

[16] This formula can be derived either by packing ε balls into the space spanned by Z or by computing the number of bits needed to quantize the SVD of Z subject to the precision; see [MDHW07] for proofs.

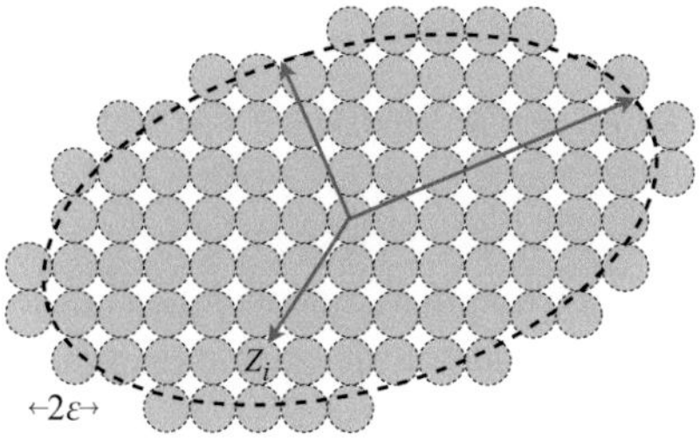

Figure 16.3 Lossy coding scheme. Given a precision ε, we pack the space/volume spanned by the data $\boldsymbol{Z}$ with small balls of diameter 2ε. The number of balls needed to pack the space gives the number of bits needed to record the location of each data point z^i, up to the given precision.

choice of $\log\det(\cdot)$ seems to be rather fundamental and we will reveal many of its magical properties soon.

Rate Distortion of Data with a Mixed Distribution

In general, the features $\boldsymbol{Z}$ of multi-class data may belong to multiple low-dimensional subspaces. To evaluate the rate distortion of such mixed data *more accurately*, we may partition the data $\boldsymbol{Z}$ into multiple subsets, $\boldsymbol{Z} = \boldsymbol{Z}^1 \cup \cdots \cup \boldsymbol{Z}^k$, with each in one low-dimensional subspace. So the above coding rate (16.2.2) is accurate for each subset. For convenience, let $\boldsymbol{\Pi} = \{\boldsymbol{\Pi}^j \in \mathbb{R}^{m\times m}\}_{j=1}^k$ be a set of diagonal matrices whose diagonal entries encode the membership of the m samples in the k classes.[17] Then, according to [MDHW07], with respect to this partition, the average number of bits per sample (the coding rate) is

$$R^c(\boldsymbol{Z}, \varepsilon \mid \boldsymbol{\Pi}) \doteq \sum_{j=1}^{k} \frac{\operatorname{trace}\left(\boldsymbol{\Pi}^j\right)}{2m} \log\det\left(\boldsymbol{I} + \frac{d}{\operatorname{trace}\left(\boldsymbol{\Pi}^j\right)\varepsilon^2} \boldsymbol{Z}\boldsymbol{\Pi}^j\boldsymbol{Z}^*\right). \tag{16.2.3}$$

Notice that when $\boldsymbol{Z}$ is given, $R^c(\boldsymbol{Z}, \varepsilon \mid \boldsymbol{\Pi})$ is a concave function of $\boldsymbol{\Pi}$. The function $\log\det(\cdot)$ in the above expressions has long been known as an effective heuristic for rank minimization problems [FHB03], as we have explored in the exercises of Chapter 7. As it tightly characterizes the rate distortion of Gaussian or subspace-like distributions, finding the clustering $\boldsymbol{\Pi}$ that minimizes

$$\min_{\boldsymbol{\Pi}} R^c(\boldsymbol{Z}, \varepsilon \mid \boldsymbol{\Pi}) \tag{16.2.4}$$

has been shown to be very effective in clustering or classification of data with mixed low-dimensional (linear) structures [MDHW07, WTL$^+$08, KPCC15]. We will soon reveal a few surprisingly good properties of this function in the new context.

[17] More precisely, the diagonal entry $\boldsymbol{\Pi}^j(i,i)$ of $\boldsymbol{\Pi}^j$ indicates the probability of sample i belonging to class j. So $\boldsymbol{\Pi}$ lies in a simplex: $\Omega \doteq \{\boldsymbol{\Pi} \mid \boldsymbol{\Pi}^j \geq \boldsymbol{0},\ \boldsymbol{\Pi}^1 + \cdots + \boldsymbol{\Pi}^k = \boldsymbol{I}_{m\times m}\}$.

16.2.2 Principle of Maximal Coding Rate Reduction

On the one hand, in the supervised learning setting, $\boldsymbol{\Pi}$ is given in advance, and we would like to learn a good representation $\boldsymbol{Z}$. For learned features to be discriminative, features of different classes/clusters are preferred to be *maximally incoherent* to each other, similar to the notion of "incoherence" that we have studied in Chapter 3. Hence together they should span a space of the largest possible volume (or dimension) and the coding rate of the whole set $\boldsymbol{Z}$ should be as large as possible. On the other hand, learned features of the same class/cluster should be highly correlated and coherent. Hence, each class/cluster should only span a space (or subspace) of a very small volume and the coding rate should be as small as possible. Therefore, a good representation $\boldsymbol{Z}$ of $\boldsymbol{X}$ is one that, given a partition $\boldsymbol{\Pi}$ of $\boldsymbol{Z}$, achieves a large difference between the coding rate for the whole and the average rate for all the subsets:

$$\Delta R(\boldsymbol{Z}, \boldsymbol{\Pi}, \varepsilon) \doteq R(\boldsymbol{Z}, \varepsilon) - R^c(\boldsymbol{Z}, \varepsilon \mid \boldsymbol{\Pi}). \tag{16.2.5}$$

If we choose the feature mapping $\boldsymbol{z} = f(\boldsymbol{x}, \boldsymbol{\theta})$ to be a deep neural network, the overall process of the feature representation and the resulting rate reduction with respect to a certain partition $\boldsymbol{\Pi}$ can be illustrated by the following:

$$\boldsymbol{X} \xrightarrow{\ f(\boldsymbol{x}, \boldsymbol{\theta})\ } \boldsymbol{Z}(\boldsymbol{\theta}) \xrightarrow{\ \boldsymbol{\Pi}, \varepsilon\ } \Delta R(\boldsymbol{Z}(\boldsymbol{\theta}), \boldsymbol{\Pi}, \varepsilon). \tag{16.2.6}$$

Note that ΔR is *monotonic* in the scale of the features $\boldsymbol{Z}$. So to make the amount of reduction comparable between different representations,[18] we need to *normalize the scale* of the learned features, either by constraining the Frobenius norm of each class $\boldsymbol{Z}^j$ to scale with the number of features in $\boldsymbol{Z}^j \in \mathbb{R}^{d \times m_j}$, i.e., $\|\boldsymbol{Z}^j\|_F^2 = m_j$, or by normalizing each feature to be on the unit sphere, i.e., $\boldsymbol{z}^i \in \mathbb{S}^{d-1}$. This formulation offers a natural justification for the need of "batch normalization" in the practice of training deep neural networks [IS15]. An alternative, arguably simpler, way to normalize the scale of learned representations is to ensure that the mapping of each layer of the network is approximately *isometric* [QYW+20], as we have discussed in the previous subsection.

Once the representations are comparable, our goal becomes to learn a set of features $\boldsymbol{Z}(\boldsymbol{\theta}) = f(\boldsymbol{X}, \boldsymbol{\theta})$ and their partition $\boldsymbol{\Pi}$ (if not given in advance) such that they maximize the reduction between the coding rate of all features and that of the sum of features with respect to their classes:

$$\max_{\boldsymbol{\theta}, \boldsymbol{\Pi}} \Delta R\big(\boldsymbol{Z}(\boldsymbol{\theta}), \boldsymbol{\Pi}, \varepsilon\big) \doteq R(\boldsymbol{Z}(\boldsymbol{\theta}), \varepsilon) - R^c(\boldsymbol{Z}(\boldsymbol{\theta}), \varepsilon \mid \boldsymbol{\Pi}), \quad \text{s.t. } \boldsymbol{Z} \subset \mathbb{S}^{d-1}, \ \boldsymbol{\Pi} \in \Omega. \tag{16.2.7}$$

We refer to this as the principle of *maximal coding rate reduction* (MCR^2), an embodiment of a famous saying:

> "*The whole is greater than the sum of the parts.*" – Aristotle.

[18] Here different representations can be either representations associated with different network parameters or representations learned after different layers of the same deep network.

Note that for the clustering purpose alone, one may only care about the sign of ΔR for deciding whether to partition the data or not, which leads to the greedy clustering algorithm in [MDHW07].[19] Here to seek or learn the most discriminative representation, we further desire:

The whole is *maximally* greater than the sum of the parts!

REMARK 16.1. (Relationship to information gain) *The maximal coding rate reduction can be viewed as a generalization to* information gain *(IG), which aims to maximize the reduction of entropy of a random variable, say z, with respect to an observed attribute, say π:* $\max_{\pi}$ *$IG(z, \pi) \doteq H(z) - H(z \mid \pi)$, i.e., the* mutual information *between z and π [CT91]. Maximal information gain has been widely used in areas such as decision trees [Qui86]. However, MCR^2 is used differently in several ways: (1) One typical setting of MCR^2 is when the data class labels are given, i.e., Π is known; MCR^2 focuses on learning representations $z(\theta)$ rather than fitting labels. (2) In traditional settings of IG, the number of attributes in z cannot be so large and their values are discrete (typically binary). Here the "attributes" Π represent the probability of a multi-class partition for all samples and their values can even be continuous. (3) As mentioned before, entropy $H(z)$ or mutual information $I(z, \pi)$ [HFLM$^+$18] is not well defined for degenerate continuous distributions whereas the rate distortion $R(z, \epsilon)$ is and can be accurately and efficiently computed for (mixed) subspaces, at least.*

16.2.3 Properties of the Rate Reduction Function

In theory, the MCR^2 principle (16.2.7) benefits from great generalizability and can be applied to representations $\boldsymbol{Z}$ of *any* distributions with *any* attributes Π as long as the rates R and R^c for the distributions can be accurately and efficiently evaluated. The optimal representation $\boldsymbol{Z}_\star$ and partition $\Pi_\star$ should have some interesting geometric and statistical properties. We here reveal nice properties of the optimal representation with the special case of subspaces, which have many important uses in machine learning. When the desired representation for $\boldsymbol{Z}$ is multiple subspaces, the rates R and R^c in (16.2.7) are given by (16.2.2) and (16.2.3), respectively. Let us assume the maximal rate reduction is achieved at the optimal representation, denoted as $\boldsymbol{Z}_\star = \boldsymbol{Z}_\star^1 \cup \cdots \cup \boldsymbol{Z}_\star^k \subset \mathbb{R}^d$, with the dimension of each subspace $\operatorname{rank}\left(\boldsymbol{Z}_\star^j\right) \le d_j$. Then, one can show that $\boldsymbol{Z}_\star$ has the following desired properties (see [YCY$^+$20] for a formal statement and detailed proofs).

THEOREM 16.2. (Optimal representation (informal statement)) *Suppose $\boldsymbol{Z}_\star = \boldsymbol{Z}_\star^1 \cup \cdots \cup \boldsymbol{Z}_\star^k$ is the optimal solution that maximizes the rate reduction* (16.2.7). *We have the following.*

[19] Strictly speaking, in the context of clustering *finite* samples, one needs to use the more precise measure of the coding length mentioned earlier; see [MDHW07] for more details.

- Between-class discriminative*: As long as the ambient space is adequately large ($d \geq \sum_{j=1}^{k} d_j$), the subspaces are all orthogonal to each other, i.e., $(\mathbf{Z}_\star^i)^* \mathbf{Z}_\star^j = \mathbf{0}$ for $i \neq j$.*
- Maximally diverse representation*: As long as the coding precision is adequately high, i.e., $\varepsilon^4 < \min_j \left\{(m_j/m)(d^2/d_j^2)\right\}$, each subspace achieves its maximal dimension, i.e., $\operatorname{rank}\left(\mathbf{Z}_\star^j\right) = d_j$. In addition, the largest $d_j - 1$ singular values of $\mathbf{Z}_\star^j$ are equal.*

In other words, in the case of subspaces, the MCR^2 principle promotes embedding of data into multiple independent subspaces, with features distributed nearly *isotropically* in each subspace (except for possibly one dimension). In addition, among all such discriminative representations, it prefers the one with the highest dimensions in the ambient space.

REMARK 16.3. (Rate distortion $\log\det(\cdot)$ versus the nuclear norm) *To encourage the learned features to be incoherent between classes, the work of [LQMS18] has proposed to maximize the difference between the nuclear norm of the whole* $\mathbf{Z}$ *and its subsets* $\mathbf{Z}^j$, *called the* orthogonal low-rank embedding *(OLE) loss,*

$$\max_{\theta} \; OLE(\mathbf{Z}(\boldsymbol{\theta}), \boldsymbol{\Pi}) \doteq \|\mathbf{Z}(\boldsymbol{\theta})\|_* - \sum_{j=1}^{k} \|\mathbf{Z}^j(\boldsymbol{\theta})\|_*, \tag{16.2.8}$$

added as a regularizer to the cross-entropy loss (16.1.4). *As we have learned from Chapter 4, the nuclear norm* $\|\cdot\|_*$ *is a* nonsmooth convex *surrogate for low-rankedness, whereas* $\log\det(\cdot)$ *is* smooth concave *instead. One can show that, unlike the rate reduction* ΔR, *OLE is always* negative *and achieves the maximal value* 0 *when the subspaces are orthogonal, regardless of their dimensions. So in contrast to* ΔR, *this loss serves as a geometric heuristic for discriminativeness but does not promote diversity of the representation. In fact, OLE typically promotes learning one-dimensional representations per class [LQMS18], whereas MCR^2 encourages learning subspaces with maximal dimensions.*

REMARK 16.4. (Relation to contrastive learning) *If samples are* evenly *drawn from* k *classes, a randomly chosen pair* $(\boldsymbol{x}^i, \boldsymbol{x}^j)$ *has a high probability of belonging to different classes if* k *is large.*[20] *We may view the learned features of two samples together with their augmentations* $\mathbf{Z}^i$ *and* $\mathbf{Z}^j$ *as two classes. Then the rate reduction*

$$\Delta R^{ij} = R\left(\mathbf{Z}^i \cup \mathbf{Z}^j, \varepsilon\right) - \frac{1}{2}\left(R(\mathbf{Z}^i, \varepsilon) + R(\mathbf{Z}^j, \varepsilon)\right) \tag{16.2.9}$$

gives a "distance" measure for how far apart the two sample sets are. We may try to further "expand" pairs that likely belong to different classes. From Theorem 16.2, the (averaged) rate reduction ΔR^{ij} *is maximized when features from different samples are uncorrelated,* $(\mathbf{Z}^i)^* \mathbf{Z}^j = \mathbf{0}$ *(see Figure 16.4), and features* $\mathbf{Z}^i$ *from the same sample are highly correlated. Hence, when applied to sample pairs, MCR^2 naturally conducts the so-called* contrastive learning *[HCL06, OLV18, HFW$^+$19]. But MCR^2*

[20] For example, when $k \geq 100$, a random pair has a probability of 99% of belonging to different classes.

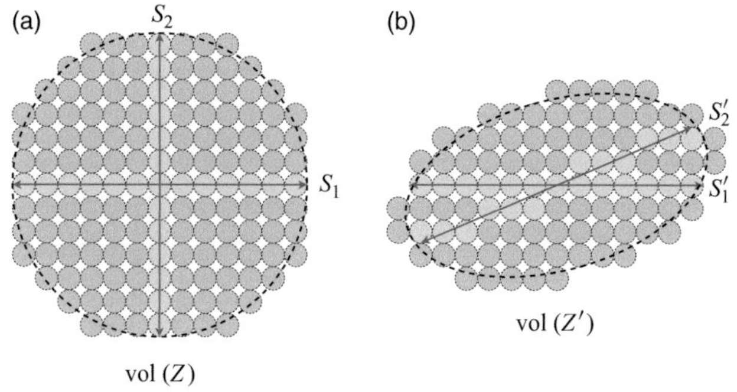

Figure 16.4 Comparison of two learned representations $\boldsymbol{Z}$ and $\boldsymbol{Z}'$ via reduced rates. R is the number of ε balls packed in the joint distribution and R^c is the sum of the numbers for all the subspaces (the green balls). ΔR is their difference (the number of blue balls). The MCR^2 principle prefers $\boldsymbol{Z}$ (the left one).

is not *limited to expand (or compress) pairs of samples and can uniformly conduct "contrastive learning" for a subset with* any number *of samples as long as we know they likely belong to different (or the same) classes, say by randomly sampling subsets from a large number of classes or with a good clustering method.*

16.2.4 Experiments on Real Data

When class labels are provided during training, we assign the membership (diagonal) matrix $\boldsymbol{\Pi} = \{\boldsymbol{\Pi}^j\}_{j=1}^k$ as follows: for each sample $\boldsymbol{x}^i$ with label j, set $\boldsymbol{\Pi}^j(i,i) = 1$ and $\boldsymbol{\Pi}^l(i,i) = 0$, for all $l \neq j$. Then the mapping $f(\cdot, \boldsymbol{\theta})$ can be learned by optimizing (16.2.7), where $\boldsymbol{\Pi}$ remains constant. We apply stochastic gradient descent to optimize MCR^2, and for each iteration we use mini-batch data $\{(\boldsymbol{x}^i, \boldsymbol{y}^i)\}_{i=1}^m$ to approximate the MCR^2 loss.

As we will see, in the supervised setting, the learned representation has very clear subspace structures. So to evaluate the learned representations, we consider a natural nearest subspace classifier. For each class of learned features $\boldsymbol{Z}^j$, let $\boldsymbol{\mu}_j \in \mathbb{R}^d$ be its mean and $\boldsymbol{U}_j \in \mathbb{R}^{d \times r_j}$ be the first r_j principal components for $\boldsymbol{Z}^j$, where r_j is the estimated dimension of class j. The predicted label of test data $\boldsymbol{x}'$ is given by[21] $j' = argmin_{j \in \{1,\dots,k\}} \|(\boldsymbol{I} - \boldsymbol{U}_j \boldsymbol{U}_j^*)(f(\boldsymbol{x}', \boldsymbol{\theta}) - \boldsymbol{\mu}_j)\|_2^2$.

We consider the CIFAR10 dataset [Kri09] and ResNet-18 [HZRS16] for $f(\cdot, \boldsymbol{\theta})$. We replace the last linear layer of ResNet-18 by a two-layer fully connected network with ReLU activation function such that the output dimension is 128. We set the mini-batch size as $m = 1000$ and the precision parameter $\varepsilon^2 = 0.5$.

[21] This is definitely not the best one can do to use the learned subspaces for classification. This particular classifier is chosen only for its simplicity.

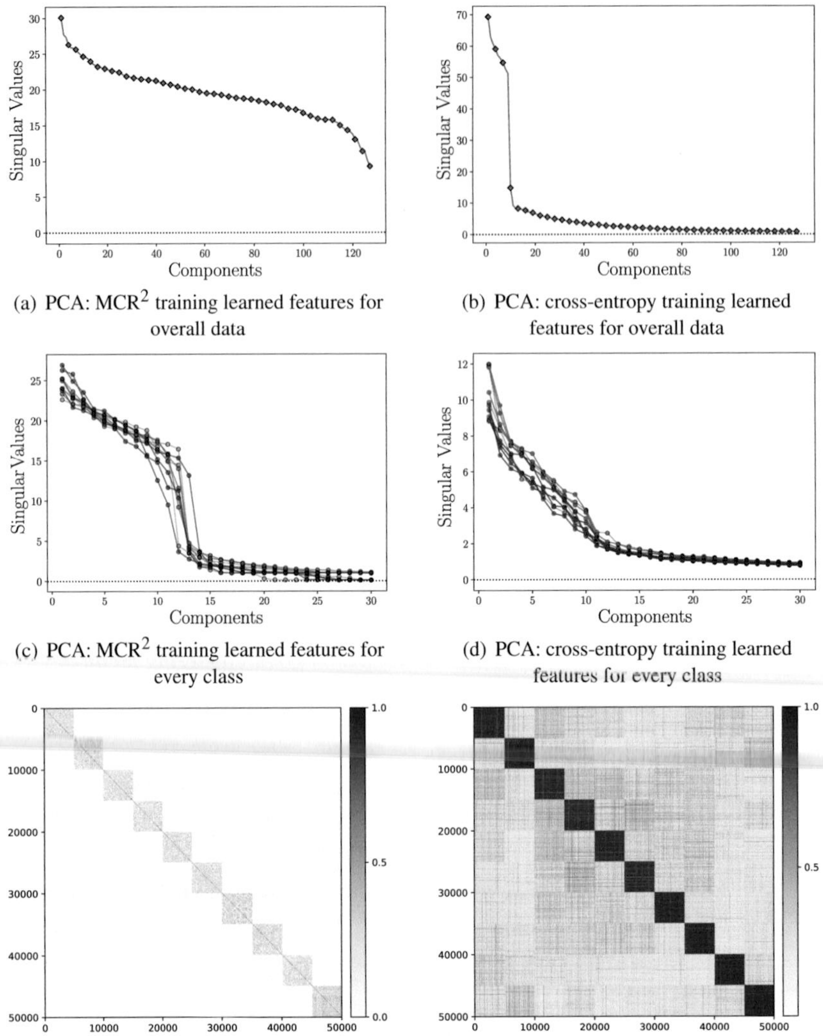

(a) PCA: MCR^2 training learned features for overall data

(b) PCA: cross-entropy training learned features for overall data

(c) PCA: MCR^2 training learned features for every class

(d) PCA: cross-entropy training learned features for every class

(e) Cosine similarity between features learned with the MCR^2 objective

(f) Cosine similarity between features learned with the CE loss

Figure 16.5 (a), (b) Principal component analysis (PCA) of features learned with the MCR^2 objective or the cross-entropy. (c), (d) Principal components of features in individual classes. (e), (f) Cosine similarity between learned features of all samples.

Discriminative and Diverse Linear Features

We calculate the principal components of representations learned by MCR^2 training and cross-entropy training (16.1.5). For cross-entropy training, we take the output of the second last layer as the learned representation. The results are summarized in Figure 16.5. As shown in Figure 16.5(a)–(d), we observe that representations learned by MCR^2 are much more diverse, the dimension of learned features (each class) is around a dozen, the dimension of the overall features is nearly 120, and the output

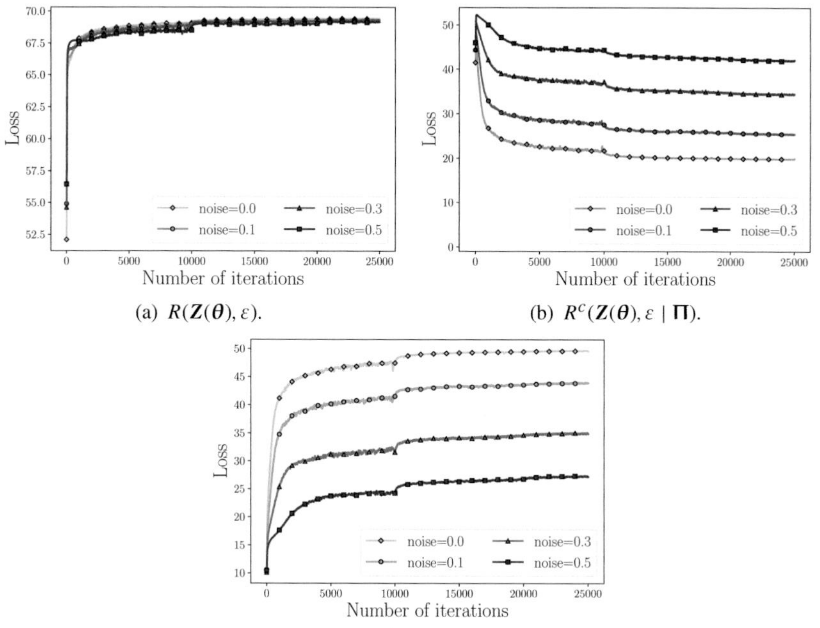

(a) $R(\boldsymbol{Z}(\boldsymbol{\theta}), \varepsilon)$.

(b) $R^c(\boldsymbol{Z}(\boldsymbol{\theta}), \varepsilon \mid \boldsymbol{\Pi})$.

(c) $\Delta R\big(\boldsymbol{Z}(\boldsymbol{\theta}), \boldsymbol{\Pi}, \varepsilon\big)$.

Figure 16.6 Evolution of rates R, R^c, and ΔR of MCR^2 during training with corrupted labels.

dimension is 128. In contrast, the dimension of the overall features learned using entropy is slightly greater than 10,[22] which is much smaller than that learned by MCR^2. For visualization purposes, we also compare the cosine similarity between learned representations for both MCR^2 training and cross-entropy training, and the results are presented in Figure 16.5(e) and (f). From Figure 16.5, for MCR^2, we find that the features of different classes are almost orthogonal and yet features of the same class are distributed rather evenly inside its subspace.

Robustness to Corrupted Labels

Because MCR^2 by design encourages richer representations that preserve intrinsic structures from the data $\boldsymbol{X}$, training relies less on class labels than traditional loss such as cross-entropy (CE). To verify this, we train the same network[23] using both CE and MCR^2 with certain ratios of *randomly corrupted* training labels. Figure 16.6 illustrates the learning process: for different levels of corruption, while the rate for the whole set always converges to the same value, the rates for the classes are inversely proportional to the ratio of corruption, indicating that the method only compresses samples with valid labels. The classification results are summarized in Table 16.1. By applying *exactly the same* training parameters, MCR^2 is significantly more robust than CE, especially with a higher ratio of corrupted labels. This can be an advantage

22 This observation is consistent with the *neural collapsing* phenomenon associated with a conventional loss function like cross-entropy reported in the recent work [PHD20].

23 Both CE and MCR^2 can have better performance by choosing larger models for the mapping.

Table 16.1. Classification results with features learned with labels corrupted at different levels.

Corrupt ratio	10%	20%	30%	40%	50%
CE training	90.91%	86.12%	79.15%	72.45%	60.37%
MCR^2 training	**91.16%**	**89.70%**	**88.18%**	**86.66%**	**84.30%**

in the settings of self-supervised learning or constrastive learning when the grouping information can be very noisy.

16.3 Deep Networks from First Principles

In the previous section, we have shown that the optimal representation $\mathbf{Z}_\star$ that maximizes the rate reduction would indeed be both maximally discriminative and informative. Nevertheless, we do not know what the optimal feature mapping $z = f(\boldsymbol{x}, \boldsymbol{\theta})$ is and how to obtain it. In the above experiments, we have adopted a conventional deep network (e.g., the ResNet) as a black box to model the mapping and learned its parameters via back propagation. It has empirically shown that, with such a choice, one can effectively optimize the MCR^2 objective and obtain discriminative and diverse representations for classifying real image datasets.

However, there are several unanswered questions. Although the objective is more intrinsic and the learned feature representation is arguably more interpretable, the network itself is still not interpretable. It is *not* clear why any chosen network is able to optimize the desired MCR^2 objective: would there be any potential limitations? The good empirical results (say with a ResNet) do not necessarily justify the particular choice in architectures and operators of the network: why is a layered deep model necessary in the first place? How wide and deep is adequate? And is there any rigorous justification for the particular convolutional and nonlinear operators used?

16.3.1 Deep Networks from Optimizing Rate Reduction

To simplify the presentation, we assume for now that the feature z and the input $\boldsymbol{x}$ have the same dimension $d = n$. But in general they can be different as we will soon see, say in the case z are multi-channel features extracted from $\boldsymbol{x}$.

Let us consider maximizing the rate reduction objective defined in (16.2.5):

$$\max_{\mathbf{Z}} \Delta R(\mathbf{Z}, \boldsymbol{\Pi}, \varepsilon) \doteq \underbrace{\frac{1}{2} \log\det\left(\boldsymbol{I} + \alpha \mathbf{Z}\mathbf{Z}^*\right)}_{R(\mathbf{Z},\varepsilon)} - \underbrace{\sum_{j=1}^{k} \frac{\gamma_j}{2} \log\det\left(\boldsymbol{I} + \alpha_j \mathbf{Z}\boldsymbol{\Pi}^j \mathbf{Z}^*\right)}_{R^c(\mathbf{Z},\varepsilon\mid\boldsymbol{\Pi})}, \tag{16.3.1}$$

where to simplify the notation we define $\alpha = n/(m\varepsilon^2)$, $\alpha_j = n/(\mathrm{tr}(\boldsymbol{\Pi}^j)\varepsilon^2)$, and $\gamma_j = \mathrm{tr}(\boldsymbol{\Pi}^j)/m$ for $j = 1, \ldots, k$.

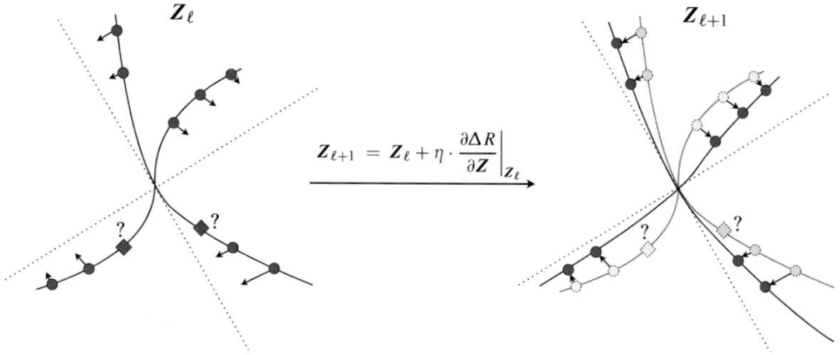

Figure 16.7 Incremental deformation of the training data, marked as "∘," via gradient flow. Notice that for points whose memberships are unknown, those marked as "⋄," their gradient cannot be directly calculated yet.

Gradient Ascent for Rate Reduction on the Training Samples

First let us directly try to optimize the objective $\Delta R(Z)$ as a function in the training samples $Z \subset \mathbb{S}^{n-1}$. To this end, we may adopt the simplest (projected) *gradient ascent* scheme (introduced in Chapter 2), for some step size $\eta > 0$:

$$Z_{\ell+1} \;\propto\; Z_\ell + \eta \cdot \frac{\partial \Delta R}{\partial Z}\bigg|_{Z_\ell} \quad \text{subject to} \quad Z_{\ell+1} \subset \mathbb{S}^{n-1}. \tag{16.3.2}$$

This scheme can be interpreted as how one should incrementally adjust locations of the current features Z_ℓ in order for the resulting $Z_{\ell+1}$ to improve the rate reduction $\Delta R(Z)$, as illustrated in Figure 16.7.

Simple calculation shows that the gradient $\partial \Delta R / \partial Z$ entails evaluating the following derivatives of the terms in (16.3.1) (we leave the derivation as an exercise for the reader):

$$\frac{1}{2}\frac{\partial \log\det(I + \alpha Z Z^*)}{\partial Z}\bigg|_{Z_\ell} = \underbrace{\alpha(I + \alpha Z_\ell Z_\ell^*)^{-1}}_{E_\ell \,\in \mathbb{R}^{n\times n}} Z_\ell, \tag{16.3.3}$$

$$\frac{1}{2}\frac{\partial\left(\gamma_j \log\det(I + \alpha_j Z \Pi^j Z^*)\right)}{\partial Z}\bigg|_{Z_\ell} = \gamma_j \underbrace{\alpha_j (I + \alpha_j Z_\ell \Pi^j Z_\ell^*)^{-1}}_{C_\ell^j \,\in \mathbb{R}^{n\times n}} Z_\ell \Pi^j. \tag{16.3.4}$$

Then the complete gradient $(\partial \Delta R / \partial Z)\big|_{Z_\ell}$ is of the following form:

$$\frac{\partial \Delta R}{\partial Z}\bigg|_{Z_\ell} = \underbrace{E_\ell}_{\text{expansion}} Z_\ell - \sum_{j=1}^{k} \gamma_j \underbrace{C_\ell^j}_{\text{compression}} Z_\ell \Pi^j \quad \in \mathbb{R}^{n\times m}. \tag{16.3.5}$$

Notice that in the above, the matrix E_ℓ only depends on Z_ℓ and it aims to *expand* all the features to increase the overall coding rate; the matrix C_ℓ^j depends on features from each class and aims to *compress* them to reduce the coding rate of each class.

Interpretation of the Two Linear Operators

For any z_ℓ we have

$$(\boldsymbol{I} + \alpha \boldsymbol{Z}_\ell \boldsymbol{Z}_\ell^*)^{-1} z_\ell = z_\ell - \boldsymbol{Z}_\ell \widehat{\boldsymbol{q}}_\ell, \tag{16.3.6}$$

where

$$\widehat{\boldsymbol{q}}_\ell \doteq \underset{\boldsymbol{q}_\ell}{argmin}\, \alpha \|z_\ell - \boldsymbol{Z}_\ell \boldsymbol{q}_\ell\|_2^2 + \|\boldsymbol{q}_\ell\|_2^2. \tag{16.3.7}$$

Notice that $\widehat{\boldsymbol{q}}_\ell$ is exactly the solution to the ridge regression of z_ℓ with all the data points $\boldsymbol{Z}_\ell$ as regressors. Therefore, $\boldsymbol{E}_\ell$ is approximately (i.e., when m is large enough) the projection onto the orthogonal complement of the subspace spanned by columns of $\boldsymbol{Z}_\ell$. Another way to interpret the matrix $\boldsymbol{E}_\ell$ is through eigenvalue decomposition of the covariance matrix $\boldsymbol{Z}_\ell \boldsymbol{Z}_\ell^*$. Assuming that $\boldsymbol{Z}_\ell \boldsymbol{Z}_\ell^* \doteq \boldsymbol{U}_\ell \boldsymbol{\Lambda}_\ell \boldsymbol{U}_\ell^*$, where $\boldsymbol{\Lambda}_\ell \doteq \mathrm{diag}\{\sigma_1, \ldots, \sigma_d\}$, we have

$$\boldsymbol{E}_\ell = \alpha\, \boldsymbol{U}_\ell\, \mathrm{diag}\left\{\frac{1}{1+\alpha\sigma_1}, \ldots, \frac{1}{1+\alpha\sigma_d}\right\} \boldsymbol{U}_\ell^*. \tag{16.3.8}$$

Therefore, the matrix $\boldsymbol{E}_\ell$ operates on a vector z_ℓ by stretching in such a way that directions of large variance are shrunk while directions of vanishing variance are kept. These are exactly the directions (16.3.3) in which we move the features so that the overall volume expands and the coding rate will increase, hence the positive sign in (16.3.5). $\boldsymbol{C}_\ell^j$ has a similar interpretation to $\boldsymbol{E}$. But to the opposite effect, the directions in (16.3.4) are "residuals" showing how the features of each class deviate from that class's subspace. These are exactly the directions in which the features need to be compressed back onto their respective subspace, hence the negative sign in (16.3.5). This is illustrated in Figure 16.8.

Essentially, the two linear operations are determined by data conducting "autoregressions" among themselves. The reader may recall that in the Introduction Chapter 1, we mentioned the importance of regressions, especially the ridge regression. As we now see, regression is very likely to be one of the ruling operations inside deep (neural) networks too. The recent renewed understanding about ridge

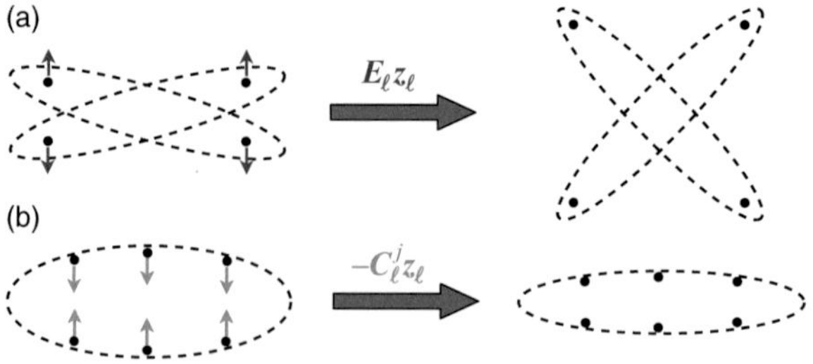

Figure 16.8 A little exaggerated interpretation of $\boldsymbol{E}_\ell$ and $\boldsymbol{C}_\ell^j$: $\boldsymbol{E}_\ell$ expands all features by contrasting and repelling features across different classes; $\boldsymbol{C}_\ell^j$ compresses each class by contracting the features to a low-dimensional subspace.

regression in an overparameterized setting [YYY+20, WX20] indicates that using seemingly redundantly sampled data (from each subspace) as regressors does not lead to overfitting.

Gradient Flow Guided Feature Map Increment

Notice that in the above, the gradient ascent considers all the features $Z_\ell = [z_\ell^1, \dots, z_\ell^m]$ as free variables. The increment $Z_{\ell+1} - Z_\ell = \eta(\partial \Delta R/\partial Z)\big|_{Z_\ell}$ does not yet give a transform on the entire feature domain $z_\ell \in \mathbb{R}^n$. This is because gradients at points not in the training cannot be computed from (16.3.5), as illustrated by points marked as "$\diamond$" in Figure 16.7. Hence, in order to find the optimal feature mapping $f(x, \theta)$ explicitly, we may consider constructing a small increment transform $g(\cdot, \theta_\ell)$ on the ℓ-th layer feature z_ℓ to emulate the above (projected) gradient scheme:

$$z_{\ell+1} \propto z_\ell + \eta \cdot g(z_\ell, \theta_\ell) \quad \text{subject to} \quad z_{\ell+1} \in \mathbb{S}^{n-1} \tag{16.3.9}$$

such that $\left[g(z_\ell^1, \theta_\ell), \dots, g(z_\ell^m, \theta_\ell)\right] \approx (\partial \Delta R/\partial Z)\big|_{Z_\ell}$. That is, we need to approximate the gradient flow $\partial \Delta R/\partial Z$ that locally deforms each (training) feature $\{z_\ell^i\}_{i=1}^m$ with a continuous mapping $g(z)$ defined on the entire feature space $z_\ell \in \mathbb{S}^{n-1}$.

By inspecting the structure of the gradient (16.3.5), it suggests that a natural candidate for the increment transform $g(z_\ell, \theta_\ell)$ is of the form

$$g(z_\ell, \theta_\ell) \doteq E_\ell z_\ell - \sum_{j=1}^{k} \gamma_j C_\ell^j z_\ell \pi^j(z_\ell) \quad \in \mathbb{R}^n, \tag{16.3.10}$$

where $\pi^j(z_\ell) \in [0, 1]$ indicates the probability of z_ℓ belonging to the j-th class.[24] Notice that the increment depends on: (1) a set of linear maps represented by E_ℓ and $\{C_\ell^j\}_{j=1}^k$ that depend only on statistics of all features Z_ℓ of the training; and (2) membership $\{\pi^j(z_\ell)\}_{j=1}^k$ of any feature z_ℓ.

Since we only have the membership π^j for the training samples, the function $g(\cdot)$ defined in (16.3.10) can only be evaluated on the training samples. To extrapolate the function $g(\cdot)$ to the entire feature space, we need to estimate $\pi^j(z_\ell)$ in its second term. In the conventional deep learning, this map is typically modeled as a deep network and learned from the training data, say via *back propagation*. Nevertheless, our goal here is not to learn a precise classifier $\pi^j(z_\ell)$ already. Instead, we only need a good enough estimate of the class information in order for $g(\cdot)$ to approximate the gradient $\partial \Delta R/\partial Z$ well.

From the previous geometric interpretation of the linear operators E_ℓ and C_ℓ^j, the term $p_\ell^j \doteq C_\ell^j z_\ell$ can be viewed as the projection of z_ℓ onto the orthogonal complement of each class j. Therefore, $\|p_\ell^j\|_2$ is small if z_ℓ is in class j and large otherwise. This motivates us to estimate its membership based on the following "softmax" function:

[24] Notice that on the training samples Z_ℓ, for which the memberships Π^j are known, the so-defined $g(z_\ell, \theta)$ gives exactly the values for the gradient $(\partial \Delta R/\partial Z)\big|_{Z_\ell}$.

$$\widehat{\pi}^j(z_\ell) \doteq \frac{\exp\left(-\lambda \|\boldsymbol{C}_\ell^j z_\ell\|\right)}{\sum_{j=1}^k \exp\left(-\lambda \|\boldsymbol{C}_\ell^j z_\ell\|\right)} \in [0,1]. \tag{16.3.11}$$

Hence the second term of (16.3.10) can be approximated by this estimated membership:[25]

$$\sum_{j=1}^{k} \gamma_j \boldsymbol{C}_\ell^j z_\ell \pi^j(z_\ell) \approx \sum_{j=1}^{k} \gamma_j \boldsymbol{C}_\ell^j z_\ell \cdot \widehat{\pi}^j(z_\ell) \doteq \sigma\Big([\boldsymbol{C}_\ell^1 z_\ell, \ldots, \boldsymbol{C}_\ell^k z_\ell]\Big), \tag{16.3.12}$$

which is denoted as a nonlinear operator $\sigma(\cdot)$ on outputs of the feature z_ℓ through k banks of filters: $[\boldsymbol{C}_\ell^1, \ldots, \boldsymbol{C}_\ell^k]$. Notice that the nonlinearity arises due to a "soft" assignment of class membership based on the feature responses from those filters. Overall, combining (16.3.9), (16.3.10), and (16.3.12), the increment feature transform from z_ℓ to $z_{\ell+1}$ now becomes

$$z_{\ell+1} \;\propto\; z_\ell + \eta \cdot \boldsymbol{E}_\ell z_\ell - \eta \cdot \sigma\Big([\boldsymbol{C}_\ell^1 z_\ell, \ldots, \boldsymbol{C}_\ell^k z_\ell]\Big) \quad \text{s.t.} \quad z_{\ell+1} \in \mathbb{S}^{n-1}, \tag{16.3.13}$$

with the nonlinear function $\sigma(\cdot)$ defined above and $\boldsymbol{\theta}_\ell$ collecting all the layer-wise parameters including $\boldsymbol{E}_\ell, \boldsymbol{C}_\ell^j, \gamma_j$, and λ. Note that features at each layer are always "normalized" onto a sphere $\mathbb{S}^{n-1}$, denoted as $\mathcal{P}_{\mathbb{S}^{n-1}}$. The form of increment in (16.3.13) can be illustrated by the diagram in Figure 16.9(a).

Deep Network from Rate Reduction

Notice that the increment is constructed to emulate the gradient ascent for the rate reduction ΔR. Hence by transforming the features iteratively via the above process, we expect the rate reduction to increase, as we will see in the experimental section. This iterative process, once converged say after L iterations, gives the desired feature map $f(\boldsymbol{x}, \boldsymbol{\theta})$ on the input $z_0 = \boldsymbol{x}$, precisely in the form of a *deep network*, in which each layer has the structure shown in Figure 16.9(a):

$$f(\boldsymbol{x}, \boldsymbol{\theta}) = \phi^L \circ \phi^{L-1} \circ \cdots \circ \phi^0(\boldsymbol{x}) \tag{16.3.14}$$

with

$$\phi^\ell(z_\ell, \boldsymbol{\theta}_\ell) \doteq \mathcal{P}_{\mathbb{S}^{n-1}}[z_\ell + \eta \cdot g(z_\ell, \boldsymbol{\theta}_\ell)]. \tag{16.3.15}$$

As this deep network is derived from maximizing the rate **reduc**ed, we call it the ReduNet. Notice that all parameters of the network are explicitly constructed layer by layer in a *forward propagation* fashion. Once constructed, there is no need of any additional supervised learning, say via back propagation. As we will see in the experiments, the so-learned features can be directly used for classification, say via a nearest subspace classifier.

[25] The choice of the softmax is mostly for its simplicity, as it is widely used in other (forward components of) deep networks for selection purposes, such as gating [SMM+17, FZS21] and routing [SFH17]. In principle, this term can be approximated by other operators, say using ReLU that is more amenable to training with back propagation; see Exercise 16.3.

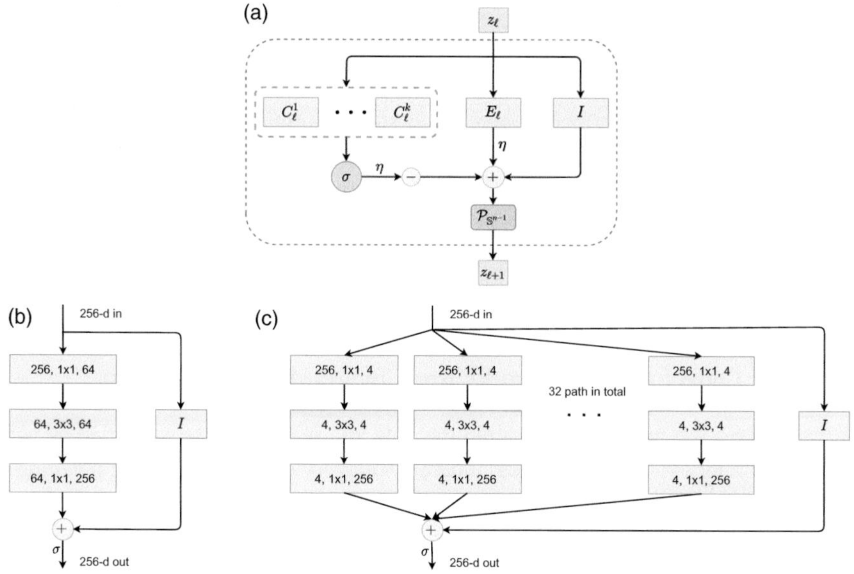

Figure 16.9 Comparison of network architectures. (a) Layer structure of the ReduNet derived from one iteration of gradient ascent for optimizing rate reduction. (b) A layer of ResNet [HZRS16]. (c) A layer of ResNeXt [XGD+17]. As we will see in the next section, the linear operators $\boldsymbol{E}_\ell$ and $\boldsymbol{C}_\ell^j$ of the ReduNet naturally become (multi-channel) convolutions when shift invariance is imposed.

Comparison with Other Approaches and Architectures

As we have mentioned earlier, structural similarities between deep networks and iterative optimization schemes, especially those for solving sparse coding, have long been observed. For example, in the work of learned ISTA [GL10], one may view a fixed number of iterations of the ISTA Algorithm 8.1 as layers of a network. One can then use the back propagation to refine the parameters (say $\boldsymbol{A}$ in each layer) to improve the convergence or accuracy of the resulting sparse codes. Later [GEBS18, MLE19, SNT20] proposed a similar interpretation of deep networks as unrolling algorithms for sparse coding.

Like all networks that are inspired by unfolding certain iterative optimization schemes, the structure of the ReduNet naturally contains a skip connection between adjacent layers as in the ResNet [HZRS16] (see Figure 16.9(b)). Nevertheless, the remaining $K+1$ parallel channels $\boldsymbol{E}, \{\boldsymbol{C}^j\}_{j=1}^K$ of the ReduNet actually draw resemblance to the parallel structures that people later found empirically beneficial for deep networks, e.g., ResNeXt [XGD+17] (see Figure 16.9(c)) or the mixture of experts (MoE) module adopted in the latest large-scale language models [SMM+17, FZS21], in which the number of parallel banks (or experts) K can be in the thousands and the number of parameters can be in the billions and even trillions.

A major difference here is that these conventional networks are all found empirically or designed heuristically whereas all components (layers, operators, and parameters) of the ReduNet architecture are by explicit construction from the objective of maximizing the rate reduction ΔR. All operators have precise optimization, statistical, and geometric interpretation consistent with the objective. Notice that even values of the parameters in the ReduNet can be constructed in a forward propagation manner, although in principle one could still fine-tune the ReduNet with back propagation if needed (as we will discuss more in the epilogue, Section 16.5 of this chapter). Furthermore, as the ReduNet architecture is based on choosing arguably the simplest gradient ascent scheme (16.3.2), we can expect that the more advanced optimization schemes introduced in Chapters 8 and 9 can lead to new architectures with improved efficiency (see Exercise 16.6 for a possible extension).

16.3.2 Convolutional Networks from Invariant Rate Reduction

So far, we have considered the data and features to be classified as vectors. In many applications, such as serial data or imagery data, the semantic meaning (labels) of the data and their features are *invariant* to certain transformations $\mathfrak{g} \in \mathbb{G}$ (for some group $\mathbb{G}$). For example, the meaning of an audio signal is invariant to shift in time; and the identity of an object in an image is invariant to translation in the image plane.[26] Hence, we prefer the feature mapping $f(\boldsymbol{x}, \boldsymbol{\theta})$ to be invariant to such transformations:

$$\textit{group invariance} \quad f(\boldsymbol{x} \circ \mathfrak{g}, \boldsymbol{\theta}) \sim f(\boldsymbol{x}, \boldsymbol{\theta}), \quad \forall\, \mathfrak{g} \in \mathbb{G}, \tag{16.3.16}$$

where "$\sim$" indicates two features belonging to the same equivalence class. The submanifolds associated with such equivalence classes are known to have sophisticated geometric and topological structures [WDCB05]. This may explain why it has been very challenging for empirically designed deep networks to ensure invariance to even simple transformations such as translation and rotation [AW18, ETT+17].[27]

In this section, we show that the MCR^2 principle is compatible with invariance in a very natural and rigorous way: we only need to assign all transformed versions $\{\boldsymbol{x} \circ \mathfrak{g} \mid \mathfrak{g} \in \mathbb{G}\}$ into the same class as $\boldsymbol{x}$ and map them all to the same subspace $\mathcal{S}$.[28] See Figure 16.10 for an illustration of the examples of 1D rotation and 2D translation. Then one can show that, when the group $\mathbb{G}$ is (discrete) circular 1D shifting or 2D translation, the resulting deep network, the ReduNet, naturally becomes a *multi-channel convolutional network*!

1D Serial Data and Shift Invariance

For one-dimensional data $\boldsymbol{x} \in \mathbb{R}^n$ under shift symmetry, we take $\mathbb{G}$ to be the group of circular shifts. Each observation $\boldsymbol{x}^i$ generates a family $\{\boldsymbol{x}^i \circ \mathfrak{g} \mid \mathfrak{g} \in \mathbb{G}\}$ of shifted copies, which are the columns of the circulant matrix $\mathsf{circ}(\boldsymbol{x}^i) \in \mathbb{R}^{n \times n}$ (see Appendix A.7 or [KS12] for the properties of circulant matrices).

[26] The transform-invariant textures (TILT) studied in the previous Chapter 15 are examples with more general groups of transformations, such as 2D affine transform or homography.

[27] Recent study has started to reveal necessary conditions for a deep network to be invariant or equivariant to certain group transforms [CW16, CGW19].

[28] Hence, any subsequent classifiers defined on the resulting set of subspaces will be automatically invariant to such transformations.

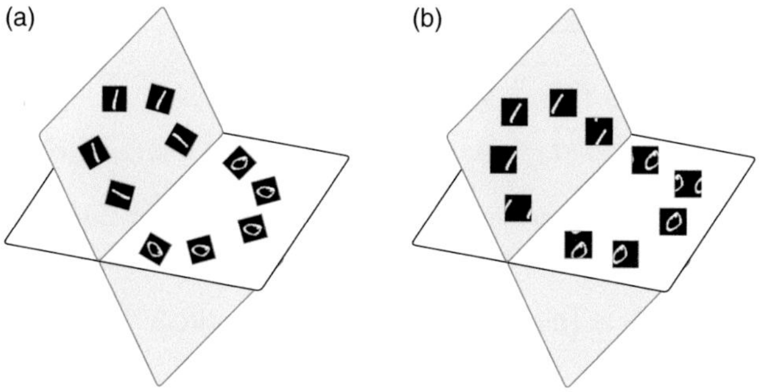

Figure 16.10 Illustration of the sought representation that is equivariant/invariant to image rotation (a) or translation (b). All transformed images of each class are mapped into the same subspace that is incoherent to other subspaces. The features embedded in each subspace are equivariant to transformation group whereas each subspace is invariant to such transformations.

What happens if we construct the ReduNet from these families:

$$\boldsymbol{Z}_1 = \Big[\mathrm{circ}(\boldsymbol{x}^1), \ldots, \mathrm{circ}(\boldsymbol{x}^m)\Big]?$$

The data covariance matrix

$$\begin{aligned}\boldsymbol{Z}_1\boldsymbol{Z}_1^* &= \Big[\mathrm{circ}(\boldsymbol{x}^1), \ldots, \mathrm{circ}(\boldsymbol{x}^m)\Big]\Big[\mathrm{circ}(\boldsymbol{x}^1), \ldots, \mathrm{circ}(\boldsymbol{x}^m)\Big]^* \\ &= \sum_{i=1}^{m} \mathrm{circ}(\boldsymbol{x}^i)\mathrm{circ}(\boldsymbol{x}^i)^* \ \in \mathbb{R}^{n\times n}\end{aligned}$$

associated with this family of samples is *automatically* a (symmetric) circulant matrix. Moreover, because the circulant property is preserved under sums, inverses, and products (see Appendix A.7), the matrices $\boldsymbol{E}_1$ and $\boldsymbol{C}_1^j$ are also automatically circulant matrices, whose application to a feature vector $\boldsymbol{z}$ can be implemented using cyclic convolution "$\circledast$." Specifically, we have the following proposition.

PROPOSITION 16.5. (Convolution structures of $\boldsymbol{E}_1$ and $\boldsymbol{C}_1^j$) *The matrix* $\boldsymbol{E}_1 = \alpha\big(\boldsymbol{I} + \alpha\boldsymbol{Z}_1\boldsymbol{Z}_1^*\big)^{-1}$ *is a circulant matrix and represents a circular convolution,*

$$\boldsymbol{E}_1\boldsymbol{z} = \boldsymbol{e}_1 \circledast \boldsymbol{z},$$

where $\boldsymbol{e}_1 \in \mathbb{R}^n$ *is the first column vector of* $\boldsymbol{E}_1$ *and "*$\circledast$*" is cyclic convolution defined as*

$$(\boldsymbol{e}_1 \circledast \boldsymbol{z})_i \doteq \sum_{j=0}^{n-1} e_1(j)x(i+n-j \bmod n). \tag{16.3.17}$$

Similarly, the matrices $\boldsymbol{C}_1^j$ *associated with any subsets of* $\boldsymbol{Z}_1$ *are also circular convolutions.*

From Proposition 16.5, we have

$$\begin{aligned} z_2 &\propto z_1 + \eta \cdot g(z_1, \boldsymbol{\theta}_1) \\ &= z_1 + \eta \cdot \boldsymbol{e}_1 \circledast z_1 - \eta \cdot \sigma\Big([\boldsymbol{c}_1^1 \circledast z_1, \ldots, \boldsymbol{c}_1^k \circledast z_1]\Big). \end{aligned} \tag{16.3.18}$$

Because $g(\cdot, \boldsymbol{\theta}_1)$ consists only of operations that co-vary with cyclic shifts, the features $\boldsymbol{Z}_2$ at the next level again consist of families of shifts:

$$\boldsymbol{Z}_2 = \big[\mathsf{circ}(\boldsymbol{x}^1 + \eta g(\boldsymbol{x}^1, \boldsymbol{\theta}_1)), \ldots, \mathsf{circ}(\boldsymbol{x}^m + \eta g(\boldsymbol{x}^m, \boldsymbol{\theta}_1))\big]. \tag{16.3.19}$$

Continuing inductively, we see that all matrices $\boldsymbol{E}_\ell$ and $\boldsymbol{C}_\ell^j$ based on such $\boldsymbol{Z}_\ell$ are circulant. By virtue of the equivariant properties of the data, the ReduNet has taken the form of a convolutional network, *with no need to explicitly choose this structure!*

The Role of Multiple Channels

There is one problem though: in general, the set of all circular permutations of a vector $\boldsymbol{x}$ give a full-rank matrix. That is, the n "augmented" features associated with each sample (hence each class) typically already span the entire space $\mathbb{R}^n$. The MCR^2 objective (16.3.1) will not be able to distinguish classes as different subspaces.

One natural remedy is to improve the separability of the data by "lifting" the signals $\boldsymbol{x}$ to a higher-dimensional space,[29] e.g., by taking their responses to multiple filters $\boldsymbol{k}_1, \ldots, \boldsymbol{k}_C \in \mathbb{R}^n$:

$$z[c] = \boldsymbol{k}_c \circledast \boldsymbol{x} = \mathsf{circ}(\boldsymbol{k}_c)\boldsymbol{x} \in \mathbb{R}^n, \quad c = 1, \ldots, C. \tag{16.3.20}$$

The filters can be predesigned invariance-promoting filters,[30] or adaptively learned from the data,[31] or randomly selected as we do in the experiments. This operation lifts each original signal (vector) $z \in \mathbb{R}^n$ to a C-channel feature vector, denoted $\bar{z} \doteq [z[1], \ldots, z[C]]^* \in \mathbb{R}^{C \times n}$. If we stack the multiple channels of a feature $\bar{z}$ as a column vector $\mathrm{vec}(\bar{z}) \in \mathbb{R}^{nC}$, the associated circulant version $\mathsf{circ}(\bar{z}) \in \mathbb{R}^{nC \times n}$ and its data covariance matrix, denoted as $\bar{\boldsymbol{\Sigma}} \in \mathbb{R}^{nC \times nC}$, for all its shifted versions are given as

$$\mathsf{circ}(\bar{z}) \doteq \begin{bmatrix} \mathsf{circ}(z[1]) \\ \vdots \\ \mathsf{circ}(z[C]) \end{bmatrix}, \quad \bar{\boldsymbol{\Sigma}} \doteq \begin{bmatrix} \mathsf{circ}(z[1]) \\ \vdots \\ \mathsf{circ}(z[C]) \end{bmatrix} \big[\mathsf{circ}(z[1])^*, \ldots, \mathsf{circ}(z[C])^*\big], \tag{16.3.21}$$

where $\mathsf{circ}(z[c]) \in \mathbb{R}^{n \times n}$ with $c \in [C]$ is the circulant version of the c-th channel of the feature $\bar{z}$. Then the columns of $\mathsf{circ}(\bar{z})$ will only span at most an n-dimensional proper subspace in $\mathbb{R}^{nC}$.

[29] There is evidence in neuroscience that suggests such an expansion of dimension brings benefits to cognition [FMR16].

[30] For 1D signals like audio, one may consider the conventional short-time Fourier transform (STFT); for 2D images, one may consider 2D wavelets as in the ScatteringNet [BM13].

[31] For learned filters, one can learn filters from the given data as the principal components of samples as in the PCANet [CJG+15] or from convolution dictionary learning [LB19, QLZ19].

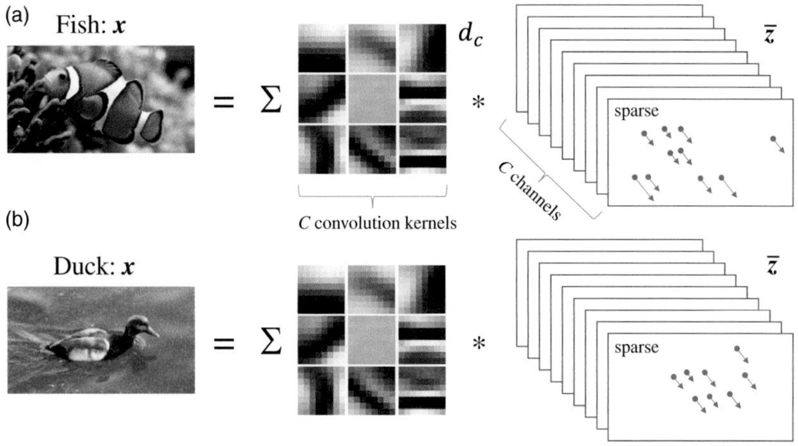

Figure 16.11 Each input signal $\boldsymbol{x}$ (an image here) can be represented as a superposition of sparse convolutions with multiple kernels $\boldsymbol{d}_c$ in a dictionary $\boldsymbol{D}$.

Tradeoff between Invariance and Sparsity

However, this simple (linear) lifting operation is not sufficient to render the classes separable still – features associated with other classes will likely span the *same* n-dimensional subspace in the lifted space. This reflects a fundamental conflict between linear (subspace) modeling and invariance: on the one hand, we desire the resulting representation to be linear, hence superposition of features of signals (including their shifted versions) in the same class remain in the same subspace (in the lifted feature space); on the other hand, we want that features of signals in different classes can be separated and belong to different (incoherent) subspaces.

One way, and probably the only way, to resolve this conflict is to impose additional structures on signals in each class, in the form of *sparsity*. We may assume that all signals $\boldsymbol{x}$ (including their shifted versions) within each class j are generated by only *sparse* combinations of shifted atoms (or motifs) in a dictionary $\boldsymbol{D}_j$:

$$\boldsymbol{x} = \mathsf{circ}(\boldsymbol{D}_j)\boldsymbol{z}_j \tag{16.3.22}$$

for some sparse $\boldsymbol{z}_j$, as shown in Figure 16.11.[32]

Furthermore, we assume the dictionaries $\boldsymbol{D} = \{\boldsymbol{D}_j\}_{j=1}^k$ between the k classes are mutually incoherent. Hence signals in one class are unlikely to be sparsely represented by atoms in any other class. Then, all signals in the k classes can be sparsely represented by all the dictionaries together:

$$\boldsymbol{x} = \left[\mathsf{circ}(\boldsymbol{D}_1), \mathsf{circ}(\boldsymbol{D}_2), \ldots, \mathsf{circ}(\boldsymbol{D}_k)\right]\bar{\boldsymbol{z}}, \tag{16.3.23}$$

for some sparse $\bar{\boldsymbol{z}}$ which encodes the membership of the signal $\boldsymbol{x}$ with respect to the k classes. The reader may have recognized that this model is very similar to the face

[32] In practice, one can further assume the atoms are "short" (or have small supports) so that the generative model is similar to the "short-and-sparse" model that we have studied in Chapter 12.

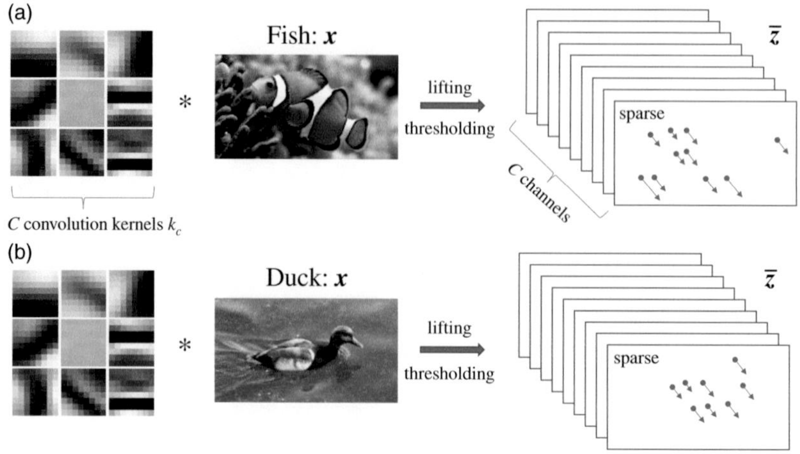

Figure 16.12 Estimate the sparse code $\bar{z}$ of an input signal $\boldsymbol{x}$ (an image here) by taking convolutions with multiple kernels $\boldsymbol{k}_c$ and then sparsifying.

recognition setting that we have seen in Chapter 13. There is a vast literature on how to learn the most compact and optimal sparsifying dictionaries from sample data, as we have touched upon before in Chapters 7, 9, and 12. One may also refer to [LB19, QLZ19] for more references on this subject.

Nevertheless, here we are not interested in the precise optimal sparse code for every individual signal. We are only interested in whether the set of sparse codes for each class are collectively separable from those of other classes.[33] Under the assumption of the sparse generative model, if the convolution kernels $\{\boldsymbol{k}_c\}$ match well with the "transpose" or "inverse" of the above sparsifying dictionaries, also known as the *analysis filters* [NDEG13, RE14], signals in one class will only have high responses to a small subset of those filters and low responses to others (due to the incoherence assumption). Figure 16.12 illustrates the basic ideas. Nevertheless, in practice, often a sufficient number of random filters suffice for the purpose of ensuring that features of different classes have different response patterns to different filters, hence make different classes separable [CJG$^+$15]. We will use the simple random filter design in the experiments to verify the concept.[34]

Hence the multi-channel responses $\bar{z}$ should be sparse. So to approximate the sparse code $\bar{z}$, we may take an entry-wise *sparsity-promoting nonlinear thresholding*, say $\tau(\cdot)$, on the filter outputs by setting low (say absolute value below ε) or negative responses to be zero:[35]

[33] Note that this is rather different from our goal of computing sparse codes in earlier chapters of this book.

[34] Better sparse coding schemes may surely lead to better classification performance, though at a higher computational cost for learning or designing the filters and computing the sparse codes more precisely.

[35] The reader should be aware that, besides the feature scale normalization and membership assignment operation, this is the third, and final, type of nonlinear operation that we have encountered.

$$\bar{z} = \tau\big[\text{circ}(\boldsymbol{k}_1)\boldsymbol{x}, \ldots, \text{circ}(\boldsymbol{k}_C)\boldsymbol{x}\big] \quad \in \mathbb{R}^{n\times C}. \tag{16.3.24}$$

One may refer to [RE14] for a more systematic study on the design of the sparsifying thresholding operator. Nevertheless, here we are not so interested in obtaining the best sparse codes as long as the codes for different classes are sufficiently separable. Hence the nonlinear operator $\boldsymbol{\tau}(\cdot)$ can be simply chosen to be a soft thresholding or a ReLU. These presumably highly sparse features $\bar{z}$ can be assumed to lie on a lower-dimensional submanifold in $\mathbb{R}^{n\times C}$, which can be linearized and separated from the other classes by subsequent ReduNet layers.

The ReduNet constructed from the circulant version of these multi-channel features $\bar{z}$ retains the good invariance properties described above: the linear operators, now denoted as $\bar{\boldsymbol{E}}$ and $\bar{\boldsymbol{C}}^j \in \mathbb{R}^{nC\times nC}$ as they are computed from the lifted and sparsified features $\bar{z}$, remain block circulant. Hence, they represent *multi-channel 1D circular convolutions* (see [CYY+20] for a rigorous statement and proof):

$$\bar{\boldsymbol{E}}(\bar{z}) = \bar{\boldsymbol{e}} \circledast \bar{z}, \quad \bar{\boldsymbol{C}}^j(\bar{z}) = \bar{\boldsymbol{c}}^j \circledast \bar{z} \quad \in \mathbb{R}^{n\times C}, \quad j = 1, \ldots, k, \tag{16.3.25}$$

where $\bar{\boldsymbol{e}}, \bar{\boldsymbol{c}}^j \in \mathbb{R}^{C\times C\times n}$ are the associated multi-channel convolution kernels. Hence by virtue of the equivariant data structures, the resulting ReduNet is naturally a deep convolutional network for multi-channel 1D signals. Notice that the number of channels remains constant through the layers (or iterations).

Fast Computation in the Spectral Domain

Since all circulant matrices can be simultaneously diagonalized by the discrete Fourier transform (DFT) matrix[36] $\boldsymbol{F}$, $\text{circ}(z) = \boldsymbol{F}^*\boldsymbol{D}\boldsymbol{F}$ (see Theorem A.32 in Appendix A.7), all $\bar{\boldsymbol{\Sigma}}$ of the form (16.3.21) can be converted to a standard "blocks of diagonals" form:

$$\bar{\boldsymbol{\Sigma}} = \begin{bmatrix} \boldsymbol{F}^* & \boldsymbol{0} & \boldsymbol{0} \\ \boldsymbol{0} & \ddots & \boldsymbol{0} \\ \boldsymbol{0} & \boldsymbol{0} & \boldsymbol{F}^* \end{bmatrix} \begin{bmatrix} \boldsymbol{D}_{11} & \cdots & \boldsymbol{D}_{1C} \\ \vdots & \ddots & \vdots \\ \boldsymbol{D}_{C1} & \cdots & \boldsymbol{D}_{CC} \end{bmatrix} \begin{bmatrix} \boldsymbol{F} & \boldsymbol{0} & \boldsymbol{0} \\ \boldsymbol{0} & \ddots & \boldsymbol{0} \\ \boldsymbol{0} & \boldsymbol{0} & \boldsymbol{F} \end{bmatrix} \in \mathbb{R}^{nC\times nC}, \tag{16.3.26}$$

where each block $\boldsymbol{D}_{kl}$ is an $n \times n$ diagonal matrix. The middle of the right-hand side of (16.3.26) is a block diagonal matrix after a permutation of rows and columns. There are n blocks of size $C \times C$. Hence, to compute $\bar{\boldsymbol{E}}$ and $\bar{\boldsymbol{C}}^j \in \mathbb{R}^{nC\times nC}$, we only have to compute in the frequency domain the inverse of $C \times C$ blocks for n times and the overall complexity would be $O(nC^3)$ instead of $O((nC)^3)$ for inverting a generic $nC \times nC$ matrix. Notice that the advantage of the spectral domain would not have been as significant had the computation of the operators $\bar{\boldsymbol{E}}$ and $\bar{\boldsymbol{C}}^j$ not involved the matrix inverse. We leave this as an exercise for the reader (Exercise 16.5).

2D Images and Translation Invariance

In the case of classifying images invariant to arbitrary 2D translation, we may view the image (feature) $\bar{z} \in \mathbb{R}^{(W\times H)\times C}$ as a function defined on a torus $\mathcal{T}^2$ (discretized as a

[36] Here we scaled the matrix $\boldsymbol{F}$ to be unitary, hence it differs from the conventional DFT matrix by a factor $1/\sqrt{n}$.

$W \times H$ grid) and consider $\mathbb{G}$ to be the (Abelian) group of all 2D (circular) translations on the torus. See Figure 16.18 for an illustration and example. Analogous to the 1D case, the associated linear operators $\bar{\boldsymbol{E}}$ and the $\bar{\boldsymbol{C}}^j$ act on the image feature $\bar{z}$ as *multi-channel 2D circular convolutions*. The resulting network will be a deep convolutional network that shares the same multi-channel convolution structures as conventional convolutional neural networks (CNNs) for 2D images [LJB$^+$95, KSH12]. The difference is that, again, the architecture of the network and parameters of the convolutions are all derived from the rate reduction objective, including the (layer) normalization and the nonlinear activations $\widehat{\pi}^j$ and τ. Again, one can show that this multi-channel 2D convolutional network can be constructed more efficiently in the spectral domain (see [CYY$^+$20] for a rigorous statement and proof). One may see [CYY$^+$20] for implementation details of such a ReduNet in the spectral domain, for translation invariance of both 1D serial data and 2D imagery data.

Connections to Convolutional and Recurrent Sparse Coding

We see from above that, in order to find a discriminative linear representation for multiple classes of signals/images that is invariant to translation, sparse coding via lifting, a multilayer architecture with multi-channel convolutions, and spectrum computing all become necessary components for achieving the objective effectively and efficiently. Figure 16.13 illustrates the whole process of learning such a representation via invariant rate reduction on the input sparse codes. Conceptual and algorithmic similarities between sparse coding and deep networks have long been observed, especially in the work of learned ISTA [GL10]. It was later extended to be convolutional for imagery data or recurrent networks for serial data, e.g., [WPPA16, PRE16, SPRE18, MLE19]. Although both sparsity and convolution have been widely advocated as desired characteristics for deep networks, their precise roles for the classification task have never been clearly revealed nor justified. For instance, using convolutional operators to ensure equivarience has been common practice in deep networks [LB95a,

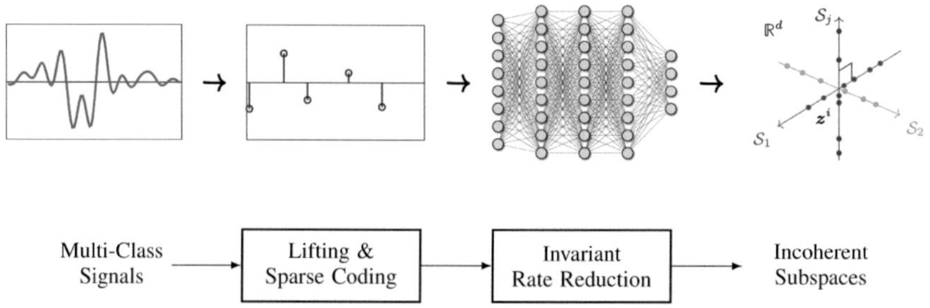

Figure 16.13 Overview of the process for classifying multi-class signals with shift invariance: multi-channel lifting and sparse coding followed by a (convolutional) ReduNet for invariant rate reduction. These operations are *necessary* to map shift-invariant multi-class signals to incoherent (linear) subspaces. Note that the architectures of most modern deep neural networks resemble this process.

CW16], but the number of convolutions needed is not clear and their parameters need to be learned via back propagation from randomly initialized ones. Of course, one may also predesign convolution filters of each layer to ensure translational invariance for a wide range of signals, say using wavelets as in ScatteringNet [BM13] and many follow-up works [WB18]. However, the number of convolutions needed usually grows exponentially with the number of layers. That is the reason why ScatteringNet type networks cannot be so deep, usually only 2–3 layers. It has never been clear in these frameworks how to design multi-channel convolutions. In contrast, in the rate reduction framework, we see that the roles of the multi-channel convolutions $(\bar{\boldsymbol{E}}, \bar{\boldsymbol{C}}^j)$ are explicitly derived and justified, the number of filters (channels) remains constant through all layers, and their parameters are determined by the data of interest.[37] As we see from the above derivation, both the convolution filters and sparsity requirements are *necessary* for success in the objective: incrementally learning a discriminative linear representation that is invariant to translation.

16.3.3 Simulations and Experiments

We now *verify* whether the so-constructed ReduNet achieves its design objectives through some basic experiments on synthetic data and real images. The datasets and experiments are chosen to clearly demonstrate the behaviors of the networks obtained this way, in terms of learning the correct discriminative representation and achieving invariance. Although these basic and early experiments are very promising, it remains active and exciting research to further improve the performance and scalability of such networks in practice. We will leave some of the discussions to the epilogue of this chapter.

Simulation: Learning Mixture of Gaussians in $\mathbb{S}^2$

We consider a mixture of three Gaussian distributions in $\mathbb{R}^3$ with means $\boldsymbol{\mu}_1, \boldsymbol{\mu}_2, and \boldsymbol{\mu}_3$ uniformly in $\mathbb{S}^2$, and variance $\sigma_1 = \sigma_2 = \sigma_3 = 0.1$. We sample $m = 500$ points from the distribution and all data points are projected onto $\mathbb{S}^2$ (see Figure 16.14). To construct the network (computing $\boldsymbol{E}$ and $\boldsymbol{C}^j$ for each layer), we set the number of iterations/layers $L = 2000$,[38] step size $\eta = 0.5$, and precision $\varepsilon = 0.1$. As shown by the two plots in Figure 16.14(a) and (b), we can observe that after the mapping $f(\cdot, \boldsymbol{\theta})$, samples from the same class converge to a single cluster and the angle between different clusters is nearly orthogonal, which agrees with the properties of the optimal solution $\boldsymbol{Z}_\star$ of the MCR^2 objective, characterized by Theorem 16.2. The values associated with the MCR^2 objective for features on different layers can be found in Figure 16.14(c). Empirically, we find that the constructed ReduNet is able

[37] Of course, the values of the parameters can be further fine-tuned if needed.

[38] It is remarkable to see how easily this framework leads to working deep networks with thousands of layers! But this also indicates that the efficiency of the layers is not so high. Given the optimization nature of the deep network, it would then be natural to expect that the acceleration techniques introduced in the earlier optimization chapters can be used to improve the efficiency of the layers (iterations). We leave this as an exercise for the reader.

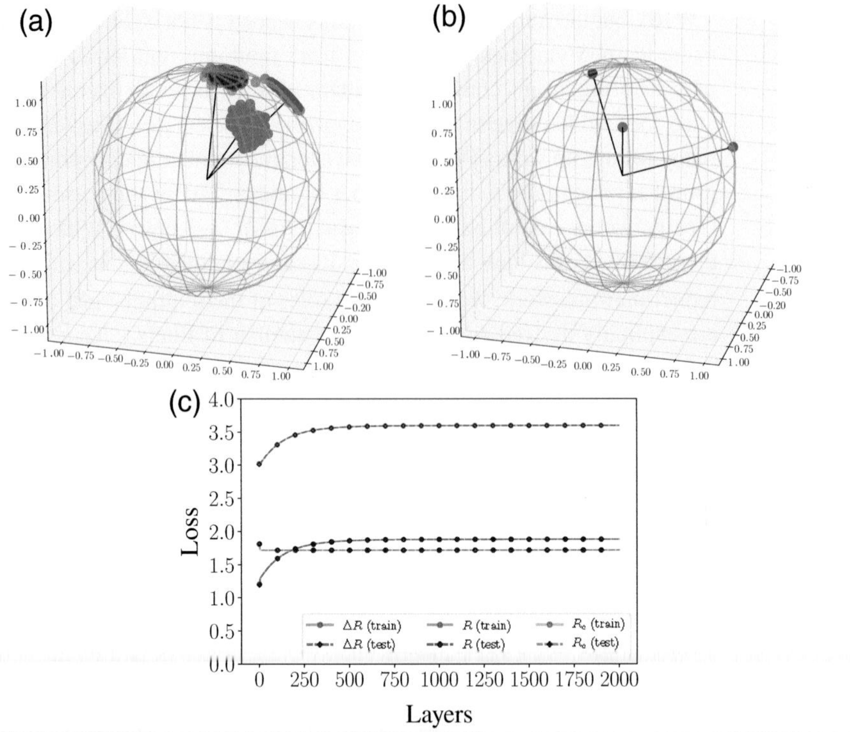

Figure 16.14 Original samples and learned representations for a mixture of three Gaussians in $\mathbb{R}^3$. We visualize data points $\boldsymbol{X}$ (before mapping) and features $\boldsymbol{Z}$ (after mapping) by scatter plots in (a) and (b), respectively. In each scatter plot, each color represents one class of samples. We also show in panel (c) the plots for the progression of values of the objective function, for both training and testing data.

to maximize MCR^2 loss and converges stably. Moreover, we sample new data points from the same distributions and find that new samples from the same class consistently converge to the same cluster as the training samples.

Experiment I: 1D Rotational Invariance on MNIST Digits

We study the ReduNet on learning *rotation*-invariant features on the MNIST dataset [LeC98]. Examples of rotated images are shown in Figure 16.15. We impose a polar grid on the image $\boldsymbol{x} \in \mathbb{R}^{H \times W}$, with its geometric center being the center of the 2D polar grid. For each radius r_i, $i \in [C]$, we can sample Γ pixels with respect to each angle $\gamma_l = l \cdot (2\pi/\Gamma)$ with $l \in [\Gamma]$. Then given an image sample $\boldsymbol{x}$ from the dataset, we represent the image in a polar coordinate representation $\boldsymbol{x}(p) = (\gamma_{l,i}, r_{l,i}) \in \mathbb{R}^{\Gamma \times C}$.

Our goal is to learn rotation-invariant features, i.e., we expect to learn $f(\cdot, \boldsymbol{\theta})$ such that $\{f(\boldsymbol{x}(p) \circ \mathfrak{g}, \boldsymbol{\theta})\}_{\mathfrak{g} \in \mathbb{G}}$ lie in the same subspace, where $\mathfrak{g}$ is the shift transformation in polar angle. By performing polar coordinate transformation for images from digit “0” and digit “1” in the training dataset, we can obtain the data matrix $\boldsymbol{X}(p) \in \mathbb{R}^{(\Gamma \cdot C) \times m}$. We use $m = 2000$ training samples, set $\Gamma = 200$ and $C = 5$ for polar transformation,

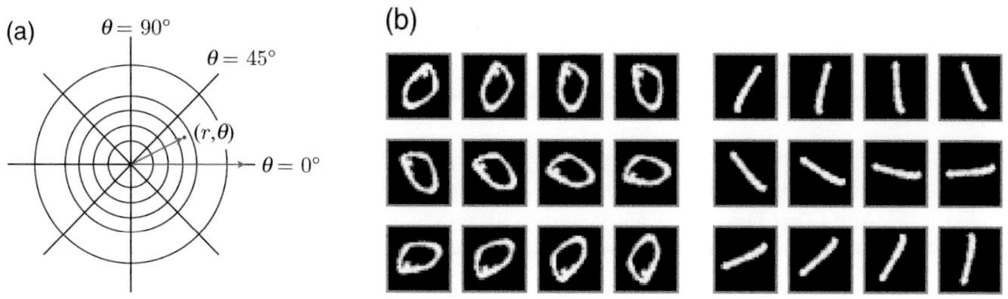

Figure 16.15 Examples of rotated images of MNIST digits for testing rotation invariance, each rotated by 18°: (a) diagram for polar coordinate representation; and (b) rotated digit “0” and digit “1”.

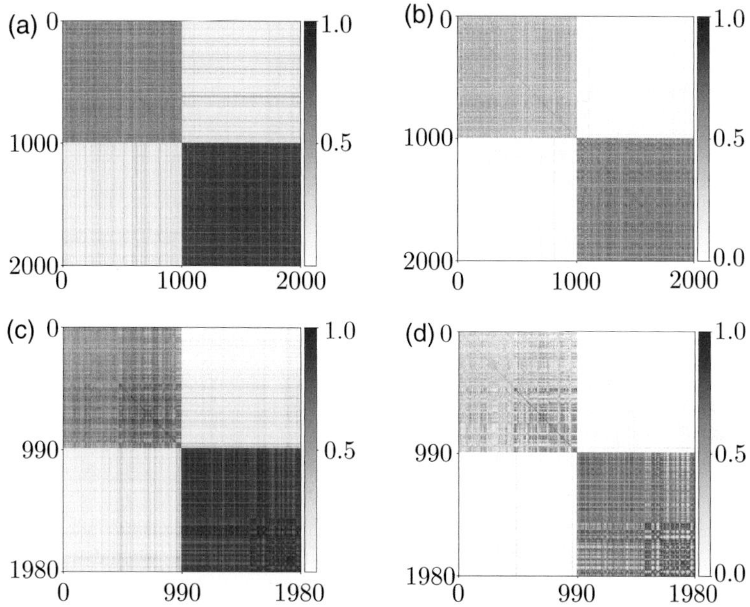

Figure 16.16 Cosine similarity (absolute value) of training/test data as well as training/test representations for learning rotation-invariant representations on MNIST: (a) $\boldsymbol{X}_{\text{train}}$, (b) $\boldsymbol{Z}_{\text{train}}$, (c) $\boldsymbol{X}_{\text{test}}$, and (d) $\boldsymbol{Z}_{\text{test}}$.

and set the number of iterations (or layers) $L = 3500$, precision $\varepsilon = 0.1$, and step size $\eta = 0.5$. We randomly generate test samples with random rotations followed by the same procedure.

To visualize the effect of the feature mapping, we show cosine similarity (absolute value) of training/test data in Figure 16.16. We can see that the ReduNet is able to map nearly all random samples from different classes to orthogonal subspaces. To verify that the resulting representation is truly invariant for *all* rotations, we pick one sample from each class and augment the sample with all possible shifted ones, then calculate the cosine similarity between these augmented samples, shown in Figure 16.17(a) and (b). Furthermore, we augment each sample in the dataset with every one of its possible shifted ones, then we evaluate the cosine similarity (in absolute value) between pairs

Table 16.2. Comparing network performance on learning rotation-invariant representations on MNIST.

	ReduNet	ReduNet (invariant)
Acc (Original Test Data)	0.983	0.996
Acc (Test Data with All Possible Shifts)	0.707	0.993

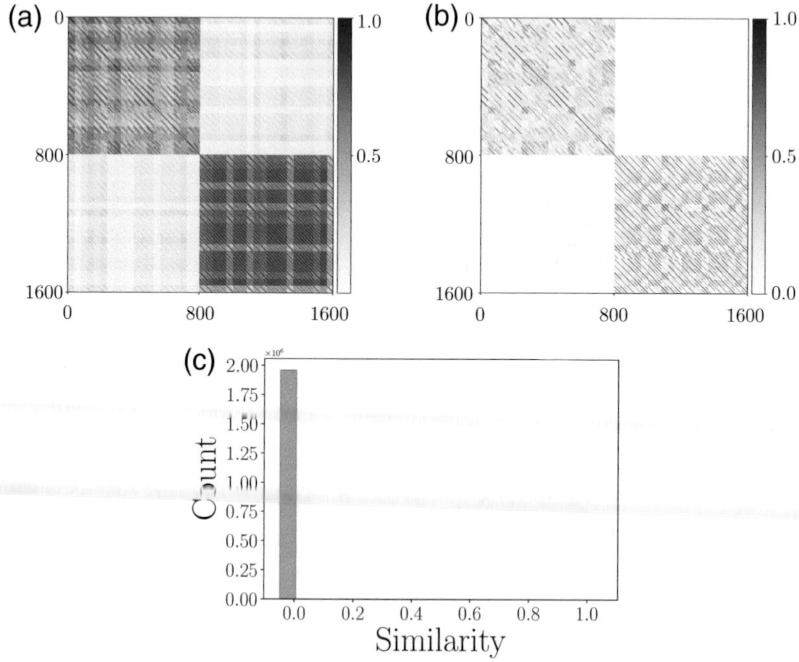

Figure 16.17 (a) and (b) Heat maps of cosine similarity between data $\boldsymbol{X}_{\text{shift}}$/learned features $\bar{\boldsymbol{Z}}_{\text{shift}}$ and (c) histogram of cosine distance between shifted samples between the two classes.

across classes: for each pair, one sample is from training and one sample is from test which belong to different classes. The histogram of the cosine similarity is plotted in Figure 16.17(c). We can clearly see that the learnt features are invariant to all shift transformation in polar angle (i.e., arbitrary rotation in $\boldsymbol{x}$).

We compare the accuracy (on both the original test data and the shifted test data) of the ReduNet (without considering invariance) and the shift invariant ReduNet. For the ReduNet (without considering invariance), we use the same training dataset as the shift-invariant ReduNet, we set iteration $L = 3500$, step size $\eta = 0.5$, and precision $\varepsilon = 0.1$. The results are summarized in Table 16.2. With the invariant design, we can see from Table 16.2 that the shift-invariant ReduNet achieves better performance in terms of invariance on the MNIST binary classification task.

Experiment II: 2D Cyclic Translation Invariance on MNIST Digits

In this part, we provide experimental results for verifying the invariance property of the ReduNet under 2D translations. We construct (1) a ReduNet (without considering

Table 16.3. Comparing network performance on learning 2D translation-invariant representations on MNIST.

	ReduNet	ReduNet (invariant)
Acc (Original Test Data)	0.980	0.975
Acc (Test Data with All Possible Shifts)	0.540	0.909

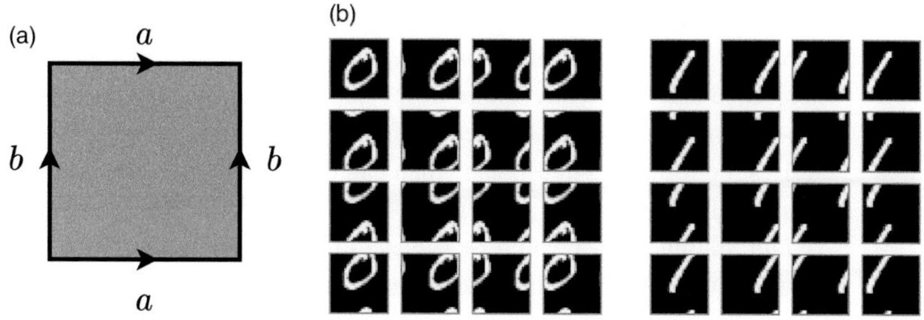

Figure 16.18 Examples of (cyclically) translated images of MNIST digits (with stride=7) for testing cyclic translation invariance of the ReduNet: (a) for cyclic 2D translation, we view a rectangular image as on a torus by identifying their opposite sides; (b) cyclic translated digit "0" and digit "1."

invariance) and (2) a 2D translation-invariant ReduNet for classifying digit "0" and digit "1" on the MNIST dataset. We use $m = 1000$ samples (500 samples from each class) for training the models, and use another 500 samples (250 samples from each class) for evaluation. To evaluate the 2D translational invariance, for each test image $\boldsymbol{x}_{\text{test}} \in \mathbb{R}^{H \times W}$, we consider *all* translation augmentations of the test image with a stride=7. More specifically, for the MNIST dataset, we have $H = W = 28$. So for each image, the total number of all cyclic translation augmentations (with stride=7) is $4 \times 4 = 16$. Examples of translated images are shown in Figure 16.18. Notice that such translations are considerably larger than normally considered in the literature since we consider invariance to the entire group of cyclic translations on the $H \times W$ grid as a torus. See Figure 16.18 for some representative test samples.

For the ReduNet (without considering translation invariance), we set iteration $L = 2000$, step size $\eta = 0.1$, and precision $\varepsilon = 0.1$. For the translation-invariant ReduNet, we set $L = 2000$, step size $\eta = 0.5$, precision $\varepsilon = 0.1$, number of channels $C = 5$, and kernel size for the random lifting kernels in (16.3.24) is set as 3×3.[39] We summarize the results in Table 16.3. Similar to the 1D rotational results on the MNIST dataset, the translation-invariant ReduNet achieves better performance under translations compared with the ReduNet without considering invariance. The accuracy drop of the translation-invariant ReduNet is much less than the one of the ReduNet without invariance design.

[39] Using more channels or better designed filters may certainly improve the performance. Here we choose the very basic ones just to verify the concept.

16.4 Guaranteed Manifold Classification by Deep Networks

The previous sections have shown how to construct (nonlinear) deep networks that embed labeled data into a union of incoherent subspaces, one per class. In contrast to our previous studies of linear and piecewise linear structure, these models can accommodate data that reside on *nonlinear* manifolds, by iteratively linearizing them. To a large extent, the constructive approach in the previous section reveals why a deep network architecture and many commonly adopted processes and operators are *necessary* for the classification task. However, due to the nonconvex nature of the objective and the greedy nature of the construction, there is still no guarantee for the so-obtained network to succeed in finding the optimal representation. This naturally raises the following questions: when can data residing on nonlinear submanifolds be accurately classified by a deep network? What resources (data, network depth and width, training time) would be *sufficient* to correctly label the data? These questions are motivated both by the observed successes of deep networks in coping with nonlinear data, and by the prevalence of nonlinear, low-dimensional structure in real data.

16.4.1 Minimal Case: Two 1D Submanifolds

In this section, we study this problem in what is arguably the simplest possible case: *two one-dimensional submanifolds on a high-dimensional sphere.* The experiment of classifying two digits, "0" and "1," with arbitrary rotation that we saw in Figure 16.15, can be viewed as an example of this problem. This is analogous to our discussion of dictionary learning in Chapter 7, where we illustrated the basic ideas in the simplistic setting of one-sparse vectors, and extracted intuitions that carry over to more general situations.[40]

The precise setup is illustrated in Figure 16.19: we observe a finite set of labeled samples $\{(\boldsymbol{x}^i, y^i)\}_{i=1}^N$ residing on two one-dimensional submanifolds $\mathcal{M}_+$ and $\mathcal{M}_-$ on a high-dimensional sphere, and wish to understand what resources are needed to correctly label *every* point on $\mathcal{M}_+$ and $\mathcal{M}_-$. This is a strong form of *generalization* since it guarantees that the learned (or constructed) classifier $f(\boldsymbol{x}, \boldsymbol{\theta})$ outputs the correct label on every possible input.

Clearly, the resources required depend on the geometry of the manifolds, which here we capture through their curvature κ and separation Δ. We will describe how this question can be studied through the lens of supervised learning, where one fits a network to data by minimizing the loss on the training data:

$$\min_{\boldsymbol{\theta}} L(\boldsymbol{\theta}, \boldsymbol{X}, \boldsymbol{Y}) = \frac{1}{N} \sum_{i=1}^{N} \ell\big(f(\boldsymbol{x}^i, \boldsymbol{\theta}), y^i\big), \tag{16.4.1}$$

[40] Any fundamental ideas that work for general cases must be explained, arguably more clearly, for the most basic case first. Typically, going from 0 to 1 is the key step in advancing our knowledge, and after that, from 1 to n is merely natural extension.

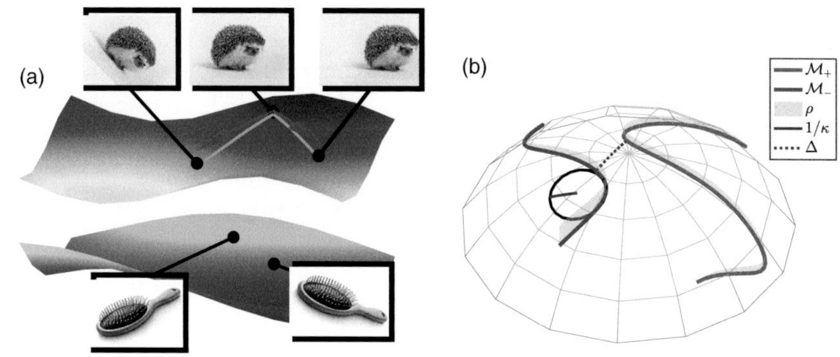

Figure 16.19 (a) Data in image classification with standard augmentations, as well as other domains in which neural networks are commonly used, lie on low-dimensional manifolds – in this case those generated by the action of continuous transformations, say rotation, on images in the training set. The dimension of the manifold is determined by the dimension of the symmetry group, and is typically small. (b) The *multiple manifold problem*. Our model problem, capturing this low-dimensional structure, is the classification of low-dimensional submanifolds of a sphere $\mathbb{S}^{n_0-1}$. The difficulty of the problem is set by the inter-manifold separation Δ and the curvature κ. The depth and width of the network required to provably reduce the generalization error efficiently are set by these parameters.

starting from a random initialization $\boldsymbol{\theta}_0$. This approach is, in a loose sense, dual to the approach taken in the previous sections. Instead of constructing networks in the *forward* direction in order to minimize a loss, we start with a random network and train it by gradient descent, which propagates information about desired outputs *backward* through the network to determine how the parameters should be adjusted. Back propagation has been the dominant method for training deep networks [RHW86]. Nevertheless, we believe ultimately that these two approaches can (and should) be combined, e.g., the analytically constructed nominal weights of the network in the previous section can be further adjusted by gradient descent, potentially reducing the number of layers needed to embed the data on orthogonal subspaces.

One major challenge in analyzing neural network training arises from the nonconvexity of the objective $L(\boldsymbol{\theta}, \boldsymbol{X}, \boldsymbol{Y})$. In the language of Chapter 7, deep networks exhibit complicated, compound symmetries (e.g., permutation or shift symmetries at each layer). We currently lack a comprehensive understanding of the optimization landscapes of deep networks. This has two implications for analysis: first, it is easier to analyze the training procedure in terms of the input–output relationship $\boldsymbol{x} \mapsto f(\boldsymbol{x}, \boldsymbol{\theta})$, rather than the weights themselves, which exhibit complicated symmetries. Second, rather than exhaustively characterizing local/global minimizers over the entire space, it is easier to analyze the dynamics of training starting from a random initial network $f(\cdot, \boldsymbol{\theta}_0)$. This enables us to bring tools from high-dimensional probability to bear on the problem: as the number of network parameters increases, the behavior of training becomes increasingly regular. Moreover, the initial distribution of the parameters can be chosen such that the layers of the network implement near-isometries.

16.4.2 Problem Formulation and Analysis

To make the above discussion more concrete, we consider a model network training problem, in which our labels take values in $\{\pm 1\}$, corresponding to the two components $\mathcal{M}_\pm$. Our goal is to fit a fully connected neural network to input data $\boldsymbol{x}^i$ of dimension n_0, with layers of width n, so that $\boldsymbol{W}_0 \in \mathbb{R}^{n \times n_0}$, $\boldsymbol{W}_\ell \in \mathbb{R}^{n \times n}$ for $\ell = 1, \dots, L-2$, and $\boldsymbol{W}_{L-1} \in \mathbb{R}^{1 \times n}$. We attempt to find these weights by minimizing the squared loss over the training data:[41]

$$\min_{\boldsymbol{\theta}} \frac{1}{2N} \sum_{i=1}^{N} \left(f(\boldsymbol{x}^i, \boldsymbol{\theta}) - y^i \right)^2 = \int_{\boldsymbol{x}} \frac{1}{2} (f(\boldsymbol{x}, \boldsymbol{\theta}) - y(\boldsymbol{x}))^2 d\mu_N(\boldsymbol{x}), \tag{16.4.2}$$

where in the final expression, we have let $\mu_N(\boldsymbol{x}) = (1/N) \sum_i \delta(\boldsymbol{x} - \boldsymbol{x}^i)$ denote the measure (distribution) associated with the training data. Let $\zeta(\boldsymbol{x})$ denote the signed error at point $\boldsymbol{x}$:

$$\zeta(\boldsymbol{x}) = f(\boldsymbol{x}, \boldsymbol{\theta}) - y(\boldsymbol{x}). \tag{16.4.3}$$

To understand how this error evolves during training, we can study a continuous-time variant of gradient descent[42] in which the parameters evolve as

$$\begin{aligned} \frac{d}{dt} \boldsymbol{\theta}_t &= -\nabla_{\boldsymbol{\theta}} L(\boldsymbol{\theta}_t, \boldsymbol{X}, \boldsymbol{Y}) = \int_{\boldsymbol{x}} (f(\boldsymbol{x}, \boldsymbol{\theta}_t) - y(\boldsymbol{x})) \left. \frac{\partial f(\boldsymbol{x}, \boldsymbol{\theta})}{\partial \boldsymbol{\theta}} \right|_t d\mu_N(\boldsymbol{x}) \\ &= -\int_{\boldsymbol{x}} \zeta_t(\boldsymbol{x}) \left. \frac{\partial f(\boldsymbol{x}, \boldsymbol{\theta})}{\partial \boldsymbol{\theta}} \right|_{\boldsymbol{\theta}_t} d\mu_N(\boldsymbol{x}). \end{aligned} \tag{16.4.4}$$

As mentioned above, characterizing the evolution of the network parameters $\boldsymbol{\theta}$ themselves is challenging; often it is easier to think in terms of the error ζ_t, which evolves as

$$\begin{aligned} \frac{d}{dt} \zeta_t(\boldsymbol{x}) &= \left. \frac{\partial f(\boldsymbol{x}, \boldsymbol{\theta})}{\partial \boldsymbol{\theta}} \right|_{\boldsymbol{\theta}_t} \frac{d}{dt} \boldsymbol{\theta}_t = -\int_{\boldsymbol{x}'} \left. \left\langle \frac{\partial f(\boldsymbol{x}, \boldsymbol{\theta})}{\partial \boldsymbol{\theta}}, \frac{\partial f(\boldsymbol{x}', \boldsymbol{\theta})}{\partial \boldsymbol{\theta}} \right\rangle \right|_{\boldsymbol{\theta}_t} \zeta_t(\boldsymbol{x}') d\mu_N(\boldsymbol{x}') \\ &\doteq -\boldsymbol{\Theta}_t \zeta_t, \end{aligned} \tag{16.4.5}$$

where $\boldsymbol{\Theta}_t$ is a (linear) integral operator that maps a function $h(\boldsymbol{x})$ to

$$\int_{\boldsymbol{x}'} \left. \left\langle \frac{\partial f(\boldsymbol{x}, \boldsymbol{\theta})}{\partial \boldsymbol{\theta}}, \frac{\partial f(\boldsymbol{x}', \boldsymbol{\theta})}{\partial \boldsymbol{\theta}} \right\rangle \right|_{\boldsymbol{\theta}_t} h(\boldsymbol{x}') d\mu_N(\boldsymbol{x}'). \tag{16.4.6}$$

This operator is positive definite: for every h, we have $\langle h, \boldsymbol{\Theta}_t h \rangle_{\mu_N} \geq 0$ where $\langle f, g \rangle_{\mu_N} = \int_{\boldsymbol{x}} f(\boldsymbol{x}) g(\boldsymbol{x}) d\mu_N(\boldsymbol{x})$. This means that the error is nonincreasing:

$$\frac{d}{dt} \| \zeta_t \|_{L^2(\mu_N)}^2 \leq 0,$$

with $\| f \|_{L^2(\mu_N)}^2 = \langle f, f \rangle_{\mu_N}$.

41 In the two-class case, it is convenient to represent the two classes as ± 1, and the choice of squared loss, instead of cross-entropy, is mainly for simplicity.

42 With the understanding that, in this setting, conclusions transfer rigorously to discrete time (finite stepping) gradient methods.

How rapidly does the error reduce? This depends on the properties of the operator $\boldsymbol{\Theta}_t$ and the error ζ_t. $\boldsymbol{\Theta}_t$ is a positive definite linear operator, sometimes referred to as the *neural tangent kernel* [JGH18].[43] The entries $\boldsymbol{\Theta}_t(\boldsymbol{x}, \boldsymbol{x}')$ measure our ability to independently modify the outputs $f(\boldsymbol{x}, \boldsymbol{\theta})$ and $f(\boldsymbol{x}', \boldsymbol{\theta})$ at points $\boldsymbol{x}$ and $\boldsymbol{x}'$. If

$$|\boldsymbol{\Theta}_t(\boldsymbol{x}, \boldsymbol{x}')| \ll \min\{\boldsymbol{\Theta}_t(\boldsymbol{x}, \boldsymbol{x}), \boldsymbol{\Theta}_t(\boldsymbol{x}', \boldsymbol{x}')\},$$

the operator $\boldsymbol{\Theta}_t$ is close to diagonal, and it is possible to independently modify the two outputs with only small changes to the parameters $\boldsymbol{\theta}$.

The operator $\boldsymbol{\Theta}_t$ can also be studied through its eigenvalue/eigenvector decomposition:

$$\boldsymbol{\Theta}_t = \sum_i \lambda_i v_i v_i^*. \tag{16.4.7}$$

Because $d\zeta_t/dt = -\boldsymbol{\Theta}_t \zeta_t$, the error will decrease rapidly as long as it is aligned with eigenvectors v_i that correspond to *large* eigenvalues λ_i. Conversely, if the error is aligned with eigenvectors that correspond to *small* eigenvalues, it will decrease slowly.

We can develop insights into both values and eigenvalues by making the following idealizations: first, we consider the behavior of $\boldsymbol{\Theta}$ at initialization (time $t = 0$). At initialization, the network parameters are independent random variables, and $\boldsymbol{\Theta}_0$ is a random operator.[44] We can study its behavior using tools from high-dimensional probability.[45] Second, we imagine that the network is wide (here, $n \gg n_0$). This means that $\boldsymbol{\Theta}_0$ is a function of *many* independent random variables. It should be no surprise that as the network width increases, this operator concentrates about its expectation. Moreover, this expectation depends on the points $\boldsymbol{x}$ and $\boldsymbol{x}'$ in a very simple way. Because of the rotational invariance of the Gaussian distribution, it is not difficult to show that $\mathbb{E}[\boldsymbol{\Theta}_0(\boldsymbol{x}, \boldsymbol{x}')]$ depends on the points $\boldsymbol{x}$ and $\boldsymbol{x}'$ only through their angle:

$$\mathbb{E}[\boldsymbol{\Theta}_0(\boldsymbol{x}, \boldsymbol{x}')] = \xi_L\Big(\angle(\boldsymbol{x}, \boldsymbol{x}')\Big), \tag{16.4.8}$$

where L is the depth of the network. Figure 16.20 plots the function ξ_L as a function of the angle $\angle(\boldsymbol{x}, \boldsymbol{x}')$ for various network depths L. Notice that ξ_L is always maximized at $\angle(\boldsymbol{x}, \boldsymbol{x}') = 0$; as L increases, $\boldsymbol{\Theta}$ becomes sharper, suggesting that the network will be able to fit more complicated functions. Here, *depth L serves as an approximation resource*: deeper networks can fit more complicated functions. In the model problem of manifold classification, this suggests that the greater the curvature κ and the smaller the separation Δ, the deeper the network needs to be.

Second, the limiting expression $\mathbb{E}[\boldsymbol{\Theta}]$ provides insights into the eigenvectors and eigenvalues of $\boldsymbol{\Theta}$. Because $\mathbb{E}[\boldsymbol{\Theta}]$ is a function of angle only, in the special case when

[43] For the sake of developing intuition, it can be thought of as an infinitely large symmetric matrix.

[44] For concreteness, here we take the initial weights to be independent $\mathcal{N}(0, 2/n)$ random variables, and the nonlinearity ϕ to be the ReLU. These particular choices ensure that each layer implements a near-isometry.

[45] In particular, because the network operations are applied sequentially, tools from Martingale theory are especially appropriate here.

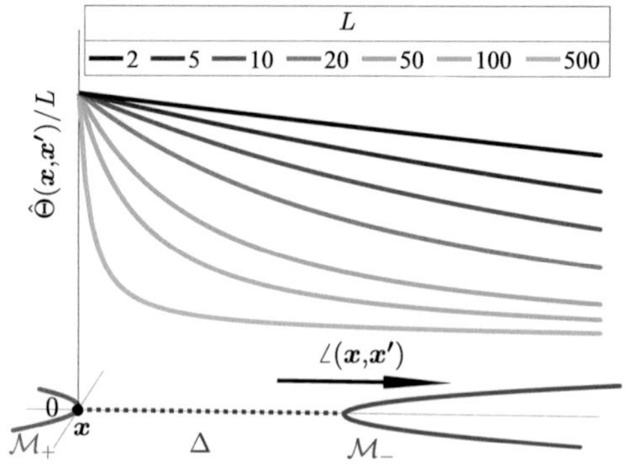

Figure 16.20 Role of Network Depth. As depth L increases, the kernel $\Theta_0(x, x')$ becomes sharper, reflecting a greater capacity to fit functions that vary spatially. In our setup, the required depth is set by the separation Δ and the curvature κ of the manifolds $\mathcal{M}_\pm$.

the data are uniformly distributed on the unit sphere, $\mathbb{E}[\Theta]$ is a (rotationally) invariant operator, which acts by *spherical convolution*. It can be diagonalized in the frequency domain,[46] with large eigenvalues corresponding to low frequencies, and small eigenvalues corresponding to high frequencies. Of course, we are interested in data that are not uniformly distributed on the sphere – rather, natural data tend to have lower-dimensional structure. However, these basic intuitions carry over to more structured situations; eigenvectors corresponding to large eigenvalues tend to be smoother or "lower frequency," while eigenvectors corresponding to small eigenvalues tend to be oscillatory or "higher frequency." Assuming the error ζ is aligned with these "lower-frequency" eigenvectors, gradient descent will rapidly drive the error towards zero.

The extent to which the error is aligned with "low-frequency" eigenvectors can be captured implicitly through a notion of "certificates": if we can exhibit ζ in the form $\zeta \approx \Theta g$, where g is some function of small L^2 norm, then ζ must not be too concentrated on directions that correspond to small eigenvectors of Θ. This construction is loosely analogous to our constructions of dual certificates in Chapters 3–5. In those chapters, we proved recovery by convex optimization, by exhibiting a subgradient in the range of a certain random operator (the row space of the measurement operators), using (random) measurements as an approximation resource. In a similar sense, here, we prove that gradient descent makes significant progress, by illustrating that the error ζ is near the range of a certain random operator Θ, using network depth and (random) parameters as approximation resources.

16.4.3 Main Conclusion

Summing up, in this setting we have the following resources:

- **Network depth** is a computation resource (via incremental approximation); deeper networks have sharper kernels Θ, which can fit more complicated functions, or adapt to more complicated geometries (larger κ, smaller Δ).

[46] More precisely, in terms of spherical harmonics.

- **Network width** is a statistical resource; as width increases, the early behavior of training becomes increasingly regular, due to two effects: (i) concentration of $\boldsymbol{\Theta}_0$ about $\mathbb{E}[\boldsymbol{\Theta}_0]$, and (ii) the ability to make large progress in the objective before $\boldsymbol{\Theta}_t$ deviates from $\boldsymbol{\Theta}_0$. The latter can be viewed as a consequence of overparameterization, analogous to our discussions of overparameterized low-rank recovery in Chapters 4–7.
- **Data samples** are a statistical resource; as the number of samples increases, the learned network $f(\cdot, \boldsymbol{\theta})$ is more likely to uniformly label the manifolds $\mathcal{M}_\pm$. The number of samples N is set by the width of the kernel ξ_L: intuitively speaking, to generalize, we need the manifold to be covered more finely than the "aperture" of the kernel.

Combining all of these considerations, it is possible to identify (tractable) conditions under which gradient descent correctly labels the manifolds. For concision, we only sketch these conditions here:

THEOREM 16.6. (Sufficient conditions for manifold classification (informal statement) [BGW20]) *Suppose that the network width* $n >$ poly$(L \log(n_0))$*, the network depth* $L > \max\{\kappa^2, \text{polylog}(n_0)\}$*, and the number of samples* $N \geq$ poly(L)*. If there exists* g *satisfying* $\|g\|_{L^2} \leq c/n$ *and* $\|\boldsymbol{\Theta}_0 g - \zeta_0\|_{L^2} < c/L$*, then with high probability randomly initialized gradient descent correctly labels every point on the manifolds* $\mathcal{M}_\pm$.

The work [BGW20] demonstrates how to construct such certificates g for simple geometries on the sphere, giving end-to-end guarantees for these simple classification problems. Although the results described in this section are limited in generality (pertaining to one-dimensional manifolds, with wide networks), they illustrate basic *sufficient conditions* for learning with structured data, and basic tensions between data properties, network architecture, and sample complexity. Both at the level of proofs and at the level of phenomena, our intuitions from the first part of this book continue to serve us well in this new setting.

16.5 Epilogue: Open Problems and Future Directions

This chapter has sketched some fundamental and substantial connections between low-dimensional models and deep neural networks. This is an active area of research, with many open problems. As an epilogue of the chapter (and of the book), we lay out a number of promising directions for future work.

Simpler and Better Networks

In practice, it is typically efficient (and even desirable from an accuracy perspective) to implement convolutional networks with very short or small (and separable) kernels [Cho17]. Identifying conditions on the data that lead naturally to short (and separable) convolutions is an interesting problem for future work. One possible conjecture is that when the data exhibit "short-and-sparse" structure, as in Chapter 12, the neural network naturally takes on a "short-and-sparse" structure. More generally, the problem of identifying simple networks is important both for efficiency of implementation and for robustness. As in the first part of this book, various notions of simplicity could be relevant, depending on the structure of the data and the processing task.

In the current straightforward implementation, the width of the ReduNet seems to grow linearly in the number of classes (i.e., the number of operators $\boldsymbol{C}^j$). Nevertheless, notice that $\boldsymbol{C}^j$ are not independent from $\boldsymbol{E}$. In fact, one can show that, near the optimal representation, the range of each $\boldsymbol{C}^j$ becomes an eigen-subspace of $\boldsymbol{E}$ [CYY+20]. This is consistent with the learning objective discussed in Section 16.2 – seeking a nonlinear mapping for independent component analysis of the given data. Hence in practice, to save both space and computation, one could approximate $\boldsymbol{C}^j$ with a subset of operations from $\boldsymbol{E}$.

At a more theoretical level, the guarantees for classification described in Section 16.4 currently demand that the network be quite wide: n should be larger than a large-degree polynomial in L. While we have motivated the need for wide networks in terms of concentration of measure, in fact it is possible to perform sharp analyses that show that the kernel $\boldsymbol{\Theta}$ concentrates uniformly over the (low-dimensional) data manifolds when the width is roughly d polylog n_0, which is optimal. Rather, the culprit in these analyses is the requirement that $\boldsymbol{\Theta}_t \approx \boldsymbol{\Theta}_0$. Relaxing this requirement seems to demand a better understanding of the (nonconvex) geometry of neural network training, in the spirit of Chapter 7.

Guaranteed Invariance

Our discussion of networks-by-design in Section 16.3 revealed a tension between sparsity (low dimensionality) and invariance (to a certain transformation group). Understanding the interplay or tradeoff between these two different, ubiquitous forms of low-dimensional structure is an important direction both for neural networks and for low-dimensional data modeling in general. An important potential impact is to help in guaranteeing uniform performance across a large family of structured transformations, such as affine transforms, homographies, general smooth deformations, or dynamics from certain differential equations. Current standard approaches to this problem combine architectural features such as convolution and pooling with learning with augmented datasets (the parameters from random initialization). However, the literature is rich with alternative "networks-by-design" proposals (the ScatteringNet [BM13], spatial transformer networks [JSZK15], capsule networks [HKW11], convolutions with respect to larger groups [CW16], etc.). A major theoretical question underlying all of these approaches is *what resources (data, network, test-time computation) are required to achieve equivarient detection or invariant classification*.

Some of the most elegant proposed approaches incur either data or computational costs that are exponential in the number of parameters of the transformation or in the number of layers/iterations. Nevertheless, there is some evidence that the problem may not be *so* difficult: in some settings such as low-rank textures in Chapter 15, the TILT algorithm (via local optimization by repeatedly linearizing the transformation) achieves a surprisingly large region of convergence; the derivation of the ReduNet suggests that if we only learn an invariant/equivalent representation for a dataset from a specific low-dimensional structure, the resources needed may scale gracefully to that of the task (say in terms of number of classes or data size). Hence, as the empirical success of TILT and ReduNet has suggested, it might be more practical to provide invariance guarantee for any given instance (rather than an entire family) of low-dimensional structures, in similar vein to Theorem 4.26 for low-rank matrix completion in Chapter 4.

Understanding Generalizability

Modern deep neural networks are often highly over-parameterized models with more parameters than necessary to perfectly fit any training data [ZBH$^+$17]. While the classical *bias–variance tradeoff* principle in statistics predicts that a large model leads to high variance error and overfitting [HTW15], modern practice with deep learning almost always favors models that are deeper, wider, and larger. Increasing studies have revealed that a fundamental reason for this is due to implicit regularization induced by the optimization algorithms [SHN$^+$18, GLSS18, GBLJ19], the low-dimensional structures of the data [MWCC18], or both [YZQM20]. We believe a clear understanding of the generalizability of deep networks relies on a full understanding of over-parameterized models for nonlinear low-dimensional data structures such as submanifolds, in a similar spirit to understanding over-complete dictionaries for sparsity studied in this book. This would require us to go well beyond the (bilinear) sparse dictionary learning or low-rank models discussed in Chapter 7.

Ensuring Robustness

Despite extensive engineering, modern deep networks remain rather vulnerable to input perturbations, label noise, or adversarial attacks [CAD$^+$18]. Empirical designs based on *trial and error* cannot provide any rigorous guarantee of robustness. Nevertheless, as we have seen throughout this book, from Boscovich's original proposal of ℓ^1 minimization, to Logan's phenomenon, to sparse error correction [CT05], and to dense error correction [WM10], surprisingly good tradeoffs between accuracy and robustness can be achieved if the corrupting errors are *incoherent* to low-dimensional structures of the data. The robust face recognition of Chapter 13 and structured texture recovery of Chapter 15 are two striking examples. It would be interesting to see whether one can generalize the notion of incoherent errors to low-dimensional submanifolds. If so, leveraging discriminative low-dimensional structures learned by the deep networks (e.g., the ReduNet) to provide strong guarantees of classification robustness (to mislabeled training data or/and to random corruptions on the input) could become a promising direction for future development.

A Unified Objective and Framework for Unsupervised Learning

This chapter sketches an approach to deriving neural networks for classification with labeled training data, based on principles from data compression and compressive sensing. Note that the lossy coding and compression approach was originally developed for (unsupervised) clustering problems [MDHW07, VMS16] (also see equation (16.2.4)) and later extended to classification [WTL$^+$08, KPCC15]: both mathematically are equivalent to maximizing the rate reduction against the membership $\boldsymbol{\Pi}$,

$$\max_{\boldsymbol{\Pi}} \Delta R(\boldsymbol{Z}, \boldsymbol{\Pi}, \varepsilon), \tag{16.5.1}$$

with the representation $\boldsymbol{Z}$ given and fixed. So the rate reduction framework can be naturally extended to unsupervised learning of both representation and class membership, or a variety of intermediate settings such as semi-supervised learning, self-supervised learning, and incremental/online learning. The main technical challenge in these settings is that the class labels are partially or entirely unknown. So the membership $\boldsymbol{\Pi}$ needs to be identified while learning the representation $\boldsymbol{Z}$:

$$\max_{\boldsymbol{Z}, \boldsymbol{\Pi}} \Delta R(\boldsymbol{Z}, \boldsymbol{\Pi}, \varepsilon), \tag{16.5.2}$$

with $\boldsymbol{Z} \subset \mathbb{S}^{n-1}$ and $\boldsymbol{\Pi} \in \Omega$ (or a constraint set based on partially known membership).

Recently, there have been promising attempts to simultaneously learn the representation $\boldsymbol{Z}$ and the class membership $\boldsymbol{\Pi}$ in the unsupervised setting with conventional deep networks [ARV20] and with contrastive learning objectives [CMM$^+$20]. The rate reduction objective (16.5.2) might be able to unify both the learning objective and network architecture in this setting: following the same idea of the ReduNet, one may construct networks that emulate the joint (gradient flow) dynamics and optimize the representation $\boldsymbol{Z}$ and the membership $\boldsymbol{\Pi}$ simultaneously or alternately:

$$\dot{\boldsymbol{Z}} = \eta \cdot \frac{\partial \Delta R}{\partial \boldsymbol{Z}}, \quad \dot{\boldsymbol{\Pi}} = \gamma \cdot \frac{\partial \Delta R}{\partial \boldsymbol{\Pi}}. \tag{16.5.3}$$

Of course, the basic gradient flow can be regularized with other additional information. For instance, the class membership $\boldsymbol{\Pi}$ can also be updated according to another (probably learned) similarity measure among the samples.[47] Success of such a scheme (or its variants) would entail understanding a nonconvex landscape with both continuous and discrete symmetries, which could potentially be studied through the lens of Chapter 7.

Forward Deep Networks as Optimization

We want to point out that it is rather insightful and beneficial to view deep (forward) networks as unfolded or *unrolled optimization* schemes for optimizing rate reduction or other intrinsic measures of compactness, as depicted in Section 16.3. This allows us to utilize the rich arsenal of techniques from optimization to design and justify a variety of deep networks. Powerful ideas that we introduced in Chapters 8 and 9 (e.g., acceleration, alternating minimization, or augmented Lagrangian, etc.) can be readily deployed to design effective optimization schemes that can in turn be emulated by deep networks. See Exercise 16.6 for a possible improvement of the ReduNet.

[47] For example, the "self-attention" or "transformer" type component [VSP$^+$17] recently incorporated into deep networks can be viewed as actively learning similarity among the samples (or their features).

Similar to the above discussion on "*Understanding Generalizability*," one could also study what *implicit regularization*

$$\mathcal{R}(\cdot) : f \mapsto \mathbb{R}_+$$

has been imposed upon the family of mappings $\mathcal{F} = \{f\}$ as they are constructed through the incremental gradient-based schemes as in the ReduNet. Or what additional regularization $\mathcal{R}(f)$ could have been imposed explicitly on the mapping f to make the representation learning problem better defined – in the sense that the optimal representation $f_\star$ would have other desired properties (e.g. smoothness) as well as be unique (or belong to a class of equivalent solutions).

Backward Propagation as Variational Fine-Tuning

The forward unrolling process depicted in Section 16.3 allows us to construct the deep network $f(\boldsymbol{x}, \boldsymbol{\theta}_0)$ – its architectures, operators, and parameters – as the *nominal* optimization path for the rate reduction ΔR. The popular back propagation for training deep networks [RHW86], analyzed in Section 16.4, can be viewed as variational methods for fine-tuning the network parameters $f(\boldsymbol{x}, \boldsymbol{\theta}_0 + d\boldsymbol{\theta}) = f(\boldsymbol{x}, \boldsymbol{\theta}_0) + \delta f$, around the nominal path $f(\boldsymbol{x}, \boldsymbol{\theta}_0)$. The fine-tuning may achieve a better tradeoff between accuracy and efficiency of the nominal network (say when only a limited number of iterations, or layers, are allowed) [GEBS18] or to better customize the network to certain subsequent tasks or new data.

Nevertheless, for networks like the ReduNet whose operators and parameters have clear geometric and statistical interpretation, it remains open how to develop new back propagation methods that respect structures and functionalities of these components (say compression or expansion) during fine-tuning. This can also be viewed as imposing certain additional regularization $\mathcal{R}$ (or constraints) onto the rate reduction objective:

$$\min_{f \in \mathcal{F}} \Delta R(f) + \lambda \cdot \mathcal{R}(f).$$

At least conceptually, by not allowing all the parameters to be set completely free for update, such regularization would help avoid overfitting or help avoid the so-called "catastrophic forgetting" in the sequential or *incremental learning* setting [MC89, WBYM21].

Another potential advantage of this variational perspective for network fine-tuning is that it opens the door to employ rigorous and powerful tools from *calculus of variations* (e.g., [Lib12]) to study properties of the optimal mapping $f_\star$ (represented by a deep network):

$$\delta \Delta R(f) + \lambda \cdot \delta \mathcal{R}(f)\big|_{f_\star} = \mathbf{0}. \tag{16.5.4}$$

This may potentially lead to new ideas and variational algorithms for fine-tuning the network besides the conventional back propagation. There is already evidence that the forward-constructed ReduNet can be fine-tuned in a *forward propagation* fashion.

Sparse Coding, Spectral Computing, and Subspace Embedding in Nature
In this chapter, we have seen both sparse coding and spectral computing (or multi-channel convolution) arise naturally as *necessary* processes for effective and efficient classification of (visual) data invariant to translation. Recall that "sparse coding," as mentioned in Chapter 1, has been hypothesized as a guiding principle for the visual cortex of primates [OF96b]. Interestingly, there is also strong scientific evidence that neurons in the visual cortex compute in the spectral domain: they encode and transmit information through the rate of spiking, hence called "spiking neurons" [SK93, EA03, BGM$^+$08]. Recent studies in neuroscience have started to reveal how these mechanisms might be integrated in the inferotemporal (IT) cortex, where neurons encode and process information about high-level object identity (e.g., face recognition), invariant to various transformations [MHSD15, CT17]. The recent studies in [CT17] went even further to hypothesize that high-level neurons encode the face space as a "linear subspace" with each cell likely encoding one axis of the subspace (rather than as previously thought "an exemplar"). The framework laid out in this chapter suggests that such a "high-level" compact (linear) representation can be efficiently and effectively learned via an arguably much simpler and more natural "forward propagation" mechanism.

So remarkably, nature might have already "learned" through millions of years of evolution to exploit benefits of the mathematical principles depicted in this chapter, in particular the computational efficiency and simplicity in sparse coding, spectral computing, and subspace embedding for achieving invariant (visual) recognition! It remains a largely open, highly intriguing question whether there will be concrete scientific evidence that suggests truly deep and broad connections between the guiding principles for perception/cognition and the computational principles for data compression/representation developed in this chapter and this book. Regardless, we, the authors, strongly believe that *the law of parsimony*, also known as Occam's razor, has always been and will always be the central governing principle for all sciences and intelligences, artificial or natural. Hence, we leave the readers with a slogan:

We learn to compress, and compress to learn!

16.6 Exercises

16.1. (Properties of OLE) *Show that the OLE objective* (16.2.8) *is always* negative *and achieves the maximal value* 0 *when the subspaces are orthogonal, regardless of their dimensions.*

16.2. (Gradient of rate reduction) *Derive equation (16.3.3) and equation (16.3.4) from the definition of the rate reduction function* (16.3.1).

16.3. (Approximation of regression residual with ReLU) *Notice that the geometric meaning of* σ *in* (16.3.12) *is to compute the regression "residual" of each feature against the subspace to which it belongs. So when we restrict all features to be in the first (positive) quadrant of the feature space,*[48] *argue that one can approximate this residual using the rectified linear units operation,* $ReLU(x) = \max(0, x)$, *on* $\boldsymbol{p}_j = \boldsymbol{C}_\ell^j z_\ell$ *or its orthogonal complement,*

$$\sigma(z_\ell) \propto z_\ell - \sum_{j=1}^{k} ReLU\big(\boldsymbol{P}_\ell^j z_\ell\big), \tag{16.6.1}$$

where $\boldsymbol{P}_\ell^j = (\boldsymbol{C}_\ell^j)^\perp$ *is the projection onto the* j*-th class.*[49] *Discuss under what conditions or assumptions the above approximation is good.*

16.4. ($\boldsymbol{E}$ and $\boldsymbol{C}^j$ as convolutions) *Prove Proposition 16.5.*

16.5. (Benefits in the spectral domain) *Show that any circulant matrix can be diagonalized by the discrete Fourier transform* $\boldsymbol{F}$*:*

$$\mathsf{circ}(z) = \boldsymbol{F}^* \operatorname{diag}\left(DFT(z)\right) \boldsymbol{F}. \tag{16.6.2}$$

Using this relationship, show that $\bar{\boldsymbol{E}}$ *in* (16.3.25) *can be computed as*

$$\bar{\boldsymbol{E}} = \begin{bmatrix} \boldsymbol{F}^* & \boldsymbol{0} & \boldsymbol{0} \\ \boldsymbol{0} & \ddots & \boldsymbol{0} \\ \boldsymbol{0} & \boldsymbol{0} & \boldsymbol{F}^* \end{bmatrix} \cdot \alpha \left(\boldsymbol{I} + \alpha \begin{bmatrix} \boldsymbol{D}_{11} & \cdots & \boldsymbol{D}_{1C} \\ \vdots & \ddots & \vdots \\ \boldsymbol{D}_{C1} & \cdots & \boldsymbol{D}_{CC} \end{bmatrix} \right)^{-1} \cdot \begin{bmatrix} \boldsymbol{F} & \boldsymbol{0} & \boldsymbol{0} \\ \boldsymbol{0} & \ddots & \boldsymbol{0} \\ \boldsymbol{0} & \boldsymbol{0} & \boldsymbol{F} \end{bmatrix}, \tag{16.6.3}$$

where $\boldsymbol{D}_{cc'}$ *are all diagonal matrices. Discuss how to exploit this structure to compute the inverse more efficiently.*

16.6. (Network architecture from accelerated gradient methods) *Empirically, people have found that additional skip connections across multiple layers may improve the network performance, e.g., highway network [SGS15] or the DenseNet [HLVDMW17]. In the ReduNet, the role of each layer is precisely interpreted as one iterative gradient ascent step for the objective function* ΔR*. In the experiments, we have observed that the basic gradient scheme sometimes converges slowly, resulting in deep networks with thousands of layers (iterations)! To improve the efficiency of the basic ReduNet, one may consider the accelerated gradient methods introduced in Chapters 8 and 9. Say to minimize or maximize a function* $h(z)$*, such accelerated methods usually take the form:*

$$\begin{cases} \boldsymbol{p}_{\ell+1} = z_\ell + \beta_\ell \cdot (z_\ell - z_{\ell-1}), \\ z_{\ell+1} = \boldsymbol{p}_{\ell+1} + \eta \cdot \nabla h(\boldsymbol{p}_{\ell+1}). \end{cases} \tag{16.6.4}$$

Sketch the resulting network architecture based on the accelerated gradient scheme, and verify empirically (say on the mixture of Gaussians or the handwritten digits) if the new architecture based on accelerated gradient would lead to faster convergence, hence networks with fewer layers (or iterations).

16.7. (Programming with deep invariant reduNet) *In Section 16.3.3, we have seen a basic example of constructing a ReduNet that is invariant to rotation (or translation)*

[48] Most current neural networks seem to adopt this regime.

[49] $\boldsymbol{P}_\ell^j$ can be viewed as the orthogonal complement to $\boldsymbol{C}_\ell^j$.

for two classes of digits, "0" and "1." Now knowing from "0" to "1," you are asked to take it from 1 to n in this exercise. This would allow you to gain some real experience with constructing ReduNets under more practical settings. Take 100 random samples from all 10 classes, 10 per class, from the MNIST dataset of 10 handwritten digits [LeC98].

(a) *First, you get a chance to construct a ReduNet that can map these 100 samples to 10 orthogonal subspaces that are invariant to* all *rotation.*
   (i) *First, convert each image to a multi-channel cyclic signal by following the same polar transforms illustrated in Figure 16.15. Here choose* $\Gamma = 200$ *and* $C = 15$.
   (ii) *Second, try to lift these signals with a number of random Gaussian filters. Try a different number of filters in the range 10 to 30; or filter kernel size from 3 to 9, etc.*
   (iii) *Construct the rest of the ReduNet. Again, try your construction with different choices of key parameters: say quantization error* $\varepsilon \in [0.01, 0.5]$, *optimization step size* $\eta \in [0.1, 1]$, *and a number of layers* $L \in [20, 100]$.

(b) *Second, finalize and evaluate your resulting ReduNet:*
   (i) *Monitor how the different rates* R, R_c, *and* ΔR *evolve with the number of layers.*
   (ii) *Compute the cosine similarity for the training set, before and after the ReduNet mapping.*
   (iii) *Randomly select an independent set of 100 samples, 10 per class, and evaluate the effect of ReduNet on these new samples.*

(c) *Finally, some bonus tasks:*
   (i) *Repeat for the task of constructing a ReduNet invariant to 2D translation for these digits. (Maybe you want to try a different range for the number of channels or layers.)*
   (ii) *Can you try to refine the so-obtained ReduNet network via back propagation by training it on the entire standard training set of MNIST? How would you evaluate what has been gained (or lost) through such refinement?*

APPENDICES

Appendix A Facts from Linear Algebra and Matrix Analysis

"Everything is linear algebra."

– attributed to Gene H. Golub

Linear algebra studies linear systems of equations and their solutions. This topic is extremely important for engineering applications. Linear models represent a simple, tractable first choice for modeling complicated systems. Moreover, many devices for measuring the physical world are designed to produce measurements that are as close as possible to linear functions of the signal to be measured, such as the MR imaging studied in Chapter 10. Even if the measurements are nonlinear or the signals of interest have nonlinear structures, a common and effective practice in engineering is to approximate any nonlinearity with a sequence of (local) linearization, as we see in Chapter 15 for recovering deformed low-rank textures and in Chapter 16 for learning submanifolds with a deep network.

In early parts of this appendix, we review several fundamental definitions, constructions, and facts from linear algebra and matrix analysis. For readers with a background in engineering, statistics, or applied mathematics, much of this material is likely to be familiar. They may use this appendix and the next few to refresh their memory and get familiar with the notation used in this book. Section A.9 contains a brief review of norms on matrices and spectral functions of matrices, two more advanced topics which we use extensively throughout the book. We have attempted to make this introduction as simple and self-contained as possible; readers looking for a more thorough introduction to this area could consult the excellent books of Horn and Johnson [HJ85], Golub and Van Loan [GVL96], or Bhatia [Bha96].[1]

A.1 Vector Spaces, Linear Independence, Bases, and Dimension

We use the notation $\mathbb{R}$ for the real numbers, and $\mathbb{R}^n$ for the n-dimensional real vectors of the form:

[1] Or Boyd and Vandenberghe [BV18] for a more elementary introduction.

$$\boldsymbol{x} \equiv \begin{bmatrix} x_1 \\ \vdots \\ x_n \end{bmatrix} \in \mathbb{R}^n, \quad \boldsymbol{x}^* = [x_1, \dots, x_n] \in \mathbb{R}^n, \tag{A.1.1}$$

where in this book, we use $\boldsymbol{x}^*$ to denote the transpose of a column vector $\boldsymbol{x}$. If the vector is complex, it represents the conjugate transpose. The space $\mathbb{R}^n$ is an example of a vector space – a space in which we can perform addition and scalar multiplication in a way that conforms to our intuition from $\mathbb{R}^3$. More formally:

DEFINITION A.1. (Vector space) *A vector space $\mathbb{V}$ over a field of scalars $\mathbb{F}$ is a set $\mathbb{V}$ (with a special distinguished zero element $\mathbf{0} \in \mathbb{V}$) endowed with two operations:*

- **vector addition** $+$, *which takes two vectors $\boldsymbol{v}, \boldsymbol{w} \in \mathbb{V}$ and produces another vector $\boldsymbol{v} + \boldsymbol{w} \in \mathbb{V}$, and*
- **scalar multiplication**, *which takes a vector $\boldsymbol{v} \in \mathbb{V}$ and a scalar $\alpha \in \mathbb{F}$, and produces a vector $\alpha\boldsymbol{v} \in \mathbb{V}$.*

The following hold: (1) addition is associative, $\boldsymbol{v}+(\boldsymbol{w}+\boldsymbol{x}) = (\boldsymbol{v}+\boldsymbol{w})+\boldsymbol{x}$; (2) addition is commutative, $\boldsymbol{v} + \boldsymbol{w} = \boldsymbol{w} + \boldsymbol{v}$; (3) zero is the additive identity, $\boldsymbol{v} + \mathbf{0} = \boldsymbol{v}$; (4) every element has an additive inverse, so for each $\boldsymbol{v} \in \mathbb{V}$, there exists an element "$-\boldsymbol{v}$" $\in \mathbb{V}$ such that $\boldsymbol{v} + (-\boldsymbol{v}) = \mathbf{0}$; (5) $\alpha(\beta\boldsymbol{v}) = (\alpha\beta)\boldsymbol{v}$; (6) multiplicative identity, $1\boldsymbol{v} = \boldsymbol{v}$, where $1 \in \mathbb{F}$ is the multiplicative identity in $\mathbb{F}$; (7) $\alpha(\boldsymbol{v} + \boldsymbol{w}) = \alpha\boldsymbol{v} + \alpha\boldsymbol{w}$; and (8) $(\alpha + \beta)\boldsymbol{v} = \alpha\boldsymbol{v} + \beta\boldsymbol{v}$.

EXAMPLE A.2. *The following are examples of vector spaces (check this!).*

- *The n-dimensional real vectors $\mathbb{R}^n$, over the scalar field $\mathbb{F} = \mathbb{R}$.*
- *The $m \times n$ real matrices*

$$\mathbb{R}^{m\times n} \doteq \left\{ \boldsymbol{X} = \begin{bmatrix} X_{11} & \cdots & X_{1n} \\ \vdots & \ddots & \vdots \\ X_{m1} & \cdots & X_{mn} \end{bmatrix} \middle| \; X_{ij} \in \mathbb{R} \right\}, \tag{A.1.2}$$

over the scalar field $\mathbb{F} = \mathbb{R}$.
- *The complex vectors $\mathbb{C}^n$ or complex matrices $\mathbb{C}^{m\times n}$, over the scalar field $\mathbb{F} = \mathbb{C}$.*
- *Function spaces, e.g.,*

$$C^0[0,1] \doteq \{f : [0,1] \to \mathbb{R} \mid f \text{ continuous}\}, \tag{A.1.3}$$

over $\mathbb{R}$. Vector spaces of functions defined on the continuum arise naturally in the study sampling problems, in which we wish to derive information about the physical world from digital measurements.

By itself, the notion of a vector space is not particularly rich: it is simply a space in which linear operations make sense. A vector space can be viewed as the "playing field" on which much more interesting models can be built, and much richer questions can be asked. As a step in this direction, we can note that it makes sense to take linear combinations of elements of a vector space. A *linear combination* is an expression of the form

$$\alpha_1 \boldsymbol{v}_1 + \alpha_2 \boldsymbol{v}_2 + \cdots + \alpha_k \boldsymbol{v}_k,$$

where $\alpha_1, \dots, \alpha_k \in \mathbb{F}$ and $\boldsymbol{v}_1, \dots, \boldsymbol{v}_k \in \mathbb{V}$.

DEFINITION A.3. (Linear independence) *A set of vectors* $\boldsymbol{v}_1, \dots, \boldsymbol{v}_k$ *are* linearly independent *if*

$$\sum_{i=1}^{k} \alpha_i \boldsymbol{v}_i = \boldsymbol{0} \quad \Longrightarrow \quad \alpha_1 = 0, \dots, \alpha_k = 0.$$

If a collection of vectors are not linearly independent, then there exists some choice of (α_i) not all zero, for which $\sum_i \alpha_i \boldsymbol{v}_i = \boldsymbol{0}$. In this case, we say that the set $\{\boldsymbol{v}_1, \dots, \boldsymbol{v}_k\}$ is *linearly dependent.*

DEFINITION A.4. (Basis for a vector space) *A* basis B *for the vector space* $\mathbb{V}$ *is defined as a* maximal, linearly independent set.

Here, *maximal* means that B is not contained in any larger linearly independent set. Any basis B for $\mathbb{V}$ *spans* $\mathbb{V}$, in the sense that every element of $\mathbb{V}$ can be written as a linear combination of elements of B:

$$\forall\, \boldsymbol{v} \in \mathbb{V},\ \exists\, \boldsymbol{b}_1, \dots, \boldsymbol{b}_k \in \mathsf{B},\ \alpha_1, \dots, \alpha_k \in \mathbb{F}, \quad \text{such that} \quad \boldsymbol{v} = \sum_{i=1}^{k} \alpha_i \boldsymbol{b}_i. \tag{A.1.4}$$

Moreover, if B is a basis, the coefficients $\alpha_1, \dots, \alpha_k$ in the above expression are unique.

EXAMPLE A.5. *In* $\mathbb{R}^n$*, we often use the* standard basis $\mathsf{B} = \{\boldsymbol{e}_1, \dots, \boldsymbol{e}_n\}$ *of coordinate vectors*

$$\boldsymbol{e}_1 = \begin{bmatrix} 1 \\ 0 \\ 0 \\ \vdots \\ 0 \end{bmatrix}, \quad \boldsymbol{e}_2 = \begin{bmatrix} 0 \\ 1 \\ 0 \\ \vdots \\ 0 \end{bmatrix}, \quad \dots, \quad \boldsymbol{e}_n = \begin{bmatrix} 0 \\ 0 \\ 0 \\ \vdots \\ 1 \end{bmatrix}. \tag{A.1.5}$$

In $\mathbb{R}^{m \times n}$ *we may work with the standard basis of coordinate matrices* $\boldsymbol{E}_{ij}$ *that are 1 in entry* (i, j) *and 0 elsewhere.*

Every vector space $\mathbb{V}$ has a basis.[2] One very fundamental result in linear algebra states that every basis has the same size:

[2] This statement may seem obvious, but it is tricky: it turns out to be equivalent to the *axiom of choice* in set theory, and hence is best viewed as an assumption. For the vector spaces we consider in this course ($\mathbb{R}^n$, $\mathbb{C}^n$, etc.), it will be very easy to construct a basis, and so for our purposes, the question is essentially moot.

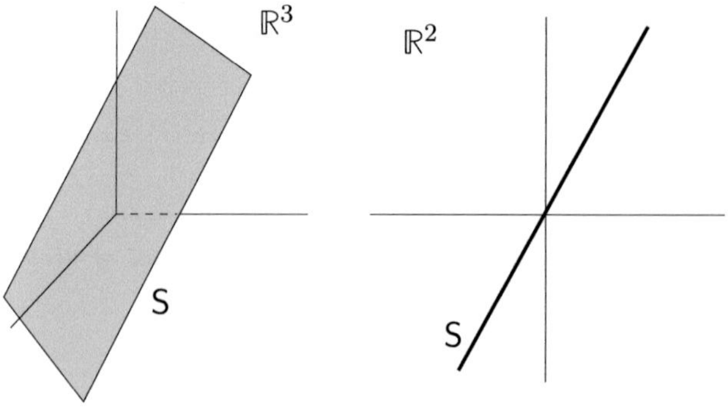

Figure A.1 Linear subspaces of $\mathbb{R}^2$ and $\mathbb{R}^3$.

THEOREM A.6. (Invariance of dimension) *For any vector space* $\mathbb{V}$, *every basis* B *has the same cardinality, which we denote* $\dim(\mathbb{V})$, *and call the* dimension *of* $\mathbb{V}$.

The notion of dimension is especially useful for talking about subspaces of the vector space $\mathbb{V}$.

DEFINITION A.7. (Linear subspace) *A* linear subspace *of a vector space* $\mathbb{V}$ *is a set* $\mathsf{S} \subseteq \mathbb{V}$ *that is also a vector space.*

For $\mathsf{S} \subseteq \mathbb{V}$ to be a linear subspace, it is necessary and sufficient that S be stable under linear combinations: for all $\alpha, \beta \in \mathbb{F}$ and $\boldsymbol{v}_1, \boldsymbol{v}_2 \in \mathsf{S}$, $\alpha \boldsymbol{v}_1 + \beta \boldsymbol{v}_2 \in \mathsf{S}$. Linear subspaces play a very important dual role, both as cleanly characterizing the solvability of linear equations, and as geometric data models. Geometrically, we can visualize a subspace as a generalization of a line, or plane, which must pass through the origin: $\mathbf{0} \in \mathsf{S}$ (see Figure A.1).

A.2 Inner Products

The most important geometric relationship between subspaces is that of *orthogonality*. To describe it clearly, we need the notion of an inner product. Below, we will assume that we are working with a vector space over either the real or complex numbers, and so the complex conjugate $\bar{\alpha}$ of $\alpha \in \mathbb{F}$ is well defined.

DEFINITION A.8. (Inner product) *A function* $\langle \cdot, \cdot \rangle : \mathbb{V} \times \mathbb{V} \to \mathbb{F}$ *is an* inner product *if it satisfies:*

- **linearity** $\langle \alpha \boldsymbol{v} + \beta \boldsymbol{w}, \boldsymbol{x} \rangle = \alpha \langle \boldsymbol{v}, \boldsymbol{x} \rangle + \beta \langle \boldsymbol{w}, \boldsymbol{x} \rangle$;
- **conjugate symmetry** $\langle \boldsymbol{v}, \boldsymbol{w} \rangle = \overline{\langle \boldsymbol{w}, \boldsymbol{v} \rangle}$;
- **positive definiteness** $\langle \boldsymbol{v}, \boldsymbol{v} \rangle \geq 0$, *with equality* $\boldsymbol{v} = \mathbf{0}$.

We then say that $\boldsymbol{v}$ and $\boldsymbol{w}$ are *orthogonal* (with respect to inner product $\langle \cdot, \cdot \rangle$) if $\langle \boldsymbol{v}, \boldsymbol{w} \rangle = 0$. In this case, we write $\boldsymbol{v} \perp \boldsymbol{w}$. For a given set $\mathsf{S} \subseteq \mathbb{V}$, we define its orthogonal complement as the set of all vectors that are orthogonal to every element of S:

DEFINITION A.9. (Orthogonal complement) *For* $\mathsf{S} \subseteq \mathbb{V}$,

$$\mathsf{S}^{\perp} = \left\{ \boldsymbol{v} \in \mathbb{V} \mid \langle \boldsymbol{v}, \boldsymbol{s} \rangle = 0 \ \forall \ \boldsymbol{s} \in \mathsf{S} \right\}.$$

It is worth noting that for any set S, $\mathsf{S}^{\perp} \subseteq \mathbb{V}$ is a linear subspace. This holds even if S is not a subspace itself.

We will use (and return to) two main examples of inner products. The first is the canonical inner product on $\mathbb{R}^n$, which simply sets

$$\langle \boldsymbol{x}, \boldsymbol{z} \rangle = \sum_{i=1}^{n} x_i z_i. \tag{A.2.1}$$

This extends to a canonical inner product on $\mathbb{R}^{m \times n}$, which is sometimes called the Frobenius inner product:

$$\langle \boldsymbol{X}, \boldsymbol{Z} \rangle \doteq \sum_{i=1}^{m} \sum_{j=1}^{n} X_{ij} Z_{ij}. \tag{A.2.2}$$

Recall that the trace of a square matrix is simply the sum of its diagonal elements:

DEFINITION A.10. *For* $\boldsymbol{M} \in \mathbb{R}^{n \times n}$, $\operatorname{trace}(\boldsymbol{M}) = \sum_{i=1}^{n} M_{ii}$.

Using the trace, we can give an expression for the Frobenius inner product which appears more complicated, but actually turns out to be tremendously useful:

$$\langle \boldsymbol{X}, \boldsymbol{Z} \rangle = \operatorname{trace}\left(\boldsymbol{X}^* \boldsymbol{Z}\right) = \operatorname{trace}\left(\boldsymbol{X} \boldsymbol{Z}^*\right). \tag{A.2.3}$$

For manipulating this expression, it is worth noting that the trace is invariant under a cyclic permutation of its argument:

THEOREM A.11. *For any matrices* $\boldsymbol{A}$ *and* $\boldsymbol{B}$ *of compatible size,* $\operatorname{trace}(\boldsymbol{A}\boldsymbol{B}) = \operatorname{trace}(\boldsymbol{B}\boldsymbol{A})$. *More generally, if* $\boldsymbol{A}_1, \dots, \boldsymbol{A}_n$ *are matrices of compatible size, and* π *is a cyclic permutation on* $\{1, \dots, n\}$, *then*

$$\operatorname{trace}(\boldsymbol{A}_1 \boldsymbol{A}_2 \cdots \boldsymbol{A}_n) = \operatorname{trace}\left(\boldsymbol{A}_{\pi(1)} \boldsymbol{A}_{\pi(2)} \cdots \boldsymbol{A}_{\pi(n)}\right). \tag{A.2.4}$$

A.3 Linear Transformations and Matrices

A mapping $\mathcal{L}$ between vector spaces $\mathbb{V}$ and $\mathbb{V}'$ over a common field $\mathbb{F}$ is a *linear transformation* (or linear map) if it respects the vector space operations:

DEFINITION A.12. (Linear map) *A* linear map *is a function* $\mathcal{L} : \mathbb{V} \to \mathbb{V}'$ *such that for all* $\alpha, \beta \in \mathbb{F}$ *and* $\boldsymbol{v}, \boldsymbol{w} \in \mathbb{V}$, $\mathcal{L}[\alpha \boldsymbol{v} + \beta \boldsymbol{w}] = \alpha \mathcal{L}[\boldsymbol{v}] + \beta \mathcal{L}[\boldsymbol{w}]$.

If $\mathbb{V}' = \mathbb{V}$ then we call $\mathcal{L}$ a *linear operator.*

EXAMPLE A.13. *Let* $\mathbb{V} = \mathbb{R}^{m\times n}$ *and* $\Omega \subseteq \{1,\dots,m\}\times\{1,\dots,n\}$. *Let* $\mathcal{P}_\Omega : \mathbb{R}^{m\times n} \to \mathbb{R}^{m\times n}$ *via*

$$(\mathcal{P}_\Omega[\boldsymbol{X}])_{ij} = \begin{cases} X_{ij} & (i,j)\in\Omega, \\ 0 & \textit{else}, \end{cases} \tag{A.3.1}$$

i.e., the restriction of $\boldsymbol{X}$ *to* Ω. *Then* $\mathcal{P}_\Omega$ *is a linear operator.*

The special case of $\mathbb{V} = \mathbb{R}^n$, $\mathbb{V}' = \mathbb{R}^m$ is of special importance. It turns out that there is a bijective correspondence between linear operators $\mathcal{L} : \mathbb{R}^n \to \mathbb{R}^m$ and $m \times n$ matrices:

THEOREM A.14. *For* $\boldsymbol{x} \in \mathbb{R}^n$ *and* $\boldsymbol{A} \in \mathbb{R}^{m\times n}$, *let*

$$(\boldsymbol{A}\boldsymbol{x})_i = \sum_j A_{ij} x_j. \tag{A.3.2}$$

Then for every $\boldsymbol{A} \in \mathbb{R}^{m\times n}$, *the mapping* $\boldsymbol{x} \mapsto \boldsymbol{A}\boldsymbol{x}$ *is a linear map from* $\mathbb{R}^n$ *to* $\mathbb{R}^m$. *Conversely for every linear map* $\mathcal{L} : \mathbb{R}^n \to \mathbb{R}^m$ *there exists a unique* $\boldsymbol{A} \in \mathbb{R}^{m\times n}$ *such that for every* $\boldsymbol{x}$, $\mathcal{L}[\boldsymbol{x}] = \boldsymbol{A}\boldsymbol{x}$.

This fact justifies the seemingly awkward standard definition of matrix multiplication – it is simply the correct way of representing the composition of two linear maps:

THEOREM A.15. *If* $\mathcal{L} : \mathbb{R}^n \to \mathbb{R}^p$ *and* $\mathcal{L}' : \mathbb{R}^p \to \mathbb{R}^m$ *are linear maps, with corresponding matrix representations* $\boldsymbol{A} \in \mathbb{R}^{p\times n}$ *and* $\boldsymbol{A}' \in \mathbb{R}^{m\times p}$, *and* $\mathcal{L}' \circ \mathcal{L}$ *denotes the composition* $\mathcal{L}' \circ \mathcal{L}(\boldsymbol{x}) = \mathcal{L}'[\mathcal{L}[\boldsymbol{x}]]$, *then* $\mathcal{L}' \circ \mathcal{L}$ *is a linear map, and its matrix representation is given by the matrix product* $\boldsymbol{A}'\boldsymbol{A}$ *whose* (i,j) *entry is*

$$\left(\boldsymbol{A}'\boldsymbol{A}\right)_{ij} = \sum_{k=1}^{p} a'_{ik} a_{kj}. \tag{A.3.3}$$

The (conjugate) transpose of a matrix $\boldsymbol{A} \in \mathbb{C}^{m\times n}$ is the $n \times m$ matrix $\boldsymbol{A}^* \in \mathbb{C}^{n\times m}$ given by

$$\boldsymbol{A} = \begin{bmatrix} A_{11} & \cdots & A_{1n} \\ \vdots & \ddots & \vdots \\ A_{m1} & \cdots & A_{mn} \end{bmatrix} \Rightarrow \boldsymbol{A}^* = \begin{bmatrix} \overline{A_{11}} & \cdots & \overline{A_{m1}} \\ \vdots & \ddots & \vdots \\ \overline{A_{1n}} & \cdots & \overline{A_{mn}} \end{bmatrix}. \tag{A.3.4}$$

When $\boldsymbol{A}$ is real, this is just the transpose. Transposition is a very simple operation on the entries of a matrix, but it has a basic reason for existing:

THEOREM A.16. *Let* $\mathcal{L} : \mathbb{R}^n \to \mathbb{R}^m$, *with corresponding matrix* $\boldsymbol{A}$. *Its adjoint map is the unique linear map* $\mathcal{L}^* : \mathbb{R}^m \to \mathbb{R}^n$ *satisfying*

$$\forall\, \boldsymbol{x}, \boldsymbol{y}, \qquad \langle \boldsymbol{y}, \mathcal{L}[\boldsymbol{x}]\rangle = \left\langle \mathcal{L}^*[\boldsymbol{y}], \boldsymbol{x}\right\rangle. \tag{A.3.5}$$

The matrix $\boldsymbol{A}^*$ *is the matrix representation of the adjoint map* $\mathcal{L}^*$.

A linear map $\mathcal{L} : \mathbb{V} \to \mathbb{V}'$ is *invertible* if for every $\boldsymbol{y} \in \mathbb{V}'$, there is a unique $\boldsymbol{x} \in \mathbb{V}$ such that $\mathcal{L}[\boldsymbol{x}] = \boldsymbol{y}$. In particular, if $\mathbb{V} = \mathbb{V}' = \mathbb{R}^n$, we call $\boldsymbol{A} \in \mathbb{R}^{n \times n}$ invertible if it corresponds to an invertible linear map. This means that the system of equations

$$\boldsymbol{A}\boldsymbol{x} = \boldsymbol{y} \tag{A.3.6}$$

always has a unique solution

$$\boldsymbol{x} = \boldsymbol{A}^{-1}\boldsymbol{y}. \tag{A.3.7}$$

It is not too difficult to show that if $\mathcal{L}$ is a linear map, its inverse $\mathcal{L}^{-1}$ is also linear. So, the notation $\boldsymbol{A}^{-1}$ above can be taken to mean "the matrix representation of the inverse mapping $\mathcal{L}^{-1}$." Fortunately, there are much more concrete criteria for determining if a given matrix $\boldsymbol{A}$ is invertible, and if so, for calculating $\boldsymbol{A}^{-1}$.

DEFINITION A.17. (Determinant) *The determinant of $\boldsymbol{A} \in \mathbb{R}^{n \times n}$ is the signed volume of the parallelepiped defined by the columns of $\boldsymbol{A}$:*

$$\det(\boldsymbol{A}) = \sum_{\pi \text{ a permutation on } \{1,\dots,n\}} \operatorname{sgn}(\pi) \times \prod_{i=1}^{n} A_{i,\pi(i)}. \tag{A.3.8}$$

The explicit expression (A.3.8) is not usually of direct use. More important is the geometric intuition: if $\det(\boldsymbol{A})$ is zero, the columns of $\boldsymbol{A}$ span a parallelepiped of zero volume, and so they lie on some lower-dimensional subspace of $\mathbb{R}^n$. Vectors $\boldsymbol{y}$ that do not reside in this subspace cannot be generated as linear combinations of the columns of $\boldsymbol{A}$, and $\boldsymbol{A}$ is not invertible. Conversely, if $\det \boldsymbol{A} \neq 0$, the columns of $\boldsymbol{A}$ span all of $\mathbb{R}^n$, and $\boldsymbol{A}$ is invertible. Making this reasoning formal, one obtains:

THEOREM A.18. (Matrix inverse) *A matrix $\boldsymbol{A} \in \mathbb{R}^{n \times n}$ is invertible if and only if $\det \boldsymbol{A} \neq 0$. If $\boldsymbol{A}$ is invertible, we can express its inverse as $\boldsymbol{A}^{-1} = (1/\det(\boldsymbol{A}))\boldsymbol{C}$, where $\boldsymbol{C} \in \mathbb{R}^{n \times n}$ is the companion matrix:*

$$\boldsymbol{C} \doteq \begin{bmatrix} (-1)^{1+1}\det(\boldsymbol{A}_{\setminus 1,\setminus 1}) & (-1)^{1+2}\det(\boldsymbol{A}_{\setminus 2,\setminus 1}) & \cdots & (-1)^{1+n}\det(\boldsymbol{A}_{\setminus n,\setminus 1}) \\ (-1)^{2+1}\det(\boldsymbol{A}_{\setminus 1,\setminus 2}) & (-1)^{2+2}\det(\boldsymbol{A}_{\setminus 2,\setminus 2}) & \cdots & (-1)^{2+n}\det(\boldsymbol{A}_{\setminus n,\setminus 2}) \\ \vdots & \vdots & \ddots & \vdots \\ (-1)^{n+1}\det(\boldsymbol{A}_{\setminus 1,\setminus n}) & (-1)^{n+2}\det(\boldsymbol{A}_{\setminus 2,\setminus n}) & \cdots & (-1)^{n+n}\det(\boldsymbol{A}_{\setminus n,\setminus n}) \end{bmatrix},$$

where the matrix $\boldsymbol{A}_{\setminus i,\setminus j}$ is constructed from $\boldsymbol{A}$ by removing the i-th row and j-th column.

Again, the above expression for $\boldsymbol{A}^{-1}$ is of little use computationally, but is conceptually helpful, since it shows that the entries of the inverse are rational functions of the entries of $\boldsymbol{A}$.

It is worth noting that for any matrices $\boldsymbol{A}$ and $\boldsymbol{B}$,

$$\det(\boldsymbol{A}\boldsymbol{B}) = \det(\boldsymbol{A})\det(\boldsymbol{B}). \tag{A.3.9}$$

This corroborates the fact that the product of invertible linear maps is invertible, and the product of invertible matrices is invertible. In particular,

$$(\boldsymbol{AB})^{-1} = \boldsymbol{B}^{-1}\boldsymbol{A}^{-1}. \tag{A.3.10}$$

It is also useful to note that for every matrix $\boldsymbol{A}$,

$$\det(\boldsymbol{A}) = \det(\boldsymbol{A}^*). \tag{A.3.11}$$

A.4 Matrix Groups

Because the product of two $n \times n$ matrices is again an $n \times n$ matrix, this operation can produce objects with interesting algebraic structure. We will not emphasize the algebra of matrix groups – or even formally define a group. Rather, we just recall the names of several groups that will recur throughout the course.

- **The general linear group** $\mathsf{GL}(n, \mathbb{R})$ consists of the invertible matrices:

$$\mathsf{GL}(n, \mathbb{R}) = \left\{ \boldsymbol{A} \in \mathbb{R}^{n \times n} \mid \det(\boldsymbol{A}) \neq 0 \right\}. \tag{A.4.1}$$

  Similarly, $\mathsf{GL}(n, \mathbb{C})$ denotes the $n \times n$ invertible matrices with complex entries.
- **The orthogonal group** $\mathsf{O}(n)$ consists of the real $n \times n$ matrices that satisfy $\boldsymbol{A}^*\boldsymbol{A} = \boldsymbol{A}\boldsymbol{A}^* = \boldsymbol{I}$:

$$\mathsf{O}(n) = \left\{ \boldsymbol{A} \in \mathbb{R}^{n \times n} \mid \boldsymbol{A}^*\boldsymbol{A} = \boldsymbol{I} \right\}. \tag{A.4.2}$$

  The expression $\boldsymbol{A}^*\boldsymbol{A} = \boldsymbol{I}$ implies that $\boldsymbol{A}$ is invertible, and that $\boldsymbol{A}^{-1} = \boldsymbol{A}^*$. Hence, $\mathsf{O}(n) \subset \mathsf{GL}(n, \mathbb{R})$. Two notes are in order: first, since $\boldsymbol{I} = \boldsymbol{I}^* = (\boldsymbol{A}^*\boldsymbol{A})^* = \boldsymbol{A}\boldsymbol{A}^*$, it is enough to keep only the expression $\boldsymbol{A}^*\boldsymbol{A}$ in the definition. Second, because $\det(\boldsymbol{A}) = \det(\boldsymbol{A}^*)$, we have $\det(\boldsymbol{A})^2 = 1$, and so every $\boldsymbol{A} \in \mathsf{O}(n)$ has determinant ± 1.
- **The special orthogonal group** $\mathsf{SO}(n)$ consists of the $n \times n$ matrices that satisfy $\boldsymbol{A}^*\boldsymbol{A} = \boldsymbol{A}\boldsymbol{A}^* = \boldsymbol{I}$, *and* $\det(\boldsymbol{A}) = +1$:

$$\mathsf{SO}(n) = \left\{ \boldsymbol{A} \in \mathbb{R}^{n \times n} \mid \boldsymbol{A}^*\boldsymbol{A} = \boldsymbol{I},\ \det(\boldsymbol{A}) = +1 \right\}. \tag{A.4.3}$$

  Clearly, $\mathsf{SO}(n) \subset \mathsf{O}(n) \subset \mathsf{GL}(n, \mathbb{R})$. In $\mathbb{R}^3$, the group $\mathsf{SO}(3)$ corresponds to the rotation matrices; $\mathsf{O}(3)$ contains rotations and reflections.
- **The unitary and special unitary groups** are subgroups of $\mathsf{GL}(n, \mathbb{C})$. The unitary group $\mathsf{U}(n)$ contains those matrices $\boldsymbol{A} \in \mathbb{C}^{n \times n}$ satisfying $\boldsymbol{A}^*\boldsymbol{A} = \boldsymbol{I}$. The special unitary group $\mathsf{SU}(n)$ contains those $\boldsymbol{A} \in \mathbb{C}^{n \times n}$ satisfying $\boldsymbol{A}^*\boldsymbol{A} = \boldsymbol{I}$ and $\det(\boldsymbol{A}) = 1$. So, $\mathsf{SU}(n) \subset \mathsf{U}(n) \subset \mathsf{GL}(n, \mathbb{C})$.

A.5 Subspaces Associated with a Matrix

To each linear operator $\mathcal{L} : \mathbb{V} \to \mathbb{V}'$, we associate two important subspaces, the range and the null space:

DEFINITION A.19. (Range, null space) *For* $\mathcal{L} : \mathbb{V} \to \mathbb{V}'$,

$$\mathrm{range}(\mathcal{L}) = \{\mathcal{L}[\boldsymbol{x}] \mid \boldsymbol{x} \in \mathbb{V}\} \subseteq \mathbb{V}', \tag{A.5.1}$$

$$\mathrm{null}(\mathcal{L}) = \{\boldsymbol{x} \in \mathbb{V} \mid \mathcal{L}[\boldsymbol{x}] = \boldsymbol{0}\} \subseteq \mathbb{V}. \tag{A.5.2}$$

The range is a linear subspace of $\mathbb{V}'$, *while the null space is a linear subspace of* $\mathbb{V}$.

Specializing these definitions to $\mathcal{L} : \mathbb{R}^n \to \mathbb{R}^m$, represented by a matrix $\boldsymbol{A}$, we obtain

$$\mathrm{null}(\boldsymbol{A}) = \{\boldsymbol{x} \mid \boldsymbol{A}\boldsymbol{x} = \boldsymbol{0}\}, \tag{A.5.3}$$

$$\mathrm{range}(\boldsymbol{A}) = \left\{\boldsymbol{A}\boldsymbol{x} \mid \boldsymbol{x} \in \mathbb{R}^n\right\} = \mathrm{col}(\boldsymbol{A}), \tag{A.5.4}$$

$$\mathrm{row}(\boldsymbol{A}) = \left\{\boldsymbol{w}^*\boldsymbol{A} \mid \boldsymbol{w} \in \mathbb{R}^m\right\}. \tag{A.5.5}$$

The sets $\mathrm{null}(\boldsymbol{A})$, $\mathrm{range}(\boldsymbol{A})$, and $\mathrm{row}(\boldsymbol{A})$ are all linear subspaces. They satisfy several very important relationships:

THEOREM A.20. *For* $\boldsymbol{A} \in \mathbb{R}^{m\times n}$, *the following relationships hold:*

- $\mathrm{null}(\boldsymbol{A})^\perp = \mathrm{range}(\boldsymbol{A}^*)$.
- $\mathrm{range}(\boldsymbol{A})^\perp = \mathrm{null}(\boldsymbol{A}^*)$.
- $\mathrm{null}(\boldsymbol{A}^*) = \mathrm{null}(\boldsymbol{A}\boldsymbol{A}^*)$.
- $\mathrm{range}(\boldsymbol{A}) = \mathrm{range}(\boldsymbol{A}\boldsymbol{A}^*)$.

From this, we obtain that $\dim(\mathrm{row}(\boldsymbol{A})) + \dim(\mathrm{null}(\boldsymbol{A})) = n$.

THEOREM A.21. (Matrix rank) *For any* $\boldsymbol{A} \in \mathbb{R}^{m\times n}$, $\dim(\mathrm{row}(\boldsymbol{A})) = \dim(\mathrm{range}(\boldsymbol{A}))$. *We call the common value the* rank *of* $\boldsymbol{A}$. *It is equal to the maximum size of a set of linearly independent rows, which is in turn equal to the maximum size of a set of linearly independent columns.*

The rank satisfies many useful properties:

THEOREM A.22. (Facts about rank) *The rank satisfies:*

- $\mathrm{rank}\,(\boldsymbol{A}\boldsymbol{B}) \le \min\{\mathrm{rank}\,(\boldsymbol{A}), \mathrm{rank}\,(\boldsymbol{B})\}$.
- **Sylvester's inequality**. *For* $\boldsymbol{A} \in \mathbb{R}^{m\times p}$, $\boldsymbol{B} \in \mathbb{R}^{p\times n}$,

$$\mathrm{rank}\,(\boldsymbol{A}\boldsymbol{B}) \ge \mathrm{rank}\,(\boldsymbol{A}) + \mathrm{rank}\,(\boldsymbol{B}) - p.$$

- **Subadditivity**. *For all* $\boldsymbol{A}, \boldsymbol{B} \in \mathbb{R}^{m\times n}$, $\mathrm{rank}\,(\boldsymbol{A}+\boldsymbol{B}) \le \mathrm{rank}\,(\boldsymbol{A}) + \mathrm{rank}\,(\boldsymbol{B})$.
- $\mathrm{rank}\,(\boldsymbol{A}) = \mathrm{rank}\,(\boldsymbol{A}\boldsymbol{A}^*) = \mathrm{rank}\,(\boldsymbol{A}^*\boldsymbol{A})$.

A.6 Linear Systems of Equations

Using the range and null space, we can decide if the system $\boldsymbol{y} = \boldsymbol{A}\boldsymbol{x}$ has a solution, and how many solutions it has:

THEOREM A.23. *Consider a linear system of equations* $\boldsymbol{y} = \boldsymbol{A}\boldsymbol{x}$.

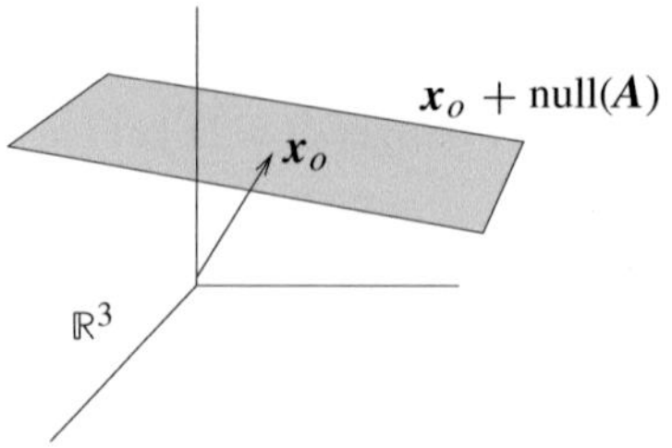

Figure A.2 Geometry of solution sets for linear equations.

- **Existence**. *The system* $y = Ax$ *has a solution* x *if and only if* $y \in \text{range}(A)$.
- **Uniqueness**. *Suppose that* x_o *satisfies* $y = Ax_o$. *Every solution to the equation* $y = Ax$ *can be generated as* $x_o + v$, *where* $v \in \text{null}(A)$. *The solution* x_o *is* unique *if and only if the null space is trivial* ($\text{null}(A) = \{\mathbf{0}\}$).

The last point means that whenever $y = Ax$ has a solution x_o, the solution set has the form

$$x_o + \text{null}(A). \tag{A.6.1}$$

The "+" here is "in the sense of Minkowski," which just means that $x + \mathsf{S} = \{x + s \mid s \in \mathsf{S}\}$. Since $\text{null}(A)$ is a linear subspace, the resulting set is a translate of a linear subspace. We call such a set an *affine subspace*. Unlike a linear subspace, an affine subspace need not contain $\mathbf{0}$.

DEFINITION A.24. (Affine combination and affine subspace) *Let* $v_1, \dots, v_k \in \mathbb{V}$. *An* affine combination *is an expression of the form* $\sum_i \alpha_i v_i$, *with* $\sum_i \alpha_i = 1$. *An* affine subspace *is a set* $\mathsf{A} \subset \mathbb{V}$ *which is stable under affine combinations.*

It is easy to check that A is an affine subspace if and only if $\mathsf{A} = x + \mathsf{S}$ for some linear subspace S. So, geometrically, we can visualize the solution set of $y = Ax$ as living on a plane which does not contain $\mathbf{0}$ – see Figure A.2.

Invertible Systems and Conjugate Gradient

If $A \in \mathbb{R}^{m \times m}$ is square, and has full rank m, then for every $y \in \mathbb{R}^m$, the system $y = Ax$ has exactly one solution $\hat{x} = A^{-1}y$, where A^{-1} can be computed according to Theorem A.18. However, when the matrix A is large, computing the inverse is very expensive. A much more efficient numerical method to compute the solution to the above linear system is the so-called *conjugate gradient method*. For completeness, we here only describe the method but refer readers to the detailed derivation and analysis in [She94, NW06].

The conjugate gradient is essentially an accelerated optimization method that solves the quadratic minimization problem

$$\min_{x} \|y - Ax\|_2^2 \tag{A.6.2}$$

with an iterative procedure. Let $r_i \in \mathbb{R}^m$ denote the residual and $d_i \in \mathbb{R}^m$ be the direction of incremental descent. The iterative process starts from any given initial state $\boldsymbol{x}_0 \in \mathbb{R}^m$, and the residual and descent direction are initialized as

$$\boldsymbol{d}_0 = \boldsymbol{r}_0 = \boldsymbol{y} - \boldsymbol{A}\boldsymbol{x}_0.$$

The conjugate gradient descent process is given by the following iteration: for $i = 0, 1, 2, \ldots,$

$$\text{conjugate gradient} \quad \begin{cases} \alpha_i = \dfrac{\boldsymbol{r}_i^* \boldsymbol{r}_i}{\boldsymbol{d}_i^* \boldsymbol{A} \boldsymbol{d}_i}, \\ \boldsymbol{x}_{i+1} = \boldsymbol{x}_i + \alpha_i \boldsymbol{d}_i, \\ \boldsymbol{r}_{i+1} = \boldsymbol{r}_i - \alpha_i \boldsymbol{A} \boldsymbol{d}_i, \\ \beta_{i+1} = \dfrac{\boldsymbol{r}_{i+1}^* \boldsymbol{r}_{i+1}}{\boldsymbol{r}_i^* \boldsymbol{r}_i}, \\ \boldsymbol{d}_{i+1} = \boldsymbol{r}_{i+1} + \beta_{i+1} \boldsymbol{d}_i. \end{cases} \tag{A.6.3}$$

The process terminates when the error reaches a prescribed accuracy: $\|\boldsymbol{y} - \boldsymbol{A}\boldsymbol{x}_i\|_2 \le \varepsilon$. The precise complexity of the conjugate gradient descent is characterized in Theorem 9.11, which plays a crucial role in achieving the optimal rate for the Newton descent scheme studied there.

In practice, we very frequently encounter linear systems of equations $\boldsymbol{y} = \boldsymbol{A}\boldsymbol{x}$ for which $\boldsymbol{A}$ is not invertible. We describe two important cases below.

Overdetermined Systems

Suppose that $\boldsymbol{A} \in \mathbb{R}^{m \times n}$ and $m > n$. Since $\operatorname{rank}(\boldsymbol{A}) \le \min\{m, n\} < m$, the range of $\boldsymbol{A}$ is a lower-dimensional subspace of $\mathbb{R}^m$. Hence, in general, the system of equations $\boldsymbol{y} = \boldsymbol{A}\boldsymbol{x}$ will not have a solution. Hence, we resort to seeking an approximate solution. Classically, this was often done via the method of *least squares*. Define the Euclidean length $\|\boldsymbol{z}\|_2 = \sqrt{\sum_i z_i^2}$ of a vector $\boldsymbol{z} \in \mathbb{R}^n$. A least-squares solution solves

$$\min_{\boldsymbol{x}} \|\boldsymbol{y} - \boldsymbol{A}\boldsymbol{x}\|_2^2. \tag{A.6.4}$$

If $\boldsymbol{A}$ has full column rank n, the solution $\hat{\boldsymbol{x}}_{LS}$ to this problem is unique, and is given by

$$\hat{\boldsymbol{x}}_{LS} = (\boldsymbol{A}^*\boldsymbol{A})^{-1}\boldsymbol{A}^*\boldsymbol{y}. \tag{A.6.5}$$

We sometimes write $\boldsymbol{A}^\dagger = (\boldsymbol{A}^*\boldsymbol{A})^{-1}\boldsymbol{A}^*$, and call this matrix the *pseudo-inverse* of $\boldsymbol{A}$. Notice that

$$\boldsymbol{A}\hat{\boldsymbol{x}}_{LS} = \boldsymbol{A}(\boldsymbol{A}^*\boldsymbol{A})^{-1}\boldsymbol{A}^*\boldsymbol{y} \tag{A.6.6}$$

$$= \boldsymbol{P}_{\operatorname{range}(\boldsymbol{A})}\boldsymbol{y} \tag{A.6.7}$$

is the orthogonal projection of $\boldsymbol{y}$ onto $\operatorname{range}(\boldsymbol{A})$; the matrix

$$\boldsymbol{P}_{\operatorname{range}(\boldsymbol{A})} = \boldsymbol{A}(\boldsymbol{A}^*\boldsymbol{A})^{-1}\boldsymbol{A}^*$$

is the projection matrix onto this space. The optimal value of the least-squares problem is

$$\left\| \boldsymbol{y} - \boldsymbol{A}\hat{\boldsymbol{x}}_{LS} \right\|_2^2 = \left\| (\boldsymbol{I} - \boldsymbol{P}_{\mathrm{range}(\boldsymbol{A})})\boldsymbol{y} \right\|_2^2 \tag{A.6.8}$$

$$= \left\| \boldsymbol{P}_{\mathrm{range}(\boldsymbol{A})^\perp} \boldsymbol{y} \right\|_2^2. \tag{A.6.9}$$

This is just the squared (Euclidean) distance from the observation $\boldsymbol{y}$ to range($\boldsymbol{A}$).

Underdetermined Systems

If on the other hand $m < n$, as discussed above, the solution is not unique – if any solution $\boldsymbol{x}_o$ exists, then there is an entire affine space $\boldsymbol{x}_o + \mathrm{null}(\boldsymbol{A})$ of solutions. A classical approach to handling such underdetermined systems is to look for the $\boldsymbol{x}$ of smallest length that is consistent with the system. Formally,

$$\min \quad \|\boldsymbol{x}\|_2^2 \quad \text{subject to} \quad \boldsymbol{y} = \boldsymbol{A}\boldsymbol{x}. \tag{A.6.10}$$

If $\boldsymbol{A}$ has full row rank (i.e., rank($\boldsymbol{A}$) $= m$), this problem has a unique solution:

THEOREM A.25. *Let $\boldsymbol{A} \in \mathbb{R}^{m \times n}$ have full row rank (i.e.,* rank $(\boldsymbol{A}) = m$*). Then for any $\boldsymbol{y} \in \mathbb{R}^m$, the optimization problem*

$$\min \quad \|\boldsymbol{x}\|_2^2 \quad \textit{subject to} \quad \boldsymbol{y} = \boldsymbol{A}\boldsymbol{x} \tag{A.6.11}$$

has a unique optimal solution,

$$\hat{\boldsymbol{x}}_{\ell^2} = \boldsymbol{A}^*(\boldsymbol{A}\boldsymbol{A}^*)^{-1}\boldsymbol{y}. \tag{A.6.12}$$

Proof The following inequality can be checked by directly expanding the right-hand side:

$$\forall \boldsymbol{x}, \boldsymbol{x}' \in \mathbb{R}^n, \quad \left\|\boldsymbol{x}'\right\|_2^2 = \left\|\boldsymbol{x} + (\boldsymbol{x}' - \boldsymbol{x})\right\|_2^2$$
$$= \|\boldsymbol{x}\|_2^2 + \langle 2\boldsymbol{x}, \boldsymbol{x}' - \boldsymbol{x}\rangle + \left\|\boldsymbol{x}' - \boldsymbol{x}\right\|_2^2. \tag{A.6.13}$$

If $\boldsymbol{x}$ and $\boldsymbol{x}'$ are feasible for our problem, then $\boldsymbol{A}\boldsymbol{x} = \boldsymbol{A}\boldsymbol{x}' = \boldsymbol{y}$, and so $\boldsymbol{x}' - \boldsymbol{x} \in \mathrm{null}(\boldsymbol{A})$. For any feasible $\boldsymbol{x}' \neq \hat{\boldsymbol{x}}_{\ell^2}$, we have

$$\begin{aligned}
\left\|\boldsymbol{x}'\right\|_2^2 &\geq \left\|\hat{\boldsymbol{x}}_{\ell^2}\right\|_2^2 + 2\langle \hat{\boldsymbol{x}}_{\ell^2}, \boldsymbol{x}' - \hat{\boldsymbol{x}}_{\ell^2}\rangle + \left\|\boldsymbol{x}' - \hat{\boldsymbol{x}}_{\ell^2}\right\|_2^2 \\
&= \left\|\hat{\boldsymbol{x}}_{\ell^2}\right\|_2^2 + 2\left\langle \boldsymbol{A}^*(\boldsymbol{A}\boldsymbol{A}^*)^{-1}\boldsymbol{y}, \boldsymbol{x}' - \hat{\boldsymbol{x}}_{\ell^2}\right\rangle + \left\|\boldsymbol{x}' - \hat{\boldsymbol{x}}_{\ell^2}\right\|_2^2 \\
&= \left\|\hat{\boldsymbol{x}}_{\ell^2}\right\|_2^2 + \underbrace{2\left\langle (\boldsymbol{A}\boldsymbol{A}^*)^{-1}\boldsymbol{y}, \boldsymbol{A}(\boldsymbol{x}' - \hat{\boldsymbol{x}}_{\ell^2})\right\rangle}_{=0} + \left\|\boldsymbol{x}' - \hat{\boldsymbol{x}}_{\ell^2}\right\|_2^2 \\
&> \left\|\hat{\boldsymbol{x}}_{\ell^2}\right\|_2^2.
\end{aligned} \tag{A.6.14}$$

□

The matrix $\boldsymbol{A}^*(\boldsymbol{A}\boldsymbol{A}^*)^{-1}$ is also called a pseudo-inverse of $\boldsymbol{A}$, and also denoted by $\boldsymbol{A}^\dagger$.[3]

[3] The fact that we have apparently used the notation $\boldsymbol{A}^\dagger$ for two different things is resolved if we consider the general form of the pseudo-inverse, which is written in terms of the singular value decomposition (SVD). We will do this after reviewing the SVD in Section A.8.

In the above, we have assumed that the matrix $\boldsymbol{A}$ is of full column or row rank. In practice, the system of equations $\boldsymbol{y} = \boldsymbol{A}\boldsymbol{x}$ can be ill-posed or the equations are corrupted by some random (Gaussian) noise $\boldsymbol{y} = \boldsymbol{A}\boldsymbol{x}+\boldsymbol{\varepsilon}$. In this case, we may consider solving a regularized version, say the popular *ridge regression*:

$$\min_{\boldsymbol{x}} \|\boldsymbol{y} - \boldsymbol{A}\boldsymbol{x}\|_2^2 + \lambda\|\boldsymbol{x}\|_2^2. \tag{A.6.15}$$

We leave as an exercise for the reader to find the optimal solution to the above problem (see Exercise 1.8).

A.7 Eigenvectors and Eigenvalues

DEFINITION A.26. (Eigenvalue and eigenvector) *Let $\boldsymbol{A} \in \mathbb{C}^{n\times n}$. We say that $\lambda \in \mathbb{C}$ is an eigenvalue of $\boldsymbol{A}$ if there exists some nonzero vector $\boldsymbol{v} \in \mathbb{C}^n \setminus \{\boldsymbol{0}\}$ such that*

$$\boldsymbol{A}\boldsymbol{v} = \lambda\boldsymbol{v}. \tag{A.7.1}$$

If we view $\boldsymbol{A}$ as corresponding to a linear map $\mathcal{L} : \mathbb{C}^n \to \mathbb{C}^n$, the definition says that $\mathcal{L}$ preserves the direction of the vector $\boldsymbol{v}$. If λ is an eigenvalue of $\boldsymbol{A}$, with corresponding eigenvector $\boldsymbol{v}$, then $\boldsymbol{v} \in \text{null}(\boldsymbol{A} - \lambda\boldsymbol{I})$, and hence $\text{rank}\,(\boldsymbol{A} - \lambda\boldsymbol{I}) < n$. Using the determinant criterion for singularity, we obtain:

THEOREM A.27. *We have that $\lambda \in \mathbb{C}$ is an eigenvalue of $\boldsymbol{A} \in \mathbb{C}^{n\times n}$ if and only if it is a root of the characteristic polynomial*

$$\chi(\lambda) = \det(\boldsymbol{A} - \lambda\boldsymbol{I}), \tag{A.7.2}$$

i.e., $\chi(\lambda) = 0$.

This implies that every matrix $\boldsymbol{A} \in \mathbb{C}^{n\times n}$ has n complex eigenvalues, counted with multiplicity. Often we are interested in real matrices $\boldsymbol{A} \in \mathbb{R}^{n\times n}$.

Real Symmetric Matrices

It is important to note that *the eigenvalues of a real matrix are not necessarily real.* There is one important special case in which the eigenvalues are guaranteed to be real: symmetric matrices. A matrix $\boldsymbol{A} \in \mathbb{R}^{n\times n}$ is *symmetric* if

$$\boldsymbol{A} = \boldsymbol{A}^*. \tag{A.7.3}$$

The eigenvalues of a symmetric matrix are necessarily real, with corresponding real eigenvectors. Moreover, it is not difficult to prove that if $\boldsymbol{v}$ and $\boldsymbol{v}'$ are eigenvectors of a symmetric matrix corresponding to *distinct* eigenvalues $\lambda \neq \lambda'$, then they are orthogonal: $\boldsymbol{v} \perp \boldsymbol{v}'$. From this, we obtain the eigenvector decomposition of a symmetric matrix:

THEOREM A.28. (Eigenvector decomposition) *Let $\boldsymbol{A} \in \mathbb{R}^{n\times n}$ be symmetric. Then there exist orthonormal vectors $\boldsymbol{v}_1, \dots, \boldsymbol{v}_n \in \mathbb{R}^n$ and real scalars $\lambda_1 \geq \cdots \geq \lambda_n$, such that if we write*

$$V = [v_1 \mid \cdots \mid v_n] \in \mathsf{O}(n), \qquad \Lambda = \begin{bmatrix} \lambda_1 & & & \\ & \lambda_2 & & \\ & & \ddots & \\ & & & \lambda_n \end{bmatrix} \in \mathbb{R}^{n \times n}, \quad \text{(A.7.4)}$$

we have

$$A = V \Lambda V^*. \quad \text{(A.7.5)}$$

The expression $A = V\Lambda V^*$ is sometimes written as $A = \sum_{i=1}^n \lambda_i v_i v_i^*$. Theorem A.28 leads to the following variational characterization of the eigenvalues, which is useful both for analytical purposes and for identifying optimization problems that can be solved directly via eigenvector decomposition:

THEOREM A.29. (Variational characterization of eigenvalues) *The first eigenvalue* λ_1 *of a symmetric matrix* A *is the optimal value of the problem*

$$\begin{array}{ll} \max & x^* A x \\ \text{subject to} & \|x\|_2^2 = 1. \end{array} \quad \text{(A.7.6)}$$

Moreover, every optimizer v_1 *is an eigenvector corresponding to* λ_1. *Similarly, the optimal value of*

$$\begin{array}{ll} \min & x^* A x \\ \text{subject to} & \|x\|_2^2 = 1 \end{array} \quad \text{(A.7.7)}$$

is λ_n. *For the intermediate eigenvalues, if* $v_1, \dots, v_{k-1}$ *are any mutually orthogonal eigenvectors corresponding to* $\lambda_1, \dots, \lambda_{k-1}$, *we have that* λ_k *is the optimal value for*

$$\begin{array}{ll} \max & x^* A x \\ \text{subject to} & \|x\|_2^2 = 1, \; x \perp v_1, \dots, v_{k-1}. \end{array} \quad \text{(A.7.8)}$$

From the previous result, it seems the eigenvector decomposition is a very useful tool for studying quadratic forms $q(x) = x^* A x$. Matrices A for which $q(x)$ is always positive are especially important:

DEFINITION A.30. (Positive definiteness) *A symmetric matrix* $A \in \mathbb{R}^{n \times n}$ *is* positive definite *if for all nonzero* $x \in \mathbb{R}^n$, $x^* A x > 0$. *It is* positive semidefinite *if for all* $x \in \mathbb{R}^n$, $x^* A x \geq 0$.

If A is positive definite, we write

$$A \succ \mathbf{0}. \quad \text{(A.7.9)}$$

If A is positive semidefinite, we write

$$A \succeq \mathbf{0}. \quad \text{(A.7.10)}$$

More generally, for symmetric matrices A and B, we write $A \succeq B$ if $A - B$ is semidefinite, i.e., $A - B \succeq \mathbf{0}$. This defines a *partial order* on the symmetric matrices, which we call the *semidefinite order*.

THEOREM A.31. *A symmetric matrix A is positive definite (respectively semidefinite) if and only if all of its eigenvalues are positive (respectively nonnegative).*

Circulant Matrix and Convolution

Given a vector $\boldsymbol{a} = [a_0, a_1, \ldots, a_{n-1}]^* \in \mathbb{R}^n$, we may arrange all its circularly shifted versions in a circulant matrix form as

$$\boldsymbol{A} \doteq \mathrm{circ}(\boldsymbol{a}) = \begin{bmatrix} a_0 & a_{n-1} & \cdots & a_2 & a_1 \\ a_1 & a_0 & a_{n-1} & \cdots & a_2 \\ \vdots & a_1 & a_0 & \ddots & \vdots \\ a_{n-2} & \vdots & \ddots & \ddots & a_{n-1} \\ a_{n-1} & a_{n-2} & \cdots & a_1 & a_0 \end{bmatrix} \in \mathbb{R}^{n \times n}. \tag{A.7.11}$$

It is easy to see that the multiplication of such a circulant matrix $\boldsymbol{A}$ with a vector $\boldsymbol{x}$ gives a (circular) convolution $\boldsymbol{A}\boldsymbol{x} = \boldsymbol{a} \circledast \boldsymbol{x}$ with

$$(\boldsymbol{a} \circledast \boldsymbol{x})_i = \sum_{j=0}^{n-1} x_j a_{i+n-j \bmod n}. \tag{A.7.12}$$

One remarkable property of circulant matrices is that *they all share the same set of eigenvectors that form a unitary matrix*. Let $\mathrm{i} = \sqrt{-1}$ and $\omega_n := \exp(-2\pi\mathrm{i}/n)$ be the roots of unity (as $\omega^n = 1$) and define the matrix

$$\boldsymbol{F}_n \doteq \frac{1}{\sqrt{n}} \begin{bmatrix} \omega_n^0 & \omega_n^0 & \cdots & \omega_n^0 & \omega_n^0 \\ \omega_n^0 & \omega_n^1 & \cdots & \omega_n^{n-2} & \omega_n^{n-1} \\ \vdots & \vdots & \ddots & \vdots & \vdots \\ \omega_n^0 & \omega_n^{n-2} & \cdots & \omega_n^{(n-2)^2} & \omega_n^{(n-2)(n-1)} \\ \omega_n^0 & \omega_n^{n-1} & \cdots & \omega_n^{(n-2)(n-1)} & \omega_n^{(n-1)^2} \end{bmatrix} \in \mathbb{C}^{n \times n}. \tag{A.7.13}$$

The matrix $\boldsymbol{F}_n$ is a unitary matrix: $\boldsymbol{F}_n \boldsymbol{F}_n^* = \boldsymbol{I}$ and is the well-known *Vandermonde matrix*. Multiplying a vector with $\boldsymbol{F}_n$ is known as the *discrete Fourier transform* (DFT). More precisely, we have the following well-known fact [KS12]:

THEOREM A.32. (Eigenvectors of circulant matrix) *An $n \times n$ matrix $\boldsymbol{A} \in \mathbb{C}^{n \times n}$ is a circulant matrix if and only if it is diagonalizable by the unitary matrix:*

$$\boldsymbol{F}_n^* \boldsymbol{A} \boldsymbol{F}_n = \boldsymbol{D}_{\boldsymbol{a}} \quad \text{or} \quad \boldsymbol{A} = \boldsymbol{F}_n \boldsymbol{D}_{\boldsymbol{a}} \boldsymbol{F}_n^*, \tag{A.7.14}$$

where $\boldsymbol{D}_{\boldsymbol{a}}$ is a diagonal matrix of eigenvalues.[4]

From the above fact, we can easily derive the following properties of circulant matrices:

- The transpose of a circulant matrix is circulant.
- Multiplication of two circulant matrices is circulant.

[4] The eigenvalues can be complex even for real circulant matrices.

- For a nonsingular circulant matrix, its inverse is also circulant (hence representing a circular convolution).
- Since all circulant matrices can be simultaneously diagonalized by the same unitary matrix $\boldsymbol{F}_n$, their summation and inversion can be reduced to the same operations on their diagonal forms, hence much faster and scalable.

Location of Eigenvalues

It is often useful to be able to characterize, in terms of the properties of $\boldsymbol{A}$, where the eigenvalues $\lambda \in \mathbb{C}$ are located. For example, we saw that if $\boldsymbol{A}$ is a symmetric matrix, the eigenvalues lie on the real axis. For general $\boldsymbol{A}$, the situation is more complicated. However, we do have the following result of Gershgorin, which states that the eigenvalues must live in a union of disks, centered about the diagonal elements A_{ii} of $\boldsymbol{A}$:

THEOREM A.33. (Gershgorin disk theorem) *Let $\boldsymbol{A} \in \mathbb{C}^{n\times n}$, and let $\lambda \in \mathbb{C}$ and $\boldsymbol{v} \in \mathbb{C}^n$ be an eigenvalue–eigenvector pair. Then there exists some $i \in \{1,\dots,n\}$ such that*

$$|\lambda - A_{ii}| \leq \sum_{j\neq i} |A_{ij}|. \tag{A.7.15}$$

This result is called the Gershgorin disk theorem, because it implies that in the complex plane $\mathbb{C}$, each eigenvalue λ lies in a union of disks D_i with centers A_{ii} and radii $r_i = \sum_{j\neq i} |A_{ij}|$. It is most powerful when the off-diagonal elements of $\boldsymbol{A}$ are small. Numerous variants and refinements are known.

A.8 The Singular Value Decomposition (SVD)

Definitions

The eigenvector decomposition $\boldsymbol{S} = \boldsymbol{V}\boldsymbol{\Lambda}\boldsymbol{V}^*$ defined in Theorem A.28 provides an essential tool for studying symmetric matrices $\boldsymbol{S}$. In particular, it shows that with an appropriate rotation of the space, a symmetric matrix acts like a diagonal matrix. It would be very useful to have a similar representation for general matrices, including nonsymmetric square matrices, and rectangular matrices. The *singular value decomposition* goes much of the way, allowing us to find bases for the domain and range of a linear map with respect to which it becomes quite simple:

THEOREM A.34. (Compact SVD, existence) *Let $\boldsymbol{A} \in \mathbb{R}^{m\times n}$, with* rank$(\boldsymbol{A}) = r$. *There exist scalars $\sigma_1 \geq \sigma_2 \geq \cdots \geq \sigma_r > 0$ and matrices $\boldsymbol{U} \in \mathbb{R}^{m\times r}$ and $\boldsymbol{V} \in \mathbb{R}^{n\times r}$ with orthonormal columns ($\boldsymbol{U}^*\boldsymbol{U} = \boldsymbol{I}$, $\boldsymbol{V}^*\boldsymbol{V} = \boldsymbol{I}$) such that if we set*

$$\boldsymbol{\Sigma} = \begin{bmatrix} \sigma_1 & & & \\ & \sigma_2 & & \\ & & \ddots & \\ & & & \sigma_r \end{bmatrix} \in \mathbb{R}^{r\times r}, \tag{A.8.1}$$

we have

$$A = U\Sigma V^*. \tag{A.8.2}$$

The σ_i *are called* singular values *of* A, *while the columns of* U *and* V *are called the (left and right, respectively) singular vectors.*

The expression in Theorem A.34 can be used to express A as a sum of r orthogonal rank-1 matrices:

$$A = \sum_{i=1}^{r} \sigma_i u_i v_i^*. \tag{A.8.3}$$

The compact SVD immediately reveals several important properties of A:

THEOREM A.35. (Properties of compact SVD) *Let* $A \in \mathbb{R}^{m\times n}$, *with compact SVD* $A = U\Sigma V^*$. *Then the following hold.*

- range(A) $=$ range(U). *The columns of* U *are an orthonormal basis for the range of* A.
- range(A^*) $=$ range(V). *The columns of* V *are an orthonormal basis for the row space of* A.

Occasionally it is useful to extend U and V to orthogonal matrices, giving the full singular value decomposition:

THEOREM A.36. (Full SVD) *Let* $A \in \mathbb{R}^{m\times n}$. *Then there exist* $U \in \mathsf{O}(m)$, $V \in \mathsf{O}(n)$, *and* $\Sigma \in \mathbb{R}^{m\times n}$ *such that*

$$A = U\Sigma V^*, \tag{A.8.4}$$

Σ *is diagonal (i.e.,* $\Sigma_{ij} = 0$ *for* $i \neq j$*), and*

$$\Sigma_{11} \geq \Sigma_{22} \geq \cdots \geq \Sigma_{\min\{m,n\},\ \min\{m,n\}} \geq 0.$$

With a full SVD, we may write the pseudo-inverse of a matrix, introduced in Section A.6, in a unified form:

$$A^\dagger = V\Sigma^\dagger U^*, \tag{A.8.5}$$

where $\Sigma^\dagger \in \mathbb{R}^{n\times m}$ is the pseudo-inverse of the diagonal matrix $\Sigma \in \mathbb{R}^{m\times n}$.[5]

It is sometimes a point of confusion that the notation for the full SVD and the compact SVD coincide. In this course, we will mostly work with the compact SVD, unless stated otherwise.

Approximation Properties

The SVD provides an immediate solution to several approximation problems. Most fundamentally, it gives a way of forming a best rank-r approximation to A:

[5] That is, $\Sigma^\dagger$ is a diagonal matrix with the diagonal entries Σ_{ii}^{-1} for all $\Sigma_{ii} > 0$.

THEOREM A.37. (Best rank-r approximation) *Let $\boldsymbol{A} \in \mathbb{R}^{m \times n}$ have singular value decomposition*

$$\boldsymbol{A} = \sum_{i=1}^{\min\{m,n\}} \sigma_i \boldsymbol{u}_i \boldsymbol{v}_i^*. \tag{A.8.6}$$

Then an optimal solution to the rank-r approximation problem

$$\begin{array}{ll} \min & \|\boldsymbol{X} - \boldsymbol{A}\|_F \\ \text{subject to} & \operatorname{rank}(\boldsymbol{X}) \leq r \end{array} \tag{A.8.7}$$

is the truncated SVD

$$\widehat{\boldsymbol{A}}_r = \sum_{i=1}^{r} \sigma_i \boldsymbol{u}_i \boldsymbol{v}_i^*. \tag{A.8.8}$$

If $\sigma_r(\boldsymbol{A}) > \sigma_{r+1}(\boldsymbol{A})$, then the solution is unique.

Interestingly, if we change $\|\cdot\|_F$ to other unitary invariant matrix norms (such as the operator norm), the above result remains unchanged. The SVD also gives a way of optimally approximating a given square matrix with an orthogonal matrix:

THEOREM A.38. (Best orthogonal approximation) *Let $\boldsymbol{A} \in \mathbb{R}^{n \times n}$, and let $\boldsymbol{A} = \boldsymbol{U}\boldsymbol{\Sigma}\boldsymbol{V}^*$ be any full singular value decomposition of $\boldsymbol{A}$. Then an optimal solution to the problem*

$$\begin{array}{ll} \min & \|\boldsymbol{X} - \boldsymbol{A}\|_F \\ \text{subject to} & \boldsymbol{X} \in \mathsf{O}(n) \end{array} \tag{A.8.9}$$

is given by $\boldsymbol{X} = \boldsymbol{U}\boldsymbol{V}^*$.

A.9 Vector and Matrix Norms

Norms on Vector Spaces

A *norm* on a vector space $\mathbb{V}$ gives a way of measuring lengths of vectors that conforms in important ways to our intuition from lengths in $\mathbb{R}^3$. Formally:

DEFINITION A.39. (Norm) *A norm on a real vector space $\mathbb{V}$ is a function $\|\cdot\| : \mathbb{V} \to \mathbb{R}$ that is*

1. **nonnegatively homogeneous**: *$\|\alpha \boldsymbol{x}\| = |\alpha| \|\boldsymbol{x}\|$ for all vectors $\boldsymbol{x} \in \mathbb{V}$, scalars $\alpha \in \mathbb{R}$;*
2. **positive definite**: *$\|\boldsymbol{x}\| \geq 0$, and $\|\boldsymbol{x}\| = 0$ if and only if $\boldsymbol{x} = \boldsymbol{0}$;*
3. **subadditive**: *$\|\cdot\|$ satisfies the triangle inequality $\|\boldsymbol{x} + \boldsymbol{y}\| \leq \|\boldsymbol{x}\| + \|\boldsymbol{y}\|$ for all $\boldsymbol{x}, \boldsymbol{y} \in \mathbb{V}$.*

One very important family of norms are the ℓ^p norms. If we take $\mathbb{V} = \mathbb{R}^n$, and $p \in [1, \infty)$, we can write

$$\|\boldsymbol{x}\|_p = \left(\sum_i |x_i|^p \right)^{1/p}. \tag{A.9.1}$$

The most familiar example is the ℓ^2 norm or "Euclidean norm"

$$\|\boldsymbol{x}\|_2 = \sqrt{\sum_i x_i^2} = \sqrt{\boldsymbol{x}^* \boldsymbol{x}},$$

which coincides with our usual way of measuring lengths. Two other cases are of almost equal importance: $p = 1$, and $p \to \infty$. Setting $p = 1$ in (A.9.1), we obtain

$$\|\boldsymbol{x}\|_1 = \sum_i |x_i|. \tag{A.9.2}$$

Finally, as p becomes larger, the expression in (A.9.1) accentuates large $|x_i|$. As $p \to \infty$, $\|\boldsymbol{x}\|_p \to \max_i |x_i|$. We extend the definition of the ℓ^p norm to $p = \infty$ by defining

$$\|\boldsymbol{x}\|_\infty = \max_i |x_i|. \tag{A.9.3}$$

However, the ℓ^p norms are far from the only norms on vectors.

EXAMPLE A.40. *The following are examples of norms:*

- *For $p \ge 1$, $\|\boldsymbol{x}\|_p$ is a norm.*
- *Every positive definite matrix $\boldsymbol{P} \succ \boldsymbol{0}$ defines a norm, via $\|\boldsymbol{x}\|_{\boldsymbol{P}} = \sqrt{\boldsymbol{x}^* \boldsymbol{P} \boldsymbol{x}}$.*
- *For $\boldsymbol{x} \in \mathbb{R}^n$, let $[\boldsymbol{x}]_{(k)}$ denote the k-th largest element of the sequence $|\boldsymbol{x}_1|, |\boldsymbol{x}_2|, \ldots, |\boldsymbol{x}_n|$. Then*

$$\|\boldsymbol{x}\|_{[K]} = \sum_{k=1}^{K} [\boldsymbol{x}]_{(k)} \tag{A.9.4}$$

  is a norm.
- *For $\boldsymbol{X} \in \mathbb{R}^{m \times n}$, the Frobenius norm $\|\boldsymbol{X}\|_F = \sqrt{\langle \boldsymbol{X}, \boldsymbol{X} \rangle}$ is a norm.*

One fundamental result in the theory of normed spaces is that in finite dimensions, all norms are comparable:

THEOREM A.41. (Equivalence of norms) *Let $\|\cdot\|_a$ and $\|\cdot\|_b$ be two norms on a finite-dimensional vector space $\mathbb{V}$. Then there exist $\alpha, \beta > 0$ such that for every $\boldsymbol{v} \in \mathbb{V}$,*

$$\alpha \|\boldsymbol{v}\|_a \le \|\boldsymbol{v}\|_b \le \beta \|\boldsymbol{v}\|_a. \tag{A.9.5}$$

It is important not to over-interpret this result. "Equivalence" here means that the values of the norms can be compared up to constants, as in (A.9.5). It does not mean that the norms behave in the same way – they may produce very different results when selected to define constraint sets, or as objective functions for optimization. For purposes of analysis, it is useful to note the following comparisons:

LEMMA A.42. (Comparisons between ℓ^p norms) *For all* $\boldsymbol{x} \in \mathbb{R}^n$,

- $\|\boldsymbol{x}\|_2 \le \|\boldsymbol{x}\|_1 \le \sqrt{n}\,\|\boldsymbol{x}\|_2$,
- $\|\boldsymbol{x}\|_\infty \le \|\boldsymbol{x}\|_2 \le \sqrt{n}\,\|\boldsymbol{x}\|_\infty$,
- $\|\boldsymbol{x}\|_\infty \le \|\boldsymbol{x}\|_1 \le n\,\|\boldsymbol{x}\|_\infty$.

To each norm, we can associate a *dual norm*. To do this precisely, we need to define a normed linear space. If $\mathbb{V}$ is a vector space and $\|\cdot\|$ is a norm on $\mathbb{V}$, we call the pair $(\mathbb{V}, \|\cdot\|)$ a *normed linear space*. A *linear functional* is a linear map $\phi : \mathbb{V} \to \mathbb{R}$. Since linear combinations of linear functionals are again linear functionals, the space of all linear functionals on a given vector space $\mathbb{V}$ is itself a vector space (called the "topological dual" of $\mathbb{V}$). On this space, we can define another function

$$\left\|\phi\right\|^* = \sup_{\boldsymbol{v}\in\mathbb{V},\ \|\boldsymbol{v}\|\le 1} |\phi(\boldsymbol{v})|. \tag{A.9.6}$$

As the notation suggests, $\left\|\phi\right\|^*$ is a norm, if we restrict to ϕ for which the supremum is finite:

DEFINITION A.43. (Dual space and dual norm) *The normed dual of the space* $(\mathbb{V}, \|\cdot\|)$ *is the space* $(\mathbb{V}^*, \|\cdot\|^*)$, *where the dual norm* $\|\cdot\|^*$ *of a linear functional* $\phi : \mathbb{V} \to \mathbb{R}$ *is defined as in* (A.9.6) *and*

$$\mathbb{V}^* = \left\{\phi : \mathbb{V} \to \mathbb{R} \text{ linear} \mid \left\|\phi\right\|^* < +\infty\right\}. \tag{A.9.7}$$

This definition may seem somewhat abstract; for our purposes, the dual spaces and dual norms we encounter will have fairly concrete descriptions:

THEOREM A.44. *Let* $\langle\cdot,\cdot\rangle$ *denote the standard inner product on* $\mathbb{R}^n$ *(and by extension on* $\mathbb{R}^{m\times n}$*). Every linear functional* $\phi : \mathbb{R}^n \to \mathbb{R}$ *can be written as*

$$\phi(\boldsymbol{x}) = \langle \boldsymbol{v}, \boldsymbol{x}\rangle, \tag{A.9.8}$$

for some vector $\boldsymbol{v} \in \mathbb{R}^n$. *Similarly, every linear functional* $\phi : \mathbb{R}^{m\times n} \to \mathbb{R}$ *can be written as*

$$\phi(\boldsymbol{X}) = \langle \boldsymbol{V}, \boldsymbol{X}\rangle, \tag{A.9.9}$$

for some matrix $\boldsymbol{V} \in \mathbb{R}^{m\times n}$.

The implication of this is that if we are considering a space $(\mathbb{R}^n, \|\cdot\|_\sharp)$, the dual space can be identified with $(\mathbb{R}^n, \|\cdot\|_\sharp^*)$, where

$$\|\boldsymbol{v}\|_\sharp^* = \sup_{\|\boldsymbol{x}\|_\sharp \le 1} \langle \boldsymbol{v}, \boldsymbol{x}\rangle. \tag{A.9.10}$$

In particular, we have the following examples:

EXAMPLE A.45. (Duals of common norms) *Check the following:*

- *The dual of the* ℓ^∞ *norm is the* ℓ^1 *norm.*
- *The dual of the* ℓ^1 *norm is the* ℓ^∞ *norm.*

- *The ℓ^2 and Frobenius norms are self-dual; i.e.,* $\|\cdot\|_2^* = \|\cdot\|_2$ *and* $\|\cdot\|_F^* = \|\cdot\|_F$.
- *If* $p,q \in [1,\infty)$, *with* $p^{-1} + q^{-1} = 1$, *then* $\|\cdot\|_p^* = \|\cdot\|_q$ *and* $\|\cdot\|_q^* = \|\cdot\|_p$.

It is immediate from the definition that for any $\boldsymbol{x}, \boldsymbol{x}'$, and any norm $\|\cdot\|$,

$$\langle \boldsymbol{x}, \boldsymbol{x}' \rangle \;\le\; \|\boldsymbol{x}\| \, \|\boldsymbol{x}'\|^* . \tag{A.9.11}$$

If we take $\|\boldsymbol{x}\| = \|\boldsymbol{x}\|_2$, we obtain the Cauchy–Schwarz inequality.

Matrix and Operator Norms

Even more interesting structure can arise when $\mathbb{V}$ is a space of matrices, e.g., $\mathbb{V} = \mathbb{R}^{m \times n}$, due to the interpretation of a matrix as a linear operator. For square matrices, many authors reserve the term "matrix norm" for a function $\|\cdot\|$ that satisfies the three criteria in Definition A.39, *and is submultiplicative*,

$$\|\boldsymbol{A}\boldsymbol{B}\| \;\le\; \|\boldsymbol{A}\| \, \|\boldsymbol{B}\| . \tag{A.9.12}$$

They use the term "vector norm on matrices" for functions on $\mathbb{V}$ that only satisfy Definition A.39. We will not emphasize this distinction in terminology. Nevertheless, the submultiplicative property (A.9.12) is often useful, and we will note it where it occurs.

The most important source of norms on matrices comes from the notion of a matrix as a linear operator:

DEFINITION A.46. (Operator norm) *Let* $(\mathbb{W}, \|\cdot\|_a)$ *and* $(\mathbb{W}', \|\cdot\|_b)$ *be two normed linear spaces, and let* $\mathcal{L} : \mathbb{W} \to \mathbb{W}'$. *The* operator norm *of* $\mathcal{L}$ *is*

$$\|\mathcal{L}\|_{a \to b} = \sup_{\|\boldsymbol{w}\|_a \le 1} \|\mathcal{L}[\boldsymbol{w}]\|_b . \tag{A.9.13}$$

Specializing the definition a bit, for an $m \times n$ matrix $\boldsymbol{A}$, if $\|\cdot\|_a$ and $\|\cdot\|_b$ are norms on $\mathbb{R}^n$ and $\mathbb{R}^m$, respectively, we write

$$\|\boldsymbol{A}\|_{a \to b} = \sup_{\|\boldsymbol{x}\|_a \le 1} \|\boldsymbol{A}\boldsymbol{x}\|_b . \tag{A.9.14}$$

The most important special case is the following.

THEOREM A.47. *The norm of a matrix* $\boldsymbol{A}$ *as an operator from* $\ell_n^2 = (\mathbb{R}^n, \|\cdot\|_2)$ *to* $\ell_m^2 = (\mathbb{R}^m, \|\cdot\|_2)$ *is*

$$\|\boldsymbol{A}\|_{2 \to 2} = \sigma_1(\boldsymbol{A}). \tag{A.9.15}$$

Several other cases are of interest:

THEOREM A.48. *The norm of any matrix as an operator from* $(\mathbb{R}^n, \|\cdot\|_1)$ *to any normed space* $(\mathbb{R}^m, \|\cdot\|_\sharp)$ *is simply the largest* $\|\cdot\|_\sharp$ *of any column of* $\boldsymbol{A}$:

$$\|\boldsymbol{A}\|_{1 \to \sharp} = \max_{j=1,\dots,n} \left\|\boldsymbol{A}\boldsymbol{e}_j\right\|_\sharp . \tag{A.9.16}$$

The norm of any matrix as an operator from $(\mathbb{R}^n, \|\cdot\|_\flat)$ *for any norm* $\|\cdot\|_\flat$ *into* $(\mathbb{R}^m, \|\cdot\|_\infty)$ *is the largest dual norm of any of the rows:*

$$\|A\|_{\flat\to\infty} = \max_{i=1,\dots,m} \left\|e_i^* A\right\|_\flat^*, \tag{A.9.17}$$

where the dual norm $\|\cdot\|_\flat^*$ *is*

$$\|v\|_\flat^* = \sup_{\|u\|_\flat \le 1} \langle u, v\rangle . \tag{A.9.18}$$

For example, $\|A\|_{1\to1}$ is just the largest ℓ^1 norm of any column of A.

Unitary Invariant Matrix Norms

It is interesting to note that the operator norm of a matrix A depends only on the singular values of A:

$$\|A\|_{2,2} = \sigma_1(A) = \|\sigma(A)\|_\infty , \tag{A.9.19}$$

where $\sigma(A)$ is the vector of singular values. In fact, the Frobenius norm $\|A\|_F$ depends only on the singular values as well:

$$\|A\|_F = \sqrt{\sum_{i=1}^{\min\{m,n\}} \sigma_i(A)^2} = \|\sigma(A)\|_2 . \tag{A.9.20}$$

This fact is not too difficult to observe from the orthogonal invariance of $\|\cdot\|_F$:

$$\forall\, A \in \mathbb{R}^{m\times n},\ P \in \mathsf{O}(m),\ Q \in \mathsf{O}(n), \quad \|PAQ\|_F = \|A\|_F . \tag{A.9.21}$$

This suggests a pattern. In fact, any ℓ^p norm of the singular values is a norm on matrices A:

DEFINITION A.49. (Schatten p-norm) *For* $A \in \mathbb{R}^{m\times n}$, *let* $\sigma(A) \in \mathbb{R}^{\min\{m,n\}}$ *denote the vector of singular values. For* $p \in [1,\infty]$, *the function*

$$\|A\|_{S_p} = \|\sigma(A)\|_p \tag{A.9.22}$$

is a norm on $\mathbb{R}^{m\times n}$.

It is easy to recognize the operator norm and Frobenius norm as special cases. One other special case is of great interest – the Schatten 1-norm

$$\|A\|_{S_1} = \sum_i \sigma_i(A). \tag{A.9.23}$$

This is also sometimes called the *trace norm* or *nuclear norm*. We reserve a special notation

$$\|A\|_* = \sum_i \sigma_i(A) \tag{A.9.24}$$

for this norm. The operator norm $\|\cdot\|_{2,2}$ and the nuclear norm $\|\cdot\|_*$ are dual norms.

We have defined several interesting, useful norms on matrices $\boldsymbol{A}$, by applying different vector norms to the singular values $\sigma(\boldsymbol{A})$. Because the singular values are orthogonal invariant, i.e., for $\boldsymbol{P} \in \mathsf{O}(m)$, $\boldsymbol{Q} \in \mathsf{O}(n)$, $\sigma(\boldsymbol{P}\boldsymbol{A}\boldsymbol{Q}) = \sigma(\boldsymbol{A})$, norms defined in this way are also orthogonal invariant. It is natural to ask whether every function $\|\sigma(\boldsymbol{A})\|$ generates a valid norm on $\mathbb{R}^{m\times n}$. It turns out that, with several restrictions, this is true.

DEFINITION A.50. (Symmetric gauge function) *A function* $f : \mathbb{R}^n \to \mathbb{R}$ *is a* symmetric gauge function *if it satisfies the following three conditions:*

- **norm:** f *is a norm on* $\mathbb{R}^n$*;*
- **permutation invariance:** *for every* $\boldsymbol{x} \in \mathbb{R}^n$ *and permutation matrix* $\boldsymbol{\Pi}$, $f(\boldsymbol{\Pi}\boldsymbol{x}) = f(\boldsymbol{x})$*;*
- **symmetry:** *for every* $\boldsymbol{x} \in \mathbb{R}^n$ *and diagonal sign matrix* $\boldsymbol{\Sigma}$ *(i.e., matrix with diagonal entries* ± 1*),* $f(\boldsymbol{\Sigma}\boldsymbol{x}) = f(\boldsymbol{x})$.

THEOREM A.51. (Von Neumann's characterization of unitary invariant norms) *Fix* $m \geq n$. *For* $\boldsymbol{M} \in \mathbb{C}^{m\times n}$, *let* $\sigma(\boldsymbol{M}) \in \mathbb{R}^n$ *denote its vector of singular values. Then for every symmetric gauge function* $f_\sharp$,

$$\|\boldsymbol{M}\|_\sharp \doteq f_\sharp(\sigma(\boldsymbol{M})) \tag{A.9.25}$$

defines a unitary invariant matrix norm on $\mathbb{C}^{m\times n}$. *Conversely, for every unitary invariant matrix norm* $\|\boldsymbol{M}\|_\flat$ *there exists a symmetric gauge function* $f_\flat$ *such that* $\|\boldsymbol{M}\|_\flat = f_\flat(\sigma(\boldsymbol{M}))$.

Appendix B Convex Sets and Functions

The notion of convexity arises when we try to formalize the property that "good local decisions lead to globally optimal solutions." Consider a generic unconstrained optimization problem

$$\min \quad f(\boldsymbol{x}). \tag{B.0.1}$$

Here $\boldsymbol{x} \in \mathbb{R}^n$ is the variable of optimization, and $f : \mathbb{R}^n \to \mathbb{R}$ is the objective function, which we are trying to make as small as possible using a numerical algorithm. Figure B.1 displays two objective functions f. The one in panel (b) has many peaks and valleys – it may be very difficult to find the lowest valley, corresponding to the global optimum $\boldsymbol{x}_\star$. Moreover, for the function f in panel (b), local information around a point $\boldsymbol{x}$ is not particularly helpful for determining what direction to move to reach the global optimum. In contrast, the bowl-shaped function in panel (a) is much more amenable to global optimization – a "gradient-descent"-type algorithm, which simply determines which direction to move by considering the slope of the graph of the function, would easily "ski" down to the global minimum.

The notion of *convexity* formalizes this property. Convexity is a geometric property. It is convenient to first introduce the notion of a convex set, and then extend this definition to functions.

B.1 Convex Sets

A set C is said to be *closed* if it contains its boundary. More precisely, for any converging sequence of points $\{\boldsymbol{x}_k\}$ in C, we must have

$$\boldsymbol{x}_k \to \bar{\boldsymbol{x}} \quad \Rightarrow \quad \bar{\boldsymbol{x}} \in \mathsf{C}.$$

A set $\mathsf{C} \subseteq \mathbb{R}^n$ is *convex* if for every pair of points $\boldsymbol{x}, \boldsymbol{x}' \in \mathsf{C}$, the line segment obtained by joining the two points also lies entirely in C:

DEFINITION B.1. (Convex set) *The set* $\mathsf{C} \subseteq \mathbb{R}^n$ *is* convex *if*

$$\forall\, \boldsymbol{x}, \boldsymbol{x}' \in \mathsf{C}, \quad \alpha \in [0,1], \qquad \alpha \boldsymbol{x} + (1-\alpha)\boldsymbol{x}' \in \mathsf{C}. \tag{B.1.1}$$

Figure B.2 gives an example of two sets, one of which is convex and one of which is not.

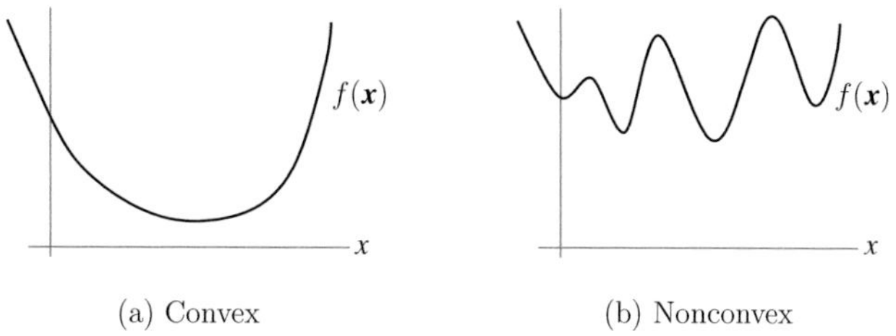

Figure B.1 Two optimization problems $\min f(\boldsymbol{x})$. The objective f in (a) appears to be amenable to global optimization, while the one in (b) appears to be more challenging.

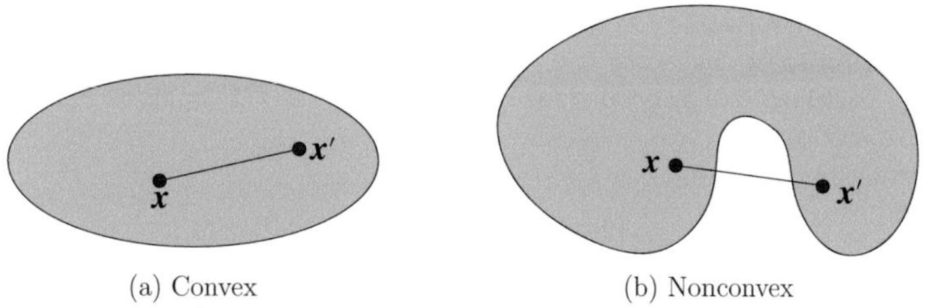

Figure B.2 Convex and nonconvex sets. A set is convex if we can select any pair of points $\boldsymbol{x}, \boldsymbol{x}'$ in the set, and the line segment joining them lies entirely within the set. The set in (a) has this property, while the set in (b) does not.

EXAMPLE B.2. (Convex sets) *Show that the following are convex:*

- *Every affine subspace.*
- *Every norm ball* $\mathsf{B}_{\|\cdot\|} = \{\boldsymbol{x} \mid \|\boldsymbol{x}\| \le 1\}$.
- *The empty set.*
- *Any intersection* $\mathsf{C} = \mathsf{C}_1 \cap \mathsf{C}_2$ *of two convex sets* C_1 *and* C_2.

PROPOSITION B.3.

1 *The intersection of a collection of convex sets* $\bigcap_i \mathsf{C}_i$ *is convex.*
2 *The image of a convex set under an affine transformation is convex.*

DEFINITION B.4. (Convex hull) *The* convex hull *of any given set* S *is the minimal convex set containing* S*, denoted as* conv(S). *If* S *contains a finite number of points* $\mathsf{S} = \{\boldsymbol{x}_i\}_{i=1}^n$*, we have*

$$\operatorname{conv}(\mathsf{S}) \doteq \left\{ \sum_{i=1}^{n} \alpha_i \boldsymbol{x}_i \;\middle|\; \forall\, \alpha_i \ge 0 \text{ with } \sum_{i=1}^{n} \alpha_i = 1 \right\}. \tag{B.1.2}$$

B.2 Convex Functions

For a function $f : \mathcal{D} \to \mathbb{R}$ defined on a (convex) domain $\mathcal{D} \subseteq \mathbb{R}^n$, its *graph* is the set of pairs $(\boldsymbol{x}, f(\boldsymbol{x}))$ that can be generated by evaluating the function f at every point:

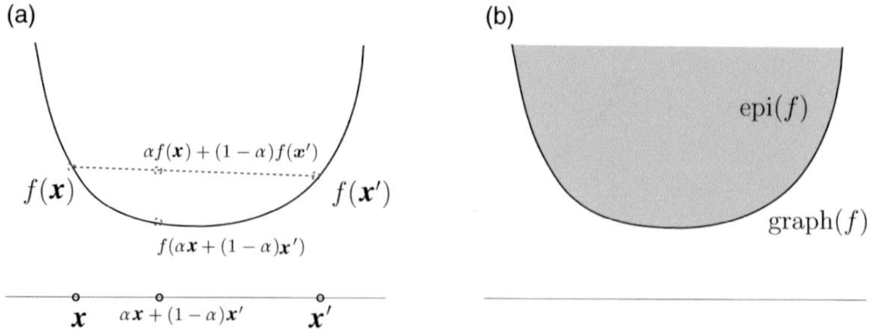

Figure B.3 Convexity of functions. A function f is convex if its epigraph epi$(f) = \{(x,t) \mid t \ge f(x)\}$ is a convex set (b). This is true if and only if for every pair of points x, x' and scalar $\alpha \in [0,1]$, $f(\alpha x + (1-\alpha)x') \le \alpha f(x) + (1-\alpha) f(x')$. The picture (a) illustrates this inequality: the segment joining $(x, f(x))$ and $(x', f(x'))$ lies above the graph of f.

$$\mathrm{graph}(f) \doteq \{(x, f(x)) \mid x \in \mathcal{D}, f(x) < +\infty\} \subseteq \mathbb{R}^{n+1}. \tag{B.2.1}$$

We give another name to everything that lies above the graph, the *epigraph*:

$$\mathrm{epi}(f) \doteq \{(x,t) \mid x \in \mathcal{D}, t \in \mathbb{R}, f(x) \le t\} \subseteq \mathbb{R}^{n+1}. \tag{B.2.2}$$

We say that f is a *convex function* if its epigraph is a convex set. Figure B.3(b) illustrates this property. Figure B.3(a) suggests an equivalent definition, which is sometimes easier to work with: f is convex if for any pair of points x and x', the line segment joining $(x, f(x))$ and $(x', f(x'))$ lies entirely above the graph of f:

DEFINITION B.5. (Convex function) *A function* $f : \mathcal{D} \to \mathbb{R}$ *is* convex *if for all* $x, x' \in \mathcal{D}$ *and* $\alpha \in [0,1]$,

$$\alpha f(x) + (1-\alpha) f(x') \ge f(\alpha x + (1-\alpha)x'). \tag{B.2.3}$$

Notice that the above definitions do not require f to be differentiable. If f is differentiable, the notion of convexity can be characterized in terms of its derivatives. Since the epigraph is convex, then the tangent plane at each point of the graph should lie beneath the graph. The following statement makes this precise:

PROPOSITION B.6. (First-Order condition) *Let* $f : \mathcal{D} \to \mathbb{R}$ *be differentiable. Then* f *is convex if and only if it satisfies the condition:*

$$f(x') \ge f(x) + \nabla f(x)^*(x' - x)$$

for all $x, x' \in \mathcal{D}$.

This is precisely the geometry of the "nice" function in Figure B.1(a). From this picture, it is clear that convexity is very favorable for global optimization.[1] There

[1] Once you have internalized the definition a bit, you may begin to wonder to what extent the implication "convexity $\implies$ easy-to-optimize" is actually true. The convex functions that we encounter in this book will all possess special structure that makes them very amenable to efficient algorithms. However, this is not true of all convex functions – there exist convex functions that are NP-hard to optimize.

also exist nonconvex functions that are easy to optimize – Chapter 7 provides a brief introduction to this emerging literature. However, if we want to talk about a class of functions, rather than a particular one, then there is a very beautiful motivation for studying convex functions. To appreciate this motivation, we need to first observe a useful fact: if $f(\boldsymbol{x})$ and $g(\boldsymbol{x})$ are convex functions, then for any $\alpha, \beta \geq 0$, $h(\boldsymbol{x}) = \alpha f(\boldsymbol{x}) + \beta g(\boldsymbol{x})$ is also convex. If we let $\mathcal{F}$ be the largest class of continuously differentiable functions that satisfy the following three demands:

- every linear function $\phi(\boldsymbol{x}) = \boldsymbol{a}^* \boldsymbol{x} + b$ is in $\mathcal{F}$,
- every nonnegative combination $\alpha f_1(\boldsymbol{x}) + \beta f_2(\boldsymbol{x})$ of $f_1, f_2 \in \mathcal{F}$ is in $\mathcal{F}$, and
- for every $f \in \mathcal{F}$, the stationarity condition $\nabla f(\boldsymbol{x}_\star) = \mathbf{0}$ implies that $\boldsymbol{x}_\star$ is a global optimizer of f,

then it turns out that the $\mathcal{F}$ is precisely the class of **convex**, continuously differentiable functions. You can interpret this as suggesting that for *global* solutions, convex functions really are the right general class of functions to study. For more details, see the book of Nesterov [Nes03].

You may also notice that in Figure B.3, the function $f(\boldsymbol{x})$ "curves upward": its second derivative is nonnegative at every point of the domain. For twice differentiable functions, this leads to a simpler condition for convexity: the function is convex if and only if its second derivative at any point and in any direction is positive. The following makes this precise:

PROPOSITION B.7. (Second-Order conditions) *Let $f : \mathcal{D} \to \mathbb{R}$ be twice differentiable. Then f is convex if and only if its Hessian is positive semidefinite:*

$$\nabla^2 f(\boldsymbol{x}) \succeq \mathbf{0}$$

for all $\boldsymbol{x} \in \mathcal{D}$.

The class of convex functions includes important examples such as linear functions and norms:

EXAMPLE B.8. (Convex functions) *Show that the following are convex functions:*

- *Every affine function $f(\boldsymbol{x}) = \boldsymbol{a}^* \boldsymbol{x} + b$.*
- *Every norm $f(\boldsymbol{x}) = \|\boldsymbol{x}\|$.*
- *Every semidefinite quadratic $f(\boldsymbol{x}) = \boldsymbol{x}^* \boldsymbol{P} \boldsymbol{x}$, with $\boldsymbol{P} \succeq \mathbf{0}$.*

Before continuing, we note one nice property of convex functions which will be useful for deriving an appropriate tractable replacement for the ℓ^0 norm.

DEFINITION B.9. (Convex combination) *A convex combination of a set of points $\boldsymbol{x}_1, \ldots, \boldsymbol{x}_k$ is an expression of the form $\lambda_1 \boldsymbol{x}_1 + \cdots + \lambda_k \boldsymbol{x}_k$, with $\lambda_i \geq 0$ for each i and $\sum_i \lambda_i = 1$.*

LEMMA B.10. (Jensen's inequality) *Let $f : \mathbb{R}^n \to \mathbb{R}$ be a convex function. For any k, $\boldsymbol{x}_1, \ldots, \boldsymbol{x}_k \in \mathbb{R}^n$, $\lambda_1, \ldots, \lambda_k \in \mathbb{R}_+$, with $\sum_i \lambda_i = 1$,*

$$f\left(\sum_i \lambda_i \boldsymbol{x}_i\right) \le \sum_i \lambda_i f(\boldsymbol{x}_i). \tag{B.2.4}$$

Proof The proof is by induction on k. For $k = 1$, there is nothing to show. Now suppose the claim is true for $1, \ldots, k-1$. Then

$$f\left(\sum_{i=1}^{k} \lambda_i \boldsymbol{x}_i\right) \le \left(\sum_{i=1}^{k-1} \lambda_i\right) f\left(\frac{\sum_{i=1}^{k-1} \lambda_i \boldsymbol{x}_i}{\sum_{i=1}^{k-1} \lambda_i}\right) + \lambda_k f(\boldsymbol{x}_k) \tag{B.2.5}$$

$$\le \sum_{i=1}^{k} \lambda_i f(\boldsymbol{x}_i) \tag{B.2.6}$$

as desired. Above, the first step uses the definition of convexity, and the second uses the inductive hypothesis. □

With this lemma, it is easy to show that any α-sublevel set of a convex function $f : \mathcal{D} \to \mathbb{R}$,

$$\mathsf{C}_\alpha = \{\boldsymbol{x} \in \mathcal{D} \mid f(\boldsymbol{x}) \le \alpha\} \tag{B.2.7}$$

is a convex set. However, a function with all its sublevel sets being convex is not necessarily a convex function![2] A function is said to be a *closed* function, if each sublevel set is a closed set. We typically only consider closed convex functions, unless otherwise stated.

PROPOSITION B.11. *We can use convex functions to generate other associated convex functions:*

1 *A function is convex if and only if it is convex when restricted to any line that intersects its domain.*
2 *A weighted sum of convex functions with nonnegative weights is convex.*
3 *If f, g are convex functions and g is nondecreasing in its univariate domain, then $h(\boldsymbol{x}) = g(f(\boldsymbol{x}))$ is convex.*
4 *Given a collection of convex functions $f_\alpha : \mathcal{D} \to \mathbb{R}$, $\alpha \in \mathsf{A}$, their pointwise supremum*

$$f(\boldsymbol{x}) \doteq \sup_{\alpha \in \mathsf{A}} f_\alpha(\boldsymbol{x})$$

is also convex.

EXAMPLE B.12. *The maximal eigenvalue of a symmetric matrix is a (closed) convex function.*

Proof To see that, the maximal eigenvalue function can be written as

$$\lambda_{\max}(\boldsymbol{X}) = \sup\{\boldsymbol{y}^* \boldsymbol{X} \boldsymbol{y}\}, \quad \|\boldsymbol{y}\|_2 = 1.$$

[2] Such functions are called *quasi-convex*. Please find an example for yourself.

Since the function is the pointwise supremum of a set of linear functions with respect to $\boldsymbol{X}$, it is a convex function. □

Convex Envelope and Conjugate

For any nonconvex (closed) function $g : \mathcal{D} \to \mathbb{R}$ defined on a convex domain $\mathcal{D}$, it has a naturally associated convex function that bounds it from below:

DEFINITION B.13. (Convex envelope) *The convex envelope of a closed function g is defined as*

$$\operatorname{conv} g(\boldsymbol{x}) = \sup\{h(\boldsymbol{x}) \mid h(\boldsymbol{x}) \text{ convex } \& \ h(\boldsymbol{x}) \leq g(\boldsymbol{x}) \ \ \forall\, \boldsymbol{x} \in \mathcal{D}\}. \tag{B.2.8}$$

Let us define the (Fenchel) *conjugate* of a function $g(\boldsymbol{x})$ (not necessarily convex) as

$$g^*(\boldsymbol{\lambda}) = \sup_{\boldsymbol{x}} \boldsymbol{\lambda}^* \boldsymbol{x} - g(\boldsymbol{x}). \tag{B.2.9}$$

This is an extended real-valued function of a vector λ of "dual variables." The conjugate of a function g is essentially the negated dual function of g that we often see in the method of Lagrange multipliers (see Section C.3).

PROPOSITION B.14. *Assuming the conjugate is well defined, we have the following:*

1. *The conjugate $g^*(\boldsymbol{\lambda})$ is always a convex function.*
2. $g^{**}(\boldsymbol{x}) = \operatorname{conv} g(\boldsymbol{x})$.

Strong Convexity

In this book, we sometimes are interested in a stronger notion of convexity.

DEFINITION B.15. (Strongly convex function) *A function $f : \mathcal{D} \to \mathbb{R}$ is* strongly convex *if f is convex and for all $\boldsymbol{x}, \boldsymbol{x}' \in \mathcal{D}$ and $\alpha \in [0, 1]$,*

$$\alpha f(\boldsymbol{x}) + (1-\alpha) f(\boldsymbol{x}') \geq f(\alpha \boldsymbol{x} + (1-\alpha)\boldsymbol{x}') + \mu \frac{\alpha(1-\alpha)}{2} \|\boldsymbol{x} - \boldsymbol{x}'\|_2^2 \tag{B.2.10}$$

for some $\mu > 0$.

Notice that the above definition does not require f to be differentiable. If f is first- or second-order differentiable, we have the following sufficient conditions for f being strongly convex.

PROPOSITION B.16. *For a differentiable convex function f over $\mathcal{D}$, we have that f is strongly convex if either of the following conditions hold:*

1. $f(\boldsymbol{x}') \geq f(\boldsymbol{x}) + \nabla f(\boldsymbol{x})^*(\boldsymbol{x}' - \boldsymbol{x}) + \mu \|\boldsymbol{x}' - \boldsymbol{x}\|_2^2$*, for all* $\boldsymbol{x}, \boldsymbol{x}' \in \mathcal{D}$*;*
2. $\nabla^2 f(\boldsymbol{x}) \succeq \mu \cdot \boldsymbol{I}$*, for all* $\boldsymbol{x} \in \mathcal{D}$*;*

for some $\mu > 0$.

However, as we see in Section 3.3.2, we are interested in strong convexity in a restricted sense.

Lipschitz Continuous Gradients

The functions we encounter in many optimization problems are often "smooth" in their landscape in the sense that their gradients do not vary so dramatically. One way to characterize such smoothness is the notion of Lipschitz continuous gradients.

DEFINITION B.17. (Lipschitz continuous gradient) *A differentiable function* $f : \mathcal{D} \to \mathbb{R}$ *has* L-Lipschitz continuous gradients *if* $\nabla f(\boldsymbol{x})$ *satisfies*

$$\|\nabla f(\boldsymbol{x}') - \nabla f(\boldsymbol{x})\|_2 \leq L\|\boldsymbol{x}' - \boldsymbol{x}\|_2, \quad \forall\, \boldsymbol{x}', \boldsymbol{x} \in \mathcal{D}, \tag{B.2.11}$$

for some constant $L > 0$. *The constant* L *is called the Lipschitz constant of* ∇f.

When the function f is twice differentiable, then it is not difficult to prove from fundamental theorems of calculus (also see proof of Lemma 8.2) that f has L-Lipschitz continuous gradients (over the domain $\mathcal{D}$) if we have

$$\|\nabla^2 f(\boldsymbol{x})\| \leq L, \quad \forall\, \boldsymbol{x} \in \mathcal{D}. \tag{B.2.12}$$

As we will see, when a convex function f over a domain $\mathcal{D}$ is both strongly convex and smooth (in the sense of having Lipschitz continuous gradients), then it can be efficiently minimized over $\mathcal{D}$ by a simple gradient descent algorithm of the type

$$\boldsymbol{x}_{k+1} = \boldsymbol{x}_k - t_k \nabla f(\boldsymbol{x}_k), \tag{B.2.13}$$

where the step size t_k can be chosen to be between $1/L$ and $2/(L + \mu)$. Somewhat surprisingly, one can easily show (see Theorem D.4) that such a vanilla algorithm enjoys ℓ^2 error contraction around the (global) minimum $\boldsymbol{x}_\star$:

$$\|\boldsymbol{x}_{k+1} - \boldsymbol{x}_\star\|_2 \leq \rho\|\boldsymbol{x}_k - \boldsymbol{x}_\star\|_2 \tag{B.2.14}$$

for some $\rho \leq 1 - \mu/L < 1$. That is, the estimate error drops exponentially with the number of iterations.

B.3 Subdifferentials of Nonsmooth Convex Functions

For smooth convex functions f, the local information encoded in the gradient ∇f and Hessian $\nabla^2 f$ characterize both the local and global behavior of f, allowing us to give optimality conditions and construct minimization algorithms. Familiar classical algorithms such as gradient ascent, Newton's method, and their variants are all constructed using differential information. Moreover, as we saw in the previous section, these quantities play a critical role in characterizing convexity for smooth functions f.

It is a curious fact, then, that many of the most useful convex objective functions arising in high-dimensional data analysis are nondifferentiable: *their gradients and Hessians do not exist.* For example, the ℓ^1 norm $\|\boldsymbol{x}\|_1 = \sum_{i=1}^n |x_i|$ is nondifferentiable at any point $\boldsymbol{x} \in \mathbb{R}^n$ with fewer than n nonzero entries. These are precisely the points that we care about for sparse estimation! This nonsmooth behavior is actually desirable from the statistical perspective. However, it forces us to make recourse to analytical tools that are general enough to handle nondifferentiable functions. Fortunately, for

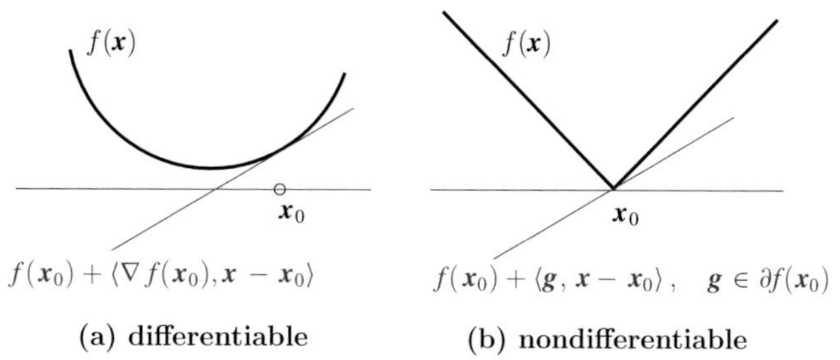

Figure B.4 Differential and subdifferentials of convex functions.

convex functions, the nondifferentiable theory rests on simple, geometrically intuitive ideas, which we describe in this section. For accessible introductions to the general theory of convexity, we recommend [Nem95, Nem07, Nes03, BV04].

The most important notion is that of a *subgradient* of a convex function, which provides a very satisfactory replacement for the gradient, when the function is not differentiable. Recall from Proposition B.6 that for convex *differentiable* f,

$$f(\boldsymbol{y}) \;\geq\; f(\boldsymbol{x}) + \langle \nabla f(\boldsymbol{x}), \boldsymbol{y} - \boldsymbol{x} \rangle, \quad \forall\, \boldsymbol{x}, \boldsymbol{y} \in \mathcal{D}. \tag{B.3.1}$$

This inequality has a simple geometric interpretation, which we visualize in Figure B.4. We visualize the graph of the function $f : \mathbb{R}^n \to \mathbb{R}$. The graph is the collection of points of the form $(\boldsymbol{x}, f(\boldsymbol{x})) \in \mathbb{R}^{n+1}$. The graph of

$$h(\boldsymbol{y}) = f(\boldsymbol{x}) + \langle \nabla f(\boldsymbol{x}), \boldsymbol{y} - \boldsymbol{x} \rangle$$

is a hyperplane, which is tangent to the graph of $\boldsymbol{f}$ at $(\boldsymbol{x}, f(\boldsymbol{x}))$. The inequality (B.3.1) says that at all points $\boldsymbol{y}$ in the domain of the function f this tangent hyperplane lies below (or more precisely, not above) the graph of f.

Figure B.4(b) visualizes the graph of another convex function f, which is not differentiable at point $\boldsymbol{x}$. The gradient of f *does not* exist at $\boldsymbol{x}$. Nevertheless, we can still define a nonvertical hyperplane $\mathcal{H} \subseteq \mathbb{R}^{n+1}$ that passes through $(\boldsymbol{x}, f(\boldsymbol{x}))$, and lies below the graph of f. This hyperplane has normal vector $(\boldsymbol{v}, -1)$, and can be expressed in notation as

$$\mathcal{H} = \{(\boldsymbol{y}, t) \mid t = f(\boldsymbol{x}) + \langle \boldsymbol{v}, \boldsymbol{y} - \boldsymbol{x} \rangle\}. \tag{B.3.2}$$

We say that $\boldsymbol{v} \in \mathbb{R}^n$ is a *subgradient* of f at $\boldsymbol{x}$ if it defines a hyperplane that supports the graph of f at $\boldsymbol{x}$, and lies below the graph everywhere:

DEFINITION B.18. (Subgradient) *Let $f : \mathcal{D} \subset \mathbb{R}^n \to \mathbb{R} \cup \{+\infty\}$ be a convex function. A vector $\boldsymbol{v}$ is a* subgradient *of f at $\boldsymbol{x} \in \mathcal{D}$ if for all $\boldsymbol{y} \in \mathcal{D}$,*

$$f(\boldsymbol{y}) \;\geq\; f(\boldsymbol{x}) + \langle \boldsymbol{v}, \boldsymbol{y} - \boldsymbol{x} \rangle. \tag{B.3.3}$$

When f is differentiable, from Proposition B.6 it is clear that $\boldsymbol{v} = \nabla f(\boldsymbol{x})$ satisfies (B.3.3). When f is *nondifferentiable*, at a given point $\boldsymbol{x}$ there can be multiple distinct hyperplanes that support the graph of f, and hence there can be multiple subgradients $\boldsymbol{v}$ (see Figure B.4). The collection of all subgradients is called the *subdifferential* of f at $\boldsymbol{x}$, and is denoted $\partial f(\boldsymbol{x})$. Formally:

DEFINITION B.19. (Subdifferential) *Let* $f : \mathcal{D} \subseteq \mathbb{R}^n \to \mathbb{R} \cup \{+\infty\}$ *be a convex function. The* subdifferential $\partial f(\boldsymbol{x})$ *is the collection of all subgradients of* f *at* $\boldsymbol{x}$*:*

$$\partial f(\boldsymbol{x}) = \{\boldsymbol{v} \mid f(\boldsymbol{y}) \geq f(\boldsymbol{x}) + \langle \boldsymbol{v}, \boldsymbol{y} - \boldsymbol{x} \rangle, \ \forall\, \boldsymbol{y} \in \mathcal{D}\}. \tag{B.3.4}$$

Notice that if $f : \mathbb{R}^n \to \mathbb{R}$ is differentiable at $\boldsymbol{x}$, its subdifferential at $\boldsymbol{x}$ is a singleton: $\partial f(\boldsymbol{x}) = \{\nabla f(\boldsymbol{x})\}$. This coincides with the classical definition of differentials.

A number of functions of interest have relatively simple subdifferentials.

EXAMPLE B.20. *As good exercises, the reader may try to verify the subdifferentials for the following functions:*

1 *The subdifferential for* $f(\boldsymbol{x}) = \|\boldsymbol{x}\|_1$ *with* $\boldsymbol{x} \in \mathbb{R}^n$.
2 *The subdifferential for* $f(\boldsymbol{x}) = \|\boldsymbol{x}\|_\infty$ *with* $\boldsymbol{x} \in \mathbb{R}^n$.
3 *The subdifferential for* $f(\boldsymbol{X}) = \sum_{j=1}^{n} \|\boldsymbol{X}\boldsymbol{e}_j\|_2$ *with* $\boldsymbol{X}$ *a matrix in* $\mathbb{R}^{n\times n}$.
4 *The subdifferential for* $f(\boldsymbol{x}) = \|\boldsymbol{X}\|_*$ *with* $\boldsymbol{X}$ *a matrix in* $\mathbb{R}^{n\times n}$.

Below are some basic properties of subdifferentials.

LEMMA B.21. (Monotonicity property) *Given a convex function* $f : \mathbb{R}^n \to \mathbb{R} \cup \{+\infty\}$ *and any* $\boldsymbol{x}, \boldsymbol{x}', \boldsymbol{v}, \boldsymbol{v}' \in \mathbb{R}^n$ *such that* $\boldsymbol{v} \in \partial f(\boldsymbol{x})$ *and* $\boldsymbol{v}' \in \partial f(\boldsymbol{x}')$, *we have*

$$\langle \boldsymbol{x} - \boldsymbol{x}', \boldsymbol{v} - \boldsymbol{v}' \rangle \geq 0. \tag{B.3.5}$$

Proof From the definition of subgradient (B.19), we have

$$f(\boldsymbol{x}') \geq f(\boldsymbol{x}) + \langle \boldsymbol{v}, \boldsymbol{x}' - \boldsymbol{x} \rangle, \quad f(\boldsymbol{x}) \geq f(\boldsymbol{x}') + \langle \boldsymbol{v}', \boldsymbol{x} - \boldsymbol{x}' \rangle. \tag{B.3.6}$$

Adding these two inequalities together we obtain:

$$f(\boldsymbol{x}) + f(\boldsymbol{x}') \geq f(\boldsymbol{x}) + f(\boldsymbol{x}') + \langle \boldsymbol{v} - \boldsymbol{v}', \boldsymbol{x}' - \boldsymbol{x} \rangle. \tag{B.3.7}$$

Canceling $f(\boldsymbol{x}) + f(\boldsymbol{x}')$ from both sides obtains the desired result. □

LEMMA B.22. *If a convex function* $f(\boldsymbol{x})$ *has Lipschitz continuous gradients with constant L, then for any* $\boldsymbol{x}_1$ *and* $\boldsymbol{x}_2$, *we have*

$$\langle \nabla f(\boldsymbol{x}_1) - \nabla f(\boldsymbol{x}_2), \boldsymbol{x}_1 - \boldsymbol{x}_2 \rangle \geq \frac{1}{L} \|\nabla f(\boldsymbol{x}_1) - \nabla f(\boldsymbol{x}_2)\|_2^2 \geq 0. \tag{B.3.8}$$

Proof Let us define a function $h(z) \doteq f(z) - z^* \nabla f(\boldsymbol{x})$. Then $h(z)$ is convex and is minimized at $z = \boldsymbol{x}$ (as $\nabla h(\boldsymbol{x}) = \boldsymbol{0}$). Hence for any z, we have

$$h(\boldsymbol{x}) \leq h\left(z - \frac{1}{L}\nabla h(z)\right) \leq h(z) + \left\langle \nabla h(z), -\frac{1}{L}\nabla h(z) \right\rangle + \frac{L}{2}\left\| \frac{1}{L}\nabla h(z) \right\|_2^2.$$

The last inequality comes from the fact that the function $f(\boldsymbol{x})$ (and hence $h(z)$) has Lipschitz continuous gradients with constant L. This gives

$$h(\boldsymbol{x}) \leq h(z) - \frac{1}{2L}\|\nabla h(z)\|_2^2. \tag{B.3.9}$$

Now applying the inequality to $\boldsymbol{x} = \boldsymbol{x}_1, z = \boldsymbol{x}_2$ as well as the reverse case $\boldsymbol{x} = \boldsymbol{x}_2$, $z = \boldsymbol{x}_1$, we get

$$f(\boldsymbol{x}_1) - \boldsymbol{x}_1^* \nabla f(\boldsymbol{x}_1) \leq f(\boldsymbol{x}_2) - \boldsymbol{x}_2^* \nabla f(\boldsymbol{x}_1) - \frac{1}{2L}\|\nabla f(\boldsymbol{x}_2) - \nabla f(\boldsymbol{x}_1)\|_2^2,$$

$$f(\boldsymbol{x}_2) - \boldsymbol{x}_2^* \nabla f(\boldsymbol{x}_2) \leq f(\boldsymbol{x}_1) - \boldsymbol{x}_1^* \nabla f(\boldsymbol{x}_2) - \frac{1}{2L}\|\nabla f(\boldsymbol{x}_1) - \nabla f(\boldsymbol{x}_2)\|_2^2.$$

Adding these two together gives the desired bound (B.3.8). □

Appendix C Optimization Problems and Optimality Conditions

"Since the fabric of the universe is most perfect and the work of a most wise Creator, nothing at all takes place in the universe in which some rule of maximum or minimum does not appear."

– Leonhard Euler

C.1 Unconstrained Optimization

The mathematical model of an (unconstrained) optimization problem can be generally described by a domain or constraint set $\mathcal{D}$ in $\mathbb{R}^n$ and an objective function $f : \mathcal{D} \to \mathbb{R}$ that maps an element of $\mathcal{D}$ to a real value. The optimization problem seeks an optimal solution $\boldsymbol{x}_\star \in \mathcal{D}$ such that the value of f is minimized:

$$f(\boldsymbol{x}_\star) \leq f(\boldsymbol{x}), \quad \text{for all } \boldsymbol{x} \in \mathcal{D}.$$

In particular, if $\mathcal{D} = \mathbb{R}^n$, it is called an unconstrained optimization problem.

DEFINITION C.1. (Local and global minima) *A variable $\boldsymbol{x}_\star$ is a local minimum of f if there exists a neighborhood $\mathsf{B}(\varepsilon, \boldsymbol{x}_\star) \doteq \{\boldsymbol{x} \in \mathcal{D} \mid \|\boldsymbol{x} - \boldsymbol{x}_\star\|_2 < \varepsilon\}$ for some $\varepsilon > 0$ such that*

$$f(\boldsymbol{x}_\star) \leq f(\boldsymbol{x}), \quad \textit{for all } \boldsymbol{x} \in \mathsf{B}(\varepsilon, \boldsymbol{x}_\star).$$

The variable $\boldsymbol{x}_\star$ is a global minimum of f if $\mathsf{B}(\varepsilon, \boldsymbol{x}_\star) = \mathcal{D}$. The above local and global minima are said to be strict if the corresponding inequalities are also strict for $\boldsymbol{x} \neq \boldsymbol{x}_\star$.

If the objective function f is differentiable, then conditions for the optimality can be expressed in terms of its derivatives. In particular, if $\boldsymbol{x}_\star$ is a local minimum, then within a small neighborhood $\mathsf{B}(\varepsilon, \boldsymbol{x}_\star)$, for any given vector $\boldsymbol{v} \in \mathbb{R}^n$, we have

$$f(\boldsymbol{x}_\star + t \cdot \boldsymbol{v}) \geq f(\boldsymbol{x}_\star)$$

for sufficiently small $t > 0$ such that $t \cdot \boldsymbol{v} \in \mathsf{B}(\varepsilon, \boldsymbol{0})$. Hence we have

$$\lim_{t \to 0} \frac{f(\boldsymbol{x}_\star + t \cdot \boldsymbol{v}) - f(\boldsymbol{x}_\star)}{t} = \nabla f(\boldsymbol{x}_\star)^* \boldsymbol{v} \geq 0.$$

Notice that this must be true for both $\boldsymbol{v}$ and $-\boldsymbol{v}$. Then for the inequality to hold for all $\boldsymbol{v} \in \mathbb{R}^n$, we must have

$$\nabla f(\boldsymbol{x}_\star) = \mathbf{0}. \tag{C.1.1}$$

DEFINITION C.2. (Stationary point or critical point) *A point $\boldsymbol{x}_\star$ that satisfies the condition $\nabla f(\boldsymbol{x}_\star) = \mathbf{0}$ is referred to as a stationary point of $f(\boldsymbol{x})$. A stationary point is also known as a critical point.*

If f is twice continuously differentiable and $\boldsymbol{x}_\star$ is a stationary point with $\nabla f(\boldsymbol{x}_\star) = \mathbf{0}$, we have

$$f(\boldsymbol{x}_\star + t \cdot \boldsymbol{v}) \approx f(\boldsymbol{x}_\star) + \frac{1}{2}\boldsymbol{v}^* \nabla^2 f(\boldsymbol{x}_\star) \boldsymbol{v} t^2 + o(t^2).$$

If $\boldsymbol{x}_\star$ is a local minimum, we have

$$f(\boldsymbol{x}_\star + t \cdot \boldsymbol{v}) - f(\boldsymbol{x}_\star) \geq 0 \quad \Rightarrow \quad \frac{1}{2}\boldsymbol{v}^* \nabla^2 f(\boldsymbol{x}_\star) \boldsymbol{v} t^2 \geq 0$$

for all $\boldsymbol{v} \in \mathbb{R}^n$. This implies that the matrix $\nabla^2 f(\boldsymbol{x}_\star)$ is necessarily positive semidefinite, namely,

$$\nabla^2 f(\boldsymbol{x}_\star) \succeq \mathbf{0}. \tag{C.1.2}$$

A stationary point satisfying the above condition is also called a *second-order* stationary point.

It is then not difficult to show the following sufficient condition for local minima:

PROPOSITION C.3. (Second-Order sufficient optimality condition) *Let $f : \mathcal{D} \to \mathbb{R}$ be twice continuously differentiable. If $\boldsymbol{x}_\star$ satisfies the conditions*

$$\nabla f(\boldsymbol{x}_\star) = \mathbf{0} \quad \text{and} \quad \nabla^2 f(\boldsymbol{x}_\star) \succ \mathbf{0},$$

then $\boldsymbol{x}_\star$ is a strict local minimum of $f(\boldsymbol{x})$.

In general, a local minimum is not necessarily a global minimum in the domain of $f(\boldsymbol{x})$. Therefore, the global minimum can be found by exhaustively comparing the values of f at all local minima. However, when the objective function f is convex, the following proposition shows that any local minimum is also a global minimum.

PROPOSITION C.4. (Global optimality of convex functions) *Let $f : \mathcal{D} \to \mathbb{R}$ be a convex function over convex set $\mathcal{D}$. Then the following hold.*

1. *A local minimum of f is also a global minimum. Furthermore, if f is strictly convex, then the global minimum, if it exists, is unique.*
2. *A point $\boldsymbol{x}_\star \in \mathcal{D}$ is a global minimum of f if $\mathbf{0} \in \partial f(\boldsymbol{x}_\star)$. In the case that f is differentiable, $\nabla f(\boldsymbol{x}_\star) = \mathbf{0}$ implies that $\boldsymbol{x}_\star$ is a global minimum.*

Finally, we note that given an objective function f, a local minimum need not exist. For example, the simple scalar function $f(x) = x$ does not have a minimal value in the domain of real numbers, as $\inf_{x \in \mathbb{R}} f(x) = -\infty$. Therefore, a sufficient condition for f to have at least one local minimum is that the set $\{f(\boldsymbol{x}) \mid \boldsymbol{x} \in \mathcal{D}\}$ is bounded below. Alternatively, according to the Weierstrass theorem, if f is continuous and the domain set $\mathcal{D} \subseteq \mathbb{R}^n$ is compact (i.e., closed and bounded), then f has at least one local minimum.

C.2 Constrained Optimization

In the previous section, the constraint set of the optimization problems is assumed to be any general set. However, in most optimization problems considered in this book, the constraints are formulated as equality or inequality conditions. For example, the domain $\mathcal{D} \subset \mathbb{R}^n$ of a polyhedron can be specified by a set of equality and inequality conditions. *Lagrange multipliers* are a set of supportive variables to facilitate the derivation of optimality conditions for such constrained optimization problems. Arguably, Lagrange multiplier theory is the most influential theory in constrained optimization. In duality theory, which we will discuss in the next section, the same Lagrange multiplier variables are also called *dual variables*, which will play a central role as the optimization variables of the *dual problems*.

First, we consider the optimization problem with equality constraints:

$$\min f(\boldsymbol{x}) \quad \text{subject to} \quad h_i(\boldsymbol{x}) = 0, \ i = 1, \dots, m, \tag{C.2.1}$$

where f and each h_i are assumed to be continuously differentiable.[1] Conveniently, we further assume that the gradients of the equality conditions at any feasible solution $\boldsymbol{x}'$ (that satisfies the equality constraints),

$$\nabla h_1(\boldsymbol{x}'), \nabla h_2(\boldsymbol{x}'), \dots, \nabla h_m(\boldsymbol{x}'),$$

are linearly independent. Such a solution $\boldsymbol{x}'$ is also called *regular*.

The optimality conditions for (C.2.1) can be conveniently derived in terms of the Lagrangian function $\mathcal{L} : \mathbb{R}^{n+m} \to \mathbb{R}$ as

$$\mathcal{L}(\boldsymbol{x}, \boldsymbol{\lambda}) \doteq f(\boldsymbol{x}) + \sum_{i=1}^{m} \lambda_i h_i(\boldsymbol{x}) = f(\boldsymbol{x}) + \langle \boldsymbol{\lambda}, \boldsymbol{h}(\boldsymbol{x}) \rangle, \tag{C.2.2}$$

where λ_i are the Lagrange multipliers for the equality conditions, and $\boldsymbol{\lambda} = [\lambda_1, \lambda_2, \dots, \lambda_m]^* \in \mathbb{R}^m$ is the corresponding Lagrange multiplier vector; and for brevity, we denote $\boldsymbol{h} = [h_1, h_2, \dots, h_m]^*$ as a map from $\mathbb{R}^n$ to $\mathbb{R}^m$.

The basic Lagrange multiplier theory states the following necessary condition for the optimality of a regular solution.

PROPOSITION C.5. (Necessary conditions for optimality) *Let $\boldsymbol{x}_\star$ be a local minimum of function $f(\boldsymbol{x})$ subject to $h_i(\boldsymbol{x}) = 0$, $i = 1, \dots, m$. Further assume $\boldsymbol{x}_\star$ is regular. Then there exists a Lagrange multiplier vector $\boldsymbol{\lambda}_\star = (\lambda_{\star,1}, \lambda_{\star,2}, \dots, \lambda_{\star,m}) \in \mathbb{R}^m$, such that*

[1] In the main text, we need to generalize to cases when f is not differentiable.

$$\begin{aligned} \nabla_{\boldsymbol{x}} \mathcal{L}(\boldsymbol{x}_\star, \boldsymbol{\lambda}_\star) &= \nabla f(\boldsymbol{x}_\star) + \sum_{i=1}^{m} \lambda_{\star,i} \nabla h_i(\boldsymbol{x}_\star) = \mathbf{0}, \\ \nabla_{\boldsymbol{\lambda}} \mathcal{L}(\boldsymbol{x}_\star, \boldsymbol{\lambda}_\star) &= \boldsymbol{h}(\boldsymbol{x}_\star) = \mathbf{0}. \end{aligned} \tag{C.2.3}$$

Furthermore, if f and $\mathbf{h}$ are twice continuously differentiable, we have

$$\begin{aligned} \boldsymbol{v}^* \nabla^2_{\boldsymbol{x}\boldsymbol{x}} \mathcal{L}(\boldsymbol{x}_\star, \boldsymbol{\lambda}_\star) \boldsymbol{v} &= \boldsymbol{v}^* \left(\nabla^2 f(\boldsymbol{x}_\star) + \sum_{i=1}^{m} \lambda_{\star,i} \nabla^2 h_i(\boldsymbol{x}_\star) \right) \boldsymbol{v} \\ &\geq 0, \quad \forall\, \boldsymbol{v} : \boldsymbol{v}^* \nabla h_i(\boldsymbol{x}_\star) = 0,\ i = 1, \dots, m. \end{aligned} \tag{C.2.4}$$

In (C.2.4), the conditions for vector $\boldsymbol{v} \in \mathbb{R}^n$ that satisfies $\boldsymbol{v}^* \nabla h_i(\boldsymbol{x}_\star) = 0$ can be understood as follows. If we consider a new point $\boldsymbol{x}' = \boldsymbol{x}_\star + t \cdot \boldsymbol{v}$ for some small $t \in \mathbb{R}$, due to the fact that $\boldsymbol{v}^* \nabla h_i(\boldsymbol{x}_\star) = 0$, a small variation along $\boldsymbol{v}$ will not change the value of $\boldsymbol{h}(\boldsymbol{x}') \approx \mathbf{0}$. Therefore, we can define

$$\mathsf{V}(\boldsymbol{x}_\star) = \{ \boldsymbol{v} \mid \boldsymbol{v}^* \nabla h_i(\boldsymbol{x}_\star) = 0,\ i = 1, \dots, m \} \tag{C.2.5}$$

as the *subspace of first-order feasible variations*.

In summary, the first-order condition (C.2.3) implies the gradient $\nabla f(\boldsymbol{x}_\star)$ is orthogonal to $\mathsf{V}(\boldsymbol{x}_\star)$, which resembles the first-order condition $\nabla f(\boldsymbol{x}_\star) = \mathbf{0}$ in unconstrained optimization. The second-order condition (C.2.4) implies the Hessian of the Lagrangian function $\mathcal{L}(\boldsymbol{x}_\star, \boldsymbol{\lambda}_\star)$ is positive semidefinite when constrained in $\mathsf{V}(\boldsymbol{x}_\star)$.

PROPOSITION C.6. (Sufficient conditions) *Assume f and $\mathbf{h}$ are twice continuously differentiable. Let $(\boldsymbol{x}_\star, \boldsymbol{\lambda}_\star) \in \mathbb{R}^{n+m}$ satisfy*

$$\begin{aligned} \nabla_{\boldsymbol{x}} \mathcal{L}(\boldsymbol{x}_\star, \boldsymbol{\lambda}_\star) &= \mathbf{0}, \\ \nabla_{\boldsymbol{\lambda}} \mathcal{L}(\boldsymbol{x}_\star, \boldsymbol{\lambda}_\star) &= \mathbf{0}, \\ \boldsymbol{v}^* \nabla^2_{\boldsymbol{x}\boldsymbol{x}} \mathcal{L}(\boldsymbol{x}_\star, \boldsymbol{\lambda}_\star) \boldsymbol{v} &> 0, \quad \forall\, \boldsymbol{v} \in \mathsf{V}(\boldsymbol{x}_\star), \boldsymbol{v} \neq \mathbf{0}. \end{aligned} \tag{C.2.6}$$

Then $\boldsymbol{x}_\star$ is a strict local minimum of $f(\boldsymbol{x})$ subject to $\boldsymbol{h}(\boldsymbol{x}) = \mathbf{0}$.

C.3 Basic Duality Theory

Recall the Lagrangian function for the above equality constrained optimization problem:

$$\mathcal{L}(\boldsymbol{x}, \boldsymbol{\lambda}) \doteq f(\boldsymbol{x}) + \sum_{i=1}^{m} \lambda_i h_i(\boldsymbol{x}) = f(\boldsymbol{x}) + \langle \boldsymbol{\lambda}, \boldsymbol{h}(\boldsymbol{x}) \rangle, \tag{C.3.1}$$

where $\boldsymbol{\lambda} = [\lambda_1, \lambda_2, \dots, \lambda_m]^* \in \mathbb{R}^m$ are the Lagrange multipliers.

In duality theory, the vector $\boldsymbol{\lambda}$ is also called the *dual variables* for the so-called *dual function*:

$$q(\boldsymbol{\lambda}) \doteq \inf_{\boldsymbol{x} \in \mathcal{D}} \mathcal{L}(\boldsymbol{x}, \boldsymbol{\lambda}). \tag{C.3.2}$$

Correspondingly, $f(\boldsymbol{x})$ is referred to as the *primal function* and $\boldsymbol{x}$ the *primal variables*.

A simple property of the dual function q is that it is a concave function regardless of whether the primal problem is convex or not, since q is the point-wise infimum of a family of affine functions with respect to $(\boldsymbol{\lambda})$.

Another important property of the dual function is that $q(\boldsymbol{\lambda})$ is a lower bound of $f(\boldsymbol{x}')$ for any feasible solution $\boldsymbol{x}'$. In particular, $q(\boldsymbol{\lambda})$ is a lower bound of the optimal value $f(\boldsymbol{x}_\star)$. This can be easily verified since, for a feasible $\boldsymbol{x}'$ satisfying $\boldsymbol{h}(\boldsymbol{x}') = \boldsymbol{0}$, we have

$$q(\boldsymbol{\lambda}) = \inf_{\boldsymbol{x}\in\mathcal{D}} f(\boldsymbol{x}) + \langle \boldsymbol{\lambda}, \boldsymbol{h}(\boldsymbol{x})\rangle \leq \inf_{\boldsymbol{x}\in\mathcal{D},\, \boldsymbol{h}(\boldsymbol{x})=\boldsymbol{0}} f(\boldsymbol{x}) \leq f(\boldsymbol{x}').$$

For the dual function $q(\boldsymbol{\lambda})$ to provide a meaningful lower bound for $f(\boldsymbol{x}_\star)$, it is natural to avoid trivial cases when $q(\boldsymbol{\lambda}) = -\infty$. So we normally restrict the domain of the dual function q to

$$\mathcal{C} \doteq \{\boldsymbol{\lambda} \mid q(\boldsymbol{\lambda}) > -\infty\}. \tag{C.3.3}$$

More specifically, the dual variables $(\boldsymbol{\lambda})$ that satisfy the above conditions are called *dual feasible solutions*.

A very useful concept in duality theory is the so-called *duality gap* between the primal and dual functions,

$$f(\boldsymbol{x}) - q(\boldsymbol{\lambda}), \tag{C.3.4}$$

since the dual function $q(\boldsymbol{\lambda})$ is a lower bound of the primal function $f(\boldsymbol{x})$, in particular of its minimal value $f(\boldsymbol{x}_\star)$. The duality gap is always nonnegative (over the set of feasible solutions). More importantly, when the duality gap is zero, namely, there exists a feasible solution $\boldsymbol{x}_\star$ and $\boldsymbol{\lambda}_\star$ such that $f(\boldsymbol{x}_\star) = q(\boldsymbol{\lambda}_\star)$, then $\boldsymbol{x}_\star$ is the optimal primal solution and $\boldsymbol{\lambda}_\star$ is the optimal dual solution.

Naturally, when we want to achieve the best lower-bound estimation of the minimal value, we can consider the following optimization problem in the dual space:

$$\max_{\boldsymbol{\lambda}} q(\boldsymbol{\lambda}). \tag{C.3.5}$$

The problem (C.3.5) is called the *Lagrange dual problem* associated with the original *primal problem* (C.2.1).

Since the optimal solution $q(\boldsymbol{\lambda}_\star)$ is the best lower-bound approximation of the global minimum $f(\boldsymbol{x}_\star)$, the following inequality condition holds trivially:

$$q(\boldsymbol{\lambda}_\star) \leq f(\boldsymbol{x}_\star). \tag{C.3.6}$$

The condition is known as the *weak duality condition*. Furthermore, when the equality can be obtained in (C.3.6), the duality gap between f and q becomes zero, and we say the primal and dual function pair satisfy the *strong duality condition*.

The strong duality condition can be achieved for convex objective functions subject to linear constraints.

THEOREM C.7. (Strong duality theorem) *Let the objective function* $f(\boldsymbol{x})$ *in* (C.2.1) *be convex and* $\boldsymbol{h}(\boldsymbol{x})$ *be linear. If the optimal value* $f_\star$ *is finite, then the optimal solution for its dual problem exists and there is no duality gap.*

Under the strong duality condition, the minimal value of f can be found by optimizing the dual problem $q(\boldsymbol{\lambda})$, and the optimal primal solution can also be obtained by minimizing the Lagrangian function $\mathcal{L}(\boldsymbol{x}, \boldsymbol{\lambda}_\star)$ over $\boldsymbol{x}$. In other words, the optimal $(\boldsymbol{x}_\star, \boldsymbol{\lambda}_\star)$ is the saddle point of the Lagrangian function $\mathcal{L}(\boldsymbol{x}, \boldsymbol{\lambda})$ that solves the following program:

$$\max_{\boldsymbol{\lambda}} \min_{\boldsymbol{x}} \mathcal{L}(\boldsymbol{x}, \boldsymbol{\lambda}). \tag{C.3.7}$$

In the above, we have assumed all functions are differentiable. In this book, we often need to optimize a convex function that is not differentiable and the type of constraints are in the form $\boldsymbol{A}\boldsymbol{x} = \boldsymbol{y}$.

LEMMA C.8. (Dual certificate) *Let* $f : \mathbb{R}^n \to \mathbb{R}$ *be convex,* $\boldsymbol{y} \in \mathbb{R}^m$*,* $\boldsymbol{A} \in \mathbb{R}^{m \times n}$*, and let* $\boldsymbol{x}_\star$ *be some point satisfying* $\boldsymbol{A}\boldsymbol{x}_\star = \boldsymbol{y}$*. If there exists* $\boldsymbol{\nu}$ *such that*

$$\boldsymbol{A}^* \boldsymbol{\nu} \in \partial f(\boldsymbol{x}_\star), \tag{C.3.8}$$

then $\boldsymbol{x}_\star$ *is a solution to the optimization problem*

$$\begin{array}{ll} \min & f(\boldsymbol{x}) \\ \text{subject to} & \boldsymbol{A}\boldsymbol{x} = \boldsymbol{y}. \end{array} \tag{C.3.9}$$

Proof Consider any $\boldsymbol{x}'$ satisfying $\boldsymbol{A}\boldsymbol{x}' = \boldsymbol{y}$. By the subgradient inequality (B.3.3),

$$\begin{aligned} f(\boldsymbol{x}') &\geq f(\boldsymbol{x}_\star) + \left\langle \boldsymbol{A}^* \boldsymbol{\nu}, \boldsymbol{x}' - \boldsymbol{x}_\star \right\rangle \\ &= f(\boldsymbol{x}_\star) + \left\langle \boldsymbol{\nu}, \boldsymbol{A}(\boldsymbol{x}' - \boldsymbol{x}_\star) \right\rangle \\ &= f(\boldsymbol{x}_\star), \end{aligned} \tag{C.3.10}$$

since $\boldsymbol{A}\boldsymbol{x}' = \boldsymbol{A}\boldsymbol{x}_\star$. Thus, $\boldsymbol{x}_\star$ is optimal. □

Appendix D Methods for Optimization

In this chapter, we review classical approaches to solving optimization problems of the form

$$\min_{x \in \mathcal{D}} f(\boldsymbol{x}), \tag{D.0.1}$$

in which we seek to minimize an objective function f over some domain $\mathcal{D}$. All of the algorithms we describe are *iterative methods* of optimization, which produce a sequence of points

$$\boldsymbol{x}_0, \boldsymbol{x}_1, \dots, \boldsymbol{x}_k, \dots \tag{D.0.2}$$

starting from some initialization $\boldsymbol{x}_0$. The goal is to generate a sequence $\{\boldsymbol{x}_k\}$ which quickly converges to a minimizer $\boldsymbol{x}_\star$ of f over $\mathcal{D}$. The total time an iterative method requires to produce an acceptable answer depends chiefly on two quantities:

1 **Per iteration cost**: how much computation it takes to generate the next point $\boldsymbol{x}_{k+1}$ given the previous points $\boldsymbol{x}_0, \dots, \boldsymbol{x}_k$.

2 **Convergence rate**: how quickly the iterate $\boldsymbol{x}_k$ improves in quality. This dictates how many iterations are required to produce a sufficiently accurate solution. This may be measured either in terms of the distance of the iterate $\boldsymbol{x}_k$ to a minimizer,

$$\|\boldsymbol{x}_k - \boldsymbol{x}_\star\|_2, \tag{D.0.3}$$

or in terms of the suboptimality in objective value,

$$|f(\boldsymbol{x}_k) - f(\boldsymbol{x}_\star)|, \tag{D.0.4}$$

or its gradient,[1]

$$\|\nabla f(\boldsymbol{x}_k) - \nabla f(\boldsymbol{x}_\star)\|_2 = \|\nabla f(\boldsymbol{x}_k)\|_2. \tag{D.0.5}$$

The above two cost quantities are usually in tension: we can have fast convergence rate at the price of very expensive iterations, or we can have very cheap iterations at the price of a relatively slow convergence. Hence, the overall complexity of an optimization algorithm is typically measured as

[1] When we are only interested in converging to a stationary point of the objective function with $\nabla f(\boldsymbol{x}_\star) = \boldsymbol{0}$.

$$\text{complexity} = \text{per iteration cost} \times \#\text{ of iterations}, \tag{D.0.6}$$

subject to a prescribed accuracy in $\boldsymbol{x}$ or the objective value $f(\boldsymbol{x})$.

In the era of big data or large models, many practical problems involve optimizing over a very large number of model parameters or training over large-scale datasets. Due to computation limitations, we typically can only afford to do fairly simple calculations in each iteration. Hence we are mainly interested in methods that achieve the fastest possible convergence rate out of methods that only work with *first-order* information (values of $f(\boldsymbol{x})$ and $\nabla f(\boldsymbol{x})$). Sometimes due to memory limitation and time requirement, we need to store the data and conduct the calculation over many *parallel* processes or a *distributed* network of machines. To reduce communication cost and delay, we often prefer algorithms that are amenable to parallel or distributed implementation and require minimal exchange of data and information across different processes or machines. In this appendix, we sketch basic ideas of some of the most popular and effective techniques that enhance the performance of first-order methods, especially those that are suitable for solving large-scale problems. We also provide references where the reader can find more complete exposition and analysis of these techniques.

D.1 Gradient Descent

Perhaps the simplest iterative method of optimization is *gradient descent*, also known as the gradient method, which applies to *differentiable* functions $f : \mathbb{R}^n \to \mathbb{R}$. The method was first introduced by Cauchy in 1847 to solve systems of equations [Cau47]. It comes from the simplest idea that from the current state $\boldsymbol{x}_k$, one would like to take a small step $t \geq 0$ in the direction $\boldsymbol{v} \in \mathbb{R}^n$ to $\boldsymbol{x}_{k+1} = \boldsymbol{x}_k + t \cdot \boldsymbol{v}$ such that the value of f decreases:

$$f(\boldsymbol{x}_{k+1}) < f(\boldsymbol{x}_k).$$

Since f is differentiable, we know that up to first-order approximation:

$$f(\boldsymbol{x}_{k+1}) - f(\boldsymbol{x}_k) = f(\boldsymbol{x}_k + t \cdot \boldsymbol{v}) - f(\boldsymbol{x}_k) \approx t \cdot \nabla f(\boldsymbol{x}_k)^* \boldsymbol{v}.$$

The gradient $\nabla f(\boldsymbol{x}_k)$ points in the direction of steepest increase of the objective f; the negative gradient is the direction of steepest decent. So in order for $f(\boldsymbol{x}_{k+1})$ to be smaller than $f(\boldsymbol{x}_k)$, it is natural to take the direction in which the value of f drops the fastest: $\boldsymbol{v} \propto -\nabla f(\boldsymbol{x}_k)$. Hence the *gradient descent* is also known as the *steepest descent*.

Therefore, gradient descent generates its next iterate by stepping in the direction of the negative gradient:

$$\boldsymbol{x}_{k+1} = \boldsymbol{x}_k - t_k \nabla f(\boldsymbol{x}_k). \tag{D.1.1}$$

Here, $t_k \geq 0$ is a scalar, often called the *step size*.[2] The step size t_k can either be determined analytically from the properties of the function f, or numerically by performing a *line search*, which produces an approximate solution[3] to the one-dimensional problem:

$$\min_{t \geq 0} \ f\left(\boldsymbol{x}_k - t \nabla f(\boldsymbol{x}_k)\right). \tag{D.1.2}$$

Convergence of Gradient Descent

A principal virtue of gradient descent is that for many problems, ∇f can be computed efficiently. To understand the overall properties of the method, we need to know how many iterations it requires to obtain a solution of a given desired quality. This depends in turn on the properties of the objective function f.

We begin by assuming that f is a convex, differentiable function, and that the gradient $\nabla f(\boldsymbol{x})$ is L-Lipschitz:

$$\left\|\nabla f(\boldsymbol{x}) - \nabla f(\boldsymbol{x}')\right\|_2 \leq L \left\|\boldsymbol{x} - \boldsymbol{x}'\right\|_2, \quad \forall \boldsymbol{x}, \boldsymbol{x}'. \tag{D.1.3}$$

This condition states that the gradient does not change too rapidly as we move from point to point. Intuitively, this means that a first-order model for the objective function generated by taking a Taylor expansion at point $\boldsymbol{x}$ will be valid over a relatively large portion of the space. Indeed, it turns out that under these hypotheses, we can take t_k to be uniform,

$$t_k = \frac{1}{L},$$

and smaller L allows larger steps. Moreover, it can be shown that with this choice,

$$\begin{aligned} f(\boldsymbol{x}_{k+1}) &\leq f(\boldsymbol{x}_k) - \frac{1}{2L} \|\nabla f(\boldsymbol{x}_k)\|_2^2 \\ &\leq f(\boldsymbol{x}_k). \end{aligned} \tag{D.1.4}$$

Thus, with this choice, the gradient method is a *descent method*: it strictly decreases the objective at each iteration, until $\boldsymbol{x}_k$ reaches a minimizer. The following theorem gives an overall control on the rate of convergence, measured in function values:

THEOREM D.1. *Let $f : \mathbb{R}^n \to \mathbb{R}$ be a differentiable function with $\nabla f(\boldsymbol{x})$ L-Lipschitz. Let $\mathsf{X}_\star \neq \varnothing$ denote the set of minimizers of f, and $f_\star$ the minimum value of f over $\mathbb{R}^n$. Consider the gradient method with constant step size $t_k = 1/L$. Then*

$$f(\boldsymbol{x}_k) - f_\star \leq \frac{L}{2} \frac{\|\boldsymbol{x}_0 - \boldsymbol{x}_\star\|_2^2}{k}. \tag{D.1.5}$$

Moreover, as $k \to \infty$, $\boldsymbol{x}_k \to \mathsf{X}_\star$.

A proof of this theorem (actually a more generalized version) can be found in Chapter 8, Section 8.2.

[2] Or the *learning rate* in learning algorithms.

[3] Typically, this is done by *backtracking*: starting from some nominal value of t, we reduce t until the function value decreases adequately, say satisfying the Armijo rule.

Several aspects of this result are worth noting. First, the suboptimality in function values decreases as $1/k$. In particular, as $k \to \infty$, $f(\boldsymbol{x}_k) \to f_\star$. Second, the rate of convergence depends on the Lipschitz constant L – the smaller L is, the faster f approaches $f_\star$. Finally, the rate of convergence depends on the distance of the initialization to $\boldsymbol{x}_\star$. A strength of this result is that it is nonasymptotic (the bound works for all k, not just k large) and does not depend on dimension n. For applications, we care not just about function values, but about the quality of the iterates $\{\boldsymbol{x}_k\}$. Here, we are guaranteed that $\boldsymbol{x}_k$ approaches $\mathsf{X}_\star$. However, no general, dimension-independent bound on the rate of convergence is known.

D.2 Rates of Convergence and Acceleration

How good is the gradient method? More generally, if we restrict ourselves to relatively simple methods that only use gradient and function value information, what rate can we obtain? This fundamental question motivates the study of lower bounds for the computational efficiency of methods. This requires a model of computation. One simple model for first-order methods assumes that, at each iteration, the next point $\boldsymbol{x}_{k+1}$ is generated based only on the previous points $\boldsymbol{x}_0, \dots, \boldsymbol{x}_k$, their function values $f(\boldsymbol{x}_0), \dots, f(\boldsymbol{x}_k)$, and gradients $\nabla f(\boldsymbol{x}_0), \dots, \nabla f(\boldsymbol{x}_k)$:

$$f(\boldsymbol{x}_{k+1}) = \mathcal{F}_{k+1}\big(\boldsymbol{x}_0, \dots, \boldsymbol{x}_k, f(\boldsymbol{x}_0), \dots, f(\boldsymbol{x}_k), \nabla f(\boldsymbol{x}_0), \dots, \nabla f(\boldsymbol{x}_k)\big). \quad \text{(D.2.1)}$$

This is sometimes referred to as a *black box model*, since the method only accesses the function f through its value and gradient at a finite discrete set of points.[4]

It has been shown that (see [Nes03]):

THEOREM D.2. (Convergence rate of gradient descent) *For every L and R, there exists a convex differentiable function f with ∇f L-Lipschitz, and an initial point $\boldsymbol{x}_0$ satisfying $\|\boldsymbol{x}_0 - \boldsymbol{x}_\star\|_2 \le R$ such that*

$$f(\boldsymbol{x}_k) - f_\star \ge c\frac{LR^2}{k^2}, \quad \text{(D.2.2)}$$

where $c > 0$ is a numerical constant.

This result can be read as saying that for the class of functions with Lipschitz continuous gradients, the best generic rate of convergence that any gradient-like method can achieve is $O(1/k^2)$. Notice that Theorem D.1 implies that the gradient method converges at a rate of $O(1/k)$. For large k, this is *much* worse!

[4] This is fundamentally different from having access to those values over a continuous set, since any algorithm that relies on such an assumption is in fact, strictly speaking, not computable. Sometimes we may use the continuous-time dynamics such as the negated gradient flow $\dot{\boldsymbol{x}} = -\nabla f(\boldsymbol{x})$ to study qualitative behaviors of certain algorithms, such as what type of critical points they converge to. Such dynamics, however, do not directly translate to implementable algorithms through naive discretization of the time, because many of the quantitative properties of the dynamics would not necessarily be preserved by such discretization.

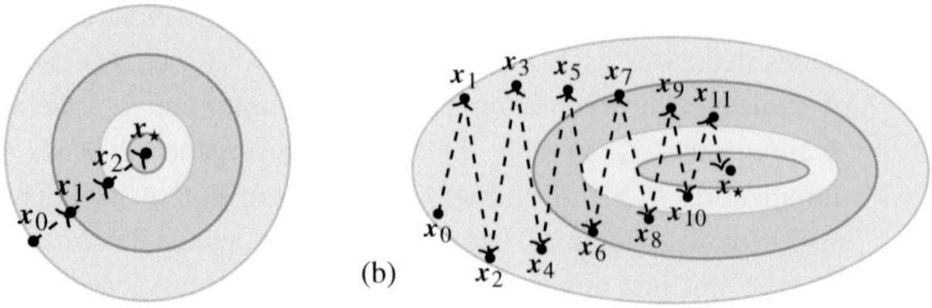

Figure D.1 Illustration of the iteration behaviors of gradient descent. (a) A quadratic function with spherical level sets. (b) A quadratic function with more ellipsoidal level sets.

Could the gradient method be suboptimal? Figure D.1 shows the behavior of gradient descent on two different problems. The figure plots the level sets $S_\beta = \{\boldsymbol{x} \mid f(\boldsymbol{x}) = \beta\}$ of the objective f as well as the iterates $\{\boldsymbol{x}_k\}$. Because the gradient $\nabla f(\boldsymbol{x})$ is orthogonal to the level set containing $\boldsymbol{x}$, the gradient method moves orthogonal to the level sets. In (a), we show a function $f(\boldsymbol{x})$ whose level sets are nearly circular. The gradient method makes rapid progress. In (b) is a function $f(\boldsymbol{x})$ whose level sets are more elongated. The iterates "chatter" repeatedly changing direction and making slow progress towards $\boldsymbol{x}_\star$.

The Heavy Ball Method

The bad behavior in Figure D.1 can be mitigated by preventing the steps $\boldsymbol{x}_{k+1} - \boldsymbol{x}_k$ from changing direction too rapidly. An intuitive way to accomplish this is to treat the iterate $\boldsymbol{x}_k$ as the trajectory of a particle with some amount of momentum, which causes it to continue moving in the same direction. This suggests an update of the form

$$\boldsymbol{x}_{k+1} = \boldsymbol{x}_k - t_k \nabla f(\boldsymbol{x}_k) + \beta_k \left(\boldsymbol{x}_k - \boldsymbol{x}_{k-1}\right). \tag{D.2.3}$$

Because this emulates the trajectory of a particle with nonzero mass, this method is aptly called the *heavy ball method*, first introduced by Polyak in 1964 [Pol64]. This method is also sometimes known as the *momentum method*, as the second term can be viewed as carrying some momentum from the previous iteration. This is the basis for the popular momentum-based ADAM algorithm for training modern neural networks [KB14]. Figure D.2 compares the heavy ball method to the gradient method on an ill-conditioned quadratic. Notice that the heavy ball method takes far fewer iterations to reach the vicinity of $\boldsymbol{x}_\star$.

Nesterov's Accelerated Method

Although the heavy ball method improves over the gradient method, its worst-case rate of convergence is still $O(1/k)$. However, by using momentum in a clever way, it *is* possible to achieve a better rate of convergence of $O(1/k^2)$, which matches the lower bound in Theorem D.2. This means, perhaps surprisingly, that there is a gradient-like method that is fundamentally better than gradient descent!

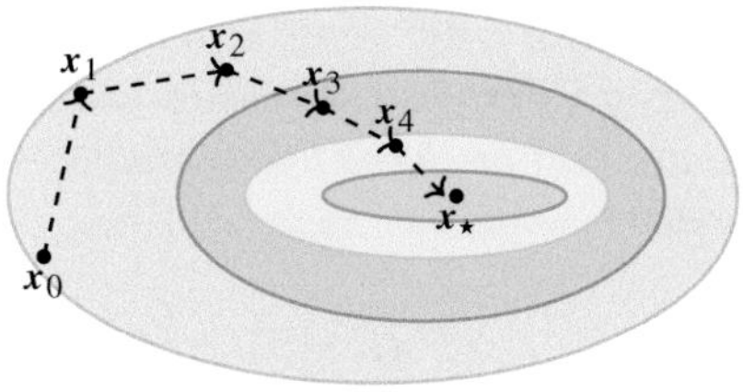

Figure D.2 Illustration of gradient descent with the heavy ball method.

The method that achieves this optimal rate is known as *Nesterov's accelerated gradient method.* Strictly speaking, it is not a momentum method. Rather, it uses two sequences of iterates $\{\boldsymbol{x}_k\}$ and $\{\boldsymbol{p}_k\}$. The auxiliary point $\boldsymbol{p}_k$ is extrapolated from $\boldsymbol{x}_k$ in a form similar to that in the heavy ball method:

$$\boldsymbol{p}_{k+1} \doteq \boldsymbol{x}_k + \beta_k(\boldsymbol{x}_k - \boldsymbol{x}_{k-1}).$$

At each iteration, we move to this new point, compute the gradient at this point, and descend from it (instead of $\boldsymbol{x}_k$):

$$\boldsymbol{x}_{k+1} = \boldsymbol{p}_{k+1} - \alpha \nabla f(\boldsymbol{p}_{k+1}). \tag{D.2.4}$$

As we have shown in Section 8.3 of Chapter 8, with properly chosen weights β_k and α, the gradient method is indeed accelerated and can achieve the optimal convergence rate of $O(1/k^2)$, for the class of functions with Lipschitz continuous gradients.

THEOREM D.3. (Convergence rate of accelerated gradient method) *Let $f : \mathbb{R}^n \to \mathbb{R}$ be a differentiable function with $\nabla f(\boldsymbol{x})$ being L-Lipschitz. Let $\mathsf{X}_\star \neq \varnothing$ denote the set of minimizers of f and $f_\star$ the minimum value of f over $\mathbb{R}^n$. The iterates $\{\boldsymbol{x}_k\}$ produced by the accelerated gradient method satisfy*

$$f(\boldsymbol{x}_k) - f_\star \leq \frac{L}{2} \frac{\|\boldsymbol{x}_0 - \boldsymbol{x}_\star\|_2^2}{(k+1)^2}. \tag{D.2.5}$$

Moreover, as $k \to \infty$, $\boldsymbol{x}_k \to \boldsymbol{x}_\star$.

Recently several works have tried to understand such acceleration by characterizing the stability of continuous ordinary differential equations associated with such iterations [SBC14] (and subsequent work [KBB16, KBB15, WWJ16]). A more detailed survey and discussion can be found in Section 8.3 of Chapter 8.

Strongly Convex Functions

Notice that Theorem D.2 characterizes the best possible rate of convergence for gradient-like methods for the class of functions with Lipschitz continuous gradients; and Theorem D.3 states that this rate can be achieved with the accelerated gradient methods. Nevertheless, this does not mean that this is the best one can do for more restricted classes of functions with better properties. If, in addition to Lipschitz continuous gradients, the functions satisfy additional properties such as being strongly convex as defined in Appendix B, it has long been known in the optimization literature that gradient-descent-type methods can converge at a *linear rate* [BV04].

THEOREM D.4. *Let $f : \mathbb{R}^n \to \mathbb{R}$ be a differentiable strongly convex function with constant μ and let $\nabla f(\boldsymbol{x})$ be L-Lipschitz. Let $f_\star$ be the minimum value of f over $\mathbb{R}^n$. Then the iterates $\{\boldsymbol{x}_k\}$ produced by the gradient descent $\boldsymbol{x}_{k+1} = \boldsymbol{x}_k - t\nabla f(\boldsymbol{x}_k)$ with $t = 1/L$ satisfy*

$$f(\boldsymbol{x}_k) - f_\star \leq \frac{L}{2} e^{-\alpha k} \|\boldsymbol{x}_0 - \boldsymbol{x}_\star\|_2^2 \tag{D.2.6}$$

for some constant $\alpha > 0$.

Proof We here give a proof to this simple fact as it helps explain why gradient descent converges very fast for many statistical learning problems in practice – the objective (loss) functions often concentrate on a function that is both strongly convex and smooth, as the size of random samples increases.

First, notice that at the optimal solution $\boldsymbol{x}_\star$ we have $\nabla f(\boldsymbol{x}_\star) = \mathbf{0}$. According to Lemma 8.2, we have

$$f(\boldsymbol{x}_k) - f(\boldsymbol{x}_\star) \leq \frac{L}{2} \|\boldsymbol{x}_k - \boldsymbol{x}_\star)\|_2^2.$$

Also, due to the strong convex and smooth assumption, we have

$$\mu \cdot \boldsymbol{I} \prec \nabla^2 f(\boldsymbol{x}) \preceq L \cdot \boldsymbol{I}, \quad \forall \boldsymbol{x}. \tag{D.2.7}$$

From the gradient descent rule, and with the fundamental theorem of calculus, we have

$$\begin{aligned}
\boldsymbol{x}_{k+1} - \boldsymbol{x}_\star &= \boldsymbol{x}_k - t\nabla f(\boldsymbol{x}_k) - \boldsymbol{x}_\star \\
&= \boldsymbol{x}_k - \boldsymbol{x}_\star - t\left(\int_0^1 \nabla^2 f(\boldsymbol{x}_\star + \tau(\boldsymbol{x}_k - \boldsymbol{x}_\star))d\tau\right)(\boldsymbol{x}_k - \boldsymbol{x}_\star).
\end{aligned}$$

This gives:

$$\begin{aligned}
\|\boldsymbol{x}_{k+1} - \boldsymbol{x}_\star\|_2 &\leq \left\|\boldsymbol{I} - t\int_0^1 \nabla^2 f(\boldsymbol{x}_\star + \tau(\boldsymbol{x}_k - \boldsymbol{x}_\star))d\tau\right\| \|\boldsymbol{x}_k - \boldsymbol{x}_\star\|_2 \\
&\leq (1 - t\mu)\|\boldsymbol{x}_k - \boldsymbol{x}_\star\|_2.
\end{aligned}$$

If we choose $t = 1/L$, then $(1 - \mu/L) < 1$, we have contraction of $\boldsymbol{x}_k - \boldsymbol{x}_\star$ in ℓ^2 norm. So we have

$$\|\boldsymbol{x}_k - \boldsymbol{x}_\star\|_2 \leq \left(1 - \frac{\mu}{L}\right)^k \|\boldsymbol{x}_0 - \boldsymbol{x}_\star\|_2, \quad \forall k,$$

or equivalently

$$\|\boldsymbol{x}_k - \boldsymbol{x}_\star\|_2^2 \leq \left(1 - \frac{\mu}{L}\right)^{2k} \|\boldsymbol{x}_0 - \boldsymbol{x}_\star\|_2^2, \quad \forall k.$$

Now, letting $\alpha = -\log(1 - \mu/L)^2 > 0$, we obtain the desired result. □

As we see from the above proof, we may also set the step size to be $t = 2/(L + \mu)$ and get a slightly better contraction factor.

According to the above theorem, $f(\boldsymbol{x}_k) - f_\star$ converges to zero exponentially in the order of $O(e^{-\alpha k})$, much faster than $O(1/k^2)$. In this book, the class of functions that we often encounter are not necessarily globally strongly convex. Nevertheless, they may satisfy a certain weaker notion of strong convexity, such as *restricted strong convexity* or local strong convexity. We will see that under such conditions, one may also expect gradient-like methods to achieve a linear rate of convergence around the global minimum.

Nondifferentiable Functions

The main assumption of gradient descent methods is that the objective function $f(\boldsymbol{x})$ is differentiable in $\boldsymbol{x}$. In this book, we often need to minimize functions that are not everywhere differentiable, such as functions involving the ℓ^1 norm $\|\boldsymbol{x}\|_1$. In such cases, we need to generalize the notion of gradient to "subgradients" (see Definition 2.3.20 in Chapter 2). Essentially, the subgradient at a point $\boldsymbol{x}$ is the set of vectors $\boldsymbol{u} \in \mathbb{R}^n$ such that

$$f(\boldsymbol{y}) \geq f(\boldsymbol{x}) + \langle \boldsymbol{u}, \boldsymbol{y} - \boldsymbol{x} \rangle, \quad \forall\, \boldsymbol{y}.$$

We often denote the set of subgradients as $\partial f(\boldsymbol{x})$. To minimize such a function $f(\boldsymbol{x})$, we may generalize the gradient descent method by replacing the gradient $\nabla f(\boldsymbol{x})$ with any subgradient:

$$\boldsymbol{x}_{k+1} = \boldsymbol{x}_k - t_k \boldsymbol{g}_k, \quad \boldsymbol{g}_k \in \partial f(\boldsymbol{x}).$$

A main disadvantage of such subgradient descent methods is their relatively poor convergence rate. In general, the convergence rate of subgradient descent for nonsmooth objective functions is

$$f(\boldsymbol{x}_k) - f_\star = O\big(1/\sqrt{k}\big).$$

The reader can refer to [Nem95, Nem07, Nes03] for more detailed analysis of subgradient descent algorithms.

It is worth noticing the significant difference in convergence rates for the same gradient descent algorithm being applied to two extreme subclasses of convex functions: the strongly convex functions versus nondifferentiable ones. For the former, gradient descent converges linearly, $O(e^{-\alpha k})$, and yet for the latter it converges much slower with a rate $O(1/\sqrt{k})$.

Nevertheless, as we will see in Chapter 8, in many of our problems, the objective function $f(\boldsymbol{x})$ is of the form $f_1(\boldsymbol{x}) + f_2(\boldsymbol{x})$ with f_1 being smooth and f_2 nonsmooth. If for the nonsmooth part f_2, the so called *proximal operator*

$$\min_{\boldsymbol{x}} f_2(\boldsymbol{x}) + \frac{1}{2}\|\boldsymbol{x} - \boldsymbol{w}\|_2^2 \tag{D.2.8}$$

has a closed-form solution or can be solved efficiently, then the subgradient descent method can be properly modified so that it would enjoy the same convergence rate as the smooth case. See the *proximal gradient* method in Section 8.2 of Chapter 8.

D.3 Constrained Optimization

It is very common in practice that we want to minimize a function $f(\boldsymbol{x})$ while the desired solution $\boldsymbol{x}_\star$ is constrained to some subset $\mathsf{C} \subset \mathbb{R}^n$:

$$\begin{array}{ll} \min & f(\boldsymbol{x}) \\ \text{subject to} & \boldsymbol{x} \in \mathsf{C}. \end{array} \tag{D.3.1}$$

Solutions in the subset C are called *feasible* solutions. Notice that we still apply the gradient descent method to minimize $f(\boldsymbol{x})$. Then, after each descent iteration,

$$\boldsymbol{p}_{k+1} = \boldsymbol{x}_k - t_k \nabla f(\boldsymbol{x}_k),$$

even if $\boldsymbol{x}_k$ is feasible, the new state $\boldsymbol{p}_{k+1}$ may step outside of the constrained set: $\boldsymbol{p}_{k+1} \notin \mathsf{C}$. A natural and simple fix to this issue is to "project" $\boldsymbol{p}_{k+1}$ back to the set C:

$$\boldsymbol{x}_{k+1} = \mathcal{P}_{\mathsf{C}}[\boldsymbol{p}_{k+1}] = \arg\min_{\boldsymbol{x} \in \mathsf{C}} \tfrac{1}{2} \left\| \boldsymbol{x} - \boldsymbol{p}_{k+1} \right\|_2^2, \tag{D.3.2}$$

where $\boldsymbol{x}_{k+1}$ is the point in C closest to $\boldsymbol{p}_{k+1}$. This will ensure the new iterate $\boldsymbol{x}_{k+1}$ is always feasible. This method is called *projected gradient descent*, and we use it to provide a simplest algorithm for minimizing the ℓ^1 norm in Chapter 2. This simple method is also the inspiration for other first-order constrained optimization methods such as the classic *Frank–Wolfe* method [FW56] that we studied in Section 8.6 of Chapter 8.

One disadvantage of such projected gradient descent methods is their relatively poor convergence rate or computational efficiency per iteration.[5] In the case the constraints are equality constraints, $\mathsf{C} = \{\boldsymbol{x} \mid \boldsymbol{h}(\boldsymbol{x}) = \boldsymbol{0}\}$, one could try to convert the constrained optimization

$$\begin{array}{ll} \min & f(\boldsymbol{x}) \\ \text{subject to} & \boldsymbol{h}(\boldsymbol{x}) = \boldsymbol{0} \end{array} \tag{D.3.3}$$

to an unconstrained one by penalizing any deviation of $\boldsymbol{h}(\boldsymbol{x})$ from $\boldsymbol{0}$:

$$\min f(\boldsymbol{x}) + \frac{\mu}{2} \|\boldsymbol{h}(\boldsymbol{x})\|_2^2. \tag{D.3.4}$$

This is known as the *penalty method*. One can show that as $\mu \to +\infty$, the solution to the unconstrained optimization approaches that of the constrained one. However, in practice, as μ becomes large, the unconstrained problem becomes increasingly harder to solve, as its gradient Lipschitz constant becomes increasingly large. See Section 8.4 of Chapter 8 for an example.

As we have discussed in Appendix C, another way to convert the constrained optimization problem is through the Lagrangian formulation. The optimal (feasible) solution $\boldsymbol{x}_\star$ to the above constrained optimization is also the optimal solution $(\boldsymbol{x}_\star, \boldsymbol{\lambda}_\star)$ to the unconstrained optimization:

[5] Unless the constraint set C is nice so that projection onto it or optimization over it is easy. That is precisely the assumption of the Frank–Wolfe method.

$$\max_{\Lambda} \min_{x} \; \mathcal{L}(x, \Lambda), \tag{D.3.5}$$

where the Lagrangian function is defined as

$$\mathcal{L}(x, \Lambda) \doteq f(x) + \langle \Lambda, h(x) \rangle.$$

It is natural to consider solving the above min–max problem through the following alternating optimization scheme:

$$x_{k+1} = \arg\min_{x} \; \mathcal{L}(x, \Lambda_k), \tag{D.3.6}$$

$$\Lambda_{k+1} = \arg\max_{\Lambda} \; \mathcal{L}(x_{k+1}, \Lambda). \tag{D.3.7}$$

Although the saddle point of the Lagrangian is the desired optimal solution, there is no guarantee that each step of the above iteration would produce feasible iterates nor is the process guaranteed to converge. As we see in Section 8.4 of Chapter 8, even for some simple problems, the above subproblems might fail to have a solution (the value of the objective function can be unbounded).

To remedy this problem, one could augment the Lagrangian $\mathcal{L}(x, \Lambda)$ with an extra quadratic penalty term for the constraint:

$$\mathcal{L}_\mu(x, \Lambda) \doteq f(x) + \langle \Lambda, h(x) \rangle + \frac{\mu}{2} \|h(x)\|_2^2,$$

which is known as the *augmented Lagrangian* [Hes69, Roc73, Pow69]. As we will see in Section 8.4 of Chapter 8, the augmented Lagrangian leads to much better conditioned subproblems for the alternating scheme:

$$x_{k+1} = \arg\min_{x} \; \mathcal{L}_\mu(x, \Lambda_k), \tag{D.3.8}$$

$$\Lambda_{k+1} = \arg\max_{\Lambda} \; \mathcal{L}_\mu(x_{k+1}, \Lambda), \tag{D.3.9}$$

and the sequence of iterates $\{(x_k, \Lambda_k)\}$ typically converges to the desired optimal solution $(x_\star, \Lambda_\star)$ for a properly chosen μ or a sequence $\{\mu_k\}$.

D.4 Block Coordinate Descent and ADMM

In many of the optimization problems that we may encounter in practice, the dimension of x could be so high that we might not even afford to conduct gradient descent to minimize $f(x)$ for all the variables together. Very often the objective function $f(x)$ has certain decomposable structures such as a finite sum:

$$\min f(x) = \sum_{i=1}^{m} f_i(x^i). \tag{D.4.1}$$

For example, the ℓ^1 norm function $\|x\|_1 = \sum_{i=1}^{n} |x_i|$ is such a decomposable function. In such cases, we may conduct the so-called *block coordinate descent* to take advantage of such decomposable structures by iteratively minimizing the objective function with respect to one block of variables at a time.

More specifically, assume the domain $\mathcal{D}$ can be written as a Cartesian product,

$$\mathcal{D} = \mathcal{D}_1 \times \mathcal{D}_2 \times \cdots \times \mathcal{D}_m,$$

where each $\mathcal{D}_i \subseteq \mathbb{R}^{n_i}$, $n_1 + n_2 + \cdots + n_m = n$. The variables can be also partitioned into m blocks as $\boldsymbol{x} = (\boldsymbol{x}^1, \boldsymbol{x}^2, \ldots, \boldsymbol{x}^m) \in \mathbb{R}^n$ with each $\boldsymbol{x}^i \in \mathcal{D}_i$. The block coordinate descent scheme proceeds as follows:

1 Initialize $\boldsymbol{x}_0 = (\boldsymbol{x}_0^1, \boldsymbol{x}_0^2, \ldots, \boldsymbol{x}_0^m)$.
2 In the k-th iteration, for every $i = 1, \ldots, m$,

$$\boldsymbol{x}_k^i = \arg\min_{\bar{\boldsymbol{x}} \in \mathcal{D}_i} f\left(\boldsymbol{x}_k^1, \ldots, \boldsymbol{x}_k^{i-1}, \bar{\boldsymbol{x}}, \boldsymbol{x}_{k-1}^{i+1}, \ldots, \boldsymbol{x}_{k-1}^m\right).$$

3 Repeat step 2 until the solution converges.

In the literature, the convergence of block coordinate descent methods can be proven under different conditions. A most natural condition is when the objective function $f(\boldsymbol{x}^1, \ldots, \boldsymbol{x}^{i-1}, \boldsymbol{x}^i, \boldsymbol{x}^{i+1}, \ldots, \boldsymbol{x}^m)$ is *strictly convex* with respect to each block $\boldsymbol{x}^i$. This guarantees that the minimal solution $\boldsymbol{x}_\star^i$ is also unique. For a more detailed discussion about conditions under which such methods converge, the reader is referred to [Ber03].

In compressive sensing or statistical learning,[6] very often we need to deal with an objective function $f(\boldsymbol{x})$ that is a sum of multiple terms:

$$f(\boldsymbol{x}) = f_1(\boldsymbol{x}) + f_2(\boldsymbol{x}) + \cdots + f_m(\boldsymbol{x}). \tag{D.4.2}$$

To obtain more scalable algorithms such that we can optimize each term in a parallel or distributed fashion, we could rewrite this problem in terms of a set of local variables $\boldsymbol{x}^i \in \mathbb{R}^n$ and one global variable z:

$$\min \sum_{i=1}^m f_i(\boldsymbol{x}^i) \quad \text{subject to} \quad \boldsymbol{x}^i = z, \quad i = 1, \ldots, m. \tag{D.4.3}$$

In the literature, this is also known as the *consensus optimization*. To solve such a constrained optimization problem, we could apply the above block descent method to its augmented Lagrangian:

$$\mathcal{L}(\boldsymbol{x}^1, \ldots, \boldsymbol{x}^m, z, \boldsymbol{\lambda}) = \sum_{i=1}^m f_i(\boldsymbol{x}^i) + \langle \boldsymbol{\lambda}^i, \boldsymbol{x}^i - z \rangle + \frac{\mu}{2} \|\boldsymbol{x}^i - z\|_2^2. \tag{D.4.4}$$

This leads to the following iterative process:

$$\begin{aligned}
\boldsymbol{x}_{k+1}^i &= \arg\min_{\boldsymbol{x}^i} f_i(\boldsymbol{x}^i) + \langle \boldsymbol{\lambda}^i, \boldsymbol{x}^i - z \rangle + \frac{\mu}{2} \|\boldsymbol{x}^i - z\|_2^2, \\
z_{k+1} &= \frac{1}{m} \sum_{i=1}^m \left(\boldsymbol{x}_{k+1}^i + \frac{1}{\mu} \boldsymbol{\lambda}_k^i\right), \\
\boldsymbol{\lambda}_{k+1}^i &= \boldsymbol{\lambda}_k^i + \mu\left(\boldsymbol{x}_{k+1}^i - z_{k+1}\right).
\end{aligned}$$

[6] Say training a deep neural network over a very large set of training samples, where $\boldsymbol{x}$ are the network parameters.

This is known as the *alternating direction method of multipliers* (ADMM). Notice that the above scheme is rather amenable to distributed implementation as each local process can solve in parallel a subproblem for $\boldsymbol{x}^i$ and then share the information through the common variable $\boldsymbol{z}$.

Although ADMM has been a very popular scheme widely used by practitioners, the analysis for its convergence and convergence rate is far from trivial. In Chapter 8, we studied the ADMM scheme for the case with $m = 2$ in great detail, as it is closely applicable to our problems (such as the robust PCA problem considered in Chapter 5). Convergence analyses for more general cases remain largely open research topics. For a more detailed exposition of ADMM and more general variants, the reader may refer to the recent manuscript of [BPC$^+$11].

Appendix E Facts from High-Dimensional Statistics

"God tirelessly plays dice under laws which he has himself prescribed."
– Albert Einstein

In this appendix, we recount a few facts about high-dimensional statistics and concentration of measure which are used throughout the text. The results that we quote are examples of a pervasive phenomenon: functions of many independent random variables often concentrate sharply about their expectations. In this section we give only a brief account of a few concentration inequalities that are used throughout the text, starting with classical scalar inequalities in Section E.1 and their counterparts for matrices in Section E.2. We refer the reader to the recent texts [BLM13, Ver08, Ver18, Wai19] for deeper and more thorough accounts of high-dimensional probability and its applications.

E.1 Basic Concentration Inequalities

Our first concentration inequality pertains to sums of independent bounded random variables $X_1, \dots, X_m$. For simplicity, we assume that the X_i have zero mean.

THEOREM E.1. (Hoeffding's inequality) *Let $X_1, \dots, X_m$ be independent random variables, with $\mathbb{E}[X_i] = 0$ and $|X_i| \le R$ almost surely. Then*

$$\mathbb{P}\left[\left| \sum_{i=1}^{m} X_i \right| > t \right] \le 2 \exp\left(-\frac{t^2}{2mR^2} \right). \tag{E.1.1}$$

This theorem implies that the sum $\sum_i X_i$ exhibits a *sub-Gaussian* tail: the tail probability decays as e^{-ct^2}. The proof is an application of the *exponential moment method* (sometimes referred to the Cramer–Chernoff method), in which we apply Markov's inequality[1] to the nonnegative random variable $\exp(\lambda \sum_i X_i)$. This general approach yields not only Hoeffding's inequality, but many other classical concentration inequalities. We illustrate the method by proving Theorem E.1 below:

[1] Recall that Markov's inequality states that for a nonnegative random variable Y, $\mathbb{P}[Y > t] < \mathbb{E}[Y]/t$.

Proof We calculate

$$\begin{aligned}\mathbb{P}\left[\sum_{i=1}^{m} X_i > t\right] &= \mathbb{P}\left[\exp\left(\lambda \sum_{i=1}^{m} X_i\right) > \exp(\lambda t)\right] \\ &\le e^{-\lambda t}\mathbb{E}\left[\exp\left(\lambda \sum_{i=1}^{m} X_i\right)\right] \\ &= e^{-\lambda t}\mathbb{E}\left[\prod_{i=1}^{m} e^{\lambda X_i}\right] \\ &= e^{-\lambda t}\prod_{i=1}^{m}\mathbb{E}\left[e^{\lambda X_i}\right]. \end{aligned} \tag{E.1.2}$$

Using that for $s \in [-R, R]$, $e^{\lambda s} \le 1 + \lambda s + \frac{1}{2}\lambda^2 R^2$, we have that

$$\begin{aligned}\mathbb{E}\left[e^{\lambda X_i}\right] &\le \mathbb{E}\left[1 + \lambda X_i + \tfrac{1}{2}\lambda^2 R^2\right] \\ &= 1 + \tfrac{1}{2}\lambda^2 R^2 \\ &\le \exp\left(\tfrac{1}{2}\lambda^2 R^2\right). \end{aligned} \tag{E.1.3}$$

Plugging in to (E.1.2), we get that

$$\mathbb{P}\left[\sum_{i=1}^{m} X_i > t\right] \le \exp\left(-\lambda t + \frac{m}{2}\lambda^2 R^2\right). \tag{E.1.4}$$

Minimizing the exponent, by setting $\lambda = t/mR^2$, we obtain the claimed result, (E.1.1). □

Hoeffding's inequality gives a convenient tool for controlling sums of bounded random variables, which we use several times throughout the text. As mentioned above, it shows that the sum exhibits a sub-Gaussian tail. In many cases the "variance" suggested by this tail, mR^2, is larger than the true variance if, for example, $\mathbb{E}[X_i^2] = \sigma^2$ with $\sigma \ll R$. The classical Bernstein inequality also accounts for variance information:

THEOREM E.2. (Bernstein's inequality) *Let $X_1, \ldots, X_m$ be independent random variables, with $\mathbb{E}[X_i] = 0$, $|X_i| \le R$ almost surely, and $\mathbb{E}[X_i^2] \le \sigma^2$. Then*

$$\mathbb{P}\left[\left|\sum_{i=1}^{m} X_i\right| > t\right] \le 2\exp\left(-\frac{t^2/2}{m\sigma^2 + 3Rt}\right). \tag{E.1.5}$$

In essence, it says that for small t, the tail behaves like $e^{-ct^2/m\sigma^2}$, i.e., Gaussian with standard deviation $m\sigma^2$, while for large t, the tail is *subexponential*, $e^{-ct/R}$. The proof of Bernstein's inequality proceeds under exactly the same lines as the proof of Hoeffding's inequality, up to line (E.1.2), but uses slightly different calculations to control the moment generating function $\mathbb{E}[e^{\lambda X_i}]$.

Concentration for Norms of Gaussian Vectors

Using similar reasoning, we can obtain the following useful bound on the ℓ^2 norm of a Gaussian vector, which is used throughout Chapter 3 to establish embedding results such as the Johnson–Lindenstrauss lemma and the restricted isometry property:

LEMMA E.3. *Let $\boldsymbol{g} = (g_1, \dots, g_m)$ with the g_i independent $\mathcal{N}(0, 1/m)$ random variables. Then for any $t \in [0, 1]$,*

$$\mathbb{P}\left[\left|\|\boldsymbol{g}\|_2^2 - 1\right| > t\right] \le 2\exp\left(-\frac{t^2 m}{8}\right). \tag{E.1.6}$$

This lemma again follows from the proof scheme of Theorem E.1, noting that $\|\boldsymbol{g}\|_2^2 = \sum_{i=1}^m g_i^2$ is a sum of independent random variables and using the following expression for the moment generating function of the random variable $h_i = g_i^2$:

$$\mathbb{E}\left[e^{\lambda h_i}\right] = \left(1 - \frac{2\lambda}{m}\right)^{-1/2}, \quad \lambda < \frac{m}{2}, \tag{E.1.7}$$

and making an appropriate choice of λ.

General Concentration Results for Lipschitz Functions

The basic concentration results described above show that sums $f(X_1, \dots, X_m) = \sum_{i=1}^m X_i$ of independent random variables concentrate sharply about their expectations $\mathbb{E}[f(X_1, \dots, X_m)] = \sum_{i=1}^m \mathbb{E}[f(X_i)]$. Depending on the assumptions on the random variables X_i the tail probability of the random variable $f(X_1, \dots, X_m) - \mathbb{E}[f(X_1, \dots X_m)]$ is either sub-Gaussian or subexponential, i.e., it is dominated by either e^{-ct^2} or e^{-ct}. In fact, this behavior can be observed not only for sums of random variables, but for much more general functions $f(X_1, \dots, X_m)$. At the slogan level, *sufficiently "nice" functions of many random variables* concentrate sharply about their expectations.

For example, suppose that f satisfies a Lipschitz condition

$$\left|f(\boldsymbol{x}) - f(\boldsymbol{x}')\right| \le L\|\boldsymbol{x} - \boldsymbol{x}'\|_2 \quad \text{for all} \quad \boldsymbol{x}, \boldsymbol{x}' \in \mathbb{R}^m, \tag{E.1.8}$$

which controls how rapidly f changes as the vector $\boldsymbol{x}$ changes. Then if $g_1, \dots, g_m$ are Gaussian random variables, $f(g_1, \dots, g_m)$ concentrates about its expectation:

THEOREM E.4. (Gauss–Lipschitz concentration) *Let $f : \mathbb{R}^m \to \mathbb{R}$ be an L-Lipschitz function, and let $g_1, \dots, g_m \sim_{\text{iid}} \mathcal{N}(0, 1)$. Then*

$$\mathbb{P}\left[\left|f(g_1, \dots, g_m) - \mathbb{E}\left[f(g_1, \dots, g_m)\right]\right| > t\right] < 2\exp\left(-\frac{t^2}{2L}\right). \tag{E.1.9}$$

This theorem states that the random variable $f(g_1, \dots, g_m)$ has a sub-Gaussian tail, which acts like a Gaussian random variable with variance L. The smaller the Lipschitz constant L (i.e., the nicer the function f), the sharper the concentration about the expectation. The orientation of the random vector $\boldsymbol{g} = (g_1, \dots, g_m)$ is uniform: $\boldsymbol{u} = \boldsymbol{g}/\|\boldsymbol{g}\|_2$ is uniformly distributed on the sphere $\mathbb{S}^{m-1}$. It should be no surprise, then, that Lipschitz functions of uniformly distributed random vectors on the sphere also concentrate:

THEOREM E.5. (Concentration on the sphere) *Let* $f : \mathbb{S}^{m-1} \to \mathbb{R}$ *be an L-Lipschitz function and let* $\boldsymbol{u} \sim \mathrm{uni}(\mathbb{S}^{m-1})$ *be uniformly distributed on the sphere. Then*

$$\mathbb{P}\left[\, |f(\boldsymbol{u}) - \mathrm{median}\, f(\boldsymbol{u})| > t \,\right] < 2\exp\left(-\frac{mt^2}{8L}\right). \tag{E.1.10}$$

This result again shows sub-Gaussian concentration with variance proportional to the Lipschitz constant L. The result happens to be phrased in terms of the median, rather than the mean. However, brief calculations using (E.1.10) show that the median is close to the mean ($|\mathrm{median}(f) - \mathbb{E}[f]| \le C/\sqrt{L}$) and so $f(\boldsymbol{u})$ is typically within $O(1/\sqrt{L})$ of its expectation as well. In our book, this result has been used to construct incoherent matrices in Chapter 3.

These results on Lipschitz concentration have generalizations to other spaces [Led01]. They also have generalizations to other distributions. One powerful related result is Talagrand's inequality for convex Lipschitz functions on the cube [Tal95]. Finally, it is possible to show concentration under other hypotheses on the function f – see [BLM13].

E.2 Matrix Concentration Inequalities

The basic concentration inequalities in Section E.1 have natural generalizations from sums of independent random scalars to sums of independent random *matrices*. The basic concentration in equalities in Section E.1 are obtained by the exponential moment method, illustrated in the proof of Theorem E.1. This elegant approach can be used to derive a number of classical probability inequalities, by using different assumptions to get different bounds on the moment generating function. However, our interest is not just in scalar random variables, but in matrices, or even operators. Is there any natural way to generalize this approach? Remarkably, the answer is yes. Since the crucial step above is exponentiating and then applying Markov's inequality, we might hope to simply replace the scalar exponential with the matrix exponential. Surprisingly, it is *almost* that easy.

Facts about the Matrix Exponential

Before carrying the above argument over to the matrix case, let us recall a few facts about matrices and matrix exponentials. Recall that a symmetric matrix $\boldsymbol{M}$ is semi-definite ($\boldsymbol{M} \succeq \mathbf{0}$) for all $\boldsymbol{x}$, $\boldsymbol{x}^* \boldsymbol{M} \boldsymbol{x} \ge 0$. We write

$$\boldsymbol{A} \succeq \boldsymbol{B},$$

whenever

$$\boldsymbol{A} - \boldsymbol{B} \succeq \mathbf{0}.$$

The matrix exponential is the function

$$\exp(\boldsymbol{M}) \;=\; \sum_{n=0}^{\infty} \frac{\boldsymbol{M}^n}{n!} \;=\; \boldsymbol{I} + \boldsymbol{M} + \boldsymbol{M}^2/2 + \cdots . \tag{E.2.1}$$

Since a symmetric matrix $\boldsymbol{M}$ has a complete orthonormal basis of eigenvectors, $\boldsymbol{M} = \boldsymbol{V}\boldsymbol{\Lambda}\boldsymbol{V}^*$, with $\boldsymbol{\Lambda} = \operatorname{diag}(\lambda_1, \dots, \lambda_n)$, the exponential of a symmetric matrix has a particularly simple form:

$$\exp(\boldsymbol{M}) \;=\; \boldsymbol{V}\exp(\boldsymbol{\Lambda})\boldsymbol{V}^* = \boldsymbol{V} \begin{bmatrix} e^{\lambda_1} & & \\ & \ddots & \\ & & e^{\lambda_n} \end{bmatrix} \boldsymbol{V}^* \succeq \boldsymbol{0}. \tag{E.2.2}$$

The exponential of a symmetric matrix is always semidefinite.

The matrix exponential satisfies many of the natural properties also satisfied by the scalar exponential. It differs in important ways, however, because matrix multiplication is not precisely analogous to scalar multiplication. In particular, in general, matrix multiplication does not commute: $\boldsymbol{AB} \neq \boldsymbol{BA}$. This causes the property $\exp(s+t) = \exp(s)\exp(t)$ to fail for matrices: in general,

$$\exp(\boldsymbol{A} + \boldsymbol{B}) \neq \exp(\boldsymbol{A})\exp(\boldsymbol{B}). \tag{E.2.3}$$

The only exception occurs when $\boldsymbol{A}$ and $\boldsymbol{B}$ do commute: $\boldsymbol{AB} = \boldsymbol{BA}$.

If our imagined program is to replace the scalar exponential with the matrix exponential in the proof of Bernstein's inequality, this fact is very bad news. The proof used, in a very critical way, the fact that $\exp(s+t) = \exp(s)\exp(t)$. Fortunately, there is a weak analog of this property that does hold for matrices, given by the following result of Golden [Gol65] and Thompson [Tho04]:

THEOREM E.6. (Golden–Thompson inequality) *Let* $\boldsymbol{A}$ *and* $\boldsymbol{B}$ *be self-adjoint matrices. Then*

$$\operatorname{trace}[\exp(\boldsymbol{A} + \boldsymbol{B})] \;\le\; \operatorname{trace}[\exp(\boldsymbol{A})\exp(\boldsymbol{B})]. \tag{E.2.4}$$

Before proceeding, we also note that for symmetric matrices $\boldsymbol{A}$ and $\boldsymbol{B}$,

$$\operatorname{trace}[\boldsymbol{AB}] \;\le\; \|\boldsymbol{A}\| \operatorname{trace}[\boldsymbol{B}]. \tag{E.2.5}$$

Matrix Bernstein Inequality

Let us apply the above results to demonstrate a probability inequality for matrices:

THEOREM E.7. (Matrix bernstein inequality) *Let* $\boldsymbol{X}_1, \dots, \boldsymbol{X}_n$ *be* $d \times d$ *independent, identically distributed self-adjoint random matrices, with* $\mathbb{E}\boldsymbol{X}_i = \boldsymbol{0}$ *and* $\|\boldsymbol{X}_i\| \le 1$ *almost surely. Then*

$$\mathbb{P}\left[\lambda_{\max}\left(\sum_{i=1}^{n} \boldsymbol{X}_i \right) > t \right] \le d \exp\left(-\min\left\{ \frac{t^2}{4n}, \frac{t}{2} \right\} \right). \tag{E.2.6}$$

Proof Note that

$$\lambda_{\max}\left(\sum_{i=1}^{n} \boldsymbol{X}_i\right) > t \iff \lambda_{\max}\left(\lambda \sum_i \boldsymbol{X}_i\right) > e^{\lambda t}$$
$$\implies \operatorname{trace}\left(\exp\left(\lambda \sum_i \boldsymbol{X}_i\right)\right) > e^{\lambda t}.$$

So,

$$\begin{aligned}
\mathbb{P}\left[\lambda_{\max}\left(\sum_{i=1}^{n} \boldsymbol{X}_i\right) > t\right] &\le \mathbb{P}\left[\operatorname{trace}\left(\exp\left(\lambda \sum_i \boldsymbol{X}_i\right)\right) > e^{\lambda t}\right] \\
&\le e^{-\lambda t}\, \mathbb{E}\operatorname{trace}\left(\exp\left(\lambda \sum_{i=1}^{n} \boldsymbol{X}_i\right)\right) \\
&\le e^{-\lambda t}\, \mathbb{E}\operatorname{trace}\left(\exp\left(\lambda \boldsymbol{X}_n\right) \exp\left(\lambda \sum_{i=1}^{n-1} \boldsymbol{X}_i\right)\right) \\
&\le e^{-\lambda t} \operatorname{trace}\left(\mathbb{E}\left[\exp(\lambda \boldsymbol{X}_n)\right] \mathbb{E}\left[\exp\left(\lambda \sum_{i=1}^{n-1} \boldsymbol{X}_i\right)\right]\right) \\
&\le e^{-\lambda t} \left\|\mathbb{E}\left[\exp(\lambda \boldsymbol{X}_n)\right]\right\| \operatorname{trace}\left(\mathbb{E}\left[\exp\left(\lambda \sum_{i=1}^{n-1} \boldsymbol{X}_i\right)\right]\right) \\
&\le e^{-\lambda t} \left\|\mathbb{E}\left[\exp(\lambda \boldsymbol{X}_n)\right]\right\| \mathbb{E}\operatorname{trace}\left(\exp\left(\lambda \sum_{i=1}^{n-1} \boldsymbol{X}_i\right)\right) \\
&\le e^{-\lambda t} \prod_{i=2}^{n} \left\|\mathbb{E}\left[\exp(\lambda \boldsymbol{X}_i)\right]\right\| \mathbb{E}\operatorname{trace}\left(\exp(\lambda \boldsymbol{X}_1)\right) \\
&\le d e^{-\lambda t} \left\|\mathbb{E}\exp(\lambda \boldsymbol{X})\right\|^n .
\end{aligned} \tag{E.2.7}$$

To bound the "matrix moment generating function"

$$M_{\boldsymbol{X}}(\lambda) = \mathbb{E}\left[\exp(\lambda \boldsymbol{X})\right], \tag{E.2.8}$$

we use a matrix variant of the scalar inequality $1 + s \le \exp(s) \le 1 + s + s^2$; namely, for any self-adjoint matrix $\boldsymbol{S}$ satisfying $-\boldsymbol{I} \preceq \boldsymbol{S} \preceq \boldsymbol{I}$, we have

$$\boldsymbol{I} + \boldsymbol{S} \preceq \exp(\boldsymbol{S}) \preceq \boldsymbol{I} + \boldsymbol{S} + \boldsymbol{S}^2. \tag{E.2.9}$$

Thus,

$$\mathbb{E}\left[\exp(\lambda \boldsymbol{X})\right] \preceq \mathbb{E}\left[\boldsymbol{I} + \lambda \boldsymbol{X} + \lambda^2 \boldsymbol{X}^2\right] \tag{E.2.10}$$
$$\preceq \boldsymbol{I} + \lambda^2 \mathbb{E}[\boldsymbol{X}^2] \tag{E.2.11}$$
$$\preceq \boldsymbol{I} + \lambda^2 \boldsymbol{I}. \tag{E.2.12}$$

So, $\|\mathbb{E}\exp(\lambda \boldsymbol{X})\| \le \left\|\boldsymbol{I} + \lambda^2 \boldsymbol{I}\right\| = 1 + \lambda^2 \le \exp(\lambda^2)$. From this, we obtain

$$\mathbb{P}\left[\lambda_{\max}\left(\sum_{i=1}^{n} \boldsymbol{X}_i\right) > t\right] \le d e^{-\lambda t} e^{\lambda^2 n}. \tag{E.2.13}$$

The proof then concludes as in the scalar case. □

The matrix Bernstein inequality can also be expressed in the following form that we will use in the book.

THEOREM E.8. (Matrix bernstein inequality [Tro12]) *Suppose that* $\mathbf{W}_1, \mathbf{W}_2, \ldots$ *are independent random matrices of dimension* $n_1 \times n_2$*, with* $\mathbb{E}[\mathbf{W}_j] = \mathbf{0}$ *and* $\left\|\mathbf{W}_j\right\| \le R$ *almost surely. Define*

$$\sigma^2 = \max\left\{\left\|\sum_j \mathbb{E}[\mathbf{W}_j \mathbf{W}_j^*]\right\|, \left\|\sum_j \mathbb{E}[\mathbf{W}_j^* \mathbf{W}_j]\right\|\right\}. \tag{E.2.14}$$

Then

$$\mathbb{P}\left[\left\|\sum_j \mathbf{W}_j\right\| \ge t\right] \le (n_1 + n_2) \exp\left(\frac{-t^2/2}{\sigma^2 + Rt/3}\right). \tag{E.2.15}$$

References

[AAZB+16] N. Agarwal, Z. Allen-Zhu, B. Bullins, E. Hazan, and T. Ma. Finding approximate local minima for nonconvex optimization in linear time. *arXiv:1611 .01146v2*, 2016.

[AB99] M. Anthony and P.L. Bartlett. *Neural Network Learning: Theoretical Foundations*. Cambridge University Press, 1999.

[AB09] S. Arora and B. Barak. *Computational Complexity: A Modern Approach*. Cambridge University Press, 1st edition, 2009.

[ABSS93] S. Arora, L. Babai, J. Stern, and Z. Sweedyk. The hardness of approximate optima in lattices, codes, and systems of linear equations. In *Proceedings of the 34th Annual Symposium on Foundations of Computer Science*, pages 724–733. IEEE, 1993.

[ADG+16] M. Andrychowicz, M. Denil, S. Gomez, et al. Learning to learn by gradient descent by gradient descent. In *Advances in Neural Information Processing Systems*, pages 3981–3989, 2016.

[AGH+14] A. Anandkumar, R. Ge, D. Hsu, S.M. Kakade, and M. Telgarsky. Tensor decompositions for learning latent variable models. *Journal of Machine Learning Research*, 15:2773–2832, 2014.

[AHP06] T. Ahonen, A. Hadid, and M. Pietikainen. Face description with local binary patterns: Application to face recognition. *IEEE Transactions on Pattern Analysis and Machine Intelligence*, 28(12):2037–2041, 2006.

[AK95] E. Amaldi and V. Kann. The complexity and approximability of finding maximum feasible subsystems of linear relations. *Theoretical Computer Science*, 147:181–210, 1995.

[AK98] E. Amaldi and V. Kann. On the approximability of minimizing nonzero variables or unsatisfied relations in linear systems. *Theoretical Computer Science*, 209:237–260, 1998.

[AKS98] N. Alon, M. Krivelevich, and B. Sudakov. Finding a large hidden clique in a random graph. In *Proceedings of the Ninth Annual ACM-SIAM Symposium on Discrete Algorithms*, pages 594–598, 1998. Society for Industrial and Applied Mathematics.

[ALMT13] D. Amelunxen, M. Lotz, M.B. McCoy, and J.A. Tropp. Living on the edge: A geometric theory of phase transitions in convex optimization. *CoRR, abs/1303.6672*, 2013.

[ALMT14] D. Amelunxen, M. Lotz, M.B. McCoy, and J.A. Tropp. Living on the edge: Phase transitions in convex programs with random data. *Information and Inference: A Journal of the IMA*, 3(3):224–294, 2014.

[Ame11] D. Amelunxen. *Geometric analysis of the condition of the convex feasibility problem*. PhD Thesis, University of Paderborn, 2011.

[AMS09] P.-A. Absil, R. Mahoney, and R. Sepulchre. *Optimization Algorithms on Matrix Manifolds*. Princeton University Press, 2009.

[ANR74] N. Ahmed, T. Natarajan, and K. Rao. Discrete cosine transform. *IEEE Transactions on Computers*, 23(1):90–93, 1974.

[ANW10] A. Agarwal, S. Negahban, and M.J. Wainwright. Fast global convergence rates of gradient methods for high-dimensional statistical recovery. In *Advances in Neural Information Processing Systems*, pages 37–45, 2010.

[ANW12] A. Agarwal, S. Negahban, and M.J. Wainwright. Noisy matrix decomposition via convex relaxation: Optimal rates in high dimensions. *The Annals of Statistics*, 40(2):1171–1197, 2012.

[ARR14] A. Ahmed, B. Recht, and J. Romberg. Blind deconvolution using convex programming. *IEEE Transactions on Information Theory*, 60(3):1711–1732, 2014.

[ARV20] Y.M. Asano, C. Rupprecht, and A. Vedaldi. Self-labelling via simultaneous clustering and representation learning. In *International Conference on Learning Representations*, 2020.

[AW18] A. Azulay and Y. Weiss. Why do deep convolutional networks generalize so poorly to small image transformations? *arXiv:1805.12177*, 2018.

[AZ17] Z. Allen-Zhu. Katyusha: The first direct acceleration of stochastic gradient methods. *The Journal of Machine Learning Research*, 18(1):8194–8244, 2017.

[AZLS19] Z. Allen-Zhu, Y. Li, and Z. Song. A convergence theory for deep learning via over-parameterization. In *International Conference on Machine Learning*, pages 242–252, 2019.

[Bub15] S. Bubeck. Convex optimization: Algorithms and complexity. *Foundations and Trends in Machine Learning*, 8(3–4):231–357, 2015.

[BMR+20] T. Brown, B. Mann, N. Ryder, et al. Language models are few-shot learners. *arXiv:2005.14165v4*, 2020.

[Bal10] R.V. Balan. On signal reconstruction from its spectrogram. In *Information Sciences and Systems (CISS), 44th Annual Conference on*, pages 1–4. IEEE, 2010.

[Bar72] H.B. Barlow. Single units and sensation: A neuron doctrine for perceptual psychology? *Perception*, 1:371–394, 1972.

[BB20] M. Brennan and G. Bresler. Reducibility and statistical-computational gaps from secret leakage. *arXiv:2005.08099*, 2020.

[BBC09] S. Becker, J. Bobin, and E. Candès. NESTA: A fast and accurate first-order method for sparse recovery. Preprint, 2009.

[BBE17] T. Bendory, R. Beinert, and Y.C. Eldar. Fourier phase retrieval: Uniqueness and algorithms. In *Compressed Sensing and Its Applications*, pages 55–91. Springer, 2017.

[BBV16] A.S. Bandeira, N. Boumal, and V. Voroninski. On the low-rank approach for semidefinite programs arising in synchronization and community detection. In *Conference on Learning Theory*, pages 361–382, 2016.

[BC14] J. Ba and R. Caruana. Do deep nets really need to be deep? In *Advances in Neural Information Processing Systems*, pages 2654–2662, 2014.

[BCE06] R. Balana, P. Casazzab, and D. Edidin. On signal reconstruction without phase. *Applied and Computational Harmonic Analysis*, 20(3):345–356, 2006.

[BCN18] L. Bottou, F.E. Curtis, and J. Nocedal. Optimization methods for large-scale machine learning. *SIAM Review*, 60(2):223–311, 2018.

[BDDW08] R. Baraniuk, M. Davenport, R. DeVore, and M. Wakin. A simple proof of the restricted isometry property for random matrices. *Constructive Approximation*, 28(3):253–263, 2008.

[BDP$^+$07] O. Bunk, A. Diaz, F. Pfeiffer, et al. Diffractive imaging for periodic samples: Retrieving one-dimensional concentration profiles across microfluidic channels. *Acta Crystallographica A*, 63(4):306–314, 2007.

[BEGK11] A. Bovier, M. Eckhoff, V. Gayrard, and M. Klein. Metastability in reversible diffusion processes I: Sharp asymptotics for capacities and exit times. *Journal of the European Mathematical Society*, 6(4):399–424, 2011.

[Bel73] E. Beltrami. Sulle funzioni bilineari. *Giornale di Mathematiche di Battaglini*, 11:98–106, 1873.

[Ber82] D. Bertsekas. *Constrained Optimization and Lagrange Multiplier Methods*. Athena Scientific, 1982.

[Ber03] D. Bertsekas. *Nonlinear Programming*. Athena Scientific, 2003.

[BGM$^+$08] A. Belitski, A. Gretton, C. Magri, et al. Low-frequency local field potentials and spikes in primary visual cortex convey independent visual information. *Journal of Neuroscience*, 28(22):5696–5709, 2008.

[BGNR17] B. Baker, O. Gupta, N. Naik, and R. Raskar. Designing neural network architectures using reinforcement learning. *arXiv:1611.02167*, 2017.

[BGW20] S. Buchanan, D. Gilboa, and J. Wright. Deep networks and the multiple manifold problem. *arXiv:2008.11245*, 2020.

[Bha96] R. Bhatia. *Matrix Analysis*. Springer, 1996.

[BHK97] P. Belhumeur, J. Hespanda, and D. Kriegman. Eigenfaces vs. Fisherfaces: Recognition using class specific linear projection. *IEEE Transactions on Pattern Analysis and Machine Intelligence*, 19(7):711–720, 1997.

[Bir11] H. Birkholz. A unifying approach to isotropic and anisotropic total variation denoising models. *Journal of Computational and Applied Mathematics*, 235(8):2502–2514, 2011.

[BJ03] R. Basri and D. Jacobs. Lambertian reflectance and linear subspaces. *IEEE Transactions on Pattern Analysis and Machine Intelligence*, 25(3):218–233, 2003.

[BJMO12] F. Bach, R. Jenatton, J. Mairal, and G. Obozinski. Optimization with sparsity-inducing penalties. *Foundations and Trends in Machine Learning*, 4(1):1–106, 2012.

[BJPD17] A. Bora, A. Jalal, E. Price, and A.G. Dimakis. Compressed sensing using generative models. In *Proceedings of the 34th International Conference on Machine Learning*, volume 70, pages 537–546. JMLR.org, 2017.

[BJS19] Y. Bai, Q. Jiang, and J. Sun. Subgradient descent learns orthogonal dictionaries. In *7th International Conference on Learning Representations*, 2019.

[BJT19] A.S. Berahas, M. Jahani, and M. Takáč. Quasi-Newton methods for deep learning: Forget the past, just sample. *arXiv:1901.09997*, 2019.

[BK96] P.N. Belhumeur and D.J. Kriegman. What is the set of images of an object under all possible lighting conditions? In *Proceedings of the IEEE International Conference on Computer Vision and Pattern Recognition*, pages 270–277, 1996.

[BKH16] J.L. Ba, J.R. Kiros, and G.E. Hinton. Layer normalization. *arXiv:1607.06450*, 2016.

[BKLN08] S.C. Blaakmeer, E.A.M. Klumperink, D.M.W. Leenaerts, and B. Nauta. Wideband balun-LNA with simultaneous output balancing, noise-canceling and distortion-canceling. *IEEE Journal of Solid-State Circuits*, 43(6):1341–1350, June 2008.

[BKM67] E.M.L. Beale, M.G. Kendall, and D.W. Mann. The discarding of variables in multivariate analysis. *Biometrika*, 54(3/4):357–366, 1967.

[BKM16] D. Bertsimas, A. King, and R. Mazumder. Best subset selection via a modern optimization lens. *The Annals of Statistics*, 44(2):813–852, April 2016.

[BKN04] F. Bruccoleri, E.A.M. Klumperink, and B. Nauta. Wide-band CMOS low-noise amplifier exploiting thermal noise canceling. *IEEE Journal of Solid-State Circuits*, 39(2):275–282, 2004.

[BKS15] B. Barak, J.A. Kelner, and D. Steurer. Dictionary learning and tensor decomposition via the sum-of-squares method. In *Proceedings of the Forty-Seventh Annual ACM Symposium on Theory of Computing*, pages 143–151, 2015.

[BLM13] S. Boucheron, G. Lugosi, and P. Massart. *Concentration Inequalities: A Nonasymptotic Theory of Independence*. Oxford University Press, 2013.

[BLO05] J.V. Burke, A.S. Lewis, and M.L. Overton. A robust gradient sampling algorithm for nonsmooth, nonconvex optimization. *SIAM Journal on Optimization*, 15(3):751–779, 2005.

[BLWY06] P. Biswas, T.-C. Lian, T.-C. Wang, and Y. Ye. Semidefinite programming based algorithms for sensor network localization. *ACM Transactions on Sensor Networks (TOSN)*, 2(2):188–220, 2006.

[BM03] S. Burer and R.D.C. Monteiro. A nonlinear programming algorithm for solving semidefinite programs via low-rank factorization. *Mathematical Programming*, 95(2):329–357, 2003.

[BM04] S. Baker and I. Matthews. Lucas-Kanade 20 years on: A unifying framework. *International Journal on Computer Vision*, 56(3):221–255, 2004.

[BM13] J. Bruna and S. Mallat. Invariant scattering convolution networks. *IEEE Transactions on Pattern Analysis and Machine Intelligence*, 35(8):1872–1886, 2013.

[BMC+06] R. Bagheri, A. Mirzaei, S. Chehrazi, et al. An 800-MHz-6-GHz software-defined wireless receiver in 90-nm CMOS. *IEEE Journal of Solid-State Circuits*, 41(12):2860–2876, 2006.

[BNJ03] D.M. Blei, A.Y. Ng, and M.I. Jordan. Latent Dirichlet allocation. *Journal of Machine Learning Research*, 3:993–1022, 2003.

[BNO03] D. Bertsekas, A. Nedic, and A. Ozdaglar. *Convex Analysis and Optimization*. Athena Scientific, 2003.

[BNS16] S. Bhojanapalli, B. Neyshabur, and N. Srebro. Global optimality of local search for low rank matrix recovery. *arXiv:1605.07221*, 2016.

[BO69] R.L. Bishop and B. O'Neill. Manifolds of negative curvature. *Transactions of the American Mathematical Society*, 145:1–49, 1969.

[Bos50] R. Boscovich. *De calculo probabilitatum que respondent diversis valoribus summe errorum post plures observationes, quarum singule possient esse erronee certa quadam quantitate*. 1750.

[Bot82] R. Bott. Lectures on Morse theory, old and new. *Bulletin of the American Mathematical Society*, 7(2):331–358, 1982.

[Bot10] L. Bottou. Large-scale machine learning with stochastic gradient descent. In *Proceedings of COMPSTAT'2010*, pages 177–186. Springer, 2010.

[Bou] J.-Y. Bouguet. Camera calibration toolbox for Matlab. `http://www.vision.caltech.edu/bouguetj/calib_doc/`.

[Bou16] N. Boumal. Nonconvex phase synchronization. *arXiv:1601.06114*, 2016.

[Bou20] N. Boumal. An introduction to optimization on smooth manifolds. Available online: `http://sma.epfl.ch/ nboumal/book/IntroOptimManifolds_Boumal_2020.pdf`, 2020.

[BPC$^+$11] S. Boyd, N. Parikh, E. Chu, B. Peleato, and J. Eckstein. Distributed optimization and statistical learning via the alternating direction method of multipliers. *Foundations and Trends in Machine Learning*, 3(1):1–122, 2011.

[BR83] G. Binnig and H. Rohrer. Surface imaging by scanning tunneling microscopy. *Ultramicroscopy*, 11(2–3):157–160, 1983.

[Bro71] D.C. Brown. Close-range camera calibration. *Photogrammetric Engineering*, 37(8):855–866, 1971.

[BRT09] P.J. Bickel, Y. Ritov, and A.B. Tsybakov. Simultaneous analysis of Lasso and Dantzig selector. *The Annals of Statistics*, 37(4):1705–1732, 2009.

[BSBC00] M. Bertalmio, G. Sapiro, C. Ballester, and V. Caselles. Image inpainting. In *Proceedings of the 27th Annual Conference on Computer Graphics and Interactive Techniques (SIGGRAPH'00)*, pages 417–424, 2000.

[BSFG09] C. Barnes, E. Shechtman, A. Finkelstein, and D.B. Goldman. PatchMatch: A randomized correspondence algorithm for structural image editing. *ACM Transactions on Graphics*, 28(3):24, 2009.

[BSGF10] C. Barnes, E. Shechtman, D.B. Goldman, and A. Finkelstein. The generalized PatchMatch correspondence algorithm. *European Conference on Computer Vision (ECCV)*, 2010.

[BT09] A. Beck and M. Teboulle. A fast iterative shrinkage-thresholding algorithm for linear inverse problems. *SIAM Journal on Imaging Science*, 2(1):183–202, 2009.

[BTR12] B.N. Bhaskar, G. Tang, and B. Recht. Atomic norm denoising with applications to line spectral estimation. *CoRR, abs/1204.0562*, 2012.

[BUF07] K. Block, M. Uecker, and J. Frahm. Undersampled radial MRI with multiple coils. Iterative image reconstruction using a total variation constraint. *Magnetic Resonance in Medicine*, 57:1086–1098, 2007.

[BV04] S. Boyd and L. Vandenberghe. *Convex Optimization*. Cambridge University Press, 2004.

[BV18] S. Boyd and L. Vandenberghe. *Introduction to Applied Linear Algebra: Vectors, Matrices, and Least Squares*. Cambridge University Press, 2018.

[BWY17] S. Balakrishnan, M.J. Wainwright, and B. Yu. Statistical guarantees for the EM algorithm: From population to sample-based analysis. *The Annals of Statistics*, 45(1):77–120, 2017.

[CAB$^+$16] G. Cruz, D. Atkinson, C. Buerger, T. Schaeffter, and C. Prieto. Accelerated motion corrected three-dimensional abdominal MRI using total variation regularized SENSE reconstruction. *Magnetic Resonance in Medicine*, 75:1484–1498, 2016.

[CAD$^+$18] A. Chakraborty, M. Alam, V. Dey, A. Chattopadhyay, and D. Mukhopadhyay. Adversarial attacks and defences: A survey. *arXiv:1810.00069*, 2018.

[Can06] E. Candès. Compressive sampling. In *Proceedings of the International Congress of Mathematicians*, 2006.

[Can08] E. Candès. The restricted isometry property and its implications for compressed sensing. *Compte Rendus de l'Academie des Sciences, Paris, Serie I*, 346:589–592, 2008.

[Cau47] A. Cauchy. Méthode générale pour la résolution des systèmes d'équations simultanées. *Compte Rendus de l'Academie des Sciences, Paris*, 25:536–538, 1847.

[CB19] C. Criscitiello and N. Boumal. Efficiently escaping saddle points on manifolds. In *Advances in Neural Information Processing Systems*, pages 5987–5997, 2019.

[CC17] Y. Chen and E.J. Candès. Solving random quadratic systems of equations is nearly as easy as solving linear systems. *Communications on Pure and Applied Mathematics*, 70(5):822–883, 2017.

[CCD+19] V. Charisopoulos, Y. Chen, D. Davis, et al. Low-rank matrix recovery with composite optimization: Good conditioning and rapid convergence. *arXiv:1904.10020*, 2019.

[CCFM18] Y. Chen, Y. Chi, J. Fan, and C. Ma. Gradient descent with random initialization: Fast global convergence for nonconvex phase retrieval. *Mathematical Programming*, 176:1–33, 2018.

[CCS08] J. Cai, E. Candès, and Z. Shen. A singular value thresholding algorithm for matrix completion. *arXiv:0810.3286*, 2008.

[CD91] M. Frank Callier and A. Charles Desoer. *Linear System Theory*. Springer, 1991.

[CD13] E. Candès and M. Davenport. How well can we estimate a sparse vector? *Applied and Computational Harmonic Analysis*, 34(2):317–323, 2013.

[CD16] Y. Carmon and J.C. Duchi. Gradient descent efficiently finds the cubic-regularized non-convex Newton step. *arXiv:1612.00547*, 2016.

[CD19] Y. Carmon and J. Duchi. Gradient descent finds the cubic-regularized nonconvex Newton step. *SIAM Journal on Optimization*, 29(3):2146–2178, 2019.

[CDDD19] V. Charisopoulos, D. Davis, M. Díaz, and D. Drusvyatskiy. Composite optimization for robust blind deconvolution. *arXiv:1901.01624*, 2019.

[CDHS17] Y. Carmon, J.C. Duchi, O. Hinder, and A. Sidford. Lower bounds for finding stationary points I. *arXiv:1710.11606*, 2017.

[CDHS18] Y. Carmon, J.C. Duchi, O. Hinder, and A. Sidford. Accelerated methods for nonconvex optimization. *SIAM Journal on Optimization*, 28(2):1751–1772, 2018.

[CDS98] S. Chen, D. Donoho, and M. Saunders. Atomic decomposition for basis pursuit. *SIAM Journal on Scientific Computing*, 20(1):33–61, 1998.

[CDS01] S. Chen, D. Donoho, and M. Saunders. Atomic decomposition by basis pursuit. *SIAM Review*, 43(1):129–159, 2001.

[CESV13] E.J. Candès, Y.C. Eldar, T. Strohmer, and V. Voroninski. Phase retrieval via matrix completion. *SIAM Journal on Imaging Sciences*, 6(1), 2013.

[CF80] T.M. Cannon and E.E. Fenimore. Coded aperture imaging: Many holes make light work. *Optical Engineering*, 19(3):283–289, 1980.

[CGT00] A.R. Conn, N.I.M. Gould, and P.L. Toint. *Trust Region Methods*, volume 1. *SIAM*, 2000.

[CGW19] T.S. Cohen, M. Geiger, and M. Weiler. A general theory of equivariant CNNs on homogeneous spaces. In *Advances in Neural Information Processing Systems*, pages 9142–9153, 2019.

[Che95] S. Chen. *Basis pursuit*. PhD Thesis, Stanford University, 1995.

[Che13] Y. Chen. Incoherence-optimal matrix completion. *IEEE Transactions on Information Theory*, 61(5):2909–2923, 2013.

[CHM+14] A. Choromanska, M. Henaff, M. Mathieu, G.B. Arous, and Y. LeCun. The loss surface of multilayer networks. *arXiv:1412.0233*, 2014.

[Cho17] F. Chollet. Xception: Deep learning with depthwise separable convolutions. *arXiv:1610.02357*, 2017.

[CHS87] T.S. Chiang, C.R. Hwang, and S.J. Sheu. Diffusions for global optimization in $\mathbb{R}^n$. *SIAM Journal of Control and Optimization*, 25:737–752, 1987.

[CJG+15] T.-H. Chan, K. Jia, S. Gao, et al. PCANet: A simple deep learning baseline for image classification? *IEEE Transactions on Image Processing*, 24(12):5017–5032, 2015.

[CJSC13] Y. Chen, A. Jalali, S. Sanghavi, and C. Caramanis. Low-rank matrix recovery from errors and erasures. *IEEE Transactions on Information Theory*, 59(7):4324–4337, 2013.

[CLC19] Y. Chi, Y.M. Lu, and Y. Chen. Nonconvex optimization meets low-rank matrix factorization: An overview. *IEEE Transactions on Signal Processing*, 67(20):5239–5269, 2019.

[CLMW11] E.J. Candès, X. Li, Y.Ma, and J. Wright. Robust principal component analysis? *Journal of the ACM (JACM)*, 58(3):11, 2011.

[CLS15a] E.J. Candès, X. Li, and M. Soltanolkotabi. Phase retrieval from coded diffraction patterns. *Applied and Computational Harmonic Analysis*, 39(2):277–299, 2015.

[CLS15b] E.J. Candès, X. Li, and M. Soltanolkotabi. Phase retrieval via Wirtinger flow: Theory and algorithms. *IEEE Transactions on Information Theory*, 61(4):1985–2007, 2015.

[CM73] J.F. Claerbout and F. Muir. Robust modeling of erratic data. *Geophysics*, 38(5):826–844, 1973.

[CMH+17] J. Cavazza, P. Morerio, B.D. Haeffele, et al. Dropout as a low-rank regularizer for matrix factorization. *CoRR*, *abs/1710.05092*, 2017.

[CMH+18] J. Cavazza, P. Morerio, B. Haeffele, et al. Dropout as a low-rank regularizer for matrix factorization. In *International Conference on Artificial Intelligence and Statistics*, pages 435–444, 2018.

[CMM+20] M. Caron, I. Misra, J. Mairal, et al. Unsupervised learning of visual features by contrasting cluster assignments. In *Advances in Neural Information Processing Systems*, volume 33, pages 9912–9924. Curran Associates, 2020.

[CMP10] A. Chai, M. Moscoso, and G. Papanicolaou. Array imaging using intensity-only measurements. *Inverse Problems*, 27(1):015005, 2010.

[Cor06] J.V. Corbett. The Pauli problem, state reconstruction and quantum-real numbers. *Reports on Mathematical Physics*, 57(1):53–68, 2006.

[CP86] T.F. Coleman and A. Pothen. The null space problem I. Complexity. *SIAM Journal on Algebraic Discrete Methods*, 7(4):527–537, 1986.

[CP10] E. Candès and Y. Plan. Matrix completion with noise. *Proceedings of the IEEE*, 98(6):925–936, 2010.

[CP11] E. Candès and Y. Plan. Tight oracle inequalities for low-rank matrix recovery from a minimal number of noisy random measurements. *IEEE Transactions on Information Theory*, 57(4):2342–2359, 2011.

[CPW12] V. Chandrasekaran, P. Parrilo, and A. Willsky. Latent variable graphical model selection via convex optimization. *The Annals of Statistics*, 40(4):1935–1967, 2012.

[CR09] E.J. Candès and B. Recht. Exact matrix completion via convex optimization. *Foundations of Computational Mathematics*, 9(6):717, 2009.

[Cro78] L. Cromme. Strong uniqueness: A far-reaching criterion for the convergence analysis of iterative procedures. *Numerische Mathematik*, 29:179–193, 1978.

[CRPW12] V. Chandrasekaran, B. Recht, P. Parrilo, and A. Willsky. The convex geometry of linear inverse problems. *Foundations of Computational Mathematics*, 12(6):805–849, 2012.

[CRT06a] E. Candès, J. Romberg, and T. Tao. Robust uncertainty principles: Exact signal reconstruction from highly incomplete frequency information. *IEEE Transactions on Information Theory*, 52(2):489–509, 2006.

[CRT06b] E. Candès, J. Romberg, and T. Tao. Stable signal recovery from incomplete and inaccurate measurements. *Communications on Pure and Applied Mathematics*, 59(8):1207–1223, 2006.

[CSD+09] V. Cevher, A. Sankaranarayanan, M. Duarte, et al. Compressive sensing for background subtraction. In *Proceedings of European Conference on Computer Vision (ECCV)*, 2009.

[CSL+20] S. Cheung, J. Shin, Y. Lau, et al. Dictionary learning in Fourier-transform scanning tunneling spectroscopy. *Nature Communications*, 11:1081, 2020.

[CSPW09] V. Chandrasekaran, S. Sanghavi, P. Parrilo, and A. Willsky. Sparse and low-rank matrix decompositions. In *IFAC Symposium on System Identification*, 2009.

[CSV13] E.J. Candès, T. Strohmer, and V. Voroninski. Phaselift: Exact and stable signal recovery from magnitude measurements via convex programming. *Communications on Pure and Applied Mathematics*, 66(8):1241–1274, 2013.

[CT81] R.L. Cook and K.E. Torrance. A reflectance model for computer graphics. *Computer Graphics*, 15(3):307–316, 1981.

[CT91] T. Cover and J. Thomas. *Elements of Information Theory*. Wiley Series in Telecommunications, John Wiley, 1991.

[CT05] E. Candès and T. Tao. Decoding by linear programming. *IEEE Transactions on Information Theory*, 51(12):4203–4215, 2005.

[CT07] E. Candès and T. Tao. The Dantzig selector: Statistical estimation when p is much larger than n. *The Annals of Statistics*, 35(6):2313–2351, 2007.

[CT09] E. Candes and T. Tao. The power of convex relaxation: Near-optimal matrix completion. *IEEE Transactions on Information Theory*, 56(5):2053–2080, 2009.

[CT17] L. Chang and D. Tsao. The code for facial identity in the primate brain. *Cell*, 169:1013–1028, 2017.

[CW98] T.F. Chan and C.-K. Wong. Total variation blind deconvolution. *IEEE Transactions on Image Processing*, 7(3):370–375, 1998.

[CW05] P. Combettes and V. Wajs. Signal recovery by proximal forward-backward splitting. *SIAM Multiscale Modeling and Simulation*, 4:1168–1200, 2005.

[CW16] T. Cohen and M. Welling. Group equivariant convolutional networks. In *International Conference on Machine Learning*, pages 2990–2999, 2016.

[CYY+20] K.H.R. Chan, Y. Yu, C. You, et al. Deep networks from the principle of rate reduction. *arXiv:2010.14765*, 2020.

[DBLJ14] A. Defazio, F. Bach, and S. Lacoste-Julien. Saga: A fast incremental gradient method with support for non-strongly convex composite objectives. In *Advances in Neural Information Processing Systems*, pages 1646–1654, 2014.

[DD18] D. Davis and D. Drusvyatskiy. Graphical convergence of subgradients in nonconvex optimization and learning. *arXiv:1810.07590*, 2018.

[DDF+90] S. Deerwester, S. Dumais, G. Furnas, T. Landauer, and R. Harshman. Indexing by latent semantic analysis. *Journal of the American Society for Information Science*, 41(6):391–407, 1990.

[DDM04] I. Daubechies, M. Defrise, and C. Mol. An iterative thresholding algorithm for linear inverse problems with a sparsity constraint. *Communications on Pure and Applied Mathematics*, 57:1413–1457, 2004.

[DDMP18] D. Davis, D. Drusvyatskiy, K.J. MacPhee, and C. Paquette. Subgradient methods for sharp weakly convex functions. *Journal of Optimization Theory and Applications*, 179(3):962–982, 2018.

[DDP17] D. Davis, D. Drusvyatskiy, and C. Paquette. The nonsmooth landscape of phase retrieval. *arXiv:1711.03247*, 2017.

[DDT+08] M.F. Duarte, M.A. Davenport, D. Takhar, et al. Single-pixel imaging via compressive sampling. *IEEE Signal Processing Magazine*, 25(2):83–91, 2008.

[DE03] D. Donoho and M. Elad. Optimally sparse representation in general (nonorthogonal) dictionaries via ℓ^1 minimization. *Proceedings of the National Academy of Sciences of the USA*, 100(5):2197–2202, 2003.

[DF87] C. Dainty and J.R. Fienup. Phase retrieval and image reconstruction for astronomy. *Image Recovery: Theory and Application*, pages 231–275, 1987.

[DFL+88] S.T. Dumais, G.W. Furnas, T.K. Landauer, S. Deerwester, and R. Harshman. Using latent semantic analysis to improve access to textual information. In *Proceedings of the Conference on Human Factors in Computing Systems, CHI*, pages 281–286, 1988.

[DIIM04] M. Datar, N. Immorlica, P. Indyk, and V.S. Mirrokni. Locality-sensitive hashing scheme based on p-stable distributions. In *Proceedings of the Twentieth Annual Symposium on Computational Geometry*, SCG '04, pages 253–262, 2004. ACM.

[DJL+17] S. Du, C. Jin, J. Lee, et al. Gradient descent can take exponential time to escape saddle points. In *Proceedings of the 31st International Conference on Neural Information Processing Systems (NIPS 2017)*, 2017.

[DLL+19] S. Du, J. Lee, H. Li, L. Wang, and X. Zhai. Gradient descent finds global minima of deep neural networks. In *International Conference on Machine Learning*, pages 1675–1685, 2019.

[DMA97] G. Davis, S. Mallat, and M. Avellaneda. Adaptive greedy approximations. *Journal of Constructive Approximation*, 13:57–98, 1997.

[DO19] J. Diakonikolas and L. Orecchia. The approximate duality gap technique: A unified theory of first-order methods. *SIAM Journal on Optimization*, 29(1):660–689, 2019.

[Don00] D. Donoho. High-dimensional data analysis: The curses and blessings of dimensionality. AMS Math Challenges Lecture, 2000. Available online: `http://www-stat.stanford.edu/~donoho/Lectures/AMS2000/AMS2000.html`, 2000.

[Don05] D.L. Donoho. Neighborly polytopes and sparse solutions of underdetermined linear equations. *Stanford Technical Report 2005–04*, 2005.

[Don06a] D. Donoho. Compressed sensing. *IEEE Transactions on Information Theory*, 52(4):1289–1306, 2006.

[Don06b] D. Donoho. For most large underdetermined systems of linear equations the minimal ℓ_1-norm solution is also the sparsest solution. *Communications on Pure and Applied Mathematics*, 59(6):797–829, 2006.

[DR16] M.A. Davenport and J. Romberg. An overview of low-rank matrix recovery from incomplete observations. *IEEE Journal of Selected Topics in Signal Processing*, 10(4):608–622, 2016.

[DR19] J.C. Duchi and F. Ruan. Solving (most) of a set of quadratic equalities: Composite optimization for robust phase retrieval. *Information and Inference: A Journal of the IMA*, 8(3):471–529, 2019.

[DS07] S. Dasgupta and L. Schulman. A probabilistic analysis of EM for mixtures of separated, spherical Gaussians. *Journal of Machine Learning Research*, 8(Feb):203–226, 2007.

[DT09] D. Donoho and J. Tanner. Counting faces of randomly projected polytopes when the projection radically lowers dimension. *Journal of the American Mathematical Society*, 22(1):1–53, 2009.

[DT10] D.L. Donoho and J. Tanner. Exponential bounds implying construction of compressed sensing matrices, error-correcting codes, and neighborly polytopes by random sampling. *IEEE Transactions on Information Theory*, 56(4):2002–2016, 2010.

[DTZ16] C. Daskalakis, C. Tzamos, and M. Zampetakis. Ten steps of EM suffice for mixtures of two Gaussians. *arXiv:1609.00368*, 2016.

[DY16] W. Deng and W. Yin. On the global and linear convergence of the generalized alternating direction method of multipliers. *Journal of Scientific Computing*, 66:889–916, 2016.

[EA03] C. Eliasmith and C. Anderson. *Neural Engineering: Computation, Representation and Dynamics in Neurobiological Systems*. MIT Press, 2003.

[EA06] M. Elad and M. Aharon. Image denoising via sparse and redundant representations over learned dictionaries. *IEEE Transactions on Image Processing*, 15(12):3736–3745, 2006.

[EB92] J. Eckstein and D.P. Bertsekas. On the Douglas-Rachford splitting method and the proximal point algorithm for maximal monotone operators. *Mathematical Programming*, 55(1–3):293–318, 1992.

[Eck12] J. Eckstein. Augmented Lagrangian and alternating direction methods for convex optimization: A tutorial and some illustrative computational results. *RUTCOR Technical Report*, 2012.

[Efr66] M. Efroymson. Stepwise regression – A backward and forward look. In *Eastern Regional Meetings of the Institute of Mathematical Statistics*, 1966.

[Ela10] M. Elad. *Sparse and Redundant Representations: From Theory to Applications in Signal and Image Processing*. Springer Science & Business Media, 2010.

[EMS18] M.A. Erdogdu, L. Mackey, and O. Shamir. Global non-convex optimization with discretized diffusions. In *Advances in Neural Information Processing Systems*, pages 9671–9680, 2018.

[ESQD05] M. Elad, J. Starck, P. Querre, and D. Donoho. Simultaneous cartoon and texture image inpainting using morphological component analysis (MCA). *Applied and Computational Harmonic Analysis*, 19:340–358, 2005.

[ETT+17] L. Engstrom, B. Tran, D. Tsipras, L. Schmidt, and A. Madry. A rotation and a translation suffice: Fooling CNNs with simple transformations. *arXiv:1712.02779*, 2017.

[Ext] The Extended Yale Face Database B. See `http://vision.ucsd.edu/~leekc/ExtYaleDatabase/ExtYaleB.html`

[EY36] C. Eckart and G. Young. The approximation of one matrix by another of lower rank. *Psychometrika*, 1(3):211–218, 1936.

[FB81] M. Fischler and R. Bolles. Random sample consensus: A paradigm for model fitting with applications to image analysis and automated cartography. *Communications of the ACM*, 24(6):381–385, 1981.

[FHB01] M. Fazel, H. Hindi, and S. Boyd. A rank minimization heuristic with application to minimum order system approximation. In *American Control Conference (ACC)*, 2001.

[FHB03] M. Fazel, H. Hindi, and S.P. Boyd. Log-det heuristic for matrix rank minimization with applications to Hankel and Euclidean distance matrices. In *Proceedings of the American Control Conference, 2003*, volume 3, pages 2156–2162. IEEE, 2003.

[FHB04] M. Fazel, H. Hindi, and S. Boyd. Rank minimization and applications in system theory. In *American Control Conference*, 2004.

[Fie87] D.J. Field. Relations between the statistics of natural images and the response properties of cortical cells. *Journal of the Optical Society of America A*, 4(12):2379–2394, 1987.

[Fie13] J.R. Fienup. Phase retrieval algorithms: A personal tour. *Applied Optics*, 52(1):45–56, 2013.

[FJZT17] S. Feizi, H. Javadi, J. Zhang, and D. Tse. Porcupine neural networks: (Almost) all local optima are global. *arXiv:1710.02196*, 2017.

[FKT15] D. Foster, H. Karloff, and J. Thaler. Variable selection is hard. In *Conference on Learning Theory*, pages 696–709, 2015.

[FSM09] M.J. Fadılı, J.L. Starck, and F. Murtagh. Inpainting and zooming using sparse representations. *The Computer Journal*, 52(1):64–79, 2009.

[FLZZ20] J. Fan, R. Li, C.-H. Zhang, and H. Zou. *Statistical Foundations of Data Science*. CRC Press, 2020.

[FMR16] S. Fusi, E. Miller, and M. Rigotti. Why neurons mix: High dimensionality for higher cognition. *Current Opinion in Neurobiology*, 37:66–74, 2016.

[FR13] S. Foucart and H. Rauhut. *A Mathematical Introduction to Compressive Sensing*. Birkhauser, 2013.

[FS20] A. Fannjiang and T. Strohmer. The numerics of phase retrieval. *arXiv:2004.05788*, 2020.

[Fuc04] J. Fuchs. On sparse representation in arbitrary redundant bases. *IEEE Transactions on Information Theory*, 50(6):1341–1344, 2004.

[FW56] M. Frank and P. Wolfe. An algorithm for quadratic programming. *Naval Research Logistics Quarterly*, 3:95–110, 1956.

[FZS21] W. Fedus, B. Zoph, and N. Shazeer. Switch transformers: Scaling to trillion parameter models with simple and efficient sparsity. *arXiv:2101.03961*, 2021.

[Gab78] K.R. Gabriel. Least squares approximation of matrices by additive and multiplicative models. *Journal of the Royal Statistical Society B*, 40:186–196, 1978.

[Gau09] C.F. Gauss. *Theoria motus corporum coelestium in sectionibus conicis solem ambientium*. F. Perthes et I. H. Besser, 1809.

[GB10] X. Glorot and Y. Bengio. Understanding the difficulty of training deep feedforward neural networks. In *Proceedings of the Thirteenth International Conference on Artificial Intelligence and Statistics*, pages 249–256, 2010.

[GB14] M. Grant and S. Boyd. CVX: MATLAB software for disciplined convex programming (web page and software). 2009. Available online: `http://stanford.edu/~boyd/cvx`, 2014.

[GBC16] I. Goodfellow, Y. Bengio, and A. Courville. *Deep Learning*. MIT Press, 2016. `http://www.deeplearningbook.org`.

[GBK01] A. Georghiades, P. Belhumeur, and D. Kriegman. From few to many: Illumination cone models for face recognition under variable lighting and pose. *IEEE Transactions on Pattern Analysis and Machine Intelligence*, 23(6):643–660, 2001.

[GBLJ19] G. Gidel, F. Bach, and S. Lacoste-Julien. Implicit regularization of discrete gradient dynamics in linear neural networks. In *Advances in Neural Information Processing Systems*, pages 3196–3206, 2019.

[GBW19] D. Gilboa, S. Buchanan, and J. Wright. Efficient dictionary learning with gradient descent. *Proceedings of the 36th International Conference on Machine Learning*, 2019.

[GCW18] C. Garcia-Cardona and B. Wohlberg. Convolutional dictionary learning: A comparative review and new algorithms. *IEEE Transactions on Computational Imaging*, 4(3):366–381, 2018.

[GEBS18] R. Giryes, Y.C. Eldar, A.M. Bronstein, and G. Sapiro. Tradeoffs between convergence speed and reconstruction accuracy in inverse problems. *IEEE Transactions on Signal Processing*, 66(7):1676–1690, 2018.

[GH86] S. Geman and C.R. Hwang. Diffusions for global optimization. *SIAM Journal on Control and Optimization*, 24:1031–1043, 1986.

[GHJY15] R. Ge, F. Huang, C. Jin, and Y. Yuan. Escaping from saddle points – online stochastic gradient for tensor decomposition. In *Proceedings of the 28th Conference on Learning Theory*, pages 797–842, 2015.

[GHY14] G. Gu, B. He, and X. Yuan. Customized proximal point algorithms for linearly constrained convex minimization and saddle-point problems: A unified approach. *Computational Optimization and Applications*, 59(1–2):135–161, 2014.

[GJ79] M.R. Garey and D.S. Johnson. *Computers and Intractability*. W. H. Freeman, 1979.

[GJ90] M.R. Garey and D.S. Johnson. *Computers and Intractability; A Guide to the Theory of NP-Completeness*. W. H. Freeman, 1990.

[GJP95] F. Girosi, M. Jones, and T. Poggio. Regularization theory and neural networks architectures. *Neural Computation*, 7(2):219–269, 1995.

[GJZ17] R. Ge, C. Jin, and Y. Zheng. No spurious local minima in nonconvex low rank problems: A unified geometric analysis. In *Proceedings of the 34th International Conference on Machine Learning*, pages 1233–1242, 2017.

[GK12] C. Grienberger and A. Konnerth. Imaging calcium in neurons. *Neuron*, 73(5):862–885, 2012.

[GKXS18] A. Gotmare, N.S. Keskar, C. Xiong, and R. Socher. A closer look at deep learning heuristics: Learning rate restarts, warmup and distillation. In *International Conference on Learning Representations*, 2018.

[GL10] K. Gregor and Y. LeCun. Learning fast approximations of sparse coding. In *Proceedings of the 27th International Conference on Machine Learning*, pages 399–406, 2010.

[GLM16] R. Ge, J.D. Lee, and T. Ma. Matrix completion has no spurious local minimum. *arXiv:1605.07272*, 2016.

[GLM17] R. Ge, J.D. Lee, and T. Ma. Learning one-hidden-layer neural networks with landscape design. *arXiv:1711.00501*, 2017.

[GLSS18] S. Gunasekar, J.D. Lee, D. Soudry, and N. Srebro. Implicit bias of gradient descent on linear convolutional networks. In *Advances in Neural Information Processing Systems*, pages 9461–9471, 2018.

[GM90] S.B. Gelfand and S.K. Mitter. Recursive stochastic algorithms for global optimization in $\mathbb{R}^d$. *Technical Report LIDS-P-1937, Massachusetts Institute of Technology*, 1990.

[GM09] D. Goldfarb and S. Ma. Convergence of fixed point continuation algorithms for matrix rank minimization. Preprint, 2009.

[GM17] R. Ge and T. Ma. On the optimization landscape of tensor decompositions. In *Advances in Neural Information Processing Systems*, 2017.

[GMOV18] W. Gao, A.V. Makkuva, S. Oh, and P. Viswanath. Learning one-hidden-layer neural networks under general input distributions. *arXiv:1810.04133*, 2018.

[GN03] R. Gribonval and M. Nielsen. Sparse representations in unions of bases. *IEEE Transactions on Information Theory*, 49(12):3320–3325, 2003.

[GN16] L.-A. Gottlieb and T. Neylon. Matrix sparsification and the sparse null space problem. *Algorithmica*, 76(2):426–444, 2016.

[Gol65] S. Golden. Lower bounds for the Helmholtz function. *Physical Review*, 137(4B):B1127, 1965.

[Gol67] R. Gold. Optimal binary sequences for spread spectrum multiplexing (corresp.). *IEEE Transactions on Information Theory*, 13(4):619–621, 1967.

[Gol80] D. Goldfarb. Curvilinear path steplength algorithms for minimization which use directions of negative curvature. *Mathematical Programming*, 18(1):31–40, 1980.

[GPAM$^+$14] I. Goodfellow, J. Pouget-Abadie, M. Mirza, et al. Generative adversarial nets. In *Advances in Neural Information Processing Systems*, pages 2672–2680, 2014.

[Gro10] D. Gross. Recovering low-rank matrices from few coefficients in any basis. *IEEE Transactions on Information Theory*, 57(3):1548–1566, 2010.

[GS12] S. Ganguli and H. Sompolinsky. Compressed sensing, sparsity, and dimensionality in neuronal information processing and data analysis. *Annual Review of Neuroscience*, 35:485–508, 2012.

[GVL96] G. Golub and C. Van Loan. *Matrix Computations*. Johns Hopkins University Press, 3rd edition, 1996.

[GVR12] L. Ghaoui, V. Viallon, and T. Rabbani. Safe feature elimination for the lasso and sparse supervised learning problems. *Pacific Journal of Optimization*, 8:667–698, 2012.

[GWL⁺10] A. Ganesh, J. Wright, X. Li, E. Candès, and Y. Ma. Dense error correction for low-rank matrices via principal component pursuit. In *International Symposium on Information Theory (ISIT)*, 2010.

[GZ19] D. Gamarnik and I. Zadik. The landscape of the planted clique problem: Dense subgraphs and the overlap gap property. *arXiv:1904.07174*, 2019.

[Haj90] P. Hajela. Genetic search – An approach to the nonconvex optimization problem. *AIAA Journal*, 28(7):1205–1210, 1990.

[Hay94a] H. Hayakawa. Photometric stereo under a light source with arbitrary motion. *Journal of the Optical Society of America A*, 11(11):3079–3089, 1994.

[Hay94b] S.S. Haykin. *Blind Deconvolution*. Prentice Hall, 1994.

[HBZ⁺17] T. Haque, M. Bajor, and Y. Zhang. et al. A direct RF-to-information converter for reception and wideband interferer detection employing pseudo-random LO modulation. In *IEEE Radio Frequency Integrated Circuits Symposium (RFIC)*, 2017.

[HCL06] R. Hadsell, S. Chopra, and Y. LeCun. Dimensionality reduction by learning an invariant mapping. In *2006 IEEE Computer Society Conference on Computer Vision and Pattern Recognition, CVPR 2006*, pages 1735–1742, 2006.

[Hes69] M.R. Hestenes. Multiplier and gradient methods. *Journal of Optimization Theory and Applications*, 4(5):303–320, 1969.

[HFLM⁺18] R. Devon Hjelm, A. Fedorov, S. Lavoie-Marchildon, et al. Learning deep representations by mutual information estimation and maximization. *arXiv:1808.06670*, 2018.

[HFW⁺19] K. He, H. Fan, Y. Wu, S. Xie, and R. Girshick. Momentum contrast for unsupervised visual representation learning. *arXiv:1911.05722*, 2019.

[HH08] F. Herrmann and G. Hennenfent. Non-parametric seismic data recovery with curvelet frames. *Geophysical Journal International*, 173(1):233–248, 2008.

[HHS17] E. Hoffer, I. Hubara, and D. Soudry. Train longer, generalize better: Closing the generalization gap in large batch training of neural networks. In *Advances in Neural Information Processing Systems*, pages 1731–1741, 2017.

[HJ85] R. Horn and C. Johnson. *Matrix Analysis*. Cambridge University Press, 1985.

[HKSS15] D.J. Herzfeld, Y. Kojima, R. Soetedjo, and R. Shadmehr. Encoding of action by the purkinje cells of the cerebellum. *Nature*, 526(7573):439, 2015.

[HKSS18] D.J. Herzfeld, Y. Kojima, R. Soetedjo, and R. Shadmehr. Encoding of error and learning to correct that error by the purkinje cells of the cerebellum. *Nature Neuroscience*, 21(5):736, 2018.

[HKV19] F. Hutter, L. Kotthoff, and J. Vanschoren, editors. *Automatic Machine Learning: Methods, Systems, Challenges*. Springer, 2019.

[HKW11] G.E. Hinton, A. Krizhevsky, and S. Wang. Transforming auto-encoders. In *International Conference on Artificial Neural Networks*, 2011.

[HL67] R.R. Hocking and R.N. Leslie. Selection of the best subset in regression analysis. *Technometrics*, 9(4):531–540, 1967.

[HL13] C.J. Hillar and L.-H. Lim. Most tensor problems are NP-hard. *Journal of the ACM (JACM)*, 60(6):45, 2013.

[HL16] E. Hazan and H. Luo. Variance-reduced and projection-free stochastic optimization. In *Proceedings of the 33rd International Conference on Machine Learning*, volume 48, pages 1263–1271. JMLR.org, 2016.

[HLVDMW17] G. Huang, Z. Liu, L. Van Der Maaten, and K.Q. Weinberger. Densely connected convolutional networks. In *2017 IEEE Conference on Computer Vision and Pattern Recognition (CVPR)*, pages 2261–2269, 2017.

[HLWY19] J. Hu, X. Liu, Z. Wen, and Y. Yuan. A brief introduction to manifold optimization. *arXiv:1906.05450*, 2019.

[HMH00] L. Hubert, J. Meulman, and W. Heiser. Two purposes for matrix factorization: A historical appraisal. *SIAM Review*, 42(1):68–82, 2000.

[HMW13] T. Heinosaari, L. Mazzarella, and M.M. Wolf. Quantum tomography under prior information. *Communications in Mathematical Physics*, 318(2):355–374, 2013.

[Hof99] T. Hofmann. Probabilistic latent semantic indexing. In *Proceedings of the 22nd Annual International ACM SIGIR Conference on Research and Development in Information Retrieval*, pages 50–57, 1999.

[Hof04] T. Hofmann. Latent semantic models for collaborative filtering. *ACM Transactions on Information Systems*, 22(1):89–115, 2004.

[Hol07] J.K. Holmes. *Spread Spectrum Systems for GNSS and Wireless Communications*. Artech House, 2007.

[Hot33] H. Hotelling. Analysis of a complex of statistical variables into principal components. *Journal of Educational Psychology*, 24(6):417–441, 1933.

[HRRS86] F. Hampel, E. Ronchetti, P. Rousseeuw, and W. Stahel. *Robust Statistics – The Approach Based on Influence Functions*. John Wiley, 1986.

[HTF09] T. Hastie, R. Tibshirani, and J. Friedman. *The Elements of Statistical Learning*. Springer, 2nd edition, 2009.

[HTT09] T. Hey, S. Tansley, and K. Tolle. *The Fourth Paradigm: Data-Intensive Scientific Discovery*. Microsoft Research, 2009.

[HTW15] T. Hastie, R. Tibshirani, and M. Wainwright. *Statistical Learning with Sparsity: The Lasso and Generalizations*. Chapman & Hall, 2015.

[Hub81] P. Huber. *Robust Statistics*. John Wiley, 1981.

[Hub92] P.J. Huber. Robust estimation of a location parameter. In *Breakthroughs in Statistics*, pages 492–518. Springer, 1992.

[HV17] B.D. Haeffele and R. Vidal. Global optimality in neural network training. In *Proceedings of the IEEE Conference on Computer Vision and Pattern Recognition*, pages 7331–7339, 2017.

[HXP20] W. Hu, L. Xiao, and J. Pennington. Provable benefit of orthogonal initialization in optimizing deep linear networks. In *International Conference on Learning Representations*, 2020.

[HY38] A.S. Householder and G. Young. Matrix approximation and latent roots. *The American Mathematical Monthly*, 45:165–171, 1938.

[HY01] M.H. Hansen and B. Yu. Model selection and the principle of minimum description length. *Journal of the American Statistical Association*, 96:746–774, 2001.

[HY12] B. He and X. Yuan. On the $O(1/n)$ convergence rate of the Douglas–Rachford alternating direction method. *SIAM Journal on Numerical Analysis*, 50(2):700–709, 2012.

[HYP+15] T. Haque, R.T. Yazicigil, K.J.L. Pan, J. Wright, and P.R. Kinget. Theory and design of a quadrature analog-to-information converter for energy-efficient wideband spectrum sensing. *IEEE Transactions on Circuits and Systems I*, 62(2):527–535, 2015.

[HYZ08] E. Hale, W. Yin, and Y. Zhang. Fixed-point continuation for ℓ^1-minimization: Methodology and convergence. *SIAM Journal on Optimization*, 19(3):1107–1130, 2008.

[HZ00] R. Hartley and A. Zisserman. *Multiple View Geometry in Computer Vision*. Cambridge University Press, 2000.

[HZRS15] K. He, X. Zhang, S. Ren, and J. Sun. Delving deep into rectifiers: Surpassing human-level performance on imagenet classification. In *Proceedings of the IEEE International Conference on Computer Vision*, pages 1026–1034, 2015.

[HZRS16] K. He, X. Zhang, S. Ren, and J. Sun. Deep residual learning for image recognition. In *Proceedings of the IEEE Conference on Computer Vision and Pattern Recognition*, pages 770–778, 2016.

[IS15] S. Ioffe and C. Szegedy. Batch normalization: Accelerating deep network training by reducing internal covariate shift. *arXiv:1502.03167*, 2015.

[JCM12] K. Jia, T.-H. Chan, and Y. Ma. Robust and practical face recognition via structured sparsity. In *Proceedings of the European Conference on Computer Vision*, 2012.

[JEH15] K. Jaganathan, Y.C. Eldar, and B. Hassibi. Phase retrieval: An overview of recent developments. *arXiv:1510.07713*, 2015.

[JEH16] K. Jaganathan, Y.C. Eldar, and B. Hassibi. STFT phase retrieval: Uniqueness guarantees and recovery algorithms. *IEEE Journal of Selected Topics in Signal Processing*, 10(4):770–781, 2016.

[JEH17] K. Jaganathan, Y.C. Eldar, and B. Hassibi. Phase retrieval: An overview of recent developments. In *Optical Compressive Imaging*, pages 263–296. CRC Press, 2017.

[JG15] T.B. Johnson and C. Guestrin. Blitz: A principled meta-algorithm for scaling sparse optimization. In *Proceedings of the International Conference on Machine Learning*, 2015.

[JGH18] A. Jacot, F. Gabriel, and C. Hongler. Neural tangent kernel: Convergence and generalization in neural networks. *arXiv:1806.07572*, 2018.

[JGKA19] M. Janzamin, R. Ge, J. Kossaifi, and A. Anandkumar. Spectral learning on matrices and tensors. *Foundations and Trends in Machine Learning*, 12(5–6):393–536, 2019.

[JGN+17] C. Jin, R. Ge, P. Netrapalli, S.M. Kakade, and M.I. Jordan. How to escape saddle points efficiently. In *Proceedings of the 34th International Conference on Machine Learning, ICML 2017*, pages 2727–2752. International Machine Learning Society (IMLS), 2017.

[JK17] P. Jain and P. Kar. Non-convex optimization for machine learning. *Foundations and Trends in Machine Learning*, 10(3–4):142–336, 2017.

[JMFU17] K.H. Jin, M.T. McCann, E. Froustey, and M. Unser. Deep convolutional neural network for inverse problems in imaging. *IEEE Transactions on Image Processing*, 26(9):4509–4522, 2017.

[JNJ18] C. Jin, P. Netrapalli, and M.I. Jordan. Accelerated gradient descent escapes saddle points faster than gradient descent. In *Conference on Learning Theory*, pages 1042–1085, 2018.

[JNRS10] M. Journée, Y. Nesterov, P. Richtárik, and R. Sepulchre. Generalized power method for sparse principal component analysis. *Journal of Machine Learning Research*, 11:517–553, 2010.

[JO80] K. Jittorntrum and M. Osborne. Strong uniqueness and second order convergence in nonlinear discrete approximation. *Numerische Mathematik*, 34:439–455, 1980.

[Jol86] I. Jolliffe. *Principal Component Analysis*. Springer, 1986.

[Jol02] I. Jolliffe. *Principal Component Analysis*. Springer, 2nd edition, 2002.

[Jor74] M.C. Jordan. Mémoire sur les formes bilinéaires. *Journal de Mathématiques Pures et Appliqués*, 19:35–54, 1874.

[Jor97] M.I. Jordan. Serial order: A parallel distributed processing approach. In *Advances in Psychology*, 121:471–495, 1997.

[Jor03] M. Jordan. *An Introduction to Probabilistic Graphical Models*. Unpublished, 2003.

[JSA15] M. Janzamin, H. Sedghi, and A. Anandkumar. Beating the perils of non-convexity: Guaranteed training of neural networks using tensor methods. *arXiv:1506.08473*, 2015.

[JSZK15] M. Jaderberg, K. Simonyan, A. Zisserman, and K. Kavukcuoglu. Spatial transformer networks. *CoRR, abs/1506.02025*, 2015.

[JZ13] R. Johnson and T. Zhang. Accelerating stochastic gradient descent using predictive variance reduction. In *Advances in Neural Information Processing Systems*, pages 315–323, 2013.

[JZB+16] C. Jin, Y. Zhang, S. Balakrishnan, M.J. Wainwright, and M.I. Jordan. Local maxima in the likelihood of Gaussian mixture models: Structural results and algorithmic consequences. In *Advances in Neural Information Processing Systems*, pages 4116–4124, 2016.

[Kar72] R.M. Karp. *Reducibility among Combinatorial Problems*. Springer, 1972.

[Kaw16] K. Kawaguchi. Deep learning without poor local minima. In *Advances in Neural Information Processing Systems*, pages 586–594, 2016.

[KB09] T.G. Kolda and B.W. Bader. Tensor decompositions and applications. *SIAM Review*, 51(3):455–500, 2009.

[KB14] D.P. Kingma and J. Ba. ADAM: A method for stochastic optimization. *CoRR, abs/1412.6980*, 2014.

[KBB15] W. Krichene, A. Bayen, and P.L. Bartlett. Accelerated mirror descent in continuous and discrete time. In *Advances in Neural Information Processing Systems*, pages 2845–2853, 2015.

[KBB16] W. Krichene, A. Bayen, and P.L. Bartlett. Adaptive averaging in accelerated descent dynamics. In *Advances in Neural Information Processing Systems*, pages 2991–2999, 2016.

[KBRW19] M.R. Kellman, E. Bostan, N.A. Repina, and L. Waller. Physics-based learned design: Optimized coded-illumination for quantitative phase imaging. *IEEE Transactions on Computational Imaging*, 5(3):344–353, 2019.

[KCYT05] J. Kim, J. Choi, J. Yi, and M. Turk. Effective representation using ICA for face recognition robust to local distortion and partial occlusion. *IEEE Transactions on Pattern Analysis and Machine Intelligence*, 27(12):1977–1981, 2005.

[KDSA+15] R. Kumar, C. Da Silva, O. Akalin, et al. Efficient matrix completion for seismic data reconstruction. *Geophysics*, 80(5):V97–V114, 2015.

[KGV83] S. Kirkpatrick, C.D. Gelett, and M.P. Vecchi. Optimization by simulated annealing. *Science*, 220:621–630, 1983.

[KH92] A. Krogh and J.A. Hertz. A simple weight decay can improve generalization. In *Advances in Neural Information Processing Systems*, pages 950–957, 1992.

[KH96] D. Kundur and D. Hatzinakos. Blind image deconvolution. *IEEE Signal Processing Magazine*, 13(3):43–64, 1996.

[KKP+18] A. Kyrillidis, A. Kalev, D. Park, et al. Provable compressed sensing quantum state tomography via non-convex methods. *npj Quantum Information*, 4(1):1–7, 2018.

[KM89] S. Kontogiorgis and R. Meyer. A variable-penalty alternating direction method for convex optimization. *Mathematical Programming*, 83:29–53, 1989.

[KMK97] D.C. Knill, P. Mamassian, and D. Kersten. The geometry of shadows. *Journal of the Optical Society of America A*, 14(12):3216–3232, 1997.

[KMR14] F. Krahmer, S. Mendelson, and H. Rauhut. Suprema of chaos processes and the restricted isometry property. *Communications on Pure and Applied Mathematics*, 67(11):1877–1904, 2014.

[Koo31] B.O. Koopman. Hamiltonian systems and transformation in Hilbert space. *Proceedings of the National Academy of Sciences of the USA*, 17:315–318, 1931.

[Kor09] Y. Koren. The BellKor solution to the Netflix grand prize. See `https://www.netflixprize.com/assets/GrandPrize2009_BPC_BellKor.pdf`, 2009.

[KPCC15] Z. Kang, C. Peng, J. Cheng, and Q. Cheng. LogDet rank minimization with application to subspace clustering. *Computational Intelligence and Neuroscience*, 2015:824289, 2015.

[KQC+19] J. Kwon, W. Qian, C. Caramanis, Y. Chen, and D. Davis. Global convergence of the EM algorithm for mixtures of two component linear regression. In *Conference on Learning Theory*, pages 2055–2110, 2019.

[Kri09] A. Krizhevsky. Learning multiple layers of features from tiny images. Available online: `http://citeseerx.ist.psu.edu/viewdoc/download?doi=10.1.1.222.9220&rep=rep1&type=pdf`, 2009.

[Kru77] J.B. Kruskal. Three-way arrays: Rank and uniqueness of trilinear decompositions, with application to arithmetic complexity and statistics. *Linear Algebra and Its Applications*, 18(2):95–138, 1977.

[KS12] I. Kra and S.R. Simanca. On circulant matrices. *Notices of the American Mathematical Society*, 59:368–377, 2012.

[KSH12] A. Krizhevsky, I. Sutskever, and G.E. Hinton. Imagenet classification with deep convolutional neural networks. In *Advances in Neural Information Processing Systems*, pages 1097–1105, 2012.

[Kuč95] L. Kučera. Expected complexity of graph partitioning problems. *Discrete Applied Mathematics*, 57(2–3):193–212, 1995.

[Kus87] H.J. Kushner. Asymptotic global behavior for stochastic approximation and diffusions with slowly decreasing noise effects: Global minimization via Monte Carlo. *SIAM Journal of Applied Mathematics*, 47:165–189, 1987.

[KW92] J. Kuczynski and H. Wozniakowski. Estimating the largest eigenvalue by the power and Lanczos algorithms with a random start. *SIAM Journal on Matrix Analysis and Applications*, 13(4):1094–1122, 1992.

[KZLW19] H.-W. Kuo, Y. Zhang, Y. Lau, and J. Wright. Geometry and symmetry in short-and-sparse deconvolution. In *International Conference on Machine Learning (ICML)*, 2019.

[Lan67] H.J. Landau. Necessary density conditions for sampling and interpolation of certain entire functions. *Acta Mathematica*, 117:37–52, 1967.

[Lan01] S. Lang. *Fundamentals of Differential Geometry*. Springer, 2001.

[Lap74] P. Laplace. Mémoire sur la probabilité des causes par les événemens. *Mémoires de Mathematique et de Physique, Presentés à l'Académie Royale des Sciences par divers Savans & lus dans ses Assemblées, Tome Sixieme*, pages 621–656, 1774.

[LB95a] Y. LeCun and Y. Bengio. Convolutional networks for images, speech, and time series. In *The Handbook of Brain Theory and Neural Networks*. MIT Press, 1995.

[LB95b] M.H. Loke and R.D. Barker. Least-squares deconvolution of apparent resistivity pseudosections. *Geophysics*, 60(6):1682–1690, 1995.

[LB00] A. Leonardis and H. Bischof. Robust recognition using eigenimages. *Computer Vision and Image Understanding*, 78(1):99–118, 2000.

[LB18] Y. Li and Y. Bresler. Global geometry of multichannel sparse blind deconvolution on the sphere. *arXiv:1805.10437*, 2018.

[LB19] Y. Li and Y. Bresler. Multichannel sparse blind deconvolution on the sphere. *IEEE Transactions on Information Theory*, 65(11):7415–7436, 2019.

[LBBH98] Y. LeCun, L. Bottou, Y. Bengio, and P. Haffner. Gradient-based learning applied to document recognition. *Proceedings of the IEEE*, 86(11):2278–2324, 1998.

[LBH15] Y. LeCun, Y. Bengio, and G. Hinton. Deep learning. *Nature*, 521(7553):436–444, 2015.

[LBOM12] Y.A. LeCun, L. Bottou, G.B. Orr, and K.-R. Müller. Efficient backprop. In *Neural Networks: Tricks of the Trade*, pages 9–48. Springer, 2012.

[LCBD20] T. Liu, A. Chaman, D. Belius, and I. Dokmanić. Interpreting U-Nets via task-driven multiscale dictionary learning. *arXiv:2011.12815*, 2020.

[LCD+19] X. Li, S. Chen, Z. Deng, et al. Nonsmooth optimization over Stiefel manifold: Riemannian subgradient methods. *arXiv:1911.05047*, 2019.

[LCWM09] Z. Lin, M. Chen, L. Wu, and Y. Ma. The augmented Lagrange multiplier method for exact recovery of corrupted low-rank matrices. *Technical Report, arXiv:1009.5055*, 2009.

[LCWY19] J. Liu, X. Chen, Z. Wang, and W. Yin. ALISTA: Analytic weights are as good as learned weights in LISTA. In *International Conference on Learning Representations*, 2019.

[LDP07] M. Lustig, D. Donoho, and J. Pauly. Sparse MRI: The application of compressed sensing for rapid MR imaging. *Magnetic Resonance in Medicine*, 58(6):1182–1195, 2007.

[LDSP08] M. Lustig, D.L. Donoho, J.M. Santos, and J.M. Pauly. Compressed sensing MRI. *IEEE Signal Processing Magazine*, 25(2):72–82, 2008.

[LeC98] Y. LeCun. The MNIST database of handwritten digits. `http://yann.lecun.com/exdb/mnist/`, 1998.

[Led01] M. Ledoux. *The Concentration of Measure Phenomenon*, Mathematical Surveys and Monographs 89. American Mathematical Society, 2001.

[Leg05] A.M. Legendre. *Nouvelles méthodes pour la détermination des orbites des comètes*. Nineteenth Century Collections Online (NCCO): Science, Technology, and Medicine: 1780–1925. F. Didot, 1805.

[Lev44] K. Levenberg. A method for the solution of certain problems in least squares. *Quarterly of Applied Mathematics*, 2:164–168, 1944.

[LGW$^+$09] Z. Lin, A. Ganesh, J. Wright, et al. Fast convex optimization algorithms for exact recovery of a corrupted low-rank matrix. In *International Workshop on Computational Advances in Multi-Sensor Adaptive Processing*, 2009.

[LH16] I. Loshchilov and F. Hutter. SGDR: Stochastic gradient descent with warm restarts. *arXiv:1608.03983*, 2016.

[LHGT04] L. Li, W. Huang, I. Gu, and Q. Tian. Statistical modeling of complex backgrounds for foreground object detection. *IEEE Transactions on Image Processing*, 13(11):1459–1472, 2004.

[LHZC01] S. Li, X. Hou, H. Zhang, and Q. Cheng. Learning spatially localized, parts-based representation. In *Proceedings of the IEEE International Conference on Computer Vision and Pattern Recognition*, pages 1–6, 2001.

[Li13] X. Li. Compressed sensing and matrix completion with constant proportion of corruptions. *Constructive Approximation*, 37(1):73–99, 2013.

[Lib12] D. Liberzon. *Calculus of Variations and Optimal Control Theory: A Concise Introduction*. Princeton University Press, 2012.

[Liu11] Y.K. Liu. Universal low-rank matrix recovery from Pauli measurements. *Proceedings of the International Conference on Neural Information Processing Systems*, 2011.

[LJ16] S. Lacoste-Julien. Convergence rate of Frank–Wolfe for non-convex objectives. *arXiv:1607.00345*, 2016.

[LJB$^+$95] Y. LeCun, L.D. Jackel, L. Bottou, et al. Learning algorithms for classification: A comparison on handwritten digit recognition. In J.H. Oh, C. Kwon, and S. Cho, editors, *Neural Networks*, pages 261–276. World Scientific, 1995.

[LK81] B. Lucas and T. Kanade. An iterative image registration technique with an application to stereo vision. In *Proceedings of Imaging Understanding Workshop*, 1981.

[LKB18] B. Lusch, J.N. Kutz, and S.L. Brunton. Deep learning for universal linear embeddings of nonlinear dynamics. *Nature Communications*, 9:4950, 2018.

[LKG$^+$19] C. Liu, K. Kim, J. Gu, Y. Furukawa, and J. Kautz. PlaneRCNN: 3D plane detection and reconstruction from a single image. *2019 IEEE/CVF Conference on Computer Vision and Pattern Recognition (CVPR)*, pages 4445–4454, 2019.

[LLA+19] X. Li, J. Lu, R. Arora, et al. Symmetry, saddle points, and global optimization landscape of nonconvex matrix factorization. *IEEE Transactions on Information Theory*, 65(6):3489–3514, 2019.

[LLB16] Y. Li, K. Lee, and Y. Bresler. Identifiability in blind deconvolution with subspace or sparsity constraints. *IEEE Transactions on Information Theory*, 62(7):4266–4275, 2016.

[LLT18] B.M. Lake, N. Lawrence, and J. Tenenbaum. The emergence of organizing structure in conceptual representation. *Cognitive Science*, 42 Suppl. 3:809–832, 2018.

[LLY+13] G. Liu, Z. Lin, S. Yan, J. Sun, and Y. Ma. Robust recovery of subspace structures by low-rank representation. *IEEE Transactions on Pattern Analysis and Machine Intelligence*, 35(1):171–184, 2013.

[LM79] P. Lions and B. Mercier. Splitting algorithms for the sum of two nonlinear operators. *SIAM Journal on Numerical Analysis*, 16:964–979, 1979.

[LM16] K. Li and J. Malik. Fast k-nearest neighbour search via dynamic continuous indexing. In *Proceedings of International Conference on Machine Learning*, 2016.

[LM18] G. Lerman and T. Maunu. An overview of robust subspace recovery. *Proceedings of the IEEE*, 106(8):1380–1410, 2018.

[LMH15] H. Lin, J. Mairal, and Z. Harchaoui. A universal catalyst for first-order optimization. In *Advances in Neural Information Processing Systems*, pages 3384–3392, 2015.

[LMZ18] Y. Li, T. Ma, and H. Zhang. Algorithmic regularization in over-parameterized matrix sensing and neural networks with quadratic activations. In *Conference on Learning Theory*, pages 2–47. PMLR, 2018.

[LNC+11] Q.V. Le, J. Ngiam, A. Coates, et al. On optimization methods for deep learning. In *Proceedings of the International Conference on Machine Learning*, 2011.

[Log65] B. Logan. *Properties of high-pass signals*. PhD Thesis, Columbia University, 1965.

[LPP+17] J.D. Lee, I. Panageas, G. Piliouras, et al. First-order methods almost always avoid saddle points. *arXiv:1710.07406*, 2017.

[LPP+19] J.D. Lee, I. Panageas, G. Piliouras, et al. First-order methods almost always avoid strict saddle points. *Mathematical Programming*, 176(1–2):311–337, 2019.

[LPW+17] Z. Lu, H. Pu, F. Wang, Z. Hu, and L. Wang. The expressive power of neural networks: A view from the width. In *Advances in Neural Information Processing Systems*, pages 6231–6239, 2017.

[LQK+19] Y. Lau, Q. Qu, H.-W. Kuo, et al. Short-and-sparse deconvolution – a geometric approach. *arXiv:1908.10959*, 2019.

[LQMS18] J. Lezama, Q. Qiu, P. Musé, and G. Sapiro. OLE: Orthogonal low-rank embedding – A plug and play geometric loss for deep learning. In *Proceedings of the IEEE Conference on Computer Vision and Pattern Recognition*, pages 8109–8118, 2018.

[LRZM12] X. Liang, X. Ren, Z. Zhang, and Y. Ma. Repairing sparse low-rank texture. In *Proceedings of the European Conference on Computer Vision*, 2012.

[LS17] S. Ling and T. Strohmer. Blind deconvolution meets blind demixing: Algorithms and performance bounds. *IEEE Transactions on Information Theory*, 63(7):4497–4520, 2017.

[LSJR16] J.D. Lee, M. Simchowitz, M.I. Jordan, and B. Recht. Gradient descent only converges to minimizers. In *Conference on Learning Theory*, pages 1246–1257, 2016.

[LSPJ18] T. Lin, S.U. Stich, K.K. Patel, and M. Jaggi. Don't use large mini-batches, use local SGD. *arXiv:1808.07217*, 2018.

[Lus13] M. Lustig. Compressed sensing MRI resources. `http://www.eecs.berkeley.edu/mlustig/CS.html`, 2013.

[LV09] Z. Liu and L. Vandenberghe. Semidefinite programming methods for system realization and identification. In *Proceedings of the 48th IEEE Conference on Decision and Control (CDC) Held Jointly with 2009 28th Chinese Control Conference*, pages 4676–4681, 2009.

[LV10] Z. Liu and L. Vandenberghe. Interior-point method for nuclear norm approximation with application to system identification. *SIAM Journal on Matrix Analysis and Applications*, 31(3):1235–1256, 2010.

[LVB+93] M. Lades, J. Vorbruggen, J. Buhmann, et al. Distortion invariant object recognition in the dynamic link architecture. *IEEE Transactions on Computers*, 42(3):300–311, 1993.

[LWDF11] A. Levin, Y. Weiss, F. Durand, and W.T. Freeman. Understanding blind deconvolution algorithms. *IEEE Transactions on Pattern Analysis and Machine Intelligence*, 33(12):2354–2367, 2011.

[LXB18] S. Ling, R. Xu, and A.S. Bandeira. On the landscape of synchronization networks: A perspective from nonconvex optimization. *arXiv:1809.11083*, 2018.

[LZSV20] X. Li, Z. Zhu, A.M.-C. So, and R. Vidal. Nonconvex robust low-rank matrix recovery. *SIAM Journal on Optimization*, 30(1):660–686, 2020.

[LZT18] Q. Li, Z. Zhu, and G. Tang. The non-convex geometry of low-rank matrix optimization. *Information and Inference: A Journal of the IMA*, 8(1):51–96, 2018.

[MA89a] R. Monteiro and I. Adler. Interior path following primal-dual algorithms. Part I: Linear programming. *Mathematical Programming*, 44:27–41, 1989.

[MA89b] R. Monteiro and I. Adler. Interior path following primal-dual algorithms. Part II: Convex quadratic programming. *Mathematical Programming*, 44:43–66, 1989.

[Mar63] D. Marquardt. An algorithm for least-squares estimation of nonlinear parameters. *SIAM Journal on Applied Mathematics*, 11:431–441, 1963.

[Mar02] A. Martinez. Recognizing imprecisely localized, partially occluded, and expression variant faces from a single sample per class. *IEEE Transactions on Pattern Analysis and Machine Intelligence*, 24(6):748–763, 2002.

[Mar14] J. Martens. New insights and perspectives on the natural gradient method. *arXiv:1412.1193*, 2014.

[Mat02] J. Matousek. *Lectures on Discrete Geometry*. Springer, 2002.

[MAV18] P. Mianjy, R. Arora, and R. Vidal. On the implicit bias of dropout. *arXiv:1806.09777*, 2018.

[MB98] A. Martinez and R. Benavente. The AR face database. *Technical Report 24, Computer Vision Center, Universitat Autonoma de Barcelona*, 1998.

[MC89] M. McCloskey and N.J. Cohen. Catastrophic interference in connectionist networks: The sequential learning problem. In *Psychology of Learning and Motivation*, volume 24, pages 109–165. Elsevier, 1989.

[McC83] S. McCormick. *A combinatorial approach to some sparse matrix problems*. PhD Thesis, Stanford University, 1983.

[MDHW07] Y. Ma, H. Derksen, W. Hong, and J. Wright. Segmentation of multivariate mixed data via lossy coding and compression. *IEEE Transactions on Pattern Analysis and Machine Intelligence*, 29(9), 2007.

[MDL+09] A. Mirzaei, H. Darabi, J.C. Leete, et al. Analysis and optimization of current-driven passive mixers in narrowband direct-conversion receivers. *IEEE Journal of Solid-State Circuits*, 44(10):2678–2688, 2009.

[ME10] M. Mishali and Y.C. Eldar. From theory to practice: Sub-Nyquist sampling of sparse wideband analog signals. *IEEE Journal of Selected Topics in Signal Processing*, 4(2):375–391, 2010.

[ME11] M. Mishali and Y.C. Eldar. Wideband spectrum sensing at sub-Nyquist rates. *IEEE Signal Processing Magazine*, 28(4):102–135, 2011.

[Meg89] N. Megiddo. Pathways to the optimal set in linear programming. In *Progress in Mathematical Programming: Interior-Point and Related Methods*, pages 131–158. Springer, 1989.

[MES08] J. Mairal, M. Elad, and G. Sapiro. Sparse representation for color image restoration. *IEEE Transactions on Image Processing*, 17(1):53–69, 2008.

[MG15] J. Martens and R. Grosse. Optimizing neural networks with Kronecker-factored approximate curvature. In *International Conference on Machine Learning*, pages 2408–2417, 2015.

[MHI10] D. Miyazaki, K. Hara, and K. Ikeuchi. Median photometric stereo as applied to the Segonko tumulus and museum objects. *International Journal on Computer Vision*, 86(2):229–242, 2010.

[MHSD15] N.J. Majaj, H. Hong, E.A. Solomon, and J.J. DiCarlo. Simple learned weighted sums of inferior temporal neuronal firing rates accurately predict human core object recognition performance. *Journal of Neuroscience*, 35(39):13402–13418, 2015.

[MHWG13] C. Mu, B. Huang, J. Wright, and D. Goldfarb. Square deal: Lower bounds and improved relaxations for tensor recovery. *arXiv:1307.5870*, 2013.

[MIJ+02] J. Miao, T. Ishikawa, B. Johnson, et al. High resolution 3D X-ray diffraction microscopy. *Physical Review Letters*, 89(8):088303, 2002.

[Mil63] J.W. Milnor. *Morse Theory*, volume 1. Princeton University Press, 1963.

[Mil90] R.P. Millane. Phase retrieval in crystallography and optics. *Journal of the Optical Society of America A*, 7(3):394–411, 1990.

[MIS07] Y. Mukaigawa, Y. Ishii, and T. Shakunaga. Analysis of photometric factors based on photometric linearization. *Journal of the Optical Society of America A*, 24(10):3326–3334, 2007.

[MJU17] M.T. McCann, K.H. Jin, and M. Unser. Convolutional neural networks for inverse problems in imaging: A review. *IEEE Signal Processing Magazine*, 34(6):85–95, 2017.

[MK87] K.G. Murty and S.N. Kabadi. Some NP-complete problems in quadratic and nonlinear programming. *Mathematical Programming*, 39(2):117–129, 1987.

[MKD06] J.F. Murray and K. Kreutz-Delgado. Learning sparse overcomplete codes for images. *Journal of VLSI Signal Processing Systems for Signal, Image and Video Technology*, 45(1–2):97–110, 2006.

[MKKY18] T. Miyato, T. Kataoka, M. Koyama, and Y. Yoshida. Spectral normalization for generative adversarial networks. *arXiv:1802.05957*, 2018.

[ML18] D. Masters and C. Luschi. Revisiting small batch training for deep neural networks. *arXiv:1804.07612*, 2018.

[MLE19] V. Monga, Y. Li, and Y.C. Eldar. Algorithm unrolling: Interpretable, efficient deep learning for signal and image processing. *arXiv:1912.10557*, 2019.

[MM18] M. Mondelli and A. Montanari. On the connection between learning two-layers neural networks and tensor decomposition. *arXiv:1802.07301*, 2018.

[MMMO17] S. Mei, T. Misiakiewicz, A. Montanari, and R.I. Oliveira. Solving SDPs for synchronization and MaxCut problems via the Grothendieck inequality. *arXiv:1703.08729*, 2017.

[MMMS01] Y. Mukaigawa, H. Miyaki, S. Mihashi, and T. Shakunaga. Photometric image-based rendering for image generation in arbitrary illumination. In *Proceedings of the IEEE International Conference on Computer Vision*, pages 652–659, 2001.

[Mor62] J. Moreau. Fonctions convexes duales et points proximaux dans un espace hilbertien. *Compte Rendus de l'Academie des Sciences, Paris, Série A, Mathématique*, 255:2897–2899, 1962.

[Mor78] J.J. Moré. The Levenberg-Marquardt algorithm: Implementation and theory. In G.A. Watson, editor, *Numerical Analysis*, pages 105–116. Springer, 1978.

[MP43] W. McCulloch and W. Pitts. A logical calculus of the ideas immanent in nervous activity. *Bulletin of Mathematical Biology*, 5:115–133, 1943.

[MP97] M. Mesbahi and G.P. Papavassilopoulos. On the rank minimization problem over a positive semidefinite linear matrix inequality. *IEEE Transactions on Automatic Control*, 42(2):239–243, 1997.

[MS81] F. MacWilliams and N. Sloane. *The Theory of Error-Correcting Codes*. North-Holland, 1981.

[MSG18] M. Massias, J. Salmon, and A. Gramfort. Celer: A fast solver for the lasso with dual extrapolation. In *Proceedings of the International Conference on Machine Learning*, 2018.

[MSKS04] Y. Ma, S. Soatto, J. Košecká, and S. Sastry. *An Invitation to 3-D Vision: From Images to Models*. Springer, 2004.

[MS07] M. Mahajan and J.M.N. Sarma. On the complexity of matrix rank and rigidity. In V. Diekert, M.V. Volkov, and A. Voronkov, editors, *Computer Science – Theory and Applications*, pages 269–280. Springer, 2007.

[MWCC18] C. Ma, K. Wang, Y. Chi, and Y. Chen. Implicit regularization in nonconvex statistical estimation: Gradient descent converges linearly for phase retrieval and matrix completion. In *Proceedings of the 35th International Conference on Machine Learning*, volume 80, pages 3345–3354. PMLR, 2018.

[MYW$^+$10] K. Min, L. Yang, J. Wright, et al. Compact projection: Simple and efficient near neighbor search with practical memory requirements. In *2010 IEEE*

Computer Society Conference on Computer Vision and Pattern Recognition, pages 3477–3484, 2010.

[MYZC08] S. Ma, W. Yin, Y. Zhang, and A. Chakraborty. An efficient algorithm for compressed MR imaging using total variation and wavelets. In *Proceedings of the IEEE International Conference on Computer Vision and Pattern Recognition*, 2008.

[MZ93] S. Mallat and Z. Zhang. Matching pursuits with time-frequency dictionaries. *IEEE Transactions on Signal Processing*, 41(12):3397–3415, 1993.

[MZWM10] K. Min, Z. Zhang, J. Wright, and Y. Ma. Decomposing background topics from keywords by principal component pursuit. In *Proceedings of the 19th ACM International Conference on Information and Knowledge Management*, 2010.

[MZYM11] H. Mobahi, Z. Zhou, A. Yang, and Y. Ma. Holistic 3D reconstruction of urban structures from low-rank textures. In *ICCV Workshop on 3D Representation and Recognition*, 2011.

[Nes18] Y. Nesterov. *Lectures on Convex Optimization*, Springer Optimization and Its Applications, volume 137. Springer, 2018.

[Nat95] B. Natarajan. Sparse approximate solutions to linear systems. *SIAM Journal of Computing*, 24(2):227–243, 1995.

[NDEG13] S. Nam, M.E. Davies, M. Elad, and R. Gribonval. The cosparse analysis model and algorithms. *Applied and Computational Harmonic Analysis*, 34(1):30–56, 2013.

[Nem95] A. Nemirovski. *Information-Based Complexity for Convex Programming*. Lecture Notes, 1995.

[Nem04] A. Nemirovski. Prox-method with rate of convergence $O(1/t)$ for variational inequalities with Lipschitz continuous monotone operators and smooth convex-concave saddle point problems. *SIAM Journal on Optimization*, 15(1):229–251, 2004.

[Nem07] A. Nemirovski. *Efficient Methods for Convex Optimization*. Lecture Notes, 2007.

[Nes83] Y. Nesterov. A method of solving a convex programming problem with convergence rate $O(1/k^2)$. *Soviet Mathematics Doklady*, 27(2):372–376, 1983.

[Nes00] Y. Nesterov. Squared functional systems and optimization problems. In *High Performance Optimization*, pages 405–440. Springer, 2000.

[Nes03] Y. Nesterov. *Introductory Lectures on Convex Optimization: A Basic Course*. Springer, 2003.

[Nes05] Y. Nesterov. Smooth minimization of non-smooth functions. *Mathematical Programming*, 103(1):127–152, 2005.

[Nes07] Y. Nesterov. Gradient methods for minimizing composite objective function. *ECORE Discussion Paper*, 2007.

[NFGS15] E. Ndiaye, O. Fercoq, A. Gramfort, and J. Salmon. Gap safe screening rules for sparse multi-task and multi-class models. In *Proceedings of the 28th International Conference on Neural Information Processing Systems*, volume 1, pages 811–819. MIT Press, 2015.

[NIGM18] C. Nwankpa, W. Ijomah, A. Gachagan, and S. Marshall. Activation functions: Comparison of trends in practice and research for deep learning. *arXiv:1811.03378*, 2018.

[NP06] Y. Nesterov and B.T. Polyak. Cubic regularization of Newton method and its global performance. *Mathematical Programming*, 108(1):177–205, 2006.

[NT09] D. Needell and J. Tropp. CoSaMP: Iterative signal recovery from incomplete and inaccurate samples. *Applied and Computational Harmonic Analysis*, 26(3):301–321, 2009.

[NW06] J. Nocedal and S. Wright. *Numerical Optimization*. Springer, 2nd edition, 2006.

[NWMS18] E. Nehme, L.E. Weiss, T. Michaeli, and Y. Shechtman. Deep-STORM: Super-resolution single-molecule microscopy by deep learning. *Optica*, 5(4):458–464, 2018.

[OF96a] B. Olshausen and D. Field. Natural image statistics and efficient coding. *Network: Computation in Neural Systems*, 7:333–339, 1996.

[OF96b] B.A. Olshausen and D.J. Field. Emergence of simple-cell receptive field properties by learning a sparse code for natural images. *Nature*, 381(6583):607, 1996.

[OF97] B. Olshausen and D. Field. Sparse coding with an overcomplete basis set: A strategy employed by V1? *Vision Research*, 37(23):3311–3325, 1997.

[OF04] B. Olshausen and D. Field. Sparse coding of sensory inputs. *Current Opinion in Neurobiology*, 14:481–487, 2004.

[OH10] S. Oymak and B. Hassibi. New null space results and recovery thresholds for matrix rank minimization. *arXiv:1011.6326*, 2010.

[OJM+20] G. Ongie, A. Jalal, C.A. Metzler, et al. Deep learning techniques for inverse problems in imaging. *IEEE Journal on Selected Areas in Information Theory*, 1(1):39–56, 2020.

[OJF+15] S. Oymak, A. Jalali, M. Fazel, Y.C. Eldar, and B. Hassibi. Simultaneously structured models with application to sparse and low-rank matrices. *IEEE Transactions on Information Theory*, 61(5):2886–2908, 2015.

[OJFH13] S. Oymak, A. Jalali, M. Fazel, and B. Hassibi. Noisy estimation of simultaneously structured models: Limitations of convex relaxation. In *IEEE Conference on Decision and Control*, pages 6019–6024, 2013.

[OLV18] A. van den Oord, Y. Li, and O. Vinyals. Representation learning with contrastive predictive coding. *arXiv:1807.03748*, 2018.

[OSB99] A.V. Oppenheim, R.W. Schafer, and J.R. Buck. *Discrete-Time Signal Processing*. Prentice Hall, 1999.

[OX18] Y. Ouyang and Y. Xu. Lower complexity bounds of first-order methods for convex-concave bilinear saddle-point problems. *arXiv:1808.02901*, 2018.

[Pat34] A.L. Patterson. A Fourier series method for the determination of the components of interatomic distances in crystals. *Physical Review*, 46(5):372, 1934.

[Pat44] A.L. Patterson. Ambiguities in the X-ray analysis of crystal structures. *Physical Review*, 65(5–6):195, 1944.

[Pea01] K. Pearson. On lines and planes of closest fit to systems of points in space. *Philosophical Magazine*, 2(6):559–572, 1901.

[Pea00] J. Pearl. *Causality: Models, Reasoning and Inference*. Cambridge University Press, 1st edition, 2000.

[Pfe18] F. Pfeiffer. X-ray ptychography. *Nature Photonics*, 12(1):9–17, 2018.

[PGW⁺12] Y. Peng, A. Ganesh, J. Wright, W. Xu, and Y. Ma. RASL: Robust alignment by sparse and low-rank decomposition for linearly correlated images. *IEEE Transactions on Pattern Analysis and Machine Intelligence*, 34(11):2233–2246, 2012.

[PHD20] V. Papyan, X.Y. Han, and D.L. Donoho. Prevalence of neural collapse during the terminal phase of deep learning training. *arXiv:2008.08186*, 2020.

[Pho75] B.T. Phong. Illumination for computer generated pictures. *Communications of the ACM*, 18(6):311–317, 1975.

[PKCS16] D. Park, A. Kyrillidis, C. Caramanis, and S. Sanghavi. Non-square matrix sensing without spurious local minima via the Burer-Monteiro approach. *arXiv:1609.03240*, 2016.

[Pla72] R.L. Plackett. Studies in the history of probability and statistics. XXIX The discovery of the method of least squares. *Biometrika*, 59(2):239–251, 1972.

[PLVH20] A. Pal, C. Lane, R. Vidal, and B.D. Haeffele. On the regularization properties of structured dropout. In *Proceedings of the IEEE/CVF Conference on Computer Vision and Pattern Recognition*, pages 7671–7679, 2020.

[PMS94] A. Pentland, B. Moghaddam, and T. Starner. View-based and modular eigenspaces for face recognition. In *Proceedings of the IEEE Conference on Computer Vision and Pattern Recognition*, pages 84–91, 1994.

[Pol64] B.T. Polyak. Some methods of speeding up the convergence of iteration methods. *USSR Computational Mathematics and Mathematical Physics*, 4(5):1–17, 1964.

[Pow69] M. Powell. A method for nonlinear constraints in minimization problems. In *Optimization*, pages 283–298. Academic Press, 1969.

[Pre98] L. Prechelt. Early stopping – But when? In *Neural Networks: Tricks of the Trade*, pages 55–69. Springer, 1998.

[PRE16] V. Papyan, Y. Romano, and M. Elad. Convolutional neural networks analyzed via convolutional sparse coding. *Journal of Machine Learning Research*, 18(1):2887–2938, 2016.

[PRK93] Y. Pati, R. Rezaiifar, and P. Krishnaprasad. Orthogonal matching pursuit: Recursive function approximation with application to wavelet decomposition. In *Asilomar Conference on Signals, Systems and Computers*, 1993.

[PRSE18] V. Papyan, Y. Romano, J. Sulam, and M. Elad. Theoretical foundations of deep learning via sparse representations: A multilayer sparse model and its connection to convolutional neural networks. *IEEE Signal Processing Magazine*, 35(4):72–89, 2018.

[PS16] T. Pock and S. Sabach. Inertial proximal alternating linearized minimization (iPALM) for nonconvex and nonsmooth problems. *SIAM Journal on Imaging Sciences*, 9(4):1756–1787, 2016.

[PSG⁺16] E.A. Pnevmatikakis, D. Soudry, Y. Gao, et al. Simultaneous denoising, deconvolution, and demixing of calcium imaging data. *Neuron*, 89(2):285–299, 2016.

[PSM82] R. Pickholtz, D. Schilling, and L. Milstein. Theory of spread-spectrum communications – A tutorial. *IEEE Transactions on Communications*, 30(5):855–884, 1982.

[PSV77] G.C. Papanicolaou, D. Stroock, and S.R.S. Varadhan. Martingale approach to some limit theorems. In *Proceedings of Duke Turbulence Conference in*

Statistical Mechanics, Dynamical Systems (ed. D. Ruelle), Duke University Mathematics Series, volume 3, 1977.

[PTRV98] C.H. Papadimitriou, H. Tamaki, P. Raghavan, and S. Vempala. Latent semantic indexing: A probabilistic analysis. In *Proceedings of the Seventeenth ACM Symposium on Principles of Database Systems*, pages 159–168, 1998.

[PV08] P. Prandoni and M. Vetterli. *Signal Processing for Communications*. EPFL Press, 2008.

[QLZ19] Q. Qu, X. Li, and Z. Zhu. A nonconvex approach for exact and efficient multichannel sparse blind deconvolution. In *Advances in Neural Information Processing Systems*, pages 4017–4028, 2019.

[QSW14] Q. Qu, J. Sun, and J. Wright. Finding a sparse vector in a subspace: Linear sparsity using alternating directions. In *Advances in Neural Information Processing Systems*, pages 3401–3409, 2014.

[Qui86] J.R. Quinlan. Induction of decision trees. *Machine Learning*, 1(1):81–106, 1986.

[QYW+20] H. Qi, C. You, X. Wang, Y. Ma, and J. Malik. Deep isometric learning for visual recognition. In *Proceedings of the International Conference on Machine Learning*, 2020.

[QZC19] W. Qian, Y. Zhang, and Y. Chen. Global convergence of least squares EM for demixing two log-concave densities. In *Advances in Neural Information Processing Systems*, pages 4795–4803, 2019.

[QZC20] W. Qian, Y. Zhang, and Y. Chen. Structures of spurious local minima in k-means. *arXiv:2002.06694*, 2020.

[QZEW17] Q. Qu, Y. Zhang, Y. Eldar, and J. Wright. Convolutional phase retrieval. In *Advances in Neural Information Processing Systems*, pages 6086–6096, 2017.

[QZL+19] Q. Qu, Y. Zhai, X. Li, Y. Zhang, and Z. Zhu. Analysis of the optimization landscapes for overcomplete representation learning. *arXiv:1912.02427*, 2019.

[QZL+20a] Q. Qu, Y. Zhai, X. Li, Y. Zhang, and Z. Zhu. Analysis of the optimization landscapes for overcomplete representation learning. In *International Conference on Learning Representations*, 2020.

[QZL+20b] Q. Qu, Z. Zhu, X. Li, et al. Finding the sparsest vectors in a subspace: Theory, algorithms, and applications. *arXiv:2001.06970*, 2020.

[Rau09] H. Rauhut. Circulant and Toeplitz matrices in compressed sensing. *arXiv:0902.4394*, 2009.

[Raz98] B. Razavi. *RF Microelectronics*. Prentice Hall, 1998.

[Raz01] B. Razavi. *Design of Analog CMOS Integrated Circuits*. McGraw Hill, 2001.

[RB16] E.K. Ryu and S. Boyd. A primer on monotone operator methods: Survey. *Applied and Computational Mathematics*, 15(1):3–43, 2016.

[RBZ06] M.J. Rust, M. Bates, and X. Zhuang. Sub-diffraction-limit imaging by stochastic optical reconstruction microscopy (STORM). *Nature Methods*, 3(10):793, 2006.

[RC93] T. Rapcsák and T. Csendes. Nonlinear coordinate transformations for unconstrained optimization II. Theoretical background. *Journal of Global Optimization*, 3(3):359–375, 1993.

[RE14] R. Rubinstein and M. Elad. Dictionary learning for analysis-synthesis thresholding. *IEEE Transactions on Signal Processing*, 62(22):5962–5972, 2014.

[Rec11] B. Recht. A simpler approach to matrix completion. *Journal of Machine Learning Research*, 12:3413–3430, 2011.

[Rei65] H. Reichenbach. *Philosophic Foundations of Quantum Mechanics*. University of California Press, 1965.

[RFB15] O. Ronneberger, P. Fischer, and T. Brox. U-net: Convolutional networks for biomedical image segmentation. In *International Conference on Medical Image Computing and Computer-Assisted Intervention*, pages 234–241. Springer, 2015.

[RFP10] B. Recht, M. Fazel, and P. Parillo. Guaranteed minimum rank solution of matrix equations via nuclear norm minimization. *SIAM Review*, 52(3):471–501, 2010.

[RHW86] D.E. Rumelhart, G.E. Hinton, and R.J. Williams. Learning representations by back-propagating errors. *Nature*, 323(6088):533–536, 1986.

[Ris78] J. Rissanen. Modeling by shortest data description. *Automatica*, 14:465–471, 1978.

[RM51] H. Robbins and S. Monro. A stochastic approximation method. *The Annals of Mathematical Statistics*, 22(3):400–407, 1951.

[Rob93] W. Harrison Robert. Phase problem in crystallography. *Journal of the Optical Society of America A*, 10(5):1046–1055, 1993.

[Roc73] R.T. Rockafellar. The multiplier method of Hestenes and Powell applied to convex programming. *Journal of Optimization Theory and Applications*, 12(6):555–562, 1973.

[Ros58] F. Rosenblatt. The perceptron: A probabilistic model for information storage and organization in the brain. *Psychological Review*, 65(6):386–408, 1958.

[RS05] J.D.M. Rennie and N. Srebro. Fast maximum margin matrix factorization for collaborative prediction. In *Proceedings of the 22nd International Conference on Machine Learning*, pages 713–719, 2005.

[RT96] G.O. Roberts and R.L. Tweedie. Exponential convergence of Langevin distributions and their discrete approximations. *Bernoulli*, 2(4):341–363, 1996.

[RV08] M. Rudelson and R. Vershynin. On sparse reconstruction from Fourier and Gaussian measurements. *Communications on Pure and Applied Mathematics*, 61(8):1025–1045, 2008.

[RW09] R.T. Rockafellar and R.J.-B. Wets. *Variational Analysis*, volume 317. Springer Science & Business Media, 2009.

[RW18] C.W. Royer and S.J. Wright. Complexity analysis of second-order line-search algorithms for smooth nonconvex optimization. *SIAM Journal on Optimization*, 28(2):1448–1477, 2018.

[Sas83] S. Sastry. The effects of small noise on implicitly defined nonlinear dynamical systems. *IEEE Transactions on Circuits and Systems*, 30(9):651–663, 1983.

[Sas99] S. Sastry. *Nonlinear Systems: Analysis, Stability, and Control*. Springer, 1999.

[SBC14] W. Su, S. Boyd, and E. Candès. A differential equation for modeling Nesterov's accelerated gradient method: Theory and insights. In *Advances in Neural Information Processing Systems*, pages 2510–2518, 2014.

[SBOR06] P. Sinha, B. Balas, Y. Ostrovsky, and R. Russell. Face recognition by humans: Nineteen results all computer vision researchers should know about. *Proceedings of the IEEE*, 94(11):1948–1962, 2006.

[SBRL19] M. Sanjabi, S. Baharlouei, M. Razaviyayn, and J.D. Lee. When does non-orthogonal tensor decomposition have no spurious local minima? *arXiv:1911.09815*, 2019.

[SC19] L. Shi and Y. Chi. Manifold gradient descent solves multi-channel sparse blind deconvolution provably and efficiently. *arXiv:1911.11167*, 2019.

[SDC03] J.-L. Starck, D.L. Donoho, and E.J. Candès. Astronomical image representation by the curvelet transform. *Astronomy & Astrophysics*, 398(2):785–800, 2003.

[SDLF$^+$17] N.D. Sidiropoulos, L. De Lathauwer, X. Fu, et al. Tensor decomposition for signal processing and machine learning. *IEEE Transactions on Signal Processing*, 65(13):3551–3582, 2017.

[SEC$^+$15] Y. Shechtman, Y.C. Eldar, O. Cohen, et al. Phase retrieval with application to optical imaging: A contemporary overview. *IEEE Signal Processing Magazine*, 32(3):87–109, 2015.

[SED05] J.-L. Starck, M. Elad, and D.L. Donoho. Image decomposition via the combination of sparse representations and a variational approach. *IEEE Transactions on Image Processing*, 14(10):1570–1582, 2005.

[Ser06] T. Serre. *Learning a dictionary of shape-components in visual cortex: Comparison with neurons, humans and machines*. PhD Thesis, Massachusetts Institute of Technology, 2006.

[SFF19] Y. Sun, N. Flammarion, and M. Fazel. Escaping from saddle points on Riemannian manifolds. In *Advances in Neural Information Processing Systems*, pages 7276–7286, 2019.

[SFH17] S. Sabour, N. Frosst, and G.E. Hinton. Dynamic routing between capsules. *CoRR, abs/1710.09829*, 2017.

[SGHK03] C. Stosiek, O. Garaschuk, K. Holthoff, and A. Konnerth. In vivo two-photon calcium imaging of neuronal networks. *Proceedings of the National Academy of Sciences of the USA*, 100(12):7319–7324, 2003.

[SGS15] R.K. Srivastava, K. Greff, and J. Schmidhuber. Highway networks. *arXiv:1505.00387*, 2015.

[Sha92] A. Shashua. *Geometry and photometry in 3D visual recognition*. PhD Thesis, Massachusetts Institute of Technology, 1992.

[She94] J.R. Shewchuk. An introduction to the conjugate gradient method without the agonizing pain. *Technical Report, Carnegie Mellon University*, 1994.

[SHK$^+$14] N. Srivastava, G. Hinton, A. Krizhevsky, I. Sutskever, and R. Salakhutdinov. Dropout: A simple way to prevent neural networks from overfitting. *Journal of Machine Learning Research*, 15(1):1929–1958, 2014.

[SHN$^+$18] D. Soudry, E. Hoffer, M.S. Nacson, S. Gunasekar, and N. Srebro. The implicit bias of gradient descent on separable data. *Journal of Machine Learning Research*, 19(1):2822–2878, 2018.

[Sho85] N. Shor. *Minimization Methods for Non-Differentiable Functions*. Springer, 1985.

[Sil80] W.M. Silver. *Determining shape and reflectance using multiple images*. Master's Thesis, Massachusetts Institute of Technology, 1980.

[Sim50] T. Simpson. *Doctrine and Application of Fluxions*. J. Nourse, 1750.

[SJL18] M. Soltanolkotabi, A. Javanmard, and J.D. Lee. Theoretical insights into the optimization landscape of over-parameterized shallow neural networks. *IEEE Transactions on Information Theory*, 65(2):742–769, 2018.

[SJM19] C. Song, Y. Jiang, and Y. Ma. Towards unified acceleration of high-order algorithms under Hölder continuity and uniform convexity. *Technical Report, arXiv:1906.00582*, 2019.

[SJM20a] C. Song, Y. Jiang, and Y. Ma. Breaking the $O(1/\varepsilon)$ optimal rate for a class of minimax problems. *arXiv:2003.11758*, 2020.

[SJM20b] C. Song, Y. Jiang, and Y. Ma. Stochastic variance reduction via accelerated dual averaging for finite-sum optimization. *arXiv:2006.10281*, 2020.

[SK93] W.R. Softky and C. Koch. The highly irregular firing of cortical cells is inconsistent with temporal integration of random EPSPs. *Journal of Neuroscience*, 13(1):334–350, 1993.

[SLJ+15] C. Szegedy, W. Liu, Y. Jia, et al. Going deeper with convolutions. In *Proceedings of the IEEE Conference on Computer Vision and Pattern Recognition*, pages 1–9, 2015.

[SLLB17] A. Sinha, J. Lee, S. Li, and G. Barbastathis. Lensless computational imaging through deep learning. *Optica*, 4(9):1117–1125, 2017.

[SMB10] D. Scherer, A. Müller, and S. Behnke. Evaluation of pooling operations in convolutional architectures for object recognition. In *International Conference on Artificial Neural Networks*, pages 92–101. Springer, 2010.

[SMM+17] N. Shazeer, A. Mirhoseini, K. Maziarz, et al. Outrageously large neural networks: The sparsely-gated mixture-of-experts layer. In *International Conference on Learning Representations*, 2017.

[SNT20] X. Sun, N.M. Nasrabadi, and T.D. Tran. Supervised deep sparse coding networks for image classification. *IEEE Transactions on Image Processing*, 29:405–418, 2020.

[SPM02] J.-L. Starck, E. Pantin, and F. Murtagh. Deconvolution in astronomy: A review. *Publications of the Astronomical Society of the Pacific*, 114(800):1051, 2002.

[SPRE18] J. Sulam, V. Papyan, Y. Romano, and M. Elad. Multilayer convolutional sparse modeling: Pursuit and dictionary learning. *IEEE Transactions on Signal Processing*, 66(15):4090–4104, 2018.

[SQW15] J. Sun, Q. Qu, and J. Wright. When are nonconvex problems not scary? *arXiv:1510.06096*, 2015.

[SQW17a] J. Sun, Q. Qu, and J. Wright. Complete dictionary recovery over the sphere I: Overview and the geometric picture. *IEEE Transactions on Information Theory*, 63(2)853–884, 2017.

[SQW17b] J. Sun, Q. Qu, and J. Wright. Complete dictionary recovery over the sphere II: Recovery by Riemannian trust-region method. *IEEE Transactions on Information Theory*, 63(2):885–914, 2017.

[SQW18] J. Sun, Q. Qu, and J. Wright. A geometric analysis of phase retrieval. *Foundations of Computational Mathematics*, 18(5):1131–1198, 2018.

[SS86] F. Santosa and W.W. Symes. Linear inversion of band-limited reflection seismograms. *SIAM Journal on Scientific and Statistical Computing*, 7(4):1307–1330, 1986.

[SS17] I. Safran and O. Shamir. Spurious local minima are common in two-layer ReLU neural networks. *arXiv:1712.08968*, 2017.

[SSL06] F. Sanja, D. Skocaj, and A. Leonardis. Combining reconstructive and discriminative subspace methods for robust classification and regression by subsampling. *IEEE Transactions on Pattern Analysis and Machine Intelligence*, 28(3):337–350, 2006.

[STDV18] F. Sheldon, F.L. Traversa, and M. Di Ventra. Taming a non-convex landscape with dynamical long-range order: Memcomputing the Ising spin-glass. *arXiv:1810.03712*, 2018.

[Sto09] M. Stojnic. Various thresholds for ℓ_1-optimization in compressed sensing. *arXiv:0907.3666*, 2009.

[Sun19a] J. Sun. Provable nonconvex methods/algorithms. `https://sunju.org/research/nonconvex/`, 2019.

[Sun19b] R. Sun. Optimization for deep learning: Theory and algorithms. *arXiv:1912.08957*, 2019.

[SW08] R. Schneider and W. Weil. *Stochastic and Integral Geometry*. Springer, 2008.

[SWW12] D.A. Spielman, H. Wang, and J. Wright. Exact recovery of sparsely-used dictionaries. In *Conference on Learning Theory*, 2012.

[SXZ+20] Y. Shen, Y. Xue, J. Zhang, K.B. Letaief, and V. Lau. Complete dictionary learning via ℓ^p-norm maximization. *arXiv:2002.10043*, 2020.

[SY07] A.M.-C. So and Y. Ye. Theory of semidefinite programming for sensor network localization. *Mathematical Programming*, 109(2–3):367–384, 2007.

[SYJS05] J. Sun, L. Yuan, J. Jia, and H.-Y. Shum. Image completion with structure propagation. *ACM Transactions on Graphics*, 24(3):861–868, 2005.

[SZ14] K. Simonyan and A. Zisserman. Very deep convolutional networks for large-scale image recognition. *arXiv:1409.1556*, 2014.

[Tal95] M. Talagrand. Concentration of measure and isoperimetric inequalities in product spaces. *Publications Mathematiques de l'I.H.E.S.*, 81:73–205, 1995.

[TBF+12] R. Tibshirani, J. Bien, J. Friedman, et al. Strong rules for discarding predictors in lasso-type problems. *Journal of the Royal Statistical Society B*, 74(2):245–266, 2012.

[TG07] J. Tropp and A. Gilbert. Signal recovery from random measurements via orthogonal matching pursuit. *IEEE Transactions on Information Theory*, 53(12):4655–4666, 2007.

[Tho04] C.J. Thompson. Inequality with applications in statistical mechanics. *Journal of Mathematical Physics*, 6(11):1812–1813, 2004.

[Tib96] R. Tibshirani. Regression shrinkage and selection via the LASSO. *Journal of the Royal Statistical Society B*, 58(1):267–288, 1996.

[TM01] D. Taubman and M. Marcellin. *JPEG 2000: Image Compression Fundamentals, Standards and Practice*. Kluwer Academic, 2001.

[TP91] M. Turk and A. Pentland. Eigenfaces for recognition. In *Proceedings of the IEEE International Conference on Computer Vision and Pattern Recognition*, 1991.

[Tro10] J. Tropp. Beyond Nyquist: Efficient sampling of sparse bandlimited signals. *IEEE Transactions on Information Theory*, 56(1):520–544, 2010.

[Tro12] J.A. Tropp. User-friendly tail bounds for sums of random matrices. *Foundations of Computational Mathematics*, 12(4):389–434, 2012.

[Tuc66] L. Tucker. Some mathematical notes on three-mode factor analysis. *Psychometrika*, 31(3):279–311, 1966.

[TV18] M.C. Tsakiris and R. Vidal. Dual principal component pursuit. *Journal of Machine Learning Research*, 19(1):684–732, 2018.

[TW15] L. Tian and L. Waller. 3D intensity and phase imaging from light field measurements in an LED array microscope. *Optica*, 2(2):104–111, 2015.

[TY09] K.-C. Toh and S. Yun. An accelerated proximal gradient algorithm for nuclear norm regularized least squares problems. Preprint, 2009. Available online: `http://math.nus.edu.sg/~matys/apg.pdf`.

[UVL16] D. Ulyanov, A. Vedaldi, and V. Lempitsky. Instance normalization: The missing ingredient for fast stylization. *arXiv:1607.08022*, 2016.

[Val77] L.G. Valiant. Graph-theoretic arguments in low-level complexity. *Lecture Notes in Computer Science*, 53:162–176, 1977.

[Van16] S. Van De Geer. *Estimation and Testing Under Sparsity*. Springer, 2016.

[VBGS17] R. Vidal, J. Bruna, R. Giryes, and S. Soatto. Mathematics of deep learning. *arXiv:1712.04741*, 2017.

[VOdM96] P. Van Overschee and B. de Moor. *Subspace Identification for Linear Systems*. Kluwer Academic, 1996.

[Ver08] R. Vershynin. Spectral norms of products of random and deterministic matrices. *arXiv:0812.2432*, 2008.

[Ver18] R. Vershynin. *High-Dimensional Probability*. Cambridge University Press, 2018.

[VHC08] G. Vogiatzis C. Hernández, and R. Cipolla. Multi-view photometric stereo. *IEEE Transactions on Pattern Analysis and Machine Intelligence*, 30(3):548–554, 2008.

[VK95] M. Vetterli and J. Kovačević. *Wavelets and Subband Coding*. Prentice Hall, 1995.

[VMS16] R. Vidal, Yi Ma, and S.S. Sastry. *Generalized Principal Component Analysis*. Springer, 1st edition, 2016.

[VSP$^+$17] A. Vaswani, N. Shazeer, N. Parmar, et al. Attention is all you need. In *Proceedings of the 31st International Conference on Neural Information Processing Systems*, NIPS'17, 6000–6010, Curran Associates, 2017.

[Wai09a] M. Wainwright. Information-theoretic limits on sparsity recovery in the high-dimensional and noisy setting. *IEEE Transactions on Information Theory*, 55(12):5728–5741, 2009.

[Wai09b] M.J. Wainwright. Sharp thresholds for high-dimensional and noisy sparsity recovery using ℓ_1-constrained quadratic programming. *IEEE Transactions on Information Theory*, 55(5):2183–2202, 2009.

[Wai19] M.J. Wainwright. *High-Dimensional Statistics: A Non-Asymptotic Viewpoint*. Cambridge Series in Statistical and Probabilistic Mathematics. Cambridge University Press, 2019.

[Wal63] A. Walther. The question of phase retrieval in optics. *Journal of Modern Optics*, 10(1):41–49, 1963.

[Wal91] G. Wallace. The JPEG still picture compression standard. *Communications of the ACM*, 34(4):30–44, 1991.

[WB18] T. Wiatowski and H. Bölcskei. A mathematical theory of deep convolutional neural networks for feature extraction. *IEEE Transactions on Information Theory*, 64(3):1845–1866, 2018.

[WBYM21] Z. Wu, C. Baek, C. You, and Y. Ma. Incremental learning via rate reduction. In *IEEE Computer Society Conference on Computer Vision and Pattern Recognition*, 2021.

[WDCB05] M.B. Wakin, D.L. Donoho, H. Choi, and R.G. Baraniuk. The multiscale structure of non-differentiable image manifolds. In *Proceedings of SPIE, the International Society for Optical Engineering*, 59141B–1, 2005.

[WdM15] I. Waldspurger, A. d'Aspremont, and S. Mallat. Phase recovery, MaxCut and complex semidefinite programming. *Mathematical Programming*, 149(1–2):47–81, 2015.

[WGE17] G. Wang, G.B. Giannakis, and Y.C. Eldar. Solving systems of random quadratic equations via truncated amplitude flow. *IEEE Transactions on Information Theory*, 64(2):773–794, 2017.

[WGMM13] J. Wright, A. Garnesh, K. Min, and Y. Ma. Compressive principal component pursuit. *IMA Journal on Information and Inference*, 2(1):32–68, 2013.

[WGS$^+$10] L. Wu, A. Ganesh, B. Shi, et al. Robust photometric stereo via low-rank matrix completion and recovery. In *Asian Conference on Computer Vision*, 2010.

[WH18] Y. Wu and K. He. Group normalization. In *Proceedings of the European Conference on Computer Vision (ECCV)*, pages 3–19, 2018.

[WJ08] M. Wainwright and M. Jordan. Graphical models, exponential families, and variational inference. *Foundations and Trends in Machine Learning*, 1:1–305, 2008.

[WLY$^+$15] Z. Wang, D. Liu, J. Yang, W. Han, and T. Huang. Deep networks for image super-resolution with sparse prior. In *Proceedings of the IEEE International Conference on Computer Vision*, 2015.

[WM10] J. Wright and Y. Ma. Dense error correction via ℓ^1-minimization. *IEEE Transactions on Information Theory*, 56(7):3540–3560, 2010.

[WMM$^+$10] J. Wright, Y. Ma, J. Mairal, et al. Sparse representation for computer vision and pattern recognition. *Proceedings of the IEEE*, 98(6):1031–1044, 2010.

[WNF08] S. Wright, R. Nowak, and M. Figueiredo. Sparse reconstruction by separable approximation. In *IEEE International Conference on Acoustics, Speech and Signal Processing*, 2008.

[WNF09] S.J. Wright, R.D. Nowak, and M.A.T. Figueiredo. Sparse reconstruction by separable approximation. *IEEE Transactions on Signal Processing*, 57(7):2479–2493, 2009.

[Woo80] R. Woodham. Photometric method for determining surface orientation from multiple images. *Optical Engineering*, 19(1):139–144, 1980.

[WPPA16] S. Wisdom, T. Powers, J. Pitton, and L. Atlas. Interpretable recurrent neural networks using sequential sparse recovery. *arXiv:1611.07252*, 2016.

[Wri87] S. Wright. *Primal-Dual Interior Point Methods*. SIAM, 1987.

[Wri97] G. Wright. Magnetic resonance imaging. *IEEE Signal Processing Magazine*, 14(1):56–66, 1997.

[WTL$^+$08] J. Wright, Y. Tao, Z. Lin, Y. Ma, and H.-Y. Shum. Classification via minimum incremental coding length (MICL). In *Advances in Neural Information Processing Systems*, pages 1633–1640, 2008.

[Wun12] H. Wunderlich. On a theorem of Razborov. *Computational Complexity*, 21(3):431–477, 2012.

[WWG+09] A. Wagner, J. Wright, A. Ganesh, Z. Zhou, and Y. Ma. Toward a practical face recognition: Robust pose and illumination via sparse representation. In *Proceedings of the IEEE International Conference on Computer Vision and Pattern Recognition*, 2009.

[WWG+12] A. Wagner, J. Wright, A. Ganesh, et al. Towards a practical face recognition system: Robust alignment and illumination via sparse representation. *IEEE Transactions on Pattern Analysis and Machine Intelligence (PAMI)*, 34(2):372–386, 2012.

[WWJ16] A. Wibisono, A.C. Wilson, and M.I. Jordan. A variational perspective on accelerated methods in optimization. *Proceedings of the National Academy of Sciences of the USA*, 113(47):E7351–E7358, 2016.

[WX20] D. Wu and J. Xu. On the optimal weighted ℓ_2 regularization in overparameterized linear regression. *arXiv:2006.05800*, 2020.

[WYD20] K. Wang, Y. Yan, and M. Diaz. Efficient clustering for stretched mixtures: Landscape and optimality. *arXiv:2003.09960*, 2020.

[WYG+09] J. Wright, A. Yang, A. Ganesh, S. Sastry, and Y. Ma. Robust face recognition via sparse representation. *IEEE Transactions on Pattern Analysis and Machine Intelligence*, 31(2):210–227, 2009.

[WYYZ08] Y. Wang, J. Yang, W. Yin, and Y. Zhang. A new alternating minimization algorithm for total variation image reconstruction. *SIAM Journal on Imaging Sciences*, 1(3):248–272, 2008.

[WZL+14] J. Wang, J. Zhou, J. Liu, P. Wonka, and J. Ye. A safe screening rule for sparse logistic regression. In *Proceedings of the 27th International Conference on Neural Information Processing Systems* volume 1, pages 1053–1061. MIT Press, 2014.

[XBSD+18] L. Xiao, Y. Bahri, J. Sohl-Dickstein, S. Schoenholz, and J. Pennington. Dynamical isometry and a mean field theory of CNNs: How to train 10,000-layer vanilla convolutional neural networks. In *International Conference on Machine Learning*, pages 5393–5402, 2018.

[XCS10] H. Xu, C. Caramanis, and S. Sanghavi. Robust PCA via outlier pursuit. In *Advances in Neural Information Processing Systems*, pages 2496–2504, 2010.

[XCS12] H. Xu, C. Caramanis, and S. Sanghavi. Robust PCA via outlier pursuit. *IEEE Transactions on Information Theory*, 58(5):3047–3064, May 2012.

[XGD+17] S. Xie, R. Girshick, P. Dollár, Z. Tu, and K. He. Aggregated residual transformations for deep neural networks. In *2017 IEEE Conference on Computer Vision and Pattern Recognition (CVPR)*, pages 5987–5995, 2017.

[XHM16] J. Xu, D. Hsu, and A. Maleki. Global analysis of expectation maximization for mixtures of two Gaussians. In *Advances in Neural Information Processing Systems 29*, 2016.

[Xu17] Y. Xu. Accelerated first-order primal-dual proximal methods for linearly constrained composite convex programming. *SIAM Journal on Optimization*, 27(3):1459–1484, 2017.

[XWCL15] B. Xu, N. Wang, T. Chen, and M. Li. Empirical evaluation of rectified activations in convolutional network. *arXiv:1505.00853*, 2015.

[XZ13] L. Xiao and T. Zhang. A proximal-gradient homotopy method for the sparse least-squares problem. *SIAM Journal on Optimization*, 23(2):1062–1091, 2013.

[XZ14] L. Xiao and T. Zhang. A proximal stochastic gradient method with progressive variance reduction. *SIAM Journal on Optimization*, 24(4):2057–2075, 2014.

[Yau74] S.-T. Yau. Non-existence of continuous convex functions on certain Riemannian manifolds. *Mathematische Annalen*, 207(4):269–270, 1974.

[YCY+20] Y. Yu, K.H.R. Chan, C. You, C.-B. Song, and Y. Ma. Learning diverse and discriminative representations via the principle of maximal coding rate reduction. In *Conference on Neural Information Processing Systems*, 2020.

[YDZ+15] L.-H. Yeh, J. Dong, J. Zhong, et al. Experimental robustness of Fourier ptychography phase retrieval algorithms. *Optics Express*, 23(26):33214–33240, 2015.

[YHK+16] R.T. Yazicigil, T. Haque, M. Kumar, et al. A compressed sampling time-segmented quadrature analog-to-information converter that exploits adaptive thresholding and virtual extension of physical hardware for rapid interferer detection. In *IEEE International Solid-State Circuits Conference*, 2016.

[YHW+15] R.T. Yazicigil, T. Haque, M.R. Whalen, et al. Wideband rapid interferer detector exploiting compressed sampling with a quadrature analog-to-information converter. In *IEEE International Solid-State Circuits Conference*, pages 3047–3064, December 2015.

[YMO13] Y. Yang, J. Ma, and S. Osher. Seismic data reconstruction via matrix completion. *Inverse Problems & Imaging*, 7(4):1379, 2013.

[YOGD08] W. Yin, S. Osher, D. Goldfarb, and J. Darbon. Bregman iterative algorithms for ℓ_1-minimization with applications to compressed sensing. *SIAM Journal on Imaging Science*, 1(1):143–168, 2008.

[YRC07] Y. Yao, L. Rosasco, and A. Caponnetto. On early stopping in gradient descent learning. *Constructive Approximation*, 26(2):289–315, 2007.

[YSLX16] Y. Yang, J. Sun, H. Li, and Z. Xu. Deep ADMM-Net for compressive sensing MRI. In *Advances in Neural Information Processing Systems*, pages 10–18, 2016.

[YWHM08] J. Yang, J. Wright, T. Huang, and Y. Ma. Image super-resolution as sparse representation of raw image patches. In *Proceedings of the IEEE International Conference on Computer Vision and Pattern Recognition*, 2008.

[YWHM10] J. Yang, J. Wright, T. Huang, and Y. Ma. Image super-resolution via sparse representation. *IEEE Transactions on Image Processing*, 19(11):2861–2873, 2010.

[YY09] X. Yuan and J. Yang. Sparse and low-rank matrix decomposition via alternating direction method. *Pacific Journal of Optimization*, 9(1):167–180, 2009.

[YYY+20] Z. Yang, Y. Yu, C. You, J. Steinhardt, and Y. Ma. Rethinking bias-variance trade-off for generalization of neural networks. In *International Conference on Machine Learning (ICML)*, 2020.

[YZQM20] C. You, Z. Zhu, Q. Qu, and Y. Ma. Robust recovery via implicit bias of discrepant learning rates for double over-parameterization. *arXiv:2006.08857*, 2020.

[YZY10] J. Yang, Y. Zhang, and W. Yin. A fast alternating direction method for TVL1-L2 signal reconstruction from partial Fourier data. *IEEE Journal of Selected Topics in Signal Processing*, 4(2):288, 2010.

[ZB18] Y. Zhong and N. Boumal. Near-optimal bounds for phase synchronization. *SIAM Journal on Optimization*, 28(2):989–1016, 2018.

[ZBH+17] C. Zhang, S. Bengio, M. Hardt, B. Recht, and O. Vinyals. Understanding deep learning requires rethinking generalization. In *International Conference on Learning Representations*, 2017.

[ZCPR03] W. Zhao, R. Chellappa, J. Phillips, and A. Rosenfield. Face recognition: A literature survey. *ACM Computing Surveys*, pages 399–458, 2003.

[ZGLM12] Z. Zhang, A. Ganesh, X. Liang, and Y. Ma. TILT: Transform-invariant low-rank textures. *International Journal of Computer Vision (IJCV)*, 99(1):1–24, 2012.

[Zha00] Z. Zhang. A flexible new technique for camera calibration. *IEEE Transactions on Pattern Analysis and Machine Intelligence*, 22(11):1330–1334, 2000.

[ZKW18] Y. Zhang, H.-W. Kuo, and J. Wright. Structured local minima in sparse blind deconvolution. In *Advances in Neural Information Processing Systems 31*, pages 2328–2337, 2018.

[ZL17] B. Zoph and Q.V. Le. Neural architecture search with reinforcement learning. *arXiv:1611.01578*, 2017.

[ZLC17] Y. Zhang, P. Liang, and M. Charikar. A hitting time analysis of stochastic gradient Langevin dynamics. In S. Kale and O. Shamir, editors, *Proceedings of the 2017 Conference on Learning Theory*, volume 65 of Proceedings of Machine Learning Research, pages 1980–2022 PMLR, 2017.

[ZLGM10] Z. Zhang, X. Liang, A. Ganesh, and Y. Ma. TILT: Transform invariant low-rank textures. In *Proceedings of Asian Conference on Computer Vision*, 2010.

[ZLK+17] Y. Zhang, Y. Lau, H.-W. Kuo, et al. On the global geometry of sphere-constrained sparse blind deconvolution. In *2017 IEEE Conference on Computer Vision and Pattern Recognition (CVPR)*, pages 4381–4389. IEEE, 2017.

[ZLM11] Z. Zhang, X. Liang, and Y. Ma. Unwrapping low-rank textures on generalized cylindrical surfaces. In *Proceedings of the IEEE International Conference on Computer Vision*, 2011.

[ZLM20] Y. Zhou, S. Liu, and Y. Ma. Learning to detect 3D reflection symmetry for single-view reconstruction. *arXiv:2006.10042*, 2020.

[ZLTW18] Z. Zhu, Q. Li, G. Tang, and M.B. Wakin. Global optimality in low-rank matrix optimization. *IEEE Transactions on Signal Processing*, 66(13):3614–3628, 2018.

[ZM20] Z. Zhou and Y. Ma. Comments on efficient singular value thresholding computation. *arXiv:2011.06710*, 2020.

[ZMKW13] Y. Zhang, C. Mu, H. Kuo, and J. Wright. Toward guaranteed illumination models for non-convex objects. In *2013 IEEE International Conference on Computer Vision*, pages 937–944, 2013.

[ZMM11] Z. Zhang, Y. Matsushita, and Y. Ma. Camera calibration with lens distortion from low-rank textures. In *Proceedings of the IEEE International Conference on Computer Vision and Pattern Recognition*, 2011.

[ZMZM20] Y. Zhai, H. Mehta, Z. Zhou, and Y. Ma. Understanding ℓ^4-based dictionary learning: Interpretation, stability, and robustness. In *International Conference on Learning Representations*, 2020.

[ZQHM19] Y. Zhou, H. Qi, J. Huang, and Y. Ma. NeurVPS: Neural vanishing point scanning via conic convolution. In *Conference on Neural Information Processing Systems*, 2019.

[ZQM19] Y. Zhou, H. Qi, and Y. Ma. End-to-end wireframe parsing. In *2019 IEEE/CVF International Conference on Computer Vision (ICCV)*, pages 962–971, 10 2019.

[ZQZ$^+$19] Y. Zhou, H. Qi, Y. Zhai, et al. Learning to reconstruct 3D Manhattan wireframes from a single image. In *2019 IEEE/CVF International Conference on Computer Vision (ICCV)*, pages 7697–7706, 2019.

[ZWJ14] Y. Zhang, M.J. Wainwright, and M.I. Jordan. Lower bounds on the performance of polynomial-time algorithms for sparse linear regression. In *Conference on Learning Theory*, pages 921–948, 2014.

[ZWMM09] Z. Zhou, A. Wagner, H. Mobahi, and Y. Ma. Face recognition with contiguous occlusion using Markov random fields. In *Proceedings of International Conference on Computer Vision*, 2009.

[ZWR$^+$18] Z. Zhu, Y. Wang, D. Robinson, et al. Dual principal component pursuit: Improved analysis and efficient algorithms. In *Advances in Neural Information Processing Systems*, pages 2171–2181, 2018.

[ZYL$^+$20] Y. Zhai, Z. Yang, Z. Liao, J. Wright, and Y. Ma. Complete dictionary learning via ℓ^4-norm maximization over the orthogonal group. *Journal of Machine Learning Research*, 21(165):1–68, 2020.

[ZYZY14] X. Zhou, C. Yang, H. Zhao, and W. Yu. Low-rank modeling and its applications in image analysis. *ACM Computing Surveys (CSUR)*, 47(2):1–33, 2014.

[ZZWM14] X. Zhang, Z. Zhou, D. Wang, and Y. Ma. Hybrid singular value thresholding for tensor completion. In *Proceedings of the AAAI Conference on Artificial Intelligence (AAAI-14)*, 2014.

List of Symbols

$\mathbb{R}$	The real numbers.
$\mathbb{C}$	The complex numbers.
$\mathfrak{i} = \sqrt{-1}$	The unit imaginary number as a solution to $x^2 + 1 = 0$.
$\mathbb{R}^n, \mathbb{C}^n$	The n-dimensional real or complex space.
$\mathbb{R}^{m\times n}, \mathbb{C}^{m\times n}$	The space of $m \times n$ real or complex matrices.
$\mathbb{S}^{n-1}$	A unit sphere in $\mathbb{R}^n$.
$\mathbb{G}$	A general (matrix) group.
$[k]$	The set $\{1, \ldots, k\}$.
I	A subset of indices usually indicating the support of a sparse vector.
Ω	A subset of indices for entries of a matrix.
S	A subspace.
$\mathsf{O}(n)$	The orthogonal group.
$\mathsf{GL}(n)$	The general linear group.
$\mathsf{SL}(n)$	The special linear group.
$\mathsf{SP}(n)$	The sign permutation group.
a, b, c, x, y, A, B, C	Scalars.
$C_1, C_2, \ldots$	Large constants.
$c_1, c_2, \ldots$	Small constants.
$\boldsymbol{x}, \boldsymbol{y}$	Vectors, always represented as columns.
$\operatorname{supp}(\boldsymbol{x})$	For $\boldsymbol{x} \in \mathbb{R}^n$, the indices of the nonzero entries, $\subseteq [n]$.
$\operatorname{sign}(\boldsymbol{x})$	The signs of a vector $\boldsymbol{x} \in \mathbb{R}^n$, in $\{-1, 0, 1\}^n$.
$\boldsymbol{X}, \boldsymbol{Y}$	Matrices.
$\boldsymbol{L}, \boldsymbol{S}$	$\boldsymbol{L}$ indicates a low-rank matrix, and $\boldsymbol{S}$ a sparse matrix.
$\mathcal{X}$	Tensors (of order > 2).
$\boldsymbol{A} \succeq \boldsymbol{B}$	The semidefinite order, i.e., $\boldsymbol{A} - \boldsymbol{B}$ is semidefinite.
$\boldsymbol{A} \succ \boldsymbol{B}$	Strict semidefinite order, i.e., $\boldsymbol{A} - \boldsymbol{B}$ is positive definite.
$\mathcal{S}^n_+$	The cone of symmetric positive semidefinite matrices of size $n \times n$.
$\boldsymbol{e}_1, \ldots, \boldsymbol{e}_n$	The standard basis vectors for $\mathbb{R}^m$.
$\boldsymbol{E}_{i,j}$	The standard basis vectors for the space of matrices $\mathbb{R}^{m\times n}$.
$\mathbf{0}$	The zero vector or matrix, depending on context.
$\mathbf{1}$	The all ones vector or matrix, depending on context.

$\boldsymbol{I}$	The identity matrix.
$\boldsymbol{a}^*$, $\boldsymbol{A}^*$	The (conjugate) transpose of a vector $\boldsymbol{a}$ or a matrix $\boldsymbol{A}$.
$\boldsymbol{A}^{-1}$	The inverse of a nonsingular matrix $\boldsymbol{A}$.
$\boldsymbol{A}^{\dagger}$	The pseudo-inverse of an arbitrary matrix $\boldsymbol{A}$.
$\operatorname{null}(\boldsymbol{A})$	The null space of $\boldsymbol{A}$.
$\operatorname{range}(\boldsymbol{A})$	The range (column space) of $\boldsymbol{A}$.
$\operatorname{range}(\boldsymbol{A}^*)$	The row space of $\boldsymbol{A}$.
$\boldsymbol{X}_{i,j}$	The (i, j) element of matrix $\boldsymbol{X}$; where possible, use i for the first index, j for the second index.
$\boldsymbol{X}_{\mathsf{I},\mathsf{J}}$	For $\boldsymbol{X} \in \mathbb{R}^{m\times n}$, the square submatrix index by $\mathsf{I} \subseteq [m]$, $\mathsf{J} \subseteq [n]$.
$\boldsymbol{X}_{*,\mathsf{J}}$	Shorthand for the column submatrix indexed by J.
$\boldsymbol{X}_{\mathsf{I},*}$	Shorthand for the row submatrix indexed by I.
$\boldsymbol{P}_{\mathsf{I}}$	Abuse of notation for the projection (matrix) of a vector onto the coordinate subspace indexed by I.
$\boldsymbol{A} = \boldsymbol{U}\boldsymbol{\Sigma}\boldsymbol{V}^*$	The singular value decomposition of $\boldsymbol{A}$; prefer the "compact" form; if $\boldsymbol{A} \in \mathbb{R}^{m\times n}$ and $\operatorname{rank}(\boldsymbol{A}) = r$, $\boldsymbol{U} \in \mathbb{R}^{m\times r}$, $\boldsymbol{\Sigma} \in \mathbb{R}^{r\times r}$, and $\boldsymbol{V} \in \mathbb{R}^{n\times r}$.
$\boldsymbol{P} = \boldsymbol{U}\boldsymbol{\Lambda}\boldsymbol{U}^*$	The eigenvector decomposition of a symmetric matrix $\boldsymbol{P} \in \mathbb{R}^{m\times m}$; here, $\boldsymbol{\Lambda}$ is diagonal, and $\boldsymbol{U} \in \mathbb{R}^{m\times m}$ with $\boldsymbol{U}^*\boldsymbol{U} = \boldsymbol{I}$.
$[\boldsymbol{x}]_k$	A best k-term approximation to $\boldsymbol{x}$.
$\operatorname{soft}(\cdot, \tau)$	Entry-wise soft-thresholding operator on a scalar, vector, or a matrix, with a threshold $\tau \geq 0$.
$\mathcal{S}_\tau(\cdot)$	A shorthand for the entry-wise soft-thresholding operator, with the threshold τ.
$\mathcal{D}_\tau(\boldsymbol{A})$	The soft-thresholding operator on the singular values of the matrix $\boldsymbol{A}$, with the threshold τ.
$\boldsymbol{a} \circledast \boldsymbol{x}$	The convolution of two signals $\boldsymbol{a}$ and $\boldsymbol{x}$; when both are of finite length, it can represent either circulant convolution or a truncated one, depending on the context.
$\lVert\boldsymbol{x}\rVert_p$	The vector ℓ^p norm.
$\lVert\boldsymbol{X}\rVert$	The ℓ^2 operator norm, $\sigma_1(\boldsymbol{X})$.
$\lVert\boldsymbol{X}\rVert_F$	The Frobenius norm.
$\lVert\boldsymbol{X}\rVert_*$	The nuclear norm.
$\lVert\mathcal{A}\rVert_{V\to W}$	The operator norm of $\mathcal{A}$, as an operator from normed space V to normed space W.
$\lVert\boldsymbol{X}\rVert_{\ell^1\to\ell^p}$	The $\ell^1 \to \ell^p$ operator norm, $\max_j \lVert\boldsymbol{X}\boldsymbol{e}_j\rVert_p$.
$\lVert\boldsymbol{X}\rVert_{\ell^2\to\ell^\infty}$	The $\ell^2 \to \ell^\infty$ operator norm, $\max_i \lVert\boldsymbol{e}_i^*\boldsymbol{X}\rVert_2$.
$\lVert\cdot\rVert_\diamond^*$	The dual norm of $\lVert\cdot\rVert_\diamond$.
$\lVert\boldsymbol{X}\rVert_{\ell^1\to\ell^2}^*$	The dual norm of the $\ell^1 \to \ell^2$ operator norm, $\sum_j \lVert\boldsymbol{X}\boldsymbol{e}_j\rVert_2$.
$O(n)$	"Big-O" means upper-bounded by $C \cdot n$ for some constant C.

$\Omega(n)$	"Big-Omega" means lower-bounded by $C \cdot n$ for some constant C.
$\Theta(n)$	"Big-Theta" means lower-bounded by $c \cdot n$ for some constant c and upper-bounded by $C \cdot n$ for some constant $C > c$.
$o(n)$	"Little-o" means ultimately smaller than n.
$\partial f(\boldsymbol{x})$	Subdifferential of a function $f(\cdot)$ at $\boldsymbol{x}$.
$\nabla f(\boldsymbol{x})$	The gradient of a differentiable function f at $\boldsymbol{x}$.
$\nabla^2 f(\boldsymbol{x})$	The Hessian of a twice-differentiable function f at $\boldsymbol{x}$.
$\mathcal{A}, \mathcal{B}, \mathcal{P}$	General linear maps; these act on elements of their domain via square brackets, e.g., $\mathcal{A}[\boldsymbol{X}]$.
$\mathcal{P}_{\mathsf{S}}$	Orthonormal projector onto a subspace of a vector space.
$\mathcal{P}_{\Omega}$	The projection operator of a matrix onto the coordinate subspace indexed by Ω.
$\min\ (x+1)^2$	Unconstrained minimization.
$\max\ -(x+1)^2$	Unconstrained maximization.
$\min\ f(\boldsymbol{x})$ subject to $h(\boldsymbol{x}) \le 0.$	Constrained minimization.
$\boldsymbol{x}_{\text{true}}, \boldsymbol{X}_{\text{true}}$	Ground-truth solutions.
$\boldsymbol{x}_o, \boldsymbol{X}_o$	Shorthand for ground-truth solutions and objective for any algorithm.
$\boldsymbol{x}_0, \boldsymbol{x}_k, \boldsymbol{x}_{k+1}$	Initial point, and estimates at the k-th and the $(k+1)$-th iteration of an algorithm.
$\{\boldsymbol{x}_i\}$	A sequence of (vector) iterates in optimization or a set of samples in statistics.
$\boldsymbol{X}_0, \boldsymbol{X}_k, \boldsymbol{X}_{k+1}$	Initial point, and estimates at the k-th and the $(k+1)$-th iteration of an algorithm.
$\{\boldsymbol{X}_i\}$	A sequence of (matrix) iterates in optimization or a set of samples in statistics.
$\hat{\boldsymbol{x}}, \hat{\boldsymbol{X}}$	Estimated approximate solutions (to an estimation or optimization problem).
$\boldsymbol{x}_\star, \boldsymbol{X}_\star$	Converged solutions of an iterative algorithm.
$\hat{\boldsymbol{x}} \in \arg\min\ f(\boldsymbol{x}).$	Set of minimizers of a function $f(\cdot)$.
$\boldsymbol{x}_\star = \arg\min\ f(\boldsymbol{x}).$	Shorthand when the minimizer of $f(\cdot)$ is unique.
$\mathbb{P}[X > t] < \exp(-t^2/2)$	Probability.
$\mathbb{P}[X > 1 \mid X < 2] = 0$	Conditional probability.
$\mathbb{E}[\cdot]$	Expectation.
$\mathbb{E}[\cdot \mid \cdot]$	Conditional expectation.
$\mathbb{1}_{x \le 3}$	Indicator for an event.
$\boldsymbol{e}, \boldsymbol{E}$	A gross error vector or matrix.
$\boldsymbol{z}, \boldsymbol{Z}$	A vector or matrix of noise.
$\mathcal{N}(\boldsymbol{\mu}, \boldsymbol{\Sigma})$	The Gaussian or normal distribution with mean $\boldsymbol{\mu}$ and covariance $\boldsymbol{\Sigma}$.
$\mathrm{Ber}(\rho)$	The Bernoulli distribution with the probability $\rho \in [0,1]$.

Index